**The Legend. The History. The Pride.**
The Satellit 800 Millennium continues the
tradition. Our goal was to create the dream.
We listened to shortwave enthusiasts from every
part of the globe who owned Grundig and other
brands. We listened to what they wanted in a high-
end shortwave portable:

A big, easy to read, beautifully lit display. A large,
traditional analog signal strength meter. A tuning
knob they could really get a grip on. The option
of push-button tuning and direct
frequency entry. A tuner with absolutely
no audible muting during tuning knob use.

We listened. It's here.
**The Dream. The Legend. The History. The
Tradition.**

Whether you are cruising offshore, enjoying
the cottage, or relaxing on an extended
vacation in some distant land, the Satellit
800 Millennium is the most powerful and
precise radio in the World. Search the globe,
you can discover the hottest news first
hand... listen to and witness the ongoing
fascination with our evolving world today...
tomorrow the universe.

The Satellit 800 Millennium.

**GRUNDIG**

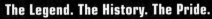

etón Corporation, 1015 Corporation Way, Palo Alto, CA 94303 • Tel: 650-903-3866 • Fax: 650-903-3867
Shortwave Hotlines: (US) 1-800-872-2228 (CN) 1-800-637-1648 • Web: www.grundigradio.com

# 2003 Passport® to

# World Band Radio

International Broadcasting Services, Ltd.

ISSN 0897-0157

## OUR READER IS THE MOST IMPORTANT PERSON IN THE WORLD!

## Editorial

| | |
|---|---|
| **Editor in Chief** | Lawrence Magne |
| **Editor** | Tony Jones |
| **Assistant Editor** | Craig Tyson |
| **Consulting Editor** | John Campbell |
| **Founder Emeritus** | Don Jensen |
| PASSPORT REPORTS | George Heidelman, Chuck Rippel, Dave Zantow, George Zeller |
| **WorldScan® Contributors** | Gabriel Iván Barrera (Argentina), James Conrad (U.S.), David Crystal (Israel), Alok Dasgupta (India), Nicolás Eramo (Argentina), Jose Jacob (India), Jembatan DX/Juichi Yamada (Japan), Anatoly Klepov (Russia), Marie Lamb (U.S.), Radio Nuevo Mundo (Japan), Célio Romais (Brazil), David Walcutt (U.S.) |
| **WorldScan® Software** | Richard Mayell |
| **Laboratory** | Robert Sherwood |
| **Artwork** | Gahan Wilson, cover |
| **Graphic Arts** | Bad Cat Design; Mike Wright, layout |
| **Printing** | Tri-Graphic Printing |

## Administration

| | |
|---|---|
| **Publisher** | Lawrence Magne |
| **Associate Publisher** | Jane Brinker |
| **Offices** | IBS North America, Box 300, Penn's Park PA 18943, USA; www.passband.com Phone +1 (215) 598-9018; Fax +1 (215) 598 3794; mktg@passband.com |
| **Advertising & Media Contact** | Jock Elliott, IBS Ltd., Box 300, Penn's Park PA 18943, USA; Phone +1 (215) 598-9018; Fax +1 (215) 598 3794; media@passband.com |

## Bureaus

| | |
|---|---|
| **IBS Latin America** | Tony Jones, Casilla 1844, Asunción, Paraguay; schedules@passband.com; Fax +1 (215) 598 3794 |
| **IBS Australia** | Craig Tyson, Box 2145, Malaga WA 6062; Fax +61 (8) 9342 9158; addresses@passband.com |
| **IBS Japan** | Toshimichi Ohtake, 5-31-6 Tamanawa, Kamakura 247-0071; Fax +81 (467) 43 2167; ibsjapan@passband.com |

## Library of Congress Cataloging-in-Publication Data

Passport to World Band Radio.
1. Radio Stations, Shortwave—Directories. I. Magne, Lawrence
TK9956.P27 2002 384.54'5 02-22739
ISBN 0-914941-83-6

PASSPORT, PASSPORT TO WORLD BAND RADIO, WorldScan, Radio Database International, RDI White Papers and White Papers are among the registered trademarks of International Broadcasting Services, Ltd., in the United States, Canada, United Kingdom and various other parts of the world.

Copyright © 2002 International Broadcasting Services, Ltd.

All rights reserved. No part of this publication may be reproduced, stored in a retrieval system, or transmitted in any form or by any means without the prior written consent of the publisher.

## IC-PCR1000
### The original black box

The IC-PCR1000 turns your PC into a Wide Band Receiver! Compatible with most PC's and laptops, the 'PCR1000 connects externally – in minutes!

- 100 kHz – 1.3 GHz†
- AM, FM, WFM, USB, LSB, CW
- Unlimited Memory Channels
- Real Time Band Scope
- IF Shift
- Noise Blanker
- Digital AFC
- Attenuator
- Tunable Bandpass Filters
- AGC Function
- S Meter Squelch
- CTCSS Tone Squelch
- Large Selection of Tuning Steps and Scans
- External Speaker Level Control

*Now with*
**BONITO SOFTWARE!**

*computer not included*

## IC-R75  Pull out the weak signals

The IC-R75 covers a wide frequency range allowing you to listen in to a world of information. With innovative features like twin passband tuning, synchronous AM detection, DSP capabilites, remote PC control and more – shortwave listening is easier than ever.

- 30 kHz - 60.0 MHz
- AM, FM, S-AM, USB, LSB, CW, RTTY
- 101 Alphanumeric Memory Channels
- Twin Passband Tuning (PBT)
- Commercial Grade
- Synchronous AM Detection (S-AM)
- Optional DSP with Auto Notch Filter
- Triple Conversion
- PC Remote Control with ICOM Software for Windows® (RSR75)

# TUNE IN THE WORLD WITH ICOM

## IC-R8500 The experts choice

ICOM technology brings you super wide band, all mode coverage from HF to 2GHz, including shortwave and VHF/UHF, while maintaining a constant receive sensitivity. The IC-R8500 is not simply a scanner – it's a professional quality communications receiver with versatile features from high speed scanning to computer control.

- 100 kHz - 2.0 GHz†
- AM, FM, WFM, USB, LSB, CW
- 1000 Alphanumeric Memories
- Commercial Grade
- IF Shift
- Noise Blanker
- Audio Peak Filter (APF)
- Selectable AGC Time Constant
- Digital Direct Synthesis (DDS)
- RS-232C Port for PC Remote Control with ICOM Software for Windows®

## IC-R3
### See & Hear all the action

Wide tuning range allows you to see and hear the excitement behind the scenes. Large, easy to read color display for frequency settings *and* video reception.

- 500 kHz – 2.45 GHz†
- AM, FM, WFM, AM-TV, FM-TV
- 450 Alphanumeric Memories
- CTCSS with Tone Scan
- 4 Level Attenuator
- Telescoping Antenna with BNC Connector
- 2" Color TFT Display with Video/Audio Output
- Lithium Ion Power

US version NTSC compatable only

## IC-R10
### Advanced performance

With the 'R10 you can tune in the world where ever you go. With a Real-time bandscope and Voice Scan Control to make it easy to find all the action.

- 500 kHz – 1.3 GHz†
- AM, FM, WFM, USB, LSB, CW
- 1000 Alphanumeric Memories
- Attenuator
- Alphanumeric Backlit Display
- VSC (Voice Scan Control)
- 7 Different Scan Modes
- Beginner Mode
- Band Scope
- Includes AA Ni-Cds & Charger

**The world is waiting**

www.icomamerica.com

©2002 ICOM America, Inc. 2380 116th Ave NE, Bellevue, WA 425-454-8155. †Cellular frequencies blocked; unblocked versions available to FCC approved users. The ICOM logo is a registered trademark of ICOM, Inc. All specifications are subject to change without notice or obligation. RXFAMPASSPORT702

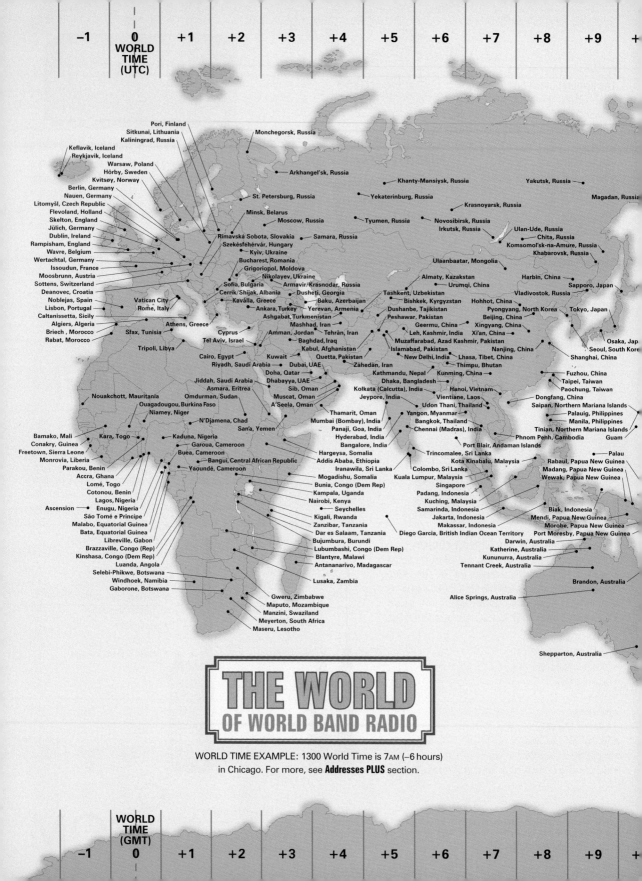

THE WORLD
OF WORLD BAND RADIO

WORLD TIME EXAMPLE: 1300 World Time is 7AM (−6 hours)
in Chicago. For more, see **Addresses PLUS** section.

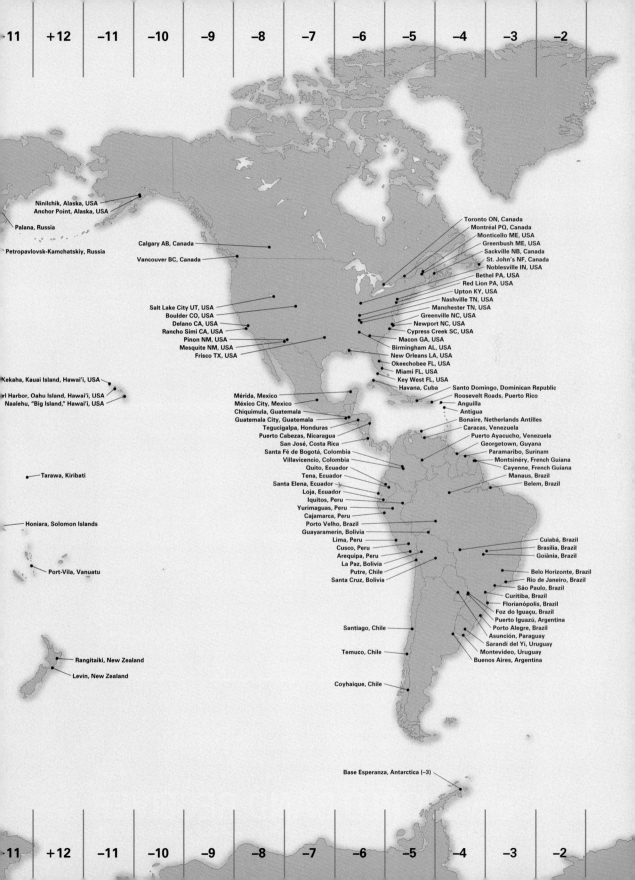

# SONY

## Enjoy Memory Scan tuning!
## Search available stations from presets.

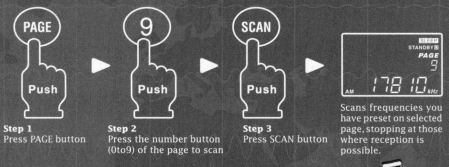

**Step 1**
Press PAGE button

**Step 2**
Press the number button
(0 to 9) of the page to scan

**Step 3**
Press SCAN button

Scans frequencies you have preset on selected page, stopping at those where reception is possible.

◎Each of 10 pages can hold 10 frequencies for a total of 100 presets.
◎By storing frequencies that differ depending on the time and period on a page,
  the available frequency can be received by scanning that page.
◎ATT control permits to adjust the reception sensitivity for scanning.
◎Built-in timer operation gives you tuning into the station
  of your choice at the two different times of your choice.

# Sony WORLD BAND RECEIVER
## FM Stereo/LW/MW/SW PLL Synthesized Receiver ICF-SW7600GR

# SONY

## Just one chip gives you a whole new world.

98 - 99

*Digital Dream Kids*

### 3000 Frequencies Packed into a Replaceable ROM Chip.
### Annual Updates Keep Your World Information Current.

●One-touch tuning for up to 8 stations: BBC, VOA, DW, and others.
Find stations without a guidebook, using SW Station Call to access 3,000
frequencies stored in ROM. ●My Memory presets for 100 favorite station
names & frequencies ●Large EL backlit LCD. ●Compact, highly portable
design ●New loop antenna supplied--band setting unnecessary.

●ROM chip updates available annually (separate purchase).

FM Stereo/LW/MW/SW  PLL Synthesized Receiver ICF-SW07

## Sony WORLD BAND RECEIVER

## Land of the Horn

# Ethiopia: Exiles Zap Media Monopoly

*by Hans Johnson*

For better or worse, the three largest nations of the Horn of Africa—Somalia, Ethiopia and Eritrea—are dependent on each other, as they are with neighboring Sudan which borders Ethiopia and Eritrea. When these links are strained, as they have been for years, nations suffer. Without the ties Ethiopia once had with Eritrea, it lost a vibrant outlet to the Red Sea. Without peace in Somalia, Islamic and other unrest spilled over into Ethiopia.

Here, no nation hangs separately. What affects one country impacts others in the region, and world band radio is in the thick of it. World band has served as a calming voice of education and peace, but governments have also used it to air their version of the "truth." These broadcasts have not always been benign.

The big wrinkle has been leased-time programming by exile groups. Since the end of the Cold War, powerful long-range transmitters have been available for hire in Germany, the former Soviet Union and beyond. This has created vast new opportunities for dissident groups and news sources which otherwise would have remained voiceless. The result has been, as with the Internet in other regions, a diminution of official power.

## World Band Sputters to Life

The heart of what is known as the Horn of Africa is ancient Ethiopia, the only country that shares a border with all others. Ethiopia is vast—almost twice the size of Texas—with over 65 million inhabitants, primarily ethnic Oromos and Amharas. Its size and strategic location have long tempted European and American powers.

**The Hamar inhabit southwestern Ethiopia.**
Irma Turtle, Turtle Tours, Inc.

The earliest record of shortwave broadcasting from Ethiopia appears in 1935, when transmitter ETB at Akaki served as a program relay for America's CBS. Invading Italians later took it over, renaming it IUD, whereupon the Americans fired up transmitter ETA from inside their embassy for point-to-point communication, along with the occasional program feed and broadcast. There was also a portable American transmitter used to feed news commentary to the United States about the Italian bombing of Addis Ababa, the Ethiopian capital, among other things reporting that of the 500 bombs dropped, over 100 were duds.

That same year, Emperor Haile Selassie used an assembled radio station, using 3.5 kW transmitters, to rally his people. Reportedly jammed by the Italians, this Imperial Ethiopian Radio was short-lived, having to be destroyed when the Ethiopian army fled Addis Ababa in 1936. In 1941 the British helped return Selassie to the throne, and a point-to-point transmitter was pressed into broadcast service for His Majesty.

> The big wrinkle has been leased-time programming by exile groups.

**Shy Ethiopian girls smile for the camera.**   C. Grant

**Radio UNMEE team in Asmara.**

Radio UNMEE

Italian point-to-point operations IUA, IUB, IUC, IUD and IUG were reported as still being active in 1937. However, it was not until the middle of next year that Ethiopian broadcasting truly got underway. Station IABA appeared on 9650 kHz at 1 kW, changing its call letters to I2AA in 1939. By 1942 the frequency had shifted to 9620 kHz.

## Religious Ministries Add Variety

In 1948, the kilowatt transmitter of Radio Addis Ababa, the Voice of Ethiopia, although airing a domestic service, was still being heard over great distances on that same frequency. It operated throughout much of the afternoon and evening from Addis Ababa in Amharic, plus English and some Arabic. From March 1950, the Adventist Hour carried the American-based program, "Voice of Prophecy" with Dr. H.M.S. Richards each Sunday. At that time the Adventist Church was actively experimenting with shortwave in several different countries; this led to the eventual formation of Adventist World Radio, which exists worldwide to this day.

In 1950 a second transmitter, 7.5 kW, was added on 15062 kHz, with another unit of

around 2.5-3.0 kW being brought on board shortly thereafter. By 1958 four transmitters were active: two at 2.5 kW, and one each at 0.5 kW and 7.5 kW. Also in the 1950s, the Imperial Palace Guard reportedly had its own 1 kW transmitter.

In 1960, thanks to an American aid package, a major upgrade took place, with 10 kW for the domestic service and 10 kW or 20 kW for the new international service directed to Europe, the Middle East and West Africa. That international service lasted only a year, but in 1964 a 100 kW transmitter was added to enhance reception in the region.

World band was further diversified in 1963 with the launch of ETLF-Radio Voice of the Gospel (RVOG), a Lutheran missionary station [see sidebar]. In the last half of 1965, Radio Addis Ababa-the Voice of Ethiopia was given the new title of Radio Ethiopia.

## Selassie Overthrown by Marxists

In 1974 Emperor Haile Selassie was overthrown and replaced by a harsh Marxist regime, which renamed Radio Ethiopia as the Voice of Ethiopia. Known as the Derg—Amharic for "committee"—the new govern-

## FROM GOSPEL OUTREACH TO DEVIL'S VOICE

In 1957 the Ninth Conference of Commission of World Mission of Lutheran World gave its approval for setting up an Ethiopian international world band station. Plans were completed in 1959, and in 1961 the station, ETLF—ET for Ethiopia, LF for Lutheran Federation—began test transmissions from a 1 kW transmitter.

On February 26, 1963, ETLF-Radio Voice of the Gospel (RVOG) formally went on the air, using a 100 kW unit located at Gedja, plus on the fifth of May a second 100 kW transmitter was activated. In all, the construction project ran some $1.8 million, a tidy sum in those days, and by the mid-seventies the annual operating budgets had reached $1.2 million.

**At RVOG's inauguration on February 26, 1963, technical director Erich Kraemer was tour guide to (from left) LWF president Dr. Franklin Clark Fry, station director Dr. Sigurd Aske, and Emperor Haile Selassie.**   LWF

None of the more than 200 staffers at the station were surprised when it was nationalized in 1977. Indeed, most were thankful that it lasted a full 14 years, given the hostile circumstances under which it labored. For example, Arabic news had to be dropped in 1965 because of tensions in the Middle East, then the Ethiopian government attempted to further rein in the station in 1967. This resulted in tighter government control of Amharic programming and news items concerning Ethiopia. The Lutheran operatives nonetheless insisted on reporting on famine and drought in the early seventies, but the Ethiopian government threatened to shut down the station unless the reports ceased.

The resulting programming prompted the Nigerian government to nickname the station the "Voice of the Devil" during that country's civil war in the late 1960s. Armed troops opposed to the government occupied the station briefly in 1974, but they departed peacefully after RVOG broadcast the rebel's call for public support.

Tensions resurfaced in 1976. The Ethiopian revolution grew more militant, and at times station personnel were arrested and interrogated. The 1977 coup brought a freezing of RVOG's assets and the return of troops. RVOG personnel, including expatriates, were briefly dragooned into operating the station under its new identification—Radio Voice of Revolutionary Ethiopia. Today, it operates as a nationalized state mouthpiece, with nary a trace of the peaceful missionary impulse which gave rise to it.

**An interview with a farmer is conducted at RVOG's area studio, "Sawtu Linjiila," in Ngaoundéré, Cameroon.**   LWF

The Lutherans had to flee Ethiopia, but did not give up on Africa. In 1983 their station was reborn as "Voice of the Gospel," this time using leased airtime over the mighty Afrique Numero Un in Gabon.

# GRUNDIG The Ultim

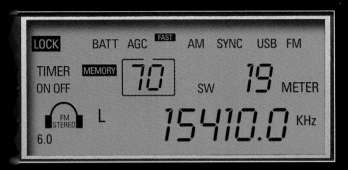

**The LCD Big!** Bold! Brightly Illuminated 6" x 3¹/₂".
Liquid Crystal Display shows all important data:
Frequency, Meter band, Memory position, Time,
LSB/USB, Synchronous Detector and more.

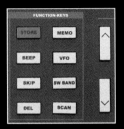

- For Fixed-step Tuning: Big, responsive Up/Down tuning buttons.
- For direct frequency entry: a responsive, intuitive numeric keypad.

**The Signal Strength Meter**
Elegant in its traditional Analog design, like the gauges in the world's finest sports cars. Large. Well Lit. Easy to read.

SATELLIT 800
MILLENNIUM

**The Tuning Controls**
For the traditional-ist: a smooth, precise tuning knob, produces no audio muting during use. Ultra fine-tuning of 50Hz on LSB/USB, 100Hz in SW, AM and Aircraft Band and 20 KHz in FM.

Dimensions: 20.5" L x 9" H x 8" W
Weight: 14.50 lbs.

*"Outstanding Performance...Unbeatable Audio Quality...Unbeatable Price"*

## The Frequency Coverage

Longwave, AM and shortwave: continuous 100-30,000 KHz.
FM: 87-108 MHz
VHF Aircraft Band: 118-137 MHz.

## The Operational Controls

Knobs where you want them; Buttons where they make sense. The best combination of traditional and high-tech controls.

## The Sound

Legendary Grundig Audio Fidelity with separate bass and treble controls, big sound from its powerful speaker and FM-stereo with the included high-quality headphones.

## The Technology

Today's latest engineering:
• Dual conversion superheterodyne circuitry.
• PLL synthesized tuner.

## The Many Features

• 70 user-programmable memories.
• Two 24-hour format clocks.
• Two ON/OFF sleep timers.
• Massive, built-in telescopic antenna.
• Connectors for external antennas – SW, AM, FM and VHF Aircraft Band.
• Line-out, headphone and external speaker jacks.

## The Power Supply

A multi-voltage (110V) AC adapter is included. Also operates on 6 size D batteries.
(not included)

# GRUNDIG

etón Corporation, 1015 Corporation Way, Palo Alto, CA 94303 • Tel: 650-903-3866 • Fax: 650-903-3867
Shortwave Hotlines: (US) 1-800-872-2228 (CN) 1-800-637-1648 • Web: www.grundigradio.com

**A traditional basketweaver practices her craft.**

C. Grant

ment was headed by the iron-fisted Major Mengistu Haile Mariam. The Derg bloodily suppressed all opposition and terrorized the population, making it widely despised.

Finally, in May of 1991, the Derg was overthrown by a coalition of forces. The Tigrayan People's Liberation Front (TPLF), representing the mainly Christian Tigrayan population of northern Ethiopia, took over Addis Ababa. Meanwhile, the Eritrean People's Liberation Front (EPLF) marched victoriously into the Eritrean capital of Asmara.

### Eritrea Gains Independence

Vast changes soon occurred, including an independent Eritrea in 1993 as the result of a UN-supervised referendum allowed by the government. This caused Ethiopia to lose its important trading and military outlet to the sea, a fact that remains a sore point with

many Ethiopians. Soon after, the fundamentalist Eritrean Islamic Jihad, based in Sudan, began attacking Eritrea, which fought back with assistance from the United States, as well as possibly Israel and others. A 1998 border war between Ethiopia and Eritrea further aggravated the situation.

Ethiopia began to be ruled more along ethnic lines. The country was divided into regions, with various indigenous groups being given greater autonomy. This did not sit well with many Amharas, the group that had traditionally ruled Ethiopia.

### Radio Ethiopia Airs Two Services

Nevertheless, the Ethiopian People's Revolutionary Democratic Front (EPRDF), which includes the TPLF, continues to rule Ethiopia. While there is some press freedom, the government has a stranglehold on broadcasting within Ethiopia proper, operating Radio Ethiopia, Radio Fana and Voice of the Tigray Revolution.

Radio Ethiopia, the station's name since 1994, broadcasts a national service using three 100 kW transmitters on 5990, 7110 and 9704 kHz. Broadcasts are in a variety of languages at 0300-0600 (0800 Sundays), 0900-1100 (1400 weekends) and 1500-2000 World Time. English, the lingua franca of East Africa, is heard weekdays at 1030-1100.

The station also operates an external service that goes back to March 12, 1977, the day the government nationalized Radio Voice of the Gospel. Promotional material still includes old RVOG antenna coverage maps, so two of the three external service channels apparently transmit from the old RVOG site south of Addis Ababa.

English is on the external service, too, at 1600-1700, plus French 1700-1800 and Arabic at 1400-1500 on 7165, 9560 and 11800 kHz; national-service broadcasts in Somali and Afar are simulcast on these frequencies at 1200-1400. Some of the external channels were also used in the 1990s for a United Nations service known as the Voice of Peace, targeted at Somalia.

## Ruling Party Stretches Rules

Radio Fana (Torch) started in 1994 as the station of the governing EPRDF party. As Ethiopia changed its media ownership laws in 1999, the station was turned over to MegaNet, a corporation owned by the party. In effect, Radio Fana provides the EPRDF with a national service on world band, even though the country's broadcast laws forbid political parties from owning radio stations.

Broadcasts are from two 10 kW transmitters at Addis Ababa. Programs in various national languages go out weekdays at 0330-0430, 0900-1200 and 1500-1700 World Time on 6210 and 6940 kHz; weekends, it's 0330-0800 and 1100-1800. The lineup ranges from news to entertainment, interspersed with commercials.

## Exiles Go Mainstream

Voice of the Tigray Revolution began in the 1980s as the broadcasting arm of the TPLF. It initially operated from Sudan, but when the TPLF gained power in 1991 the station was moved to Mekele, capital of the Tigray region.

The station continues as the regional voice of the TPLF, and it also airs programs for Eritrea. Two 10 kW units operate, mostly in Tigrinya, on 5500 and 6350 kHz weekdays at 0400-0500, 0930-1030 and 1500-1900 World Time, weekends at 0400-0900 and 1100-1600.

## Cold War's End Brings Opportunity

Part of the Cold War's legacy is the availability of high-powered world band transmitters for hire. Once used for blanketing the airwaves, these leased-time transmitters especially abound in the European Union and former Soviet Union, but are found in other countries, as well.

Exiles around the world have taken advantage of this to get their messages out to a wide audience, and Ethiopians are no exception. They are the most prolific, with nine groups producing professional-caliber programs and raising money to pay for airtime.

## Oromos Beam in from Russia

Take "Radio Voice of Oromiyaa," headed by Mahdi Muudee. This Atlanta, Georgia, software maven uses world band to serve Oromos, the nation's largest ethnic group, in a country otherwise limited to government-controlled media. The program is aired from a hired Russian transmitter every Monday and Thursday at 1730-1800 World Time on 12115 or 12125 kHz.

"Radio Voice of Oromiyaa" has no apparent ties to any particular political party—"We are free and independent," claims Muudee. The station works closely with a similarly named program over American public radio station KFAI-FM in Minneapolis, Minnesota. Its producer, Jelil Abdella, points out that they provide segments for the world band operation.

**Radio UNMEE staff conduct a field interview.**
Radio UNMEE

**Happy children.**

C. Grant

"Radio Voice of Oromiyaa" pays for airtime by passing the hat among the Oromo diaspora in the United States. This has become tougher than at the outset. "It is difficult," Abdella laments, as the initial enthusiasm has worn off.

## Oromo Front Transmits from Germany

"Voice of Oromo Liberation" (VOL) has operated from a number of locations, including Sudan in the early 1990s. It is the mouthpiece of the Oromo Liberation Front (OLF), a rebel group seeking independence for the Oromo region of Ethiopia. The Front continues to fight a low-level guerilla war against the Ethiopian government.

VOL currently purchases airtime on a transmitter in Germany, rather than operating from territory they control in Ethiopia. OLF spokesman Lencho Bati explains, "The liberated zone is not protected enough to broadcast from there."

> **Exiles can compete with the government for audience share.**

Programs are in Oromo, as well as Amharic, the national language of Ethiopia. This allows the OLF to explain its position not only to kinsmen, but also to other ethnic groups. Broadcasts air Wednesdays, Fridays and Sundays at 1700-1800 World Time on 15670 kHz, but this frequency changes periodically—historically, it has been within 15650 and 15795 kHz. At three hours per week, the "Voice of Oromo Liberation" has a more extensive schedule than any other opposition radio.

## Struggle Triggers Dissident Radios

"Dejen Radio" ("Base Radio" in English) was born out of political strife in March 2001, when 12 members of the TPLF's Central Committee were ousted after having challenged the Prime Minister. "Dejen Radio" sided with the dissidents, then inaugurated world band transmissions a few months later.

**Radio Voice of the Gospel administration and studio building, Addis Ababa, Ethiopia.** LWF

**Radio UNMEE presenters read the news.**
Radio UNMEE

Initial broadcasts via Nashville's WWCR under two monikers failed to provide good reception. The group then switched to facilities in western Russia and changed the name to "Dejen Radio," now heard Saturdays at 1700-1800 World Time on 12115 or 12125 kHz. "Having the radio has made such a difference," exults Haile Abeda, senior publisher of the Ethiopian Commentator, parent organization for the programs. "We can now expose the activities of the government."

The station may put a goliath signal into Ethiopia, but the sponsoring group is lilliputian. Ethiopian Commentator has only about ten members, all in the American Midwest, according to Dr. Ghelawdewos Araia, who once wrote for the *Ethiopian Commentator* and is the author of *Ethiopia, A Political Economy of Transition*. Still, somehow they manage to scrape up the funds needed to stay on the air.

"Radio Solidarity" grew out of the same TPLF split as "Dejen Radio," but is tied to the Tigrean International Solidarity for Justice and Democracy (TISJD). Although the two groups cooperate and share many goals, the TISJD allows members of political parties to join. The TISJD is growing rapidly, and its radio program has a substantial audience in Ethiopia. "[That's because] most of the Tigrean people are angry with the government," relates Araia.

The TISJD got over $10,000 from its initial fund-raiser for the station. Its "Radio Solidarity" programs are heard Wednesdays and Saturdays via German facilities at 1600-1630 World Time on 15530 kHz, and they also hope to purchase airtime on a private FM station in Ethiopia, according to station spokesman Dade Desta.

## Station Conceived in Disunity

"Netsanet Radio" was the program of Netsanet-Le, a self-described civic organization. It was essentially identical to a program aired over WUST-AM in Washington, D.C., according to spokesman Bezuwrk Getachew.

"Netsanet Radio" aspired to inform ethnic kinsfolk of events in their country. When asked why so many other groups had been doing the same thing, Getachew replied, "[It] is the lack of unity." Programs were broadcast from a Russian transmission site on Sundays and Wednesdays at 1700-1800 World Time on 12115 or 12110 kHz.

**The Treasury of the Arc of the Covenant, Axum, Ethiopia.**

Sacredsites.com

"Netsanet Radio" stopped broadcasting in June of 2002, as they ran out of money. However, Getachew says that if funding can be put together they are likely to reappear, albeit not necessarily using the same schedule or Russian transmission facilities.

## Broadcasts Linked to Hated Regime

The Medhin party, founded by Goshu Wolde in the mid 1980s, has been rejected by some, as Wolde was foreign minister in the hated Mengistu regime. The party has about 60 Amhara members, according to Dr. Araia.

"Voice of Ethiopian Medhin" is the party's official organ. It can be heard via discreetly leased facilities in Germany on Thursdays and Sundays at 1600-1700 World Time on 15530 or 15670 kHz.

Dr. Ejigou Demissie is also a Medhin member, and has no problem with Wolde's past. In Demissie's view, Medhin and Wolde have the same right to broadcast to Ethiopia as anyone else.

## Red Terror Terrorizes Reds

The Maoist Ethiopian People's Revolutionary Party (EPRP), founded in 1972, suffered mightily during Mengistu's brand of Red Terror in the late seventies. The party's angry remnants, supported by Sudan, then fought the government in a 1980s guerilla war. It now has an estimated 3,000 to 4,000 members, primarily Amharas.

The EPRP's "Voice of Ethiopian Unity"—also known as "Voice of the Democratic Path of Ethiopian Unity"—has a substantial following in the country. It is closely involved with a Washington, D.C., area program, "Hibrit Radio," according to Bellette Fassika, the party's North American representative.

In Fassika's view, the EPRP is a multi-ethnic party struggling against a Tigrayan-dominated society. The broadcasts, via German facilities, can be heard Sundays at 0700-0800 World Time on 21550 kHz, and again on Wednesdays at 1830-1930, winter on 11840 kHz and summer on 15565 kHz.

## Rainbow in Exile

The Amharic station "Keste Demena"—Radio Rainbow—calls itself "the voice of peace and brotherhood." Its parent organization has an equally benign mouthful of a rubric, the "Research and Action Group for

Peace in Ethiopia and the Horn of Africa (RAGPEHA).

RAGPEHA is headed by Dr. Negede Gobezie. He lives in exile in Brussels, and is better known for his involvement in the Coalition of Ethiopian Democratic Forces, which is made up of several Ethiopian opposition parties.

While "Radio Rainbow" does not yet operate a website, it does have more extensive geographical coverage than other opposition radios. It targets Europe as well as Ethiopia, and at one time there were even broadcasts for North America. The schedule is 1900-2000 World Time Fridays on (winter) 11840 and (summer) 15565 kHz for Ethiopia, and for Europe on Saturdays at 0900-1000 (0800-0900 summer) on 6180 kHz, all via judiciously leased transmitters in Germany.

## Ogaden Warriors Seek Split

"Radio Xoriyo"—Radio Freedom—is the voice of the Ogadenia National Liberation Front (ONLF), which is in armed opposition to the Ethiopian government. The ONLF wants the Ogaden region, largely inhabited by ethnic Somalis, to break away from Ethiopia and become part of Somalia. Indeed, Somalia invaded and briefly held the region during a 1977 border war.

"Radio Xoriyo" broadcasts from discreetly leased facilities in Germany on Tuesdays and Fridays at 1630-1700 World Time on 15530 or 15580 kHz. All transmissions are in Somali.

## Robust Outlook for Leased Airtime

World band appears to have a promising future in Ethiopia. It is the only medium that covers the entire country, and almost certainly will remain so for some time unless transmission authorities pull the plugs. It is popular among listeners in neighboring countries, as well, which gives impetus to Radio Ethiopia's external service.

Before the end of the Cold War, Ethiopian exiles couldn't hope to reach listeners throughout their native land, much less Ethiopians abroad. But now, thanks to leased airtime and the dispersal qualities of shortwave, they compete head to head with the Ethiopian government for audience share. Given the assertiveness among Ethiopians expatriates, even more Ethiopian stations may eventually populate the world band airwaves.

---

*A tip of the hat to Adrian Peterson, Adventist World Radio, for his valuable input.*

**www.passband.com**

**This Mursi woman's lip plate is considered a sign of beauty.**   Irma Turtle, Turtle Tours, Inc.

# When Information

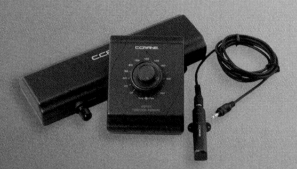

## Justice AM (MW) Antenna

### Twin Coil Ferrite™ – Works With Any Portable Or Stereo Receiver

Doubles Daytime Reception • Reduces Nighttime Fade & Signal Distortion • Antenna Element Can Be Mounted Away From RF Noise

## FM Transmitter

### Transmits Stereo Audio From Any Source To Any Radio

Broadcast From Your Computer, MP3 Player, Portable CD, Cassette, Electric Guitar ... The Possibilities Are Endless

## C.Crane Solar Panel

### Powerful Enough To Run A Radio In Overcast Weather

Works With Most Sangean Radios And RadioShack® Equivalents • Lightweight And Durable • Weatherproof

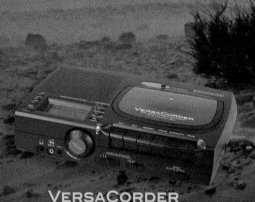

## VersaCorder

### Versatile Dual Speed Tape Recorder

Programmable • Records 4 Hours On One Side Of A Cassette Tape • Built-In Monitor Speaker, Microphone & VOX

# Listen And You'll Know™

RadioShack® is a registered trade mark of RadioShack Corporation; Sangean is a registered trademark of Sangean America, Inc.; 'Listen And You'll Know' and C.Crane are trademarks of C. Crane Company Inc. All rights reserved

# Is Important ...

## SANGEAN ATS505P

### MOST FEATURES & BEST PERFORMANCE FOR THE PRICE!

SUPERB AUDIO QUALITY
• AM/FM/SW/SSB
• 45 MEMORY PRESETS • AUTO MEMORY SEARCH & STORE
• DUAL TIME CLOCK WITH ALARM
• AC ADAPTER & SW ANTENNA INCL.

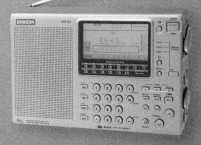

## SANGEAN ATS909

### THE ULTIMATE FEATURES & PERFORMANCE IN A PORTABLE SW RECEIVER!

306 MEMORY PRESETS
• AM/FM/SW/TRUE UPPER & LOWER SSB • AM/FM STEREO THROUGH HEADPHONES • DUAL TIME CLOCK WITH ALARM

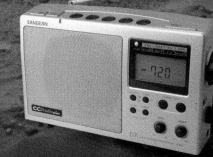

## CCRADIO 'plus'

### THE BEST AM RADIO MADE TODAY!

LONG RANGE AM RECEPTION WITH FM/ TV AUDIO/ WX & NOAA ALERT • ALARM • RECORD TIMER • AM EXTERNAL ANTENNA JACK • AUDIO IN/OUT

## SANGEAN ATS818ACS

### HIGH PERFORMANCE SW WITH BUILT-IN CASSETTE RECORDER/PLAYER

54 MEMORY PRESETS • AM/FM/SW/ SSB • PROGRAMMABLE CASSETTE RECORDER • AM/FM STEREO THROUGH HEADPHONES

## SANGEAN
sangean.com

**C. CRANE COMPANY INC.**
ccrane.com

## FREE
### CATALOG
### 1-800-522-8863

# Eritrea: Africa's Newest Nation

## by Hans Johnson

Eritrea sailed into the 20th century as a palmy Italian colony, complete with period European architecture and a strong infrastructure. By the early 1930s the number of Italian immigrants had risen to more than 70,000, but this was not enough for Italy's *duce*, Benito Mussolini. In 1935, in a precursor to later Axis conquests, he used his colony as a springboard for the invasion and occupation of Ethiopia. The successful campaign resulted in both countries being combined with Italian Somaliland to form Italian East Africa.

Ironically, it was World War II which brought liberation of a sort, thanks to the efforts of British and indigenous forces. Later, in 1947, a peace agreement between Ethiopia and

Italy was to decide the status of Eritrea within a year, but nothing came of it.

The decision thus fell to the United Nations, which in 1952 decided that federation with Ethiopia was the best course. The shotgun marriage lasted only ten years, after which Eritrea became a mere province of Ethiopia. Their patience worn thin, Eritreans stepped up the fight for independence.

## Strategic Location Attracts Outsiders

In the mid-1930s, the Mussolini regime established Radio Marina, a naval station in the Eritrean capital of Asmara. Because radio signals propagate unusually well into and from Eritrea, in 1943 the United States began to use Radio Marina as a military-intelligence post to relay military radio signals, as well as to receive radio signals from afar—eventually including outer space.

Later called Kagnew Station, but originally still operating as Radio Marina, this 2,200-3,400 acre facility saw service until April 29, 1977, when the Americans were shown the door. Although much of Kagnew's mission revolved around military communications, from July 1, 1951 it included the mediumwave AM station AFSA, part of the United States Armed Forces Radio Service. Initial power was a mere 50 Watts, rising in 1958 to 150 Watts, then 200 Watts in 1963, down to 100 Watts in 1964, and up to a full kilowatt in 1971. Later came KANU-TV and FM.

## Struggle Unites Disparate Groups

Eritrea is approximately the size and population of Louisiana, roughly 4.5 million, and is comparably divided between Christians and Muslims. Numerous ethnic groups inhabit the country, but Eritrean nationalism

**The President, Isaias Afewerki, strolls into the street. Immediate traffic jam.**   B. Holdsworth

**Mussolini Started Eritrea's First Station.**

Opposite: At the Asmara Stadium, schoolgirls celebrate the anniversary of the 30 year Revolution.
B. Holdsworth

Revolutionary murals celebrate Eritrea's struggle for independence.
B. Holdsworth

## "VOICE OF PEACE AND DEMOCRACY OF ERITREA"

Unlike Ethiopia, where several disestablishmentarian stations broadcast into the country from abroad, Eritrea has just two opposition radios beaming in from beyond its borders.

"Voice of Peace and Democracy of Eritrea" airs its programs over a 10 kW facility at Mekele, Ethiopia, used at other times for domestic broadcasts of the local station, Voice of the Tigray Revolution.

One group behind these broadcasts is thought to be the Democratic Movement for the Liberation of Eritrea (DMLE), a resistance force that broke away from the Eritrean Libera-

tion Front (ELF). According to John Young, author of an authoritative history of the Tigre People's Liberation Front (TPLF), the DMLE was organized in the mid-1980s with extensive backing from the TPLF, which then continued to work closely with its new ally.

"Voice of Peace and Democracy of Eritrea" has used the Mekele facility since February 1999, and is a tough catch outside East Africa. It transmits Mondays to Saturdays in Tigrinya and Kunamigna at 0315-0400 and 1415-1500 World Time on 5500 and 6350 kHz.

**The Danakil Depression—hotter than Death Valley.**  B. Holdsworth

### "Voice of Democratic Eritrea"

With a burst of staccato machine-gun fire for effect, the "Voice of Democratic Eritrea" (VODE) surfaced in the fall of 1997. World band listeners regularly heard the station from as far away as California, as the VODE was using powerful transmitters in Sudan. In all likelihood, these were part of the Sudanese national radio station.

VODE was the official voice of the Eritrean Liberation Front-Revolutionary Council (ELF-RC), a large Eritrean opposition group. Several years earlier, the ELF-RC had lost out when the Eritrean People's Liberation Front seized power in 1991 and two years later gained independence for Eritrea.

The ELF-RC, seeking a fresh role, became a convenient proxy for Sudan when its relations with Eritrea deteriorated in the mid-1990s. This marriage of convenience ended on May 2, 1999, when Sudan and Eritrea signed a peace treaty requiring both countries to end clandestine broadcasts directed at one another.

**The EPLF fortified Mt. Denden with some 400 kilometers of trenches.**  B. Holdsworth

A low-level ELF-RC presence continues to be tolerated by the Sudanese government, but the group stresses that it no longer receives any Sudanese support. Reduced to the status of bystander, the ELF-RC took nearly a year to resume its world band transmissions, using leased airtime on a German transmitter starting in June 2000. The machine gun dramatics were dropped, and the program's name was tweaked to "Voice of Democratic Eritrea International."

**The Catholic Cathedral on Asmara's Liberty Avenue, the main drag.**  B. Holdsworth

This operation is funded exclusively by ELF-RC members and supporters, according to Seyoum O. Michael, ELF-RC International Relations Chief. Apparently the ELF-RC also produces the programs, as they sound less professional than when they were from Sudanese facilities.

Michael insists that the ELF-RC has not broadcast from Ethiopia. However, the ELF-RC is not a monolithic block. Although Michael's faction apparently has not operated from Ethiopia, other factions may have.

Feedback is mostly by email, although some comes in by post. In addition to their world band broadcasts, the ELF-RC is involved in a number of local radio shows in Europe and the United States. These include the Alliance of Eritrean National Forces programs over a Washington, D.C. AM station—the Alliance is an opposition front made up of a number of groups, including the ELF-RC.

Broadcasts, in Arabic and Tigrinya, are for Eritrea, the Middle East and North Africa, as well as Europe. Eritrea, Africa and the Middle East are served on Mondays and Thursdays at 1700-1800 World Time on 15670 kHz, while those for western Europe are on Saturdays at 1500-1600 winter (1400-1500 summer) on 5925 kHz. Ironically, renting a 100 kW transmitter provides the ELF-RC with more sophisticated world band facilities than the Eritrean government has at its disposal.

**High noon, siesta time in the Red Sea port of Massawa.**
B. Holdsworth

**Women celebrate the shooting down of an Ethiopian jet that attempted to bomb Asmara's airport.**

B. Holdsworth

united them in their goal to achieve independence.

For many years, the leading group opposing Ethiopian rule was the Eritrean Liberation Front (ELF). Inevitably there were splits within the organization, most notably in 1970 when the group which was to become the Eritrean People's Liberation Front (EPLF) broke away from the ELF. It was the EPLF which then became the driving force for Eritrean independence.

## Radio on the Run

The Voice of the Broad Masses of Eritrea (VOBME), now the country's official and only broadcaster, started life as a clandestine station transmitting from the Eritrean bush. Known locally by its Tigrinyan name of Dimtsi Hafash, its maiden broadcast took to the air in January 1979. In those early days VOBME was often literally on the run in order to escape Ethiopian shelling.

The EPLF found the VOBME to be a decisive tool capable of reaching almost every Eritrean. As a goodwill gesture, it also aired programs from kindred groups opposed to the Mengistu regime in Ethiopia, such as

the Tigre People's Liberation Front (TPLF). Yet, there were tensions between the EPLF and the TPLF. So, in the spirit of no good deed going unpunished, it wasn't unheard of for the TPLF to criticize the EPLF over the EPLF's own VOBME transmitter.

In the early 1990s the remaining Ethiopian-held territory in Eritrea fell to opposition forces. Once *de facto* independence was achieved in 1991, VOBME moved out of the bush and into more permanent quarters in the Eritrean capital of Asmara.

## Station Boosts Power

Transmitter powers were modest at first, 2 kW and 10 kW, but the mid-1990s brought relief in the form of two 100 kW units. These greatly improved reception in neighboring countries.

The new transmitters were needed, as relations with Sudan were becoming tense. Each accused the other of trying to destabilize it, with Sudan supporting groups trying to install an Islamic state in Eritrea. Eritrea, for its part, supported groups in southern Sudan that opposed the Arab-Muslim dominated government in Khartoum.

## Independence Leads to Ethiopian Jamming

The United Nations quickly recognized Eritrea after a 1993 nationwide referendum where the Eritreans chose independence. However, Eritrea's falling from the grasp of Ethiopia was resented by a number of Ethiopians. Like Mussolini in mirror-image, they saw Eritrea as an integral part of their country.

There was also concern that the "loss" of Eritrea would be, like falling dominoes, the first step in a wider dismemberment of Ethiopia. Relations between the two countries grew worse, with clashes in 1998 escalating into a full-scale war the next year.

During that border war, VOBME began to be the target of jamming by Ethiopia, which broadcast simultaneously on VOBME frequencies. The Eritrean station apparently did not respond with the usual countermeasures, even though world band excels at overcoming jamming. Ethiopia's deliberate interference came to an abrupt end in 2000, right after a cease-fire was declared. Two years later, the United Nations formally demarcated the border.

In spite of the end of hostilities, there still isn't much media freedom in Eritrea—the VOBME remains the only broadcaster on national soil. It transmits in Amharic, Oromo, Tigre, Arabic and Tigrinya at 0300-0600 and 1400-1830 World Time on 7100 and 7175 kHz. It is widely heard in Europe, and occasionally is picked up by DXers in North America.

## UN Creates Radio UNMEE

Eritrea and Ethiopia agreed to a cease-fire in mid-2000, and United Nations peacekeepers entered the region soon afterwards. The UN Mission in Eritrea and Ethiopia (UNMEE) has several objectives, including monitoring of the cease-fire and delimiting the border. Over 4,000 troops from some 40-odd countries make up the force.

Radio UNMEE is part of that mission. Its broadcasts started from the local facilities of the Voice of the Broad Masses of Eritrea in January 2001, and were free of charge. World band transmissions were twice a week in English, Tigrinya, Tigre and Arabic on 7100 and 7175 kHz.

The original agreement was that Radio UNMEE would also broadcast, free of charge, via Radio Ethiopia's facilities. However, the Ethiopian government and UNMEE have yet to come to terms, so these facilities have never been used.

In time, VOBME started insisting on payment because of wear and tear to the station's facilities, and also hit up UNMEE for spare transmitter parts. The UN demurred, so the broadcasts were terminated in October, 2001. UNMEE continued to negotiate with both countries to return the program to the air, but only on the basis that it would be transmitted free of charge.

Unsuccessful in its negotiations with either government, in April 2002 Radio UNMEE went through VT Merlin Communications to lease a facility in the United Arab Emirates. Merlin, privatized and spun off from Britain's BBC, is now a subsidiary of VT Group plc, and is the largest broker for leased-time shortwave transmissions throughout the world. Not long after the Merlin agreement, VOBME saw the light and resumed carrying Radio UNMEE. Negotiations continue with Radio Ethiopia.

Radio UNMEE airs via the UAE Tuesdays at 0430-0530 World Time on 15235 kHz (15215 kHz summer), and Fridays at 1900-2000 on 13670 kHz (13735 kHz summer); in addition to the languages inaugurated in 2001, the station has added Oromo. UNMEE also uses VOBME facilities Wednesdays at 0700-0800 on 7100 kHz. Plans call for the UN to remain in the region until all border demarcation issues are wrapped up, so Radio UNMEE should remain active until at least that time.

# GRUNDIG  Keeps

## The Best AM/FM/SW Radio on the Planet!

**Satellit 800**

### Yacht Boy 400PE

This is a true high-performance receiver offering the best performance available in its class. You will hear international broadcasts from around the world on shortwave, including broadcasts and communications requiring SSB circuitry. Listen to shortwave on its built-in telescopic antenna or connect it your favorite external antenna. But do not think it is just for shortwave. Its superior sensitivity and selectivity make it the best choice for anyone needing superior AM and FM performance in weak-signal and fringe areas. Perfect for pulling in those distant, hard to get AM talk shows that are so popular today.
DIMENSIONS: 7.75˝ L x 4.5˝ H x 1.5˝ W
WEIGHT: 1 lb. 5 oz.

Suggested list price:  US $ 149.99

### Yacht Boy 300PE

Designed with remarkable performance at an incredibly low price, the YB300PE receives world wide international short-wave broadcasts as well as your local AM and FM-stereo stations. Great for either travel or home use, it is small enough for large pockets or carry-on luggage and takes up little space on your desk. Use the alarm clock feature to wake you up in the morning and the sleep timer to lull you asleep at night.
DIMENSIONS: 5.75˝ L x 3.5˝ H x 1.25˝ W
WEIGHT: 12 oz.

Suggested list price:  US $ 79.99

### Grundig Porsche Design G2000A AM/FM/SW Radio

Wake up to sports and talk radio on AM, soothing stereo (with earphones) on FM or fascinating shortwave from around the world… select from 13 International bands from 2.3 - 7.4 and 9.4 - 26.1 MHz. Punch in any station or lock your favorites into 20 memories… other features include digital clock and alarm with Quartz accuracy… earphones… butter-soft handcrafted leather case. Designed by F.A.Porsche, the G2000A is a pleasure to own and operate. Uses 3 AA batteries (not included).
DIMENSIONS:  5.5˝ L x 3.5˝ H x 1.375˝ W
WEIGHT:  11.52 oz.

Suggested list price:  US $ 99.99

# the World Informed!

The Satellit 800. In the history of shortwave receivers, no other manufacturer has maintained a continuously evolving series of high-end portable radios, decade after decade.

**Extensive frequency coverage.**
- Long wave, AM-broadcast and Shortwave, 100-30,000 KHz, continuous.
- FM broadcast, 87-108 MHz.
- VHF aircraft band, 118-137 MHz.
- Multi-mode reception – AM, FM-stereo, Single Sideband USB/LSB and VHF aircraft band.

**The right complement of high-tech features.**
- Three built-in bandwidths, using electronically switched IF filters: 6.0, 4.0, 2.3 KHz.
- Synchronous detector for improved quality of AM and shortwave broadcast signals, minimizes fading, distortion and adjacent frequency interference.
- Selectable AGC in fast and slow mode.
  Auto Backlight shutoff to conserve battery life. Low Battery Indicator.

**Engineered for the best possible reception.**
- High Dynamic Range, allowing for detection of weak signals in the presence of strong signals.
- Excellent sensitivity and selectivity.

**Legendary Grundig audio.**
- Outstanding audio quality, with separate bass and treble tone control.
- FM Stereo with headphones or external amplified stereo speakers.
- Includes high quality stereo headphones.
- Multiple audio outputs: line level output for recording, stereo headphone output.

**Information displayed the way it should be.**
- Large, illuminated, informational LCD display of operational parameters, measuring a massive 6˝ x 3½˝, easy to read.
- An elegant, calibrated, analog signal strength meter, in the finest tradition.
- Digital frequency display to 100 Hertz accuracy on AM, SW and VHF aircraft bands. 50 Hz when SSB used.

**Traditional and high-tech tuning controls.**
- A real tuning knob, like on traditional radios, but with ultra-precise digital tuning, with absolutely no audio muting when used.
- A modern, direct-frequency-entry keypad for instant frequency access, and push buttons for fixed-step tuning.

**Plenty of user programmable memory.**
- 70 programmable memories, completely immune to loss due to power interruptions. • Memory scan feature.

**Clocks and timers.**
- Dual, 24 hour format clocks. • Dual programmable timers.

**Antenna capabilities that really make sense.**
- Built in telescopic antenna for use on all bands.
- External antenna connections for the addition of auxiliary antennas, e.g. professionally engineered shortwave antennas; long-wire shortwave antennas; specialized AM broadcast band antennas for enthusiasts of AM DX'ing; FM broadcast band antennas; VHF air band antennas.

**Power, dimensions, weight.**
- Operation on six internal "D" cell batteries or the included 110V AC adapter (a 220V AC adapter is available upon request).
- Big dimensions and weight. A real radio.
  20.5˝ L × 9.4˝ H × 8˝ W., 14.5 lb.

Suggested list price: US $ 499.99

## CLASSIC 960 AM/FM/SW RADIO

FM Stereo/AM/Shortwave Radio. Remember when radio sounded so real that voices were almost with you in the room? When music had a warm, rich, full-bodied tone? Those wonderful days are back! Grundig has revived its legendary Model 960. The long-lost sound is back. The 3˝ side speakers, left and right, spread a spacious stereo image, while a front-firing 4˝ speaker reinforces the bass and fills your listening room with glorious Grundig sound. The cabinet is solid wood.

The Grundig New Classic 960 is your listening post that lets you travel the globe without ever leaving home.
DIMENSIONS: 15.5"W x 11.25"H x 7"D
WEIGHT: 9 lbs. 10 oz

Suggested list price: US $ 199.99

## FR200 EMERGENCY AM/FM/SW RADIO

Be prepared and stay informed with the FR200 from Grundig. If the power goes out and batteries aren't available, the FR200 can operate for one hour with just one minute of cranking. Its built-in generator means that even in the most desperate situations, you can still have access to local news and information as wells as to news from around the world.
DIMENSIONS: 6.75"W x 5.75"H x 2.125"D
WEIGHT: 1 lbs. 5 oz. Suggested list price: US $ 39.99

**(R) RadioShack.**®
You've got questions. We've got answers.
1-800-843-7422 or www.radioshack.com

# Sudan: Millions Perish in Strife

*by Hans Johnson*

Nearly half again as large as Alaska, Sudan is immense and varied, with 30 million inhabitants geographically clustered by ethnicity. To the north are Arab Muslims who traditionally dominate the country, while in the south it is solidly black—some Muslim, others Christian or animist.

After independence from the United Kingdom in 1956, coups and counter-coups became a way of life for Sudan. In one such instance, in 1969, Colonel Gaafar Nimeiri seized power. This resulted in an exacerbation of the off-and-on guerilla struggle in the south, which originated in 1955 and lasted until a 1972 peace agreement was signed in Addis Ababa.

The second conflict started in 1983. The triggers were the then-Nimeiri government's imposition of Islamic law, and the division of the south into three provinces ruled from Khartoum. This balkanization was especially egregious, as it violated the 1972 accords stipulating that the south would be a single autonomous region. The discovery of oil in the area only raised the stakes.

Nimeiri was overthrown in 1985. His overthrowers were, in turn, themselves overthrown in 1989 by the National Islamic Front (NIF), which to this day maintains a shaky hold on power from Khartoum.

Civil strife has showed signs of ending, possibly motivated in part by American interest in Sudan's oil reserves. The rebels and government recently agreed on a framework for a comprehensive peace settlement, but how this will ultimately work out remains to be seen.

Southern insurgents have been powerful enough to hold the country-side, but not the major towns. Like the government, they lack the military might to take over the entire country—a situation compounded by intense infighting among rebel forces. The result has been a bloody stalemate in which two million have perished and twice that number have been displaced while the world has averted its gaze. Sudan's economy, potentially wealthy, remains a basket case—the "African disease," writ in dystopian chapters.

## Shelters Bin Laden, Supports Saddam

In recent years Sudan has been a thorn in the side of the American government. It was a quasi-ally of Iraq during the Gulf War, and also snuggled up to Iran. Harboring Osama bin Laden until 1996 and supporting international terrorism for much of the 1990s further alienated Sudan from exasperated American policymakers.

The Clinton administration finally spent some $20 million trying to overthrow the NIF regime in the mid and late 1990s, and Sudan's

**Some of the Dinka people are still slaves.**

Insart.com

**Sudan has been a bloody stalemate in which two million have perished.**

**Opposite: These women personify the desperate straits of the Sudan.**

Radio Voice of Hope

**Slave group Wedweil.**

Insart.com

In Sudan, where war is a part of life, it pays to be prepared. Here a man demonstrates the use of his "hiding hole," also known as a bomb shelter.

BASIC Ministries, Inc.

continuing involvement in terrorism resulted in an American cruise missile strike in 1998. The American government also provided some $3 million in logistical aid to the opposition National Democratic Alliance in early 2001.

Sudan finally moved away from its terrorist links in the wake of the World Trade Center and Pentagon attacks. The current Bush administration has taken an active role in trying to solve the civil war, appointing a special envoy and promising to take a balanced approach. So far, a partial cease-fire has been achieved, but an end to the conflict continues to be elusive.

## Radio Neglects Southern Concerns

Radio Omdurman, sited in a city adjacent to the capital of Khartoum, emerged in 1940 with two hours of broadcasts daily. In 1960, according to *Broadcasting in Africa*, the U.S. Agency for International Development gave the station two 50 kW world band transmitters, but these reached only part of the country. (The Transmitter Documentation Project does not allude to this but states, instead, that two 20 kW Marconi transmitters were activated by Radio Omdurman in 1957.)

Worse, Radio Omdurman acted not as a national voice, but rather as an Arab Muslim outlet that deigned to transmit in languages of the black south only once, during the first civil war. With peace in 1972, Radio Omdurman returned to its exclusively Arabic roots, according to Sudan expert Wendy James at Oxford University.

It took the start of the second civil war in 1983 to awaken Radio Omdurman out of its Arab-centric slumber. John Gerang, an ethnic Dinka and southerner, formed the Sudan People's Liberation Army (SPLA), which took up arms against the government.

Gerang also started "Radio SPLA." With a powerful signal and slick programming, the station gave the government a real scare. The Sudanese authorities attempted to jam the signals, as well to air "black" propaganda by airing similar-sounding music mixed with a very different message. They also created National Unity Radio, which transmitted in English and southern languages in direct response to "Radio SPLA."

"Radio SPLA" died a slow death in the mid-1990's; when it went off, so did National Unity Radio. Although Khartoum has jammed other anti-Sudanese clandestines, it has not created any comparable radio services in response to them.

Radio Omdurman also played a role in the second civil war, attempting to motivate the population against the SPLA. This peaked in 1991 when Radio Omdurman put a 100 kW Harris transmitter on the air. Another transmitter of unknown power also appeared at this time, allowing the station to be easily heard on 7200 and 9165 kHz.

In 1992, the NIF started enforcing a long-ignored decree limiting the types of music that could be played. Songs not glorifying Islam or the NIF were banned, and the popular program "Good Morning My Country" was yanked off the air. Ironically, it was that same Radio Omdurman which had given rise to the prominence of Sudanese popular music during World War II.

Age and a lack of maintenance have taken their toll—Radio Omdurman is now harder to hear on world band than most of the anti-Sudanese clandestines. One transmitter formerly on 9200 kHz appears to be off, while on 7200 kHz the signal has become enfeebled. The station is officially on at 0200-0730 and 1600-2200 World Time in Arabic, save for an hour each of French and English at 1600-1800.

## "Millennium Voice"/"Voice of the Horn"

In addition to Radio Omdurman, a number of Sudanese opposition stations are alive and kicking.

Take one shadowy anti-Sudanese government operation which took to the air in November 2001, identifying in English as "Millennium Voice" and in Arabic as "Voice of the Horn." The strange English identification results not from adamantine concerns, but rather from inventive translation.

Sources close to the operation claim that content is primarily religious in nature, intended for much of Africa. While there was some general African programming

initially, this line ultimately doesn't square with the anti-Sudanese-government programs being broadcast now. For example, it airs interviews with officials of the National Democratic Alliance (NDA) and other leading lights of the Sudanese opposition—scarcely religious fare. The "religious" claim also doesn't jibe with the station's initial email address at a German-based newspaper, *Voice of Eritrea*, which appears to side with the Eritrean government.

*Voice of Eritrea's* editor, Abdulkadir Hamdan, agrees that he had helped the station by hosting an email address, but hasn't explained why his organization had ties to an anti-Sudanese-government station. When queried by PASSPORT, he initially reiterated the claim that "Voice of the Horn" is a service for all of Africa, but eventually admitted that anti-Sudanese-government forces operating out of London have ties to the service, and offered to contact them. Nevertheless, the exact backing and funding of "Millennium Voice" continue to lie hidden in the shadows.

Programs are predominantly in Sudanese Arabic, although occasionally there can be

**These Sudanese insurgents are Christians.**

In Jesus' Name Ministries

**Cassava flour offered for sale in the open market, Yei, Sudan.**  BASIC Ministries, Inc.

Asmara. He adds that the station suffers sporadic deliberate interference from Sudanese government transmitters.

The station changed its name to "Voice of New Sudan" in the spring of 2002. More than just a new appellation, it purports to reflect the philosophy of a Sudan free of ethnic, religious and similar divisions. The station's staff, after all, comes from an admixture of Sudanese opposition groups, including the SPLA, the Federal Party and the Beja Congress.

"Voice of New Sudan" airs Saturdays through Thursdays at 0300-0400 and 1400-1500 World Time, Fridays at 0500-0700. Although all transmissions are nominally on 7000 kHz, the frequency sometimes moves slightly to give government jammers the slip.

smatterings of English. These are aired Monday and Friday at 1330-1430 World Time on 21550 kHz from a transmitter at one of the various VT Merlin Communications sites in the United Kingdom.

### "Voice of New Sudan"

The Sudan Alliance Forces (SAF) is led by Abdel Aziz Khalid, an ex-Sudanese army paratrooper. It occupies territory in eastern Sudan, and has close ties to John Gerang's SPLA. The SAF also airs "Voice of New Sudan," known as "Voice of Freedom and Renewal" when it first went on the air in 1998.

The SAF purchased a 10 kW world band transmitter from Enery-Onix in New York, where station engineers received their training, according to Bernie Wise, the company's president. SAF claims that the transmitter is in Sudanese territory occupied by them, but Wise insists that it was actually installed in Asmara, Eritrea.

"Our broadcasts are in Arabic and local languages, and are intended for Sudan, the Horn and eastern Africa," according to Tijani Al-Hajd, SAF policy secretary in

### "Radio SPLA"

Beginning in 1983, the SPLA had access to the old Voice of the Gospel world band facilities in Addis Ababa, Ethiopia. Thanks to these, "Radio SPLA" put out a tremendous signal. Programs were in the languages of southern Sudan, and were very professional sounding.

This came to a halt when the Mengistu regime in Ethiopia was overthrown in 1991. According to Sudan experts Wendy James and Douglas Johnson, "Radio SPLA" then sporadically used its own modest mobile transmitter in Sudan until 1995, when they gained access to more powerful NDA facilities in Asmara which were used until 2000. Official SPLA communiqués have vowed to bring back "Radio SPLA," and John Gerang stated that the station would return in 2002. However, thus far there has been no sign of it.

### "Voice of Sudan" *vs.* al Qaeda

The National Democratic Alliance (NDA) grew out of the 1989 coup in Sudan. It is an umbrella group of several Sudanese opposition parties, and had a large operation on world band radio from 1995 until 2000.

"Voice of Sudan" grew out of an American and Eritrean attempt to destabilize the Sudanese government, which was sheltering al Qaeda operatives. From facilities in Asmara, the "Voice of Sudan" used as many as three different transmitters, simply overwhelming government attempts to jam.

The station vanished in 2000 with the end of American aid and the loss of its support base as Eritrea improved relations with Sudan. The NDA approved a plan to resume broadcasting from "liberated areas of Sudan" in April 2002, but the date came and went in silence. What the future holds remains to be seen, but the group has managed to receive limited funding from the Bush Administration.

**Starvation is an ongoing problem in the Sudan.**

In Jesus' Name Ministries

## "Radio Voice of Hope"

One man's humanitarian station is another's clandestine, and so it is with "Radio Voice of Hope." It is funded by the Dutch government and various Dutch Christian and media groups, while the New Sudan Council of Churches actually runs the station.

Supporters see the broadcasts as giving a "voice to the voiceless," as the official government station in Khartoum doesn't broadcast in languages of the south or address their concerns. Ironically, "Radio Voice of Hope," billed as a peace station, sees itself as a replacement for the rebel "Radio SPLA," which although the station of an insurgent group is the best mouthpiece Sudanese southerners ever had. Yet, even while supporters insist "RVOH" is an honest broker attempting to achieve peace, critics see it as a mere puppet of the SPLA.

"Radio Voice of Hope" can be heard Saturday in Arabic, English and vernaculars at 0330-0430 World Time on 12060 and 15320 kHz. Broadcasts emanate from Radio Netherlands facilities in Madagascar.

## Foggy Future

Sudan's move away from sponsoring terrorism may have saved the Khartoum government from military intervention led by the United States. With Sudan's shift away from support of terrorism, the Bush Administration has appeared to be lightening up. But although it has more important issues on its plate, there are still signs that the American government would like to see a lasting peace in Sudan.

World band will probably continue to be active in the region, and possibly expand. For starters, the NDA and SPLA are likely to return to the world band airwaves, and the government would not be far behind if that happens.

Professor James has noted that stations involved in the conflict have been directing their programs away from a mass listenership and towards the elite power players of the world. Given the length of this conflict, this may make sense. Although the Sudanese people have suffered exceptionally, they have little ability to end the turbulence. It is the powerful in Sudan who must achieve lasting peace.

Special thanks to *Clandestine Radio Watch*, Mathias Kropf and Ludo Maes/TDP.

# GRUNDIG

## YACHT BOY 300PE AM/FM/SW RADIO

Designed with remarkable performance at an incredibly low price, the YB300PE receives world wide international shortwave broadcasts as well as your local AM and FM-stereo stations. Great for either travel or home use, it is small enough for large pockets or carry-on luggage and takes up little space on your desk. Use the alarm clock feature to wake you up in the morning and the sleep timer to lull you to sleep at night.

- Coverage: SW 2.3-7.8 MHz and 9.1-26.1 MHz, covering all 13 international short-wave broadcast bands. FM: 87.5 - 108MHz. AM: 520 - 1710 KHz.

- LCD displays time, frequency, and memory station.

- Display light for momentary illumination.

- Digital PLL synthesized receiver.

- Direct frequency entry system for instant access to stations.

- 24 station memory presets.

- Sleep timer and alarm.

- FM/SW 360 degree rotary telescopic antenna / MW ferrite far antenna.

- External antenna jack for improved shortwave reception.

- Includes: AC adaptor, carrying strap, case, earphones, and three AA batteries.

DIMENSIONS: 5 3/4"W x 3 1/2"H x 1 1/8"D

WEIGHT: 10 oz.

THE WORLD AT YOUR FINGERTIPS.

Y A C H T   B O Y   3 0 0 P E

*"Outstanding Performance...Unbeatable Audio Quality...Unbeatable Price"*
Lawrence Magne, *Editor-in-Chief, Passport to World Band Radio*

## YACHT BOY 400PE AM/FM/SW RADIO

This is a true high-performance receiver offering the best performance available in its class. You will hear international broadcasts from around the world on shortwave, including broadcasts and communications requiring SSB circuitry. Listen to shortwave on its built-in telescopic antenna or connect it to your favorite external antenna. But do not think it is just for shortwave. Its superior sensitivity and selectivity make it the best choice for anyone needing superior AM and FM performance in weak-signal and fringe areas. Perfect for pulling in those distant, hard-to-get AM talk shows that are so popular today.

- PLL synthesized tuning for rock-solid frequency stability.
- FM-stereo with headphones or external powered speakers.
- No tuning gaps in its shortwave receiver mean that all frequencies can be accessed.
- Single sideband (SSB) circuitry for reception of shortwave long distance two-way communication such as amateur radio, marine and aeronautical.
- Randomly programmable memory presets allow for quick access to favorite stations.
- The LCD shows display of time, frequency, band, automatic turn-on, and sleep timer.
- Liquid crystal display (LCD) shows time and clock/timer modes / Dual alarm modes: beeper & radio / Dual clocks show time in 24 hour format /Sleep timer programmable in 10 minute increments to 60 minutes.
- Phase-lock-loop tuning.
- Tunes both upper and lower sideband with infinite tuning.
- User selectable tuning steps: 1khz/5khz in SW; 1khz/9khz/10khz in MW; 1khz/9khz in LW.
- User selectable wide/narrow bandwidth filter.
- DX/Local switch.
- Hi/Low tone option.
- Switchable 9khz/10khz scan rates on MW (the AM broadcast band) for use in both North America and Europe.
- FM-stereo with mono option.
- Telescopic antenna for FM and shortwave reception / Built-in ferrite antenna for MW and LW /External antenna for shortwave can be connected via the built-in receptacle.
- Includes: carrying case, earphones and AC adaptor for North American use.

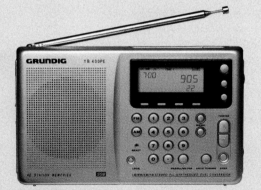

DIMENSIONS: 7 3/4"W x 4 5/8"H x 1 3/8"D

WEIGHT: 1 lbs. 5 oz.

UNSURPASSED POWER, PERFORMANCE & PORTABILITY.

Y A C H T   B O Y   4 0 0 P E

## GRUNDIG

etón Corporation, 1015 Corporation Way, Palo Alto, CA 94303  •  Tel: 650-903-3866  •  Fax: 650-903-3867
Shortwave Hotlines: (US) 1-800-872-2228  (CN) 1-800-637-1648  •  Web: www.grundigradio.com

# Somalia: Clans Clash by Radio

*by Hans Johnson*

With a strategic location at the junction of the Red Sea and Indian Ocean, Texas-sized Somalia has long been of interest to foreign colonizers and occupiers. The Portuguese and the Sultan of Zanzibar established coastal bases as early as the 15th and 16th century, while in 1886 the British founded a protectorate centered around the city of Hargeysa. The Italians were only a couple of decades behind, setting up a nearby separate colony with Mogadishu as its capital.

The onset of World War II brought brief Italian rule to both the British and Italian colonies, but it was short-lived. The British quickly returned in 1941, threw out the Italians and occupied both colonies. After the war ended, the Allies were supposed to decide the fate of Somalia. They didn't, so the matter was turned over to the United Nations, which reestablished Italian rule during a transition period.

## Rival Warlords Squash Democracy

In 1960, British Somaliland became independent, and five days later it joined with the newly independent Italian Somaliland to become the unified nation of Somalia. Democracy lasted until a 1969 coup by Major General Siyad Barre, who declared Somalia to be a socialist state the following year.

Somalia invaded Ethiopia in 1977 as part of a campaign to support ethnic Somalis in the Ogaden region of Ethiopia. Ethiopia, backed by Cuban troops and Soviet aid, recaptured Ogaden a year later. But as Barre's rule grew more despotic in the 1980s, competing tribal clans became openly defiant. By 1990, leading figures in Mogadishu were calling for Barre's resignation, and the next year he fled in exile to Nigeria. Somalia plunged into chaos.

Factional fighting commenced between transitional President Ali Muhammad and General Muhammad Farah Aydid, a former army chief of staff who also saw himself as president. Normal life in Mogadishu came to a standstill, while regions such as Somaliland and Puntland simply broke away from the country and became de facto autonomous regions. The country fractured along clan boundaries, then crumbled further along sub-clan lines.

## American Troops Sustain Casualties

The threat of mass starvation prompted an American-led UN intervention in 1992, but the grisly death of U.S. Army Rangers a year later prompted a withdrawal. Numerous cease-fires have since been declared, but never obeyed.

**The decorative art of henna.** U.N. Somalia

**Somalia plunged into chaos.**

**This Somali Air Force MiG-21 fighter appears to be airworthy.** M. Toal

**Sam Voron, one of the founders of Radio Galkayo, at its original location in the dingy Galkayo Police Station.**

S. Voron

A Transitional National Government (TNG) was set up in 2000, but it still lacks a firm grip on the country. Indeed, without a world band transmitter the government has no means of reaching the population, so it makes do with an FM transmitter in Mogadishu. That effort has been less than successful.

## Radio Mogadishu, Veteran Player

World band radio is in a constant state of flux, with stations coming and going. A group dominated by a warlord or other political faction will obtain equipment, make a sudden appearance, then disappear. These brief cycles seemingly result from equipment failure and a lack of funding.

But some stations have been around for decades. The Italians set up "Experimental Radio of Mogadishu" in 1951 with a 0.2 kW transmitter. This unit was unreliable, so a 4 kW PTT unit was often used instead.

Italy also installed a 5 kW unit in 1959, while Russia provided a 50 kW transmission facility in 1965. This provided good overseas reception, but the Soviet antennas weren't as effective for domestic coverage, so the 5 kW transmitter remained in service. In addition to programs in Somali, the station had two-hour program blocks in English, Arabic, Amharic and Oromifa.

Suleiman M. Adam, who wrote the seminal work on the early years of Radio Mogadishu and Radio Hargeysa, *Gather Round the Speakers*, states that during the Barre regime Radio Mogadishu was used as a propaganda tool to promote socialism. After Barre fled, the facilities were captured and operated by self-declared president Muhammad Aydid. He eventually settled on the name of Radio Mogadishu, Voice of the People (Masses).

## U.S. Air Force Avenges Pakistani Killings

Aydid's strong opposition to the UN intervention in Somalia eventually made the station a target. U.S. Air Force AC-130 gunships destroyed it with cannon fire after the death of 24 Pakistani UN peacekeepers. Aydid rigged up a telephone exchange in Mogadishu as a replacement station, and by July was on the air with a 1 kW transmitter in reduced-carrier upper sideband. This mode is audible on ordinary cheap portables, so it was quickly emulated by other groups.

After General Aydid died in 1996, his son took over the faction and continued to use the station. As with other Somali outlets, operation was irregular. Press reports indicate that the facility was refurbished in early 2001, with a new manager being appointed to put greater emphasis on world band broadcasts.

Radio Mogadishu can be heard at 0300-0500, 0900-1100 and 1500-1900 World Time in the vicinity of 6750 kHz.

## Rival Warlords Air "People's Voice"

Not to be outdone, Mogadishu warlord Muse Sudi Yalahow also has a station, located in the Medina section of the city. Known as "The People's Voice," it started test trans-missions in 2000. While all sorts of claims have been made about the prowess of this station, it was actually captured from Ali Mahdi Muhammad, who in 1992 started its operation from the Kaaran district of north Mogadishu. Once an ally of Yalahow, Muhammad allowed his station to fall into Yalahow's lap during a clash in 1999.

The exact schedule for "The People's Voice" is uncertain, but appears to be 1600-1900 World Time somewhere between 6500 and 6900 kHz.

## Radio Banadir Now Commercial

Radio Banadir Broadcasting (RBB) bills itself as a non-partisan commercial station, and publicizes the usual boilerplate about supporting democracy and human rights. It is located in north Mogadishu, but *Banadir* is the Somali word for the greater Mogadishu region. Commercial rival HornAfrik maintains that Banadir started as the voice of warlord Hussein Haji Bod, and has only recently become a commercial operation.

RBB claims to have taken to the air in 1997, but that apparently refers to the FM part of the station. Enterprising Somalis living in Canada took an initial world band transmitter to Somalia in 1999 after first testing it from Germany. Along the way, the station also obtained a second world band transmitter.

RBB states that it operates at 0600-2200 World Time in both the 6 and 7 MHz segments (49 and 41 meters), but it has only been heard operating on an oft-changed frequency around the edges of the 7 MHz segment.

Currently, it is heard at 1530-1900 on 7002 kHz. The 6 MHz segment is too crowded for effective monitoring of this transmission, and the station manager claims to have no idea of what frequency is being used. At 2.5 kW, the main transmitter is impressive by Somali standards, but in reality it operates at only 0.5 kW.

## Chieftain Seizes Transmitter

Rounding out the roster of stations in Mogadishu is "Radio Voice of Pacification," located in the city's south. In spite of the lofty moniker, it is controlled by warlord Uthman Ali Ato, who made his money off an earlier Somali oil boom. He initially sided with the Aydid faction, but by 1995 they were openly feuding.

Ato's station came on the air that same year. According to the article "Broadcasting in East Africa," it has neither a proper studio nor its own transmitter. Instead, it uses Racal equipment captured from the military

**From the balcony of Edna Aden Hospital in Hargeysa is Edna Aden herself, founder of the very successful hospital.**  U.N. Somalia

# GRUNDIG

## Satellit 800 The Best AM/FM/SW Radio on the Planet!

The Satellit 800. In the history of shortwave receivers, no other manufacturer has maintained a continuously evolving series of high-end portable radios, decade after decade.

**Extensive frequency coverage.**
- Long wave, AM-broadcast and Shortwave, 100-30,000 KHz, continuous.
- FM broadcast, 87-108 MHz.
- VHF aircraft band, 118-137 MHz.
- Multi-mode reception – AM, FM-stereo, Single Sideband USB/LSB and VHF aircraft band.

**The right complement of high-tech features.**
- Three built-in bandwidths, using electronically switched IF filters: 6.0, 4.0, 2.3 KHz.
- Synchronous detector for improved quality of AM and shortwave broadcast signals, minimizes fading, distortion and adjacent frequency interference.
- Selectable AGC in fast and slow mode.
  Auto Backlight shutoff to conserve battery life. Low Battery Indicator.

**Engineered for the best possible reception.**
- High Dynamic Range, allowing for detection of weak signals in the presence of strong signals.
- Excellent sensitivity and selectivity.

**Legendary Grundig audio.**
- Outstanding audio quality, with separate bass and treble tone control.
- FM Stereo with headphones or external amplified stereo speakers.
- Includes high quality stereo headphones.
- Multiple audio outputs: line level output for recording, stereo headphone output.

**Information displayed the way it should be.**
- Large, illuminated, informational LCD display of operational parameters, measuring a massive 6″ x 3½″, easy to read.

- An elegant, calibrated, analog signal strength meter, in the finest tradition.
- Digital frequency display to 100 Hertz accuracy on AM, SW and VHF aircraft bands. 50 Hz when SSB used.

**Traditional and high-tech tuning controls.**
- A real tuning knob, like on traditional radios, but with ultra-precise digital tuning, with absolutely no audio muting when used.
- A modern, direct-frequency-entry keypad for instant frequency access, and push buttons for fixed-step tuning.

**Plenty of user programmable memory.**
- 70 programmable memories, completely immune to loss due to power interruptions. • Memory scan feature.

**Clocks and timers.**
- Dual, 24 hour format clocks. • Dual programmable timers.

**Antenna capabilities that really make sense.**
- Built in telescopic antenna for use on all bands.
- External antenna connections for the addition of auxiliary antennas, e.g. professionally engineered shortwave antennas; long-wire shortwave antennas; specialized AM broadcast band antennas for enthusiasts of AM DX'ing; FM broadcast band antennas; VHF air band antennas.

**Power, dimensions, weight.**
- Operation on six internal "D" cell batteries or the included 110V AC adapter (a 220V AC adapter is available upon request).
- Big dimensions and weight. A real radio. 20.5″ L × 9.4″ H × 8″ W., 14.5 lb.

Suggested list price: CAN $599.99

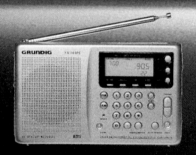

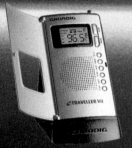

## Yacht Boy 400PE

This is a true high-performance receiver offering the best performance available in its class. You will hear international broadcasts from around the world on shortwave, including broadcasts and communications requiring SSB circuitry. Listen to shortwave on its built-in telescopic antenna or connect it your favorite external antenna. But do not think it is just for shortwave. Its superior sensitivity and selectivity make it the best choice for anyone needing superior AM and FM performance in weak-signal and fringe areas. Perfect for pulling in those distant, hard to get AM talk shows that are so popular today.
DIMENSIONS: 7.75″ L x 4.5″ H x 1.5″ W
WEIGHT: 1 lb. 5 oz.

Suggested list price: CAN $ 199.99

## eTRAVELLER VII AM/FM/SW RADIO

With its superior dual conversion superheterodyne circuitry for optimal sensitivity and selectivity, all-band continuous shortwave coverage, AM/FM and FM stereo, the eTraveller VII is the smallest fully digital radio in its class. Measuring only 2 1/2" x 4 1/2" x 7/8", its sleek smooth design fits into your pocket, briefcase or purse. And, at only 5.3 ounces, it will never weigh you down. Its beautiful platinum color with black accents, combined with practical rubberized side panels, make it both practical and pleasurable to own and operate.
DIMENSIONS: 2.5"W x 4.5"H x .825"D
WEIGHT: 5 lbs. 3 oz.

Suggested list price: CAN $ 99.99

## Grundig Porsche Design G2000A AM/FM/SW Radio

Wake up to sports and talk radio on AM, soothing stereo (with earphones) on FM or fascinating shortwave from around the world… select from 13 International bands from 2.3 - 7.4 and 9.4 - 26.1 MHz. Punch in any station or lock your favorites into 20 memories… other features include digital clock and alarm with Quartz accuracy… earphones… butter-soft handcrafted leather case. Designed by F.A.Porsche, the G2000A is a pleasure to own and operate. Uses 3 AA batteries (not included).
DIMENSIONS: 5.5" L x 3.5" H x 1.375" W
WEIGHT: 11.52 oz.

Suggested list price: CAN $ 129.99

## CLASSIC 960 AM/FM/SW RADIO

*New*

FM Stereo/AM/Shortwave Radio. Remember when radio sounded so real that voices were almost with you in the room? When music had a warm, rich, full-bodied tone? Those wonderful days are back! Grundig has revived its legendary Model 960. The long-lost sound is back. The 3" side speakers, left and right, spread a spacious stereo image, while a front-firing 4" speaker reinforces the bass and fills your listening room with glorious Grundig sound. The cabinet is solid wood.

The Grundig Classic 960 is your listening post that lets you travel the globe without ever leaving home.
DIMENSIONS: 15.5"W x 11.25"H x 7"D
WEIGHT: 9 lbs. 10 oz

Suggested list price: CAN $ 249.99

## FR200 EMERGENCY AM/FM/SW RADIO

Be prepared and stay informed with the FR200 from Grundig. If the power goes out and batteries aren't available, the FR200 can operate for one hour with just one minute of cranking. Its built-in generator means that even in the most desperate situations, you can still have access to local news and information as wells as to news from around the world.
DIMENSIONS: 6.75"W x 5.75"H x 2.125"D
WEIGHT: 1 lbs. 5 oz    Suggested list price: CAN $ 49.99

 **RadioShack**®
You've got questions. We've got answers.™
1-800-668-4433 or www.radioshack.ca

A 1997 Somaliland exchange between staff at Galkayo and Hargeysa. The van contains the original Radio Hargeysa valve operated station, active during the war in which Hargeysa was overrun by Mogadishu government troops.

S. Voron

or police, and is powered by a generator in Ato's compound.

In addition to programs in Somali, mainly for Ato's clan and followers, the station has short segments in Arabic and English. "RVOP" has an irregular schedule, but is usually heard at 1500-1900 World Time on 6847 kHz.

## Enthusiasts, Oxfam Assist "Radio Galkayo"

Broadcasting from north-central Somali is "Radio Galkayo," located in the autonomous state of Puntland established in 1998. Puntland does not recognize the TNG.

"Radio Galkayo" owes a lot to foreign assistance. It was set up in 1993 by the enigmatic Australian Sam Voron and his International Amateur Radio Network (IARN), a controversial organization within the amateur radio community. Voron installed a transmitter with a 0.8 kW amplifier and fed it into a log periodic antenna.

The whole arrangement worked splendidly for a number of years, but by 2000 the station was down to a feeble 125 Watts. High winds and wear had rendered the log

periodic antenna inoperable, putting "Radio Galkayo" in danger of going off of the air.

Cumbre DX, a shortwave radio club, teamed up with IARN to purchase spare parts for the station. Voron traveled to Galkayo after the spares arrived, installed them and performed other maintenance to allow the transmitter to function reliably at 125 Watts.

Oxfam Canada has also contributed $34,000, according to Ramon Genesse, Horn of Africa Capacity Builder Program Manager. Additionally, Oxfam provides training support and sends staff to international community radio conferences.

IARN returned in 2002 to purchase and install a 0.8 kW linear amplifier to boost transmitter output. However, the station's manager for many years, Hassan Mohammed Jama, doesn't believe that a mere 800 Watts is adequate for covering all of Puntland. This low power may not provide adequate coverage, but without such outside assistance "Radio Galkayo" would never have been on the air, let alone lasted ten years.

A leadership struggle broke out in the spring of 2002. Jama Ali Jama, selected by clan elders as the leader of Puntland, was thrown out by Colonel Abdullahi Yusuf Ahmed. One of Ahmed's first actions was to close down a

Bossasso station he disagreed with, but "Radio Galkayo" has backed Ahmed, as he is originally from Galkayo.

"Radio Galkayo" is on the air at 1000-1200 and 1600-1700 World Time on 6985 kHz. Like all Somali stations, it changes frequency slightly from time to time.

## Radio Hargeysa, Somalia's Original Station

In 1941, the British set up Radio Kudu, a 0.1 kW radio station in Hargeysa with programs in English, Arabic and Somali. A 0.6 kW transmitter was installed in 1944, whereupon the station renamed Radio Somali. Four years later this was replaced by a 1 kW unit, but reception was still limited until a 5 kW transmitter was installed in 1957. As most Somalis couldn't afford a radio, the colonial authorities built up the audience by establishing public listening centers in major towns.

Operating on 7120 kHz, the original Radio Hargeysa was destroyed in fighting in 1988. However, the Somali National Movement (SNM) operated a station which eventually morphed into a reincarnated Radio Hargeysa for the self-declared "Republic of Somaliland." Originally it used an amateur radio transmitter of about 1 kW, but it has been slightly easier to hear since receiving unspecified technical assistance from Yemen in 1999 (the BBC World Service has also been providing training and assistance).

In the spring of 2002, the government banned all private broadcasting, making Radio Hargeysa the only legal station in "Somaliland." Radio Omdurman, Sudan's state broadcaster, also offered to set up an FM station in Hargeysa to carry Radio Omdurman and Radio Hargeysa.

Radio Hargeysa can be heard at 0330-0530, 1000-1200 and 1430-1900 World Time on 7530 kHz in the reduced-carrier upper sideband mode.

**Some of Radio Galkayo's staff pose in front of the station's transmitting equipment.**   S. Voron

## "Radio Baidoa" Short of Funds

Somalia's south has been home to "Radio Baidoa," mouthpiece of the Rahaweyn Resistance Army (RRA). First noted in 1999, the station used equipment imported from Australia, according to Mohammed Rashid, who provides an Internet presence for the station. Rashid claims that the transmitter is still on the air, but it hasn't been noted in over a year by Western monitors. Historically, the station has had trouble finding money to run its generators.

It was last heard on 6810 kHz at 1500-1800 World Time.

**Putting up Radio Galkayo's directional antenna in 1994.**
S. Voron

**Sam Voron reports a 100% pass rate at the Somali ham exams. All technical staff and announcers passed, resulting in 24 new Somali hams.**   S. Voron

World band will almost certainly continue to play a role, but Somalis seem to be increasingly willing to set up private FM stations within the country, rather than broadcast from abroad as do Ethiopian exiles. This inherently diminishes the political role of radio, as Somali FM stations exist mostly to advertise to a local market. For any force to exert an influence over the entire country, it will need world band. Somalia is just too large and poor for any other medium to reach all Somalis anytime soon.

A likely candidate for world band would appear to be the TNG, but for now it has enough problems trying to control Mogadishu without worrying about the rest of the country. Should it receive international support to help it have power over the whole country, look for it to initially lease world band airtime abroad, followed by construction of indigenous facilities.

### FM Shows Near-Term Promise

Short of a major Western intervention or backing of the TNG, Somalia will probably continue to plod along. Enterprising Somalis can provide infrastructure improvements, but it remains to be seen whether they can also provide political stability.

_____

*Special thanks to Suleiman M. Adam, Wolf Harranth, Radio Austria International; also, Chris Greenway/BBC Monitoring and Sam Voron.*

## UNICEF SOMALI RADIO'S BEST CUSTOMER

UNICEF has a strong relationship with a number of Somali radio outlets. With the demise of UNICEF's Voice of Peace service for Somalia, these ties have only strengthened.

UNICEF places paid spot ads and radio programs on several stations, educating the public on such topics as immunization. "It is part of our social mobilization campaign," explains Julia Spry-Leverton, UNICEF Somalia Communications Officer. Paying hard currency not only for spots, but also for entire blocks of airtime, UNICEF is Somali radio's best paying customer.

Radio Hargeysa, "Radio Galkayo," "Radio Banadir" and "Voice of the People" are the world band broadcasters that currently work with UNICEF. "While a lot of stations come and go, these are the most stable," relates Juma Magara, Program Communications Officer. UNICEF has also conducted training courses in radio journalism for employees of some of these stations.

While UNICEF pays for the airtime, they are not anyone's fool. Monitors in Somalia check to ensure that spots and programs are actually played, according to Magara.

# Quality Communications Equipment Since 1942

## COMMERCIAL RECEIVERS

**TEN-TEC**

The Ten-Tec RX-340 is *the* ultimate receiver! Advanced D.S.P. technology at under $4000.

## WIDEBAND RECEIVERS & SCANNERS

**YAESU**   **AOR**   **uniden** Bearcat

**ALINCO**

**ICOM**

Universal offers an extensive line of new and used scanners and wideband receivers from all major manufacturers including: Alinco, AOR, ICOM, Yaesu and Uniden-Bearcat. The AOR AR8200MkIIB and Yaesu VR5000 are shown.

## UNIVERSAL M-450v1.5

The **Universal M-450v1.5** reader displays: **RTTY, SITOR, FEC-A, ASCII, SWED-ARQ** and **Weather FAX** (to the printer port) plus the **ACARS** aviation teletype mode. DTMF, CTCSS and DCS are also supported. Features a big two-line, 20 character LCD and parallel port. Operates from 12 VDC or with the supplied AC adapter. No computer or monitor is required. Made in the U.S.A. *#0450*   **$399.95**

## AMATEUR RADIO EQUIPMENT

**ICOM**   **ALINCO**

**YAESU**

**KENWOOD**   **JRC**

Universal has been selling the finest new and used amateur radio equipment since 1942 and is an authorized sales and service center for all major lines.

## HUGE FREE CATALOG

The **Universal Communications Catalog** covers everything for the shortwave, amateur and scanner enthusiast. With prices, photos and informative descriptions. This 100 page catalog is **FREE** by bookrate or for $3 by Priority mail (5 IRCs airmail outside N. America). Rising postage costs prevent us from sending this catalog out automatically so request your copy today!

## Universal Radio, Inc.
**6830 Americana Pkwy.**
**Reynoldsburg, Ohio**
**43068-4113 U.S.A.**

☎ 800 431-3939   Orders & Prices
☎ 614 866-4267   Information
→ 614 866-2339   FAX Line
✉ dx@universal-radio.com

## COMMUNICATIONS RECEIVERS

**JRC**   **YAESU**

**DRAKE**

**AOR**

**ICOM**

Universal Radio carries an excellent selection of new and used communications receivers. JRC NRD-545 shown.

## PORTABLE RECEIVERS

**GRUNDIG**
**SONY**
**ICOM**
**SANGEAN**

Universal Radio offers over 40 portable receivers from $50 to over $500. The Sangean ATS-909 is shown. Universal also carries **factory reconditioned Grundig** shortwave radios at a substantial savings.

## BOOKS

**Shortwave Receivers Past & Present** *By F. Osterman*
This huge 473 page guide covers over 770 receivers from 98 manufacturers, made from 1942-1997. Entry information includes: receiver type, date sold, photograph, size & weight, features, reviews, specifications, new & used values, variants, value rating & availability. Become an instant receiver expert. *#0003*   **$24.95**

**Passport To Worldband Radio** *By L. Magne*
Graphic presentation of all shortwave broadcast stations. Equipment reviews, too. A *must have* book. *#1000* **$19.95**

**World Radio TV Handbook**
All shortwave broadcast stations organized by country with schedules, addresses, power, etc. *#2000*   **$24.95**

**Worldwide Aeronautical Frequency Dir.** *By R. Evans*
The definitive guide to commercial and military, HF and VHF-UHF aero comms. including ACARS. *#0042*   **$14.98**

**Guide to Utility Stations** *By J. Klingenfuss*
Simply the best guide to non-broadcast stations. 11,600 frequencies CW, SSB, AM, RTTY & FAX. *#4363*   **$39.95**

**Discover DXing!** *By J. Zondlo*
An introduction to DXing AM, FM and TV. *#0019*   **$5.95**

**Joe Carr's Receiving Antenna Handbook** *By J. Carr*
Arguably the best book devoted to receiving antennas for longwave through shortwave. *#3113*   **$19.95**

U.S. orders under $100 ship for $4.95, under $500 for $9.95.

**www.RFfun.com** *or*
**www.universal-radio.com**

- Mastercard   • Prices and specs. are subject to change.
- Visa • JCB   • Returns subject to a 15% restocking fee.
- Discover      • Used equipment list available.

**Visit our operational showroom near Columbus, Ohio**

# Ten of the Best: 2003's Top Shows

World band is a feast for news hounds, but there are also one-of-a-kind shows rarely found elsewhere. Here are ten of the best, as selected by PASSPORT's monitors. "What's On Tonight," farther back in this edition, details all world band programs in English.

Times and days are in World Time, while "winter" and "summer" refer to seasons in the Northern Hemisphere.

**"NewsLink"**
**Deutsche Welle**

Deutsche Welle's "NewsLink" gathers no moss. Its 24 minutes trot along briskly, with easily digested reports on German and European topics often not covered elsewhere—sometimes with a European press review. Interviews and reports get straight to the point, and presentation is top notch. If you have an interest in Europe—or just want to hear worthwhile news that's not boring—this is where to park your dial.

For *North America* the show airs Tuesday through Saturday (local weekday evenings in the Americas). First slot is 0105, winter on 6040, 6145, 9640, 9700 and 9765 kHz; and summer on 6040, 9640, 11810 and 13720 kHz. A second airing is at 0305, winter on 6020, 6045, 9640, 9700 and 11985 kHz; and summer on 9535, 9640, 11935 and 15105 kHz. The third and final opportunity (best for western North America) is at 0505, winter on 5960, 6120, 9670 and 11795 kHz; and summer on 9670, 9785 and 11985 kHz. For night owls, the 0905 edition for Australasia on 9510 kHz is also heard throughout much of North America.

*Europe* has four weekday slots: 0905, 1105 and 1605 on 6140 kHz; and 2005 on (winter) 6180 or (summer) 6140 kHz.

There's nothing specifically aimed at the *Middle East*, but try 21560 kHz at 0905 Monday through Friday winter.

*Southern Africa* has three choices. The first is at 0405 Tuesday through Saturday, winter on 9565 and 9710 kHz; and midyear on 6180, 7225, 12045 and 13690 kHz. A second can be heard Monday through Friday at 0905, winter on 15410 and 17860 kHz; and midyear on 12035, 15410, 17800 and 21780 kHz. The final edition goes out weekdays at 1605, winter on 15455 and 21840 kHz; and midyear on 9735, 11665 and 21840 kHz.

> **With Charlie Gillett at the helm, the BBC's "World of Music" is now a great earful.**

Best for *East Asia* is 0905 weekdays, winter on 9770 kHz and summer on 15470 kHz. *Southeast Asia* gets three bites. The first is at 0905 Monday through Friday, winter on 17820, 17845 and 21790 kHz; and summer on 17715, 17770, 17820 and 21790 kHz. The second airing is 12 hours later at 2105 (Tuesday through Saturday in the target area), winter on 9765 and 15275 kHz; and summer on 9670, 9765 and 12035 kHz. The third and final opportunity is at 2305, winter on 9470, 9815, 9940 and 13690 kHz; and summer on 9815, 12000, 17560 and 21790 kHz.

In *Australasia* tune in weekdays at 0905, winter on 6160, 9510 and 17820 kHz; and midyear on 6160, 9510, 17715, 17770 and 21790 kHz. A second broadcast goes out at 2105 (Tuesday through Saturday in the target area), winter on 9690, 9765, 15275 and 17560 kHz; and midyear on 9670, 9765 and 12035 kHz.

## "World of Music"/"Charlie Gillett"
## BBC World Service

The ultimate extravaganza of world music is still the Canadian Broadcasting Corporation's "Global Village" (PASSPORT 2002, pp. 46-47), but

**Charlie Gillett chooses a selection for the BBC's "World of Music," while journalist Paul Fisher looks on.**

Philip Ryalls, BBC

the BBC World Service's "World of Music" offers a different twist. After years under the baton of the venerable Andy Kershaw, the program then lost its way when it was changed to a mix of music and documentary.

"World of Music" has now bounced back with Charlie Gillett at the helm. Unlike "Global Village," the tone is subdued, and there are no interviews, backup stories or excerpts from live events. All music is taken off CDs, including unreleased demos, and the result is arguably even more eclectic than its Canadian counterpart.

Whether it's Arto Tuncboyaciyan, The African Divas or a little Cybertropic Chilango Power, it's a great earful. When Gillett takes an occasional break, Kershaw steps in with his own brand of excellence.

Decisions by World Service program planners are almost always incomprehensible to listeners trying to keep track of favorite shows. For those already confused by seven different program streams—and seasonal adjustments for Daylight Saving Time in three streams—a major program reshuffle for summer 2002 probably left them in a complete daze. And this was less

than a year after drastic transmission cutbacks to the Americas and Australasia.

Gillett came out better than most. His show was switched to different days, but many times remained the same. There's no guarantee there won't be yet another BBC juggling act for 2003, but for now this is the schedule:

Best for eastern *North America* are 1430 Monday on 15190 kHz; 0130 Tuesday (Monday evening local American date, and one hour earlier in summer) on 5975 and 12095 kHz; and 0405 Wednesday (0305 in summer) on 5975 kHz. In western North America, try the Tuesday edition on 9525 kHz winter and 11835 kHz summer; and the Wednesday slot on 6135 kHz winter, and 11835 kHz summer. Another option for the West Coast is 1530 Monday on 9740 kHz.

*Europe* has three picks—all one hour earlier in summer, but on the same channels year round. Winter times are 0930 Monday on 12095 and 15485 kHz; 1930 Monday on 6195 and 9410 kHz; and 0405 Wednesday on 9410 kHz.

The *Middle East* gets two opportunities, with the same setup as Europe; both are one hour earlier in summer, with the same frequencies. Winter airings are 0830 Monday on 17640 kHz, and 1730 the same day on 15565 kHz.

*Southern Africa* gets two Monday slots: 0730 on 6190 and 11940 kHz; and 1930 on 3255, 6190 and 12095 kHz.

In *East Asia*, tune in at 0230 Monday on 15280 and 15360 kHz; 1530 Monday on 6135, 6195 and 9740 kHz; and 0630 Tuesday on 15360, 17760 and 21660 kHz. For *Southeast Asia* it's 0230 Monday on 15360 kHz; 1530 the same day on 6195 and 9740 kHz; and 0630 Tuesday on 11955 and 15360 kHz.

There's officially nothing for *Australasia*, but reception at 1530 Monday on 9740 kHz, and 0630 Tuesday on 11955 kHz usually provides decent reception.

# UPDATE YOUR LISTENING SCHEDULES MONTHLY WITH MONITORING TIMES, *the* leading shortwave magazine.

### If it's on the radio, it's in *Monitoring Times*!

Do you own a radio, a shortwave receiver, a scanning receiver, or a ham radio? Then *Monitoring Times*® is your magazine! Open a copy of *MT*, and you will find 92 pages packed with news, information, and tips on getting more out of your radio listening. In fact, it's the most comprehensive radio hobby magazine in the U.S., and you can have it all for only $26.95 per year!

*But that's not all...* if you have a computer, then you need...

### ... *MT EXPRESS!*

Now you can receive the world's favorite monitoring magazine over the Internet! No postal delays and no lost or torn issues. And you can get every issue faster – anywhere in the world – than U.S. postal subscribers!

For a mere $19.95 (U.S. funds), or only $11 if you have a print subscription, MT Express delivers to your computer – in brilliant color – the entire Monitoring Times magazine in PDF format.

Free software lets you navigate through the magazine or click from the index, even search by keywords! Print it out on your computer printer, or use compatible text readers for the visually impaired.

**MT EXPRESS** on-line subscription: US **$19.95** (or US **$11** for current print subscribers)

*Receive your free sample now by visiting http://www.monitoringtimes.com*

### Annual Subscription Rates to Print Version

U.S. Second Class Mail, US $26.95
U.S. First Class Mail, US $57.95
Canadian Surface Mail, US $39.50
Canadian Air Mail, US $51.50
Foreign International, US $58.50
Foreign Air Mail, US $88.95

6 month, 2 year, and 3 year subscriptions available.

Sample copy available in Europe for US$4.75 (allow six weeks for delivery).

* International broadcasting program schedules
* World hotbed frequencies
* Shortwave and Longwave DXing
* Satellite broadcasting
* Pirate and clandestine stations
* Two-way communications
* Listening tips from the experts
* Frequency lists and loggings
* News-breaking articles
* Exclusive interviews
* New product reviews
* Feature articles
...and much, much more!

**CALL NOW!**

Published by Grove Enterprises, Inc.

# 800-438-8155

**www.grove-ent.com**
828-837-9200  fax: 828-837-2216
7540 Highway 64 West
Brasstown, NC  28902

Or you can order by emailing order@grove-ent.com with a Visa, Mastercard or Discover

## "Aural Tapestry"
## Radio Netherlands

Culture is never going to get top spot in any listeners' survey, but it has a tireless following among a noteworthy segment of international listeners. The BBC World Service and the Voice of Russia are known for their cultural shows, but Radio Netherlands has the winning format. It has garnered prestigious awards from radio festivals from New York to China, and for good reason.

"Aural Tapestry" is not for mass audiences, but if you're interested in exotica like Livonian poetry, the letters of Van Gogh or a Dutch author addicted to Greek music, you'll feel as if you finally found a home. The deft hand of producer David Swatling brings subjects to life, blurs traditional boundaries and—to quote the show's opening words—interweaves art, history and culture.

"Report from Austria" producer Kerry Skyring and reporter Joanna King at the Johann Strauss monument in Vienna.    ROI

Downside? "Aural Tapestry" has traditionally been aired only from April to October, but for 2003 it starts on the last Sunday in March.

In *North America*, easterners can tune in at 1100 Sunday or 1130 Thursday on 5965 kHz; and 0030 Sunday and 0000 Thursday (Saturday and Wednesday evenings, local date) on 6165 and 9845 kHz. For *western North America* choose from 1530 Sunday or 1500 Thursday on 15220 kHz; and 0500 Friday on 6165 and 9590 kHz.

Slots for *Europe* are at 1100 Sunday and 1130 Thursday on 6045 and 9860 kHz.

In *Southern Africa,* expect a rock-solid signal at 1900 Sunday and 1930 Thursday on 6020 kHz.

For *East* and *Southeast Asia* it's 1100 Sunday and 1000 Thursday on 12065 and 13710 kHz. *Australasia* has the same slot, but on 9790 kHz. Channels for Asia also provide good reception in parts of Australasia.

## "Report from Austria"
## Radio Austria International

Reporting of national news is nearly a rule among international broadcasters. Indeed, stations like Radio Australia and Radio Canada International tend to overdo it, while others go into statistical overload trying to drumbeat their country's progress.

"Report from Austria," an in-depth look at events in this Central European country, avoids these pitfalls. This long-running program, formerly daily, now airs only five days a week, and content is strictly national. However, regional news is covered weekends by "Inside Central Europe," a joint production of Radio Austria International, Radio Prague, Radio Polonia, Radio Budapest and Radio Slovakia International.

Start times vary, but are usually around three minutes into the broadcast.

Sadly, in *North America* the show is only available for the East. Winter, tune in at

0230 Tuesday through Saturday (local weekday evenings in North America) on 7325 kHz; summer, one hour earlier, it's on 9870 kHz.

*Europe* has a total of five opportunities: Monday through Friday winter at 1230 and 1430 on 6155 and 13730 kHz, and 1930 and 2130 on 5945 and 6155kHz; with an additional airing at 0630 Tuesday through Saturday on 6155 and13730 kHz. Summer, all are one hour earlier, but on the same winter frequencies.

There is no broadcast for Southern Africa, but listeners in the *Middle East* can listen at 0630 Tuesday through Saturday (one hour earlier in summer) on 17870 kHz.

For *East Asia* and *Australasia*, it's 1230 Monday through Friday winter on 21770 kHz, and one hour earlier summer on 21780 kHz.

**Paul Rans, author of "Music from Flanders."**

Radio Flanders International

## "Music from Flanders"
## Flanders Radio International

Flanders Radio International is like a favorite car: predictable, comfortable, an old friend. So it's no surprise that its weekend "Music from Flanders" is an unostentatious 25 minutes of pleasure.

The Flemish have a long and diverse musical heritage, including classical, jazz and folk. Belgian folk music is little known outside of western Europe, but "Music from Flanders" gives it welcome airplay. Work songs, sea songs, centuries-old ballads, dance tunes and drinking songs—these all have a surprising appeal, and you won't hear them on MTV. Although the fiddle and accordion are heard most, there's no shortage of other instruments like the mandolin, dulcimer, flute, tambourine—even bagpipes and the hurdy-gurdy!

Timing for eastern *North America* is 2230 Saturday, winter on 13700 kHz and summer on 15565 kHz. Listeners farther west get their opportunity five and a half hours later at 0400 Sunday, winter on 11985 kHz and summer on 15565 kHz.

Broadcasts for *Europe* are Saturday: winter at 0800 on 5985, 13685 and 15195 kHz; and 1830 on 9925 and 13685 kHz. In summer, 0700 on 5985 kHz; and 1730 and 1930 on 9925 and 13690 kHz. For the *Middle East* there's a Saturday slot on 13710 kHz, winter at 1830 and summer one hour earlier.

Saturday is also the day in *East* and *Southeast Asia*: 1230 winter and 1130 summer on 9865 kHz. Reception is sometimes possible in western parts of Australia.

**John Peel came to the BBC by way of Texas, Oklahoma and a pirate radio station.** BBC

## "The Alternative"/"John Peel"
## BBC World Service

Few realize that the BBC's John Peel, with his trademark British accent, cut his broadcasting teeth at WRR radio in Dallas, Texas. He

# GRUNDIG

## YB 550PE AM/FM/SW RADIO

The Yacht Boy 550PE combines form and function to deliver an excellent shortwave listening experience. This radio is designed to make listening to shortwave broadcasts as quick and simple as possible. With 100 memory presets available to store international frequencies, the Yacht Boy 550PE makes it simple to access broadcasts within seconds.

- Receives shortwave continuously FM: 87.0-108 MHz, AM: 531-1602 KHz and 520-1710 KHz, SW: 1711-29999 KHz.
- Signal strength indicator.
- Six tuning methods.
- Auto turn off at low battery/battery indicator.
- Direct digital keypad tuning.
- Illuminated multifunction LCD display.
- 100 user-set station memories.
- Shortwave autoscan tuning.
- AM/FM (FM stereo with earphones).
- Clocks/Sleep timer.
- Radio or buzzer alarm.
- Titanium-look finish.
- Telescopic antenna.
- Dynamic micro speaker.
- Earphone jack.
- Handy travel case.
- 9-volt Grundig AC adapter.

DIMENSIONS: 3 1/2"W x 5 3/4"H x 1 3/8"D

WEIGHT: 1 lbs. 5 oz.

THE ULTIMATE PORTABLE SHORTWAVE RADIO.

Y A C H T    B O Y    5 5 0 P E

*"Outstanding Performance...Unbeatable Audio Quality...Unbeatable Price"*
Lawrence Magne, *Editor-in-Chief, Passport to World Band Radio*

# eTRAVELLER VII AM/FM/SW RADIO

With its superior dual conversion superheterodyne circuitry for optimal sensitivity and selectivity, all-band continuous shortwave coverage, AM/FM and FM stereo, the eTraveller VII is the smallest fully digital radio in its class. Measuring only 2 1/2" x 4 1/2" x 7/8", its sleek smooth design fits into your pocket, briefcase or purse. And, at only 5.3 ounces, it will never weigh you down. Its beautiful platinum color with black accents, combined with practical rubberized side panels, make it both practical and pleasurable to own and operate.

- Frequency Range: FM 87.5 - 108 MHz, AM 530-1710 KHz, SW 2-10 MHz & 11-30 MHz.

- Tuning controls: Up/Down tuning buttons, autoscan & manual tuning.

- 30 Memory presets with memory scan.

- Ferrite bar (internal) for AM, telescopic for FM.

- Dual conversion superheterodyne AM and SW circuitry.

- 24-Hour clock, alarm (radio or beep), and sleep timer.

- Included: 2 AA batteries, AC Adapter, travel pouch, desk stand, shortwave listening guide, earphones.

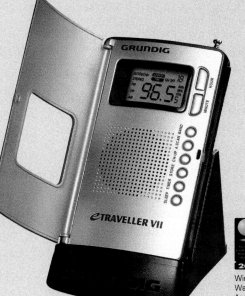

DIMENSIONS: 2 1/2"W x 4 1/2"H x 7/8"D

WEIGHT: 5 lbs. 3 oz.

TRAVEL THE WORLD.

Winner of the Design and Engineering Ward from the Consumer Electronic Association 2002

eTRAVELLER VII

# GRUNDIG

etón Corportation, 1015 Corporation Way, Palo Alto, CA 94303 • Tel: 650-903-3866 • Fax: 650-903-3867
Shortwave Hotlines: (US) 1-800-872-2228 (CN) 1-800-637-1648 • Web: www.grundigradio.com

later worked at other American stations—including KMEN near Los Angeles and Oklahoma's KOMA—before returning to the United Kingdom in 1967. He then joined a ship-based pirate, Radio London, where "The Perfumed Garden" show made him a celebrity.

Radio London left the airwaves in 1967, after the British government passed a law banning North Sea radio pirates. A month later, the BBC launched a popular music channel, Radio 1, and John Peel was hired as one of its first jocks. The rest is history.

Today, the sixtysomething Peel still has the same wry humor and enthusiasm for innovation that he possessed in his youth. He now airs pop punk, experimental bands, reggae, rock groups working the college circuit—whatever is looking to the future. Not surprisingly, most listeners are young, but there are others who, like Peel, are older but still edgy for the fresh and the raw.

Peel's show was one of the big winners to come out of the World Service's 2002 summer schedule: airings to the Americas went from one to three. Barring any further shuffling for 2003, listeners in eastern *North America* can expect to hear Peel at 0405 Thursday (Wednesday evening local American date, and one hour earlier in summer) on 5975 kHz; 1430 Thursday on 15190 kHz; and 0130 Friday (0030 in summer) on 5975 and 12095 kHz, this despite the fact there are no longer any transmissions officially targeted at North America. Farther west, try 0405 Thursday on 6135 kHz (one hour earlier in summer on 11835 kHz); the Friday slot on 9525 kHz (11835 kHz in summer), and Thursday at 1530 on 9740 kHz.

*Europe* has three Thursday editions, all one hour earlier in summer—these use the same channels all year. Winter, the show is at 0405 on 9410 kHz; 0930 on 12095 and 15485 kHz; and 1930 on 6195 and 9410 kHz.

The *Middle East* also has three airings, which like Europe are one hour earlier in summer but use the same frequencies year round. Winter times are 0830 Thursday on 17640 kHz; 1730 the same day on 15565 kHz; and 1230 Friday on 11760, 15575 and 17640 kHz.

*Southern Africa* gets two Thursday slots: 0730 on 6190 and 11940 kHz; and 1930 on 3255, 6190 and 12095 kHz.

In *East Asia*, tune in at 0230 Thursday on 15280 and 15360 kHz, and 1530 on 6135, 6195 and 9740 kHz; also, 0630 Friday on 15360, 17760 and 21660 kHz. For *Southeast Asia* it's 0230 Thursday on 15360 kHz; 1530 Thursday on 6195 and 9740 kHz; and 0630 Friday on 11955 and 15360 kHz.

There's officially nothing for *Australasia*, but you can still tune in at 1530 Thursday on 9740 kHz and 0630 Friday on 11955 kHz.

## "Jazz Show"
## Voice of Russia

Why listen to a jazz show on shortwave, with its substandard audio?

Simple. You're not going to hear a local station airing a gypsy vocalist "scatting like Anita O'Day on amphetamines," in the words of an American jazz critic. Nor will you find ethno jazz from Central Asia, or fusion from the Caucasus. Or even foot-stomping syncopation from the early days of sound recording.

The Voice of Russia's "Jazz Show" is as much a journey of discovery as a listening experience, although artists like Valentina Ponomareva and Rishad Shafi sound good under any conditions.

Winter in *North America*, tune 0231 Wednes-day (Tuesday evening local American date) on 7180, 7250, 7335, 9765, 12020 and 13665 kHz; or 0531 Monday on 7125, 7180, 12010, 12020, 15595 and 17595 kHz. In summer, one hour earlier, it's either 0131

**"Jazz Show"** is prepared by Elena Biryukova (left) and Larisa Avrutina, and is presented by Carl Watts.   VOR

Wednesday on 9665, 9725, 11825, 12000 and 17595 kHz; or 0431 Monday on 9665, 11750, 12000, 17565, 17650, 17660 and 17690 kHz.

*Europe* has just one winter slot, at 2131 Friday on 5940, 5950, 6175, 7300, 7340 and 7390 kHz. Summer, one hour earlier, it's on 9480, 9775, 11675, 12030, 12070 and 15455 kHz. One slot is better than no slot, which is what the Middle East and Southern Africa get.

In *Southeast Asia* winter, tune in at 1531 Wednesday on 6205 and 11500 kHz; or 0931 Thursday on 11770, 17495 and 21485 (or 21810) kHz. Summer slots are 1431 Wednesday on 7390 (also heard in East Asia), 12055, 15560 and 17645 kHz; and 0831 Thursday on 15490, 17495, 17525, 17675, 17685 and 17795 kHz.

*Australasia*, like Europe, has just the one opportunity: winter at 0931 Thursday on 15275, 15470, 17525 and 17665 kHz; and midyear, one hour earlier, on 17495, 17525, 17635, 17685 and 17795 kHz.

## "Health Matters"
## BBC World Service

The global HIV/AIDS epidemic has underscored that conquering disease involves more than just treating patients once they have become infected. More attention is now being paid to social factors like poverty and education, as well as to self-medication and the overprescription of drugs.

This shift is reflected in the evolution of the BBC World Service's "Health Matters." This influential program now focuses not just on health care and medical research, but takes a wider look at health in its larger context. Yet, it continues to include such bread-and-butter issues as the dangers of taking too much paracetamol.

The show is not specifically targeted to North America, but it is well heard there, anyway, thanks to the dispersal qualities of shortwave. Winter, listeners in eastern *North America* have three opportunities to tune "Health Matters": 0205 Tuesday (Monday evening local American date) on 5975 and 12095 kHz; 2105 Tuesday on 5975 and 12095 kHz; and 1505 Wednesday on 15190 kHz. Listeners out west can try 9525 kHz at 0205 Tuesday, and for night owls there's 9740 kHz at 1105 Monday. In summer, best slots for eastern North America are 0105 Tuesday on 5975 and 12095 kHz; and 1505 Wednesday on 15190 kHz. In western North America, tune in at 0105 Tuesday on 11835 kHz, or 1105 Monday on 9740 kHz.

*Europe* has three airings. Winter, it's at 2005 Monday on 6195 and 9410 kHz, and 1505 Tuesday and 1005 Wednesday on 12095 and 15485 kHz. Summer slots are an hour earlier, same frequencies.

The *Middle East* gets an even better deal, with four choices in winter and three in summer. The first winter slot is at 1805 Monday on 9410 kHz. Repeats go out at 0205 Tuesday on 9410 and 12095 kHz; 1405 the same day on 15575 and 17640 kHz; and 0905 Wednesday on 11760, 15575 and 17640 kHz. Summer times are 1705 Monday on 12095 and 15575 kHz; 1305 Tuesday on 11760, 15575 and 17640 kHz; and 0805 Wednesday on 17640 kHz.

In *Southern Africa* it's 1805 Monday on 3255, 6190 and 21470 kHz; or 0805 Wednesday on 6190, 11940 and 21470 kHz.

For *East Asia* there is 1105 Monday on 6195, 9740, 15360 and (summer) 17760 kHz; 0705 Tuesday on 15360, 17760 and 21660 kHz; and 0305 Wednesday on 15280, 15360, 17760 and 21660 kHz. The same three slots are also available for *Southeast Asia*: 1105 Monday on 6195 and 9740 kHz; 0705 Tuesday on 11955 and 15360 kHz; and 0305 Wednesday on 15360 kHz.

*Australasia*, like North America, is not an official target for the BBC World Service, but there's regular reception, anyway, at 1105 Monday on 9740 kHz, and 0705 Tuesday on 11955 kHz.

## "Russian Treasures"
## Voice of Russia

World band audio is far from ideal for music; yet, paradoxically, it offers up some of the finest classical music to be found. And it doesn't come any finer than "Russian Treasures," a gem squirreled away between two other shows. It runs a mere 11 minutes, but gives full credence to the adage that good things come in small packages.

"Russian" is not restricted just to singers and musicians from within Russia's frontiers; it is also applied to those from abroad with family or other connections to the country. One example: Nikolai Gedda, born in Sweden of a Russian father.

Commercial recordings from Edison's days to the present are complemented by treasures from the Voice of Russia's vast Soviet-era archives. To hear Rachmaninoff playing music by Scriabin in a rare early recording borders on a religious experience. This is music that stirs the juices, no matter what the medium, and with some of today's world band receivers the audio quality can be more pleasant than in the past.

On any given day, the Voice of Russia program lineup may not correspond to the official schedule. Days and times listed are those observed just prior to PASSPORT's deadline, but could change. Officially, times are 2030 (except Thursday) and 0730 (except Friday), both slots one hour earlier in summer.

The winter slot for *Europe* is 2039 Monday, Tuesday and Thursday through Saturday on 5940, 5950, 6175, 7335, 7340, 7390 and 9775 kHz. In summer, one hour earlier, choose from 7440, 9480, 9775, 9890, 11675, 12030 and 12070 kHz.

There is no specific airing for *North America*, but East Coast listeners should try the frequencies for Europe. There are no airings scheduled for either the Middle East or Southern Africa.

The winter timing for *Southeast Asia* is 0739 Monday, Tuesday, Wednesday, Friday and Saturday on 11770 and 21485 (or 21810) kHz. Summer at 0639, it's on 15490, 17685 and 17795 kHz.

*Australasia* has the same slot as Southeast Asia, winter on 15275, 15470, 17525 and 17665 kHz; and midyear on 17495, 17635, 17685, 17795 and 21790 kHz.

## "From Our Own Correspondent"
## BBC World Service

Some shows have been around for such a long time, they seem to have become permanent fixtures. So it is with the BBC World Service's "From Our Own Correspondent," which went through a period of revitalization in 2002.

Its reports emanate from correspondents "out in the field." Yet, they tend to be more like short essays than background reports or dry news stories, often painting vivid audio pictures of local conditions and customs. One might be a tale of the tribulations of traveling in the Philippines, another the poignant reflection on a family destined to die from starvation. Mainly, it's always personal.

This was one of the programs most affected by the World Service's schedule changes in the summer of 2002; its new times bear little resemblance to those that existed before. Since the program comes in two distinct sizes—15 and 30 minutes—there may be even more adjustments to come.

For now, though, listeners in eastern *North America* can expect to hear it at 2230 Saturday and 2245 Wednesday (2145 in summer) on 5975 and 12095 kHz; 0345 Thursday (Wednesday evening local American date, and one hour earlier in summer) on 5975 and (summer) 12095 kHz; and 1130 Thursday on 6195 and 15190 kHz. Listeners on the West Coast should try 0345 Thursday on 9525 kHz (one hour earlier on 11835 kHz in summer).

*Europe* has an even more complicated schedule: 1805 Saturday (one hour earlier in summer) on 6195, 9410 and (summer) 15480 kHz; 2230 Saturday (summer only) on 6195 kHz; 0805 Sunday and 1645 Wednesday (1545 in summer) on 12095 and 15485 kHz; 0745 Thursday (one hour earlier in summer) on 9410, 12015 and 15480 kHz; and 1130 Thursday on 12095 and 15480 kHz.

In the *Middle East*, try 0230 Sunday on 9410 and 12095 kHz; 0805 the same day on 15575 and 17640 kHz; 1945 Wednesday winter on 9740 kHz (one hour earlier in summer on 12095 and 15575 kHz); and 0345 Thursday on 9410, 12095 and 15575 kHz.

**Producer Mike Popham orchestrates the BBC's "From Our Own Correspondent" from Bush House. More a series of informed musings than hard reports, it brings perspective and a sense of direction to current events.**
BBC Audience Relations

*Southern Africa* has three opportunities: 0805 Sunday on 6190, 11940 and 21470 kHz; 2145 Wednesday on 3255, 6005 and 6190 kHz; and 1030 Thursday on 6190, 11940 and 21470 kHz.

In *East Asia*, tune in at 2230 Saturday (local Sunday in the target area) on 5965 and 6195 kHz; 0230 Sunday on 15280 and 15360 kHz; 0805 Sunday on 15360, 17760 and 21660 kHz; 2145 Wednesday on 5965, 6195 and 11945 kHz; and 0045 Thursday on 15280 and 15360 kHz.

The lineup for *Southeast Asia* is 1705 Saturday (summer only) on 3915 and 7160 kHz; 2230 Saturday on 6195, 7105, 9660 and 11685 kHz; 0230 Sunday on 15360 kHz; 0805 Sunday on 11955 and 15360 kHz; 2145 Wednesday on 3915 and 6195 kHz; and 0045 Thursday on 15360 kHz.

*Australasia* is no longer an official target for the BBC World Service, but reception is decent at 0805 Sunday on 11955 kHz.

_____

*Prepared by Tony Jones and the staff of* PASSPORT TO WORLD BAND RADIO.

# GRUNDIG

## CLASSIC 960 AM/FM/SW RADIO

**FM Stereo/AM/Shortwave Radio.** Remember when radio sounded so real that voices were almost with you in the room? When music had a warm, rich, full-bodied tone? Those wonderful days are back! Grundig has revived its legendary Model 960. The long-lost sound is back. The 3" side speakers, left and right, spread a spacious stereo image, while a front-firing 4" speaker reinforces the bass and fills your listening room with glorious Grundig sound.

**Experience the Renaissance of Radio.** You need a great radio to enjoy great radio! More stations. More news and more music. Get yourself a 960 with full, rich sound and enjoy. The Grundig Classic 960 is your listening post that lets you travel the globe without ever leaving home.

**Connect your CD or cassette player.** It's your entertainment center. Auxiliary input takes the audio signal from your CD, cassette player, or TV... and turns it into spacious, room-filling, glorious Grundig sound! This special 50th-Anniversary Edition faithfully replicates the dimensions and styling of the original Model 960. The cabinet is solid wood. The gold-tone illuminated dial and knobs are accented with solid brass.

DIMENSIONS: 15 1/2"W x 11 1/4"H x 7"D

WEIGHT: 9 lbs. 10 oz.

UNFORGETTABLE STYLING AND CLASSIC GRUNDIG SOUND.

CLASSIC 960

*"Outstanding Performance...Unbeatable Audio Quality...Unbeatable Price"*
*Lawrence Magne, Editor-in-Chief, Passport to World Band Radio*

# GRUNDIG G2000A AM/FM/SW RADIO
## Design by F.A. Porsche

Timeless Elegance - Inspired by the legendary Porsche 911, the Grundig G2000A Design by F.A. Porsche, exhibits the same purity of line that has made the 911 a timeless classic. The smell of new car leather and the expertly stitched case embodies the meticulously crafted control panel with its smooth, recessed speaker grill and deeply sculptured buttons.

- Direct digital keypad tuning.
- Illuminated multifunction LCD display.
- 20 user-set station memories.
- Shortwave tuning from 2.30-7.4 MHz and 9.4-26.1 MHz.
- FM stereo with included earphones.
- Radio or buzzer alarm.
- Sleep timer.
- Snap-on leather case.
- Telescopic antenna.
- Dynamic 2" wide-range speaker.
- 3 AA batteries / AC Adapter (not included).

DIMENSIONS: 5 1/2"W x 3 1/2"H x 1 1/4"D

WEIGHT: 7 oz.

TRAVEL THE WORLD WITH A G2000A.

GRUNDIG G2000A AM/FM/SW RADIO

# GRUNDIG

etón Corporation, 1015 Corporation Way, Palo Alto, CA 94303 • Tel: 650-903-3866 • Fax: 650-903-3867
Shortwave Hotlines: (US) 1-800-872-2228 (CN) 1 800 637 1648 • Web: www.grundigradio.com

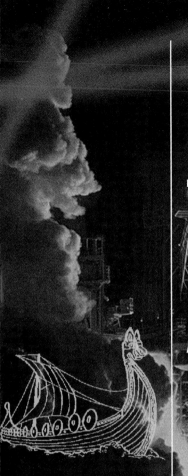

# Compleat Idiot's Guide to Getting Started

## Ramping Up: Three World Band "Musts"

World band radio isn't conventional radio, so it calls for some new approaches. Here are the three key "musts" to hear the world successfully.

### *"Must" #1:* World Time and Day

**World band schedules use a single time, *World Time*.** World band radio is global, with stations broadcasting around-the-clock from virtually every time zone. Imagine the chaos if each station used its local time to indicate when you should tune in. Ergo, World Time.

World Time, or Coordinated Universal Time (UTC), is also known as Greenwich Mean Time (GMT) or, in the military, "Zulu." It is announced in 24-hour format, so 2 PM is 1400 ("fourteen hundred") hours. Most major international broadcasters announce World Time at the hour. On the Internet World Time is given at various sites, including tycho.usno.navy.mil/what.html and www.nrc.ca/inms/time/cesium.shtml.

Around North America, you can also hear World Time over standard time stations WWV in Colorado, WWVH in Hawaii and CHU in Ottawa. WWV and WWVH are on 5000, 10000 and 15000 kHz, with WWV also on 2500 and 20000 kHz. CHU is on 3330, 7335 and 14670 kHz.

See PASSPORT's sidebar to set your 24-hour clock. For example, if you live on the East Coast of the United States, *add* five hours winter (four hours summer) to your local time to get World Time. So, if it is 8 PM EST (the 20th hour of the day) in New York, it is 0100 hours World Time.

Adjust your radio's 24-hour clock. No clock? Get one now unless you enjoy doing weird computations in your head (it's 6:00 PM here, so add five hours to make it 11:00 PM, which on a 24-hour clock converts to 23:00 World Time—but, whoops, it's summer so I should have added four hours instead of five . . .). The best money you'll ever spend.

Don't forget to "wind your calendar," because at midnight a new *World Day* arrives. This can trip up even experienced listeners—sometimes radio stations, too. So if it is 9 PM EST Wednesday in New York, it is 0200 hours World Time *Thursday*.

> **With one of the better-rated portables, you'll be able to hear much of what world band has to offer.**

### *"Must" #2:* Finding Stations

**PASSPORT shows station schedules three ways: by country, time of day and frequency.** By-country is best to tune to a given station. "What's On Tonight," the time-of-day section, is like *TV Guide* and has program descriptions. The by-frequency Blue Pages help tell you what you're hearing when you're dialing around the bands.

## PASSPORT'S THREE-MINUTE START

Too swamped to read the manual? Try this:

1. Night is the right time, so wait until evening when signals are strongest. In a concrete-and-steel building put your radio by a window or balcony.

2. Make sure your radio is plugged in or has fresh batteries. Extend the telescopic antenna fully and vertically. Set the DX/local switch (if there is one) to "DX," but otherwise leave the controls the way they came from the factory.

3. Turn on your radio. Set it to 5900 kHz and begin tuning slowly toward 6200 kHz; you can also try 9400-9990 kHz. You should hear stations from around the world.

*Other times?* Read "Best Times and Frequencies for 2003."

## SETTING YOUR WORLD TIME CLOCK

PASSPORT's "Addresses PLUS" lets you arrive at the local time in another country by adding or subtracting from World Time. Use that section to determine the time within a country you are listening to.

This box, however, gives it from the other direction—what to add or subtract from your local time so you can determine World Time. Use this to set your World Time clock.

Wherever in the world you live, you can also use Addresses PLUS, instead of this sidebar, to determine World Time simply by reversing the time difference. For example, Addresses PLUS states that Burundi's local time is "World Time +2." So if you're in Burundi, to set your World Time clock you would take Burundi time *minus* two hours.

| *WHERE YOU ARE* | *TO DETERMINE WORLD TIME* |
|---|---|
| **North America** | |
| **Newfoundland** St. John's NF, St. Anthony NF | Add 3½ hours, 2½ summer |
| **Atlantic** St. John NB, Battle Harbour NF | Add 4 hours, 3 summer |
| **Eastern** New York, Atlanta, Toronto | Add 5 hours, 4 summer |
| **Central** Chicago, Mexico City, Nashville, Winnipeg | Add 6 hours, 5 summer |
| **Mountain** Denver, Salt Lake City, Calgary | Add 7 hours, 6 summer |
| **Pacific** San Francisco, Vancouver | Add 8 hours, 7 summer |
| **Alaska** | Add 9 hours, 8 summer |
| **Hawaii** | Add 10 hours |
| **Central America & Caribbean** | |
| **Bermuda** | Add 4 hours, 3 summer |
| **Barbados, Puerto Rico, Virgin Islands** | Add 4 hours |
| **Bahamas, Cuba** | Add 5 hours, 4 summer |
| **Jamaica** | Add 5 hours |
| **Costa Rica** | Add 6 hours |
| **Europe** | |
| **United Kingdom, Ireland, Portugal** | Same time as World Time winter, subtract 1 hour summer |

| | |
|---|---|
| **Continental Western Europe; parts of Central and Eastern Continental Europe** | Subtract 1 hour, 2 hours summer |
| **Lithuania** | Subtract 2 hours year round |
| **Elsewhere in Continental Europe:** Belarus, Bulgaria, Cyprus, Estonia, Finland, Greece, Latvia, Moldova, Romania, Russia (Kaliningradskaya Oblast), Turkey, Ukraine | Subtract 2 hours, 3 summer |
| **Moscow** | Subtract 3 hours, 4 summer |

## Mideast & Africa

| | |
|---|---|
| **Côte d'Ivoire, Ghana, Guinea, Liberia, Mali, Morocco, Senegal, Sierra Leone** | World Time exactly |
| **Angola, Benin, Chad, Congo, Nigeria, Tunisia** | Subtract 1 hour |
| **Egypt, Israel, Jordan, Lebanon, Syria** | Subtract 2 hours, 3 summer |
| **South Africa, Zambia, Zimbabwe** | Subtract 2 hours |
| **Ethiopia, Kenya, Kuwait, Saudi Arabia, Tanzania, Uganda** | Subtract 3 hours |
| **Iran** | Subtract 3½ hours, 4½ summer |

## Asia & Australasia

| | |
|---|---|
| **Pakistan** | Subtract 5 hours, 6 summer |
| **India** | Subtract 5½ hours |
| **Bangladesh, Sri Lanka** | Subtract 6 hours |
| **Laos, Thailand, Vietnam** | Subtract 7 hours |
| **China (including Taiwan), Malaysia, Philippines, Singapore** | Subtract 8 hours |
| **Japan, Korea** | Subtract 9 hours |
| **Australia: *Victoria, New South Wales, Tasmania*** | Subtract 11 hours local summer, 10 local winter (midyear) |
| **Australia: *South Australia*** | Subtract 10½ hours local summer, 9½ hours local winter (midyear) |
| **Australia: *Queensland*** | Subtract 10 hours |
| **Australia: *Northern Territory*** | Subtract 9½ hours |
| **Australia: *Western Australia*** | Subtract 8 hours |
| **New Zealand** | Subtract 13 hours local summer, 12 hours local winter (midyear) |

# GRUNDIG

## MINI 100 PE AM/FM/SW RADIO

Travel with the world in your pocket. Another exciting breakthrough in world band technology. A well-built radio that fits in the palm of your hand. AM/FM stereo/SW radio with LED indicator, six shortwave broadcast bands, telescopic antenna, earphones and belt clip make listening easy. Comes with soft carrying case.

TUNER FREQUENCY RANGES

| | |
|---|---|
| FM | 88-108 MHz |
| AM | 525-1710 MHz |
| SW1 | 5.80-6.40 MHz |
| SW2 | 6.90-7.50 MHz |
| SW3 | 9.40-10.00 MHz |
| SW4 | 11.65-12.15 MHz |
| SW5 | 15.00-15.65 MHz |
| SW6 | 17.50-18.14 MHz |

DIMENSIONS: 2 3/4"W x 4"H x 3/4"D

WEIGHT: 4.5 oz.

THE WORLD IN YOUR HAND.

MINI 100 PE

*"Outstanding Performance...Unbeatable Audio Quality...Unbeatable Price"*
Lawrence Magne, *Editor-in-Chief, Passport to World Band Radio*

# FR200 EMERGENCY
# AM/FM/SW RADIO

Be prepared and stay informed with the FR200 from Grundig. If the power goes out and batteries aren't available, the FR200 can operate for one hour with just one minute of cranking. Its built-in generator means that even in the most desperate situations, you can still have access to local news and information as wells as to news from around the world.

- Four Band Tuning – AM/FM/SW1/SW2.
- Built in power generator.
- Rechargeable battery pack.
- 2 1/2" diameter speaker.
- Emergency light.
- Fine tuning knob.
- DC jack, earphone jack.

DIMENSIONS: 6 3/4"W x 5 3/4"H x 2 1/8"D

WEIGHT: 1 lbs. 5 oz.

SOS EMERGENCY RADIO.

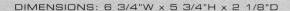

G R U N D I G   F R 2 0 0

**GRUNDIG**

etón Corporation, 1015 Corporation Way, Palo Alto, CA 94303 • Tel: 650-903-3866 • Fax: 650-903-3867
Shortwave Hotlines: (US) 1-800-872-2228 (CN) 1-800-637-1648 • Web: www.grundigradio.com

## BEST TIMES AND FREQUENCIES FOR 2003

With world band, if you dial randomly you're just as likely to get dead air as a program. That's because some world band segments are alive and kicking only by day, while others spring to life at night. Others fare better at certain times of the year.

This guide is most accurate if you're listening from north of Africa or South America. Even then, what you'll actually hear will vary—depending upon your location, where the station transmits from, the time of year and your radio (*see* Propagation in the glossary). Although world band is active around the clock, signals are usually best from an hour or two before sunset until sometime after midnight. Too, try a couple of hours on either side of dawn. **Nighttime** refers to your local hours of darkness, plus dawn and dusk.

### Possible Reception Nighttime

2 MHz (120 meters) **2300-2495 kHz**—overwhelmingly domestic stations, with 2496-2504 kHz for time stations only.

### Limited Reception Nighttime

3 MHz (90 meters) **3200-3400 kHz**—overwhelmingly domestic stations.

### Good-to-Fair in Europe and Asia except Summer Nights; Elsewhere, Limited Reception Nighttime

4 MHz (75 meters) **3900-4050 kHz**—international and domestic stations, primarily not in or beamed to the Americas; 3900-3950 kHz mainly Asian and Pacific transmitters; 3950-4000 kHz also includes European and African transmitters; 4001-4050 kHz currently out-of-band.

### Some Reception Nighttime; Regional Reception Daytime

5 MHz (60 meters) **4750-4995 kHz** and **5005-5100 kHz**—mostly domestic stations, with 4996-5004 kHz for time stations only and 5061-5100 kHz currently out-of-band.

### Excellent Nighttime; Regional Reception Daytime

6 MHz (49 meters) **5730-6300 kHz**—5730-5899 kHz and 6201-6300 kHz currently out-of-band.

### Good Nighttime; Regional Reception Daytime

7 MHz (41 meters) **6890-6990 kHz** and **7100-7600 kHz**—6890-6990 kHz and 7351-7600 kHz currently out-of-band; 7100-7300 kHz no American-based transmitters and few transmissions targeted to the Americas.

9 MHz (31 meters) **9250-9995 kHz**—9250-9399 kHz and 9901-9995 kHz currently out-of-band; 9996-10004 kHz for time stations only.

### Good Nighttime except Mid-Winter; Some Reception Daytime and Winter Nights; Good Asian and Pacific Reception Mornings in America

11 MHz (25 meters) **11500-12200 kHz**—11500-11599 kHz and 12101-12200 kHz currently out-of-band.

**Esmail Amid-Hozour (glasses), CEO of Grundig's Lextronix affiliate, discusses Satellit 800 quality control issues.**
Lextronix

World band frequencies are usually given in kilohertz (kHz), but some stations use Megahertz (MHz). The only difference is three decimal places, so 6170 kHz is the same as 6.17 MHz, 6175 kHz identical to 6.175 MHz, and so on.

You're used to hearing FM and other stations at the same spot on the dial, day and night, or Webcasts at the same URLs.

But things are a lot different when you roam the international airwaves.

World band radio is like a global bazaar where a variety of merchants come and go at different times of the day and night. Where you once tuned in, say, a French station, hours later you might find a Russian or Chinese broadcaster roosting on that same spot.

**Good Daytime; Good Summer Nighttime**

13 MHz (22 meters) **13570-13870 kHz**

15 MHz (19 meters) **15005-15800 kHz**—14996-15004 kHz for time stations only; 15005-15099 kHz currently out-of-band.

**Good Daytime; Variable, Limited Reception Summer Nighttime**

17 MHz (16 meters) **17480-17900 kHz**

19 MHz (15 meters) **18900-19020 kHz**

21 MHz (13 meters) **21450-21850 kHz**

**Some Reception Daytime**

25 MHz (11 meters) **25670-26100 kHz**

There are more stations than there is space, so they try to outshout each other.

George Poppin, shown with wife Dottie, has been actively assisting world band stations since he first contacted Israel Radio 25 years back.    G. Poppin

Or on a nearby perch. If you suddenly hear interference from a station on an adjacent channel, it doesn't mean something is wrong with your radio; it probably means another station has begun broadcasting on a nearby frequency. There are more stations on the air than there is space for them, so sometimes they try to outshout each other.

To cope with this, purchase a radio with superior adjacent-channel rejection—selectivity—and lean towards radios with synchronous selectable sideband. PASSPORT REPORTS, a major section of this book, tells you which stand out.

Because world band is full of surprises from one listening session to the next, experienced listeners do a lot of surfing of the airwaves. Daytime, you'll find most stations above 11500 kHz; at night, below 16000 kHz.

If a station can't be found or fades out, there is probably nothing wrong with your radio. The atmosphere's sky-high ionosphere deflects world band signals down to earth, where they bounce off water or land back up to the ionosphere, then back up and back down again like a dribbled basketball until they get to your radio. This is why world band radio is so unencumbered—its signals don't rely on cables or satellites or the Internet, just layers of ionized gases which have enveloped our planet for millions of years. World band is free from regulation,

## WORLD TIME CLOCKS

Some radios include a World Time clock displayed fulltime—this is best. Other radios may have World Time clocks, but to see the time you have to press a button when the radio is in use. Because World Time uses the 24-hour format, digital clocks are easier to read than hands.

MFJ Enterprises manufactures several 24-hour clocks—conventional or atomic-synchronized, some with seconds displayed numerically—from $9.95 to $79.95. Sharper Image also offers three clocks in the $39.95–49.95 range.

Other 24-hour clocks run up to $2,000, including models designed primarily for professional applications. Nearly all the pricier models display seconds and even split-seconds numerically, while many synchronize with an official atomic clock standard.

Sharper Image's World Time "Woody Clock" shows date, day and temperature. Hourly chime and announcement, too.

**PASSPORT's Toshimichi Ohtake sports appropriate head gear while en route to the 2002 World Cup soccer championships in Japan.** T. Ohtake

free from taxes, free from fees—and largely free from ads, as well.

But nature's ionosphere, like the weather, changes constantly, so world band stations have to adjust accordingly. The result is that broadcasters operate within different frequency ranges, depending upon the time of day and season of the year.

That same changeability can work in your favor, especially if you like to eavesdrop on signals not intended for your part of the world. Sometimes stations from exotic locales—places you would not ordinarily hear—become surprise arrivals at your radio, thanks to the shifting characteristics of nature's ionosphere.

### "Must" #3: The Right Radio

**Choose carefully, but you shouldn't need a costly set.** Avoid cheap radios, as they suffer from one or more major defects. With one of the better-rated portables you'll be able to hear much more of what world band has to offer.

Look for a radio with digital frequency display, which is the easiest to tune—all radios tested for PASSPORT REPORTS have digital displays, but analog (slide-rule-tuning) models are still sold. Also, get a radio that tunes at least 4750-21850 kHz with no significant gaps or "holes." Otherwise, you may not be able to tune in some stations.

You won't need an exotic outside antenna unless you're using a tabletop model. All portables, and to some extent portatops, are designed to work well off the built-in telescopic antenna—or, if you want it to perform a bit better, with several yards or meters of insulated wire clipped on.

If you just want to hear the major stations, you'll do fine with a moderately priced portable. Beyond that, portatop models have a better chance of bringing in faint and difficult signals, and they usually sound better, too. Tabletop receivers are aimed at experienced DX enthusiasts, so they tend to be unnecessarily costly and complex for most program listeners to operate.

---

*Prepared by Jock Elliott, Tony Jones and Lawrence Magne.*

# GRUNDIG Stay Alert! Be Informed!

# SATELLIT 800 MILLENNIUM

The Satellit 800 Millennium. In the history of short-wave receivers, no other manufacturer has maintained a continuously evolving series of high-end portable radios, decade after decade.

**Extensive frequency coverage.**
- Long wave, AM-broadcast and Shortwave, 100-30,000 KHz, continuous.
- FM broadcast, 87-108 MHz.
- VHF aircraft band, 118-137 MHz.
- Multi-mode reception – AM, FM-stereo, Single Sideband USB/LSB and VHF aircraft band.

**The right complement of high-tech features.**
- Three built-in bandwidths, using electronically switched IF filters: 6.0, 4.0, 2.3 KHz.
- Synchronous detector for improved quality of AM and shortwave broadcast signals, minimizes fading, distortion and adjacent frequency interference.
- Selectable AGC in fast and slow mode. Auto Backlight shutoff to conserve battery life. Low Battery Indicator.

**Performance engineered for the best possible reception.**
- High Dynamic Range, allowing for detection of weak signals in the presence of strong signals.
- Excellent sensitivity and selectivity.

**Legendary Grundig audio.**
- Outstanding audio quality, with separate bass and treble tone control - in the Grundig tradition.
- FM Stereo with headphones or external amplified stereo speakers.
- Includes high quality stereo headphones.
- Multiple audio outputs: line level output for recording, stereo headphone output.

**Information displayed the way it should be.**
- Large, illuminated, informational LCD display of operational parameters, measuring a massive 6″ x 3½″, easy to read.
- An elegant, calibrated, analog signal strength meter, in the finest tradition.
- Digital frequency display to 100 Hertz accuracy on AM, SW and VHF aircraft bands. 50 Hz when SSB used.

**Traditional and high-tech tuning controls.**
- A real tuning knob, like on traditional radios, but with ultra-precise digital tuning, with absolutely no audio muting when used.
- A modern, direct-frequency-entry keypad for instant frequency access, and push buttons for fixed-step tuning.

**Plenty of user programmable memory.**
- 70 programmable memories, completely immune

to loss due to power interruptions.
- Memory scan feature.

**Clocks and timers.**
- Dual, 24 hour format clocks.
- Dual programmable timers.

**Antenna capabilities that really make sense.**
- Built in telescopic antenna for portable use on all bands.
- External antenna connections for the addition of auxiliary antennas, e.g. professionally engineered shortwave antennas; long-wire shortwave antennas; specialized AM broadcast band antennas for enthusiasts of AM DX'ing; FM broadcast band antennas; VHF air band antennas.

**Power, dimensions, weight.**
- Operation on six internal "D" cell batteries or the included 110V AC adapter (a 220V AC adapter is available upon request).
- Big dimensions and weight. A real radio. 20.5″L x 9.4″ H x 8″ W., 14.5 lb.

Suggested list price: US $ 499.95

**THE WIZ**
**1-800-2THEWIZ**
www.thewiz.com

**West Marine**
We make boating more fun!™
**1-800-BOATING**
www.westmarine.com

**g!**
good guys
**1-800-866-GUYS**
www.goodguys.com

# The Ultimate in Digital Technology

## Yacht Boy 400PE

This is a true high-performance receiver offering the best performance available in its class. You will hear international broadcasts from around the world on shortwave, including broadcasts and communications requiring SSB circuitry. Listen to shortwave on its built-in telescopic antenna or connect it your favorite external antenna. But do not think it is just for short-wave. Its superior sensitivity and selectivity make it the best choice for anyone needing superior AM and FM performance in weak-signal and fringe areas. Perfect for pulling in those distant, hard to get AM talk shows that are so popular today.
Dimensions: 7.75″ L x 4.5″ H x 1.5″ W
Weight:      1 lb. 5 oz.
Suggested list price:  US $ 149.95

## Yacht Boy 300PE

Designed with remarkable performance at an incredibly low price, the YB300PE receives world wide international shortwave broadcasts as well as your local AM and FM-stereo stations. Great for either travel or home use, it is small enough for large pockets or carry-on luggage and takes up little space on your desk. Use the alarm clock feature to wake you up in the morning and the sleep timer to lull you asleep at night.
Dimensions: 5.75″ L x 3.5″ H x 1.25″W.
Weight:      12 oz.
Suggested list price:  US $ 79.95

## Grundig Porsche Design G2000A
### AM/FM/SW Radio

Wake up to sports and talk radio on AM, soothing stereo (with earphones) on FM or fascinating shortwave from around the world... select from 13 International bands from 2.3 - 7.4 and 9.4 - 26.1 MHz. Punch in any station or lock your favorites into 20 memories... other features include digital clock and alarm with Quartz accuracy... earphones... butter-soft handcrafted leather case. Designed by F. A.Porsche, the G2000A is a pleasure to own and operate. Uses 3 AA batteries (not included).
Dimensions: 5.5″ L x 3.5″ H x 1.375″ W
Weight:      11.52 oz.
Suggested list price:  US $ 99.95

etón Corporation, 1015 Corporation Way, Palo Alto, CA 94303 • Tel: 650-903-3866 • Fax: 650-903-3867
Shortwave Hotlines: (US) 1-800-872-2228 (CN) 1-800-637-1648 • Web: www.grundigradio.com

# First Tries:
# Ten Easy Catches

Here are ten fortissimo stations that you should be able to hear almost anywhere. All are in English, often with first-rate programs.

Times and days are in World Time, while "winter" and "summer" refer to seasons in the Northern Hemisphere, where summer is in the middle of the year.

**EUROPE**
**France**

**Radio France Internationale** now concentrates on audiences in Africa, the Middle East and southern Asia. Former broadcasts to Europe and North America were unceremoniously dumped in 2000, leaving listeners to scramble for alternatives.

Fortunately, shortwave's dispersal qualities mean that RFI's informative programs are also heard in regions outside the targeted areas.

☞ RECOMMENDED PROGRAM: All—none is less than first rate.

*North America:* Nothing targeted to there, but try 11710 kHz at 0600-0630 weekdays; 15605 kHz at 0700-0800 weekdays; 15540 kHz at 1200-1230; and 11995 kHz winter at 1600-1700. These transmissions from RFI's Gabon relay are for West Africa, but are heard well beyond.

*Middle East:* 1400-1500 on 17620 kHz; also 1600-1730 winter on 11615 kHz and summer on 15605 kHz, though this slot is intended mainly for East Africa.

*South Asia:* 1400-1500 on 11610kHz, also for western parts of *Southeast Asia* and *Australia*.

*Africa:* RFI's broadcasts to Africa have a large audience, and deservedly so. Audible at 0400-0430 weekdays on any two frequencies from 11910, 11995, 13610 and 15155 kHz; 0500-0530 weekdays on 13610 (winter), 15155 and (summer) 17800 kHz; 0600-0630 weekdays on 11710, 15155 and/or 17800 kHz; 0700-0800 on 15605 kHz; 1200-1230 on 15540 and 25820 kHz; 1600-1700 on 11615, 11995, 12015, 15605, 17605 and 17850 kHz; and at 1700-1730 on 11615, 15605 and/or 17605 kHz.

**Erlends Calabuig oversees all foreign-language transmissions for Radio France Internationale.**
RFI

## Germany

**Deutsche Welle**, the Voice of Germany believes in sticking to a proven, successful format. Its 45-minute English broadcasts focus heavily on German and European news, plus features on German life and culture. Highly respected by its peers, DW also has a large and loyal listenership.

☞ RECOMMENDED PROGRAM: "NewsLink" (*see* "Ten of the Best").

**Radio France Internationale focuses on Asia, Africa and the Middle East.**

**Deutsche Welle's "NewsLink" staff produces top-notch reports on developments in Germany and Europe.**
DW

Radio Netherlands was among the first to cast doubts on the viability of world band broadcasting in the face of evolving technologies. Yet, after years of experimentation they are now committed to world band more strongly than ever before.   RNW

*North and Central America:* 0100-0145 winter on 6040, 6145, 9640, 9700 and 9765 kHz; summer on 6040, 9640, 11810 and 13720 kHz. The second edition goes out at 0300-0345, winter on 6020, 6045, 9640, 9700 and 11985 kHz; summer on 9535, 9640, 11935 and 15105 kHz. The third and final broadcast is at 0500-0545, winter on 5960, 6120, 9670 and 11795 kHz; and summer on 9670, 9785 and 11985 kHz. This last offering is best for western North America.

*Europe:* 0600-1900 year-round on 6140 kHz; and 2000-2045 winter on 6180 kHz, replaced summer by 6140 kHz.

*Southern Africa:* 0400-0445 winter—summer in the Southern Hemisphere—on 9565 and 9710 kHz; summer on 6180, 7225, 12045 and 13690 kHz. The second slot is available 0900-0945 winter on 15410 and 17860 kHz; and midyear on 12035, 15410, 17800 and 21780 kHz. A third broadcast goes out at 1100-1145 on 15410 kHz; and the fourth and final edition airs at 1600-1645 winter on 15455 and 21840 kHz; and midyear on 9735, 11665 and 21840 kHz.

*East Asia:* 0900-0945 winter on 9770 kHz, summer on 15470 kHz.

*Southeast Asia and Australasia:* 0900-0945 winter on 6160, 9510, 17820, 17845 and 21790 kHz; summer on 6160, 9510, 17715, 17770, 17820 and 21790 kHz. A second broadcast—nominally to Australasia but also well heard in Southeast Asia—airs at 2100-2145 winter on 9690, 9765, 15275 and 17560 kHz; summer on 9670, 9765 and 12035 kHz. There's an additional transmission for Southeast Asia at 2300-2345: winter on 9470, 9815 and 13690 kHz; summer on 9815, 12000, 17560 and 21790 kHz.

## Netherlands

**Radio Netherlands**, after years of fine-tuning its identity, is now on a roll. Immensely popular with listeners, it is busy garnering a host of international awards. This station is strong on self-belief, so is not afraid to tackle thorny subjects. No dumbing down for marginal audiences, no wet fingers to the wind.

☞ RECOMMENDED PROGRAMS: "Aural Tapestry" (*see* "Ten of the Best") and "Documentary."

*Eastern North America:* 1130-1325 (one hour earlier in summer) on 5965 kHz, and 2330-0125 on 6165 and 9845 kHz.

*Western North America:* 1430-1625 on 15220 kHz, and 0430-0530 on 6165 and 9590 kHz.

*Europe:* 1130-1325(one hour earlier in summer) on 6045 and 9860 kHz.

*Southern Africa:* 1730-1925 on 6020 kHz.

*East and Southeast Asia:* 0930-1125 winter on 7260 and 12065 kHz, and summer on 12065 and 13710 kHz.

*Australia and the Pacific:* 0930-1125 on 9790 kHz. Frequencies for East and Southeast Asia are also widely heard within the region.

# NRD-545

## *Legendary Quality. Digital Signal Processing. Awesome Performance.*

**W**ith the introduction of the NRD-545, Japan Radio raises the standard by which high performance receivers are judged.

Starting with JRC's legendary quality of construction, the NRD-545 offers superb ergonomics, virtually infinite filter bandwidth selection, steep filter shape factors, a large color liquid crystal display, 1,000 memory channels, scan and sweep functions, and both double sideband and sideband selectable synchronous detection. With high sensitivity, wide dynamic range, computer control capability, a built-in RTTY demodulator, tracking notch filter, and sophisticated DSP noise control circuitry, the NRD-545 redefines what a high-performance receiver should be.

**JRC** *Japan Radio Co., Ltd.*

Japan Radio Company, Ltd., New York Office —
2125 Center Ave., Suite 208, Fort Lee, NJ 07024
Voice: 201-242-1882   Fax: 201-242-1885

Japan Radio Company, Ltd. — Akasaka Twin Tower (main), 17-22,
Akasaka 2-chome, Minato-ku, Tokyo 107, Japan   Fax: (03) 3584-8878

- LSB, USB, CW, RTTY, FM, AM, AMS, and ECSS (Exalted Carrier Selectable Sideband) modes.
- Continuously adjustable bandwidth from 10 Hz to 9.99 kHz in 10 Hz steps.
- Pass-band shift adjustable in 50 Hz steps up or down within a ±2.3 kHz range.
- Noise reduction signal processing adjustable in 256 steps.
- Tracking notch filter, adjustable within ±2.5 kHz in 10 Hz steps, follows in a ±10 kHz range even when the tuning dial is rotated.
- Continuously adjustable AGC between 0.04 sec and 5.1 sec in LSB, USB, CW, RTTY, and ECSS modes.
- 1,000 memory channels that store frequency, mode, bandwidth, AGC, ATT, and (for channels 0–19) timer on/off.
- Built-in RTTY demodulator reads ITU-T No. 2 codes for 170, 425, and 850 Hz shifts at 37 to 75 baud rates. Demodulated output can be displayed on a PC monitor through the built-in RS-232C interface.
- High sensitivity and wide dynamic range achieved through four junction-type FETs with low noise and superior cross modulation characteristics.
- Computer control capability.
- Optional wideband converter unit enables reception of 30 MHz to 2,000 MHz frequencies (less cellular) in all modes.

## Russia

The **Voice of Russia** has resisted the temptation to be trendy instead of effective. Instead, its program lineup includes cultural gems welcomed by audiences weary of cookie-cutter offerings. With a dedicated staff and vast sound archives, it makes exceptional use of the limited finances at its disposal.

☞ RECOMMENDED PROGRAM: "Russian Treasures" (*see* Ten of the Best).

*Eastern North America:* 0200-0600 winter on 7125 (0400-0600), 7180, 7250 (0200-0400), and (0200-0300) 9765 kHz; summer, one hour earlier, it's 9665 kHz at 0100-0500, 9725 kHz at 0100-0300, 11750 kHz at 0300-0500, and 11825 at 0100-0200. During winter afternoons, try frequencies beamed to Europe—some make it to eastern North America.

*Western North America:* Best for winter are: 0200-0400 on 7335, 12020 and 13665 kHz; and 0400-0600 on 7330, 12010, 12020, 13665 (till 0500), 15595 and 17595 kHz. For summer reception, one hour earlier, use 12000 and 17595 kHz at 0100-0300; and 12000, 17565, 17650, 17660 and 17690 kHz at 0300-0500.

*Europe:* Winter, it's 1800-2000 on 5940, 5950 (from 1900), 6175, 7335, 7340 and 9775 kHz; and 2000-2200 on 5940, 5950, 6175, 7300 (from 2100), 7335, 7340 and (2030-2100) 9775 kHz. Summer options are 1700-1900 on 9480, 9775, 9890, 11630

(from 1800) and 11675 kHz; and 1900-2100 on 9480, 9775, 9890 11675, 12030, 12070 and (from 2000) 15455 kHz. Note that 5940 and 6175 kHz (winter) and 9480 and 11675 kHz (summer) are only available weekends during the first hour.

*Middle East:* 1600-1900 (1500-1800 in summer). Winter, there's 6005 kHz (1600-1700), 9470 kHz (1700-1800), and 9830 kHz (1600-1900). In summer, use 7325 kHz at 1500-1600, 15540 kHz at 1600-1700, and 11985 kHz at 1500-1800.

*Southern Africa:* Officially, there's nothing beamed this way, but winter try 9875 kHz at 1500-1600, and 9875 and 11510 kHz at 1900-2000. Midyear, go for 9495 kHz at 1700-1900 and 11510 kHz at 1800-1900. These are targeted at East Africa, but make it farther south.

*Southeast Asia:* 0600-1000 winter on 11770, 17495 (from 0800) and 21485 (or 21810) kHz; and 0600-0900 summer on 15490, 17495 (from 0700), 17525, 17675, 17685 and 17795 kHz; 1500-1600 winter on 6205 and 11500 kHz; 1400-1500 summer on 7390, 12055, 15560 and 17645 kHz; and 1500-1600 summer on 11500 kHz.

*Australasia:* 0600-0800 winter on 15275, 15470, 17525, 17665 and 21790 kHz; and 0800-1000 on 9905 (from 0830), 15460, 15470, 17495, 17570 (till 0900) and 17525 kHz. Midyear, 0500-0900 on 17495 (from 0700), 17525 (from 0700), 17635 (from 0530), 17685 and (till 0700) 21790 kHz.

**Voice of Russia staff (from left): Elena Baskakova, Anastasia Mironova and Svetlana Yekimenko.** VoR

## United Kingdom

**BBC World Service's** management leaves the impression that the listener is the last person who matters. Indeed, its current director even sniffs that the station is not interested in being heard by the likes of Michigan automobile workers.

A combination of lower-quality productions and seven different program streams has strained audience patience. Some effort is being made to repair the damage, but this doesn't originate at the top so major improvement is unlikely anytime soon. Nevertheless, there remain a number of superb programs, which thanks to the dispersal properties of shortwave can be enjoyed almost anywhere.

**Jane Hanser of the BBC World Service's informative "Health Matters."**

BBC World Service

☞ RECOMMENDED PROGRAM: "Health Matters" (*see* Ten of the Best).

*North America:* Since July 2001, there have no longer been any broadcasts officially targeted at the United States and Canada. Nevertheless, the BBC is still heard well throughout much of the United States and Canada.

Best for eastern North America is the service for the Caribbean: 1000-1100 on 6195 kHz, 1100-1400 on 6195 and 15190 kHz, 1400-1700 on 15190 kHz, and 2100-0500 on 5975 kHz. The transmission for South America at 2100-0300 on 12095 kHz is also heard in parts of the region, but tends to suffer from teletype interference unless your radio has synchronous selectable sideband (choose the lower sideband). Too, some daytime frequencies for Europe and the Mideast can be heard— particularly during summer—but times vary, depending on your location and the time of year.

For nighttime and early morning reception in western North America, tune to the BBC's East Asia stream on 9740 kHz (1000-1600); reception is especially good on the West Coast. Winter evenings, try 9525 kHz (0100-0400) and 6135 kHz (0400-0600), replaced summer by 11835 kHz at 0100-0500; these transmissions are nominally for Mexico.

*Europe:* A powerhouse 0300-2300 on 6195, 9410, 12095, 15485, 15565 and 17640 kHz, with times varying for each channel. Three frequencies—12095 (part of the time), 15565 and 17640 kHz— carry the program stream intended for the Mideast.

*Middle East:* 0200-2000. Key frequencies—times for each vary according to whether it is winter or summer—are 9410, 11760, 12095, 15565, 15575 and 17640 kHz. Frequencies of 12095, 15565 and 17640 kHz are mainly intended for Eastern Europe, but provide acceptable reception in northern parts of the Mideast.

*Southern Africa:* 0300-2200 on, among others, 3255, 6005, 6190, 11940, 12095, 21470 and 21660 kHz—times vary for each channel.

*East and Southeast Asia:* 0000-0300 on 6195 (till 0200), 15280 and 15360 kHz; 0300-0500 on 15280, 15360 (till 0330), 17760 and 21660 kHz; 0500-0900 on 11955, 15280 (till 0530), 15360, 17760 and 21660; 0900-1030 on 6195, 9605, 9740, 11945, 15360, 17760 and 21660 kHz; 1030-1100 on 6195, 9740, 15360, 17760 (summer) and (weekends) 21660 kHz; 1100-1400 on 6195, 9740 and 15360 or 17760 kHz; 1400-1600 on 6135 (winter), 6195 and 9740 kHz; 1600-1700 on 3915, 6195 and 7160 kHz; and 1700-1800 (to Southeast Asia) on 3915 and 7160 kHz. Local mornings, it's 2100-2200 on 3915, 5965, 6195 and 11945 kHz; 2200-2300 on 5965, 6195, 7105 and 11685 kHz; and 2300-2400 on 3915, 5965, 6035 (or 9580), 6195, 7105, 11685 11945, 11955 and 15280 kHz.

*Australasia:* Like North America, Australasia is no longer an official target for BBC broadcasts. Fortunately, the back door of the candy store is still open—transmissions for Southeast Asia are easily heard in Australia and New Zealand. Best bets: 0500-0900 on 11955 and 15360 kHz; 1100-1600 on 9740 kHz; and 2200-2400 on 11685 kHz. At 2200-2300, 12080 kHz is also available for the southwestern Pacific.

## ASIA
### China

**China Radio International** is technically among the best, and has grown to become a serious international broadcaster. Expect some interesting news coverage in 2003 as the country makes important political and economic adjustments. CRI has a worldwide network of relays to complement powerful transmitters on home soil, so reception is good just about everywhere.

☞ RECOMMENDED PROGRAM: "Voices from Other Lands."

*Eastern North America:* 0100-0200 on 9580 and 9790 kHz, 0300-0400 on 9690 kHz, 0400-0500 on 9730 kHz, 1300-1400 on 9570 kHz, and 2300-2400 on 5990 (better to the south) and 13680 kHz.

*Western North America:* 0300-0400 on 9690 kHz, 0400-0500 on 9730 kHz, 0500-0600 (0400-0500 in summer) on 9560 kHz, 1400-1600 on 7405 (1300-1500 in summer) and 17720 kHz, and 2300-2400 on 13680 kHz.

*Europe:* 2000-2200 winter on 5965 and 9840 kHz, and summer on 11790 and 15110 kHz. A relay via Moscow can be heard winter at 2200-2300 on 7170 kHz, and summer on 9880 kHz (replaced by 7175 kHz in autumn).

*Middle East:* Officially, there are no broadcasts for this area, but try 1700-1800 on 9670 kHz; 1900-2000 winter on 9585 kHz (summer on 13790 kHz); and 1900-2100 on 9440 kHz, intended for North Africa.

*Southern Africa:* 1400-1600 on 13685 and 15125 kHz; 1600-1700 winter on 13650 kHz, and summer on 9565 kHz ; 1700-1800 on 9570, 9695 and (summer) 15265 kHz; and 2000-2130 on 11640 and 13630 kHz.

*Asia: (Southeast)* 1200-1300 on 9730 and 11980 kHz; and 1300-1400 on 11980 and 15180 kHz; *(South)* 1400-1500 winter on 9700, 11675 and 11765 kHz; and summer on 9700, 11675 and 15110 kHz; and 1500-1600 on 7160 and 9785 kHz.

*Australasia:* 0900-1100 on 11730 and 15210 kHz; 1200-1300 on 9760, 11760 and 15415 kHz; and 1300-1400 on 11760 and 11900 kHz.

### China (Taiwan)

**Radio Taipei International** is very much a window on Taiwan and all things Taiwanese, with lighter programming than that of its colleagues across the Strait. Europe and North America are served by relays, but Asia and Australasia receive their broadcasts direct from Taiwan.

☞ RECOMMENDED PROGRAM: "Jade Bells and Bamboo Pipes."

*Eastern North America:* 0200-0400 on 5950 kHz.

# Experience Events and Places Around the World...
## ...while in the comfort of your own chair.

**Drake's world band communication receivers preserve their history of excellence, with something for every level of skill or interest. You will appreciate the high standards of craftsmanship, quality, and performance, built into each receiver.**

### R8B Communications Receiver

For the avid enthusiast, the top of the line R8B offers serious performance with Selectable Sideband Synchronous Detection and five built-in filters.

### Also Available From Drake -

For the listener on the go, the Grundig Satellite 800 world band receiver provides all the advanced features of a table top unit. It is battery powered, portable, and includes an AC adapter and FM stereo headphones.
Size: 20.5" L x 9" H x 8" D.

## Order Now Risk Free! 15 Day Money Back Trial.

We are so confident you'll be impressed with the performance of our radios, we'll give you a full refund on your factory direct order, less shipping and handling charges, if the receiver doesn't meet your expectations. Call for complete details.

### Order Today, From Your Local Dealer or Factory Direct By Calling 1-800-568-3426.

 *The Finest Line of Products For The Shortwave Enthusiast.*

**R.L. Drake Company**
**phone:** 937-746-4556

230 Industrial Dr.
**fax:** 937-743-4510

Franklin, OH 45005 U.S.A.
**on-line:** www.rldrake.com

*Western North America:* 0200-0300 on 9680 kHz; 0300-0400 on 5950 and 9680 kHz; and 0700-0800 on 5950 kHz.

*Central America:* 0200-0300 on 11740 kHz; 0300-0400 and 0700-0800 on 5950 kHz.

*Europe:* 1800-1900 on 3955 kHz; and 2200-2300 on (winter) 5810 and 9355 kHz, and (summer) 15600 kHz.

*Middle East:* There is nothing specifically targeted to the Mideast, but if you have a superior receiver try the 2200-2300 broadcast to Europe via the Florida relay.

*Southern Africa:* Another area which is not officially targeted, but the 1600-1800 broadcast for South Asia on 11550 kHz is the best bet.

*Asia: (East)* 0200-0300 on 15465 kHz; 1100-1200 on 11985 kHz; and 1200-1300 on 7130 kHz; *(Southeast)* 0200-0300 on 15320 kHz; 0300-0400 on 11875 and 15320 kHz; 1100-1200 on 7445 kHz; and 1400-1500 on 15265 kHz; *(South)* 1600-1800 on 11550 kHz.

*Australasia:* 1200-1300 on 9610 kHz.

## Japan

**Radio Japan** is a respected source of Asian news, and airs a rich variety of Japanese music. Its worldwide relay network makes it easily heard just about anywhere.

☞ RECOMMENDED PROGRAM: "Music Beat."

*Eastern North America:* Best are 1100-1200 on 6120 kHz and 0000-0100 on 6145 kHz, both via the Canada relay in New Brunswick.

*Western North America:* 0500-0600 on 6110 and (winter) 9835 or (summer) 13630 kHz; 0600-0700 winter on 9835 kHz, and summer on 13630 kHz; 1400-1500 and 1700-1800 on 9505 kHz; and 2100-2200 on 17825 kHz. In Hawaii, tune in at 0600-0700 on 17870 kHz and 2100-2200 on 21670 kHz. For Central America there's 0300-0400 on 17825 kHz.

*Europe:* 0500-0600 on 5975 kHz; 0500-0700 on 7230 kHz; 1700-1800 on 11970 kHz; 2100-2200 on 6115, 6180 and 11830 kHz.

*Middle East:* 0100-0200 on 11870 (winter), 11880 and (summer) 17560 kHz; and 1400-1500 on 17755 kHz.

*Southern Africa:* 1700-1800 on 15355 kHz.

*Asia:* 0000-0015 on 13650 and 17810 kHz; 0100-0200 on 11860, 15325, 17810 and 17845 kHz; 0500-0600 on 11715, 11760, 15195 and 17810 kHz; 0600-0700 on 11740 and 15195 kHz; 1000-1200 on 9695 and 15590 kHz; 1400-1500 on 7200, 9845 (winter) and (summer) 11730 kHz; and 1500-1600 on 7200, 9750, 9845 (winter) and (summer) 11730 kHz. Transmissions to Asia are often heard in other parts of the world, as well.

*Australasia:* 0100-0200 on 17685 kHz; 0300-0400 on 21610 kHz; 0500-0700 and 1000-1100 on 21755 kHz; and 2100-2200 winter on 11850 and 11920 kHz, replaced midyear by 6035 and 17860 kHz.

## AMERICAS
### Canada

**Radio Canada International** formerly vied with the BBC World Service for the largest audience in the United States, and had a major impact in other countries, as well. However, in recent years it has been caught up in bureaucratic turf wars and union disputes, and now relays many existing programs from the domestic CBC. For Canadian exiles and peacekeeping troops this provides a welcome link to home, but the original audience of foreigners has largely wandered off to more interesting pastures.

Still, many of these CBC programs are first rate, and help serve to introduce the world to oft-underestimated Canadian artistic talent.

☞ RECOMMENDED PROGRAM: "Global Village."

# Listening is only half the fun...
# POPULAR
# COMMUNICATIONS
## *is the other half*

**If you enjoy radio communications, you'll love**

**POPULAR COMMUNICATIONS** — the largest, most authoritative monthly magazine for Shortwave Listening and Scanner Monitoring. Get fast home delivery and find out why **POPULAR COMMUNICATIONS** is read by more active listeners than all other communications publications combined! Subscribe today and SAVE over 58% off the newsstand price (Save even more off 2- and 3-year subscriptions).

## FOR FASTER SERVICE FAX 1-516-681-2926

Name_____Call_____

Address _____

City _____State _____Zip _____

☐ **1 year 12 issues........$28.95**    ☐ **2 years 24 issues........$51.95**    ☐ **3 years 36 issues........$74.95**
*Save $30.93*                                *Save $67.81*                                *Save $104.69*
Canada/Mexico–one year $38.95,  two years $71.95,  three years $104.95. **U.S Dollars**
Foreign Air post–one year $48.95,  two years $91.95,  three years $134.95. **U.S Dollars**

Credit Card #_____Exp. Date _____

☐ Check        ☐ Money Order        ☐ MasterCard        ☐ VISA        ☐ AMEX        ☐ Discover
Allow 6 to 8 weeks for delivery                                                    PASSWBR 03

## Popular Communications, 25 Newbridge Road, Hicksville, NY 11801 Telephone (516) 681-2922

Radio Canada International now carries many programs from the domestic CBC, a number of which originate at the CBC's Toronto headquarters. A. Mujunen

*Europe:* 2100-2200 winter on 9770, 11600, 12015 and 13650 kHz; and 2000-2100 summer on 5850, 5995, 11690, 15325 and 17870 kHz.

*Middle East:* Best bets are 2100-2200 winter on 7425 kHz, and 2000-2100 summer on 11690 or 15470 kHz.

*Asia:* To East Asia at 1200-1300 winter on 9660 and 11730 kHz, and summer on 9660 and 15190 kHz; to Southeast Asia at 0000-0100 on 9640 (summer), 9680 (winter) and 11895 kHz; and 1200-1300 on (winter) 11730 and (summer) 15190 kHz; to South Asia at 0200-0300 on 15150 (winter), 15260 (summer) and 17860 kHz; and 1500-1600 winter on 15360 and 17820 kHz, replaced summer by 15455 and 17720 kHz.

## United States

The **Voice of America** has become something of a political hot potato. Its editorial independence has been questioned, it has few friends in Congress, and for years it has been hopelessly mismanaged at the highest level. It is now but a shadow of its former self.

On the positive side, several music shows have been introduced to break the monotony of the former rolling-news format, and news programs are now broader-based. Too, a new director was appointed at the end of August 2002, so there remains the possibility of eventual improvement.

The VOA's biggest problem is that politicians and others with little or no experience in international broadcasting are increasingly dictating how the station should be run. This has led to certain of its language services being treated like commercial music operations to attract advertiser-friendly youthful demographics rather than dependable vehicles for information and influence. It's hardly surprising, as the *au courant* mantra is, "If American advertising can sell Coca-Cola, why can't the Voice of America sell the USA"?

*North America:* Morning reception is much better in eastern North America than farther west, but evening broadcasts fare somewhat better. Winter, morning broadcasts air at 1300-1400 weekdays, 1400-1600 (daily) and 1600-1700 Sunday, all on 9515, 9640 and 17710 kHz. In summer, transmissions are an hour earlier: 1200-1500 Monday-Friday on 9515, 13655 and 17820 kHz; and 1300-1600 weekends on 9515, 13655 and 17800 kHz. Winter evening broadcasts air at 2300-0100 on 5960, 6175, 9590 and 9755 kHz; and 0200-0300 on 6040, 9755 and 11990 kHz. Summer is 2200-2400 on 6175, 9590, 13670 and 17695 kHz; and 0100-0200 on 5960, 13670, 15170 and 15305 kHz.

☞ RECOMMENDED PROGRAM: "Music Time in Africa."

*North America:* There is a widespread misconception that because the VOA isn't beamed to an American audience, it can't be heard within the United States. In reality, it comes in quite well on world band, allowing American taxpayers to hear firsthand what their government is telling the world in their name. The two best times to listen are when the VOA broadcasts to South America and the Caribbean. The morning schedule is 1000-1100 daily on 5745, 7370 and 9590 kHz; and evening broadcasts are at 0000-0200 Tuesday through Saturday—local weekday evenings in the Americas—on 5995, 6130, 7405, 9455, 9775, 11695 (till 0100), 13740 (0130-0200) and (0000-0130) 13790 kHz. The African Service can also be heard in parts of North America; try 0300-0500 on 9575 kHz; 0500-0630 (till 0700 weekends) on 6035 kHz; 1800-2200 on 15580 kHz; and 2000-2200 on 17895 kHz.

There's not much for *Europe*, but try 0400-0700 winter on 7170 kHz, and summer on 9530 kHz; 0500-0700 winter on 11825 kHz; 1500-1700 winter on 15205 kHz; 1700-2100 summer on 9760 kHz; and 2100-2200 year-round on 6040 and 9760 kHz.

*Middle East:* 0400-0700 winter on 11825 (from 0500) and 15205 kHz; 0400-0700 summer on 11965 and 15205 kHz; 1400-1500 (winter) on 15205 kHz; 1500-1700 on 9575 (winter), 9700 (summer) and 15205 kHz; 1700-1800 winter on 6040, 9760 and 15205 kHz; summer on 9700 and 9760 kHz; 1800-2100 winter on 6040 (till 1900), 9690 (from 1900) and 9760 kHz; summer on 6095 (from 1900), 6160 (1900-2000), 9760 and (till 1900) 9770; and 2100-2200 on 6040, 6095 (summer), 9595 (winter) and 9760 kHz.

*Southern Africa:* 0300-0500 on 5855 (midyear), 6080, 7105 (till 0400), 7340 (to 0330), 7415 (winter), 9575, 9885 (till 0430), and (midyear) 17895 kHz; 0500-0630 (to 0700 weekends) on 11835 (or 13670) and 12080 (or 13710) kHz; 1600-1700 on 13710, 15225 (or 15485), 15240 (or 15410) and 17895 kHz; 1700-1800 on 15240 (or 15410) and 17895 kHz; and 1800-2200 on 7415 (from 1900 winter), 15240 (or 15410), 15445 (midyear, from 1900), 15580 and 17895 kHz.

*East and Southeast Asia:* 0800-1000 winter on 11995, 13615 and 15150 kHz; summer on 11930, 13620, 13760 and 15150 kHz; 1000-1100 winter on 15250 and 15455 kHz; summer on 13620, 15240 and 15425 kHz; 1100-1300 winter on 6110, 9760, 11705, 15250 and 15455 kHz; summer on 6160, 9760, 13610, 15160, 15240 and 15425 kHz; 1300-1500 winter on 6110, 9760, 11705 and 15480 kHz; summer on 6160, 15160 and 15425 kHz; 1700-1800 weekdays, winter on 6045, 9525, 9670, 9795 and 11955 kHz; summer on 6045, 7215, 9770 and 9785 kHz; 1900-2000 on 15180 kHz; 2100-2200 on 15185 and 17820 kHz; 2200-2400 on 7215, 9770, 9890 (winter), 15185, 15290, 15305 and 17820 kHz; and 0000-0100 on 7215, 9770 (summer), 9890 (winter), 15185, 15290 and 17820 kHz.

*Australasia:* 1000-1200 on 5985 (winter), 9645 (from 1100), 9770 (midyear), 11720 and 15425 kHz; 1200-1500 on 9645 (till 1400), 11715 (till 1300) and 15425 kHz; 1700-1800 weekdays on 5990 and (mid-year) 7170 or (winter) 15255 kHz; 1900-2000 on 9525 and 11770 (or 11870) kHz; 2100-2200 on 9670 (winter), 9705 (mid-year), 11870 and 17735 (or 17740) kHz; 2200-2400 on 9705 (midyear), 9770 (winter), 11760 and 17735 (or 17740) kHz; and 0000-0100 on 11760 and 17740 kHz.

*Prepared by Tony Jones and the staff of* PASSPORT TO WORLD BAND RADIO.

www.passband.com

# GRUNDIG STAY

# SATELLIT 800 MILLENNIUM

The Satellit 800 Millennium. In the history of shortwave receivers, no other manufacturer has maintained a continuously evolving series of high-end portable radios, decade after decade.

**Extensive frequency coverage.**
- Long wave, AM-broadcast and Shortwave, 100-30,000 KHz, continuous.
- FM broadcast, 87-108 MHz.
- VHF aircraft band, 118-137 MHz.
- Multi-mode reception – AM, FM-stereo, Single Sideband USB/LSB and VHF aircraft band.

**The right complement of high-tech features.**
- Three built-in bandwidths, using electronically switched IF filters: 6.0, 4.0, 2.3 KHz.
- Synchronous detector for improved quality of AM and shortwave broadcast signals, minimizes fading, distortion and adjacent frequency interference.
- Selectable AGC in fast and slow mode. Auto Backlight shutoff to conserve battery life. Low Battery Indicator.

**Performance engineered for the best possible reception.**
- High Dynamic Range, allowing for detection of weak signals in the presence of strong signals.
- Excellent sensitivity and selectivity.

**Legendary Grundig audio.**
- Outstanding audio quality, with separate bass and treble tone control - in the Grundig tradition.
- FM Stereo with headphones or external amplified stereo speakers.
- Includes high quality stereo headphones.
- Multiple audio outputs: line level output for recording, stereo headphone output.

**Information displayed the way it should be.**
- Large, illuminated, informational LCD display of operational parameters, measuring a massive 6˝ x 3½˝, easy to read.
- An elegant, calibrated, analog signal strength meter, in the finest tradition.
- Digital frequency display to 100 Hertz accuracy on AM, SW and VHF aircraft bands. 50 Hz when SSB used.

**Traditional and high-tech tuning controls.**
- A real tuning knob, like on traditional radios, but with ultra-precise digital tuning, with absolutely no audio muting when used.
- A modern, direct-frequency-entry keypad for instant frequency access, and push buttons for fixed-step tuning.

**Plenty of user programmable memory.**
- 70 programmable memories, completely immune to loss due to power interruptions.
- Memory scan feature.

**Clocks and timers.**
- Dual, 24 hour format clocks.
- Dual programmable timers.

**Antenna capabilities that really make sense.**
- Built in telescopic antenna for portable use on all bands.
- External antenna connections for the addition of auxiliary antennas, e.g. professionally engineered shortwave antennas; long-wire shortwave antennas; specialized AM broadcast band antennas for enthusiasts of AM DX'ing; FM broadcast band antennas; VHF air band antennas.

**Power, dimensions, weight.**
- Operation on six internal "D" cell batteries or the included 110V AC adapter (a 220V AC adapter is available upon request).
- Big dimensions and weight. A real radio. 20.5˝ L x 9.4˝ H x 8˝ W., 14.5 lb.

# ALERT! BE INFORMED!

## Yacht Boy 400PE

This is a true high-performance receiver offering the best performance available in its class. You will hear international broadcasts from around the world on shortwave, including broadcasts and communications requiring SSB circuitry. Listen to shortwave on its built-in telescopic antenna or connect it your favorite external antenna. But do not think it is just for shortwave. Its superior sensitivity and selectivity make it the best choice for anyone needing superior AM and FM performance in weak-signal and fringe areas. Perfect for pulling in those distant, hard to get AM talk shows that are so popular today.
Dimensions: 7.75″ L x 4.5″ H x 1.5″ W.
Weight:   1 lb. 5 oz.

## Yacht Boy 300PE

Designed with remarkable performance at an incredibly low price, the YB300PE receives world wide international shortwave broadcasts as well as your local AM and FM-stereo stations. Great for either travel or home use, it is small enough for large pockets or carry-on luggage and takes up little space on your desk. Use the alarm clock feature to wake you up in the morning and the sleep timer to lull you asleep at night.
Dimensions: 5.75″ L x 3.5″ H x 1.25″ W.
Weight:   12 oz.

**universal radio inc.**

6830 Americana Pkwy.
Reynoldsburg, Ohio
43068-4113 U.S.A.

| | |
|---|---|
| **Orders & Prices phone:** | **800 431-3939** |
| **Information phone:** | **614 866-4267** |
| **Fax:** | **614 866-2339** |
| **Web:** | dx@universal-radio.com |
| | www.DXing.com |
| | www.universal-radio.com |

# How to Choose a World Band Radio

Some electronic products are almost commodities—with a little common sense you can get what you want without fuss or bother.

Not so world band receivers, which vary greatly from model to model. As usual, money talks, but even that's a fickle barometer. Fortunately, many perform well and we rate them accordingly. Yet, even among models with comparable star ratings it helps to choose a radio that fits your requirements.

### No Elbow Room

World band radio is a jungle: 1,100 channels, with stations scrunched cheek-by-jowl. It's much more crowded than FM or mediumwave AM, and to make matters worse a global voyage can make signals weak and quavery. To cope, a radio has to perform exceptional electronic gymnastics. Some succeed, others don't.

This is why PASSPORT REPORTS was created. At IBS we've tested hundreds of world band radios and accessories since 1977. These evaluations include rigorous hands-on use by listeners, plus specialized lab tests we've developed over the years. These form the basis of PASSPORT REPORTS, and for some popular premium receivers and antennas there are also the soup-to-nuts Radio Database International White Papers®.

## Four-Point Checklist

✔ **Price.** Do you want to hear big stations, or flush out soft voices from exotic lands? Powerful evening signals, or weaker signals by day? Decide, then choose a radio that surpasses your needs by a good notch or so—this helps ensure against disappointment without wasting money.

**Grundig's pocket-sized eTraveller VII.** Grundig/Lextronix

Once the novelty wears thin, most people give up on cheap radios—they're clumsy to tune, often receive poorly and can sound terrible. That's why we don't cover analog-tuned models, but even some digitally tuned models can disappoint.

Most find satisfaction with portables selling for $100-200 in the United States or £90-130 in the United Kingdom with a rating of ✪✪⅞ or more. If you're looking for elite performance, shoot for a portable or portatop rated ✪✪✪¾ or better—at least $350 or £300—or consider a five-star tabletop model.

---

## PASSPORT'S STANDARDS

At International Broadcasting Services we have been analyzing shortwave equipment since 1977. Our reviewers, and no one else, write everything in PASSPORT REPORTS. These include our laboratory findings, all of which are done by an independent laboratory recognized as the world's leader. (For more on this, please see the Radio Database International White Paper, *How to Interpret Receiver Lab Tests and Measurements*.)

Our review process is completely separate from equipment advertising, which is not allowed within PASSPORT REPORTS. Our team members may not accept review fees from manufacturers, nor may they "permanently borrow" radios. International Broadcasting Services does not manufacture, sell or distribute world band radios or related hardware.

> **We have been analyzing shortwave equipment since 1977.**

PASSPORT recognizes superior products regardless of when they first appear on the market. We don't bestow annual awards, but instead designate each exceptional model, regardless of its year of introduction, as *Passport's Choice.*

# FEATURES FOR SOLID PERFORMANCE

A signal should not just be audible, but actually sound pleasant. Radios can have several features which help bring this about—some keep out unwanted sounds, others enhance audio quality. Of course, just because a feature exists doesn't mean it functions properly, but we check for this in PASSPORT REPORTS.

## "Must" Features for Quality Reception

*Full world band coverage* from 2300-26100 kHz is best, although 3200-21850 kHz or even 4750-21850 kHz is usually adequate. If coverage is less, look at "Best Times and Frequencies for 2003" elsewhere in this book to ensure that important world band segments are completely covered.

*Synchronous selectable sideband* greatly enhances rejection of adjacent-channel interference while reducing fading distortion. It is found on some models selling for $150 or £110 and up.

Especially if a receiver doesn't have synchronous selectable sideband, it helps to have two or more *bandwidths* for superior adjacent-channel rejection. Some premium models incorporate this *and* synchronous selectable sideband—a killer combo. Multiple band-widths are found on a number of models over $140 or £95.

*Multiple conversion* or *double conversion* helps reject spurious "image" signals— unwanted growls, whistles, dih-dah sounds and the like. Few models under $100 or £70 have it; nearly all over $150 or £100 do.

## Other Helpful Attributes

High-quality speakers are an aural plus, as are *tone controls*—preferably continuously tunable with separate bass and treble adjustments. For world band reception, *single-sideband* (SSB) reception capability is only marginally relevant, but it is essential for utility or "ham" signals, as well as reception of low-powered signals from the U.S. Armed Forces Radio & Television Network. On costlier models you'll get it whether you want it or not.

Heavy-hitting tabletop models are designed to flush out virtually the most stubborn signal, but they usually require experience to operate and are overkill for casual listening. Among these look for a tunable *notch filter* to zap howls; *passband offset* (a/k/a *passband tuning* and *IF shift*) for superior adjacent-channel rejection and audio contouring, especially in conjunction with synchronous selectable sideband; and multiple *AGC* decay rates. At electrically noisy locations a *noise blanker* is essential; some work much better than others.

*Digital signal processing (DSP)* is the latest attempt to enhance mediocre signal quality. Until recently it has been much smoke, little fire, but the technology is improving. Watch for more DSP receivers in the years to come, but don't worship at their altar.

With portables and portatops an *AC adaptor* reduces operating costs and may improve weak-signal performance. Some of these are poorly made and cause hum, but most are quite good. With tabletop models an *inboard AC power supply* is preferable but not essential.

Looking ahead, *digital shortwave transmission* is being tested by Digital Radio Mondiale (www.drm.org). However these tests fare, it will be years, if then, before existing analog transmissions are phased out in favor of digital.

**If mounted correctly, an outdoor wire antenna will withstand even near-Arctic conditions.**

S. Soininen

✔ **Location.** Signals tend to be strongest in and around Europe, next-strongest in eastern North America. Elsewhere in the Americas, or in Hawaii or Australasia, you'll need a receiver that's unusually sensitive to weak signals—some sort of accessory antenna helps, too.

✔ **Which features?** Divide features between those which affect performance and those that impact operation (see sidebars), but be wary of judging a radio mainly by its features. A radio with few features may outperform one laden with goodies.

✔ **Where to buy?** Whether you buy in a store, by phone or on the Web makes little difference. That's because world band receivers don't test well in stores except in the handful of world band showrooms with proper outdoor antennas. Even then, long-term satisfaction is hard to gauge from a spot test, so visits at different times are advisable.

One thing a store lets you get a feel for is ergonomics—how intuitive a radio is to operate. You can also get a thumbnail idea of world band fidelity by listening to mediumwave AM stations or a superpower world band station.

**www.passband.com**

## USEFUL OPERATING FEATURES

*Digital frequency readout* is a "must" to find stations quickly. A *24-hour World Time clock* helps to know when to tune in; many receivers have them, or you can buy them separately.

Also: direct-access tuning via *keypad* and *presets* ("memories"); and any combination of a *tuning knob*, up/down *slewing* controls or *"signal-seek" scanning* to hunt around for stations. Some radios have handy *one-touch presets* buttons, like a car radio.

Depending on your listening habits, you may be interested in an *on/off timer* or built-in cassette recording. Also, look for an *illuminated display* and a good *signal-strength indicator*. Travelers prefer portables with power-lock switches that keep the radio from going on accidentally, but the lock on some Chinese-made portables doesn't disable the display illumination.

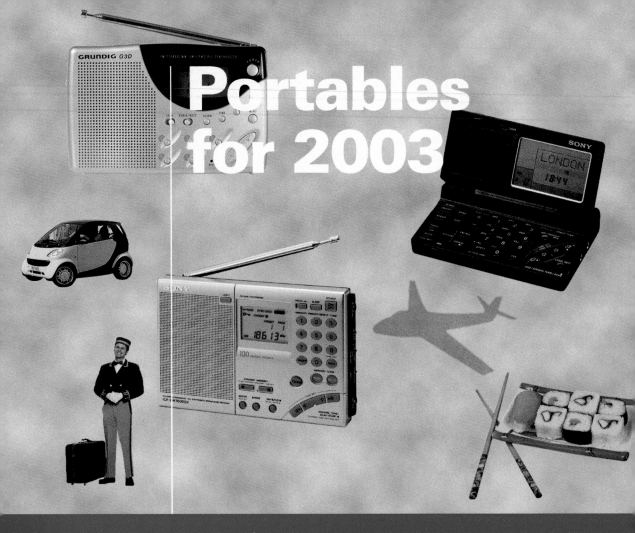

# Portables for 2003

Portables are what most of us purchase, even if we also own something fancier. They are handy, affordable and usually do the trick.

In Europe and along the east coast of North America, evening signals come in so well that virtually any well-rated portable should be all you'll need. Even if you live elsewhere or listen during the day, when signals are weaker—or are

into chasing anemic signals—a top-ranked portable can do surprisingly well just by being coupled to a simple outdoor wire antenna.

### World Band on the Go

World band makes for unbeatable outdoor entertainment, as well as a global link when you're traveling. For these and emergency situations, only a portable will do.

Compact and pocket portables are the radio equivalents of Palm-type handhelds, while some larger portables are more like smaller laptop computers. There are compact models with three or more stars that sell for around the equivalent of $150 to $200—you can't go wrong with these workhorses. But there are also compacts that sell for much less which are good enough for occasional use. These are excellent values for trips, although even travel warriors should think twice before going mini. A pocket model makes sense only if weight is paramount and you have a larger radio at home.

Not surprisingly, top-rated portables are also among the largest, but they're not huge. PASSPORT staffers routinely use Sony ICF-2010 lap portables while globetrotting, for example.

## Sales Rise

Since the Gulf war there has been a shift in the world band radio landscape in North America, and to a lesser degree Europe and Australasia. All but vanished are cheap analog radios with such dismal performance that they drove newcomers away from world band. At the same time demand has slackened for tabletop receivers, although this may be turning around.

## Marketing Creates Dominance

The lion's share of world band radios are now priced from $99.95 to $499.95, and it is that market segment which has grown the most in recent years. The manufacturer lineup has become much more focused, as well. Grundig's Lextronix, a marketing powerhouse based in California, is now the 600-pound world band gorilla in North America—especially since Radio Shack dropped its line of world band portables in mid-2002. These have been replaced by Grundig units, which thanks to Lextronix's savvy promotion have reportedly outsold Radio Shack's former house-brand models.

Fortunately, the best of those erstwhile Radio Shack portables continue to be available from the original manufacturer, Sangean, whose branded products are sold by world band specialty firms, mail-order catalogs and other retail outlets. As a bonus, native Sangean versions sometimes come standard with accessories that cost extra under the Radio Shack imprimatur.

## Sony De-emphasizes Consumer Electronics

Also important for 2003 is the unfolding history of Sony, whose dominant presence in world band was personally overseen for years by the company's late founder, the legendary Akio Morita. According to press reports, Sony is now moving away from consumer electronics products of all types, closing factories and emphasizing minimization of inventories. Additionally, marketing managers have had their

Find major updates to the 2003 PASSPORT REPORTS at www. passband.com.

workloads increased to the point where there is a paucity of human and other marketing resources to devote to any one product type.

Thus it is that when 9/11 caused demand to rise in North America, Sony continued to maintain old levels of production so as not to risk having additional inventory. Moreover, according to a Sony spokesperson, in 2003 they plan to drop their best-performing model, the ICF-2010, at the very time when demand is at its highest.

The future? Grundig's Lextronix arm, possibly in liaison with other firms, may be planning to take advantage of world band's relatively high profit margins by expanding its marketing outside North America. However, with over half a billion shortwave listeners worldwide, this is too large an opportunity to be dominated by any one company for long. As the decade unfolds, look for hungry new players from China to step to the plate and restore competition lost by the fading profiles of others.

## Longwave Useful for Some

The longwave band is still used for some domestic broadcasts in Europe, North Africa and Russia. If you live or travel there, longwave coverage may be a slight plus. Otherwise, forget it.

## Who's the Toughie?

Thankfully, the days of poorly made world band portables appear to be largely behind us. At the same time, truly robust models are becoming harder to find as production and design economies take their toll. With any brand of world band radio, experience suggests that you should avoid models which have been recently introduced and are technologically sophisticated.

Most Sony world band radios are made in Japan, whereas all Grundig and all but one of Sangean's models are now made in China. "Made in China" was once enough to raise a caution flag on high. However, build quality from Chinese plants, although still

---

### TIPS FOR GLOBETROTTING

Air travel with a world band radio, even post-9/11, has proven not to be a problem so long as you take some common-sense steps. To avoid hassles with airline security personnel:

- Bring a portable, not a portatop or tabletop model—terrorists like big radios. Best is a pocket or compact model, although we've encountered no security problems with lap portables.
- Stow your radio in a carry-on bag, not in checked luggage or on your person.
- Take along fresh batteries so you can demonstrate that the radio actually works.
- If asked what the radio is for, say for personal use.
- If traveling in zones of war or civil unrest, or off the beaten path in much of Africa or parts of South America, take along a radio you can afford to lose and which fits inconspicuously in a pocket.
- If traveling to Bahrain, avoid taking a radio which has the word "receiver" on its cabinet. Security personnel may think you're a spy.

Theft? Radios, cameras, binoculars, laptop computers and the like are almost always stolen to be resold. The more worn the item looks—affixing scuffed stickers helps—the less likely it is to be confiscated by corrupt inspectors or stolen by thieves.

rarely equal to Japanese or Taiwanese standards, is now much better and continues to improve.

## Fix It?

Portables aren't meant to be friends for life, and are priced accordingly. The most robust models are usually not ready for the landfill until after years of use, whereas some pedestrian models may give no more than a few years of regular service. At that point, they aren't worth fixing.

If you purchase a genuinely defective new portable, insist upon an immediate exchange without a restocking fee—manufacturers' repair facilities tend to have a disappointing record. That having been said, Grundig in Europe and North America, and Sangean America in the United States and Canada appear to be providing better in-warranty service on portables than most, but even their post-warranty service can seriously disappoint. If quality of service is important to you, consider a tabletop model, instead.

## Shelling Out

Street prices are given, including British and Australian VAT/GST where applicable. These vary plus or minus, so take them as the general guide they are meant to be. Shortwave specialty outlets and a growing number of other retailers have attractive prices, whereas duty-free shopping is not always the bargain you might expect.

We try to stick to plain English, but some specialized terms have to be used. If you come across something that's not clear, check with this edition's glossary.

## Findings Apply Worldwide

PASSPORT REPORTS evaluates virtually every digitally tuned portable that meets reasonable minimum standards. We go wherever in the world it is necessary to obtain radios, and our findings are applicable worldwide, with

geographical provisos given as appropriate. Here, then, are the results of our hands-on and laboratory tests of current models.

## What PASSPORT's Ratings Mean

**Star ratings:** ✪✪✪✪✪ is best. Stars reflect overall performance and meaningful features, plus to some extent ergonomics and build quality. Price, appearance, country of manufacture and the like are not taken into account. Nevertheless, to facilitate comparison, the portable rating standards are very similar to those used for the portatop, tabletop and professional models reviewed elsewhere in this PASSPORT.

A rating of at least ✪✪½ should please most who listen to major stations regularly during the evening. However, for casual use on trips virtually any small portable may suffice.

*Passport's Choice.* La crème de la crème. Our test team's personal picks of the litter—digitally tuned portables we would buy or have bought for our personal use.

✪: A relative bargain, with decidedly more performance than the price would suggest.

## How Portables Are Listed

Models are listed by size; and, within size, in order of world band listening suitability. Street prices are cited, including VAT/GST where applicable. Versions designed for certain few countries might not receive single-sideband signals and/or may have reduced tuning ranges.

Unless otherwise indicated, each digital model has:

- Tuning by keypad, up/down slewing keys, station presets and signal-seek tuning.
- Digital frequency readout to the nearest kilohertz.
- Coverage of the world band shortwave spectrum from at least 3200-26100 kHz.
- Coverage of the usual 87.5-108 MHz FM band.

## WHAT TO LOOK FOR

• **Tuning features.** Digitally tuned models are so superior to analog that these are now the only models tested by PASSPORT. Look for such handy tuning aids as direct-frequency access via keypad, station presets (programmable channel memories), up-down tuning via tuning knob and/or slewing keys, band/segment selection, and signal-seek or other scanning. These make the radio easier to tune—no small point, given that a hundred or more channels may be audible at any one time.

• **Audio quality.** Unlike many portatop and tabletop models, portables don't have rich, full audio. However, some are better than others.

• **Adjacent-channel rejection I:** *selectivity, bandwidth*. World band stations are packed together about twice as closely as ordinary mediumwave AM stations, so they tend to slop over and interfere with each other. Radios with superior selectivity are better at rejecting this. However, enhanced selectivity also means less high-end ("treble") audio response and muddier sound. So, having more than one bandwidth allows you to choose between superior selectivity ("narrow bandwidth") when it is warranted, and more realistic audio ("wide bandwidth") when it is not.

• **Adjacent-channel rejection II:** *synchronous selectable sideband*. This is the first major advance in world band listening quality in decades. With powerful stations "out in the clear," it has little audible impact. However, for tougher signals it improves audio quality by minimizing selective-fading distortion, while reducing adjacent-channel interference by selecting the "better half" of a signal. *Bonus:* this feature also helps considerably in reducing distortion with fringe mediumwave AM stations—mid-distance stations also audible by day—at twilight and even at night.

• **Single-sideband demodulation.** If you are interested in hearing non-broadcast short-wave signals—"hams" and utility signals—single-sideband circuitry is *de rigeur*. Too, the popular low-powered U.S. Armed Forces Radio-Television Service (AFRTS/AFN) can only be heard intelligibly on receivers with single-sideband capability. No portable excels, but those that stand out are cited in PASSPORT REPORTS.

• **Weak-signal sensitivity.** Important if you live in a weak-signal location or tune to DX or daytime stations. Since the BBC's cutbacks in 2001, this also has become relevant for hearing the World Service within North America and Australasia. On the other hand, most portables have enough sensitivity to pull in major stations evenings if you're in such places as Europe or North Africa—even the east coast of North America.

☞ A simple outboard antenna enhances sensitivity, as well as the signal-to-noise ratio, on nearly any good portable.

• **Ergonomics.** Some radios are easy to use because they don't have complicated features. But even complex models can be designed to operate intuitively.

• **World Time clock.** A World Time clock—24-hour format—is a "must." You can obtain these separately, but many radios have them built in; the best display time whether the radio is on or off.

• **AC adaptor.** An outboard AC adaptor is virtually a necessity except on trips. Those provided by the manufacturer are usually best and should be free from hum and noise.

- Coverage of the AM (mediumwave) band in selectable 9 and 10 kHz channel increments from about 530-1700 kHz.
- Adequate spurious-signal ("image") rejection.
- No synchronous selectable sideband or single-sideband demodulation. However, when there is synchronous selectable sideband, the unwanted sideband is rejected approximately 25 dB via phasing, not IF filtering.

## POCKET PORTABLES

### Perfect for Travel, Marginal for Home

Pocket portables weigh under a pound, or half-kilogram, and are between the size of an audio cassette jewel box and a handheld calculator. They operate off two to four ordinary small "AA" (UM-3 penlite) batteries. These diminutive models do one job well: provide news and entertainment when you're traveling.

Don't expect much more. Listening to tiny speakers can be tiring, so pocket portables aren't great for everyday listening except through earpieces.

There is a superior choice among compact models. Their bigger speakers sound better, and they're still small enough for carry-on bags.

✪✪✪ *Passport's Choice*
### Sony ICF-SW100S

**Price:** $359.95 in the United States. CAN$599.00 as available in Canada. £199.95 in the United Kingdom. €333.00 in Germany.

**Pro:** Tiny. Superior overall world band performance for size category. High-tech synchronous selectable sideband generally performs well, reducing adjacent-channel interference and selective-fading distortion on world band, longwave and mediumwave AM signals, while adding slightly to weak-signal sensitivity and audio crispness (*see* Con). Single bandwidth, especially when

**Soldier's Friend: Sony's ICF-SW100 is ultra-sophisticated, yet only the size of a cassette box. Don't leave Langley without it.**

synchronous selectable sideband is used, exceptionally effective at adjacent-channel rejection. Relatively good audio, provided supplied earbuds or outboard audio are used (*see* Con). FM stereo through earbuds. Numerous helpful tuning features, including keypad, two-speed slewing, signal-seek-then-resume scanning (*see* Con), five handy "pages" with ten presets each. Presets can display station name. Tunes in relatively precise 0.1 kHz increments. Good single-sideband performance (*see* Con). Good dynamic range. Worthy ergonomics for size and features. Illuminated display. Clock for many world cities, which can be made to work as a *de facto* World Time clock (*see* Con). Timer/snooze. Travel power lock. Japanese FM (most versions) and longwave bands. Amplified outboard antenna, in addition to usual built-in antenna (*see* Con). Weak-battery indicator; about 16 hours from a set of batteries (*see* Con). High-quality travel case for radio. *Except for North America:* AC adaptor comes with American and European plugs and adjusts automatically to local voltages worldwide.

**Con:** Tiny speaker, although innovative, has mediocre sound, limited loudness and little tone shaping. Closing clamshell reduces speaker loudness and high-frequency response. Weak-signal sensitivity could be better, although supplied outboard active antenna helps. Expensive. No tuning knob. Clock not readable when station frequency displayed. As "London Time" is used by the clock for World Time, the summertime clock adjustment cannot be used if World Time is to be displayed accurately. Rejection of certain spurious signals ("images"), and 10 kHz "repeats" when synchronous selectable sideband off, could be better. In some urban locations, FM signals from 87.5 to 108 MHz can break through into world band segments with distorted sound, e.g. between 3200 and 3300 kHz. Synchronous selectable sideband tends to lose lock if batteries weak, or if NiCd cells are used. Synchronous selectable sideband alignment can vary with temperature, factory alignment and battery voltage, causing synchronous selectable sideband reception to be slightly more muffled in one sideband than the other. Some readers report BFO pulling causes audio quavering, not found in our test units. Batteries run down faster than usual when radio off. Tuning in 0.1 kHz increments means that non-synchronous single-sideband reception can be mistuned by up to 50 Hz, so audio quality varies. Signal-seek scanner sometimes stops 5 kHz before a strong "real" signal. No meaningful signal-strength indicator. Supplied accessory antenna performs less well than another Sony accessory antenna, the AN-LP1. Mediumwave AM reception only fair. Mediumwave AM channel spacing adjusts peculiarly. Flimsy battery cover. No batteries (two "AA" required). *North America:* AC adaptor only 120 Volts.

☞ In early production samples, the cable connecting the two halves of the "clamshell" case tended to lose continuity with extended use because of a very tight radius and an unfinished edge; this was successfully resolved with a design change in early 1996. Those with early units who encounter this problem should go to www.tesp.com/sw100faq.htm for repair information.

**Verdict:** Mighty midget, a shoehorning *tour de force*. Its synchronous selectable sideband and effective bandwidth filter make this tops in its size class for rejecting adjacent-channel interference. Speaker and, to a lesser extent, weak-signal sensitivity keep it from being all it could have been, and the accessory antenna isn't Sony's latest or best. Yet, this Japanese-made model still is the handiest pocket portable around, and a nifty gift idea.

✪✪✪    *Passport's Choice*
## Sony ICF-SW100E

**Price:** *ICF-SW100E:* £179.95 in the United Kingdom. €269.95 in Germany. *ACE-30 AC adaptor:* £24.95 in the United Kingdom. €25.50 in Germany.

**Verdict:** This version, not available in North America, includes only a case, tape-reel-type passive antenna and earbuds. Otherwise, it is identical to the Sony ICF-SW100S, above.

✪✪✪    *Passport's Choice*
## Sangean ATS 606AP, Sanyo MB-60A, Roberts R617, Roberts R876

**Price:** *ATS 606AP:* $139.95 in the United States. CAN$179.00 in Canada. £104.95 in the United Kingdom. €101.50 in Germany. *MB-60A:* R1,000.00 in South Africa. *R617:* £119.95 (€196) in the United Kingdom. *R876:* £129.95 (€212) in the United Kingdom.

**Pro:** Speaker audio quality less bad than most pocket models—comparable to a mediocre-sounding compact model (*see* Con). Speaker audio unusually intelligible. Single bandwidth reasonably effective at adjacent-channel rejection, while providing reasonable audio bandwidth. Weak-signal sensitivity, although not optimum, a bit above average. Various helpful tuning features, including keypad, 54 presets, slewing, signal-seek tuning and meter band selection. Keypad has superior feel and tactile response. Longwave. Dual-zone 24-hour clock. Illuminated LCD. Alarm. 15/30/45/60-

minute snooze. Travel power lock (*see* Con). Multi-level battery strength indicator; also, weak-battery warning. Stereo FM through earphones or earbuds. Above-average FM sensitivity, selectivity and capture ratio. Memory scan (*see* Con). Rubber feet reduce sliding while elevation panel in use. *R876 and ATS 606AP:* UL-approved 120/230V AC adaptor, with American and European plugs, adjusts to proper AC voltage automatically; also ANT-60 reel-in outboard wire antenna. *ATS 606AP:* In North America, service provided by Sangean America to models sold under its name.

**Con:** No tuning knob. Audio quality, although superior for size class, lacks low-frequency ("bass") response. Clock not readable while frequency displayed. No meaningful signal-strength indicator. Keypad not in telephone format. Power lock doesn't disable LCD illumination button. No carrying strap or handle. No batteries (three "AA" needed). On our unit, clock initially refused to be set. *ATS 606AP:* Country of manufacture (China) not specified on radio or box.

**Verdict:** Easily the best buy in a pocket model—an excellent value, with the best sound among pocket models.

Choosing between the Sony ICF-SW100 series and this model is a no-brainer. If maximum freedom from adjacent-channel interference and/or smallness of size are paramount, the innovative little Sony wins. If audio quality, affordability and ease of use are primary, spring for this Sangean-made mini.

## ★★½ ✪
### Grundig eTraveller VII

**Price:** $99.95 in the United States. CAN$99.00 in Canada.

**Pro:** Good rejection of spurious "image" signals, unusual at this price. Single bandwidth reasonably effective at adjacent-channel rejection, while providing adequate audio bandwidth. Audio quality above average for size class (*see* Con). Auto scan/

**Best buy in a pocket model: Sangean ATS 606AP. Superior audio, too.**

slew-tuning works better than most—thankfully, as there are almost no other tuning features (*see* Con). Hinged protective travel cover, like on a Flip Phone, protects front of radio (*see* Con). World Time clock, with snooze and two-event timer that activates last-tuned frequency. Power/standby switch not easy to turn on accidentally while packed away in luggage (*see* Con). FM stereo through earbuds, included. Also comes with 117V AC adapter, desk stand, soft travel case and two "AA" alkaline batteries. *North America:* Toll-free tech support.

**Con:** Paucity of helpful tuning facilities, including no keypad or tuning knob and only ten world band presets (plus 20 more for FM and mediumwave AM). Audio quality, although decent for size class, lacks low-frequency ("bass") response. Antenna does not rotate or swivel. Almost large and heavy enough to qualify as a compact model. Tunes world band only in 5 kHz steps and displays in nonstandard XX.XX MHz/XX.XX5 MHz format. No signal-strength indicator. Hinged front cover can get in the way, although it may be removed. Clock not readable while frequency displayed, although time replaces frequency briefly if button is pushed. No travel power lock, although power/standby function provides considerable protection. Turning radio on for the first time is thor-

**Grundig's eTraveller VII has some quirks and no keypad, but is attractive and performs agreeably.**

oughly counterintuitive. No LCD illumination. No carrying strap or handle.

**Verdict:** A handsome, affordable package with pleasant performance. Yet, the eTraveller's hinged front cover and paucity of tuning features make it more appropriate for traveling than for routine daily use—hardly surprising, given its name. Like all Grundig radios of recent times, it is made in China.

### ✪½
### Kaiwa KA-818, Tecsun R-818

**Price:** $34.95 or less in the United States; up to $40 elsewhere.

**Tecsun R-818, cheapest portable with digital frequency readout.**

**Pro:** Sensitivity to weak world band signals at least average for pocket model. Clock with alarm (see Con). Carrying pouch and belt clip.

**Con:** Analog radio with a digital frequency counter, so lacks tuning except by knob. Does not tune 90, 60, 22, 13 or 11 meter segments. Frequency counter completely omits last digit so, say, 9575 kHz appears as either 9.57 or 9.58 MHz. Clock in 12-hour format only. Poor image rejection. Mediocre audio quality. Telescopic antenna does not rotate or swivel. Mediumwave AM lacks weak-signal sensitivity. Pedestrian FM, with spurious signals. On one of our new units the telescopic antenna immediately fell apart. Two "AA" batteries not included. Few vendors in America and Europe. Warranty only 90 days in United States and various other countries.

**Verdict:** Performance brings up the rear, but price, size and alarm make it worth consideration for casual use on trips.

## COMPACT PORTABLES
### Nice for Travel, Okay for Home

Compact portables are the most popular because of their intersection of price, performance, size and speaker audio. They tip in at one to two pounds, under a kilogram, and are typically sized 8 × 5 × 1.5 inches, or 20 × 13 × 4 cm. Like pocket models, they feed off "AA" (UM-3 penlite) batteries—but, usually, more of them. They travel almost as well as pocket models, but sound better and usually receive better, too. They can also suffice as home sets.

### ✪✪✪¼   *Passport's Choice*
### Sony ICF-SW07

**Price:** $399.95 in the United States. CAN$699.00 in Canada. £249.95 in the United Kingdom. €309.00 in Germany.

**Pro:** Best non-audio performance among travel portables. Eye popper. High-tech synchronous selectable sideband generally performs very well; reduces adjacent-channel interference and selective-fading distortion on world band, longwave and mediumwave AM signals while adding slightly to weak-signal sensitivity. Unusually small and light for a compact model. Numerous tuning aids, including pushbutton access of frequencies for four stations stored on a replaceable ROM, keypad, two-speed up/down slewing, 20 presets (ten for world band) and "signal-seek, then resume" tuning. Clamshell design aids in handiness of operation, and is further helped by illuminated LCD readable from a wide variety of angles. Hump on the rear panel places the keypad at a convenient operating angle. Comes with AN-LP2 outboard "tennis racquet" antenna, effective in enhancing weak-signal sensitivity on world band; this antenna, unlike the AN-LP1, has automatic preselector tuning. Good single sideband performance (*see* Con). Clock covers most international time zones, as well as World Time. Outstanding reception of weak and crowded FM stations, with limited urban FM overloading resolved by variable-level attenuator. FM stereo through earpieces, supplied. Japanese FM (most versions) and longwave bands. Above-average reception of mediumwave AM band. Travel power lock. Closing clamshell does not interfere with speaker. Low-battery indicator. Presets information is non-volatile, can't be erased when batteries changed. Two turn-on times for alarm/clock radio. Sixty-minute snooze. Hinged battery cover can't be misplaced. AC adaptor.

**Con:** Pedestrian audio quality, made worse by the lack of a second, wider, bandwidth and meaningful tone control. Lacks tuning knob. Display shows time and tuned frequency, but not both at the same time. Tuning resolution of 0.1 kHz above 1620 kHz means that non-synchronous single-sideband reception can be mis-tuned by up to 50 Hz, so audio quality varies. Synchronous selectable sideband tends to lose lock if batteries weak, or if NiCd cells are used. Synchronous selectable sideband alignment can vary with temperature, factory alignment

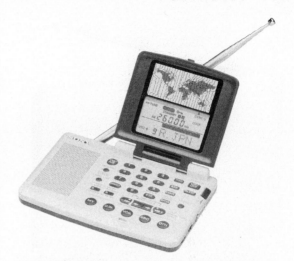

The Sony ICF-SW07 is the top-performing travel radio, except for pedestrian speaker.

and battery voltage, causing synchronous selectable sideband reception to be slightly more muffled in one sideband than the other. No meaningful signal-strength indicator. LCD frequency/time numbers relatively small for size of display, with only average contrast. AN-LP2 accessory antenna has to be physically disconnected for proper mediumwave AM reception. 1621-1700 kHz portion of American AM band is erroneously treated as shortwave, although this does not harm reception quality. Low battery indicator misreads immediately after batteries installed; clears up when radio is turned on. No batteries (two "AA" required). UTC, or World Time, displays as "London" time even during the summer, when London is an hour off from World Time. DST key can change UTC in error.

**Verdict:** Speaker audio aside, this Japanese-made model is the best available for travel—and a killer eyeful.

### ✪✪✪⅛ ☾ *Passport's Choice*
### Sony ICF-SW7600GR

**Price:** $169.95 in the United States. CAN$299.00 in Canada. £149.95 in the United Kingdom. €185.00 in Germany. AUS$509.00 in Australia. *AC-E60HG 120V*

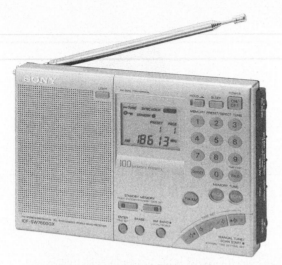

Sony's value-priced ICF-7600GR offers three-star
performance, advanced technology and
robust construction.

*AC adaptor (as available):* $19.95 in the
United States.

**Pro:** One of the great values in world band
radio. Far and away the least-costly model
available with high-tech synchronous
selectable sideband; this generally performs
well, reducing adjacent-channel interference and selective-fading distortion on
world band, longwave and mediumwave AM
signals (*see* Con). Single bandwidth,
especially when synchronous selectable
sideband is used, exceptionally effective at
adjacent-channel rejection. Seemingly
robust—similar predecessor had superior
quality of components and assembly for

price class, and held up unusually well.
Numerous helpful tuning features, including
keypad, two-speed up/down slewing, 100
presets and "signal-seek, then resume"
tuning. For those with limited hearing of
high-frequency sounds, such as some men
over the half-century mark, audio quality
may be preferable to that of Grundig Yacht
Boy 400PE (*see* Con). Single-sideband
performance arguably the best of any
portable; analog clarifier, combined with
LSB/USB switch, allow single-sideband
signals (e.g., AFRTS, utility, amateur) to be
tuned with uncommon precision, and thus
with superior carrier phasing and the
resulting natural-sounding audio. Dual-zone
24-hour clock with single-zone readout,
easy to set. Reel-in outboard passive
antenna accessory aids slightly with weak-
signal reception. Snooze/timer. Illuminated
LCD has high contrast when read head-on
or from below. Travel power lock. Superior
reception of difficult mediumwave AM
stations. Superior FM capture ratio helps
separate co-channel stations. FM stereo
through earpieces or headphones. Japanese
FM (most versions) and longwave bands.
Superior battery life. Weak-battery indicator. Stereo line output for taping. Hinged
battery cover can't be mislaid.

**Con:** Audio lacks tonal quality for pleasant
world band or mediumwave AM music
reproduction, and speaker audio tiring for
any type of FM program. Weak-signal
sensitivity, although respectable, not equal

## COMING UP

In 2003 Sangean will introduce the ATS 636 pocket
portable, similar to the larger ATS 909.

Tecsun, associated with Grundig, will also introduce the
RMB400 ($50) BCL-2000 (photo).

Emergencies? Look for the forthcoming appearance of a
new digitally tuned windup/solar-powered travel portable,
reportedly engineered for serious performance.

to that of the top handful of top-rated portables; helped considerably by extra-cost Sony AN-LP1 active antenna reviewed elsewhere in this edition. Image rejection adequate, but not excellent. Three switches, including those for synchronous selectable sideband, located unhandily at the side of the cabinet. No tuning knob. When using up/down slewing buttons, muting slows down manual bandscanning. No meaningful signal-strength indicator. Synchronous selectable sideband holds lock decently, but less well on weak signals than in Sony's larger models; too, it tends to lose lock even more if batteries weak or if NiCd cells used. Synchronous selectable sideband alignment can vary with temperature, factory alignment and battery voltage, causing synchronous selectable sideband reception to be slightly more muffled in one sideband than the other. 1621-1700 kHz portion of American AM band is erroneously treated as shortwave, although this does not harm reception quality. Even though it has a relatively large LCD, same portion of display is used for clock and frequency digits; thus, clock not readable when radio is switched on. No earphones or earpieces. No batteries (four "AA" needed).

**Verdict:** The robust Sony ICF-SW7600GR provides excellent bang for the buck, even though it is manufactured in high-cost Japan. Its advanced-tech synchronous selectable sideband helps greatly in rejecting adjacent-channel interference and selective-fading distortion. Top drawer single-sideband reception for a portable, too, along with superior tough-signal FM and mediumwave reception. However, musical audio quality is only *ordinaire*.

★★★ ✪ *Passport's Choice*
**Grundig Yacht Boy 400PE**

**Price:** *YB-400PE:* $149.95 in the United States. CAN$199.99 in Canada. £99.95 (€163) in the United Kingdom. AUS$279.00 in Australia. *YB-400PE refurbished units, as*

The affordable Grundig Yacht Boy 400 is popular because of its straightforward, solid performance and pleasant audio.

*available:* $99.95 in the United States. CAN$169.00 in Canada.

**Pro:** Audio quality tops in size category for those with sharp hearing. Two bandwidths, both well-chosen. Ergonomically superior, a pleasure to operate. A number of helpful tuning features, including keypad, up/down slewing, 40 station presets, "signal seek" frequency scanning and scanning of station presets. Signal-strength indicator. Dual-zone 24-hour clock, with one zone shown at all times; however, clock displays seconds only when radio is off. Illuminated display. Alarm/ snooze. Tunable BFO allows for superior signal phasing during single-sideband reception (*see* Con). Reel-in outboard wire antenna supplements telescopic antenna. Generally superior FM performance. FM in stereo through headphones. Longwave. AC adaptor. *North America:* Toll-free tech support.

**Con:** Circuit noise ("hiss") can be slightly intrusive with weak signals. No tuning knob. At many locations there can be break-through of powerful AM or FM stations into the world band spectrum. Keypad not in telephone format. No LSB/USB switch, and single-sideband reception not all it could be. No batteries (six "AA" needed).

☞ Refurbished units reportedly include gift and similar returns from department stores and other outlets where customers tend to be unfamiliar with world band radio.

Everything but the radio itself is supposed to be replaced. Limited availability.

**Verdict:** This popular receiver is one of the top values for hearing world band programs. Superior audio quality, dual bandwidths and simplicity of operation set this Chinese-made compact receiver apart—even though circuit noise with weak signals could be lower.

### Retested for 2003
### ✪✪✪
### Sangean ATS 909, Sangean ATS 909 "Deluxe," Roberts R861

**Price:** *ATS 909:* $259.95 in the United States. CAN$369.00 in Canada. £199.95 in the United Kingdom. €191.50 in Germany. AUS$399.00 in Australia. *ATS 909 "Deluxe":* $289.90 in the United States. *AC adaptor:* £16.95 (€28) in the United Kingdom. *R861:* £179.95 (€293) in United Kingdom.

**Pro:** Exceptionally wide range of tuning facilities and hundreds of world band presets, including one which works with a single touch. "Page" tuning system uses 29 pages and alphanumeric station descriptors for world band. Two voice bandwidths. Tunes single-sideband signals in unusually precise 0.04 kHz increments, making this one of the best portables for listening to these signals (*see* Con). Shortwave dynamic

**Sangean's ATS 909 uses high-tech tuning and excels with utility signals.**

range slightly above average for portable. Travel power lock. 24-hour clock shows at all times, and can display local time in various cities of the world (*see* Con). 1-10 digital signal-strength indicator. Low-battery indicator. Clock radio feature offers three "on" times for three discrete frequencies. Snooze. FM sensitive to weak signals (see Con) and performs well overall, has RDS feature, and is in stereo through earpieces, supplied. Illuminated display. Superior ergonomics, including tuning knob with tactile detents. Longwave. *ATS 909 (North American units), ATS 909 "Deluxe" and Roberts:* Superb, but relatively heavy, multivoltage AC adaptor with North American and European plugs. ANT-60 reel-in outboard wire antenna. Sangean service provided by Sangean America on models sold under its name. *ATS 909 "Deluxe," available only from C. Crane Company):* Enhanced tuning knob operation and elimination of muting between stations.

**Con:** Weak-signal sensitivity with built-in telescopic antenna not equal to that of comparable models. Tuning knob tends to mute stations during bandscanning (C. Crane Company offers a "Deluxe" modification to remedy this). Larger and heavier than most compact models. Signal-seek tuning, although flexible and relatively sophisticated, tends to stop on few active shortwave signals. Although scanner can operate out-of-band, reverts to default (in-band) parameters after one pass. Two-second wait between when preset is keyed and station becomes audible. Although synthesizer tunes in 0.04 kHz increments, frequency readout only in 1 kHz increments. Software oddities; e.g., under certain conditions, alphanumeric station descriptor may stay on full time. Page tuning system enjoyed by some users, but cumbersome for others. Audio quality only so-so, not aided by three-level treble-cut tone control. No carrying handle or strap. 24-hour clock set up to display home time, not World Time, although this is easily overcome by not using world-cities-time feature. Clock does not compensate for daylight (summer) time in each displayed city. FM can overload in high-signal-strength environments, causing false "repeat" signals to appear; capture ratio average. Heterodyne interference, possibly related to the digital display, sometimes interferes with reception of strong mediumwave AM signals. Battery consumption well above average; would profit from lower current draw or larger (e.g., "C") cell size. No batteries (four "AA" required). Elevation panel flimsy. *Sangean:* AC adaptor lacks UL approval.

☞ Frequencies pre-programmed into "pages" vary by country of sale. It is useful to keep a couple of empty pages to aid in editing, deleting or changing pre-programmed page information.

**Verdict:** Like the tabletop Icom IC-R75, this travel-sized portable is a favorite among those who regularly tune utility and ham signals. It includes a wide range of operating features and relatively precise tuning of single-sideband signals, but weak-signal sensitivity with the built-in telescopic antenna is not what it should be. The RDS feature now works better than in early production units. This is the only Sangean model still made in Taiwan, rather than China.

**Observation on Latest Unit:** Improved RDS performance, but otherwise unchanged.

**✪✪⅞ ⓒ**
### Sangean ATS-808A, Roberts R809

**Price:** *Sangean:* $119.95 in the United States. CAN$159.00 in Canada. £84.95 in the United Kingdom. €101.50 in Germany. *ADP-808 120V AC adaptor:* $10.95 in the United States. *Roberts:* £99.95 (€163) in the United Kingdom.

**Pro:** The best value on the thrifty side of the Sony ICF-SW7600GR and Grundig Yacht Boy 400. Dual bandwidths, a major plus that's exceptional anywhere near this price class (*see* Con). Relatively simple to operate for

technology class. Various helpful tuning features include two-speed tuning knob, although only 18 presets for world band. Weak-signal sensitivity a bit better than most. Keypad has exceptional feel and tactile response. Longwave. Dual-zone 24-hour clock, displayed separately from frequency. Alarm/snooze. Seven-level signal strength and battery indicator. Travel power lock. Stereo FM via earpieces, supplied. Superior FM reception.

**Con:** Fast tuning tends to mute receiver when tuning knob is turned quickly. Narrow bandwidth performance only fair. Spurious-signal ("image") rejection, although above average, not equal to that of top-rated portables. Pedestrian audio quality with two-level tone switch. Display not illuminated. Keypad not in telephone format. No carrying strap or handle. AC adaptor extra. No batteries (six "AA" needed). Country of manufacture (now China) not specified on radio or box.

**Verdict:** This Sangean offering is the best value in an under-$145 world band radio, with relative simplicity of operation and superior overall performance. If you don't need single-sideband capability, the ATS-808A is a better overall choice than the sibling ATS 505, below, for reception of weak or interfered world band signals.

**The Sangean ATS-808A has tuning features and performance usually found only at higher prices.**

**Sangean's ATS 505P is the lowest-cost way to receive single-sideband signals.**

✪✪¾
## Sangean ATS 505P, Roberts R9914

**Price:** *ATS 505P:* $129.95 in the United States. CAN$179.00 in Canada. €99.00 in Germany. AUS$229.00 in Australia. *R9914:* £99.95 (€163) in the United Kingdom.

**Pro:** Numerous helpful tuning features, including two-speed tuning knob, keypad, presets (*see* Con), up/down slewing, meter-band carousel selection, signal-seek tuning and scanning of presets (*see* Con). Automatic-sorting feature arranges presets in frequency order. Analog clarifier with center detent

and stable circuitry allows single-sideband signals to be tuned with uncommon precision and to stay properly tuned, thus allowing for superior audio phasing for a portable (*see* Con). Illuminated LCD. Dual-zone 24/12-hour clock. Alarm/snooze. Modest battery consumption. Nine-level battery-reserve indicator. Travel power lock (*see* Con). FM stereo through earbuds, supplied. Longwave. AC adaptor. Tape measure antenna.

**Con:** Bandwidth slightly wider than appropriate for a single-bandwidth receiver. Large for a compact. Only 18 world band presets, divided up between two "pages" with nine presets apiece. Tuning knob tends to mute stations during bandscanning by knob, especially when tuning rate is set to fine (1 kHz); muting with coarse (5 kHz) tuning is much less objectionable. Keys respond slowly, needing to be held down momentarily rather than simply tapped. Stop-listen-resume scanning of presets wastes time. Pedestrian overall single-sideband reception because of excessively wide bandwidth and occasional distortion caused by AGC timing. Clock does not display independent of frequency. No meaningful signal-strength indicator. No carrying handle or strap. Country of manufacture (China) not specified on radio or box. Travel power lock does not deactivate LCD illumination key. No batteries (four "AA" needed).

**Verdict:** The best bet in a low-cost portable that demodulates single-sideband signals, but you should also consider other models if this feature is not needed.

✪✪¾ ✒
## Sony ICF-SW35

**Price:** $89.95 in the United States. CAN$179.95 as available in Canada. £79.95 in the United Kingdom. €117.00 in Germany. AUS$269.00 in Australia. *AC-E45HG 120V AC adaptor:* $19.95 in the United States.

**Pro:** Superior reception quality, with excellent adjacent-channel rejection

**Sony's ICF-SW35 lacks tuning features.**

(selectivity) and spurious-signal rejection. Fifty world band presets, which can be scanned within five "pages." Signal-seek-then-resume scanning works unusually well. Two-speed slewing. Illuminated display. Dual-zone 24-hour clock. Dual-time alarm. Snooze (60/45/30/15 minutes). Travel power lock. FM stereo through headphones, not supplied. Weak-battery indicator. Japanese FM (most versions) and longwave bands.

**Con:** No keypad or tuning knob. Synthesizer muting and poky slewing degrade bandscanning. Audio quality clear, but lacks low-frequency response ("bass"). Clock not displayed independent of frequency. LCD lacks contrast when viewed from above. AC adaptor is extra and pricey. No batteries (three "AA" required).

**Verdict:** The Sony ICF-SW35 has superior rejection of spurious image signals that are the bane of nearly all other under-$100 models. This Chinese-made compact lacks a keypad, which is partially overcome by the large number of presets and effective scanning. Overall, a decent low-cost choice only if you listen to a predictable roster of stations.

### ✪✪½
### Sony ICF-SW40

**Price:** $119.95 in the United States. £84.95 (€138) in the United Kingdom. *AC-E45HG 120V AC adaptor:* $19.95.

**Pro:** Relatively affordable. Technologically unintimidating for analog traditionalists, as its advanced digital tuning circuitry is disguised to look like slide-rule, or analog, tuning. 24-hour clock. Two "on" timers and snooze. Travel power lock. Illuminated LCD. Japanese FM band (most versions).

**Con:** Single bandwidth is relatively wide, reducing adjacent-channel rejection. No keypad. Lacks coverage of 1625-1705 kHz portion of North American mediumwave AM band. AC adaptor, much-needed, is extra and overpriced. No batteries (three "AA" required).

Sony ICF-SW40: digital receiver in analog drag.

**Verdict:** If you're turned off by things digital and complex, Sony's Japanese-made ICF-SW40 will feel like an old friend. Otherwise, forget it.

### ✪✪½
### Sangean ATS 404, Roberts R881

**Price:** *Sangean:* $99.95 in the United States. CAN$129.00 in Canada. £59.95 in the United Kingdom. €76.50 in Germany. AUS$162.00 in Australia. *ADP-808 120V AC adaptor:* $10.95 in the United States. *Roberts:* £79.95 (€130) in the United Kingdom.

**Pro:** Superior weak-signal sensitivity. Several handy tuning features. Stereo FM

The value-priced Sangean ATS 404 is also sold in the United Kingdom as the Roberts R881.

through earpieces, supplied. Dual-zone 24/ 12-hour clock displays seconds numerically. Alarm/snooze. Travel power lock. Illuminated LCD. Battery indicator.

**Con:** Poor spurious-signal ("image") rejection. No tuning knob. Overloading, controllable by shortening telescopic antenna on world band and collapsing it on mediumwave AM band. Picks up some internal digital hash. Tunes only in 5 kHz increments. No signal-strength indicator. Frequency and time cannot be displayed simultaneously. Power lock does not disable LCD illumination. No handle or carrying strap. AC adaptor extra. Country of manufacture (China) not specified on radio or box. No batteries (four "AA" needed).

**Verdict:** Value priced.

## ✪✪½
## Grundig Yacht Boy 300PE, Tecsun PL757

**Price:** *YB-300PE:* $79.95 in the United States. CAN$99.99 in Canada. *YB-300PE refurbished units, as available:* $59.95 in the United States.

**Pro:** Sensitive to weak world band and FM signals. Various helpful tuning features. World Time clock with alarm, clock radio and 10-90 minute snooze (*see* Con).

**The Grundig Yacht Boy 300PE stands out for travel, weak-signal reception.**

Illuminated LCD (*see* Con). 120V AC adaptor (North America) and supplementary antenna. Travel power lock (*see* Con). Stereo FM through earbuds, supplied. *North America:* Toll-free tech support.

**Con:** Mediocre spurious-signal ("image") rejection. No tuning knob. Few presets; e.g., only six for 2300-7800 kHz range. Tunes world band only in 5 kHz steps and displays in nonstandard XX.XX MHz/XX.XX5 MHz format. Keypad entry of even channels with all digits (e.g., 6 - 1 - 9 - 0, Enter) tunes radio 5 kHz higher (e.g., 6195); remedied by not entering trailing zero (e.g., 6 - 1 - 9, Enter). Unhandy carouseling "MW/SW1/SW2/FM" control required for tuning within 2300-7800 kHz *vs.* 9100-26100 kHz range or *vice versa*. Clock not displayed independent of frequency; button alters which one is visible. Nigh-useless signal-strength indicator. LCD illumination not disabled by travel power lock.

**Verdict:** Except for LCD illumination being permanently enabled, this Chinese-made model is priced and sized for air travel, especially where signals are weak.

## *New for 2003*
## ✪✪  Ⓒ
## Kchibo KK-E200

**Price:** $64.95 in the United States.

**Pro:** Pleasant audio for size and price. Various helpful tuning features, including keypad (*see* Con), 12 world band presets (*see* Con), up/down slewing, meter-band carousel selection and signal-seek tuning. High-contrast illuminated LCD (*see* Con) indicates which preset is in use. Agreeable selectivity and weak-signal sensitivity for price class. Snooze, shutoff selectable from 10-90 minutes. World Time clock. Travel power lock (*see* Con). AC adaptor (*see* Con). FM stereo through earbuds, supplied. Pleasant FM performance for price and size class. Control to reset scrambled microprocessor. Hinged battery cover to prevent misplacing (*see* Con).

**Con:** Spurious-signal ("image") rejection only fair. Dynamic range mediocre, sometimes overloads even with built-in antenna. Does not receive important 7305-9495 kHz chunk of world band spectrum. Does not receive 1621-1705 kHz portion of expanded AM band in the Americas. No tuning knob. Tunes world band only in 5 kHz steps and displays in nonstandard XX.XX MHz/XX.XX5 MHz format. Unhandy carouseling "MW/SW1/SW2/FM" control required when shifting from tuning within 2300-7300 kHz *vs.* 9500-26100 kHz range or *vice versa*. No signal-strength indicator. Annoying one-second pause when tuning from one channel to the next. Only six presets for each of the four "bands" (FM/MW-AM/SW1/SW2). Dreadful mediumwave AM performance, with circuit noise drowning out weak stations and degrading stronger ones. AC adaptor sometimes produces slight hum. Elevation panel flimsy; also, hard to open with short fingernails. Clock doesn't display when frequency is shown, although pushbutton allows time to replace frequency. No alarm or other awakening function. Keypad not in telephone format. Fragile battery-cover hinge pins snap off easily. LCD illumination only fair. Power lock doesn't disable LCD light button. Using 9/10 kHz mediumwave AM channel switch erases presets and clock setting. No weak-battery indicator; radio goes abruptly silent when batteries weaken. No batteries (three "AA" needed). Box claims "fancy leather cover," but it is ordinary vinyl. No indication of county of manufacture (China) on product, box or manual. "Chinglish" owner's manual occasionally puzzles. Warranty only 90 days in North America.

**Verdict:** The boldly styled Kchibo KK-E200 comes with useful accessories omitted on models costing substantially more, and its audio quality is pleasant for its size and price. Although it lacks full frequency coverage, has no alarm and is overly muted for bandscanning, it is a bargain and an eyeful. As an affordable gift, it's hard to beat.

New for 2003 is the Kchibo KK-E200. Inexpensive, but performs decently.

**Evaluation of New Model:** Since 1988 Kchibo has been manufacturing a wide variety of world band portables in Shenzhen under the brand names Kchibo and Kaide, as well as OEM for other firms. The Kchibo KK-E200 we tested is not only among the cheapest reasonably performing digital world band radios, but also it is tricked out with a number of useful accessories: AC adaptor with an "on" LED, vinyl carrying pouch, stereo earbuds and 15-foot (5-meter) accessory wire antenna. Another bonus is its razzle-dazzle retro appearance. Its three-tone cabinet with stylish sweeps and chrome buttons make it look like it belongs inside a 1957 Chevy convertible.

The AC adaptor is especially welcome, as these often cost extra. It works reasonably well, although it generates a slight hum on some strong world band signals. Three "AA" batteries can also be used, but they do not insert or remove with ease. The battery cover is hinged to prevent loss, but the flimsy hinge pins break easily, defeating the purpose.

## Mystery: Country of Origin

The reasonably large, illuminated LCD has good contrast and is easily viewed, but the frequency is displayed in the unconventional

XX.XX/XX.XXx MHz format concocted several years ago by some ivory tower theoretician in China. This is a powerful indication to the savvy consumer that the radio is made in China—a point you'd likely not know otherwise, as Kchibo, like Sangean, doesn't indicate the country of origin on the radio, carton or owner's manual ("China" is marked on the AC adaptor, but Chinese AC adaptors are routinely supplied with products made elsewhere). This practice isn't quite so misleading as when some post-War Japanese products, labeled "MADE IN USA," were actually from the Japanese island of Usa. Yet, it is pointless, as by now Chinese electronics have pretty much become world class.

The radio's Chinese origin is also evident in the owner's manual, which although instructive is written in what might qualify as Chinese Ebonics: "For keeping good performance to avoid fierce lash, or fall into the ground from high." For those with a developed sense of humor, this should be regarded as an inadvertent bonus.

## Numerous Features for Price

Sharing that display is a World Time clock with a snooze function that can turn off the radio anywhere from 10-90 minutes later. However, contrary to what the manufacturer's sales office indicates, there is no alarm or clock-radio feature, a drawback for travel—no signal-strength indicator, either. The clock readout replaces the frequency display when the radio is off, or with the radio on by pressing a button. Other features include a travel power lock and a microprocessor reset in case the microprocessor crashes. However, the power lock does not disable the LCD illumination button— another earmark of Chinese-made portables.

Unlike some other low-cost models, the KK-E200 comes with a keypad. This is nothing to sniff at—there are tabletop models that lack this essential feature, yet sell for

hundreds of dollars more. As the Kchibo has no tuning knob, this keypad is especially important for quick tuning.

There is no tuning knob, which is normal at this price point, but there are 24 presets (six each for SW1, SW2, FM and MW-AM), up/down slew buttons which tune world band in 5 kHz increments, signal-seek tuning and a meter-band carousel button. However, when tuning from one channel to the next with the slew control, you have to wait one second before there is any sound. This makes bandscanning a tortosian chore.

World band coverage is from 2300-26100 kHz, except for a "Great Hole of China" tuning gap between 7305-9495 kHz where nothing can be received. A perusal of PASSPORT's Blue Pages shows just how many stations lie within the edges of this untuned range, which is a pity—7700-9000 kHz or even 7600-9300 kHz would have made more sense. This same circuit design also requires that a button be pushed when you want to go from tuning within the 2300-7300 kHz range to the 9500-26100 kHz range, and *vice versa*.

## Superior Audio Quality and Sensitivity

A major virtue is world band audio quality, which is unusually pleasant for a receiver of this size—even if for aging ears it lacks crispness. Another important area where the 'E200 does nicely is adjacent-channel rejection, or selectivity—this helps shoo away the annoying squeals and squawks of shortwave. However, as with all models in this price class, single-conversion IF circuitry is used. This allows "images" of powerful signals to repeat at reduced strength 900 kHz lower in frequency.

Another plus is weak-signal sensitivity, which is above average for this price class— an important factor in such weak-signal parts of the world as central and western North America and Australasia. However, a downside to weak-signal sensitivity in a low-cost radio is overloading, and the KK-E200 is no exception. It sometimes overloads with its built-in antenna when there are strong signals on nearby frequencies, and an external antenna just makes matters worse—especially in such high-signal parts of the world as Europe. Switching in the attenuator or shortening the telescopic antenna resolves the mishmash of overloading, but simultaneously reduces sensitivity.

FM performance is decent, with good weak-signal sensitivity and an average capture ratio. Mediumwave AM reception fares worse. It is seriously compromised by high circuit noise that drowns out weak stations and disrupts the fidelity of many stronger stations.

Seventy bucks and change doesn't get you a radio for all seasons. The Kchibo KK-E200 doesn't demodulate utility or ham signals, so it is of no use for the AFRTS's USB transmissions that are valued more than CNN by many American globetrotters. Its limited dynamic range makes it suboptimal for use in Europe, North Africa and the Near East, and single-conversion circuitry and other factors keep it from being a DX gem.

Yet, in the Americas, the Pacific and much of Asia, the KK-E200 is a solid bargain for enjoying news, music and entertainment for hours on end.

**If there is such a thing as a "ladies' world band radio," it is the tasteful Grundig Porsche P2000.**

⊙⊙

### Grundig G2000A "Porsche Design," Grundig Porsche P2000, Grundig Yacht Boy P2000

**Price:** *G2000A:* $99.95 in the United States. CAN$99.00 in Canada. *P2000:* £79.95 (€130) in the United Kingdom. AUS$199.00 in Australia. *G2ACA 120V AC adaptor:* $12.95 in the United States.

**Pro:** One of the most functionally attractive world band radios on the market, with generally superior ergonomics that include an effective and handy lambskin protective case. Superior adjacent-channel rejection—selectivity—for price and size class. Keypad (in proper telephone format), handy meter-band carousel control, signal-seek and up/down slew tuning. Twenty station presets, of which ten are for world band and the rest for FM and mediumwave AM stations. FM stereo through earpieces, supplied. World Time clock. Timer/snooze/alarm. Illuminated display. Travel power lock. Microprocessor reset control. *North America:* Toll-free tech support.

**Con:** Pedestrian audio. Weak-signal sensitivity mediocre between 9400-26100 kHz, improving slightly between 2300-7400 kHz. Poor spurious-signal ("image") rejection. Does not tune such important world band ranges as 7405-7550 and 9350-9395 kHz. Tunes world band only in 5 kHz steps and displays in nonstandard XX.XX MHz/XX.XX5 MHz format. No tuning knob. Annoying one-second pause when tuning from one channel to the next. Old-technology SW1/SW2 switch complicates tuning. Protruding power button can get in the way of nearby slew-tuning and meter-carousel keys. Leather case makes it difficult to retrieve folded telescopic antenna. Magnetic catches weak on leather case. No carrying strap. Signal-strength indicator nigh useless. Clock not displayed separately from frequency. No batteries (three "AA" required).

**Verdict:** This German-styled, Chinese-manufactured portable is the ultimate in tasteful design, but performance is of a decidedly lesser caliber.

### New for 2003
✪⅝
### Kchibo KK-S320

**Price:** $ 54.99 plus shipping in the United States.

**Pro:** Even more compact than its costlier KK-E200 cousin, with better mediumwave AM performance and greater audio crispness. Agreeable weak-signal sensitivity. Snooze, shutoff selectable up to 90 minutes (*see* Con) and single-event on/off timer. High contrast LCD indicates which preset is in use. AC adaptor. FM stereo via earbuds, supplied.

**Con:** No coverage of 120, 90, 75, 60, 16, 15, 13 and 11 meter (2, 3, 4, 5, 17, 19, 21 and 25 MHz) segments, with only partial coverage of 49 and 19 meters (6 and 15 MHz). No keypad or tuning knob; other tuning alternatives cumbersome, especially with "out-of-band" frequencies. Only five presets for each of the three "bands" (FM/MW-AM/SW). "Signal seek" scanning works only within limited frequency segments. Snooze function cannot be turned off. After radio powers up, slewing buttons cannot be used nor the frequency displayed, until the user presses a preset or band key once, or presses the display key three times. Poor dynamic range, with overloading a major problem at night. Poor adjacent-channel selectivity. "Floating birdie" sometimes appears in various world band segments. Mediocre spurious-signal ("image") rejection. Poor dynamic range for nighttime listening in many parts of the world. Does not receive 1621-1710 kHz portion of expanded mediumwave AM band in the Americas. Tunes world band only in 5 kHz steps. Displays only in nonstandard XX.XX/XX.XX5 MHz format. Display not illuminated. Clock uses 12-hour format, not suitable for

World Time. Elevation panel hard to open. Clock doesn't display when frequency is shown, although pushbutton allows time to replace frequency. No travel power lock. No signal-strength indicator. No weak-battery indicator; radio goes abruptly silent when batteries start to flag. No batteries included (three "AA" needed). Microprocessor sometimes freezes up, requiring activation of reset button; this also erases the presets and clock setting stored in memory. No indication of county of manufacture (China) on product, box or manual. "Chinglish" owner's manual occasionally puzzles. FM performance pedestrian. Not easily purchased in the Americas or most other parts of the world. Warranty period not yet apparent.

**Verdict:** Conveniently smaller than its KK-E200 cousin, and priced to move. Yet, the KK-S320's cumbersome tuning, inadequate shortwave coverage and rudimentary world band performance make it a dubious choice.

**Evaluation of New Model:** The first thing that strikes you when you remove the two-tone Kchibo KK-S320 from its box is, "Isn't that cute"? It is attractive and handily sized for traveling, with a thrifty price tag, to boot—especially considering that it comes equipped with AC adaptor, travel case, earbuds and a clip-on wire antenna.

Audio is reasonably pleasant, too, considering the radio's size and price. Indeed, audio is even better than that of the kindred Kchibo KK-E200, and produces more high-end response without sacrificing bass response.

### Cumbersome Tuning

Tuning is limited to dual-speed up/down slewing, along with a handful of presets for each "band" (five for world band, five each for FM and mediumwave AM). The slewing circuitry has none of the annoying muting found on the 'E200, but tuning is only in 5 kHz steps and there is no tuning knob. Signal-seek scanning works properly, but is only usable within certain relatively narrow frequency parameters listed in the owners manual.

With no keypad and limited scanning functions, tuning is a pain. The "fast" setting helps, but if you are tuning within an "out-of-band" range you have to press the slew button once for each 5 kHz increment, as the scanning function is disabled. If you attempt to use the scanner by letting up on the up-down button, it will leap to the next preset band. Either you will get used to it, or you'll wind up gulping Maalox.

There is no shortwave "band selector" either, so the only way to get from one world band segment to another is to push and wait. Again the "fast" button helps.

## Radio Narcolepsy

The KK-E320 is the first radio PASSPORT has tested that always turns off after a given time, like a coin-operated washer. When the radio is turned on, its snooze ("sleep") mode is always activated; there is no way to switch it off. It is set at the maximum of 90 minutes, so no matter what you do the radio will always shut off after 90 minutes of operation. Or less—if you hold down the power button as you turn on the radio, it will allow for shorter operation times before it turns off. But do what you will, it will invariably shut off by itself.

When the radio turns on, the clock continues to display as it does when the radio is off. It reads out only 12-hour time, not 24-hour as used by World Time. Worse, in order to show the frequency display, a button must first be pressed three times to toggle through the various clock functions.

This also means that not only are the 'S320's tuning options limited, simply activating them can be convoluted. In order to use the up/down slewing function, for example, after the radio is turned on you must first either must press one of the five

**The Kchibo KK-S320 is strictly K-cheapo.**

preset buttons or hit the display button three times. Otherwise, no cigar.

Once this "boot up" exercise has been completed, the LCD finally shows the tuned frequency. However, it then displays only in the nonstandard XX.XX/XX.XX5 MHz format.

Why? Several years ago, while China was still relatively hidden from the rest of the world, some Chinese engineer apparently looked in a textbook and found that frequencies above 3 MHz should be expressed in Megahertz, with trailing kilohertz zeroes being suppressed (e.g., 4.83 MHz). Ah, so, but for decades the shortwave norm in consumer electronics has been to use the kilohertz standard (4830 kHz), although where manufacturers have used Megahertz most have displayed the trailing zero (4.830 MHz). To this day, many Chinese world band radios still omit the trailing zero.

## Tunes 5950-15600 kHz

The essence of a world band receiver is that it receives world band signals. The KK-S320 does indeed continuously tune 5950-15600 kHz, once you get the knack of it, and this includes the 7305-9495 kHz frequency range missed by the costlier 'E200. Too, it doesn't have the annoying SW band switch found on the 'E200.

But the 'S320 completely misses the 120, 90, 75, 60, 16, 15, 13 and 11 meter (2, 3, 4,

5, 17, 19, 21 and 25 MHz) segments, along with important chunks of 49 and 19 meters (6 and 15 MHz). Look over PASSPORT's Blue Pages, and you'll see just how much of world band's offerings the 'S320 misses from 2300-5945 and 15605-26100 kHz. Also absent is mediumwave AM from 1621-1710 kHz, most of the American "X-band."

## Dismal Performance

World band sensitivity using the built-in telescopic antenna is above average, important for listeners in many parts of the world. More good news is that mediumwave AM performance is improved over that of the sibling 'E200. FM performance, although pedestrian, is acceptable, too.

However, dynamic range is dismal. During nighttime listening in higher-signal-strength parts of the world, especially with the AC adaptor connected, overloading in and around the 6 MHz segment can sometimes be controlled only by collapsing the telescopic antenna. Thus, the included wire antenna accessory is of little use at night, although it can provide a helpful boost by day.

Selectivity is nearly as disappointing. A strong signal can bleed two or three channels (10-15 kHz) on either side. As with the other Kchibo, there is a single IF of 450 kHz, so spurious "images," or repeat signals, appear 900 kHz below a transmission's real

frequency. An unusual variation of this is a "floating birdie" which often, but not always, appears on various frequencies, only to disappear, then reappear on other frequencies within the 41, 31 and 19 meter (7, 9 and 15 MHz) segments.

There is a microprocessor-reset button on the front panel, and unlike on most receivers it is genuinely needed. For example, when we removed the batteries and immediately changed over to the AC adaptor, the set would not come on until this button was pressed, which in turn erased the presets and stored time data. (Alternatively, if the batteries are removed for at least one minute before the adaptor is connected, the reset button doesn't need to be used.)

The Kchibo KK-S320 looks great and is temptingly priced, but its overall performance and tuning scheme make it significantly inferior to the KK-E200, which costs little more but is worth every extra farthing.

## ✪½
## Bolong HS-490

**Price:** ¥360 in China.

**Pro:** Inexpensive for a model with digital frequency display, ten world band station presets, and ten station presets for mediumwave AM and FM. World Time clock (*see* Con). Reel-type outboard passive antenna accessory. AC adaptor. Illuminated display. Alarm/snooze. FM stereo (*see* Con) via earbuds, included.

**Con:** Seemingly nearly impossible to find outside China. Requires patience to get a station, as it tunes world band only via 10 station presets and multi-speed up/down slewing/scanning. Tunes world band only in 5 kHz steps and displays in nonstandard XX.XX MHz/XX.XX5 MHz format. Poor spurious-signal ("image") rejection. So-so adjacent-channel rejection (selectivity). World Time clock not displayed independent of frequency. Does not receive relatively

**If you long for a Bolong, try their HS-490.**

## NEW FOR 2003

### Freeplay Windup/Solar Digital Portable

At first blush, the Chinese-made Freeplay Summit seems to be the perfect radio for today. It is powered four ways: built-in solar panel, replaceable NiMH batteries charged by solar, supplied AC adaptor and Freeplay's famous hand-cranked generator.

Thirty seconds of cranking provides half an hour of playtime, and when fully charged it runs something like 20 hours, depending on volume. When power fades, the Summit shuts off before losing time and frequency data stored for the 12/24-hour clock and 30 presets—ten each for mediumwave AM and FM, plus five each for world band (5950-15600 kHz) and longwave. There is no keypad or control to jump from one world band segment to another, but the slew controls also trigger a signal-seek scanner.

### Thousands of Battery Hours

Freeplay claims batteries should deliver 80 percent power after 400-600 full charges, or 8000-12000 hours of use. At two hours daily, that's roughly 11-16 years, which is why Freeplay spokesperson Nicola Hoare asserts that their batteries will last "for the life of the product." Even after a battery refuses to take a charge, Freeplay says the radio will still run from direct sunlight or the AC adaptor.

The Summit comes with a 23-foot (7 meter) windup antenna, international plug adaptors, a frequency guide, a cloth tote bag and a two-year warranty. With all this, at $99.99 or £84.99 (€139) it is a sensible value provided you don't expect too much.

### Limited Tuning Range and Performance

It doesn't tune the 120, 90, 75, 60, 16, 15, 13 and 11 meter (2, 3, 4, 5, 17, 19, 21 and 25 MHz) world band segments, and also misses parts of 49 and 19 meters. Look at PASSPORT's Blue Pages from 2300-5945 and 15605-26100 kHz, and you'll see just how much is missed. On the other hand, mediumwave AM goes to 1710 kHz in 9 or 10 kHz steps; world band uses 5 kHz steps.

Selectivity and spurious-signal ("image") rejection are poor, and weak-signal sensitivity is so mediocre that the windup antenna is needed for all but the strongest signals. Too, on mediumwave AM local stations slop 20 kHz on either side, making DXing difficult. FM's okay, though, and the audio is surprisingly pleasant.

☞ C. Crane plans to offer a version with two shortwave "bands" covering either 2300-7300/9500-26100 kHz or, better, 3200-10000/9500-26100 kHz, instead of one shortwave and one longwave.

**Verdict:** If world band performance counts, stick with a conventional battery-powered portable. Otherwise, check out the two-band version when it comes out.

*—James Careless*

**Freeplay Summit, cranky but useful.**

unimportant 6200-7100 kHz portion of world band spectrum. Does not receive 1615-1705 kHz portion of expanded AM band in the Americas. No signal-strength indicator. No travel power lock. Mediumwave AM 9/10 kHz tuning increments not selectable, which may make for inexact tuning in some parts of the world other than where the radio was purchased. FM selectivity and capture ratio mediocre. FM stereo did not trigger on our unit.

**Verdict:** Made by a joint venture between Xin Hui Electronics and Shanghai Huaxin Electronic Instruments. No prize, but as good you'll find among the truly cheap, which probably accounts for this model's having been the #1 seller among digital world band radios in China.

## LAP PORTABLES

### Pleasant for Home, Acceptable for Travel

A lap portable is probably your best bet for use primarily around the home and yard, plus on occasional trips. They are large enough to perform well, usually sound better than compact models, yet are not too big to fit into a carry-on or briefcase. Most take 3-4 "D" (UM-1) or "C" (UM-2) cells, plus sometimes a couple of "AA" (UM-3) cells for memory backup.

Sony's ICF-2010 is still the best portable, but old-school quality makes it a cost accountant's nightmare. It is about to fade into history.

These are typically just under a foot wide—that's 30 cm—and weighing in around 3-4 pounds, or 1.3-1.8 kg. For air travel, that's okay if you are a dedicated listener, but a bit much otherwise.

Two models stand out for most listeners: the Sony ICF-2010 and Sony ICF-SW77, which unfortunately have become increasingly hard to find. They have the same overall rating, but many who favor one don't much care for the other. The Sangean ATS-818 is hardly in the same league, but at its current American pricing it is a tempting option.

According to the manufacturer, the '2010 is to be discontinued in March, 2003. As with other Sony models, production has recently been lagging behind demand, so be prepared to go on a waiting list.

✪✪✪¾  📄  *Passport's Choice*
### Sony ICF-2010

**Price:** *ICF-2010:* $349.95 in the United States. Not distributed by Sony elsewhere, but available worldwide by mail order or email from major American world band specialty firms. *Padded carrying case #0395:* $29.95 from Universal Radio in the United States. *Franzus F11 240-to-120 V AC,50 Watt, travel transformer:* about $10 at airports, travel shops and online merchants.

**Pro:** High-tech synchronous selectable sideband, thanks to Sony's proprietary chip with sideband phase canceling; this well-executed feature has superior deep-fade lock, allowing the receiver to perform, overall, better for program listening than on any other portable in reducing adjacent-channel interference and selective-fading distortion on world band, longwave and mediumwave AM signals; it can also add slightly to weak-signal sensitivity (*see* Con). This is further aided by two bandwidths (10.4 kHz and 4.3 kHz) which offer a listener-oriented tradeoff between genuinely wideband audio fidelity and relatively tighter adjacent-channel rejection (selectivity), especially when used in concert with synchronous selectable sideband. Use of 32 separate one-touch station preset keys in rows and columns is ergonomically the best to be found on any model, portable or tabletop, at any price—simply pushing one key brings in your station, a major convenience (*see* Con). Numerous other helpful tuning features. Excellent weak-signal sensitivity above 4 MHz (noise floor typically -131 dBm, sensitivity typically 0.15 microvolts) (*see* Con). Superior dynamic range (DR-20 = 80 dB, DR-5 = 68 dB) and third-order intercept point (IP3-20 = –9 dBm, IP3-5 = –21 dBm). Good overall distortion (under 3.5 percent). Tunes and displays in relatively precise 0.1 kHz increments (*see* Con). Generally superior performance with single-sideband signals ( *see* Con). Separate

World Time clock, easily set, displays continuously and keeps exact time for months on end. Exceptionally robust, with superior quality of construction underscored by the huge numbers in use worldwide over the past many years; only exception, battery-spring contact, easily remediable by user (*see* Con). First IF rejection excellent, 85 dB. Excellent AGC threshold, 0.6 microvolts. Alarm/snooze, with four-event timer. Illuminated LCD. Travel power lock. Excellent ten-LED digital signal-strength indicator much better than those on most other portables; also seconds as a useful indication of battery strength. Overall reception of fringe and distant mediumwave AM signals is as good as it gets in a portable, thanks to the combination of synchronous selectable sideband, dual bandwidths and splendid field sensitivity (with its built-in ferrite-rod antenna; an

## LAST CALL FOR RADIO LEGEND

Sony's ICF-2010 is the world's finest portable, irrespective of cost or size. Yet, it first came on the market all the way back in 1985, when Reagan and Thatcher were at their apex of power. This legendary receiver has been the choice of shortwave cognoscenti ever since.

### Sony Changes Focus

Sony's excellence in world band technology resulted from personal attention lavished on it by the company's founder, Akio Morita, and several top-flight engineers at the Shibaura Technology Center. Now, the firm has grown into a diversified institution that is cutting back on all consumer electronics production so resources can be focused elsewhere.

Thus it is that after 18 years Sony's flagship world band receiver is about to get the axe, a Sony spokesperson informs PASSPORT. In March the ICF-2010 is scheduled to fade into the sunset as arguably the most influential and long-lived shortwave portable of all time. No replacement appears to be in the offing.

So, get it while you can, and also grab a service manual and spare antenna (800/488-7669 or sony.dapc@am.sony.com). Your '2010 should be a tireless companion—two of our monitors' units are still soldiering away after 15 punishing years.

**The Sony ICF-2010 debuted in 1985,
when "Out of Africa" was winning Oscars.**

external AM antenna may disappoint). Japanese FM (most versions) and longwave bands. FM very sensitive to weak signals, making it well suited for fringe reception (*see* Con). Passable reception of air band signals. Hum-free 120 V AC adaptor (center-pin negative, unlike other Sony models; *see* Con). Comes with length of outboard wire antenna that attaches to a separate antenna connector, also supplied.

**Con:** Distributed by Sony only in North America, and even then only until March of 2003; however, it is routinely exported worldwide from American world band specialty firms. Audio quality lacks solid bass, with only a simple three-level treble-cut tone control. Station presets and clock/timer features immediately erase whenever microprocessor/memory batteries are replaced, and also sometimes when set is jostled (changing to a different brand of "AA" batteries may help). Similarly, when the "D" cells lose contact an "Error 3" message appears; stretching the battery springs helps. On some new and aging samples, positive battery spring sometimes does not make contact with jack PC board, preventing operation on batteries ("Error 3"); easily remediable, see sidebar. Wide bandwidth unusually broad, although this is typically a problem only when the synchronous selectable sideband is not in use; traveling DXers sometimes prefer the tighter bandwidths of the ICF-SW77, or equip their '2010 with replacement bandwidth filters offered by such aftermarket firms as Kiwa; this results in less interference when both sidebands suffer from heavy interference or for reception of "utility" signals, but at the cost of relatively muffled audio with world band and mediumwave AM signals. Signal-seek tuning works poorly. Telescopic antenna swivel gets slack with heavy use, requiring periodic adjustment of tension screw. Synchronous selectable sideband tends to lose lock if batteries weak, or if NiCd cells are used (NiCd cells put out relatively low voltage). Synchronous selectable sideband alignment can vary with temperature, factory alignment and battery voltage, causing synchronous selectable sideband reception to be slightly more muffled in one sideband than the other—notably with the narrow bandwidth. Synchronous selectable sideband adds minor digital hash to weak signals. On some, especially older, samples, or with depleted batteries, frequency readout can be off by up to 0.6 kHz in "lower" sync mode. Lacks up/down slewing controls. Keypad not in telephone format. LCD not clearly visible when radio viewed from above. Tuning resolution in 0.1 kHz increments means that non-synchronous single-sideband reception can be out of phase by up to 50 Hz, so audio quality varies. Image rejection, although 62 dB (good), is 18 dB less than on ICF-SW77. Blocking (109 dB) only fair. Weak-signal sensitivity (noise floor –118 dBm, sensitivity 0.75 microvolts) only fair within 120 meter tropical segment. Superior dynamic range invites use of external antennas, which if left connected when storms nearby can cause a transistor to blow; fortunately, it is not difficult for a technician to replace. Only 32 presets offered. Shoulder strap instead of handle, but this can be user-replaced. In high-signal-strength environments, FM band can overload, causing false "repeat" signals to appear. FM capture ratio only fair, limiting ability to separate co-channel stations. Air band insensitive to weak signals. No 240V AC adaptor known to be offered by Sony; best bet is to plug the Sony 120V AC adaptor into a Franzus F11 travel transformer or other 2:1 transformer. No batteries (three "D" and two "AA" required).

**Verdict:** Get it while you can, as Sony is set to drop the '2010 in March. Except for everyday audio quality and urban FM, the '2010 is the favorite portable of most PASSPORT panelists, as well as myriad radio monitors and DXers. It is among the best for rejection of one of world band's major bugaboos, adjacent-channel interference, thanks in part to its synchronous selectable sideband circuit that allows for broadband audio even if only one sideband is free from adjacent-channel interference. Alone among sophisticated receivers, it allows dozens of stations to be brought up at the single touch of a key.

📄 An *RDI WHITE PAPER* is available for this model.

## FREE FIX FOR SONY ICF-2010

A Sony ICF-2010 may soldier on for 15 years or more without acting up. Yet, sometimes an intermittent tab contact can cause it to quit operating from batteries and show an "Error 3" message. With older receivers, this is caused by oxidation and wear, but some newer units act up because tabs were not adequately bent at the factory.

Too, sometimes jiggling the radio will cause the presets and clock/timer settings to erase. This is inherent in the radio's design, but can be minimized with a little tweaking.

### Fifteen Minutes, Give or Take

We tried a fix from Universal Radio, the world's largest seller and exporter of '2010s. This remedies both problems in 10-20 minutes with no parts, using needle-nose pliers and a #2 Phillips screwdriver. Recommended, but not essential, are ethyl alcohol, a Q-Tip and a white eraser (reddish erasers, often on wooden pencils, corrode metal).

- Remove all batteries and the AC adaptor.

- Remove seven Phillips screws from the back panel, where they are marked by arrows—one in the battery cavity, one in each lower corner and four at the top (including three under the antenna shaft, which needs to be angled up).

- Lift off the back—it should come loose easily—placing the speaker to the right. Blow out cobwebs and dust.

- Optional: Near the DC jack, where the AC adaptor plugs in, is a small circuit board marked BATT+ in tiny letters. Rub a white eraser clean on paper, then use it to burnish the half-inch, or 10 mm, solder blob just above "BATT+." Blow away eraser dust, then wipe the blob with a clean cloth.

- Stretch the "AA" battery spring slightly with needle-nose pliers, but don't break the plastic base.

- Hold the back panel so the inside is facing you and the antenna mount is in the upper-left corner. Near the lower-left corner is a stainless-steel "D" cell battery tab; it has a pointed tip with a small hole and points up slightly. Use pliers to bend that tip to the right about 1/8 inch, or 3 mm.

- Hold the lowest coil of the "D" battery spring firmly in place with a finger, then use pliers to stretch the spring slightly.

- Optional: Dip one end of Q-Tip into straight alcohol, rub off excess, then wipe positive and negative battery-holder contacts (two springs and two tabs) for "AA" and "D" cells. Immediately burnish those same contacts with dry end of Q-Tip.

- Replace the back panel, inserting the short screw within the "D" battery cavity.

- The radio should now work off batteries. If not, repeat this procedure, but in the sixth step tweak the pointed tip an additional 1/16 inch or so—a millimeter or two.

When the ICF-2010 moves to emeritus status, the ICF-SW77 will become Sony's flagship model.

## ✪✪✪¾
## Sony ICF-SW77, Sony ICF-SW77E

**Price:** $469.95 in the United States. £329.95 as available in the United Kingdom. €485.00 in Germany. ¥8,000 in China. *Padded carrying case #0395:* $29.95 from Universal Radio in the United States.

**Pro:** A rich variety of tuning and other features, including sophisticated "page" tuning that some enjoy but others dislike; includes 162 presets, two-speed tuning knob, signal-seek tuning (*see* Con), keypad tuning and meter-band access. Synchronous selectable sideband is exceptionally handy to operate; it significantly reduces selective-fading distortion and adjacent-channel interference on world band, longwave and mediumwave AM signals; although the sync chip part number was changed not long back, its performance is virtually unchanged (*see* Con). Two well-chosen bandwidths (6.0 kHz and 3.3 kHz) provide superior adjacent-channel rejection. Excellent image rejection and first-IF rejection, both 80 dB. Excellent-to-superb weak-signal sensitivity (noise floor –133 dBm, sensitivity 0.16 microvolts) in and around lower-middle portion of shortwave spectrum where most listening is done (*see* Con). Superb overall distortion, almost always under one percent. Dynamic range (82 dB) and third-order intercept point (–10 dBm) fairly good and only slightly less than those of the ICF-2010 at 20 kHz separation (*see* Con). Tunes in very precise 0.05 kHz increments; displays in 0.1 kHz increments; these and other factors make this model superior to any other portable for single-sideband reception, although portatop and tabletop models usually fare better yet. Continuous bass and treble tone controls, a rarity. Two illuminated multi-function liquid crystal displays. Dual-zone clock, displays separately from frequency. Station name appears on LCD when station presets used. 10-level signal-strength indicator (*see* Con). Excellent stability, less than 20 Hz drift after ten-second warmup. Excellent weak-signal sensitivity (noise floor –130 dBm, sensitivity 0.21 microvolts) within little-used 120 meter segment (*see* Con). Flip-up chart for calculating time differences. VCR-type five-event timer controls radio and optional outboard recorder alike. Superior FM audio quality. Stereo FM through earpieces, supplied. Japanese FM (most versions) and longwave bands. AC adaptor, hum-free, and reel-in outboard antenna. Rubber strip helps prevent sliding.

**Con:** "Page" tuning system relatively complex to operate; many find that station presets can't be accessed simply. World band and mediumwave AM audio slightly muffled even when wide bandwidth in use. Synthesizer chugging degrades reception quality during bandscanning by knob. Dynamic range (64 dB) and third-order intercept point (–37 dBm) only fair at 5 kHz separation. Weak-signal sensitivity varies from fair to superb, depending on where between 2 and 30 MHz receiver is being tuned. Synchronous selectable sideband holds lock less well than ICF-2010 model. Synchronous selectable sideband tends to lose lock if batteries weak, or if NiCd cells are used. Synchronous selectable sideband alignment can vary with temperature, factory alignment and battery voltage, causing synchronous selectable sideband reception to be slightly more muffled in one sideband than the other. Signal-seek tuning skips over weaker signals. Flimsy 11-element telescopic antenna (the older version of the 'SW77 had nine elements). LCD characters small for size of receiver. Display illumination does not stay on with AC power. Unusual tuning knob design disliked by some. On mediumwave AM band, relatively insensitive, sometimes with spurious sounds during single-sideband reception; this doesn't apply to world band reception, however. Mundane reception of difficult FM signals. Signal-strength indicator grossly overreads, covering only a 20 dB range with maximum reading at only 3 microvolts. AGC threshold, 2 microvolts (good), inferior to that of ICF-2010. Painted surfaces can wear off with heavy use. Getting harder to find outside the United States. No batteries (four "C" required).

☞ For those seeking to have their ICF-SW77 repaired, a helpful source at Sony of America suggests: Sony Service Center, 1504 Grundy's Lane, MD #12, Bristol PA 19007 USA.

**Verdict:** The Japanese-made '77 has been a strong contender among portables since it was improved some time back, and for single-sideband reception it is the best portable by a skosh. It's also one of the very few models with continuously tuned bass and treble controls. Ergonomics, however, are a mixed bag, so if you're interested consider trying it out first.

## NUMBERS: TOP TWO PORTABLES

| | Sony ICF-2010 | Sony ICF-SW77 |
|---|---|---|
| Max. Sensitivity/Noise Floor | 0.15 $\mu$V, **S**/–131 dBm, **E** [1] | 0.16 $\mu$V, **S**/–133 dBm, **E** [2] |
| Blocking | 109 dB, **F** | 121 dB, **G** |
| Bandwidths *(Shape Factors)* | 10.4 *(1:1.8,* **E***)*, 4.3 *(1:2.0,* **G***)* kHz | 6.0 *(1:1.9,* **E***)*, 3.3 *(1:2.0,* **G***)* kHz |
| Ultimate Rejection | 70 dB, **G** | 70 dB, **G** |
| Front-End Selectivity | **F** | — [3] |
| Image Rejection | 62 dB, **G** | 80 dB, **E** |
| First IF Rejection | 85 dB, **E** | 80 dB, **E** |
| Dynamic Range/IP3 (5 kHz) | 68 dB, **F**/–21 dBm, **G** | 64 dB, **F**/–37 dBm, **F** |
| Dynamic Range/IP3 (20 kHz) | 80 dB, **F**/–9 dBm, **G** | 82 dB, **F**/–10 dBm, **G** |
| Phase Noise | 114 dBc, **G** | 122 dBc, **E** |
| AGC Threshold | 0.6 $\mu$V, **E** | 2.0 $\mu$V, **G** |
| Overall Distortion, sync | 2.9%, **G**/3.5%, **G** [4] | 2.3%, **E**/3.3%, **G** [4] |

**IBS Lab Ratings:**   **S** Superb   **E** Excellent   **G** Good   **F** Fair   **P** Poor

(1) Measurements flat from 5-29 MHz, but drop to 0.75 $\mu$V, **F**/-118 dBm, **F** at 2 MHz.

(2) Sensitivity varies considerably by frequency at 2 MHz and between 10-29.9 MHz; *viz.*, from 0.16 $\mu$V to 1.40 $\mu$V, **S** - **F**. Noise floor varies by frequency from –133 dBm to –117 dBm, **E** - **G**. Neither measurement could be made at 5 MHz because of spurious responses, noise and leakage.

(3) Cannot be determined.

(4) Wide/narrow bandwidths.

Sangean's ATS-818 brings value to lap portables. Also sold as the Roberts R827, it is often chosen for audio quality and single-sideband reception.

★★½
### Sangean ATS-818, Roberts R827

**Price:** *Sangean:* $174.95 in the United States. CAN$239.00 in Canada. £139.95 (€228) in the United Kingdom. *AC adaptor:* £16.95 (€28) in the United Kingdom. *Roberts:* £159.95 (€261) in the United Kingdom.

**Pro:** Superior overall world band performance. Numerous tuning features, including 18 world band station presets. Two bandwidths for good fidelity/interference tradeoff. Analog clarifier with center detent and stable circuitry allows single-sideband signals to be tuned with uncommon precision, thus allowing for superior audio phasing for a portable (*see* Con). Illuminated display. Signal-strength indicator. Dual-zone 24-hour clock, with one zone displayed separately from frequency. Alarm/snooze/timer. Travel power lock. FM stereo through headphones. Longwave. AC adaptor.

**Con:** Tends to mute when tuning knob turned quickly, making bandscanning difficult (the C. Crane Company offers a $20.00/$29.95 modification to remedy this). Wide bandwidth a bit broad for world band reception. Unconfirmed reader reports suggest that the front end is unusually prone to malfunctioning from static discharge into the antenna,

such as from fingertips during dry winter periods. Keypad not in telephone format. Touchy variable control for single-sideband fine tuning. Does not come with tape-recorder jack. No batteries (four "D" and three "AA" needed). Country of manufacture (now China) not specified on radio or box.

**Verdict:** This is a decent, predictable radio—performance and features, alike—and for 2003 it has been priced to move. However, unless modified it is mediocre for bandscanning.

# LARGE ("FIELD") PORTABLES
### Excellent for Home, Poor for Travel

Large, or "field," shortwave analog portables were common in the days of the Zenith Transoceanic and other bygone tube-type models that required huge special batteries. Today, smaller digital portables provide improved operation and superior reception except for audio quality.

However, this category is far from gone. Now, large portables are derived from sophisticated tabletop receiver designs. These have superior audio quality, along with the potential to offer exceptional difficult-signal and single-sideband performance. Accordingly, these are now classified as "portatop" receivers—portable versions of tabletop receivers.

PASSPORT devotes a separate chapter to portatop models.

# WORLD BAND CASSETTE RECORDERS

What happens if your favorite show comes on at an inconvenient time? Why, tape it, of course, with a world band cassette recorder—just like on your VCR.

Two models are offered, and there's no question which is better: the Sony. Smaller, too, so it is less likely to raise eyebrows among airport security personnel. But there's a whopping price difference over the Sangean.

## ✪✪✪⅛ *Passport's Choice*
### Sony ICF-SW1000T

Like jewelry, the Sony ICF-SW1000T is good stuff in a small package. Priced like jewelry, too.

**Price:** *ICF-SW1000T:* $449.95 in the United States. CAN$779.00 as available in Canada. £359.95 as available in the United Kingdom. €489.00 in Germany. *AC-E30HG 120V AC adaptor:* $19.95.

**Pro:** Built-in recorder in rear of cabinet, with two events of up to 90 minutes each, selectable in ten-minute increments. Relatively compact for travel, also helpful to avoid airport security hassles. High-tech synchronous selectable sideband; this generally performs well, reducing adjacent-channel interference and selective-fading distortion on world band, longwave and mediumwave AM signals while adding slightly to weak-signal sensitivity (*see* Con). Single bandwidth, especially when synchronous selectable sideband is used, exceptionally effective at adjacent-channel rejection. Numerous helpful tuning features, including keypad, two-speed up/down slewing, 32 presets and signal-seek scanning. Thirty of the 32 presets are within three easy-to-use "pages" so stations can be clustered. Weak-signal sensitivity above average up to about 16 MHz. Demodulates single-sideband signals (*see* Con). World Time clock, easy to set (*see* Con). Snooze, 10-90 minutes. Illuminated LCD readable from a wide variety of angles. Travel power lock, also useful to keep recorder from being inadvertently switched on while cabinet being grasped (*see* Con). Easy on batteries. Records on both sides of tape without having to flip cassette (provided FWD is selected along with the "turning-around arrow"). Auto record level (*see* Con). "ISS" switch helps radio avoid interference from recorder's bias circuitry. FM stereo through earphones; earbuds supplied. Japanese FM (most versions) and longwave bands. Tape-reel-type outboard passive antenna accessory. Dead-battery indicator. Lapel mic (*see* Con).

**Con:** Pedestrian audio quality. Synchronous selectable sideband tends to lose lock if batteries not fresh, or if NiCd cells are used. Synchronous selectable sideband alignment can vary with temperature, factory alignment and battery voltage, causing synchronous selectable sideband reception to be slightly more muffled in one sideband than the other. No tuning knob. Clock not readable when radio switched on except for ten seconds when key is pushed. No meaningful signal-strength indicator, which negates its otherwise obvious role for traveling technical monitors. No recording-level indicator or tape counter. Slow rewind. Fast forward and reverse use buttons that have to be held down. No built-in mic; outboard (lapel) mic is mono. Reception is interrupted for a good two seconds when recording first commences. No pause control. Single lock deactivates controls for radio and recorder alike; separate locks would have been preferable. Tuning resolution of 0.1 kHz allows single-sideband signals to be mis-tuned by up to 50 Hz. Frequency readout to 1 kHz, rather than 0.1 kHz tuning increment. Lacks flip-out

# MAKE YOUR PORTABLE "HEAR" BETTER

Regardless of which portable you own, you can boost weak-signal sensitivity on the cheap. How cheap? Nothing, for starters.

Look for "sweet spots" to place your radio: near windows, appliances, telephones, I-beams and the like. If your portable has an AC adaptor, try that, then batteries; sometimes the adaptor does better, sometimes not. Places to avoid are near computers or appliances with microprocessors, dimmers, non-incandescent lighting and cable-TV lines.

## Outdoor Antenna Can Help

An outdoor antenna isn't necessary, but it can help. Good news: With compact and smaller portable receivers, simplest is often best, as sophisticated wire antennas can cause "overloading." Run several meters or yards of ordinary insulated wire to a tree, then clip one end to your set's telescopic antenna with an alligator or claw clip available from Radio Shack and such. It's fast and cheap, yet effective.

If you are in a weak-signal location, such as central or western North America or Australia, and want stronger signals, even better is to erect an inverted-L (so-called "longwire") antenna. These are available at Radio Shack (278-758, $9.99) and other radio specialty outlets, or may be constructed from detailed instructions found in the RDI White Paper, PASSPORT *Evaluation of Popular Outdoor Antennas*. Antenna length is not critical, but keep the lead-in wire reasonably short.

Use an outdoor antenna only when needed—disconnect during thunder, snow or sand storms and when the radio is off. And don't touch any antenna during dry weather, as you may discharge static electricity into your radio's vulnerable innards.

## Creative Indoor Solutions

All antennas work best outdoors, away from electrical noises inside your home. If your supplementary antenna has to be indoors, run it along the middle of a window with Velcro, tape or suction cups. In a reinforced-concrete building which absorbs radio signals, you can affix a long whip or telescopic car antenna sticking outdoors, like a flag wall mast, onto a windowsill or balcony rail. Antennas like these are all but invisible, but work well because they reach away from the building.

Amplified ("active") antennas are small and handy, but cost more. Best for portables is the Sony AN-LP1 that because of high demand has recently been in short supply. It is reviewed in PASSPORT REPORTS' article on active antennas, and despite what Sony's literature says it works with the Sony ICF-SW77.

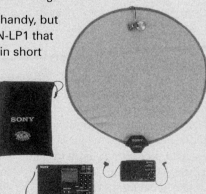

**If you want your portable to snare more weak stations, look into the Sony AN-LP1 portable active antenna.**

elevation panel; instead, uses less handy plug-in elevation tab. FM sometimes overloads. Telescopic antenna exits from the side, which limits tilting choices for FM. Misleading location of battery springs makes it easy to insert one of the two "AA" radio batteries in the wrong direction, albeit to no ill effect. No batteries (three "AA" required, two for radio and one for recorder). AC adaptor costs extra. Increasingly hard to find outside United States.

**Verdict:** Strictly speaking, the Sony ICF-SW1000T is the world's only true world band cassette recorder. Made in Japan, this is an innovative little package with surprisingly good battery life and build quality.

The Sangean ATS-818ACS and Roberts RC828 cost half as much as Sony's offering, but are less sophisticated.

★★½  ⓒ
### Sangean ATS-818ACS, Roberts RC828

**Price:** *Sangean:* $224.95 in the United States. CAN$269.00 in Canada. £199.95 in the United Kingdom. €198.00 in Germany. *AC adaptor:* £16.95 (€28) in the United Kingdom. *Roberts:* £199.95 (€326) in the United Kingdom.

**Pro:** Built-in cassette recorder. Price low relative to competition. Superior overall world band performance. Numerous tuning features, including 18 world band station presets. Two bandwidths for good fidelity/interference tradeoff. Analog clarifier with center detent and stable circuitry allows single-sideband signals to be tuned with uncommon precision, thus allowing for superior audio phasing for a portable (*see* Con). Illuminated display. Signal-strength indicator. Dual-zone 24-hour clock, with one zone displayed separately from frequency. Alarm/snooze/timer. Travel power lock. Stereo through headphones. Longwave. Built-in condenser mic. AC adaptor.

**Con:** Recorder has no multiple recording events, just one "on" time (quits when tape runs out). Tends to mute when tuning knob turned quickly, making bandscanning difficult (the C. Crane Company offers a $20.00/$29.95 modification to remedy this). Wide bandwidth a bit broad for world band reception without synchronous selectable sideband. Speaker smaller, with slightly less fidelity, than on regular 818 model without recorder. Unconfirmed reader reports suggest that the front end is unusually prone to malfunctioning from static discharge into the antenna, such as from fingertips during dry winter periods. Keypad not in telephone format. Touchy single-sideband clarifier. Recorder has no level indicator and no counter. Fast-forward and rewind controls installed facing backwards. No batteries (four "D" and three "AA" needed). Country of manufacture (now China) not specified on radio or box.

**Verdict:** A great buy, although recording is only single-event with no timed "off."

---

*The* PASSPORT *portable-radio review team includes Lawrence Magne, Tony Jones and David Zantow; also, James Careless, with laboratory measurements performed independently by Rob Sherwood. Additional feedback from Hanno Olinger, Lars Rydén, Craig Tyson, Danny Wu and George Zeller.*

www.passband.com

# Is A Portatop for You?

Most of us buy a world band radio not for just a room, but for our entire home property. Yet, portables rarely sound as pleasant as tabletop models, nor can most cut the mustard with really tough signals. Solution: Combine various characteristics of portables and tabletops into one high-performance package—a portatop—which can be serviced, like tabletops, for years to come.

Drawbacks? A portatop is larger and costlier than a portable, and goes through batteries with abandon. If you're comfortable with that, you'll find performance and fidelity approaching that of a good tabletop receiver.

"New" for 2003 is the Tecsun HAM-2000, sold in China. Well, sort of—Tecsun also manufactures the

Satellit 800 for Grundig, so this is merely "badge engineering" for sales within the Chinese market.

But what a dismal choice of a name. Shortwave listening was once widely confused with ham radio, so for years receiver manufacturers and specialty publishers have taken measures to clear the air. Tecsun, in one fell swoop, has managed to undo much that had been accomplished.

## What PASSPORT's Rating Symbols Mean

**Star ratings:** ✪✪✪✪✪ is best. Stars reflect overall performance and meaningful features, plus to some extent ergonomics and build quality. Price, appearance, country of manufacture and the like are not taken into account. With portatop models there is a balanced emphasis on listening quality, on one hand, and the ability to flush out tough, hard-to-hear signals on the other. Nevertheless, to facilitate comparison the portatop rating standards are very similar to those used for the professional, tabletop and portable models reviewed elsewhere in this PASSPORT.

*Passport's Choice. La crème de la crème.* Our test team's personal picks of the litter—models we would buy or have bought for our personal use.

✪**:** A relative bargain, with decidedly more performance than the price would suggest.

**Portatop models have superior audio by world band standards.**

✪✪✪✪⅛ ✪ 📖 *Passport's Choice*

## Grundig Satellit 800, Grundig Satellit 800 EU, Tecsun HAM-2000

**Price:** *S-800:* $499.95 including 120 V AC adaptor and headphones in the United States. CAN$599.99 including 120 V AC adaptor and headphones in Canada. *S-800 refurbished units, as available:* $399.95 in the United States. *S-800 EU:* £549.00 including 240V AC adaptor and headphones in the United Kingdom. €698.00 including 240V AC adaptor and headphones in Germany. *HAM-2000:* ¥3,500 in China.

**Pro:** Outstanding price, especially in North America and China, for level of performance. Superior, room-filling tonal quality by world band, even if not audiophile, standards—whether with the internal speaker, outboard speakers or headphones; only receiver tested that comes with full-size audiophile-style padded headphones. Tonal shaping aided by continuous separate bass and treble tone controls, a rarity among world band receivers at any price. Excellent-performing synchronous selectable sideband, with 27 dB of unwanted-sideband rejection; this reduces adjacent-channel interference and selective-fading distortion with world band, longwave and mediumwave AM signals. Synchronous selectable sideband also boosts recoverable audio from some of the weakest of signals, and halves overall distor-

**Opposite: Portatop circuits undergo analysis at Tecsun R&D in China.**

Tecsun

tion from 5.3% in the ordinary AM mode to 2.4% on audio frequencies from 100-3,000 Hz. Three voice/music bandwidths; wide measures around 7 kHz, while medium and narrow measure in the vicinity of 5.8 kHz and 2.6 kHz (*see* Con). Bandwidths generally have excellent shape factors (*see* Con) and excellent ultimate rejection; all bandwidths are selectable independent of mode (or dependent, if the user prefers), and work in concert with the synchronous selectable sideband feature to provide superior adjacent-channel rejection. Slow/fast AGC decay (*see* Con). Numerous helpful tuning aids, including 70 tunable station presets that store many variables (*see* Con); also, presets may be scanned (*see* Con). Excellent ergonomics, including many dedicated, widely spaced controls; exceptionally smooth knob tuning aided by ball bearings (*see* Con); and foolproof frequency entry. Superb LCD with huge, bold characters has high contrast and can be viewed clearly from virtually any angle; it is even readable by many with faltering eyesight (*see* Con). Analog signal-strength indicator, a rarity at this price, has gradations in useful S1-9/+60 dB standard (*see* Con). Single-sideband reception above the portable norm (*see* Con), with rock-solid frequency stability and 50 Hz tuning increments. High- and low-impedance inputs for 0.1-30 MHz external antennas. Weak-signal shortwave sensitivity with built-in telescopic antenna equal to or better than that of best-rated portables. Weak-signal shortwave sensitivity with an external antenna can be boosted by setting antenna switch to "whip," thus adding preamplification (and, in such locations as Europe evenings, sometimes generating overloading as well). Superior blocking performance aids consistency of weak-signal sensitivity. Generally superior dynamic range and third-order intercept

## NUMBERS: GRUNDIG SATELLIT 800/TECSUN HAM-2000

| | |
|---|---|
| Max. Sensitivity/Noise Floor | 0.43 µV, **G**/–124 dBm, **G** [1] |
| Blocking | 132 dB, **E** |
| Bandwidths *(Shape Factors)* | 7.1 *(1:1.6,* **E***)*, 5.8 *(1:1.6,* **E***)*, 2.6 *(1:2.2,* **G***)* kHz |
| Ultimate Rejection | 75 dB, **E** |
| Front-End Selectivity | **F** |
| Image Rejection | 65 dB, **G** |
| First IF Rejection | 83 dB, **E** |
| Dynamic Range/IP3 (5 kHz) | 67 dB, **F**/–26 dBm, **G** [2] |
| Dynamic Range/IP3 (20 kHz) | 92 dB, **E**/+11 dBm, **S** [2] |
| Phase Noise | 111 dBc, **G** |
| AGC Threshold | 0.8 µV, **S** |
| Overall Distortion, sync | 2.4%, **E** |

| **IBS Lab Ratings:** | **S** Superb | **E** Excellent | **G** Good | **F** Fair | **P** Poor |
|---|---|---|---|---|---|

(1) Sample-to-sample variation from 0.23 to 0.43 µV, –129 to –124 dBm.

(2) Estimated, as ability to measure limited by birdies, phase noise and other mixing products.

Based on the much costlier Drake SW8 receiver, this beefy portatop is the Jolly Gray Giant of world band radios.

point to the extent they can be measured amidst receiver phase noise and such. Two-event on/off timer and two 24-hour clocks (*see* Con). Large, tough telescopic antenna includes spring-loaded detents for vertical, 45-degree and 90-degree swiveling; also rotates freely 360 degrees (*see* Con). Clever display and signal strength meter illumination—with batteries in use, light automatically comes on for 15 seconds either at the touch of any button or when receiver is knob or slew tuned; 15-second illumination cycle can be aborted by pushing the light button a second time. FM—mono through built-in speaker, stereo through outboard speakers, headphones and line output—performs well, although capture ratio only average and nearby FM transmitters may cause some overloading. Covers longwave down to 100 kHz. Built-in ferrite rod antenna may be used for 0.1-1.8 MHz. Covers the 118-137 MHz aeronautical band, but only in the AM mode without synchronous selectable sideband; performs about as well as a simple handheld scanner. Excellent, long carrying handle. Comes with AC adaptor—120 V AC or 220 V AC, depending upon where radio is sold; otherwise, alkaline batteries need changing every 35 hours or so, about 25 cents per hour. Battery-strength indicator (*see* Con). Rack-type handles protect front panel should radio fall over. *North America:* Repairs in and out of one-year warranty are performed by the R.L. Drake Company, long known for superior service (*see* Con). Excellent toll-free tech support.

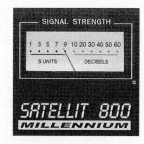

An analog signal-strength indicator is a welcome feature, but this one greatly underreads.

**Con:** Huge (20 3/8 inches—517 mm—wide) and weighty (15 pounds or 6.8 kg with batteries). Plastic cabinet and other components are of portable-radio quality, not in the same radiophile-hardware league as found on tabletop models. Synthesizer phase noise, only fair, slightly impacts reception of weak-signals adjacent to powerful signals and in

**Chinese experts check out a Tecsun portatop aboard a Chinese ship.**
Fanzhongxiong

other circumstances; also, limits ability to make certain laboratory measurements accurately. Lacks notch filter, noise blanker, passband tuning and digital signal process-ing (DSP) found on some tabletop models. When ungrounded (e.g., AC adaptor is not connected) and powered by batteries, there is vigorous "hash" while the tuning knob is being handled within some portions of the mediumwave AM band; this ceases when the tuning knob is released, and reception quality of the received station is not affected. Each key push must each be done within three seconds, lest receiver wind up being mis-tuned or placed into an unwanted operating mode. No signal-seek frequency scanning. Signal-strength indicator greatly underreads, although arguably this is preferable to the overreading often found with other models. Outboard AC adaptor in lieu of inboard power supply. Single sideband's 50 Hz synthesizer increments allow tuning to be out of phase by up to 25 Hz, diminishing audio fidelity. Fast AGC decay setting is handy for bandscanning, but sometimes causes distortion with powerful signals; remedied by going to slow AGC when no longer actively bandscanning.

Numerous modest birdies on longwave, mediumwave AM, shortwave and FM bands; these rarely cause heterodyne interference to world band signals, approximately one time in 250 they might heterodyne utility, ham and Eastern Hemisphere mediumwave signals. Spurious signal on 20,000 kHz obscures WWV reception. Ergonomics, although excellent, are not ideal; e.g., no rows and columns of dedicated buttons for station presets, as is found on the Sony ICF-2010. Sharp bevel on tuning knob. Neither clock displays when frequency is shown; however, pushbutton allows time to replace frequency on the display for three seconds. Both clocks in 24-hour format and neither displays seconds numerically; 12-hour format not selectable for local time. For faint-signal DXing, recoverable audio with an outboard antenna, although good, not fully equal to that of most tabletop and professional models. Using the built-in antenna, sensitivity to weak signals is not of DX caliber in the mediumwave AM band; remedied by using Terk AM Advantage or similar accessory antenna. Some frontal (only) radiation of digital noise from LCD, rarely causes problem in actual use. No adjustable feet or elevation rod to angle receiver upwards for handy operation. When receiver leaned backward, the telescopic antenna, if angled, spins to the rear. Battery-strength indicator doesn't come on until immediately before radio mutes from low battery voltage. Misleading location of battery spring clips makes it easy to insert half the batteries in the wrong direction, albeit to no permanent ill effect. Battery cover may come loose if receiver bumped in a specific and unusual manner. Antenna switches located unhandily on rear panel. "USB" on LCD displays as "LISB." No schematic or repair manual available, making service difficult except at authorized repair facilities. No batteries (6 "D" needed). *Tecsun:* "HAM" a confusing name, as world band radio has nothing to do with hams, who are licensed to transmit to each other.

☞ Refurbished Grundig units reportedly include gift and similar types of returns from department stores and other outlets where customers tend to be unfamiliar with world band radio. Refurbishing is done at Drake's facility in Ohio.

**Verdict:** The Grundig Satellit 800/Tecsun HAM-2000 is a benchmark receiver, being the first ever to offer such a level of near-tabletop performance at a near-portable price. Its audio quality and ergonomics are also among the best of any world band receiver on the market.

📄 An *RDI WHITE PAPER* is available for this model.

―――――――――――

*The* PASSPORT *portatop review team includes Lawrence Magne, Tony Jones, Craig Tyson and George Zeller, with Avery Comarow, George Heidelman, John Wagner. Laboratory measurements by Robert Sherwood.*

# Reading Last Week's *TV Guide*?

Probably not, and world band changes much more than TV. There are hundreds of new schedules and programs each year—new radios, too!

If you want your next PASSPORT right off the press, drop us a line at New Passport, Box 300, Penn's Park, PA 18943 USA, fax 1 (215) 598 3794 or e-mail mktg@passband.com. When the new edition is being readied for shipment to dealers, we'll notify you by postcard, or you can check at www.passband.com.

**www.passband.com**

# Tabletop Receivers for 2003

Tabletop receivers flush out tough game—faint stations swamped by competing signals. That's why they are prized by radio aficionados known as "DXers," an old telegraph term meaning long distance. But tabletop models aren't for everybody, and it shows. Even in prosperous North America and Europe, tabletop unit sales are minimal even while the roster of choices is as great as ever.

Most models are pricier than portables or portatops, yet less expensive than the professional supersets also reviewed in PASSPORT REPORTS. For that money you tend to get not only excellent performance, but also a fairly robust device. Tabletop models are not only manufactured to a higher standard than portables and portatops, but also are relatively easy to service and are backed up by knowledgeable repair facilities. What you rarely find in a tabletop is reception of the everyday 87.5-108 MHz FM band—for this coverage in a premium receiver, look to a portatop.

## Where in the World Is San Diego, Carmen?

Tabletop sets, like portatop and professional models, are heavy artillery for where signals are routinely weak—places like the North American Midwest and West, or Australia and New Zealand. Even elsewhere there can be a problem when signals pass over or near the geomagnetic North Pole. To check, place a string on a globe—a conventional map won't do—between you and the station's transmitter, as given in the Blue Pages. If the string passes near or above latitude 60° north, beware.

## Daytime Signals Weaker

Some programs formerly heard at prime time are now audible only during your local daytime. These signals tend to be weaker, especially when not beamed to your part of the world. However, thanks to the scattering properties of shortwave, you can still eavesdrop on many of these "off-beam" signals. But it's harder, and that's where a superior receiver's longer reach comes in.

However, if you are already using a portable with an outdoor antenna and it is being disrupted by electrical noise from nearby motors, dimmers and such, you probably won't benefit from a tabletop model. Its superior circuitry boosts local noise as much as signals.

## New and Improved for 2003

For 2003 the big news is the introduction of a potentially superb receiver from the American firm of Ten-Tec. This model, the RX-350, lives up to its potential in many ways, and sometimes does even better. Yet, it is still several steps away from having reached the mountaintop.

We also retested the Icom IC-R75 with its DSP option that wasn't available when we did our first test in 1999, as well as the Drake R8b. Both get high marks.

Too, we reanalyzed the Drake R8B, and were pleased to find that silent internally generated signals—"birdies"—have been reduced and stability has been improved. It remains the best tabletop, at least until it becomes clear how Ten-Tec's RX-350 evolves.

## Many Antennas Available

In high-rise buildings, portables can disappoint. Reinforced buildings soak up signals, while local broadcast and cellular transmitters can interfere.

Here, a good bet for tough stations is a well-rated tabletop or portatop model fed by a homebrew insulated-wire antenna along, or just outside, a window or balcony. Also, try an ordinary telescopic car antenna that juts out, like a wall flag mast, out a window or balcony ledge.

Another alternative is to amplify these homebrew antennas with an active preselector. You can also try amplified ("active") antennas that have reception elements and amplifiers in separate modules. Several such devices are evaluated in this PASSPORT REPORTS.

If you don't live in an apartment, go with a first-rate passive (unamplified) outdoor wire antenna, usually under $100. Performance findings and installation tips are in the Radio Database International White Paper, *Popular Outdoor Antennas*, and are summarized in this PASSPORT REPORTS.

## Complete Findings Now Available

Our unabridged laboratory and hands-on test results for each receiver are too exhaustive to reproduce here. However, they are available for selected models as PASSPORT's Radio Database International

White Papers—details on availability are elsewhere in this book. More are planned, and will be listed at www.passband.com as they become available.

## Tips for Using this Section

Receivers are listed in order of suitability for listening to difficult-to-hear world band stations; important secondary consideration is given to audio fidelity and ergonomics. Street prices are cited, with British and Australian VAT/GST where applicable. Prices vary, so take them as the general guide they are meant to be.

Unless otherwise stated, all tabletop models have:

- Digital frequency synthesis and display.
- Full coverage of at least the 155-29999 kHz longwave, mediumwave AM and short-wave spectra—including all world band frequencies—but no coverage of the FM broadcast band (87.5-108 MHz). Models designed for sale in certain countries have reduced shortwave tuning ranges.
- A wide variety of helpful tuning features.
- Synchronous selectable sideband via high-rejection IF filtering (not lower-rejection phasing), which greatly reduces adjacent-channel interference and selective-fading distortion.

☞ **ECSS:** Many tabletop models can tune to the nearest 10 Hz or even 1 Hz, allowing the user to use the receiver's single-sideband circuitry to manually phase its BFO (internally generated carrier) with the station's transmitted carrier. Called "ECSS" (exalted-carrier, selectable-sideband) tuning, this can be used in lieu of synchronous selectable sideband. However, in addition to the relative inconvenience of this technique, unlike synchronous selectable sideband, which re-phases continually and perfectly, ECSS is always slightly out of phase. This causes at least some degree of harmonic distortion to music and speech, while tuning to the nearest Hertz can generate slow-sweep fading (for this reason, mis-phasing by two or three Hertz may provide better results).

- Proper demodulation of modes used by non-world-band shortwave signals, except for models designed to be sold in certain countries. These modes include single sideband (LSB/USB) and CW ("Morse code"); also, with suitable ancillary devices, radioteletype (RTTY), frequency shift key (FSK) and radiofax (FAX).
- Meaningful signal-strength indication.
- Illuminated display.

## What PASSPORT's Rating Symbols Mean

**Star ratings:** ✪✪✪✪✪ is best. Stars reflect overall performance and meaningful features, plus to some extent ergonomics and build quality. Price, appearance, country of manufacture and the like are not taken into account. With tabletop models there is a slightly greater emphasis on the ability to flush out tough, hard-to-hear signals, as this is one of the main reasons these sets are chosen. Nevertheless, to facilitate comparison the tabletop rating standards are very similar to those used for the professional, portatop and portable models reviewed elsewhere in this PASSPORT.

*Passport's Choice. La crème de la crème.* Our test team's personal picks of the litter—models we would buy or have bought for our personal use.

**∅:** A relative bargain, with decidedly more performance than the price would suggest. However, none of these receivers is cheap.

## Retested for 2003

✪✪✪✪✪ 📃 *Passport's Choice*
**Drake R8B**

**Price:** *R8B:* $1,379.00 in the United States. CAN$2,199.00 in Canada. *MS8 Speaker:* US$49.00 in the United States. CAN$75.00 in Canada. *VHF Converter:* US$249.00 plus $20 installation in the United States.

CAN$399.00 plus installation in Canada. *R8B Technical Manual:* $39.95 in the United States.

**Pro:** Superior all-round performance for listening to world band programs and hunting DX catches, as well as utility, amateur and mediumwave AM signals. Mellow, above-average audio quality, especially with suitable outboard speaker or headphones (*see* Con). Synchronous selectable sideband excels at reducing distortion caused by selective fading, as well as at diminishing or eliminating adjacent-channel interference; also has synchronous double sideband. Five well-chosen bandwidths, four suitable for world band. Highly flexible operating controls, including a powerful tunable AF notch filter (tunes to 5,300 Hz AF, but *see* Con) and an excellent passband offset control. Best ergonomics of any five-star model (*see* Con).

The Drake R8B does almost everything well, yet has no significant flaws.

Tunes and displays in precise 10 Hz increments. Slow/fast/off AGC with superior performance characteristics. Exceptionally effective noise blanker. Helpful tuning features include 1,000 presets and sophisticated scanning functions; presets can be quickly accessed via the tuning knob and slew buttons. Built-in switchable preamplifier. Accepts two antennas, selectable via front panel. Two 24-hour clocks, with

| NUMBERS: TOP TWO TABLETOPS | | |
| --- | --- | --- |
| | **Drake R8B** | **AOR AR7030** |
| Max. Sensitivity/Noise Floor | 0.21 μV, Ⓔ[1]/–130 dBm, Ⓔ[1] | 0.2 μV, Ⓔ/–128 dBm, Ⓖ |
| Blocking | 136 dB, Ⓢ | >130 dB, Ⓔ |
| Shape Factors, voice BWs | 1:1.96–1:2.70, Ⓖ | 1:1.52–1:1.96, Ⓔ |
| Ultimate Rejection | 75 dB, Ⓔ | 90 dB, Ⓢ |
| Front-End Selectivity | Half octave, Ⓔ | High/low pass, Ⓕ |
| Image Rejection | >90 dB, Ⓢ | >100 dB, Ⓢ |
| First IF Rejection | >90 dB, Ⓢ | 95 dB, Ⓢ |
| Dynamic Range/IP3 (5 kHz) | 77 dB, Ⓔ/–17 dBm, Ⓔ | 82 dB, Ⓔ/+1 dBm, Ⓢ |
| Dynamic Range/IP3 (20 kHz) | 93 dB, Ⓔ/+8 dBm, Ⓔ | 100 dB, Ⓢ/+28 dBm, Ⓢ |
| Phase Noise | 113 dBc, Ⓖ | 130 dBc, Ⓢ |
| AGC Threshold | 0.55 μV, Ⓔ | 2.25 μV, Ⓖ |
| Overall Distortion, sync | 0.6%, Ⓢ | 2.0%, Ⓔ |
| Notch filter depth | 55 dB, Ⓢ | 55 dB, Ⓢ |
| **IBS Lab Ratings:** Ⓢ Superb  Ⓔ Excellent  Ⓖ Good  Ⓕ Fair  Ⓟ Poor | | |
| (1) Preamp on; 0.45 μV Ⓖ/–124 dBm Ⓖ with preamp off. | | |

seconds displayed numerically and two-event timer (*see* Con). Helpful operating manual. Power cord detaches handily from receiver, making it easy to replace. Fifteen-day money-back trial period if ordered from factory. Superior factory service.

**Con:** Virtually requires a good outboard speaker for non-headphone listening, although the optional Drake MS8 outboard speaker not equal to the receiver's audio potential; try a good amplified computer speaker or high-efficiency passive speaker instead. Slight bassiness in audio, remediable through careful choice of the right outboard speaker. Neither clock shows when frequency displayed. Lightweight tuning knob lacks any trace of flywheel effect; this, along with thin cabinet metal and mechanical frequency encoder in lieu of optical encoder used in original R8, exude an aura of cheesiness; nevertheless, years-long track record indicates that reliability is at least average. No IF output. Otherwise-excellent tilt bail difficult to open. Notch filter does not tune below 500 Hz (AF). Virtually impossible to find at dealers outside North America. When changing from 90-132V to 180-264V AC, a resistor must be removed from receiver, which for some users will require a technician. Optional VHF converter difficult to install; best is to have this done when receiver is purchased.

**Verdict:** The American-made Drake R8B is the only non-professional receiver we have ever tested that gets everything right, where something important isn't missing or sputtering and ergonomics are worthy. This means there's little point spending money on such performance-enhancing accessories as the Sherwood SE-3, although a better—outboard—speaker can allow the receiver to live up to its fidelity potential.

**Observations with Latest Sample:** Our latest unit had fewer and weaker "birdies" than in the past—less than a dozen, mostly between 13.0 and 13.8 MHz and under one microvolt. Drift has been halved, too, to 25

Hz after a ten-second warmup. Otherwise, test numbers (sidebar) fell within the expected range of sample-to-sample variation from past units.

Overall, the Drake R8B continues to be the logical choice in a tabletop for most world band listeners. Our latest tests suggest that while it remains fundamentally unchanged, its performance has been every-so-slightly tweaked in recent production.

📄 An *RDI WHITE PAPER* is available for this model.

## ✪✪✪✪✪ *Passport's Choice*
### AOR AR7030, AOR AR7030+3

**Price:** *AR7030:* £799.00 in the United Kingdom. €1,148.00 in Germany. AUS$2,890.00 in Australia. *AR7030+3:* $1,469.95 in the United States. £949.00 in the United Kingdom. €1,298.00 in Germany. AUS$3,250.00 in Australia.

**Pro:** In terms of sheer performance for program listening, as good a radio as we've ever tested. Except for sensitivity to weak signals (*see* Con), easily overcome, the same comment applies to DX reception. Exceptionally quiet circuitry. Superior audio quality when used with a first-rate outboard speaker or audio system. Synchronous selectable sideband performs exceptionally well at reducing distortion caused by selective fading, as well as at diminishing or eliminating adjacent-channel interference; also has synchronous double sideband. Best dynamic range of any consumer-grade radio tested. Nearly all other lab measurements are top-drawer. Four voice bandwidths (2.3, 7.0, 8.2 and 10.3 kHz), with cascaded ceramic filters, come standard; up to six, either ceramic or mechanical, upon request (*see* Con). Advanced tuning and operating features aplenty, including passband tuning. Tunable audio (AF) notch and noise blanker now available, albeit as an option; notch filter extremely effective, with little loss of audio fidelity. Built-in preamplifier (*see*

Con). Automatically self-aligns and centers all bandwidth filters for optimum performance, then displays the actual measured bandwidth of each. Remote keypad (*see* Con). Accepts two antennas. IF output. Optional improved processor unit now has 400 memories, including 14-character alphanumeric readout for station names. World Time clock, which displays seconds, calendar and timer/snooze features. Superior mediumwave AM performance. Superior factory service.

**Con:** Unusually convoluted ergonomics, including tree-logic operating scheme, especially in +3 version; once the initial glow of ownership has passed, this can become tiresome. Remote control unit, which has to be aimed carefully at either the front or the back of the receiver, is required to use certain features, such as direct frequency entry; not all panelists were enthusiastic about this arrangement, wishing that a mouse-type umbilical cable had been used instead. Although the remote keypad can operate from across a room, the LCD characters are too small to be seen from such a distance. LCD omits certain important information, such as signal strength, when radio in various status modes. Sensitivity to weak signals good, as are related noise-floor measurements, but could be a bit better; a first-rate antenna, as indicated elsewhere in this PASSPORT, overcomes this. Because of peculiar built-in preamplifier/attenuator design in which the two are linked, receiver noise rises slightly when preamplifier used in +10 dB position, or attenuator used in –10 dB setting; however, +3 version remedies this. When six bandwidths used (four standard ceramics, two optional mechanicals), ultimate rejection, although superb with widest three bandwidths, cannot be measured beyond –80/–85 dB on narrowest three bandwidths because of phase noise; still, ultimate rejection is excellent or better with these narrow bandwidths. Lacks, and would profit from, a bandwidth of around 4 or 5 kHz; a

Collins mechanical bandwidth filter of 3.5 kHz (nominal at –3 dB, measures 4.17 kHz at –6 dB) is an option worth considering. Such Collins filters, in the two optional bandwidth slots, measure as having poorer shape factors (1:1.8 to 1:2) than the standard-slot MuRata ceramic filters (1:1.5 to 1:1.6). LCD emits some digital electrical noise, potentially a problem only if an amplified (active) antenna is used with its pickup element (e.g. telescopic rod) placed near the receiver. Minor microphonics (audio feedback), typically when internal speaker is used, noted in laboratory; in actual listening, however, this is not noticeable; in any event, this is moot when an outboard speaker is used. Uses outboard AC adaptor instead of built-in power supply.

☞ Mechanical encoders on the '7030 used to have an above-average failure rate, seemingly because of corrosion on contacts. Starting from serial number 102050, with production as of late July, 1999, AOR has replaced the original Bourns mechanical encoder with a metal-encased version from Alps—the AR7030 now uses only Alps mechanical encoders, whereas the AR7030+3 uses Alps mechanical and Bourns optical encoders. A conversion kit for earlier units is available for £20 plus shipping, although it requires skill to install. Similarly, features of the +3 version can be incorporated into existing regular models by skilled technicians.

**The AOR AR7030+3 is an outstanding performer, though menu operation limits popularity.**

**Verdict:** This is definitely not your grandfather's radio. The AR7030, designed and manufactured in England, is an even better performer and more robust in the +3 variation. Alas, ergonomics, already peculiar and cumbersome in the "barefoot" version, are even more hostile in the +3 incarnation. For some, this is not a problem—indeed, it can even be a satisfying challenge, at least in the short run. But for many others it's just not worth the bother.

Ergonomics and slightly limited sensitivity to weak signals aside, the '7030 is arguably the best choice—certainly among the best choices—for serious DX available on the scotch side of a professional-grade model. This is a receiver you'll really need to lay your hands on before you'll know whether it's love or hate—or something between.

## ✪✪✪✪½
## Japan Radio NRD-545

**Price:** $1,799.95 in the United States. £1,395.00 in the United Kingdom. €2,147.00 in Germany. AUS$3,950.00 in Australia. *NVA-319 external speaker:* $210.00 in the United States. £189 in the United Kingdom. €295.00 in Germany. *CHE-199 VHF-UHF converter:* $399.95 in the United States. £269 in the United Kingdom. €449.00 in Germany.

**Pro:** Superior build quality, right down to the steel cabinet with machined screws. Easily upgraded by changing software ROMs. Fully 998 bandwidths provide unprecedented flexibility. Razor-sharp skirt selectivity, especially with voice bandwidths. Outstanding array of tuning aids, including 1,000 presets (*see* Con). Wide array of reception aids, including passband offset, excellent manual/automatic tunable notch, and synchronous selectable sideband having good lock. Superb reception of single-sideband and other "utility" signals. Demodulates C-Quam AM stereo signals, which then need to be fed through an external audio amplifier, not provided (the

headphone jack can't be used for this, as it is monaural). Highly adjustable AGC in all modes requiring BFO (*see* Con). Tunes in ultra-precise 1 Hz increments, although displays only in 10 Hz increments. Ergonomics, including the physical quality of tuning knob and other controls, among the very best. Some useful audio shaping. Computer interface with NRD Win software (*see* Con); among other things, is effective at processing RTTY signals. Virtually no spurious radiation of digital "hash." Hiss-free audio-out port for recording or feeding low-power FM transmitter to hear world band around the house. Internal AC power supply is quiet and generates little heat. Power cord detaches handily from receiver, like on a PC, making it easy to replace. Includes a "CARE package" of all needed metric plugs and connectors, along with a 12V DC power cord.

**Con:** Ultimate rejection only fair, although average ultimate rejection equivalent is 10-15 dB better; this unusual gap comes about from intermodulation (IMD) inside the digital signal processor, and results in audible "monkey chatter" under certain reception conditions. Audio quality sometimes tough sledding in the unvarnished AM mode—using synchronous selectable sideband helps greatly. No AGC adjustment in AM mode or with synchronous selectable sideband, and lone AGC decay rate too fast. Dynamic range only fair. Synchronous selectable sideband sometimes slow to kick in. Notch filter won't attenuate heterodynes (whistles) any higher in pitch than 2,500 Hz AF. Noise reduction circuit only marginally useful. Signal-strength indicator overreads at higher levels. Frequency display misreads by up to 30 Hz, especially at higher tuned frequencies, and gets worse as the months pass by. Presets don't store synchronous-AM settings. Audio amplifier lacks oomph with some poorly modulated signals. No IF output, nor can one be retrofitted. NRD Win software, at least the current v1.00, handles only uploads, not downloads, and works only on com port 1 that is usually already in use. World Time clock doesn't show when frequency displayed. No tilt bail or feet. Anti-reflective paint on buttons and knobs becomes shiny with wear.

**Verdict:** In many ways Japan Radio's NRD-545 is a remarkable performer, especially for utility and tropical-bands DXing. With its first-class ergonomics and the fine feel of superior construction quality, it is always a pleasure to operate. Yet, more is needed to make this the ultimate receiver it could be. By now Japan Radio should have issued a ROM upgrade to remedy at least some of these long-standing issues, but *nada* as yet.

Whether "monkey chatter" and other manifestations of DSP overload are an issue varies markedly from one listening situation to another. It depends on the type of signals being received, what part of the world you are in, and your own aural perceptions. Among our panelists, all noticed it eventually, but reaction varied from "no big deal" to howls of derision.

### ✪✪✪✪⅜
### Japan Radio "NRD-545SE"

**Price:** *NRD-545SE:* $1,899.00 in the United States. *Retrofit to change an existing receiver to "SE":* $104.00 plus receiver shipping both ways.

**Pro:** Dynamic range, 5 kHz, improves from 66 dB to 73 dB.

**Con:** Not available outside North America. *With 8 kHz replacement filter:* Audio bandwidth reduced by 20 percent at the high end. *With 6 kHz replacement filter (not tested):* Audio bandwidth reduced by about 40 percent at the high end.

☞ For all except those who confine their listening to tough DX or utility catches, the 8 kHz filter is a preferable choice over the 6 kHz option.

**Verdict:** Sherwood Engineering, an American firm, replaces the stock DSP protection filter

The Japan Radio NRD-545, though pricey, is still the best DSP tabletop receiver.

with one of two narrower filters of comparable quality. In principle, this should provide beaucoup decibels of audible improvement in the "monkey chatter" encountered on the '545 from adjacent-channel signals. Alas, our listening panel couldn't hear the difference, but did notice an unwelcome reduction in audio crispness with world band signals—as well as, of course, with mediumwave AM reception.

The "SE" modification yields a slight improvement in close-in dynamic range, but bottom line is nice try, no cigar. Adventurous DXers may wish to consider the 6 kHz filter-replacement option in lieu of the 8 kHz option tested.

For utility DXing, as well as intense world band DXing, the reduction in high-end audio response is not a real issue. For these applications, the "SE" may represent a marginal improvement over the stock '545.

### *Retested for 2003*
### ✪✪✪✪⅜  ✐
### Icom IC-R75/Icom IC-R75E

**Price:** *Receiver only:* Under $800.00 in the United States, the exact price depending on factory rebates, if any, available at the time; sometimes the UT-106 DSP unit has been thrown in for free, as well. CAN$1,399.00 in Canada. £649.00 in the United Kingdom. €798.00 in Germany. AUS$1,680.00 in Australia. *UT-106 DSP unit:* $139.95 in the United States. CAN$250.00 in Canada.

£79.95 in the United Kingdom. €117.10 in Germany. AUS175.00 in Australia. *Icom Replacement Bandwidth Filters (e.g., 3.3 kHz):* $160-200 or equivalent worldwide. *SP-20 amplified audio-shaping speaker:* $219.95 in the United States. CAN$470.00 in Canada. £164.95 (€264) in the United Kingdom.

**Pro:** Dual passband offset acts as variable bandwidth and a form of IF shift (*see* Con). Reception of faint signals alongside powerful competing ones aided by excellent ultimate selectivity and good blocking. Excellent front-end selectivity, with seven filters for the shortwave range and more for elsewhere. Two levels of preamplification, 10 dB and 20 dB, can be switched off. Excellent weak-signal sensitivity and good AGC threshold with +20 dB preamplification. Superior rejection of spurious signals. Excellent stability, essential for unattended reception of RTTY and certain other types of utility transmissions. Excels in reception of utility and ham signals, as well as world band signals tuned via "ECSS" technique. Ten tuning steps. Can tune and display in exacting 1Hz increments (*see* Con). Adjustable UT-106 DSP audio accessory with automatic variable notch filter, normally an extra-cost option, helps to a degree in improving intelligibility, but not pleasantness, of some tough signals; also, it reduces heterodyne ("whistle") interference. Fairly good ergonomics, including smooth-turning weighted tuning knob; nice touch is spinning finger dimple, even if it doesn't spin very well. "Control Central" LCD easy to read and evenly illuminated by 24 LEDs with dimmer. Adjustable AGC—fast, slow, off. Tuning knob uses reliable optical encoder normally found only on professional receivers, rather than everyday mechanical variety. Low overall distortion. Pleasant and hiss-free audio with suitable outboard speaker; audio-shaping amplified Icom SP-20, although pricey, works well for a number of applications. 101 presets. Two antenna inputs, switchable. Digital bar graph signal-strength indicator, although not as desirable as an analog meter, is unusually linear above S-9 and can be set to hold a peak reading briefly. Audio-out port for recording or feeding low-power FM transmitter to hear world band around the house (*see* Con). World Time clock, timer and snooze (*see* Con). Tunes to 60 MHz, including 6 meter VHF ham band. Tilt bail (*see* Con).

**Con:** Synchronous detector virtually nonfunctional; operates only with modification by user or specialty firm, or by addition of a specialized auxiliary device. Dual passband offset usually has little impact on received world band signals and is inoperative when synchronous detection is in use. DSP's automatic variable notch tends not to work with AM-mode signals not received via "ECSS" technique (tuning AM-mode signals as though they were single sideband). Mediocre audio through internal speaker, and no tone control to offset slightly bassy reproduction that originates prior to the audio stage; audio improves to pleasant with an appropriate external speaker, especially one that offsets the receiver's slight bassiness. Suboptimal audio recovery with weak AM-mode signals having heavy fading; largely remediable by "ECSS" tuning and switching off AGC. Display misreads up to 20 Hz, somewhat negating the precise 1 Hz tuning. Keypad requires frequencies to be entered in MHz format with decimal or trailing zeroes, a pointless inconvenience. Some knobs small. Uses outboard "floor brick" AC adaptor in lieu of internal power supply; adaptor's emission field may be picked up by nearby indoor antennas or unshielded antenna lead-in wiring, which can cause minor hum on received signals (remediable by moving antenna or using shielded lead-in cable). Can read clock or presets IDs or frequency, but no more than one at the same time. RF/AGC control operates peculiarly. Tilt bail lacks rubber protection for furniture surface. Keyboard beep appears at audio line output. No schematic provided.

**Verdict:** The Japanese-made Icom IC-R75 is a first-rate receiver for unearthing tough utility and ham signals, as well as world band signals received via manual "ECSS" tuning. Nothing else equals it on the sunny side of a kilobuck.

Its hopeless synchronous detector performance is much improved by a simple modification from such specialty firms as Kiwa. Alternatively, the Sherwood SE-3 outboard fidelity-enhancing device can be used to entirely replace the 'R75's synchronous and audio circuits. Yet, one can but marvel at Icom's corporate culture which allows a simple fix be shunned by the factory year after year, while at the same time they invalidate the warranty if a set is modified to operate properly; during the warranty it may help to have upgrades performed by an authorized Icom dealer. Thankfully, the 'R75's exacting frequency steps allow for easy "ECSS" tuning of world band signals as though they were single sideband.

**Observations with Latest Sample:** As in PASSPORT's initial tests of an early unit in 1999, our lab measurements show the Icom IC-R75 to be a commendable performer; with maximum preamplification every measurement is good, excellent or superb. This puts it ahead of a number of costlier models, which is possible in part because it is not a true DSP receiver, which at this level of performance would cost considerably more.

Overall, it performs best with the full 20 dB of preamplification, although in some very-high-signal areas with high-gain antennas this can stress dynamic range. At 5 kHz separation points (phase noise prevented 20 kHz measurements) DR/IP3 measure 65 dB/–25 dBm—good, but 20 dB of preamp gain can tax subsequent circuitry.

Performance is only slightly reduced with preamplification off—noise floor drops from –135 dBm, excellent, to –122 dBm, good; sensitivity from 0.11 µV, superb, to 0.6 µV, fair; and AGC threshold from 0.4 µV, good,

The Icom IC-R75's sync is virtually useless. Otherwise, it's an excellent receiver and sensibly priced.

to 3.5 µV, fair. The corresponding 10 dB preamplification numbers are noise floor –129 dBm, good, sensitivity 0.25 µV, excellent, and AGC threshold 1.3 µV, fair.

Audio quality with the internal speaker is pedestrian, but with the right outboard speaker it can become quite pleasant, thanks in part to low overall distortion. Indeed, with SSB/ECSS distortion is under one *tenth* of one percent, a level that would put many CD players to shame. There is a hint of excessive bassiness and no tone control to overcome it, but the appropriate outboard speaker can clean it up.

Our 'R75 included the adjustable UT-106 audio DSP accessory that wasn't available for our original tests in 1999. It borders on being a "must have" for DXing, dropping unwanted noise as much as 15 dB. Nevertheless, on very weak signals the '106 gives residual noise a flanging or ringing sound. On stronger signals it tends to kill off high audio frequencies, leaving a quiet but somewhat restricted recovered audio. So, like most controls that help out when reception gets tough, the '106 is something you'll welcome at times, but generally leave switched off. It can be tricky to install, so this is best left to your dealer.

The '106 also includes an automatic notch filter. It works well, although its depth falls off at range extremes—for example, 37 dB at 1000 Hz, 26 dB at 400 & 2000 Hz, and a feeble 15 dB at 100 and 5000 Hz.

The 'R75 would have significantly more appeal if it had properly performing synchronous selectable sideband. Indeed, it comes equipped with something along these lines, but for all practical purposes it doesn't work. That's bad enough, but what puzzles is that it is relatively easy to fix. The factory should have made this simple change in production years ago, but for whatever reason Icom insists there is no problem. Fortunately, the receiver's ECSS tuning is almost as effective as synchronous selectable sideband, and you can check with specialty firms to consider a modification or synchronous selectable sideband accessory.

### New for 2003
✪✪✪¼
### Ten-Tec RX-350

**Price:** *RX-350:* $1,199.00 in the United States. £1,099.00 (€1725) in the United Kingdom. *302R external keypad/tuning knob:* $139.00 in the United States. £129.00 (€203) in the United Kingdom. *307B external speaker:* $98.00 in the United States. £89.00 (€140) in the United Kingdom.

**Pro:** Receiver is unlikely to become dated for some time, as many aspects of performance and operation can be readily updated, thus far and presumably always for free, by downloading revised firmware from the manufacturer's website (*see* Con); except for clock, all memory, including for firmware, is non-volatile and thus not dependent on battery backup. Lowest-cost tabletop model available with genuine DSP bandwidth filtering. A superb choice of no less than 34 bandwidths, including at least a dozen suitable for world band reception. Numerous helpful tuning features—front-panel tuning knob; up/down frequency and band slewing; 1024 presets divided into eight banks with alphanumeric station indicators; sophisticated scanning; optional keypad/tuning knob; and two VFOs. Optional external keypad/tuning knob is handy, comfortable and works well (*see* Con); it allows for frequency entry not only in Megahertz, but also in kilohertz via the enter key if the leading zero is entered first for frequencies under 10000 kHz. Tuning knobs on receiver and outboard keypad both use a reliable optical encoder normally found only on professional receivers, rather than the everyday mechanical variety. Tunes and displays in ultra-precise 1 Hz increments (*see* Con). Superior close-in (5 kHz separation) dynamic range/IP3. Excellent passband offset works in all non-FM modes, providing (in addition to the handy AML/AMU settings) selectable sideband for the synchronous detector (*see* Con). Generally worthy ergonomics with large display and seven useful tuning steps; also, bandwidths and presets conveniently selectable by knob (*see* Con), and controls have good tactile "feel"—especially the large, weighted metal tuning knob with rubber edging (*see* Con). Punchy, above-average audio with low overall distortion adds to enjoyment of music and enhances intelligibility, especially with suitable external speaker (*see* Con). Audio-out port for recording or feeding low-power FM transmitter to hear world band around the house. Unlike a number of other DSP receivers, does not make static crashes sound harsh; additionally, DSP noise reduction feature can moderate static noise a bit more. DSP noise reduction also of some use in improving aural quality of certain received signals (*see* Con). Receiver emits very little radiated digital "hash," so inverted-L antennas with single-wire feedlines and proximate loop antennas don't suffer from noise pickup. Rock stable, essential for unattended reception of RTTY and certain other types of utility transmissions. Notch filter automatic, effective over a wide range (0.1 to over 8.0 kHz AF), and can attenuate more than one heterodyne at a time (*see* Con). AGC threshold, originally poor, improved to excellent in latest version. Signal-strength indicator unusually accurate (*see* Con). More likely than most other models to be adaptable to possible future digital world band transmissions. Soft and hard microprocessor resets provide useful flexibility in case receiver's "computer" gets its knickers in a twist. AC power supply is inboard, where it belongs, and does not run hot. Tilt bail places receiver at handy angle for operation (*see* Con). Timer. Manufacturer has an exemplary record for customer support and factory repair.

**Con:** As tested in the revised-hardware version that came out to improve front-end selectivity, sensitivity is poor on mediumwave AM and even worse on longwave. RF preamplifier cannot be switched off to help prevent overloading. Our receiver froze up periodically; also, when going from memory channels back to a VFO, display showed invalid frequencies in the 45 to 94 MHz range (*see* ☞). Significant phase noise kept us from meaningfully measuring dynamic range/IP3 at 20 kHz separation; it also precluded plausible skirt-selectivity and ultimate rejection measurements. Synchronous selectable sideband loses lock easily during fades, albeit without causing whistling. Circuit hiss with widest bandwidths, a common syndrome with DSP receivers, although the noise reduction feature helps. Spectrum display of marginal utility—limited visual indication, poor contrast, significant time lag and it mutes the receiver during sweep; potentially the most useful range shown in the owner's manual is 120 kHz, but this does not appear in the menu. Keypad costs extra, even though it is virtually a necessity; it also comes with a remote tuning knob that some may find redundant and which adds to size and cost. Optional outboard keypad has intermittent frequency-entry hesitation. On one unit the display misread up to 30 Hz, somewhat negating the precise 1 Hz tuning; other samples did better. Ineffective noise blanker—DSP, not IF—unnecessarily complicated to turn on as instructed via menu (not indicated in the owner's manual, but the key combination of Alt NR can turn it on more simply), and its 1-7 adjustment

Ten-Tec's new RX-350 has enormous potential. Will it be realized?

needs to be at 5 or above to really work. AM-mode signals, whether received in the conventional AM mode or synchronous, sound harsh with fast AGC. No AGC off. Friction when turning knobs; remediable by easing knobs slightly away from front panel (with tuning knob, remove rubber edging to access hex screw). Passband offset requires many knob turns to shift the setting significantly with AM-mode or synchronous (SAM) reception, although not in other modes. Automatic notch filter can't be tuned manually in CW and RTTY reception modes, so the notch automatically impacts the desired signal along with any heterodyne(s). Signal-strength indicator's format, using numeric decibels and a short displayed scale, generally disliked by panelists. Noise reduction not adjustable, and solitary setting sometimes reduces intelligibility. Audio control in original version required more than three turns from soft to loud, although revised version uses the traditional single turn; however, as a result the audio scale display now shows 25 percent when the control is set to 100 percent. Unusual 9-pin-to-9-pin serial cable needed to download software not included with receiver. A number of commonly used controls are on the left, inconvenient for northpaws. No IF output. Tilt bail lacks protective rubber sheathing. Neither speaker wire can connect to ground, so an external speaker should not have a grounded cabinet (the 307B is appropriate in this regard).

☞ Two of our three units tested suffered from periodic freezing, or lockup, and occasional peculiar display readings. All were resolved by turning the receiver off, then back on again after no more than ten minutes, but re-downloading the firmware made no difference. The manufacturer insists these are sample defects, although to us it appears to have the earmarks of an inherent, but remediable, firmware cause.

**Verdict:** A solid winner in the making, with any number of advanced-technology advantages. Nonetheless, it's not quite there yet, especially for mediumwave AM and longwave.

**Evaluation of New Model:** The new Ten-Tec RX-350 has gone a long way towards setting a new standard in non-professional tabletop receivers, and it's hardly surprising. Their RX-340 professional rig is a superlative receiver, so these folks from Tennessee know their stuff.

Yet, thus far the '350, like Drake's initial R8, is really a work in progress. Drake advanced to the R8A, which turned out also to be in need of tweaking, then finally the R8B before they finally got it right. Ten-Tec appears to be following the same course.

## Forever Young

But there's a major difference between the '350 and most other receivers: It's a true DSP device, being specifically designed so it can be upgraded over the years simply by downloading the latest firmware off the Internet. In principle, this also makes it more likely than most other models to be able to process digital world band transmissions, should these ever materialize. Right off, this continual technical reincarnation puts the '350 into a class nearly unto itself.

We got a taste of this firsthand, after our receiver arrived with a variety of apparent design shortcomings. As is our custom, we contacted the manufacturer to see whether we had a sample defect, or if they planned

to make improvements anytime soon. They noted our concerns, came up with a number of fixes, then posted revised firmware, v1.15 b28 and b32, for all to download—these are what we used for our final series of tests.

Yet, not everything can be corrected by bits and bytes. A major problem we encountered was local mediumwave AM stations cross-modulating with other local stations, and even world band stations 4 MHz and below. Ten-Tec resolved this by adding a high-pass filter to attenuate mediumwave and longwave signals. This is a hardware fix (see photo), which goes to show that there are limits to how much online downloads can update a receiver.

## Precise Tuning, Bountiful Bandwidths

The '350 tunes in exacting 1 Hz increments, which is as good as it gets, although on one of our units the frequency misread by 20 Hz at 10 MHz and 30 Hz at 15 MHz (other units did better).

Our lab findings unearthed no unwelcome surprises, except that phase noise was such that we were unable to properly ascertain certain readings, such as 20 kHz dynamic range/IP3, skirt selectivity and ultimate rejection.

The '350 offers a superb choice of no less than 34 bandwidths, including at least a dozen suitable for world band—the rest are for utility and ham signals. We were unable to measure their skirt selectivity or ultimate rejection because of phase noise, and there is some audible hiss with wider bandwidths. But, overall, they appear to work well, even if some settings are actually audibly wider than indicated on the receiver.

Choosing among many bandwidths can be an ergonomic nightmare on some receivers, but on the '350 it is a pleasure thanks to the choice being made by a knob. Once you've used it you'll never want to go back to any other method.

## Excellent Tuning Features

There are no less than 1024 presets that display alphanumeric station names. These are grouped into eight banks of 128 scannable memory presets handily accessible by knob. Additional tuning aids include a front-panel tuning knob, up/down frequency and band slewing, sophisticated scanning and two VFOs. There's no front-panel keypad, though. Instead, it's outboard and costs extra.

This keypad, the 302R, is like a computer mouse on steroids. If its delightful ergonomics weren't enough, it also frees up front-panel space for the large LCD and numerous controls. It also has F1, F2 and F3 keys to select tuning step, mode, VFO and spectrum display, and there's a second weighted tuning knob for laid-back tuning; it uses the same type of optical tuning encoder as the receiver.

The outboard keypad/knob combo works so well, it's virtually inconceivable to own the receiver without it, even if the frequency-entry button occasionally has to be pushed twice to "take."

## Solid Controls

The '350's cabinet is of reasonable-gauge steel affixed to the sheet-aluminum chassis by self-tapping screws, while the front panel is of plastic. In all, mechanical construction quality is better than that of some other tabletop models, even if it's not the stuff of professional rigs.

All buttons are hard plastic and have good tactile "feel"—some are single-function, others double-function. However, some rotatable controls are stiff to turn. This is quickly overcome by removing the rubber edging or shiny outer ring, then loosening the knob with a hex key. Move the knob slightly away from the cabinet, re-tighten, then replace the ring or edging and you're done.

The main tuning knob, like the one on the outboard keypad, is excellent. It is large and weighted, with a finger hole and "rubber tire"

outer edge. It activates an optical encoder, not the less-dependable mechanical variety typically found on non-professional receivers. Made by Agilent Technologies, it is the same that's used by Watkins-Johnson for some of its professional receivers.

## Most Lab Findings Good or Excellent

Even with phase-noise limitations, we were able to obtain accurate readings of dynamic range and IP3 at the critical 5 kHz separation points. Basically, the numbers are excellent. Image and first IF rejection, both 65 dB, are good, as is blocking at 121 dB, although below the norm for tabletop models. On the other hand, notch depth, at 25-30 dB, is merely adequate.

Sensitivity fares better, but there's a rub. This is achieved in part through the use of an RF preamplifier which can't be switched off. Because of this and the original front-end design, there was considerable cross-modulation from local mediumwave AM stations. Ten-Tec came up with a quick fix and has promised to look into something better, but an "always on" RF amp is not a hallmark of good receiver design.

Other measurements fare nicely. The AGC threshold was originally a dismal 17 microvolts, but Ten-Tec changed it in firmware v1.15 to an excellent 1.7 micro-

**RX-350's high-pass filter. A better front-end fix may be coming.**

volts. However, if the preamp is ever made switchable, the AGC threshold should be readjusted to around one microvolt.

## Superior Audio Quality

Audio quality is something best judged by the human ear, and by that subjective yardstick the '350 sounds surprisingly good not just for a DSP model—sometimes these can sound tiring and harsh—but by any standard. Intelligibility is especially impressive, equal to that of Ten Tec's professional RX-340. Music fares well, too, but those who focus on musical programs will probably continue to favor the mellow throat of the Drake R8B.

Overall distortion is low, usually under two percent with slow or medium AGC decay—fast AGC increases distortion. The upward-firing internal speaker is decent enough, but better is to use a first-rate outboard speaker instead (heed the manual's warning about the grounding of speaker leads).

One advantage of DSP is that it can sometimes be used to enhance audio intelligibility. As expected, the '350's DSP noise reduction circuitry helps reduce such aural annoyances as thunderstorm static. However, it is not adjustable, and its lone setting tends to reduce intelligibility along with the noise.

The '350's DSP bag of goodies also includes an effective automatic heterodyne-reduction notch filter that acts on not just one, but all interfering carriers. Those who prowl the tropical segments below 5.1 MHz will especially appreciate its ability to tone down annoying whistles by a single command. However, with such non-voice modes, such as CW and RTTY, the auto notch impacts the desired signal, along with the targeted heterodyne interference. Were it also manually tunable this would not be the case.

Many who purchase receivers in the over-kilobuck category use them for more than hearing world band broadcasts. They also tune utility transmissions, where Gibraltar-

like frequency stability is needed for unattended reception. Here, the '350 shines. The most we could get it to drift after being on for ten-seconds was five Hertz. It just doesn't get any better than this.

## Sync Loses Lock

The '350 includes a passband offset control, although it requires many tiresome turns to be shifted significantly during AM-mode or synchronous (SAM) reception. That control and the synchronous detector, like the handy AML and AMU settings, allow for genuine synchronous selectable sideband reception, which is important not only to relieve fading distortion, but also to help overcome adjacent-channel interference.

However, in order for this to function properly a sync circuit needs to maintain lock during signal fades. The '350 does not do this well, especially when the passband control is offset significantly.

Hopefully this will be improved upon, as it was recently with the Ten-Tec RX-340. In the meantime, those exacting 1 Hz tuning steps allow for easy tuning of world band signals as though they were single sideband. This technique, "ECSS," works almost as well as synchronous selectable sideband on a receiver with this degree of tuning resolution and stability.

## Strength and Spectrum Displays

You probably won't buy the '350 for its signal-strength indicator, even though it is unusually accurate. Its bar graph is short, supplemented by a numeric readout of decibels that one our panelists called, "as jumpy as grasshoppers in a wheat field."

You're not likely to buy this receiver for its spectrum display, either. It has little vertical rise even for powerful signals, doesn't operate in real time and mutes the receiver. Only if the displayed frequency range has few strong signals and the proper sweep range is chosen is it of tangible use; best is to decrease the bandwidth to its minimum (300 Hz), press the "Sweep" key, then return to a wider bandwidth.

The '350's DSP noise blanker gets no blue ribbon. Any number of other tabletop models do better by operating within the IF stage.

### First-Rate World Time Clock

The World Time clock on the '350 is nigh ideal. It not only shows seconds numerically, it also displays time, day, month and year independent of the frequency readout. Nit: To set minutes for World Time, you must go to the 12-hour format, input minutes, then return to the 24-hour format.

The '350's microprocessor can be reset either "soft" or "hard." The 38-page owner's manual is essential for understanding menu functions, but sometimes it has contradictory information on the "hard" reset procedure. The manual could also be more detailed, and includes no schematics or block diagrams. Fortunately, some schematics are on Ten Tec's website.

### A Work in Progress

Bottom line, the Ten-Tec RX-350 is a work in progress, very much like the Drake R8 series. What we first tested the '350 in the summer of 2002 was, like the original R8, in need of considerable tweaking. The upgraded receiver we tested in the fall of that same year was more along the lines of the R8A—better, but not yet quite all it should be.

The manufacturer tells us that they will attend to outstanding issues when they can pull engineering talent away from their backlog of essential projects. But promises are promises, results are results. This is, after all, the type of receiver from which buyers expect top-notch mediumwave AM performance, sometimes longwave too, in addition to shortwave. Should the '350 eventually be fitted with an improved front end—the key upgrade, as this is mainly a hardware change—we'll go over it afresh

and post the findings at our website, www.passband.com.

Ten-Tec has a long track record of providing exceptional customer support online and by phone. They also offer first-rate factory service, and their long-established company looks solid for the future. Add to that the ability to keep the '350 up-to-date through online firmware downloads, and this receiver is something to consider for the long haul.

### ✪✪✪✪
### Icom IC-R8500A

**Price:** *IC-R8500A-02 (no cellular reception):* Under $1,700.00 in the United States, the exact price depending on factory rebates, if any, available at the time. *IC-R8500A:* $1,749.95 for government use or export in the United States. CAN$2,849.00 in Canada. £1,349.00 in the United Kingdom. €1,689.00 in Germany. AUS$3,480.00 in Australia. *External speakers:* Up to three Icom speakers available worldwide, with prices ranging from under $65 to over $300 or equivalent.

**Pro:** Wide-spectrum multimode coverage from 0.1-2000 MHz includes longwave, mediumwave AM, shortwave and scanner frequencies. Physically very rugged, with professional-grade cast-aluminum chassis and impressive computer-type innards. Generally superior ergonomics, with generous-sized front panel having large and well-spaced controls, plus outstanding tuning knob with numerous tuning steps. 1,000 presets and 100 auto-write presets

The Icom IC-R8500A provides wide-spectrum multimode coverage, all in one box.

have handy naming function. Superb weak-signal sensitivity. Pleasant, low-distortion audio aided by audio peak filter. Passband tuning ("IF shift"). Unusually readable LCD. Tunes and displays in precise 10 Hz increments. Three antenna connections. Clock-timer, combined with record output and recorder-activation jack, make for superior hands-off recording of favorite programs, as well as for feeding a low-power FM transmitter to hear world band around the house.

**Con:** No synchronous selectable sideband. Bandwidth choices for world band and other AM-mode signals leap from a very narrow 2.7 kHz to a broad 7.1 kHz with nothing between, where something is most needed; third bandwidth is 13.7 kHz, too wide for world band, and no provision is made for a fourth bandwidth filter. Only one single-sideband bandwidth. Unhandy carousel-style bandwidth selection with no permanent indication of which bandwidth is in use. Poor dynamic range, surprising at this price point. Passband tuning ("IF shift") does not work in the AM mode, used by world band and mediumwave AM-band stations. No tunable notch filter. Built-in speaker mediocre. Uses outboard AC adaptor instead of inboard power supply.

☞ The Icom IC-R8500 is available in two similarly priced versions. That sold to the public in the United States is blocked so it cannot receive the 824-849 and 869-894 MHz cellular bands. In the U.S., the un-blocked version is sold only to government-approved organizations, although Canadian mail-order firms will ship this version to customers in the United States.

☞ Also tested with Sherwood SE-3 non-factory accessory, which proved to be outstanding at adding selectable synchronous sideband. It also provides passband tuning in the AM mode used by nearly all world band stations. Adding the SE-3 and replacing the widest bandwidth with a 4 to 5 kHz bandwidth filter dramatically improve performance on shortwave, mediumwave AM and longwave.

**Verdict:** The large Icom IC-R8500 is really a scanner that happens to cover world band, rather than *vice versa*. As a standalone world band radio, it makes little sense, but it is well worth considering if you want an all-in-one scanner/shortwave receiver. Made in Japan.

## ✪✪✪✪
## AOR AR5000+3

**Price:** *AR5000+3 receiver:* $2,099.95 in the United States. CAN$3,799.00 in Canada. £1,799.00 in the United Kingdom. €2,099.00 in Germany. AUS$4,360.00 in Australia. *Collins 6 kHz mechanical filter (recommended):* $99.95 in the United States. £76.00 in the United Kingdom.

**Pro:** Ultra-wide-spectrum multimode coverage from 0.1-2,600 MHz includes longwave, mediumwave AM, shortwave and scanner frequencies. Helpful tuning features include 2,000 presets. Narrow bandwidth filter and optional Collins wide filter both have superb skirt selectivity (standard wide filter's skirt selectivity unmeasurable because of limited ultimate rejection). Synchronous selectable and double sideband (*see* Con). Front-end selectivity, image rejection, IF rejection, weak-signal sensitivity, AGC threshold and frequency stability all superior. Exceptionally precise frequency readout to nearest Hertz. Most accurate displayed frequency measurement of any receiver tested to date. Superb circuit shielding

**The AOR wide-spectrum AR5000+3 is primarily for world band, secondarily VHF and up.**

results in virtually zero radiated digital "hash." IF output (*see* Con). Automatic Frequency Control (AFC) works on AM-mode, as well as FM, signals. Owner's manual, important because of operating system, unusually helpful.

**Con:** Synchronous detector loses lock easily, especially if selectable sideband feature in use, greatly detracting from the utility of this high-tech feature. Substandard rejection of unwanted sideband with selectable synchronous sideband. Overall distortion rises when synchronous detector used. Ultimate rejection of "narrow" 2.7 kHz bandwidth filter only 60 dB. Ultimate rejection mediocre (50 dB) with standard 7.6 kHz "wide" bandwidth filter, improves to an uninspiring 60 dB when replaced by optional 6 kHz "wide" Collins mechanical filter. Installation of optional Collins filter requires expertise, patience and special equipment. Poor dynamic range. Cumbersome ergonomics. No passband offset. No tunable notch filter. Needs good external speaker for good audio quality. World Time clock does not show when frequency displayed. IF output frequency 10.7 MHz instead of standard 455 kHz.

**Verdict:** Unbeatable in some respects, inferior in others—it comes down to what use you will be putting the radio. The optional 6 kHz Collins filter is strongly recommended, but it should be installed by your dealer at the time of purchase. Although some AOR receivers are engineered and made in the United Kingdom, this model is designed and manufactured in Japan.

★★★★
### Palstar R30/R30C/R30CC, Lowe HF-350

**Price:** *R30:* $495.00 in the United States. £399.95 in the United Kingdom. *R30C (not tested):* $575.00 in the United States. *R30CC (not tested):* $650.00 in the United States. *HF-350 (not tested):* £375.00 in the United Kingdom. €399.00 in Germany.

Palstar's R30CC uses Collins filters, possibly important as MuRata is discontinuing many filters.

☞ We tested the R30, but there are variations. The R30C is identical, except that a Collins mechanical filter is used for the narrow bandwidth—puzzling, in that the standard version already has superb skirt selectivity and ultimate rejection; the new R30CC goes one step farther uses Collins mechanical filters for both bandwidths. The HF-350, like the R30, uses two MuRata ceramic filters, but the wide bandwidth is narrower—nominally 4 kHz, but in practice it could be closer to 5 kHz. Regardless, adjacent-channel interference would be reduced, but at the cost of audio bandwidth.

**Pro:** Superb skirt selectivity (1:1.4) and ultimate rejection (90 dB); bandwidths measure 7.7 kHz (*see* Con) and 2.7 kHz, using MuRata ceramic filters (*see* Con). Generally good dynamic range. Pleasant audio quality with 7.7 kHz bandwidth (*see* Con). Overall distortion averages 0.5 percent, superb, in single-sideband mode (in AM mode, averages 2.9 percent, good, at 60% modulation and 4.4 percent, fair, at 95% modulation). Every other performance variable measures either good or excellent in PASSPORT's lab. Features include selectable slow/fast AGC decay; 20-100 Hz/100-500 Hz VRIT (slow/fast variable-rate incremental tuning) knob; 1 MHz slewing; and 100 non-volatile station presets that store frequency, bandwidth, mode, AGC setting and attenuator setting. Analog signal-strength indicator reads in useful S1-9/+60 dB standard and is reasonably accurate (*see* Con). Also operates from ten firmly secured "AA" internal batteries (*see* Con). Lightweight and small (*see* Con). Good AM-mode sensitivity within longwave and mediumwave AM bands. Switchable illumination of LCD and signal-strength indicator. Self-resetting circuit breaker. Optional AA30A and AM-30 active antennas, evaluated elsewhere in this PASSPORT REPORTS.

**Con:** No keypad for direct frequency entry, not even as an outboard mouse-type option; virtually all other receivers over $130 come with or offer a keypad. No synchronous selectable sideband. Wide bandwidth slightly broad for a model lacking synchronous selectable sideband, often allowing adjacent-channel (5 kHz) heterodyne whistles to be heard; the HF-350 version's narrower wide bandwidth should resolve this, albeit by reducing audio bandwidth. Lacks features found in top-gun receivers, such as tunable notch filter, noise blanker, passband tuning and adjustable RF gain. No visual indication of which bandwidth is being used. No tone controls. Our unit's frequency readout off by 100 Hz. Signal-strength indicator drops about two "S" units when going from wide to narrow bandwidths. Several significant birdies, including one on 20,002 kHz; numerous other and faint birdies don't impact reception. Minor digital "hash" radiates about six inches or 15 centimeters from the front panel. Tiny identical front-panel buttons, including the MEM button which if accidentally pressed can erase a preset. Presets not as intuitive or easy to select as with various other models; lacks frequency information on existing presets during memory storage. Uses AC adaptor instead of built-in power supply. High battery consumption. Batteries uniquely difficult to install, requiring partial disassembly of the receiver and care not to damage speaker connections or confuse polarities. Receiver's lightness allows it to slide around, especially when tuning knob is pushed in to change VRIT increments; the added weight of batteries helps slightly.

☞ Works best when grounded.

**Verdict:** Although the Ohio-made Palstar R30 family of receivers is woefully lacking in tuning and performance features, what it sets out to do, it does to a high standard. If you can abide the convoluted battery installation procedure, it can also be used as a quasi-portable.

Nevertheless, this receiver lacks a distinct identity. Although the audio is pleasant, it doesn't have synchronous selectable sideband, needed to make it a premium listener's radio; it even omits tuning features found on portables costing a fourth as much. At the same time, its commendable electronic performance serves a limited purpose because the receiver lacks important features which help snare DX the way sophisticated tabletop models can.

But not everybody fits neatly into these either-or categories. One size doesn't fit all, and to that end the R30's straightforward concept and quality performance adds diversity and choice to the roster of available models.

✪✪✪¾ 📄
### Yaesu FRG-100

**Price:** $549.95 in the United States. CAN$999.00 in Canada. £449.00 in the United Kingdom.

**Pro:** Excellent performance in many respects. Includes three bandwidths, a noise blanker, selectable AGC, two attenuators, the ability to select 16 pre-programmed

Yaesu's affordable FRG-100: Rumors of its death have been greatly exaggerated.

world band segments, two clocks, on-off timers, 52 tunable station presets that store frequency and mode data, a variety of scanning schemes and an all-mode squelch.

**Con:** No keypad for direct frequency entry. No synchronous selectable sideband. Lacks features found in "top-gun" receivers: passband tuning, notch filter, adjustable RF gain. Simple controls and display, combined with complex functions, can make certain operations confusing. Dynamic range only fair. Uses AC adaptor instead of built-in power supply.

**Verdict:** While sparse on features, in many respects the Yaesu FRG-100 succeeds in delivering worthy performance within an attractive price class. Reportedly this model was discontinued in mid-1999, but as of late 2002 it is still very much a part of Yaesu's product line.

📄 An *RDI WHITE PAPER* is available for this model.

### ✪✪✪
### Yaesu VR-5000

**Price:** *VR-5000 Receiver, including single-voltage AC adaptor:* Under $890.00 in the United States, the exact price depending on factory rebates, if any, available at the time. CAN$1,499.00 in Canada. £599.00 in the United Kingdom. €849.00 in Germany. *DSP-1 digital notch, bandpass and noise reduction unit:* $119.95 in the United States. €101.30 in Germany. *DVS-4 16-second digital audio recorder:* $47.00 in the United States. CAN$80.00 in Canada. €40.50 in Germany. *FVS-1A voice synthesizer:* $43.00 in the United States. CAN$75.00 in Canada. £38.00 in the United Kingdom. €50.00 in Germany.

**Pro:** Unusually wide frequency coverage, 100 kHz through 2.6 GHz (U.S. version omits cellular frequencies 869-894 MHz). Two thousand alphanumeric-displayed presets, which can be linked to any of up to 100 groupings of presets. Up to 50 programmable start/stop search ranges. Large and

For a wide-spectrum receiver, the Yaesu VR-5000 is priced remarkably low.

potentially useful "band scope" spectrum display (*see* Con). Bandwidths have superb skirt selectivity, with shape factors between 1:1.3 and 1:1.4. Wide AM bandwidth (17.2 kHz) allows local mediumwave AM stations to be received with superior fidelity (*see* Con). Flexible software settings provide a high degree of control over selected parameters. Sophisticated scanning choices, although of limited use because of false signals generated by receiver's inadequate dynamic range (*see* Con). Dual-receive function, with sub-receiver circuitry feeding "band scope" spectrum display; when spectrum display not in use, two signals may be monitored simultaneously, provided they are within 20 MHz of each other. Sensitivity to weak signals excellent-to-superb within shortwave spectrum, although combined with receiver's inadequate dynamic range this tends to cause overloading when a worthy antenna is used (*see* Con). Appears to be robustly constructed. External spectrum display, fed by receiver's 10.7 MHz IF output, can perform very well for narrow-parameter scans (*see* Con). Two 24-hour clocks, both of which are shown except when spectrum display mode not in use; one clock tied into an elementary map display and database of time in a wide choice of world cities. On-off timer allows for up to 48 automatic events. Snooze/alarm timers. Lightweight and compact. Multi-level display dimmer (*see* Con). Optional DSP unit includes adjustable notch filtering, a bandpass feature and noise reduction. Tone control. Built-in "CAT" computer control interface.

**Con:** Exceptionally poor dynamic range (49 dB at 5 kHz separation, 64 dB at 20 kHz) and IF/image rejection (as low as 30 dB) for a tabletop model; for listeners in such high-signal parts of the world as Europe, North Africa and eastern North America, this shortcoming all but cripples reception of shortwave signals; the degree to which VHF-UHF is degraded depends *inter alia* upon the extent of powerful transmissions in the vicinity of the receiver. No synchronous selectable sideband, a major drawback for world band and mediumwave AM listening, but not for shortwave utility/ham, VHF or UHF reception. Has only one single-sideband bandwidth, a relatively broad 4.0 kHz. Wide AM bandwidth (17.2 kHz) of no use for shortwave reception. For world band listening, the middle (8.7 kHz) AM bandwidth lets through adjacent-channel 5 kHz heterodyne, while narrow bandwidth (consistently 3.9 kHz, not the 4.0 kHz of the SSB bandwidth) produces muffled audio. Line output level low. Audio distorts at higher volume settings. Limited bass response. Audio hissy without DSP option, especially noticeable with a good outboard speaker; according to unconfirmed reports, this is to be improved in future production. Phase noise measures 94 dBc, poor. AGC threshold measures 11 microvolts, poor. No adjustment of AGC decay. Single-sideband AGC decay too slow. Signal-strength indicator has only five levels and overreads; an alternative software-selectable signal-strength indicator—not easy to get in and out of—has no markings other than a single reference level. Built-in spectrum display's dynamic range only 20 dB (–80 to –100 dBm), with a very slow scan rate. Long learning curve: Thirty buttons (often densely spaced, lilliputian and multifunction)—along with carouseling mode/tune-step selection and a menu-driven command scheme—combine to produce ergonomics that are not intuitive. Marginally informative owner's manual; an improved manual continues to be promised by the manufacturer. Mediocre tuning-knob "feel." Only one low-impedance antenna connector, inadequate for a wideband device that calls for multiple antennas. Longwave sensitivity mediocre. Clocks don't display seconds numerically. Marginal display contrast. Display bright even when dimmed. Although four LEDs used for backlighting, the result is unevenly distributed. Uses AC adaptor instead of built-in power supply. AC adaptor and receiver both tend to run warm. Tilt feet have inadequate rise.

**Verdict:** A basic VHF/UHF scanner with basic shortwave, the new Japanese-made Yaesu VR-5000 wideband receiver falls shy for world band reception in strong-signal parts of the world. Elsewhere, it fares better on shortwave, but VHF/UHF performance depends on the number and strength of local transmitters.

### Enhanced for 2003
✪✪✪  ⊘
### AKD Target HF-3M, NASA HF-4/HF-4E, SI-TEX NAV-FAX 200

**Price:** *HF-3M/HF-4/HF-4E:* £149.95 in the United Kingdom. *HF-4E/S:* €299.00 in Germany. *PA30 antenna:* €35.30 in Germany. *NAV-FAX 200 (www.si-tex.com):* $399.00 in the United States. *SI-TEX ACNF 120V AC adaptor:* $19.95 in the United States.

**Pro:** Superior rejection of spurious "image" signals. Third-order intercept point for superior strong-signal handling capability.

**An enhanced version of the Target HF-3M is available from Si-Tex in North America.**

Bandwidths have superb ultimate rejection. *HF-4/HF-4E/HF-4E/S:* Two AM-mode bandwidths. Illuminated LCD. *Except NAV-FAX 200:* Comes with DOS software for weatherfax ("WEFAX") reception using a PC; software upgrade may be in the offing. *NAV-FAX 200:* Comes with Mscan Meteo Pro Lite software (www.mscan.com) for WEFAX, RTTY and NAVTEX reception using a PC with Windows XP or earlier. Comes with wire antenna and audio patch cable. Two-year warranty, with repair facility in Florida.

**Con:** No keypad, and variable-rate tuning knob is difficult to control. Broad skirt selectivity. Single-sideband bandwidth relatively wide. Volume control fussy to adjust. Synthesizer tunes in relatively coarse 1 kHz increments, supplemented by an analog fine-tuning "clarifier" control. Only ten presets. Single sideband requires both tuning controls to be adjusted. No synchronous selectable sideband, notch filter or passband tuning. Frequency readout off by 2 kHz in single-sideband mode. Uses AC adaptor instead of built-in power supply. No clock, timer or snooze feature. *HF3M:* Bandwidths not selectable independent of mode. Only AM-mode bandwidth functions for world band reception. LCD not illuminated. *Except NAV-FAX 200:* Apparently not available outside United Kingdom.

**Verdict:** Pleasant world band performance at a surprisingly affordable price, although various features are absent and operation is more frustrating than on many other models. A treat for yachting.

**Observations for 2003:** For North Americans, the big news is the introduction of the SI-TEX version, now available throughout the United States and Canada. As a bonus for utility DXers and mariners, it includes WEFAX, RTTY and NAVTEX reception under Windows. SI-TEX confirms that they plan to keep the '200 in their line indefinitely, and it comes with a two-year warranty with repairs at their easily reached St. Petersburg, Florida facility.

---

*The PASSPORT tabletop-model review team consists of Lawrence Magne, David Zantow and George Zeller; also, George Heidelman, Tony Jones, Chuck Rippel and David Walcutt, with Craig Tyson. Laboratory measurements by J. Robert Sherwood.*

## ROLL YOUR OWN

Most shortwave kits are novelties, but there is one exception: Ten-Tec's small 1254 world band radio, $195. Parts quality appears to be excellent, and assembly runs at least 24 hours. It has 15 presets, but lacks keypad, signal-strength indicator, synchronous selectable sideband, tilt bail, LSB/USB settings and adjustable AGC. Tuning increments are 500 Hz for single sideband and 5 kHz for AM-mode, and an analog clarifier for tweaking between these increments.

Phase noise, front-end selectivity and longwave/mediumwave AM sensitivity are poor. Bandwidth is 5.6 kHz, and there is worthy ultimate rejection, image rejection, world band sensitivity, blocking, AGC threshold and frequency stability. Dynamic range and first IF rejection are fair, while overall distortion is good—with an external speaker, audio is pleasant.

**When Ike was president, kit building was "the most." Ten-Tec stokes the embers with its 1254 kit.**

The Ten-Tec 1254 is a fun weekend project, and the manufacturer's track record for hand-holding means that when you're through the radio will really work.

# Professional Receivers for 2003

Like Cray computers, the root market for professional receivers is not the public. Rather, these are targeted to commercial, maritime, surveillance and military organizations with deep pockets. Their requirements have much in common with the needs of world band listening, but there are a number of differences, as well.

Some of these variants make for better results, others worse. But when it all comes together, this is the hardware that is most likely to scale the toughest, most extreme heights of DX reception.

## Receivers in Three Flavors

There are numerous categories of professional receivers, but these boil down to three basics: easy for human operation, complex for human operation, and no human operation.

The first are designed so laymen can tune "utility" signals with minimal training. After all, if a B-52 takes shrapnel and the radioman is out, the more straightforward a radio is to operate, the more likely it is that other crew members will be able to carry on. Trouble is, simplicity of operation can also result in performance compromises, making these potentially inferior choices for world band cognoscenti.

The second category goes to the other extreme, with features and performance that are "no holds barred." These assume a high degree of operator skill, and are the type of professional receiver we analyze in PASSPORT REPORTS. They are well worth considering if you aren't put off by their complexity of operation and sticker shock.

Simplest are "black box" professional receivers, which have virtually no controls. These are operated remotely or by computers, often at hush-hush surveillance facilities. We don't cover this category, as some of the best models are available only to U.S. Federal agencies or NATO organizations. However, consumer-grade versions are evaluated elsewhere within PASSPORT REPORTS.

The Icom IC-R9000L is not included in this year's reviews, as it is no longer in production. However, a small quantity may still be available in Australia for AUS$21,800. It is thoroughly reviewed in its own RDI White Paper report.

**Find major updates to the 2003 PASSPORT REPORTS at www.passband.com.**

## Major Shared Characteristics

All professional receivers should be physically and electrically robust, with resistance to hostile environments and rough handling, as well as a high mean time between failures (MTBF). Additionally, their components need to be unusually consistent so board swapping and other field repairs can be accomplished without disturbing alignment and the like.

The two best models PASSPORT REPORTS has tested were developed to replace the nonprofessional Icom IC-R71A. This was being used by the U.S. National Security Agency in offshore surveillance, but it had limitations. The reclusive folks at Fort Meade choose carefully, so their implied endorsement amounts to something of a "Good Housekeeping Seal of Approval."

## Good Antenna Essential

Top-rated, properly erected antennas are an absolute "must" if these receivers are to reach their full potential. For test results and installation information, see the Radio Database International White Paper, *Evaluation of Popular Outdoor Antennas*, as well as reviews of antennas found elsewhere in PASSPORT REPORTS.

If reception at your location is already disrupted by electrical noises even when a suitable antenna is in use, a better receiver would be a waste of money. Before buying, try eliminating the source of noise or reorienting your antenna.

## Volts with Jolts

Professional receivers tend to be unusually rugged, and in fact tend to include MOV surge protection before the power supply. Nevertheless, it helps to plug your pricey receiver into a non-MOV surge arrestor, such as Zero-Surge (www.zerosurge.com) or Brick Wall (www.brickwall.com).

Any receiver's outdoor antenna always should be fed through a suitable static arrestor, but this is especially important with the Watkins-Johnson WJ-8711A if it isn't equipped with the 8711/PRE option.

## Audio with DSP Receivers

In principle, there is no reason DSP (digital signal processing) receivers can't produce audio quality equal to, and in some ways better than, conventional models. Witness the audio quality of digital CDs, for example.

But a multi-stage receiver is much more complex than a CD, so it requires a great deal of processing horsepower. Today's DSP receivers still fall short in this regard, one result being that audio quality is not all it could be. In particular, static crashes tend to sound harsher.

Helping offset this is that hard-core DXers often find recoverable audio to be slightly greater with DSP receivers. Of course, this same benefit would continue to accrue should overall audio quality be improved through greater microprocessor power.

Unlike with top-rated tabletop receivers, which don't need the Sherwood SE-3 accessory, it is nearly a "must" for all professional receivers except the Ten-Tec

RX-340—DSP or not—being used to tune world band stations. Indeed, even the '340 profits from the SE-3 to some extent. While this device doesn't fundamentally resolve the DSP audio issue, it tames it considerably while also providing high-quality synchronous selectable sideband. These are enormous pluses, but there are downsides, too: extra cost, operating complexity and a BFO that is not fully as stable as those on the top two professional receivers.

## Ready for Digital Broadcasts?

Today's DSP receivers process analog radio signals digitally. However, analog world band broadcasts may eventually be superceded by digital. Even if this comes to pass, digital transmission should remain in the realm of the experimental for years to come, followed by a transition period in which both analog and digital operate in parallel.

With conventional portable, portatop and tabletop receivers this hardly matters, as these are not intended to be friends for life. However, professional models are designed to keep humming for decades, not just years. What happens if digital transmissions begin to appear while your second-mortgage receiver is still in its prime?

Manufacturers are not yet in a position to promise future upgrades to receive digital. Nevertheless, among professional models tested by Passport, those that look most encouraging for eventual digital reception are the Watkins-Johnson WJ-8711A and Ten-Tec RX-340. Indeed, a digital signal output board is already being offered for the '8711A.

## Tips for Using this Section

Professional receivers are listed in order of suitability for listening to difficult-to-hear world band stations. Important secondary consideration is given to audio fidelity, ergonomics and reception of utility signals.

We cite actual selling prices as of when we go to press, including European VAT and Australian GST where applicable.

Unless otherwise stated, all professional models have:

- Digital frequency synthesis and display.
- Full coverage of at least the 155-29999 kHz longwave, mediumwave AM and shortwave spectra—including all world band frequencies—but no coverage of the FM broadcast band (87.5-108 MHz).
- A wide variety of helpful tuning features.
- Synchronous selectable sideband via high-rejection IF filtering (not lower-rejection phasing), which greatly reduces adjacent-channel interference and fading distortion. On some units this is referred to as "SAM" (synchronous AM).
  ☞ **ECSS:** Professional models can tune to the nearest 10 Hz or even 1 Hz, allowing the user to use the receiver's single-sideband circuitry to manually phase its BFO (internally generated carrier) with the station's transmitted carrier. Called "ECSS" (exalted-carrier, selectable-sideband) tuning, this can be used with AM-mode signals in lieu of synchronous selectable sideband. However, in addition to the relative inconvenience of this technique, unlike synchronous detection, which re-phases continually and essentially perfectly, ECSS is always slightly out of phase. This causes at least some degree of harmonic distortion to music and speech, while tuning to the nearest Hertz can generate slow-sweep fading (for this reason, high-pass audio filtering or mis-phasing by two or three Hertz may provide better results).
- Proper demodulation of modes used by non-world-band shortwave signals. These modes include single sideband (LSB/USB and sometimes ISB) and CW ("Morse code"); also, with suitable ancillary devices, radioteletype (RTTY), frequency shift key (FSK) and radiofax (FAX).
- Meaningful signal-strength indication.

- Illuminated display.
- Superior build quality, robustness and sample-to-sample consistency as compared to consumer-grade tabletop receivers.
- Audio output for recording or low-power FM retransmission to hear world band around your domicile.

## What PASSPORT's Rating Symbols Mean

**Star ratings:** ✪✪✪✪✪ is best. Stars reflect overall performance and meaningful features, plus to some extent ergonomics and build quality. Price, appearance, country of manufacture and the like are not taken into account. With professional models there is a strong emphasis on the ability to flush out tough, hard-to-hear signals, as this is usually the main reason these sets are chosen by world band enthusiasts. Nevertheless, to facilitate comparison professional receiver rating standards are very similar to those used for the tabletop, portatop and portable models reviewed elsewhere in this PASSPORT.

*Passport's Choice. La crème de la crème.* Our test team's personal picks of the litter—models we would buy or have bought for our personal use.

✪✪✪✪✪ *Passport's Choice*
### Watkins-Johnson WJ-8711A

**Price (receiver, factory options; prices change often):** *WJ-8711A:* $5,295.00 plus shipping worldwide. *871Y/SEU DSP Speech Enhancement Unit:* $1,130.00. *8711/PRE Sub-Octave Preselector:* $1,030.00. *871Y/DSO1 Digital Signal Output Unit:* $1,070.00.

**Price (aftermarket options):** *Ten-Tec #19-0525 cabinet:* $217.24 in the United States. *Sherwood SE-3 MK III accessory:* $549.00 plus shipping worldwide.

**Pro:** Proven robust. BITE diagnostics and physical layout allows technically qualified users to make most repairs on-site. Users

**Best is the Watkins-Johnson WJ-8711A, but it has become a chore to purchase and repair as corporate changes take place.**

can upgrade receiver performance over time by EPROM replacement. Exceptional overall performance. Unsurpassed reception of feeble world band DX signals, especially when mated to the Sherwood SE-3 synchronous selectable sideband device and the WJ-871Y/SEU noise-reduction unit (*see* Con). Unusually effective "ECSS" reception, tuning AM-mode signals as though they were single sideband. Superb reception of non-AM mode "utility" stations. Generally superior audio quality when coupled to the Sherwood SE-3 fidelity-enhancing accessory, the W-J speech enhancement unit and a worthy external speaker (*see* Con). Unparalleled bandwidth flexibility, with no less than 66 outstandingly high-quality bandwidths. Tunes and displays in ultra-precise 1 Hz increments; trimmer inside radio allows frequency readout to be user-aligned against a known frequency standard, such as WWV/WWVH or a laboratory device. Extraordinary operational flexibility—virtually every receiver parameter is adjustable. One hundred station presets. Synchronous detection, called "SAM" (synchronous AM), reduces selective-fading distortion with world band, mediumwave AM and longwave signals, and works even on very narrow voice bandwidths (*see* Con). Rock stable. Built-in preamplifier. Tunable notch filter. Effective noise blanking. Highly adjustable scanning of both frequency ranges and channel presets. Easy-to-read displays. Large tuning knob. Can be fully and effectively computer and remotely controlled. Passband shift (*see* Con).

Numerous outputs for data collection and ancillary hardware, including 455 kHz IF-out which makes for instant installation of Sherwood SE-3 accessory and balanced line outputs (connect to balanced hookup to minimize "hash" radiation). Remote control and dial-up data collection; Windows control software available from manufacturer. Among the most likely of all world band receivers tested to be able to be retrofitted for eventual reception of digital world band broadcasts. Inboard AC power supply, which runs unusually cool, senses incoming current and automatically adjusts to anything from 90-264 VAC, 47-440 Hz—a plus during brownouts or with line voltage or frequency swings. Superior-quality factory service (*see* Con). Comprehensive and well-written operating manual, packed with technical information and schematic diagrams.

**Con:** Static crashes and modulation-splash interference sound noticeably harsher than on analog receivers, although this has been improved in latest operating software. Synchronous detection not sideband-selectable, so it can't reduce adjacent-channel interference (remediable by Sherwood SE-3). Basic receiver has mediocre audio in AM mode; "ECSS" tuning or synchronous detection, along with the speech enhancement unit (W1 noise-reduction setting), required to alleviate this. Some clipping distortion in the single-sideband mode. Complex to operate to full advantage. Circuitry puts out a high degree of digital noise ("hash"), relying for the most part on the panels for electrical shielding; one consequence is that various versions emanate hash through the nonstandard rear-panel audio terminals, as well as through the signal-strength meter and front-panel headphone jack—this problem is lessened when the Sherwood SE-3 is used. Antennas with shielded (e.g., coaxial) feedlines are less likely to pick up receiver-generated hash. Passband shift operates only in CW mode. Jekyll-and-Hyde ergonomics: sometimes wonderful, sometimes awful. Front-panel rack "ears" protrude, with the right "ear" getting in the way of the tuning knob; fortunately, these are easily removed. Mediocre front-end selectivity, remediable by 8711/PRE option (with minor 2.5 dB insertion loss); e.g. for those living near mediumwave AM transmitters. 871Y/SEU option reduces audio gain and is extremely difficult to install; best to have all options factory-installed. Most recent sample's tuning knob has rotational play that causes a very slight pause when reversing direction. Signal-strength indicator's gradations in dBm only. No DC power input. Factory service can take as much as two months. Cabinet extra, available from Ten-Tec. Plastic feet have no front elevation and allow receiver to slide around. Available only through U.S. manufacturer (+1-301/948-7550); receiver and factory options have been subjected to a number of price increases since British Aerospace takeover.

☞ In 1999 Watkins-Johnson was taken over by Marconi, the British electronics goliath, which only months later was swallowed up by British Aerospace. As a result, Watkins-Johnson is now "BAE Systems."

**Verdict:** The American-made WJ-8711A is, by a hair, the ultimate machine for down-and-dirty world band DXing when money is no object; after all, fully tricked out this receiver costs as much as some cars. Had there not been digital hash, inexcusable at this price—and had there been better audio quality, a tone control, passband shift and synchronous selectable sideband—the '8711A would have been even better, especially for program listening. Fortunately, the Sherwood SE-3 accessory remedies virtually all these problems and improves DX reception, to boot; W-J's 871Y/SEU complements, rather than competes with, the SE-3 for improving recovered audio.

Overall, the WJ-8711A DSP receiver is exceptionally well-suited to demanding aficionados with suitable financial where-withal—provided they want an exceptional degree of manual receiver control.

### Enhanced for 2003
### ★★★★★ *Passport's Choice*
### Ten-Tec RX-340

**Price:** $3,950.00 in the United States. £3,995.00 (€6,512) in the United Kingdom. *Hammond RCBS1900513GY2 or RCBS1900513BK1 13" deep cabinet (www.hammondmfg.com/rackrcbs.htm):* $99.95 in the United States. *Ten-Tec #307G external speaker:* $98.95 in the United States. *Sherwood SE-3 MK III accessory:* $549.00 plus shipping worldwide.

**Pro:** Appears to be robust (*see* Con). BITE diagnostics and physical layout allows technically qualified users to make most repairs on-site. Users can upgrade receiver performance over time by replacing one or another of three socketed EPROM chips (currently v1.10A). Superb overall performance, including for reception of feeble world band DX signals, especially when mated to the Sherwood SE-3 device; in particular, superlative image and IF rejection, both >100 dB. Few birdies. Audio quality usually worthy when receiver coupled to the Sherwood SE-3 accessory and a good external speaker. Average overall distortion in single-sideband mode a breathtakingly low 0.2 percent; in other modes, under 2.7 percent. Exceptional bandwidth flexibility, with no less than 57 outstandingly high-quality bandwidths

**Ten-Tec is unusually consumer-friendly, even though the RX-340 is mainly for governments.**

having shape factors of 1:1.33 or better; bandwidth distribution exceptionally good for world band listening and DXing, along with other activities (*see* Con). Tunes and displays accurately in ultra-precise 1 Hz increments. Extraordinary operational flexibility—virtually every receiver parameter is adjustable; for example, the AGC's various time constants have 118 million possible combinations, plus pushbutton AGC "DUMP" to temporarily deactivate AGC (*see* Con). Worthy front-panel ergonomics, valuable given the exceptional degree of manual operation; includes easy-to-read displays (*see* Con). Also, large, properly weighted rubber-track tuning knob with fixed dimple and Oak Grigsby optical encoder provide superior tuning "feel" and reliability. Attractive front panel. Two

hundred station presets, 201 including the scratchpad. Synchronous selectable sideband, called "SAM" (synchronous AM), reduces selective-fading distortion, as well as at diminishing or eliminating adjacent-channel interference, with world band, mediumwave AM and longwave signals; with earlier software lock was easily lost, but from v1.10A it now holds lock acceptably (*see* Con). Built-in half-octave preselector comes standard. Built-in preamplifier (*see* Con). Adjustable noise blanker, works well in most situations (*see* Con). Stable as Gibraltar, as good as it gets. Tunable DSP notch filter with exceptional depth of 58 dB (*see* Con). Passband shift (passband tuning) works unusually well (*see* Con). Unusually effective "ECSS" reception by tuning AM-mode signals as though they

## NUMBERS: TOP TWO PROFESSIONAL RECEIVERS

|  | Watkins-Johnson WJ-8711A | Ten-Tec RX-340 |
|---|---|---|
| Max. Sensitivity/Noise Floor | 0.13 $\mu$V, **S**/–136 dBm, **E** | 0.17 $\mu$V, **S**/–132 dBm, **E**[1] |
| Blocking | 123 dB, **G** | 109 dB, **F** |
| Shape Factors, voice BWs | 1:1.21-1:1.26, **S** | 1:1.15-1:1.33, **S** |
| Ultimate Rejection | >80 dB, **E** | 70 dB, **G** |
| Front-End Selectivity | Wideband, **F**/Half octave, **E**[2] | Half octave, **E** |
| Image Rejection | 80 dB, **E** | >100 dB, **S** |
| First IF Rejection | — [3] | >100 dB, **S** |
| Dynamic Range/IP3 (5 kHz) | 74 dB, **G**/–18 dBm, **E** | 46 dB, **P**/–53 dBm, **P** |
| Dynamic Range/IP3 (20 kHz) | 99 dB, **S**/+20 dBm, **S** | 84 dB, **G**/+4 dBm, **E** |
| Phase Noise | 115 dBc, **G** | 113 dBc, **G** |
| AGC Threshold | 0.1 $\mu$V, **P** | 0.3 $\mu$V, **G** [4] |
| Overall Distortion, sync | 8.2%, **P** | 2.6%, **G** |
| Notch filter depth | 58 dB, **S** | 58 dB, **S** |

**IBS Lab Ratings:**   **S** Superb    **E** Excellent    **G** Good    **F** Fair    **P** Poor

(1) Preamp on. With preamp off, 0.55 $\mu$V, **G** /–122 dBm, **G**.
(2) **F** standard/**E** with optional preselector.
(3) Adequate, but could not measure precisely.
(4) Preamp on. With preamp off, 1.3 $\mu$V, **E**.

were single sideband. Superb reception of "utility" (non-AM mode) stations using a wide variety of modes and including fast filters for delay-critical digital modes. Highly adjustable scanning of both frequency ranges and channel presets. Can be fully and effectively computer and remotely controlled. Numerous outputs for data collection and ancillary hardware, including 455 kHz IF-out for instant hookup of Sherwood SE-3 accessory. Remote control and dial-up data collection. Superb analog signal-strength indicator (see Con). Among the most likely of all world band receivers tested to be able to be retrofitted for eventual reception of digital world band broadcasts. Inboard AC power supply senses incoming current and automatically adjusts to anything from 90-264 VAC, 48-440 Hz—a plus during brownouts or with line voltage or frequency swings. Superior control of fluorescent display dimming (see Con). Superior-quality factory service, reasonably priced by professional standards, with helpful online/phone tech support. Comprehensive and well-written operating manual, packed with technical information and schematic diagrams.

**Con:** Synchronous selectable sideband loses lock relatively easily; e.g., if listening to one sideband and there is a strong signal impacting the other sideband, lock can be momentarily lost; resolved by Sherwood SE-3 fidelity device. DSP microprocessor limitations result in poor dynamic range/IP3 at 5 kHz signal spacing. Blocking, phase noise and ultimate rejection all pretty good, but not of professional caliber. Complex to operate to full advantage. Static crashes sound harsher than on analog receivers. Not all bandwidths available in all modes. Spurious signals noted around 6 MHz segment (49 meters) at night at one test location having superb antennas. Synchronous selectable sideband, although recently improved, doesn't hold lock quite as well as some other models. When 9-10 dB preamplifier turned on, AGC acts on noise unless IF gain reduced by 10 dB. Notch filter does not work in AM, synchronous selectable sideband or ISB modes. Passband shift tunes only plus or minus 2 kHz and does not work in the ISB or synchronous selectable sideband modes; remediable with Sherwood SE-3. Audio quality and synchronous selectable sideband's lock both profit from Sherwood SE-3 accessory and good outboard speaker. Occasional "popping" sound, notably when synchronous selectable sideband or ISB in use—DSP overload? No AGC off except by holding down DUMP button. Noise blanker not effective at some test locations; for example, other receivers work better in reducing noise from electric fences. Audio power, especially through headphones, could be greater. On our unit, right-channel headphone audio cuts out at full volume. On our unit, occasional minor buzz from internal speaker. Keypad not in telephone format. Some ergonomic clumsiness when going back and forth between the presets and VFO tuning; too, "Aux Parameter" and "Memory Scan" knobs touchy to adjust. Signal-strength indicator illuminated less than display. Digital hash from fluorescent display emits from front of receiver, although not elsewhere. On our latest unit, stick-on decal with front-panel markings has peeled loose above the main display, and pushing it back into place hasn't helped; this has not been a problem on other units. No DC power input. Cabinet extra. Cabinet excessively deep, requiring operator to reach in far to get to rear panel.

**Verdict:** With an extreme degree of manual control, the Ten-Tec RX-340, when coupled to fidelity-enhancing hardware, is a superb DSP receiver for those who want no-compromise performance for years to come. It's a sensible value, too—with bells and whistles, it costs considerably less than a fully equipped WJ-8711A.

**Improvement in Latest Version:** With the latest software improvements, synchronous selectable sideband finally works acceptably.

**There are many high-performance receivers, but only the Japan Radio NRD-301 is built like the Pyramids. Easy on-the-spot repair, too.**

## ✪✪✪✪½
## Japan Radio NRD-301A

**Price:** Under $8,000 in the United States—actual price varies considerably. *Cabinet #MPBX10832:* $449.95 if ordered with receiver, $749.95 if ordered separately, in the United States. *Aftermarket voice bandwidth filters:* approximately $150 each, installed ($139.95 uninstalled), in the United States. *Sherwood SE-3:* $549 plus shipping worldwide.

**Pro:** Uncommonly easy to repair on the spot—aided by built-in test equipment (BITE), plug-in circuit boards and a spare-parts kit. Superior overall performance in nearly all respects. Superior ergonomics. Passband shift, operates in AM mode. Tunes in ultra-precise 1 Hz increments. Three hundred presets, and VFO operates from presets' channels. Effective noise blanker. Adjustable AGC decay. Sophisticated scanning system. AF (audio) filter narrows high- and low-frequency audio response. Comes with spare parts for on-site repair. Operates from a wide range of AC voltages, using an easily adjusted inboard power supply and 24 VDC ship's power. Can be computer controlled. Room for additional bandwidths. Unlike other professional models, the actual selling price varies enormously—attractive pricing can be found in some quarters.

**Con:** Usually available only on special order. Lacks the operating flexibility of such professional supersets as the Watkins-Johnson WJ-8711A. Only two voice bandwidths (*see* Pro), although both perform nicely and are well chosen. No keypad tuning, a major omission. No synchronous selectable sideband; remediable by adding Sherwood SE-3 outboard accessory, which uses off-tuning to select sidebands. No tunable notch filter. Unusual audio, antenna and AC cord jacks. Signal-strength indicator not illuminated. Slight whine from LED display at high brightness after receiver has been on for over an hour. Slight AC "tingle" when touching cabinet, remediable by grounding the receiver or, for receive-only applications, by removing marine-oriented C1 and C2 capacitors from across the back of the AC socket. AC power transformer runs very hot and sometimes buzzes. Distribution limited to Japan Radio dealers, offices, and a few specialty organizations such as shipyards. Rack mounted, so cabinet is extra and pricey.

☞ The above star rating is for the receiver "as is" from the factory. With the addition of at least one more AM-mode voice filter and the Sherwood SE-3, the rating improves by a quarter star.

**Verdict:** Japan Radio's NRD-301A receiver is exceptional. It is probably fit to be handed down from one generation to the next, what with its seemingly bulletproof construction, ease of repair and superior overall performance. Yet, as it comes from the factory it lacks certain features of use for everyday world band listening and DXing.

---

*The PASSPORT professional-model review team consists of Tony Jones, Lawrence Magne, Chuck Rippel, David Walcutt, David Zantow and George Zeller. Laboratory measurements by J. Robert Sherwood.*

# Choosing a Premium Receiver?

## *Get premium advice before you buy!*

If you could, you'd spend weeks with each receiver, learning its charms and foibles. Seeing for yourself how it handles—*before* you spend.

Now, you can do the next best thing—better, some folks insist. Radio Database International White Papers®, from the PASSPORT® TO WORLD BAND RADIO library of in-depth test reports, put the facts right into your hands. We test run each receiver for you. Put it through comprehensive laboratory and bench tests to find out where it shines. And where it doesn't.

Then our panel takes over: DXers, professional monitors, program listeners. They're mean, grumpy, hypercritical . . . and take lots of notes. They spend weeks with each receiver, checking ergonomics and long-run listening quality with all kinds of stations. Living with it day and night.

With PASSPORT's RDI White Papers®, these findings—the good, the bad and the ugly—are yours, along with valuable tips on how to operate your radio to best advantage. Each receiver report covers one model in depth, and is US$6.95 postpaid in the United States and Canada; $9.95 airmail elsewhere.

PASSPORT RDI White Papers for current models:
    Drake R8B
    Grundig Satellit 800
    Sony ICF-2010/ICF-2001D
    Yaesu FRG-100
    How to Interpret Receiver Lab Tests & Measurements
    Popular Outdoor Antennas, including installation

PASSPORT RDI White Papers for earlier receivers:
    AOR AR3030
    Drake R8/R8E
    Drake R8A

Drake SW8
Grundig Satellit 500
Grundig Satellit 650 (and Satellit 600)
Icom IC-R71
Icom IC-R9000/'R9000A
Kenwood R-5000
Japan Radio NRD-93
Japan Radio NRD-525 (includes summary evaluation of Japan Radio NRD-515)
Japan Radio NRD-535D/NRD-535
Lowe HF-125
Lowe HF-150
Lowe HF-225 and Lowe HF-235
Sony CRF-V21
Ten-Tec RX325
Yaesu FRG-8800

Available direct or from dealers. For VISA/ MasterCard orders, click on www.passband.com or call our 24-hour autovoice order line: +1 (215) 598-9018; also, fax +1 (215) 598 3794. Or send your check or money order, specifying which reports you want, to:

**Passport RDI White Papers**
**Box 300**
**Penn's Park, PA 18943 USA**

More RDI White Papers are planned. These will be listed at www.passband.com as they become available.

"We strongly recommend the PASSPORT RDI White Papers before purchasing any receiver over $100. The *Consumer Reports* of shortwave radio."

—What's New, *Monitoring Times*

**www.passband.com**

# Receivers for PCs

Much of the enjoyment of world band comes from using a variety of knobs and buttons to unearth stations and enhance their reception quality. But one size doesn't fit all. A small but visible group prefers to have their receivers controlled by a PC.

These receivers have no physical controls, so only computers can operate them. Marrying shortwave receivers to PCs allows the performance of each to enhance the capabilities of the other. Yet, benefits are offset by drawbacks, such as convoluted hardware configurations and radio interference from PC hardware—monitors and cables are prime culprits, so you may need to experiment with alternatives for best results. Professional operations are set up to avoid these issues, but for a person at home it's a lot tougher.

Sales reflect this. Although proponents of PC-controlled receivers are enthusiastic and voluble, especially on the Internet, it turns out there's far more smoke than fire. Reliable industry sources report that actual sales levels have been consistently negligible following the initial months after product introduction.

PASSPORT's tests show that only one offering really cuts the mustard for world band: the $295 Ten-Tec RX-320, which earns four stars and is scheduled to remain in Ten-Tec's lineup indefinitely. Runner-up is the three-star Icom IC-PCR1000, which works equally well as a VHF+ scanner. The two-star WiNRADiO 1500e has been replaced by the 1550e that reportedly incorporates some degree of improvement; the 1500e has performed much better as a scanner than as a world band receiver.

## ✪✪✪✪ ✇ *Passport's Choice*
### Ten-Tec RX-320

**Price:** *RX-320:* $295.00 plus shipping worldwide. *Third-party control software:* Free-$99 worldwide.

**Pro:** Superior dynamic range. Apparently superb bandwidth shape factors (*see* Con). In addition to the supplied factory control software, third-party software is available, often for free, and may improve operation. Up to 34 bandwidths with third-party software. Tunes in extremely precise 1 Hz increments (10 Hz with tested factory software); displays to the nearest Hertz, and frequency readout is easily user-aligned. Large, easy-to-read digital frequency display and faux-analog frequency bar. For PCs with sound cards, outstanding freedom from distortion aids in providing good audio quality with most but not all cards and speakers. Fairly good audio, but with limited treble, also available through radio for PCs without sound cards. Superb blocking

performance helps maintain consistently good world band sensitivity. Passband offset (*see* Con). Spectrum display with wide variety of useful sweep widths (*see* Con). World time on-screen clock (*see* Con). Adjustable AGC decay. Thousands of memories (presets), with first-rate memory configuration, access and sorting—including by station name and frequency. Only PC-controlled model tested which returns to last tuned frequency when PC turned off. Superior owner's manual. Outstanding factory help and repair support.

**Con:** No synchronous selectable sideband, although George Privalov's Control Panel Program now automates retuning of drifty AM-mode signals received as "ECSS." Some characteristic "DSP roughness" in the audio under certain reception conditions. Synthesizer phase noise measures only fair; among the consequences are that bandwidth shape factors cannot be measured exactly. Some tuning ergonomics only fair as compared with certain standalone receivers. No tunable notch filter. Passband offset doesn't function in AM mode. Signal-strength indicator, calibrated 0-80, too sensitive, reading 20 with no antenna connected and

**The best consumer grade PC-controlled shortwave receiver is the $295 Ten-Tec RX-320.**

30 with only band noise being received. Mediocre front-end selectivity can allow powerful mediumwave AM stations to "ghost" into the shortwave spectrum, thus degrading reception of world band stations. Uses AC adaptor instead of built-in power supply. Spectrum display does not function with some third-party software and is only a so-so performer. Mediumwave AM reception below 1 MHz suffers from reduced sensitivity, and longwave sensitivity is atrocious. No internal speaker on receiver module. World Time clock tied into computer's clock, which may not be accurate without periodic adjustment. Almost no retail sources outside the United States.

☞ PASSPORT's four-star rating is for the RX-320 with third-party control software. With factory software the rating is slightly lower.

**Verdict:** No contest, the American-made Ten-Tec RX-320 is the star of the PC show when it is coupled to solid control software. Unless you live near a mediumwave AM station, this receiver runs circles around most receivers of any sort near its price class.

## ✪✪✪
## Icom IC-PCR1000

**Price:** *IC-PCR1000:* $399.95 in the United States. CAN$799.00 in Canada. £319.95 in the United Kingdom. AUS$890.00 in

Icom's IC-PCR1000 provides solid wide-spectrum performance at low cost.

Australia. €449.00 in Germany. *UT-106 DSP Unit:* $139.95 in the United States. £82.00 in the United Kingdom. US$175 in Australia.

**Pro:** Wideband frequency coverage. Spectrum display with many useful sweep widths for shortwave, as well as good real-time performance. Tunes and displays in extremely precise 1 Hz increments. Comes with reasonably performing control software (*see* Con). Excellent sensitivity to weak signals. AGC, adjustable, performs well in AM and single-sideband modes. Nineteen banks of 50 memories each, with potential for virtually unlimited number of memories. Passband offset (*see* Con). Powerful audio with good weak-signal readability and little distortion (*see* Con).

**Con:** Poor dynamic range. Audio quality, not pleasant, made worse by presence of circuit hiss. No line output to feed PC sound card and speakers, so no alternative to using receiver's audio. No synchronous selectable sideband. Only two AM-mode bandwidths—8.7 kHz (nominal 6 kHz) and 2.4 kHz (nominal 3 kHz)—both with uninspiring shape factors. Synthesizer phase noise, although not measurable, appears to be only fair; among the effects of this are that bandwidth shape factors cannot be exactly measured. Mediocre blocking slightly limits weak-signal sensitivity when frequency segment contains powerful signals. Tuning ergonomics only fair as compared with some standalone receivers. Automatic tunable notch filter with DSP audio processing (UT-106, not tested) an extra-cost option. Lacks passband offset in AM mode. Uses AC adaptor instead of built-in power supply. Spectrum display mutes audio when single-sideband or CW signal being received. No clock. Mediocre inboard speaker, remediable by using outboard speaker. Sparse owner's manual.

☞ In the last half of 2002, Icom began including Bonito RadioCom 4.0 software with "select packages" of the 'PCR1000. This nominally provides more flexible audio shaping and the ability to record programs onto hard drive.

**Verdict:** Among tested PC-controlled receivers, the Japanese-made Icom IC-PCR1000 is the most appropriate for wideband frequency coverage and first-rate shortwave spectrum display.

✪✪
## WiNRADiO 1500e

**Price:** $549.95 in the United States. CAN$899.00 in Canada. £369.00 in the United Kingdom. AUS$899.00 in Australia. €587.00 in Germany.

**Pro:** Wideband frequency coverage. AM-mode bandwidth has superb shape factor and good ultimate rejection. Spectrum display with good real-time performance (*see* Con). Tunes in precise 10 Hz increments; display has 1 Hz resolution, but of course can show only tuned 10 Hz increments. Comes with reasonably performing control software (*see* Con). Excellent sensitivity to weak signals, generally best among PC-controlled receivers tested (*see* Con). Passband offset (*see* Con). World time on-screen clock (*see* Con). High quality of assembly and construction.

**Con:** Dreadful dynamic range, a crucial shortcoming for world band (*see* ☞ below). Only one AM-mode bandwidth (6.5 kHz). Audio lacks power quality. No decent line output to feed PC sound card and speakers, so receiver's audio has to be used. Microphonics from internal speaker, making outboard speaker *de rigeur*. No synchronous selectable sideband. AGC not adjustable. No tunable notch filter. Poor blocking limits weak-signal sensitivity when band contains powerful signals. Long learning curve due to complexity. Tuning ergonomics only fair as compared with some standalone receivers. Lacks passband offset in AM mode. Uses AC adaptor instead of built-in power supply. Spectrum display of limited utility because of numerous spurious signals (*see* ☞,

As tested, WiNRADiO models are less disappointing as scanners than as world band receivers.

below). World Time clock tied into computer's clock, which may not be accurate. Comes with 9/25-pin cable and 25/9 adaptor, which doesn't fit onto some laptops, rather than usual 9/9 cable. Sparse owner's manual.

**Verdict:** As tested, this model is ill suited to world band applications.

☞ The 1500e has been replaced by the similar WR-1550e, which the manufacturer claims has improved dynamic range and spurious-signal rejection. Their official emailed product-release announcement also claims better sensitivity, although the WiNRADiO Website says improved selectivity with no mention of sensitivity.

☞ The pricey WiNRADiO 3100e we tested is very similar to the 1500e, above, but with improved dynamic range and reduced sensitivity to weak shortwave signals. $1,849.95 in the United States, CAN$3,199.00 in Canada, £1,169.00 in the United Kingdom and AUS$2,629.44 in Australia. It has been replaced by the WR-3150e with what the manufacturer calls "similar improvements."

---

*Chuck Rippel, Robert Sherwood and David Zantow, with Lawrence Magne; also, Craig Tyson.*

www.passband.com

# Passive Antennas: Wires That Work

Part of the allure of world band as opposed to Webcasts is no wires. Yet, for those seeking the best in world band performance, an outdoor antenna can be surprisingly effective—and most are made from wire.

If you decide to spring for a serious outdoor wire antenna, there are three "musts" for optimum results:

- Mate the type of antenna to the type of receiver.
- Purchase the best antenna of the type you want which fits outdoors.
- Erect the antenna safely and for best performance.

## Signal-to-Noise

An outdoor antenna will almost always help with weaker signals by providing more signal and overcoming local electrical noises and receiver circuit noise. The result—more signal, less noise—is an improvement in the *signal-to-noise ratio*. It's like getting rid of crackling and hiss on a noisy telephone line.

The signal-to-noise ratio is important because increasing signal strength means little if you also increase background noise by a similar amount. These noises can be from local sources—appliances, fluorescent lights, computers, dimmers and the like—as well as from "hiss" and other circuit noises generated within your receiver.

## When an Antenna Won't Help

Nevertheless, muscular stations already coming in well probably won't sound better. Your receiver's signal-strength indicator may read higher, but its automatic-gain control (AGC) ensures that what you hear probably won't sound much different than it does with your existing antenna.

If you are using a simple portable, forget sophisticated antennas—outdoor or indoor, passive or active. Rather, either make do with the built-in telescopic antenna, or for more oomph stick to a simple inverted-L wire outdoor antenna or the Sony AN-LP1 active loop. Among the best inverted-L antennas in the United States is Radio Shack's ten-buck "SW Antenna Kit" with wire, insulators and other goodies, plus $2 for a claw/alligator clip or other connector. In Australia Dick Smith Electronics offers the comparable K 3490 Short Wave Antenna.

These inverted-L antennas may be too long for your radio, causing "overload" from too much incoming signal; yet, you can always shorten it. Experiment, but as a rough rule of thumb the less costly the portable, the shorter the antenna.

At the other extreme, tabletop world band receivers usually don't even come with built-in antennas, as these can't begin to do justice to their exceptional potential. A good antenna is as essential to these elite receivers as high-octane gasoline is to a Maserati.

## Location, Location

Antenna location is as important as the type of antenna chosen. An antenna placed out in the fresh air—high up, and away from electrical lines, communications cables and other sources of noise—will excel in improving the "noise" portion of the signal-to-noise ratio.

## Unamplified *vs.* Amplified Antennas

There are two basic types of outboard antennas: "unamplified" (typically outdoor) and "amplified" or "active" (indoor, outdoor or both).

An unamplified antenna consists of a healthy length of wire or other metal receiving element to provide a radio signal directly to the receiver. It has no electrical amplification. An amplified or active antenna, on the other hand, typically uses a much shorter rod or wire receiving element, plus one or more stages of electrical amplification to make up for the relatively modest signal input of the diminutive receiving element.

Amplified antennas are popular because they are compact—for apartments, ideal. Even some homeowners prefer them because they can be easy to erect and relatively inconspicuous.

But amplified antennas have four drawbacks. First, their short receiving elements don't provide the signal-to-noise enhancement that comes when longer elements are used. Second, the antenna's amplifier can generate noise of its own. Third, the antenna's amplifier can itself overload, with results comparable to those found when a receiver overloads . . . a mishmash of jumbled-sounding stations up and down the dial; indeed, if amplifier gain is excessive it can also overload the receiver. Fourth, most amplified antennas have mediocre front-end selectivity, and thus are prone to commingling signals from local mediumwave AM stations with those from world band radio stations. This makes them potentially bad news for the very urban areas in which apartment dwellers and powerful radio/TV signals coexist in close proximity.

So, while there are a few good amplified antennas on the market today, these are not the antennas of choice except when installation of a first-rate unamplified antenna is simply not feasible.

Of course, if you're an apartment dweller with high-quality receiving gear, there is really precious little choice—it's dictated by where you live and the whims of your landlord or tenants' association. Unless you have access to a long roof or parcel of ground and the blessing of your landlord or tenants' association, you'll usually have to make do with an amplified antenna simply because there's no legit way to erect a long outdoor antenna.

Still, determined apartment dwellers have put their creative juices to full use with a wide variety of hidden or camouflaged outdoor wire antennas, such as phoney "clotheslines." Or they have simply capital-ized on urban apathy by erecting a good outdoor wire antenna, then seeing whether any adverse reaction materializes. For these circumstances, the alternative least likely to attract attention is an inverted-L of moder-ate length, using wire that's not too thick or brightly colored.

## Static Protection

An effective static protector is essential during thunderstorms, windy snowfalls and sandstorms. These storms tend to generate static charges, "sparks" strong enough to send your radio to the repair shop. Among the best protectors are those made by Alpha Delta Communications.

## Installation

Thanks to the tireless activities of amateur radio organizations, Americans have traditionally been unlikely to encounter legal restrictions on erecting world band antennas. However, covenants or deed restrictions, increasingly common in "gated" communities, may limit what you can do. In general, though, the rule of reason applies: Outdoor wire antennas should be neither unsightly nor particularly visible.

Most antennas are robustly constructed to withstand ice buildup during storms. However, those which require guying need hardware comparable in strength to that of the antenna. Also give consideration to the use of bungee cords to provide elasticity in the event of heavy ice buildup.

Safety is paramount during installation, especially to avoid falls or making contact with potentially lethal electrical utility and other lines. There's much more to this than we can cover here, but you can find specif-ics in the RADIO DATABASE INTERNATIONAL report, *Evaluation of Popular Outdoor Antennas*, as well as at www.universal-radio.com/catalog/sw_ant/safeswl.html.

## Which Are Best?

For that RDI White Paper, we tested a number of popular outdoor wire antennas for shortwave listening. The best of those are reported on here. All are dipoles, most of which rely on traps for frequency reso-nance. Three layouts are used: end-fed sloper, with the antenna pitched about 30 degrees from horizontal; center-fed tapered wing, with a tall (about 20 feet or 6 meters) center mounting and two end mountings which are lower; and center-fed horizontal, hung between two points of comparable height.

Passive antennas are among the most difficult devices to evaluate properly. First, the quality of reception is frequency-dependent, so any overall rating is only a generalization. Second, performance depends to a noticeable extent on how well the antenna is erected, and even the type of soil, moisture and bedrock immediately underneath.

## Star Ratings

PASSPORT now awards star ratings based on any and all types of antennas—three stars, for example, means the same thing regardless of whether an antenna is active or passive. This facilitates comparison of a given passive antenna with an active antenna that might otherwise seem equally suitable.

## Inverted-L Alternatives

What about inverted-L antennas, sometimes referred to as "longwires"? They are simple and inexpensive, and for most radios they provide excellent results, even doing reasonably well on mediumwave AM.

Simple inverted-L antennas of moderate length are available at radio stores—these usually rate three stars, sometimes four, and are much too short to be called "longwires." Huge homemade versions, detailed in the RDI White Paper on outdoor antennas, can run over 200 feet, or 60 meters—Universal Radio and others sell the necessary specialized parts.

These long inverted-L antennas can perform fully as well as the Alpha Delta DX-Ultra, sometimes better because their enormous capture wavelength tends to improve the signal-to-noise ratio. But they are a nightmare to keep erect during ice storms and other extremes of weather, which can also cause sagging because of stretched wire.

### ✪✪✪✪¾ *Passport's Choice*
### Alpha Delta DX-Ultra

**Price:** $119.95 in the United States.

**Pro:** Best overall performer of any antenna tested, passive or active. Little variation in performance from one world band segment to another. Rugged construction. Comes with built-in static protection. Wing design appropriate for certain yard layouts. Covers mediumwave AM band.

**Con:** Assembly a major undertaking, with stiff wire having to be bent and fed through spacer holes, then affixed. Unusually lengthy, 80 feet or 25 meters. Does not include needed coaxial cable lead-in. Relatively heavy, adding to erection effort. Warranty only six months.

**The Alpha Delta DX-Ultra takes time, care and patience to put up, but works very well.**

**Alpha Delta's DX-SWL
Sloper makes sense
where there is only one
high mounting point.**

**Verdict:** The Alpha Delta DX-Ultra rewards sweat equity—it is really more of a kit than a finished product. First, you have to purchase the needed lead-in cable and other hardware bits, then assemble, bend and stretch the many stiff wires, section-by-section.

Because the wire used should outlast the Pyramids, assembly is a trying and unforgiving exercise. Each wire needs to be rigorously and properly affixed, lest it slip loose and the erected antenna comes tumbling down, as it did at one of our test sites.

While all outdoor antennas require yard space, the Ultra is the longest manufactured antenna tested. It is also relatively heavy, making installation an even more tiresome chore than it already is. In ice-prone climates, be sure any trees or poles attached to the antenna are sturdy.

But if you have the yard space and don't object to leaping assembly and erection hurdles, you are rewarded with a robust antenna that is outperformed only by hugely long inverted-L antennas and professional-grade antennas beyond the financial reach of even the most enthusiastic listener.

✪✪✪✪½ *Passport's Choice*
## Alpha Delta DX-SWL Sloper

**Price:** $79.95 in the United States.

**Pro:** Rugged construction. Sloper design, using traps to save space, unusually practical for some yard layouts. Covers mediumwave AM band.

**Con:** Requires assembly, a significant exercise. Does not include static protection. Does not include needed coaxial cable lead-in. Warranty only six months.

☞ A shortened version, the 40-foot (12 meter) DX-SWL-S, not tested by us, is available for $69.95. Its nominal coverage is 3.2-22 MHz, omitting the 2 MHz (120 meter) world band segment. Although both Sloper versions nominally don't cover the 25 MHz (11 meter) world band segment, our measurements of the full-length Sloper show excellent results at 25650-26100 kHz.

**Verdict:** An excellent choice if you find that a 60-foot (18 meter) sloper will fit better into your yard than the Ultra or a very long inverted-L wire. However, it is a chore to assemble.

✪✪✪✪⅛ *Passport's Choice*

## Eavesdropper Model T, Eavesdropper Model C

**Price:** *Models T and C:* $89.95 in the United States.

**Pro:** Exceptionally compact, only 43 feet or 13 meters, making it relatively likely to fit into a yard. Comes with built-in static protection. One-year warranty, after which repairs made "at nominal cost." *Model T:* Easiest to install of any Passport's Choice antenna—just unpack it and it's ready to hang. Comes with ribbon lead-in wire, which tends to have less signal loss than coaxial cable. *Model C:* Easier than most to install, with virtually everything included and assembled but the coaxial cable lead-in.

**Con:** Some performance drop in 2 MHz (120 meter) and 3 MHz (90 meter) tropical segments. *Model C:* Coaxial cable not included.

☞ Eavesdropper also makes a fully assembled $89.95 sloper antenna, not tested by us, similar to the Alpha Delta DX-SWL Sloper. It comes with lead-in wire and a static arrestor.

**Verdict:** There's no getting around the rule that the longer the antenna, the more likely it is to do well at low frequencies. The Eavesdropper's designer told PASSPORT some years back that their research showed little tuning taking place below 4.7 MHz, while on the other hand many folks had problems with yard space, or just wanted a shorter antenna less likely to come down in an ice storm. So he designed the Eavesdropper to be relatively compact, yet perform optimally above 4.7 MHz while still doing decent service lower down.

Our tests confirm this. The Eavesdropper horizontal trap dipoles perform quite nicely above 4.7 MHz, with a notch less gain in the 2 MHz and 3 MHz tropical segments.

The Eavesdropper T comes "ready to go" and is straightforward to erect. In practice the ribbon lead-in wire used by the T works very well, using phasing to cancel out much electrical noise. Too, it stands up to weather and usually has less signal loss than the coaxial cable used by its C sibling. The C version is helpful when there is significant electrical noise in the immediate vicinity of the feedline.

---

*Prepared by Stephen Bohac, Jock Elliott, Tony Jones, Lawrence Magne and David Walcutt.*

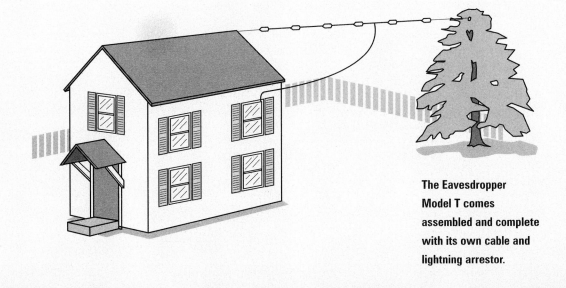

**The Eavesdropper Model T comes assembled and complete with its own cable and lightning arrestor.**

# Active Antennas: Where Space Is Limited

Do you listen during the day, when signals are harder to hear? Do you like to flush out weaker, more unusual stations?

If so, a good outboard antenna can be your radio's best friend. Problem is, the most effective world band antennas are passive—unamplified—and require yard space. If you have little or no room outdoors, or are in an apartment or hotel, something else is needed.

That "something else" is an active antenna. These include a small rod ("whip") or loop, or a short wire—the receiving element—to snare signals from the airwaves. But because these elements are not lengthy, signals they pass on to the receiver tend to be weak. If something weren't done to overcome this, it would be like powering a car with a golf cart engine.

Active antennas resolve this by electrically amplifying signals before they get to the receiver. Although a lengthy passive wire antenna has inherent advantages, compact active antennas can do a surprisingly good job. The challenge is to sort out winners from losers.

## Improved Performance

Active antennas used to be considered strictly as also-rans. Early models were noisy, overloaded easily, generated harmonic "false" signals and suffered from the ravages of outdoor use. They quickly earned a reputation for failing to perform even close to what serious listeners demanded.

In recent years, and again for 2003, this has been changing for the better. The introduction of robust, well-engineered models has changed the game considerably. While none yet equals the performance of a proper outdoor wire antenna, the gap has closed considerably.

We've limited our testing to designs likely to perform satisfactorily under a wide range of circumstances. However, simpler amplified antennas are available at low cost for portables. In general, the weaker the overall signal strengths at your location, the greater the chances these budget offerings will suffice.

## Proximate *vs.* Remote

Active antennas can be either proximate or remote. A proximate model requires that the receiving element be located near the receiver, as it is mounted on a control box which must be close to the radio. Remote models allow the receiving element to be placed a considerable distance away—either indoors or, with some models, out in the open weather where reception is superior.

> **PASSPORT's tests now include months of hands-on use.**

The rugged Yaesu G-5550 twin-axis rotor tilts and turns. This helps outdoor loop antennas give optimum results on mediumwave AM DX—sometimes shortwave, too.

Photos: pp. 181–182 Chuck Rippel; pp. 183–192 Robert Sherwood.

Remote units are almost always the better bet, as they allow a receiving element to be placed where electrical noise is low and incoming signals are strong. Proximate models give you no choice unless you are willing to move the entire receiver to where reception happens to be optimum, which may not be a satisfactory place to listen.

Nevertheless, proximate loop antennas, such as the new AOR LA-350, have an advantage in that they can be aimed away from the source of any disruptive local electrical noise. This can improve reception considerably under the right circumstances.

If you do choose a proximate model, keep in mind that many radios put out some degree of electrical "hash," or noise. Typically, this radiates forward from the receiver's digital display, so it is best to locate a proximate antenna behind or to either side of the radio.

## Preselection vs. Broadband

Broadband electronic amplifiers have the potential for all sorts of mischief. Some add noise and spurious signals, especially from the mediumwave AM band; others may overload a receiver with too much gain.

A partial solution is to have effective tunable or switchable preselection. Preselection limits the band of frequencies which get full amplification, and in so doing reduces the odds of spurious signals being created by the antenna or the receiver.

Problem is, preselection adds to manufacturing cost. And because it usually requires manual tuning, it can increase operating complexity—although it doesn't have to. As indicated in our review of the Sony ICF-SW07 elsewhere in PASSPORT REPORTS, preselection can be automated if the antenna and receiver are designed to work together. So far only the 'SW07 can do this.

A simplified variant of preselection is to substantially reduce gain at frequencies below around two Megahertz with a high-pass filter, or within a given (mediumwave AM) frequency range with a band rejection filter. This is a great help in keeping powerful local mediumwave AM stations from disrupting world band reception.

## Amplified Wire Affordable, Works Well

If you don't have space outdoors for a full-fledged passive wire antenna, but have enough room for a short outdoor wire, consider the MFJ-1020. It performs only modestly with its little built-in antenna. However, it does unusually well as an active preselector when used with a short inverted-L wire antenna, especially if the wire is placed outdoors. If this is feasible at your location, the combo can provide superior performance at an affordable price.

## How Much Is Too Much?

Newcomers sometimes judge an active antenna by how much gain it provides, as shown on a receiver's signal-strength indicator. This can be misleading.

For one thing, with a first-rate receiver and passive outdoor wire antenna, there is rarely any need for electrical gain between the antenna and receiver. In principle, a good active antenna should replicate that "natural" level of gain—or, better, the signal-to-noise ratio. Too little gain, then overall circuit noise appears, if only from the receiver. Too much gain and the receiver's dynamic range, and possibly that of the antenna's amplifier, is strained unnecessarily.

## AC Can Cause Hum, Buzz

Active antennas work best when powered by battery. This eliminates all possibility of hum and buzzing caused, directly or indirectly, by an AC-to-DC power supply or adaptor. Problem is, using batteries, instead, is impractical with most models.

Hum and buzzing was found in a number of models of AC-powered unbalanced active antennas. The best practical solution: Keep AC adaptors and cords as far as possible from an antenna's receiving element and feedline.

## Steps You Can Take

Antenna performance is roughly one part technology, one part geography and geology, and one part installation. This report covers the first, with tips on the third, but in the end all we can do is boost your odds of success. After all, much of the outcome depends on where you live and what you do once the antenna arrives.

Antenna location and installation details can make all the difference. Consider experimenting with different locations before doing a permanent installation, and if your receiver has multiple antenna inputs don't be afraid to see which works best.

## Results for 2003

Proper testing of antennas includes not only careful laboratory analysis, but also months of hands-on field testing to know, in general, how an antenna performs. But given a year or more, seasonal characteristics can also be evaluated and more test locations included.

### WHERE TO INSTALL A REMOTE ANTENNA

The good news is that if an excellent active antenna is installed properly, it can perform very well. The bad news is that if you have room outdoors to mount it optimally, you may also have room for a passive wire antenna that will perform better, yet. Probably cheaper, too.

Still, here are a few practical tips on placement of weather-resistant remote models. As always with antennas, creativity rules—don't be afraid to experiment.

- If you can mount your antenna's receiving element outdoors, try to do it in the clear, especially away from anything metal. Use a nonconductive mast or capped PVC pipe, as metal masts or pipes are likely to degrade performance. Optimum height from ground is usually around 10-25 feet or 3-8 meters, but keep in mind that "ground" refers to electrical ground, which includes non-wooden roofs and the like.

  If this is not feasible, try a nearby tree. This works less well because tree sap is electrically conductive, but is a reasonable fallback, especially with hardwood deciduous varieties. Ensure that leaves and branches can't brush against the element under most weather conditions.

- If outdoor mounting is impractical, then have the receiving element protrude out into the fresh air as much as possible. Even if you are in a high-rise building, this can work so long as a window opens or there is a balcony. For example, if your antenna's receiving element is a whip you can stick it away from the building 45 degrees or so, like a flag mast. If that is too visible, try using a string or rope to pull it up, out of view, by day.

  If you are in a house with an attic, especially one with no foil-lined insulation along the pitched roof, and the roof is not metal, this can often work in lieu of an outdoor placement. Indeed, with the large Wellbrook models this is a tempting alternative to placement within a room, especially if a rotor is used.

- If all these choices are impractical, then at least place the receiving element up against a large window. Glass blocks signals much less than masonry or metal, including to a limited extent insulation foil and aluminum siding.

Over the past months of testing, we've found that the Wellbrook ALA 330 is even better than it seemed at first blush. On the other hand, our expanded testing has also revealed that the Dressler ARA 100 DX can overload badly in environments awash with powerful local mediumwave AM and low-band VHF-TV signals.

The two RF Systems antennas given low marks in Passport 2001 have both been discontinued, and replaced by the new DX-One Professional Mark II. The new version is much improved, and is now one of the best.

Also new for 2003 is the AOR LA-350 indoor loop antenna. It requires more human interaction than any other model tested in recent years, and at some locations is prone to pick up electrical noise. But for the growing ranks of listeners who can't place a receiving element outdoors, the '350 is a welcome addition that also offers directional longwave and mediumwave AM DX reception.

Most active antennas are designed for use with tabletop models, but not all. The Sony AN-LP1 continues to be an exceptional value for use with portable receivers. We have tested several samples, but since late 2001 it has been in short supply in North America. Indeed, Americans have sometime taken to ordering from European sources just to get past the wait.

## What Passport's Ratings Mean

**Star ratings:** ✪✪✪✪✪ is best for any type of antenna, but in reality even the best of active antennas don't yet merit more than four stars when compared against passive antennas. To help with in making a purchase decision, star ratings for active antennas may now be compared directly against those for passive antennas found elsewhere in this Passport Reports. Stars reflect overall performance on shortwave and meaningful features, plus to some extent ergonomics and build quality. Price,

appearance, country of manufacture and the like are not taken into account.

*Passport's Choice*. La crème de la crème. Our test team's personal picks of the litter—models we would buy or have bought for our personal use.

✪: A relative bargain, with decidedly more performance than the price would suggest.

Active antennas are listed in descending order of merit. Unless otherwise indicated each has a one-year warranty.

### Retested for 2003
✪✪✪✪  *Passport's Choice*
**Wellbrook ALA 330**

**Remote, broadband, outdoor-indoor, 2.3-30 MHz**

**Price:** £119.95 plus £10.00 shipping in the United Kingdom. £129.95 plus £25.00 shipping to North America.

**Pro:** Best signal-to-noise ratio, including reduced pickup of thunderstorm static, on all shortwave frequencies, of any active model tested. Low-noise/low-static pickup characteristic most noticeable during summer, when it sometimes outperforms sophisticated outdoor wire antennas. Its aluminum loop receiving element allows it to be affixed to a low-cost TV rotor to improve reception by directionally nulling local electrical noise and static. Sometimes, rotatability also can slightly reduce co-channel shortwave interference; as is to be expected, this modest nulling of co-channel skywave interference is best at frequencies below 5 MHz. Superior build quality, including rigorous weatherproofing (*see* Con). Supplied AC adaptor, regulated, is among the best tested for not causing hum or buzzing, likely because of the antenna's balanced design. Although any large loop is inherently susceptible to inductive pickup of local thunderstorm static, during our tests the antenna's amplifier never suffered static damage during storms; indeed, even nearby one kilowatt shortwave transmissions did no damage to the antenna amplifier. Protected circuitry, using an easily replaced 315 mA slow-blow fuse.

**Con:** Moderate gain for reception within the Western Hemisphere, Asia and Australasia. Marginally less gain than ALA 1530 within 2.3-2.5 MHz (120 meter) tropical segment. Mediumwave AM coverage is possible, even though the antenna is designed only for shortwave; as expected, reception suffers from low sensitivity, while longwave sensitivity is insignificant, being down more than 30 dB compared to the '1530. Balanced loop receiving element, about one meter across, not easy to mount and is large and cumbersome to ship. Mounting mast and optional rotor add to cost. BNC connector at the receiving element's base is open to the weather and thus needs to be user-sealed with Coax Seal, electrical putty or similar. Encapsulated amplifier makes repair impossible. Manufacturer cautions against allowing high winds to stress mounting flange or sunlight to damage head amplifier; however, after a summer of wind and sun at one outdoor test location, nothing untoward has materialized. Adaptor supplied for 117V AC runs hot after being plugged in for a few hours, while amplifier tends to run slightly warm. No coaxial cable supplied. Available for purchase or export only two ways: via cheque through the English manufacturer (www.wellbrook.uk.com), or with credit card via a dealer's unsecured email address in England, although a secure order page is being considered.

☞ If your receiver has antenna inputs with varying impedances, experiment to see which provides the greatest signal strength. Also, at times an antenna tuner can improve signal level as much as 6 dB.

**Verdict:** If its dimensions and purchase hurdles don't deter you, you will not find a better active antenna for shortwave reception than the U.K.-made Wellbrook

Wellbrook's loop antennas are top performers. They are available worldwide, but only through the manufacturer in the U.K.

ALA 330. While the tough ALA 330 usually does not equal the recovered-signal performance of a good outdoor wire antenna, it is once again the best-performing active antenna we have tested. Indeed, DXers may find the '330 to be an appropriate auxiliary antenna to cope with noises and static that can disrupt signals brought in by a passive wire antenna when atmospheric signal-to-noise is the limiting factor.

Optimally, mounting should be outdoors with a rotor, although this is more important with the ALA 1530 model (*see* below) when used for longwave and mediumwave AM reception. However, worthy results on shortwave can be expected indoors sans rotor or with manual rotation, provided the usual caveats are followed for placement of the reception element.

**Observations for 2003:** The '330's ability to keep down static and electrical noise is something that DXers can appreciate when circumstances are appropriate. This is an antenna that the more you use it for challenging reception, the more you come to appreciate its virtues.

The Wellbrook ALA 330 and ALA 1530 work nicely if simply mounted, but at one of our test locations results were even better at great height.

**★★★★** *Passport's Choice*

*(conditional, see first ☞)*

### Wellbrook ALA 1530, Wellbrook ALA 1530P

**Remote, broadband, outdoor-indoor, 0.15-30 MHz**

**Price:** *ALA 1530:* £119.95 plus £10.00 shipping in the United Kingdom. £129.95 plus £25.00 shipping to North America. *ALA 1530P (not tested):* £109.95 plus £10.00 shipping in the United Kingdom. £109.95 plus £25.00 shipping elsewhere. *Yaesu G-5550 twin-axis rotor:* $599.95 in the United States. CAN$1060.00 in Canada.

☞ The Wellbrook ALA 1530 is prone to overloading in locations rich with strong mediumwave AM signals. Star rating does not apply to use in these locations.

☞ Mediumwave AM and longwave performance directionality may suffer if the '1530 is not mounted well away from other antennas.

☞ The "P" version, not tested by us, uses a semi-rigid plastic loop rather than aluminum. It is intended for indoor use only.

**Verdict:** Virtually identical to the Wellbrook ALA 330 (*see* review, above), but also covers mediumwave AM and longwave nominally down to 150 kHz, but with reduced performance down to 50 kHz—and does so brilliantly. This is thanks in no small part to the effectiveness of directional reception on frequencies below the shortwave spectrum. Mediumwave AM reception is particularly aided by the Yaesu G-5500 rotor, used in our tests, which has twin-axis capability. Although costly, it allows the receiving element to be both rotated and tilted to enhance nulling of co-channel interference below 1.7 MHz.

However, the '1530's extended frequency range also can result in mediumwave AM signals surfacing within the shortwave spectrum, degrading reception—this is usually a more significant issue in urban and suburban North America than elsewhere. Yet, for this, too, a rotor can help, as it allows the problem to be minimized by turning the antenna perpendicular to an offending mediumwave AM signal's axis.

### *New for 2003*

**★★★½** *Passport's Choice*

### RF Systems DX-One Professional Mark II

**Remote, broadband, outdoor-indoor, 0.02-60 MHz**

**Price:** $669.95 in the United States. £295.00 in the United Kingdom. €498.00 in Germany. AUS$1,170.00 in Australia.

**Pro:** Outstanding dynamic range. Very low noise. Outputs for two receivers. Comes standard with switchable band rejection filter to reduce the chances of mediumwave AM signals ghosting into the shortwave spectrum. Receiving element has outstanding build quality. Coaxial connector at head amplifier is completely shielded from the weather by a clever mechanical design. Superior low noise, high gain performance on mediumwave AM.

**Con:** Unbalanced design makes antenna susceptible to importing buzz at some locations; this is especially noticeable because of otherwise-excellent performance. AC power supply not bypassed as well as it could be, causing slight hum on some signals. More likely than most antennas to exacerbate fading, even though design nominally reduces fading effects. No coaxial cable supplied. Output position for 10 dB gain measures +6 dB. Warranty only six months.

**Verdict:** Substantially improved over the discontinued original version, the pricey new RF Systems DX-One Professional Mark II is now a superior performer. As with any antenna with a small capture area that has an unbalanced design, at some locations it will be prone to pick up local electrical noise. Made in the Netherlands.

**Evaluation of New Model:** No question—the new DX-One Pro Mark II is much improved over the original version PASSPORT tested two years back.

For starters, gain is now adequate throughout the entire radio spectrum from longwave through 30 MHz. While the original version was almost dead on shortwave, the Mark II's gain is much improved, even though it remains less than the lively Dressler ARA 100 HDX. Mechanically, there is little obvious difference in the design, although the internal head amplifier has higher gain and nominally improved static protection—greatly welcomed, as the original amplifier was prone to "blow" from static charges.

The connection box of the DX-One Pro, normally situated near the receiver, has also been upgraded. It now includes a maximum-gain position of 10 dB, although we measured actual maximum gain as 6 dB.

A mediumwave AM band rejection filter continues to be included, although it is situated after the head amplifier. This means that it can't protect the antenna from potential overload—only the receiver. The Mark II's superior dynamic range all but

rules out antenna overload, but the filter's being to protect receivers from overloading by strong local signals is a useful feature.

The most glaring problem with this unit, like the Dressler ARA 100 HDX, is that, at some locations, it can import buzz or hash from local electrical sources. This almost certainly results from the use of an unbalanced design, rather than the balanced design used in the AC-fed Wellbrook and our reference antenna, a passive outdoor balun-fed dipole.

Long outdoor wire antennas have relatively great capture lengths that ameliorate local noises, plus they have no electronic circuitry connected to household current. So even though most also have unbalanced designs, they are much less inclined to

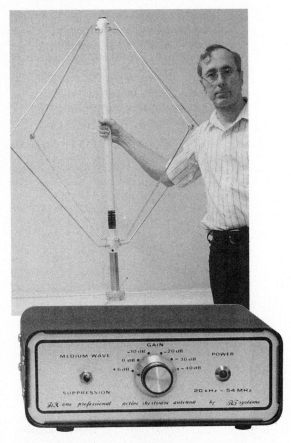

**Robert Sherwood with the RF Systems DX-One Professional.**

introduce or reproduce local electrical noise from whatever origin. Active antennas, on the other hand, have relatively tiny capture areas. They benefit much more from the noise-cancelling effect of a balanced design.

The DX-One Pro Mark II, unlike the original version, produces respectable signal levels. Indeed, on some signals the Mark II comes out ahead of the top-rated Wellbrook, and if you don't encounter significant buzzing at your location you should be pleased, indeed. But where buzzing is encountered, the signal-to-noise ratio is likely to be worse than that of the Wellbrook, but not always.

RF Systems claims that the antenna's "eggbeater" design allows it to receive both horizontally and vertically polarized signals comparably well. Because of phase rotation in the ionosphere, the manufacturer states that this polarization flexibility allows the Mark II to soften the effects of fading. However, in our tests of the earlier version, receivers produced more, not less, fading with the RF Systems offering than, for example, the Dressler ARA 100 HDX and Wellbrook loops. With the Mark II, we encountered the same syndrome.

For non-AM mode signals, and with receivers having proper AM-mode synchronous detection, this is only a minor drawback. But it goes to underscore the gulf that can exist between a theoretical concept and real-world use.

Overall, the RF Systems DX-One Professional Mark II is as good a performer as you can find this side of the Wellbrook offerings. And, unlike those, it is made to withstand the rigors of outdoor climactic challenges.

### Retested for 2003
### ★★★¼  (conditional, see ☞)
### Dressler ARA 100 HDX

**Remote, broadband, outdoor-indoor, 0.04-40 MHz**

**Price:** $529.95 in the United States. £325.00 on special order in the United Kingdom.

**Pro:** Superior build quality, with fiberglass whip and foam-encapsulated head amplifier to resist the weather (*see* Con). Very good gain below 20 MHz (*see* Con). Superior signal-to-noise ratio. Handy detachable "N" connector on bottom. AC adaptor with regulated DC output is better than most.

**Con:** Even with an amplifier having superior dynamic range, tends to overload in urban/ suburban environments awash in powerful mediumwave AM signals unless antenna element mounted close to the ground. Encapsulated design makes most repairs impossible. Above 20 MHz gain begins to fall off slightly. Body of antenna runs slightly warm. "N" connector at the head amplifier/ receiving element exposed to weather, needs to be sealed with Coax Seal, electrical putty or similar by user. Gain control cumbersome to adjust; fortunately, in practice it is rarely needed. Reader reports suggest that ordering direct from the factory can be a frustrating experience.

☞ Star rating applies only when used where there is not significant ambient mediumwave RF, as the Dressler ARA 100

**Dressler's ARA 100 HDX and ARA 60 S work well if not near powerful transmitters.**

HDX, unless mounted close to the ground, is prone to overloading at locations rich with strong mediumwave AM signals or low-band VHF-TV stations. At some locations, even mounting the antenna on the ground did not eliminate overloading.

**Verdict:** The robust Dressler ARA 100 HDX, made in Germany, is an excellent but costly low-noise antenna so long as you are not located near one or more powerful medium-wave AM or low-band VHF-TV transmitters.

**Observations for 2003:** No change for most applications, but this year's testing procedure unearthed considerable over-loading when used in certain urban/suburban environments where there are powerful nearby mediumwave AM or low-band VHF-TV stations.

★★★  (conditional, see ☞)
### Dressler ARA 60 S

**Remote, broadband, outdoor-indoor, 0.04-60/100 MHz**

**Price:** $289.95 in the United States. £169.00 in the United Kingdom. €184.00 in Germany.

**Pro:** Superior build quality, with fiberglass whip and foam-encapsulated head amplifier to resist weather (*see* Con). Very good and consistent gain, even above 20 MHz. AC adaptor with regulated DC output is better than most.

**Con:** Encapsulated design makes most repairs impossible. RG-58 coaxial cable permanently attached on antenna end, making user replacement impossible. Gain control cumbersome to adjust; fortunately, in practice it is rarely needed. Reader reports suggest that ordering direct from the factory can be a frustrating experience.

☞ Not retested for 2003, but comments about overloading in the above 2003 review of the ARA 100 HDX likely apply to the '60 S, as well.

**Verdict:** Very similar to the ARA 100 HDX in tests for 2001—even its dynamic range and overloading performance were virtually identical. This makes the German-made ARA 60 S an excellent lower-cost alternative to the ARA 100 HDX.

★★★ *ⓒ* *Passport's Choice*
### MFJ-1020B

**This rating only for when used with short outdoor inverted-L antenna.**

See review towards the end of this article.

★★¾ *ⓒ* *Passport's Choice*
### Sony AN-LP1

**Remote, manual preselection, indoor/portable, 3.9-4.3 + 4.7-25 MHz**

**Price:** $79.95 in the United States. CAN$185.00 in Canada. £69.99 in the United Kingdom. €101.75 in Germany.

**Pro:** Tops for use with portable receivers. Very good overall performance, including generally superior gain (*see* Con), especially within world band segments—yet surprisingly free from side effects. Battery operation, so no internally caused buzzing (*see* Con). Compact folding design for airline and other travel; also handy for hospital, prison or other institutional use where an antenna must be stashed away periodically. Can be used even with portables that have no antenna input jack (*see* Con). Plug-in filter to reduce local electrical noise (*see* Con). Low battery consumption (*see* Con). Powered by the radio when used with Sony ICF-SW7600G or ICF-SW1000T portables.

**Con:** Only remote model tested which can't be mounted outdoors during inclement weather. Functions acceptably on short-wave only between 3.9-4.3 MHz and 4.7-25 MHz, with no mediumwave AM coverage. Gain varies markedly throughout the shortwave spectrum, in large part because the preselector's step-tuned resonances

For portables, no other active antenna beats the Sony AN-LP1. It is much better than Sony's other offerings, but doesn't work on mediumwave AM.

Jane Brinker

lack variable peaking. Preselector bandswitching complicates operation slightly. Battery operation only—no AC power supply, not even a socket for an AC adaptor—although battery drain is minimal. Consumer-grade plastic construction with no shielding. When clipped onto a telescopic antenna instead of fed through an antenna jack, the lack of a ground connection reduces performance. Plug-in noise filter unit reduces signal strength by several decibels.

☞ Sony recommends that the AN-LP1 not be used with the Sony ICF-SW77 receiver. However, our tests indicate that so long as the control box and loop receiving element are kept reasonably away from the radio, the antenna performs well.

☞ The Sony ICF-SW07 compact portable comes with an AN-LP2 antenna. This is virtually identical in concept and performance to the AN-LP1, except that because it is designed solely for use with the 'SW07 it has automatic preselection to simplify

operation. At present the AN-LP2 cannot be used with other radios, even those from Sony.

**Verdict:** A real winner if the shoe fits and you can find one—it has been in short supply in North America since late 2001, although it has been relatively available in the United Kingdom. Hands down, this is the best model for world band reception on portables. It is often a worthy choice for portatop and tabletop models, as well, provided you don't mind battery-only operation. This Japanese-made model has generally excellent gain, low noise and few side effects. The price is right, too.

Yet, there is limited frequency coverage— 90/120 meter DXers should look elsewhere—and the loop receiving element cannot be mounted permanently outdoors. Too, the lack of variable preselector peaking causes gain to vary greatly by frequency; this especially limits utility DX performance. Otherwise, the Sony AN-LP1 is nothing short of a bargain.

## New for 2003
✪✪¾
## AOR LA-350

### Proximate, manual preselection, indoor, 0.2-1.6 MHz and 2.5-33 MHz

**Price:** *LA-350 antenna, with two shortwave elements:* $299.95 in the United States. *350L longwave element, 350M mediumwave AM element:* $72.95 each in the United States.

**Pro:** Above-average gain. Some directivity below 10 MHz, directionally nulling local electrical noise and static. Sometimes, rotatability can also slightly reduce co-channel shortwave interference; as is the norm with loop antennas, this modest nulling of co-channel skywave interference is best at frequencies below 5 MHz. Rotatability can also improve reception by directionally nulling local electrical noise. Small, easy to rotate. Antenna elements easy to swap (*see* Con). Relatively easy to peak by ear or signal-strength indicator (*see* Con).

**Con:** Proximate model, so receiving element has to be placed near receiver. Unbalanced design results in local electrical noise being passed into receiver at some locations; owner's manual says a better AC adaptor can reduce this, but a $300 product should come equipped with the proper adaptor. Requires change of antenna elements when going from 3-9 MHz range to 9-33 MHz range or *vice versa*; separate (optional) elements for mediumwave AM and longwave also require shuffling. Requires manual peaking when significantly changing received frequency. Phone plug, which connects antenna elements to the head amplifier, lacks lock washer and thus may loosen; easily remedied with Loctite. User has to supply BNC female-to-PL239 male adaptor, needed to connect antenna to many models of tabletop receivers. Owner's manual says BNC-to-BNC cable comes with antenna, but was not packed with our unit.

**Verdict:** The '350's unbalanced design makes it more susceptible to local electrical

noise pickup than either Wellbrook model, and the supplied AC adaptor doesn't help. It also requires manual swapping of loop heads and circuit peaking. This having been said, where local electrical noise doesn't intrude the '350's superior gain, handy size and ease of rotation make it an effective choice for indoor use.

**Evaluation of New Model:** The AOR LA-350 is a fully rotatable indoor tuned loop, only one foot (30 cm) in diameter, which sits near the operator where it can be easily rotated. It has to be manually peaked as you tune up and down the radio spectrum, but this helps prevent overloading. Finding the peak is obvious and easy.

It comes standard with two rotatable loop elements—one for 3-9 MHz, another nominally for 9-30 MHz—that plug into the power supply/amplifier. (The tuning capacitor operates about ten percent beyond the quoted range, so it actually peaks up to 33 MHz.) Options include a plug-in element for longwave 0.2-0.54 MHz, and another for mediumwave AM 0.54-1.6 MHz—slightly shy of the new 1.7 MHz band limit in the Western Hemisphere.

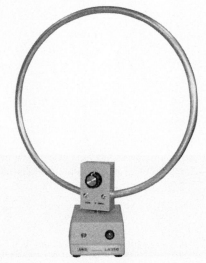

**New for 2003 is the AOR LA-350. Compact, with good gain.**

The '350 loop has an unbalanced design, unlike Wellbrook models. This allows the '350 to suffer from man-made-noise pickup at some locations, just like active whips but to a lesser extent. If this is a problem at your location, the owner's manual says to buy a better adaptor from a third party. Sensible advice, but for over $500, including optional antenna elements, the manufacturer should provide a proper adaptor in the first place.

Also useful is to take advantage of one of the '350's major virtues, directionality, by turning the loop until local noise is maximally reduced. This works especially well with stations in the international world band segments, which go upwards from 5.73 MHz. Rotation will often attenuate local noise without weakening the received signal.

On average, the '350 has slightly more gain than either Wellbrook loop, but the '350's susceptibility to pickup of local noise degrades its signal-to-noise ratio at some locations. Where this is not an issue, the '350 gives the Wellbrook a good run for its money.

The '350 uses a stereo phone plug to attach each loop to the amplifier. This design allows for 360-degree rotation of the loop.

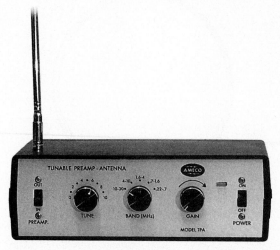

Ameco has been around longer than most people have been alive. Shown, their TPA active antenna.

There is no lock washer securing the phone plug, but a dollop of Loctite resolves this. As with all loops, the '350 shows significant directionality on low frequencies, although this diminishes as the tuned frequency increases within the shortwave spectrum.

The '350 requires swapping of heads and frequent retuning, and is susceptible to pickup of local electrical noise. Add a relatively steep price tag, and either Wellbrook comes off as a more attractive choice. But the '350 shines indoors: It is smaller, has above-average gain and is handy to rotate manually.

## ✪✪½ ⊘
## Ameco TPA

**Proximate, manual preselection, indoor, 0.22-30 MHz**

**Price:** $69.95 in the United States.

**Pro:** Highest recovered signal with the longest supplied whip of the four proximate models tested. Most pleasant unit to tune to proper frequency. Superior ergonomics, including easy-to-read front panel with good-sized metal knobs (*see* Con). Superior gain below 10 MHz.

**Con:** Proximate model, so receiving element has to be placed near receiver. Above 15 MHz gain slips to slightly below average. Overloads with external antenna; because gain potentiometer is in the first stage, decreasing gain may increase overloading as current drops through the FET. Preselector complicates operation, compromising otherwise-superior ergonomics. No rubber feet, slides around in use; user-remediable. No AC adaptor. Consumer-grade plastic construction with no shielding. Comes with no printed information on warranty; however, manufacturer states by telephone that it is the customary one year.

**Verdict:** The Ameco TPA, made in the United States, is the best proximate model tested for bringing in usable signals with the factory-supplied whip—signal recovery was excellent. However, when connected to an external antenna it overloads badly, and reducing gain doesn't help.

## ✪✪½
## McKay Dymek DA100E, McKay Dymek DA100EM, Stoner Dymek DA100E, Stoner Dymek DA100EM

**Remote, broadband, indoor-outdoor-marine, 0.05-30 MHz**

**Price:** *DA100E:* $179.95 in the United States. *DA100EM (marine version, not tested):* $199.95 in the United States.

**Pro:** Respectable gain and noise. Generally good build quality, with worthy coaxial cable and an effectively sealed receiving element; marine version (not tested) appears to be even better yet for resisting weather. Jack for second antenna when turned off. Minor gain rolloff at higher shortwave frequencies. *DA100EM (not tested):* Weather-resistant fiberglass whip and brass fittings help ensure continued optimum performance.

**Con:** Slightly higher noise floor compared to other models. Some controls may confuse initially. Dynamic range among the lowest of any model tested; for many applications in the Americas this is adequate, but for use near local transmitters, or in Europe and other strong-signal parts of the world, the antenna is best purchased on a returnable basis. *DA100E:* Telescopic antenna allows moisture and avian waste penetration between segments, and thus potential resistance and/or spurious signals; user should seal these gaps with Coax Seal, electrical putty or similar. Telescopic antenna could, in principle, be de-telescoped by birds, ice and the like, although we did not actually encounter this. Warranty only 30 days.

**Verdict:** The DA100E is a proven "out of the box" choice, with generally excellent

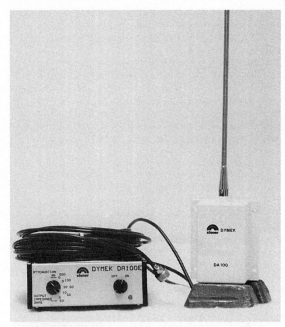

California's George McKay created radio products in the early 1980s. His Dymek DA100, now in the "E" version, is still offered.

weatherproofing and coaxial cable. Because its dynamic range is relatively modest, it is more prone than some other models to overload, especially in an urban environment or other high-signal-strength location. In principle the extra twenty bucks for the marine version should be a good investment, provided its fiberglass whip is not too visible for your location.

## ✪✪¼
## MFJ 1024

**Remote, broadband, indoor-outdoor, 0.05-30 MHz**

**Price:** $139.95 in the United States. CAN$220.00 in Canada.

**Pro:** Overall good gain and low noise. A/B selector for quick connection to another receiver. "Aux" input for passive antenna. 30-day money-back guarantee if purchased from manufacturer.

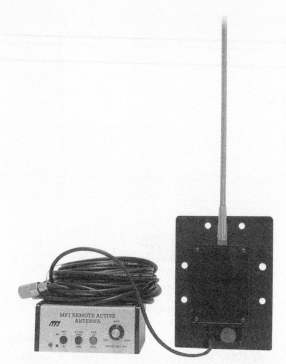

The MFJ 1024 remote antenna is similar to, but cheaper than, the slightly better Dymek equivalent.

**Con:** Significant hum with supplied AC adaptor; remedied when we substituted a suitable aftermarket adaptor. Non-standard power socket complicates substitution of AC adaptor; also, adaptor's sub-mini plug can spark when inserted while the adaptor is plugged in; adaptor should be unplugged beforehand. Dynamic range among the lowest of any model tested; for many applications in the Americas it is adequate, but for use near local transmitters, or in Europe and other strong-signal parts of the world, antenna is best purchased on a returnable basis. Slightly increased noise floor compared to other models. Telescopic antenna allows moisture and avian waste penetration between segments, and thus potential resistance and/or spurious signals; user should seal these gaps with Coax Seal, electrical putty or similar. Telescopic antenna could, in principle, be

de-telescoped by birds, ice and the like after installation, although we did not actually encounter this. Control box/amplifier has no external weather sealing to protect from moisture, although the printed circuit board nominally comes with a water-resistant coating. Coaxial cable to receiver not provided. Mediocre coaxial cable provided between control box and receiving element. On our unit, a coaxial connector came poorly soldered from the factory.

**Verdict:** The MFJ 1024, made in America, performs almost identically to the Stoner Dymek DA100E, but sells for $40 less. However, that gap lessens if you factor in the cost of a worthy AC adaptor—assuming you can find or alter one to fit the unusual power jack—and the quality of the 1024's coaxial cable is not in the same league.

### ✪✪
### Vectronics AT-100

**Proximate, manual preselection, indoor, 0.3-30 MHz**

**Price:** $79.95 in the United States. CAN$109.00 in Canada.

**Pro:** Good—sometimes excellent—gain (see Con), especially in the mediumwave AM band. Good dynamic range. Most knobs are commendably large.

**Con:** Proximate model, so receiving element has to be placed near receiver. No AC power; although it accepts an AC adaptor, the lack of polarity markings complicates adaptor choice (it is center-pin positive). Preselector complicates operation, especially as it is stiff to tune and thus awkward to peak. Our unit oscillated badly with some receivers, limiting usable gain—although it was more stable with other receivers, and thus appears to be a function of the load presented by a given receiver.

**Verdict:** If ever there were a product that needs to be purchased on a returnable basis, this is it. With one receiver, this

American-made model gives welcome gain and worthy performance; with another, it goes into oscillation nearly at the drop of a hat.

## ✪¾
## Sony AN-1

**Remote, broadband, indoor-outdoor, 0.15-30 MHz**

**Price:** $89.95 in the United States. CAN$160.00 in Canada. £64.95 in the United Kingdom. €101.75 in Germany.

**Pro:** Connects easily to any portable or other receiver, using supplied cables and inductive coupler. Unusually appropriate for low-cost portables lacking an outboard antenna input. Only portable-oriented model tested with weather resistant remote receiving element. Unlike Sony AN-LP1, it covers entire shortwave spectrum, plus mediumwave AM and longwave. AC adaptor jack, although antenna designed to run on six "AA" batteries. Good quality coaxial cable. Coaxial cable user-replaceable once head unit is disassembled. Switchable high-pass filter helps reduce intrusion of mediumwave AM signals into shortwave spectrum; rolloff begins at 3 MHz. Receiving element's bracket allows for nearly any mounting configuration (*see* Con).

**Con:** Poor gain, with pronounced reduction as frequency increases. Mediocre mediumwave AM performance. Clumsy but versatile mounting bracket makes installation tedious. No AC adaptor.

☞ Sony offers a number of active antennas in various world markets. All appear to be similar to the AN-1, except for the very different AN-LP1.

**Verdict:** The Japanese-made Sony AN-1 has feeble gain, rendering it practically useless on higher frequencies and little better below. However, for outdoor mounting and use on lower frequencies it provides passable performance.

The Vectronics AT-100 works nicely on some receivers, poorly on others.

## ✪¾
## Palstar AA30A/AA30P/AM-30

**Proximate, manual preselection, indoor, 0.3-30 MHz**

**Price:** *AA30A:* $69.95 in the United States. *AA30P (not tested):* €96.50 in Germany. *AM-30 (not tested):* £69.95 in the United Kingdom.

**Pro:** Moderate-to-good gain. Tuning control easily peaked. Can be powered directly by

Except for mediumwave AM, Sony's AN-1 is inferior to its newer AN-LP1.

**The Palstar AA30 series of active antennas works properly below 14 MHz, but there can be problems higher up.**

the Palstar R30/R30C and Lowe HF-350 tabletop receivers (reviewed elsewhere in PASSPORT REPORTS), an internal battery or an AC adaptor.

**Con:** Spurious oscillation throughout 14-30 MHz range. Overloads with external antenna. Proximate model, so receiving element has to be placed near receiver. Preselector complicates operation. No AC adaptor.

☞ At present, the AA30A's cabinets are silk screened simply as "AA30," although the accompanying owner's manual refers to the "AA30A."

☞ The Palstar AM-30, not tested, is sold in Europe. It appears to be comparable to the AA30A.

**Verdict:** Oscillation makes this a dubious choice except for reception below 14 MHz. Manufactured in the United States.

### ✪¾
### MFJ-1020B

**Proximate, manual preselection, indoor, 0.3-30 MHz**

**Price:** $79.95 in the United States. CAN$125.00 in Canada.

**Pro:** Superior dynamic range. Rating rises to three stars if converted from a proximate to a remote model by removing the built-in antenna and connecting the active preselector module to a user-purchased inverted-L antenna. Choice of PL-259 or RCA connections. 30-day money-back guarantee if purchased from manufacturer.

**Con:** Proximate model, so receiving element has to be placed near receiver (*see* Pro). Low gain, excessive noise. Preselector complicates operation and tuning capacitor hard to peak. Knobs small and not easy to adjust. Confusing markings on front panel. Two manufacturing flaws found on our unit: a defective lowest frequency inductor or switch, as the unit would not tune below 530 kHz; also, crooked front panel. No AC adaptor.

☞ The '2010B has been replaced by the similar '1020C that covers 0.3-40 MHz.

**Verdict:** The MFJ-1020B, made in the United States, is uninspiring with its own telescopic antenna. However, it works very well when coupled to a short wire in lieu of the built-in telescopic antenna.

**The MFJ-1020B is a sleeper. With its built-in antenna, it is blah. Yet, as an active preselector affixed to a short wire, it becomes an excellent choice.**

*Prepared by Robert Sherwood, with George Heidelman, Chuck Rippel and David Zantow; also, Lawrence Magne, with Carl Silberman.*

# WHERE TO FIND IT: INDEX TO RADIOS & ANTENNAS

PASSPORT REPORTS evaluates nearly every digitally tuned receiver and many antennas on the market. Here's where they are found, with those that are new, forthcoming, revised, rebranded or retested in **bold**.

Comprehensive PASSPORT® Radio Database International White Papers® are available for the many popular premium receivers and outdoor antennas. Each RDI White Paper®—$6.95 in North America, $9.95 airmail elsewhere—contains virtually all our panel's findings and comments during hands-on testing, as well as laboratory measurements and what these mean to you. These unabridged reports are available from key world band dealers, or you can contact our 24-hour VISA/MC order channels (www.passband.com, autovoice +1 215/598-9018, fax +1 215/598 3794), or write us at PASSPORT RDI White Papers, Box 300, Penn's Park, PA 18943 USA.

📖 *Radio Database International White Paper®* available.

# What's On Tonight?

## *PASSPORT's Hour-by-Hour Guide to World Band Shows*

There are few commercial stations on world band, so most are free from market pressures and rigid formats. That means there's an awful lot of unusual and creative programs. To find them, here is an hour-by-hour selection from all over. For best bets, look for icons:

■ Station superior, most shows excellent

● Show worth hearing

Some stations provide schedules, others don't. Yet, even among those that do, data isn't always credible or complete. To resolve this, PASSPORT monitors stations around the world, firsthand, to detail schedule activity throughout the year. Additionally, to be as useful as possible, PASSPORT's schedules consist not just of observed activity, but also that which we have creatively opined will appear well into the year ahead. This predictive material is based on decades of experience, and is original from us. Although this is inherently less exact than real-time data, it has proven to be a real help over the years.

Primary frequencies are given for North America, Western Europe, East Asia and Australasia, plus the Middle East, Southern Africa and Southeast Asia. If you want secondary and seasonal channels, or frequencies for other parts of the world, check out "Worldwide Broadcasts in English" and the Blue Pages.

To eliminate confusion, World Time and World Day are used—both are explained in "Compleat Idiot's Guide to Getting Started" and the glossary. Seasons are those in the Northern Hemisphere ("summer" July, etc.; "winter" January, etc.).

**A teacher has her kindergarten students pose for a class photo before a Taipei shrine.**  T. Ohtake

## 0000–0559
## North America—Evening Prime Time
## Europe & Mideast—Early Morning
## Australasia & East Asia—Midday and Afternoon

### 00:00

■**BBC World Service for the Americas.** Tuesday through Saturday winter (weekday evenings in the Americas), opens with five minutes of *news*. Next comes the long-running *Outlook*, and the hour is rounded off with a 15-minute feature (very much a mixed bag). Best of the weekend shows is Sunday's ●*Play of the Week* (world theater at its best), and Monday's replacements are *World Briefing*, ●*Sports Roundup* and *The World Today*. Summer, starts with five minutes of *news*, then Tuesday through Saturday there's a series of arts programs. The second half hour is given over to popular music—try ●*Charlie Gillett* (world music, Tuesday) and the eclectic ●*John Peel* (Friday). Weekends, there's the final part of Sunday's ●*Play of the Week* (or *World Briefing* and ●*Sports Roundup*) followed by ●*Agenda*; replaced Monday by the same lineup as in winter. Continuous programming to North America and the Caribbean on 5975

kHz. Listeners in eastern North America can also try 12095 kHz, targeted at South America; a radio with synchronous selectable sideband helps reduce teletype interference. Farther west, try 11835 kHz in summer.

■**BBC World Service for East and Southeast Asia.** Starts with 20 minutes of *World Briefing*, followed by ●*Sports Roundup*. Except for Sunday, ●*World Business Report/Review* can then be heard on the half-hour. The final 15-minute slot is taken by ●*Analysis* (Tuesday, Wednesday, Friday and Saturday), ●*From Our Own Correspondent* (Thursday) and ●*Letter from America* on Monday. The only 30-minute show is *Agenda* at 0030 Sunday. Audible in East Asia on 15280, 15360 and (till 0030) 17615 kHz; and in Southeast Asia on 3915 (to 0030), 6195, 7105 (to 0030) and 15360 kHz.

**Radio Bulgaria.** Winter only at this time. *News*, music and features. Tuesday through Saturday (weekday evenings in North America), the news is followed by *Events and*

**00:00–00:00**

The serene countryside of Ghinda, Eritrea, betrays decades of civil strife. Things have calmed down with the imposition of a ceasefire monitored by the UN, which also operates Radio UNMEE.

Mike Metras

*Developments*, replaced Sunday by *Views Behind the News* and Monday by the delightfully exotic ●*Folk Studio*. The next slot consists of weekly features. Take your pick from *Plaza/Walks and Talks* (Monday), *Magazine Economy* (Tuesday), *Arts and Artists* (Wednesday), *History Club* (Thursday), *The Way We Live* (Friday), *DX Programme* (Saturday) and *Answering Your Letters*, a listener-response show, on Sunday. Tuesday through Sunday, the broadcast ends with *Keyword Bulgaria*. Sixty minutes to eastern North America and Central America on 7400 and 9400 kHz. One hour earlier in summer.

**Radio Canada International.** Winter only at this time. Tuesday through Saturday (weekday evenings in North America), it's the final hour of the CBC domestic service news program ●*As It Happens*, which features international stories, Canadian news and general human interest features. Weekends, you can hear two of Canada's best radio shows—Sunday's ●*Quirks and Quarks* (science) and Monday's ●*Global Village* (world music), both from the CBC's domestic output. To North America on 5960, 9590 and 9755 kHz. One hour earlier in summer. For a separate year-round broadcast to Asia, see the next item.

**Radio Canada International.** Tuesday through Saturday, it's ●*The World At Six*; and a shortened version of ●*As It Happens*, both news-oriented programs. These are replaced Sunday by ●*Quirks and Quarks* (a science show) and Monday by *Tapestry*. One hour to Southeast Asia on 11895 kHz, and also heard in much of East Asia, especially during summer.

**Radio Japan.** *News*, then Tuesday through Saturday (weekday evenings local American date) it's *Japan and the World 44 Minutes* (an in-depth look at current trends and events in Japan and elsewhere). This is replaced Sunday by *Hello from Tokyo*, and Monday by *Weekend Square*. One hour to eastern North America on 6145 kHz via the powerful relay facilities of Radio Canada International in Sackville, New Brunswick. A separate 15-minute news bulletin for Southeast Asia is aired on 13650 and 17810 kHz.

**Radio Exterior de España ("Spanish National Radio").** *News*, then Tuesday through Saturday (local weekday evenings in the Americas) it's *Panorama*, which features a recording of popular Spanish music, a commentary or a report, a review of the Spanish press, and weather. The remainder of the program is a mixture of literature, science, music and general programming. Tuesday (Monday evening in North America), there's *Sports Spotlight* and *Cultural Encounters*, replaced Wednesday by *People of Today* and

*Entertainment in Spain*; Thursday brings *As Others See Us* and, biweekly, *The Natural World* or *Science Desk*; Friday has *Economic Report* and *Cultural Clippings*; and Saturday offers *Window on Spain* and *Review of the Arts*. The broadcast ends with a language course, *Spanish by Radio*, considered by many to be the best on the air. The Sunday lineup is *Hall of Fame* and *Gallery of Spanish Voices*, replaced Monday by *Window on Spain*, then a feature on Spanish music (well worth hearing) and *Radio Club*, a listener-response program. Sixty minutes to eastern North America winter on 6055 kHz, and summer on 6055 or 15385 kHz. Popular with many listeners.

**Radio for Peace International,** Costa Rica. Continues with a six-hour cyclical block of social-conscience and counterculture programming audible in Europe and the Americas on 15039 kHz.

**Radio Ukraine International.** Summer only at this time. Ample coverage of local issues, including news, sports, politics and culture. Worth hearing is ●*Music from Ukraine*, which fills most of the Monday (Sunday evening in the Americas) broadcast. Sixty minutes to Europe on 5905 kHz, to eastern North America on 12040 kHz, and to West Asia on 7320 kHz. One hour later in winter. Budget and technical limitations have reduced audibility of this station to only a fraction of what it used to be.

**Radio Australia.** *World News*, then a feature. Monday's offering—unusual, to say the least— is *Awaye*, a program dealing with indigenous affairs. This is replaced Tuesday by *Science Show* and Wednesday by *The National Interest* (topical events). Thursday's *Background Briefing* (investigative journalism) and Friday's historical *Hindsight* complete the weekday lineup. *Feedback* (a listener-response show) and *Country Breakfast* fill the Saturday slots, and Sunday's feature is *The Europeans*. Targeted at Asia and the Pacific on 9660, 12080, 15240, 15415, 17580, 17750 (from 0030), 17775, 17795 and 21740 kHz. In North America (best during summer) try 17580, 17795 and 21740 kHz; and in East Asia go for 15240 kHz. For Southeast Asia there's 15415, 17750 and 17775 kHz.

**Radio Prague,** Czech Republic. Summer only at this time; see 0100 for specifics. Thirty minutes to eastern North America and the Caribbean on 7345 and 11615 kHz. One hour later in winter.

**Voice of America.** The first 60 minutes of a two-hour broadcast to the Caribbean and Latin America which is aired Tuesday through Saturday (weekday evenings in the Americas). *News Now*, a rolling news format covering political, business and other developments. On 5995, 6130, 7405, 9455, 9775, 11695 and 13740 kHz. The final hour of a separate service to East and Southeast Asia and Australasia (see 2200) can be heard on 7215, 9770, 11760, 15185, 15290, 17735 and 17820 kHz.

**Radio Thailand.** *Newshour*. Thirty minutes to eastern and southern parts of Africa (who listens at this hour?), winter on 9680 kHz and summer on 9690 kHz.

**All India Radio.** The final 45 minutes of a much larger block of programming targeted at East and Southeast Asia, and heard well beyond. To East Asia on 9950, 11620 and 13605 kHz; and to Southeast Asia on 9705, 11620 and 13605 kHz.

**Radio Cairo,** Egypt. The final half hour of a 90-minute broadcast to eastern North America. *Arabic by Radio* can be heard on the hour, and there's a daily *news* bulletin at 0015. See 2300 for more specifics. Easy reception on 9900 kHz.

**Radio New Zealand International.** A friendly package of *news* and features sometimes replaced by live sports commentary. Part of a much longer broadcast for the South Pacific, but also heard in parts of North America (especially during summer) on 17675 kHz.

**WJIE,** Upton, Kentucky. Twenty-four hours of Christian music targeted at North America on 7490 kHz. For more religious broadcasting at this hour, try **WYFR-Family Radio** on 6085 and 9505 kHz, and **KTBN** on (winter) 7510 or (summer) 15590 kHz. For something a little more controversial, tune to Dr. Gene Scott's University Network, via **WWCR** on 5935 (or 13845) kHz or **KAIJ** on 5755 (or 13815) kHz. Traditionalist Catholic programming can be heard via **WEWN** on 5825 kHz.

## 00:00–01:00

**AFRTS Shortwave,** USA. Network news, live sports, music and features in the upper-sideband mode from the Armed Forces Radio & Television Service. Transmitted from modestly powered U.S. Navy stations around the globe. Try 4319, 5765, 6350, 6458.5, 10320, 12579, 12689.5 and 13362 kHz.

### 00:30

■**Radio Netherlands.** Opens with a feature, then Tuesday through Saturday (weekday evenings in North America) there's ●*Newsline* (current events). Take your pick from ●*EuroQuest* (Tuesday), ●*A Good Life* (Wednesday), *Dutch Horizons* (Thursday), ●*Research File* (Friday), and Saturday's award-winning ●*Documentary*. Weekend fare is a mixed bag, but ●*Aural Tapestry* on summer Mondays is a must for culture buffs The second of two hours to North America on 6165 and 9845 kHz.

**Radio Vilnius,** Lithuania. A half hour that's heavily geared to news and background reports about events in Lithuania. Of broader appeal is *Mailbag*, aired every other Sunday (Saturday evenings local American date). For some Lithuanian music, try the next evening, towards the end of the broadcast. To eastern North America winter on 7325 kHz and summer on 11690 kHz.

**Voice of the Islamic Republic of Iran.** A one-hour package of news, commentary and features with the accent heavily on Islam and Islamic culture. Not the lightest of programming, but an interesting alternative to what is heard from Western media (even if you disagree). One hour to eastern North America and Central America winter on 6015, 6065 and 6135 kHz, and summer on 9610 and 11970 kHz.

**Radio Thailand.** *Newshour*. Thirty minutes to central and eastern North America, winter on 13695 kHz and summer on 15395 kHz.

### 01:00

■**BBC World Service for the Americas.** Tuesday through Saturday winter (weekday evenings in the Americas), five minutes of

news are followed by a series of arts programs. The second half hour brings popular music, including Tuesday's ●*Charlie Gillett* (world music) and Friday's ●*John Peel*. The weekend lineup consists of *World Briefing*, ●*Sports Roundup* and current events. In summer, opens with five minutes of *news*, then it's some of the best of the BBC's output. The best double bill is undoubtedly Tuesday (Monday evening local American date), when ●*Health Matters* shares the stage with ●*Everywoman*. Also recommended are ●*Omnibus* (0130 Wednesday), *Discovery* and *Sports International* (Thursday), ●*One Planet* (0105 Friday), and *Science in Action* (0105 Saturday). On Sunday, 30 minutes of *The World Today* are followed by *Music Review*, and Monday there's five minutes of *news* and 55 minutes of *Wright Round the World*. Continuous programming to North America and the Caribbean on 5975 kHz, and to western North America and Central America winter on 9525 kHz, and summer on 11835 kHz. In parts of eastern North America, 12095 kHz (nominally to South America) is also audible; a radio with synchronous selectable sideband helps reduce teletype interference.

■**BBC World Service for East and Southeast Asia.** Monday through Saturday, there's five minutes of *World News*, replaced Sunday by a half hour of *The World Today*. Tuesday through Saturday at 0105, look for *Outlook*, one of the BBC's longest running shows (though not as good as it used to be). Monday, this gives way to *Talking Point* (a call-in show). On weekdays, the final 15 minutes carry ●*Off the Shelf*, serialized readings from the best of world literature. At the same time Saturday you can hear *Write On* (a listener-response program), and the religious *In Praise of God* can be heard at 0130 Sunday. Continuous to East Asia on 15280 and 15360 kHz, and to Southeast Asia on 6195 and 15360 kHz.

**Radio Canada International.** Summer only at this time. *News*, followed Tuesday through Saturday (weekday evenings local American date) by *Canada Today*. The Sunday opener is *Business Sense*, replaced Monday by a listener-response show, *The Mailbag*. On the half-hour, it's *Canada in the World* on Sunday and

# GRUNDIG The Ultimate in Digital Technology

High-quality headphones included.

## SATELLIT 800

The Satellit 800. In the history of shortwave receivers, no other manufacturer has maintained a continuously evolving series of high-end portable radios, decade after decade.

### Extensive frequency coverage.
• Long wave, AM-broadcast and Shortwave, 100-30,000 KHz, continuous.
• FM broadcast, 87-108 MHz.
• VHF aircraft band, 118-137 MHz.
• Multi-mode reception – AM, FM-stereo, Single Sideband USB/LSB and VHF aircraft band.

### The right complement of high-tech features.
• Three built-in bandwidths, using electronically switched IF filters: 6.0, 4.0, 2.3 KHz.
• Synchronous detector for improved quality of AM and shortwave broadcast signals, minimizes fading, distortion and adjacent frequency interference.
• Selectable AGC in fast and slow mode. Auto Backlight shutoff to conserve battery life. Low Battery Indicator.

### Engineered for the best possible reception.
• High Dynamic Range, allowing for detection of weak signals in the presence of strong signals.
• Excellent sensitivity and selectivity.

### Legendary Grundig audio.
• Outstanding audio quality, with separate bass and treble tone control.
• FM Stereo with headphones or external amplified stereo speakers.
• Includes high quality stereo headphones.
• Multiple audio outputs: line level output for recording, stereo headphone output.

### Information displayed the way it should be.
• Large, illuminated, informational LCD display of operational parameters, measuring a massive 6˝ x 3¹/₂˝, easy to read.
• An elegant, calibrated, analog signal strength meter, in the finest tradition.
• Digital frequency display to 100 Hertz accuracy on AM, SW and VHF aircraft bands. 50 Hz when SSB used.

### Traditional and high-tech tuning controls.
• A real tuning knob, like on traditional radios, but with ultra-precise digital tuning, with absolutely no audio muting when used.
• A modern, direct-frequency-entry keypad for instant frequency access, and push buttons for fixed-step tuning.

### Plenty of user programmable memory.
• 70 programmable memories, completely immune to loss due to power interruptions.
• Memory scan feature.

### Clocks and timers.
• Dual, 24 hour format clocks.
• Dual programmable timers.

### Antenna capabilities that really make sense.
• Built in telescopic antenna for use on all bands.
• External antenna connections for the addition of auxiliary antennas, e.g. professionally engineered shortwave antennas; long-wire shortwave antennas; specialized AM broadcast band antennas for enthusiasts of AM DX'ing; FM broadcast band antennas; VHF air band antennas.

### Power, dimensions, weight.
• Operation on six internal "D" cell batteries or the included 110V AC adapter (a 220V AC adapter is available upon request).
• Big dimensions and weight. A real radio. 20.5˝ L x 9.4˝ H x 8˝ W., 14.5 lb.

Suggested list price:  US $ 499.95

---

## Grundig's Most Powerful Portable...

This is a true high-performance receiver offering the best performance available in its class. You will hear international broadcasts from around the world on shortwave, including broadcasts and communications requiring SSB circuitry. Listen to shortwave on its built-in telescopic antenna or connect it your favorite external antenna. But do not think it is just for shortwave. Its superior sensitivity and selectivity make it the best choice for anyone needing superior AM and FM performance in weak-signal and fringe areas. Perfect for pulling in those distant, hard to get AM talk shows that are so popular today.

Dimensions: 7.75˝ L x 4.5˝ H x 1.5˝ W
Weight:   1 lb. 5 oz.
Suggested list price:  US $ 149.95

---

### Ham Radio Outlet Stores:  12 STORE BUYING POWER

| | | | |
|---|---|---|---|
| Phoenix, AZ | (602) 242-3515 | Denver, CO | (303) 745-7373 |
| Anaheim, CA | (714) 533-7373 | New Castle, DE | (302) 322-7092 |
| Burbank, CA | (818) 842-1786 | Atlanta, GA | (770) 263-0700 |
| Oakland, CA | (510) 534-5757 | Salem, NH | (603) 898-3750 |
| San Diego, CA | (858) 560-4900 | Portland, OR | (503) 598-0555 |
| Sunnyvale, CA | (408) 736-9496 | Woodbridge, VA | (703) 643-1063 |

*www.hamradio.com*

## 01:00–01:00

*Spotlight* on Monday. Sixty minutes to North, Central and South America on 5960, 13670, 15170 and 15305 kHz. One hour later in winter.

■**Deutsche Welle,** Germany. *News,* followed Tuesday through Saturday (weekday evenings in the Americas) by the comprehensive ●*NewsLink*—commentary, interviews, background reports and analysis. This is followed by ●*Insight* (analysis, Tuesday); ●*Man and Environment* (ecology, Wednesday); *Living in Germany* (Thursday), *Spotlight on Sport* (Friday), or Saturday's *German by Radio*. Sunday fare is *Talking Point* and ●*Inside Europe*, replaced Monday by *Religion and Society* and *Arts on the Air*. Forty-five minutes of very good reception in North America and the Caribbean, winter on 6040, 6145, 9640, 9700 and 9765 kHz; and summer on 6040, 9640, 11810 and 13720 kHz.

**Radio Slovakia International.** Wednesday through Saturday (Tuesday through Friday evenings in the Americas), *News* is followed by *Topical Issue* and a feature. These include Wednesday's *Business News* (and *Currency Update*), Friday's *Culture News* and Saturday's *Regional News.* Tuesday and Sunday, the news is followed by *Insight Central Europe*; and Monday's lineup is *Sunday Newsreel* and *Listeners' Tribune.* A friendly half hour to eastern North America and the Caribbean on 5930 and 6190 (or 7230) kHz, and to South America on 9440 kHz.

**Radio Budapest,** Hungary. Summer only at this time. *News* and features, most of which are broadcast on a non-regular basis. Thirty minutes to North America on 9560 kHz. One hour later in winter.

**Radio Prague,** Czech Republic. *News,* then Tuesday through Saturday (weekday evenings in the Americas), there's the in-depth *Newsview* and one or more features: *One on One* (informal interviews, Tuesday); *Witness* and *Talking Point* or *Central Europe Today* (Wednesday); *ABC of Czech* and either *Profile* or *Czechs in History* (Thursday); *Economics Report* (Friday); and *Magazine* ("the show that starts where the news ends") on Saturday. Winter, the Sunday *news* is followed by

*Spotlight* (visits to different locations in the Czech Republic) and *Readings from Czech Literature* or *Saturday Music.* In summer, these are replaced by *Insight Central Europe.* Monday, there's *A Letter from Prague, The Arts* and *Mailbox.* Thirty minutes to eastern and central North America and the Caribbean on 6200 and 7345 kHz.

**Radio Exterior de España ("Spanish National Radio").** Repeat of the 0000 transmission. Sixty minutes to eastern North America winter on 6055 kHz, and summer on 6055 or 15385 kHz. One of the better broadcasts aired at this hour.

**RAI International—Radio Roma,** Italy. Actually starts at 0055. *News* and Italian music make up this 20-minute broadcast to North America on 9675 and 11800 kHz.

**Radio Japan.** *News,* then Tuesday through Saturday there's *Japan and the World 44 Minutes* (an in-depth look at trends and events in Japan and beyond). This is replaced Sunday by *Pop Joins the World,* and Monday by *Hello from Tokyo.* One hour to East Asia on 17845 kHz; to South Asia on 15325 kHz; to Southeast Asia on 11860 and 17810 kHz; to Australasia on 17685 kHz; to South America on 17835 kHz; and to the Mideast on 11880 and 17560 kHz. The broadcast on 17685 kHz may differ somewhat from the other transmissions, and may include alternative features.

**Radio for Peace International,** Costa Rica. Continues with a six-hour cyclical block of social-conscience and counterculture programming audible in Europe and the Americas on 15039 kHz.

**China Radio International.** Starts with *News,* followed Tuesday through Saturday (weekday evenings in the Americas) by special reports. The rest of the broadcast is devoted to features. Regulars include *People in the Know* (Tuesday), *Biz China* (Wednesday), *China Horizons* (Thursday), *Voices from Other Lands* (Friday), and *Life in China* on Saturday. Sunday's lineup includes *Global Review* and *Listeners' Garden* (has some interesting Chinese music) and the Monday menu offers *Report from Developing Countries* and *In the Spotlight.* One hour to North America on 9580 and 9790 kHz, via CRI's Cuban and Canadian relays.

**Voice of Vietnam.** A relay via the facilities of Radio Canada International. Begins with *news*, then there's *Commentary* or *Weekly Review*, followed by short features and some pleasant Vietnamese music (especially at weekends). Thirty minutes to eastern North America, with reception better to the south. On 6175 kHz. Repeated at 0230 on the same channel.

**Voice of Russia World Service.** Summer only at this hour, and the start of a four-hour block of programming for North America. *News*, then Tuesday through Saturday (weekday evenings in North America), there's *Commonwealth Update*, replaced Sunday by *News and Views*, and Monday by *Sunday Panorama* and *Russia: People and Events*. The second half-hour contains some interesting fare, with just about everyone's favorite being Tuesday's ●*Folk Box*. Other popular shows include Friday's ●*Music at Your Request* (may alternate with *Yours for the Asking* or ●*Music Around Us*), ●*Moscow Yesterday and Today* (Sunday), Wednesday's ●*Jazz Show*, and Saturday's evocative ●*Christian Message from Moscow*. Best for eastern North America are 9665, 9725 and 11825 kHz; farther west, use 12000 and 17595 kHz.

**Radio Habana Cuba.** The start of a two-hour cyclical broadcast to North America. Tuesday through Sunday (Monday through Saturday evenings in North America), the first half hour consists of international and Cuban *news* followed by *RHC's Viewpoint*. The next 30 minutes consist of a *news* bulletin and the sports-oriented *Time Out* (five minutes each) plus a feature: *Caribbean Outlook* (Tuesday and Friday), *DXers Unlimited* (Wednesday and Sunday), the *Mailbag Show* (Thursday) and *Weekly Review* (Saturday). Monday, the hour is split between *Weekly Review* and *Mailbag Show*. To eastern and central North America on 6000 and 9820 kHz. Also available to Europe on 11705 kHz upper sideband, though not all radios, unfortunately, can process such signals.

**Voice of Korea,** North Korea. For the time being, of curiosity value only. But with North

**Black Christians and animists in southern Sudan have been shortchanged by Omdurman's Arab-oriented Muslim rule.** churchworldservice.org

Korea showing signs of emerging from years of self-imposed isolation, this broadcasting dinosaur could provide some surprises. In the meantime, it's an hour of old-style communist programming. One hour to East Asia on 3560, 6195, 7140 and 9345 kHz; and to Central and South America on any three channels from 6520, 7580, 11735, 13760 and 15180 kHz.

**Radio Australia.** Part of a 24-hour service to Asia and the Pacific, but which can also be heard at this time in parts of North America (better to the west). Begins with world *news*, then Tuesday through Saturday there's *Asia Pacific* (regional current events), replaced Sunday by *Correspondents' Report*. Weekdays on the half-hour, there's yet more reporting: *Health Report* (Monday), *Law Report* (Tuesday), *Religion Report* (Wednesday) and *Media Report* (Thursday). Friday brings some relief, with *Sports Factor*. Weekend fare consists of Saturday's *Arts Talk* and Sunday's musical *Oz Sounds*. Targeted at Asia and the Pacific on 9660, 12080, 15240, 15415, 17580, 17750, 17775 (till 0130), 17795 and 21725 kHz. In North America (best during summer) try 17580 and 17795 kHz; in East Asia go for 15240 and 21725 kHz; and best for Southeast Asia are 15415, 17750 and 17775 kHz. Some channels may carry a separate sports service on winter Saturdays.

**Voice of Croatia.** Summer only at this time, and actually starts three minutes into a predominantly Croatian broadcast. Approxi-

## 01:00–02:00

World band succeeds in Ethiopia, as it allows the government and dissidents to reach the rural majority. Here in Lalibela, families live much as did their forebears centuries ago.

C. Grant

mately 15 minutes of news from and about Croatia. To eastern North America on 9925 kHz. One hour later in winter.

**HCJB—Voice of the Andes,** Ecuador. Tuesday through Saturday (weekday evenings in North America) there's *News* followed by *Studio 9*— including *Inside HCJB* (Tuesday), *Ham Radio Today* (Thursday), *Did you Hear?* (Wednesday and Friday), and the delightful ●*Música del Ecuador* on Saturday. On Sunday (Saturday evening in the Americas) it's *DX Partyline*, and Monday, *Musical Mailbag*. Religious programs make up the second half-hour Monday through Saturday, with the friendly *Saludos Amigos* occupying the Sunday slot. The first of five hours of continuous programming to North America on 9745 and 11960 kHz.

**Voice of America.** The second and final hour of a two-hour broadcast to the Caribbean and Latin America which is aired Tuesday through Saturday (weekday evenings in the Americas). *News Now*, a rolling news format covering political, business and other developments. On the half-hour, a program in "Special" (slow-speed) English is carried on 7405, 9775 and 13740 kHz; with mainstream programming continuing on 5995, 6130 and 9455 kHz.

**Radio Ukraine International.** Winter only at this time; see 0000 for specifics. Sixty minutes of informative programming targeted at Europe, eastern North America and West Asia. Poor reception in most areas due to limited transmitter availability. Try 7375 kHz for eastern North America, 7420 kHz for West Asia, and 9610 kHz in eastern Europe. One hour earlier in summer.

**Radio New Zealand International.** Continues with *news* and features sometimes replaced by live sports commentary. Part of a much longer broadcast for the South Pacific, but also heard in parts of North America (especially during summer) on 17675 kHz.

**Radio Tashkent,** Uzbekistan. *News* and features with a strong Uzbek flavor; some exotic music, too. A half hour to West and South Asia and the Mideast, occasionally heard in North America; winter on 5955, 5975 and 7215 kHz; and summer on 7190 and 9715 kHz.

**WJIE,** Upton, Kentucky. Continues with Christian music for North American listeners on 7490 kHz. Also with religious programs to North America at this hour are **WYFR-Family Radio** on 6065 and 9505 kHz, **WWCR** on 5935 (or 13845) kHz and **KTBN** on 7510 kHz. For traditionalist Catholic programming, tune to **WEWN** on 5825 kHz.

**AFRTS Shortwave,** USA. Network news, live sports, music and features in the upper-

sideband mode from the Armed Forces Radio & Television Service. Transmitted from modestly powered U.S. Navy stations around the globe. Try 4319, 5765, 6350, 6458.5, 10320, 12579, 12689.5 and 13362 kHz.

## 01:30

**Radio Austria International.** Summer only at this time. Tuesday through Saturday (weekday evenings in North America) there's a brief bulletin of *news*, then the informative ●*Report from Austria*. This is replaced Sunday by *Insight Central Europe* and Monday by *Network Europe*, both of which are joint productions with other European stations. Thirty minutes to eastern North America on 9870 kHz. One hour later in winter.

**Radio Sweden.** Tuesday through Saturday, it's *news* and features in *Sixty Degrees North*, concentrating heavily on Scandinavian topics. Several of the features rotate from week to week, but a few are fixtures. Tuesday's *SportScan* is replaced Wednesday by *Close Up* or an alternative feature, and Thursday by *Money Matters*. Friday's carousel is *Nordic Report*, *GreenScan* (the environment), *Heart Beat* (health), and *S-Files*, with *Weekly Review* filling the Saturday slot. The Sunday rotation is *Weekend*, *Spectrum*, *Sweden Today* and *Studio 49*, while Monday's offering is *In Touch with Stockholm* (a listener-response program) or the musical *Sounds Nordic*. Thirty minutes to South Asia and beyond, winter on 7430 kHz and summer on 13625 kHz.

**RTE Overseas,** Ireland. A half-hour information bulletin from Radio Telefís Éireann's domestic Radio 1. To Central America (and well heard in parts of North America) on 6155 kHz.

## 01:45

**Radio Tirana,** Albania. Tuesday through Sunday (Monday through Saturday evenings in North America) and summer only at this time. Approximately 15 minutes of *news* and commentary from this small Balkan country. To North America on 6115 and 7160 kHz. One hour later in winter.

## 02:00

■**BBC World Service for the Americas.** Tuesday through Saturday winter (weekday evenings in the Americas), starts with five minutes of *news*, then it's some of the best of the BBC's output. Pick of an excellent litter are ●*Health Matters* and ●*Everywoman* (Tuesday), ●*Omnibus* (0130 Wednesday), *Discovery* (science) and *Sports International* (Thursday), ●*One Planet* (0105 Friday), and *Science in Action* (0105 Saturday). On Sunday, 30 minutes of *The World Today* are followed by *Music Review*, and Monday there's five minutes of *news*, with *Wright Round the World* occupying the remainder of the hour. Summer, opens with 30 minutes of *The World Today*, then Tuesday through Saturday there's a quarter hour of ●*World Business Report* followed most days by ●*Analysis* (current events). The exception is Thursday's ●*From Our Own Correspondent*. Sunday's ●*World Business Review* and ●*Letter from America* are replaced Monday by ●*Assignment*. Continuous programming to North America and the Caribbean on 5975 kHz, and to western North America and Central America winter on 9525 kHz and summer on 11835 kHz. In parts of eastern North America, 12095 kHz (nominally to South America) is also audible; a radio with synchronous selectable sideband helps reduce teletype interference.

■**BBC World Service for the Mideast.** Summer only at this time. News and current events in *The World Today*. One hour weekdays but reduced to 30 minutes at weekends, when Saturday's *Global Business* and Sunday's ●*From Our Own Correspondent* complete the hour. On 9410 and 11760 kHz.

■**BBC World Service for East Asia.** Weekdays, the first half hour consists of *News* and an arts show, *Meridian*. In a brutal switch from highbrow to lowbrow, the next 30 minutes are a mixed bag of popular music and *Westway*, a soap. Weekends there's 30 minutes of *The World Today*, with Saturday's *Global Business* or Sunday's ●*From Our Own Correspondent* completing the hour. Continuous to East Asia on 15280 and 15360 kHz, and to Southeast Asia on 15360 kHz.

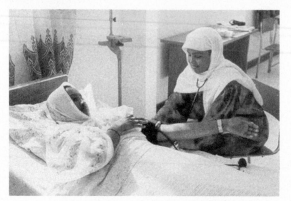

**A trainee nurse takes a patient's blood pressure at the Edna Aden Hospital in Hargeisa, Somalia.**

UN

**Radio Cairo,** Egypt. Repeat of the 2300 broadcast, and the first hour of a 90-minute potpourri of *news* and features about Egypt and the Arab world. Now uses a 500-kilowatt transmitter, so reception is considerably better than in the past. To North America on 9475 kHz.

**Radio Argentina al Exterior—RAE** Tuesday through Saturday only (local weekday evenings in the Americas). A freewheeling presentation of news, press review, short features and local Argentinian music. The press review is possibly unique, since the items are often translated on-air as the announcer reads the newspaper in the studio. Not the easiest station to tune, but popular with many of those who can hear it. Fifty-five minutes nominally to North America on 6060 and 11710 kHz, but tends to be best heard in the southern U.S. and the Caribbean. Sometimes pre-empted by live soccer commentary in Spanish.

**Radio Budapest,** Hungary. Winter only at this time. *News* and features, most of which are broadcast on a non-regular basis. Thirty minutes to North America on 9835 kHz. One hour earlier in summer.

**Wales Radio International.** This time summer Saturdays (Friday evenings American date) only. News, reports and music from the land of the castles. Thirty minutes to North America on 9795 kHz, and one hour later in winter.

**Radio Canada International.** *News*, followed Tuesday through Saturday (weekday evenings local American date) by *Canada Today* and then, on the half-hour, theme programs. On the remaining days, there's Sunday's *Business Sense* and *Canada in the World*, replaced Monday by *The Mailbag* (a listener-response show) and *Spotlight*. One hour winter to North America on 6040 and 11725 kHz; and year round to South Asia on 15150 (winter), 15260 (summer) and 17860 kHz.

■**Deutsche Welle,** Germany. *News*, then Tuesday through Saturday there's the excellent ●*NewsLink*—commentary, interviews, background reports and analysis. The final part of the broadcast consists of a feature. Choose from ●*Insight* (analysis, Tuesday); ●*Man and Environment* (ecology, Wednesday); *Living in Germany* (Thursday); *Spotlight on Sport* (Friday); and Saturday's *German by Radio*. The Sunday offerings are *Weekend Review* and *Mailbag*, replaced Monday by *Weekend Review* (second part) and ●*Marks and Markets*. Forty-five minutes nominally targeted at South Asia, but widely heard elsewhere. Winter on 7285, 9765, 11965 and 13605 kHz; and summer on 11965, 13720 and 15370 kHz.

**Radio Bulgaria.** Summer only at this time. Starts with *news*, then Tuesday through Saturday (weekday evenings in North America) there's *Events and Developments*, replaced Sunday by *Views Behind the News* and Monday by 15 minutes of Bulgarian exotica in ●*Folk Studio*. Additional features include *Answering Your Letters* (a listener-response show, Monday), *Plaza/Walks and Talks* (Tuesday), *Magazine Economy* (Wednesday). *Arts and Artists* (Thursday), *History Club* (Friday), *The Way We Live* (Saturday) and *DX Programme*, a Sunday show for radio enthusiasts. Wednesday through Monday, the broadcast ends with *Keyword Bulgaria*. Sixty minutes to eastern North America and Central America on 9400 and 11700 kHz. One hour later in winter.

**Radio Prague,** Czech Republic. Winter only at this time. Repeat of the 0100 broadcast (see

# A World of Listening from Sangean and Universal!

# SANGEAN

## ATS-909

The **ATS-909** is the flagship of the Sangean line. It packs features and performance into a very compact and stylish package. Coverage includes all long wave, medium wave and shortwave frequencies. FM and FM stereo to the headphone jack is also available. Shortwave performance is enhanced with a wide-narrow bandwidth switch and excellent single side band performance (SSB tuning to 40 Hz steps via fine tuning). Five tuning methods are featured: keypad entry, auto scan, manual up-down tuning, memory recall or manual knob tuning. The alphanumeric memory lets you store 306 presets (260 shortwave, 18 AM, 18 FM and 9 LW plus priority). The three event clock-timer displays even when the radio is tuning and has 42 world city zones stored. The large backlit LCD also features a signal strength and battery bar graph. The ATS-909 will display RDS on PL, PS and CT for station name and clock time in areas where this service is available. Also features a record jack and tone switch. Includes AC adapter, carry case, stereo ear buds, wave guide and Sangean ANT-60 roll-up antenna. 8½"x5½"x1½" 2 Lbs. Requires four AA cells (not supplied).

## ATS-818 and ATS-818ACS

Have you been waiting for a quality digital world band radio with a built-in cassette recorder? Now you have it in the exciting **Sangean ATS-818ACS**. This no-compromise receiver has full dual-conversion shortwave coverage (1.6 - 30 MHz) plus long wave, AM and FM (stereo to headphone jack). A BFO control is included for smooth S.S.B. or CW reception. A big LCD display with dial lamp shows: frequency (1 kHz on SW), 24 hour time, battery indicator and signal strength. The receiver features an RF gain, tone, wide-narrow selectivity, keypad entry, manual tuning knob, plus 54 memories (18 for shortwave). Includes: AC adapter, external antenna adapter and wave guide. The recorder has a built-in mic and auto-shutoff. Requires four D cells and three AA cells (not supplied). 11¼" x 7" x 2½" (296x192x68 mm).

The **Sangean ATS-818** is the same as above except with only 45 memories and no cassette recorder. The ATS-818 also includes the AC adapter. Both models are available in either black or titanium-silver.

## ATS-505P

The **Sangean ATS-505P** covers long wave 153-279 kHz, AM 520-1710, shortwave solid from 1711-29999 kHz plus FM 87.5-108 MHz. The backlit display can show either the frequency or the time (12/24 format). Tune via the tuning knob, Up-Down buttons, automatic tuning, keypad entry or from the 45 memories. The ATS-505P even tunes Morse code and single sideband (SSB) using a separate Clarify knob on the side of the radio. You may press in the tuning knob to select between normal and fine tuning (1 or 10 kHz on AM/LW and 1 or 5 kHz on SW). Other features include: FM stereo to headphone jack, 9/10 kHz AM step, beep on/off, dial lock, stereo-mono switch, alarm by radio or buzzer, auto-scan, auto memory, sleep-timer, tune LED, stereo-mono switch, tilt-stand, external antenna input and 6 VDC jack. With: AC adapter, ANT-60 wind-up antenna, case, earphones and wave guide. Titanium matte finish. 8.5"x5.3"x1.6" Requires four AA cells.

## ATS-404

The **Sangean ATS-404** is one of most attractive and capable radios ever offered in the under $100 price range. Coverage includes AM, FM and 14 shortwave bands, or continuous shortwave 2.3-26.1 MHz. Tune via the Up-Down buttons, auto tune, keypad entry or from the 45 memories. Other features include: FM stereo to headphone jack, 12/24 hour clock, low-battery indicator, dial lock, 9/10 kHz MW step, dial lamp, stereo-mono switch, alarm by radio or buzzer, sleep-timer, tune LED, tilt-stand and 6 VDC jack. With: case, earphones and wave guide. Silver-gray matte finish. 6½"x4"x1½" 10 oz. Requires four AA cells or optional ADP-808 AC adapter.

**universal radio inc.**

**Universal Radio, Inc.**
6830 Americana Pkwy.
Reynoldsburg, Ohio
43068-4113 U.S.A.

☎ 800 431-3939 Orders & Prices
☎ 614 866-4267 Information
→ 614 866-2339 FAX Line
✉ dx@universal-radio.com

The amazing **Sangean DT-300VW** digital radio fits in your shirt pocket yet receives: AM, FM, FM stereo, NOAA weather and VHF TV audio (channels 2 to 13).

**www.RFfun.com** or
**www.universal-radio.com**

• Visa • JCB • Prices and specs. are subject to change.
• Mastercard • Returns subject to a 15% restocking fee.
• Discover • Huge **free catalog** available on request.
**Visit our operational showroom near Columbus, Ohio**

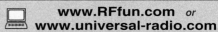

**02:00–02:00**

there for specifics), with *Insight Central Europe* occupying the Sunday slot. A half hour to North America on 6200 and 7345 kHz.

**HCJB—Voice of the Andes,** Ecuador. A mixed bag of religious programming, depending on the day of the week. Continuous to North America on 9745 and 11960 kHz.

**Voice of Croatia.** Winter only at this time, and actually starts around 0203. Approximately six minutes of news from and about Croatia. To eastern North America on 7280 (or 9925) kHz. One hour earlier in summer.

The Sumela Monastery in Trabzon, Turkey was built to be difficult to conquer. It should also be ideal for world band DXing.   G. Poppin

**Radio Taipei International,** Taiwan. Opens with 15 minutes of *News*, and weekdays closes with *Let's Learn Chinese*, which has a series of segments for beginning, intermediate and advanced learners. In between, there are either one or two features, depending on which day it is. Monday (Sunday evening in North America) listen to the pleasurable and exotic ●*Jade Bells and Bamboo Pipes* (Taiwanese music); Tuesday's pairing is *Culture Express* and *Trends*; Wednesday's slots are *Taiwan Today* and the esoterically titled *Confucius and Inspiration Beyond*; Thursday's double bill is *Discover Taiwan* and *New Music Lounge*; and Friday's combo brings together *Taipei Magazine* and *People*. These are replaced Saturday by *Groove Zone* and *Kaleidoscope*, and Sunday by *Great Wall Forum* and *Mailbag Time*. One hour to North and Central America on 5950, 9680 and 11740 kHz; and to Southeast Asia on 15320 kHz. For a separate service to East Asia, see the next item.

**Radio Taipei International,** Taiwan. Like the broadcast for Southeast Asia and the Americas, opens with 15 minutes of *News*, and weekdays closes with *Let's Learn Chinese*. However, the features are different: *Taiwan Economic Journal* and *People* (Monday), ●*Jade Bells and Bamboo Pipes* (Tuesday), *New Music Lounge* and *Confucius and Inspiration Beyond* (Wednesday), *Taipei Magazine* and *Life Unusual* (Thursday), and Friday's *Taiwan Gourmet* and *Discover Taiwan*. Saturday's pairing of *Kaleidoscope* and *Mailbag Time* is replaced Sunday by *Great Wall Forum* and *Asia Pacific*. Sixty minutes to East Asia on 15465 kHz.

**Voice of Russia World Service.** Winter, the start of a four-hour block of programming to North America; summer, it's the beginning of the second hour. *News*, features and music to suit all tastes. Winter fare includes *Commonwealth Update* (0211 Tuesday through Saturday), replaced Sunday by *News and Views* and Monday by *Sunday Panorama*. The second half hour includes ●*Folk Box* (Tuesday), ●*Jazz Show* (Wednesday), ●*Music at Your Request* or ●*Music Around Us* (Friday), ●*Christian Message from Moscow* (Saturday), ●*Moscow Yesterday and Today* (Sunday) and *Timelines* (Monday). In summer, take your pick from *Moscow Mailbag*

(0211 Sunday, Monday and Thursday), *Newmarket* (business, same time Wednesday and Saturday), and *Science and Engineering* (0211 Tuesday and Friday). There's a news summary on the half-hour, then ●*Audio Book Club* (Saturday), *Songs from Russia* (Sunday), *This is Russia* (Monday), *Kaleidoscope* (Tuesday), *Musical Portraits from the Twentieth Century* and *Russia: People and Events* (Wednesday), ●*Moscow Yesterday and Today* (Thursday) or Friday's *Russian by Radio*. Note that these days are World Time; locally in North America it will be the previous evening. For eastern North America winter, tune to 7180, 7250 and 9765 kHz; summer, it's 9665 and 9725 kHz. Listeners in western states should go for 12020 and 13665 kHz in winter; and 12000 and 17595 kHz in summer.

**Radio Habana Cuba.** The second half of a two-hour broadcast to eastern and central North America. Tuesday through Sunday (Monday through Saturday evenings in North America), opens with 10 minutes of international *news*. Next comes *Spotlight on the Americas* (Tuesday through Saturday) or Sunday's *The World of Stamps*. The final 30 minutes consists of news-oriented programming. The Monday slots are *From Havana* and ●*The Jazz Place* or *Breakthrough* (science). On 6000 and 9820 kHz. Also available to Europe on 11705 kHz upper sideband.

**Radio Station Belarus/Radio Minsk.** Monday, Wednesday and Friday through Sunday, summer only at this time. See 0300 for details. Thirty minutes to Europe on 5970 and 7210kHz. One hour later in winter. Sometimes audible in eastern North America.

**Radio Australia.** Continuous programming to Asia and the Pacific, but well heard in parts of North America (especially to the west). Begins with *World News*, then Monday through Friday it's *The World Today* (comprehensive coverage of world events). Weekends, there's Saturday's *Background Briefing* and *Earthbeat*, replaced Sunday by *Margaret Throsby* (interviews and music). Targeted at Asia and the Pacific on 9660, 12080, 15240, 15415, 15515, 17580, 17750 and 21725 kHz. Best heard in North America (especially during summer) on 15515 and 17580 kHz; in East Asia on 15240 and

21725 kHz; and in Southeast Asia on 15415 and 17750 kHz. Some of these channels carry a separate sports service on summer (mid-year) weekends and winter Saturdays.

**Radio for Peace International,** Costa Rica. Continues with a six-hour cyclical block of social-conscience and counterculture programming audible in Europe and the Americas on 7445 and 15039 kHz.

**Radio Korea International,** South Korea. Opens with *news* and commentary, followed Tuesday through Thursday (Monday through Wednesday evenings in the Americas) by *Seoul Calling*. Weekly features include *Echoes of Korean Music* and *Shortwave Feedback* (Monday), *Tales from Korea's Past* (Tuesday), *Korean Cultural Trails* (Wednesday), *Pulse of Korea* (Thursday), *From Us to You* (a listener-response program) and *Let's Learn Korean* (Friday), *Let's Sing Together* and *Korea Through Foreigners' Eyes* (Saturday), and Sunday's *Discovering Korea*, *Korean Literary Corner* and *Weekly News*. Sixty minutes to North America on 9560 and 15575 kHz.

**Voice of Korea,** North Korea. Repeat of the 0100 broadcast; see there for specifics. Abominably bad programs, but improvement may be on the way now that the country is beginning to accept outside help. One hour to South East Asia on any two channels from 9325, 11335, 11845 and 15230 kHz. Also audible in parts of East Asia on 4405 kHz.

**Radio Romania International.** *News*, commentary, press review and features on Romania. Regular spots include Wednesday's *Youth Club* (Tuesday evening, local American date), Thursday's *Romanian Musicians*, and Friday's *Listeners Letterbox* and ●*Skylark* (Romanian folk music). Fifty-five minutes to North America winter on 9550 and 11830 kHz, and summer on 9510 and 11940 kHz; to East Asia winter on 11740 and 15290 kHz, and summer on 11810 and 15105 kHz; and to Australasia winter on 11940 and 15370 kHz, and midyear on 15180 and 17815 kHz.

**WJIE,** Upton, Kentucky. Continues with Christian music for North American listeners on 7490 kHz. Also with religious broadcasts to North America at this hour are **WYFR-Family**

## 02:00–03:00

"Moscow Yesterday and Today" director Vladimir Dyomin. His Voice of Russia program was selected by PASSPORT 2002 as one of the best programs on the air.
VoR

**Radio** on 6065 and 9505 kHz, **WWCR** on 5935 kHz, **KAIJ** on 5755 kHz, and **KTBN** on 7510 kHz. Traditionalist Catholic programming can be heard via **WEWN** on 5825 kHz.

**AFRTS Shortwave,** USA. Network news, live sports, music and features in the upper-sideband mode from the Armed Forces Radio & Television Service. Transmitted from modestly powered U.S. Navy stations around the globe. Try 4319, 5765, 6350, 6458.5, 10320, 12579, 12689.5 and 13362 kHz.

### 02:30

**Radio Austria International.** Winter only at this time; see 0130 for specifics. Thirty minutes to eastern North America on 7325 kHz. One hour earlier in summer.

**Radio Sweden.** Tuesday through Saturday (weekday evenings in North America), it's *news* and features in *Sixty Degrees North*, with the accent heavily on Scandinavian topics. See 0330 for full program details. Sunday, there's *Spectrum* (the arts), *Weekend, Sweden Today* or *Studio 49*. A listener-response program, *In Touch with Stockholm*, is aired on the first Monday of each month, and replaced by *Sounds Nordic* on the remaining weeks. Thirty minutes to eastern North America on 9490 kHz.

**Radio Tirana,** Albania. Tuesday through Sunday (Monday through Saturday evenings in North America) and summer only at this time. Thirty minutes of Balkan news and music to North America on 6115 and 7160 kHz. One hour later during winter.

**Radio Budapest,** Hungary. Summer only at this time. *News* and features, not many of which are broadcast on a regular basis. Thirty minutes to North America on 9570 kHz. One hour later in winter.

**Voice of Vietnam.** Repeat of the 0100 broadcast; see there for specifics. A relay to eastern North America via the facilities of Radio Canada International on 6175 kHz. Reception is better to the south.

### 02:45

**Radio Tirana,** Albania. Tuesday through Sunday (Monday through Saturday local American date) and winter only at this time. Approximately 15 minutes of *news* and commentary from one of Europe's least known countries. To North America on 6115 and 7160 kHz. One hour earlier in summer.

**Vatican Radio.** Actually starts at 0250. Concentrates heavily, but not exclusively, on issues affecting Catholics around the world.

Twenty minutes to eastern North America on 7305 and 9605 kHz.

## 03:00

**■BBC World Service for the Americas.**
Winter, there's some newsy but interesting fare, with *World Briefing* and ●*Sports Roundup* filling the first half hour. These are followed Tuesday through Saturday (weekday evenings local American date) by 15 minutes of ●*World Business Report* and (most days) ●*Analysis* (current events). The exception is Thursday's ●*From Our Own Correspondent*. On the remaining days, there are features. Tuesday through Saturday summer, five minutes of *news* are followed by popular music—try ●*Charlie Gillet* (world music, Wednesday) and ●*John Peel* (eclectic, Thursday). There's another feature at 0330, and ●*Off the Shelf* (readings from the best of world literature) completes the hour. *World Briefing* and ●*Sports Roundup* fill the first 30 minutes on Sunday and Monday, and are followed by ●*Reporting Religion* and *Westway* (a soap), respectively. Continuous programming to North America and the Caribbean on 5975 kHz, and to western North America and Central America winter on 9525 kHz and summer on 11835 kHz.

**■BBC World Service for Eastern Europe and the Mideast.** Starts with *World Briefing* and ●*Sports Roundup*, then Monday through Saturday there's top-notch financial reporting in ●*World Business Report/Review*. The final 15-minute slot goes to ●*Analysis* (Tuesday, Wednesday, Friday and Saturday), *Write On* or *Waveguide* (Monday), and ●*From Our Own Correspondent* on Thursday. A full half hour of ●*Science in Action* airs at 0330 Sunday. To Eastern Europe on 6195 and (summer) 9410 kHz, and to the Mideast on 9410, 11760 and 11955 kHz.

**■BBC World Service for Southern Africa.**
Same as the service for the Mideast until 0330, then Monday through Friday it's *Network Africa*, a fast-moving breakfast show. This is replaced Saturday by *African Quiz* or *This Week and Africa*, and Sunday by *Postmark Africa*. The first 60 minutes of a 19-hour block

of programming. On 3255, 6005, 6190 and 7125 kHz.

**■BBC World Service for East and Southeast Asia.** Monday through Saturday, starts with five minutes of *news*. Best of the weekday features which follow are ●*One Planet* and *People and Places* (Monday), *Discovery* and *Essential Guide* (Tuesday), Wednesday's excellent combo of ●*Health Matters* and ●*Everywoman*, Thursday's ●*Focus on Faith* (0330) and Friday's *Sports International* and *Pick of the World*. On Saturday, the news is followed by 55 minutes of *Wright Round the World*. The Sunday lineup consists of *World Briefing*, ●*Sports Roundup* and *Science in Action*. Audible in East Asia on 15280, 15360 (to 0330), 17760 and 21660 kHz. For Southeast Asia there's only 15360 kHz until 0330.

**Voice of Croatia.** Summer only at this time, and actually starts several minutes into a predominantly Croatian broadcast. Approximately six minutes of news from and about Croatia. To western North America on 9925 kHz. One hour later in winter.

**Wales Radio International.** This time winter Saturdays (Friday evenings American date) only. News, interviews and music from the home of the eisteddfod. Thirty minutes to North America on 9735 kHz, and one hour earlier in summer.

**Radio Taipei International,** Taiwan. Opens with 15 minutes of *News*, and closes weekdays with *Let's Learn Chinese*. The remaining airtime is taken up by features. Monday (Sunday evening in North America) there's *Taiwan Economic Journal* followed by *People*; Tuesday brings ●*Jade Bells and Bamboo Pipes*; Wednesday's lineup is *New Music Lounge* and *Confucius and Inspiration Beyond*; Thursday's combo is *Taipei Magazine* and *Life Unusual*; and Friday's menu consists of *Taiwan Gourmet* and *Discover Taiwan*. The Saturday slots go to *Kaleidoscope* and *Mailbag Time*, replaced Sunday by *Great Wall Forum* and *Asia Pacific*. One hour to North and Central America on 5950 and 9680 kHz, and to Southeast Asia on 11875 and 15320 kHz.

**China Radio International.** Starts with *News,* then Tuesday through Saturday (weekday evenings in the Americas) there's in-depth reporting. The rest of the broadcast is devoted to features. Regular shows include *People in the Know* (Tuesday), *Biz China* (Wednesday), *China Horizons* (Thursday), *Voices from Other Lands* (Friday), and *Life in China* on Saturday. The Sunday lineup includes *Global Review* and *Listeners' Garden* (reports, music and Chinese language lessons), while Monday's menu is *Report from Developing Countries* and *In the Spotlight*. One hour to North America on 9690 kHz.

■**Deutsche Welle,** Germany. *News*, then Tuesday through Saturday (weekday evenings in North America) it's ●*NewsLink*—an impressive package of commentary, interviews, background reports and analysis. The final slot is a feature:●*Insight* (Tuesday), ●*Man and Environment* (Wednesday), *Living in Germany* (Thursday), *Spotlight on Sport* (Friday) and *German by Radio* on Saturday. The Sunday offerings are *Weekend Review* and ●*Spectrum* (science); while Monday brings *Weekend Review* (second part) and *Arts on the Air*. Forty-five minutes to North America and the Caribbean winter on 6020, 6045, 9640, 9700 and 11985 kHz; and summer on 9535, 9640, 11935 and 15105 kHz.

**Radio Ukraine International.** Summer only at this time, and a repeat of the 0000 broadcast; see there for specifics. Sixty minutes to northern Europe on 7150 kHz, and to eastern North America on 12040 kHz. One hour later in winter. Generally poor reception due to budget and technical limitations.

**Voice of America.** Three and a half hours (four at weekends) of continuous programming aimed at an African audience. Monday through Friday, there's the informative and entertaining ●*Daybreak Africa*, with the remaining airtime taken up by *News Now*—a mixed bag of sports, science, business and other news and features. Although beamed to Africa, this service is widely heard elsewhere, including parts of the United States. Try 6035 (winter), 6080, 6115 (summer), 7105, 7275 (summer), 7290, 7415 (winter), 9575 (winter) and 9885 kHz.

**Voice of Russia World Service.** Continuous programming to North America at this hour.

*News*, then winter it's a listener-response program, *Moscow Mailbag* (Monday, Thursday and Sunday), the business-oriented *Newmarket* (Wednesday and Saturday), or *Science and Engineering* (Tuesday and Friday). At 0331, there's ●*Audio Book Club* (Saturday), *This is Russia* (Monday), *Kaleidoscope* (Tuesday), *Musical Portraits from the Twentieth Century* and *Russia: People and Events* (Wednesday), ●*Moscow Yesterday and Today* (Thursday), *Russian by Radio* (Friday) and *Songs from Russia* on Sunday. Note that these days are World Time, so locally in North America it will be the previous evening. In summer, look for *News and Views* at 0311 Tuesday through Sunday, replaced Monday by *Sunday Panorama* and *Russia: People and Events*. After a brief news summary on the half-hour, there's Sunday's *Kaleidoscope*, Monday's ●*Audio Book Club*, and a changing roster of features on the remaining days. In eastern North America, use 7180 and 7250 kHz in winter, and 9665 and 11750 kHz in summer. In western North America, the situation is a little better—for winter, try 12020 and 13665 kHz; in summer, take your pick from 12000, 17565, 17650, 17660 and 17690 kHz.

**Radio Station Belarus/Radio Minsk.** Monday, Wednesday and Friday through Sunday, winter only at this time. Thirty minutes of local *news* and interviews, plus a little Belarusian music. All transmissions at this hour are repeats of broadcasts originally aired Tuesday or Thursday evenings. To Europe on 5970 and 7210 kHz, and one hour earlier in summer. Sometimes heard in eastern North America.

**XERMX—Radio México Internacional.** Summer only at this time. Tuesday through Saturday (weekday evenings in North America) there's an English summary of the Spanish-language *Antena Radio*, replaced Sunday by *Mailbox*, a listener-response show. Monday's programming is in Spanish. Thirty minutes to North America on 9705 and 11770 kHz. One hour later in winter.

**Radio Australia.** *World News*, then Monday through Friday there's *Regional Sports*, *Pacific Focus* and a 20-minute music feature—*Oz*

Music Show (Monday), *Music Deli* (music from different cultures, Tuesday), *Blacktracker* (indigenous music and stories, Wednesday), *Australian Country Style* (Thursday), and *Jazz Notes* (Friday). Saturday, the out-of-town *Rural Reporter* is paired with *In the Pipeline*, and Sunday's *Feedback* (a listener-response show) is followed by some cutting scientific commentary in ●*Ockham's Razor*. Continuous to Asia and the Pacific on 9660, 12080, 15240, 15415, 15515, 17580, 17750 and 21725 kHz. Also heard in North America (best in summer) on 15515 and 17580 kHz. In East Asia, tune to 15240 or 21725 kHz; for Southeast Asia, there's 15415 and 17750 kHz. Some of these channels carry a separate sports service at weekends.

**Radio Habana Cuba.** Repeat of the 0100 broadcast. To eastern and central North America on 6000 and 9820 kHz, and also available to Europe on 11705 kHz upper sideband.

**Radio Thailand.** *News Magazine*. Thirty minutes to western North America winter on 15460 kHz, and summer on 15395 kHz.

**HCJB—Voice of the Andes,** Ecuador. Predominantly religious programming at this hour. Try *Inspirational Classics* at 0300 Sunday (local Saturday evening in North America). Continuous to the United States and Canada on 9745 and (winter) 11960 kHz.

**Radio Prague,** Czech Republic. Summer only at this hour. *News*, then Tuesday through Saturday (weekday evenings in the Americas), there's the in-depth *Newsview* and one or two features: *One on One* (informal interviews, Tuesday); *Witness* and *Talking Point* or *Central Europe Today* (Wednesday); *ABC of Czech* and either *Profile* or *Czechs in History* (Thursday); *Economics Report* (Friday); and *Magazine* ("the show that starts where the news ends") in the Saturday slot. Sunday, the *news* is followed by *Spotlight* (a jaunt around the Czech Republic) and *Readings from Czech Literature* or *Saturday Music*. These are replaced Monday by *A Letter from Prague*, *The Arts* and *Mailbox*. A half hour to North America on 7345 and 9870 kHz. This is by far the best opportunity for listeners in western states. One hour later in winter.

Carcasses of MiG fighters, detritus from Somalia's 1977 invasion of Ethiopia.   M. Toal

**Radio Cairo,** Egypt. The final half-hour of a 90-minute broadcast to North America on 9475 kHz.

**Radio Bulgaria.** Winter only at this time; see 0200 for specifics. A distinctly Bulgarian potpourri of news, commentary, interviews and features, plus a fair amount of music. Not to be missed is the musical ●*Folk Studio* at 0310 Monday (Sunday evening local American date). Sixty minutes to eastern North America and Central America on 7400 and 9400 kHz. One hour earlier in summer.

**Radio Japan.** *News*, then weekdays there's *Asian Top News*. This is followed by a 35-minute feature. Choose between Monday's *Japan Musical Log*, Japanese language lessons (Tuesday and Thursday), *Japan Musical Treasure Box* (Wednesday), and *Music Beat* (Japanese popular music, Friday). *Weekend Square* fills the Saturday slot, and *Hello from Tokyo* is aired Sunday. Sixty minutes to Australasia on 21610 kHz, and to Central America on 17825 kHz.

**Radio New Zealand International.** Continues with *news* and features targeted at a regional audience. Part of a much longer transmission for the South Pacific, but also heard in parts of North America (especially during summer) on

## 03:00–04:00

17675 kHz. Often carries commentaries of local sporting events. Popular with many listeners.

**Voice of Korea,** North Korea. Just about the last of the old-time communist stations, with quaint terms like "Great Leader" and "Unrivaled Great Man" seemingly destined for immortality. Starts with *"news,"* with much of the remainder of the broadcast devoted to revering the late Kim Il Sung. Abominably bad programs, but worth the occasional listen just to hear how awful they are. One hour to East Asia on 3560, 6195, 7140 and 9345 kHz.

**Voice of Turkey.** Summer only at this time. *News*, followed by *Review of the Turkish Press* and features (some of them unusual) with a strong local flavor. Selections of Turkish popular and classical music complete the program. Fifty minutes to eastern North America on 9650 and 11655 kHz, and to the Mideast on 7270 kHz. One hour later during winter.

**WJIE,** Upton, Kentucky. Continues with Christian music for North American listeners on 7490 kHz. Also with religious programs to North America at this hour are **WYFR-Family Radio** on 6065 and 9505 kHz, **WWCR** on 5935 kHz, **KAIJ** on 5755 kHz and **KTBN** on 7510 kHz. For traditionalist Catholic fare, try **WEWN** on 5825 kHz.

**Radio for Peace International,** Costa Rica. Continues with a variety of counterculture and social-conscience features. Audible in Europe and the Americas on 7445 and 15039 kHz.

**AFRTS Shortwave,** USA. Network news, live sports, music and features in the upper-sideband mode from the Armed Forces Radio & Television Service. Transmitted from modestly powered U.S. Navy stations around the globe. Try 4319, 5765, 6350, 6458.5, 10320, 12579, 12689.5 and 13362 kHz.

### 03:30

**United Arab Emirates Radio,** Dubai. *News*, then a feature devoted to Arab and Islamic history or culture. Twenty minutes to North America on 12005, 13675 and 15400 kHz; heard best during the warm-weather months.

**Radio Sweden.** Tuesday through Saturday (weekday evenings local American date), it's *news* and features in *Sixty Degrees North*, concentrating heavily on Scandinavian topics. Several of the features rotate from week to week, but a few are fixtures. Tuesday's *SportScan* is replaced Wednesday by *Close Up* or an alternative feature, and Thursday by *Money Matters*. Friday's roundabout is *Nordic Report*, *GreenScan* (the environment), *Heart Beat* (health), and *S-Files*, and *Weekly Review* fills the Saturday slot. The Sunday rotation is *Weekend*, *Spectrum*, *Sweden Today* and *Studio 49*, while Monday's offering is *In Touch with Stockholm* (a listener-response program) or the musical *Sounds Nordic*. Thirty minutes to western North America on 9490 kHz.

**Radio Prague,** Czech Republic. Summer only at this time. Identical to the 0300 broadcast for North America; see there for specifics. Thirty minutes to the Mideast and South Asia on 11600 and 15620 kHz. One hour later in winter.

**Radio Budapest,** Hungary. This time winter only. *News* and features, most of which are broadcast on a non-regular basis. Thirty minutes to North America on 9835 kHz. One hour earlier in summer.

**Voice of Vietnam.** A relay via the facilities of Radio Canada International. Begins with *news*, then there's *Commentary* or *Weekly Review*, followed by short features and some pleasant Vietnamese music (particularly at weekends). A half hour to western North America on 6175 kHz.

**Radio Tirana,** Albania. Tuesday through Monday (Monday through Saturday evenings local American date) and winter only at this time. *News*, features and lively Albanian music. Thirty minutes to North America on 6115 and 7160 kHz. One hour earlier in summer.

### 04:00

■**BBC World Service for the Americas.** Tuesday through Saturday winter, five minutes of *news* are followed by popular music—best are ●*Charlie Gillet* (world music, Wednesday) and ●*John Peel* (eclectic, Thursday). There's another feature at 0330, and ●*Off the Shelf* (readings from the best of world literature) completes the hour. *World Briefing* and ●*Sports Roundup* fill the first 30 minutes on Sunday and Monday, and are followed by ●*Reporting Religion* and *Westway* (a soap), respectively. Monday through Friday summer (Sunday through Thursday evenings in North America), it's 50 minutes of news and current events in *The World Today*, with ●*Sports Roundup* closing the hour. On the remaining days, *The World Today* is cut to 30 minutes, and is followed by Saturday's ●*Assignment* (or another documentary), and Sunday's *Global Business* and ●*Sports Roundup*. Continuous programming to western North America and Central America on 5975, (winter) 6135 and (summer) 11835 kHz.

■**BBC World Service for Europe.** Identical to the service for the Americas, except for 0430 summer Saturdays, when ●*Weekend* replaces ●*Assignment*. Continuous to Europe and North Africa on 6195, 9410 and (summer) 12035 kHz.

■**BBC World Service for the Mideast.** Similar to the service for the Americas, but *In Praise of God* replaces *Global Business* at 0430 Sunday. Continuous programming on 11760 and 15575 kHz.

■**BBC World Service for Southern Africa.** Thirty minutes of ●*The World Today*, followed Monday through Friday by *Network Africa*. Weekends at 0430, look for Saturday's *Talkabout Africa* or Sunday's *African Perspective*. Continues on 3255, 6190, 7125 and (winter) 11765 kHz.

■**BBC World Service for East Asia.** Monday through Friday, it's 50 minutes of news and current events in *The World Today*, then ●*Sports Roundup* closes the hour. On the remaining days, *The World Today* is cut to 30 minutes, and is followed by Saturday's ●*Assignment* (or another documentary), and Sunday's ●*Omnibus* or light entertainment (including the unique ●*Brain of Britain* for part of the year). Continuous to East Asia on 15280, 17760 and 21660 kHz.

**Voice of Croatia.** Winter only at this time, and actually starts several minutes into a predominantly Croatian broadcast. Approximately six minutes of news from and about Croatia. To western North America on 6130 (or 7285) kHz. One hour earlier in summer.

**Radio Habana Cuba.** Repeat of the 0200 broadcast. To east and central North America on 6000 and 9820 kHz. Also available to Europe on 11705 kHz upper sideband.

**Flanders Radio International,** Belgium. Tuesday through Saturday (weekdays evenings in North America), the format is *News*, feature(s), *Soundbox*. Take your pick from *Focus on Europe* and *Sports* (Tuesday), *Green Society* (Wednesday), *The Arts* (Thursday and Saturday), *Around Town* (Thursday), *Economics* and *International Report* (Friday) and Saturday's *Tourism*. These are replaced Sunday by ●*Music from Flanders*, and Monday by *Radio World*, *Tourism*, *Brussels 1043* (a listener-response program) and *Soundbox*. A half hour to western North America winter on 11985 kHz, and summer on 15565 kHz.

**Radio Prague,** Czech Republic. Winter only at this time; see 0300 for specifics. Thirty minutes to North America on 7345 and 9435 kHz. By far the best opportunity for western states. One hour earlier in summer.

■**Radio France Internationale.** Weekdays only at this time. Starts with a bulletin of African *news* and an international newsflash. Next, there's a review of the French dailies, an in-depth look at events in Africa, the main news event of the day in France, and sports. Thirty information-packed minutes to East Africa on any two channels from 11910, 11995, 13610 and 15155 kHz. Heard well beyond the intended target area.

**Radio Ukraine International.** Winter only at this time, and a repeat of the 0100 broadcast. Ample coverage of local issues, including news, sports, politics and culture. Well worth a listen is ●*Music from Ukraine*, which fills most of the Monday (Sunday evening in the Americas) broadcast. Sixty minutes to Europe on 7285 and 9610 kHz; to eastern North America on 7375 kHz, and to West Asia on 7420 kHz. One hour earlier in summer. Budget and technical limitations have greatly reduced the audibility of this station.

## 04:00–04:30

**Among the casualties of Ethiopia's instability has been tourism. All but unknown are such magnificent sights as Tissisat Falls.**    M. Stockdale

**XERMX—Radio México Internacional.** Tuesday through Saturday winter (weekday evenings in North America) there's an English summary of the Spanish-language *Antena Radio*, replaced Sunday by a listener-response program, *Mailbag*. Monday's programming is in Spanish. The summer lineup consists of *Regional Roots and Rhythms* (Tuesday), *Mosaic of Mexico* (Wednesday), *Mailbox* (Thursday), *Magical Trip* (Friday), *Mirror of Mexico* (Saturday) and *DXperience* (a show for radio enthusiasts, Sunday). There are no programs on Monday. Thirty minutes to North America on 9705 and 11770 kHz.

**HCJB—Voice of the Andes,** Ecuador. Tuesday through Saturday (weekday evenings in North America), *News* is followed by *Studio 9*—including *Inside HCJB* (Tuesday), *Ham Radio Today* (Thursday), *Did You Hear?* (Wednesday and Friday), and the unique and enjoyable ●*Música del Ecuador* on Saturday. The second half-hour is given over exclusively to religious programs. On Sunday (Saturday evening in the Americas), the news is followed by *DX Partyline* and *Saludos Amigos*, and Monday by *Musical Mailbag* and *Mountain Meditations*. Continuous programming to North America on 9745 and 11960 kHz.

**Radio Australia.** *World News*, then Monday through Friday it's music and interviews with *Margaret Throsby*. Weekend fare consists of *Pacific Focus* followed by Saturday's *The Buzz* or Sunday's *Arts Talk*. Continuous to Asia and the Pacific on 9660, 12080, 15240, 15415, 15515, 17580, 17750 (from 0530) and 21725 kHz. Should also be audible in parts of North America (best during summer) on 15515 and 17580 kHz. In East Asia, choose between 15240 and 21725 kHz; for Southeast Asia, there's 15415 and 17750 kHz. Some channels carry separate sports programming at weekends.

■**Deutsche Welle, Germany.** *News*, followed Tuesday through Saturday by ●*NewsLink* and *Hallo Africa* (except Saturday, when there's *German by Radio*). The Sunday lineup is *Weekend Review* and ●*Inside Europe*, and the Monday menu features *Weekend Review* (second edition) and ●*Marks and Markets*. A 45-minute broadcast aimed primarily at eastern and southern Africa, but also heard in parts of the Mideast. Winter on 6180, 7195, 9565 and 9710 kHz; and summer on 6180, 7225, 12045 and 13690 kHz.

**Voice of America.** Directed to Africa and the Mideast, but widely heard elsewhere. *News Now*—a mixed bag of sports, science, business and other news and features. Weekdays on the half-hour, the African service leaves the mainstream programming and carries its own ●*Daybreak Africa*. To North Africa year round on 7170 kHz, and to the Mideast summer on 11965 kHz. The African service is available on 6035 (winter), 6080, 7265 and 7275 (summer), 7415 (winter), 9575, 9775 (winter) and 9885 kHz. Some of these are only available until 0430. Reception of some of these channels is also possible in North America.

**Radio Romania International.** Similar to the 0200 transmission (see there for specifics). Fifty-five minutes to North America winter on 9550 and 11830 kHz, and summer on 9510 and 11940; and to South Asia winter on 15335 and 17735 kHz, and summer on 17735 and 21480kHz.

**Voice of Turkey.** Winter only at this time. See 0300 for specifics. Fifty minutes to Europe and

North America on 6020 kHz, and to the Mideast on 7240 kHz. One hour earlier in summer.

**WJIE,** Upton, Kentucky. Continues with Christian music for North American listeners on 7490 kHz. Also with religious programs to North America at this hour are **WYFR-Family Radio** on 6065 and 9505 kHz, **WWCR** on 5935 kHz, **KAIJ** on 5755 kHz and **KTBN** on 7510 kHz. Traditionalist Catholic programming is available via **WEWN** on 5825 kHz.

**Kol Israel.** Summer only at this time. *News* for 15 minutes from Israel Radio's domestic network. To Europe and eastern North America on 9435 and 15640 kHz, and to Australasia on 17545 kHz. One hour later in winter.

**China Radio International.** Repeat of the 0300 broadcast; one hour to North America on 9730 and (summer only) 9560 kHz.

**Radio New Zealand International.** Continues with regional programming for the South Pacific. Part of a much longer broadcast, which is also heard in parts of North America (especially during summer) on 15340 or 17675 kHz. Sometimes carries commentaries of local sports events.

**Radio for Peace International,** Costa Rica. Part of a six-hour cyclical block of predominantly social-conscience and counterculture programming. Audible in Europe and the Americas on 7445 and 15039 kHz.

**Voice of Russia World Service.** Continues to North America at this hour. Tuesday through Sunday winter (Monday through Saturday evenings local American date), it's *News and Views*, replaced Monday by *Sunday Panorama* and *Russia: People and Events*. During the second half hour, the Sunday slot goes to *Kaleidoscope*, replaced Monday by ●*Audio Book Club*. The rest of the lineup is variable, and often chosen at short notice. The summer schedule has plenty of variety, and includes ●*Jazz Show* (0431 Monday), ●*Music at Your Request* or an alternative (same time Tuesday), the business-oriented *Newmarket* (0411 Thursday), *Science and Engineering* (same time Wednesday and Saturday), ●*Folk Box* (0431 Thursday), ●*Audio Book Club* (0431 Friday), *Moscow Mailbag* (0411 Tuesday and Friday) and the retrospective ●*Moscow Yesterday and Today* (0431 Sunday). In eastern North America, tune to 7125 and 7180 kHz in winter, and 9665 and 11750 kHz in summer. Best winter bets for the west coast are 12010, 12020, 13665, 15595 and 17595 kHz; in summer, choose from 12000, 17565, 17650, 17660 and 17690 kHz.

**AFRTS Shortwave,** USA. Network news, live sports, music and features in the upper-sideband mode from the Armed Forces Radio & Television Service. Transmitted from modestly powered U.S. Navy stations around the globe. Try 4319, 5765, 6350, 6458.5, 10320, 12579, 12689.5 and 13362 kHz.

## 04:30

■**Radio Netherlands.** Tuesday through Saturday (weekday evenings in North America), starts with ●*Newsline*, then a feature program. The lineup includes ●*Research File* (science, Tuesday); *Music 52-15* (eclectic, Wednesday); the excellent award-winning ●*Documentary* (Thursday); *Sound Fountain* (winter) or ●*Aural Tapestry* (summer) on Friday; and ●*A Good Life* (Saturday). The Sunday fare includes *Europe Unzipped* and *Insight*, and Monday there's *Sincerely Yours* and *Dutch Horizons*. One hour to western North America on 6165 and 9590 kHz.

**Radio Prague,** Czech Republic. Winter only at this time. *News*, then Tuesday through Saturday there's the in-depth *Newsview* and one or two features: *One on One* (informal interviews, Tuesday); *Witness* and *Talking Point* or *Central Europe Today* (Wednesday); *ABC of Czech* and either *Profile* or *Czechs in History* (Thursday); *Economics Report* (Friday); and *Magazine* in the Saturday slot. Sunday, the *news* is followed by *Spotlight* (visits to different locations in the Czech Republic) and *Readings from Czech Literature* or *Saturday Music*. These are replaced Monday by *A Letter from Prague*, *The Arts* and *Mailbox*. Thirty minutes to the Mideast and South Asia on 9865 and 11600 kHz. One hour earlier in summer.

## 05:00

**■BBC World Service for the Americas.**
Winter only at this time. Monday through
Friday (Sunday through Thursday evenings in
North America), it's 50 minutes of news and
current events in *The World Today*, with
●*Sports Roundup* closing the hour. On the
remaining days, *The World Today* is cut to 30
minutes, and is followed by Saturday's
●*Assignment* (or another documentary), and
Sunday's *Global Business* and ●*Sports
Roundup*. The final hour to western North
America and Central America on 6135 kHz.

**■BBC World Service for Europe.** Monday
through Friday, a full hour of news in ●*The
World Today*. Weekends, the second half hour
is replaced Saturday by ●*Weekend* (winter) or
*Arts in Action* (summer), and Sunday by
●*Reporting Religion* and ●*Letter from America*.
Continuous to Europe and North Africa on
6195, 9410 and (summer) 12095 kHz.

**■BBC World Service for the Mideast.** Same
as for Europe, except that the 0530 Sunday
slot is occupied by *Global Business*.

**■BBC World Service for Africa.** ●*The World
Today*, then weekdays on the half-hour there's
a continuation of *Network Africa*. Weekends,
the final 30 minutes are filled by Saturday's
*African Quiz* or *This Week and Africa*, and
Sunday's *Artbeat*. Continuous programming on
3255 (midyear), 6190, 11765 and (winter)
11940 kHz.

**■BBC World Service for East and Southeast
Asia and the Pacific.** Starts with 30 minutes
of ●*The World Today*. Thereafter, it's a mixed
bag of features. Favorites are ●*Off the Shelf*
(serialized readings from world literature,
0545 weekdays) and ●*Reporting Religion* and
●*Letter from America* (0130 and 0145 Sunday).
Continuous to East Asia on 15280 (till 0530),
15360, 17760 and 21660 kHz; and to Southeast Asia on 9740 and 15360 kHz. Heard in
Australasia on 15360 kHz.

**■Deutsche Welle,** Germany. Repeat of the
45-minute 0100 transmission to North America,
except that Sunday's *Inside Europe* is replaced
by ●*Marks and Markets*; and Monday's *Arts on
the Air* gives way to *Cool*. Winter on 5960,

6120, 9670 and 11795 kHz; and summer on
9670, 9785, and 11985 kHz. This slot is by far
the best for western North America.

**Radio Exterior de España ("Spanish
National Radio").** *News*, then Tuesday
through Saturday (local weekday evenings in
the Americas) it's *Panorama*, which features a
recording of popular Spanish music, a
commentary or a report, a review of the
Spanish press, and weather. The remainder of
the program is a mixture of literature, science,
music and general programming. Tuesday
(Monday evening in North America), there's
*Sports Spotlight* and *Cultural Encounters*;
Wednesday features *People of Today* and
*Entertainment in Spain*; Thursday brings *As
Others See Us* and, biweekly, *The Natural World*
or *Science Desk*; Friday has *Economic Report*
and *Cultural Clippings*; and Saturday offers
*Window on Spain* and *Review of the Arts*. A
language course, *Spanish by Radio*, closes the
hour. On the remaining days, you can listen to
Sunday's *Hall of Fame* and *Gallery of Spanish
Voices*; and Monday's *Visitors' Book*, a feature
on Spanish music and *Radio Club*. Sixty
minutes to the eastern and southern United
States on 6055 kHz.

**■Radio France Internationale.** Monday
through Friday only at this time. Similar to the
0400 broadcast, but without the international
newsflash. A half hour to East Africa (and
heard well beyond) on 13610 (winter), 15155
and (summer) 17800 kHz.

**Vatican Radio.** Summer only at this time.
Twenty minutes of programming oriented to
Catholics. To Europe on 4005, 5890 and 7250
kHz. One hour later in winter.

**Voice of Croatia.** Summer only at this time,
and actually starts about three minutes into a
predominantly Croatian broadcast. Approximately six minutes of news from and about
Croatia. To Australasia on 9470 kHz. One hour
later in winter.

**XERMX—Radio México Internacional.**
Tuesday through Saturday (weekday evenings
local American date) and winter only at this
time. Take your pick from *Regional Roots and
Rhythms* (Tuesday), *Mosaic of Mexico* (Wednesday), *Mailbox* (Thursday), *Magical Trip* (Friday),

*Mirror of Mexico* (Saturday) and Sunday's *DXperience*, a program for radio enthusiasts. The station is off the air on Monday. Thirty minutes to North America on 9705 and 11770 kHz. One hour earlier in summer.

**Radio Japan.** *News*, then Monday through Friday there's *Japan and the World 44 Minutes* (an in-depth look at current trends and events). This is replaced Saturday by *Hello from Tokyo* and Sunday by *Pop Joins the World*. One hour to Europe on 5975 and 7230 kHz; to East Asia on 11715, 11760 and 15195 kHz; to Southeast Asia on 17810 kHz; to Australasia on 21755 kHz; and to western North America on 6110 and (winter) 9835 or (summer) 13630 kHz.

**China Radio International.** This time winter only. Repeat of the 0300 broadcast; one hour to North America on 9560 kHz via a Canadian relay.

**HCJB—Voice of the Andes,** Ecuador. Predominantly religious programming at this hour. For a general audience, try Sunday's *Inspirational Classics* (Saturday night in North America). The final 60 minutes of five hours of continuous programming to North America on 9745 and 11960 kHz.

**Voice of America.** Continues with the morning broadcast to Africa and the Mideast. *News Now*—a mixed bag of sports, science, business and other news and features. To North Africa on 7170 and (winter only) 5995 and 11805 kHz; to the Mideast on 11825 (winter) or (summer) 11965 kHz; and to the rest of Africa on 5970, 6035, 6080, 7195 (summer), 7295 (winter), 9630 (summer) and 12080 kHz. Some of these channels are audible in parts of North America.

**Radio Habana Cuba.** The start of a two-hour broadcast for the East Coast and western North America. Tuesday through Sunday (Monday through Saturday evenings in North America), the first half hour consists of international and Cuban news followed by *RHC's Viewpoint*. The next 30 minutes consist of a news bulletin and the sports-oriented *Time Out* (five minutes each) plus a feature: *Caribbean Outlook* (Tuesday and Friday), *DXers Unlimited* (Wednesday and Sunday), the *Mailbag Show* (Thursday) and *Weekly Review* (Saturday).

Monday, the hour is split between *Weekly Review* and *Mailbag Show*. In the east, use 9550 kHz; in the west, 9820 kHz (also audible in parts of Australasia). Additionally available to Europe on 9830 kHz upper sideband.

**Voice of Nigeria.** Monday through Friday, opens with the lively *Wave Train* followed by *VON Scope*, a half hour of *news* and press comment. Pick of the weekend programs is ●*African Safari*, a musical journey around the African continent, which can be heard Saturdays at 0500. This is replaced Sunday by five minutes of *Reflections* and 25 minutes of music in *VON Link-Up*, with the second half-hour taken up by *News*. The first 60 minutes of a longer broadcast to West Africa (and heard in parts of North America, especially in winter) on 7255 kHz, and to North Africa and Europe on 15120 kHz.

**Radio New Zealand International.** Continues with regional programming for the South Pacific. Part of a much longer broadcast, which is also heard in parts of North America (especially during summer) on 11820 or 15340 kHz.

**Radio Australia.** *World News*, then Monday through Friday there's *Pacific Beat* (background reporting on events in the Pacific)—look for a sports bulletin at 0530. Weekends, the news is followed by *Pacific Focus* and Saturday's *Lingua Franca* and *Business Weekend* or Sunday's *Fine Music Australia*. Continuous to Asia and the Pacific on 9660, 12080, 15240, 15415, 15515, 17580, 17750 (from 0530) and 21725 kHz. In North America (best during summer) try 15515 and 17580 kHz. Best for East Asia are 15240 and 21725 kHz; in Southeast Asia use 15415 or 17750 kHz. Some channels carry alternative sports programming at weekends.

**Voice of Russia World Service.** Winter, the *news* is followed by a wide variety of programs. These include *Jazz Show* (0531 Monday), ●*Music at Your Request* or an alternative (same time Tuesday), the business-oriented *Newmarket* (0511 Thursday), *Science and Engineering* (same time Wednesday and Saturday), ●*Folk Box* (0531 Thursday), ●*Audio Book Club* (0531 Friday), *Moscow Mailbag*

**05:00–06:00**

(0511 Tuesday and Friday), and the retrospective ●*Moscow Yesterday and Today* (0531 Sunday). Note that these days are World Time; locally in North America it will be the previous evening. Tuesday through Saturday summer, there's *Focus on Asia and the Pacific*, replaced Sunday by *Science and Engineering* and Monday by *Moscow Mailbag*. On the half-hour, look for *This is Russia* (Wednesday and Friday), ●*Audio Book Club* (Sunday), ●*Moscow Yesterday and Today* (Thursday), ●*Christian Message from Moscow* (Saturday) and *Russian by Radio* Monday and Wednesday. Winter only to eastern North America on 7125 and 7180 kHz, and to western parts on 12010, 12020, 15595 and 17595 kHz. Available summer to Australasia on 17635, 17685, 17795 (also heard in Southeast Asia) and 21790 kHz.

**Radio for Peace International,** Costa Rica. Continues with a six-hour cyclical block of social-conscience and counterculture programming. Audible in Europe and the Americas on 7445 kHz.

**Kol Israel.** Winter only at this time. *News* for 15 minutes from Israel Radio's domestic network. To Europe and eastern North America on any two channels from 6280, 7475, 9435 and 11605 kHz, and to Australasia on 15640 or 17600 kHz. One hour earlier in summer.

**WJIE,** Upton, Kentucky. Continues with Christian music for North American listeners on 7490 kHz. Also with religious programs to North America at this hour are **WYFR-Family Radio** on 5985 kHz, **WWCR** on 5935 kHz, **KAIJ** on 5755 kHz and **KTBN** on 7510 kHz. For traditionalist Catholic programming, tune to **WEWN** on 5825 kHz.

**AFRTS Shortwave,** USA. Network news, live sports, music and features in the upper-sideband mode from the Armed Forces Radio & Television Service. Transmitted from modestly powered U.S. Navy stations around the globe. Try 4319, 5765, 6350, 6458.5, 10320, 12579, 12689.5 and 13362 kHz.

## 05:30

**Radio Austria International.** Summer only at this time. Tuesday through Saturday, there's a brief bulletin of *news*, then the informative ●*Report from Austria*. The remaining days feature two European co-productions: Sunday's *Insight Central Europe* and Monday's *Network Europe*. Thirty minutes to Europe on 6155 and 13730 kHz, and to the Mideast on 17870 kHz.

**United Arab Emirates Radio,** Dubai. See 0330 for program details. Twenty minutes to East Asia and Australasia on 15435, 17830 and 21700 kHz. Frequencies tend to vary a little.

**Radio Thailand.** Thirty minutes of *news* and short features relayed from one of the station's domestic services. To Europe winter on 13780 kHz, and summer on 21795 kHz.

Officials of Tibet's Xizang People's Broadcasting Station visit with representatives of Tecsun and Grundig, which manufacture and distribute world band portables and portatops.

E.A. Hozour

**0600–1159
Australasia & East Asia—Evening Prime Time
Western North America—Late Evening
Europe & Mideast—Morning and Midday**

## 06:00

■**BBC World Service for Europe.** Monday through Friday winter, a full hour of *The World Today* (news and current events). Weekends, it's reduced to 30 minutes and followed by Saturday's ●*People and Politics* or Sunday's ●*Agenda*. Summer weekdays, you can hear 20 minutes of *World Briefing* followed by ●*Sports Roundup*, ●*World Business Report* and ●*Analysis* (replaced Monday by ●*Letter from America* and Thursday by ●*From Our Own Correspondent*). Saturday and Sunday, the first half hour is the same as during the week, with the final 30 minutes being filled with the same features as winter. Continuous to Europe and North Africa on 6195, 9410, 12095 and (summer) 15485 kHz.

■**BBC World Service for Eastern Europe and the Mideast.** Tuesday through Saturday, starts with *News*, then the popular ●*Outlook* (except Monday, when there's *Talking Point*, a call-in show). Weekdays, the final 15 minutes are filled by ●*Off the Shelf* (readings from the best of world literature). The Saturday slot goes to *Write On* or *Waveguide*, and Sunday's lineup is *World Briefing*, ●*Sports Roundup* and ●*Agenda* (current events). Continues on 11760, 15565 and 15575 kHz.

■**BBC World Service for Southern Africa.** Identical to the service for the Mideast at this hour. Continuous programming on 6190, 11765 and 11940 kHz.

■**BBC World Service for East and Southeast Asia and the Pacific.** Five minutes of *news*, then Monday through Friday there's an arts show, *Meridian*. The next half hour consists mostly of a mixed bag of music and light entertainment. Exceptions are winter Thursdays (●*Omnibus*) and summer Mondays (●*Omnibus* and *Composer of the Month*). Weekends, starts with *World Briefing* and ●*Sports Roundup*, then it's either Saturday's

●*People and Politics* or Sunday's *Westway* (a soap). Continuous to East Asia on 15360, 17760 and 21660 kHz; to Southeast Asia on 9740 and 15360 kHz; and to Australasia on 15360 kHz.

■**Deutsche Welle, Germany.** Repeat of the 0400 broadcast. Forty-five minutes to West Africa (and often heard in Europe), winter on 7225, 9565 and 11785 kHz; and summer on 11925, 13790 and 17860 kHz. The same programs also form part of a separate one hour broadcast to Europe on 6140 kHz. The bonus for Europeans is an extra 15-minute feature: *Business German* (Monday), *People in Europe* (Tuesday), *German by Radio* (Wednesday), ●*Insight* (Thursday), ●*Man and Environment* (Friday), *Women on the Move* or *Development Forum* (Saturday) and Sunday's *Around Germany*.

**Radio Habana Cuba.** The second half of a two-hour broadcast for the East Coast and western North America. Tuesday through Sunday (Monday through Saturday evenings in North America), opens with 10 minutes of international news. Next comes *Spotlight on the Americas* (Tuesday through Saturday) or Sunday's *The World of Stamps*. The final 30 minutes consists of news-oriented programming. The Monday slots are *From Havana* and ●*The Jazz Place* or *Breakthrough* (science). Tune to 9550 kHz in the east, and 9820 kHz out west. Also available to Europe on 9830 kHz upper sideband. Listeners in Australasia can try 9820 kHz, as it's also beamed their way.

**Radio Japan.** *News*, then weekdays there's *Asian Top News*. This is followed by a 35-minute feature: *Japan Music Log* (Monday), Japanese language lessons (Tuesday and Thursday), *Japan Musical Treasure Box* (Wednesday), and *Music Beat* (Japanese popular music, Friday). On the remaining days, *Pop Joins the World* fills the Saturday slot and *Weekend Square* is aired on Sunday. One hour to Europe on 7230 kHz;

to East Asia on 15195 kHz; to Southeast Asia on 11740 kHz; to Australasia on 21755 kHz; to western North America on (winter) 9835 or (summer) 13630 kHz; and to Hawaii and Central America on 17870 kHz. This last broadcast may differ somewhat from the other transmissions, and may include alternative features.

**Voice of Croatia.** Winter only at this time, and actually starts around 0603. Approximately six minutes of news from and about Croatia. To Australasia on 9470 (or 11970) kHz. One hour earlier in summer.

■**Radio France Internationale.** Weekdays only at this time. Similar to the 0400 broadcast (see there for specifics), but includes a report on the day's main international story. A half hour to East Africa on two or more channels from 11710, 15155 and 17800 kHz.

**Technicians prepare to perform preventive maintenance on IBB antennas at Biblis, Germany.** A. Mujunen

**Voice of America.** Final segment of the transmission to Africa and the Mideast. Monday through Friday, the mainstream African service carries just 30 minutes of ●*Daybreak Africa*, with other channels carrying a full hour of *News Now*—a mixed bag of sports, science, business and other news and features. Weekend programming is the same to all areas—60 minutes of *News Now*. To North Africa on 5995 (winter), 7170, 9680 (summer) and 11805 kHz; to the Mideast on 11825 (winter) or (summer) 11965 kHz; and to mainstream Africa on 5970, 6035, 6080, 7195 (summer), 7285 (winter), 9630 (summer), 11950 (winter), 11995 (summer), 12080 and (winter) 15600 kHz. Some of these channels are audible in North America.

**Radio Australia.** Opens with *News*, then the weekday lineup is *Regional Sports*, *Pacific Focus* and a 20-minute feature—*Oz Music Show* (Monday), *Music Deli* (music from different cultures, Tuesday), *Blacktracker* (indigenous music and stories, Wednesday), *Australian Country Style* (Thursday), and *Jazz Notes* (Friday). Saturday's pairing is *Feedback* (a listener-response program) and *Oz Sounds*, replaced Sunday by *The Europeans*. Continuous to Asia and the Pacific on 9660, 12080, 15240, 15415, 15515, 17580, 17750 and 21725 kHz. Listeners in western North America should try 15515 and 17580 kHz. In East Asia, tune to 15240 or 21725 kHz; for Southeast Asia, use 15415 or 17750 kHz. Some channels carry an alternative sports program until 0700 on weekends (0800 midyear).

**Radio New Zealand International.** Continues with regional programming for the South Pacific. Part of a much longer broadcast, which is also heard in parts of North America (especially during summer) on 11820 or 15340 kHz.

**Voice of Russia World Service.** *News*, then winter it's *Focus on Asia and the Pacific* (Tuesday through Saturday), *Science and Engineering* (Sunday), and *Moscow Mailbag* (Monday). On the half-hour, look for *This is Russia* (Friday), ●*Audio Book Club* (Sunday), ●*Moscow Yesterday and Today* (Thursday), ●*Christian Message from Moscow* (Saturday) and *Russian by Radio* on Monday and Wednesday. In summer, the news is followed by *Science and Engineering* (Monday and Friday), the business-oriented *Newmarket* (Wednesday and Saturday), and a listener-response program, *Moscow Mailbag*, on the remaining days. The second half hour is mostly a combination of *Russia: People and Events*, ●*Russian Treasures* (a gem of a classical music program) and the religious *Daily Reflections*. Continuous programming to Australasia and Southeast Asia. Winter in Australasia (local summer in the Southern Hemisphere), tune to 15275, 15470, 17655, 17665 and 21790 kHz; midyear, go for 15490, 17635, 17685, 17795 and 21790 kHz. For Southeast Asia, there's 11770, 17655 and 21485 kHz in winter, and 15490 and 17795 kHz in summer.

**Radio for Peace International,** Costa Rica. Continues with counterculture and social-conscience programs. Audible in Europe and the Americas on 7445 kHz (may also use 15039 kHz).

**Vatican Radio.** Winter only at this time. Twenty minutes with a heavy Catholic slant. To Europe on 4005, 5890 and 7250 kHz. One hour earlier in summer.

**WJIE,** Upton, Kentucky. Continues with Christian music to North America on 7490 kHz. Also with religious programs for North American listeners at this hour are **WYFR-Family Radio** on 5985 kHz, **WWCR** on 5935 kHz, **KAIJ** on 5755 kHz, **KTBN** on 7510 kHz, and **WHRI-World Harvest Radio** on 5760 and 7315 kHz. Traditionalist Catholic fare is available on 5825 kHz.

**Voice of Malaysia.** *News*, followed Monday, Wednesday, Friday and Sunday by a two-minute Malayan language lesson (replaced by a local pop hit on Tuesday). The next 33 minutes are given over to *Hits All the Way*. Saturday, it's the 35-minute *Mailbag*. The hour is rounded off with a feature: *New Horizon* (Monday), *ASEAN Focus* (Tuesday), *Malaysia in Perspective* (Wednesday), *Personality* (Thursday), *News and Views* (Friday), and *Weekly Roundup* and *Current Affairs* on the weekend. The first hour of a 150-minute broadcast to Southeast Asia and Australasia on 6175, 9750 and 15295 kHz.

**HCJB—Voice of the Andes,** Ecuador. Summer only at this time. Monday through Friday it's *News* and *Studio 9*—including *Inside HCJB* (Monday), *Ham Radio Today* (Wednesday), *Did You Hear?* (Tuesday and Thursday), and the delightful ●*Música del Ecuador* on Friday. The second half-hour is solid religious programming. Weekend fare consists of Saturday's *DX Partyline* and *Saludos Amigos* and Sunday's *Musical Mailbag* and *Mountain Meditations*. The first of two hours to Europe on 11680 kHz. One hour later in winter.

**AFRTS Shortwave,** USA. Network news, live sports, music and features in the upper-sideband mode from the Armed Forces Radio & Television Service. Transmitted from modestly powered U.S. Navy stations around the globe. Try 4319, 5765, 6350, 6458.5, 10320, 12579, 12689.5 and 13362 kHz.

## 06:30

**Radio Austria International.** Winter only at this time; see 0530 for specifics. Thirty minutes to Europe on 6155 and 13730 kHz, and to the Mideast on 17870 kHz. One hour earlier in summer.

## 06:40

**Radio Romania International.** Actually starts at 0636. A 17-minute broadcast to western Europe winter on 7145, 9510, 9570, 11790 and 11940 kHz; and summer on 7105, 9625, 9550 and 11775 kHz.

## 07:00

■**BBC World Service for Europe.** Winter, you can hear 20 minutes of *World Briefing* followed by ●*Sports Roundup*, then weekdays there's ●*World Business Report* and ●*Analysis* (replaced Monday by ●*Letter from America* and Thursday by ●*From Our Own Correspondent*). Weekends, these give way to Saturday's *Arts in Action* and Sunday's ●*Assignment* (or substitute documentary). Monday through Saturday summer, starts with *News*, then the long-running *Outlook* (except Monday, when there's

**07:00–07:00**

*Talking Point*, a call-in show). Weekdays, the final 15 minutes go to ●*Off the Shelf* (readings from the best of world literature); Saturday, the slot is filled by *Write On*. Sunday's lineup is *World Briefing*, ●*Sports Roundup* and ●*Assignment* (or an alternative documentary). Continuous to Europe and North Africa on 6195, 9410, 12095, 15485 and 15565 kHz.

■**BBC World Service for Eastern Europe and the Mideast.** Five minutes of *News*, then it's either the weekday *Meridian* (an arts program), Saturday's *The Edge* (a 110-minute youth show) or Sunday's *The Alternative* (popular music). Monday through Friday, the second half hour is a mixed bag of mostly popular music, replaced Sunday by ●*Assignment* or its temporary replacement. Continuous programming on 11760, 15565, 15575 and 17640 kHz.

Along the overflowing Shabelle River near the Somali village of Gojogojo, a boy watches villagers arrive by boat from neighboring Bulomamo.

Radhika Chalasani, UNICEF

■**BBC World Service for East and Southeast Asia and the Pacific.** Monday through Saturday, starts with five minutes of *news*, then it's all features. Best of the bunch are *Discovery* (science, 0705 Monday), Tuesday's pairing of ●*Health Matters* and ●*Everywoman*, Wednesday's ●*Focus on Faith* (0730) and Friday's ●*One Planet* (0705). The Sunday lineup consists of *World Briefing*, ●*Sports Roundup* and ●*Assignment* (or its temporary replacement). Continuous to East Asia on 15360, 17760 and 21660 kHz; to Southeast Asia on 9740 and 15360 kHz; and to Australasia on 15360 kHz.

■**Deutsche Welle, Germany.** An hour of hybrid programming for Europe. No news, just features—some of which are heard on shortwave at other hours, and some that are normally broadcast only on satellite and the internet. Monday's combo is ●*Spectrum* (science) and *Around Germany*; Tuesday, there's an international joint production, *Women on the Move* (or *Development Forum*) and ●*Insight*; Wednesday is trade oriented, with ●*Marks and Markets*, *Business Germany* and *People in Europe*; Thursday features *Arts on the Air* and ●*Great Performers*; Friday, there's *Cool* and *Focus on Folk*; Saturday, it's ●*Inside Europe*; and Sunday's presentation is *Concert Hour*. On 6140 kHz.

■**Radio France Internationale.** Starts with a bulletin of African *news*. Next, there's a review of the French dailies, an in-depth look at events in Africa, the main news event of the day in France, and sports. The broadcast ends with a 25-minute feature— *French Lesson*, *Crossroads*, *Voices*, *Rendez-Vous*, *World Tracks*, *Weekend* or *Club 9516* (a listener-response program). One hour to West Africa on 15605 kHz, via RFI's Gabon relay.

■**Flanders Radio International,** Belgium. Summer only at this time. Weekdays, starts with *News*, then one or more features, and closes with *Soundbox*. The lineup includes *The Arts* (Monday and Thursday), *Tourism* (Monday), *Focus on Europe* and *Sports* (Tuesday), *Green Society* (Wednesday), *Around Town* (Thursday), and *Economics* and *International Report* (Friday).These are replaced Saturday by ●*Music from Flanders*, and Sunday by *Radio*

# The Shortwave Store

A Wide Selection of Products, Great Pricing and Secure Online Shopping!

**GRUNDIG**

**SONY**

**MFJ**

**AOR**

**SANGEAN**

**ALPHA DELTA**

**VECTRONICS**

**Justice AM Antenna**

Improves AM Reception on
any portable or home stereo

**C. C. Radio** *plus*

The Best Radio for Long
Range AM Reception

**Versacorder**

Record up to 8 hours on a
single cassette! Built-in timer

## Visit us on the web or call toll-free for pricing.

**USA:** http://usa.shortwavestore.com - **Canada:** http://www.shortwavestore.com

AOR AR-7030PLUS

Sony SW7600GR

Grundig YB400 PE

Car Stereos with
Shortwave Reception.

Finally an **inexpensive** and **simple** way to improve your shortwave reception!

Order Part #LIM

Simply connect any random length of wire to the terminal and
connect the coax to your radio's antenna jack. No tuning
required! Lowers noise and provides up to 6dB of gain over a
random wire alone. Completely passive and weatherproof for
years of reliable service. Only $29.95 USD! See product
details and download the complete owner's manual on our
site at www.shortwavestore.com/lim

**The Shortwave Store**

1380 Hopkins St., Unit 10
Whitby, Ontario L1N 2C3

Toll-free: 1-888-426-1688
Tel: (905) 665-5466
Fax: (905) 665-5460
e-mail:questions@shortwavestore.com

**07:00–08:00**

**Marie Lamb is a jazz announcer at WAER-FM and a familiar voice on world band.**

James Scherzi

**AFRTS is a tough catch, but ideal for traveling Yanks.**

*World*, *Tourism*, *Brussels 1043* (a listener-response program) and *Soundbox*. A half hour to western Europe on 5985 kHz. One hour later in winter.

**Radio Prague,** Czech Republic. Summer only at this time. See 0800 for specifics. Thirty minutes to Europe on 9880 and 11600 kHz. One hour later in winter.

**Voice of Croatia.** Summer only at this time, and actually starts about three minutes into a predominantly Croatian broadcast. Approximately six minutes of news from and about Croatia. To Australasia on 13820 kHz. One hour later in winter.

**Radio Slovakia International.** Tuesday through Friday, *News* is followed by *Topical Issue* and a feature. These include Wednesday's *Business News* (and *Currency Update*), Friday's *Culture News* and Saturday's *Regional News*. Monday and Saturday, the news is followed by *Insight Central Europe*; and Monday's combo is *Sunday Newsreel* and *Listeners' Tribune*. A friendly half hour to Australasia on 9440 (summer), 15460, 17550 (or 11990) and (winter) 21705 kHz.

**Radio Australia.** *World News*, then Monday through Friday it's *Pacific Beat* (background reporting on events in the Pacific)—look for the latest sports news at 0730. *Asia Pacific* and *Business Report* are aired Saturday, with *Correspondents' Report* and *In Conversation* filling the Sunday slots. Continuous to Asia and the Pacific on 9660, 12080, 15240, 15415, 17580, 17750 and 21725 kHz. Listeners in western North America can try 15240 and 17580 kHz (best during summer), while East Asia is served by 15240 and 21725 kHz. For Southeast Asia, take your pick from 15415 and 17750 kHz.

**Voice of Malaysia.** Starts weekdays with 45 minutes of *Fascinating Malaysia*, replaced Saturday by *Malaysia Rama* and *Malaysia in Perspective*, and Sunday by *ASEAN Melody* and *Destination Malaysia*. Not much doubt about where the broadcast originates! The hour ends with a 15-minute feature. Continuous to Southeast Asia and Australasia on 6175, 9750 and 15295 kHz.

**Radio for Peace International,** Costa Rica. Continues with a six-hour cyclical block of social-conscience and counterculture programming. Audible in Europe and the Americas on 7445 kHz (may also use 15039 kHz).

**Voice of Russia World Service.** Continuous programming to Southeast Asia and Australasia. *News*, then a variety of features. The winter lineup includes *Science and Engineering* (Monday and Friday), the business-oriented *Newmarket* (Wednesday and Saturday), and a listener-response program, *Moscow Mailbag*, on the remaining days. The second half hour is mostly a combination of *Russia: People and Events*, ●*Russian Treasures* and the religious *Daily Reflections*. Summer, the news is followed by the informative ●*Update* on Tuesday, Thursday and Saturday. Other offerings include *Science and Engineering* (Wednesday), *Moscow Mailbag* (Friday) and Monday's masterpiece, ●*Music and Musicians*. On the half-hour, there's some of the Voice of Russia's best—●*Audio Book Club* (Wednesday), ●*Moscow Yesterday and Today* (Friday), *Songs from Russia* (Sunday), ●*Folk Box* (Tuesday) and *This is Russia* on Thursday. Mondays, it's a continuation of ●*Music and Musicians*. Well heard in Australasia winter (local summer) on 15275, 15470, 17655, 17665 and 21790 kHz; and midyear on 17495,

17525, 17635, 17675, 17685 and 17795 kHz. For Southeast Asia, there's 11770, 17655 and 21485 kHz in winter, and 15490, 17685 and 17795 kHz in summer.

**WJIE,** Upton, Kentucky. Continues with Christian music for North American listeners on 7490 kHz. Also with religious programs to North America at this hour are **WWCR** on 5935 kHz, **KAIJ** on 5755 kHz, **KTBN** on 7510 kHz, and **WHRI-World Harvest Radio** on 5745 kHz. For traditionalist Catholic programming, tune to **WEWN** on 5825 kHz.

**Radio New Zealand International.** Continues with regional programming for the South Pacific. Part of a much longer broadcast, which is also heard in parts of North America (especially during summer) on 9885 or 11675 kHz.

**Radio Taipei International,** Taiwan. Opens with 15 minutes of *News*, and weekdays closes with *Let's Learn Chinese*, which has a series of segments for beginning, intermediate and advanced learners. In between, there are either one or two features, depending on which day it is. Monday (Sunday evening in North America) it's the exotic ●*Jade Bells and Bamboo Pipes* (Taiwanese music); Tuesday's combo is *Culture Express* and *Trends*; Wednesday's slots are *Taiwan Today* and *Confucius and Inspiration Beyond*; Thursday's pairing is *Discover Taiwan* and *New Music Lounge*; and Friday brings together *Taipei Magazine* and *People*. These are replaced Saturday by *Groove Zone* and *Kaleidoscope*, and Sunday by *Great Wall Forum* and *Mailbag Time*. One hour to western North America and Central America on 5950 kHz.

**HCJB—Voice of the Andes,** Ecuador. Monday through Friday winter there's *News* and *Studio 9*, featuring *Inside HCJB* (Monday), *Ham Radio Today* (Wednesday), *Did You Hear?* (Tuesday and Thursday) and a long-time favorite, ●*Música del Ecuador* on Friday. These are replaced Saturday by *DX Partyline*, and Sunday by *Musical Mailbag*. The second half-hour is predominantly religious, though Saturday's *Saludos Amigos* and Sunday's *Mountain Meditations* are listener favorites. Summer programming is solidly religious To Europe

winter on 5965 kHz, and summer on 11680 kHz. The first hour of a separate block of programming—the first 30 minutes are identical to the winter lineup for Europe—airs to Australasia on 11755 kHz.

**AFRTS Shortwave,** USA. Network news, live sports, music and features in the upper-sideband mode from the Armed Forces Radio & Television Service. Transmitted from modestly powered U.S. Navy stations around the globe. Try 4319, 5765, 6350, 6458.5, 10320, 12579, 12689.5 and 13362 kHz.

## 07:30

**Swiss Radio International.** *Newsnet*—news and analysis of Swiss and world events. Look for lighter fare on Saturday, when the biweekly *Capital Letters* (a listener-response program) alternates with *Name Game* (first Saturday) and *Sounds Good* (music and interviews, third Saturday). A half hour to North and West Africa winter on 9885 and 13790 kHz, and summer on 15545 and 17685 kHz; also to southern Africa winter on 17665 kHz, and 21750 kHz midyear.

**KTWR-Trans World Radio,** Guam. The first half hour of a 90-minute evangelical broadcast targeted at Southeast Asia on 15200 (or 15510) kHz.

## 08:00

■**BBC World Service for Europe.** Monday through Saturday winter, starts with *News*, then the long-running *Outlook* (except Monday, when there's *Talking Point*, a call-in show). Weekdays, the final 15 minutes are given to ●*Off the Shelf* (readings from the best of world literature), replaced Saturday by *Write On*. Sunday's lineup is ●*From Our Own Correspondent* and *The Greenfield Collection* (classical music). Summer weekdays, opens with five minutes of *News*, then *Meridian* (an arts program). The second half hour is a mixed bag of popular music or *Westway* (a soap). Saturday has youth-oriented programming, and Sunday's lineup is the same as winter. Continuous to Europe and North Africa on 9410 (winter), 12095, 15485 and 15565 kHz.

**08:00–08:00**

With creative energy, chutzpah and lots of wire, the "Bosasso Relay Station" has been known to pick up Somalia's "Radio Galkayo" on 6985 kHz and retransmit it on 9615 kHz.

S. Voron

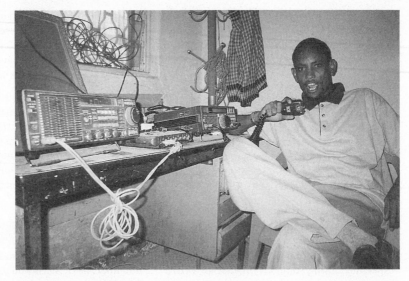

■**BBC World Service for Eastern Europe and the Mideast.** *News*, then weekdays there's an interesting collection of features: ●*One Planet* and *People and Places* (Monday), *Discovery* and *Essential Guide* (Tuesday), ●*Health Matters* and ●*Everywoman* (Wednesday), *Science View* and ●*Focus on Faith* (Thursday) and *Sports International* and *Pick of the World* on Friday. Saturday airs the final part of *The Edge* (a youth show), replaced Sunday by ●*From Our Own Correspondent* and *Arts in Action*. Continues on 15565, 15575 and 17640 kHz.

■**BBC World Service for East and Southeast Asia and the Pacific.** Starts with *news*, then weekdays, a feature: ●*Omnibus* (winter Mondays), alternative pop (Tuesday), *The Greenfield Collection* (classical music, Wednesday), jazz (Thursday), *Composer of the Month* (summer Fridays) and light entertainment on winter Fridays and summer Mondays. *World Learning* (an educational program) follows on the half-hour. The Saturday lineup is variable, but tends to have youth-oriented programming most of the year. Sunday spots are ●*From Our Own Correspondent* and *Arts in Action*. Continuous to East Asia on 15360, 17760 and 21660 kHz; to Southeast Asia on 9740 and 15360 kHz; and to Australasia on 15360 kHz.

■**Deutsche Welle, Germany.** A shortwave relay of Deutsche Welle's satellite service.

Monday, there's *Cool* and *Focus on Folk*; Tuesday's cultural combo is *Arts on the Air* and ●*Great Performers*; Wednesday's musical spots are *Classical Showcase* and *Hits* (or *Melody Time*); Thursday brings ●*Spectrum* (science), ●*Man and Environment* (ecology) and *Living in Germany*; Friday has *People in Europe*, *Around Germany*, *Business German* and *German History*; Saturday's pairing is ●*Weekend* and *Around Germany*; and Sunday there's an international joint production, *Women on the Move* (or *Development Forum*) and ●*Insight*. An hour of news-free programming for Europe on 6140 kHz.

**HCJB—Voice of the Andes,** Ecuador. Continuous programming (mostly religious) to Europe and Australasia. To Europe winter on 5965kHz, and to Australasia year round on 11755 kHz.

**Flanders Radio International,** Belgium. This time winter only. See 0700 for specifics. Thirty minutes to Europe on 5985, 13685 and 15195 kHz. One hour earlier in summer.

**Voice of Croatia.** Winter only at this time, and actually starts around 0803. Approximately six minutes of news from and about Croatia. To Australasia on 13820 kHz. One hour earlier in summer.

**Voice of Malaysia.** *News* and commentary, then *Golden Oldies*. The final half hour of a much longer transmission targeted at Southeast Asia and Australasia on 6175, 9750 and 15295 kHz.

**Radio Prague,** Czech Republic. Winter only at this time. *News,* then weekdays it's the in-depth *Newsview* and one or more features: *One on One* (informal interviews, Monday); *Witness* and *Talking Point* or *Central Europe Today* (Tuesday); *ABC of Czech* and either *Profile* or *Czechs in History* (Wednesday); *Economics Report* (Thursday); and *Magazine* ("the show that starts where the news ends") on Friday. Weekend fare consists of Saturday's *Insight Central Europe* and Sunday's *A Letter from Prague, The Arts* and *Mailbox.* Thirty minutes to Europe on 11600 and 15255 kHz. One hour earlier in summer.

**Radio Australia.** Part of a 24-hour service to Asia and the Pacific, but which can also be heard at this time throughout much of North America. Begins with a bulletin of *World News,* then Monday through Friday there's an in-depth look at current events in *PM.* Weekends, the news is followed by *Grandstand Wrap,* a roundup of the latest Australian sports action, with Saturday's *Earthbeat* or Sunday's *Innovations* filling the second half hour. On 5995, 9580, 9710, 12080, 13605, 15240, 15415, 17750 (from 0830) and 21725 kHz. Audible in parts of North America on 9580 and 15240 kHz. Best for East Asia is 21725 kHz, with 15415 and 17750 kHz the channels for Southeast Asia.

**WJIE,** Upton, Kentucky. Continues with Christian music to North America on 7490 kHz. Other U.S. religious broadcasters operating at this hour include **WWCR** on 5935 kHz, **KAIJ** on 5755 kHz, **KTBN** on 7510 kHz, and **WHRI-World Harvest Radio** on 5745 kHz. Traditionalist Catholic programming can be heard via **WEWN** on 5825 kHz.

**Voice of Russia World Service.** Continuous programming to Southeast Asia and Australasia. Winter, *News* is followed by ●*Update* on Tuesday, Thursday and Saturday. Other features include *Science and Engineering* (Wednesday), *Moscow Mailbag* (Friday) and Monday's outstanding ●*Music and Musicians* (classical music). On the half-hour, there's some of the Voice of Russia's best—●*Audio Book Club* (Wednesday), ●*Moscow Yesterday and Today* (Friday), ●*Folk Box* (Tuesday), *Songs from Russia* (Sunday), *Kaleidoscope* (Saturday), and Thursday's *This is Russia.* In summer, ●*Update* is only available on Wednesday and Friday. It is replaced Monday by *Science and Engineering,* Tuesday by *Focus on Asia,* Thursday by *Newmarket* and Saturday by *Moscow Mailbag.* Sunday's offering is the 45-minute ●*Music and Musicians*—a jewel among classical music shows. Choice pickings from the second half hour include ●*Moscow Yesterday and Today* (Monday), ●*Folk Box* (Thursday), ●*Jazz Show* (Friday) and Saturday's ●*Christian Message from Moscow.* For Australasia winter (local Oz summer), use 15275, 15470, 17495, 17525, 17655 and 17665 kHz; midyear, take your pick from 17495, 17525, 17635, 17675, 17685 and 17795 kHz. In Southeast Asia, there's 11770, 17655 and 21485 (or 21810) kHz in winter, and 15490, 17495, 17675, 17685 and 17795 kHz in summer.

**KTWR-Trans World Radio,** Guam. Continuation of evangelical programming to Southeast Asia on 15200 (or 15510) kHz. At 0815, a separate 75-minute block to Australasia begins on 15330 kHz.

**Radio New Zealand International.** Continues with regional programming for the South Pacific. Part of a much longer broadcast, which is also heard in parts of North America (especially during summer) on 9885 or 11675 kHz.

**Radio Korea International,** South Korea. Opens with *news* and commentary, followed Monday through Wednesday by *Seoul Calling.* Weekly features include *Echoes of Korean Music* and *Shortwave Feedback* (Sunday), *Tales from Korea's Past* (Monday), *Korean Cultural Trails* (Tuesday), *Pulse of Korea* (Wednesday), *From Us to You* (a listener-response program) and *Let's Learn Korean* (Thursday), *Let's Sing Together* and *Korea Through Foreigners' Eyes* (Friday), and Saturday's *Discovering Korea, Korean Literary Corner* and *Weekly News Focus.* Sixty minutes to Europe on 7550 and 13670 kHz, and to Asia and Australasia on 9570 kHz.

**AFRTS Shortwave,** USA. Network news, live sports, music and features in the upper-

**08:00–09:00**

sideband mode from the Armed Forces Radio & Television Service. Transmitted from modestly powered U.S. Navy stations around the globe. Try 4319, 5765, 6350, 6458.5, 10320, 12579, 12689.5 and 13362 kHz.

## 08:10

**Voice of Armenia.** Summer Sundays only. Twenty minutes of Armenian *news* and culture. To Europe on 15270 kHz, and to the Mideast on 4810 kHz. One hour later in winter.

## 08:30

**Swiss Radio International.** *Newsnet*—news and background reports on world and Swiss events. Look for some lighter fare on Saturdays, when *Capital Letters* (a biweekly listener-response program) alternates with *Name Game* (first Saturday) and *Sounds Good* (third Saturday). To southern Africa on 21770 kHz.

## 09:00

■**BBC World Service for Europe.** Monday through Saturday winter, opens with five minutes of *News*, then weekdays it's *Meridian* (an arts show). The second half hour is a mixed bag of popular music or *Westway* (a soap). Saturday has youth-oriented programming, replaced Sunday by *World Briefing*, ●*Reporting Religion* and *In Praise of God*. Summer (except Sunday), starts with *News*, then weekdays there's an interesting collection of features: ●*One Planet* and *People and Places* (Monday), *Discovery* and *Essential Guide* (Tuesday), ●*Health Matters* and ●*Everywoman* (Wednesday),●*Focus on Faith* (0930 Thursday) and *Sports International* and *Pick of the World* on Friday. Saturday brings *World Briefing*, ●*Letter from America* and *Global Business*, and Sunday's programming is the same as winter. Continuous to Europe and North Africa on 12095, 15485 and 15565 kHz.

■**BBC World Service for Eastern Europe and the Mideast.** Weekdays, identical to the service for Asia and the Pacific. On the weekends, *World Briefing* is followed by Saturday's ●*Letter from America* and *Global Business*, or Sunday's *Reporting Religion* and ●*People and Politics*. Continuous programming on 11760, 15565, 15575 and 17640 kHz.

■**BBC World Service for East and Southeast Asia and the Pacific.** Winter, starts with *World Briefing*, then weekdays it's ●*Sports Roundup*. The lineup for the 0945 feature is ●*Analysis* (Tuesday, Wednesday and Friday), ●*From Our Own Correspondent* (Thursday) and *Write On* (a listener-response program, Monday). Saturday features are ●*Analysis* and *Global Business*, and Sunday there's ●*Reporting Religion* and *In Praise of God*. Monday through Friday summer, there's one hour of *World Update*; Saturday, it's *World Briefing* followed by ●*Letter from America* and *Global Business*; and Sunday's programs are the same as winter. To East Asia on 9740, 11945, 15360, 17760 and 21660 kHz; to Southeast Asia on 6195, 9740 and 15360 kHz; and to Australasia on 15360 kHz.

■**Deutsche Welle,** Germany. *News*, followed Monday through Friday by ●*NewsLink*, and then a feature. Monday, it's *Development Forum* or *Women on the Move*; Tuesday brings ●*Insight*; Wednesday has the interesting ●*Man and Environment*; Thursday, there's *Living in Germany*; and Friday's slot is *Spotlight on Sport*. Weekend fare consists of Saturday's *Talking Point* and ●*Marks and Markets*; and Sunday's *Religion and Society* and *Cool*. Forty-five minutes to East Asia winter on 9770 kHz, replaced summer by 15470 kHz; and to Southeast Asia and Australasia, winter on 6160, 9510, 17820 and 17845 kHz; and summer on 6160, 9510 17715, 17770, 17820 and 21790 kHz. For a separate service to Africa, see the next item.

■**Deutsche Welle,** Germany. Similar to the service for Asia and the Pacific, except that Saturday's *Marks and Markets* is replaced by *African Kaleidoscope*. Forty-five minutes to eastern and southern Africa, winter on 11785, 15410 and 21560 kHz; and midyear on 12035, 15410, 17800 and 21790 kHz. This service is also available to West Africa on (winter) 17800 or (summer) 21560 kHz. For yet another service, to Europe, see the next entry.

■**Deutsche Welle,** Germany. Same as for Asia and the Pacific, but with an extra 15-minute feature: *Business German* (Monday), *German History* (Tuesday), *German by Radio* (Wednesday), ●*Insight* (Thursday), ●*Man and Environment* (Friday), *Women on the Move* or *Development Forum* (Saturday) and Sunday's *Living in Germany*. One hour to Europe on 6140 kHz.

**HCJB—Voice of the Andes,** Ecuador. Monday through Friday, *News* is followed by *Studio 9*, featuring *Inside HCJB* (Monday), *Ham Radio Today* (Wednesday), *Did You Hear?* (Tuesday and Thursday), and the unique ●*Música del Ecuador* on Friday. Saturday's *DX Partyline* is replaced Sunday by *Musical Mailbag*. The second half-hour is heavily religious, although Saturday's friendly *Saludos Amigos* has a more general appeal. Continuous to Australasia on 11755 kHz.

**China Radio International.** Starts with *News*, then weekdays there are background reports. The rest of the broadcast is devoted to features. Regular shows include *People in the Know* (Monday), *Biz China* (Tuesday), *China Horizons* (Wednesday), *Voices from Other Lands* (Thursday), and *Life in China* on Friday. Saturday's features are *Global Review* and *Listeners' Garden* (reports, music and Chinese language lessons), and Sunday there's *Report from Developing Countries* and *In the Spotlight*. One hour to Australasia on 11730 and 15210 kHz.

**Radio New Zealand International.** Continuous programming for the islands of the South Pacific, where the broadcasts are targeted. On 9885 or 11675 kHz. Audible in much of North America, especially in summer.

**Voice of Russia World Service.** Winter only at this time. *News*, followed by ●*Update* on Wednesday and Friday. This is replaced Monday by *Science and Engineering*, Tuesday by *Focus on Asia*, Thursday by *Newmarket* and Saturday by *Moscow Mailbag*. Sunday's offering is the 45-minute ●*Music and Musicians*—not to be missed if you are an aficionado of classical music. Choice pickings from the second half hour include ●*Moscow Yesterday and Today* (Monday), ●*Folk Box* (Thursday) ●*Jazz Show* (Friday) and Saturday's ●*Christian Message from Moscow*. The Tuesday and Wednesday slots are also worth a listen. To Australasia on 15275, 15470, 17495, 17525 and 17665 kHz; and to Southeast Asia on 11770, 17495 and 21485 (or 21810) kHz.

**Radio Prague,** Czech Republic. Summer only at this time. See 1000 for specifics. Thirty minutes to South Asia and West Africa on 21745 kHz, and heard well beyond. One hour later in winter.

**Radio Australia.** *World News*, then weekdays it's a call-in show, *Australia Talks Back*. This is replaced Saturday by *Science Show* and *Business Weekend*, and Sunday by *The National Interest* (topical events). Continuous to Asia and the Pacific on 9580, 11880 or 17750 (from 0930) and 21820 kHz; and heard in North America on 9580 kHz. Best for East and Southeast Asia is 11880 (or 17750) kHz, and listeners in Europe should try 21820 kHz.

**The International Telecommunication Union (ITU) is headquartered in Geneva, Switzerland. It is the nerve center of worldwide frequency management.**

A. Mujunen

## 09:00–10:00

**KTWR-Trans World Radio,** Guam. Final 30 minutes of evangelical programming to Australasia on 15330 kHz.

**WJIE,** Upton, Kentucky. Continues with Christian music to North America on 7490 kHz. Other U.S. religious broadcasters operating at this hour include **WWCR** on 5935, **KAIJ** on 5755, **KTBN** on 7510 kHz, and **WHRI-World Harvest Radio** on 5745 kHz. Traditionalist Catholic programming is aired via **WEWN** on 5825 kHz.

**AFRTS Shortwave,** USA. Network news, live sports, music and features in the upper-sideband mode from the Armed Forces Radio & Television Service. Transmitted from modestly powered U.S. Navy stations around the globe. Try 4319, 5765, 6350, 6458.5, 10320, 12579, 12689.5 and 13362 kHz.

### 09:10

**Voice of Armenia.** Winter Sundays only. Twenty minutes of Armenian *news* and culture. To Europe on 15270 kHz, and to the Mideast on 4910 kHz. One hour earlier in summer.

### 09:30

■**Radio Netherlands.** Monday through Friday it's ●*Newsline*, then a feature. Top picks are ●*Research File* (science, Monday), ●*Aural Tapestry* (summer Thursdays), ●*A Good Life* (Friday), and Wednesday's well produced ●*Documentary*. Tuesday, you can hear the eclectic *Music 52-15*. Weekend fare is a mixed bag, with Sunday's *Sincerely Yours* (a listener-response program) most suited to a general audience. The first of two hours to East and Southeast Asia and Australasia on 7260 (winter), 9790, 12065 and (summer) 13710 kHz. Recommended listening.

**Radio Vilnius,** Lithuania. A half hour that's mostly *news* and background reports about events in Lithuania. Of broader appeal is *Mailbag*, aired every other Sunday. For a little Lithuanian music, try the second half of Monday's broadcast. To western Europe on 9710 kHz.

**Voice of the Straits, China.** Thursday and Friday only. The 30-minute *Focus on China* covers cultural, economic and social developments in the country. Priority is given to business news, but there are often interesting items on environmental and other legislation—from broadcasting to family planning. Formerly on Friday and Sunday, the program moved to a new schedule in summer 2002. To East and Southeast Asia on 6115 and 11590 kHz, and well heard in much of Australasia and beyond.

### 10:00

■**BBC World Service for the Americas.** Monday through Friday winter, opens with a half hour of *World Update* (news and current events) and closes with 15 minutes of ●*Sports Roundup*. In between, you can hear ●*Letter from America* (Monday), ●*Analysis* (Tuesday, Wednesday and Friday) and ●*From Our Own Correspondent* on Thursday. Weekends, the first 30 minutes are divided between *World Briefing* and ●*Sports Roundup*, with the second half hour consisting of Saturday's *Science in Action* or Sunday's ●*Agenda*. In summer, the weekday lineup is *World Briefing*, ●*World Business Report* and ●*Sports Roundup*, with weekend programs the same as in winter. To the Caribbean on 6195 kHz, and audible in much of the southern and eastern United States. Listeners farther west can tune to the Asian stream on 9740 kHz.

■**BBC World Service for Europe.** Winter weekdays, opens with *News*, then there's an interesting collection of features: ●*One Planet* and *People and Places* (Monday), *Discovery* and *Essential Guide* (Tuesday), ●*Health Matters* and ●*Everywoman* (Wednesday),●*Focus on Faith* (0930 Thursday) and *Sports International* and *Pick of the World* on Friday. Saturday brings *World Briefing*, ●*Letter from America* and *Global Business*; and Sunday there's *World Briefing*, ●*Sports Roundup* and ●*Agenda*. In summer, starts with *World Briefing*, then Monday through Friday there's ●*World Business Report* and ●*Sports Roundup*. Weekends, ●*Sports Roundup* moves to 1020 and is followed by Saturday's ●*Science in*

# GRUNDIG TUNES IN THE WORLD

Satellit 800 Millennium

## The World's Most Powerful Radio for the Serious Listener...

The Grundig Satellit legend continues. The pinnacle of over three decades of continually evolving Satellit series radios, it embodies the dreams and wishes of serious shortwave listeners the world over. Its continuous frequency coverage of 100-30,000 KHz means that broadcasts from every corner of the globe are at your finger tips. London, Tokyo, Moscow and many, many more. Listen to ham radio operators communicating across the continent and around the world. Outstanding AM performance. Beautiful FM-stereo with the included high quality headphones. And, just for fun, hear those planes as they take off and land at your local airport on the VHF 118-136 MHz aircraft band. Even if you're new to shortwave, you'll find it a breeze to operate. The experienced hobbyist will appreciate its host of advanced high-tech features. Use its built-in antennas, or connect to your favorite external ones. From its massive, easy-to-read, fully illuminated 6″ × 3.5″ Liquid Crystal Display, elegant traditional analog signal strength meter, modern PLL circuit designs, to the silky smooth tuning knob which creates absolutely no audio muting during use, this radio defines the Grundig tradition. This is the advanced radio for you. Includes a 110V AC adapter (a 220V AC adapter is available upon request) and high quality headphones. Operates on 6 D cells (not included). 20.5″ L × 9.4″ H × 8″ W.

# LISTENING HAS NEVER BEEN MORE ENJOYABLE...

## MOST ADVANCED YB 400PE

Advance Hi-Tech features, easy to use, exceptional performance in Shortwave, AM and FM. Hear broadcasts from around the world. Catch those hard to receive AM and FM stations at home. Turn on the SSB and listen to ham operators. Digital PLL and Display. Direct Frequency Entry. Auto Tuning. Manual Step Tuning. FM-stereo. 40 memories. 2 Clocks. Alarms. Sleep Timer. Dimensions: 7.75″ L × 4.5″ H × 1.5″ W    Weight:  1 lb. 5 oz.

## BEST VALUE NEW YB 300PE

Hear broadcasts from every continent. Has all 13 shortwave international broadcast bands. Local AM and FM-stereo too. Fully digital PLL. Direct frequency entry. Auto scan. Push-button tuning. Clock, alarm and 10 to 90 minute sleep timer. 24 memories. Titanium color. Easy-read LCD. Display light. External SW antenna socket. Carrying strap. Includes AC adapter, case, earphones, batteries, supplementary SW antenna. Compact. Measures  5.75″L × 3.5″H × 1.25″ W    Weight:  12 oz.

## by GRUNDIG

**AMATEUR ELECTRONIC SUPPLY**
5710 West Good Hope Road
Milwaukee, WI 53223
(414) 358-0333 Toll Free: 1-800-558-0411
Web: http://www.aesham.com

BRANCH LOCATIONS:
Orlando, FL          (407) 894-3238
 Toll Free:        1-800-327-1917
Las Vegas, NV      (702) 647-3114
 Toll Free:        1-800-634-6227
Cleveland, OH      (440) 585-7388
 Toll Free:        1-800-321-3594

**10:00–10:30**

*Action* or Sunday's ●*Weekend*. Continuous to Europe and North Africa on 12095, 15485 and 15565 kHz.

■**BBC World Service for Eastern Europe and the Mideast.** Starts with a half hour of *World Briefing* (shorter at weekends, when the final ten minutes are taken by ●*Sports Roundup*). The 1030 weekday slot goes to *The Learning Zone*, an educational program. Saturday and Sunday, it's the same as for the Americas. Continues on 11760, 15565, 15575 and 17640 kHz.

■**BBC World Service for East and Southeast Asia and the Pacific.** Monday through Friday, the format is *World Update* (*World Briefing* in summer), ●*World Business Report* and ●*Sports Roundup*. Saturday's *news* bulletin is followed by *Jazzmatazz* and *The Greenfield Collection* (a classical music request show), and Sunday's feature is a first-rate concert of classical music—not to be missed if you appreciate top-notch performances. Continuous to East Asia on 9740 and (till 1030) 15360, 17760 and 21660 kHz; to Southeast Asia on 6195, 9740 and (till 1030) 15360 kHz. For Australasia there's 15360 kHz. Well heard in western North America on 9740 kHz.

■**Deutsche Welle, Germany.** A partial relay of the station's satellite service, consisting of just features. Monday's pairing is ●*Spectrum* (science) and *Around Germany*; Tuesday has an international joint production, *Women on the Move* (or *Development Forum*) and ●*Insight*; Wednesday there's ●*Marks and Markets*, *Business Germany* and *German by Radio*; Thursday features *Arts on the Air* and ●*Great Performers*; and Friday's lineup is *Cool* and *Hits* (or *Melody Time*). Weekends, the Saturday airing is ●*Inside Europe*, replaced Sunday by *Concert Hour*. Sixty minutes to Europe on 6140 kHz.

**Radio Australia.** *World News*, then weekdays there's *Asia Pacific* and a feature on the half-hour. Monday, it's health; Tuesday, law; Wednesday, religion; Thursday, media; and Friday, sport. Saturday's lineup consists of *Pacific Review* and *In Conversation*, replaced Sunday by *The Buzz* and *Rural Reporter*. Continuous to Asia and the Pacific on 9580,

11880 (or 17750) and 21820 kHz; and heard in North America on 9580 kHz. Listeners in East and Southeast Asia should tune to 11880 (or 17750) kHz, and 21820 kHz is often heard in Europe.

**Radio Jordan.** Summer only at this time. A 60-minute partial relay of the station's domestic broadcasts, beamed to western Europe and eastern North America on 11690 or 17580 kHz. One hour later in winter. Tends to be irregular.

**Radio Prague,** Czech Republic. Winter only at this time. *News*, followed Monday through Friday by the in-depth *Newsview* and one or two features. Take your pick from *One on One* (informal interviews, Monday); *Witness* and *Talking Point* or *Central Europe Today* (Tuesday); *ABC of Czech* and *Profile* or *Czechs in History* (Wednesday); *Economics Report* (Thursday); and *Magazine* on Friday. Weekend fare consists of Saturday's *Insight Central Europe* and Sunday's *A Letter from Prague*, *The Arts* and *Mailbox*. Thirty minutes to South Asia and West Africa on 21745 kHz, but audible well beyond. One hour earlier in summer.

**Radio Japan.** *News*, then Monday through Friday there's *Japan and the World 44 Minutes* (an in-depth look at current trends and events). This is replaced Saturday by *Hello from Tokyo*, and Sunday by *Weekend Square*. One hour to Asia on 15590 kHz, to Southeast Asia on 9695 kHz, and to Australasia on 21755 kHz.

**RTE Overseas,** Ireland. A half-hour information bulletin from Radio Telefís Éireann's domestic Radio 1. To Australasia on 15280 kHz.

**Voice of Mongolia.** Most days, it's *news*, reports and short features, all with a local flavor. The entire Sunday broadcast is devoted to exotic Mongolian music. Thirty minutes to Southeast Asia and Australasia on 12015 or 12085 kHz. Tends to be well heard in parts of the United States during March and September.

**Voice of Vietnam.** Begins with *news*, then there's *Commentary* or *Weekly Review* followed by short features and pleasant Vietnamese music (especially at weekends). Thirty minutes to Southeast Asia on 9840 and 12020 kHz.

**10:00–10:30**

"Hello from Tokyo" announcer Ms. Hisako Tomisawa, with Radio Japan producer Akira Sato (standing). PASSPORT's Toshimichi Ohtake explains the half-century history of the Japan Short Wave Club.

T. Ohtake

**Voice of America.** The start of the VOA's daily broadcasts to the Caribbean. *News Now*—a mixed bag of sports, science, business and other news and features. On 6165, 7405 and 9590 kHz. For a separate service to Australasia, see the next item.

**Voice of America.** The ubiquitous *News Now*, but unlike the service to the Caribbean, this is part of a much longer broadcast. To Australasia on 5985, 11720, and 15425 kHz.

**China Radio International.** Repeat of the 0900 broadcast, but with news updates. One hour to Australasia on 11730 and 15210 kHz.

**All India Radio.** *News*, then a composite program of commentary, press review and features, interspersed with exotic Indian music. One hour to East Asia on 15235 and 17800 kHz, and to Australasia on 17510 and 17895 kHz. Also beamed to Sri Lanka on 15260 kHz.

**Voice of Korea,** North Korea. The last of the old-time communist stations, but with the country showing signs of emerging from years of isolation, changes could be in the offing. For now, it's a living fossil of a bygone era in international broadcasting. One hour to Central America on 9335 and 11710 kHz; and to Southeast Asia on 9850 (or 13650) and 11735 kHz. Also audible in parts of East Asia on 3560 kHz.

**WJIE,** Upton, Kentucky. Continues with Christian music to North America on 7490 kHz. Other U.S. religious broadcasters operating at this hour include **WWCR** on 5935 kHz, **KTBN** on 7510 kHz, **WYFR-Family Radio** on 5950 kHz, and **WHRI-World Harvest Radio** on 6040 and 9495 kHz. For traditionalist Catholic programming, try **WEWN** on 5825 (or 7425) kHz.

**HCJB—Voice of the Andes,** Ecuador. The final sixty minutes of four hours of mostly religious programming to Australasia on 11755 kHz.

**AFRTS Shortwave,** USA. Network news, live sports, music and features in the upper-sideband mode from the Armed Forces Radio & Television Service. Transmitted from modestly powered U.S. Navy stations around the globe. Try 4319, 5765, 6350, 6458.5, 10320, 12579, 12689.5 and 13362 kHz.

## 10:30

**Radio Prague,** Czech Republic. This time summer only. Repeat of the 0700 broadcast but with different programming on Saturday; see 1130 for program specifics. A half hour to northwestern Europe on 9880 and 11615 kHz. One hour later during winter.

## 10:30–11:00

**Radio Netherlands.** The second of two hours targeted at East and Southeast Asia and Australasia. Opens with a feature. Quality shows include ●*EuroQuest* (Monday), ●*A Good Life* (Tuesday), ●*Research File* (science, Thursday) and Friday's excellent ●*Documentary*. Other offerings include *Dutch Horizons* (Wednesday) and Sunday's *Sound Fountain* (winter) or ●*Aural Tapestry* (summer). Monday through Friday, the final 25 minutes go to ●*Newsline*, replaced weekends by a simple *news* bulletin and a feature. On 7260 (winter), 9790, 12065 and (summer) 13710 kHz. For a separate summer broadcast to western Europe and eastern North America, see the next item.

**Radio Netherlands.** Summer only at this time, and the first 60 minutes of an approximately two-hour broadcast. Weekdays, opens with ●*Newsline* (current events), which is replaced weekends by a *news* bulletin. The second half hour (more at weekends) is devoted to features. Choice pickings include ●*EuroQuest* (Monday), ●*A Good Life* (Tuesday), ●*Research File* (science, Thursday) and Friday's excellent ●*Documentary*. Other offerings include Wednesday's *Dutch Horizons*, Saturday's *Europe Unzipped* and *Insight*, and Sunday's *Wide Angle* and ●*Aural Tapestry*. To western Europe on 6045 and 9860 kHz, and to eastern North America on 5965 kHz.

**Kol Israel.** Summer only at this time. Fifteen minutes from Israel Radio's domestic network. To Europe and eastern North America on 15640 and 17545 kHz. One hour later in winter.

**United Arab Emirates Radio,** Dubai. *News*, then a feature dealing with one or more aspects of Arab life and culture. Weekends, there are replies to listeners' letters. To Europe and North Africa on 13675, 15370, 15395 and 21605 kHz. Some frequencies tend to be a little variable

## 11:00

**BBC World Service for the Americas.** Starts weekends with *World Briefing* and *British News* (replaced weekdays by special programming for the Caribbean) and most days ends with ●*Sports Roundup*. The remaining programs change according to season. Continuous programming to eastern North America and the Caribbean on 6195 and 15190 kHz. Listeners farther west should tune to the Asian stream on 9740 kHz.

**BBC World Service for Europe.** Winter, identical to the service for the Americas, except that *Arts in Action* replaces ●*Agenda* at 1130 Sunday. Monday through Saturday summer, there's *World Briefing*, *British News*, ●*Analysis* (replaced Monday be ●*Letter from America* and Thursday by ●*From Our Own Correspondent*) and ●*Sports Roundup* (preempted Friday by *Football Extra*). Sunday, there's more of the same during the first 30 minutes, with *Arts in Action* completing the hour. Continuous to Europe and North Africa on 12095, 15485 and 15565 kHz.

**BBC World Service for Eastern Europe and the Mideast.** *News*, then Monday through Friday there's an arts show, *Meridian*. The next half hour consists of a mixed bag of music and light entertainment, except for Thursday's ●*Omnibus*. On Saturday, the news if followed by *Wright Round the World*, and Sunday fare consists of *World Briefing*, *British News* and *Arts in Action*. Continues on 11760, 15565, 15575 and 17640 kHz.

**BBC World Service for East and Southeast Asia and the Pacific.** Weekdays there's five minutes of *news*, then a pair of features: ●*Health Matters* and ●*Everywoman* (Monday), *Science View* and ●*Focus on Faith* (Tuesday), *Sports International* and *Pick of the World* (Wednesday), ●*One Planet* and *People and Places* (Thursday), and *Discovery* and *Essential Guide* on Friday. Some of the BBC's better offerings. Weekends, opens with *World Briefing* and *British News*, then it's Saturday's ●*Science in Action* or Sunday's first half hour of ●*Play of the Week* (the best in world theater). Continuous to East Asia on 9740, 9815 and 15280 kHz; to Southeast Asia on 6195 and 9740 kHz; and to Australasia on 9740 kHz (also heard in western North America).

**Radio Taipei International,** Taiwan. Opens with 15 minutes of *News*, and closes weekdays with *Let's Learn Chinese*. The remaining airtime is taken up by features. Monday, there's *Taiwan Economic Journal* followed by *People*; Tuesday brings ●*Jade Bells and Bamboo Pipes*; Wednesday's lineup is *New Music Lounge* and *Confucius and Inspiration Beyond*; Thursday's combo is *Taipei Magazine* and *Life Unusual*; and Friday's menu consists of *Taiwan Gourmet* and *Discover Taiwan*. The Saturday slots go to *Kaleidoscope* and *Mailbag Time*, replaced Sunday by *Great Wall Forum* and *Asia Pacific*. Sixty minutes to Southeast Asia on 7445 kHz. For a separate transmission to East Asia, see the next item.

**Radio Taipei International,** Taiwan. Opens with 15 minutes of *News*, and weekdays closes with *Let's Learn Chinese*, which has a series of segments for beginning, intermediate and advanced learners. In between, there are either one or two features, depending on which day it is. Monday, you can listen to the pleasurable and exotic ●*Jade Bells and Bamboo Pipes* (Taiwanese music); and Tuesday to *Culture Express* and *Trends*. Wednesday's slots are *Taiwan Today* and *Confucius and Inspiration Beyond*; Thursday's pairing is *Discover Taiwan* and *New Music Lounge*; and Friday brings together *Taipei Magazine* and *People*. These are replaced Saturday by *Groove Zone* and *Kaleidoscope*, and Sunday by *Great Wall Forum* and *Mailbag Time*. One hour to East Asia on 11985 kHz.

**■Deutsche Welle,** Germany. *News*, then weekdays it's ●*NewsLink* and *Hallo Africa* (not Monday). These are replaced Saturday by *Talking Point* and *African Kaleidoscope*, and Sunday by *Religion and Society* and *Cool*. Forty-five minutes to Africa winter on 15410, 17800, 21550 and 21780 kHz; and summer on 11785, 15410, 17860, 21525 and 21665 kHz. Best for southern Africa is 15410 kHz. For a separate service to Europe, see the next item.

**■Deutsche Welle,** Germany. Similar to the service for Africa, but with an additional 15-minute feature: *Business German* (Monday), *People in Europe* (Tuesday), *German by Radio* (Wednesday), ●*Insight* (Thursday), ●*Man and Environment* (Friday), *Women on the Move* or *Development Forum* (Saturday) and Sunday's *Around Germany*. One hour to Europe on 6140 kHz.

**Radio Australia.** *World News*, with the remainder of the first half hour going to *Asia Pacific* (replaced Sunday by *Correspondents' Report*). Monday through Friday, the next 30 minutes consist of a sports bulletin and *Life Matters* (personal and social issues). Weekends, there's *Fine Music Australia* (classical music) at 1130 Saturday, and *Business Report* at the same time Sunday. Continuous to East Asia and the Pacific on 5995, 6020, 9580, 11880, 12080 and 21820 kHz; and heard in much of North America on 6020 and 9580 kHz. Listeners in Europe should try 21820 kHz.

**Radio Bulgaria.** Summer only at this time. Starts with *news*, then Tuesday through Saturday there's *Events and Developments* (preceded Saturday by *In Focus*). The remaining lineup includes *Answering Your Letters* (a listener-response show, Sunday), the enjoyable and exotic ●*Folk Studio* (Monday), *Magazine Economy* (Tuesday). *Arts and Artists* (Wednesday), *History Club* (Thursday), *The Way We Live* (Friday) and *DX Programed*, a Saturday show for radio enthusiasts. Tuesday through Sunday, the broadcast ends with *Keyword Bulgaria*. Sixty minutes to Europe on 15700 and 17500 kHz. One hour later during winter.

**Radio Ukraine International.** Summer only at this time. An hour's ample coverage of just about all things Ukrainian, including news, sports, politics and culture. Well worth a listen is ●*Music from Ukraine*, which fills most of the Sunday broadcast. Sixty minutes to northern Europe on 15520 kHz, and to West Asia on 11840 kHz. One hour later in winter. Tends to be irregular due to financial limitations.

**HCJB—Voice of the Andes,** Ecuador. First 60 minutes of more than three hours of religious programming to the Americas on 12005 and 15115 kHz.

**Voice of America.** A mixed bag of sports, science, business and other news and features. To East Asia on 6110 (or 6160), 9760, 11705 (winter) and 15160 kHz, and to Australasia on 5985 (or 9770), 9645, 11720 and 15425 kHz.

**Radio Jordan.** A 60-minute partial relay of the station's domestic broadcasts, beamed to western Europe and eastern North America on 11690 or 17580 kHz. Tends to be irregular.

## 11:00–11:30

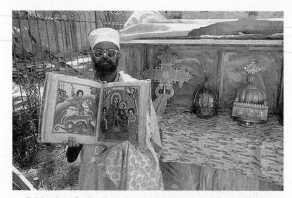

**Ethiopian Orthodox priest shows an ancient Bible and crowns of Ethiopian kings, St. Mary of Zion, Axum.**

sacredsites.com

**Radio Japan.** *News*, then weekdays there's *Asian Top News* and a 35-minute feature: *Japan Music Log* (Monday), Japanese language lessons (Tuesday and Thursday), *Japan Musical Treasure Box* (Wednesday), and Friday's *Music Beat* (Japanese popular music—old and new). *Pop Joins the World* fills the Saturday slot, and is replaced Sunday by *Hello from Tokyo*. One hour to eastern North America on 6120 kHz; to Asia on 15590 kHz; and to Southeast Asia on 9695 kHz.

**Xizang [Tibet] People's Broadcasting Station, China.** Monday through Saturday only. *Holy Tibet* describes itself as "a window to life in Tibet," and is a 20-minute package of information and local music—mountains, monasteries, local customs, and even Tibetan hip hop! Sometimes acknowledges listeners' reception reports at the end of the program. Original editions are aired on Monday, Wednesday and Friday, and repeated at the same time the next day. Well heard in East and Southeast Asia and parts of Australasia (South America, too). On 4905, 4920, 5240, 6110, 6130, 6200, 7385 and 9490 kHz.

**Radio Singapore International.** A three-hour package for Southeast Asia, and widely heard beyond. Starts with ten minutes of *news* (five at weekends), then Monday through Friday there's *Business and Market Report*, replaced Saturday by *Insight*, and Sunday by *Business World*. These are followed on the quarter-hour by several mini-features, including a daily news and weather bulletin on the half-hour. Monday's lineup is *Young Expressions*, *The Write Stuff*, *Youth Beat* and *E-Z Beat*; Tuesday brings *A World of Our Own*, *On the Line from Silicone Valley*, *Hong Kong: Dragon City*, and *E-Z Beat*; Wednesday offers *Perspective*, *Eco Watch*, *On Second Thought* and *Classic Gold*; Thursday has *Frontiers, Eco-Watch*, *Potluck*, *Singapore Scene* and *Love Songs*; and Friday's list includes *Asian Journal*, *Indonesian Media Watch*, *Arts Arena*, *Science and Technology Watch* and *Classic Gold*. Saturday, expect *Insight*, *Regional Press Review*, *Frontiers*, *A Current Affair*, *Family Ties* and *Straight Talk*; replaced Sunday by *Comment*, *Youth Beat*, *Snapshots*, *A Current Affair* and *Instrumentals*. On 6150 and 9600 kHz.

**CBC North-Québec,** Canada. Summer only at this time; see 1200 for specifics. Intended for a domestic audience, but also heard in the northeastern United States on 9625 kHz.

**Voice of Vietnam.** Repeat of the 1000 transmission. A half hour to Southeast Asia on 7285 kHz.

**Voice of the Islamic Republic of Iran.** The first hour of a 90-minute block of news, commentary and features, plus a little Iranian music. Strongly reflects an Islamic point of view. To West, South and Southeast Asia, but widely heard elsewhere. Winter on 15265, 15375, 15385, 15480, 15585, 21470 and 21730 kHz; and summer on 15215, 15585, 15600, 21470 and 21730 kHz.

**WJIE,** Upton, Kentucky. Continues with Christian music to North America on 7490 kHz. Other U.S. religious broadcasters operating at this hour include **WWCR** on 5935 kHz, **KTBN** on 7510 kHz, **WYFR-Family Radio** on 5950 kHz, and **WHRI-World Harvest Radio** on 6040 and 9495 kHz. Traditionalist Catholic programming can be found on **WEWN** on 5825 (or 7425) kHz.

**AFRTS Shortwave,** USA. Network news, live sports, music and features in the upper-

sideband mode from the Armed Forces Radio & Television Service. Transmitted from modestly powered U.S. Navy stations around the globe. Try 4319, 5765, 6350, 6458.5, 10320, 12579, 12689.5 and 13362 kHz.

## 11:30

**Radio Austria International.** Summer only at this time; see 1230 for program specifics. Thirty minutes to Europe on 6155 and 13730 kHz, and to South and Southeast Asia and Australasia on 21780 kHz. One hour later in winter.

**Radio Korea International,** South Korea. Opens with *news* and commentary, followed Monday through Wednesday by *Seoul Calling*. Weekly features include *Echoes of Korean Music* and *Shortwave Feedback* (Sunday), *Tales from Korea's Past* (Monday), *Korean Cultural Trails* (Tuesday), *Pulse of Korea* (Wednesday), *From Us to You* (a listener-response program) and *Let's Learn Korean* (Thursday), *Let's Sing Together* and *Korea Through Foreigners' Eyes* (Friday), and Saturday's *Discovering Korea*, *Korean Literary Corner* and *Weekly News Focus*. Sixty minutes to eastern North America on 9650 kHz via their Canadian relay.

■**Radio Netherlands.** Winter weekdays, opens with ●*Newsline* (current events), which is replaced weekends by a *news* bulletin. The second half hour (more at weekends) is given to features. The lineup includes ●*EuroQuest* (Monday), ●*A Good Life* (Tuesday), ●*Research File* (science, Thursday) and Friday's excellent ●*Documentary*. Other offerings include *Dutch Horizons* (Wednesday), *Europe Unzipped* and *Insight* (Saturday), and *Wide Angle* and *Sound Fountain* on Sunday. Summer, starts with a feature and ends with ●*Newsline* (Monday through Friday) or a *news* bulletin (Saturday and Sunday). Pick of the litter are ●*Research File* (science, Monday), ●*Aural Tapestry* (Thursday), ●*A Good Life* (Friday) and Wednesday's award-winning ●*Documentary*. On the remaining days, you can hear *Music 52-15* (Tuesday), *Europe Unzipped* (Saturday) and *Dutch Horizons* and *Sincerely Yours* on Sunday. To western Europe on 6045 and 9860 kHz, and to eastern North America on 5965 kHz.

**Flanders Radio International,** Belgium. Summer only at this time. Weekdays, the *News* is followed by one or more features, with *Soundbox* closing the broadcast. The lineup includes *The Arts* (Monday and Thursday), *Tourism* (Monday), *Focus on Europe* and *Sports* (Tuesday), *Green Society* (Wednesday), *Around Town* (Thursday), and *Economics* and *International Report* (Friday). Closes with *Soundbox*. These are replaced Saturday by ●*Music from Flanders*, and Sunday by *Radio World*, *Tourism*, *Brussels 1043* (a listener-response program) and *Soundbox*. Thirty minutes to East Asia and Australasia on 9865 kHz. One hour later in winter.

**Radio Prague,** Czech Republic. Winter only at this time. *News*, then Monday through Friday it's *Newsview* plus one or two features. Monday's *One on One* (a series of informal interviews) is replaced Tuesday by *Witness* and *Talking Point* or *Central Europe Today*; and Wednesday by *ABC of Czech* and either *Czechs in History* or *Profile*. The business-oriented *Economic Report* fills the Thursday slot, and *Magazine* is Friday's show. Weekends, the news is followed by Saturday's *Spotlight* (Czech regional issues) and *Readings from Czech Literature* or *Saturday Music*; and Sunday by *A Letter from Prague*, *The Arts* and *Mailbox*. Thirty minutes to northwestern Europe on 11640 kHz, and to East Africa on 21745 kHz. The latter channel is also audible in parts of the Mideast. The European broadcast is one hour earlier in summer, but there is no corresponding transmission for East Africa.

**Kol Israel.** Winter only at this time. Fifteen minutes from Israel Radio's domestic network. To Europe and eastern North America on 17545 kHz. One hour earlier in winter.

**Wales Radio International.** Winter Saturdays only at this time. Thirty minutes of news, interviews and music for Australasia on 17625 kHz. One hour later in summer (Oz winter).

**Radio Sweden.** Summer only at this time; see 1230 for program details. Thirty minutes to eastern North America (one hour later in winter) on 18960 kHz, and to East Asia and Australasia (two hours later in winter) on 17505 kHz.

## 1200–1759
### Western Australia & East Asia—Evening Prime Time
### North America—Morning and Lunchtime
### Europe & Mideast—Afternoon and Early Evening

### 12:00

■**BBC World Service for the Americas.** A full hour of news and current events in ●*Newshour*, except for the first 20 minutes Monday through Friday, when there's alternative programming for the Caribbean. Continuous to North America and the Caribbean on 6195 and 15190 kHz. Listeners in western states may get a better signal from the Asian stream on 9740 kHz.

■**BBC World Service for Europe.** Winter, you can hear the daily ●*Newshour*—60 minutes of news and current events. Monday through Friday summer, starts with a *news* bulletin and is followed by *Outlook* and a 15-minute feature. Weekends, the news is followed by Saturday's *Wright Round the World* or Sunday's *The Alternative* (popular music) and *Global Business*. Continuous to Europe and North Africa on 12095, 15485 and 15565 kHz.

■**BBC World Service for Eastern Europe and the Mideast.** ●*Newshour*—the best in news and analysis. Some general interest items, too. Continuous programming on 11760, 15565, 15575 and 17640 kHz.

■**BBC World Service for East and Southeast Asia and the Pacific.** Monday through Friday, five minutes of *news* are followed by *Outlook* (news and human interest stories). The hour ends with a 15-minute feature. Saturday fare consists of a *news* bulletin, some light entertainment (●*Brain of Britain* part of the year) and the excellent ●*Assignment* (or alternative documentary). Sunday, it's the final part of ●*Play of the Week*, which runs till 1230 or 1300. If the former, ●*Agenda* takes over the second half hour. Continuous to East Asia on 6195, 9740, 9815 (summer) and 15280 kHz; to Southeast Asia on 6195 and 9740 kHz; and to Australasia on 9740 kHz. Also audible in western North America on 9740 kHz.

**Radio Canada International.** Summer weekdays only at this time. The first 60 minutes of a three-hour block of the Canadian Broadcasting Corporation's *This Morning*. To eastern North America and the Caribbean on 9515, 13655 and 17820 kHz. For a separate year-round service to Asia, see the next item.

**Radio Canada International.** *News*, then Tuesday through Saturday it's ●*This Morning, Tonight*. This is replaced Sunday by ●*Global Village* (an extravaganza of world music) and Monday by ●*Quirks and Quarks* (an irreverent look at science). One hour to East and Southeast Asia winter on 9660 and 11730 kHz, and summer on 9660 and 15190 kHz.

**Radio Tashkent,** Uzbekistan. *News* and commentary, followed by features such as *Life in the Village* (Wednesday), a listeners' request program (Monday), and local music (Thursday). Heard better in Asia, Australasia and Europe than in North America. Thirty minutes winter on 5060, 5975, 6025 and 9715 kHz; and summer on 7285, 9715, 15295 and 17775 kHz.

■**Radio France Internationale.** Opens with a *news* bulletin, then there's a 25-minute feature— *French Lesson, Crossroads, Voices, Rendez-Vous, World Tracks, Weekend* or *Club 9516* (a listener-response program). A half hour to West Africa (and audible in parts of eastern North America) on 15540 kHz, and to East Africa on 25820 kHz.

**Radio Bulgaria.** This time winter only; see 1100 for specifics. Unlike most other stations, Radio Bulgaria continues to feature folk music in its program lineup. Particularly worthy of note is the 15-minute ●*Folk Studio* aired at 1210 Monday. Sixty minutes to Europe on 15700 and 17500 kHz. One hour earlier in summer.

**Radio Polonia,** Poland. This time summer only. Sixty minutes of news, commentary, features and music—all with a Polish accent. Monday through Friday, it's *News from Poland*—a potpourri of news, reports and

# GRUNDIG TUNES IN THE WORLD

**SATELLIT 800**

## The World's Most Powerful Radio for the Serious Listener...

The Grundig Satellit legend continues. The pinnacle of over three decades of continually evolving Satellit series radios, it embodies the dreams and wishes of serious shortwave listeners the world over. Its continuous frequency coverage of 100-30,000 KHz means that broadcasts from every corner of the globe are at your finger tips. London, Tokyo, Moscow and many, many more. Listen to ham radio operators communicating across the continent and around the world. Outstanding AM performance. Beautiful FM-stereo with the included high quality headphones. And, just for fun, hear those planes as they take off and land at your local airport on the VHF 118-136 MHz aircraft band. Even if you're new to shortwave, you'll find it a breeze to operate. The experienced hobbyist will appreciate its host of advanced high-tech features. Use its built-in antennas, or connect to your favorite external ones. From its massive, easy-to-read, fully illuminated 6″ x 3.5″ Liquid Crystal Display, elegant traditional analog signal strength meter, modern PLL circuit designs, to the silky smooth tuning knob which creates absolutely no audio muting during use, this radio defines the Grundig tradition. This is the advanced radio for you. Includes a 110V AC adapter (a 220V AC adapter is available upon request) and high quality headphones. Operates on 6 D cells (not included). 20.5″ L x 9.4″ H x 8″ W.

## MOST ADVANCED YB 400PE

Advance Hi-Tech features, easy to use, exceptional performance in Shortwave, AM and FM. Hear broadcasts from around the world. Catch those hard to receive AM and FM stations at home. Turn on the SSB and listen to ham operators. Digital PLL and Display. Direct Frequency Entry. Auto Tuning. Manual Step Tuning. FM-stereo. 40 memories. 2 Clocks. Alarms. Sleep Timer. Dimensions: 7.75″ L x 4.5″ H x 1.5″ W    Weight: 1 lb. 5 oz.

## BEST VALUE NEW YB 300PE

Hear broadcasts from every continent. Has all 13 shortwave international broadcast bands. Local AM and FM-stereo too. Fully digital PLL. Direct frequency entry. Auto scan. Push-button tuning. Clock, alarm and 10 to 90 minute sleep timer. 24 memories. Titanium color. Easy-read LCD. Display light. External SW antenna socket. Carrying strap. Includes AC adapter, case, earphones, batteries, supplementary SW antenna. Compact. Measures  5.75″ L  x  3.5″ H  x 1.25″ W    Weight:  12 oz.

## GRUNDIG PORSCHE DESIGN G2000A AM/FM/SW RADIO

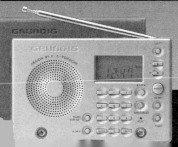

Wake up to sports and talk radio on AM, soothing stereo (with earphones) on FM or fascinating shortwave from around the world… select from 13 International bands from 2.3 - 7.4 and 9.4 - 26.1 MHz. Punch in any station or lock your favorites into 20 memories… other features include digital clock and alarm with Quartz accuracy… earphones… butter-soft handcrafted leather case. Designed by F.A.Porsche, the G2000A is a pleasure to own and operate. Uses  3 AA batteries (not included). Dimensions: 5.5″ L x 3.5″ H x 1.375″ W    Weight:  11.52 oz.

**LCM**

24 Foxwarren Dr., Willowdale
Ontario, Canada  M2K 1L3
Tel. (416) 225-8961 / Fax (416) 730-1977

**FOR THE NEWEST
GRUNDIG SHORTWAVE
RADIOS SHOP LCM**

## 12:00–12:30

Somali village women are primary targets for UNICEF radio's educational programs and spot ads.

UN

interviews. This is followed by an arts program, *Focus*, and *Chart Show* (a cultural clash, Monday); *Day in the Life* and *Request Concert* (Tuesday); *Cookery Corner* and *The Best of Polish Radio* (Wednesday); *Letter from Poland* and *Multimedia Show* (Thursday); and Friday's *Business Week* and *Discovering Chopin* (or an alternative classical music feature). The Saturday broadcast begins with a bulletin of *news*, then there's *Panorama* (investigative reporting) and *Soundcheck*. Sundays, you can hear *The Weeklies*, *Europe East* and *Postbag*, a listener-response program. To Europe on 6095, 7145, 7270, 9525 and 11820 kHz. One hour later in winter.

**Radio Australia.** *World News*, then Monday through Thursday it's *Late Night Live* (round-table discussion). On the remaining days, there's Friday's *Sound Quality* (music), Saturday's *The Spirit of Things*, and Sunday's *Country Club* (not all country music comes from Nashville!). Continuous to Asia and the Pacific on 5995, 6020, 9580, 11650, 11880 and 21820 kHz; and well heard in much of North America on 6020 and 9580 kHz. Listeners in Europe should try 21820 kHz.

**Radio Jordan.** A 60-minute partial relay of the station's domestic broadcasts, beamed to western Europe and eastern North America on 11690 or 17580 kHz. Tends to be irregular.

**Radio Ukraine International.** Winter only at this time. See 1100 for specifics. Sixty minutes to Europe on 11720 and 15520 kHz, and to Central Asia on 11825 kHz. One hour earlier in summer. Tends to be irregular due to financial limitations.

**CBC North-Québec,** Canada. Part of an 18-hour multilingual broadcast for a domestic audience, but which is also heard in the northeastern United States. Weekend programming at this hour is in English, and features *news* followed by the enjoyably eclectic ●*Good Morning Québec* (Saturday) or *Fresh Air* (Sunday). Starts at this time winter, but summer it is already into the second hour. On 9625 kHz.

**HCJB—Voice of the Andes,** Ecuador. Continuous religious programming to the Americas on 12005 and 15115 kHz.

**Radio Singapore International.** Continuous programming to Southeast Asia and beyond. Starts with five minutes of *news*, then it's mostly the same programs as the previous hour (see 1100) but on different days of the week. On 6150 and 9600 kHz.

**Radio Taipei International,** Taiwan. Repeat of the 1100 broadcast for East Asia; see there for program details. One hour to East Asia on 7130 kHz, and to Australasia on 9610kHz.

**Voice of the Islamic Republic of Iran.** Final half hour of a 90-minute broadcast with the accent firmly on Islam and Islamic culture. To West, South and Southeast Asia, but widely heard beyond. Winter on 15265, 15375, 15385, 15480, 15585, 21470 and 21730 kHz; and summer on 15215, 15585, 15600, 21470 and 21730 kHz.

**Voice of America.** A mixed bag of current events, sports, science, business and other news and features. To East Asia on 6110 (or 6160), 9760, 11715, 11705 (winter) and 15160 kHz; and to Australasia on 9645, 11715 and 15425 kHz.

**China Radio International.** *News*, then weekdays there are in-depth reports. The rest of the broadcasts consists of features, including regular shows *People in the Know* (Monday), *Biz China* (Tuesday), *China Horizons* (Wednesday), *Voices from Other Lands* (Thursday) and Friday's *Life in China*. The weekend lineup includes Saturday's *Global Review* and *Listeners' Garden*, and Sunday's *Report from Developing Countries* and *In the Spotlight*. One hour to Southeast Asia on 9730 and 11980 kHz, and to Australasia on 9760, 11760 and 15415 kHz.

**WJIE,** Upton, Kentucky. Continues with Christian music to North America on 7490 kHz. Other U.S. religious broadcasters operating at this hour include **WWCR** on 5935 (or 13845) kHz, **KTBN** on 7510 kHz, **WYFR-Family Radio** on 5950, 11830 (winter) and 11970 (or 17750) kHz, and **WHRI-World Harvest Radio** on 6040 and 9495 kHz. For traditionalist Catholic programming, tune **WEWN** on 5825 (or 7425) kHz.

**AFRTS Shortwave,** USA. Network news, live sports, music and features in the upper-sideband mode from the Armed Forces Radio & Television Service. Transmitted from modestly powered U.S. Navy stations around the globe. Try 4319, 5765, 6350, 6458.5, 10320, 12579, 12689.5 and 13362 kHz.

### 12:15

**Radio Cairo,** Egypt. The start of a 75-minute package of news, religion, culture and entertainment, much of it devoted to Arab and Islamic themes. The initial quarter hour consists of virtually anything, from quizzes to Islamic religious talks, then there's *news* and commentary, followed by political and cultural items. To Asia on 17595 kHz.

### 12:30

**Radio Austria International.** Winter only at this time. Starts with a brief bulletin of *news*, then weekdays there's the informative ●*Report from Austria*. The weekend replacements are two European co-productions: Saturday's *Insight Central Europe* and Sunday's *Network Europe*. Thirty minutes to Europe on 6155 and 13730 kHz, and to South and Southeast Asia and Australasia on 21770 kHz. One hour earlier in summer.

**Radio Bangladesh.** *News*, followed by Islamic and general interest features and pleasant Bengali music. Thirty minutes to Southeast Asia, also heard in Europe, on 7185 and 9550 kHz. Frequencies may vary slightly.

■**Radio Netherlands.** Winter only at this time. The second of two hours for listeners in western Europe and eastern North America. Starts with a feature and ends with ●*Newsline* (Monday through Friday) or a *news* bulletin (weekends). Quality shows include ●*Research File* (science, Monday), ●*Encore* (Thursday) ●*A Good Life* (Friday) and Wednesday's award-winning ●*Documentary*. On the remaining days, you can hear *Music 52-15* (Tuesday), *Sound Fountain* (Thursday) and *Dutch Horizons* and *Sincerely Yours* on Sunday. To western Europe on 6045 and 9860 kHz, and to eastern North America on 5965 kHz.

**Flanders Radio International,** Belgium. Winter only at this time; see 1130 for specifics. A half hour to East Asia and Australasia on 9865 kHz. One hour earlier in summer.

**Voice of Vietnam.** Repeat of the 1000 transmission. A half hour to Southeast Asia on 9840 and 12020 kHz. Frequencies may vary slightly.

**Radio Thailand.** Thirty minutes of *news* and short features. To Southeast Asia and

## 12:30–13:00

Australasia, winter on 9810 kHz and summer on 9885 kHz.

**Voice of Turkey.** This time summer only. Fifty-five minutes of *news*, features and Turkish music. To Europe on 17830 kHz, and to Southeast Asia and Australasia on 17615 kHz. One hour later in winter.

**Radio Sweden.** Monday through Friday, it's *news* and features in *Sixty Degrees North*, concentrating heavily on Scandinavian topics. The Monday slot goes to *SportScan*, replaced Tuesday by *Close Up* or an alternative feature, and Wednesday by *Money Matters*. Thursday features a different show each week of the month—*Nordic Report*, *GreenScan*, *Heart Beat* or *S-Files*, while Friday offers a review of the week's news. Saturday's slot is filled by

**The president of Puntland State in northern Somalia inspects the old Radio Galkayo room prior to relocation.**

S. Voron

*Weekend*, *Spectrum* (the arts), *Sweden Today* or *Studio 49*, and Sunday fare consists of *In Touch with Stockholm* (a listener-response program) or the musical *Sounds Nordic*. A year-round half hour to North America on 18960 kHz; and summer to Asia and Australasia on 17505 and 21530 kHz.

**Wales Radio International.** Summer Saturdays only at this time. News, interviews and local music from Britain's westernmost region. Thirty minutes to Australasia on 17845 kHz, and one hour earlier in winter.

## 13:00

■**BBC World Service for the Americas.** Weekdays, a five-minute *news* bulletin is followed by the long-running *Outlook* and the enjoyable ●*Off the Shelf* (readings from world literature). Saturday fare consists of *World Football* (soccer) and a music feature, replaced Sunday by jazz or other music and the religious *In Praise of God*. Continuous programming to North America and the Caribbean on 6195 and 15190 kHz. The Asian stream on 9740 kHz is likely to provide better reception in western North America.

■**BBC World Service for Europe.** Monday through Friday winter, starts with a *news* bulletin, then it's *Outlook* (news and human interest stories) and a 15-minute feature. Weekends, the news is followed by Saturday's *Wright Round the World* or Sunday's *The Alternative* (popular music) and *Global Business*. Summer weekdays, five minutes of *news* are followed by an arts show, *Meridian* (except Monday, when ●*Omnibus* is aired in its place). The next half hour consists of a mixed bag of music and light entertainment. Saturday, there's 60 minutes of news and current events in ●*Newshour*, reduced Sunday to a half hour, and complemented by *Sportsworld*. Continuous to Europe and North Africa on 12095, 15485 and 15565 kHz.

■**BBC World Service for Eastern Europe and the Mideast.** Starts with *News*, then it's all features. Pick of the weekday litter are *Discovery* (science, 0705 Monday), Tuesday's pairing of ●*Health Matters* and ●*Everywoman*,

Wednesday's ●*Focus on Faith* (0730) and Friday's ●*One Planet* (0705). Weekend fare consists of Saturday's *Jazzmatazz* and ●*People and Politics*, and Sunday's quiz or panel game followed by *Global Business*. Continuous programming on 11760, 15565, 15575 and 17640 kHz.

■**BBC World Service for East and Southeast Asia and the Pacific.** Fifty minutes of ●*Newshour* (a full hour on weekends), with ●*World Business Report* occupying the remaining 10-minute weekday slot. To East and Southeast Asia on 6195 and 9740 kHz, and to Australasia on 9740 kHz (also audible in western North America).

**Radio Canada International.** Monday through Friday winter, and daily in summer. Winter, it's the first 60 minutes of a three-hour block of the Canadian Broadcasting Corporation's *This Morning*; summer weekdays, the second hour thereof. Summer Saturdays, there's a look at Canadian politics in *The House*, and Sunday it's the start of yet another three-hour show, *The Sunday Edition*. To eastern North America and the Caribbean winter weekdays on 9515, 13655 and 17710 kHz. The summer schedule is a little more complicated: Monday through Friday on 9515, 13655 and 17820 kHz; and weekends on 9515, 13655 and 17800 kHz.

**China Radio International.** Repeat of the 1200 broadcast; see there for specifics. One hour to Southeast Asia on 11980 and 15180 kHz; and to Australasia on 11760 and 11900 kHz. Also available to eastern North America on 9570 kHz; and summer only to western North America on 7405 kHz.

**Radio Polonia,** Poland. This time winter only. *News*, commentary, music and a variety of features. See 1200 for specifics. Sixty minutes to Europe on 6095, 7270, 9525 and 11820 kHz. Listeners in southeastern Canada and the northeastern United States should also try 11820 kHz. One hour earlier during summer.

**Radio Prague,** Czech Republic. Summer only at this hour. *News*, then Monday through Friday there's the in-depth *Newsview* and one or two features: *One on One* (informal interviews, Monday); *Witness* and *Talking Point*

or *Central Europe Today* (Tuesday); *ABC of Czech* and either *Profile* or *Czechs in History* (Wednesday); *Economics Report* (Thursday); and *Magazine* ("the show that starts where the news ends") in the Friday slot. The Saturday show is *Insight Central Europe*, and is replaced Sunday by *A Letter from Prague*, *The Arts* and *Mailbox*. Thirty minutes to northern Europe on 13580 kHz, and to South Asia (audible in parts of the Mideast) on 21735 or 21745 kHz. There is no corresponding broadcast in winter.

**Radio Jordan.** A partial relay of the station's domestic broadcasts, beamed to Europe on 11690 kHz. Continuous till 1630 (1730 in winter). Also audible in parts of eastern North America, especially during winter. Tends to be irregular.

**Radio Korea International,** South Korea. Opens with *news* and commentary, followed Monday through Wednesday by *Seoul Calling*. Weekly features include *Echoes of Korean Music* and *Shortwave Feedback* (Sunday), *Tales from Korea's Past* (Monday), *Korean Cultural Trails* (Tuesday), *Pulse of Korea* (Wednesday), *From Us to You* (a listener-response program) and *Let's Learn Korean* (Thursday), *Let's Sing Together* and *Korea Through Foreigners' Eyes* (Friday), and Saturday's *Discovering Korea*, *Korean Literary Corner* and *Weekly News Focus*. Sixty minutes to Southeast Asia on 9570 and 13670 kHz.

**Radio Cairo,** Egypt. The final half-hour of the 1215 broadcast, consisting of listener participation programs, Arabic language lessons and a summary of the latest news. To Asia on 17595 kHz.

**CBC North-Québec,** Canada. Continues with multilingual programming for a domestic audience. *News*, then winter Saturdays it's the second hour of ●*Good Morning Québec*, replaced Sunday by *Fresh Air*. In summer, the news is followed by *The House* (Canadian politics, Saturday) or the highly professional ●*Sunday Morning*. Weekday programs are mainly in languages other than English. Audible in the northeastern United States on 9625 kHz.

**Radio Australia.** Monday through Friday, there's a quarter-hour of *news* followed by 45

**13:00–14:00**

minutes of World Music in ●*The Planet*. Weekends, after five minutes of *news*, it's either Saturday's *Science Show* or the second part of Sunday's *Country Club*. Continuous programming to Asia and the Pacific on 5995, 6020, 9580, 11650, 11660 (from 1330), 11880 (till 1330) and 21820 kHz; and easily audible in much of North America on 6020 and 9580 kHz. In Europe, try 21820 kHz.

**Radio Singapore International.** The third and final hour of a daily broadcasting package to Southeast Asia and beyond. Starts with a five-minute bulletin of the latest *news*, then most days it's music: *Singapop* (local talent, Monday and Thursday); *Rhythm in the Sun* (Tuesday and Sunday); *Spin the Globe* (world music, Wednesday and Saturday); and *Hot Trax* (new releases, Friday). There's more news on the half-hour, then a short feature. Monday's offering is *Family Ties*, replaced Tuesday by *The Write Stuff*. Wednesday's feature is *Potluck*; Thursday has *Call from America*; and Friday it's *Snapshot*. These are followed by the 15-minute *Newsline*. Weekend fare is made up of Saturday's *On the Line from Silicone Valley*, *On Second Thought* and *Arts Arena*; and Sunday's *A World of Our Own* and *Limelight*. The broadcast ends with yet another five-minute news update. On 6150 and 9600 kHz.

**Voice of Korea,** North Korea. Just about the last of the old-time communist stations, with quaint terms like "Great Leader" and "Unrivaled Great Man" seemingly destined for immortality. Starts with *"news,"* with much of the remainder of the broadcast devoted to revering the late Kim Il Sung. Abominably bad programs, but worth the occasional listen just to hear how awful they are. One hour to Europe on any two channels from 7505, 11335, 13760 and 15245 kHz; and to North America on 9335 and 11710 kHz. Also audible in parts of East Asia on 4405 kHz.

**WJIE,** Upton, Kentucky. Continues with Christian music to North America on 7490 kHz. Other U.S. religious broadcasters operating at this hour include **WWCR** on 5935 (or 13845) kHz, **KTBN** 7510 kHz, **WYFR-Family Radio** on 11740, 11830, 11970, 13695 and 17750 kHz, and **WHRI-World Harvest Radio** on 6040 and 15105 kHz.

Traditionalist Catholic programming is available via **WEWN** on 11875 kHz.

**HCJB—Voice of the Andes,** Ecuador. A further 60 minutes of religious broadcasting to the Americas on 12005 and 15115 kHz.

**Voice of America.** A mix of current events and sports, science, business and other news and features. To East Asia on 6110 (or 6160), 9760, 11705 (winter) and 15160 kHz; and to Australasia on 9645 and 15425 kHz. Both areas are also served by 11715 kHz until 1330.

**AFRTS Shortwave,** USA. Network news, live sports, music and features in the upper-sideband mode from the Armed Forces Radio & Television Service. Transmitted from modestly powered U.S. Navy stations around the globe. Try 4319, 5765, 6350, 6458.5, 10320, 12579, 12689.5 and 13362 kHz.

## 13:30

**United Arab Emirates Radio,** Dubai. *News*, then a feature on an Arab or Islamic theme. Twenty minutes to Europe and North Africa (also audible in eastern North America) on 13630, 13675, 15395 and 21605 kHz. The higher frequencies tend to vary somewhat.

**Radio Austria International.** Summer only at this time, and a repeat of the 1130 broadcast. See 1230 for program specifics. Thirty minutes to Europe on 6165 and 13730 kHz. One hour later in winter.

**Voice of Turkey.** This time winter only. *News*, then *Review of the Turkish Press* and features (some of them unusual) with a strong local flavor. Selections of Turkish popular and classical music complete the program. Fifty-five minutes to Europe on 17815 kHz, and to Southeast Asia and Australasia on 17690 kHz. One hour earlier in summer.

**Radio Sweden.** See 1230 for program details. Thirty minutes to North America summer on 18960 kHz. Also to Asia and Australasia winter on 9430 and year round on 17505 kHz.

**Voice of Vietnam.** Begins with *news*, then there's *Commentary* or *Weekly Review*, followed by short features and pleasant Vietnamese

**13:00–14:00**

Radio Vlaanderen Internationaal's broadcasting studio in Brussels, Belgium. Its "Music from Flanders" has been chosen by PASSPORT as being an exceptional program.
RVi

music (particularly at weekends). A half hour to Europe winter on 7145 (or 11575) and 9730 kHz, and summer on 11640 and 13740 kHz.

**All India Radio.** The first half hour of a 90-minute block of regional and international *news*, commentary, exotic Indian music, and a variety of talks and features of general interest. To Southeast Asia and beyond on 9690, 11620 and 13710 kHz.

**Radio Tashkent,** Uzbekistan. *News* and commentary, then features. Look for an information and music program on Tuesdays, with more music on Sundays. Apart from Wednesday's *Business Club*, most other features are broadcast on a non-weekly basis. Heard in Asia, Australasia, Europe and occasionally in North America; winter on 5060, 5975, 6025 and 9715 kHz; and summer on 7285, 9715, 15295 and 17775 kHz.

## 14:00

**■BBC World Service for the Americas.** *News*, then weekdays it's a series of 25-minute arts programs. The second half hour is much more lowbrow—popular music. By far the best are Monday's ●*Charlie Gillett* (world music) and Thursday's ●*John Peel* (eclectic and raw). Weekend programming consists of a five-

minute *news* bulletin followed by Saturday's live *Sportsworld* or a Sunday call-in show, *Talking Point*. Continuous to North America and the Caribbean on 15190 kHz. Listeners in the western United States may get better reception from the Asian stream on 9740 kHz.

**■BBC World Service for Europe.** Winter weekdays, five minutes of *news* are followed by an arts show, *Meridian*. The next half hour consists of a mixed bag of music and light entertainment. Same time summer, the *news* is followed by two features, including some of the BBC's better offerings—*Discovery* and *Essential Guide* (Monday), ●*Health Matters* and ●*Everywoman* (Tuesday), ●*Focus on Faith* (1430 Wednesday), *Sports International* and *Pick of the World* (Thursday) and Friday's ●*One Planet* and *People and Places*. Weekend programs are the same all year: five minutes of *news* followed by Saturday's *Sportsworld* or Sunday's *Talking Point*, a call-in show. Continuous to Europe and North Africa on 12095, 15485 and 15565 kHz.

**■BBC World Service for Eastern Europe and the Mideast.** Similar to the service for Asia and the Pacific, except for the first half hour weekdays, when *World Briefing* and ●*World Business Report* take the place of *East Asia Today*. Continuous programming on 15565, 15575 and 17740 kHz.

■**BBC World Service for East and Southeast Asia and the Pacific.** The weekday lineup is *East Asia Today*, *British News* and ●*Sports Roundup*. Weekends, starts with *news*, then it's either Saturday's live *Sportsworld* or Sunday's call-in show, *Talking Point*. Continuous to East and Southeast Asia on 6195 and 9740 kHz, and to Australasia on 9740 kHz (also audible in western North America).

**Radio Japan.** *News*, then Monday through Friday there's *Japan and the World 44 Minutes* (an in-depth look at current trends and events). This is replaced Saturday by *Weekend Square*, and Sunday by *Pop Joins the World*. One hour to the Mideast on 17755 kHz; to western North America on 9505 kHz; to South Asia on (winter) 9845 or (summer) 11730 kHz; and to Southeast Asia on 7200 kHz.

■**Radio France Internationale.** Weekdays, opens with international and Asian *news*; then come in-depth reports, a look at the main news event of the day in France, and sports. *Asia-Pacific*, replaces the international report on Saturday, and Sunday fare includes a weekly report on cultural events in France and a phone-in feature. These are followed on the half-hour by a 25-minute feature— *French Lesson*, *Crossroads*, *Voices*, *Rendez-Vous*, *World Tracks*, *Weekend* or *Club 9516* (a listener-response program). An hour of interesting and well-produced programming to the Mideast and beyond on 17620 kHz; and to South Asia on 11610 kHz.

**Radio Romania International.** First afternoon broadcast for European listeners. *News*, commentary, press review, and features about Romanian life and culture, interspersed with lively Romanian folk music. Fifty-five minutes winter on 11940, 15365 and 17790 kHz; and summer on 15250 and 17735 kHz.

**Voice of Russia World Service.** Summer only at this time. Eleven minutes of *News*, followed Monday through Saturday by much of the same in *News and Views*. Completing the lineup is *Sunday Panorama* and *Russia: People and Events*. On the half-hour, the lineup includes some of the station's better entertainment features. Try ●*Folk Box* (Monday), ●*Music at Your Request* or an alternative (Tuesday and Thursday), ●*Jazz Show* (Wednesday) and Friday's retrospective ●*Moscow Yesterday and Today*, all of which should please. Making up the roster are Saturday's *Timelines* and Sunday's *Kaleidoscope*. Targeted at South and Southeast Asia at this hour. In the Southeast, choose from 7390, 12055, 15560 and 17645 kHz.

**Radio Australia.** *World News* is followed Monday through Friday by a continuation of ●*The Planet* (world music), Saturday's *New Dimensions* or Sunday's *Books and Writing*. Continuous to Asia and the Pacific on 5995, 6080, 9580, 11650 and 11660 kHz (5995 and 9580 kHz are audible in North America, especially to the west). In Southeast Asia, use 6080 or 11660 kHz.

**Radio Prague,** Czech Republic. Winter only at this time. *News*, then weekdays there's the in-depth *Newsview* and one or more features: *One on One* (informal interviews, Monday); *Witness* and *Talking Point* or *Central Europe Today* (Tuesday); *ABC of Czech* and *Profile* or *Czechs in History* (Wednesday); *Economics Report* (Thursday); and *Magazine* ("the show that starts where the news ends") on Friday. The Saturday show is *Insight Central Europe*, replaced Sunday by *A Letter from Prague*, *The Arts* and *Mailbox*. A friendly half hour to eastern North America and East Africa on 21745 kHz. There is no corresponding summer broadcast.

**Voice of America.** This time winter only. The first of several hours of continuous programming to the Mideast. *News*, current events and short features covering sports, science, business, entertainment and other topics. On 15205 kHz.

**XERMX—Radio México Internacional.** Summer only at this time. Monday through Friday, there's an English summary of the Spanish-language *Antena Radio*, replaced Saturday by *Mirror of Mexico*, and Sunday by *Regional Roots and Rhythms*. Thirty minutes, best heard in western and southern parts of the United States on 9705 and 11770 kHz. One hour later in winter.

**Radio Taipei International,** Taiwan. Opens with 15 minutes of *News*, and weekdays closes

# www.Radioworld.ca

## Canada's Radio Superstore!

# GRUNDIG

## Satellit 800

- Fx Range: 100-30000 KHz, 87-108 & 118-136 MHz
- Direct Keypad entry Multi-Mode: AM-FM-SSB-LSB
- 3 Filters Built-in, Large LCD display
- C/W AC adapter and communication headphones

## YB-300PE*

- Receives MW, SW & FM broadcast
- 24 Memory Channels - PLL Technology
- Direct Keypad Entry, Digital readout
- Compact size, 8 x 5 x 1.25 in.,
- Telescopic antenna included

## YB-400PE

- Receives MW, SW & FM broadcast
- 40 Memory Channels
- SSB reception - Direct Keypad Entry
- Narrow AM filter - Compact size
- includes AC adapter

## SANGEAN

### ATS-818ACS

$179 us

Deluxe full featured shortwave radio Plus FM-Stereo- MW- LW- SW with built-in Cassette.

Cont. AM coverage from 150 to 29999 kHz
Direct key entry - Digital Tuning - 45 Mem
Wide/Narrow Filters - Fine Tuning - Scan
SSB & CW - RF Gain Control - Dual Time

### ATS-808A

$109 us

### ATS-606AP

$119 us

*Lowest Prices on Sangean*

## ICOM

**R10    R3    R2**

We stock all Icom Scanners & Receivers too!

**PCR-100
PCR-1000**

## AOR

We stock all AOR Scanners & Receivers incl.:  AR-8200MKII
AR-3000, AR-5000+, AR-8600, etc

## YUPITERU

We carry all
Yupiteru Scanners too!

## Visit our web site for all our specials: www.radioworld.ca

# AOR    ICOM    ALINCO    GRUNDIG
# YAESU    ICOM    SONY    YUPITERU
# SANGEAN    OPTOELECTRONICS    Bearcat    DRAKE

| Alpha-Delta | ARRL | Comet | Daiwa | Diamond | Garmin | Maha | MFJ |
| Passport | Premier | RF Limited | Timewave | Unadilla | Valor | Van Gordon | Vectronics | WRTH |

## Sold and Serviced by the most experienced staff in Canada

**Store Address:**
4335 Steeles Ave. W.,
Toronto, ON, Canada   M3N 1V7

**Store Hours :**
Monday, Tuesday, Wednesday & Friday: 10am - 5pm --- Thursday: 10am - 7pm --- Saturday: 10am - 3pm

**Phone Number:** **(416) 667-1000**

**FAX :** (416) 667-9995      **E-Mail:** sales @ radioworld.ca

with *Let's Learn Chinese*. In between, there are either one or two features, depending on the day of the week. Monday's offering is the pleasurable and exotic ●*Jade Bells and Bamboo Pipes* (Taiwanese music); Tuesday's pairing is *Culture Express* and *Trends*; the Wednesday slots are *Taiwan Today* and *Confucius and Inspiration Beyond*; Thursday has *Discover Taiwan* and *New Music Lounge*; and Friday's combo brings together *Taipei Magazine* and *People*. These are replaced Saturday by *Groove Zone* and *Kaleidoscope*, and Sunday by *Great Wall Forum* and *Mailbag Time*. One hour to Southeast Asia on 15265 kHz.

**China Radio International.** Starts with *News*, then weekdays there are background reports. The rest of the broadcast is devoted to features. Regular shows include *People in the Know* (Monday), *Biz China* (Tuesday), *China Horizons* (Wednesday), *Voices from Other Lands* (Thursday), and *Life in China* on Friday. The Saturday lineup includes *Global Review* and *Listeners' Garden* (reports, music and Chinese language lessons), and Sunday's broadcast has *Report from Developing Countries* and *In the Spotlight*. One hour to western North America on 7405 and 17720 kHz; to South

Asia on 9700, 11675, and (winter) 11765 or (summer) 15110 kHz; and to East Africa on 13685 and 15125 kHz.

**All India Radio.** The final hour of a 90-minute composite program of commentary, press review, features and exotic Indian music. To Southeast Asia and beyond on 9690, 11620 and 13710 kHz.

**Radio Canada International.** Winter weekdays, it's the second of three hours of *This Morning*; summer, the final 60 minutes of the same. Winter Saturdays, there's a look at Canadian politics in *The House*; summer, it's the entertaining ●*Vinyl Café*. On the remaining day, there's 60 minutes of another three-hour show, *The Sunday Edition*. To eastern North America and the Caribbean winter on 9515, 13655 and 17710 kHz; and summer on 9515, 13655 and (Monday through Friday) 17820 kHz. Weekends, 17820 kHz is replaced by 17800 kHz.

**HCJB—Voice of the Andes,** Ecuador. The final half hour of a 210-minute block of religious programs to the Americas on 12005 and 15115 kHz.

**CBC North-Québec,** Canada. Continues with multilingual programming for a domestic audience. *News*, followed winter Saturdays by *The House* (Canadian politics). In summer, it's *The Great Eastern*, a magazine for Newfoundlanders. Sundays, there's 60 minutes of the three-hour *Sunday Morning*. Weekday programs are in languages other than English. Audible in the northeastern United States on 9625 kHz.

**Radio Jordan.** A partial relay of the station's domestic broadcasts, beamed to Europe on 11690 kHz. Continuous till 1630 (1730 in winter).Also audible in parts of eastern North America, especially during winter. Tends to be irregular.

**Voice of America.** *News* and reports on a variety of topics. To East Asia on 6110 (or 6160), 9760, 11705 (winter) and 15160 kHz; and to Australasia on 15425 kHz.

**Radio Thailand.** Thirty minutes of tourist features for Southeast Asia and Australasia; winter on 9530 kHz, and summer on 9830 kHz.

**Radio New Zealand International's news team. This delightful station has a surprisingly long reach, even being audible part of the year in Eastern North America.**

RNZI

**WJIE,** Upton, Kentucky. Continues with Christian music to North America on 7490 kHz. Other U.S. religious broadcasters operating at this hour include **WWCR** on 13845 and 15685 kHz, **KTBN** on 7510 kHz, **WYFR-Family Radio** on 11740, 11830, 11970 (or 17760) and 17750 kHz, and **WHRI-World Harvest Radio** on 6040 and 15105 kHz. For traditionalist Catholic fare, try **WEWN** on 11875 kHz.

**CFRX-CFRB,** Toronto, Canada. Audible throughout much of the northeastern United States and southeastern Canada during the hours of daylight with a modest, but clear, signal on 6070 kHz. This pleasant, friendly station carries news, sports, weather and traffic reports—most of it intended for a local audience. Call in if you'd like at +1 (514) 790-0600—comments from outside Ontario are welcomed. Weekdays at this hour, you can hear *The Charles Adler Show*.

**AFRTS Shortwave,** USA. Network news, live sports, music and features in the upper-sideband mode from the Armed Forces Radio & Television Service. Transmitted from modestly powered U.S. Navy stations around the globe. Try 4319, 5765, 6350, 6458.5, 10320, 12579, 12689.5 and 13362 kHz.

## 14:30

■**Radio Netherlands.** The first 60 minutes of a two-hour block of programming. Monday through Friday it's ●*Newsline* (current events) and a feature. Pick of an excellent pack are ●*Research File* (science, Monday), ●*Encore* (Thursday), ●*A Good Life* (Friday) and Wednesday's award-winning ●*Documentary*. Making up the roster is Tuesday's *Music 52-15*, (good at its best). Weekend programming opens with *News*, then it's either Saturday's *Europe Unzipped*, *Insight* and *Sound Fountain* (replaced summer by ●*Aural Tapestry)*; or Sunday's *Sincerely Yours*, a program preview and *Dutch Horizons*. To South Asia winter on 12070, 12080 and 15595 kHz; and summer on 9890, 11835 and 12075 kHz. Also year round to western North America on 15220 kHz.

**Radio Austria International.** Winter only at this time. Monday through Friday there's a brief bulletin of *news*, then the informative ●*Report from Austria*. The weekend shows are two European co-productions: *Insight Central Europe* on Saturday, and *Network Europe* on Sunday. Thirty minutes to Europe on 6155 and 13730 kHz. One hour earlier in summer.

**Radio Sweden.** Winter only at this time. Monday through Friday, it's *news* and features in *Sixty Degrees North*, concentrating heavily on Scandinavian topics. Several of the features rotate from week to week, but a few are fixtures. Monday's *SportScan* is replaced Tuesday by *Close Up* or an alternative feature, and Wednesday by *Money Matters*. Thursday's carousel is *Nordic Report*, *GreenScan* (the environment), *Heart Beat* (health), and *S-Files*, with *Weekly Review* filling the Saturday slot. The Sunday rotation is *Weekend*, *Spectrum*, *Sweden Today* and *Studio 49*, while Monday's offering is *In Touch with Stockholm* (a listener-response program) or the musical *Sounds Nordic*. Thirty minutes to North America on 18960 kHz, and to Asia and Australasia on 17505 kHz.

## 15:00

■**BBC World Service for the Americas.** Starts with five minutes of *news*, then features, including some of the BBC's better offerings—●*One Planet* (1505 Monday), *Science in Action* (same time Tuesday), ●*Health Matters* and ●*Everywoman* (Wednesday), ●*Omnibus* (1530 Thursday), *Discovery* (science) and *Sports International* (Friday). Saturday has live action in *Sportsworld*, and Sunday programming is either more sport or the finest in classical music. Continuous programming to the Caribbean and North America on 15190 kHz. In western states, try the Asian stream on 9740 kHz—you may well get better reception.

■**BBC World Service for Europe.** Winter, identical to the service for the Americas. In summer, the format is *World Briefing*, *British News* and ●*Analysis* (except Wednesday, when you can hear ●*From Our Own Correspondent*). Saturday, it's a continuation of *Sportsworld*, and Sunday there's some fine classical music (features vary). Continuous to Europe and

**15:00–15:00**

Radio Galkayo's antenna was upgraded with the support of the International Amateur Radio Club, Rotary Boulder in Western Australia and an Australian government grant. S. Voron

North Africa on 9410 (winter), 12095, 15485 and 15565 kHz.

■**BBC World Service for Eastern Europe and the Mideast.** The weekday lineup is *News*, ●*Outlook* and a 15-minute feature (very much a mixed bag). The Saturday news is followed by a continuation of *Sportsworld*, and Sunday it's time for the BBC's weekly concert of classical music (definitely worth hearing). On 15575 kHz (additional frequencies may be available winter).

■**BBC World Service for East and Southeast Asia and the Pacific.** *News*, then Monday through Friday, *Meridian* (the arts). The second half hour is totally different— either a soap or popular music. These are replaced Saturday by the live *Sportsworld*, and Sunday by *The Alternative* (popular music) and ●*Omnibus* (winter) or *Composer of the Month* (summer). Continuous to East and Southeast Asia on 6195 and 9740 kHz, and to Australasia on 9740 kHz (also heard in western North America).

**China Radio International.** See 1400 for program details. Sixty minutes to western North America on 7405 (winter) and 17720 kHz. Also available year round to South Asia on 7160 and 9785 kHz; and to East Africa on 13685 and 15125 kHz.

**Radio Australia.** *World News*, then weekdays there's *Asia Pacific* and a feature on the half-hour. Monday, it's health; Tuesday, law; Wednesday, religion; Thursday, media; and Friday, sport. These are replaced Saturday by *Melisma* (classical music), and Sunday by *Encounter* and *Business Weekend*. Continuous programming to the Pacific on 5995, 9580 and 11650 kHz (also well heard in western North America). Additionally available to Southeast Asia on 6080 and 11660 kHz.

**Voice of America.** Continues with programming to the Mideast. A mixed bag of current events and sports, science, business and other news and features. Winter on 9575 and 15205 kHz, and summer on 9700 and 15205 kHz. Also heard in much of Europe.

**Radio Canada International.** Daily in winter, but weekends only in summer. Winter weekdays, it's the final 60 minutes of *This Morning*; replaced Saturday by the unique ●*Vinyl Café* (readings and music). Summer, the Saturday slot goes to ●*Quirks and Quarks* (a science show with a difference). On the remaining day it's *The Sunday Edition* both winter and summer. To North America and the Caribbean, winter on 9515, 13655 and 17710 kHz; and summer on 9515, 13655 and 17800 kHz. For a separate broadcast to South Asia, see the next item.

**Radio Canada International.** *News*, then Tuesday through Saturday it's ●*This Morning Tonight*. Sunday's feature is ●*Global Village* (world music at its best) and Monday there's ●*Quirks and Quarks*, a unique science show. Sixty minutes to South Asia winter on 15360 and 17820 kHz, and summer on 15455 and 17720 kHz. Heard well beyond the intended target area, especially to the west.

**XERMX—Radio México Internacional.** Winter weekdays, there's an English summary of the Spanish-language *Antena Radio*, replaced Saturday by *Mirror of Mexico*, and Sunday by *Regional Roots and Rhythms*. The summer lineup consists of *Mirror of Mexico* (Monday), *Mailbox* (Tuesday and Sunday), *Magical Trip* (Wednesday), *DXperience* (for radio enthusiasts, Thursday), *Regional Roots and Rhythms* (Friday) and *Mosaic of Mexico* (Saturday). Thirty minutes to North America, best heard in western and southern parts of the United States on 9705 and 11770 kHz.

**Radio Japan.** *News*, then Monday through Friday there's *Asian Top News* and a 35-minute feature. Pick from *Japan Music Log* (Monday), Japanese language lessons (Tuesday and Thursday), *Japan Musical Treasure Box* (Wednesday), and *Music Beat* (Japanese popular music, Friday). *Pop Joins the World* fills the Saturday slot, replaced Sunday by *Hello from Tokyo*. One hour to East Asia on 9750 kHz; to South Asia on (winter) 9845 or (summer) 11730 kHz; and to Southeast Asia on 7200 kHz.

**Voice of Russia World Service.** Predominantly news-related fare for the first half-hour, then a mixed bag, depending on the day and season. At 1531 winter, look for ●*Folk Box* (Monday), ●*Jazz Show* (Wednesday), ●*Music at Your Request* or an alternative (Tuesday and Thursday), *Kaleidoscope* (Sunday) and Friday's retrospective ●*Moscow Yesterday and Today*. Summer at this time, look for some listener favorites. The lineup includes *This is Russia* (Monday), ●*Moscow Yesterday and Today* (Tuesday), ●*Audio Book Club* (dramatized reading, Wednesday), the incomparable ●*Folk Box* (Thursday), and *Songs from Russia* on Friday. Weekend fare is split between Saturday's *Kaleidoscope* and Sunday's *Russian*

*by Radio*. To the Mideast summer on 7325 and 11985 kHz; and to Southeast Asia winter on 6205 an 11500 kHz, and summer on 7390 and 11500 kHz.

**Voice of Mongolia.** *News*, reports and short features dealing with local issues, with Sunday featuring lots of exotic Mongolian music. Thirty minutes to eastern Europe and West and Central Asia on 12015 kHz, and sometimes heard beyond.

**WJIE,** Upton, Kentucky. Continues with Christian music to North America on 7490 kHz. Other U.S. religious broadcasters operating at this hour include **WWCR** on 13845 kHz, **KTBN** on 7510 (or 15590) kHz, and **WYFR-Family Radio** on 11830 and 17750 (or 17760) kHz. Traditionalist Catholic programming is available from **WEWN** on 11875 kHz.

**Radio Jordan.** A partial relay of the station's domestic broadcasts, beamed to Europe on 11690 kHz. Continuous till 1630 (1730 in winter). Audible in parts of eastern North America, especially during winter. Has tended to be irregular in recent years.

**Voice of Korea,** North Korea. Repeat of the 1300 broadcast; see there for specifics. Abominably bad programs, but improvement may be on the way now that the country is beginning to accept outside help. One hour to Europe on any two channels from 7505, 11335, 13760 and 15245 kHz; and to North America on 9335 and 11710 kHz. Also audible in parts of East Asia on 4405 kHz.

**CFRX-CFRB,** Toronto, Canada. See 1400. Monday through Friday, it's a continuation of *The Charles Adler Show*. Look for *News and Commentary* summer at 1550. Weekend fare consists of *The CFRB Gardening Show* (Saturday) replaced the following day by *CFRB Sunday*. On 6070 kHz.

**AFRTS Shortwave,** USA. Network news, live sports, music and features in the upper-sideband mode from the Armed Forces Radio & Television Service. Transmitted from modestly powered U.S. Navy stations around the globe. Try 4319, 5765, 6350, 6458.5, 10320, 12579, 12689.5 and 13362 kHz.

**15:30–16:00**

## 15:30

■**Radio Netherlands.** The second of two hours targeted at western North America and South Asia. Monday through Friday, starts with a feature and ends with ●*Newsline* (current events). Choice pickings include ●*EuroQuest* (Monday), ●*A Good Life* (Tuesday), ●*Research File* (science, Thursday) and Friday's ●*Documentary* (winner of several prestigious awards). The weekend format is feature-news-feature. Saturday fare includes *Europe Unzipped*; Sunday, there's *Sound Fountain* (replaced summer by ●*Aural Tapestry*) and *Wide Angle*. To South Asia winter on 12070, 12080 and 15595 kHz; and summer on 9890, 11835 and 12075 kHz. Also year round to western North America on 15220 kHz.

**Voice of the Islamic Republic of Iran.** A one-hour broadcast of news, commentary and features, strongly reflecting an Islamic point of view. To South and Southeast Asia and Australasia winter on four of more channels from 7115, 7180, 9605, 11640, 11775, 11835 and 11870 kHz; and summer on 7245, 9635 and 11775 kHz. Frequency usage tends to be a little erratic, though not as much as in the past.

## 16:00

■**BBC World Service for the Americas.** Monday through Friday winter, it's *World Briefing, British News,* ●*Analysis* (except Wednesday's ●*From Our Own Correspondent*) and ●*Sports Roundup*; summer, there's ●*Europe Today,* ●*World Business Report* and ●*Sports Roundup*. Weekends, year round, there's a short *news* bulletin followed by live sports. The final hour to the Caribbean and North America on 15190 kHz.

■**BBC World Service for Europe.** Monday through Saturday, is identical to the service for East and Southeast Asia. Sunday, the winter offering is a concert of classical music (well worth hearing); summer, there's live sports. Continuous to Europe and North Africa on 9410, 12095 and 15565 kHz.

■**BBC World Service for Eastern Europe and the Mideast.** *News*, then Monday through Friday, *Meridian* (the arts) and a soap or popular music. Weekends, there's live sports. Continuous programming on 15565 and 15575 kHz.

■**BBC World Service for East and Southeast Asia.** Winter weekdays, there's *World Briefing, British News,* ●*Analysis* (except for Thursday's ●*From Our Own Correspondent*), and ●*Sports Roundup*. These are replaced in summer by ●*Europe Today,* ●*World Business Report* and ●*Sports Roundup*. Saturdays and summer Sundays, a five-minute *news* bulletin is followed by live sports. In winter, the Sunday lineup is *World Briefing, British News,* ●*Reporting Religion* and ●*Sports Roundup*. The final hour to East Asia on 6195 kHz; and continuous to Southeast Asia on 3915 and 7160 kHz.

■**Radio France Internationale.** The first half hour includes *news* and reports from across Africa, international newsflashes and news about France. Next is a 25-minute feature— *French Lesson, Crossroads, Voices, Rendez-Vous, World Tracks, Weekend* or *Club 9516* (a listener-response program). A fast-moving hour to Africa and the Mideast on 11615, 11995, 12015, 15605, 17605 and 17850 kHz. Best for the Mideast is 11615 kHz in winter, and 15605 kHz in summer. For southern Africa, 12015 and 17850 kHz should be more than enough.

**United Arab Emirates Radio,** Dubai. A 15-minute feature on Arab history or culture, and preceded and followed by programming in Arabic. A little later, around 1630, there's a short bulletin of *news*. To Europe and North Africa (also heard in eastern North America) on 13630, 13675, 15395 and 21605 kHz (the last two frequencies tend to vary a little).

■**Deutsche Welle,** Germany. *News*, then Monday through Friday it's ●*NewsLink* followed by *Africa Report*. Weekends, the Saturday news is followed by *Talking Point* and ●*Spectrum*, with *Religion and Society* and *Arts on the Air* filling the Sunday slots. Forty-five minutes aimed primarily at eastern, central and southern parts of Africa, but also audible outside the continent. Winter on 9735, 15455 and 21840 kHz; and summer on 9735, 11665

**15:30–16:00**

Canadian teacher Neil Carleton brings the joy of shortwave to his students. His latest: the world band radio and ham club at the R. Tait McKenzie Public School in Almonte, Ontario.

N. Carleton

and 21840 kHz. For a separate service to South Asia and beyond, see the next entry.

■**Deutsche Welle,** Germany. Similar to the broadcast for Africa (see previous entry), except that *Asia-Pacific Report* replaces *Africa Report*, and *Cool* is aired in place of Sunday's *Arts on the Air*. Nominally to South Asia, but heard well beyond. Winter on 7225, 11695 and 13605 kHz; and summer on 6170, 7225 and 17595 kHz.

**Radio Korea International,** South Korea. Opens with *news* and commentary, followed Monday through Wednesday by *Seoul Calling*. Weekly features include *Echoes of Korean Music* and *Shortwave Feedback* (Sunday), *Tales from Korea's Past* (Monday), *Korean Cultural Trails* (Tuesday), *Pulse of Korea* (Wednesday), *From Us to You* (a listener-response program) and *Let's Learn Korean* (Thursday), *Let's Sing Together* and *Korea Through Foreigners' Eyes* (Friday), and Saturday's *Discovering Korea*, *Korean Literary Corner* and *Weekly News Focus*. One hour to East Asia on 5975 kHz, and to the Mideast and much of Africa on 9515 and 9870 kHz.

**Radio Taipei International,** Taiwan. Opens with 15 minutes of *News*, and weekdays closes with *Let's Learn Chinese*. In between, there are either one or two features, depending on the day of the week. Monday, you can listen to the

pleasurable and exotic ●*Jade Bells and Bamboo Pipes* (Taiwanese music); and Tuesday to *Culture Express* and *Trends.* Wednesday's slots are *Taiwan Today* and *Confucius and Inspiration Beyond*; Thursday fare is *Discover Taiwan* and *New Music Lounge*; and Friday brings together *Taipei Magazine* and *People.* These are replaced Saturday by *Groove Zone* and *Kaleidoscope*, and Sunday by *Great Wall Forum* and *Mailbag Time.* The first of two hours to South Asia on 11550 kHz, and heard well beyond.

**Voice of Korea,** North Korea. Repeat of the 1500 broadcast. Just about the last of the old-time communist stations. One hour to the Mideast and Africa on 9975 and 11735 kHz; and also heard in parts of East Asia on 3560 kHz.

**Radio Pakistan.** Winter only at this time. Fifteen minutes of *news* from the Pakistan Broadcasting Corporation's domestic service. Intended for the Mideast and Africa, but heard well beyond. Try 11570, 15335 and 15725 kHz.

**Radio Prague,** Czech Republic. Summer only at this time. Monday's *One on One* (a series of informal interviews) is replaced Tuesday by *Witness* and *Talking Point* or *Central Europe Today*; and Wednesday by *ABC of Czech* and either *Czechs in History* or *Profile.* The business-oriented *Economic Report* fills the Thursday slot, and *Magazine* is Friday's show. Weekends, the news is followed by Saturday's *Spotlight* (Czech regional issues) and *Readings from Czech Literature* or *Saturday Music*; and Sunday's *A Letter from Prague*, *The Arts* and *Mailbox*. A half hour to Europe on 5930 kHz, and to East Africa on 21745 kHz. The transmission for Europe is one hour later in winter, but there is no corresponding broadcast for East Africa.

**Radio Algiers,** Algeria. *News*, then western and Arab popular music, with an occasional feature thrown in. One hour of so-so reception in Europe, and sometimes heard in eastern North America. On 11715 and 15160 kHz. Tends to be irregular.

**Radio Australia.** Continuous programming to Asia and the Pacific. At this hour *World News* is followed by *Margaret Throsby* (interviews and music, Monday), *The Comfort Zone* (Tuesday), *Verbatim* (personal experiences) and *Earshot* (Wednesday), *Hindsight* (a look back into history, Thursday), and Friday's show of Australian indigenous music and stories, *Awaye* Saturday brings a continuation of *Melisma*, replaced Sunday by *The National Interest* (topical events). Beamed to the Pacific on 5995, 9580 and 11650 kHz (and well heard in western North America). Additionally available to East and Southeast Asia on 6080, 9475 and 11660 kHz.

**Radio Ethiopia.** An hour-long broadcast divided into two parts by the 1630 *news* bulletin. Regular weekday features include *Kaleidoscope* and *Women's Forum* (Monday), *Press Review* and *Africa in Focus* (Tuesday), *Guest of the Week* and *Ethiopia Today* (Wednesday), *Ethiopian Music* and *Spotlight* (Thursday) and *Press Review* and *Introducing Ethiopia* on Friday. For weekend listening, there's *Contact* and *Ethiopia This Week* (Saturday), or Sunday's *Listeners' Choice* and *Commentary*. Best heard in parts of Africa and the Mideast, but sometimes audible in Europe. On 7165, 9560 and 11800 kHz.

**Radio Jordan.** A partial relay of the station's domestic broadcasts, beamed to Europe on 11690 kHz. The final half hour in summer, but a full 60 minutes in winter. Audible in parts of eastern North America, especially during winter. Tends to be irregular.

**Voice of Russia World Service.** Continuous programming to the Mideast and West Asia at this hour. *News*, then very much a mixed bag, depending on the day and season. Winter weekdays, there's *Focus on Asia and the Pacific*, with Saturday's *Newmarket* and Sunday's *Moscow Mailbag* making up the week. On the half-hour, choose from *This is Russia* (Monday), ●*Moscow Yesterday and Today* (Tuesday), ●*Audio Book Club* (dramatized reading, Wednesday), the exotic and eclectic ●*Folk Box* (Thursday), and Friday's *Songs from Russia*. Weekend fare is split between Saturday's *Kaleidoscope* and Sunday's *Russian by Radio*. Summer, the news is followed by the business-oriented *Newmarket* (Monday and Thursday), *Science and Engineering* (Tuesday and Sunday), *Moscow Mailbag* (Wednesday and Friday), and Saturday's showpiece, ●*Music and Musicians*. The features after the half-hour tend to be variable. Audible in the Mideast winter on 6005 and 9830 kHz, and summer on 11985 and 15540 kHz.

**Radio Canada International.** Winter weekends only at this hour. Saturday, there's ●*Quirks and Quarks* (science), and Sunday it's the final hour of *The Sunday Edition*. To North America and the Caribbean on 9515, 13655 and 17710 kHz.

**XERMX—Radio México Internacional.** Winter only at this time. Take your pick from *Mirror of Mexico* (Monday), *Mailbox* (Tuesday and Sunday), *Magical Trip* (Wednesday), *DXperience* (a show for radio enthusiasts, Thursday), *Regional Roots and Rhythms* (Friday) and *Mosaic of Mexico* (Saturday). Thirty minutes to western and southern parts of the United States on 9705 and 11770 kHz. One hour earlier in summer.

**China Radio International.** Starts with *News*, then weekdays continues with in-depth reports. The remainder of the broadcast is made up of features. Regular shows include *People in the Know* (Monday), *Biz China* (Tuesday), *China Horizons* (Wednesday), *Voices from Other Lands* (Thursday) and Friday's *Life in China*. Saturday, there's *Global Review* and *Listeners' Garden* (reports, music and a Chinese language lesson), replaced Sunday by *Report from Developing Countries* and *In the*

*Spotlight.* One hour to eastern and southern Africa winter on 13650 kHz, and midyear on 9565 kHz.

**Voice of America.** Several hours of continuous programming aimed at an African audience. At this hour, there's a split between mainstream programming and news and features in "Special" (slow-speed) English. The former can be heard on 6035, 13710, 15225 and 15410 kHz, and the "Special" programs on 13600, 15445 and (summer) 17895 kHz. For a separate service to the Mideast, see the next item.

**Voice of America.** *News Now*—a mixed bag of news and reports on current events, sports, science, business and more. To the Mideast winter on 9575 and 15205 kHz, and summer on 9700 and 15205 kHz. Also heard in much of Europe.

**WJIE,** Upton, Kentucky. Continues with Christian music to North America on 7490 kHz. Other U.S. religious broadcasters operating at this hour include **WWCR** on 13845 and 15685 kHz, **KTBN** on 15590 kHz, and **WYFR-Family Radio** on 11830 and 17750 (or 17760) kHz. Traditionalist Catholic programming can be heard via **WEWN** on 11875 and 13615 kHz.

**CFRX-CFRB,** Toronto, Canada. See 1400. Winter weekdays, it's the final part of *The Charles Adler Show*, with *The CFRB Gardening Show* and *CFRB Sunday* the weekend offerings. Summer, look for *The Motts* Monday through Friday, and ●*The World at Noon* on weekends.

**AFRTS Shortwave,** USA. Network news, live sports, music and features in the upper-sideband mode from the Armed Forces Radio & Television Service. Transmitted from modestly powered U.S. Navy stations around the globe. Try 4319, 5765, 6350, 6458.5, 10320, 12579, 12689.5 and 13362 kHz.

### 16:30

**Radio Slovakia International.** Summer only at this time; see 1730 for specifics. Thirty minutes of friendly programming to western Europe on 5920, 6055 and 7345 kHz. One hour later in winter.

**Voice of Vietnam.** *News*, then *Commentary* or *Weekly Review* followed by short features and pleasant Vietnamese music (especially at weekends). A half hour to Europe winter on 7145 (or 11575) and 9730 kHz, and summer on 11640 and 13740 kHz.

**Kol Israel.** Summer only at this time. Fifteen minutes from Israel Radio's domestic network. To Europe and eastern North America on 17545 kHz. One hour later in winter.

**Xizang [Tibet] People's Broadcasting Station, China.** Monday through Saturday only. *Holy Tibet*, which describes itself as "a window to life in Tibet," is a 20-minute package of information and local music—mountains, monasteries, local customs, and (mostly) Tibetan popular music. Sometimes acknowledges listeners' reception reports at the end of the program. Original editions are aired on Monday, Wednesday and Friday, and repeated at the same time the next day. Well heard in East Asia, and sometimes provides fair reception in Europe. On 4905, 4920, 5240, 6110, 6130, 6200, 7385 and 9490 kHz.

**Radio Cairo,** Egypt. The first 30 minutes of a two-hour mix of Arab music and features on Egyptian and Islamic themes, with *news*, commentary, quizzes, mailbag shows, and answers to listeners' questions. To southern Africa on 15255 kHz.

### 17:00

■**BBC World Service for Europe.** Identical to the service for Southeast Asia. Continuous to Europe and North Africa on 6195 and 9410 kHz.

■**BBC World Service for Eastern Europe and the Mideast.** Starts weekdays with five minutes of *news*, then there's a pair of features: ●*Health Matters* and ●*Everywoman* (Monday), *Science View* and ●*Focus on Faith* (Tuesday), *Sports International* and *Pick of the World* (Wednesday), ●*One Planet* and *People and Places* (Thursday), and *Discovery* and *Essential Guide* on Friday. Some of the BBC's best. Saturday's lineup consists of *World Briefing*, *British News* and *Westway* (a soap); Sunday, it's the first hour of ●*Play of the Week*. On 11980 (winter), 12095 and 15575 kHz.

**17:00–17:00**

High-stepping Dinka youth
march off to attend a
regional peace conference.
New Sudan Council of Churches

■**BBC World Service for Southern Africa.**
*News*, *Focus on Africa*, and ●*Sports Roundup*.
Part of a 19-hour daily service on a variety of
channels. At this hour, on 3255, 6190 and
15400 kHz.

■**BBC World Service for Southeast Asia.**
Monday through Friday winter, there's
●*Europe Today*, ●*World Business Report* and
●*Sports Roundup*. Summer replacements are a
five-minute *news* bulletin, *Outlook* (news and
human interest stories) and a 15-minute
feature (very much a mixed bag). Winter
Saturdays, it's *World Briefing*, *British News* and
●*Sportsworld*, replaced summer by ●*From Our
Own Correspondent* and ●*Agenda*. Sunday's
winter offerings are *Global Business* and
●*Agenda*, with ●*Play of the Week* filling the
summer slot. The final hour to Southeast Asia,
on 3915 and 7160 kHz.

**Radio Prague,** Czech Republic. Similar to the
1600 broadcast (see there for program
specifics), but summer Saturdays, *Insight
Central Europe* replaces *Spotlight* and *Readings
from Czech Literature* or *Saturday Music*. A half
hour year round to Europe on 5930 kHz; also
winter to West and Central Africa on 17485
kHz, and summer to central and southern
Africa on 21745 kHz.

**Radio Romania International.** *News*,
commentary, a press review, and several short
features. Music, too. Thirty minutes to Europe
winter on 9625 11830, 11940 and 15245 kHz;
and summer on 11740, 15365, 15380, 17735
and 17805 kHz.

**Radio Australia.** Continuous programming to
Asia and the Pacific. Starts with *World News*,
then Monday through Friday there's *Bush
Telegraph*, a light-hearted look at rural and
regional issues in Australia. Replaced Satur-
day by *The Spirit of Things*, and Sunday by *New
Dimensions*. Beamed to the Pacific on 5995,
9580, 9815 and 11880 kHz; and to East and
Southeast Asia on 6080 and 9475 kHz.
Listeners in Japan should tune to 9815 kHz.
Also audible in parts of western North America
on 5995, 9580 and 11880 kHz.

**Radio Polonia,** Poland. This time summer
only. Monday through Friday, it's *News from
Poland*—a compendium of news, reports and
interviews. This is followed by *Cookery Corner*
and *The Best of Polish Radio* (Monday), *Letter
from Poland* and *Multimedia Show* (Tuesday),
*Day in the Life* and *Discovering Chopin* (Wednesday), *Focus* (the arts in Poland) and *Soundcheck*
(Thursday), and Friday's *Business Week*
followed by *Postbag*, a listener-response show.
The Saturday broadcast begins with a bulletin
of *news*, then there's *Europe East, The Weeklies*
and *Chart Show*. Sundays, it's five minutes of
*news* followed by *Panorama* and *Request
Concert*. Sixty minutes to Europe on 6000 and
7285 kHz. One hour later during winter.

**Radio Jordan.** Winter only at this time. The
last 30 minutes of a partial relay of the
station's domestic broadcasts, beamed to
Europe on 11690 kHz. Tends to be irregular.

**Voice of Russia World Service.** *News*, then
it's a mixed bag, depending on the day and

season. Winter, the news is followed by the business-oriented *Newmarket* (Monday and Thursday), *Science and Engineering* (Tuesday and Sunday), and *Moscow Mailbag* (Wednesday and Friday). The choice of features for the second half hour is somewhat variable. In summer, the news is followed by a series of features: *Moscow Mailbag* (Monday, Thursday and Saturday), *Newmarket* (Tuesday and Friday), *Science and Engineering* (Wednesday) and Sunday's jewel, *Music and Musicians* On the half-hour, the lineup includes *Kaleidoscope* (Monday), ●*Music at Your Request* or an alternative (Tuesday), ●*Moscow Yesterday and Today* (Wednesday), Friday's ●*Folk Box* and Saturday's *Songs from Russia*. Summer only to Europe on 9775 and 9890 kHz, plus weekends on 9480 and 11675 kHz. For the Mideast, tune to 9470 and 9830 kHz in winter, and 11985 kHz in summer. In Southern Africa, try 11510 kHz midyear.

**Kol Israel.** Winter only at this time. Thirty minutes from Israel Radio's domestic network. To Europe and eastern North America on 17545 kHz. One hour earlier in summer.

**Radio Japan.** *News*, then weekdays look for some in-depth reporting in *Japan and the World 44 Minutes*. Saturday's feature is *Hello From Tokyo*, replaced Sunday by *Pop Joins the World*. One hour to Europe on 11970 kHz; to southern Africa on 15355 kHz; and to western North America on 9505 kHz.

**Radio Taipei International,** Taiwan. The final 60 minutes of a two-hour block of programs to South Asia. Opens with 15 minutes of *News*, and closes weekdays with *Let's Learn Chinese*. The remaining airtime is taken up by features. Monday, there's *Taiwan Economic Journal* followed by *People*; Tuesday offers ●*Jade Bells and Bamboo Pipes*; Wednesday's lineup is *New Music Lounge* and *Confucius and Inspiration Beyond*; Thursday's combo is *Taipei Magazine* and *Life Unusual*; and Friday's menu consists of *Taiwan Gourmet* and *Discover Taiwan*. The Saturday slots go to *Kaleidoscope* and *Mailbag Time*, replaced Sunday by *Great Wall Forum* and *Asia Pacific*. On 11550 kHz.

**China Radio International.** Repeat of the 1600 transmission; see there for specifics.

One hour to eastern and southern parts of Africa winter on 7150, 9570 and 9695 kHz; and midyear on 9570, 9695, 11920 and 15265 kHz. Also available year round to the Mideast on 9670 kHz.

**Voice of Vietnam.** Summer only at this time. Thirty minutes to western Europe via an Austrian relay on 9725 kHz. See 1800 for specifics. One hour later in winter.

**Voice of America.** Continuous programming to the Mideast and North Africa. *News*, then Monday through Friday it's the interactive *Talk to America*. Weekends, there's the ubiquitous *News Now*. Winter on 6040, 9760 and 15205 kHz; and summer on 9760, 15135 and 15255 kHz. Also heard in much of Europe. For a separate service to Africa, see the next item.

**Voice of America.** Programs for Africa. Monday through Saturday, identical to the service for Europe and the Mideast (see previous item). Sunday on the half-hour, look for the entertaining ●*Music Time in Africa*. Audible well beyond where it is targeted. On 6035, 7415, 11920, 11975, 12040, 13710, 15410, 15445 and 17895 kHz, some of which are seasonal. For yet another service (to East Asia and the Pacific), see the next item.

**Voice of America.** Monday through Friday only. *News*, followed by the interactive *Talk to America*. Sixty minutes to Asia on 5990, 6045, 6110/6160, 7125, 7215, 9525, 9645, 9670, 9770, 11945, 12005 and 15255 kHz, some of which are seasonal. For Australasia, try 9525 and 15255 kHz in winter, and 7150 and 7170 kHz in summer.

■**Radio France Internationale.** An additional half-hour (see 1600) of predominantly African fare. Monday through Friday, focuses on *news* from the eastern part of Africa. Weekends, there's *Spotlight on Africa*, health issues, features on French culture, sports, media in Africa, and a phone-in feature, *On-Line*. To East Africa and the Mideast on any two channels from 11615, 15605 and 17605 kHz. Occasionally heard in North America.

**Radio Cairo,** Egypt. See 1630 for specifics. Continues with a broadcast to southern Africa on 15255 kHz.

**17:00–18:00**

**WJIE,** Upton, Kentucky. Continues with Christian music to North America on 7490 kHz. Other U.S. religious broadcasters operating at this hour include **WWCR** on 13845 and 15685 kHz, **KTBN** on 15590 kHz, and **WHRI-World Harvest Radio** on 13760 and 15105 kHz.

**CFRX-CFRB,** Toronto, Canada. See 1400. Winter weekends at this time, there's ●*The World at Noon*; summer, it's *The Mike Stafford Show*. Monday through Friday, look for *The Motts*. On 6070 kHz.

**AFRTS Shortwave,** USA. Network news, live sports, music and features in the upper-sideband mode from the Armed Forces Radio & Television Service. Transmitted from modestly powered U.S. Navy stations around the globe. Try 4319, 5765, 6350, 6458.5, 10320, 12579, 12689.5 and 13362 kHz.

## 17:30

■**Radio Netherlands.** The first of three hours targeted at Africa, and heard well beyond. Monday through Friday, the initial 30 minutes are taken up by ●*Newsline* (current events), with a feature occupying the second half hour. Best of a good bunch are ●*Research File* (Monday), ●*Documentary* (Wednesday), ●*Aural Tapestry* (summer Thursdays, and replaced by *Sound Fountain* in winter) and ●*A Good Life* on Friday. For a change of pace, try the eclectic *Music 52-15* aired each Tuesday. Weekend fare consists of *news* followed by Saturday's *Europe Unzipped*, *Insight* and *Sound Fountain* (●*Aural Tapestry* midyear); and Sunday's *Sincerely Yours* (a listener-response show) and *Dutch Horizons*. Sixty minutes on 6020 (best for southern Africa), 7120 (summer) and 11655 kHz.

**Radio Slovakia International.** Monday through Friday, *News* is followed by *Topical Issue* and a feature. These include Wednesday's *Business News* (and *Currency Update*), Thursday's *Culture News* and Friday's *Regional News*. Saturday (and sometimes Monday), the news is followed by *Insight Central Europe*; and Monday's lineup is *Sunday Newsreel* and *Listeners' Tribune*. A friendly half hour to western Europe on 5915, 6055 and 7345 kHz. One hour earlier in summer.

**Radio Sweden.** Summer only at this hour; see 1830 for program details. Thirty minutes of Scandinavian fare for Europe Monday through Saturday on 6065 kHz, and for Europe and West Africa Sunday on 13580 kHz. One hour later during winter.

**Swiss Radio International.** *Newsnet*—news and background reports on world and Swiss events. Some lighter fare on Saturdays, when the biweekly *Capital Letters* (a listener-response program) alternates with *Name Game* (first Saturday) and *Sounds Good* (third Saturday). Thirty minutes to the Mideast and East Africa winter on 9605 (or 9600), 13790 and 15555 kHz; and summer on 15220, 17735 and 21720 kHz.

**Flanders Radio International,** Belgium. Summer only at this time. Weekdays, starts with *News*, then come one or more features and *Soundbox*. The lineup includes *Focus on Europe* and *Sports* (Monday), *Green Society* (Tuesday), *The Arts* (Wednesday and Friday), *Around Town* (Wednesday), *Economics* and *International Report* (Thursday), and Friday's *Tourism*. These are replaced Saturday by ●*Music from Flanders*, and Sunday by *Radio World*, *Tourism*, *Brussels 1043* (a listener-response program) and *Soundbox*. Thirty minutes to Europe on 9925 and 13690 kHz; and to the Mideast on 13710 kHz. One hour later in winter.

**Kol Israel.** Winter only at this time. Fifteen minutes from Israel Radio's domestic network. To Europe and eastern North America on one or more frequencies from 11605, 17525 and 17545 kHz. One hour earlier in winter

## 17:45

**All India Radio.** The first 15 minutes of a two-hour broadcast to Europe, Africa and the Mideast, consisting of regional and international *news*, commentary, a variety of talks and features, press review and exotic Indian music. Continuous till 1945. To Europe on 7410, 9950 and 11620 kHz; to West Africa on 9445, 13605 and 15155 kHz; and to East Africa on 11935, 15075 and 17670 kHz.

## 1800–2359
## Europe & Mideast—Evening Prime Time
## East Asia—Early Morning
## Australasia—Morning
## Eastern North America—Afternoon and Suppertime
## Western North America—Midday

### 18:00

**BBC World Service for Europe.** Monday through Friday winter, *News* is followed by *Outlook* (news and human interest stories) and a mixed bag of 15-minute features. Weekend fare is *World Briefing*, *British News* and either Saturday's ●*Agenda* or Sunday's ●*Assignment*. Summer weekdays, there's *news*, *Meridian* (the arts) and a soap or popular music. These are replaced Saturday by *World Briefing*, *British News*, *World Business Review* and *Letter from America*. Sunday, it's the final part of ●*Play of the Week*. If it ends at 1820, you also get *British News* and *Assignment* (or an alternative documentary); if it makes it to 1830, you get just the documentary; and if it goes the full hour, just sit back and enjoy it! Continuous to Europe and North Africa on 6195 and 9410 kHz.

**BBC World Service for Eastern Europe and the Mideast.** Except Sunday, starts with 20 minutes of *World Briefing*, with *British News* making up the half hour. Weekdays, the next 30 minutes bring ●*World Business Report* and ●*Analysis* (except 1845 Wednesday, when it's ●*From Our Own Correspondent*). At the same time Saturday, there's ●*World Business Review* and ●*Letter from America*. Sunday, it's a continuation of ●*Play of the Week*. Continuous programming on 11980 (winter), 12095 and (summer) 15575 kHz.

**■BBC World Service for Southern Africa.** Starts weekdays with five minutes of *News*, then it's a couple of features: ●*Health Matters* and ●*Everywoman* (Monday), *Science View* and ●*Focus on Faith* (Tuesday), *Sports International* and *Pick of the World* (Wednesday), ●*One Planet* and *People and Places* (Thursday), and *Discovery* and *Essential Guide* on Friday. Not a bad one among them. Weekends, the first 30 minutes are taken by *World Briefing* and *British News*. After the half-hour, it's Saturday's

●*World Business Review* and ●*Letter from America* or Sunday's ●*Assignment* (sometimes replaced by an alternative documentary). Continuous programming on 3255, 6190 and 15400 kHz.

**Radio Kuwait.** The start of a three-hour package of *news*, Islamic-oriented features and western popular music. Some interesting features, even if you don't particularly like the music. There is a full program summary at the beginning of each transmission, to enable you to pick and choose. To Europe and eastern North America on 11990 kHz.

**Voice of Vietnam.** Begins with *news*, which is followed by *Commentary* or *Weekly Review*, short features and some pleasant Vietnamese music (especially at weekends). A half hour to Europe winter on 5955, 7145 (or 11575) and 9730 kHz; and summer on 11640 and 13740 kHz. The 5955 kHz channel is via an Austrian relay, and should provide good reception.

**All India Radio.** Continuation of the transmission to Europe, Africa and the Mideast (see 1745). *News* and commentary, followed by programming of a more general nature. To Europe on 7410, 9950 and 11620 kHz; to West Africa on 9445, 13605 and 15155 kHz; and to East Africa on 11935, 15075 and 17670 kHz.

**Radio Prague,** Czech Republic. Winter only at this time. *News*, then Monday through Friday there's *Newsview* and one or two features. Monday's *One on One* (informal interviews) is replaced Tuesday by *Witness* and *Talking Point* or *Central Europe Today*; and the Wednesday shows are *ABC of Czech* followed by *Profile* or *Czechs in History*. *Economic Report* fills the Thursday slot, and Friday's feature is *Magazine* ("the show that starts where the news ends"). The weekend lineup consists of Saturday's *Insight Central Europe*, and Sunday's *A Letter from Prague*, *The Arts* and *Mailbox*. A half hour

**18:00–18:30**

A Tecsun lab technician
checks for quality during
production of world band
radios.   Tecsun

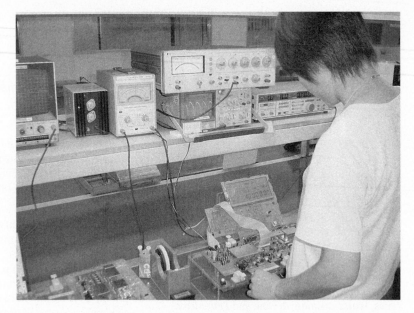

to Europe on 5930 kHz, and to Australasia on
7315 kHz. Europe's broadcast is one hour
earlier in summer, but for Australasia it's two
hours later.

**RTE Overseas,** Ireland. A half-hour information bulletin from Radio Telefís Éireann's
domestic Radio 1. To the Mideast, winter on
9895 kHz and summer on 15585 kHz.

**Radio Australia.** Sunday through Friday,
*World News* is followed by *Pacific Beat* (a news
magazine), replaced Saturday by *Lifelong
Learning*. As we went to press, the future
content of the second half hour was yet to be
decided. Part of a continuous 24-hour service,
and at this hour beamed to the Pacific on
6080, 7240, 9580, 9815 and 11880 kHz.
Additionally available to East Asia on 9475
and 9815 kHz. In western North America, try
9580 and 11880 kHz.

**Radio Polonia,** Poland. This time winter only.
See 1700 for program specifics. *News*, features
and music reflecting Polish life and culture.
Sixty minutes to Europe on 6000 and 7285
kHz. One hour earlier in summer.

**Voice of Russia World Service.** Continuous
programming to Europe and beyond. Predominantly news-related fare during the initial half

hour in summer, but the winter schedule offers
a more varied diet. Winter, the *news* is
followed by a series of features: *Moscow
Mailbag* (Monday, Thursday and Saturday),
*Newmarket* (Tuesday and Friday), *Science and
Engineering* (Wednesday) and the outstanding
●*Music and Musicians* on Sunday. On the half-
hour, the lineup includes *Kaleidoscope*
(Monday), ●*Music at Your Request* or an
alternative (Tuesday), ●*Moscow Yesterday and
Today* (Wednesday), *Folk Box* (Friday) and
Saturday's *Songs from Russia*. Summer
weekdays, the first half hour consists of news
followed by *Commonwealth Update*, while the
features that follow tend to be somewhat
variable. The Saturday slots are filled by
*Science and Engineering* and *This is Russia*,
replaced Sunday by *Musical Portraits of the
Twentieth Century* and ●*Christian Message from
Moscow* (an insight into Russian Orthodoxy).
Best winter bets are 5940 and 6175 (weekends), 7335, 7340 and 9775 kHz; likely
summer channels include 7300, 9480, 9775,
9890, 11630 11675 and 11870 kHz. Also
available winter only to the Mideast on 9830
kHz. In Southern Africa, try 11510 kHz.

**Radio Argentina al Exterior—R.A.E.** Monday
through Friday only. *News* and short features
on Argentina and its people. One of only a

handful of stations which still give prominence to folk music. Tangos, too, if you're nostalgic. Fifty-five minutes to Europe on 9690 and 15345 kHz.

**Voice of America.** Continuous programming to the Mideast and North Africa. *News Now*—reports and features on a variety of topics. On 6040 (winter) and 9760 kHz. For a separate service to Africa, see the next item.

**Voice of America.** Monday through Friday, it's *News Now* and *Africa World Tonight*. Weekends, there's a full hour of the former. To Africa—but heard well beyond—on 7275, 11920, 11975, 12040, 13710, 15410, 15580 and 17895 kHz, some of which are seasonal.

**Radio Cairo,** Egypt. See 1630 for specifics. The final 30 minutes of a two-hour broadcast to southern Africa on 15255 kHz.

**Radio Taipei International,** Taiwan. Opens with 15 minutes of *News*, and weekdays closes with *Let's Learn Chinese*. In between, there are either one or two features, depending on the day of the week. Monday's exotic ●*Jade Bells and Bamboo Pipes* (Taiwanese music) is replaced Tuesday by *Culture Express* and *Trends,* and Wednesday by *Taiwan Today* and *Confucius and Inspiration Beyond*. The Thursday lineup is *Discover Taiwan* and *New Music Lounge*; and Friday's combo brings together *Taipei Magazine* and *People*. These are replaced Saturday by *Groove Zone* and *Kaleidoscope*, and Sunday by *Great Wall Forum* and *Mailbag Time*. One hour to western Europe on 3955 kHz.

**WJIE,** Upton, Kentucky. Continues with Christian music to North America on 7490 kHz. Other U.S. religious broadcasters operating at this time include **WWCR** on 13845 and 15685 kHz, **KTBN** on 15590 kHz, and **WHRI-World Harvest Radio** on 13760 and 15105 kHz. For traditionalist Catholic programming, tune **WEWN** on 11875 and 13615 kHz.

**CFRX-CFRB,** Toronto, Canada. Audible throughout much of the northeastern United States and southeastern Canada during the hours of daylight with a modest, but clear, signal on 6070 kHz. This pleasant, friendly

station carries news, sports, weather and traffic reports—most of it intended for a local audience. Winter weekdays at this hour, it's *The Motts*; summer, look for *The John Oakley Show*. Weekends feature *The Mike Stafford Show*.

**AFRTS Shortwave,** USA. Network news, live sports, music and features in the upper-sideband mode from the Armed Forces Radio & Television Service. Transmitted from modestly powered U.S. Navy stations around the globe. Try 4319, 5765, 6350, 6458.5, 10320, 12579, 12689.5 and 13362 kHz.

## 18:15

**Radio Bangladesh.** *News*, followed by Islamic and general interest features; some nice Bengali music, too. Thirty minutes to Europe on 7190 and 9550 kHz, and irregularly on 15520 kHz. Frequencies may be slightly variable.

## 18:30

■**Radio Netherlands.** The second part of a three-hour block of programming for Africa, but also well heard in parts of North America at this hour. Monday through Friday, the first half hour is occupied by ●*Newsline*, then there's a 30-minute feature. Some excellent shows, including ●*EuroQuest* (Monday), ●*A Good Life* (Tuesday), ●*Research File* (science, Thursday) and Friday's excellent ●*Documentary*. The weekend menu consists of a bulletin of *news* followed by two or more features. Saturday's lineup includes *Europe Unzipped* and *Insight*, while *Wide Angle* and *Sound Fountain* (●*Aural Tapestry* midyear) are the Sunday offerings. On 6020, 7120 (midyear), 9895, 11655, 13700, 17605 and (midyear) 21590 kHz. The last two frequencies, via a relay in the Netherlands Antilles, are widely heard in the United States. In southern Africa, tune to 6020 kHz.

**Radio Austria International.** Summer only at this time; see 1930 for program details. Thirty minutes to Europe on 5945 and 6155 kHz, and one hour later in winter.

## 18:30–19:00

**Radio Slovakia International.** Summer only at this time; see 1930 for program specifics. Thirty minutes of *news* and features with a strong Slovak flavor. To western Europe on 5920, 6055 and 7345 kHz. One hour later in winter.

**RTE Overseas,** Ireland. A half-hour information bulletin from Radio Telefís Éireann's domestic Radio 1. To North America on 13640 kHz, and to Central and Southern Africa on 21630 kHz.

**Flanders Radio International,** Belgium. Winter only at this time. See 1730 for program details. Thirty minutes to Europe on 9925 and 13685 kHz; and to the Mideast on 13710 kHz. One hour earlier in summer.

**Voice of Turkey.** This time summer only. *News*, followed by *Review of the Turkish Press*, then features on Turkish history, culture and international relations, interspersed with enjoyable selections of the country's popular and classical music. Fifty minutes to Western Europe on 11960 kHz. One hour later in winter.

**Radio Sweden.** Winter only at this time. Monday through Friday, it's *news* and features in *Sixty Degrees North*, concentrating heavily

on Scandinavian topics. The Monday slot goes to *SportScan*, replaced Tuesday by *Close Up* or an alternative feature, and Wednesday by *Money Matters*. Thursday features a different show each week of the month—*Nordic Report*, *GreenScan*, *Heart Beat* or *S-Files*, while Friday offers a review of the week's news. Saturday's slot is filled by *Weekend*, *Spectrum* (the arts), *Sweden Today* or *Studio 49*, and Sunday fare consists of *In Touch with Stockholm* (a listener-response program) or the musical *Sounds Nordic*. Thirty minutes to Europe, Monday through Saturday on 6065 kHz, and Sunday on 5840 kHz. One hour earlier in summer.

## 19:00

**■BBC World Service for Europe.** Monday through Friday winter, there's *news*, *Meridian* (the arts) and a soap or popular music. Weekends, the first half hour consists of *World Briefing* and ●*Sports Roundup*, with the final 30 minutes going to Saturday's ●*World Business Review* and ●*Letter from America* or Sunday's *Science in Action*. Summer weekdays, opens with five minutes of *news*, and then it's features: ●*Health Matters* and ●*Everywoman* (Monday), ●*Focus on Faith* (1930 Tuesday), *Sports International* and *Pick of the World* (Wednesday), ●*One Planet* and *People and Places* (Thursday), and *Discovery* and *Essential Guide* on Friday. Some of the BBC's better offerings. Weekend fare is similar to that in winter, except for 1930 Saturday, when there's a 30-minute soap. Continuous to Europe and North Africa on 6195 and 9410 kHz.

**■BBC World Service for Eastern Europe and the Mideast.** Weekdays, starts with *World Briefing* and ●*Sports Roundup*, and ends with ●*Off the Shelf* (readings from world literature). In between, there's a 15-minute feature. On the weekend, a five-minute *news* bulletin is followed by Saturday's *Classical Request* and ●*Omnibus*, or Sunday's *Jazzmatazz* and ●*From Our Own Correspondent*.

**■BBC World Service for Southern Africa.** Monday through Friday, *News* is followed by 25 minutes of *Focus on Africa*. The second half hour consists of popular music or *Westway*, a soap. Weekend programming opens with

**Somali technicians receive their official licenses at a newly established radio station.** S. Voron

*World Briefing*, Saturday's ●*Sports Roundup* ●*Science in Action* or Sunday's news bulletin followed by *Wright Round the World*. Continuous on 3255, 6190 and 15400 kHz. The last frequency can often be heard in eastern North America during summer.

**Radio Australia.** Begins with *World News*, then Sunday through Thursday it's *Pacific Beat* (in-depth reporting on the region). Friday's slots go to *Pacific Focus* and *In Conversation*, replaced Saturday by *Earthbeat* (the environment) and *Lingua Franca*. Continuous to Asia and the Pacific on 6080, 7240, 9500, 9580, 9815 and 11880 kHz. Listeners in western North America should try 9580 and 11880 kHz, and best for East Asia are 6080 and 9500 kHz.

**Radio Kuwait.** See 1800; continuous to Europe and eastern North America on 11990 kHz.

**Kol Israel.** Summer only at this time. Twenty-five minutes of even-handed and comprehensive news reporting from and about Israel. To Europe and North America on 11605, 15615 and 17545 kHz; and to Africa and South America on 15640 kHz. One hour later in winter.

**All India Radio.** The final 45 minutes of a two-hour broadcast to Europe, Africa and the Mideast (see 1745). Starts off with *news*, then continues with a mixed bag of features and Indian music. To Europe on 7410, 9950 and 11620 kHz; to West Africa on 9445, 13605 and 15155 kHz; and to East Africa on 11935, 15075 and 17670 kHz.

**Radio Bulgaria.** Summer only at this time. Starts with *news*, then Monday through Friday there's *Events and Developments*, replaced Saturday by *Views Behind the News* and Sunday by 15 minutes of Bulgarian exotica in ●*Folk Studio*. Additional features include *Magazine Economy* (Monday), *Arts and Artists* (Tuesday), *History Club* (Wednesday), *The Way We Live* (Thursday) and *DX Programed*, a Friday slot for radio enthusiasts. Saturday is interactive day, with *Answering Your Letters*, a listener-response show, and *Walks and Talks* fills the Sunday slot. Monday through Friday, the broadcast ends with *Keyword Bulgaria*. Sixty minutes to Europe on 9400 and 11700 kHz. One hour later during winter.

**Radio Budapest,** Hungary. Summer only at this time. *News* and features, few of which are broadcast on a regular basis. Thirty minutes to Europe on 6025 and 7130 kHz. One hour later in winter.

■**Deutsche Welle,** Germany. *News*, then Monday through Friday it's ●*NewsLink* followed by *Africa Report*. Weekends, the Saturday news is followed by *Talking Point* and ●*Spectrum* (science); Sunday, by *Religion and Society* and *Arts on the Air*. Forty-five minutes to Africa, but also well heard in parts of eastern North America. Winter channels are 11765, 11810, 13780, 15275, and 15455 kHz; summer, choose from 11805, 11965, 13720, 15390 and 17810 kHz. Best winter options for North America are 11810 and 15275 kHz; and summer, 15390 kHz.

**Voice of Russia World Service.** Continuous programming to Europe at this hour. *News*, then winter weekdays there's *Commonwealth Update* (news and reports from and about the CIS), replaced Saturday by *Science and Engineering*, and Sunday by *Musical Portraits of the Twentieth Century*. Monday through Saturday summer, it's *News and Views*, with *Sunday Panorama* and *Russia: People and Events* filling the Sunday slots. Winter weekends at 1931, there's Saturday's *This is Russia*, and Sunday's emotive ●*Christian Message from Moscow*. During the week, the feature lineup is somewhat variable. Summer offerings at this time are mostly a combination of *Russia: People and Events*, the aptly-titled ●*Russian Treasures* and the religious *Daily Reflections*. Winter choices are 5940, 5950, 6175, 7340, 7360, 7440 and 9775 kHz; in summer, try 7440, 9480, 9685, 9775, 9890, 11675, 12030 and 12070 kHz.

**China Radio International.** Repeat of the 1600 transmission. One hour to North Africa and the Mideast on 9440, 9585 (winter), and (summer) 11750 and 13790 kHz.

**Radio Thailand.** A 60-minute package of *news*, features and (if you're lucky) enjoyable Thai music. To Northern Europe winter on 9535 kHz, and summer on 7155 kHz.

**Voice of Korea,** North Korea. Strictly of curiosity value only. An hour of old-style

**19:00–19:30**

Voice of Turkey engineer
Sedef Somaltin is
responsible for the
station's frequency usage.

VoT

communist programming to Europe on any two channels from 7505, 11335, 13760 and 15245 kHz; and to North America on 11710 kHz. Also heard in parts of East Asia on 4405 kHz.

**Voice of Vietnam.** Repeat of the 1800 transmission (see there for specifics). A half hour to Europe winter on 7145 (or 11575) and 9730 kHz, and summer on 11640 and 13740 kHz.

**Voice of America.** Continuous programming to the Mideast and North Africa. *News Now*—news and reports on a wide variety of topics. On 9760 and (summer) 9770 kHz. Also heard in Europe. For a separate service to Africa, see the next item.

**Voice of America.** *News Now*, then Monday through Friday it's *World of Music*. Best of the weekend programs is ●*Music Time in Africa* at 1930 Sunday. Continuous to most of Africa on 6035, 7375, 7415, 11920, 11975, 12040, 15410, 15445 and 15580 kHz, some of which are seasonal. For yet another service, to Australasia, see the following item.

**Voice of America.** Sixty minutes of news and reports covering a variety of topics. One hour to Australasia on 9525, 11870 and 15180 kHz.

**Radio Korea International,** South Korea. Opens with *news* and commentary, followed Monday through Wednesday by *Seoul Calling*. Weekly features include *Echoes of Korean Music* and *Shortwave Feedback* (Sunday), *Tales from Korea's Past* (Monday), *Korean Cultural Trails* (Tuesday), *Pulse of Korea* (Wednesday), *From Us to You* (a listener-response program) and *Let's Learn Korean* (Thursday), *Let's Sing Together* and *Korea Through Foreigners' Eyes* (Friday), and Saturday's *Discovering Korea*, *Korean Literary Corner* and *Weekly News Focus*. Sixty minutes to East Asia on 5975 kHz, and to Europe on 7275 kHz.

**WJIE,** Upton, Kentucky. Continues with Christian music to North America on 7490 kHz. Other U.S. religious broadcasters operating at this time include **WWCR** on 13845 and 15685 kHz, **KTBN** on 15590 kHz, and **WHRI-World Harvest Radio** on 13760 kHz. For traditionalist Catholic programming, try **WEWN** on 11875 and 13615 kHz.

**CFRX-CFRB,** Toronto, Canada. See 1800. Weekdays at this time, you can hear *The John Oakley Show*; weekends, it's replaced by *The Mike Stafford Show*. On 6070 kHz.

**AFRTS Shortwave,** USA. Network news, live sports, music and features in the upper-sideband mode from the Armed Forces Radio & Television Service. Transmitted from modestly powered U.S. Navy stations around the globe. Try 4319, 5765, 6350, 6458.5, 10320, 12579, 12689.5 and 13362 kHz.

The Japan Short Wave
Club's bulletins continue
with vigor after 50 years.

T. Ohtake

## 19:30

**Radio Polonia,** Poland. Summer only at this time. Monday through Friday, it's *News from Poland*—news, reports and interviews on the latest events in the country. This is followed by *Cookery Corner* and *The Best of Polish Radio* (Monday), *Letter from Poland* and *Multimedia Show* (Tuesday), *Day in the Life* and *Discovering Chopin* (Wednesday), *Focus* (the arts in Poland) and

*Soundcheck* (Thursday), and Friday's *Business Week* followed by *Postbag*, a listener-response show. The Saturday broadcast begins with a bulletin of *news*, then there's *Europe East, The Weeklies* and *Chart Show*. Sundays, look for five minutes of *news* followed by *Panorama* and *Request Concert*. Sixty minutes to Europe on 6035, 7185, 7265 and 9525 kHz. One hour later during winter.

**Radio Austria International.** Winter only at this time. Starts with a short bulletin of *news*, then weekdays it's ●*Report from Austria*, an in-depth look at this central European country. Weekends, there's Saturday's *Insight Central Europe* and Sunday's *Network Europe*, both joint-productions with other European stations. To Europe on 5945 and 6155 kHz, and one hour earlier in summer.

**Radio Slovakia International.** Monday through Friday, there's *News*, *Topical Issue* and a feature. These include Wednesday's *Business*

*News* (and *Currency Update*), Thursday's *Culture News* and Friday's *Regional News*. Saturday (and sometimes Monday), the news is followed by *Insight Central Europe*; and the Sunday pairing is *Sunday Newsreel* and *Listeners' Tribune*. A friendly 30 minutes to Western Europe on 5915, 6055 and 7345 kHz. One hour earlier in summer.

**Swiss Radio International.** *Newsnet*—news and background reports on world and Swiss events. Some lighter fare on Saturdays, when the biweekly *Capital Letters* (a listener-response program) alternates with *Name Game* (first Saturday) and *Sounds Good* (third Saturday). Thirty minutes to Africa winter on 9605, 13660, 15485 and 17660 kHz; and summer on 13645, 15220 and 17580 and 17735 kHz. Easy reception in southern Africa on 17660/17735 kHz.

**Voice of Turkey.** Winter only at this time. See 1830 for program details. Some unusual

# No other antenna combines all these features:

- Includes Zap Trapper™ Gas Tube Lightning Arrestor
- Completely assembled, ready to use
- Includes 100 feet of 72-ohm transmission line
- Includes 50 feet of 450-pound test nylon support rope
- Automatic bandswitching by trap circuits, which electrically separate the antenna segments—just tune your receiver to the desired band!
- Balanced input minimizes local noise pickup
- Heavy 14-gauge antenna wire to survive those severe storms that bring down lesser antennas
- Ultrasonically-welded, sealed, weather-resistant trap covers
- May be installed in the attic
- Overall length less than 43 feet
- Full year warranty
- Also available, Model C equipped with a center connector to accept coax—same low price

In stock at selected dealers worldwide. Send for complete information on all our products, including our Eavesdropper™ SWL Sloper. MasterCard and Visa accepted.

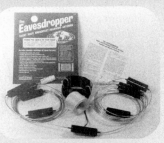

Receive the world's short wave bands with only one antenna and one feed line!

11 meters (25.6 to 26.1 MHz)
13 meters (21.46 to 21.85 MHz)
16 meters (17.55 to 17.9 MHz)
19 meters (15.1 to 15.6 MHz)
22 meters (13.6 to 13.8 MHz)
25 meters (11.65 to 12.05 MHz)
31 meters (9.5 to 9.9 MHz)
41 meters (7.1 to 7.3 MHz)
49 meters (5.95 to 6.2 MHz)
60 meters (4.75 to 5.06 MHz)
75 meters (3.9 to 4.0 MHz)

*Only*
**$89.95**
*plus $6.00 shipping (USA)*
*Export shipping quoted*

P.O. Box 563-P, Palatine, Illinois 60078 USA    Made in USA
(847) 359-7092 • Fax (847) 359-8161
Manufacturers of Quality Short Wave Listening Antenna Systems

**19:30–20:00**

Transmitter hall, Biblis, Germany. During the Cold War, this facility was effective in helping bring about the downfall of communism in Europe and the Soviet Union.

Nick Olguin

programs and friendly presentation make for worthy listening. Fifty minutes to Europe on 7125 kHz. One hour earlier in summer.

**Voice of the Islamic Republic of Iran.** A one-hour broadcast of news, commentary and features with a strong Islamic influence. To Europe winter on 6110, 7215 and 7320 kHz; and summer on 11670 and 11855 kHz. Also to southern Africa winter on 11695 and 15140 kHz, and summer on 9800 and 11750 kHz.

**Flanders Radio International,** Belgium. Summer only at this time. Weekdays, there's *News* followed one or two features, and *Soundbox*. The lineup includes *Focus on Europe* and *Sports* (Monday), *Green Society* (Tuesday), *The Arts* (Wednesday and Friday), *Around Town* (Wednesday), *Economics* and *International Report* (Thursday), and Friday's *Tourism*. These are replaced Saturday by ●*Music from Flanders*, and Sunday by *Radio World, Tourism, Brussels 1043* (a listener-response program) and *Soundbox*. Thirty minutes to Europe on 9925 and 13690 kHz. There is no corresponding winter broadcast on shortwave, only on mediumwave AM.

**Radio Sweden.** Summer only at this time, and a repeat of the 1730 broadcast. See 1830 for

program details. Thirty minutes to Europe on 6065 kHz, and one hour later in winter.

■**Radio Netherlands.** Monday through Friday, starts with a feature and ends with ●*Newsline*, replaced weekends by a *news* bulletin and a second feature. Quality fare, including ●*Research File* (science, Monday), ●*A Good Life* (Friday) and Wednesday's award-winning ●*Documentary*. On the remaining days you can hear, among others, *Music 52-15* (Tuesday), *Europe Unzipped* (Saturday) and *Dutch Horizons* and *Sincerely Yours* (a listener-response show) on Sunday. The end of a three-hour broadcast to Africa on 6020 (best for southern parts), 7120 (midyear), 9895, 11655, 13700, 17605 and (midyear) 21590 kHz. The last two frequencies are audible in much of the United States.

**RAI International—Radio Roma,** Italy. Actually starts at 1935. Approximately 12 minutes of *news*, then some Italian music. Twenty minutes to western Europe on 5970 and 9745 kHz.

**Radio Station Belarus/Radio Minsk.** Tuesday and Thursday, summer only at this time. See 2030 for specifics. Thirty minutes to Europe on 7105 and 7210 kHz. One hour later in winter.

**19:30–20:00**

## 19:40

**Voice of Armenia.** Monday through Saturday, summer only at this time. Twenty minutes of Armenian *news* and culture. To Europe on 9960 kHz, and to the Mideast on 4810 kHz. One hour later in winter.

## 19:50

**Vatican Radio.** Summer only at this time. Twenty minutes of programming oriented to Catholics. To Europe on 4005, 5890 and 7250 kHz. One hour later in winter.

## 20:00

■**BBC World Service for Europe.** Monday through Friday winter, the format is *News* and two features. These include ●*Health Matters* and ●*Everywoman* (Monday), ●*Focus on Faith* (1930 Tuesday), *Sports International* and *Pick of the World* (Wednesday), ●*One Planet* and *People and Places* (Thursday), and *Discovery* and *Essential Guide* on Friday. Weekends, there's Saturday's ●*From Our Own Correspondent* and *Westway* (a soap), replaced Sunday by popular music and light entertainment. In summer, it's ●*Newshour*, the standard for all in-depth news shows from international broadcasters. One hour to Europe and North Africa on 6195 and 9410 kHz.

■**BBC World Service for Southern Africa.** Fifty minutes of ●*Newshour*, with ●*Sports Roundup* closing the hour. Continuous programming on 3255, 6190 and 15400 kHz. The last frequency is often audible in eastern North America during summer.

■**Deutsche Welle,** Germany. *News*, then Monday through Friday there's the in-depth ●*NewsLink* followed by a feature. Monday, it's *German by Radio*; Tuesday has the ecological ●*Man and Environment*; Wednesday brings ●*Insight*; Thursday, try *Living in Germany*; and Friday's slot is *Spotlight on Sport*. *Weekend Review* and ●*Weekend* (a European co-production) are aired Saturday, replaced Sunday by a second edition of *Weekend Review* and *Arts on the Air*. Forty-five minutes to

Europe winter on 6180 kHz, and summer on 6140 kHz.

**Radio Canada International.** Summer only at this time. *News*, then Monday through Friday there's *Canada Today*. These are followed by a theme program on the half-hour. Saturday's features are *Business Sense* and *Canada in the World*, with Sunday's slots going to *The Mailbag* (a listener-response show) and *Spotlight*. Sixty minutes to Europe, Africa and the Mideast on 5850, 5995, 11690, 11965, 12015, 15325, 15470 and 17870 kHz. One hour later during winter.

**Radio Damascus,** Syria. Actually starts at 2005. *News*, a daily press review, and different features for each day of the week. These can be heard at approximately 2030 and 2045, and include *Arab Profile* and *Palestine Talk* (Monday), *Syria and the World* and *Listeners Overseas* (Tuesday), *Around the World* and *Selected Readings* (Wednesday), *From the World Press* and *Reflections* (Thursday), *Arab Newsweek* and *Cultural Magazine* (Friday), *Welcome to Syria* and *Arab Civilization* (Saturday), and *From Our Literature* and *Music from the Orient* (Sunday). Most of the transmission, however, is given over to Syrian and some western popular music. One hour to Europe, often audible in eastern North America, on 12085 and 13610 kHz.

**Swiss Radio International.** Repeat of the 1930 broadcast. Thirty minutes to Africa winter on 9605, 13660, 15485 and 17660 kHz; and summer on 13645, 15220 and 17580 and 17735 kHz. Good reception in southern Africa on 17660/17735 kHz.

**Radio Australia.** Starts with *World News*, then Sunday through Thursday there's a continuation of *Pacific Beat* (in-depth reporting). Friday fare consists of *Pacific Review* and *Country Breakfast*, and Saturday, *Australia All Over* (a popular show from the Radio National domestic service). Continuous programming to the Pacific on 9580, 9815 and 11880 kHz; and to East and Southeast Asia on 9500 kHz. In western North America, try 9580 and 11880 kHz.

**Voice of Russia World Service.** Continuous programming to Europe at this hour. *News*, then Monday through Saturday winter it's

**20:00–20:30**

*News and Views*, with *Sunday Panorama* and *Russia: People and Events* completing the lineup. In summer, these are replaced by a variety of features. Pick from *Science and Engineering* (Monday and Thursday), *Newmarket* (Wednesday and Saturday), *Moscow Mailbag* (Tuesday and Friday), and the 47-minute ●*Music and Musicians* on Sunday. Winter on the half-hour, it's mostly a combination of *Russia: People and Events*, ●*Russian Treasures* (gems of classical music) and the religious *Daily Reflections*. Best of the summer offerings at this time are Thursday's ●*Folk Box*, Friday's ●*Jazz Show* and Tuesday's ●*Music at Your Request* or its alternative. Other features include *Songs from Russia* (Monday), *Musical Portraits of the Twentieth Century* (Wednesday) and Saturday's *Russian by Radio*. Winter on 5940, 5950, 6175, 7335, 7340, 7390 and 9775 kHz; and summer on 9480, 9775, 9890, 11675, 12030, 12070 and 15455 kHz. Some channels are audible in eastern North America.

**Radio Kuwait.** The final sixty minutes of a three-hour broadcast to Europe and eastern North America (see 1800). Regular features at this time include *Theater in Kuwait* (2000), *Saheeh Muslim* (2030) and *News in Brief* at 2057. On 11990 kHz.

**Radio Bulgaria.** This time winter only. See 1900 for specifics. Often includes exotic Bulgarian folk music. Sixty minutes to Europe, and sometimes audible in parts of eastern North America, on 5800 and 7500 kHz. One hour earlier during summer.

**Radio Exterior de España ("Spanish National Radio").** Weekdays only at this time. *News*, followed Monday through Friday by *Panorama* (Spanish popular music, commentary, press review and weather), then a couple of features: *Sports Spotlight* and *Cultural Encounters* (Monday); *People of Today* and *Entertainment in Spain* (Tuesday); *As Others See Us* and, biweekly, *The Natural World* or *Science Desk* (Wednesday); *Economic Report* and *Cultural Clippings* (Thursday); and *Window on Spain* and *Review of the Arts* (Friday). A language course, *Spanish by Radio*, ends the broadcast. Sixty minutes to Europe winter on 9690 kHz, and summer on 15290 kHz; and to North and West Africa winter on 9595 kHz, and summer on 9570 kHz.

**Radio Budapest,** Hungary. Winter only at this time. *News* and features, most of which are broadcast on a non-regular basis. Thirty minutes to Europe on 6125 and 7135 kHz. One hour earlier in summer.

**Radio Algiers,** Algeria. *News*, then western and Arab popular music, with an occasional feature thrown in. One hour of so-so reception in Europe, and sometimes heard in eastern North America. On 11715 and 15160 kHz. Tends to be irregular.

**China Radio International.** Starts with *News*, then weekdays there are special reports. The rest of the broadcast consists of features. Regular shows include *People in the Know* (Monday), *Biz China* (Tuesday), *China Horizons* (Wednesday), *Voices from Other Lands* (Thursday), and *Life in China* on Friday. The Saturday lineup includes *Global Review* and *Listeners' Garden* (reports, music and Chinese language lessons), and Sunday's broadcast has *Report from Developing Countries* and *In the Spotlight*. One hour to Europe winter on 5965 and 9840 kHz, and summer on 11790 and 15110 kHz. Also available to eastern and southern Africa on 11640 (or 11735) and 13630 (or 13640) kHz; and to North Africa (audible in the Mideast) on 9440 kHz.

**Voice of Mongolia.** *News*, reports and short features dealing with local topics. Some exotic Mongolian music, too, especially on Sundays. Thirty minutes to eastern Europe on 12015 kHz. Sometimes makes it farther west.

**Kol Israel.** Winter only at this time. Twenty-five minutes of *news* and in-depth reporting from and about Israel. To Europe and North America on any three channels from 6280, 7520, 9435 and 11605 kHz; and to Southern Africa and South America on 15640 kHz. One hour earlier in summer.

**HCJB—Voice of the Andes,** Ecuador. Monday through Friday winter there's *News* and *Studio 9*, featuring *Inside HCJB* (Monday), *Ham Radio Today* (Wednesday), *Did You Hear?* (Tuesday and Thursday) and long-time favorite ●*Música del Ecuador* on Friday. These are replaced

**20:00–20:30**

Saturday by *DX Partyline*, and Sunday by *Musical Mailbag*. The second half-hour is predominantly religious, though Saturday's *Saludos Amigos* and Sunday's *Mountain Meditations* are listener favorites. The first of two hours for Europe, winter on 11895 kHz and summer on 17660 kHz.

**Voice of America.** Continuous programming to the Mideast and North Africa. *News*, reports and capsulated features covering everything from politics to entertainment. On 6095 (winter), 9760, and (summer) 9770 kHz. For African listeners there's the weekday *Africa World Tonight*, replaced weekends by *Nightline Africa*, on 6035, 7275, 7375, 7415, 11715, 11855, 15410, 15445, 15580, 17725 and 17755 kHz, some of which are seasonal. Both transmissions are heard well beyond their target areas, including parts of North America.

**WJIE,** Upton, Kentucky. Continues with Christian music to North America on 7490 kHz. Other U.S. religious broadcasters which operate at this time include **WWCR** on 13845 and 15685 kHz, **KTBN** on 15590 kHz, and **WHRI-World Harvest Radio** on 13760 kHz. For traditionalist Catholic programming, tune **WEWN** on 11875 and 13615 kHz.

**Radio Prague,** Czech Republic. Summer only at this time. *News*, then weekdays there's the in-depth *Newsview* and one or more features: *One on One* (informal interviews, Monday); *Witness* and *Talking Point* or *Central Europe Today* (Tuesday); *ABC of Czech* and either *Profile* or *Czechs in History* (Wednesday); *Economics Report* (Thursday); and *Magazine* on Friday. Weekends, the news is followed Saturday by *Spotlight* (a jaunt around the Czech Republic) and *Readings from Czech Literature* or *Saturday Music*; and Sunday by *A Letter from Prague*, *The Arts* and *Mailbox*. Thirty minutes to western Europe on 5930 kHz, and to Southeast Asia and Australasia on 11600 kHz. One hour later in winter.

**CFRX-CFRB,** Toronto, Canada. See 1800. Summer weekdays at this time, you can hear ●*The World Today*, three hours of news, interviews, sports and commentary. On 6070 kHz.

**AFRTS Shortwave,** USA. Network news, live sports, music and features in the upper-sideband mode from the Armed Forces Radio & Television Service. Transmitted from modestly powered U.S. Navy stations around the globe. Try 4319, 5765, 6350, 6458.5, 10320, 12579, 12689.5 and 13362 kHz.

## 20:30

**Radio Polonia,** Poland. This time winter only. See 1930 for program specifics. *News*, music and features, covering multiple aspects of Polish life and culture. Sixty minutes to Europe on 6035, 6095, 7285 and 9525 kHz. One hour earlier in summer.

**Radio Sweden.** Winter only at this time. Monday through Friday, it's *news* and features in *Sixty Degrees North*, concentrating heavily on Scandinavian topics. Monday there's *SportScan*, replaced Tuesday by *Close Up* or an alternative feature, and Wednesday by *Money Matters*. Thursday features a different show each week of the month—*Nordic Report*, *GreenScan*, *Heart Beat* or *S-Files*, while Friday offers a review of the week's news. Saturday's slot is filled by *Weekend*, *Spectrum* (the arts), *Sweden Today* or *Studio 49*, and the Sunday lineup is *In Touch with Stockholm* (a listener-response program) or the musical *Sounds Nordic*. Thirty minutes to Europe (one hour earlier in summer) on 6065 kHz, and to Asia and Australasia (one hour later in summer) on 9445 kHz.

**Voice of Vietnam.** *News*, then it's either *Commentary* or *Weekly Review*, which in turn is followed by short features. Look for some pleasant Vietnamese music towards the end of the broadcast (more at weekends). A half hour to Europe winter on 7145 (or 11575) and 9730 kHz, and summer on 11640 and 13740 kHz.

**Radio Thailand.** Fifteen minutes of *news* targeted at Europe. Winter on 9535 kHz, and summer on 9680 kHz.

**Voice of Turkey.** This time summer only. *News*, followed by *Review of the Turkish Press* and features (some of them unusual) with a strong local flavor. Selections of Turkish popular and classical music complete the program. Fifty minutes to Southeast Asia and Australasia on 9525 kHz. One hour later during winter.

**Radio Station Belarus/Radio Minsk.** Tuesday and Thursday only at this time. Thirty minutes of local *news* and interviews, plus a little Belarusian music. To Europe on 7105 and 7210 kHz. Occasionally heard in eastern North America during winter.

**Wales Radio International.** Summer Fridays only at this time. News, interviews and music from the Welsh hills and valleys. Thirty minutes to Europe on 7325 kHz, and one hour later in winter.

**Radio Habana Cuba.** The first half of a 60-minute broadcast to Europe. Monday through Saturday, there's international and Cuban news followed by *RHC's Viewpoint*. This is replaced Sunday by *Weekly Review*. On 13750 kHz. Also on 13660 kHz upper sideband, though not all radios, unfortunately, can process such signals.

**Radio Tashkent,** Uzbekistan. Thirty minutes of news, commentary and features, with some exotic Uzbek music. To Europe on 5025 and 11905 kHz, and to West Asia and the Mideast on 9540 (or 9545) kHz.

**RAI International—Radio Roma,** Italy. Actually starts at 2025. Twenty minutes of *news* and music targeted at the Mideast on 9710 (winter), 9670 (summer) and 11880 kHz.

### 20:45

**Voice of Armenia.** Monday through Saturday, winter only at this time. Actually starts at 2040. Twenty minutes of Armenian *news* and culture. To Europe on 9960 kHz, and to the Mideast on 4910 kHz. The channel for Europe sometimes produces fair reception in parts of eastern North America. One hour earlier in summer.

**All India Radio.** The first 15 minutes of a much longer broadcast, consisting of a press review, Indian music, regional and international *news*, commentary, and a variety of talks and features of general interest. Continuous till 2230. To Western Europe on 7410,

9445, 9950 and 11620 kHz; and to Australasia on 9575, 9910, 11620 and 11715 kHz. Early risers in Southeast Asia can try the channels for Australasia.

**Vatican Radio.** Winter only at this time, and actually starts at 2050. Twenty minutes of predominantly Catholic fare. To Europe on 4005, 5890 and 7250 kHz. One hour earlier in summer.

### 21:00

**■BBC World Service for the Americas.** Winter weekdays, opens with five minutes of *news*, then a features double-bill (except on 5975 kHz, which has *Caribbean Report* until 2130). Pick of the features are *Science in Action* (2005 Monday), ●*Health Matters* and ●*Everywoman* (Tuesday), ●*Omnibus* (2030 Wednesday), *Discovery* (science) and *Sports International* (Thursday) and ●*One Planet* (Friday). Summer at the same time the lineup is *News*, ●*World Business Report*, *British News*, ●*Sports Roundup* and ●*Analysis* (replaced Wednesday by ●*From Our Own Correspondent*). Winter weekends, look for 60 minutes of ●*Newshour*, which is replaced summer by a bulletin of *news* and several short features. The Saturday slots are ●*World Business Review*, *British News*, ●*Sports Roundup* and *Patterns of Faith*; and the Sunday lineup is *Global Business*, ●*Sports Roundup* and *Write On*. To the Caribbean and eastern and southern parts of the United States on 5975 kHz. 12095 kHz, targeted at South America, is also audible in some areas; a radio with synchronous selectable sideband helps reduce teletype interference.

**BBC World Service for Europe.** Winter programming consists of ●*Newshour*, the BBC's flagship in-depth news show. In summer, weekday format is *News*, ●*World Business Report*, *British News*, ●*Sports Roundup* and ●*Off the Shelf* (readings from world literature). Saturday, the news is followed by *Jazzmatazz* and *Composer of the Month*; Sunday, by popular music and light entertainment. Continuous to Europe and North Africa on 6195 and 9410 kHz.

**BBC World Service for Southern Africa.** Winter, there's a full 60 minutes of ●*Newshour*. In summer, the weekday lineup is *News*, ●*World Business Report*, *British News*, ●*Sports Roundup* and ●*Analysis* (replaced Wednesday by ●*From Our Own Correspondent*). Weekends, opens with five minutes of *News*, then Saturday it's ●*World Business Review*, *British News*, ●*Sports Roundup* and ●*Letter from America*. These are replaced Sunday by *Global Business*, ●*Sports Roundup* and ●*Reporting Religion*. The final 60 minutes of a 19-hour block of programming. On 3255, 6005 and 6190 kHz.

■**BBC World Service for East and Southeast Asia.** Identical to the service for Southern Africa. To East Asia on 5965, 6195 and (summer) 11945 kHz; and to Southeast Asia on 3915 and 6195 kHz.

**Radio Exterior de España ("Spanish National Radio").** Summer weekends only at this time. *News* and features with a friendly touch. Not to be missed is Sunday's feature on Spanish music. One hour to Europe on 9840 kHz, and to North and West Africa on 9570 kHz. One hour later in winter.

**Radio Ukraine International.** Summer only at this time. *News*, commentary, reports and interviews, covering multiple aspects of Ukrainian life. Saturdays feature a listener-response program, and most of Sunday's broadcast is a showpiece for Ukrainian music. Sixty minutes to Europe on 5905, 6020, 9950, 11705 and 11950 kHz. One hour later in winter. Should be easily heard despite the station's technical limitations.

**Radio Canada International.** A full hour winter, but only 30 minutes in summer. Winter weekdays there's *Canada Today*, and a theme program on the half-hour. Saturday's features are *Business Sense* and *Canada in the World*, with Sunday's slots going to *The Mailbag* (a

# Receiver Modifications for Icom, Drake and JRC

Improve your high-end receiver with time-proven Sherwood modifications. Icom's R-9000 can be dramatically improved with the famous SE-3 Synchronous Detector. Additional filters provide 12, 9, 6, 4, and 3 kHz AM bandwidths. Whisper quiet "Cool Kit" provides replacement rear panel with muffin fan that reduces internal temperature to near ambient.

Modifications for Drake R8 and R8A to improve AGC and add an upconverter for the SE-3 Synchronous Detector.

JRC NRD 515, 525, 535 and 345 owners can enjoy the SE-3 Synchronous Detector plus add additional extra-filter bandwidths. See Website for details.

**Sherwood Engineering Inc.**
1268 South Ogden Street
Denver, CO 80210
Voice: (303) 722-2257
Fax: (303) 744-8876
Web: www.sherweng.com
E-mail: robert@sherweng.com

**21:00–21:00**

listener-response show) and *Spotlight*. Sixty minutes to Europe, Africa and the Mideast on 5850, 7235, 7425, 9770, 9805 and 13650 kHz; and one hour earlier during summer. In summer, the weekday ●*World at Six* is replaced Saturday by *Media Zone* and Sunday by *Canada in the World*, and goes out on 5850, 7235, 13690, 15325 and 17870 kHz. One hour later in winter.

**Radio Prague,** Czech Republic. Winter only at this time. See 2000 for program details. *News* and features on Czech life and culture. A half hour to western Europe (and easily audible in parts of eastern North America) on 5930 kHz, and to Southeast Asia and Australasia on 9430 kHz. One hour earlier in summer.

**Radio Bulgaria.** This time summer only. Starts with *news*, then Monday through Friday there's *Events and Developments*, replaced Saturday by *Views Behind the News* and Sunday by 15 minutes of Bulgarian exotica in ●*Folk Studio*. Additional features include *Walks and Talks* (Monday), *Magazine Economy* (Tuesday), *Arts and Artists* (Wednesday), *History Club* (Thursday), *The Way We Live* (Friday) and *DX Programed*, a Saturday slot for radio enthusiasts. Sunday, look for *Answering Your Letters*, a listener-response show. Tuesday through Saturday, the broadcast ends with *Keyword Bulgaria*. Sixty minutes to Europe on 9400 and 11700 kHz. One hour later during winter.

**China Radio International.** Repeat of the 2000 transmission; see there for specifics. One hour to Europe winter on 5965 and 9840 kHz, and summer on 11790 and 15110 kHz. A 30-minute shortened version is also available to eastern and southern Africa on 11640 (or 11735) and 13630 (or 13640) kHz.

**Voice of Russia World Service.** Winter only at this time. *News*, then *Science and Engineering* (Monday and Thursday), the business-oriented *Newmarket* (Wednesday and Saturday), *Moscow Mailbag* (Tuesday and Friday) or Sunday's excellent ●*Music and Musicians*. Best of the second half hour are Thursday's ●*Folk Box*, Friday's ●*Jazz Show* and Tuesday's ●*Music at Your Request* or its alternative. Other features include *Songs from Russia* (Monday) and Saturday's *Russian by Radio*. The final 60

minutes for Europe on 5940, 5950, 6175, 7300, 7335, 7340 and 7390 kHz, and one hour earlier in summer. Some channels are audible in eastern North America.

**Radio Budapest,** Hungary. Summer only at this time. *News* and features, few of which are broadcast on a regular basis. Thirty minutes to Europe on 3975 and 6025 kHz. One hour later in winter.

**Radio Japan.** *News*, then Monday through Friday (Tuesday through Saturday local date in Australasia) there's *Asian Top News* and a 35-minute feature: *Japan Music Log* (Monday), Japanese language lessons (Tuesday and Thursday), *Japan Treasure Box* (Wednesday) and *Music Beat* (Japanese popular music, Friday). *Weekend Square* fills the Saturday slot, and *Hello from Tokyo* is aired Sunday. Sixty minutes to Europe on 6055 (summer), 6090 (winter), 6180 and 11830 kHz; to Australasia winter on 11850 and 11920 kHz, and midyear on 6035 and 17860 kHz; to western North America on 17825 kHz; to Hawaii on 21670 kHz; and to Central Africa on 11855 kHz. The broadcast on 17825 kHz may differ somewhat from the other transmissions, and may include alternative features.

**Radio Australia.** *World News*, then Sunday through Thursday there's a look at current events in *AM* (replaced Friday by a listener-response program, *Feedback*). Next, on the half-hour, there's a daily feature—*In the Pipeline* (Sunday), *Health Report* (Monday), *Innovations* (Tuesday), *Religion Report* (Wednesday), and the musical *Oz Sounds* on Thursday. Saturday, it's the final part of *Australia All Over* plus the 15-minute *Asia Sunday*. Continuous to the Pacific on 7240, 9580 (till 2130), 9660, 11880, 12080, 17715 and 21740 kHz; and to East and Southeast Asia (till 2130) on 9500 kHz. Listeners in North America should try 11880, 17715 and 21740 kHz.

■**Deutsche Welle,** Germany. *News*, then weekdays (Tuesday through Saturday in the target areas) it's ●*NewsLink* followed by a feature. Monday, it's either *Development Forum* or *Women on the Move*; Tuesday, there's a look at ●*Man and Environment*; Wednesday's

**Antennas for the IBB transmitters at scenic Biblis, Germany.**

Nick Olguin

slot is ●*Insight*; Thursday, there's *Living in Germany*; and Friday's offering is *Spotlight on Sport*. Saturday's slots are *Weekend Review* (first edition) and *Mailbag*, replaced Sunday by *Weekend Review* (second edition) and *Arts on the Air*. Forty-five minutes to Southeast Asia and Australasia winter on 9690, 9765, 15275 and 17560 kHz; and midyear on 9670, 9765 and 12035 kHz. An almost identical broadcast (except that Saturday's *Mailbag* is replaced by *African Kaleidoscope*) goes out simultaneously to West Africa, and is audible in much of eastern North America. Winter on 9615, 11645 15410 and 17765 kHz; and summer on 9830, 11865 and 15135 kHz. In North America, try 15410 and 17765 kHz in winter, and 15135 kHz in summer.

**Radio Romania International.** *News*, commentary, press review and features. Regular spots include *Youth Club* (Tuesday), *Romanian Musicians* (Wednesday), and Thursday's *Listeners' Letterbox* and ●*Skylark* (Romanian folk music). Fifty-five minutes to Europe winter on 5955, 7105, 7215 and 9690 kHz; and summer on 9510, 9725, 11740 and 11940 kHz.

**Radio México Internacional.** Summer only at this time, when there's a daily 30-minute feature. The lineup consists of *Mosaic of Mexico* (Monday and Friday), *DXperience* (for radio enthusiasts, Tuesday and Sunday),

*Regional Roots and Rhythms* (Wednesday), *Mirror of Mexico* (Thursday) and Saturday's *Magical Trip*. Best heard in western and southern parts of the United States on 9705 and 11770 kHz.

**Radio Korea International,** South Korea. Starts with *news*, followed Monday through Wednesday by *Economic News Briefs*. The remainder of the broadcast is taken up by a feature: *Shortwave Feedback* (Sunday), *Seoul Calling* (Monday and Tuesday), *Pulse of Korea* (Wednesday), *From Us to You* (Thursday), *Let's Sing Together* (Friday) and *Weekly News Focus* (Saturday). Thirty minutes to Europe summer on 3955 kHz, and one hour later in winter. Also at this time, a repeat of the 1900 one-hour broadcast, aired year round on 15575 kHz.

**Voice of Korea,** North Korea. For the time being, of curiosity value only. But with North Korea showing signs of emerging from years of self-imposed isolation, this broadcasting dinosaur could provide some surprises. In the meantime, it's an hour of old-style communist programming. One hour to Europe on any two channels from 7505, 11335, 13760 and 15245 kHz. Also audible in parts of East Asia on 4405 kHz.

**HCJB—Voice of the Andes,** Ecuador. The second of two hours of predominantly religious programming to Europe, winter on 11895 kHz, and summer on 17660 kHz.

**21:00–22:00**

**Radio Habana Cuba.** The final 30 minutes of a one-hour broadcast. Monday through Saturday, there's a *news* bulletin and the sports-oriented *Time Out* (five minutes each), then a feature: *Caribbean Outlook* (Monday and Thursday), *DXers Unlimited* (Tuesday and Saturday), the *Mailbag Show* (Wednesday) and *Weekly Review* (Friday). These are replaced Sunday by a longer edition of *Mailbag Show*. To Europe on 13750 kHz. Also available on 13660 kHz upper sideband.

**Voice of America.** For Africa and Australasia, it's *News Now*—a series of reports and features covering a multitude of topics. Also available to the Mideast and North Africa on 6040, 9535 (summer) and 9760 kHz. In Africa, tune to 6035, 7375, 7415, 11715, 11975, 13710, 15410, 15445, 15580 and 17725 kHz (some of which are seasonal); and in Southeast Asia and the Pacific to 11870, 15185 and 17735 (or 17740) kHz.

**All India Radio.** Continues to Western Europe on 7410, 9445, 9950 and 11620 kHz; and to Australasia on 9575, 9910, 11620 and 11715 kHz. Look for some authentic Indian music from 2115 onwards. The European frequencies are audible in parts of eastern North America, while those for Australasia are also heard in Southeast Asia.

**Master control for the former American shortwave facility at Playa de Pals, Spain. It was shut down recently in favor of youth-oriented pop music over Arab FM stations.** Nick Olguin

**CFRX-CFRB,** Toronto, Canada. If you live in the northeastern United States or southeastern Canada, try this pleasant little local station, usually audible for hundreds of miles/kilometers during daylight hours on 6070 kHz. Winter weekdays at this time, you can hear ●*The World Today* (summer, starts at 2000)—three hours of news, sport and interviews.

## 21:15

**Radio Damascus,** Syria. Actually starts at 2110. *News*, a daily press review, and a variety of features (depending on the day of the week) at approximately 2130 and 2145. These include *Arab Profile* and *Economic Affairs* (Sunday), *Camera and Masks* and *Selected Readings* (Monday), *Reflections* and *Back on the Stage* (Tuesday), *Listeners Overseas* and *Palestine Talking* (Wednesday), *From the World Press* and *Arab Women in Focus* (Thursday), *Arab Newsweek* and *From Our Literature* (Friday), and *Human Rights* and *Syria and the World* (Saturday). The transmission also contains Syrian and some western popular music. Sixty minutes to North America and Australasia on 12085 and 13610 (or 15095) kHz.

**BBC World Service for the Caribbean.** *Caribbean Report*, although intended for listeners in the area, can also be clearly heard throughout much of eastern North America. This brief, 15-minute program provides comprehensive coverage of Caribbean economic and political affairs, both within and outside the region. Monday through Friday only, on 11675 and 15390 kHz.

**Radio Cairo,** Egypt. The start of a 90-minute broadcast highlighting Arab and Egyptian themes. The initial quarter-hour of general programming is followed by *news*, commentary and political items. This in turn is followed by a cultural program until 2215, when the station again reverts to more general fare. A big signal to Europe on 9990 kHz.

**WJIE,** Upton, Kentucky. Continuous Christian music to North America on 7490 kHz. Other U.S. religious broadcasters operating at this hour include **WWCR** on 13845 and 15685 and kHz, **KTBN** on 15590 kHz, and **WHRI-World**

**21:00–22:00**

**Harvest Radio** on 13760 kHz. Traditionalist Catholic programming is available from **WEWN** on 11875 and 13615 kHz.

**AFRTS Shortwave,** USA. Network news, live sports, music and features in the upper-sideband mode from the Armed Forces Radio & Television Service. Transmitted from modestly powered U.S. Navy stations around the globe. Try 4319, 5765, 6350, 6458.5, 10320, 12579, 12689.5 and 13362 kHz.

## 21:30

**BBC World Service for the Falkland Islands.** *Calling the Falklands* has been running for such a long time, it's a little surprising it's still on the air. This twice-weekly transmission for a small community in the South Atlantic consists of news and short features, and is one of the curiosities of world band radio. Audible for 15 minutes Tuesday and Friday on 11680 kHz, and easily heard in parts of eastern North America.

**Radio Austria International.** Summer only at this time. Starts with a brief bulletin of *news*, then weekdays it's the informative ●*Report from Austria*. The weekend replacements are two European co-productions: Saturday's *Insight Central Europe* and Sunday's *Network Europe*. To Europe on 5945 and 6155 kHz, and one hour later during winter.

**Radio Prague,** Czech Republic. Summer only at this time. See 2230 for specifics, except that the Saturday programs are reversed, with *Insight Central Europe* aired in summer. A half hour to Southeast Asia and Australasia on 11600 kHz, and to West Africa on 15545 kHz.

**Radio Station Belarus/Radio Minsk.** Tuesday and Thursday only at this time, and one hour earlier in summer. See 2030 for specifics. Thirty minutes to Europe on 7105 and 7210 kHz.

**Wales Radio International.** Winter Fridays only at this time. News, interviews and music from westernmost Britain. Thirty minutes to Europe on 6010 or 7325 kHz, and one hour earlier in summer.

**Radio Tashkent,** Uzbekistan. Thirty minutes of news, commentary and features, plus some exotic Uzbek music. To Europe on 5025 and 11905 kHz, and to West Asia and the Mideast on 9540 (or 9545) kHz.

**Radio Tirana,** Albania. Monday through Saturday, summer only at this time. *News*, short features and some lively Albanian music. Thirty minutes to Europe on 7130 and 9540 kHz. One hour later in winter.

**Voice of Turkey.** This time winter only. *News*, followed by *Review of the Turkish Press* and features (some of them unusual) with a strong local flavor. Selections of Turkish popular and classical music complete the program. Fifty minutes to Southeast Asia and Australasia on 9525 kHz. One hour earlier in summer.

**Radio Sweden.** Summer only at this time. Thirty minutes of predominantly Scandinavian fare (see 2230 for specifics). To Europe on 6065 kHz, and to Southeast Asia and Australasia on 15255 kHz.

**Voice of the Islamic Republic of Iran.** A one-hour package of news, commentary and features with a distinctly Islamic slant. Not the lightest of programming, but an interesting alternative to what is heard from Western media (even if you disagree). To Australasia winter on 9780 and 11740 kHz, and summer on 9570 and 13665 kHz.

## 22:00

■**BBC World Service for the Americas.** Monday through Friday winter, five minutes of *news* are followed by ●*World Business Report*, *British News*, ●*Sports Roundup* and ●*Analysis* (replaced Wednesday by ●*From Our Own Correspondent*). Summer, it's a full hour of *The World Today*, with the exception of Friday, when the final 30 minutes are taken up by ●*People and Politics*. Weekend programs are year round, with *The World Today* filling the first half hour, followed by Saturday's ●*From Our Own Correspondent* or Sunday's ●*Agenda*. Continuous programming to the Caribbean and eastern North America on 5975 kHz. Also audible in some areas on 12095 kHz, beamed to South America; a radio with synchronous selectable sideband helps reduce teletype interference.

**22:00–22:00**

A mountain train cheats gravity above the Python Valley in Eritrea.    Mike Metras

**BBC World Service for Europe.** Winter weekdays, there's *News*, ●*World Business Report*, British News, ●*Sports Roundup* and ●*Off the Shelf* (readings from world literature). Weekends, *News* is followed by *Jazzmatazz* and ●*Omnibus* (Saturday), and *Meridian* (the arts) and ●*Weekend* on Sunday. Summer, it's news and current events in *The World Today*, reduced to 30 minutes Friday and Saturday, when it is followed by ●*People and Politics* and ●*From Our Own Correspondent*, respectively. The final 60 minutes of a 19-hour block of programming to Europe and North Africa. On 6195 kHz.

**■BBC World Service for East and Southeast Asia and the Pacific.** Sunday through Thursday (local Asian weekdays), it's a full hour of news and current events in ●*The World Today*. Friday and Saturday, there's 30 minutes of the same, followed by ●*People and Politics* and ●*From Our Own Correspondent*, respectively. Continuous to East Asia on 5965 and 6195 kHz; to Southeast Asia on 6195, 7110, 9660 and 11955 kHz; and to Australasia on 9660, 11955 and 12080 kHz.

**Radio Bulgaria.** This time winter only. See 2100 for specifics. News and culture from the Balkans—don't miss ●*Folk Studio* (Bulgarian music) at 2210 Sunday. Sixty minutes to Europe, also heard in parts of eastern North America, on 5800 and 7500 kHz. One hour earlier in summer.

**Radio Cairo,** Egypt. The second half of a 90-minute broadcast to Europe on 9990 kHz; see 2115 for program details.

**Radio Exterior de España ("Spanish National Radio").** Winter weekends only at this time. A popular package of *news* and features. Sunday's series on Spanish music is highly recommended. One hour to Europe on 9680 kHz, and to North and West Africa on 9595 kHz. One hour earlier in summer.

**China Radio International.** Repeat of the 2000 transmission (see there for specifics), but with news updates. One hour to Europe winter on 7170 kHz, summer on 9880 kHz, and autumn on 7175 kHz.

**Voice of America.** The beginning of a three-hour block of programs to East and Southeast Asia and the Pacific. The ubiquitous *News Now*—news and reports on current events, sports, science, business, entertainment and more. To East and Southeast Asia on 7215, 9705, 9770, 11760, 15185, 15290, 15305, 17735 (or 17740) and 17820 kHz; and to Australasia on 15185, 15305 and 17735 kHz. The first half hour is also available weekday evenings to Africa on 7340, 7375 and 7415 kHz.

**Radio Australia.** *News*, followed Sunday through Thursday by *AM* (current events) and, on the half-hour, a feature. The lineup starts with Sunday's *Australian Music Show* (contemporary music) and ends with Thursday's *Jazz Notes*. In between, there's *Music Deli* (samplings from different cultures, Monday); *Blacktracker* (contemporary aboriginal music, Tuesday); and *Australian Country Style* (Oz's response to Nashville, Wednesday). Friday's features are *Asia Pacific* and a later-than-usual edition of *AM*; and Saturday's pairing is *Correspondents' Report* and *Business Report*. Continuous programming to the Pacific on 17715, 17795 and 21740 kHz (audible in parts of North America, especially during summer), and to Southeast Asia on 13620, 15230 and 15240 kHz.

**Radio Taipei International,** Taiwan. Opens with 15 minutes of *News*, and weekdays closes with *Let's Learn Chinese*, which has a series of segments for beginning, intermediate and advanced learners. The remainder of the broadcast is given over to features. Monday, you can listen to the pleasurable and exotic ●*Jade Bells and Bamboo Pipes* (Taiwanese music); and Tuesday to *Culture Express* and *Trends*. Wednesday's slots are *Taiwan Today* and *Confucius and Inspiration Beyond*; Thursday's pairing is *Discover Taiwan* and *New Music Lounge*; and Friday airs *Taipei Magazine* and *People*. These are replaced Saturday by *Groove Zone* and *Kaleidoscope*, and Sunday by *Great Wall Forum* and *Mailbag Time*. Sixty minutes to western Europe, winter on 5810 and 9355 kHz, and summer on 15600 kHz.

**Radio Tirana,** Albania. Monday through Saturday, winter only at this time. Thirty minutes of news, short features and Albanian music. To Europe on 7130 and 9540 kHz. One hour earlier in summer.

**Radio Habana Cuba.** Monday through Saturday, the first half hour consists of international and Cuban news followed by commentary in *RHC's Viewpoint*. The next 30 minutes consist of a news bulletin and the sports-oriented *Time Out* (five minutes each) followed by a feature: *Caribbean Outlook* (Monday and Thursday), *DXers Unlimited* (Tuesday and Saturday), the *Mailbag Show* (Wednesday) and *Weekly Review* (Friday). Sunday, the hour is split between *Weekly Review* and *Mailbag Show*. Sixty minutes to the Caribbean and southern United States on 9550 kHz.

**Radio Budapest,** Hungary. Winter only at this time. *News* and features, most of which are broadcast on a non-regular basis. Thirty minutes to Europe on 3975 and 6025 kHz. One hour earlier in summer.

**Voice of Turkey.** Summer only at this time. *News*, followed by *Review of the Turkish Press* and features with a strong local flavor. Selections of Turkish popular and classical music complete the program. Fifty minutes to Europe and eastern North America on 11960 and 12000 kHz. One hour later during winter.

**Radio Canada International.** Summer only at this hour, and a relay of CBC domestic programming. Monday through Friday, opens

with ●*The World at Six*; Saturday and Sunday, *The World This Weekend*. On the half-hour there's the weekday ●*As It Happens*, Saturday's *Madly Off in All Directions* (sometimes replaced by another comedy show), and Sunday's *The Inside Track*. Sixty minutes to North America on 6175, 9590, 13670 and 17695 kHz. The first half hour is also available to the Caribbean and South America on 11920, 15170 and 17880 kHz. One hour later in winter. For a separate winter service to Europe, see the next item.

**Radio Canada International.** Winter only at this time. Weekdays, it's ●*The World at Six*; Saturday, *Media Zone;* and Sunday, *Canada in the World*. Thirty minutes to Europe and North Africa on 5850, 6045, 9770 and 9805 kHz. One hour earlier in summer.

**Radio Korea International,** South Korea. Winter only at this hour. See 2100 for specifics Thirty minutes to Europe on 3955 kHz, and one hour earlier in summer.

**Radio Ukraine International.** Winter only at this time. A potpourri of things Ukrainian, with the Sunday broadcast often featuring some excellent music. Sixty minutes to Europe and beyond on 5905, 7240 and 9560 kHz. Often mediocre reception due to financial and technical limitations. One hour earlier in summer.

**Radio for Peace International,** Costa Rica. Counterculture and social-conscience programs. to Europe and North America on 15039 kHz.

**XERMX—Radio México Internacional.** Monday through Friday summer, there's an English summary of the Spanish-language *Antena Radio* (weekend programs are in Spanish). Winter, there's a daily feature: *Mosaic of Mexico* (Monday and Friday), *DXperience* (a show for radio enthusiasts, Tuesday and Sunday), *Regional Roots and Rhythms* (Wednesday), *Mirror of Mexico* (Thursday) and Saturday's *Magical Trip*. Best heard in western and southern parts of the United States on 9705 and 11770 kHz.

**All India Radio.** The final half-hour of a transmission to Western Europe and Australasia, consisting mainly of news-related

**22:00–23:00**

fare. To Western Europe on 7410, 9445, 9950 and 11620 kHz; and to Australasia on 9575, 9910, 11620 and 11715 kHz. Frequencies for Europe are audible in parts of eastern North America, while those for Australasia are also heard in Southeast Asia.

**WJIE,** Upton, Kentucky. Continues with Christian music to North America on 7490 kHz. Other U.S. religious broadcasters heard at this hour include **WWCR** on 13845 kHz, **KAIJ** on 13815 kHz, **KTBN** on 15590 kHz, and **WHRI-World Harvest Radio** on 5745 kHz. For traditionalist Catholic programming, try **WEWN** on 9355 and 13615 kHz.

**CFRX-CFRB,** Toronto, Canada. See 2100.

**AFRTS Shortwave,** USA. Network news, live sports, music and features in the upper-sideband mode from the Armed Forces Radio & Television Service. Transmitted from modestly powered U.S. Navy stations around the globe. Try 4319, 5765, 6350, 6458.5, 10320, 12579, 12689.5 and 13362 kHz.

### 22:30

**Radio Sweden.** Monday through Friday, it's *news* and features in *Sixty Degrees North*, concentrating heavily on Scandinavian topics. The Monday slot goes to *SportScan*, replaced Tuesday by *Close Up* or an alternative feature, and Wednesday by *Money Matters*. Thursday features a different show each week of the month—*Nordic Report*, *GreenScan*, *Heart Beat* or *S-Files*, while Friday offers a review of the week's news. Saturday's slot is filled by *Weekend*, *Spectrum* (the arts), *Sweden Today* or *Studio 49*, and Sunday fare consists of *In Touch with Stockholm* (a listener-response program) or the musical *Sounds Nordic*. Thirty minutes to Europe on 6065 and 7325 kHz, with the latter frequency also audible in Africa and the Mideast. One hour earlier in summer.

**Radio Austria International.** Winter only at this time; see 2130 for program specifics. Thirty minutes to Europe on 5945 and 6155 kHz, and one hour earlier in summer.

**Flanders Radio International,** Belgium. Weekdays, it's *News*, feature(s) and *Soundbox*.

The lineup includes *Focus on Europe* and *Sports* (Monday), *Green Society* (Tuesday), *The Arts* (Wednesday and Friday), *Around Town* (Wednesday), *Economics* and *International Report* (Thursday), and Friday's *Tourism*. These are replaced Saturday by ●*Music from Flanders*, and Sunday by *Radio World*, *Tourism*, *Brussels 1043* (a listener-response program) and *Soundbox*. Thirty minutes to North America winter on 13700 kHz, and summer on 15565 kHz.

**Radio Prague,** Czech Republic. *News*, then Monday through Friday there's *Newsview* and one or two features. Monday's *One on One* (informal interviews) is replaced Tuesday by *Witness* and *Talking Point* (issues shaping people's lives in the Czech Republic) or *Central Europe Today*. Wednesday's lineup is *ABC of Czech* followed by *Profile* or *Czechs in History*. *Economic Report* fills the Thursday slot, and Friday's feature is *Magazine*. Weekend fare consists of Saturday's *Insight Central Europe* (winter) or *Spotlight* followed by *Saturday Music* or *Readings from Czech Literature* (summer); and Sunday's *A Letter from Prague*, *The Arts* and *Mailbox*. A half hour to eastern North America winter on 7345 kHz, and summer on 11600 and 15545 kHz; also to West Africa winter on 9435 kHz.

### 22:45

**All India Radio.** The first 15 minutes of a much longer broadcast, consisting of Indian music, regional and international *news*, commentary, and a variety of talks and features of general interest. Continuous till 0045. To East Asia on 9950, 11620 and 13605 kHz; and to Southeast Asia on 9705, 11620 and 13605 kHz.

### 23:00

■**BBC World Service for the Americas.** Monday through Thursday winter, a full hour of *The World Today*. On the remaining days, it's reduced to 30 minutes and followed by *Global Business* (Friday), *Arts in Action* (Saturday) or Sunday's *Pick of the Week*. Summer weekdays, opens with five minutes of *news*. Next comes the long-running *Outlook*, and the hour is rounded off with a 15-minute feature (very much a mixed bag). Saturday brings ●*Play of the Week* (world theater at its best), replaced Sunday by the same programs as in winter. Continuous to the Caribbean and eastern North America on 5975 kHz. Also audible in some areas on 12095 kHz, targeted at South America; a radio with synchronous selectable sideband helps reduce teletype interference.

■**BBC World Service for East and Southeast Asia and the Pacific.** Sunday through Thursday (weekday mornings in Asia), it's the second hour of *The World Today*, a breakfast news show for the region. On the remaining days there's 30 minutes of the same, followed by Friday's *Global Business* or Saturday's *Arts in Action*. Continuous to East Asia on 5965, 6035, 6195, 11945, 11955 and 15280 kHz; to Southeast Asia on 3915, 6195, 7105 and 11955 kHz; and to Australasia on 11955 kHz.

**Voice of Turkey.** Winter only at this hour. See 2200 for program details. Fifty minutes to Europe on 6020 kHz, and to eastern North America on 9655 kHz. One hour earlier in summer.

■**Deutsche Welle,** Germany. Repeat of the 2100 broadcast to Southeast Asia and Australasia (see there for specifics). Forty-five minutes to South and Southeast Asia, winter on 9470, 9815 and 13690 kHz; and summer on 9815, 12000, 17560 and 21790 kHz.

**Radio Australia.** *World News*, followed Sunday through Thursday by *Asia Pacific* (replaced Friday by *Lingua Franca*, and Saturday by some sharp scientific commentary in ●*Ockham's Razor*). On the half-hour, look for a feature. *Earthbeat* (the environment) occupies the Sunday slot, and is replaced Monday by *The Buzz*. Then come Tuesday's *Arts Talk*, Wednesday's *Rural Reporter*, Thursday's *Media Report*, Friday's *Sports*

**YAESU** VR-5000

The **Yaesu VR-5000** provides sophisticated wideband reception covering 100 kHz to 2600 MHz (2.6 GHz) less cellular, in AM, FM-N, FM-W, LSB, USB and CW. This radio features a real-time bandscope and you get 2000 memories. Optional aids such as a DSP unit, voice synthesizer and digital voice recorder are available. The VR-5000 is only 7.1x2.75x8". **Contact Universal for full details and pricing.** Universal also offers the full range of Yaesu amateur radio products.

## VR-500

The **VR-500** is the first radio to provide wideband coverage plus SSB reception in such a small and capable package. Coverage is from 100 kHz to 1300 MHz (less cellular) in AM, FM-N/W and SSB-CW. Features include: 1000 memories, priority, dual watch, dial lamp, alpha numeric recall, band scope and Smart Search. The VR-500 is an amazing 2.3x3.7x1" 8 oz. (58x95x25mm 220 g) and operates from two AA cells. With BNC type antenna. Yaesu also now offers the incredible *and* affordable **VR-120D**. You can put nearly the entire radio spectrum in your shirt pocket for under $200! **Please visit our website or call for pricing.**

## Universal Radio, Inc.
### 6830 Americana Pkwy.
### Reynoldsburg, OH 43068
☎ **800 431-3939** Orders & Prices
☎ 614 866-4267 Information
→ 614 866-2339 FAX Line
 dx@universal-radio.com

◆ **HUGE FREE CATALOG** ◆

Universal offers a huge 100 page catalog covering everything for the shortwave, amateur or scanner enthusiast. Available FREE on request (or five IRC's outside of North America).

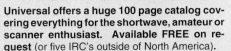 **www.RFfun.com** or **www.universal-radio.com**

## 23:00–23:30

*Factor*, and Saturday's *Innovations*. Continuous to the Pacific on 9660, 12080, 17715, 17795 and 21740 kHz; and to Southeast Asia on 13620, 15230 and 15240 kHz. Listeners in North America should try 17715, 17795 and 21740 kHz, especially during summer.

**Radio Canada International.** Summer weekdays, the final hour of ●*As It Happens*; winter, the first 30 minutes of the same, preceded by the up-to-the-minute news program ●*World at Six*. Summer weekends, look for ●*Quirks and Quarks* (science, Saturday) and ●*Global Village* (world music, Sunday). These are replaced winter by *The World This Weekend* (both days), a comedy

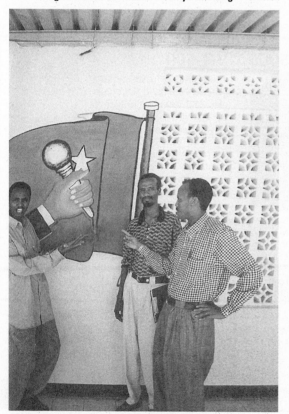

Station director Burhan (center), with announcers Goombear (left) and Isak, show off the newly painted logo outside the Radio Galkayo building.   S. Voron

show (Saturday) and *The Inside Track* (Sunday). To North America on (winter) 5960, (summer) 6175, 9590, (winter) 9755, and (summer) 13670 and 17695 kHz.

**China Radio International.** Starts with *News*, and weekdays continues with in-depth reports. The remainder of the broadcast is made up of features. Regular shows include *People in the Know* (Monday), *Biz China* (Tuesday), *China Horizons* (Wednesday), *Voices from Other Lands* (Thursday) and Friday's *Life in China*. Saturday, there's *Global Review* and *Listeners' Garden* (reports, music and a Chinese language lesson), replaced Sunday by *Report from Developing Countries* and *In the Spotlight*. One hour to the United States and Caribbean on 5990 and 13680 kHz via CRI's Cuban and Canadian relays.

**Radio for Peace International,** Costa Rica. Continues with a six-hour cyclical block of social-conscience and counterculture programming audible in Europe and the Americas on 15039 kHz.

**Radio Cairo,** Egypt. The first hour of a 90-minute broadcast to eastern North America. A ten-minute *news* bulletin is aired at 2315, with the remaining time taken up by short features on Egypt, the Middle East and Islam. For the intellectual listener there's *Literary Readings* at 2345 Monday, and *Modern Arabic Poetry* at the same time Friday. More general fare is available in *Listener's Mail* at 2325 Thursday and Saturday. Easy reception on 9900 kHz.

**Radio Romania International.** *News*, commentary and features, plus some enjoyable Romanian music. Fifty-five minutes to Europe on 7195 (winter), 9570 and (summer) 11775 kHz; also to eastern North America winter on 9510 and 11940 kHz, and summer on 11740 and 15105 kHz.

**Radio Bulgaria.** Summer only at this time. *News*, music and features. Monday through Friday (weekday evenings in North America), the news is followed by *Events and Developments*, replaced Saturday by *Views Behind the News* and Sunday by the enjoyable and exotic ●*Folk Studio*. The next slot consists of weekly features. Take your pick from *Plaza/Walks and Talks* (Sunday), *Magazine Economy* (Monday),

**23:00–23:30**

*Arts and Artists* (Tuesday), *History Club* (Wednesday), *The Way We Live* (Thursday), *DX Programed* (Friday) and *Answering Your Letters*, a listener-response show, on Saturday. Monday through Saturday, the broadcast ends with *Keyword Bulgaria*. Sixty minutes to eastern North America on 9400 and 11700 kHz. One hour later during winter.

**XERMX—Radio México Internacional.** Winter weekdays only. An English summary of the Spanish-language *Antena Radio*. Weekend programs are in Spanish. One hour earlier in summer. Thirty minutes to North America on 9705 and 11770 kHz, and best heard in western and southern parts of the United States.

**Voice of America.** Continues with programs aimed at East Asia and the Pacific on the same frequencies as at 2200.

**WJIE,** Upton, Kentucky. Continuous Christian music to North America on 7490 kHz. Other U.S. religious broadcasters heard at this time include **WWCR** on 13845 kHz, **KAIJ** on 13815 kHz, **KTBN** on 15590 kHz, and **WHRI-World Harvest Radio** on 5745 kHz. For traditionalist Catholic programming, tune **WEWN** on 9355 and 13615 kHz.

**AFRTS Shortwave,** USA. Network news, live sports, music and features in the upper-sideband mode from the Armed Forces Radio & Television Service. Transmitted from modestly powered U.S. Navy stations around the globe. Try 4319, 5765, 6350, 6458.5, 10320, 12579, 12689.5 and 13362 kHz.

## 23:30

■**Radio Netherlands.** Opens Monday through Friday with ●*Newsline*, replaced weekends by a *news* bulletin. The next 30 minutes are devoted to features: ●*Research File* (science, Monday); *Music 52-15* (Tuesday); the outstanding ●*Documentary* (Wednesday); ●*Aural Tapestry* (summer Thursdays; *Sound Fountain* in winter); and ●*A Good Life* (Friday). Saturday's lineup is *Europe Unzipped*, *Insight* and *Music 52-15*, replaced Sunday by *Sincerely Yours*, a program preview and *Dutch Horizons*. The first of two hours to North America on 6165 and 9845 kHz.

**Radio Prague,** Czech Republic. Winter only at this time. See 2230 for specifics. Saturday programming at this hour is *Spotlight* followed by *Saturday Music* or *Readings from Czech Literature*. A half hour to eastern North America on 7345 and 9435 kHz, and one hour earlier in summer.

**Radio Vilnius,** Lithuania. A half hour that's mostly *news* and background reports about events in Lithuania. Of broader appeal is *Mailbag*, aired every other Saturday. For some Lithuanian music, try the second half of Sunday's broadcast. To eastern North America on 9875 kHz.

**Swiss Radio International.** *Newsnet*—news and background reports on world and Swiss events. Some lighter fare on Saturdays, when the biweekly *Capital Letters* (a listener-response program) alternates with *Name Game* (first Saturday) and *Sounds Good* (third Saturday). Thirty minutes to South America on 9885, (winter) 11660 and (summer) 11905 kHz. As a result of SRI's decision to discontinue shortwave broadcasts to all parts of the world except the Middle East, Africa and South America (and these are also to be phased out eventually), this slot is far and away the best opportunity for listeners in North America.

**All India Radio.** Continuous programming to East and Southeast Asia. A potpourri of *news*, commentary, features and exotic Indian music. To East Asia on 9950, 11620 and 13605 kHz; and to Southeast Asia on 9705, 11620 and 13605 kHz.

**Voice of Vietnam.** *News*, then *Commentary* or *Weekly Review*. These are followed by short features and some pleasant Vietnamese music. A half hour to Southeast Asia on 9840 and 12020 kHz. Frequencies may vary slightly.

---

*Prepared by Tony Jones and the staff of* Passport to World Band Radio.

# Addresses PLUS—2003

*Station Postal and Email Addresses . . . PLUS Webcasts, Websites, Who's Who, Phones, Faxes, Bureaus, Future Plans, Items for Sale, Giveaways . . . PLUS Summer and Winter Times in Each Country!*

Much of PASSPORT shows how stations reach out to you, but Addresses PLUS shows how you can reach out to stations. It also details, country by country, how broadcasters go beyond world band radio to inform and entertain.

**Webcasts Grow Outside United States**

Addresses PLUS also provides URLs for world band stations simul-casting over the Internet. These are on the increase, as in North America alone there are tens of millions of listeners, while elsewhere the audience is expanding.

World band simulcasters have recently been given a leg up from unexpected sources. In the United States, a combination of Congressional action and actors' union demands has created a prohibitive financial burden on Webcasting, but it only impacts stations within the U.S. The effect has been to terminate nearly all American stations' Web simulcasts, except those of a religious nature.

These actions were seemingly designed to protect established American and kindred media conglomerates from home-grown competition. Yet, the main result has been to give non-American Webcasters a competitive advantage. In the United States, foreign broadcasters now have the Webcasting audience virtually unto themselves.

**Dinka tribesman leaves for the hunt.**

customtourguide.com

### "Applause" Replies

When radio broadcasting was in its infancy, listeners sent in "applause" cards to let stations how well they were being received. To say "thanks," stations would reply with a letter or illustrated card verifying ("QSLing" in Morse-code) that the station the listener heard was, in fact, theirs. While they were at it, some would throw in a free souvenir—station calendar, pennant or sticker.

This still goes on today, although obtaining QSLs is tougher than it used to be. You can learn how to provide feedback to stations by looking under "Verification" in PASSPORT's glossary. Some stations also sell goods—radios, CDs, publications, clothing, tote bags, caps, watches, clocks, pens, knives, letter openers, lighters, refrigerator magnets and keyrings.

### Paying Postfolk

Most stations reply to listener correspondence—even email—through the postal system. That way, they can send out printed schedules, verification cards and other "hands-on" souvenirs. Major stations usually do this for free, but smaller ones often seek reimbursement for postage.

Most effective, especially for Latin American and Indonesian stations, is to enclose some unused (mint) stamps from the station's country. These are available from Plum's Airmail Postage, 12 Glenn Road, Flemington NJ 08822 USA, plumdx@msn.com, phone +1 (908) 788-1020,

> **Foreign Webcasters have the American audience virtually to themselves.**

**World band portables help relieve cabin fever during cruises into the Alaskan wild.** M. Guha

**August, 2002 conference of the HFCC, ABU and ASBU in Bangkok, hosted by VT Merlin Communications.**

Jacques Bouliane, CBC Transmission

fax +1 (908) 782 2612. One way to help ensure your return-postage stamps will be put to the intended use is to affix them onto a pre-addressed return airmail envelope. The result is a self-addressed stamped envelope, or SASE as it is referred to in Addresses PLUS.

You can also prompt reluctant stations by donating one paper U.S. dollars, preferably hidden from prying eyes by a piece of foil-covered carbon paper or the like. Registration helps, too, as cash tends to get stolen. Additionally, International Reply Coupons (IRCs), which recipients may exchange locally for air or surface stamps, are available at a number of post offices worldwide. Thing is, they're increasingly hard to find, relatively costly, not fully effective, and aren't accepted by postal authorities in some countries.

## Stamp Out Crime

Yes, even nowadays mail theft is a problem in several countries. We identify these, and for each one offer proven ways to help avoid theft. Remember that a few postal employees are stamp collectors, and in certain countries they freely steal mail with unusual stamps. When in doubt, use everyday stamps or, even better, a postal meter or PC-generated postage. Another option is to use an aerogram.

## ¿Que Hora Es?

World Time, explained elsewhere in this book, is essential if you want to find out when your favorite station is on. But if you want to know what time it is in any given country, World Time and Addresses PLUS work together to give you local times within each country.

So that you don't have to wrestle with seasonal changes in your own time, we give local times for each country in terms of hours' difference from World Time, which stays the same year-round. For example, if you look below under "Algeria," you'll see that country is World Time +1; that is, one hour ahead of World Time. So, if World Time is 1200, the local time in Algeria is 1300 (1:00 PM). On the other hand, México City is World Time –6; that is, six hours behind World Time. If World Time is 1200, in México City it's 6:00 AM.

Times shown in parentheses are for the middle of the year—roughly April-October; specific dates of seasonal-time changeovers for individual countries can be obtained at www.oag.com or (U.S. callers only) by dialing the OAG toll-free at 1-800-342-5624 during working hours.

## Spotted Something New?

Has something changed since we went to press? A missing detail? Please let us know! Your update information, especially photocopies of material received from stations, is highly valued. Contact the IBS Editorial Office, Box 300, Penn's Park, PA 18943 USA, fax +1 (215) 598 3794, email addresses@passband.com.

*Muchas gracias* to the kindly folks and helpful organizations mentioned at the end of this chapter for their tireless cooperation in the preparation of this section. Without you, none of this would have been possible.

## Using PASSPORT's Addresses PLUS Section

**Stations included:** All stations are listed if known to reply, however erratically. Also, new stations which possibly may reply to correspondence from listeners.

**Leased-time programs:** Private organizations/NGOs that lease air time, but which possess no world band transmitters of their own, are usually not listed. However, they may be reached via the stations over which they are heard.

**Postal addresses.** Communications addresses are given. These sometimes differ from the physical transmitter locations given in the Blue Pages.

**Email addresses and Websites.** Given in Internet format. Periods, commas and semicolons at the end of an address listing are normal sentence punctuation, not part of the address, and "http://" is used only when there is no "www."

**Phone and fax numbers.** To help avoid confusion, telephone numbers are given with hyphens, fax numbers without. All are configured for international dialing once you add your country's International access code (011 in the United States and Canada, 010 in the United Kingdom, and so on). For domestic dialing within countries outside the United States, Canada and the Caribbean, replace the country code (1-3 digits preceded by a "+") by a zero.

**Giveaways.** If you want freebies, say so politely in your correspondence. These are usually available until supplies run out.

**Webcasting.** World band stations which simulcast and/or provide archived programming over the Internet are indicated by ▣.

**Unless otherwise indicated, stations:**
- Reply regularly within six months to most listeners' correspondence in English.
- Provide, upon request, free station schedules and verification ("QSL") postcards or letters (see "Verification" in the glossary for further information). We specify when other items are available for free or for purchase.
- Do not require compensation for postage costs incurred in replying to you. Where compensation is required, details are provided.

**Local times.** These are given in difference from World Time. For example, "World Time –5" means that if you subtract five hours from World Time, you'll get the local time in that country. Thus, if it were 1100 World Time, it would be 0600 local time in that country. Times in (parentheses) are for the middle of the year—roughly April-October. For exact changeover dates, see above explanatory paragraph.

## AFGHANISTAN    World Time + 4:30

**Radio Afghanistan**, Afghan Radio and TV, P.O. Box 544, Ansari Wat, Kabul, Afghanistan. Contact: Mir Amanullah Sharifi, Head of Planning & Foreign Relations. Commenced relays via Norway and the United Arab Emirates during summer 2002, but plans to eventually resume shortwave broadcasting from within Afghanistan.

## ALBANIA    World Time +1 (+2 midyear)

**☞Radio Tirana**, External Service, Rruga Ismail Qemali Nr. 11, Tirana, Albania. Phone: (general) +355 (42) 23-239; (Phone/fax, Technical Directorate) +355 (42) 26203. Fax: (External Service) +355 (42) 23650; (Technical Directorate) +355 (42) 27 745. Email: (general) radiotirana@radiotirana.net; radiotirana@interalb.net; (Technical Directorate) 113566.3011@compuserve.com; (Mandija) imandija@icc-al.org; or dcico@artv.tirana.al. Web: (general) www.radiotirana.net; http://rtsh.sil.at; (RealAudio from Radio Tirana 1, domestic service) http://rtsh.sil.at/online.htm. Contact: Bardhyl Pollo, Director of External Services; Adriana Bislea, English Department; Clara Ceska; Marjeta Thoma; Pandi Skaka, Producer; or Diana Koci; (Technical Directorate) Irfan Mandija, Technical Director ARTV; (Frequency Management) Mrs. Drita Cico, Head of RTV Monitoring Center. May send free stickers and postcards. Replies from the station are again forthcoming, but it is advisable to include return postage ($1 should be enough).

**Trans World Radio**—*see* Monaco.

## ALGERIA    World Time +1 (+2 midyear)

**Radio Algiers International**—same details as "Radio Algérienne," below.

**☞Radio Algérienne (ENRS)**

*NONTECHNICAL AND GENERAL TECHNICAL:* 21 Boulevard des Martyrs, Algiers 16000, Algeria. Phone: (Direction Générale) +213 (21) 230-821; (Direction Commerciale) +213 (21) 590-700; (head of international relations) +213 (21) 594-266; (head of technical direction) +213 (21) 692-867. Fax: +213 (21) 230 823. Email: (information) information@algerian-radio.dz; (Direction Générale) dg@algerian-radio.dz; (Direction Technique, including reception reports) technique@algerian-radio.dz. Web: (includes Windows Media) www.algerian-radio.dz. Contact: (nontechnical) L. Zaghlami; Chaabane Lounakil, Head of International Arabic Section; Mrs. Zehira Yahi, Head of International Relations; or Relations Extérieures; (technical) M. Lakhdar Mahdi, Head of Technical Direction. Replies irregularly. French or Arabic preferred, but English accepted.

*FREQUENCY MANAGEMENT OFFICE:* Télédiffusion d'Algérie, Centre Nsdal, Bouzareah 1850, Algeria. Phone: +213 (21) 904-512; or +213 (21) 901-717. Fax: +213 (21) 901 499 or +213 (21) 901 522. Email: tda@ist.cerist.dz. Contact: Slimane Djematene; or Karim Zitouni.

## ANGOLA    World Time +1

**Rádio Ecclésia**, Rua Comandante Bula 118, São Paulo, Luanda, Angola; or Caixa Postal 3579, Luanda, Angola. Phone: (general) +244 (2) 443-041; (studios) +244 (2) 445-484. Fax: +244 (2) 443 093. Email: ecclesia@snet.co.ao. Web: http://recclesia.org. Contact: Fr. Antônio Jaca, General Manager. A Catholic station founded in 1954 and which broadcast continuously from March 1955 until closed by presidential decree in 1978. Reestablished in March 1997, when it was granted a permit to operate on FM. Experimented with shortwave transmissions via Radio Nederland facilities during July 2000, but these were terminated for technical reasons. Restarted transmissions in April 2001 via facilities of Germany's Deutsche Telekom (*see*) and switched to a South African relay in May 2002. Eventually hopes to resume shortwave broadcasts via its own transmitter, if and when the current tight regulations in Angola are relaxed. According to press reports, the shortwave equipment has already been purchased by the Episcopal Conference of Portugal.

**☞Rádio Nacional de Angola**, Caixa Postal 1329, Luanda, Angola. Fax: +244 (2) 391 234. Email: (technical) rochapinto@rna.so Web: (includes RealAudio) www.rna.ao; if the audio link doesn't work, try www.netangola.com/p/default.htm. Contact: Júlio Mendonça, Diretor dos Serviços de Programas; Lourdes de Almeida, Chefe de Secção; or Manuel Rabelais, Diretor Geral; (technical) Cândido Rocha Pinto, Diretor dos Serviços Técnicos. Formerly replied occasionally to correspondence, preferably in Portuguese, but replies have been more difficult recently. $1, return postage or 2 IRCs most helpful.

## ANTARCTICA    World Time –3 Base Antártica Esperanza

**Radio Nacional Arcángel San Gabriel—LRA36**, Base Esperanza, 9411 Antártida Argentina, Argentina. Phone/fax: +54 (2964) 421 519. Email: lra36@infovia.com.ar. Web: (unofficial) www.fcapital.com.ar/esperanza/pagina_otras.htm; (official Base Esperanza site) www.ejercito.mil.ar/antarti/base_esperan/bas_espera.htm. Contact: Fernando José Isla, Director. Return postage required. Replies to correspondence in Spanish, and sometimes to correspondence in English and French, depending on who is at the station. If no reply, try sending your correspondence (but don't write the station's name on the envelope) and 2 IRCs via the helpful Gabriel Iván Barrera, Casilla 2868, C1000WBC Buenos Aires, Argentina.

## ANGUILLA    World Time –4

**Caribbean Beacon**, Box 690, Anguilla, British West Indies. Phone: +1 (264) 497-4340. Fax: +1 (264) 497 4311. Contact: Monsell Hazell, Chief Engineer. $2 or return postage helpful. Relays Dr. Gene Scott's University Network—*see* USA.

## ANTIGUA    World Time –4

**BBC World Service—Caribbean Relay Station**, P.O. Box 1203, St. John's, Antigua. Phone: +1 (268) 462-0994. Fax: +1 (268) 462 0436. Contact: (technical) David George. Nontechnical correspondence should be sent to the BBC World Service in London (*see*).

**Deutsche Welle—Relay Station Antigua**—same address and contact as BBC World Service, above. Nontechnical correspondence should be sent to Deutsche Welle in Germany (*see*).

## ARGENTINA    World Time –3

**Radio Baluarte**, Casilla de Correo 45, 3370 Puerto Iguazú, Provincia de Misiones, Argentina. Phone: +54 (3737) 422-557. Email: icnfuturo@hotmail.com. Contact: Hugo Eidinger, Director. Free tourist literature. Return postage helpful. The same programs are aired on 1610 kHz (Radio Maranatha) and 101.7 MHz (Radio Futuro), and all three outlets are believed to be unlicensed. However, given the current radio licensing situation in the country, this is not unusual.

**Radiodifusión Argentina al Exterior—RAE**, Casilla de Correos 555, C1000WBC Buenos Aires, Argentina. Phone/fax:

+54 (11) 4325-6368; (technical) +54 (11) 4325-5270. Email: (general) rae@radionacional.gov.ar; (technical) operativa@radionacional.gov.ar; (Marcela Campos) camposrae@fibertel.com.ar (this address is to be phased out). Contact: (general) John Anthony Middleton, Head of English Team; María Dolores López, Spanish Team; (administration) Marcela G. R. Campos, Directora; (technical) Gabriel Iván Barrera, DX Editor. Return postage or $1 appreciated.

**Radio Nacional Buenos Aires**, Maipú 555, C1006ACE Buenos Aires, Argentina. Phone: +54 (11) 4325-9100. Fax: (management—Gerencia General) +54 (11) 4325 9433; (Director) +54 (11) 4325-4590, +54 (11) 4322-4313; (technical—Gerencia Operativa) +54 (11) 4325-5270. Email: (general) info@ radionacional.gov.ar; (Director) direccion@radionacional.gov.ar, or mariogiorgi@uol.com.ar; (technical) operativa@radionacional.gov.ar. Web: www.radionacional.gov.ar. Contact: (general) Mario Giorgi, Director; (technical) Alberto Enríquez. $1 helpful. Prefers correspondence in Spanish, and usually replies via RAE (see above). If no reply, try sending your correspondence (but don't write the station's name on your envelope) and 2 IRCs via the helpful Gabriel Iván Barrera, Casilla 2868, C1000WBC Buenos Aires, Argentina.

## ARMENIA   World Time +3 (+4 midyear)

**Public Radio of Armenia/Voice of Armenia**, Radio Agency, Alek Manoukyan Street 5, 375025 Yerevan, Armenia. Phone: +374 (2) 570-970, +374 (2) 554-761 or +374 (2) 552-650. Fax: +374 (2) 151 600. Email: pubarm@armradio.am. Web: (seemingly out of date) www.expo.am/natradio. Contact: V. Voskanian, Deputy Editor-in-Chief; R. Abalian, Editor-in-Chief; Armenag Sansaryan, International Relations Bureau; Laura Baghdassarian, Deputy Manager, Radioagency; or Armen Amiryan, Director. Free postcards and stamps. Replies slowly.

## ASCENSION   World Time exactly

**BBC World Service—Atlantic Relay Station**, English Bay, Ascension (South Atlantic Ocean). Fax: +247 6117. Contact: (technical) Jeff Cant, Staff Manager; M.R. Watkins, A/Assistant Resident Engineer; or Mrs. Nicola Nicholls, Transmitter Engineer. Nontechnical correspondence should be sent to the BBC World Service in London (see).

**Radio Japan, Radio Roma and Voice of America via BBC Ascension Relay Station**—All correspondence should be directed to the regular addresses in Japan, Italy and USA (see).

## AUSTRALIA   World Time +11 (+10 midyear) Victoria (VIC), New South Wales (NSW), Australian Capital Territory (ACT) and Tasmania (TAS); +10:30 (+9:30 midyear) South Australia (SA); +10 Queensland (QLD); +9:30 Northern Territory (NT); +8 Western Australia (WA)

**Australian Broadcasting Corporation Northern Territory HF Service—ABC Radio 8DDD Darwin**, Administrative Center for the Northern Territory Shortwave Service, ABC Box 9994, GPO Darwin NT 0820, Australia. Phone: +61 (8) 8943-3222; (engineering) +61 (8) 8943-3209. Fax: +61 (8) 8943 3235 or +61 (8) 8943 3208. Contact: (general) Tony Bowden, Branch Manager; (administration) Carole Askham, Administrative Officer; (technical) Peter Camilleri or Yvonne Corby. Free stickers and postcards. "Traveller's Guide to ABC Radio" for $1. T-shirts US$20. Three IRCs or return postage helpful.

**Australian Defence Forces Radio**, Department of Defence, EMU (Electronic Media Unit) ANZAC Park West, APW 1-B-07, Reid, Canberra, ACT 2601, Australia. Phone: +61 (2) 6266-6669. Fax: +61 (2) 6266 6565. Contact: (general) Adam Iffland, Presenter; (technical) Hugh Mackenzie, Managing Presenter; or Brian Langshaw. SAE and 2 IRCs needed for a reply. Formerly broadcast irregularly using its own transmitters, but currently airs via the facilities of Radio Australia. Replies to verification inquiries only.

**BBC World Service via Radio Australia**—For verification direct from the Australian transmitters, contact John Westland, Director of English Programs at Radio Australia (see). Nontechnical correspondence should be sent to the BBC World Service in London (see).

**Radio Australia**

*STUDIOS AND MAIN OFFICES:* GPO Box 428G, Melbourne VIC 3001, Australia. Phone: ("Openline" voice mail for listeners' messages and requests) +61 (3) 9626-1825; (switchboard) +61 (3) 9626-1800; (English programs) +61 (3) 9626-1922; (marketing manager) +61 (3) 9626 1723; (engineering) +61 (3) 9626-1914. Fax and Faxpoll: (general) +61 (3) 9626 1899; (engineering) +61 (3) 9626 1917. Email: (general) english@ra.abc.net.au; (marketing manager) hutchins.andria@abc.net.au; (engineering) holmes.nigel@a2.abc.net.au; (Radio Australia transmissions and programs) raelp@radioaus.abc.net.au; (Pacific Services) rapac@radioaus.abc.net.au; (Internet and Web Coordinator) naughton.russell@a2.abc.net.au. Web: (includes RealAudio) www.abc.net.au/ra. Contact: (general) John Westland, Head, English Language Programming; Roger Broadbent, Producer "Feedback"; Tony Hastings, Director of Programs; Caroline Bilney, Information Officer; Andria Hutchins, Marketing Manager; or Jean-Gabriel Manguy, General Manager; (technical) Nigel Holmes, Transmission Manager, Transmission Management Unit. Free stickers and sometimes pennants and souvenirs available. On-air language courses available in Chinese, Indonesian, Khmer and Vietnamese. Course notes available at cost price. Radio Australia will attempt to answer listener's letters even though this will largely depend on the availability of resources and a reply may no longer be possible in all cases. All reception reports received by Radio Australia will now be forwarded to the Australian Radio DX Club for assessment and checking. ARDXC will forward completed QSLs to Radio Australia for mailing. For further information, contact John Westland, Director of English Programs at Radio Australia (Email: westland.john@a2.abc.net.au); or John Wright, Secretary/Editor, ARDXC (Email: dxer@fl.net.au). Plans to add new aerials and re-locate 250 kW transmitters.

*NEW YORK BUREAU, NONTECHNICAL:* Room 2260, 630 Fifth Avenue, New York NY 10020 USA. Phone: (representative) +1 (212) 332-2540; or (correspondent) +1 (212) 332-2545. Fax: +1 (212) 332 2546. Contact: Maggie Jones, North American Representative.

*LONDON BUREAU, NONTECHNICAL:* 54 Portland Place, London W1N 4DY, United Kingdom. Phone: +44 (20) 7631-4456. Fax: (administration) +44 (20) 7323 0059, (news) +44 (20) 7323 1125. Contact: Robert Bolton, Manager.

*BANGKOK BUREAU, NONTECHNICAL:* 209 Soi Hutayana off Soi Suanplu, South Sathorn Road, Bangkok 10120, Thailand. Fax: +66 (2) 287 2040. Contact: Nicholas Stuart.

*SAN FRANCISCO OFFICE, SCHEDULES:* 2654 17th Avenue, San Francisco CA 94116 USA. Phone: +1 (415) 564-9968. Email: GPoppin@aol.com. Contact: George Poppin. This address, a volunteer office, only provides Radio Australia schedules to listeners. All other correspondence should be sent directly to the main office in Melbourne.

**Voice International Limited** (formerly Christian Voice International Australia)

*MAIN OFFICE:* Voice International TM, P.O. Box 1104, Buderim, QLD 4556, Australia. Phone: +61 (7) 5477-1555. Fax: +61 (7) 5477 1727. Email: (general) voice@vil.com.au; info@vil.com.au; (Edmiston) mike.edmiston@vil.com.au; (Moti) raymoti@ vil.com.au. Web: www.vil.com.au. Contact: (general) Mike Edmiston, Director; or Raymond Moti, Station Manager.

*TRANSMITTER SITE:* Voice International, PMB 5777, Darwin NT 0801, Australia. Phone: +61 (8) 8981-6591. Fax: +61 (8) 8981 2846. Contact: Mrs. Lorna Manning, Site Administrator.

**Radio VNG** (official time station)

PRIMARY ADDRESS: National Standards Commission, P.O. Box 282, North Ryde, NSW 1670, Australia. Toll-free telephone (Australia only) (1800) 251-942. Phone: +61 (2) 9888-3922. Fax: +61 (2) 9888 3033. Email: rbrittain@nsc.gov.au. Contact: Dr. Richard Brittain, Secretary, National Time Committee. Station offers a free 16-page booklet about VNG and free promotional material. Free stickers and postcards. One IRC or $1 helpful. Likely to close December 31st 2002.

ALTERNATIVE ADDRESS: VNG Users Consortium, GPO Box 1090, Canberra, ACT 2601, Australia. Fax: +61 (2) 6249 9355. Contact: Dr. Marion Leiba, Honorary Secretary. Three IRCs appreciated.

# AUSTRIA    World Time +1 (+2 midyear)

☛ **Radio Afrika International**, Radio Afrika Center, Heigerleinstrasse 7, A-1160 Vienna, Austria. Phone/fax: +43 (1) 4944-033. Email: radio.afrikas@sil.at. Web: (includes RealAudio) www.radioafrika.net.

☛ **Radio Austria International**

*MAIN OFFICE:* Argentinierstrasse 31, A-1040 Vienna, Austria. Phone: (management) +43 (1) 87878-12130; (answering machine/listener's service) +43 (1) 87878-13636; (frequency management) +43 (1) 87878-12629. Fax: (management) +43 (1) 87878 14404; (frequency management) +43 (1) 87878 12773; (listener's service) +43 (1) 87878 14404. Email: (frequency schedules, comments, reception reports) roi.service@orf.at; (intermedia programme) intermedia@orf.at; (Internet programming service) roi@orf.at; (frequency management) hfbc@orf.at. Web: (includes RealAudio) http://roi.orf.at. Contact: (general) Vera Bock, Listener's Service; "Postbox"/ "Hörerbriefkasten/Flash des Ondes" listeners' letters shows; Wolf Harranth, Editor, "Intermedia"; (management) Roland Machatschke, Managing Director; or Michael Kerbler, Deputy Director, Head of German Department & Director of Programs; (English Department) David Ward; (French Department) Lucien Giordani; (Spanish Department) Jacobo Naar-Carbonell;

## TIPS FOR EFFECTIVE CORRESPONDENCE

**Write to be read.** Be interesting and helpful from the recipient's point of view, yet friendly without being chummy. Comments on specific programs are almost always appreciated, even if you are sending in what is basically a technical report.

**Incorporate language courtesies.** Using the broadcaster's tongue is always a plus— Addresses PLUS indicates when it is a requirement—but English is usually the next-best bet. When writing in any language to Spanish-speaking countries, remember that what gringos think of as the "last name" is actually written as the penultimate name. Thus, Juan Antonio Vargas García, which can also be written as Juan Antonio Vargas G., refers to Sr. Vargas; so your salutation should read, *Estimado Sr. Vargas*.

What's that "García" doing there, then? That's *mamita's* father's family name. Latinos more or less solved the problem of gender fairness in names long before Anglos.

But, wait—what about Portuguese, used by all those stations in Brazil? Same concept, but in reverse. *Mamá's* father's family name is penultimate, and the "real" last name is where English- speakers are used to it, at the end.

In Chinese, the "last" name comes first. However, when writing in English, Chinese names are sometimes reversed for the benefit of *weiguoren*—foreigners. Use your judgement. For example, "Li" is a common Chinese last name, so if you see "Li Dan," it's "Mr. Li." But if it's "Dan Li"—and certainly if it's been Westernized into "Dan Lee"—he's already one step ahead of you, and it's still "Mr. Li" (or Lee). Less widely known is that the same can also occur in Hungarian. For example, "Bartók Béla" for Béla Bartók.

If in doubt, fall back on the ever-safe "Dear Sir" or "Dear Madam," or use email, where salutations are not expected. And be patient—replies by post usually take weeks, sometimes months. Slow responders, those that tend to take many months to reply, are cited in Addresses PLUS, as are erratic repliers.

(Internet Programming Service) Marianne Veit or Oswald Klotz; (technical) Ing. Ernst Vranka, Frequency Manager; Ing. Klaus Hollndonner, Chief Engineer; Martin Cargnelli, Monitoring Department; or Listener's Service. Program schedule twice a year, as well as quiz prizes. Mr. Harranth seeks collections of old verification cards and letters for the highly organized historical archives he is maintaining.
*WASHINGTON NEWS BUREAU:* 1206 Eaton Ct. NW, Washington DC 20007 USA. Phone: +1 (202) 822-9570. Contact: Eugen Freund.

## AZERBAIJAN   World Time +3 (+4 midyear)

**Radio Dada Gorgud/Voice of Azerbaijan**, Medhi Hüseyin küçäsi 1, 370011 Baku, Azerbaijan. Phone: +994 (12) 398-585. Fax: +994 (12) 395 452. Email: root@aztv.baku.az. Web: (State TV and Radio Broadcasting Company parent organization) www.aztv.az. Contact: Mrs. Tamam Bayatli-Öner, Director; Kamil Mamedov, Director of Division of International Relations; or Arzu Abdullayev. May run station contests at various times during the year. Free postcards, and occasionally, books. $1 or return postage helpful. Replies irregularly to correspondence in English.

## BANGLADESH   World Time +6

**Bangladesh Betar**
*NONTECHNICAL CORRESPONDENCE:* External Services, Bangladesh Betar, Shahbagh Post Box No. 2204, Dhaka 1000, Bangladesh; (physical address) Betar Bhaban Sher-e-Bangla Nagar, Agargaon Road, Dhaka 1207, Bangladesh. Phone: (director general) +880 (2) 8615-294; (Rahman Khan) +880 (2) 8613-949; (external services) +880 (2) 8618-119. Fax:(director general) +880 (2) 8612 021. Email: (Office of Director General) dgbetar@bd.drik.net; (external services) ts-betar@bdonline.com. Contact: Mrs. Dilruba Begum, Director, External Services; Ashfaque-ur Rahman Khan, Director - Programmes; or (technical) Muhammed Nazrul Islam, Station Engineer. $1 helpful. For further technical contacts, *see* below.
*TECHNICAL CORRESPONDENCE:* National Broadcasting Authority, NBA Bhaban, 121 Kazi Nazrul Islam Avenue, Shahabagh, Dhaka 1000, Bangladesh. Phone: +880 (2) 500-143/7, +880 (2) 500-490, +880 (2) 500-810, +880 (2) 505-113 or +880 (2) 507-269; (Shakir) +880 (2) 818-734; (Das) +880 (2) 500-810. Fax: +880 (2) 817 850; (Shakir) +880 (2) 817 850. Email: dgradio@drik.bgd.toolnet.org, or rrc@aitlbd.net. Contact: Syed Abdus Shakir, Chief Engineer; (reception reports) Manoranjan Das, Station Engineer, Dhaka; or Muhammed Romizuddin Bhuiya, Senior Engineer (Research Wing). Verifications not common from this office.

## BELARUS   World Time +2 (+3 midyear)

**Belarusian Radio**—*see* Radio Station Belarus, below, for details.
**Radio Grodno (Hrodna)**—contact via Radio Station Belarus, below.
**Radio Mogilev (Mahiliou)**—contact via Radio Station Belarus, below.
☞**Radio Station Belarus/Radio Minsk**, vul. Chyrvonaya 4, Minsk 220807, Republic of Belarus. Phone: (domestic Belarusian Radio) +375 (17) 239-5810; (external services, general) +375 (17) 239-5830; (English Service) +375 (17) 239-5831; (German Service) +375 (17) 239-5875. Fax: (all services) +375 (17) 284 8574. Email: (domestic Belarusian Radio) tvr@tvr.by; (external services) radio-minsk@tvr.by. Web: (includes Windows Media) www.tvr.by. Contact: Natalia Khlebus, Director; Grigori

Mityushnikov, Editor, English Service; Ilia Dohel, English Program Director; Elena Khoroshevich, German Program Editor; or Jürgen Eberhardt, German Program Editor. Free Belarus stamps.

## BELGIUM   World Time +1 (+2 midyear)

☞**RTBF-International**, B-1044 Brussels, Belgium. Phone: +32 (2) 737-4024. Fax: +32 (2) 737 3032. Email: relint.r@rtbf.be, or rtbfi@rtbf.be. Web: (RTBF-International) www.rtbf.be/ri/; ("La Première") www.rtbf.be/premiere/; (RealAudio) www.rtbf.be/jp. Contact: Jean-Pol Hecq, Directeur des Relations Internationales (or "Head, International Service" if writing in English). Broadcasts are essentially a relay of news and information programs from the domestic channel "La Première" of RTBF (Radio-Télévision Belge de la Communauté Française) via facilities of Deutsche Telekom (*see*) in Jülich, Germany. Return postage not required. Accepts email reports.
☞**Radio Vlaanderen Internationaal (RVI)**
*NONTECHNICAL AND GENERAL TECHNICAL:* B-1043 Brussels, Belgium; (English Section) RVI Brussels Calling, B-1043 Brussels, Belgium. Phone: +32 (2) 741-5611, +32 (2) 741-3806/7 or +32 (2) 741-3802. Fax: (administration and Dutch Service) +32 (2) 732 6295; (other language services) +32 (2) 732 8336. BBS: +32 (3) 825-3613. Email: info@rvi.be. Web: (text and RealAudio) www.rvi.be; (RealAudio in English, French, German and Dutch) www.wrn.org/ondemand/belgium.html. Contact (general) Deanne Lehman, Producer, "Brussels 1043" letterbox program; Ximena Prieto, Head, Foreign Languages Desk; Maryse Jacob, Head, French Service; Martina Luxen, Head, German Service; or Wim Jansen, Station Manager; (general technical) Frans Vossen, Producer, "Radio World." Sells RVI T-shirts (large/extra large) for 400 Belgian francs. May send free music CD. Remarks and reception reports can also be sent c/o the following diplomatic addresses:
*NIGERIA EMBASSY:* Embassy of Belgium, 1A, Bak Road, Ikoyi-Island, Lagos, Nigeria.
*ARGENTINA EMBASSY:* Embajada de Bélgica, Defensa 113 - 8° Piso, 1065 Buenos Aires, Argentina.
*FREQUENCY MANAGEMENT OFFICE:* BRTN, August Reyerslaan 52, B-1043 Brussels, Belgium. Phone: +32 (2) 741-5020. Fax: +32 (2) 741 5567. Email: (De Cuyper) hector.decuyper@vrt.be. Contact: Hector De Cuyper, Frequency Manager.

## BENIN   World Time +1

**Office de Radiodiffusion et Télévision du Benin**, Boite Postale 366, Cotonou, Bénin. Phone: +229 300-481, +229 301-096 or +229 301-347. Fax: +229 302 184. Web: www.ortb.org. Contact: (Cotonou) Damien Zinsou Ala Hassa; Emile Desire Ologoudou, Directeur Generale; or Leonce Goohouede; (technical) Anastase Adjoko, Chef de Service Technique. Return postage, $1 or IRC required. Replies irregularly and slowly to correspondence in French.
*PARAKOU REGIONAL STATION:* ORTB-Parakou, Boite Postale 128, Parakou, Benin. Phone: +229 610-773. Fax: +229 610 881. Contact: (general) J. de Matha, Le Chef de la Station; (technical) Léon Donou, Chef des Services Techniques. Return postage required. Replies tend to be extremely irregular, and a safer option is to send correspondence to the Cotonou address.

## BHUTAN   World Time +6

**Bhutan Broadcasting Service**
*STATION:* Department of Information and Broadcasting, Ministry of Communications, P.O. Box 101, Thimphu, Bhutan.

Phone: +975 (2) 323-071/72. Fax: +975 (2) 323 073. Email: (News and Current Affairs) news@bbs.com.bt; (Kinga Singye) ks@bbs.com.bt; (Thinley Tobgay Dorji) thinley@bbs.com.bt; (Sonam Tobgay) toby@bbs.com.bt. Web: (includes news and songs in MP3) www.bbs.com.bt. Contact: (general) Thinley Tobgay Dorji, News Coordinator; or Kinga Singye, Executive Director; (technical) Dorji Wangchuk, Station Engineer. Two IRCs, return postage or $1 required. Replies irregularly; correspondence to the U.N. Mission (see following) may be more fruitful.

UNITED NATIONS MISSION: Permanent Mission of the Kingdom of Bhutan to the United Nations, Two United Nations Plaza, 27th Floor, New York NY 10017 USA. Fax: +1 (212) 826 2998. Contact: Mrs. Kunzang C. Namgyel, Third Secretary; Mrs. Sonam Yangchen, Attaché; Ms. Leki Wangmo, Second Secretary; or Hari K. Chhetri, Second Secretary. Free newspapers and booklet on the history of Bhutan.

# BOLIVIA World Time –4

NOTE ON STATION IDENTIFICATIONS: Many Bolivian stations listed as "Radio . . ." may also announce as "Radio Emisora . . ." or "Radiodifusora . . ."

Paititi Radiodifusión—see Radio Paititi, below.

Radio Ayopaya, Casilla 2433, Cochabamba, Bolivia.

Radio Abaroa, Calle Nicanor Gonzalo Salvatierra 249, Riberalta, Beni, Bolivia. Contact: René Arias Pacheco, Director. Return postage or $1 required. Replies occasionally to correspondence in Spanish.

Radio Animas, Chocaya, Animas, Potosí, Bolivia. Contact: Julio Acosta Campos, Director. Return postage or $1 required. Replies irregularly to correspondence in Spanish.

Radio Camargo—see Radio Emisoras Camargo, below.

Radio Centenario "La Nueva"

MAIN OFFICE: Casilla 818, Santa Cruz de la Sierra, Bolivia. Phone: +591 (33) 529-265. Fax: +591 (3) 524 747. Email: mision.eplabol@scbbs-bo.com. Contact: Napoleón Ardaya B., Director. May send a calendar. Free stickers. Return postage or $1 required. Audio cassettes of contemporary Christian music and Bolivian folk music $10, including postage; CDs of Christian folk music $15, including postage. Replies to correspondence in English and Spanish.

U.S. BRANCH OFFICE: LATCOM, 1218 Croton Avenue, New Castle PA 16101 USA. Phone: +1 (412) 652-0101. Fax: +1 (412) 652 4654. Contact: Hope Cummins.

Radio Eco

MAIN ADDRESS: Correo Central, Reyes, Ballivián, Beni, Bolivia. Contact: Gonzalo Espinoza Cortés, Director. Free station literature. $1 or return postage required. Replies to correspondence in Spanish.

ALTERNATIVE ADDRESS: Rolmán Medina Méndez, Correo Central, Reyes, Ballivián, Bolivia.

Radio Eco San Borja (San Borja la Radio), Correo Central, San Borja, Ballivián, Beni, Bolivia. Contact: Gonzalo Espinoza Cortés, Director. Free station poster promised to correspondents. Return postage appreciated. Replies slowly to correspondence in Spanish.

Radio Emisoras Ballivián (when operating), Correo Central, San Borja, Beni, Bolivia. Replies to correspondence in Spanish, and sometimes sends pennant.

Radio Emisora Padilla—see Radio Padilla, below.

Radio Emisora Villamontes—see Radio Villamontes, below.

Radio Emisoras Camargo, Casilla 09, Camargo, Provincia Nor-Cinti, Bolivia. Contact: Pablo García B., Gerente Propietario. Return postage or $1 required. Replies slowly to correspondence in Spanish.

Radio Emisoras Minería—see Radiodifusoras Minería.

☞Radio Fides, Casilla 9143, La Paz, Bolivia. Fax: +591 (22) 379 030. Email: rafides@fidesbolivia.com (rafides@caoba.entelnet.bo may also work). Web: (includes RealAudio) http://fidesbolivia.com. Contact: R.P. Eduardo Pérez Iribarne, S.J., Director. Replies occasionally to correspondence in Spanish.

Radio Illimani, Casilla 1042, La Paz, Bolivia. Phone: +591 (22) 376-364. Fax: +591 (22) 359 275. Email: illimani@communica.gov.bo. Contact: Gabriel Astorga Guachala. $1 required, and your letter should be registered and include a tourist brochure or postcard from where you live. Replies irregularly to friendly correspondence in Spanish.

Radio Juan XXIII [Veintitrés], Avenida Santa Cruz al frente de la plaza principal, San Ignacio de Velasco, Santa Cruz, Bolivia. Phone: +591 (3962) 2087. Phone/fax: +591 (3962) 2188. Contact: Pbro. Elías Cortezón, Director; or María Elffy Gutiérrez Méndez, Encargada de la Discoteca. Return postage or $1 required. Replies occasionally to correspondence in Spanish.

☞Radio La Cruz del Sur, Casilla 1408, La Paz, Bolivia. Phone: +591 (22) 220-541. Fax: +591 (22) 243 337. Email: cruzdelsur@zuper.net. Web: (includes Real Audio) www.geocities.com/cruzdelsur2000. Contact: Presbítero Reyes Baltazar Quispe, Director. Pennant $1 or return postage. Replies slowly to correspondence in Spanish.

Radio La Palabra, Parroquia de Santa Ana de Yacuma, Beni, Bolivia. Phone: +591 (3848) 2117. Contact: Padre Yosu Arketa, Director. Return postage necessary. Replies to correspondence in Spanish.

Radio La Plata (if reactivated), Casilla 276, Sucre, Bolivia. Phone: +591 (4691) 31-616. Fax: +591 (64) 41 400. Contact: Freddy Donoso Bleichner, Director Ejecutivo.

Radio Mallku (formerly Radio A.N.D.E.S.), Casilla No. 16, Uyuni, Provincia Antonio Quijarro, Departamento de Potosí, Bolivia. Phone: +591 (2693) 2145. Email: (FRUTCAS parent organization) frutcas@hotmail.es. Contact: Freddy Juárez Huarachi, Director; Erwin Freddy Mamani Machaca, Jefe de Prensa y Programación. Spanish preferred. Return postage in the form of two U.S. dollars appreciated, as the station depends on donations for its existence. Station owned by La Federación Unica de Trabajadores Campesinos del Altiplano Sud (FRUTCAS).

Radio Minería—see Radiodifusoras Minería.

Radio Mosoj Chaski, Casilla 4493, Cochabamba, Bolivia. Phone: +591 (442) 220-641 or +591 (442) 220-644. Fax: +591 (442) 251 041. Email: chaski@bo.net.

Radio Movima, Calle Baptista No. 24, Santa Ana de Yacuma, Beni, Bolivia. Contact: Rubén Serrano López, Director; Javier Roca Díaz, Director Gerente; or Mavis Serrano, Directora. Return postage or $1 required. Replies irregularly to correspondence in Spanish.

Radio Nacional de Huanuni, Casilla 681, Oruro, Bolivia. Contact: Rafael Linneo Morales, Director General; or Alfredo Murillo, Director. Return postage or $1 required. Replies irregularly to correspondence in Spanish.

Radio Norte, Calle Warnes 195, 2do piso del Cine Escorpio, Montero, Santa Cruz, Bolivia. Phone: +591 (3922) 20-970. Fax: +591 (3922) 21 062. Contact: Leonardo Arteaga Ríos, Director.

Radio Padilla, Padilla, Chuquisaca, Bolivia. Contact: Moisés Palma Salazar, Director. Return postage or $1 required. Replies to correspondence in Spanish.

Radio Paititi, Casilla 172, Guayaramerín, Beni, Bolivia. Contact: Armando Mollinedo Bacarreza, Director; Luis Carlos Santa Cruz Cuéllar, Director Gerente; or Ancir Vaca Cuéllar, Gerente-Propietario. Free pennants. Return postage or $3 required. Replies irregularly to correspondence in Spanish.

📻**Radio Panamericana**, Casilla 5263, La Paz, Bolivia; (physical address) Av. 16 de Julio, Edif. 16 de Julio, Of. 902, El Prado, La Paz, Bolivia. Phone: +591 (22) 312-644, +591 (22) 311-383 or +591 (22) 313-980. Fax: +591 (22) 334 271. Email: pana@panamericana-bolivia.com; if that fails, try jorge_o@megatron-bo.net. Web: (includes RealAudio) www.panamericana-bolivia.com. Contact: Daniel Sánchez Rocha, Director. Replies irregularly, with correspondence in Spanish preferred. $1 or 2 IRCs helpful.

**Radio Perla del Acre**, Casilla 7, Cobija, Departamento de Pando, Bolivia. Return postage or $1 required. Replies irregularly to correspondence in Spanish.

**Radio Pío XII [Doce]**, Siglo Veinte, Potosí, Bolivia. Phone: +591 (258) 20-250. Fax: +591 (258) 20 544. Email: radiopio@nogal.oru.entelnet.bo. Contact: Pbro. Roberto Durette, OMI, Director General; or José Blanco. Return postage necessary. As mail delivery to Siglo Veinte is erratic, latters may be sent instead to: Casilla 434, Oruro, Bolivia; to the attention of Abenor Alfaro Castillo, periodista de Radio Pío XX [Phone: +591 (252) 76-1630].

**Radio San Gabriel**, Casilla 4792, La Paz, Bolivia. Phone: +591 (22) 414-371. Phone/fax: +591 (22) 411 174. Email: rsg@fundayni.rds.org.bo. Contact: Hno. José Canut Saurat, Director General; or Sra. Martha Portugal, Dpto. de Publicidad. $1 or return postage helpful. Free book on station, Aymara calendars and *La Voz del Pueblo Aymara* magazine. Replies fairly regularly to correspondence in Spanish. Station of the Hermanos de la Salle Catholic religious order.

**Radio San Miguel**, Casilla 102, Riberalta, Beni, Bolivia. Phone: +591 (385) 8268 or +591 (385) 8363. Fax: +591 (385) 8268. Contact: Félix Alberto Rada Q., Director; or Gerin Pardo Molina, Director. Free stickers and pennants; has a different pennant each year. Return postage or $1 required. Replies irregularly to correspondence in Spanish. Feedback on program "Bolivia al Mundo" (aired 0200-0300 World Time) especially appreciated.

**Radio Santa Ana**, Calle Sucre No. 250, Santa Ana de Yacuma, Beni, Bolivia. Contact: Mario Roberto Suárez, Director; or Mariano Verdugo. Return postage or $1 required. Replies irregularly to correspondence in Spanish.

**Radio Santa Cruz**, Emisora del Instituto Radiofónico Fé y Alegría (IRFA), Casilla 672 (or 3213), Santa Cruz, Bolivia. Phone: +591 (33) 521-814. Fax: +591 (33) 532 257. Email: irfacruz@roble.scz.entelnet.bo. Contact: Padre Francisco Flores, S.J., Director General; Srta. María Yolanda Marco Escobar, Secretaria de Dirección; Señora Mirian Suárez, Productor, "Protagonista Ud."; or Lic. Silvia Nava S. Free pamphlets, stickers and pennants. Welcomes correspondence in English, French and Spanish, but return postage required for a reply.

**Radio Villamontes**, Avenida Méndez Arcos No. 156, Villamontes, Departamento de Tarija, Bolivia. Contact: Gerardo Rocabado Galarza, Director. $1 or return postage required.

**Radio Yura (La Voz de los Ayllus)**, Casilla 326, Yura, Provincia Quijarro, Departamento de Potosí, Bolivia. Phone: +591 (281) 36-216. Email: canal18@cedro.pts.entelnet.bo. Contact: Rolando Cueto F., Director.

**Radiodifusoras Minería**, Casilla de Correo 247, Oruro, Bolivia. Phone: +591 (252) 77-736. Contact: Dr. José Carlos Gómez Espinoza, Gerente Propietario; or Srta. Costa Colque Flores, Responsable del programa "Minería Cultural." Free pennants. Replies to correspondence in Spanish.

**Radiodifusoras Trópico**, Casilla 60, Trinidad, Beni, Bolivia. Contact: Eduardo Avila Alberdi, Director. Replies slowly to correspondence in Spanish. Return postage required for reply.

## BOTSWANA  World Time +2

**Radio Botswana**, Private Bag 0060, Gaborone, Botswana. Phone: +267 352-541 or +267 352-861. Fax: +267 357 138. Contact: (general) Ted Makgekgenene, Director; or Monica Mphusu, Producer, "Maokaneng/Pleasure Mix"; (technical) Kingsley Reetsang, Principal Broadcasting Engineer. Free stickers, pennants and pins. Return postage, $1 or 2 IRCs required. Replies slowly and irregularly.

**Voice of America/IBB—Botswana Relay Station**
*TRANSMITTER SITE:* Voice of America, Botswana Relay Station, Moepeng Hill, Selebi-Phikwe, Botswana; or VOA-Botswana Transmitting Station, Private Bag 38, Selebi-Phikwe, Botswana. Phone: +267 810-932. Contact: Station Manager. This address for specialized technical correspondence only, although some reception reports may be verified, depending on who is at the site. During 2001, a number of verifications were received from Gabriel Tjitjo, Supervisor, Transmission Plant. All other correspondence should be directed to the regular VOA or IBB addresses (*see* USA).

## BRAZIL  World Time –1 (–2 midyear) Atlantic Islands; –2 (–3 midyear) Eastern, including Brasília and Rio de Janeiro; –3 (–4 midyear) Western; –4 Northwestern; –5 Acre. There are often slight variations from one year to the next. Information regarding Daylight Saving Time can be found at http://pcdsh01.on.br.

*NOTE:* Postal authorities recommend that, because of the level of theft in the Brazilian postal system, correspondence to Brazil be sent only via registered mail.

**Emissora Rural A Voz do São Francisco**, Caixa Postal 8, 56300-000 Petrolina PE, Brazil. Email: emissorarural@silcons.com.br. Contact: Maria Letecia de Andrade Nunes. Return postage necessary. Replies to correspondence in Portuguese.

**Rádio Alvorada (Londrina)**, Rua Senador Souza Naves 9 - 9º andar, 86010-921 Londrina PR, Brazil. Contact: Padre José Guidoreni, Diretor; Padre Manuel Joaquim; or Sonia López. Pennants $1 or return postage. Replies to correspondence in Portuguese.

**Rádio Alvorada (Parintins)**, Rua Governador Leopoldo Neves 516, 69151-440 Parintins AM, Brazil. Email: alvorada@jurupari.com.br. Contact: Raimunda Ribeira da Motta, Diretora; or M. Braga. Return postage required. Replies occasionally to correspondence in Portuguese.

**Rádio Alvorada (Rio Branco)**, Avenida Ceará 2150—Altos de Gráfica Globo, 69900-470 Rio Branco AC, Brazil. Email: severian@mdnet.com.br. Contact: José Severiano. Occasionally replies to correspondence in Portuguese.

📻**Rádio Araguaia**—FM sister-station to Rádio Anhanguera (*see* next entry) and sometimes relayed via the latter's shortwave outlet. Web: (general) www.opopular.com.br/araguaia/; (RealAudio) www2.opopular.com.br/radio.htm. Usually identifies as "Araguaia FM."

**Rádio Anhanguera**, BR-157 Km. 1103, Zona Rural, 77804-970 Araguaína TO, Brazil. Return postage required. Occasionally replies to correspondence in Portuguese. Sometimes airs programming from sister-station Rádio Araguaia, 97.1 FM (*see* previous item) or from the Rede Somzoomsat satellite network.

📻**Rádio Anhanguera**, Caixa Postal 13, 74823-000 Goiânia GO, Brazil. Web: (RealAudio only) www2.opopular.com.br/radio.htm. Contact: Rossana F. da Silva; or Eng. Domingo Vicente Tinoco. Return postage required. Replies to correspondence in Portuguese. Although—like its namesake in Araguaína (*see*, above)—a member of the Sistema de Rádio da

Organização Jaime Câmara, this station is also an affiliate of the CBN network and often identifies as "CBN Anhanguera," especially when airing news programming.

**Rádio Aparecida**, Avenida Getulio Vargas 185, 12570-000 Aparecida SP, Brazil; or Caixa Postal 2, 12570-970 Aparecida SP, Brazil. Phone/fax: +55 (12) 564-4400. Email: (nontechnical) radioaparecida@redemptor.com.br. Web: www.radioaparecida.com.br. Contact: Padre C. Cabral; Savio Trevisan, Departamento Técnico; Cassiano Alves Macedo, Producer, "Encontro DX"; Ana Cristina Carvalho, Secretária da Direção; Padre Cesar Moreira; or João Climaco, Diretor Geral. Return postage or $1 required. Replies occasionally to correspondence in Portuguese.

**Rádio Bandeirantes**, Caixa Postal 372, Rua Radiantes 13, Morumbi, 01059-970 São Paulo SP, Brazil. Fax: +55 (11) 3743 5391. Email: rbradio@band.com.br. Web: (includes Windows Media) www.radiobandeirantes.com.br. Contact: Marcelo Parada, Diretor Geral; or Carlos Newton. Free stickers, pennants and canceled Brazilian stamps. $1 or return postage required.

**Rádio Baré** (when operating), Avenida Santa Cruz Machado 170 A, 69010-070 Manaus AM, Brazil. Contact: Fernando A.B. Andrade, Diretor Programação e Produção.

**Rádio Brasil**, Caixa Postal 625, 13000-000 Campinas, São Paulo SP, Brazil. Contact: Wilson Roberto Correa Viana, Gerente. Return postage required. Replies to correspondence in Portuguese.

**Rádio Brasil Central**, Caixa Postal 330, 74001-970 Goiânia GO, Brazil. Contact: Ney Raymundo Fernández, Diretor Administrativo; Sergio Rubens da Silva; or Arizio Pedro Soárez, Diretor Gerente. Free stickers. $1 or return postage required. Replies to correspondence in Portuguese.

**Rádio Brasil Tropical**, Caixa Postal 405, 78005-970 Cuiabá MT, Brazil (street address: Rua Joaquim Murtinho 1456, 78020-830 Cuiabá MT, Brazil). Phone: +55 (65) 321-6882 or +55 (65) 321-6226. Fax: +55 (65) 624 3455. Email: rcultura@terra.com.br. Contact: Klécius Antonio dos Santos, Diretor Comercial; or Roberto Ferreira, Gerente Comercial. Free stickers. $1 required. Replies to correspondence in Portuguese. Shortwave sister-station to Rádio Cultura de Cuiabá (see).

**Rádio Caiari**, Av. Carlos Gomes 932, 78900-030 Porto Velho RO, Brazil. Contact: Carlos Alberto Diniz Martins, Diretor Geral; or Ronaldo Rocha, Diretor Executivo. Free stickers. Return postage helpful. Replies irregularly to correspondence in Portuguese.

**Rádio Canção Nova**, Caixa Postal 57, 12630-000 Cachoeira Paulista SP, Brazil; (physical address) Rua João Paulo II s/n, Alto da Bela Vista, 12630-000 Cachoeira Paulista SP, Brazil. Phone: +55 (12) 560-2022. Fax: +55 (12) 561 2074. Email: (general) radio@cancaonova.org.br; (Director) adriana@cancaonova.org.br. Web: (includes RealAudio) www.cancaonova.org.br/cnova/radio. Contact: (general) Benedita Luiza Rodrigues; Ana Claudia de Santana; or Valera Guimarães Massafera, Secretária; (administration) Adriana Pereira, Diretora da Rádio. Free stickers, pennants and station brochure sometimes given upon request. May send magazines. $1 helpful.

**Rádio Capixaba**, Caixa Postal 509, 29000-000 Vitória ES, Brazil; or (street address) Av. Santo Antônio 366, 29025-000 Vitória ES, Brazil. Email: radiocap@terra.com.br. Contact: Jairo Gouvea Maia, Diretor; or Sr. Sardinha, Técnico. Replies occasionally to correspondence in Portuguese.

**Rádio Clube de Dourados**, Rua Ciro Mello 2045, Dourados MS, Brazil. Web: www.radioclubeam720.com.br. Replies irregularly to correspondence in Portuguese.

**Rádio Clube de Ribeirao Preto** (if reactivated), Ribeirao Preto SP, Brazil. Phone/fax: +55 (16) 610-3511. Email: scc@clube.com.br; clubeam@clube.com.br. Web: (includes RealAudio) www.clube.com.br.

**Rádio Clube de Rondonópolis** (when operating), Caixa Postal 190, 78700-000 Rondonópolis MT, Brazil. Contact: Canário Silva, Departamento Comercial; or Saúl Feliz, Gerente-Geral. Return postage helpful. Replies to correspondence in Portuguese.

**Rádio Clube de Varginha**, Caixa Postal 102, 37000-000 Varginha MG, Brazil. Email: sistemaclube@varginha.com.br. Contact: Mariela Silva Gomez. Return postage necessary. Replies to correspondence in Spanish and Portuguese.

**Rádio Clube do Pará**, Caixa Postal 533, 66000-000 Belém PA, Brazil. Email: online form. Web: (includes Windows Media) www.radioclubedopara.com.br. Contact: Edyr Paiva Proença, Diretor Geral; or José Almeida Lima de Sousa. Return postage required. Replies irregularly to correspondence in Portuguese.

**Radio Clube Paranaense**, Rua Rockefeller 1311, Prado Velho, 80230-130 Curitiba PR, Brazil. Phone: +55 (41) 332-2772. Email: clubeb2@onda.com.br. Web: www.clubeb2.com.br. Contact: Vicente Mickosz, Superintendente.

**Rádio Coari**—see Rádio Educação Rural-Coari.

**Rádio Copacabana** (when operating), Rua Visconde Inhauma 37 - 12º andar, Rio de Janeiro. Phone: +55 (21) 233-9269 or +55 (21) 263-8567. Replies slowly to correspondence in Portuguese.

Rádio Congonhas, Praça Basílica 130, 36404-000 Congonhas MG, Brazil. Replies to correspondence in Portuguese.

**Rádio Cultura Araraquara**, Avenida Feijó 583 (Centro), 14801-140 Araraquara SP, Brazil. Phone: +55 (16) 232-3790. Fax: +55 (16) 232 3475. Email: ouvintes@culturafmam.com.br (cultura@techs.com.br may also work). Web: (includes Windows Media) www.culturafmam.com.br. Contact: Antonio Carlos Rodrigues dos Santos, Diretor Artistico e Comercial. Return postage required. Replies slowly to correspondence in Portuguese.

**Rádio Cultura de Campos**, Caixa Postal 79, 28100-970 Campos RJ, Brazil. $1 or return postage necessary. Replies to correspondence in Portuguese.

**Rádio Cultura de Cuiabá**—AM sister-station of Rádio Brasil Tropical (see) and whose programming is partly relayed by RBT. Email: rcultura@terra.com.br. Web: www.grupocultura.com.br.

**Rádio Cultura Filadelfia**, Rua Antonio Barbosa 1353, Caixa Postal 89, 85851-090 Foz do Iguaçu PR, Brazil. Phone: +55 (45) 523-2930. A Finnish listener reported receiving a reply from Andre Antero (andreantero@hotmail.com); however, this person's connection with the station is unknown.

**Rádio Cultura Ondas Tropicais**, Rua Barcelos 25 - Praça 14, 69020-200 Manaus AM, Brazil. Phone: +55 (92) 633-2030. Fax: +55 (92) 633 3332. Web: (FUNTEC parent organization) www.tvculturaamazonas.br. Contact: Luíz Fernando de Souza Ferreira; or Maria Jerusalem dos Santos, Chefe da Divisão de Rádio. Replies to correspondence in Portuguese. Return postage appreciated. Station is part of the FUNTEC (Fundação Televisão e Rádio Cultura do Amazonas) network.

**Rádio Cultura São Paulo**, Rua Cenno Sbrighi 378, Agua Branca, 05036-900 São Paulo, Brazil; or Caixa Postal 11544, 05049-970 São Paulo, Brazil. Phone: (general) +55 (11) 3874-3122; (Cultura AM) +55 (11) 3874-3081; (Cultura FM) +55 (11) 3874-3082. Fax: +55 (11) 3611 2014. Email: (Cultura AM, relayed on 9615 and 17815 kHz) falecom@radiocultura.am.br; (Cultura FM, relayed on 6170 kHz) falecom@radioculturasp.fm.br. Web: (includes Windows Media) www.tvcultura.com.br. Contact: Thais de Almeida Dias, Chefe de Produção e Programação; Eduardo Weber; Sra. Maria Luíza Amaral Kfouri, Chefe de Produção; or Valvenio Martins de

Almeida, Coordenador de Produção. $1 or return postage required. Replies slowly to postal correspondence in Portuguese.

**Rádio Difusora 6 de Agosto**, Rua Pio Nazário 31, 69930-000 Xapuri AC, Brazil. Contact: Francisco Evangelista de Abreu. Replies to correspondence in Portuguese.

**Rádio Difusora Acreana**, Rua Benjamin Constant 161, 69908-520 Rio Branco AC, Brazil. Contact: Washington Aquino, Diretor Geral. Replies irregularly to correspondence in Portuguese.

**Rádio Difusora Cáceres**, Caixa Postal 297, 78200-000 Cáceres MT, Brazil. Contact: Sra. Maridalva Amaral Vignardi. $1 or return postage required. Replies occasionally to correspondence in Portuguese.

**Rádio Difusora de Aquidauana**, Caixa Postal 18, 79200-000 Aquidauana MS, Brazil. Phone: +55 (67) 241-3956 or +55 (67) 241-3957. Contact: Primaz Aldo Bertoni, Diretor; or João Stacey. Free tourist literature and used Brazilian stamps. $1 or return postage required. This station sometimes identifies during the program day as "Nova Difusora," but its sign-off announcement gives the official name as "Rádio Difusora, Aquidauana."

**Rádio Difusora de Londrina**, Caixa Postal 1870, 86000-000 Londrina PR, Brazil. Contact: Walter Roberto Manganoti, Gerente. Free tourist brochure, which sometimes seconds as a verification. $1 or return postage helpful. Replies irregularly to correspondence in Portuguese.

**Rádio Difusora de Macapá**, Caixa Postal 2929, 68900-000 Macapá AP, Brazil; or (physical address) Rua Cândido Mendes 525 - Centro, 68900-100 Macapá AP, Brazil. Phone: +55 (96) 212-1120 or +55 (96) 212-1118. Fax: +55 (96) 212 1116. Email: rdm@macapa-ap.com.br. Web: http://macapa-ap.com.br/empresas/rdm.htm. Contact: Paulo Roberto Rodrigues, Gerente. $1 or return postage required. Replies irregularly to correspondence in Portuguese. Sometimes provides stickers, key rings and—on rare occasions—T-shirts.

**Rádio Difusora de Poços de Caldas**, Caixa Postal 937, 37701-970 Poços de Caldas MG, Brazil; or (street address) Rua Rio Grande do Sul 631 - 1º andar, 37701-001 Poços de Caldas MG, Brazil. Phone/fax: +55 (35) 3722-1530. Email: difusora@difusorapocos.com.br. Web: www.difusorapocos.com.br. Contact: (general) Orlando Cioffi, Diretor; (technical) Ronaldo Cioffi, Diretor Técnico. $1 or return postage required. Replies to correspondence in Portuguese.

☞**Rádio Difusora do Amazonas**, Caixa Postal 311, 69000-000 Manaus AM, Brazil. Web: (includes Windows Media) www.difusoramanaus.com.br. Contact: J. Joaquim Marinho, Diretor. Joaquim Marinho is a keen collector and especially interested in Duck Hunting Permit Stamps, stamp booklets and stamp sheets. Will reply to correspondence in Portuguese or English. $1 or return postage helpful.

**Rádio Difusora Roraima**, Avenida Capitão Ene Garcez 830, 69304-000 Boa Vista RR, Brazil. Phone/fax: +55 (95) 623-2259. Email: radiorr@technet.com.br. Web: www.radiororaima.com.br. Contact: Galvão Soares, Diretor Geral. Return postage required. Replies occasionally to correspondence in Portuguese.

**Rádio Difusora Taubaté**, Rua Dr. Sousa Alves 960, 12020-030 Taubaté SP, Brazil. Contact: Emilio Amadei Beringhs Neto, Diretor Superintendente. May send free stickers, pens, keychains and T-shirts. Return postage or $1 helpful.

**Rádio Educação Rural—Campo Grande**, Caixa Postal 261, 79002-233 Campo Grande MS, Brazil. Phone: +55 (67) 384-3164, +55 (67) 382-2238 or +55 (67) 384-3345. Contact: Ailton Guerra, Gerente-Geral; Angelo Venturelli, Diretor; or Diácono Tomás Schwamborn. $1 or return postage required. Replies to correspondence in Portuguese.

**Rádio Educação Rural—Coari**, Praça São Sebastião 228, 69460-000 Coari AM, Brazil. Contact: Lino Rodrigues Pessoa, Diretor Comercial; Joaquim Florencio Coelho, Diretor Administrador da Comunidade Salgueiro; or Elijane Martins Correa. $1 or return postage helpful. Replies irregularly to correspondence in Portuguese.

**Rádio Educadora de Bragança** (when operating), Rua Barão do Rio Branco 1151, 68600-000 Bragança PA, Brazil. Contact: José Rosendo de S. Neto; Zelina Cardoso Gonçalves; or Adelino Borges, Aux. Escritório. $1 or return postage required. Replies to correspondence in Portuguese.

**Rádio Educadora de Guajará Mirim**, Praça Mario Correa No.90, 78957-000 Guajará Mirim RO, Brazil. Contact: Padre Isidoro José Moro. Return postage helpful. Replies to correspondence in Portuguese.

**Rádio Educadora de Limeira**, Caixa Postal 105, 13480-970 Limeira SP, Brazil. Email: (Bortolan) bab@zaz.com.br. Contact: Bruno Arcaro Bortolan, Gerente.

☞**Rádio Gaúcha**, Rua Ipiranga 1075 - 3º andar, Bairro Azenha, 90160-093 Porto Alegre RS, Brazil. Phone: +55 (51) 3218-6600. Fax: +55 (51) 3218 6680. Email: (general) gaucha@rdgaucha.com.br; (comments on program content) reportagem@rdgaucha.com.br; (technical) gilberto.kussler@rdgaucha.com.br. Web: (includes RealAudio) http://radiogaucha.clicrbs.com.br. Contact: Marco Antônio Baggio, Gerente de Jornalismo/Programação; Armindo Antônio Ranzolin, Diretor Gerente; Gilberto Kussler, Gerente Técnico; Geraldo Canali. Replies occasionally to correspondence, preferably in Portuguese.

**Rádio Gazeta**, Avenida Paulista 900, 01310-940 São Paulo SP, Brazil. Phone: +55 (11) 3170-5757. Fax: +55 (11) 3170 5630. Email: (Fundação Cásper Líbero parent organization)

# Cumbre DX

## "Firstest With The Bestest"

### www.cumbredx.org

Cumbre DX is an electronic shortwave newsletter sent our weekly over the Internet. We have exciting and new shortwave DX news and loggings from a set of worldwide contributors. Cumbre DX's research staff also gathers original shortwave news items that are not available in any other publication. But the best part about Cumbre DX is that it is absolutely FREE!

*FOR YOUR FREE SAMPLE COPY, SEND AN EMAIL TO:*

### cumbredx@yahoo.com

*Para una muestra gratis, envíenos un Email al la dirección de arriba.*

fcl@fcl.com.br. Web: (Fundação Cásper Líbero parent organization) www.fcl.com.br. Contact: Shakespeare Ettinger, Supervisor Geral de Operação; Bernardo Leite da Costa; José Roberto Mignone Cheibub, Gerente Geral; or Ing. Aníbal Horta Figueiredo. Free stickers. $1 or return postage necessary. Replies to correspondence in Portuguese. Currently relays programming from the station's mediumwave station (Gazeta AM) after several years of leasing airtime to the "Deus é Amor" Pentecostal church.

🔊**Rádio Globo**, Rua do Russel 434-Glória, 22210-210 Rio de Janeiro RJ, Brazil. Phone: +55 (21) 555-8375. Fax: +55 (21) 558 6385. Email: (administration) gerenciaamrio@radioglobo.com.br. Web: (includes RealAudio) www.radioglobo.com.br/globorio. Contact: Marcos Libretti, Diretor Geral. Replies irregularly to correspondence in Portuguese. Return postage helpful.

🔊**Rádio Globo**, Rua das Palmeiras 315, Santa Cecilia, 01226-901 São Paulo SP, Brazil. Phone: +55 (11) 3824-3217. Fax: +55 (11) 3824 3210. Email: (Rapussi) margarete@radioglobo.com.br. Web: (includes RealAudio) www.radioglobo.com.br. Contact: Ademar Dutra, Locutor, "Programa Ademar Dutra"; Margarete Rapussi; Guilherme Viterbo; or José Marques. Replies to correspondence, preferably in Portuguese.

🔊**Rádio Guaíba**, Rua Caldas Júnior 219, 90019-900 Porto Alegre RS, Brazil. Phone: +55 (51) 3215-6222. Email: (administration) diretor@radioguaiba.com.br; (technical) centraltecnica@radioguaiba.com.br. Web: (includes RealAudio) www.radioguaiba.com.br. Return postage helpful.

🔊**Rádio Guarani** (if reactivated), Avenida Assis Chateaubriand 499, Floresta, 30150-101 Belo Horizonte MG, Brazil. Phone: +55 (31) 3237-6000. Fax: +55 (31) 3237 6656. Email: guarani@guarani.com.br. Web: (includes RealAudio) www.guarani.com.br. Contact: Junara Belo, Setor de Comunicações. Replies slowly to correspondence in Portuguese. Return postage helpful.

**Rádio Guarujá**, Caixa Postal 45, 88000-000 Florianópolis SC, Brazil. Email: guaruja@radioguaruja.com.br. Web: www.radioguaruja.com.br. Contact: Mario Silva, Diretor; Joana Sempre Bom Braz, Assessora de Marketing e Comunicação; or Rosa Michels de Souza. Return postage required. Replies irregularly to correspondence in Portuguese.

*NEW YORK OFFICE:* 45 West 46 Street, 5th Floor, Manhattan, NY 10036 USA.

**Rádio Inconfidência**, Caixa Postal 1027, Belo Horizonte MG, Brazil; or (street address) Avenida Raja Gabáglia 1666, Luxemburgo, 30350-540 Belo Horizonte MG, Brazil. Phone: +55 (31) 3297-7344. Fax: +55 (31) 3297 7348. Email: inconfidencia@inconfidencia.com.br. Web: www.inconfidencia.com.br. Contact: Isaias Lansky, Diretor; Manuel Emilio de Lima Torres, Diretor Superintendente; Jairo Antolio Lima, Diretor Artístico; or Eugenio Silva. Free stickers and postcards. May send CD of Brazilian music. $1 or return postage helpful.

**Rádio Integração** (when active), Rua Alagoas 270, 69980-000 Cruzeiro do Sul AC, Brazil. Contact: Oscar Alves Bandeira, Gerente. Return postage helpful.

**Rádio IPB AM**, Rua Itajaí 473, Bairro Antonio Vendas, 79041-270 Campo Grande MS, Brazil. Contact: Iván Páez Barboza, Diretor Geral (hence, the station's name, "IPB"); Pastor Laercio Paula das Neves, Dirigente Estadual; Agenor Patrocinio S., Locutor; Pastor José Adão Hames; or Kelly Cristina Rodrigues da Silva, Secretária. Return postage required. Replies to correspondence in Portuguese. Most of the airtime is leased to the "Deus é Amor" Pentecostal church.

🔊**Rádio Itatiaia**, Rua Itatiaia 117, 31210-170 Belo Horizonte MG, Brazil. Fax: +55 (31) 446 2900. Email: itatiaia@itatiaia.com.br. Web: (includes RealAudio) www.itatiaia.com.br/am/index.html. Contact: Lúcia Araújo Bessa, Assistente da Diretória; or Claudio Carneiro.

**Rádio Jornal "A Crítica"** (when active), Caixa Postal 2250, 69061-970 Manaus AM, Brazil; or Av. Andre Araujo s/n, Aleixo, 69060-001 Manaus AM, Brazil. Contact: Sr. Cotrere, Gerente.

🔊**Rádio Liberal**, C.P 498, 66017-970 Belém PA, Brazil; (street address) Av. Nazaré 350, 66035-170 Belém PA, Brazil. Phone: +55 (91) 213-1500. Fax: +55 (91) 224 5240. Email: radio@radioliberal.com.br. Web: (includes RealAudio) www.radioliberal.com.br. Contact: Flavia Vasconcellos; Advaldo Castro, Diretor de Programação AM; João Carlos Silva Ribeiro, Coordenador de Programação AM.

**Rádio Marumby**, Caixa Postal 296, 88010-970 Florianópolis SC, Brazil; Rua Angelo Laporta 841, C. P. 62, 88020-600 Florianópolis SC, Brazil; or (missionary parent organization) Gideões Missionários da Última Hora—GMUH, Ministério Evangélico Mundial, Rua Joaquim Nunes 244, Caixa Postal 2004, 88340-000 Camboriú SC, Brazil. Email: (GMUH parent organization) gmuh@gmuh.com.br. Web: www.gmuh.com.br/aradio.htm; www.gmuh.com.br/marumby.htm. Contact: Davi Campos, Diretor Artístico; Dr. Cesario Bernardino, Presidente, GMUH; or Jair Albano, Diretor. $1 or return postage required. Free diploma and stickers. Replies to correspondence in Portuguese.

**Rádio Marumby, Curitiba**—see Rádio Novas de Paz, Curitiba, below.

🔊**Rádio Meteorologia Paulista**, Caixa Postal 91, 14940-970 Ibitinga, São Paulo SP, Brazil; or (street address) Rua Capitão João Marques 89, Jardim Centenário, 14940-000 Ibitinga, São Paulo SP, Brazil. Phone: +55 (16) 242-3388. Fax: +55 (16) 242 5056. Email: radio.ibitinga@ibinet.com.br. Web: (includes RealAudio from Ternura FM, relayed several hours each day by Rádio Meteorologia Paulista) www.ibinet.com.br/radioibitinga. Contact: Roque de Rosa, Diretora. Replies to correspondence in Portuguese. $1 or return postage required.

**Rádio Missões da Amazônia**, Travessa Ruy Barbosa 142, 68250-000 Obidos PA, Brazil. Phone: +55 (91) 544-1155 or +55 (91) 544-2103. Email: ama@orinet.org.br. Web: www.kaleb.hpg.ig.com.br. Contact: Max Hamoy; Edérgio de Moras Pinto; or Maristela Hamoy. Return postage required. Replies occasionally to correspondence in Portuguese.

**Rádio Mundial**, Av. Paulista 2198-Térreo, Cerqueira Cesar, 01310-300 São Paulo, Brazil. Phone: +55 (11) 253-0082. Phone/fax: +55 (11) 283 5833. Email: radiomundial@radiomundial.com. Web: www.radiomundial.com.br. Contact: (nontechnical) Luci Rothschild de Abreu, Diretora Presidente.

🔊**Rádio Nacional da Amazônia**, SCRN 702/3 Bloco-B, Ed. Radiobrás, 70710-750 Brasília DF, Brazil. Fax: +55 (61) 321 7602. Email: Website online form. Web: (includes Windows Media) www.radiobras.gov.br/nacional. Contact: (general) Luíz Otavio de Castro Souza, Diretor; Fernando Gómez da Câmara, Gerente de Escritório; or Januario Procopio Toledo, Diretor. Free stickers, but no verifications.

🔊**Rádio Nacional de Brasília**—same postal and Web addresses as Rádio Nacional da Amazônia, above.

**Rádio Nacional São Gabriel da Cachoeira**, Avenida Alvaro Maia 850, 69750-000 São Gabriel da Cachoeira AM, Brazil. Contact: Luíz dos Santos França, Gerente; or Valdir de Souza Marques. Return postage necessary. Replies to correspondence in Portuguese.

**Rádio Novas de Paz**, Avenida Paraná 1896, 82510-000 Curitiba PR, Brazil; or Caixa Postal 22, 80000-000 Curitiba

PR, Brazil. Phone: +55 (41) 257-4109. Contact: João Falavinha Ienzen, Gerente. $1 or return postage required. Replies irregularly to correspondence in Portuguese.

**Rádio Nova Visão**

STUDIOS: Rua do Manifesto 1373, 04209-001 São Paulo SP, Brazil. Contact: José Eduardo Dias, Diretor Executivo. Return postage required. Replies to correspondence in Portuguese. Free stickers. Relays Rádio Trans Mundial fulltime.

TRANSMITTER: Caixa Postal 551, 97000-000 Santa Maria RS, Brazil; or Caixa Postal 6084, 90000-000 Porto Alegre RS, Brazil. Reportedly issues full-data verifications for reports in Portuguese or German, upon request, from this location. If no luck, try contacting, in English or Dutch, Tom van Ewijck, via email at egiaroll@mail.iss.lcca.usp.br. For further information, see the entry for Rádio Trans Mundial.

**Rádio Oito de Setembro** (when operating), Caixa Postal 8, 13690-000 Descalvado SP, Brazil. Contact: Adonias Gomes. Replies to corrrespondence in Portuguese.

**Rádio Pioneira de Teresina**, Rua 24 de Janeiro 150 sul/centro, 64001-230 Teresina PI, Brazil. Phone: +55 (86) 222-8121. Fax: +55 (86) 222 8122. Email: pioneira@ranet.com.br. Web: www.igrejadeteresina.hpg.ig.com.br. Contact: Luíz Eduardo Bastos; or Padre Tony Batista, Diretor. $1 or return postage required. Replies slowly to correspondence in Portuguese.

**Rádio Progresso** (if reactivated), Estrada do Belmont s/n, Bº Nacional, 78903-400 Porto Velho RO, Brazil. Return postage required. Replies occasionally to correspondence in Portuguese.

**Rádio Record**

STATION: Caixa Postal 7920, 04084-002 São Paulo SP, Brazil. Email: radiorecord@rederecord.com.br. Web: www.rederecord.com.br (click on "Rádio"). Contact: Mário Luíz Catto, Diretor Geral. Free stickers. Return postage or $1 required. Replies occasionally to correspondence in Portuguese.

NEW YORK OFFICE: 630 Fifth Avenue, Room 2607, New York NY 10111 USA.

**Rádio Relógio**, Rua Paramopama 131, Ribeira, Ilha do Governador, 21930-110 Rio de Janeiro RJ, Brazil. Phone: +55 (21) 467-0201. Fax: +55 (21) 467 4656. Email: radiorelogio@ig.com.br. Web: www.radiorelogio.com.br. Contact: Olindo Coutinho, Diretor Geral; or Renato Castro. Replies occasionally to correspondence in Portuguese.

**Rádio RGS**—see Rádio Rio Grande do Sul, below.

**Rádio Ribeirão Preto**, Caixa Postal 1252, 14025-000 Ribeirão Preto SP, Brazil (physical address: Av. 9 de Julho 600, 14025-000 Ribeirão Preto SP, Brazil). Phone/fax: +55 (16) 610-3511. Contact: Lucinda de Oliveira, Secretária; Luis Schiavone Junior; or Paulo Henríque Rocha da Silva. Replies to correspondence in Portuguese.

**Rádio Rio Grande do Sul**, Rede Pampa de Comunicação, Rua Orfanatrófio 711, 90840-440 Porto Alegre RS, Brazil. Phone: +55 (51) 233-8311. Fax: +55 (51) 233 4500. Email: pampa@pampa.com.br. All the station's shortwave outlets carry programming from Sistema LBV Mundial (see), to where all program and reception related correspondence should be sent.

**Rádio Rio Mar**, Rua José Clemente 500, 69010-070 Manaus AM, Brazil. Web: www.geocities.com/radioriomar. Replies to correspondence in Portuguese. Contact: Jairo de Sousa Coelho, Diretor de Programação e Jornalismo. $1 or return postage helpful.

**Rádio Rural Santarém**, Rua São Sebastião 622, 68005-090 Santarém PA, Brazil. Contact: João Elias B. Bentes, Gerente Geral; or Edsergio de Moraes Pinto. Replies slowly to correspondence in Portuguese. Free stickers. Return postage or $1 required.

**Rádio Trans Mundial**, Caixa Postal 18300, 04626-970 São Paulo SP, Brazil. Phone: +55 (11) 5031-3533. Fax: +55 (11) 5031 5271. Email: (general) rtm@transmundial.com.br; (technical) tecnica@transmundial.com.br; ("Amigos do Rádio" DX-program) amigosdoradio@transmundial.com.br. Web: (includes RealAudio) www.transmundial.com.br. Contact: José Eduardo Dias, Diretor; or Rudolf Grimm, programa "Amigos do Rádio." Sells religious books and casettes and CDs of religious music (from choral to bossa nova). Prices, in local currency, can be found at the Website (click on "catálogo"). Program provider for Rádio Nova Visão—see, above.

**Rádio Cacique** (when operating), Caixa Postal 486, 18090-970 Sorocaba SP, Brazil. Phone: +55 (15) 231-3712 or (15) 232-2922. Web: www.radiocacique.com.br.

**Rádio Senado**. Caixa Postal 070-747, 70359-970 Brasília DF, Brazil; or (physical address) Praça dos Três Poderes, Anexo II, Bloco B, Térreo, 70165-900 Brasília DF, Brazil. Email: radio@senado.gov.br; (Maintenance Engineer) arenato@senado.gov.br. Web: (includes RealAudio) www.senado.gov.br/radio. Contact: Aldo Renato B. de Assis, Engenheiro de Manutenção.

**Rádio Tupi**, Avenida Nadir Dias Figueiredo 1329, 02110-901 São Paulo SP, Brazil. Contact: Alfredo Raymundo Filho, Diretor Geral; Montival da Silva Santos; or Elia Soares. Free stickers. Return postage required. Replies occasionally to correspondence in Portuguese.

**Rádio Universo/Rádio Tupi**, Caixa Postal 7133, 80000-000 Curitiba PR, Brazil. Contact: Luíz Andreu Rúbio, Diretor. Replies occasionally to correspondence in Portuguese. Rádio Universo's program time is rented by the "Deus é Amor" Pentecostal church, and is from the Rádio Tupi network. Identifies on the air as "Radio Tupi, Sistema Universo de Comunicação" or, more often, just as "Radio Tupi."

**Rádio Verdes Florestas**, Caixa Postal 53, 69981-970 Cruzeiro do Sul AC, Brazil. Contact: Marlene Valente de Andrade. Return postage required. Replies occasionally to correspondence in Portuguese.

**Rádio Voz do Coração Imaculado** (when operating), Caixa Postal 354, 75001-970 Anápolis GO, Brazil. Contact: P. Domingos M. Esposito A religious station which started shortwave operation in 1999 with the transmitter formerly used by Rádio Carajá. Operation tends to be irregular, as the station is funded entirely from donations.

**Rede SomZoom Sat**—a satellite network based in Fortaleza, Ceará, whose programming is sometimes carried by Brazilian world band stations (usually during night hours). Email: somzoomsat@somzoom.com.br. Web: (includes Windows Media) www.somzoom.com.br/Radio/radio.htm.

**Sistema LBV Mundial**, Legião da Boa Vontade, Av. Sérgio Tomás 740, Bom Retiro, 01131-010 São Paulo SP, Brazil; or Rua Doraci 90, Bom Retiro, 01134-020 São Paulo SP, Brazil. Phone: 3225-4500. Fax: +55 (11) 3225 4639. Web: (general) http://sistema.lbv.org; (LBV parent organization, includes RealAudio) www.lbv.org. Contact: André Tiago, Diretor; Sandra Albuquerque, Secretária; or Gizelle Almeida, Gerente do Dept. de Rádio. Replies slowly to correspondence in all main languages. Program provider for Radio Rio Grande do Sul (see).

NEW YORK OFFICE: 383 5th Avenue, 2nd Floor, New York NY 10016 USA. Phone: +1 (212) 481-1004. Fax: +1 (212) 481 1005. Email: lgw2000@aol.com.

**Voz de Libertação**. Ubiquitous programming originating from the "Deus é Amor" Pentecostal church's Rádio Universo (1300 kHz) in São Bernardo do Campo, São Paulo, and heard over several shortwave stations, especially Rádio Universo,

Curitiba (*see*). A RealAudio feed is available at the "Deus é Amor" Website, www.ipda.org.br.

**Voz do Coração Imaculado**—*see* Rádio Voz do Coração Imaculado.

## BULGARIA   World Time +2 (+3 midyear)

📧**Bulgarian National Radio**, 4 Dragan Tsankov Blvd., 1040 Sofia, Bulgaria. Phone: +359 (2) 652-871. Fax: (weekdays) +359 (2) 657 230. Web: (includes RealAudio) www.nationalradio.bg. Contact: Borislav Djamdjiev, Director; Iassen Indjev, Executive Director; or Martin Minkov, Editor-in-Chief.

📧**Radio Bulgaria**
*NONTECHNICAL AND TECHNICAL:* P.O. Box 900, BG-1000, Sofia, Bulgaria. Phone: (general) +359 (2) 985-241; (Managing Director) +359 (2) 854-604. Fax: (general, usually weekdays only) +359 (2) 871 060, +359 (2) 871 061 or +359 (2) 650 560; (Managing Director) +359 (2) 946 1576; or +359 (2) 988 5103; (Frequency Manager) +359 (2) 963 4464. Email: rcorresp1@fon15.bnr.acad.bg; or rbul1@nationalradio.bg. Web: (RealAudio in English, French and Russian) www.nationalradio.bg/real.htm. Contact: (general) Mrs. Iva Delcheva, English Section; Svilen Stoicheff, Head of English Section; (administration and technical) Anguel H. Nedyalkov, Managing Director; (technical) Atanas Tzenov, Director. Replies regularly, but sometimes slowly. Return postage helpful, as the station is financially overstretched due to the economic situation in the country. For concerns about frequency usage, contact BTC, below, with copies to Messrs. Nedyalkov and Tzenov of Radio Bulgaria.
*FREQUENCY MANAGEMENT AND TRANSMISSION OPERATIONS:* Bulgarian Telecommunications Company (BTC), Ltd., 8 Totleben Blvd., 1606 Sofia, Bulgaria. Phone: +359 (2) 88-00-75. Fax: +359 (2) 87 58 85 or +359 (2) 80 25 80. Contact: Roumen Petkov, Frequency Manager; or Mrs. Margarita Krasteva, Radio Regulatory Department.
**Radio Varna**, 22 blv. Primorski, 9000 Varna, Bulgaria. Replies irregularly. Return postage required. If no reply is forthcoming, try sending an email to rcorresp1@bnr.acad.bg.

## BURKINA FASO   World Time exactly

**Radiodiffusion-Télévision Burkina**, B.P. 7029, Ouagadougou, Burkina Faso. Phone: +226 310-441. Contact: (general) Raphael L. Onadia or M. Pierre Tassembedo; (technical) Marcel Teho, Head of Transmitting Centre. Replies irregularly to correspondence in French. IRC or return postage helpful.

## BURMA—*see* MYANMAR.

## BURUNDI   World Time +2

**La Voix de la Révolution**, B.P. 1900, Bujumbura, Burundi. Phone: +257 22-37-42. Fax: +257 22 65 47 or +257 22 66 13. Email: rtnb@cbinf.com. Contact: (general) Grégoire Barampumba, Head of News Section; or Frederic Havugiyaremye, Journaliste; (administration) Gérard Mfuranzima, Le Directeur de la Radio; or Didace Baranderetse, Directeur Général de la Radio; (technical) Abraham Makuza, Le Directeur Technique. $1 required.

## CAMBODIA   World Time +7

**National Radio of Cambodia** (when operating)
*STATION ADDRESS:* 106 Preah Kossamak Street, Monivong Boulevard, Phnom Penh, Cambodia. Phone: +855 (23) 423-369 or +855 (23) 422-869. Fax: + 855 (23) 427 319. Email: vocri@vocri.org. Web: www.vocri.org. Contact: (general) Miss Hem Bory, English Announcer; Kem Yan, Chief of External Relations; or Touch Chhatha, Producer, Art Department; (administration) In Chhay, Chief of Overseas Service; Som Sarun, Chief of Home Service; Van Sunheng, Deputy Director General, Cambodian National Radio and Television; or Ieng Muli, Minister of Information; (technical) Oum Phin, Chief of Technical Department. Free program schedule. Replies irregularly and slowly. Do not include stamps, currency, IRCs or dutiable items in envelope. Registered letters stand a much better chance of getting through. Has been increasingly off the air in recent years.

## CAMEROON   World Time +1

*NOTE:* Any CRTV outlet is likely to be verified by contacting via registered mail, in English or French with $2 enclosed, James Achanyi-Fontem, Cameroon Link, Shortwave Monitors, P.O. Box 1460, Douala, Cameroon.
**Cameroon Radio Television Corporation (CRTV)—Buea**, P.M.B., Buea (Sud-Ouest), Cameroon. Contact: Ononino Oli Isidore, Chef Service Technique. Three IRCs, $1 or return postage required.
**Cameroon Radio Television Corporation (CRTV)—Garoua**, B.P. 103, Garoua (Nord/Adamawa), Cameroon. Contact: Kadeche Manguele. Free cloth pennants. Three IRCs or return postage required. Replies irregularly and slowly to correspondence in French.
📧**Cameroon Radio Television Corporation (CRTV)—Yaoundé**, B.P. 1634, Yaoundé (Centre-Sud), Cameroon. Phone: +237 221-4035, +237 221-4077 or +237 221-4088. Fax: +237 220 4340. Email: crtv@crtv.cm. Web: (includes RealAudio and Windows Media) www.crtv.cm. Contact: (technical or nontechnical) Prof. Gervais Mendo Ze, Directeur-Général; (technical) Eyébé Tanga, Directeur Technique. $1 required. Replies slowly (sometimes extremely slowly) to correspondence in French.

## CANADA   World Time –3:30 (–2:30 midyear) Newfoundland; –4 (–3 midyear) Atlantic; –5 (–4 midyear) Eastern, including Quebec and Ontario; –6 (–5 midyear) Central; except Saskatchewan; –6 Saskatchewan; –7 (–6 midyear) Mountain; –8 (–7 midyear) Pacific, including Yukon.

📧**Canadian Broadcasting Corporation (CBC)—English Programs**, P.O. Box 500, Station A, Toronto, Ontario, M5W 1E6, Canada. Phone: (Audience Relations) +1 (416) 205-3700. Email: cbcinput@toronto.cbc.ca. Web: (includes RealAudio) www.radio.cbc.ca. CBC prepares some of the programs heard over Radio Canada International (*see*).
*LONDON NEWS BUREAU:* CBC, 43-51 Great Titchfield Street, London W1P 8DD, England. Phone: +44 (20) 7412-9200. Fax: +44 (20) 7631 3095.
*PARIS NEWS BUREAU:* CBC, 17 avenue Matignon, F-75008 Paris, France. Phone: +33 (1) 4421-1515. Fax: +33 (1) 4421 1514.
*WASHINGTON NEWS BUREAU:* CBC, National Press Building, Suite 500, 529 14th Street NW, Washington DC 20045 USA. Phone: +1 (202) 383-2900. Contact: Jean-Louis Arcand, David Hall or Susan Murray.
📧**Canadian Broadcasting Corporation (CBC)—French Programs**, Société Radio-Canada, C.P. 6000, succ. centre-ville, Montréal, Québec, H3C 3A8, Canada. Phone: (Audience Relations) +1 (514) 597-6000. Email (comments on programs): auditoire@montreal.radio-canada.ca. Welcomes correspondence sent to this address but may not reply due to shortage

of staff. Web: (includes RealAudio) www.radio-canada.ca. CBC prepares some of the programs heard over Radio Canada International (*see*).

**CBC Northern Quebec Shortwave Service**—*see* Radio Canada International, below.

**📻CFRX-CFRB**

*MAIN ADDRESS:* 2 St. Clair Avenue West, Toronto, Ontario, M4V 1L6, Canada. Phone:(main switchboard) +1 (416) 924-5711; (talk shows switchboard) +1 (416) 872-1010; (news centre) +1 (416) 924-6717; (CFRB information access line) +1 (416) 872-2372. Fax: (main fax line) +1 (416) 323 6830; (CFRB news fax line) +1 (416) 323 6816. Email: (comments on programs) cfrbcomments@cfrb.com; (News Director) news@cfrb.com; (general, nontechnical) info@cfrb.com; or opsmngr@cfrb.com; (technical) ian.sharp@cfrb.com. Web: (includes MP3) www.cfrb.com. Contact: (nontechnical) Carlo Massaro, Information Officer; or Steve Kowch, Operations Manager; (technical) Ian Sharp, Technical Supervisor. Reception reports should be sent to the verification address, below.

*VERIFICATION ADDRESS:* Ontario DX Association, P.O. Box 161, Station 'A', Willowdale, Ontario, M2N 5S8, Canada, or by email: odxa@compuserve.com. General information about CFRB/CFRX can be seen at the ODXA Website: www.odxa.on.ca. General information about CFRB/CFRX reception may be directed to the QSL Manager, Steve Canney, VA3SC (email: scanney@cogeco.ca). A free CFRB/CFRX information sheet and an ODXA brochure is enclosed with your verification card. Reports are processed quickly if sent to this address.

**CFVP-CKMX**, AM 1060, Standard Broadcasting, P.O. Box 2750, Station 'M', Calgary, Alberta, T2P 4P8, Canada. Phone: (general) +1 (403) 240-5800; (news) +1 (403) 240-5844; (technical) +1 (403) 240-5867. Fax: (general and technical) +1 (403) 240 5801; (news) +1 (403) 246 7099. Contact: (general) Gary Russell, General Manager; or Beverley Van Tighem, Exec. Ass't.; (technical) Ken Pasolli, Technical Director.

**CHU**, Time and Frequency Standards, Bldg. M-36, National Research Council, Ottawa, Ontario, K1A 0R6, Canada. Phone: (general) +1 (613) 993-5186; (administration) +1 (613) 993-1003 or +1 (613) 993-2704. Fax: +1 (613) 993 1394. Email: time@nrc.ca. Web: www.cisti.nrc.ca/inms/time/ctse.html. Contact: Dr. Rob Douglas; Dr. Jean-Simon Boulanger, Group Leader; or Ray Pelletier, Technical Officer. Official standard frequency and World Time station for Canada on 3330, 7335 and 14670 kHz. Brochure available upon request.Those with a personal computer, Bell 103 compatible modem and appropriate software can get the exact time, from CHU's cesium clock, via the telephone; details available upon request, or direct from the Website.

**📻CKZN**, CBC Newfoundland and Labrador, P.O. Box 12010, Station 'A', St. John's, Newfoundland, A1B 3T8, Canada. Phone: +1 (709) 576-5155. Fax: +1 (709) 576 5099. Email: (administration) radiomgt@stjohns.cbc.ca; (engineer) keith_durnford@cbc.ca. Web: (includes RealAudio) www.stjohns.cbc.ca. Contact: (general) Heather Elliott, Communications Officer; (technical) Shawn R. Williams, Manager, Transmission and Distribution; Keith Durnford, Station Engineer; Jerry Brett, Transmitter Department; or Janet Ferweda. Free CBC sticker and verification card with the history of Newfoundland included. Don't enclose money, stamps or IRCs with correspondence, as they will only have to be returned. Relays CBN (St. John's, 640 kHz) except at 1000-1330 World Time (one hour earlier in summer) when programming comes from CFGB Goose Bay.

*CFGB ADDRESS:* CBC Radio, Box 1029 Station 'C', Happy Valley, Goose Bay, Labrador, Newfoundland A0P 1C0, Canada.

**For decades Ian McFarland graced the airwaves over Radio Canada International and Radio Japan. Retired, he now lives with his wife, Mary, on Vancouver Island.**  H. Sellers

**📻CKZU-CBU**, CBC, P.O. Box 4600, Vancouver, British Columbia, V6B 4A2, Canada—for verification of reception reports, mark the envelope, "Attention: Engineering." Toll-free telephone (U.S and Canada only) 1-800-961-6161. Phone: (general) +1 (604) 662-6000; (engineering) +1 (604) 662-6060. Fax: +1 (604) 662 6350. Email: (general) webmaster@vancouver.cbc.ca; (Newbury) newburyd@vancouver.cbc.ca. Web: (includes RealAudio) www.vancouver.cbc.ca. Contact: (general) Public Relations; (technical) Dave Newbury, Transmission Engineer.

**📻Radio Canada International**

*NOTE: (CBC Northern Quebec Service)* The following RCI address, fax and email information for the Main Office and Transmission Office is also valid for the CBC Northern Quebec Shortwave Service, provided you make your communication to the attention of the particular service you seek to contact.

*MAIN OFFICE:* P.O. Box 6000, Montréal, Quebec, H3C 3A8, Canada; or (street address) 1400 boulevard René Lévesque East, Level B Montréal, Québec, H2L 2M2, Canada. Phone: (general) +1 (514) 597-7500; (Audience Relations, Ms. Maggy Akerblom) +1 (514) 597-7555; (Communications) +1 (514) 597-7551. Fax: (general) +1 (514) 597 7076; (Audience Relations) +1 (514) 597 7760. Email: rci@montreal.radio-canada.ca. Web: (includes Window Media & MP3) www.rcinet.ca. Contact: (general) Maggy Akerblom, Audience Relations; Stéphane Parent, Producer/Host "Le courrier mondial"; Mark Montgomery; or Ian Jones, Producer/Host "The Maple Leaf Mailbag"; (administration) Jean Larin, Director; (technical—verifications) Bill Westenhaver. Free stickers & lapel pins on request.

*TRANSMISSION OFFICE, INTERNATIONAL SERVICES, CBC TRANSMISSION:* Room: B52-70, 1400 boulevard René Lévesque East, Montréal, Québec, H2L 2M2, Canada. Phone: +1 (514) 597-7618/19. Fax: +1 (514) 284 2052. Email: (Théorêt) gerald_theoret@radio-canada.ca; (Bouliane) jacques_bouliane@

radio-canada.ca. Contact: (general) Gérald Théorêt, Frequency Manager, CBC Transmission Management; or Ms. Nicole Vincent, Frequency Management; (administration) Jacques Bouliane, Coordinator of Engineering. This office only for informing about transmitter-related problems (interference, modulation quality, etc.), especially by fax. Verifications not given out at this office; requests for verification should be sent to the main office, above.
*TRANSMITTER SITE:* CBC, P.O. Box 6131, Sackville New Brunswick, E4L 1G6, Canada. Phone: +1 (506) 536-2690/1. Fax: +1 (506) 536 2342. Email: ray_bristol@cbc.ca. Contact: Raymond Bristol, Sackville Plant Manager, CBC Transmission. All correspondence not concerned with transmitting equipment should be directed to the appropriate address in Montréal, above. Free tours given during normal working hours.
*MONITORING STATION:* P.O. Box 460, Station Main Stittsville, Ontario, K2S 1A6, Canada. Phone: +1 (613) 831-4802. Fax: +1 (613) 831 0343. Email: williamd@ottawa.cbc.ca. Contact: Derek Williams, Manager of Monitoring.
**Radio Monte-Carlo Middle East (via Radio Canada International)**—*see* France.
**Shortwave Classroom**, R. Tait McKenzie Public School, 175 Paterson Street, Almonte, Ontario, K0A 1A0, Canada. Phone: +1 (613) 256-8248. Fax: +1 (613) 256 4791. Email: carletonn@ucdsb.on.ca. Contact: Neil Carleton, VE3NCE, Editor & Publisher. *The Shortwave Classroom* newsletter was published three times per year as a nonprofit volunteer project for teachers around the world that use shortwave listening in the classroom, or as a club activity, to teach about global perspectives, media studies, world geography, languages, social studies and other subjects. Although no longer published, a set of back issues with articles and classroom tips from teachers around the globe is available for $10.

## CENTRAL AFRICAN REPUBLIC  World Time +1

**Radio Centrafrique**, Radiodiffusion-Télévision Centrafricaine, B.P. 940, Bangui, Central African Republic. Contact: (technical) Jacques Mbilo, Le Directeur des Services Techniques; or Michèl Bata, Services Techniques. Replies on rare occasions to correspondence in French; return postage required.
**Radio Ndeke Luka**, c/o PNUD, Av. de l'Indépendance, B.P. 872, Bangui, Central African Republic. Operated by the Hirondelle Foundation, and successor to the UN-run Radio MINURCA. Currently off shortwave, but eventually hopes to acquire a transmitter.

## CHAD  World Time +1

**Radiodiffusion Nationale Tchadienne—N'djamena**, B.P. 892, N'Djamena, Chad. Contact: Djimadoum Ngoka Kilamian; or Ousmane Mahamat. Two IRCs or return postage required. Replies slowly to correspondence in French.
**Radiodiffusion Nationale Tchadienne—Radio Moundou** (when operating), B.P. 122, Moundou, Logone, Chad. Contact: Dingantoudji N'Gana Esaie.

## CHILE  World Time –3 (–4 midyear)

**Radio Esperanza**
*OFFICE:* Casilla 830, Temuco, Chile. Phone: +56 (45) 213-790. Phone/fax: +56 (45) 367-070. Email: esperanza@telsur.cl. Website: www.acym.cl/radio.htm. Contact: (general) Juanita Cárcamo, Departamento de Programación; Eleazar Jara, Dpto. de Programación; Ramón P. Woerner K., Publicidad; or Alberto

Higueras Martínez, Locutor; (verifications) Rodolfo Campos, Director; Juanita Carmaco M., Dpto. de Programación; (technical) Juan Luis Puentes, Dpto. Técnico. Free pennants, stickers, bookmarks and tourist information. Two IRCs, $1 or 2 U.S. stamps appreciated. Replies, often slowly, to correspondence in Spanish or English.
*STUDIO:* Calle Luis Durand 03057, Temuco, Chile. Phone/fax: +56 (45) 240-161.
**Radio Santa María**, Apartado 1, Coyhaique, Chile. Phone: +56 (67) 232-398, +56 (67) 232-025 or +56 (67) 231-817. Fax: +56 (67) 231 306. Contact: Pedro Andrade Vera, Coordinador. $1 or return postage required. May send free tourist cards. Replies to correspondence in Spanish and Italian.
**Radio Parinacota**, Casilla 82, Arica, Chile.
**Radio Triunfal Evangélica** (if reactivated), Calle Las Araucarias 2757, Villa Monseñor Larrain, Talagante, Chile. Phone: +56 (1) 815-4765. Contact: Fernando González Segura, Obispo de la Misión Pentecostal Fundamentalista. Two IRCs required. Replies to correspondence in Spanish.
◪**Radio Voz Cristiana**
*TRANSMISSION FACILITIES:* Casilla 395, Talagante, Santiago, Chile. Phone: (Engineering) +56 (2) 855-7046. Fax: +56 (2) 855 7053. Email: (Operations Manager) gisela@vozcristiana.cl; (Engineering) vozing@interaccess.cl; (Frequency Manager) andrewflynn@christianvision.com; (Administration) vozcrist@interaccess.cl. Contact: Ms. Gisela Vergara, Operations Manager; (technical) Andrew Flynn, Head of Engineering. Free program and frequency schedules. Sometimes sends small souvenirs. All QSL requests should be sent to the Miami address, below.
*PROGRAM PRODUCTION:* P.O. Box 2889, Miami FL 33144 USA; or (street address) 15485 Eagle Nest Lane, Suite 220, Miami Lakes FL 33014 USA. Phone: +1 (305) 231-7704. Fax: +1 (305) 231 7447. Email: (comments) comentarios@vozcristiana.com; (González) david@vozcristiana.com. Web: (includes RealAudio) www.vozcristiana.com. Contact: (administration) Juan Mark Gallardo, Director Regional; (technical and nontechnical) David González, Gerente de Programación. Verifies reception reports.

## CHINA  World Time +8; still nominally +6 ("Urümqi Time") in the Xinjiang Uighur Autonomous Region, but in practice +8 is observed there, as well.

*NOTE:* China Radio International, the Central People's Broadcasting Station and certain regional outlets reply regularly to listeners' letters in a variety of languages. If a Chinese regional station does not respond to your correspondence within four months—and many will not, unless your letter is in Chinese or the regional dialect—try writing them c/o China Radio International.
◪**Central People's Broadcasting Station (CPBS)—China National Radio** (Zhongyang Renmin Guangbo Diantai), P.O. Box 4501, Beijing 100866, China. Phone: +86 (10) 6851-2435 or +86 (10) 6851-5522. Fax: +86 (10) 6851 6630. Email: zhangzr@mail.cnradio.com.cn. Web: (includes RealAudio) www.cnr.com.cn. Contact: Wang Changquan, Audience Department, China National Radio. Tape recordings of music and news $5 plus postage. CPBS T-shirts $10 plus postage; also sells ties and other items with CPBS logo. No credit cards. Free stickers, pennants and other small souvenirs. Return postage helpful. Responds regularly to correspondence in English and Standard Chinese (Mandarin). Although in recent years this station has officially been called "China National Radio" in English-language documents, all on-air identifications in Standard Chinese con-

tinue to be "Zhongyang Renmin Guangbo Dientai" (Central People's Broadcasting Station). To quote from the Website of China's State Administration of Radio, Film and TV: "The station moved to Beijing on March 25, 1949. It was renamed the Central People's Broadcasting Station (it [sic] English name was changed to China National Radio later on) . . ."

**China Huayi Broadcasting Company**, P.O. Box 251, Fuzhou, Fujian 350001, China. Contact: Lin Hai Chun, Announcer; or Wu Gehong. Replies to correspondence in English and Chinese. On-air, announces in English as "Corporation" but the correct translation from the Chinese name is "Company."

**China National Radio**—see Central People's Broadcasting Station (CPBS), above.

🔲**China Radio International**

*MAIN OFFICE, NON-CHINESE LANGUAGES SERVICE:* 16A Shijingshan Street, Beijing 100040, China; or P.O. Box 4216, CRI-2 Beijing 100040 China. Phone: (Director's office) +86 (10) 6889-1625; (Audience Relations.) +86 (10) 6889-1617 or +86 (10) 6889-1652; (English newsroom/current affairs) +86 (10) 6889-1619; (Technical Director) +86 (10) 6609-2577. Fax: (Director's office) +86 (10) 6889 1582; (English Service) +86 (10) 6889 1378 or +86 (10) 6889 1379; (Audience Relations) +86 (10) 6889 3175; (administration) +86 (10) 6851 3174; (German Service) +86 (10) 6889 1941; (Spanish Service) +86 (10) 6889 1909. Email: (English) crieng@cri.com.cn; or msg@cri.com.cn; (Chinese) chn@cri.com.cn; (German) ger@box.cri.com.cn (*see* also the entry for the Berlin Bureau, below); (Japanese) jap@cri.com.cn; (Spanish) spa@cri.com.cn; ("Voices from Other Lands" program) voices@box.cri.com.cn. Web: (official, includes RealAudio) www.cri.com.cn; (unofficial, but regularly updated) http://pw2.netcom.com/~jleq/cril.htm. Contact: Ms. Wang Anjing, Director of Audience Relations, English Service; Ying Lian, English Service; Shang Chunyan, "Listener's Garden"; Yu Meng, Editor; or Li Ping, Director of English Service; (administration) Li Dan, President, China Radio International; Xia Jixuan, Chen Minyi, Chao Tieqi and Wang Dongmei, Deputy Directors, China Radio International; Xin Liancai, Director International Relations, China Radio International. Free bi-monthly *Messenger* newsletter for loyal listeners, pennants, stickers, desk calendars, pins and handmade papercuts. Every year, China Radio International holds contests and quizzes, with the overall winner getting a free trip to China. T-shirts for $8. Two-volume, 820-page set of *Day-to-Day Chinese* language-lesson books $15, including postage worldwide; a 155-page book, *Learn to Speak Chinese: Sentence by Sentence*, plus two cassettes for $15. Two chinese music tapes for $15. Various other books (on arts, medicine, Chinese idioms etc.) in English available from Audience Relations Department, English Service, China Radio International, 100040 Beijing, China. Payment by postal money order to Mr. Li Yi. Every year, the Audience Relations Department will renew the mailing list of the *Messenger* newsletter. CRI is also relayed via shortwave transmitters in Canada, Cuba, France, French Guiana, Mali, Russia and Spain.

*FREQUENCY PLANNING DIVISION:* Radio and Television of People's Republic of China, 2 Fuxingmenwai Street, Beijing 100866, China; or P.O. Box 2144, Beijing 100866, China. Phone: (Wang Xiulan) +86 (10) 6609-2080 or +86 (10) 6609-2627; (Yang Minmin) +86 (10) 6609-2070. Fax: +86 (10) 6801 6436 or +86 (10) 6609 2176. Email: (Wang Xiulan) plc2000@btamail.net.cn; (Yang Minmin & Li Guohua) pdc@abrs.chinasartft. Contact: Ms. Wang Xiulan, Director of Frequency Planning Division; Ms. Li Guohua, Frequency Manager; Ms. Yang Minmin, Manager, Frequency Coordination; or Zheng Shuguang, Frequency Manager.

*MAIN OFFICE, CHINESE LANGUAGES SERVICE:* China Radio International, Beijing 100040, China. Prefers correspondence in Chinese (Mandarin).

*ARLINGTON NEWS BUREAU:* 2000 South Eads Street APT#712, Arlington VA 22202 USA. Phone: +1 (703) 521-8689. Contact: Mr. Yongjing Li.

*BERLIN BUREAU:* Berliner Büro, Gürtelstr. 32 B, D-10247 Berlin, Germany. Phone: +49 (30) 2966-8998. Fax: +49 (30) 2966 8997. Email: deyubu@hotmail.com. Correspondence to CRI's German Service can be sent to this office.

*CHINA (HONG KONG) NEWS BUREAU:* 387 Queen's Road East, Room 1503, Hong Kong, China. Phone: +852 2834-0384. Contact: Ms. He Jincao.

*JERUSALEM NEWS BUREAU:* Flat 16, Hagdud Ha'ivri 12, Jerusalem 92345, Israel. Phone: +972 (2) 566-6084. Contact: Ms. Liu Suyun.

*LONDON NEWS BUREAU:* 13B Clifton Gardens, Golders Green, London NW11 7ER, United Kingdom. Phone: +44 (20) 8458-6943. Contact: Ms. Wu Manling.

*NEW YORK NEWS BUREAU:* 630 First Avenue #35K, New York NY 10016 USA. Fax: +1 (212) 889 2076. Contact: Mr Qian Jun.

*SYDNEY NEWS BUREAU:* Unit 53, Block A15 Herbert Street, St. Leonards NSW 2065, Australia. Phone: +61 (2) 9436-1493. Contact: Mr. Yang Binyuan.

*SAN FRANCISCO OFFICE, SCHEDULES:* 2654 17th Avenue, San Francisco CA 94116 USA. Phone: +1 (415) 564-9968. Email: GPoppin@aol.com. Contact: George Poppin. This address, a volunteer office, only provides CRI schedules to listeners. All other correspondence should be sent directly to the main office in Beijing.

**Fujian People's Broadcasting Station**, 2 Gutian Lu, Fuzhou, Fujian 350001, China. $1 or IRC helpful. Contact: Audience Relations. Replies occasionally and usually slowly. Prefers correspondence in Chinese.

**Gannan People's Broadcasting Station**, 49 Renmin Xije, Hezuo Zhen, Xiahe, Gian Su 747000, China. Verifies reception reports written in English. Return postage not required.

**Gansu People's Broadcasting Station**, 226 Donggang Xilu, Lanzhou 730000, China. Phone: +86 (931) 841-1054. Fax: +86 (931) 882 5834. Contact: Li Mei. IRC helpful.

**Guangxi Foreign Broadcasting Station**, 12 Min Zu Avenue, Nanning, Guangxi 530022, China. Phone: +86 (771) 585-4191, +86 (771) 585-4256 or +86 (771) 585-4403. Email: 101@gxfbs.com or 103@gxfbs.com; (Thanh Mai) thanhmai@gxfbs.com. Web: www.gxfbs.com. Contact: Thanh Mai, Vietnamese Section. Free stickers and handmade papercuts. IRC helpful. Replies irregularly. Broadcasts in Vietnamese and Cantonese to listeners in Vietnam.

**Guangxi People's Broadcasting Station** (if reactivated), 75 Min Zu Avenue, Nanning, Guangxi 530022, China. Email: gxbs@public.nn.gx.cn. Web: www.gxpbs.com. IRC helpful. Replies irregularly.

**Guizhou People's Broadcasting Station**, 259 Qingyun Lu, Guiyang, Guizhou 550002, China. Phone: +86 (851) 582-2495. Fax: +86 (851) 586 9983.

**Heilongjiang People's Broadcasting Station**, 181 Zhongshan Lu, Harbin, Heilongjiang 150001, China. Phone: +86 (451) 262-7454. Fax: +86 (451) 289 3539. Email: am621@sina.com. Web: www.am621.com.cn. $1 or return postage helpful.

**Honghe People's Broadcasting Station**, 32 Jianshe Donglu, Gejiu, Yunnan 661400, China. Contact: Shen De-chun, Head of Station; or Mrs. Cheng Lin, Editor-in-Chief. Free travel brochures.

**Hubei People's Broadcasting Station**, 563 Jiefang Dadao, Wuhan, Hubei 430022, China.

**Hunan People's Broadcasting Station**, 27 Yuhua Lu, Changsha, Hunan 410007, China. Phone: +86 (731) 554-7202. Fax: +86 (731) 554 7220.

**Jiangxi People's Broadcasting Station**, 111 Hongdu Zhong Dadao, Nanchang, Jiangxi 330046, China. Email: gfzq@public.nc.jx.cn. Contact: Tang Ji Sheng, Editor, Chief Editor's Office. Free gold/red pins. Replies irregularly. Mr. Tang enjoys music, literature and stamps, so enclosing a small memento along these lines should help assure a speedy reply.

**Nei Menggu (Inner Mongolia) People's Broadcasting Station**, 19 Xinhua Darjie, Hohhot, Nei Menggu 010058, China. Web: www.nmrb.com.ch. Contact: Zhang Xiang-Quen, Secretary; or Liang Yan. Replies irregularly.

**Qinghai People's Broadcasting Station**, 96 Kunlun Lu, Xining, Qinghai 810001, China. Contact: Liqing Fangfang; or Ghou Guo Liang, Director, Technical Department. $1 helpful.

**Radio Television Hong Kong**, C.P.O Box 70200, Kowloon, Hong Kong, China. May broadcast weather reports every even two years, usually around late March, on 3940 kHz for the South China Sea Yacht Race. Website for the race is: www.rhkyc.org.hk/chinasearace/home.htm.

**CAPE D'AGUILAR HF STATION:** P.O. Box 9896, GPO Hong Kong, China. Phone: +825 2809-2434. Fax: +825 2809 2434. Contact: Lam Chi Keung, Assistant Engineer. This station provides the transmission facilities for the weather reports on the South China Sea Yacht Race. See previous entry.

**Sichuan People's Broadcasting Station**, 119-1 Hongxing Zhonglu, Chengdu, Sichuan 610017, China. Web: www.swww.com.cn/scsb. Replies occasionally.

**Voice of Jinling (Jinling zhi Sheng)**, P.O. Box 268, Nanjing, Jiangsu 210002, China. Fax: +86 (25) 413 235. Contact: Strong Lee, Producer/Host, "Window of Taiwan." Free stickers and calendars, plus Chinese-language color station brochure and information on the Nanjing Technology Import and Export Corporation. Replies to correspondence in Chinese and to simple correspondence in English. $1, IRC or 1 yuan Chinese stamp required for return postage.

**Voice of Pujiang (Pujiang zhi Sheng)**, P.O. Box 3064, Shanghai 200002, China. Phone: +86 (21) 6208-2797. Fax: +86 (21) 6208 2850. Contact: Jiang Bimiao, Editor and Reporter.

**Voice of the Strait (Haixia zhi Sheng)**, People's Liberation Army Broadcasting Centre, P.O. Box 187, Fuzhou, Fujian 350012, China. Email: hxzs@mail.radiohx.com; (English program): china@radiohx.com. Web: (includes RealAudio) www.radiohx.com. Replies irregularly.

**Wenzhou People's Broadcasting Station**, 19 Xianxue Qianlu, Wenzhou, Zhejiang 325000, China.

**Xilingol People's Broadcasting Station**, Xilin Dajie, Xilinhot, Nei Menggu 026000, China.

**Xinjiang People's Broadcasting Station**, 84 Tuanjie Lu, Urümqi, Xinjiang 830044, China. Email: mw738@21cn.com. Web: www.xjbs.com.cn. Contact: Zhao Ji-shu or Ms. Zhao Donglan, Editorial Office. Free tourist booklet, postcards and used Chinese stamps. Replies to correspondence in Chinese and to simple correspondence in English.

**Xizang People's Broadcasting Station**, 180 Beijing Zhonglu, Lhasa, Xizang 850000, China. Web: http://tibet.goldinfo.com.cn/diantai/diantai.htm. Contact: Lobsang Chonphel, Announcer; or Miss Wenxin, host of "Tonight's Appointment" program. Free stickers and brochures. Enclosing an English-language magazine may help with a reply. Sometimes announces itself in English as "China Tibet Broadcasting Station" or "Tibet China Broadcasting Station."

**Yunnan People's Broadcasting Station**, 73 Renmin Xilu, Central Building of Broadcasting and TV, Kunming, 650031 Yunnan, China. Phone: +86 (871) 531-0270. Fax: +86 (871) 531 0360. Contact: Sheng Hongpeng or F.K. Fan. Free Chinese-language brochure on Yunnan Province, but no QSL cards. $1 or return postage helpful. Replies occasionally.

**Zhejiang People's Broadcasting Station**, 111 Moganshan Lu, Hangzhou, Zhejiang 310005, China. Phone: +86 (571) 807-7050. Email: radiozjy@163.com. Contact: Yin Weiling, Editor.

# CHINA (TAIWAN)   World Time +8

**Central Broadcasting System (CBS)**, 55 Pei'an Road, Tachih, Taipei 104, Taiwan, Republic of China. Phone: +886 (2) 2591-8161 or +886 (2) 2885-6168. Email: cbs@cbs.org.tw. Web (includes RealAudio): www.cbs.org.tw. Contact: Lee Ming, Deputy Director. Free stickers.

**China Radio**, 53 Min Chuan West Road 9th Floor, Taipei 10418, Taiwan. Phone: +886 (2) 2598-1009. Fax: +886 (2) 2598 8348. Email: (Adams) readams@usa.net. Contact: Richard E. Adams, Station Director. Verifies reception reports. A religious broadcaster, sometimes referred to as "True Light Station," transmitting via leased facilities in Petropavlovsk-Kamchatskiy, Russia.

**Radio Taipei International**, P.O. Box 24-38, Taipei, Taiwan, Republic of China. Phone: +886 (2) 2885-6168. Fax: +886 (2) 2886 2294. Email: (general) cbs@cbs.org.tw; (English) prog@cbs.org.tw; (German) deutsch@cbs.org.tw. Web: (includes RealAudio and online reception report form) www.cbs.org.tw. Contact: (general) Mei-yee Chao, Chief of Listeners' Service Section; (administration) Shih-lin Ger, President; (technical) Peter Lee, Manager, Engineering Department. May send an annual diary, other publications and an occasional surprise gift. Broadcasts to the Americas are relayed via WYFR's Okeechobee site in the USA. Also uses relay facilities in France and the United Kingdom.

*BERLIN OFFICE:* Postfach 08 05 36, D-10005 Berlin, Germany.

*OSAKA NEWS BUREAU:* C.P.O. Box 180, Osaka Central Post Office, Osaka 530-091, Japan.

*TOKYO NEWS BUREAU:* P.O. Box 21, Azubu Post Office, Tokyo 106, Japan.

*SAN FRANCISCO NEWS BUREAU:* P.O. Box 192793, San Francisco CA 94119-2793 USA.

**Voice of Asia**, P.O. Box 24-777, Taipei, Taiwan, Republic of China. Phone: +886 (2) 2771-0151, X-2431. Fax: +886 (2) 2751 9277. Web: same as for Radio Taipei International, above. As of June 2001, broadcasts only in Thai, although previous languages included English.

# CLANDESTINE

Clandestine broadcasts are often subject to abrupt change or termination. Being operated by anti-establishment political and/or military organizations, these groups tend to be suspicious of outsiders' motives. Thus, they are more likely to reply to contacts from those who communicate in the station's native tongue, and who are perceived to be at least somewhat favorably disposed to their cause. Most will provide, upon request, printed matter on their cause, though not necessarily in English.

For more detailed information on clandestine stations, refer to the annual publication, *Clandestine Stations List*, about $10 or 10 IRCs postpaid by air, published by the Danish Shortwave Clubs International, Tavleager 31, DK-2670 Greve, Denmark; phone (Denmark) +45 4290-2900; fax (via Germany) +49 6371 71790; email 100413.2375@compuserve.com. For CIA media contact information, *see* USA. Available on the Internet, *The Clandestine Radio Intel Webpage* specializes in background information on these stations and is organized by region and target country. The page can be accessed at: www.ClandestineRadio.com. Another informative Web page specializing in clandestine radio information and containing a twice monthly report on the latest news and developments affecting the study of clandestine radio is *Clandestine Radio Watch*, found at www.listen.to/qip.

**"Ashur Radio"** (also known as "Qala D Ashur" and "Voice of Zowaa"). Email: info@zowaa.com; or ashur@zowaa.com. Web: (Zowaa parent organization) www.zowaa.com. Supports the Assyrian Democratic Movement (Zowaa), and is believed to broadcast via facilities in Azerbaijan.

**"Ava-ye Ashena"** (Familiar Voice), Schwarzackerstrasse 2, Leipzig D-04299 Germany. Email: redaction@avayeashena.com; or webmaster@avayeashena.com. Web: (RealAudio) www.avayeashena.com. Leases airtime over a transmitter in Lithuania.

**"Dat Radio."** Email: info@datradio.com. Web: (includes MP3) www.datradio.com. Opposed to Kazakstan president Nazarbayev.

**"Dejen Radio."** Email: (Ethiopian Commentator parent organization) articles@ethiopiancommentator.com. Web: (RealAudio) www.ethiopiancommentator.com/dejenradio/index2.html.

**"Democratic Voice of Burma"** ("Democratic Myanmar a-Than")

STATION: DVB Radio, P.O. Box 6720, St. Olavs Plass, N-0130 Oslo, Norway. Phone: +47 (22) 20-0021. Phone/fax: +47 (22) 36-2525. Email: dvbburma@online.no. Web: (includes RealAudio) www.communique.no/dvb. Contact: (general) Dr. Anng Kin, Listener Liaison; Aye Chan Naing, Daily Editor; or Thida, host for "Songs Request Program"; (administration) Harn Yawnghwe, Director; or Daw Khin Pyone, Manager; (technical) Saw Neslon Ku, Studio Technician; Petter Bernsten; or Technical Dept. Norwegian kroner requested for a reply, but presumably Norwegian mint stamps would also suffice. Programs produced by Burmese democratic movements, as well as professional and independent radio journalists, to provide informational and educational services for the democracy movement inside and outside Burma. Opposes the current Myanmar government. Transmitted originally via facilities in Norway, but more recently has broadcast from sites in Germany, Madagascar, New Zealand and Russia.

AFFINITY GROUPS:

BurmaNet. Email: (BurmaNet News editor, Free Burma Coalition, USA) strider@igc.apc.org; (Web coordinator, Free Burma Coalition, USA) freeburma@pobox.com. Web: (BurmaNet News, USA) http://sunsite.unc.edu/freeburma/listservers.html.

Free Burma Coalition, 1101 Pennsylvania Avenue SE #204, Washington DC 20003 USA Phone: +1 (202) 547-5985. Fax: +1 (202) 544 6118. Email: info@freeburmacoalition.org. Web: www.freeburmacoalition.org.

**"Fang Guang Ming Radio"**—successor to "World Falun Dafa Radio" and radio outlet of the Falun Gong movement. Web: (parent organization) www.fgmtv.org; (RealAudio/MP3) www.falundafaradio.org. Reception reports are best sent to: TDP, P.O. Box 1, 2310 Rijkevorsel, Belgium.

**"Jakada Radio International."** Email: jakint2002@yahoo.com. Web: www.geocities.com/nac6015/webs/jakada. Headed by Yaro Yusufu Mamman, former Nigerian ambassador to Spain and the Vatican, and now chairman of Nigeria's Alliance for Democracy political party. Reception reports can be verified from: TDP, P.O. Box 1, 2310 Rijkevorsel, Belgium.

**"Millenium Voice."** Email: milleniumvoice@aol.com. Transmits from the United Kingdom, and oppposes the Sudan government.

**"National Radio of the Democratic Saharan Arab Republic"**—*see* Radio Nacional de la República Arabe Saharaui Democrática, Western Sahara.

**"Netsanet Radio"** (if reactivated), Netsanet Le-Ethiopia, P.O. Box 5398, Takoma Park MD 20913 USA. Voicemail: +1 (301) 562-8597. Email: netsanet@netsanet.com. Web: (includes RealAudio) www.netsanet.com. Opposed to the Ethiopian government.

**"Qala D Ashur"**—*see* "Ashur Radio"

**"Radio Anternacional,"** BM Box 1499, London WC1N 3XX, United Kingdom. Phone: +44 (20) 8962-2707. Fax: +44 (20) 8346 2203. Email: radio7520@yahoo.com; (Majedi) azarmajedi@yahoo.com. Web: (includes Windows Media) www.anternacional.org. Contact: Ms. Azar Majedi. A broadcast in Persian sponsored by the Committee for Humanitarian Assistance to Iranian Refugees (CHAIR) and aired via facilities in Moldova. Has ties to the Worker-Communist Party of Iran.

**"Radio Barabari."** Email: info@barabari.org. Web: (includes RealAudio and MP3) www.radiobarabari.net. As of September 2002, was leasing airtime via a transmitter in Lithuania, but has used other countries in the past.

**"Radio Dat"**—*see* "Dat Radio"

**"Radio Free Afghanistan"**—*see* USA.

**"Radio Free Bougainville"** (when operating), 2 Griffith Avenue, Roseville NSW 2069, Australia. Phone/fax: +61 (2) 9417-1066. Contact: Sam Voron, Australian Director. $5, AUS$5 or 5 IRCs required. Station is operated from Panguna, Central Bougainville by members of the Mekamui Defence Force led by Francis Ona. Opposed to the Papua New Guinea government.

**"Radio Free Iraq"**—*see* USA.

**"Radio Freedom, Voice of the Ogadeni People"**—*see* Radio Xoriyo.

**"Radio Independent Makumi"** (when operating)—*see* "Radio Free Bougainville" (which is sometimes operated under this name) for contact details.

**"Radio International"**—*see* "Radio Anternacional"

**"Radio Kurdistan"**—*see* Iraq

**"Radio Nacional de la República Arabe Saharaui Democrática"**—*see* Western Sahara.

**"Radio New Sudan,"** SNA/SAF, Culture and Information Office, Neguse Street Nr. 6/8 (or P.O. Box 9257), Asmara, Eritrea. Email: infosaf@eol.com.er. Web: (Sudan Alliance Forces) www.safsudan.com. Contact: Amir Babkir, Sudan Alliance Forces Secretary for Culture and Information. The Sudan Alliance Forces are an opposition guerrilla army of ex-government northern soldiers, affiliated to the Asmara, Eritrea-based National Democratic Alliance (NDA). Opposes the current Sudan government. Claims to operate in liberated areas on the Sudanese side of the Sudan-Eritrea border, but actual site seems to be in Asmara, Eritrea. Formerly known as "Voice of Freedom and Renewal."

**"Radio Payam-e Dost"** (Bahá'í Radio International). Phone: +1 (703) 671-8888. Email: payam@bahairadio.org. Web: www.bahairadio.org.

**"Radio Rainbow"** ("Kestedamena rediyo ye selamena yewendimamach dimtse"), c/o RAPEHGA, P.O. Box 140104, D-53056 Bonn, Germany. Contact: T. Assefa. Supposedly operated by an Ethiopian opposition group called Research and Action Group for Peace in Ethiopia and the Horn of Africa. Broadcasts via hired shortwave transmitters in Germany.

**"Radio Sedaye Iran"**—*see* KRSI, USA.

☞"Radio Solidarity," P.O. Box 60040, Washington DC 20039 USA. Email: ethiopians@tisjd.net or tisforjd@aol.com. Web: (includes RealAudio) www.tisjd.net. Supports the Tigrean International Solidarity for Justice and Democracy organization.

"Radio Station Freedom, Voice of the Communist Party of Iraqi Kurdistan" ("Era ezgay azadiya, dengi hizbi shuyu'i kurdistani iraqa").
*KURDISTAN COMMUNIST PARTY-IRAQ (KCPI) PARENT ORGANIZATION:* Web: http://user.tninet.se/~lto357q/framse4.

"Radio Voice of Afghanistan"—*see* United Kingdom.

"Radio Voice of Hope"—*see* Netherlands.

"Radio Voice of the Mojahed,"—*see* "Voice of the Mojahed," later in this section.

"Radio Voice of the People." Email: voxpop@zol.co.zw (if this fails, try the online email form). Web: www.voxpop.co.zw. Airs via Radio Nederland facilities in Madagascar and is opposed to Zimbabwean president Mugabe.
*MOVEMENT FOR DEMOCRATIC CHANGE PARENT ORGANIZATION:* Harvest House, 6th Floor, N.Mandela Ave/Angwa St, Harare, Zimbabwe. Phone: +263 (91) 367-151/2/3 or +263 (4) 781-138/9. Email: support@mdc.co.zw. Web: www.mdczimbabwe.com.

"Radio VOP"—*see* "Radio Voice of the People," above.

☞"Radio Xoriyo," ("Halkani wa Radio Xoriyo, Codkii Ummadda Odageniya"). Email: radioxoriyo@ogaden.com; or ogaden@yahoo.com (some verifications received from these addresses). Web: (includes RealAudio) www.ogaden.com/Radio_Freedom.htm. Broadcasts are supportive of the Ogadenia National Liberation Front, and hostile to the Ethiopian government. Transmits via facilities of Germany's Deutsche Telekom (*see*).

"Republic of Iraq Radio, Voice of the Iraqi People" ("Idha'at al-Jamahiriya al-Iraqiya, Saut al-Sha'b al-Iraqi"). Anti-Saddam Hussein "black" clandestine supported by CIA, British Intelligence, the Gulf Cooperation Council and Saudi Arabia. The name of this station has changed periodically since its inception during the Gulf crisis. Via transmitters in Saudi Arabia.
*SPONSORING ORGANIZATION:* Iraqi National Congress, 17 Cavendish Square, London W1M 9AA, United Kingdom. Phone: +44 (20) 7665-1812; (office in Arbil, Iraq) +873 (682) 346-239. Fax: +44 (20) 7665 1201; (office in Arbil, Iraq) +873 (682) 346 240. Email: pressoffice@inc.org.uk. Web: www.inc.org.uk.

☞"SW Radio Africa"
*UNITED KINGDOM OFFICE:* Phone: +44 (20) 8387-1441. Email:views@swradioafrica.com. Web: (includes Windows Media) www.swradioafrica.com.

Opposed to Zimbabwe president Robert Mugabe. Programs are produced in London and aired via a transmitter in South Africa.

☞"Voice of Biafra International," 733 15th Street NW, Suite 700, Washington DC 20005 USA (reception reports can also be verified from: TDP, P.O. Box 1, 2310 Rijkevorsel, Belgium.) Phone: +1 (202) 347-2983. Email: biafrafoundation@yahoo.com; (Nkwocha) oguchi@pacbell.net; oguchi@mbay.net. Web (includes Windows Media): www.biafraland.com/vobi.htm. Contact: Oguchi Nkwocha, M.D. A project of the Biafra Foundation, Ekwe Nche and the Biafra Actualization Forum.

"Voice of China" ("Zhongguo zhi Yin"), P.O. Box 273538, Concord CA 94527 USA; or (sponsoring organization) Foundation for China in the 21st Century, P.O. Box 11696, Berkeley CA 94701 USA. Contact: Lily Hu, Executive Director. Mainly "overseas Chinese students" interested in the democratization of China. Financial support from the Foundation for China in the 21st Century. Has "picked up the mission" of the earlier Voice

of June 4th, but has no organizational relationship with it. Transmits via facilities of the Central Broadcasting System, Taiwan (*see*).

☞"Voice of Democratic Eritrea" ("Sawt Eritrea al-Dimuqratiya-Sawtu Jabhat al-Tahrir al-Eritrea"), ELF-RC, Postfach 200434, D-53134 Bonn, Germany. Alternative address (Michael): Postfach 1946, D-65428 Ruesselheim, Germany. Phone: +49 (228) 356-181. Email: (Eritrean political opposition) meskerem@erols.com. Web: (includes RealAudio) www.meskerem.net. Contact: Seyoum O. Michael, Member of Executive Committee, ELF-RC. Station of the Eritrean Liberation Front-Revolutionary Council, hostile to the government of Eritrea. Transmits via facilities of Deutsche Telekom (*see*), in Germany.

☞"Voice of Ethiopian Medhin," EMDP, P.O. Box 13875, Silver Spring, MD 20911 USA; Medhin Dimts, Postfach 111423 D-60049 Frankfurt/Main, Germany. Web: (includes RealAudio) www.medhin.org. Broadcast produced by overseas members of the Ethiopian Medhin Democratic Party (EMDP) based in the USA, a broad-based coalition of Ethiopians aiming to democratize their country. Transmits via the German facilities of Deutsche Telekom (*see*).
*MEDHIN INFORMATION AND PUBLIC RELATIONS DEPARTMENT:* Postfach 4432, D-90023 Nueremberg, Germany. Phone/fax: +49 (911) 209-433.

"Voice of Ethiopian Unity"—*see* "Voice of the Democratic Path of Ethiopian Unity"

"Voice of Iranian Kurdistan" ("Seda-ye Kordestan-e Iran")—Contact one of the PDKI (Democratic Party of Iranian Kurdistan parent organization) offices, below.
*PDKI INTERNATIONAL BUREAU:* AFK, Boite Postale 102, F-75623 Paris Cedex 13, France. Phone: +33 (1) 4585-6431. Fax: +33 (1) 4585 2093. Email: pdkiran@club-internet.fr; Web: www.pdk-iran.org.
*PDKI CANADA BUREAU:* P.O. Box 29010, London, Ontario N6K 4L9, Canada. Phone/fax: +1 (519) 680-7784. Email: pdkiontario@pdki.org. Web: www.pdki.org.
*PDKI REPRESENTATIVE IN USA:* Email: pdkiusa@pdki.org.

"Voice of Iraqi Kurdistan"—*see* Iraq.

"Voice of Jammu Kashmir Freedom" ("Sada-i Hurriyat-i Jammu Kashmir"), P.O. Box 102, Muzaffarabad, Azad Kashmir, via Pakistan. Contact: Islam-ud Din Butt. Pro-Moslem and favors Azad Kashmiri independence from India. Believed to transmit via facilities in Pakistan. Return postage not required.
*HARKAT-UL-MUJAHIDEEN SPONSORING ORGANIZATION:* Email: info@harkatulmujahideen.org. Web: www.ummah.net.pk/harkat.

☞"Voice of Khmer Krom," P.O. Box 121, Pensauken NJ 08110 USA. Email: vokk@khmerkrom.org. Web: (includes RealAudio) http://radio.khmerkrom.org. Targeted at the inhabitants of what used to be South Vietnam, and aired via facilities in Central Asia. Reception reports can be verified from: TDP, P.O. Box 1, 2310 Rijkevorsel, Belgium.

☞ "Voice of Komalah" ("Seda-ye Komalah"). Email: radiokom@radiokomaleh.com. Web: (includes RealAudio) www.radiokomaleh.com. Station of the Kurdish branch of the Communist Party of Iran.
*KOMALAH PARENT ORGANIZATION (KURDISTAN):* Email: komalah@hotmail.com.
*SWEDISH OFFICE:* P.O. Box 750 26, Uppsala, Sweden. Phone/fax: +46 (18) 468-493. Email: komala@cpiran.org.

"Voice of Kurdistan Toilers" ("Aira dengi zahmtkishan-e kurdistana")
*KURDISTAN TOILERS PARTY PARENT ORGANIZATION:* Email: info@ktp.nu. Web: www.ktp.nu.

**"Voice of Mesopotamia"** ("Denge Mezopotamya")
*KURDISTAN WORKERS PARTY (PKK) SPONSORING ORGANIZATION:* Email: serxwebun@serxwebun.com. Web: www.pkk.org.
*ADDRESS FOR RECEPTION REPORTS:* TDP, P.O. Box 1, 2310 Rijkevorsel, Belgium.
**"Voice of National Salvation"** ("Gugugui Sori Pangsong"), Grenier Osawa 107, 40 Nando-cho, Shinjuku-ku, Tokyo, Japan. Phone: +81 (3) 5261-0331. Fax: +81 (3) 5261 0332. Email: (National Salvation Front) kuguk@alles.or.jp. Web: (National Salvation Front parent organization) www.alles.or.jp/~kuguk. Verifications have also been received from the offices of the National Democratic Front of South Korea (successor to the former Revolutionary Party for Reunification).
*TOKYO OFFICE:* Phone: +81 (3) 5261-0331. Fax: +81 (3) 5261 0332. Email: ndfsk@campus.ne.jp. Web: www.ndfsk.dyn.to.
*PYONGYANG OFFICE:* NDFSK Mission in Pyongyang, Munsu-dong, Taedonggang District, Pyongyang, Democratic People's Republic of Korea. Phone: +850 (2) 381-4292. Fax: +850 (2) 381 4505 (valid only in those countries with direct telephone service to North Korea). Email: ndfskpy@campus.ne.jp.
Pro-North Korea, pro-Korean unification; supported by North Korean government. On the air since 1967, but not always under the same name. Via North Korean transmitters located in Pyongyang, Haeju and Wongsan.
☞**"Voice of Oromiyaa"** ("Sagalee Oromiyaa"). Email: sagaloromo@aol.com. Web: (includes RealAudio) www.voiceoforomiyaa.com.
☞**"Voice of Oromo Liberation"** ("Sagalee Bilisummaa Oromoo"), Postfach 510610, D-13366 Berlin, Germany; or SBO, Prinzenallee 81, D-13357 Berlin, Germany. Phone: +49 (30) 494-1036. Fax: +49 (30) 494 3372. Email: sbo13366@aol.com. Web: (includes RealAudio) www.oromoliberationfront.org/sbo.html. Contact: Taye Teferah, European Coordinator. Occasionally replies to correspondence in English or German. Return postage required. Station of the Oromo Liberation Front of Ethiopia, an Oromo nationalist organization. Via Deutsche Telekom facilities in Germany.
*OROMO LIBERATION FRONT USA OFFICE:* P.O. Box 73247, Washington DC 20056 USA. Phone: +1 (202) 462-5477. Fax: +1 (202) 332 7011.
**"Voice of Palestine, Voice of the Palestinian Islamic Revolution"** ("Saut al-Filistin, Saut al-Thowrah al-Islamiyah al-Filistiniyah")—for many years considered a clandestine station, but is now officially listed as part of the Arabic schedule of the Voice of the Islamic Republic of Iran, over whose transmitters the broadcasts are aired. *See* "Iran" for potential contact information. Supports the Islamic Resistance Movement, Hamas, which is anti-Arafat and anti-Israel.
**"Voice of the Communist Party of Iraqi Kurdistan"**—*see* "Radio Station Freedom"
**"Voice of the Communist Party of Iran"** ("Seda-ye Hezb-e Komunist-e Iran")
*COMMUNIST PARTY OF IRAN SPONSORING ORGANIZATION:* C.D.C.R.I., Box 704 45, S-107 25 Stockholm, Sweden. Phone/fax: +46 (8) 786-8054. Email: cpi@cpiran.org. Web: www.cpiran.org.
☞**"Voice of the Democratic Path of Ethiopian Unity,"** Finote Democracy, P.O. Box 88675, Los Angeles CA 90009 USA. Email: efdpu@finote.org. Web: (includes RealAudio) www.finote.org. Transmits via German facilities of Deutsche Telekom (*see*).
*EUROPEAN ADDRESS:* Finote Democracy, Postbus 10573, 1001 EN, Amsterdam, Netherlands.
☞**"Voice of the Iraqi People"** (when operating), BM Al-Tariq, London WC1N 3XX, United Kingdom. Web: www.iraqcp.org/

radicp; (RealAudio) http://icp42.tripod.com/icpradio; (Iraqi Communist Party sponsoring organization) www.iraqcp.org. Not to be confused with "Republic of Iraq Radio, Voice of the Iraqi People" (*see*).
**"Voice of the Islamic Revolution in Iraq,"** P.O. Box 11365/738, Tehran, Iran; P.O. Box 37155/146, Qom, Iran; or P.O. Box 36802, Damascus, Syria. Anti-Saddam Hussain, and supported by the Shi'ite-oriented Supreme Assembly of the Islamic Revolution of Iraq, led by Mohammed Baqir al-Hakim. Supported by the Iranian government and transmitted via facilities of Islamic Republic of Iran Broadcasting.
*SPONSORING ORGANIZATION:* Supreme Council for Islamic Revolution in Iraq (SCIRI), 27a Old Gloucester St, London WC1N 3XX, United Kingdom. Phone: +44 (20) 7371-6815. Fax: +44 (20) 7371 2886. Email: info@nidaa-arrafidain.com Web: www.nidaa-arrafidain.com.
**"Voice of the Kurdistan People"**—*see* Iraq.
☞**"Voice of the Mojahed"** (Seda-ye Mojahed)
*PARIS BUREAU:* Mojahedines de Peuple d'Iran, 17 rue des Gords, F-95430 Auvers-sur-Oise, France; or Mojahed, c/o CCI, 147 rue St. Martin, F-75003 Paris, France. Fax: +33 (1) 4271 5627. Email: (People's Mojahedin Organization of Iran parent organization) mojahed@mojahedin.org. Web: (RealAudio) www.mojahedin.org/Pages/seda; (People's Mojahedin Organization of Iran parent organization) www.mojahedin.org. Contact: Majid Taleghani. Station replies very irregularly and slowly. Pre-prepared verification cards and SASE helpful, with correspondence in French or Persian almost certainly preferable. Sponsored by the People's Mojahedin Organization of Iran (OMPI) and the National Liberation Army of Iran.
*OTHER BUREAUS:* Voice of the Mojahed, c/o Heibatollahi, Postfach 502107, 50981 Köln, Germany; or P.O. Box 3133, Baghdad, Iraq. Contact: B. Moradi, Public Relations.
☞**"Voice of the Worker"** ("Seda-ye Kargar"). Web: (includes historical archives in TrueSpeech) www.kvwpiran.org.
*WORKER-COMMUNIST PARTY OF IRAN (WPI) PARENT ORGANIZATION:* Email: wpi@wpiran.org. Web: www.wpiran.org.
*WPI INTERNATIONAL OFFICE:* WPI, Office of International Relations, Suite 730, 28 Old Brompton Road, South Kensington, London SW7 3SS, United Kingdom. Phone: +44 (77) 7989-8968. Fax: +44 (87) 0136 2182. Email: wpi.international.office@ukonline.co.uk.
**"Voice of the Worker-Communist Party of Iraq"** (Aira dangi kizb-e communist-e kargar-e iraqa") (when operating), WCPI Radio, Zargata, Sulaimania, Iraq. Email: radio@wpiraq.org; (WPCI parent organization) jamal@wpiraq.org. Web: (WCPI parent organization) www.wpiraq.org. Station of the Worker-Communist Party of Iraq.
*WCPI CANADIAN OFFICE:* P.O. Box 491, Don Mills Postal Station, North York, Ontario M3C 2T4, Canada.
*WCPI GERMAN OFFICE:* A.K.P.I., Postfach 160244, D-10336 Berlin, Germany.
*WCPI SWEDISH OFFICE:* W.P.C.I., Box 1211, SE-17224, Sundbyberg, Sweden.
☞**"Voice of Tibet"**
*ADMINISTRATIVE OFFICE:* Welhavensgate 1, N-0166 Oslo, Norway. Phone: (administration) +47 2211-2700; (studio) +47 2211-1209. Fax: +47 2211 5474. Email: voti@online.no; (Norbu) votibet@online.no. Web: (includes RealAudio) www.vot.org. Contact: Øystein Alme, Project Manager [sometimes referred to as "Director"]; or Chophel Norbu, Project Coordinator.
*MAIN EDITORIAL OFFICE:* Voice of Tibet, Editor-in-Chief, Narthang Building, Gangchen, Kyishong, Dharamsala-176 215 H.P., India. Phone: +91 (1892) 28179 or +91 (1892) 22384.

Fax: +91 (1892) 24913. Email: vot@nde.vsnl.net.in. Contact: Sonam Dargyay. A joint venture of the Norwegian Human Rights House, Norwegian Tibet Committee and World-View International. Programs focus on Tibetan culture, education, human rights and news from Tibet. Opposed to Chinese control of Tibet. Those seeking a verification for this program should enclose a prepared card or letter. Return postage helpful. Verifications have been received from both addresses. Broadcasts via transmitters in the former Soviet Union.

**"Voice of Tigers"** (when operating). Web: (archived news in RealAudio) www.eelamweb.com/vot. No direct contact information is known, but try the following: c/o Eelamweb, 170 Lees Avenue #902, Ottawa, Ontario K1S 5G5, Canada (email: webmaster@eelamweb.com, or feedback@eelamweb.com). Station operated by Liberation Tigers of Tamil-Eelam.

**"Voice of Zowaa"**—*see* "Ashur Radio"

**"Voz de la Resistencia"**
Email: (FARC-EP parent organization) farc-ep@comision.internal.org; or elbarcino@laneta.apc.org (updated transmission schedules and QSLs available from this address, but correspond in Spanish). Web: www.resistencianacional.org/radio.htm; www.radioresistencia.com; (FARC-EP parent organization) http://burn.ucsd.edu/~farc-ep. Contact: Olga Lucía Marín, Comisión Internacional de las FARC-EP. Station of the Fuerzas Armadas Revolucionarias de Colombia - Ejercito del Pueblo.

# COLOMBIA  World Time –5

*NOTE: Colombia, the country, is always spelled with two o's. It should never be written as "Columbia."*

**Caracol Colombia** (if reactivated)
MAIN OFFICE: Apartado Aéreo 9291, Santafé de Bogotá, D.C., Colombia. Phone: +57 (1) 337-8866. Fax: +57 (1) 337 7126. Web: (includes RealAudio) www.caracol.com.co/webasp2/homeneo.asp. Contact: Hernán Peláez Restrepo, Jefe Cadena Básica; Efraín Jiménez, Director de Operaciones; or Oscar López M., Director Musical. Free stickers. Replies to correspondence in Spanish and English.
MIAMI OFFICE: 2100 Coral Way, Miami FL 33145 USA. Phone: +1 (305) 285-2477 or +1 (305) 285-1260. Fax: +1 (305) 858 5907.

**Caracol Florencia** (if reactivated), Apartado Aéreo 465, Florencia, Caquetá, Colombia. Phone: +57 (88) 352-199. Contact: Guillermo Rodríguez Herrera, Gerente; or Vicente Delgado, Operador. Replies occasionally to correspondence in Spanish.

**Caracol Villavicencio**—*see* La Voz de los Centauros.

**Ecos del Atrato** (when operating), Apartado Aéreo 196, Quibdó, Chocó, Colombia. Phone: +57 (49) 711-450. Contact: Absalón Palacios Agualimpia, Administrador. Free pennants. Replies to correspondence in Spanish.

**La Voz de la Selva**—*see* Caracol Florencia.

**La Voz de Tu Conciencia**, Apartado Aéreo 95300, Santafé de Bogotá, D.C., Colombia.

**La Voz de los Centauros (Caracol Villavicencio)**, Cra. 31 No. 37-71 Of. 1001, Villavicencio, Meta, Colombia. Phone: +57 (986) 214-995. Fax: +57 (986) 623 954. Contact: Carlos Torres Leyva, Gerencia; or Olga Arenas, Administradora. Replies to correspondence in Spanish.

**La Voz del Guaviare**, Carrera 22 con Calle 9, San José del Guaviare, Colombia. Phone: +57 (986) 840-153/4. Fax: +57 (986) 840 102. Contact: Luis Fernando Román Robayo, Director General. Replies slowly to correspondence in Spanish.

**La Voz del Llano**, Calle 41B No. 30-11, Barrio La Grama,

Villavicencio, Meta, Colombia; or (postal address in Bogotá) Apartado Aéreo 67751, Santafé de Bogotá, Colombia. Phone: +57 (986) 624-102. Fax: +57 (986) 625 045. Contact: Manuel Buenaventura, Director; Rafael Rodríguez R., or Edgar Valenzuela Romero. Replies occasionally to correspondence in Spanish. $1 or return postage necessary.

**Ondas del Orteguaza**, Calle 16, No. 12-48, piso 2, Florencia, Caquetá, Colombia. Phone: +57 (88) 352-558. Contact: Sandra Liliana Vásquez, Secretaria; Señora Elisa Viuda de Santos; or Henry Valencia Vásquez. Free stickers. IRC, return postage or $1 required. Replies occasionally to correspondence in Spanish.

**Radio Auténtica**, Calle 38 No. 32-41, piso 7, Edif. Santander, Villavicencio, Meta, Colombia. Phone: +57 (986) 626-780. Phone/fax: +57 (986) 624-507. Web: (Cadena Radial Auténtica de Colombia parent organization) www.cmb.org.co/cra. Contact: (general) Pedro Rojas Velásquez; or Carlos Alberto Pimienta, Gerente; (technical) Sra. Alba Nelly González de Rojas, Administradora. Sells religious audio cassettes for 3,000 pesos. Return postage required. Replies slowly to correspondence in Spanish.

**Radiodifusora Nacional de Colombia**
MAIN ADDRESS: Edificio Inravisión, CAN, Av. Eldorado, Santafé de Bogotá, D.C., Colombia. Phone: +57 (1) 222-0415. Fax: +57 (1) 222 0409 or +57 (1) 222 8000. Email: radio_oc@inravision.com.gov; radiodifusora@hotmail.com. Web: (includes online reception report form) www.inravision.gov.co/seccionradiodifusora/onda1.htm. Contact: Janeth Jiménez M., Coordinadora de Onda Corta; or Dra. Athala Morris, Directora. Free lapel badges, membership in Listeners' Club and monthly program booklet.

# CONGO (DEMOCRATIC REPUBLIC)  (formerly Zaïre) World Time +1 Western, including Kinshasa; +2 Eastern

**Radio Bukavu** (when active), B.P. 475, Bukavu, Democratic Republic of the Congo. $1 or return postage required. Replies slowly. Correspondence in French preferred.

**Radio CANDIP Bunia** (formerly La Voix du Peuple, and prior to that, Radio CANDIP), B.P. 373, Bunia, Democratic Republic of Congo. Letters should preferably be sent via registered mail. $1 or return postage required. Correspondence in French preferred.

**Radio Lubumbashi** (when operating), B.P. 7296, Lubumbashi, Democratic Republic of the Congo. Letters should be sent via registered mail. $1 or 3 IRCs helpful. Correspondence in French preferred.

**Radio Okapi**
Email: info@monuc.org. Web: (includes Windows Media) www.monuc.org/radio. A joint project involving the United Nations Mission in the Democratic Republic of the Congo (MONUC) and the Swiss-based Fondation Hirondelle.
MONUC PUBLIC INFORMATION OFFICES:
(USA) P.O. Box 4653, Grand Central Station, New York NY 10163-4653 USA. Phone: +1 (212) 963-0103. Fax: +1 (212) 963 0205.
(Congo) 12 Av. des Aviateurs, Kinshasa, Gombe, Democratic Republic of the Congo; or B.P. 8811, Kinshasa 1, Democratic Republic of the Congo. Phone: +39 0831 24 5000, X-56372 or X-56374.

**Radio-Télévision Nationale Congolaise**, B.P. 3171, Kinshasa-Gombe, Democratic Republic of the Congo. Letters should be sent via registered mail. $1 or 3 IRCs helpful. Correspondence in French preferred.

## CONGO (REPUBLIC)   World Time +1

**Radiodiffusion Nationale Congolaise** (also announces as "Radio Liberté," "Radio Nationale" or "Radio Congo"), Radiodiffusion-Télévision Congolaise, B.P. 2241, Brazzaville, Congo. Contact: (general) Antoine Ngongo, Rédacteur en chef; (administration) Alphonse Bouya-Dimi, Directeur; or Zaou Mouanda. $1 required. Replies irregularly to letters in French sent via registered mail.

## COSTA RICA   World Time –6

**Faro del Caribe—TIFC**
*MAIN OFFICE:* Apartado 2710, 1000 San José, Costa Rica. Phone: +506 (226) 2573 or +506 (226) 2618. Fax: +506 (227) 1725. Email: tifc@farodelcaribe.org. Web: www.farodelcaribe.org. Contact: Carlos A. Rozotto Piedrasanta, Director Administrativo; or Mauricio Ramires; (technical) Minor Enrique, Station Engineer. Free stickers, pennants, books and bibles. $1 or IRCs helpful.
*U.S. OFFICE, NONTECHNICAL:* Misión Latinoamericana, P.O. Box 620485, Orlando FL 32862 USA.

**Radio Casino**, Apartado 287, 7301 Puerto Limón, Costa Rica. Phone: +506 758-0029. Fax: +506 758 3029. Contact: Edwin Zamora, Departamento de Notícias; or Luis Grau Villalobos, Gerente; (technical) Ing. Jorge Pardo, Director Técnico; or Geraldo Moya, Técnico.

**Radio Exterior de España—Cariari Relay Station**, Cariari de Pococí, Costa Rica. Phone: +506 767-7308 or +506 767-7311. Fax: +506 225 2938.

**☞Radio For Peace International (RFPI)**
*MAIN OFFICE:* Apartado 88, Santa Ana, Costa Rica. Phone: +506 249-1821. Fax: +506 249 1095. Email: info@rfpi.org; radiopaz@racsa.co.cr; rfpicr@sol.racsa.co.cr. Web: (includes RealAudio and MP3) www.rfpi.org. Contact: (general) Debra Latham, General Manager of RFPI, Editor of *VISTA* and co-host of "RFPI Mailbag"; (programming) Joe Bernard, English Program Coordinator; Willie Barrantes, Director, Spanish Department; or Ms. Sabine Kapuschinski, Host of German program; (nontechnical or technical) James Latham, Station Manager. Replies sometimes slow in coming because of the mail. Quarterly *VISTA* newsletter, which includes schedules and program information, $40 annual membership ($50 family/organization) in "Friends of Radio for Peace International"; station commemorative T-shirts and rainforest T-shirts $20; thermo mugs $10 (VISA/MC). Free bumper stickers. Actively solicits listener contributions. Free online verification of email reports, but $1 or 3 IRCs required for verification by QSL card. Limited number of places available for volunteer broadcasting and journalism interns; those interested should send résumé. RFPI was created by United Nations Resolution 35/55 on December 5, 1980.
*U.S. OFFICE, NONTECHNICAL:* P.O. Box 20728, Portland OR 97294 USA. Phone: +1 (503) 252-3639. Fax: +1 (503) 255 5216. Contact: Dr. Richard Schneider, Chancellor CEO, University of Global Education (formerly World Peace University). Newsletter, T-shirts and so forth, as above. University of the Air courses (such as "Earth Mother Speaks" and "History of the U.N.") $25 each, or on audio cassette $75 each (VISA/MC).

**☞Radio Reloj** (when operating), Sistema Radiofónico H.B., Apartado Postal 341-1000, San José, Costa Rica. Phone: +506 286-2636. Fax: +506 226 5579. Email: info@radioreloj.co.cr. Web: (includes live audio, but registration required) www.radioreloj.co.cr. Contact: Roger Barahona, Gerente; or Francisco Barahona Gómez. Can be very slow in replying. $1 required.

**Radio Universidad de Costa Rica**, Apartado 1-06, 2060 Universidad de Costa Rica, San Pedro de Montes de Oca, San José, Costa Rica. Phone: (general) +506 207-4727; (studio) +506 225-3936. Fax: +506 207 5459. Email: radioucr@cariari.ucr.ac.cr. Web: http://cariari.ucr.ac.cr/~radioucr/radioucr. Contact: Marco González Muñoz; Henry Jones, Locutor de Planta; or Nora Garita B., Directora. Marco González is a radio amateur, call-sign TI3AGM. Free postcards, station brochure and stickers. Replies slowly to correspondence in Spanish or English. $1 or return postage required.
**University Network**—*see* USA.

## CROATIA   World Time +1 (+2 midyear)

**☞Croatian Radio-Television (Hrvatska Radio-Televizija, HRT)**
*MAIN OFFICE:* Hrvatska Radio-Televizija (HRT), Prisavlje 3, HR-10000 Zagreb, Croatia. Phone: (operator) +385 (1) 634-3366; (Managing Director) +385 (1) 634-3308; (Technical Director) +385 (1) 634-3663. Fax: (Technical Director) +385 (1) 634 3636. Email: (Managing Director) i.lucev@hrt.hr; (Technical Director) nikola.percin@hrt.hr; (technical, including reception reports) z.klasan@hrt.hr. Web: (includes RealAudio) www.hrt.hr. Contact: (general) Ivanka Lucev, Managing Director; (Technical Director) Nikola Percin.
TRANSMITTING STATION DEANOVEC: P.O Box 3, 10313 Graberje Ivaanicko, Croatia. Phone: +385 (1) 634-3926. Fax: +385 (1) 282 0700. Email: dane.pavlic@hrt.hr. Contact: Dane Pavlic, Head of Station.
*TRANSMISSION AUTHORITY:* Odasiljaci i Veze D.O.O., Vlaska 106, HR-10000 Zagreb, Croatia. Phone: +385 (1) 464-6160. Fax: +385 (1) 464 6161. Email: Zelimir.Klasan@hrt.hr. Contact: Zelimir Klasan. This independent state-owned company replaces the former Transmitters and Communications Department of HRT.

**Voice of Croatia, External Radio Service (Glas Hrvatske)**—same address as "Hrvatska Radio," above. Phone: (Editor-in-Chief) +385 (1) 634-2602; (Shortwave Technical Coordinator) +385 (1) 634-3428; (Shortwave Technical Coordinator, mobile) +385 9857-7565. Fax: (Editor-in-Chief) +385 (1) 634 3305; (Shortwave Technical Coordinator) +385 (1) 634 3347. Email: (Editor-in-Chief) ivana.jadresic@hrt.hr; (staff) kratki.val@hrt.hr; (Shortwave Technical Coordinator) z.klasan@hrt.hr. Contact: (Editor-in-Chief) Ivana Jadresic; (Shortwave Technical Coordinator, domestic & external) Zelimir Klasan.
Croatian Radio operates two services on world band: the domestic (first) national radio program, transmitted via HRT's Deanovec shortwave station for listeners in Europe and the Mediterranean; and a special service in Croatian, with news segments in English and Spanish for Croatian expatriates, which airs via facilities of Deutsche Telekom (*see*) in Jülich, Germany and is sponsored by the Croatian Heritage Organization. The previous Croatian external broadcasting service known as "Radio Hrvatska" and produced by the Croatian Information Center (Hrvatski Informativni Centar, HIC) was discontinued on October 1st 2000. The external service resumed its transmissions on April 18th 2001 as Glas Hrvatske (Voice of Croatia) under the authority of HRT.
*WASHINGTON NEWS BUREAU:* Croatian-American Association, 2020 Pennsylvania Avenue NW, Suite 287, Washington DC 20006 USA. Phone: +1 (202) 429-5543. Fax: +1 (202) 429 5545. Email: 73150.3552@compuserve.com. Web: www.hrnet.org/CAA. Contact: Frank Brozovich, President.

## CUBA World Time –5 (–4 midyear)

**Radio Habana Cuba**, P.O. Box 6240, Habana, Cuba 10600. Phone: (general) +53 (7) 784-954 or +53 (7) 334-272; (English Department) +53 (7) 877-6628; (Coro) +53 (7) 814-243 or (home) +53 (7) 301-794. Fax: (general) +53 (7) 783 518; (English Department) +53 (7) 705 810. Email: (general) radiohc@ip.etecsa.cu; (English Service) radiohc@enet.cu; (Arnie Coro) arnie@radiohc.org. Web: (includes Windows Media and online reception report form) www.radiohc.cu; (includes archived scripts of "DXers Unlimited") www.radiohc.org. Contact: (general) Lourdes López, Head of Correspondence Dept.; Juan Jacomino, Head of English Service; or Mike La Guardia, Senior Editor; (administration) Ms. Milagro Hernández Cuba, General Director; (technical) Arnaldo Coro Antich, ("Arnie Coro"), Producer, "DXers Unlimited"; or Arturo González, Head of Technical Department. Free wallet and wall calendars, pennants, stickers, keychains and pins. DX Listeners' Club. Free sample *Granma International* newspaper. Contests with various prizes, including trips to Cuba.

**Radio Rebelde**, Departamento de Relaciones Públicas, Apartado 6277, Habana 10600, Cuba; or (street address) Calle 23 No. 258 entre L y M, El Vedado, Habana, Cuba 10600. For technical correspondence (including reception reports), substitute "Servicio de Onda Corta" in place of "Departamento de Relaciones Públicas." Reception reports can also be emailed to Radio Habana Cuba's Arnie Coro (arnie@radiohc.org) for forwarding to Radio Rebelde. Phone: +53 (7) 334-269. Fax: +53 (7) 323 514. Email: (nontechnical) rebelde@ceniai.inf.cu. Web (includes Windows Media): www.radiorebelde.cubaweb.cu. Contact: Daimelis Monzón; Noemí Cairo Marín; Iberlise González Padua; or Marisel Ramos Soca (all from "Relaciones Públicas"); or Jorge Luis Más Zabala, Director, Relaciones Públicas. Replies slowly, with correspondence in Spanish preferred.

## CYPRUS World Time +2 (+3 midyear)

📻**Bayrak Radio—BRT International**, BRTK Campus, Dr. Fazil Küçük Boulevard, P.O. Box 417, Lefkosa - T.R.N.C., via Mersin 10, Turkey. Phone: +90 (392) 225-5555. Fax: (general) +90 (392) 225 4581. Email: (general) brt@cc.emu.edu.tr; (technical, including reception reports) tosun@cc.emu.edu.tr. Web: (includes RealAudio) www.brt.gov.nc.tr. Contact: Mustafa Tosun, Head of Transmission Department.

**BBC World Service—East Mediterranean Relay Station**, P.O. Box 209, Limassol, Cyprus. Contact: Steve Welch. This address for technical matters only. Other correspondence should be sent to the BBC World Service in London (*see*).

📻**Cyprus Broadcasting Corporation**, Broadcasting House, P.O. Box 4824, Nicosia 1397, Cyprus; or (physical address) RIK Street, Athalassa, Nicosia 2120, Cyprus. Phone: +357 (2) 862-000. Fax: +357 (2) 314 050. Email: rik@cybc.com.cy. Web: (includes RealAudio) www.cybc.com.cy. Contact: (general) Pavlos Soteriades, Director General; or Evangella Gregoriou, Head of Public and International Relations; (technical) Andreas Michaelides, Director of Technical Services. Free stickers. Replies occasionally, sometimes slowly. IRC or $1 helpful.

## CZECH REPUBLIC World Time +1 (+2 midyear)

📻**Radio Prague**, Czech Radio, Vinohradská 12, 12099 Prague 2, Czech Republic. Phone: (general) +420 (2) 2409-4608; (Czech Department) +420 (2) 2422-2236; (English Department) +420 (2) 2421-8349; (German Department) +420 (2) 2422-2235. Phone/fax: (Oldrich Čip, technical) +420 (2) 2271-5005. Fax: (nontechnical and technical) +420 (2) 2421 8239 or +420 (2) 2422 2236; (English Department) +420 (2) 2421 8349. Email: (general) cr@radio.cz; (Director) Miroslav.Krupicka@radio.cz; (English Department) english@radio.cz; (Program Director) David.Vaughan@radio.cz; (free news texts) robot@radio.cz, writing "Subscribe English" (or other desired language) within the subject line; (technical, chief engineer) cip@radio.cz. Web: (includes RealAudio and MP3) www.radio.cz; (text) ftp:// ftp.radio.cz; gopher://gopher.radio.cz. Contact: (general) Markéta Atanasová; David Vaughan, Editor-in-Chief; (administration) Miroslav Krupička, Director; (technical, all programs) Oldrich Čip, Chief Engineer. Free stickers. Samples of *Welcome to the Czech Republic* and *Czech Life* available upon request from Orbis, Vinohradská 46, 120 41 Prague, Czech Republic. **RFE-RL**—*see* USA.

## DENMARK World Time +1 (+2 midyear)

📻**Radio Danmark**

*MAIN OFFICE:* Radioavisen, Rosenørns Allé 22, DK-1999 Frederiksberg C, Denmark. Phone: (office, including voice mail, voice schedules in Danish) +45 3520-5784. Fax: + 45 3520 5781. Email: (schedule and program matters) rdk@dr.dk; (technical matters and reception reports) rdktek@dr.dk. Web: (includes RealAudio) www.dr.dk/rdk. Contact: (general) Jette Hapiach, Audience Communications; (technical) Erik Køie, Technical Adviser. Replies to correspondence in English, German, French, Norwegian, Swedish or Danish. Cassette tapes, CD and MD (not returned), short RealAudio or MP3 or similar email files accepted. Will verify all correct reception reports; although not necessary, return postage ($1, EUR1 or one IRC) appreciated. Uses transmitting facilities of Radio Norway International. All broadcasts are in Danish, and are aired at xx.30-xx.55 24 hours a day. "Tune In" letterbox program aired every second Saturday, hourly 6 times from 11.48 UTC (summer; winter 12.48 UTC).

*TRANSMISSION MANAGEMENT AUTHORITY:* Broadcast Service Danmark A/S, Banestroget 21, DK-2630 Taastrup, Denmark. Phone: +45 4332-2408. Email: ihl@bsd.dk. Contact: Ib H. Lavrsen, Senior Engineer.

*NORWEGIAN OFFICE, TECHNICAL:* Details of reception quality may also be sent to the Engineering Department of Radio Norway International (*see*), which operates the transmitters currently used by Radio Danmark.

**World Music Radio**, P. O. Box 112, DK-8900 Randers, Denmark. Phone +45 70 222 222. Fax +45 70 222 888. Email: wmr@wmr.dk. URL: www.wmr.dk. Contact: Stig Hartvig Nielsen. Return postage required. An independent station, WMR first went on the air in 1967 from the Netherlands, from where broadcasting continued until August 1973. Later programs were aired via the facilities of Radio Andorra (in 1976 and 1980), Radio Milano International (1982-1983) and Radio Dublin (1983-1989). In 1997, WMR returned to the air between May 31 and August 24 from a new HQ in Denmark, leasing airtime over powerful transmitters in South Africa. These broadcasts ceased due to lack of commercial advertising. According to a reliable source, the station may resume operation during 2003.

## DOMINICAN REPUBLIC World Time –4

**Emisora Onda Musical** (when active), Pablo Hincado 204 Altos, Apartado Postal 860, Santo Domingo, Dominican Republic. Contact: Mario Báez Asunción, Director. Replies occasionally to correspondence in Spanish. $1 helpful.

**Radio Amanecer Internacional**, Apartado Postal 4680, Santo Domingo, Dominican Republic. Phone: +1 (809) 688-5600, +1 (809) 688-5609, +1 (809) 688-8067. Fax: +1 (809) 227 1869. Email: amanecer@tricom.net (may not work). Web: www.tricom.net/amanecer. Contact: (general) Señora Ramona C. de Subervi, Directora; (technical) Ing. Sócrates Domínguez. $1 or return postage required. Replies slowly to correspondence in Spanish.

**Radio Barahona** (when operating), Apartado 201, Barahona, Dominican Republic; or Gustavo Mejía Ricart No. 293, Apto. 2-B, Ens. Quisqueya, Santo Domingo, Dominican Republic. Contact: (general) Rodolfo Z. Lama Jaar, Administrador; (technical) Ing. Roberto Lama Sajour, Administrador General. Free stickers. Letters should be sent via registered mail. $1 or return postage helpful. Replies to correspondence in Spanish.

**Radio Cima Cien** (when operating), Apartado 804, Santo Domingo, Dominican Republic. Fax: +1 (809) 541 1088. Contact: Roberto Vargas, Director. Free pennants, postcards, coins and taped music. Roberto likes collecting stamps and coins.

**Radio Cristal Internacional**, Apartado Postal 894, Santo Domingo, Dominican Republic; or (street address) Calle Pepillo Salcedo No. 18, Altos, Santo Domingo, Dominican Republic. Phone: +1 (809) 565-1460 or +1 (809) 566-5411. Fax: +1 (809) 567 9107. Contact: (general) Fernando Hermón Gross, Director de Programas; or Margarita Reyes, Secretaria; (administration) Darío Badía, Director General; or Héctor Badía, Director de Administración. Seeks reception reports. Return postage of $2 appreciated.

# ECUADOR   World Time –5 (–4 sometimes, in times of drought); –6 Galapagos

*NOTE:* According to HCJB's "DX Party Line," during periods of drought, such as caused by "El Niño," electricity rationing causes periods in which transmitters cannot operate because of inadequate hydroelectric power, as well as spikes which occasionally damage transmitters. Accordingly, many Ecuadorian stations tend to be irregular, or even entirely off the air, during drought conditions.

*NOTE:* According to veteran Dxer Harald Kuhl in Hard-Core-DX of Kotanet Communications Ltd., IRCs are exchangeable only in the cities of Quito and Guayaquil. Too, overseas airmail postage is very expensive now in Ecuador; so when in doubt, enclosing $2 for return postage is appropriate.

**Emisoras Jesús del Gran Poder** (if reactivated), Casilla 17-01-133, Quito, Ecuador. Phone: +593 (2) 251-3077. Contact: Mariela Villarreal; Padre Angel Falconí, Gerente; or Hno. Segundo Cuenca OFM.

**Emisoras Luz y Vida**, Casilla 11-01-222, Loja, Ecuador. Phone: +593 (7) 570-426. Contact: Hermana (Sister) Ana Maza Reyes, Directora; or Lic. Guida Carrión H., Directora de Programas. Return postage required. Replies irregularly to correspondence in Spanish.

**Escuelas Radiofónicas Populares del Ecuador**, Juan de Velasco 4755 y Guayaquil, Casilla Postal 06-01-341, Riobamba, Ecuador. Phone: +593 (3) 961-608 or +593 (3) 960-247. Fax: +593 (3) 961 625. Email: admin@esrapoec.ecuanex.net.ec. Web: www.ded.org.ec/essapa01.htm. Contact: Juan Pérez Sarmiento, Director Ejecutivo; or María Ercilia López, Secretaria. Free pennants and key rings. "Chimborazo" cassette of Ecuadorian music for 10,000 sucres plus postage; T-shirts for 12,000 sucres plus postage; and caps with station logo for 8,000 sucres plus postage. Return postage helpful. Replies to correspondence in Spanish.

**◼HCJB World Radio, The Voice of the Andes**
*STATION:* Casilla 17-17-691, Quito, Ecuador. Phone: (general) +593 (2) 226-6808 (X-4441, 1300-2200 World Time Monday through Friday, for the English Dept.); (Frequency Management) +593 (2) 226-6808 (X-4627); (*DX Partyline* English program, toll-free, U.S. only, for reception reports, loggings and other correspondence) +1 866 343-0791. Fax: (general) +593 (2) 226 7263; (Frequency Manager) +593 (2) 226 3267. Email: (Graham) agraham@hcjb.org.ec; (Frequency Management) irops@hcjb.org.ec or dweber@hcjb.org.ec; (language sections) format is language@hcjb.org.ec; so to reach, say, the Spanish Department, it would be spanish@hcjb.org.ec. Web: (English, includes RealAudio and online reception report form) www.hcjb.org; (Spanish) www.hcjb.org.ec. Contact: (general) English [or other language] Department; (administration) Jim Estes, Director of Broadcasting; Alex Saks, Station Manager; Curt Cole, Programme Director, or Allen Graham, Ecuador National Director; (technical) Douglas Weber, Frequency Manager. Free religious brochures, calendars, stickers and pennants; free email *The Andean Herald* newsletter. *Catch the Vision* book $8, postpaid. IRC or unused U.S. or Canadian stamps appreciated for airmail reply.

*INTERNATIONAL HEADQUARTERS:* HCJB World Radio, Inc., P.O. Box 39800, Colorado Springs CO 80949-9800 USA. Phone: +1 (719) 590-9800. Fax: +1 (719) 590 9801. Email: info@hcjb.org. Contact: Andrew Braio, Public Information; (administration) Richard D. Jacquin, Director, International Operations. Various items sold via U.S. address—catalog available. This address is not a mail drop, so listeners' correspondence, except those concerned with purchasing HCJB items, should be directed to the usual Quito address.

*ENGINEERING CENTER:* 2830 South 17th Street, Elkhart IN 46517 USA. Phone: +1 (219) 294-8201. Fax: +1 (219) 294 8391. Email: info@hcjbeng.org. Web: www.hcjbeng.org. Contact: Dave Pasechnik, Project Manager; or Bob Moore, Engineering. This address only for those professionally concerned with the design and manufacture of transmitter and antenna equipment. Listeners' correspondence should be directed to the usual Quito address.

*REGIONAL OFFICES:* Although HCJB has over 20 regional offices throughout the world, the station wishes that all listener correspondence be directed to the station in Quito, as the regional offices do not serve as mail drops for the station.

*"EDXP NEWSREPORTS":* Web: www.members.tripod.com/-bpadula/edxp.html. Special news reports concentrating on shortwave broadcasts to and from Asia, the Far East, Australia, the Pacific and the Indian sub-continent, compiled by EDXP and aired once a month on the third Saturday (UTC) and repeated on the following Sunday via HCJB during the *"DX Partyline"* English program. Special EDXP QSLs will be offered for the shortwave releases (not for RealAudio). Reports of the EDXP feature should be sent to: Bob Padula, EDXP QSL Service, 404 Mont Albert Road, Surrey Hills, Victoria 3127, Australia. Return postage appreciated. Outside of Australia, 1 IRC or $1; within Australia, four 50c Australian stamps. Email reports welcome at edxp@bigpond.com, and verified with Web-delivered animated QSLs.

**La Voz de Saquisilí—Radio Libertador**, Calle 24 de Mayo, Saquisilí, Cotopaxi, Ecuador. Phone: +593 (3) 721-035. Contact: Arturo Mena Herrera, Gerente-Propietario, who may also be contacted via his son-in-law, Eddy Roger Velástegui Mena, who is studying in Quito (Email: eddyv@uio.uio.satnet.net). Reception reports actively solicited, and will be confirmed with a special commemorative QSL card. Return postage, in the form of $2 or mint Ecuadorian stamps, appreciated; IRCs difficult to exchange. Spanish strongly preferred.

**La Voz del Napo**, Misión Josefina, Tena, Napo, Ecuador. Phone: +593 (6) 886-422. Contact: Ramiro Cabrera, Director. Free pennants and stickers. $2 or return postage required. Replies occasionally to correspondence in Spanish.

**La Voz del Río Tarqui** (when operating), Manuel Vega 653 y Presidente Córdova, Cuenca, Ecuador. Phone: +593 (7) 822-132. Contact: Sra. Alicia Pulla Célleri, Gerente. Replies irregularly to correspondence in Spanish. Has ties with station WKDM in New York.

**La Voz del Upano**

*STATION:* Vicariato Apostólico de Méndez, Misión Salesiana, 10 de Agosto s/n, Macas, Ecuador. Phone: +593 (7) 700-186. Contact: P. Domingo Barrueco C., Director. Free pennants and calendars. On one occasion, not necessarily to be repeated, sent tape of Ecuadorian folk music for $2. Otherwise, $2 required. Replies to correspondence in Spanish.

*QUITO OFFICE:* Procura Salesiana, Equinoccio 623 y Queseras del Medio, Quito, Ecuador. Phone: +593 (2) 551-012.

**Radio Bahá'í** ("La Emisora de la Familia") (when operating), Casilla 10-02-1464, Otavalo, Imbabura, Ecuador. Phone: +593 (6) 920-245. Fax: +593 (6) 922 504. Contact: (general) William Rodríguez Barreiro, Coordinador; or Juan Antonio Reascos, Locutor; (technical) Ing. Tom Dopps. Free information about the Bahá'í faith, which teaches the unity of all the races, nations and religions, and that the Earth is one country and mankind its citizens. Free pennants. Return postage appreciated. Replies regularly to correspondence in English or Spanish. Enclosing a family photo may help getting a reply. Station is property of the Instituto Nacional de Enseñanza de la Fe Bahá'í (National Spiritual Assembly of the Bahá'ís of Ecuador). Although there are many Bahá'í radio stations around the world, Radio Bahá'í in Ecuador is the only one on shortwave.

**Radio Buen Pastor**—*see* Radio El Buen Pastor.

**Radio Centinela del Sur (C.D.S. Internacional)**, Casilla 11-01-106, Loja, Ecuador; or (studios) Olmedo 11-56 y Mercadillo, Loja, Ecuador. Phone: +593 (7) 561-166 or +593 (7) 570-211. Fax: +593 (7) 562 270. Contact: (general) Marcos G. Coronel V., Director de Programas; or José A. Coronel V., Director del programa "Ovación"; (technical) José A. Coronel Illescas, Gerente General. Return postage required. Replies occasionally to correspondence in Spanish.

**Radio Centro**, Casilla 18-01-574, Ambato, Ecuador. Phone: +593 (3) 822-240 or +593 (3) 841-126. Fax: +593 (3) 829 824. Contact: Luis Alberto Gamboa Tello, Director Gerente; or Lic. María Elena de López. Free stickers. Return postage appreciated. Replies to correspondence in Spanish.

**Radiodifusora Cultural Católica La Voz del Upano**—*see* La Voz del Upano, above.

**Radiodifusora Cultural, La Voz del Napo**—*see* La Voz del Napo, above.

**Radio El Buen Pastor,** Asociación Cristiana de Indígenas Saraguros (ACIS), Reino de Quito y Azuay, Correo Central, Saraguro, Loja, Ecuador. Phone: +593 (2) 00-146. Contact: (general) Dean Pablo Davis, Sub-director; Segundo Poma, Director; Mark Vogan, OMS Missionary; Mike Schrode, OMS Ecuador Field Director; Juana Guamán, Secretaria; or Zoila Vacacela, Secretaria; (technical) Miguel Kelly. $2 or return postage in the form of mint Ecuadorian stamps required, as IRCs are difficult to exchange in Ecuador. Station is keen to receive reception reports; may respond to English, but correspondence in Spanish preferred. $10 required for QSL card and pennant.

**Radio Federación Shuar (Shuara Tuntuiri)**, Casilla 17-01-1422, Quito, Ecuador. Phone/fax: +593 (2) 504-264. Contact: Manuel Jesús Vinza Chacucuy, Director; Yurank Tsapak Rubén Gerardo, Director; or Prof. Albino M. Utitiaj P., Director de Medios. Return postage or $2 required. Replies irregularly to correspondence in Spanish.

**Radio Interoceánica**, Santa Rosa de Quijos, Cantón El Chaco, Provincia de Napo, Ecuador. Email: interoceanic@hotmail.com; (Riera) edwinriera@hotmail.com. Contact: Edwin Riera, Director; Byron Medina, Gerente; or Ing. Olaf Hegmuir. $2 or return postage required, and donations appreciated (station owned by Swedish Covenant Church). Replies slowly to correspondence in Spanish, English or Swedish.

**Radio Jesús del Gran Poder**—*see* Emisoras Jesús del Gran Poder, above.

**Radio La Voz del Río Tarqui**—*see* La Voz del Rio Tarqui.

**Radio Luz y Vida**—*see* Emisoras Luz y Vida, above.

**🖳Radio María**

*GUAYAQUIL OFFICE:* P. Icaza 437 y G. Córdova, Guayaquil, Ecuador. Phone: +593 (4) 568-172. Fax: +593 (4) 568 176. Email: radiomaria@radiomariaecuador.org. Web: (includes RealAudio) www.radiomariaecuador.org.

*QUITO OFFICE:* Baquerizo Moreno 281 y Leonidas Plaza, Quito, Ecuador. Phone: +593 (2) 564-714, +593 (2) 564-719 or +593 (2) 558-702. Fax: +593 (2) 237 630. Email: radmaria@andinanet.net. A Catholic radio network currently leasing airtime over La Voz del Napo (*see*), but which is looking into the possiblity of setting up its own shortwave station.

**Radio Nacional Espejo** (when operating), Casilla 17-01-352, Quito, Ecuador. Phone: +593 (2) 21-366. Email: (Marco Caicedo) mcaicedo@hoy.net. Contact: Marco Caicedo, Gerente; Steve Caicedo; or Mercedes B. de Caicedo, Secretaria. Replies irregularly to correspondence in English and Spanish.

**Radio Nacional Progreso**, Casilla V, Loja, Ecuador. Contact: José A. Guamán Guajala, Director del programa "Círculo Dominical." Replies irregularly to correspondence in Spanish, particularly for feedback on "Círculo Dominical" program aired Sundays from 1100 to 1300. Return postage required.

**Radio Oriental**, Casilla 260, Tena, Napo, Ecuador. Phone: +593 (6) 886-033 or +593 (6) 886-388. Contact: Luis Enrique Espín Espinosa, Gerente General. $2 or return postage helpful. Reception reports welcome.

**Radio Quito**, Casilla 17-21-1971, Quito, Ecuador. Phone/fax: +593 (2) 508-301. Email: radioquito@elcomercio.com. Contact: Xavier Almeida, Gerente General; or José Almeida, Subgerente. Free stickers. Return postage normally required, but occasionally verifies email reports. Replies slowly, but regularly.

**Sistema de Emisoras Progreso**—*see* Radio Nacional Progreso, above.

# EGYPT  World Time +2 (+3 midyear)

*WARNING: MAIL THEFT.* Feedback from PASSPORT readership indicates that money is sometimes stolen from envelopes sent to Radio Cairo.

**Egyptian Radio**, P.O. Box 1186, 11511 Cairo, Egypt. Email: ertu@ertu.gov.eg. Web: www.ertu.gov.eg. For additional details, *see* Radio Cairo, below.

**Radio Cairo**

*NONTECHNICAL:* P.O. Box 566, Cairo 11511, Egypt. Phone: +20 (2) 677-8945. Fax: +20 (2) 575 9553. Contact: Mrs. Amal Badr, Head of English Programme; Mrs. Sahar Kalil, Director of English Service to North America and Producer, "Questions and Answers"; or Mrs. Magda Hamman, Secretary. Free stickers,

postcards, stamps, maps, papyrus souvenirs, calendars and *External Services of Radio Cairo* book. Free booklet and individually tutored Arabic-language lessons with loaned textbooks from Kamila Abdullah, Director General, Arabic by Radio, Radio Cairo, P.O. Box 325, Cairo, Egypt. Arabic-language religious, cultural and language-learning audio and video tapes from the Egyptian Radio and Television Union sold via Sono Cairo Audio-Video, P.O. Box 2017, Cairo, Egypt; when ordering video tapes, inquire to ensure they function on the television standard (NTSC, PAL or SECAM) in your country. Once replied regularly, if slowly, but recently replies have been increasingly scarce. Comments welcomed about audio quality—*see TECHNICAL*, below. Avoid enclosing money (*see WARNING*, above).
TECHNICAL: Broadcast Engineering Department, 24th Floor—TV Building (Maspiro), Egyptian Radio and Television Union, P.O. Box 1186, 11511 Cairo, Egypt. Phone/fax: +20 (2) 574-6840. Email: (general) rtu@idsc.gov.eg; (Lawrence) niveenl@hotmail.com; (Eldine) gihanessam@hotmail.com; (Gamich) ismailgamich@yahoo.com. Contact: Ismail Mahmoud Gamich, Head of Frequency Management; Hamdy Emara, Director of Monitoring & Frequency Management; Mrs. Hoda Helmy; Gihan Essam Eldine; Mrs. Rokaya M. Kamel; or Ms. Niveen W. Lawrence, Director of Shortwave Department. Comments and suggestions on audio quality and level especially welcomed. One PASSPORT reader reported that his letter to this address was returned by the Egyptian postal authorities, but we have not received any other reports of returned mail.

## ENGLAND—*see* UNITED KINGDOM.

## EQUATORIAL GUINEA    World Time +1

**Radio Africa**
TRANSMISSION OFFICE: Apartado 851, Malabo, Isla Bioko, Equatorial Guinea.
U.S. OFFICE FOR CORRESPONDENCE AND VERIFICATIONS: Pan American Broadcasting, 20410 Town Center Lane #200, Cupertino CA 95014 USA. Phone: +1 (408) 996-2033; (toll-free, U.S. only) 1-800-726-2620. Fax: +1 (408) 252 6855. Email: pabcomain@aol.com. Web: www.radiopanam.com. Contact: (listener correspondence) Terry Kraemer; (general) Carmen Jung, Office and Sales Administrator; or James Manero. $1 in cash or unused U.S. stamps, or 2 IRCs, required for reply.
**Radio East Africa**—same details as "Radio Africa," above.
**Radio Nacional de Guinea Ecuatorial—Bata** ("Radio Bata"), Apartado 749, Bata, Río Muni, Equatorial Guinea. Phone: +240 (8) 2592. Fax: +240 (8) 2093. Contact: José Mba Obama, Director. If no response try sending your letter c/o Spanish Embassy, Bata, enclosing $1 for return postage. Spanish preferred.
**Radio Nacional de Guinea Ecuatorial—Malabo** ("Radio Malabo"), Apartado 195, Malabo, Isla Bioko, Equatorial Guinea. Phone: +240 (9) 2260. Fax: (general) +240 (9) 2097; (technical) +240 (9) 3122. Contact: (general) Román Manuel Mané-Abaga, Jefe de Programación; Ciprano Somon Suakin; or Manuel Sobede, Inspector de Servicios de Radio y TV; (technical) Hermenegildo Moliko Chele, Jefe Servicios Técnicos de Radio y Televisión. $1 or return postage required. Replies irregularly to correspondence in Spanish.

## ERITREA    World Time +3

**Radio UNMEE**—*see* United Nations.
📻**Voice of the Broad Masses of Eritrea** (Dimtsi Hafash), Ministry of Information, Radio Division, P.O. Box 872, Asmara,

**Handbook for Radio Marina, the former American facility at Asmara, Eritrea.**

Eritrea; or Ministry of Information, Technical Branch, P.O. Box 243, Asmara, Eritrea. Phone: +291 (1) 116-084 or +291 (1) 120-497. Fax: +291 (1) 126 747. Email: nesredin1@dehai.org. Web: (including RealAudio) www.dehai.org/dhe/dhe.htm. Contact: Ghebreab Ghebremedhin; or Mehreteab Tesfagiorgis, Technical Director, Engineering Division. Return postage or $1 helpful. Free information on history of the station and about Eritrea.

## ETHIOPIA    World Time +3

**Radio Ethiopia**: (external service) P.O. Box 654; (domestic service) P.O. Box 1020—both in Addis Ababa, Ethiopia (address your correspondence to "Audience Relations"). Phone: (main office) +251 (1) 116-427 or +251 (1) 551-011; (engineering) +251 (1) 200-948. Fax: +251 (1) 552 263. Web: www.angelfire.com/biz/radioethiopia. Contact: (external service, general) Kahsai Tewoldemedhin, Program Director; Ms. Woinshet Woldeyes, Secretary, Audience Relations; Ms. Ellene Mocria, Head of Audience Relations; or Yohaness Ruphael, Producer, "Contact"; (administration) Kasa Miliko, Head of Station; (technical) Terefe Ghebre Medhin or Zegeye Solomon. Free stickers and tourist brochures. Poor replier.
**Radio Fana** (Radio Torch), P.O. Box 30702, Addis Ababa, Ethiopia. Phone: +251 (1) 516-777. Email: radio-fana@telecom.net.et. Contact: Woldu Yemessel, General Manager; Mesfin Alemayehu, Head, External Relations; or Girma Lema, Head, Planning and Research Department. Station is autonomous and receives its income from non-governmental educational sponsorship. Seeks

help with obtaining vehicles, recording equipment and training materials.

**Voice of the Tigray Revolution**, P.O. Box 450, Mek'ele, Tigray, Ethiopia. Contact: Fre Tesfamichael, Director. $1 helpful.

## FINLAND   World Time +2 (+3 midyear)

### ☞YLE Radio Finland

*MAIN OFFICE:* Box 78, FIN-00024 Yleisradio, Finland. Phone: (general, 24-hour English speaking switchboard for both Radio Finland and Yleisradio Oy) +358 (9) 14801; (international information) +358 (9) 1480-3729; (administration) +358 (9) 1480-4320 or +358 (9) 1480-4316; (Technical Customer Service) +358 (9) 1480-3213; (comments on programs) +358 (9) 1480-5490. Fax: (general) +358 (9) 148 1169; (international information) +358 (9) 1480 3391; (Technical Affairs) +358 (9) 1480 3588. Email: (general) rfinland@yle.fi, or rfinland@aol.com; (comments on programs) christina.rockstroh@yle.fi; (English section) radio.world@yle.fi; (German & French section) radio.mondo@yle.fi; (Yleisradio Oy parent organization) fbc@yle.fi; (reception reports) raimoe.makela@yle.fi. To contact individuals, the format is firstname.lastname@yle.fi; so to reach, say, Pertti Seppä, it would be pertti.seppa@yle.fi. Web: (includes RealAudio) www.yle.fi/rfinland/; (stored news audio in Finnish, Swedish, English, German, French and Russian) www.wrn.org/ondemand/finland.html; (online reception report form) www.yle.fi/sataradio/receptionreport.html. Contact—Radio Finland: (English) Eddy Hawkins; (Finnish and Swedish) Pertti Seppä; (German and French) Dr. Stefan Tschirpke; (Russian) Timo Uotila and Mrs. Eija Laitinen; (administration) Juhani Niinistö, Head of International Radio; (comments on programs) Mrs. Christina Rockstroh, Managing Editor, foreign language radio. Contact—Yleisradio Oy parent organization: (general) Marja Salusjärvi, Head of International PR; (administration) Arne Wessberg, Managing Director; or Tapio Siikala, Director for Domestic and International Radio. Sometimes provides free stickers and small souvenirs, as well as tourist and other magazines. For a free color catalog of souvenirs, clothes, toys, timepieces, binoculars, CDs, tapes and other merchandise, contact the YLE Shop, Yleisradio, Pl 77, FIN-00003 Helsinki, Finland. Phone: +358 (9) 1480-3555. Fax: +358 (9) 1480 3466 or go to www.yle.fi/yleshop. Replies to correspondence. For verification of reception reports, *see* Transmission Facility, below. YLE Radio Finland external broadcasting is a part of YLE and not a separate administrative unit. Radio Finland itself is not a legal entity. *NUNTII LATINI (Program in Latin):* P.O. Box 99, FIN-00024 Yleisradio, Finland. Fax: +358 (9) 1480 3391. Email: nuntii.latini@yle.fi. Web: www.yle.fi/fbc/nuntii.html. Six years of Nuntii Latini now available in books I to III at US$30 each from: Bookstore Tiedekirja, Kirkkokatu 14, FIN-00170 Helsinki, Finland; fax: +358 (9) 635 017. VISA/MC/EURO.
*NETWORK PLANNING:* Digita, Wireless Networks, P.O. Box 135, FIN-00521 Helsinki, Finland. Phone: (Huuhka) +358 (20) 411-7287; (Hautala) +358 (20) 411-7282. Fax: +358 (9) 148 5260. Email: esko.huuhka@digita.fi or kari.hautala@digita.fi. Contact: Esko Huuhka, Head of Network Planning; or Kari Hautala, Monitoring Engineer.
*TRANSMISSION FACILITY:* Digita Shortwave Centre, Makholmantie 79, FIN-28660 Pori; or (verifications) Pori SW Base, Preiviikki, FIN-28660 Pori, Finland—Attention: Raimo Mäkelä. (Email: raimoe.makela@yle.fi). Web: (Digita Oy) www.digita.fi; www.yle.fi/sataradio/preiviiki.html. Contact: Kalevi Vahtera, Station Manager; or Raimo Mäkelä (QSL-verifications). Issues full-data verification cards for good recep-

tion reports, and provides free illustrated booklets about the transmitting station.
*NORTH AMERICAN OFFICE—LISTENER and MEDIA LIAISON:* P.O. Box 462, Windsor CT 06095 USA. Phone: +1 (860) 688-5540 or +1 (860) 688-5098. Phone/fax: (24-hour toll-free within U.S. and Canada for recorded schedule and voice mail) 1-800-221-9539. Fax: +1 (860) 688 0113. Email: yleus@aol.com. Contact: John Berky, YLE Finland Transcriptions. Free *YLE North America* newsletter. This office does not verify reception reports.
**Scandinavian Weekend Radio**, P.O. Box 35, FIN-40321, Jyväskylä, Finland. Phone: (when on air) +358 (400) 995-559. Fax: (when on air) +358 (3) 475 5776. Email: (general) info@swradio.net; (technical) esa.saunamaki@swradio.net; (reception reports) online report form at the station's Website. Web: www.swradio.net. Two IRCs, $2 or 2 euros required for verification card.

## FRANCE   World Time +1 (+2 midyear)

### ☞Radio France Internationale (RFI)

*MAIN OFFICE:* B.P. 9516, F-75016 Paris Cedex 16, France; (street address) 116, avenue du président Kennedy, F-75016 Paris, France. Phone: (general) +33 (1) 56-40-12-12; (International Affairs and Program Placement) +33 (1) 44-30-89-32 or +33 (1) 44-30-89-49; (Service de la communication) +33 (1) 42-30-29-51; (Audience Relations) +33 (1) 44-30-89-69/70/71; (Media Relations) +33 (1) 42-30-29-85; (Développement et de la communication) +33 (1) 44-30-89-21; *(Fréquence Monde)* +33 (1) 42-30-10-86; (English Service) +33 (1) 56-40-30-62; (Spanish Department) +33 (1) 42-30-30-48. Fax: (general) +33 (1) 56 40 47 59; (International Affairs and Program Placement) +33 (1) 44 30 89 20; (Audience Relations) +33 (1) 44 30 89 99; (other nontechnical) +33 (1) 42 30 44 81; (English Service) +33 (1) 56 40 26 74; (Spanish Department) +33 (1) 42 30 46 69. Email: (Audience Relations) courrier.auditeurs@rfi.fr; (English Service) english.service@rfi.fr, english.features@rfi.fr. Web: (includes RealAudio) www.rfi.fr. Contact: John Maguire, Editor, English Language Service; J.P. Charbonnier, Producer, "Lettres des Auditeurs"; Joël Amar, International Affairs/Program Placement Department; Arnaud Littardi, Directeur du développement et de la communication; Nicolas Levkov, Rédactions en Langues Etrangères; Daniel Franco, Rédaction en français; Mme. Anne Toulouse, Rédacteur en chef du Service Mondiale en français; Christine Berbudeau, Rédacteur en chef, *Fréquence* **Monde**; or Marc Verney, Attaché de Presse; (administration) Jean-Paul Cluzel, Président-Directeur Général; (technical) M. Raymond Pincon, Producer, "Le Courrier Technique." Free *Fréquence* **Monde** bi-monthly magazine in French upon request. Free souvenir keychains, pins, lighters, pencils, T-shirts and stickers have been received by some—especially when visiting the headquarters at 116 avenue du Président Kennedy, in the 16th Arrondissement. Can provide supplementary materials for "Dites-moi tout" French-language course; write to the attention of Mme. Chantal de Grandpre, "Dites-moi tout." "Le Club des Auditeurs" French-language listener's club ("Club 9516" for English-language listeners); applicants must provide name, address and two passport-type photos, whereupon they will receive a membership card and the club bulletin. RFI exists primarily to defend and promote Francophone culture, but also provides meaningful information and cultural perspectives in non-French languages.
*TRANSMISSION OFFICE, TECHNICAL:* TéléDiffusion de France, Direction de la Production et des Méthodes, Shortwave service, 10 rue d'Oradour sur Glane, 75732 Paris Cedex 15, France.

Phone: (Bochent) +33 (1) 5595-1369; or (Meunier) +33 (1) 5595-1161. Fax: +33 (1) 5595 2137. Email: (Bochent) danielbochent@compuserve.com; (Meunier) a_meunier@compuserve.com. Contact: Daniel Bochent, Head of shortwave service; Alain Meunier, Michel Penneroux, Business Development Manager AM-HF; Mme Annick Daronian or Mme Sylvie Greuillet (short wave service). This office is for informing about transmitter-related problems (interference, modulation quality), and also for reception reports and verifications.

UNITED STATES PROMOTIONAL, SCHOOL LIAISON, PROGRAM PLACEMENT AND CULTURAL EXCHANGE OFFICES:

*NEW ORLEANS:* Services Culturels, Suite 2105, Ambassade de France, 300 Poydras Street, New Orleans LA 70130 USA. Phone: +1 (504) 523-5394. Phone/fax: +1 (504) 529-7502. Contact: Adam-Anthony Steg, Attaché Audiovisuel. This office promotes RFI, especially to language teachers and others in the educational community within the southern United States, and arranges for bi-national cultural exchanges. It also sets up RFI feeds to local radio stations within the southern United States.

*NEW YORK:* Audiovisual Bureau, Radio France Internationale, 972 Fifth Avenue, New York NY 10021 USA. Phone: +1 (212) 439-1452. Fax: +1 (212) 439 1455. Contact: Gérard Blondel or Julien Vin. This office promotes RFI, especially to language teachers and others within the educational community outside the southern United States, and arranges for bi-national cultural exchanges. It also sets up RFI feeds to local radio stations within much of the United States.

*NEW YORK NEWS BUREAU:* 1290 Avenue of the Americas, New York NY 10019 USA. Phone: +1 (212) 581-1771. Fax: +1 (212) 541 4309. Contact: Ms. Auberi Edler, Reporter; or Bruno Albin, Reporter.

*WASHINGTON NEWS BUREAU:* 529 14th Street NW, Suite 1126, Washington DC 20045 USA. Phone: +1 (202) 879-6706. Contact: Pierre J. Cayrol.

*SAN FRANCISCO OFFICE, SCHEDULES:* 2654 17th Avenue, San Francisco CA 94116 USA. Phone: +1 (415) 564-9968. Email: GPoppin@aol.com. Contact: George Poppin. This address, a volunteer office, only provides RFI schedules to listeners. All other correspondence should be sent directly to the main office in Paris.

**◘Radio Monte Carlo-Middle East**

*MAIN OFFICE:* Radio Monte Carlo-Moyen Orient, 116 avenue du président Kennedy, F-75116 Paris, France; or B.P. 371, Paris 16, France. Email: contact@rmc-mo.com. Web: (includes RealAudio) www.rmc-mo.com. A station of the RFI group whose programs are produced in Paris and aired via a mediumwave AM transmitter in Cyprus; also via FM in France and parts of the Middle East. Some Arabic programs are also broadcast on shortwave to North America via Radio Canada International's Sackville facilitities, and to North Africa as part of the RFI Arabic broadcasts.

*CYPRUS ADDRESS:* P.O. Box 2026, Nicosia, Cyprus. Contact: M. Pavlides, Chef de Station. Reception reports have sometimes been verified via this address.

**Voice of Orthodoxy**—*see* Voix de l'Orthodoxie, below.

**Voix de l'Orthodoxie**, B.P. 416-08, F-75366 Paris Cedex 08, France. Email: irinavo@wanadoo.fr. Contact: Michel Solovieff, General Secretary. An organization that has long broadcast religious programming to Russia via shortwave transmitters in various countries, most recently via Deutsche Telekom (Germany) and Kazakstan. Verifies reception reports, including those written in English.

*RUSSIAN OFFICE:* Nab. Leitenanta Shmidta 39, St. Petersburg 199034, Russia.

# FRENCH GUIANA   World Time −3

**Radio France Internationale/Swiss Radio International—Guyane Relay Station**, TDF, Montsinéry, French Guiana. Contact: (technical) Chef des Services Techniques, RFI Guyane. All correspondence concerning non-technical matters should be sent directly to the main addresses (*see*) for Radio France Internationale in France and Swiss Radio International in Berne. Can consider replies only to technical correspondence in French.

**◘RFO Guyane**, 43 bis, rue du Docteur-Gabriel-Devèze, B.P. 7013 - Cayenne Cedex, French Guiana. Phone: +595 299-900 or +594 299-907. Fax: +594 299 958. Web: (text plus news summaries in Quick-Time audio) www.rfo.fr/guyane/guyane.htm; (streaming in RealAudio, Windows Media and Quick-Time) www.rfo.fr/emissions/emis_s_radio.htm. Contact: (administration) George Chow-Toun, Directeur Régional; (editorial) Claude Joly, Rédacteur en Chef; (technical) Charles Diony, Directeur Technique. Free stickers. Replies occasionally and sometimes slowly; correspondence in French preferred, but English often okay.

# GABON   World Time +1

**Afrique Numéro Un**, B.P. 1, Libreville, Gabon. Fax: +241 742 133. Email: africagc@club-internet.fr. Web: www.africa1.com. Contact: (general) Gaston Didace Singangoye; or A. Letamba, Le Directeur des Programmes; (technical) Mme. Marguerite Bayimbi, Le Directeur [sic] Technique. Free calendars and bumper stickers. $1, 2 IRCs or return postage helpful. Replies very slowly.

**RTV Gabonaise**, B.P. 10150, Libreville, Gabon. Contact: André Ranaud-Renombo, Le Directeur Technique, Adjoint Radio. Free stickers. $1 required. Replies occasionally, but slowly, to correspondence in French.

# GEORGIA   World Time +4 (+5 midyear)

**◘Georgian Radio**, TV-Radio Tbilisi, ul. M. Kostava 68, Tbilisi 380071, Republic of Georgia. Phone: (domestic service) +995 (32) 368-362; (external service) +995 (32) 360-063. Fax: +995 (32) 955 137. Email: office@geotvr.ge. Web: (includes MP3) www.geotvr.ge. Contact: (external service) Helena Apkhadze, Foreign Editor; Tamar Shengelia; Mrs. Natia Datuaschwili, Secretary; or Maya Chihradze; (domestic service) Lia Uumlaelsa, Manager; or V. Khundadze, Acting Director of Television and Radio Department. Replies erratically and slowly, in part due to financial restrictions. Return postage or $1 helpful.

**Radio Hara**, Rustaveli Ave. 52, II Floor, Apt. 211-212, Tbilisi, Georgia. Email: league@geoconst.org.ge. Contact: Nino Berdznishvili, Program Manager; or Zourab Shengelia. Programs are produced by the Georgian-Abkhazian Relations Institute.

**Republic of Abkhazia Radio**, Abkhaz State Radio and TV Co., Aidgylara Street 34, Sukhum 384900, Republic of Abkhazia; or Zvanba Street 8, Sukhum 384900, Republic of Abkhazia. However, given the problems in getting mail to Abkhazia, the station requests that reception reports be sent to the following address: National Library of Abkhazia, Krasnodar District, P.O. Box 964, 354000 Sochi, Russia. Phone: +995 (881) 24-867 or +995 (881) 25-321. Fax: +995 (881) 21 144. Contact: Zurab Argun, Director. A 1992 uprising in northwestern Georgia drove the majority of ethnic Georgians from the region. This area remains virtually autonomous from Georgia.

**Transmission facilities are often fed programs via satellite. These IBB antennas at Lampertheim, Germany are for satellite reception and, rear, world band transmission of the VOA and others.**    A. Mujunen

# GERMANY    World Time +1 (+2 midyear)

**📻Adventist World Radio**

*AWR GERMAN LANGUAGE OFFICE:* Stimme der Hoffnung, Am Elfengrund 66, D-64297 Darmstadt, Germany. Phone: (listener services) +49 (6151) 9544-0; (technical) +49 (6151) 954-465. Fax: (listener services) +61 (6151) 954 470; (technical) +61 (6151) 539 3365. Email: (listener services) service@stimme-der-hoffnung.de; (technical) dxer@stimme-der-hoffnung.de. Web: (includes RealAudio) www.stimme-der-hoffnung.de/rs. Contact: (technical) Lothar Klepp. Note that only German should be used to contact this office; all listener mail in English should be sent to: Adventist World Radio, 39 Brendon Street, London W1H 5HD, United Kingdom. *See* other AWR listings under Guam, Guatemala, Kenya, Madagascar, United Kingdom and USA.

*AWR EUROPE FREQUENCY MANAGEMENT OFFICE:* Postfach 100252, D-64202 Darmstadt, Germany. Phone: +49 (6151) 953-151. Fax: +61 (6151) 953 152. Email: (Dedio) 102555.257@compuserve.com; or dedio@awr.org. Contact: Claudius Dedio, Frequency Coordinator.

**📻Bayerischer Rundfunk**, Rundfunkplatz 1, D-80300 München, Germany. Phone: +49 (89) 5900-01. Fax: +49 (89) 5900 2375. Email: (general) info@br-online.de; (technical) techinfo@brnet.de. Web: (includes RealAudio) www.br-online.de. Contact: Dr. Gualtiero Guidi; or Jutta Paue, Engineering Adviser. Free stickers and 250-page program schedule book.

**Christliche Wissenschaft** (Christian Science), Radiosendungen, E. Bethmann, P.O. Box 7330, D-22832

Norderstedt, Germany; or CS-Radiosendungen, Alexanderplatz 2, D-20099 Hamburg, Germany. Contact: Erich Bethmann. A program aired intermittently via the Jülich facilities of Deutsche Telekom (*see*).

**Deutsche Telekom**—*see* "Shortwave Radio Station Jülich—Deutsche Telekom AG."

**📻Deutsche Welle, Radio and TV International**

*MAIN OFFICE:* Raderbergguertel 50, D-50968 Cologne, Germany. Phone: (English Service, general) +49 (221) 389-4144; (listeners' mail) +49 (221) 389-2500; (Program Distribution) +49 (221) 389-2781; (technical) +49 (221) 389-3221 or +49 (221) 389-3208; (Technical Advisory Service) +49 (221) 389-3208; (Frequency Manager, Peter Pischalka) +49 (221) 389-3228; (Public Relations) +49 (221) 2041. Fax: (English Service) +49 (221) 389 4155, (listeners' mail) +49 (221) 389 2510; (English Service, Current Affairs) +49 (221) 389 4554; (Public Relations) +49 (221) 389 2047; (Program Distribution) +49 (221) 389 2784; (Technical Advisory Service) +49 (221) 389 3220. Email: (general) online@dw-world.de; (Technical Advisory Service) tb@dw-world.de; (specific individuals) format is normally firstname.lastname@dw-world.de, so to reach, say, Peter Senger, it would be peter.senger@dw-world.de; (Program Distribution) 100302.2003@compuserve.com; (technical) (Pischalka) 100565.1010@compuserve.com; (Schall) nschall@dw-world.de; (Scholz) 100536.2173@compuserve.com. Web: (general, including RealAudio) www.dw-world.de. Contact: (general) Ursula Fleck-Jerwin, Audience Mail Department; Dr. Ralf Siepmann, Director of Public Relations; Dr. Burkhard Nowotny, Director of Media Department; Harald Schuetz; or ("German by Radio" language course) Herrad Meese; (English Service) Margot Forbes; (administration) Erik Bettermann, Director General; (Marketing, Distribution & Technology) Peter Senger; (Programme Distribution) Heinz-G. Pianka; (technical—Radio Frequency Department) Werner Theis, Frequency Manager; (technical—Transmission Management/Technical Advisory Service) Mrs. Silke Bröker; Norbert Schall; Horst Scholz, Head of Transmission Management; Jürgen Hortenbach; Mrs. Franziska Sacher; or B. Klaumann, Transmission Management. Free pennants, stickers, key chains, pens, *Deutsch—warum nicht?* language-course book, *Germany—A European Country and its People* book. Free 40 page booklet *"Radio Worlds/Worlds of Radios"* featuring radio related articles and stories from different countries. Available from PR and Marketing. Also free DW pocket guide and booklets on shortwave reception, receivers and antennas. Local Deutsche Welle Listeners' Clubs in selected countries. Operates via shortwave transmitters in Germany, Antigua, Canada, Madagascar, Portugal, Russia, Rwanda and Sri Lanka. Deutsche Welle is scheduled to move from Cologne to Bonn in the near future.

*ELECTRONIC TRANSMISSION OFFICE FOR PROGRAM PREVIEWS:* Infomedia, 25 rue du Lac, L-8808 Arsdorf, Luxembourg. Phone: +352 649-270. Fax: +352 649 271. This office will electronically transmit Deutsche Welle program previews to you upon request; be sure to provide either a dedicated fax number or an email address so they can reply to you.

*BRUSSELS NEWS BUREAU:* International Press Center, 1 Boulevard Charlemagne, B-1040 Brussels, Belgium.

*U.S./CANADIAN LISTENER CONTACT OFFICE:* 2800 South Shirlington Road, Suite 901, Arlington VA 22206-3601 USA. Phone: +1 (703) 931-6644.

*RUSSIAN LISTENER CONTACT OFFICE:* Nemezkaja Wolna, Abonentnyj jaschtschik 596, Glawpotschtamt, 190000 St. Petersburg, Russia.

*WASHINGTON NEWS BUREAU:* P.O. Box 14163, Washington DC

20004 USA. Fax: +1 (202) 526 2255. Contact: Adnan Al-Katib, Correspondent.

**Deutschlandfunk**, Raderberggürtel 40, D-50968 Köln, Germany. Phone: +49 (221) 345-0. Fax: +49 (221) 345 4802. Email: (program information) deutschlandfunk@dradio.de. Web: www.dradio.de/dlf/themen.

**DeutschlandRadio-Berlin**, Hans-Rosenthal-Platz, D-10825 Berlin Schönberg, Germany. Phone: +49 (30) 8503-0. Fax: +49 (30) 8503 6168. Email: dlrb@dlf.de; online@dlf.de; (program information) deutschlandradioberlin@dradio.de. Web: www.dradio.de/dlrb/index.html. Contact: Dr. Karl-Heinz Stamm; or Ulrich Reuter. Correspondence in English accepted. Sometimes sends stickers, pens, magazines and other souvenirs.

**Eurosonor Radio**, Waldstrasse 30, D-63065 Offenbach, Germany. Phone: +49 (721) 151-314. Fax: +49 (721) 151 188. Email: radio@eurosonor.de or corcovado@eurosonor.de. Web: (includes online reception report form) www.eurosonor.de/radio. Contact: (general) Christian Schmid; (Listener Services) Christa Schmid. Replies to correspondence in German and English.

**Evangeliums-Rundfunk**—*see* Monaco (Trans World Radio).

**Evangeliums-Radio-Hamburg**, Postfach 920741, D-21137 Hamburg, Germany. Phone: +49 (40) 702-7025. Fax: +49 (40) 8540 8861. Email: evangeliums-radio-hamburg@t-online.de. Web: www.evr-hamburg.de. Verifies reports in German, and possibly English. Airs via Deutsche Telekom's Jülich facilities, and locally on FM and cable.

**Lutherische Stunde**, Postfach 1162, D-27363 Sottrum, Germany; or (street address) Clüversborstel 14, D-27367 Sottrum, Germany. Phone: +49 (4264) 2436. Fax: +49 (4264) 2437. Email: info@lutherischestunde.de. Web: www.lutherischestunde.de. Religious broadcast currently aired via Voice of Russia, but has used other world band facilities in the past. Verifies reception reports in German, and may also reply to correspondence in English.

**Missionswerk Werner Heukelbach**, D-51702 Bergneustadt 2, Germany. Contact: Manfred Paul or Peter Bronclik. Religious broadcast heard via the Voice of Russia and sometimes over Deutsche Telekom's Jülich facilities. Replies to correspondence in English and German.

**Mitteldeutscher Rundfunk**, Kantstrasse 71-73, Leipzig, Germany. Phone: +49 (341) 300-0. Fax: +49 (341) 300 5544. Email: (technical) techhot@mdr.de; for nontechnical correspondence, use the online email form at the station's Website. Web: (includes RealAudio) www.mdr.de. Free stickers, lapel pins, booklets and pamphlets. Relayed on shortwave during night hours via the transmitter of Bayerischer Rundfunk. Replies to correspondence in English and German; return postage not required.

**Shortwave Radio Station Jülich—Deutsche Telekom AG**
*JÜLICH ADDRESS:* Rundfunksendestelle Jülich, Merscher Höhe D-52428 Jülich, Germany. Phone: +49 (2461) 697-310; (Technical Engineer) +49 (2461) 697-330; (Technical Advisor and Sales Management) +49 (2461) 697-340. Fax: (all offices) +49 (2461) 697 372. Email: (Hirte) guenter.hirte@telekom.de; (Goslawski) roman.goslawski@telekom.de; (Brodowsky) walter.brodowsky@telekom.de; (Weyl) ralf.weyl@telekom.de. Contact: Günter Hirte, Head of Shortwave Radio Station Jülich; Roman Goslawski, Technical Engineer; Horst Tobias, Frequency Manager; (technical) Walter Brodowsky, Technical Advisor; or (nontechnical) Ralf Weyl, Sales Management. Reception reports accepted by mail or fax, and should be clearly marked to the attention of Walter Brodowsky.
*KÖLN ADDRESS:* Niederlassung 2 Köln, Service Centre Rundfunk, D-50482 Köln Germany. Phone: (Kraus) +49 (221) 575-4000; (Hufschlag) +49 (221) 575-4011. Fax: +49 (221) 575 4090. Email: info@dtag.de. Web: www.dtag.de; www.telekom.de. Contact: Egon Kraus, Head of Broadcasting Service Centre; or Josef Hufschlag, Customer Advisor for High Frequency Broadcasting. This organization operates transmitters on German soil used by Deutsche Welle, as well as those leased to various non-German world band stations.

**Radio Santec**, Marienstrasse 1, D-97070 Würzburg, Germany. Phone: (0800-1600 Central European Time, Monday through Friday) +49 (931) 3903-264. Fax: +49 (931) 3903 195. Email: info@radio-santec.com. Web: (includes RealAudio) www.radio-santec.com. Reception reports verified with QSL cards only if requested. Radio Santec, constituted as a separate legal entity in 1999, is the radio branch of Universelles Leben (*see*, below).

**Südwestrundfunk**, Neckarstrasse 230, D-70190 Stuttgart, Germany. Phone +49 (711) 929-0. Fax: +49 (711) 929 2600. Email: (general) info@swr-online.de; (technical) technik@swr-online.de. Web: (includes RealAudio) www.swr-online.de. Sometimes sends stickers and postcards. Return postage not required.

*SWR BADEN-BADEN:* Hans-Bredow-Strasse, D-76530 Baden-Baden, Germany. Phone: +49 (7221) 929-0.
This station is the result of a merger between Süddeutscher Rundfunk and Südwestfunk. Based in Stuttgart, transmissions under the new banner commenced in September 1998.

**Universelles Leben** (Universal Life)
*HEADQUARTERS:* Postfach 5643, D-97006 Würzburg, Germany. Phone: +49 (931) 3903-0. Fax: (general) +49 (931) 3903 233. Email: info@universelles-leben.org. Web: (includes RealAudio) www.universelles-leben.org. Contact: Janet Wood, English Dept; "Living in the Spirit of God" listeners' letters program; or Johanna Limley. Free stickers, publications and occasional small souvenirs. Produces "The Word, The Cosmic Wave" (Das Wort, die kosmische Welle) transmitted via the Voice of Russia, Deutsche Telekom (Jülich, Germany) and various other world band stations. Replies to correspondence in English, German or Spanish. Also, *see* Radio Santec, above.
*SALES OFFICE:* Das WORT GmbH, Im Universelles Leben, Max-Braun-Str. 2, D-97828 Marktheidenfeld/Altfeld, Germany. Phone: +49 (9391) 504-135. Fax: +49 (9391) 504 133. Email: info@das-wort.com. Web: www.das-wort.com. Sells books, audio cassettes and videos related to broadcast material.
*NORTH AMERICAN BUREAU:* Universal Life, The Inner Religion, P.O. Box 651, Guilford CT 06437 USA. Phone: +1 (203) 458-7771. Fax: +1 (203) 458 0713.

# GHANA   World Time exactly

*WARNING—CONFIDENCE ARTISTS:* Attempted correspondence with Radio Ghana may result in requests, perhaps resulting from mail theft, from skilled confidence artists for money, free electronic or other products, publications or immigration sponsorship. To help avoid this, correspondence to Radio Ghana should be sent via registered mail.

**Ghana Broadcasting Corporation**, Broadcasting House, P.O. Box 1633, Accra, Ghana. Phone: +233 (21) 221-161. Fax: +233 (21) 221 153 or +233 (21) 773 227. Web: www.gbc.com.gh. Contact: (general) Mrs. Maud Blankson-Mills, Director of Corporate Affairs; (administration) Cris Tackie, Acting Director of Radio; (technical) K.D. Frimpong, Director of Engineering; or E. Heneath, Propagation Department. Replies tend to be erratic, and reception reports are best sent to the attention of the Propagation Engineer, GBC Monitoring

Station. Enclosing an IRC, return postage or $1 and registering your letter should improve the chances of a reply.

# GREECE  World Time +2 (+3 midyear)

**📻Foni tis Helladas** (Voice of Greece)
*NONTECHNICAL:* Hellenic Radio-Television, ERA-5, The Voice of Greece, 432 Mesogion Av., 15342 Athens, Greece; or P.O. Box 60019, 15310 Aghia Paraskevi, Athens, Greece. Phone: +30 (1) 606-6298, +30 (1) 606-6308 or +30 (1) 606-6310. Fax: +30 (1) 606 6309. Email: fonel@hol.gr or era5@leon.nreps.ariadne-t.gr. Web: www.ert.gr/radio/era5. Contact: Angeliki Barka, Head of Programmes. Ioannis Koutzouradis, Managing Director; or Gina Vogiatzoglou, Progrmme Director. Free tourist literature.
*TECHNICAL:* Elliniki Radiophonia—ERA-5, General Technical Directorate, ERT/ERA Hellenic Radio Television SA, Mesogion 402, 15342 Athens, Greece. Phone: (Charalambopoulos) +30 (1) 606-6257; (Vorgias) +30 (1) 606-6256 or +30 (1) 606-6263. Fax: +30 (1) 606 6243. Email: (reception reports) era5@ert.gr; (Vorgias) svorgias@ert.gr; (Charalambopoulos) bcharalabopoulos@ert.gr. Contact: Charalambos Charalambopoulos or Sotiris Vorgias, Planning Engineer; (administration) Th. Kokossis, General Director; or Nicolas Yannakakis, Director. Technical reception reports may be sent via mail, fax or email. Taped reports not accepted.
**Radiophonikos Stathmos Makedonias—ERT-3**, Angelaki 2, 546 21 Thessaloniki, Greece. Phone: +30 (31) 244-979. Fax: +30 (31) 236 370. Email: charter3@compulink.gr. Contact: (general) Mrs. Tatiana Tsioli, Program Director; or Lefty Kongalides, Head of International Relations; (technical) Dimitrios Keramidas, Engineer. Free booklets and other small souvenirs.

# GREENLAND  World Time –3 (–2 midyear)

**Kalaallit Nunaata Radio** (Radio Greenland), P.O. Box 1007, DK-3900 Nuuk, Greenland. Phone: +299 325-333. Fax: +299 325 042. Web: www.knr.gl. Although off world band for many years, the station is reported to be considering replacing its mediumwave AM transmitters with a shortwave transmitter. Since all inhabited areas of the country are now covered by FM signals, it is believed that shortwave would be financially more viable than mediumwave to broadcast to the country's fishermen.

# GUAM  World Time +10

**Adventist World Radio—KSDA**
AWR-Asia, P.O. Box 8990, Agat, Guam 96928 USA. Phone: +1 (671) 565-2000. Fax: +1 (671) 565 2983. Email: english@awr.org. Web: www.awr.org. Contact: Elvin Vence, Chief Engineer. All listener mail should be sent to: Adventist World Radio, 39 Brendon Street, London W1H 5HD, United Kingdom. Also, *see* AWR listings under Germany, Guatemala, Kenya, Madagascar, United Kingdom and USA.
**Trans World Radio—KTWR**
*MAIN OFFICE, ENGINEERING INQUIRIES & FREQUENCY COORDINATION ONLY:* P.O. Box 8780, Agana, Gu 96928 USA. Phone: +1 (671) 828-8637. Fax: +1 (671) 828 8636. Email: cwhite@guam.twr.org or ktwrfreq@guam.twr.org. Web: (schedule) www.gospelcom.net/twr/broadcasts/guam.htm. Contact: (technical) Chuck White, Chief Engineer/Station Manager; or George Ross, Frequency Coordinator Manager. This office will also verify email reports with a QSL card. All English listener mail of a nontechnical nature should now be sent to the Aus-

tralian office (*see* next entry). Addresses for listener mail in other languages will be found in the broadcasts. Also, *see* USA.
*ENGLISH LISTENER MAIL, NONTECHNICAL:* Trans World Radio ANZ, 2-6 Albert Street, Blackburn, Victoria 3130, Australia; or P.O. Box 390, Box Hill, Victoria 3128, Australia. Phone: +61 (3) 9878-5922. Fax: +61 (3) 9878 5944. Email: info@twradio.org. Web: www.twradio.org. Contact: John Reeder, National Director.
*PROGRAMMING INQUIRES & REGIONAL HEADQUARTERS:* Trans World Radio, 75 High Street #04-00 Wisma Sugnomal, Singapore 179435, Singapore.
*CHINA (HONG KONG) OFFICE:* TWR-CMI, P.O. Box 98697, Tsimshatsui Post Office, Kowloon, Hong Kong. Phone: +852 2780-8336. Fax: +852 2385 5045. Email: (general) info@twr.org.hk; (Ko) simon_ko@compuserve.com; (Lok) joycelok@compuserve.com. Web: www.twr.org.hk. Contact: Simon Ko, Acting Area Director; or Joyce Lok, Programming/Follow -up Director.
*NEW DELHI OFFICE:* P.O. Box 4310, New Delhi-110 019, India. Contact: N. Emil Jebasingh, Vishwa Vani; or S. Stanley.
*TOKYO OFFICE:* Pacific Broadcasting Association, C.P.O. Box 1000, Tokyo 100-91, Japan. Phone +81 (3) 3295-4921. Fax: +81 (3) 3233 2650. Email: pba@path.ne.jp. Contact: (administration) Nobuyoshi Nakagawa.

# GUATEMALA  World Time –6

**Adventist World Radio—Unión Radio**, Apartado de Correo 51-C, Guatemala City, Guatemala. Phone: +502 365-2509. Fax:+502 365 9076. Email: uniradio@infovia.com.gt; mundi@guate.net. Free tourist and religious literature and Guatemalan stamps. Return postage (3 IRCs or $1) appreciated. Correspondence in Spanish preferred. Also, *see* AWR listings under Germany, Guam, Kenya, Madagascar, United Kingdom and USA.
**La Voz de Nahualá**, Nahualá, Sololá, Guatemala. Phone: +502 763-0115 or +502 763-0163. Contact: (technical) Juan Fidel Lepe Juárez, Técnico Auxiliar; or F. Manuel Esquipulas Carrillo Tzep. Return postage required. Correspondence in Spanish preferred.
**Radio Amistad**
*ADDRESS FOR RECEPTION REPORTS:* David Daniell, Asesor de Comunicaciones, Apartado Postal 25, Bulevares MX, 53140 Mexico. Phone/fax: +52 (5) 572-9633. Email: dpdaniell@aol.com. Replies to correspondence in English or Spanish.
**Radio Buenas Nuevas**, 13020 San Sebastián, Huehuetenango, Guatemala. Contact: Israel G. Rodas Mérida, Gerente. $1 or return postage helpful. Free religious and station information in Spanish. Sometimes includes a small pennant. Replies to correspondence in Spanish.
**Radio Chortís**, Centro Social, 20004 Jocotán, Chiquimula, Guatemala. Contact: Padre Juan María Boxus, Director. $1 or return postage required. Replies irregularly to correspondence in Spanish.
**Radio Cultural—TGNA**, Apartado de Correo 601, Guatemala City, Guatemala. Phone: +502 471-0807. Contact: Mariela Posadas, QSL Secretary; or Wayne Berger, Chief Engineer. Free religious printed matter. Return postage or $1 appreciated.
**Radio K'ekchi—TGVC**, 3ra Calle 7-15, Zona 1, 16015 Fray Bartolomé de las Casas, Alta Verapaz, Guatemala; (Media Consultant) David Daniell, Asesor de Comunicaciones, Apartado Postal 25, Bulevares MX, 53140 Mexico. Phone: (station) +502 950-0299; (Daniell, phone/fax) +52 (5) 572-9633. Fax: (station) +502 950 0398. Email: dpdaniell@aol.com. Contact: (gen-

eral) Gilberto Sun Xicol, Gerente; Ancelmo Cuc Chub, Director; or Mateo Botzoc, Director de Programas; (technical) Larry Baysinger, Ingeniero Jefe. Free paper pennant. $1 or return postage required. Replies to correspondence in Spanish.

**Radio Mam**, Acu'Mam, Cabricán, Quetzaltenango, Guatemala. Contact: Porfirio Pérez, Director. Free stickers and pennants. $1 or return postage required. Replies irregularly to correspondence in Spanish.

**Radio Maya de Barillas—TGBA**, 13026 Villa de Barillas, Huehuetenango, Guatemala. Contact: José Castañeda, Pastor Evangélico y Gerente. Free pennants and pins. Station is very interested in receiving reception reports. $1 or return postage required. Replies occasionally to correspondence in Spanish.

**Radio Tezulutlán—TGTZ** (when operating), Apartado de Correo 19, Cobán, Alta Verapaz 16001, Guatemala. Phone: +502 952-1928 or +502 951-2848. Fax: +502 951 3080. Email: verapaz@intelnet.net.gt. Web: www. verapaz.com/tezulutlan. Contact: Sergio W. Godoy, Director; or Hno. Antonio Jacobs, Director Ejecutivo. Pennant for donation to specific bank account. $1 or return postage required. Replies to correspondence in Spanish.

**Radio Verdad**, Apartado Postal 5, Chiquimula, Guatemala. Contact: Dr. Edgar Amílcar Madrid Morales, Gerente. May send free pennants & calendars. Replies to correspondence in Spanish and English; return postage appreciated. An evangelical and educational station.

## GUINEA    World Time exactly

**Radiodiffusion-Télévision Guinéenne**, B.P. 391, Conakry, Guinea. If no reply is forthcoming from this address, try sending your letter to: D.G.R./P.T.T., B.P. 3322, Conakry, Guinea. Phone/fax: +224 451-408. Email: (Issa Conde, Directeur) issaconde@yahoo.fr. Contact: (general) Yaoussou Diaby, Journaliste Sportif; Boubacar Yacine Diallo, Directeur Général/ORTG; Issa Conde, Directeur; or Seny Camara; (administration) Momo Toure, Chef Services Administratifs; (technical, studio) Mbaye Gagne, Chef de Studio; (technical, overall) Direction des Services Techniques. Return postage or $1 required. Replies very irregularly to correspondence in French.

## GUYANA    World Time –3

**Voice of Guyana**, Guyana Broadcasting Corporation, Broadcasting House, P.O. Box 10760, Georgetown, Guyana. Phone: +592 (2) 258-734, +592 (2) 258-083 or +592 (2) 262-691. Fax: +592 (2) 258 756, but persist as the fax machine appears to be switched off much of the time. Contact: (general) Indira Anandjit, Personnel Assistant; or M. Phillips; (technical) Roy Marshall, Senior Technician; or Shiroxley Goodman, Chief Engineer. $1 or IRC helpful. Sending a spare sticker from another station helps assure a reply. Note that when the station's mediumwave transmitter is down because of a component fault, parts of the shortwave unit are sometimes 'borrowed' until spares become available. As a result, the station is sometimes off shortwave for several weeks at a time.

## HOLLAND—*see* NETHERLANDS

## HONDURAS    World Time –6

**La Voz de la Mosquitia** (when operating)
*STATION:* Puerto Lempira, Dpto. Gracias a Dios, Honduras. Contact: Sammy Simpson, Director; or Larry Sexton. Free pennants.

*U.S. OFFICE:* Global Outreach, Box 1, Tupelo MS 38802 USA. Phone: +1 (601) 842-4615. Another U.S. contact is Larry Hooker, who occasionally visits the station, and who can be reached at +1 (334) 694-7976.

**La Voz Evangélica—HRVC**
*MAIN OFFICE:* Apartado Postal 3252, Tegucigalpa, M.D.C., Honduras. Phone: +504 234-3468/69/70. Fax: +504 233 3933. Email: info@hrvc.org. Web (includes RealAudio): www.hrvc.org. Contact: (general) Srta. Orfa Esther Durón Mendoza, Secretaria; Tereso Ramos, Director de Programación; Alan Maradiaga; or Modesto Palma, Jefe, Depto. Tráfico; (technical) Carlos Paguada, Director del Dpto. Técnico; (administration) Venancio Mejía, Gerente; or Nelson Perdomo, Director. Free calendars. Three IRCs or $1 required. Replies to correspondence in English, Spanish, Portuguese and German.

*REGIONAL OFFICE, SAN PEDRO SULA:* Apartado 2336, San Pedro Sula, Honduras. Phone: +504 557-5030. Contact: Hernán Miranda, Director.

*REGIONAL OFFICE, LA CEIBA:* Apartado 164, La Ceiba, Honduras. Phone: +504 443-2390. Contact: José Banegas, Director.

**Radio Costeña**—relays Radio Ebenezer (1220 kHz mediumwave), and all correspondence should be sent to the latter's address: Radio Ebenezer 1220 AM, Apartado 3466, San Pedro Sula, Honduras. Email: ebenezer@globalnet.hn; or pastor@ebenezer.hn. Web: www.ebenezer.hn. Contact: Germán Ponce, Gerente. According to a Swedish DXer, a reply was received from Iván Franco at casasps@yahoo.com, but it's not known what relation this person has with the station.

**Radio HRMI, Radio Misiones Internacionales**
*STATION:* Apartado Postal 20583, Comayaguela, M.D.C., Honduras. Phone: +504 233-9029. Contact: Wayne Downs, Director. $1 or return postage helpful.

*U.S. OFFICE:* IMF World Missions, P.O. Box 6321, San Bernardino CA 92412, USA. Phone +1 (909) 370-4515. Fax: +1 (909) 370 4862. Email: jkpimf@msn.com. Contact: Dr. James K. Planck, President; or Gustavo Roa, Coordinator.

**Radio Litoral—HRLW**, Apartado Postal 888, La Ceiba, Provincia Atlántida, Honduras. Phone: +504 443-0039. Email: radiolitoral@psinet.hn. Contact: José A. Mejía, Gerente-Propietario; or Antonio Jerome. Free postcards. 1$ or return postage required. Replies to correspondence in Spanish.

**Radio Luz y Vida—HRPC**, Apartado 369, San Pedro Sula, Honduras. Phone: +504 654-1221. Fax: +504 557 0394. Email: efmhonduras@globalnet.hn. Contact: Don Moore, Station Director; Cristóbal "Chris" Fleck; Ubaldo Zaldivar; or, to have your letter read over the air, "English Friendship Program." Return postage or $1 appreciated.

## HUNGARY    World Time +1 (+2 midyear)

📻**Radio Budapest**
*STATION OFFICES:* Bródy Sándor utca 5-7, H-1800 Budapest, Hungary. Phone: (general) +36 (1) 328-7339, +36 (1) 328-8328, +36 (1) 328-7357 +36 (1) 328-8588, +36 (1) 328-7710 or +36 (1) 328-7723; (voice mail, English) +36 (1) 328-8320; (voice mail, German) +36 (1) 328-7325; (administration) +36 (1) 328-7503 or +36 (1) 328-8415; (technical) +36 (1) 328-7226 or +36 (1) 328-8923. Fax: (general) +36 (1) 328 8517; (administration) +36 (1) 328 8838; (technical) +36 (1) 328 7105. Email: (English) ango11@kaf.radio.hu; (German) nemetl@kaf.radio.hu; (Spanish) espanol@kaf.radio.hu; (Hungarian Information Resources) avadasz@bluemoon.sma.com; (technical) (Füszfás) Fuszfasla@muszak.radio.hu. Web: (general) www.kaf.radio.hu/index.html; (RealAudio in English, German, Hungarian and

Russian) www.wrn.org/ondemand/hungary.html. Contact: (English Language Service) Ágnes Kevi, Correspondence; Louis Horváth, DX Editor; or Sándor Laczkó, Editor; (administration) László Krassó, Director, Foreign Broadcasting; Dr. Zsuzsa Mészáros, Vice-Director, Foreign Broadcasting; János Szirányi, President, Magyar Rádió; or János Simkó, Vice President, Magyar Rádió; (technical) László Füszfás, Deputy Technical Director, Magyar Rádió; Külföldi Adások Főszerkesztősége; or Lajos Horváth, Műszaki Igazgatősá; (Hungarian Information Resources) Andrew Vadasz. Replies irregularly to correspondence in English, but seems to answer all mail in Spanish.

COMMUNICATION AUTHORITY: P.O. Box 75, H-1525 Budapest, Hungary. Phone: +36 (1) 457-7178. Fax: +36 (1) 457 7120 or 36 (1) 356 5520. Email: czuprak@hif.hu. Contact: Ernö Czuprák.

TRANSMISSION AUTHORITY: Ministry of Transport, Communications and Water Management, P.O. Box 87, H-1400 Budapest, Hungary. Phone: +36 (1) 461-3390. Fax: +36 (1) 461 3392. Email: horvathf@cms.khvm.hu. Contact: Ferenc Horváth, Frequency Manager, Radio Communications Engineering Services.

# ICELAND   World Time exactly

📻**Ríkisútvarpid**, International Relations Department, Efstaleiti 1, IS-150 Reykjavík, Iceland. Phone: +354 515-3000. Fax: +354 515 3010. Email: isradio@ruv.is. Web: (includes RealAudio) www.ruv.is/utvarpid. Contact: Dóra Ingvadóttir, Head of International Relations; or Markús Öern Antonsson, Director.

# INDIA   World Time +5:30

WARNING—MAIL THEFT: Several PASSPORT readers report that letters to India containing IRCs and other valuables have disappeared en route when not registered. Best is either to register your letter or to send correspondence in an unsealed envelope, and without enclosures.

VERIFICATION OF REGIONAL STATIONS: All Indian regional stations can be verified via New Delhi (see All India Radio—External Services Division for contact details), but some listeners prefer contacting each station individually, in the hope of receiving a direct QSL. Well-known Indian DXer Jose Jacob makes the following suggestions: address your report to the station engineer of the respective station; specify the time of reception in both World Time (UTC) and Indian Standard Time (IST); instead of using the SINPO code, write a brief summary of reception quality; and if possible, report on local programs rather than relays of national programming from New Delhi. Jose adds that reports should be written in English, and return postage is not required (although an IRC or mint Indian stamps may sometimes help).

📻**All India Radio**

ADMINISTRATION: Directorate General of All India Radio, Akashvani Bhawan, 1 Sansad Marg, New Delhi-110 001, India. Phone: (general) +91 (11) 371-0006; (Chief Operating Officer) +91 (11) 338-6055; (Engineer-in-Chief) +91 (11) 371-0058; (Phone/fax, Frequency Assignments) +91 (11) 371-0145 or +91 (11) 371-4062; (programming) +91 (11) 371-5411, (voice mail, English) +91 (11) 376-1166, (Hindi) +91 (11) 376-1144. Fax: +91 (11) 371 1956; (Engineer-in-Chief) +91 (11) 372 5212; (programming) +91 (11) 371 0106. Email: (Frequency Assignments) faair@nda.vsnl.net.in. Contact: (general) A. Baijal, Chief Operating Officer; (technical) K.M. Paul, Engineer-in-Chief; or A.K. Bhatnagar, Director - Frequency Assignments.

AUDIENCE RESEARCH: Audience Research Unit, All India Radio, Press Trust of India Building, 2nd floor, Sansad Marg, New Delhi-110 001, India. Phone: +91 (11) 371-0033. Contact: R.S. Murthy, Director.

INTERNATIONAL MONITORING STATION—MAIN OFFICE: International Monitoring Station, All India Radio, Dr. K.S. Krishnan Road, Todapur, New Delhi-110 012, India. Phone: +91 (11) 573-5936, +91 (11) 573-5937 or +91 (11) 573-5939. Contact: B.L. Kasturiya, Deputy Director; D.P. Chhabra or R.K. Malviya, Assistant Research Engineers—Frequency Planning.

NEWS SERVICES DIVISION: News Services Division, Broadcasting House, 1 Sansad Marg, New Delhi-110 001, India. Phone: +91 (11) 371-0084 or +91 (11) 373-1510. Fax: +91 (11) 373 1510. Contact: E. Awasthi, Director General—News.

RESEARCH AND DEVELOPMENT: Office of the Chief Engineer R&D, All India Radio, 14-B Ring Road, Indraprastha Estate, New Delhi-110 002, India. Phone: (general) +91 (11) 331-1711, +91 (11) 331-1762, +91 (11) 331-3532 or +91 (11) 331-3574; (Chief Engineer) +91 (11) 331 8329 or +91 (11) 373-6255. Fax: +91 (11) 331 8329 or +91 (11) 331 6674. Email: rdair@nda.vsnl.net.in. Web: www.air.kode.net. Contact: A.S. Guin, Chief Engineer.

TRANSCRIPTION AND PROGRAM EXCHANGE SERVICES: Akashvani Bhawan, 1 Sansad Marg, New Delhi-110 001, India. Phone: +91 (11) 371-7927. Contact: D.P. Jadav, Director.

**All India Radio—Aizawl**, Radio Tila, Tuikhuahtlang, Aizawl-796 001, Mizoram, India. Phone: +91 (389) 322-415. Fax: +91 (389) 322 114. Email: airzawl@sancharnet.in. Contact: (technical) S. Nellai Nayagam, Station Engineer.

**All India Radio—Aligarh**, Anoopshahar Road, Aligarh-202 001, Uttar Pradesh, India. Phone: +91 (571) 401-993. Phone/fax: +91 (571) 400-972.

**All India Radio—Bangalore Shortwave Transmitting Centre**
HEADQUARTERS: see All India Radio—External Services Division.
AIR OFFICE NEAR TRANSMITTER: P.O. Box 5096, Bangalore-560 001, Karnataka, India. Phone/fax: +91 (80) 846-0379. Email: spt@bgl.vsnl.net.in. Contact: (technical) P.S. Bajpai, Superintending Engineer.

**All India Radio—Bhopal**, Akashvani Bhawan, Shamla Hills, Bhopal-462 002, Madhya Pradesh, India. Phone: +91 (755) 540-041. Email: airbhopal@vsnl.com. Contact: (technical) S.K. Gaur, Station Engineer.

**All India Radio—Chennai**
EXTERNAL SERVICES: see also All India Radio—External Services Division. Contact: M. Ahmad, Deputy Director General.
DOMESTIC SERVICE: Kamrajar Salai, Mylapore, Chennai-600 004, Tamil Nadu, India. Phone/fax: +91 (44) 638-3204. Email: airchennai@vsnl.com. Contact: (technical) S.R.M Sastry, Superintending Engineer.

**All India Radio—External Services Division**
MAIN ADDRESS: Broadcasting House, 1 Sansad Marg, P.O. Box 500, New Delhi-110 001, India. Phone: (general) +91 (11) 371-5411; (Director) +91 (11) 371-0057. Contact: (general) P.P. Setia, Director of External Services; or S.C. Panda, Audience Relations Officer; (technical) Rakesh Tyagi, Assistant Director Engineering (F.A.). Email (Research Dept.): rdair@giasdl01.vsnl.net.in; (comments on programs) air@kode.net. Web: (includes RealAudio in English and other languages) www.allindiaradio.com; http://air.kode.net; (unofficial, but contains updated schedule information) www.angelfire.com/in/alokdg/air.html. Free monthly India Calling magazine and stickers. Replies erratic. Except for stations listed below, correspondence to domestic stations is more likely to be responded to if it is sent via the External Services Division; request that your letter be forwarded to the appropriate domestic station.
VERIFICATION ADDRESS: Prasar Bharati Corporation of India,

Akashvani Bhawan, Room 204, Sansad Marg, New Delhi-110 001, India; or P.O. Box 500, New Delhi-110 001, India. Fax: +91 (11) 372 5212 or +91 (11) 371 4697. Email: faair@nda.vsnl.net.in; or faair@giasdl01.vsnl.net.in. Contact: Director, Frequency Assignments.

**All India Radio—Gangtok**, Old MLA Hostel, Gangtok-737 101, Sikkim, India. Phone: +91 (359) 22636. Email: airgtk@dte.vsnl.net.in. Contact: (general) Y.P. Yolmo, Station Director; (technical) A. Bhatnagar, Station Engineer.

**All India Radio—Gorakhpur**

*NEPALESE EXTERNAL SERVICE: see* All India Radio—External Services Division.

*DOMESTIC SERVICE:* Town Hall, Post Bag 26, Gorakhpur-273 001, Uttar Pradesh, India. Phone/fax: +91 (551) 337-401. Fax: +91 (551) 333 618. Contact: (technical) Dr. S.M. Pradhan, Superintending Engineer; or P.P. Shukle, Station Engineer.

**All India Radio—Guwahati**, P.O. Box 28, Chandmari, Guwahati-781 003, Assam, India. Phone/fax: +91 (361) 540-135. Fax: +91 (361) 540 378 or +91 (361) 540 426. Email: airgau@sancharnet.in. Contact: (technical) P.C. Sanghi, Superintending Engineer; or H.S. Dhillon, Station Engineer.

**All India Radio—Hyderabad**, Rocklands, Saifabad, Hyderabad-500 004, Andhra Pradesh, India. Phone: +91 (40) 323-4904. Fax: +91 (40) 323 2239 or +91 (40) 323 4282. Email: airhyd@hd2.vsnl.net.in. Contact: (technical) P. Vishwanathan, Superintending Engineer.

**All India Radio—Imphal**, Palau Road, Imphal-795 001, Manipur, India. Phone: +91 (385) 20-534. Email: airimfal@dte.vsnl.net.in. Contact: (technical) M. Jayaraman, Superintending Engineer.

**All India Radio—Itanagar**, Naharlagun, Itanagar-791 110, Arunachal Pradesh, India. Phone: +91 (360) 213-007. Fax: +91 (360) 213 008 or +91 (360) 212 933. Contact: J.T. Jirdoh, Station Director; or P. Sanghi, Superintending Engineer. Verifications direct from station are difficult, as engineering is done by staff visiting from the Regional Engineering Headquarters at AIR—Guwahati (*see*); that address might be worth contacting if all else fails.

**All India Radio—Jaipur**, 5 Park House, Mirza Ismail Road, Jaipur-302 001, Rajasthan, India. Phone: +91 (141) 366-623. Fax: +91 (141) 363 196. Email: airjpr@jp1.dot.net.in. Contact: (technical) S.C. Sharma, Station Engineer; or C.L. Goel, Assistant Station Engineer.

**All India Radio—Jammu**—*see* Radio Kashmir—Jammu.

**All India Radio—Jeypore**, Jeypore-764 005, Orissa, India. Phone: +91 (685) 432-524. Fax: +91 (685) 432 358. Email: airjeyp@dte.vsn1.net.in. Contact: M.P. Singh, Superintending Engineer; P. Subramanium, Assistant Station Engineer; A. Chanti Babu, Assistant Station Engineer; or K. Naryan Das, Assistant Station Engineer.

**All India Radio—Kohima**, P.O. Box 42, Kohima-797 001, Nagaland, India. Phone/fax: +91 (370) 22121. Fax: +91 (370) 22109. Contact: (technical) M. Tyagi, Superintending Engineer; K.K Jose, Assistant Engineer; or K. Morang, Assistant Station Engineer. Return postage, $1 or IRC helpful.

**All India Radio—Kolkata**, G.P.O. Box 696, Kolkata—700 001, West Bengal, India. Phone: +91 (33) 248-9131. Email: aircal@cal.vsnl.net.in. Contact: (technical) S.K. Pal, Superintending Engineer.

**All India Radio—Kurseong**, Mehta Club Building, Kurseong-734 203, Darjeeling District, West Bengal, India. Phone: +91 (3554) 4350. Contact: (general) George Kuruvilla, Assistant Director; (technical) R.K. Sinha, Chief Engineer; or B.K. Behara, Station Engineer.

**All India Radio—Leh**—*see* Radio Kashmir—Leh.

**All India Radio—Lucknow**, 18 Vidhan Sabha Marg, Lucknow-226 001, Uttar Pradesh, India. Phone: +91 (522) 244-130 or +91 (522) 237-476. Fax: +91 (522) 237 470. Email: airlko@sancharnet.in. Contact: Dr. S.M. Pradhan, Superintending Engineer. This station now appears to be replying via the External Services Division, New Delhi.

**All India Radio—Mumbai**

*EXTERNAL SERVICES: see* All India Radio—External Services Division.

*COMMERCIAL SERVICE (VIVIDH BHARATI):* All India Radio, P.O. Box 11497, 101 M K Road, Mumbai-400 0020, Maharashtra, India. Phone: (general) +91 (22) 203-1341 or +91 (22) 203-594; (Phone/fax, Director) +91 (22) 203-7702; (Phone/fax, Superintending Engineer) +91 (22) 882-1867. Fax: +91 (22) 287 6040. Email: (general) vbs@vsnl.com; (Manuswamy) mindiran@yahoo.co.uk. Contact: Vijayalakshmi Sinha, Director; or Indiran Munuswamy, Superintending Engineer.

*DOMESTIC SERVICE:* P.O. Box 13034, Mumbai-400 020, Maharashtra, India. Phone: +91 (22) 202-9853. Email: (general) sdairmumbai@vsnl.net; (Manuswamy) mindiran@yahoo.co.uk. Contact:Indiran Munuswamy, Superintending Engineer; or Lak Bhatnagar, Supervisor, Frequency Assignments.

**All India Radio—New Delhi**, P.O. Box 70, New Delhi-110 011, India. Phone: (general) +91 (11) 371-6249. Fax: +91 (11) 371 0113. Email: (reception reports) faair@nda.vsnl.net.in. Contact: (technical) V. Chaudhry, Superintending Engineer.

**All India Radio—Panaji Shortwave Transmitting Centre**

*HEADQUARTERS: see* All India Radio—External Services Division, above.

*AIR OFFICE NEAR TRANSMITTER:* P.O. Box 220, Altinho, Panaji-403 001, Goa, India. Phone: +91 (832) 225-623 or +91 (832) 230-696. Fax: +91 (832) 225 662 or +91 (832) 225 351. Email: airtrgoa@goatelecom.com. Contact: (technical) V.K. Singhla, Station Engineer; V. Punnose, Superintending Engineer; or G.N. Shetti, Assistant Engineer.

**All India Radio—Port Blair**, Haddo Post, Dilanipur, Port Blair-744 102, South Andaman, Andaman and Nicobar Islands, Union Territory, India. Phone: +91 (3192) 30-682. Fax: +91 (3192) 30 260. Email: airpb@dte.vsnl.net.in. Contact: (technical) S. Kumar, Station Engineer. Registering letter appears to be useful.

**All India Radio—Ranchi**, 6 Ratu Road, Ranchi-834 001, Jharkhand, India. Phone: +91 (651) 283-310 or +91 (651) 208-558. Fax: +91 (651) 301 666 or +91 (651) 301 957. Contact: (technical) H.K. Sinha, Superintending Engineer.

**All India Radio—Shillong**, P.O. Box 14, Shillong-793 001, Meghalaya, India. Phone: +91 (364) 224-443 or +91 (364) 222-781. Fax: +91 (364) 222 781. Email: air_neschillong@yahoo.com. Contact: (general) C. Lalsaronga, Director NEIS; (technical) R. Venugopal, Superintending Engineer; or H. Diengdoh, Station Engineer. Free booklet on station's history. Replies tend to be rare, due to a shortage of staff.

**All India Radio—Shimla**, Choura Maidan, Simla-171 004, Himachal Pradesh, India. Phone: +91 (177) 4809 or +91 (177) 211-355. Fax: +91 (177) 204 400. Contact: (technical) V.K. Upadhayay, Superintending Engineer; or P.K. Sood, Assistant Station Engineer. Return postage helpful.

**All India Radio—Srinagar**—*see* Radio Kashmir—Srinagar.

**All India Radio—Thiruvananthapuram**, P.O. Box 403, Bhakti Vilas, Vazuthacaud, Thiruvananthapuram-695 014, Kerala, India. Phone: +91 (471) 325-009. Fax: +91 (471) 324 406 or +91 (471) 324 982. Email: airtvpm@md4.vsnl.net.in; (Station Engineer) tvm_airtvpm@sancharnet.in. Contact: (technical) N.M Kumar, Station Engineer; or Radhakrishnan Menon, Station Engineer.

**Radio Kashmir—Leh**, Leh-194 101, Ladakh District, Jammu and Kashmir, India. Phone: +91 (198) 252-063. Fax: +91 (198) 252 234. Contact: (technical) L.K. Gandotar, Station Engineer; R. Singh, Assistant Station Engineer.

**Radio Kashmir—Srinagar**, Sherwani Road, Srinagar-190 001, Jammu and Kashmir, India. Phone: +91 (194) 71-460. Phone/fax: +91 (194) 452-100. Fax: +91 (194) 452 168. Email: akashvani@nde.com. Contact: L. Rehman, Station Director; or P.M. Bansal, Station Engineer.

**Radio Tila**—*see* All India Radio—Aizawl.

**Trans World Radio**
*STUDIO:* P.O. Box 4407, L-15, Green Park, New Delhi-110 016, India. Phone: +91 (11) 685-2568, +91 (11) 685-5674 or +91 (11) 686-1319. Fax: +91 (11) 686 8049. Contact: N. Emil Jebasingh, Director. This office is used for program production and answering listeners' correspondence, and does not have its own transmission facilities.
*ON-AIR ADDRESS:* P.O. Box 5, Andhra Pradesh, India.

# INDONESIA    World Time +7 Western: Waktu Indonesia Bagian Barat (Jawa, Sumatera); +8 Central: Waktu Indonesia Bagian Tengal (Bali, Kalimantan, Sulawesi, Nusa Tenggara); +9 Eastern: Waktu Indonesia Bagian Timur (Papua, Maluku)

*NOTE:* Except where otherwise indicated, Indonesian stations, especially those of the Radio Republik Indonesia (RRI) network, will reply to at least some correspondence in English. However, correspondence in Indonesian is more likely to ensure a reply.

**Kang Guru II Radio English**, KANGURU, JALF, Kotak Pos 3095, Denpasar 80030, Bali, Indonesia. Phone: +62 (361) 225-243. Fax: +62 (361) 263 509. Email: kangguru@ialfbali.co.id. Web: www.kanguru.org. Contact: Walter Slamer, Kang Guru Project Manager; or Ogi Yutarini, Administration Officer. Free "KANGURU" magazine. This program is aired over various RRI outlets, including Jakarta and Sorong. Continuation of this project, currently sponsored by Australia's AusAID, will depend upon whether adequate supplementary funding can be made available.

**Radio Pemerintah Daerah Kabupaten TK II—RPDK Manggarai**, Ruteng, Flores, Nusa Tenggara Timur, Indonesia. Contact: Simon Saleh, B.A. Return postage required.

**Radio Pemerintah Daerah Kabupaten Daerah TK II—RSPDKD Ngada**, Jalan Soekarno-Hatta, Bjawa, Flores, Nusa Tenggara Tengah, Indonesia. Phone: +62 (384) 21-142. Contact: Drs. Petrus Tena, Kepala Studio.

**Radio Republik Indonesia—RRI Ambon** (when operating), Jalan Jendral Akhmad Yani 1, Ambon 97124, Maluku, Indonesia. Phone: +62 (911) 52-740, +62 (911) 53-261 or +62 (911) 53-263. Fax: +62 (911) 53 262. Contact: Drs. H. Ali Amran or Pirla C. Noija, Kepala Seksi Siaran. A very poor replier to correspondence in recent years. Correspondence in Indonesian and return postage essential.

**Radio Republik Indonesia—RRI Banda Aceh** (when operating), Kotak Pos 112, Banda Aceh 23243, Aceh, Indonesia. Phone: +62 (651) 22-116/156. Contact: Parmono Prawira, Technical Director; or S.H. Rosa Kim. Return postage helpful.

**Radio Republik Indonesia—Bandar Lampung**, *see* RRI Tanjung Karang listing below.

**Radio Republik Indonesia—RRI Bandung** (when operating), Stasiun Regional 1, Kotak Pos 1055, Bandung 40122, Jawa Barat, Indonesia. Email: rribandung@yahoo.com. Web: http://www.kanguru.org/rristationprofiles.htm. Contact: Drs. Idrus Alkaf, Kepala Stasiun; Mrs. Ati Kusmiati; or Eem Suhaemi, Kepala Seksi Siaran. Return postage or IRC helpful.

**Radio Republik Indonesia—RRI Banjarmasin** (when operating), Stasiun Nusantara 111, Kotak Pos 117, Banjarmasin 70234, Kalimantan Selatan, Indonesia. Phone: +62 (511) 268-601 or +62 (511) 261-562. Fax: +62 (511) 252 238. Contact: Jul Chaidir, Stasiun Kepala; or Harmyn Husein. Free stickers. Return postage or IRCs helpful.

**Radio Republik Indonesia—RRI Bengkulu**, Stasiun Regional 1, Kotak Pos 13 Kawat, Kotamadya Bengkulu 38227, Indonesia. Phone: +62 (736) 350-811. Fax: +62 (736) 350 927. Contact: Drs. Drs. Jasran Abubakar, Kepala Stasiun. Free picture postcards, decals and tourist literature. Return postage or 2 IRCs helpful.

**Radio Republik Indonesia—RRI Biak**, Kotak Pos 505, Biak 98117, Papua, Indonesia. Phone: +62 (981) 21-211 or +62 (981) 21-197. Fax: +62 (981) 21 905. Contact: Butje Latuperissa, Kepala Seksi Siaran; or Drs. D.A. Siahainenia, Kepala Stasiun. Correspondence in Indonesian preferred.

**Radio Republik Indonesia—RRI Bukittinggi** (when operating), Stasiun Regional 1 Bukittinggi, Jalan Prof. Muhammad Yamin 199, Aurkuning, Bukittinggi 26131, Propinsi Sumatera Barat, Indonesia. Phone: +62 (752) 21-319 or +62 (752) 21-320. Fax: +62 (752) 367 132. Contact: Mr. Effendi, Sekretaris; Zul Arifin Mukhtar, SH; or Samirwan Sarjana Hukum, Producer, "Phone in Program." Replies to correspondence in Indonesian or English. Return postage helpful.

**Radio Republik Indonesia—RRI Denpasar** (when operating), Kotak Pos 3031, Denpasar 80233, Bali, Indonesia. Phone: +62 (361) 222-161 or +62 (361) 223-087. Fax: +62 (361) 227 312. Contact: I Gusti Ngurah Oka, Kepala Stasiun. Replies slowly to correspondence in Indonesian. Return postage or IRCs helpful.

**Radio Republik Indonesia—RRI Dili** (when operating), Stasiun Regional 1 Dili, Jalan Kaikoli, Kotak Pos 103, Díli 88000, Timor-Timur, Indonesia. Contact: Harry A. Silalahi, Kepala Stasiun; Arnoldus Klau; or Paul J. Amalo, BA. Return postage or $1 helpful. Replies occasionally to correspondence in Indonesian.

**Radio Republik Indonesia—RRI Fak Fak**, Jalan Kapten P. Tendean, Kotak Pos 54, Fak-Fak 98612, Papua, Indonesia. Phone: +62 (956) 22-519 or +62 (956) 22-521. Contact: Bahrun Siregar, Kepala Stasiun; Aloys Ngotra, Kepala Seksi Siaran; Drs. Tukiran Erlantdo; or Richart Tan, Kepala Sub Seksi Siaran Kata. Station plans to upgrade its transmitting facilities with the help of the Japanese government. Return postage required. Replies occasionally.

**Radio Republik Indonesia—RRI Gorontalo**, Jalan Jendral Sudirman 30, Gorontalo 96115, Sulawesi Utara, Indonesia. Fax: +62 (435) 821 590/91. Contact: Drs. Bagus Edi Asmoro; Drs. Muhammad. Assad, Kepala Stasiun; or Saleh S. Thalib, Technical Manager. Return postage helpful. Replies occasionally, preferably to correspondence in Indonesian.

**⬛Radio Republik Indonesia—RRI Jakarta**
*STATION:* Stasiun Nasional Jakarta, Kotak Pos 356, Jakarta 10110, Daerah Khusus Jakarta Raya, Indonesia; or (street address) Jalan Medan Merdeka Barat 4-5, Jakarta 10110, Indonesia. Phone: +62 (21) 384-9091 or +62 (21) 384-6817. Fax: +62 (21) 345 7132 or +62 (21) 345 7134. Email: rri@rrionline.com. Web: (includes Windows Media) www.rri.online.com. Contact: Drs. Beni Koesbani, Kepala Stasiun; or Drs. Nuryudi, MM. Return postage helpful. Replies irregularly.

*"DATELINE" ENGLISH PROGRAM: see* Kang Guru II Radio English.

*"U.N. CALLING ASIA" ENGLISH PROGRAM:* Program via RRI Jakarta Programa Ibukota Satu, every Sunday. Contact address same as United Nations Radio *(see)*.

**Radio Republik Indonesia—RRI Jambi**
STATION: Jalan Jendral A. Yani 5, Telanaipura, Jambi 36122, Propinsi Jambi, Indonesia. Contact: M. Yazid, Kepala Siaran; H. Asmuni Lubis, BA; or Byamsuri, Acting Station Manager. Return postage helpful.

**Radio Republik Indonesia—RRI Jayapura**, Kotak Pos 1077, Jayapura 99200, Papua, Indonesia. Phone: +62 (967) 33-339. Fax: +62 (967) 33 439. Contact: Harry Liborang, Direktorat Radio; Hartono, Bidang Teknik; or Dr. David Alex Siahainenia, Kepala. Return postage of $1 helpful. Replies to correspondence in Indonesian or English.

**Radio Republik Indonesia—RRI Kendari**, Kotak Pos 7, Kendari 93111, Sulawesi Tenggara, Indonesia. Phone: +62 (401) 21-464. Fax: +62 (401) 21 730. Contact: H. Sjahbuddin, BA; Muniruddin Amin, Programmer; or Drs. Supandi. Return postage required. Replies slowly to correspondence in Indonesian.

**Radio Republik Indonesia—RRI Kupang (Regional I)** (when operating), Jalan Tompello 8, Kupang 85225, Timor, Indonesia. Phone: +62 (380) 821-437 or +62 (380) 825-444. Fax: +62 (380) 833 149. Contact: Drs. P.M. Tisera, Kepala Stasiun; Qustigap Bagang, Kepala Seksi Siaran; or Said Rasyid, Kepala Studio. Return postage helpful. Correspondence in Indonesian preferred. Replies occasionally.

**Radio Republik Indonesia—RRI Madiun** (when operating), Jalan Mayjend Panjaitan 10, Madiun 63133, Jawa Timur, Indonesia. Phone: +62 (351) 464-419, +62 (351) 459-198, +62 (351) 462-726 or +62 (351) 459-495. Fax: +62 (351) 464 964. Web: http://www.kanguru.org/rristationprofiles.htm. Contact: Sri Lestari, SS or Imam Soeprapto, Kepala Seksi Siaran. Replies to correspondence in English or Indonesian. Return postage helpful.

**Radio Republik Indonesia—RRI Makassar**, Jalan Riburane 3, Makassar, 90111, Sulawesi Selatan, Indonesia. Phone: +62 (411) 321-853. Contact: H. Kamaruddin Alkaf Yasin, Head of Broadcasting Department; L.A. Rachim Ganie; Ashan Muhammad, Kepala Bidang Teknik; Salam Hormat, Head of Station; or Drs. Bambang Pudjono. Return postage, $1 or IRCs helpful. Replies irregularly and sometimes slowly.

**Radio Republik Indonesia—RRI Malang** (when operating), Kotak Pos 78, Malang 65140, Jawa Timur, Indonesia; or Jalan Candi Panggung No. 58, Mojolangu, Malang 65142, Indonesia. Email: makobu@mlg.globalxtrem.net. Contact: Drs.Tjutju Tjuar Na Adikorya, Kepala Stasiun; Ml. Mawahib, Kepala Seksi Siaran; or Dra Hartati Soekemi, Mengetahui. Return postage required. Free history and other booklets. Replies irregularly to correspondence in Indonesian.

**Radio Republik Indonesia—RRI Manado** (when operating), Kotak Pos 1110, Manado 95124 Propinsi Sulawesi Utara, Indonesia. Phone: +62 (431) 863-392. Fax: +62 (431) 863 492. Contact: Costher H. Gulton, Kepala Stasiun; or Untung Santoso, Kepala Seksi Teknik. Free stickers and postcards. Return postage or $1 required. Replies occasionally to correspondence in Indonesian.

**Radio Republik Indonesia—RRI Manokwari**, Regional II, Jalan Merdeka 68, Manokwari 98311, Papua, Indonesia. Phone: +62 (962) 21-343. Contact: Eddy Kusbandi, Manager; or Nurdin Mokogintu. Return postage helpful.

**Radio Republik Indonesia—RRI Mataram** (when operating), Stasiun Regional I Mataram, Jalan Langko 83 Ampenan, Mataram 83114, Nusa Tenggara Barat, Indonesia. Phone: +62 (370) 23-713 or +62 (370) 21-355. Contact: Drs. Hamid Djasman, Kepala; or Bochri Rachman, Ketua Dewan Pimpinan Harian. Free stickers. Return postage required. With sufficient return postage or small token gift, sometimes sends tourist information and Batik print. Replies to correspondence in Indonesian.

**Radio Republik Indonesia—RRI Medan** (when operating), Jalan Letkol Martinus Lubis 5, Medan 20232, Sumatera, Indonesia. Phone: +62 (61) 324-222/441. Fax: +62 (61) 512 161. Contact: Kepala Stasiun, Ujamalul Abidin Ass; Drs. S. Parlin Tobing, SH, Produsennya; "Kontak Pendengar"; Drs. H. Suryanta Saleh; or Suprato. Free stickers. Return postage required. Replies to correspondence in Indonesian.

**Radio Republik Indonesia—RRI Merauke**, Stasiun Regional 1, Kotak Pos 11, Merauke 99611, Papua, Indonesia. Phone: +62 (971) 21-396 or +62 (971) 21-376. Contact: (general) Drs. Buang Akhir, Direktor; Achmad Ruskaya B.A., Kepala Stasiun, Drs.Tuanakotta Semuel, Kepala Seksi Siaran; or John Manuputty, Kepala Subseksi Pemancar; (technical) Daf'an Kubangun, Kepala Seksi Tehnik. Return postage helpful.

**Radio Republik Indonesia—RRI Nabire** (when operating), Kotak Pos 110, Jalan Merdeka 74 Nabire 98811, Papua, Indonesia. Phone: +62 (984) 21-013. Contact: Muchtar Yushaputra, Kepala Stasiun. Free stickers and occasional free picture postcards. Return postage or IRCs helpful.

**Radio Republik Indonesia—RRI Padang**, Kotak Pos 77, Padang 25111, Sumatera Barat, Indonesia. Phone: +61 (751) 28-363, +62 (751) 21-030 or +62 (751) 27-482. Contact: H. Hutabarat, Kepala Stasiun; or Amir Hasan, Kepala Seksi Siaran. Return postage helpful.

**Radio Republik Indonesia—RRI Palangkaraya** (when operating), Jalan M. Husni Thamrin 1, Palangkaraya 73111, Kalimantan Tengah, Indonesia. Phone: +62 (536) 21-779. Fax: +62 (536) 21 778. Contact: Andy Sunandar; Drs.Amiruddin; S. Polin; A.F. Herry Purwanto; Meyiwati SH; Supardal Djojosubrojo, Sarjana Hukum; Dr. S. Parlin Tobing, Station Manager; Murniaty Oesin, Transmission Department Engineer; Gumer Kamis; or Ricky D. Wader, Kepala Stasiun. Return postage helpful. Will respond to correspondence in Indonesian or English.

**Radio Republik Indonesia—RRI Palembang** (when operating), Jalan Radio 2, Km. 4, Palembang 30128, Sumatera Selatan, Indonesia. Phone: +62 (711) 350-811, +62 (711) 309-977 or +62 (711) 350-927. Contact: Drs. H. Mursjid Noor, Kepala Stasiun; H.Ahmad Syukri Ahkab, Kepala Seksi Siaran; or H.Iskandar Suradilaga. Return postage helpful. Replies slowly and occasionally.

**Radio Republik Indonesia—RRI Palu**, Jalan R.A. Kartini 39, Palu 94112, Sulawesi Tengah, Indonesia. Phone: +62 (451) 21-621 or +62 (451) 94-112. Contact: Akson Boole; Nyonyah Netty Ch. Soriton, Kepala Seksi Siaran; Gugun Santoso; Untung Santoso, Kepala Seksi Teknik; or M. Hasjim, Head of Programming. Return postage required. Replies slowly to correspondence in Indonesian.

**Radio Republik Indonesia—RRI Pekanbaru** (when operating), Kotak Pos 51, Pekanbaru 28113, Kepulauan Riau, Indonesia. Phone: +62 (761) 22-081, +62 (761) 23-606 or +62 (761) 25-111. Fax: +62 (761) 23 605. Contact: (general) Hendri Yunis, ST, Kepala Stasiun, Ketua DPH; Arisun Agus, Kepala Seksi Siaran; Drs. H. Syamsidi, Kepala Supag Tata Usaha; or Zainal Abbas. Return postage helpful.

**Radio Republik Indonesia—RRI Pontianak**, Kotak Pos 1005, Pontianak 78117, Kalimantan Barat, Indonesia. Phone: +62 (561) 734-987. Fax: +62 (561) 734 659. Contact: Ruddy Banding, Kepala Seksi Siaran; Achmad Ruskaya, BA; Drs. Effendi Afati, Producer, "Dalam Acara Kantong Surat"; Subagio, Kepala Sub Bagian Tata Usaha; Augustwus Campek; Rahayu Widati; Suryadharma, Kepala Sub Seksi Programa; or Muchlis Marzuki

B.A. Return postage or $1 helpful. Replies some of the time to correspondence in Indonesian (preferred) or English.

**Radio Republik Indonesia—RRI Samarinda**, Kotak Pos 45, Samarinda, Kalimantan Timur 75110, Indonesia. Phone: +62 (541) 743-495. Fax: +62 (541) 741 693. Contact: Siti Thomah, Kepala Seksi Siaran; Tyranus Lenjau, English Announcer; S. Yati; Marthin Tapparan; or Sunendra, Kepala Stasiun. May send tourist brochures and maps. Return postage helpful. Replies to correspondence in Indonesian.

**Radio Republik Indonesia—RRI Semarang** (when operating), Kotak Pos 1073, Semarang 50241, Jawa Tengah, Indonesia. Phone: +62 (24) 831-6686, +62 (24) 831-6661 or +62 (24) 831-6330. (Phone/fax, marketing) +62 (24) 831-6330. Web: http://www.kanguru.org/rristationprofiles.htm. Contact: Djarwanto, SH; Drs. Sabeni, Doktorandus; Drs. Purwadi, Program Director; Dra. Endang Widiastuti, Kepala Sub Seksi Periklanan Jasa dan Hak Cipta; H. Sutakno, Kepala Stasiun; or Mardanon, Kepala Teknik. Return postage helpful.

**Radio Republik Indonesia—RRI Serui**, Jalan Pattimura Kotak Pos 19, Serui 98213, Papua, Indonesia. Phone: +62 (983) 31-150 or +62 (983) 31-121. Contact: Agus Raunsai, Kepala Stasiun; J. Lolouan, BA, Kepala Studio; Ketua Tim Pimpinan Harian, Kepala Seksi Siaran; Yance Yebi-Yebi; Natalis Edowai; Albertus Corputty; or Drs. Jasran Abubakar. Replies occasionally to correspondence in Indonesian. IRC or return postage helpful.

**Radio Republik Indonesia—RRI Sibolga** ( when operating), Jalan Ade Irma Suryani, Nasution No. 11, Sibolga 22513, Sumatera Utara, Indonesia. Phone: +61 (631) 21-183, +62 (631) 22-506 or +62 (631) 22-947. Contact: Mrs. Laiya, Mrs. S. Sitoupul or B.A. Tanjung. Return postage required. Replies occasionally to correspondence in Indonesian.

**Radio Republik Indonesia—RRI Sorong**

STATION: Kotak Pos 146, Sorong 98414, Papua, Indonesia. Phone: +62 (951) 21-003, +62 (951) 22-111, or +62 (951) 22-611. Contact: Drs. Sallomo Hamid; Tetty Rumbay S., Kasubsi Siaran Kata; Mrs. Tien Widarsanto, Resa Kasi Siaran; Ressa Molle; Mughpar Yushaputra, Kepala Stasiun; Umar Solle, Station Manager; or Linda Rumbay. Return postage helpful. Replies to correspondence in English.

"DATELINE" ENGLISH PROGRAM: See Kang Guru II Radio English.

**Radio Republik Indonesia—RRI Sumenep** (when operating), Jalan Urip Sumoharjo 26, Sumenep 69411, Madura, Jawa Timur, Indonesia. Phone: +62 (328) 62-317, +62 (328) 21-811, +62 (328) 21-317 or +62 (328) 66-768. Contact: Dian Irianto, Kepala Stasiun. Return postage helpful.

**Radio Republik Indonesia—RRI Surabaya**, (when operating) Stasiun Regional I, Kotak Pos 239, Surabaya 60271, Jawa Timur, Indonesia. Phone: +62 (31) 534-1327, +62 (31) 534-2327, +62 (31) 534-1327, +62 (31) 534-5474, +62 (31) 534-0478 or +62 (31) 547-3610. Fax: +62 (31) 534 2351. Contact: Zainal Abbas, Kepala Stasiun; Usmany Johozua, Kepala Seksi Siaran; Drs. E. Agus Widjaja, MM, Kasi Siaran; Pardjingat, Kepala Seksi Teknik; or Ny Koen Tarjadi. Return postage or IRCs helpful.

**Radio Republik Indonesia—RRI Surakarta** (when operating), Kotak Pos 40, Surakarta 57133, Jawa Tengah, Indonesia. Phone: +62 (271) 634-004/05, +62 (271) 638-145, +62 (271) 654-399 or +62 (271) 641-178. Fax: +62 (271) 642 208. Contact: H. Tomo, B.A., Head of Broadcasting; or Titiek Sudartik, S.H., Kepala. Return postage helpful.

**Radio Republik Indonesia—RRI Tanjungkarang**, Kotak Pos 24, Bandar Lampung 35213, Indonesia. Phone: +62 (721) 555-2280 or +62 (721) 569-720. Fax: +62 (721) 562 767. Contact: M. Nasir Agun, Kepala Stasiun; Hi Hanafie Umar; Djarot Nursinggih, Tech. Transmission; Drs. Doewadji, Kepala Seksi Siaran; Drs. Zulhaqqi Hafiz, Kepala Sub Seksi Periklanan; or Asmara Haidar Manaf. Return postage helpful. Also identifies as RRI Bandar Lampung. Replies in Indonesian to correspondence in English or Indonesian.

**Radio Republik Indonesia—RRI Tanjungpinang**, Stasiun RRI Regional II Tanjungpinang, Kotak Pos 8, Tanjungpinang 29123, Kepulauan Riau, Indonesia. Phone: +62 (771) 21-278, +62 (771) 21-540, +62 (771) 21-916 or +62 (771) 29-123. Contact: M. Yazid, Kepala Stasiun; Wan Suhardi, Produsennya, "Siaran Bahasa Melayu"; or Rosakim, Sarjana Hukum. Return postage helpful. Replies occasionally to correspondence in Indonesian or English.

**Radio Republik Indonesia—RRI Ternate** (when operating), Jalan Sultan Khairun, Kedaton, Ternate 97720 (Ternate), Maluku Utara, Indonesia. Phone: +62 (921) 21-582, +62 (921) 21-762 or +62 (921) 25-525. Contact: (general) Abd. Latief Kamarudin, Kepala Stasiun; (technical) Rusdy Bachmid, Head of Engineering; or Abubakar Alhadar. Return postage helpful.

**Radio Republik Indonesia Tual** (when operating), Watden, Pulau Kai, Tual 97661 Maluku, Indonesia.

**Radio Republik Indonesia—RRI Wamena** (when operating), RRI Regional II, Kotak Pos 10, Wamena, Papua 99511, Indonesia. Phone: +62 (969) 31-380. Fax: +62 (969) 31 299. Contact: Yoswa Kumurawak, Penjab Subseksi Pemancar. Return postage helpful.

**Radio Republik Indonesia—RRI Yogyakarta** (when operating), Jalan Amat Jazuli 4, Kotak Pos 18, Yogyakarta 55224, Jawa Tengah, Indonesia. Fax: +62 (274) 2784. Phone: +62 (274) 512-783/85 or +62 (274) 580-333. Email: rri-yk@yogya.wasantara.net.id. Contact: Phoenix Sudomo Sudaryo; Tris Mulyanti, Seksi Programa Siaran; Martono, ub. Kabid Penyelenggaraan Siaran; Mr. Kadis, Technical Department; or Drs. H. Hamdan Sjahbeni, Kepala Stasiun. IRC, return postage or $1 helpful. Replies occasionally to correspondence in Indonesian or English.

**Radio Siaran Pemerintah Daerah TK II—RSPD Halmahera Tengah, Soasio**, Jalan A. Malawat, Soasio, Maluku Tengah 97812, Indonesia. Contact: Drs. S. Chalid A. Latif, Kepala Badan Pengelola.

🔊**Voice of Indonesia**, Kotak Pos 1157, Jakarta 10001, Daerah Khusus Jakarta Raya, Indonesia. Phone: +62 (21) 720-3467, +62 (21) 355-381 or +62 (21) 349-091. Fax: +62 (21) 345 7132. Web: (Windows Media) www.rrionline.com. Contact: Anastasia Yasmine, Head of Foreign Affairs Section; or Amy Aisha, Presenter, "Listeners Mailbag." Free stickers and calendars. Be careful when addressing your letters to the station as mail sent to the Voice of Indonesia, Japanese Section, has sometimes been incorrectly delivered to NHK's Jakarta Bureau. Very slow in replying but enclosing 4 IRCs may help speed things up.

# IRAN   World Time +3:30 (+4:30 midyear)

🔊**Voice of the Islamic Republic of Iran**

MAIN OFFICE: IRIB External Services, P.O. Box 19395-6767, Tehran, Iran; or P.O. Box 19395-3333, Tehran, Iran. Phone: (IRIB Public Relations) +98 (21) 204-001/2/3 and +98 (21) 204-6894/5. Fax: (external services) +98 (21) 205 1635, +98 (21) 204 1097 or + 98 (21) 291 095; (IRIB Public Relations) +98 (21) 205 3305/7; (IRIB Central Administration) +98 (21) 204 1051; (technical) +98 (21) 654 841. Email: (general) webmaster@irib.com; irib@dci.iran.com; (Research Centre) iribrec@dci.iran.com. Web: (includes RealAudio) www.irib.com/worldservice. Contact: (general) Hamid Yasamin, Public Affairs; Ali Larijani, Head; or Hameed Barimani, Producer, "Listeners Special"; (administration) J. Ghanbari, Director General; or J. Sarafraz, Deputy Managing Director; (technical) M. Ebrahim Vassigh, Frequency Manager. Free seven-volume set of books on Islam, magazines, calendars, book markers, tourist literature and postcards. Verifications require a minimum of two days' reception data on two or more separate broadcasts, plus return postage. Station is currently asking their listeners to send in their telephone numbers so that they can call and talk to them directly. Upon request they will even broadcast your conversation on air. You can send your phone number to the postal address above or you can fax it to: + 98 (21) 205 1635. If English Service doesn't reply, then try writing the French Service in French.

*ENGINEERING ACTIVITIES, TEHRAN:* IRIB, P.O. Box 15875-4344, Tehran, Iran. Phone: +98 (21) 2196-6127. Fax: +98 (21) 204 1051, +98 (21) 2196 6268 or +98 (21) 172 924. Contact: Mrs. Niloufar Parviz.

*ENGINEERING ACTIVITIES, HESSARAK/KARAJ:* IRIB, P.O. Box 155, Hessarak/Karaj, Iran. Phone: (Frequency Control & Design Bureau) +98 (21) 216-3762; (Majid Farahmandnia) +98 (21) 216-3772; or (Yousef Ghadaksaz) +98 (21) 216-3742. Fax: (Frequency Design Bureau) +98 (21) 201 3649. Email: rezairib@dci.iran.com; (Ali Akbar Sabouri) sabouri@takta.net; (Yousef Ghadaksaz) ghadaksaz@irib.com; or (Majid Farahmandnia) farahmand@irib.com. Contact: Yousef Ghadaksaz, Manager of Shortwave Radio Department; Ali Akbar Sabouri, Head of Karaj Station; M. Ebrahim Vasigh; or Majid Farahmandnia, Manager, Frequency Control and Design Bureau.

SIRJAN TRANSMITTING STATION: P.O. Box 369, Sirjan, Iran. Phone: +98 (21) 216-3744. Contact: Ebrahim Safabahar, Head of Sirjan Station.

**Mashhad Regional Radio**, P.O. Box 555, Mashhad Center, Jomhoriye Eslame, Iran. Contact: J. Ghanbari, General Director.

# IRAQ   World Time +3 (+4 midyear)

**Radio Iraq International** (Idha'at al-Iraq al-Duwaliyah)
*MAIN OFFICE:* P.O. Box 8145 CN.12222, Baghdad, Iraq; if no reply, try: P.O. Box 8125, Baghdad, Iraq; or P.O. Box 7728, Baghdad, Iraq. Contact: M. el Wettar. State broadcasting facilities in Iraq continue to suffer from operational difficulties.
*INDIA ADDRESS:* P.O. Box 3044, New Delhi 110003, India.
**Radio Kurdistan** ("Aira dangi kurdistana, dangi hizbi socialisti democrati kurdistan") (when active). Web: (KSDP parent organization) www.ksdp.net. Station is run by the Kurdistan Socialist Democratic Party.
**Voice of Iraqi Kurdistan** ("Aira dangi Kurdestana Iraqiyah") (when active). Sponsored by the Kurdistan Democratic Party-Iraq (KDP), led by Masoud Barzani, and the National Democratic Iraqi Front. Broadcasts from its own transmitting facilities, reportedly located in the Kurdish section of Iraq. To contact the station or to obtain verification of reception reports, try going via one of the following KDP offices (the Swedish office is known to verify email reception reports):
*KURDISTAN-SALAHEDDIN CENTRAL MEDIA AND CULTURE OFFICE:* Phone: +873 (761) 610-320. Fax: +873 (761) 610 321. Email: kdppress@aol.com.
*KDP LONDON OFFICE:* KDP International Relations Committee-London, P.O. Box 7725, London SW1V 3ZD, United Kingdom. Phone: +44 (20) 7498-2664. Fax: +44 (20) 7498 2531. Email: kdpeurope@aol.com.

*KDP MADRID OFFICE:* PDK Comité de Relaciones Internacionales-España, Avenida Papa Negro, 20-1°-105ª, E-28043 Madrid, Spain. Phone: +34 (91) 759-9475. Fax: +34 (91) 300 1638. Email: pdk@futurnet.es. Web: http://usuarios.futurnet.es/p/pdk.
*KDP WASHINGTON OFFICE:* KDP International Relations Committee-Washington, 1015 18th Street, NW, Suite 704, Washington DC 20036 USA. Phone: +1 (202) 331-9505. Fax: +1 (202) 331 9506. Email: kdpusa@aol.com. Contact: Namat Sharif, Kurdistan Democratic Party.
*KDP-CANADA OFFICE:* Phone: +1 (905) 387-3759. Fax: +1 (905) 387 3756. Email: kdpcanada@hotmail.com. Web: www.geocities.com/Paris/Gallery/3209.
*KDP-DENMARK OFFICE:* Postbox 437, DK-3000 Helsingor, Denmark; or Postbox 551, DK-2620 Albertslund, Denmark. Phone/fax: +45 5577-9761. Email: kdpdenmark@hotmail.com. Web: http://members.tripod.com/kdpDenmark.
*KDP-SWEDEN OFFICE:* Box 2017, SE-145 02 Norsborg, Sweden. Phone: +46 (8) 361-446. Fax: +46 (8) 367 844. Email: party@kdp.pp.se; (Atroushi) atrushi@iname.com. Web: (includes Windows Media) www.kdp.pp.se. Contact: Alex Atroushi, who will verify email reports sent to the "party" address.
**Voice of the Kurdistan People**—*see* Voice of the People of Kurdistan, below.
**Voice of the People of Kurdistan** ("Aira dangi gelli kurdistana"). Email: said@aha.ru; or puk@puk.org. Web: www.aha.ru/~said/dang.htm; (PUK parent organization) www.puk.org. Official radio station of the Patriotic Union of Kurdistan (PUK) led by Jalal Talabani. Originally called "Voice of the Iraqi Revolution."
*PUK GERMAN OFFICE:* Patriotische Union Kurdistans (PUK), Postfach 21 0231, D-10502 Berlin, Germany. Phone: +49 (30) 3409-7850. Fax: +49 (30) 3409 7849. Email: pukoffice@pukg.de. Contact: Dara Gafori. Replies to correspondence in English and German, and verifies reception reports.

# IRELAND   World Time exactly (+1 midyear)

**Radio Telefís Éireann**, Broadcasting Developments, RTÉ, Dublin 4, Ireland. Phone: (general) +353 (1) 208-3111; (Broadcasting Developments) +353 (1) 208-2350. Audio services available by phone include concise news bulletins: (United States, special charges apply) +1 (900) 420-2411; (United Kingdom) +44 (891) 871-116; (Australia) +61 (3) 9552-1140; and concise sports bulletins: (United States, special charges apply) +1(900) 420-2412; (United Kingdom) +44 (891) 871-117; (Australia) +61 (3) 9552-1141. Fax: (general) +353 (1) 208 3082; (Broadcasting Developments) +353 (1) 208 3031. Email: (Hayde) haydej@rte.ie. Web: (general, includes RealAudio) www.rte.ie/radio/; (RealAudio, some programs) www.wrn.org/ondemand/ireland.html. Contact: Julie Hayde; or Bernie Pope, Reception. IRC appreciated. Offers a variety of video tapes (mostly PAL, but a few "American Standard"), CDs and audio cassettes for sale from RTÉ Commercial Enterprises Ltd, Box 1947, Donnybrook, Dublin 4, Ireland; (phone) +353 (1) 208-3453; (fax) +353 (1) 208 2620. A full list of what's on offer can be viewed at www.rte.ie/lib/store.html#music. Regular transmissions via facilities of VT Merlin Communications (*see* United Kingdom) in Ascension, Canada, Singapore and the United Kingdom—*see* next item—and irregularly via these and other countries for sports or election coverage.
**RTÉ Overseas (Shortwave)**—a half-hour information bulletin from RTÉ's (*see*, above) domestic Radio 1, relayed on shortwave. Web: www.rte.ie/radio/worldwide.html. Same contact details as RTÉ above.

# ISRAEL   World Time +2 (+3 midyear)

**Bezeq—Israel Telecommunication Corp. Ltd.**, Engineering and Planning Division, Radio and T.V. Broadcasting Section, P.O. Box 62081, Tel-Aviv 61620, Israel. Phone: +972 (3) 626-4562 or +972 (3) 626-4500. Fax: +972 (3) 626 4559. Email: (Oren) mosheor@bezeq.com. Web: www.bezeq.co.il. Contact: Moshe Oren, Frequency Manager. Bezeq is responsible for transmitting the programs of the Israel Broadcasting Authority (IBA), which *inter alia* parents Kol Israel. This address only for pointing out transmitter-related problems (interference, modulation quality, network mixups, etc.), especially by fax, of transmitters based in Israel. Verifications not given out at this office; requests for verification should be sent to the English Department of Kol Israel (*see* below).

**Galei Zahal (Israel Defence Forces Radio)**, Zahal, Military Mail No. 01005, Israel. Phone: +972 (3) 512-6666. Fax: +972 (3) 512 6760. Email: glz@galatz.co.il. Web: (includes Windows Media) www.msn.co.il/webinclude/redir.asp?startid=clip_108&url=http://gifs.msn.co.il/media/glz.asx.

**Kol Israel (Israel Radio, the Voice of Israel)**
*STUDIOS:* Kol Israel, P.O. Box 1082, Jerusalem 91010, Israel. Phone: (general) +972 (2) 530-2222; (Engineering Dept.) +972 (2) 501-3453; (Hebrew voice mail for Reshet Bet program "The Israel Connection") +972 (3) 765-1929. Fax: (English Service) +972 (2) 530 2424. Email: (general) ask@israel-info.gov.il; (English Service) englishradio@iba.org.il; (correspondence relating to reception problems, only) engineering@israelradio.org; (Reshet Bet program for Israelis abroad) radio1@iba.org.il. Web: (schedule, RealAudio) www.israelradio.org; (IBA parent organization, including RealAudio in Hebrew and Arabic) www.iba.org.il. Contact: Edmond Sehayeq, Head of Programming, Arabic, Persian and Yemenite broadcasts; Yishai Eldar, Reporter, English News Department; Steve Linde, Head of English News Department; or Sara Gabbai, Head of Western Broadcasting Department; (administration) Shmuel Ben-Zvi, Director of External Broadcasting; (technical, frequency management) Raphael Kochanowski, Director of Liaison and Coordination, Engineering Dept. Various political, religious, tourist, immigration and language publications. IRC required for reply.
*SAN FRANCISCO OFFICE, SCHEDULES:* 2654 17th Avenue, San Francisco CA 94116 USA. Phone: +1 (415) 564-9968. Email: GPoppin@aol.com. Contact: George Poppin. This address, a volunteer office, only provides Kol Israel schedules. All other correspondence should be sent directly to the main office in Jerusalem.

# ITALY   World Time +1 (+2 midyear)

**Italian Radio Relay Service**, IRRS-Shortwave, Nexus-IBA, C.P. 10980, I-20110 Milano, Italy. Phone: +39 (02) 266-6971. Fax: +39 (02) 7063 8151. Email: (general) info@nexus.org; (reception reports) reports@nexus.org; (Cotroneo) aec@nexus.org; (Norton) ron@nexus.org. Web:www.nexus.org/radio.htm; (MP3) http://mp3.nexus.org. Contact: (general) Ms. Anna S. Boschetti, Verification Manager; Alfredo E. Cotroneo, President; (technical) Ron Norton. For budget reasons, this station cannot assure a reply to all listeners' mail. Email correspondence and reception reports by email are answered promptly and at no charge. A number of booklets and sometimes stickers and small souvenirs are available for sale, but check their Website for further details. Two IRCs or $1 helpful.

**Radio Europe**, P.O. Box 12, 20090 Limito di Pioltello, Milan, Italy. Phone: +39 (02) 9210-0246. Fax: +39 (02) 8645 0149. Email: radioeurope@iol.it. Web: (includes RealAudio) www.alpcom.it/hamradio/freewaves/europe.htm. Contact: Dario Monferini, Foreign Relations Director; or Alex Bertini, General Manager. Pennants $5 and T-shirts $25. $30 for a life-time membership to Radio Europe's Listeners' Club. Membership includes T-shirt, poster, stickers, flags, gadgets, and so forth, with a monthly drawing for prizes. Application forms available from station. Sells airtime for $20 per hour. Two IRCs or $1 return postage appreciated. Unlicensed, but apparently left alone by the authorities.

**Radio Roma-RAI International** (external services)
*MAIN OFFICE:* External/Foreign Service, Centro RAI, Saxa Rubra, 00188 Rome, Italy; or P.O. Box 320, Correspondence Sector, 00100 Rome, Italy. Phone: +39 (06) 33-17-2360. Fax: +39 (06) 33 17 18 95 or +39 (06) 322 6070. Email: raiinternational@rai.it. Web: (shortwave) www.raiinternational.rai.it/radio/indexoc.htm. Contact: (general) Rosaria Vassallo, Correspondence Sector; or Augusto Milana, Editor-in-Chief, Shortwave Programs in Foreign Languages; Esther Casas, Servicio Español; (administration) Angela Buttiglione, Managing Director; or Gabriella Tambroni, Assistant Director. Free stickers, banners, calendars and *RAI Calling from Rome* magazine. Can provide supplementary materials, including on VHS and CD-ROM, for Italian-language video course, "Viva l' italiano," with an audio equivalent soon to be offered, as well. Is constructing "a new, more powerful and sophisticated shortwave transmitting center" in Tuscany; when this is activated, RAI International plans to expand news, cultural items and music in Italian and various other language services—including Spanish & Portuguese, plus new services in Chinese and Japanese. Responses can be very slow. Pictures of RAI's Shortwave Center at Prato Smeraldo can be found at www.mediasuk.org/rai.
*SHORTWAVE FREQUENCY MONITORING OFFICE:* RaiWay Monitoring Centre, Centro di Controllo, Via Mirabellino 1, 20052 Monza (MI), Italy. Phone: +39 (039) 388-389. Phone/fax (ask for fax): +39 (039) 386-222. Email: raiway.hfmonitoring@rai.it or cqmonza@rai.it. Contact: Mrs. Lucia Luisa La Franceschina; or Mario Ballabio.
*ENGINEERING OFFICE, ROME:* Via Teulada 66, 00195 Rome, Italy. Phone: +39 (06) 331-70721. Fax: +39 (06) 331 75142 or +39 (06) 372 3376. Email: isola@rai.it. Contact: Clara Isola.
*ENGINEERING OFFICE, TURIN:* Via Cernaia 33, 10121 Turin, Italy. Phone: +39 (011) 810-2293. Fax: +39 (011) 575 9610. Email: allamano@rai.it. Contact: Giuseppe Allamano, HF Frequency Planning.
*NEW YORK OFFICE, NONTECHNICAL:* 1350 Avenue of the Americas—21st floor, New York NY 10019 USA. Phone: +1 (212) 468-2500. Fax: +1 (212) 765 1956. Contact: Umberto Bonetti, Deputy Director of Radio Division. RAI caps, aprons and tote bags for sale at Boutique RAI, c/o the aforementioned New York address.
*SAN FRANCISCO OFFICE, SCHEDULES:* 2654 17th Avenue, San Francisco CA 94116 USA. Phone: +1 (415) 564-9968. Email: GPoppin@aol.com. Contact: George Poppin. This address, a volunteer office, only provides RAI schedules to listeners. All other correspondence should be sent directly to the main office in Rome.

**Radio Speranza, Modena** (when operating), Largo San Giorgio 91, 41100 Modena, Italy. Phone/fax: +39 (059) 230-373. Email: radiosperanza@radiosperanza.it. Web: www.radiosperanza.com. Contact: Padre Luigi Cordioli, Missionario Redentorista. Free Italian-language newsletter. Replies enthusiastically to correspondence in Italian. Return postage appreciated.

**RTV Italiana-RAI** (domestic services)
*CALTANISSETTA:* Radio Uno, Via Cerda 19, 90139 Palermo, Sic-

ily, Italy. Contact: Gestione Risorse, Transmission Quality Control. $1 required.

*ROME:* Centro RAI, Saxa Rubra, 00188 Rome, Italy. Fax: +39 (06) 322 6070. Email: grr@rai.it. Web: www.rai.it.

**Tele Radio Stereo, Roma** (when operating), Via Bitossi 18, 00136 Roma, Italy. Fax: + 39 (06) 353 48300.

## JAPAN   World Time +9

**NHK Fukuoka**, 1-1-10 Ropponmatsu, Chuo-ku, Fukuoka-shi, Fukuoka 810-8577, Japan.

**NHK Osaka**, 3-43 Bamba-cho, Chuo-ku, Osaka 540-8501, Japan. Fax: +81 (6) 6941 0612. Contact: (technical) Technical Bureau. IRC or $1 helpful.

**NHK Sapporo**, 1-1-1 Ohdori Nishi, Chuo-ku, Sapporo 060-8703, Japan. Fax: +81 (11) 232 5951. Sometimes sends postcards, stickers or other small souvenirs.

**NHK Tokyo/Shobu-Kuki**, 3047-1 Oaza-Sanga, Shobu-cho, Minamisaitama-gun, Saitama 346-0104, Japan. Fax: +81 (3) 3481 4985 or +81 (480) 85 1508. IRC or $1 helpful. Replies occasionally. Letters should be sent via registered mail.

📻**Radio Japan/NHK World** (external service)

*MAIN OFFICE:* NHK World, Nippon Hoso Kyokai, Tokyo 150-8001, Japan. Phone: +81 (3) 3465-1111. Fax: (general) +81 (3) 3481 1350; ("Hello from Tokyo" and Production Center) +81 (3) 3465 0966. Email: (general) info@intl.nhk.or.jp; ("Hello from Tokyo" program) hello@intl.nhk.or.jp; (Spanish Section) latin@intl.nhk.or.jp. Web: (includes RealAudio and Windows Media) www.nhk.or.jp/nhkworld. Contact: (administration) Isao Kitamoto, Deputy Director General; Hisashi Okawa, Senior Director International Planning; (general) Yoshiki Fushimi; H. Kawamoto, English Service; Ms. Kyoko Hirotani, Programming Division; or K. Terasaka, Programming Division.

*ENGINEERING ADMINISTRATION DEPARTMENT:* Nippon Hoso Kyokai, Tokyo 150-8001, Japan. Phone: +81 (3) 5455-5395 or +81 (3) 5455-2288. Fax: +81 (3) 3485 0952. Email: yoshimi@eng.nhk.or.jp or kurasima@eng.nhk.or.jp. Contact: Tetsuya Itsuk or Toshiki Kurashima.

*MONITORING SECTION:* NHK World/Radio Japan. Fax: +81 (3) 3481 1877.

*HONG KONG OFFICE:* Phone: +852 2577-5999.

*LONDON OFFICE:* Phone: +44 (20) 7334-0909.

*LOS ANGELES OFFICE:* Phone: +1 (310) 816-0300.

*NEW YORK OFFICE:* Phone: +1 (212) 755-3907.

*SINGAPORE OFFICE:* Phone: + 65 225-0667.

**Radio Tampa/NSB**

*MAIN OFFICE:* Nihon Shortwave Broadcasting, 9-15 Akasaka 1-chome, Minato-ku, Tokyo 107-8373, Japan. Fax: +81 (3) 3583 9062. Email: web@tampa.co.jp. Web: (includes Windows Media) www.tampa.co.jp. Contact: H. Nagao, Public Relations; M. Teshima; Ms. Terumi Onoda; or H. Ono. Sending a reception report may help with a reply. Free stickers and Japanese stamps. Radio Tampa plans to drop shortwave broadcasts in favor of satellite transmissions in the near future. $1 or 2 IRCs helpful.

*NEW YORK NEWS BUREAU:* 1325 Avenue of the Americas #2403, New York NY 10019 USA. Fax: +1 (212) 261 6449. Contact: Noboru Fukui, reporter.

## JORDAN   World Time +2 (+3 midyear)

**Radio Jordan**, P.O. Box 909, Amman, Jordan; or P.O. Box 1041, Amman, Jordan. Phone: (general) +962 (6) 477-4111; (International Relations) +962 (6) 477-8578; (English Service) +962 (6) 475-7410 or +962 (6) 477-3111; (Arabic Service) +962 (6)

463-6454; (Saleh) +962 (6) 474-8048; or (Al-Arini) +962 (6) 474-9161. Fax: (general) +962 (6) 478 8115; (English Service) +962 (6) 420 7862; (Al-Arini) +962 (6) 474 9190. Email: (general) general@jrtv.gov.jo; (programs) rj@jrtv.gov.jo; (schedule) feedback@jrtv.gov.jo; (technical) eng@jrtv.gov.jo; (Director of Radio TV Engineering) arini@jrtv.gov.jo. Web: www.jrtv.com/radio.htm. Contact: (general) Jawad Zada, Director of Foreign Service; Mrs. Firyal Zamakhshari, Director of Arabic Programs; or Qasral Mushatta; (administrative) Hashem Khresat, Director of Radio; Mrs. Fatima Massri, Director of International Relations; or Muwaffaq al-Rahayifah, Director of Shortwave Services; (technical) Youssef Al-Arini, Director of Radio TV Engineering. Free stickers. Replies irregularly and slowly. Enclosing $1 helps.

## KENYA   World Time +3

**Adventist World Radio**, AWR Africa, P.O. Box 42276, Nairobi, Kenya. Phone: +254 (2) 573-277. Fax: +254 (2) 568 433. Web: www.awr.org. Contact: (general) Samuel Misiani, Regional Director. Free home Bible study guides, program schedule and other small items. Return postage (IRCs or 1$) appreciated. This office will sometimes verify reception reports direct, but replies are slow. Also, *see* AWR listings under Germany, Guam, Guatemala, Madagascar, United Kingdom and USA.

📻**Kenya Broadcasting Corporation**, P.O. Box 30456, Harry Thuku Road, Nairobi, Kenya. Phone: +254 (2) 334-567. Fax: +254 (2) 220 675. Email: (general) kbc@swiftkenya.com; (management) mdkbc@swiftkenya.com; (technical services) kbctechnical@swiftkenya.com. Web: (general) www.kbc.co.ke; (RealAudio) www.africaonline.co.ke/AfricaOnline/netradio.html. Contact: (general) Henry Makokha, Liaison Office; (administration) Joe Matano Khamisi, Managing Director; (technical) Nathan Lamu, Senior Principal Technical Officer; Augustine Kenyanjier Gochui; Lawrence Holnati, Engineering Division; or Daniel Githua, Assistant Manager Technical Services (Radio). IRC required. Replies irregularly. If all you want is verfication of your reception report(s), you may have better luck sending your letter to: Engineer in Charge, Maralal Radio Station, P.O. Box 38, Maralal, Kenya.

## KIRIBATI   World Time +12

**Radio Kiribati** (when operating), Broadcasting & Publications Authority, P.O. Box 78, Bairiki, Tarawa, Republic of Kiribati.

ハイテックな海外短波放送情報誌
毎年発行 PWR
（パスポート・ツー・ワールドバンド・ラジオ）
あなたのレシーバーで、新しい世界が開けます

● 英文約560頁(分り易い日本語解説付き)
● 一目で分るグラフィック表示の周波数表・ブルーページ
● 国別放送局リスト、アドレス1200局以上掲載
● 大好評の受信機テスト・データ、国産受信機特価情報
● 米国IBS社発行、国内一流クラブ推賞図書
　1冊3600円(郵送料込み、日本語解説付き)
お申し込み：郵便振替・00210-7-28136　IBSジャパン
(お問合わせ先：〒247-0071 鎌倉市玉縄5-31-6 大武)

Phone: +686 21187. Fax: +686 21096. Email: bpa@tskl.net.ki. Contact: (general) Atiota Bauro, Programme Organiser; Mrs. Otiri Laboia; Batiri Bataua, News Editor; or Moia Tetoa, Radio Manager; (technical) Tooto Kabwebwenibeia, Broadcast Engineer; Martin Ouma Ojwach, Senior Superintendent of Electronics; Kautabuki Rubeiarki, Senior Technician; or T. Fakaofo, Technical Staff. Cassettes of local songs available for purchase. $1 or return postage required for a reply (IRCs not accepted). Currently off the air due to transmitter problems.

# KOREA (DPR)    World Time +9

**Voice of Korea**, External Service, Korean Central Broadcasting Station, Pyongyang, Democratic People's Republic of Korea (*not* "North Korea"). Phone: +850 (2) 381-6035. Fax: +850 (2) 381 4416. Phone and fax numbers valid only in those countries with direct telephone service to North Korea. Web: (unofficial) www.hikoryo.com/ser/vok.htm. Free publications, pennants, calendars, newspapers, artistic prints and pins. Do not include dutiable items in your envelope. Replies are irregular, as mail from countries not having diplomatic relations with North Korea is sent via circuitous routes and apparently does not always arrive. Indeed, some PASSPORT readers continue to report that mail to the sation results in their receiving anti-communist literature from *South* Korea, which indicates that mail interdiction has not ceased. One way around the problem is to add "VIA BEIJING, CHINA" to the address, but replies via this route tend to be slow in coming. Another gambit is to send your correspondence to an associate in a country—such as China, Ukraine or India—having reasonable relations with North Korea, and ask that it be forwarded. If you don't know anyone in these countries, try using the good offices of the following person: Willi Passman, Oberhausener Str. 100, D-45476, Mülheim, Germany. Send correspondence in a sealed envelope without any address on the back. That should be sent inside another envelope. Include 2 IRCs to cover the cost of forwarding.

*Regional Korean Central Broadcasting Stations*—Not known to reply, but a long-shot possibility is to try corresponding in Korean to: Korean Central Broadcasting Station, Ministry of Posts and Telecommunications, Chongsung-dong, Moranbong District, Pyongyang, Democratic People's Republic of Korea.

# KOREA (REPUBLIC)    World Time +9

📻**Korean Broadcasting System (KBS)**, 18 Yoido-dong, Youngdeungpo-ku, Seoul, Republic of Korea 150-790. Phone: +82 (2) 781-1000. Fax: +82 (2) 781 1698 or +82 (2) 781 2399. Email: pr@kbs.co.kr. Web: (includes Windows Media) www.kbs.co.kr.

📻**Radio Korea International**

*MAIN OFFICE:* Overseas Service, Korean Broadcasting System, Yoido-dong 18, Youngdeungpo-ku, Seoul, Republic of Korea 150-790. Phone: (general) +82 (2) 781-3650/60/70; (English Service) +82 (2) 781-3674/5/6; (German Service) +82 (2) 781-3682/3/9; (Japanese Service) +82 (2) 781-3654/5/6 (Spanish Service) +82 (2) 781-3679/81/97. Fax: +82 (2) 781 3694/5/6. Email: (general) rki@kbs.co.kr; (English) english@kbs.co.kr; (German) german@kbs.co.kr; (Japanese) rkijp@kbs.co.kr; (Spanish) spanish@kbs.co.kr. Web: (includes Windows Media) www.rki.kbs.co.kr. Contact: Cho Won-Suk, Executive Director; Ms. Shin Joo-Ok, Director Division 1; or Ms. Han Hee-Joo, Director Division 2, and is also the Producer/Co-Host of "*Multiwave Feedback*" show. QSLs, time/frequency schedule,

station stickers, calendars, *Let's Learn Korean* book and a wide variety of other small souvenirs. *History of Korea* is available on CD-ROM (upon request) and via the station's Website.

"*EDXP NEWS REPORTS*": Web: www.members.tripod.com/-bpadula/edxp.html. Special news reports concentrating on shortwave broadcasts to and from Asia, the Far East, Australia, the Pacific and the Indian sub-continent, compiled by EDXP and aired once a week on a Sunday (UTC) during the Radio Korea International "*Multiwave Feedback*" program in English. Special EDXP QSLs will be offered for the shortwave releases (not for RealAudio). Reports of the EDXP feature should be sent to: Bob Padula, EDXP QSL Service, 404 Mont Albert Road, Surrey Hills, Victoria 3127, Australia. Return postage appreciated. Outside of Australia, 1 IRC or $1; within Australia, four 50c Australian stamps. Email reports welcome at edxp@bigpond.com, and verified with Web-delivered animated QSLs.

# KUWAIT    World Time +3

**Ministry of Information**, P.O. Box 193, 13002 Safat, Kuwait. Phone: +965 241-5301. Fax: +965 243 4511. Web: www.moinfo.gov.kw. Contact: Sheik Nasir Al-Sabah, Minister of Information.

*FREQUENCY SECTION:* Ministry of Information, P.O. Box 967 13010 Safat, Kuwait. Phone: +965 243-6193 or +965 241-7830. Fax: +965 241 5498. Contact: Ms. Wesam Najaf, Head of Frequency Section; or Ahmad Alawdhi, Communication Engineer.

📻**Radio Kuwait**, P.O. Box 397, 13004 Safat, Kuwait; (technical) Department of Frequency Management, P.O. Box 967, 13010 Safat, Kuwait. Phone: (general) +965 242-3774; (technical) +965 241-0301. Fax: (general) +965 245 6660; (technical) +965 241 5946. Email: (technical, including reception reports) kwtfreq@hotmail.com; (frequency matters) kwtfreq@ncc.moc.kw; (general) radiokuwait@radiokuwait.org or info@moinfo.gov.kw. Web: (technical) www.moinfo.gov.kw/ENG/FREQ/; (RealAudio) www.radiokuwait.org. Contact: (general) Manager, External Service; (technical) Nasser M. Al-Saffar, Frequency Manager; or Wessam Najaf. Sometimes gives away stickers, calendars, pens or key chains.

# KYRGYZSTAN    World Time +5 (+6 midyear)

**Kyrgyz Radio**, Kyrgyz TV and Radio Center, 59 Jash Gvardiya Boulevard, 720300 Bishkek, Kyrgyzstan. Phone: (general) +996 (312) 253-404 or +996 (312) 255-741; (Director) +996 (312) 255-700 or +996 (312) 255-709; (Assemov) +996 (312) 650-7341 or +996 (312) 255-703; (Atakanova) +996 (312) 251-927; (technical) +996 (312) 257-771. Fax: +996 (312) 257 952. Note that from a few countries, the dialing code is still the old +7 (3312). Email: trk@kyrnet.kg. Contact: (administration), Moldoseyit Mambetakunov, Vice-Chairman -Kyrgyz Radio; or Eraly Ayilchiyev, Director; (general) Talant Assemov, Editor - Kyrgyz/Russian/German news; Gulnara Abdulaeva, Announcer -Kyrgyz/Russian/German news; (technical) Mirbek Uursabekov, Technical Director. Kyrgyz and Russian preferred, but correspondence in English and German can also be processed. For quick processing of reception reports, use email in German to Talant Assemov.

*TRANSMISSION FACILITIES:* Ministry of Transport and Communications, 42 Issanova Street, 720000 Bishkek, Kyrgyzstan. Phone: +996 (312) 216-672. Fax: +996 (312) 213 667. Contact: Jantoro Satybaldiyev, Minister. The shortwave transmitting station is located at Krasny-Retcha (Red River), a military encampment in the Issk-Ata region, about 40 km south of Bishkek.

# LAOS    World Time +7

**Lao National Radio, Luang Prabang** (if reactivated), Luang Prabang, Laos; or B.P. 310, Vientiane, Laos. Return postage required (IRCs not accepted). Replies slowly and very rarely. Best bet is to write in Laotian or French directly to Luang Prabang, where the transmitter is located.

**Lao National Radio, Vientiane**, Laotian National Radio and Television, B.P. 310, Vientiane, Laos. Phone: +856 (21) 212-429. Fax: +856 (21) 212 430. Email: natradio@laonet.net. Contact: Khoun Sounantha, Manager-in-Charge; Bounthan Inthasai, Director General; Mrs. Vinachine, English/French Sections; Ms. Mativarn Simanithone, Deputy Head, English Section; or Miss Chanthery Vichitsavanh, Announcer, English Section who says, "It would be good if you send your letter unregistered, because I find it difficult to get all letters by myself at the post. Please use my name, and 'Lao National Radio, P.O. Box 310, Vientiane, Laos P.D.R.' It will go directly to me." Sometimes includes a program schedule and Laotian stamps when replying. The external service of this station is currently off shortwave.

# LEBANON    World Time +2 (+3 midyear)

**◙Voice of Charity**, Rue Fouad Chéhab, B.P. 850, Jounieh, Lebanon. Phone: +961 (9) 914-901 or +961 (9) 918-090. Email: radiocharity@opuslibani.org.lb. Web: (includes RealAudio) www.radiocharity.org.lb. Contact: Frère Elie Nakhoul, Managing Director. Program aired via facilities of Vatican Radio from a station founded by the Order of the Lebanese Missionaries. Basically, a Lebanese Christian educational radio program. Replies to correspondence in English, French and Arabic, and verifies reception reports.

# LESOTHO    World Time +2

**Radio Lesotho**, P.O. Box 552, Maseru 100, Lesotho. Phone: +266 323-371 or +266 323-561. Fax: +266 323 003. Web: http://www.radioles.co.ls. Contact: (general) Mamonyane Matsaba, Acting Programming Director; or Sekhonyana Motlohi, Producer, "What Do Listeners Say?"; (administration) Ms. Mpine Tente, Principal Secretary, Ministry of Information and Broadcasting; (technical) Lebohang Monnapula, Chief Engineer; Emmanuel Rametse, Transmitter Engineer; or Motlatsi Monyane, Studio Engineer. Return postage necessary, but do not include currency notes—local currency exchange laws are very strict.

# LIBERIA    World Time exactly

NOTE: Mail sent to Liberia may be returned as undeliverable.
**Radio ELWA**, c/o SIM Liberia, 08 B.P. 886, Abidjan 08, Côte d'Ivoire. Contact: Moses T. Nyantee, Station Manager; or Chief Technician.

**Radio Liberia International** (when operating), Liberian Communications Network/KISS, P.O. Box 1103, 1000 Monrovia 10, Liberia. Phone: +231 226-963 or +231 227-593. Fax: (during working hours) +231 226 003. Contact: Issac P. Davis, Engineer-in-Charge/QSL Coordinator. $5 required for QSL card.

**Radio Veritas**, P.O. Box 3569, Monrovia, Liberia. Phone: +231 226-979. Contact: Steve Kenneh, Manager.

# LIBYA    World Time +2

**Libyan Jamahiriyah Broadcasting Corporation**, P.O. Box 9333, Soug al Jama, Tripoli, Libya. Email: info@ljbc.net. Web: www.ljbc.net.

FREQUENCY MANAGEMENT: Box 333, Soug al Jama, Tripoli, Libya. Phone: +218 (21) 361-4508. Fax: +218 (21) 489 4240. Contact: Youssef Al-Moujrab; Salah Zayani; or Abdessalem Zaglem.

**Voice of Africa**, P.O. Box 4677, Soug al Jama, Tripoli, Libya. Phone: +218 (21) 444-0112, +218 (21) 444-9106 or +218 (21) 444-9872. Fax: +218 (21) 444 9875. Email: africanvoice@hotmail.com. The external service of Libyan Jamahiriyah Broadcasting, it identifies as "Voice of Africa" in its English and French programs, while in Arabic it may use the same identification as for the domestic service or refer to itself as the "Voice of Libya." Replies slowly and irregularly.

MALTA OFFICE: P.O. Box 17, Hamrun, Malta. Replies tend to be more forthcoming from this address than direct from Libya.

# LITHUANIA    World Time +2

NOTE: A telephone renumbering plan commenced in November 2001 and is scheduled to end in March 2003. If the numbers below no longer work, contact your telephone operator for advice on how to proceed.

**Communications Regulatory Authority**, Algirdo str. 27, LT-2006 Vilnius, Lithuania. Phone: (Cesna) +370 (2) 231-550; or (Barakauskas) +370 (2) 261-177. Fax: +370 (2) 261 564. Email: (Barakauskas) rrt@rrt.lt; (Cesna) acesna@rrt.lt. Contact: Arturas Medeisis, Head of Division of Strategic Planning; Augutis Cesna, Head of Section, Radio & TV Broadcasting; or Tomas Barakauskas, Director. Replaces the former State Radio Frequency Service.

**Lietuvos Radijo ir Televizijos Centras (LRTC)**, Sausio 13-osios 10, LT-2044 Vilnius, Lithuania. Phone: +370 (2) 459-397. Fax: +370 (2) 706 919. Email: info@lrtc.net. Web: www.lrtc.net. Contact: A. Vydmontas, Director General. Operates the transmitters used by Lithuanian Radio/Radio Vilnius.

**◙Lithuanian Radio** (if reactivated on shortwave), Lietuvos Radijas, S. Konarskio 49, LT-2674 Vilnius MTP, Lithuania. Phone: (Program Director) +370 (2) 363-002; (Technical Director) +370 (2) 363-202. Fax: (administration) +370 (2) 235 333; (Technical Director) +370 (2) 363 208. Email: (Litvaitiene) litvaitiene@lrt.lt; (reception reports) peles@lrt.lt. Web: (includes RealAudio and Windows Media) www.lrt.lt. Contact: (general) Ms. Guoda Litvaitiene, Program Director; (technical) Vytautas Marozas, Technical Director.

**Radio Vilnius**, Lietuvos Radijas, Konarskio 49, LT-2674 Vilnius, Lithuania. Phone: +370 (2) 363-079. Fax: +370 (2) 233 526. Email: ravil@lrt.lt. Web: see Lithuanian Radio, above. Contact: Ms. Rasa Lukaite, "Letterbox"; Audrius Braukyla, Editor-in-Chief; or Ms. Ilonia Rukiene, Head of English Department. Free stickers, pennants, Lithuanian stamps and other souvenirs.

# MADAGASCAR    World Time +3

**Adventist World Radio**
ADMINISTRATION: B.P. 700, Antananarivo, Madagascar. Phone: +261 (2022) 404-65.
STUDIO: B.P. 460, Antananarivo, Madagascar.
TECHNICAL AND NON-TECHNICAL (e.g. comments on programs)—see United Kingdom and USA. AWR broadcasts in Malagasy and French on leased airtime from Radio Nederland's Madagascar Relay. Reception reports concerning these broadcasts are best sent to the AWR U.K. office. Also, see AWR listings under Germany, Guam, Guatemala, Kenya, United Kingdom and USA.

**Radio Madagasikara**, B.P. 442, Antananarivo 101, Madagascar. Email: radmad@dts.mg. Web: http://takelaka.dts.mg/

radmad. Contact: Mlle. Rakotonirina Soa Herimanitia, Secrétaire de Direction, a young lady who collects stamps; Mamy Rafenomanantsoa, Directeur; or J.J. Rakotonirina, who has been known to request hi-fi catalogs. $1 required, and enclosing used stamps from various countries may help. Tape recordings accepted. Replies slowly and somewhat irregularly, usually to correspondence in French.

**Radio Nederland Wereldomroep—Madagascar Relay**, B.P. 404, Antananarivo, Madagascar. Contact: (technical) Rahamefy Eddy, Technische Dienst; or J.A. Ratobimiarana, Chief Engineer. Nontechnical correspondence should be sent to Radio Nederland Wereldomreop in the Netherlands (*see*).

## MALAWI    World Time +2

**Malawi Broadcasting Corporation** (when operating), P.O. Box 30133, Chichiri, Blantyre 3, Malawi. Phone: +265 671-222. Fax: +265 671 257 or +265 671 353. Email: dgmbc@malawi.net. Contact: (general) Wilson Bankuku, Director General; J.O. Mndeke; or T.J. Sineta; (technical) Edwin K. Lungu, Controller of Transmitters; Phillip Chinseu, Engineering Consultant; or Joseph Chikagwa, Director of Engineering. Currently off air due to lack of transmitter spares. Return postage or $1 helpful, as the station is underfunded.

## MALAYSIA    World Time +8

**Asia-Pacific Broadcasting Union (ABU)**, P.O. Box 1164, 59700 Kuala Lumpur, Malaysia; or (street address) 2nd Floor, Bangunan IPTAR, Angkasapuri, 50614 Kuala Lumpur, Malay-

**RVOG programs provide Indian women and children with health advice, educational programs and scientific lectures, as well as music.**  LWF

sia. Phone: (general) +60 (3) 2282-3592; (Programme Department)+60 (3) 2282-2480; (Technical Department) +60 (3) 2282-3108. Fax: +60 (3) 2282 5292. Email: (Office of Secretary-General) sg@abu.org.my; (Programme Department) prog@abu.org.my; (Technical Department) tech@abu.org.my. Web: www.abu.org.my. Contact: (administration) David Astley, Secretary-General; (technical) Sharad Sadhu and Rukmin Wijemanne, Senior Engineers, Technical Department.

**Radio Malaysia Kota Kinabalu**, RTM Sabah, 2.4 km Jalan Tuaran, 88614 Kota Kinabalu, Sabah, Malaysia. Phone: +60 (88) 213-444. Fax: +60 (88) 223 493. Email: rtmkk@rtm.net.my. Web: www.p.sabah.gov.my/rtm. Contact: Benedict Janil, Director of Broadcasting; Hasbullah Latiff; or Mrs. Angrick Saguman. Registering your letter may help. $1 or return postage required.

📻**Radio Malaysia, Kuala Lumpur**

*MAIN OFFICE:* RTM, Angkasapuri, Bukit Putra, 50614 Kuala Lumpur, Malaysia. Phone: +60 (3) 2282-5333 or +60 (3) 2282-4976. Fax: +60 (3) 2282 4735, +60 (3) 2282 5103 or +60 (3) 2282 5859. Email: sabariah@rtm.net.my or helpdesk@rtm.net.my. Web: www.rtm.net.my. Contact: (general) Madzhi Johari, Director of Radio; (technical) Ms. Aminah Din, Deputy Director Engineering (Radio); Abdullah Bin Shahadan, Engineer, Transmission and Monitoring; or Ong Poh, Chief Engineer. May sell T-shirts and key chains. Return postage required.

*RADIO 1 (MALAY):* Wisma Radio Angkasapuri, P.O. Box 11272, 50740 Kuala Lumpur, Malaysia. Phone: +60 (3) 2288-7841 or +60 (3) 2288-7261. Fax: +60 (3) 2284 7593. Email: komit@radio1.com.my. Web: www.rtm.net.my/radio1; (includes Windows Media) www.radio1.com.my.

*RADIO 4 (ENGLISH):* Same address as Radio 1, above. Phone: +60 (3) 2288-7282/3/4/5 or +60 (3) 2288-7663. Fax: +60 (3) 2284 5750. Email: radio4@rtm.net.my. Web: www.rtm.net.my/radio4.

*RADIO 6 (TAMIL):* Same address as Radios 1 and 4, above. Phone: +60 (3) 2288-7279. Fax: +60 (3) 2284 9137. Web: www.rtm.net.my/radio6.

*TRANSMISSION OFFICE:* Controller of Engineering, Department of Broadcasting (RTM), 43000 Kajang, Selangor Darul Ehsan, Malaysia. Phone: +60 (3) 8736-1530 or +60 (3) 8736-1863. Fax: +60 (3) 8736 1227. Email: rtmkjg@rtm.net.my. Contact: Jeffrey Looi.

**Radio Malaysia Sarawak (Kuching)**, RTM Sarawak, Jalan Satok, 93614 Kuching, Sarawak, Malaysia. Phone: +60 (82) 248-422. Fax: +60 (82) 241 914. Email: rtmkuc@rtm.net.my. Contact: (general) Yusof Ally, Director of Broadcasting; Mohd. Hulman Abdollah; or Human Resources Development; (technical, but also nontechnical) Colin A. Minoi, Technical Correspondence; (technical) Kho Kwang Khoon, Deputy Director of Engineering. Return postage helpful.

**Radio Malaysia Sarawak (Miri)**, RTM Miri, Bangunan Penyiaran, 98000 Miri, Sarawak, Malaysia. Phone: +60 (85) 422-524 or +60 (85) 423-645. Fax: +60 (85) 411 430. Contact: Clement Stia. $1 or return postage helpful.

**Radio Malaysia Sarawak (Sibu)**, RTM Sibu, Bangunan Penyiaran, 96009 Sibu, Sarawak, Malaysia. Phone: +60 (84) 323-566. Fax: +60 (84) 321 717. Contact: Clement Stia, Divisional Controller, Broadcasting Department. $1 or return postage required. Replies irregularly and slowly.

**Voice of Islam**—Program of the Voice of Malaysia (*see*, below).

**Voice of Malaysia**, Suara Malaysia, Wisma Radio Angkasapuri, P.O. Box 11272, 50740 Kuala Lumpur, Malaysia. Phone: (general) +60 (3) 2288-7824; (English Service) +60 (3) 2282-7826. Fax: +60 (3) 2284 7594. Email: vom@rtm.net.my; (technical, Kajang transmitter site) rtmkjg@po.jaring.my. Web:http://

www.rtm.net.my/vom/utama.htm. Contact: (general) Mrs. Mahani bte Ujang, Supervisor, English Service; Hajjah Wan Chuk Othman, English Service; (administration) Santokh Singh Gill, Director; or Mrs. Adilan bte Omar, Assistant Director; (technical) Lin Chew, Director of Engineering; (Kajang transmitter site) Kok Yoon Yeen, Technical Assistant. Free calendars and stickers. Two IRCs or return postage helpful. Replies slowly and irregularly.

## MALI   World Time exactly

**Radiodiffusion Télévision Malienne**, B.P. 171, Bamako, Mali. Phone: +223 212-019 or +223 212-474. Fax: +223 214 205. Email: (Traore) cotraore@sotelma.ml. Contact: Karamoko Issiaka Daman, Directeur des Programmes; (administration) Abdoulaye Sidibe, Directeur General; (Technical) Nouhoum Traore. $1 or IRC helpful. Replies slowly and irregularly to correspondence in French. English is accepted.

## MALTA   World Time +1 (+2 midyear)

**Voice of the Mediterranean (Radio Melita)**, St Francis Ravelin, Floriana VLT 15, Malta; or P.O. Box 143, Valetta CMR 01, Malta. Phone: +356 240-421 or +356 248-080. Fax: +356 241 501. Email: info@vomradio.com. Web: (includes Windows Media) www.vomradio.com. Contact: (management) Richard Muscat, Managing Director; (German Service and listener contact) Ingrid Huettmann; Victoria Farrugia. Letters and reception reports welcomed. May send blank QSL cards, stickers and bookmarks.

## MAURITANIA   World Time exactly

**Radio Mauritanie**, B.P. 200, Nouakchott, Mauritania. Phone: +222 (2) 52287. Fax: +222 (2) 51264. Email: rm@mauritania.mr. Contact: Madame Amir Feu; Lemrabott Boukhary; Madame Fatimetou Fall Dite Ami, Secretaire de Direction; Mr. El Hadj Diagne; or Mr. Hane Abou. Return postage or $1 required. Rarely replies.

## MEXICO   World Time –6 (–5 midyear) Central, South and Eastern, including D.F.; –7 (–6 midyear) Mountain; –7 Sonora; –8 (–7 midyear) Pacific

**Candela FM**—see RASA Onda Corta.

**La Hora Exacta—XEQK** (if reactivated), Real de Mayorazgo 83, Barrio de Xoco, 03330-México 13, D.F., Mexico. Phone: +52 (5) 628-1731, +52 (5) 628-1700 Ext. 1648 or 1659. Fax: +52 (5) 604 8292. Web: www.imer.gob.mx. Contact: Lic. Santiago Ibarra Ferrer, Gerente.

**La Jarocha—XEFT** (if reactivated), Apartado Postal 21, 91701-Veracruz, VER, Mexico. Phone: +52 (29) 322-250. Contact: C.P. Miguel Rodríguez Sáez, Sub-Director; or Lic. Juan de Dios Rodríguez Díaz, Director. Free tourist guide to Veracruz. Return postage, IRC or $1 probably helpful. Likely to reply to correspondence in Spanish.

**Radio Educación Onda Corta—XEPPM**, Apartado Postal 21-940, 04021-México, D.F., Mexico. Phone: (general) +52 (5) 559-6169. Phone/fax: (Director's Office) +52 (5) 575-6566. Email: (general) radioe@conaculta.gob.mx; (Lidia Camacho) lidiac@conaculta.gob.mx. Web: www.cnca.gob.mx/cnca/buena/radio/temas.html; (includes Windows Media) www.radioeducacion.edu.mx. Contact: (general) Lic. María Del Carmen Limón Celorio, Directora de Producción y Planeación; (administration) Lic. Lidia Camacho Camacho, Directora General; (technical) Ing. Jesús Aguilera Jiménez, Subdirector de

Desarrollo Técnico. Free stickers, calendars and station photo. Return postage or $1 required. Replies, sometimes slowly, to correspondence in English, Spanish, Italian or French.

**Radio Huayacocotla—XEJN**
*STATION ADDRESS:* "Radio Huaya," Dom. Gutiérrez Najera s/n, Apartado Postal 13, 92600-Huayacocotla, VER, Mexico. Phone: +52 (775) 80067. Fax: +52 (775) 80178. Email: radiohua@sjsocial.org, or framos@uibero.uia.mx. Web: www.sjsocial.org/Radio/huarad.html. Contact: Martha Silvia Ortiz López, Coordinadora. Return postage or $1 helpful. Replies irregularly to correspondence in Spanish.

**Radio México Internacional—XERMX**, Instituto Méxicano de la Radio, Apartado Postal 21-300, 04021-México, D.F., Mexico. Phone: +52 (5) 604-7846 or +52 (5) 628-1720. Fax: +52 (5) 628 1710. Email: rmi@eudoramail.com. Web: www.imer.gob.mx/estaciones/rmi.html. Contact: Juan Josi Miroz, Host "Mailbag Program." Free stickers, post cards and stamps. Sometimes free T-shirts and CDs. Welcomes correspondence, including inquiries about Mexico, in Spanish, English and French. $1 helpful. A bilingual reception report form can be downloaded and printed from the website.

**Radio Mil Onda Corta—XEOI**, NRM, Avda. Insurgentes Sur 1870, Col. Florida, 01030-México, D.F., Mexico; or Apartado Postal 21-1000, 04021-México, D.F., Mexico (this address for reception reports and listeners' correspondence on the station's shortwave broadcasts, and mark the envelope to the attention of Dr. Julián Santiago Díez de Bonilla). Phone: (station) +52 (5) 662-1000 or +52 (5) 662-1100; (Núcleo Radio Mil network) +52 (5) 662-6060, +52 (5) 663-0739 or +52 (5) 663 0590. Fax: (station) +52 (5) 662 0974; (Núcleo Radio Mil network) +52 (5) 662 0979. Email: info@nrm.com.mx. Web: www.nrm.com.mx/estaciones/radiomil. Contact: (administration) Edilberto Huesca P., Vicepresidente Ejecutivo del Núcleo Radio Mil; or Lic. Gustavo Alvite Martínez, Director; (shortwave service) Dr. Julián Santiago Díez de Bonilla. Free stickers. $1 or return postage required.

**Radio Transcontinental—XERTA** (when operating), Plaza de San Juan 5, Primer piso, Despacho 2, Esquina con Ayuntamiento, Centro, 06070-México, D.F., Mexico. Phone: +52 (5) 518-4938. Web: http://www.misionradio.com. Contact: Verónica Coria Miranda, Representante Ejecutiva.

**Radio Universidad Autónoma de México (UNAM)—XEYU** (if reactivated), Adolfo Prieto 133, Colonia del Valle, 03100-México 12, D.F., Mexico. Phone: +52 (5) 523-2633. Email: radiounam@www.unam.mx. Web: (includes RealAudio) www.unam.mx/radiounam. Contact: (general) Lic. Fernando Escalante Sobrino, Directora General de Radio UNAM; (technical) Ing. Gustavo Carreño, Departamento Técnico. Free tourist literature and stickers. $1 or return postage required. Replies irregularly to correspondence in Spanish.

**RASA Onda Corta—XEQM** (when operating), Apartado Postal 217, 97001-Mérida, YUC, Mexico. Phone: +52 (99) 236-155. Fax: +52 (99) 280 680. Contact: Lic. Bernardo Laris Rodríguez, Director General del Grupo RASA Mérida. Replies irregularly to correspondence in Spanish. Currently relays programs from FM sister station "Candela Tropicaliente," but hopes eventually to produce its own programming based on the best programs of each station in the network.

## MONACO   World Time +1 (+2 midyear)

**Trans World Radio**
*STATION:* B.P. 349, MC-98007 Monte-Carlo, Monaco-Cedex. Phone: +377 (92) 16-56-00. Fax: +377 (92) 16 56 01. Web:

(transmission schedule) www.gospelcom.net/twr/broadcasts/europe.htm. Contact: (general) Mrs. Jeanne Olson; (administration) Richard Olson, Station Manager; (Technical) *see VIENNA OFFICE, TECHNICAL: see* Vienna address, below. Free paper pennant. IRC or $1 helpful. Also, *see* USA.

*GERMAN OFFICE:* Evangeliums-Rundfunk, Postfach 1444, D-35573 Wetzlar, Germany. Phone: +49 (6441) 957-0. Fax: +49 (6441) 957 120. Email: erf@erf.de; or siemens@arf.de. Web: (includes RealAudio) www.erf.de. Contact: Jürgen Werth, Direktor.

*NETHERLANDS OFFICE, NONTECHNICAL:* Postbus 176, NL-3780 BD Voorthuizen, Netherlands. Phone: +31 (0) 3429-2727. Fax: +31 (0) 3429 6727. Contact: Beate Kiebel, Manager Broadcast Department; or Felix Widmer.

*VIENNA OFFICE, TECHNICAL:* Postfach 141, A-1235 Vienna, Austria. Phone: +43 (1) 863-1233 or +43 (1) 863-1247. Fax: +43 (1) 863 1220. Email: (Menzel) 100615.1511@compuserve.com; (Schraut) twr_euro_bschraut@compuserve.com; bschraut@twr-europe.at; (Roswell) croswell@twr-europe.at; (Dobos) kdobos@twr-europe.at. Contact: Helmut Menzel, Director of Engineering; Bernhard Schraut, Frequency Manager; Charles K. Roswell, Frequency Coordinator; or Kalman Dobos, Frequency Coordinator.

*SWISS OFFICE:* Evangelium in Radio und Fernsehen, Witzbergstrasse 23, CH-8330 Pfäffikon ZH, Switzerland. Phone: +41 (951) 0500. Fax: +41 (951) 0540. Email: erf@erf.ch. Web: www.erf.ch.

## MONGOLIA   World Time +8 (+9 midyear)

*NOTE:* Due to telecommunication network expansion, it is possible that some of the numbers below will no longer work. If you encounter difficulty, try inserting an additional "1" after the country code.

**Mongolian Radio** (Postal and email addresses same as Voice of Mongolia, *see* below). Phone: (administration) +976 (1) 323-520 or +976 (1) 328-978; (editorial) +976 (1) 329-766; (MRTV parent organization) +976 (1) 326-663. Fax: +976 (1) 327 234. Email: radiomongolia@magicnet.mn. Contact: A. Buidakhmet, Director.

**⬚Voice of Mongolia**, C.P.O. Box 365, Ulaanbaatar 13, Mongolia. Phone: +976 (1) 321-624 or (English Section) +976 (1) 327-900. Fax: +976 (1) 323 096 or (English Section) +976 (1) 327 234. Email: (general) radiomongolia@magicnet.mn, radio-internet@magicnet.mn, or (International Relations Office) mrtv@magicnet.mn. Web: (includes RealAudio) www.mongol.net/vom. Contact: (general) Mrs. Narantuya, Chief of Foreign Service; D. Batbayar, Mail Editor, English Department; N. Tuya, Head of English Department; Dr. Mark Ostrowski, Consultant, MRTV International Relations Department; or Ms. Tsegmid Burmaa, Japanese Department; (administration) Ch. Surenjav, Director; (technical) Ing. Ganhuu, Chief of Technical Department. Correpondence should be directed to the relevant language section and 2 IRCs or 1$ appreciated. Sometimes very slow in replying. Accepts taped reception reports, preferably containing five-minute excerpts of the broadcast(s) reported, but cassettes cannot be returned. Free pennants, postcards, newspapers and Mongolian stamps.

## MOROCCO   World Time exactly

**⬚Radio Medi Un**

*MAIN OFFICE:* B.P. 2055, Tanger, Morocco (physical location: 3, rue Emsallah, 90000 Tanger, Morocco). Phone/fax: +212

(9) 936-363 or +212 (9) 935-755. Email: (general) medi1@medi1.com; (technical) technique@medi1.com. Web: (includes RealAudio) www.medi1.com; www.medi1.co.ma. Contact: J. Dryk, Responsable Haute Fréquence. Two IRCs helpful. Free stickers. Correspondence in French preferred.

*PARIS BUREAU, NONTECHNICAL:* 78 Avenue Raymond Poincaré, F-75016 Paris, France. Phone: +33 (1) 45-01-53-30. Correspondence in French preferred.

**Radio Mediterranée Internationale**—*see* Radio Medi Un.

**⬚Radiodiffusion-Télévision Marocaine**, 1 rue El Brihi, Rabat, Morocco. Phone: +212 (7) 766-881/83/85, +212 (7) 701-740 or +212 (7) 201-404. Fax: +212 (7) 722 047, or +212 (7) 703 208. Email: rtm@rtm.gov.ma; (technical) hammouda@rtm.gov.ma. Web: (general) www.rtm.gov.ma; (radio) www.rtm.gov.ma/Radiodiffusion/Radiodiffusion.htm; (RealAudio) www.maroc.net/rc/live.htm. Contact: (nontechnical and technical) Ms. Naaman Khadija, Ingénieur d'Etat en Télécommunication; Abed Bendalh; or Rahal Sabir; (technical) Tanone Mohammed Jamaledine, Technical Director; Hammouda Mohamed, Engineer; or N. Read. Correspondence welcomed in English, French, Arabic or Berber.

**Voice of America/IBB—Morocco Relay Station, Briech.** Phone: (office) +212 (9) 93-24-81. Fax: +212 (9) 93 55 71. Contact: Station Manager. These numbers for urgent technical matters only. Otherwise, does not welcome direct correspondence; *see* USA for acceptable VOA and IBB Washington addresses and related information.

## MOZAMBIQUE   World Time +2

**Rádio Moçambique** (when operating), Rua da Rádio no. 2, Caixa Postal 2000, Maputo, Mozambique. Phone: +258 (1) 431-679/80. Fax: +258 (1) 421 816. Web: www.teledata.mz/radiomocambique. Contact: (general) João Baptista de Sousa, Administrador de Produção; Izidine Faquira, Diretor de Programas; Orlanda Mendes, Produtor, "Linha Direta"; (technical) Eng. Eduardo Rufino de Matos, Administrador Técnico; or Daniel Macabi, Diretor Técnico. Free medallions and pens. Cassettes featuring local music $15. Return postage, $1 or 2 IRCs required. Replies to correspondence in Portuguese or English.

## MYANMAR (BURMA)   World Time +6:30

**Radio Myanmar**

*STATION:* GPO Box 1432, Yangon-11181, Myanmar; or Pyay Road, Yangon-11041, Myanmar. Phone: +95 (1) 532-814. Fax: +95 (1) 525 428. Contact: Ko Ko Htway, Director (Broadcasting).

## NAGORNO-KARABAGH   World Time +3 (+4 midyear)

**Voice of Justice**, Tigranmetz Street 23a, Stepanakert, Nagorno-Karabagh. Contact: Michael Hajiyan, Station Manager. Replies to correspondence in Armenian, Azeri, Russian and German.

## NAMIBIA   World Time +2 (+1 midyear)

**Radio Namibia/Namibian Broadcasting Corporation**, P.O. Box 321, Windhoek 9000, Namibia. Phone: (general) +264 (61) 291-3111; (National Radio—English Service) +264 (61) 291-2440; (German Service) +264 (61) 291-2330; (Schachtschneider) +264 (61) 291-2188. Fax: (general) +264 (61) 217 760; (German Service) +264 (61) 291 2291; (Duwe, technical) +264 (61) 231 881. Email: (general) webmaster@nbc.com.na. To contact individuals, the format is initiallastname@nbc.com.na; so to reach, say, Peter Schachtschneider, it would be pschachtschneider@nbc.com.na. Web: www.nbc.com.na/index.html. Contact: (technical) Peter Schachtschneider, Manager, Transmitter Maintenance; Joe Duwe, Chief Technician. Free stickers.

## NEPAL   World Time +5:45

**📻Radio Nepal**, P.O. Box 634, Singha Durbar, Kathmandu, Nepal. Phone: (general) +977 (1) 223-910; (engineering) +977 (1) 225-467. Fax: +977 (1) 221 952. Email: radio@rne.wlink.com.np; (engineering) radio@engg.wlink.com.np. Web: (includes RealAudio in English and Nepali) www.radio-nepal.com. Contact: (general) S.R. Sharma, Executive Director; M.P. Adhikari, Deputy Executive Director; Jayanti Rajbhandari, Director - Programming; or S.K. Pant, Producer, "Listener's Mail"; (technical) Ram Sharan Kharki, Director - Engineering. 3 IRCs necessary, but station urges that neither mint stamps nor cash be enclosed, as this invites theft by Nepalese postal employees.

## NETHERLANDS   World Time +1 (+2 midyear)

**📻Radio Nederland Wereldomroep (Radio Netherlands)**
*MAIN OFFICE:* P.O. Box 222, 1200 JG Hilversum, The Netherlands. Phone: (general) +31 (35) 672-4211; (English Language Service) +31 (35) 672-4242; (24-hour listener Answerline) +31 (35) 672-4222. Fax: (general) +31 (35) 672 4207, but indicate destination department on fax cover sheet; (English Language Service) +31 (35) 672 4239. Email: (English Language Service) letters@rnw.nl; ("Media Network") media@rnw.nl. Web: (English Home Page) www.rnw.nl; (Media Network) www.medianetwork.nl; (RealAudio) www.rnw.nl/distrib/realaudio. Contact: (management) Lodewijk Bouwens, Director General; Jonathan Marks, Creative Director; Jan Hoek, Director of Finance and Logistics; Freek Eland, Editor-in-Chief; Mike Shaw, Head of English Language Service; Ginger da Silva, Network Manager English; (listener correspondence) Howard Shannon or Neville Powis, hosts of listener contact programme "Sincerely Yours" (include your telephone number or email address). Full-data verification card for reception reports, following guidelines in the RNW folder, "Writing Useful Reception Reports," available on the Media Network Website. Semi-annual *On Target* newsletter also free upon request, as are stickers and booklets. Other language departments have their own newsletters. The Radio Netherlands Music Department produces concerts heard on many NPR stations in North America, as well as a line of CDs, mainly of classical, jazz, world music and the Euro Hit 40. Most of the productions are only for rebroadcasting on other stations, but recordings on the NM Classics label are for sale. More details are available at the RNW Website (a new Website for RN music is under construction). Visitors welcome, but must call in advance.
*PROGRAMME DISTRIBUTION, NETWORK AND FREQUENCY PLANNING:* P.O. Box 222, 1200 JG Hilversum, The Netherlands. Phone: +31 (35) 672-4422. Fax: +31 (35) 672 4429. Email: nfp@rnw.nl. Contact: Leo van der Woude, Frequency Manager; or Jan Willem Drexhage, Head of Programme Distribution.
*NEW DELHI OFFICE:* (local correspondence only) P.O. Box 5257, Chanakya Puri Post Office, New Delhi, 110 021, India. Forwards mail from Indian listeners to the Netherlands every three weeks.
**📻Radio Voice of Hope**, Plot No. 15, Komi Crescent, Lusira, 338829 Kampala, Uganda. Phone: +256 (41) 220-334. Email:

webmaster@radiovoiceofhope.net; hope@africaonline.co.ug; or (Namadi) jnamadi@excite.com. Web: (includes RealAudio) www.radiovoiceofhope.net. Contact: Jane Namadi, Editor. Return postage requested. Programs are produced by the New Sudan Council of Churches (NSCC) at studios in the Netherlands and Uganda. Identifies as "Radio Voice of Hope for the voiceless in southern Sudan." Transmits via the Radio Nederland relay station in Madagascar, and is a project sponsored by the Dutch public broadcaster NCRV and supported by Pax Christi and the Interchurch Organization for Development Corporation.
*KENYA ADDRESS:* P.O.Box 66168, Nairobi, Kenya. Phone: +254 (2) 446-966 or +254 (2) 448-141/2. Fax: +254 (2) 447 015. Email: nscc-nbo@maf.org.

## NETHERLANDS ANTILLES   World Time –4

**Radio Nederland Wereldomroep—Bonaire Relay**, P.O. Box 45, Kralendijk, Netherlands Antilles. Contact: Leo Kool, Manager. Nontechnical correspondence should be sent to Radio Nederland Wereldomroep in the Netherlands (*see*).

## NEW ZEALAND   World Time +13 (+12 midyear)

**📻Radio New Zealand International (Te Reo Irirangi O Aotearoa, O Te Moana-nui-a-kiwa)**, P.O. Box 123, Wellington, New Zealand. Phone: +64 (4) 474-1437. Fax: +64 (4) 474 1433 or +64 (4) 474 1886. Email: info@rnzi.com. Web: (includes RealAudio and online reception report form) www.rnzi.com. Contact: Florence de Ruiter, Listener Mail; Myra Oh, Producer, "Mailbox"; or Walter Zweifel, News Editor; (administration) Ms. Linden Clark, Manager; (technical) Adrian Sainsbury, Technical Manager. Free stickers, schedule/flyer about station, map of New Zealand and tourist literature available. English/Maori T-shirts for US$20; sweatshirts $40; interesting variety of CDs, as well as music cassettes and spoken programs, in Domestic "Replay Radio" catalog (VISA/MC). Two IRCs or $2 for QSL card, one IRC for schedule/catalog. Email reports verified by email only.
**Radio Reading Service—ZLXA**, P.O. Box 360, Levin 5500, New Zealand. Phone: (general) +64 (6) 368-2229; (engineering) +64 (25) 985-360. Fax: +64 (6) 368 7290. Email: (general) nzrpd@xtra.co.nz; (Bell) ABell@radioreading.org; (Little) Alittle@radioreading.org; (Stokoe) BStokoe@radioreading.org. Web: www.radioreading.org. Contact: (general) Ash Bell, Manager/Station Director; (administration) Allen J. Little, Executive President; (technical, including reception reports) Brian Stokoe. Operated by volunteers 24 hours a day, seven days a week. Station is owned by the "New Zealand Radio for the Print Disabled Inc." Free brochure, postcards and stickers. $1, return postage or 3 IRCs appreciated.

## NICARAGUA   World Time –6

**Radio Miskut**, Barrio Pancasan, Puerto Cabezas, R.A.A.N., Nicaragua. Phone: +505 (282) 2443. Fax: +505 (267) 3032. Contact: Evaristo Mercado Pérez, Director de Operación y de Programas; or Abigail Zúñiga Fagoth. T-shirts $10, and *Resumen Mensual del Gobierno y Consejo Regional* and *Revista Informativa Detallada de las Gestiones y Logros* $10 per copy. Station has upgraded to a new shortwave transmitter and is currently improving its shortwave antenna. Replies slowly and irregularly to correspondence in English and Spanish. $2 helpful, as is registering your letter.

# NIGER  World Time +1

**La Voix du Sahel**, O.R.T.N., B.P. 361, Niamey, Niger. Fax: +227 72 35 48. Contact: (general) Adamou Oumarou; Issaka Mamadou; Zakari Saley; Souley Boubacou; or Mounkaïla Inazadan, Producer, "Inter-Jeunes Variétés"; (administration) Oumar Tiello, Directeur; (technical) Afo Sourou Victor. $1 helpful. Correspondence in French preferred. Correspondence by males with this station may result in requests for certain unusual types of magazines and photographs.

# NIGERIA  World Time +1

*WARNING—MAIL THEFT:* For the time being, correspondence from abroad to Nigerian addresses has a relatively high probability of being stolen.

*WARNING—CONFIDENCE ARTISTS:* For years, now, correspondence with Nigerian stations has sometimes resulted in letters from highly skilled "pen pal" confidence artists. These typically offer to send you large sums of money, if you will provide details of your bank account or similar information (after which they clean out your account). Other scams are disguised as tempting business proposals; or requests for money, free electronic or other products, publications or immigration sponsorship. Persons thus approached should contact their country's diplomatic offices. For example, Americans should contact the Diplomatic Security Section of the Department of State [phone +1 (202) 647-4000], or an American embassy or consulate.

**Radio Nigeria—Enugu**, P.M.B. 1051, Enugu (Anambra), Phone: +234 (42) 254-137. Fax: +234 (42) 255 354. Nigeria. Contact: Louis Nnamuchi, Assistant Director Technical Services. Two IRCs, return postage or $1 required. Replies slowly.

**Radio Nigeria—Ibadan**, Broadcasting House, P.M.B. 5003, Ibadan, Oyo State, Nigeria. Phone: +234 (22) 241-4093 or +234 (22) 241-4106. Fax: +234 (22) 241 3930. Contact: V.A. Kalejaiye, Technical Services Department; Rev. Olukunle Ajani, Executive Director; Nike Adegoke, Executive Director; or Dare Folarin, Principal Public Affairs Officer. $1 or return postage required. Replies slowly.

**Radio Nigeria—Kaduna**, P.O. Box 250, Kaduna (Kaduna), Nigeria. Contact: Yusuf Garba, Ahmed Abdullahi, R.B. Jimoh, Assistant Director Technical Service; or Johnson D. Allen. May send sticker celebrating 30 years of broadcasting. $1 or return postage required. Replies slowly.

**Radio Nigeria—Lagos**, P.M.B. 12504, Ikoyi, Lagos, Nigeria. Phone: +234 (1) 269-0301. Fax: +234 (1) 269 0073. Contact: Willie Egbe, Assistant Director for Programmes; Babatunde Olalekan Raji, Monitoring Unit. Two IRCs or return postage helpful. Replies slowly and irregularly.

**Voice of Nigeria**, P.M.B. 40003 Falomo Post Office, Ikoyi, Lagos, Nigeria. Phone: +234 (1) 269-3075 or +234 (9) 234-4017. Fax: +234 (1) 269 1944 or +234 (9) 234 6970. Email: info@voice ofnigeria.org; dgovon@nigol.net.ng or vonlagos@fiberia.com; (Idowu) tidowu@yahoo.com. Web: www.voiceofnigeria.org. Contact: (general) Alhaji Lawal Yusuf Saulawa, Director of Programming; Mrs. Stella Bassey, Deputy Director Programmes; Ben Egbuna, Acting Director of News; or Livy Iwok, Editor; (administration) Taiwo Alimi, Director General; Alhaji Abubakar Jijiwa, Director of Administration & Finance; Mrs. Margaret Obanya, Assistant Director, Administration; Tope Idowu, Editor "Voice Of Nigeria Airwaves" program magazine & Special Assistant to the Director General; Frank Iloye, Station Manager; or Dr. Walter Ofonagoro, Minister of Information; (technical) Timothy Gyang, Deputy Direc-

tor, Engineering. Replies from station tend to be erratic, but continue to generate unsolicited correspondence from supposed "pen pals" (*see WARNING—CONFIDENCE ARTISTS*, above); faxes, which are much less likely to be intercepted, may be more fruitful. Two IRCs or return postage helpful.

# NORTHERN MARIANA ISLANDS  World Time +10

**Far East Broadcasting Company—Radio Station KFBS Saipan**

*MAIN OFFICE:* FEBC, P.O. Box 500209, Saipan, Mariana Islands MP 96950 USA. Phone: (main office) +1 (670) 322-3841. Fax: +1 (670) 322 3060. Email: saipan@febc.org. Web: www.febc.org. Contact: Chris Slabaugh, Field Director; Irene Gabbie, QSL Secretary; Mike Adams; or Robert Springer, Director. Replies sometimes take months. Also, *see* FEBC Radio International, USA.

# NORWAY  World Time +1 (+2 midyear)

⊠**Radio Norway**

*MAIN OFFICE, NONTECHNICAL:* Utenlandssendingen, NRK, N-0342 Oslo, Norway. Phone: (general) + 47 (23) 048-441 or +47 (23) 048-444; (Norwegian-language 24-hour recording of schedule information +47 (23) 048-008 (Americas, Europe, Africa), +47 (23) 048-009 (elsewhere). Fax: (general) +47 (23) 047 134 or +47 (22) 605 719. Email: radionorway@nrk.no. Web: (includes Windows Media) www.nrk.no/radionorway. Contact: (general) Kirsten Ruud Salomonsen, Head of External Broadcasting; or Grethe Breie, Consultant; (technical) Gundel Krauss Dahl, Head of Radio Projects. Free stickers and flags.

*WASHINGTON NEWS BUREAU:* Norwegian Broadcasting, 2030 M Street NW, Suite 700, Washington DC 20036 USA. Phone: +1 (202) 785-1481 or +1 (202) 785-1460. Contact: Bjorn Hansen or Gunnar Myklebust.

*SINGAPORE NEWS BUREAU:* NRK, 325 River Valley Road #01-04, Singapore.

*FREQUENCY MANAGEMENT OFFICE:* Statens Teleforvaltning, Dept. TF/OMG, Revierstredet 2, P.O. Box 447 Sentrum, N-0104 Oslo, Norway. Phone: +47 (22) 824-889 or +47 (22) 824-878. Fax: +47 (22) 824 891 or +47 (22) 824 790. Email: (Johnsbråthen) erik.johnsbraten@npt.no; (Ohta) ayumu.ohta@npt.no. Contact: Erik Johnsbråthen, Frequency Manager; or Ayumu Ohta.

**UKEsenderen**, Elgesetergate 1, N-7030 Trondheim, Norway. Email: uka@uka.no. Web: www.uka.ntnu.no. A student station which operates on 7215 kHz for approximately three weeks (mid-October to early November) in odd-numbered years.

# OMAN  World Time +4

**BBC World Service—Eastern Relay Station (BERS)**, P.O. Box 23, Wilayat Masirah, Post Code 414, Sultanate of Oman. Technical correspondence should be sent to "Senior Transmitter Engineer"; nontechnical goes to the BBC World Service in London (*see* United Kingdom). A new transmission complex at al-Ashkhara is in the process of replacing the facilities at Masirah, built in 1966.

⊠**Radio Sultanate of Oman**, Ministry of Information, P.O. Box 600, Muscat, Post Code 113, Sultanate of Oman. Phone: +968 602-494 or +968 603-222. Fax: (general) +968 602 055, +968 693 770 or +968 602 831; (technical) +968 604 629 or +968 607 239. Email: (general) tvradio@omantel.net.om; (Frequency Management) sjnomani@omantel.net.om; or abulukman@hotmail.com. Web: (includes RealAudio) www.oman-radio.gov.om. Contact: (Directorate General of Technical Affairs) Abdallah Bin Saif Al-Nabhani, Acting Chief Engineer; Salim Al-Nomani, Director of Frequency Management; or Ahmed Mohamed Al-Balushi, Head of Studio's Engineering. Replies regularly, and responses are from one to two weeks. $1, mint stamps or 3 IRCs helpful.

## PAKISTAN    World Time +5 (+6 midyear)

NOTE: Pakistan introduced Daylight Saving Time (DST) for the first time in 2002. A decision on whether or not to repeat the exercise in subsequent years is not expected until sometime in 2003.

**Azad Kashmir Radio**, Muzaffarabad, Azad Kashmir, Pakistan. Contact: (technical) M. Sajjad Ali Siddiqui, Director of Engineering; or Liaquatullah Khan, Engineering Manager. Registered mail helpful. Rarely replies to correspondence.

**Pakistan Broadcasting Corporation**—same address, fax and contact details as "Radio Pakistan," below. Web: (includes RealAudio) www.radio.gov.pk.

**Radio Pakistan**, P.O. Box 1393, Islamabad 44000, Pakistan. Phone: +92 (51) 921-0689 or +92 (51) 921-4278. Fax: +92 (51) 920 1861 or +92 (51) 922 3877. Email: (general) cnoradio@isb.comsats.net.pk; (technical) cfmpbchq@isb.comsats.net.pk (reception reports to this address have been verified with QSL cards). Web: www.radio.gov.pk/exter.html. Contact: (technical) Ahmed Nawaz, Senior Broadcast Engineer, Room No. 324, Frequency Management Cell; Syed Abrar Hussain, Controller of Frequency Management; Syed Asmat Ali Shah, Senior Broadcasting Engineer; or Nasirahmad Bajwa, Frequency Management. Free stickers, pennants and Pakistan Calling magazine. May also send pocket calendar. Replies irregularly to postal correspondence; better is to use email if you can. Plans to replace two 50 kW transmitters with 500 kW units if and when funding is forthcoming.

## PALAU    World Time +9

**Radio Station T8BZ** (formerly KHBN), P.O. Box 66, High Adventure Radio Network, Koror, Palau PW 96940. Phone: +680 488-2162. Fax: (main office) +680 488 2163; (engineering) +680 544 1008. Email: (technical) cacciatore@lineone.net. Contact: (technical) Rev. Dr. Bill Burton, Chief Engineer. IRC requested. Also, see High Adventure Ministries, USA.

## PAPUA NEW GUINEA    World Time +10

NOTE: Stations are sometimes off the air due to financial or technical problems which can take weeks or months to resolve.

**KBBN** ("Krai Bilong Baibel Bradkesting Netwok"), P.O. Box 617, Mt. Hagen W.H.P., Papua New Guinea. Email: bwells@daltron.com.pg. Contact: Brad Wells. A bible radio ministry initially broadcasting on FM, but which eventually hopes to add a shortwave transmitter.

**National Broadcasting Corporation of Papua New Guinea**, P.O. Box 1359, Boroko 111 NCD, Papua New Guinea. Phone: +675 325-5233, + 675 325-5949 or +675 325-6779. Fax: +675 323 0404, +675 325 0796 or +675 325 6296. Email: pom@nbc.com.pg. Web: www.nbc.com.pg. Contact: (general) Renagi R. Lohia, CBE, Managing Director and C.E.O.; or Ephraim Tammy, Director, Radio Services; (technical) Bob Kabewa, Sr. Technical Officer; or F. Maredey, Chief Engineer. Two IRCs or return postage helpful. Replies irregularly.

**Radio Bougainville**, P.O. Box 35, Buka, North Solomons Province (NSP), Papua New Guinea. Contact: Aloysius Rumina, Provincial Programme Manager; Ms. Christine Talei, Assistant Provincial Manager; or Aloysius Laukai, Senior Programme Officer. Replies irregularly.

**Radio Central** (when operating), P.O. Box 1359, Boroko, NCD, Papua New Guinea. Contact: Steven Gamini, Station Manager; Lahui Lovai, Provincial Programme Manager; or Amos Langit, Technician. $1, 2 IRCs or return postage helpful. Replies irregularly.

**Radio Eastern Highlands** (when operating), P.O. Box 311, Goroka, EHP, Papua New Guinea. Contact: Tonko Nonao, Program Manager; Ignas Yanam, Technical Officer; or Kiri Nige, Engineering Division. $1 or return postage required. Replies irregularly.

**Radio East New Britain** (when operating), P.O. Box 393, Rabaul, ENBP, Papua New Guinea. Contact: Esekia Mael, Station Manager; or Oemas Kumaina, Provincial Program Manager. Return postage required. Replies slowly.

**Radio East Sepik**, P.O. Box 65, Wewak, E.S.P., Papua New Guinea. Contact: Elias Albert, Assistant Provincial Program Manager; or Luke Umbo, Station Manager.

**Radio Enga**, P.O. Box 300, Wabag, Enga Province, Papua New Guinea. Phone: +675 547-1213. Contact: (general) John Lyein Kur, Station Manager; or Robert Papuvo, (technical) Gabriel Paiao, Station Technician.

**Radio Gulf** (when operating), P.O. Box 36, Kerema, Gulf, Papua New Guinea. Contact: Tmothy Akia, Station Manager; or Timothy Akia, Provincial Program Manager.

**Radio Madang**, P.O. Box 2138, Madang, Papua New Guinea. Phone: +675 852-2415. Fax: +675 852 2360. Contact: (general) Damien Boaging, Senior Programme Officer; Geo Gedabing, Provincial Programme Manager; Peter Charlie Yannum, Assistant Provincial Programme Manager; or James Steve Valakvi, Senior Programme Officer; (technical) Lloyd Guvil, Technician.

**Radio Manus**, P.O. Box 505, Lorengau, Manus, Papua New Guinea. Phone: +675 470-9029. Fax: +675 470 9079. Contact: (technical and nontechnical) John P. Mandrakamu, Provincial Program Manager. Station is seeking the help of DXers and broadcasting professionals in obtaining a second hand, but still usable broadcasting quality CD player that could be donated to Radio Manus. Replies regularly. Return postage appreciated.

**Radio Milne Bay** (when operating), P.O. Box 111, Alotau, Milne Bay, Papua New Guinea. Contact: (general) Trevor Webumo, Assistant Manager; Simon Muraga, Station Manager; or Raka Petuely, Program Officer; (technical) Philip Maik, Technician. Return postage in the form of mint stamps helpful.

**Radio Morobe**, P.O. Box 1262, Lae, Morobe, Papua New Guinea. Fax: +675 472 6423. Contact: Ken L. Tropu, Assistant Program Manager; Peter W. Manua, Program Manager; Kekalem M. Meruk, Assistant Provincial Program Manager; or Aloysius R. Nase, Station Manager.

**Radio New Ireland**, P.O. Box 140, Kavieng, New Ireland, Papua New Guinea. Contact: Otto A. Malatana, Station Manager; or Ruben Bale, Provincial Program Manager. Return postage or $1 helpful.

**Radio Northern** (when operating), Voice of Oro, P.O. Box 137, Popondetta, Oro, Papua New Guinea. Contact: Roma Tererembo, Assistant Provincial Programme Manager; or Misael Pendaia, Station Manager. Return postage required.

**Radio Sandaun**, P.O. Box 37, Vanimo, Sandaun Province, Papua New Guinea. Contact: (nontechnical) Gabriel Deckwalen, Station Manager; Zacharias Nauot, Acting Assistant Manager; Celina Korei, Station Journalist; Elias Rathley, Provincial

Programme Manager; Mrs. Maria Nauot, Secretary; (technical) Paia Ottawa, Technician. $1 helpful.

**Radio Simbu**, P.O. Box 228, Kundiawa, Chimbu, Papua New Guinea. Phone: +675 735-1038 or +675 735-1082. Fax: +675 735 1012. Contact: (general) Jack Wera, Manager; Tony Mill Waine, Provincial Programme Manager; Felix Tsiki; or Thomas Ghiyandiule, Producer, "Pasikam Long ol Pipel." Cassette recordings $5. Free two-Kina banknotes.

**Radio Southern Highlands** (when operating), P.O. Box 104, Mendi, SHP, Papua New Guinea. Contact: (general) Andrew Meles, Provincial Programme Manager; Miriam Piapo, Programme Officer; Benard Kagaro, Programme Officer; Lucy Aluy, Programme Officer; Jacob Mambi, Shift Officer; or Nicholas Sambu, Producer, "Questions and Answers"; (technical) Ronald Helori, Station Technician. $1 or return postage helpful; or donate a wall poster of a rock band, singer or American landscape.

**Radio Western**, P.O. Box 23, Daru, Western Province, Papua New Guinea. Contact: Robin Wainetti, Manager; (technical) Samson Tobel, Technician. $1 or return postage required. Replies irregularly.

**Radio Western Highlands** (when operating), P.O. Box 311, Mount Hagen, WHP, Papua New Guinea. Contact: (general) William Kie, Acting Station Manager; (technical) Esau Okole, Technician. $1 or return postage helpful. Replies occasionally. Often off the air because of theft, armed robbery or inadequate security for the station's staff.

**Radio West New Britain**, P.O. Box 412, Kimbe, WNBP, Papua New Guinea. Fax: +675 983 5600. Contact: Valuka Lowa, Provincial Station Manager; Darius Gilime, Provincial Program Manager; Lemeck Kuam, Producer, "Questions and Answers"; or Esekial Mael. Return postage required.

# PARAGUAY    World Time –3 (–4 midyear)

**Radio Encarnación** (if reactivated), Gral. Artigas casi Gral. B. Caballero, Encarnación, Paraguay. Phone: +595 (71) 4376 or +595 (71) 3345. Fax: +595 (71) 4099. Contact: Bienvenida Kriskovich Vda. de Madelaire, Propietaria. $1 or return postage helpful. On February 6, 2001—after 43 years and a lengthy legal battle which went all the way to the Paraguayan supreme court—the station was returned to its rightful owners. Unfortunately, both the mediumwave and shortwave transmitting equipment had been dismantled before being handed over, and was totally unusable. It remains to be seen if and when the station will be reactivated.

**Radio Guairá** (if reactivated), Alejo García y Presidente Franco, Villarrica, Paraguay. Phone: +595 (541) 2385 or +595 (541) 3411. Fax: +595 (541) 2130. Contact: (general) Lídice Rodríguez, Propietaria; (technical) Enrique Traversi. Welcomes correspondence in Spanish. $1 or return postage helpful.

**Radio Nacional del Paraguay** (when operating), Blas Garay 241 entre Yegros e Iturbe, Asunción, Paraguay. Phone: +595 (21) 449-213. Fax: +595 (21) 332 750. Free tourist brochure. $1 or return postage required. Replies, sometimes slowly, to correspondence in Spanish.

# PERU    World Time–5

*NOTE: Obtaining replies from Peruvian stations calls for creativity, tact, patience—and the proper use of Spanish, not form letters and the like.*

**CPN Radio**, Cadena Peruana de Noticias, Gral. Salaverry 156, Miraflores, Lima, Peru. Phone: +51 (1) 446-1554 or +51 (1) 445-7770. Email: webmastercpn@gestion.com.pe. Web: www.cpnradio.com.pe. Contact: Oscar Romero Caro, Gerente General; or Zenaida Solís, Directora de Programas.

**Estación C**, Casilla de Correo 210, Moyobamba, San Martín, Peru. Contact: Porfirio Centurión, Propietario.

**Estación Tarapoto** (if reactivated), Jirón Federico Sánchez 720, Tarapoto, Peru. Phone: +51 (94) 522-709. Contact: Luis Humberto Hidalgo Sánchez, Gerente General; or José Luna Paima, Announcer. Replies occasionally to correspondence in Spanish.

**Estación Wari**, Calle Nazareno 108, Ayacucho, Peru. Phone: +51 (64) 813-039. Contact: Walter Muñoz Ynga I., Gerente.

**Estación X (Equis)**, Calle Argentina 198, Bagua, Departamento de Amazonas, Peru.

**Frecuencia Líder (Radio Bambamarca)**, Jirón Jorge Chávez 416, Bambamarca, Hualgayoc, Cajamarca, Peru. Phone: (office) +51 (74) 713-260; (studio) +51 (74) 713-249. Contact: (general) Valentín Peralta Díaz, Gerente; Irma Peralta Rojas; or Carlos Antonio Peralta Rojas; (technical) Oscar Lino Peralta Rojas. Free station photos. *La Historia de Bambamarca* book for 5 Soles; cassettes of Peruvian and Latin American folk music for 4 Soles each; T-shirts for 10 Soles each (sending US$1 per Sol should suffice and cover foreign postage costs, as well). Replies occasionally to correspondence in Spanish. Considering replacing their transmitter to improve reception.

**Frecuencia San Ignacio**, Jirón Villanueva Pinillos 330, San Ignacio, Cajamarca, Peru. Contact: Franklin R. Hoyos Cóndor, Director Gerente; or Ignacio Gómez Torres, Técnico de Sonido. Replies to correspondence in Spanish. $1 or return postage necessary.

**Frecuencia VH**—*see* Radio Frecuencia VH.

**La Super Radio San Ignacio** (when operating), Avenida Víctor Larco 104, a un costado del campo deportivo, San Ignacio, Distrito de Sinsicap, Provincia de Otuzco, La Libertad, Peru.

**La Voz de Anta**, Distrito de Anta, Provincia de Acobamba, Departamento de Huancavelica. Phone: +51 (64) 750-201.

**La Voz de la Selva**—*see* Radio La Voz de la Selva.

**La Voz de San Juan**—*see* Radio La Voz de San Juan.

**La Voz del Campesino**—*see* Radio La Voz del Campesino.

**La Voz del Marañón**—*see* Radio La Voz del Marañón.

**Ondas del Suroriente**—*see* Radio Ondas del Suroriente, below.

**Radio Adventista Mundial—La Voz de la Esperanza**, Jirón Dos de Mayo No. 218, Celendín, Cajamarca, Peru. Contact: Francisco Goicochea Ortiz, Director; or Lucas Solano Oyarce, Director de Ventas.

**Radio Altura (Cerro de Pasco)**, Casilla de Correo 140, Cerro de Pasco, Pasco, Peru. Phone: +51 (64) 721-875, +51 (64) 722-398. Contact: Oswaldo de la Cruz Vásquez, Gerente General. Replies to correspondence in Spanish.

**Radio Altura (Huarmaca)**, Antonio Raymondi 3ra Cuadra, Distrito de Huarmaca, Provincia de Huancabamba, Piura, Peru.

**Radio Amauta del Perú**, (when operating), Jirón Manuel Iglesias s/n, a pocos pasos de la Plazuela San Juan, San Pablo, Cajamarca, Nor Oriental del Marañón, Peru.

**Radio Amistad**, Manzana I-11, Lote 6, Calle 22, Urbanización Mariscal Cáceres, San Juan de Lurigancho, Lima, Peru. Phone: +51 (1) 392-3640. Email: radioamistad@peru.com. Contact: Manuel Mejía Barboza. Accepts email reception reports.

**Radio Ancash**, Casilla de Correo 221, Huaraz, Peru. Phone: +51 (44) 721-381,+51 (44) 721-359, +51 (44) 721-487, +51 (44) 722-512. Fax: +51 (44) 722 992. Contact: Armando Moreno Romero, Gerente General. Replies to correspondence in Spanish.

**Radio Andahuaylas**, Jr. Ayacucho No. 248, Andahuaylas, Apurímac, Peru. Contact: Sr. Daniel Andréu C., Gerente. $1 required. Replies irregularly to correspondence in Spanish.

**Radio Andina (Huancabamba)**, Huáscar 201, Huancabamba, Piura, Peru. According to an on-air announcement, the station is expected to move to Avenida Ramón Castilla 254. Phone: +51 (74) 473-104. Contact: Manuel Campos Ojeda, Director.

**Radio Andina (Huancayo)**, Real 175, Huancayo, Junín, Peru. Phone: +51 (64) 231-123. Replies infrequently to correspondence in Spanish.

**Radio Apurímac** (when operating), Jirón Cusco 206 (or Ovalo El Olivo No. 23), Abancay, Apurímac, Peru. Contact: Antero Quispe Allca, Director General.

**Radio Atlántida**

STATION: Jirón Arica 441, Iquitos, Loreto, Peru. Phone: +51 (94) 234-452, +51 (94) 234-962. Contact: Pablo Rojas Bardales.

LISTENER CORRESPONDENCE: Sra. Carmela López Paredes, Directora del prgrama "Trocha Turística," Jirón Arica 1083, Iquitos, Loreto, Peru. Free pennants and tourist information. $1 or return postage required. Replies to most correspondence in Spanish, the preferred language, and some correspondence in English.

**Radio Ayaviri (La Voz de Melgar)** (if reactivated), Apartado Postal 8, Ayaviri, Puno, Peru. Fax: +51 (54) 320 207, specify on fax "Anexo 127." Contact: (general) Sra. Corina Llaiqui Ochoa, Administradora; (technical) José Aristo Solórzano Mendoza, Director. Free pennants. Sells audio cassettes of local folk music for $5 plus postage; also exchanges music cassettes. Correspondence accepted in English, but Spanish preferred.

**Radio Bahía**, Jirón Alfonso Ugarte 309, Chimbote, Ancash, Peru. Phone: +51 (44) 322-391. Contact: Margarita Rossel Soria, Administradora; or Miruna Cruz Rossel, Administradora.

**Radio Bambamarca**—see Frecuencia Líder, above.

**Radio Bethel**—see Radio Bethel Arequipa, below.

**Radio Bethel Arequipa**, Avenida Unión 215, 3er piso, Distrito Miraflores, Arequipa, Peru. Usually announces as "Radio Bethel" and belongs to the "Movimiento Misionero Mundial" evangelistic organization.

**Radio Bolívar**, Correo Central, Bolívar, Provincia de Bolívar, Departamento de La Libertad, Peru. Contact: Julio Dávila Echevarría, Gerente. May send free pennant. Return postage helpful.

**Radio Cajamarca**, Jirón La Mar 675, Cajamarca, Peru. Phone: +51 (44) 921-014. Contact: Porfirio Cruz Potosí.

**Radio Chanchamayo**, Jirón Tarma 551, La Merced, Junín, Peru.

**Radio Chaski**, Baptist Mid-Missions, Apartado Postal 368, Cusco, Peru; or Alameda Pachacútec s/n B-5, Cusco, Peru. Phone: +51 (84) 225-052. Contact: Andrés Tuttle H., Gerente; or Felipe S. Velarde Hinojosa M., Representante Legal.

**Radio Chincheros**, Jirón Apurímac s/n, Chincheros, Departamento de Apurímac, Peru.

**Radio Chota**, Jirón Anaximandro Vega 690, Apartado Postal 3, Chota, Cajamarca, Peru. Phone: +51 (44) 771-240. Contact: Aladino Gavidia Huamán, Administrador. $1 or return postage required. Replies slowly to correspondence in Spanish.

**Radio Comas**, Avenida Estados Unidos 327, Urbanización Huaquillay, km 10 de la Avenida Túpac Amaru, Distrito de Comas, Lima, Peru. Phone: +51 (1) 525-0859. Fax: +51 (1) 525 0094. Email: rtcomas@terra.com.pe. Contact: Edgar Saldaña R.; Juan Rafael Saldaña Reátegui (Relaciones Públicas) or Gamaniel Francisco Chahua, Productor-Programador General.

**Radio Comercial Naranjos** (when operating), Avenida Cajamarca 464, Distrito de Pardo Miguel Naranjos, Provincia de Rioja, San Martín, Peru. Contact: Mario Cusma Vasquez, Propietario; Esperanza Galo Gomez, Gerente Adminitivo; or Pepe Vasquez, Jefe de Producciones.

**Radio CORA**, Compañía Radiofónica Lima, S.A., Paseo de la República 144, Centro Cívico, Oficina 5, Lima 1, Peru. Phone: +51 (1) 433-5005, +51 (1) 433-1188 or +51 (1) 433-0848. Fax: +51 (1) 433 6134. Email: cora@peru.itete.com.pe; cora@lima.business.com.pe. Contact: (general) Juan Ramírez Lazo, Propietario y Director Gerente; Dra. Lylian Ramírez M., Directora de Prensa y Programación; Juan Ramírez Lazo, Director Gerente; or Srta. Angelina María Abie; (technical) Srta. Sylvia Ramírez M., Directora Técnica. Free station sticky-label pads, bumper stickers and may send large certificate suitable for framing. Audio cassettes with extracts from their programs $20 plus $2 postage; women's hair bands $2 plus $1 postage. Two IRCs or $1 required. Replies slowly to correspondence in English, Spanish, French, Italian and Portuguese.

**Radio Coremarca** (if reactivated), Jirón Jaime de Martínez, Bambamarca, Peru. Contact: Virgilio Carranza Tello, Director. A small educational station, so include return postage with your correspondence.

**Radio Cultural Amauta**, Cahuide 278, Apartado Postal 24, Huanta, Ayacucho, Peru. Phone: +51 (64) 832-153. Email: arca@terra.com.pe or montessd@terra.com.pe. Contact: Demetria Montes Sinforoso (Administradora); Vicente Saico Tinco.

**Radio Cusco**, Apartado Postal 251, Cusco, Peru. Phone: (general)+51 (84) 225-851; (management) +51 (84) 232-457. Fax: +51 (84) 223 308. Contact: Sra. Juana Huamán Yépez, Administradora; or Raúl Siú Almonte, Gerente General; (technical) Benjamín Yábar Alvarez. Free pennants, postcards and key rings. Audio cassettes of Peruvian music $10 plus postage. $1 or return postage required. Replies irregularly to correspondence in English or Spanish. Station is looking for folk music recordings from around the world to use in their programs.

**Radio del Pacífico**, Apartado Postal 4236, Lima 1, Peru. Phone: +51 (1) 433-3275. Fax: +51 (1) 433 3276. Contact: J. Petronio Allauca, Secretario, Departamento de Relaciones Públicas; or Julio Villarreal. $1 or return postage required. Replies occasionally to correspondence in Spanish.

**Radio El Sol de los Andes**, Jirón 2 de Mayo 257, Juliaca, Peru. Phone: +51 (54) 321-115. Fax: +51 (54) 322 981. Contact: Armando Alarcón Velarde.

**Radio Estación Uno**, Barrio Altos, Distrito de Pucará, Provincia Jaén, Nor Oriental del Marañón, Peru.

**Radio Estudio 2000**, Distrito Miguel Pardo Naranjos, Provincia de Rioja, Departamento de San Martín, Peru.

**Radio Frecuencia VH ("La Voz de Celendín"; "RVC")**, Jirón José Gálvez 1030, Celendín, Cajamarca, Peru. Contact: Fernando Vásquez Castro, Propietario.

**Radio Frecuencia San Ignacio**—see Frecuencia San Ignacio.

**Radio Horizonte (Chachapoyas)**, Apartado Postal 69 (or Jirón Amazonas 1177), Chachapoyas, Amazonas, Peru. Phone: +51 (74) 757-793. Fax: +51 (74) 757 004. Contact: Sra. Rocío García Rubio, Ing. Electrónico, Directora; Percy Chuquizuta Alvarado, Locutor; María Montaldo Echaiz, Locutora; Marcelo Mozambite Chavarry, Locutor; Ing. María Dolores Gutiérrez Atienza, Administradora; Juan Nancy Ruíz de Valdez, Secretaria; Yoel Toro Morales, Técnico de Transmisión; or María Soledad Sánchez Castro, Administradora. Replies to correspondence in English, French, German and Spanish. $1 required.

**Radio Horizonte (Chiclayo)**, Jirón Incanato 387 Altos, Distrito José Leonardo Ortiz, Chiclayo, Lambayeque, Peru. Phone: +51 (74) 252-917. Contact: Enrique Becerra Rojas, Owner and General Manager. Return postage required.

**Radio Hualgayoc** (when operating), Jirón San Martín s/n, Hualgayoc, Cajamarca, Peru. Contact: Máximo Zamora Medina, Director Propietario.

FCC delegation to the 2002 HFCC frequency coordination conference in Bangkok: Doug Garlinger (dark shirt), LeSEA; Tom Lucey, FCC; George Ross, KTWR; and Dennis Dempsey, WEWN.

D. Garlinger

**Radio Huamachuco** (if reactivated), Jirón Bolívar 937, Huamachuco, La Libertad, Peru. Contact: Manuel D. Gil Gil, Director Propietario.

**Radio Huanta 2000**, Jirón Gervacio Santillana 455, Huanta, Peru. Phone: +51 (64) 932-105. Fax: +51 (64) 832 105. Contact: Ronaldo Sapaico Maravi, Departmento Técnico; or Sra. Lucila Orellana de Paz, Administradora. Free photo of staff. Return postage or $1 appreciated. Replies to correspondence in Spanish.

**Radio Huarmaca**, Av. Grau 454 (detrás de Inversiones La Loretana), Distrito de Huarmaca, Provincia de Huancabamba, Región Grau, Peru. Contact: Simón Zavaleta Pérez. Return postage helpful.

**Radio Ilucán**, Jirón Lima 290, Cutervo, Región Nororiental del Marañón, Peru. Phone: +51 (44) 737-010 or +51 (44) 737-231. Contact: José Gálvez Salazar, Gerente Administrativo. $1 required. Replies occasionally to correspondence in Spanish.

**Radio Imagen**, Casilla de Correo 42, Tarapoto, San Martín, Peru; Jirón San Martín 328, Tarapoto, San Martín, Peru; or Apartado Postal 254, Tarapoto, San Martín, Peru. Phone: +51 (94) 522-696. Contact: Adith Chumbe Vásquez, Secretaria; or Jaime Ríos Tapullima, Gerente General. Replies irregularly to correspondence in Spanish. $1 or return postage helpful.

**Radio Integración**, Av. Seoane 200, Apartado Postal 57, Abancay, Departamento de Apurímac, Peru. Contact: Zenón Hernán Farfán Cruzado, Propietario.

**Radio Internacional del Perú** (when operating), Jirón Bolognesi 532, San Pablo, Cajamarca, Peru.

**Radio Jaén (La Voz de la Frontera)**, Calle Mariscal Castilla 439, Jaén, Cajamarca, Peru. Contact: Luis A. Vilchez Ochoa, Administrador.

**Radio Juliaca (La Decana)**, Jirón Ramón Castilla 949, Apartado Postal 67, Juliaca, San Román, Puno, Peru. Phone: +51 (54) 321-372. Fax: +51 (54) 332 386. Contact: Robert Theran Escobedo, Director.

**Radio JVL**, Jirón Túpac Amaru 105, Consuelo, Distrito de San Pablo, Provincia de Bellavista, Departamento de San Martín, Peru. Contact: John Wiley Villanueva Lara—a student of electronic engineering—who currently runs the station, and whose initials make up the station name. Replies to correspondence in Spanish. Return Postage required.

**Radio La Hora**, Av. Garcilaso 180, Cusco, Peru. Phone: +51 (84) 225-615 or +51 (84) 231-371. Contact: (general) Edmundo Montesinos G., Gerente; (reception reports) Carlos Gamarra

Moscoso, who is also a DXer. Free stickers, pins, pennants and postcards of Cusco. Return postage required. Replies to correspondence in Spanish. Reception reports are best sent direct to Carlos Gamarra's home address: Av. Garcilaso 411, Wanchaq, Cusco, Peru. The station hopes to increase transmitter power to 2 kw if and when the economic situation improves.

**Radio La Inmaculada**, Parroquia La Inmaculada Concepción, Frente de la Plaza de Armas, Santa Cruz, Provincia de Santa Cruz, Departamento de Cajamarca, Peru. Phone: +51 (74) 714-051. Contact: Reverendo Padre Angel Jorge Carrasco, Gerente; or Gabino González Vera, Locutor.

**Radio Lajas**, Jirón Rosendo Mendívil 589, Lajas, Chota, Cajamarca, Nor Oriental del Marañón, Peru. Contact: Alfonso Medina Burga, Gerente Propietario.

**Radio La Merced**, Junín 163, La Merced, Junín, Peru. Phone: +51 (64) 531-199. Occasionally replies to correspondence in Spanish.

**Radio La Oroya**, Calle Lima 190, Tercer Piso Of. 3, Apartado Postal 88, La Oroya, Provincia de Yauli, Departamento de Junín, Peru. Phone: +51 (64) 391-401. Fax: +51 (64) 391 440. Email: rlofigu@net.cosapidata.com.pe. Contact: Jacinto Manuel Figueroa Yauri, Gerente-Propietario. Free pennants. $1 or return postage necessary. Replies to correspondence in Spanish.

**Radio La Voz**, Andahuaylas, Apurímac, Peru. Contact: Lucio Fuentes, Director Gerente.

**Radio La Voz de Abancay**, Avenida Noviembre Lote 6, Urbanización Micaela Bastidas, Abancay, Departamento de Apurímac, Peru. Contact: Lucio Fuentes, Propietario.

**Radio La Voz de Chiriaco**, Jirón Ricardo Palma s/n, Chiriaco, Distrito de Imaza, Provincia de Bagua, Departamento de Amazonas, Peru. Contact: Hildebrando López Pintado, Director; Santos Castañeda Cubas, Director Gerente; or Fidel Huamuro Curinambe, Técnico de Mantenimiento. $1 or return postage helpful.

**Radio La Voz de Cutervo** (if reactivated), Jirón María Elena Medina 644-650, Cutervo, Cajamarca, Peru.

**Radio La Voz de Huamanga** (if reactivated), Calle El Nazareno, 2$^{do}$ Pasaje No. 161, Ayacucho, Peru. Phone: +51 (64) 812-366. Contact: Sra. Aguida A. Valverde Gonzales. Free pennants and postcards.

**Radio La Voz de la Selva**, Jirón Abtao 255, Casilla de Correo 207, Iquitos, Loreto, Peru. Phone: +51 (94) 265-245. Fax: +51 (94) 264 531. Email: lvsradio@terra.com.pe. Contact: Julia

Jáuregui Rengifo, Directora; Marcelino Esteban Benito, Director; Pedro Sandoval Guzmán, Announcer; or Mery Blas Rojas. Replies to correspondence in Spanish.

**Radio La Voz de las Huarinjas**, Barrio El Altillo s/n, Huancabamba, Piura, Peru. Phone: +51 (74) 473-126 or +51 (74) 473-259. Contact: Alfonso García Silva, Gerente Director (also the owner of the station); or Bill Yeltsin, Administrador. Replies to correspondence in Spanish.

**Radio La Voz de Oxapampa**, Av. Mullenbruck 469, Oxapampa, Pasco, Peru. Contact: Pascual Villafranca Guzmán, Director Propietario.

**Radio La Voz de San Juan**, 28 de Julio 420, Lonya Grande, Provincia de Utcubamba, Región Nororiental del Marañón, Peru. Contact: Prof. Víctor Hugo Hidrovo; or Edilberto Ortiz Chávez, Locutor. Formerly known as Radio San Juan.

**Radio La Voz de Santa Cruz** (if reactivated), Av. Zarumilla 190, Santa Cruz, Cajamarca, Peru.

**Radio La Voz del Campesino**, Av. Ramón Castilla s/n en la salida a Chiclayo, Huarmaca, Provincia de Huancabamba, Piura, Peru. Contact: Hernando Huancas Huancas.

**Radio La Voz del Marañón** (if reactivated), Jirón Bolognesi 130, Barrio La Alameda, Cajamarca, Nor Oriental del Marañón, Peru. Contact: Eduardo Díaz Coronado.

**Radio Libertad de Junín**, Cerro de Pasco 528, Apartado Postal 2, Junín, Peru. Phone: +51 (64) 344-026. Contact: Mauro Chaccha G., Director Gerente. Replies slowly to correspondence in Spanish. Return postage necessary.

**Radio Líder**, Portal Belén 115, 2do piso, Cusco, Peru. Contact: Mauro Calvo Acurio, Propietario.

**Radio Lircay** (when operating), Barrio Maravillas, Lircay, Provincia de Angaraes, Huancavelica, Peru.

**Radio Los Andes (Huamachuco)** (if reactivated), Pasaje Damián Nicolau 108-110, 2do piso, Huamachuco, La Libertad, Peru. Phone: +51 (44) 441-240 or +51 (44) 441-502. Fax: +51 (44) 441 214. Contact: Monseñor Sebastián Ramis Torerns.

**Radio Los Andes (Huarmaca)**, Huarmaca, Provincia de Huancabamba, Región Grau, Peru. Contact: William Cerro Calderón.

**Radio Luz y Sonido**, Apartado Postal 280, Huánuco, Peru; (physical address) Jirón Dos de Mayo 1286, Oficina 205, Huánuco, Peru. Phone: +51 (64) 512-394 or +51 (64) 518-500. Fax: +51 (64) 511 985. Contact: (technical) Jorge Benavides Moreno; (nontechnical) Pedro Martínez Tineo, Director Ejecutivo; Lic. Orlando Bravo Jesús; or Seydel Saavedra Cabrera, Operador/Locutor. Return postage or $2 required. Replies to correspondence in Spanish, Italian and Portuguese. Sells video cassettes of local folk dances and religious and tourist themes.

**Radio Madre de Dios**, Daniel Alcides Carrión 385, Apartado Postal 37, Puerto Maldonado, Madre de Dios, Peru. Phone: +51 (84) 571-050. Fax: +51 (84) 571 018 or +51 (84) 573 542. Contact: (administration) Padre Rufino Lobo Alonso, Director; (general) Alcides Arguedas Márquez, Director del programa "Un Festival de Música Internacional," heard Mondays 0100 to 0200 World Time. Sr. Arguedas is interested in feedback for this letterbox program. Replies to correspondence in Spanish. $1 or return postage appreciated.

**Radio Majestad** (if reactivated), Calle Real 1033, Oficina 302, Huancayo, Junín, Peru.

**Radio Marañón**, Apartado Postal 50, Jaén, Cajamarca, Peru; or (street address) Francisco de Orellana 343, Jaén, Cajamarca, Peru. Phone: +51 (44) 731-147 or +51 (44) 732-168. Fax: +51 (44) 732 580. Email: correo@radiomaranon.org.pe. Web: www.radiomaranon.org.pe. Contact: Francisco Muguiro Ibarra,

Director. Return postage necessary. May send free pennant. Replies slowly to correspondence in Spanish and (sometimes) English.

**Radio Marginal**, San Martín 257, Tocache, San Martín, Peru. Phone: +51 (94) 551-031. Rarely replies.

**Radio Máster**, Jirón 20 de Abril 308, Moyobamba, Departamento de San Martín, Peru. Contact: Américo Vásquez Hurtado, Director.

**Radio Melodía**, San Camilo 501, Arequipa, Peru. Phone: +51 (54) 232-071, +51 (54) 232-327 or +51 (54) 285-152. Fax: +51 (54) 237 312. Contact: Hermogenes Delgado Torres, Director; or Señora Elba Alvarez de Delgado. Replies to correspondence in Spanish.

**Radio Moderna**, Jirón Arequipa 323, 2do piso, Celendín, Cajamarca, Peru.

**Radio Mundial Adventista**, Colegio Adventista de Titicaca, Casilla 4, Juliaca, Peru. Currently on mediumwave (AM) only, but is expected to add shortwave sometime in the future.

**Radio Naylamp**, Avenida Andrés Avelino Cáceres 800, Lambayeque, Peru. Phone: +51 (74) 283-353. Contact: Dr. Juan José Grández Vargas, Director Gerente; or Delicia Coronel Muñoz, who is interested in receiving postcards and the like. Free stickers, pennants and calendars. Return postage necessary.

**Radio Nor Andina**, Jirón José Gálvez 602, Celendín, Cajamarca, Peru. Contact: Misael Alcántara Guevara, Gerente; or Víctor B. Vargas C., Departamento de Prensa. Free calendar. $1 required. Donations (registered mail best) sought for the Committee for Good Health for Children, headed by Sr. Alcántara, which is active in saving the lives of hungry youngsters in poverty-stricken Cajamarca Province. Replies irregularly to casual or technical correspondence in Spanish, but regularly to Children's Committee donors and helpful correspondence in Spanish.

**Radio Nor Peruana, Emisora Municipal**, Jirón Ortiz Arrieta 588, 1er. piso del Concejo Provincial de Chachapoyas, Chachapoyas, Amazonas, Peru. Contact: Carlos Poema, Administrador; or Edgar Villegas, program host for "La Voz de Chachapoyas," (Sundays, 1100-1300).

**Radio Nuevo Horizonte**, Consorcio Minero Horizonte, Minera Aurífera Retamas, Distrito de Parcoy, Provincia de Pataz, Departamento de La Libertad, Peru.

**Radio Ondas del Huallaga**, Jirón Leoncio Prado 723, Apartado Postal 343, Huánuco, Peru. Phone: +51 (64) 511-525 or +51 (64) 512-428. Contact: Flaviano Llanos Malpartida, Representante Legal. $1 or return postage required. Replies to correspondence in Spanish.

**Radio Ondas del [Río] Marañón**, Jirón Amazonas 315, Distrito de Aramango, Provincia de Bagua, Departamento de Amazonas, Región Nororiental del Marañón, Peru. Contact: Agustín Tongod, Director Propietario. "Río"—river—is sometimes, but not always, used in on-air identification.

**Radio Ondas del Río Mayo**, Jirón Huallaga 348, Nueva Cajamarca, San Martín, Peru. Phone: +51 (94) 556-006. Contact: Edilberto Lucío Peralta Lozada, Gerente; or Víctor Huaras Rojas, Locutor. Free pennants. Return postage helpful. Replies slowly to correspondence in Spanish.

**Radio Ondas del Suroriente**, Jirón Ricardo Palma 510, Quillabamba, La Convención, Cusco, Peru.

**Radio Oriente**, Vicariato Apostólico, Avenida Progreso 114, Yurimaguas, Loreto, Peru. Phone: +51 (94) 352-156. Fax: +51 (94) 352 128. Contact: (general) Sra. Elisa Cancino Hidalgo; or Juan Antonio López-Manzanares M., Director; (technical) Pedro Capo Moragues, Gerente Técnico. $1 or return postage required. Replies occasionally to correspondence in English, French, Spanish and Catalan.

**Radio Origen**, Acobamba, Departamento de Huancavelica, Peru.

**Radio Paccha** (if reactivated), Calle Mariscal Castilla 52, Paccha, Provincia de Chota, Departamento de Cajamarca, Peru.

**Radio Paucartambo, Emisora Municipal**
STATION ADDRESS: Paucartambo, Cusco, Peru.
STAFFER ADDRESS: Manuel H. Loaiza Canal, Correo Central, Paucartambo, Cusco, Peru. Return postage or $1 required.

**Radio Perú ("Perú, la Radio")**
STUDIO ADDRESS: Jirón Atahualpa 191, San Ignacio, Región Nororiental del Marañón, Peru.
ADMINISTRATION: Avenida San Ignacio 493, San Ignacio, Región Nororiental del Marañón, Peru. Contact: Oscar Vásquez Chacón, Director General; or Idelso Vásquez Chacón, Director Propietario. Sometimes relays the FM outlet, "Estudio 97."

**Radio Quillabamba**, Jirón Ricardo Palma 432, Apartado Postal 76, Quillabamba, La Convención, Cusco, Peru. Phone: +51 (84) 281-002. Fax: +51 (84) 281 771. Contact: Padre Francisco Javier Panera, Director. Replies very irregularly to correspondence in Spanish.

**Radio Reina de la Selva**, Jirón Ayacucho 944, Plaza de Armas, Chachapoyas, Región Nor Oriental del Marañón, Peru. Phone: +51 (74) 757-203. Contact: José David Reina Noriega, Gerente General; or Jorge Oscar Reina Noriega, Director General. Replies irregularly to correspondence in Spanish. Return postage necessary.

**Radio San Antonio** (Callalli), Parroquia San Antonio de Padua, Plaza Principal s/n, Callalli, Departamento de Arequipa, Peru.

**Radio San Antonio** (Villa Atalaya), Jirón Iquitos s/n, Villa Atalaya, Departamento de Ucayali, Peru. Email: (Zerdin) zerdin@terra.com.pe. Contact: Gerardo Zerdin.

**Radio San Francisco Solano**, Parroquia de Sóndor, Calle San Miguel No. 207, Distrito de Sóndor, Huancabamba, Piura, Peru. Contact: Reverendo Padre Manuel José Rosas Castillo, Vicario Parroquial. Station operated by the Franciscan Fathers. Replies to correspondence in Spanish. $1 helpful.

**Radio San Ignacio**, Jirón Victoria 277, San Ignacio, Región Nororiental del Marañón, Peru. Contact: César Colunche Bustamante, Director Propietario; or his son, Fredy Colunche, Director de Programación.

**Radio San Juan**, Distrito de Aramango, Provincia de Bagua, Departamento de Amazonas, Región Nororiental del Marañón, Peru.

**Radio San Juan**, 28 de Julio 420, Lonya Grande, Provincia de Utcubamba, Región Nororiental del Marañón, Peru. Contact: Prof. Víctor Hugo Díaz Hidrovo; or Edilberto Ortiz Chávez, Locutor.

**Radio San Miguel**, Av. Huayna Cápac 146, Huánchac, Cusco, Peru. Contact: Sra. Catalina Pérez de Alencastre, Gerente General; or Margarita Mercado. Replies to correspondence in Spanish.

**Radio San Miguel** (when operating), Jirón Bolívar 356, a media cuadra de la Plaza de Armas, Provincia de San Miguel, Cajamarca, Peru.

**Radio San Miguel de El Faique** (when operating), Distrito de El Faique, Provincia de Huancabamba, Departamento de Piura, Peru.

**Radio San Nicolás**, Jirón Amazonas 114, Rodríguez de Mendoza, Peru. Contact: Juan José Grández Santillán, Gerente; or Violeta Grández Vargas, Administradora. Return postage necessary.

**Radio Santa Rosa**, Jirón Camaná 170, Casilla 4451, Lima 01, Peru. Phone: +51 (1) 427-7488. Fax: +51 (1) 426 9219. Email: radiosantarosa@terra.com.pe. Web: http://barrioperu.terra.com.pe/radiosantarosa. Contact: Padre Juan Sokolich Alvarado, Director; or Lucy Palma Barreda. Free stickers and pennants. $1 or return postage necessary. 180-page book commemorating station's 35th anniversary $10. Replies to correspondence in Spanish.

**Radio Satélite**, Jirón Cutervo No. 543, Provincia de Santa Cruz, Cajamarca, Peru. Phone: +51 (74) 714-074, +51 (74) 714-169. Contact: Sabino Llamo Chávez, Gerente. Free tourist brochure. $1 or return postage required. Replies to correspondence in Spanish.

**Radio Sicuani**, Jirón 2 de Mayo 212, Sicuani, Canchis, Cusco, Peru; or Apartado Postal 45, Sicuani, Peru. Phone: +51 (84) 351-136 or +51 (84) 351-698. Fax: +51 (84) 351 697. Email: cecosda@mail.cosapidata.com.pe. Contact: Mario Ochoa Vargas, Director.

**Radio Soledad** (if reactivated), Centro Minero de Retama, Distrito de Parcoy, Provincia de Pataz, La Libertad, Peru. Contact: Vicente Valdivieso, Locutor. Return postage necessary.

**Radio Sudamérica**, Jirón Ramón Castilla 491, tercer nivel, Plaza de Armas, Cutervo, Cajamarca, Peru. Phone: +51 (74) 736-090 or +51 (74) 737-443. Contact: Jorge Luis Paredes Guerra, Administrador; or Amadeo Mario Muñoz Guivar, Propietario.

**Radio Superior (Bolívar)**, Jirón San Martín 229, Provincia de Bolívar, Departamento de La Libertad, Peru.

**Radio Tacna**, Aniceto Ibarra 436, Casilla de Correo 370, Tacna, Peru. Phone: +51 (54) 714-871. Fax: +51 (54) 723 745. Email: scaceres@viabcp.com. Contact: (nontechnical and technical) Ing. Alfonso Cáceres Contreras, Sub-Gerente/Jefe Técnico; (administration) Yolanda Vda. de Cáceres C., Directora Gerente. Free stickers and samples of *Correo* local newspaper. $1 or return postage helpful. Audio cassettes of Peruvian and other music $2 plus postage. Replies irregularly to correspondence in English and Spanish.

**Radio Tawantinsuyo**, Av. Sol 806, Cusco, Peru. Phone: +51 (84) 226-955 or +51 (84) 228-411. Contact: Ing. Raul Montesinos Espejo, Director Gerente. Has a very attractive QSL card, but only replies occasionally to correspondence, which should be in Spanish.

**Radio Tarma**, Jirón Molino del Amo 167, Apartado Postal 167, Tarma, Peru. Phone/fax: +51 (64) 321-167 or +51 (64) 321-510. Contact: Mario Monteverde Pomareda, Gerente General. Sometimes sends 100 Inti banknote in return when $1 enclosed. Free stickers. $1 or return postage required. Replies irregularly to correspondence in Spanish.

**Radio Tayacaja** (when operating), Correo Central, Distrito de Pampas, Tayacaja, Huancavelica, Peru. Phone: +51 (64) 220-217, Anexo 238. Contact: (general) J. Jorge Flores Cárdenas; (technical) Ing. Larry Guido Flores Lezama. Free stickers and pennants. Replies to correspondence in Spanish. Hopes to replace transmitter.

**Radio Tingo María** (when operating), Jirón Callao 115 (or Av. Raimondi No. 592), Casilla de Correo 25, Tingo María, Leoncio Prado, Departamento de Huánuco, Peru. Contact: Gina A. de la Cruz Ricalde, Administradora; or Ricardo Abad Vásquez, Gerente. Free brochures. $1 required. Replies slowly to correspondence in Spanish.

**Radio Tropical**, Casilla de Correo 31, Tarapoto, Peru. Phone: +51 (94) 522-083 or +51 (94) 524-689. Fax: +51 (94) 522 155. Contact: Mery A. Rengifo Tenazoa, Secretaria; or Luis F. Mori Reátegui, Gerente. Free stickers, occasionally free pennants, and station history booklet. $1 or return postage required. Replies occasionally to correspondence in Spanish.

**Radio Unión**, Apartado Postal 833, Lima 27, Peru; or (street address) Avenida Central 717 - Piso 12, San Isidro, Lima 27,

Peru. Phone: +51 (1) 440-2093. Fax: +51 (1) 440 7594. Email: runion@amauta.rcp.net.pe. Contact: Raúl Rubbeck Jiménez, Director Gerente; Juan Zubiaga Santiváñez, Gerente; Natividad Albizuri Salinas, Secretaria; or Juan Carlos Sologuren, Dpto. de Administración, who collects stamps. Free satin pennants and stickers. IRC required, and enclosing used or new stamps from various countries is especially appreciated. Replies irregularly to correspondence and tape recordings, with Spanish preferred.

**Radio Uno**, Av. Balta 1480, 3er piso, frente al Mercado Modelo, Chiclayo, Peru. Phone: +51 (74) 224-967. Contact: Luz Angela Romero, Directora del noticiero "Encuentros"; Plutarco Chamba Febres, Director Propietario; Juan Vargas, Administrador; or Filomena Saldívar Alarcón, Pauta Comercial. Return postage required.

**Radio Uripa**, Avenida Túpac Amaru s/n, Uripa, Provincia de Chincheros, Departamento de Apurímac, Peru. Contact: Lorenzo Quispe Nauto, Propietario.

**Radio Victoria**, Jr.Reynel 320, Mirones Bajo, Lima 1, Peru. Phone: +51 (1) 336-5448. Fax: +51 (1) 427 1195. Email: soermi@mixmail.com. Contact: Marta Flores Ushinahua. This station is owned by the Brazilian-run Pentecostal Church "Dios Es Amor," with local headquarters at Av. Arica 248, Lima; phone: +51 (1) 330-8023. Their program "La Voz de la Liberación" is produced locally and aired over numerous Peruvian shortwave stations.

**Radio Virgen del Carmen ("RVC")**, Jirón Virrey Toledo 466, Huancavelica, Peru. Phone: +51 (64) 752-740. Contact: Rvdo. Samuel Morán Cárdenas, Gerente.

**Radiodifusoras Huancabamba**, Calle Unión 409, Huancabamba, Piura, Peru. Phone: +51 (74) 473-233. Contact: Federico Ibáñez Maticorena, Director.

**Radiodifusoras Paratón**, Jirón Alfonso Ugarte 1090, contiguo al Parque Leoncio Prado, Huarmaca, Provincia de Huancabamba, Piura, Peru. Contact: Prof. Hernando Huancas Huancas, Gerente General; or Prof. Rómulo Chincay Huamán, Gerente Administrativo.

# PHILIPPINES   World Time +8

NOTE: Philippine stations sometimes send publications with lists of Philippine young ladies seeking "pen pal" courtships.

**DUR2—Philippine Broadcasting Service** (when operating), Bureau of Broadcasting Services, Media Center, Bohol Avenue, Quezon City, Philippines. Relays DZRB Radio ng Bayan and DZRM Radio Manila.

**⬛Far East Broadcasting Company—FEBC Radio International (External Service)**

MAIN OFFICE: P.O. Box 1, Valenzuela, Metro Manila, Philippines 0560. Phone: (general) +63 (2) 292-5603, +63 (2) 292-9403 or +63 (2) 292-5790; (International Broadcast Manager) +63 (2) 292-5603 ext. 158. Fax: +63 (2) 292 9430; +63 (2) 291 4982 (International Broadcast Manager) +63 (2) 292 9724, but lacks funds to provide faxed replies. Email: febcomphil@febc.org.ph; (Peter McIntyre) pm@febc.jfm.org.ph; (Larry Podmore) lpodmore@febc.jmf.org.ph; (Chris Cooper) ibm@febc.org.ph; Web: www.febc.org; www.febc.ph. Contact: (general) Peter McIntyre, Manager, International Operations Division; (administration) Carlos Peña, Managing Director; Chris Cooper, International Broadcast Manager; (engineering) Ing. Renato Valentin, Frequency Manager; Larry Podmore, IBG Chief Engineer. Free stickers and calendar cards. Three IRCs appreciated for airmail reply. Plans to add a new 100 kW shortwave transmitter.

INTERNATIONAL SCHEDULLING OFFICE: FEBC, 20 Ayer Rajah Crescent, Technopreneur Center, #09-22, Singapore 139964, Singapore. Phone: +65 6773-9017. Fax: +65 6773 9018. Email: phsu@febc.org. Contact: Peter C. Hsu, International Schedule Manager.

NEW DELHI BUREAU, NONTECHNICAL: c/o FEBA, Box 6, New Delhi-110 001, India.

**Radyo Pilipinas, the Voice of Democracy**, Philippine Broadcasting Service, 4th Floor, PIA Building, Visayas Avenue, Quezon City 1100, Metro Manila, Philippines. Phone: (general) +63 (2) 924-2620; +63 (2) 920-3963; or +63 (2) 924-2548; (engineering) +63 (2) 924-2268. Fax: +63 (2) 924 2745. Email: pbs.pao@pbs.gov.ph. Contact: (nontechnical) Evelyn Salvador Agato, Officer-in-Charge; Mercy Lumba; Leo Romano, Producer, "Listeners and Friends"; Tanny V. Rodriguez, Station Manager; or Richard G. Lorenzo, Production Coordinator; (technical) Danilo Alberto, Supervisor; or Mike Pangilinan, Engineer. Free postcards and stickers.

**Radio Veritas Asia**

STUDIOS AND ADMINISTRATIVE HEADQUARTERS: P.O. Box 2642, Quezon City, 1166 Philippines. Phone: +63 (2) 939-0011 to 14, +63 (2) 939-4465, +63 (2) 939-4692 or +63 (2) 939-7476. Fax: (general) +63 (2) 938 1940; (Frequency Planning and Monitoring) +63 (2) 939 7556. Email: (Program Dept.) rvaprogram@rveritas-asia.org; (Audience Research) rva-ars@rveritas-asia.org; (technical) info@radio-veritas.org.ph; (Frequency Management) fmrva@pworld.net.ph. Web: www.rveritas-asia.org. Contact: (administration) Ms. Erlinda G. So, Manager; (general) Ms. Cleofe R. Labindao, Audience Relations Officer; Mrs. Regie de Juan Galindez; or Msgr. Pietro Nguyen Van Tai, Program Director; (technical) Honorio L. Llavore, Technical Director; Alex M. Movilla, Assistant Technical Director; or Alfonso L. Macaranas, Frequency Planning. Free caps, T-shirts, stickers, pennants, rulers, pens, postcards and calendars. Free bi-monthly newsletter UPLINK. Return postage appreciated.

TRANSMITTER SITE: Radio Veritas Asia, Palauig, Zambales, Philippines. Contact: Fr. Hugo Delbaere, CICM, Technical Consultant.

BRUSSELS BUREAUS AND MAIL DROPS: Catholic Radio and Television Network, 32-34 Rue de l' Association, B-1000 Brussels, Belgium; or UNDA, 12 Rue de l'Orme, B-1040 Brussels, Belgium.

**Voice of Friendship**—see FEBC Radio International.

# PIRATE

Pirate radio stations are usually one-person operations airing home-brew entertainment and/or iconoclastic viewpoints. In order to avoid detection by the authorities, they tend to appear irregularly, with little concern for the niceties of conventional program scheduling. Most are found in Europe chiefly on weekends, and mainly during evenings in North America, often just above 6200 kHz, just below 7000 kHz and just above 7375 kHz. These sub rosa stations and their addresses are subject to unusually abrupt change or termination, sometimes as a result of forays by radio authorities.

A worthy source of current addresses and other information on American pirate radio activity is: A*C*E, P.O. Box 12112, Norfolk VA 23541 USA (email: pradio@erols.com; Web: www.frn.net/ace/), a club which publishes a periodical ($20/year U.S., US$21 Canada, $27 elsewhere) for serious pirate radio enthusiasts.

For Europirate DX news, try:

SRSNEWS, Swedish Report Service, Ostra Porten 29, SE-442 54 Ytterby, Sweden. Email: srs@ice.warp.slink.se. Web: www-pp.kdt.net/jonny/index.html.

*Pirate Connection*, P.O. Box 4580, SE-203 20 Malmoe, Sweden; or P.O. Box 7085, Kansas City, Missouri 64113 USA. Phone: (home, Sweden) +46 (40) 611-1775; (mobile, Sweden) +46 (70) 581-5047. Email: etoxspz@eto.ericsson.se, xtdspz@lmd.ericsson.se or spz@exallon.se. Web: www-pp.hogia.net/jonny/pc. Six issues annually for about $23. Related to SRSNEWS, above.

*FRS Goes DX*, P.O. Box 2727, NL-6049 ZG Herten, Netherlands. Email: FRSH@pi.net; or peter.verbruggen@tip.nl. Web: http://home.pi.net/~freak55/home.htm.

*Free-DX*, 3 Greenway, Harold Park, Romford, Essex, RM3 OHH, United Kingdom.

*FRC-Finland*, P.O. Box 82, FIN-40101 Jyvaskyla, Finland.

*Pirate Express*, Postfach 220342, Wuppertal, Germany.

For up-to-date listener discussions and other pirate-radio information on the Internet, the usenet URLs are: alt.radio.pirate and rec.radio.pirate.

# POLAND   World Time +1 (+2 midyear)

Office of Telecommunication Regulation, Rozyckiego 1C, PL-51-608 Wroclaw, Poland. Phone: +48 (71) 348-8866. Fax: +48 (71) 345 9043. Email: w.sega@urt.gov.pl. Web: http://www.urt.gov.pl. Contact: Wiktor Sega, Deputy Director, Frequency Management Department.

**📻 Radio Maryja**, ul. Żwirki i Wigury 80, PL-87-100 Toruń, Poland. Phone: +48 (56) 655-2361. Fax: +48 (56) 655 2362. Email: radio@radiomaryja.pl; (Kabulska) anna.kabulska@radiomaryja.pl. Web: (includes RealAudio) www.radiomaryja.pl; (Windows Media) http://nyas.radiomaria.org/Poland.asx. Contact: Father Tadeusz Rydzk, Dyrektor; Father Jacek Cydzik; Anna Kabulska, Secretary; or Malgorzata Zaniewska. Polish preferred, but also replies to correspondence in English. Transmits via facilities in western Russia.

**📻 Radio Polonia**

STATION: External Service, P.O. Box 46, PL-00-977 Warsaw, Poland. Phone: (general) +48 (22) 645-9305 or +48 (22) 444-123; (English Section) +48 (22) 645-9262; (German Section) +48 (22) 645-9333; (placement liaison) +48 (2) 645-9002. Fax: (general and administration) +48 (22) 645 5917 or +48 (22) 645 5919; (placement liaison) +48 (2) 645 5906. Email (general): piatka@radio.com.pl; (Polish Section) polonia@radio.com.pl; (English Section) english.section@radio.com.pl; (German Section) deutsche.redaktion@radio.com.pl; (Esperanto Section) esperanto.redakcio@radio.com.pl. Web: www.radio.com.pl/polonia/; (RealAudio in English and Polish) www.wrn.org/ondemand/poland.html. Contact: (general) Rafał Kiepuszewski, Head, English Section and Producer, "Postbag"; Peter Gentle, Presenter, "Postbag"; or Ann Flapan, Corresponding Secretary; (administration) Jerzy M. Nowakowski, Managing Director; Wanda Samborska, Managing Director; Bogumiła Berdychowska, Deputy Managing Director; or Maciej Lętowski, Executive Manager. On-air Polish language course with free printed material. Free stickers, pens, key rings and possibly T-shirts depending on financial cutbacks. DX Listeners' Club.

TRANSMISSION AUTHORITY: PAR (National Radiocommunication Agency), ul. Kasprzaka 18/20, PL-01-211 Warsaw, Poland. Phone: +48 (22) 608-8139/40, +48 (22) 608-8174 or +48 (22) 608-8191. Fax: +48 (22) 608 8195. Email: the format is initial.last name@par.gov.pl, so to reach, say,

Filomena Grodzicka, it would be f.grodzicka@par.gov.pl. Contact: Mrs. Filomena Grodzicka, Head of BC Section; Lukasz Trzos; Mrs. Katalin Jaros; Ms. Urszula Rzepa or Jan Kondej. Responsible for coordinating Radio Polonia's frequencies.

**📻 Radio Racja**

SHORTWAVE: P.O. Box 144, 220102 Minsk, Belarus. Email: rac@user.unibel.by, r101@user.unibel.by, or info@newsbelarus.com. Web: (includes RealAudio) www.racja.pl.

BIALYSTOK FM STATION: Osrodek Radiowy w Bialymstoku, ul. Ciapla 1/7. PL-15-472 Bialystok, Poland. Contact: Wiktor Stachwiuk, Director.

Broadcasts in Belarusian and is opposed to President Lukashenko. The shortwave broadcasts are a joint Minsk-Warsaw production, and transmitted from Warsaw. The Bialystok station is part of the same organization, but has different programs which are intended for the Belarusian community in eastern Poland.

# PORTUGAL   World Time exactly (+1 midyear); Azores World Time −1 (World Time midyear)

**📻 RDP Internacional—Rádio Portugal**, Apartado 1011, 1001 Lisbon, Portugal; (street address) Av. Eng. Duarte Pacheco 26, 1070-110 Lisbon, Portugal. Phone: (general) +351 (21) 382-0000; (engineering) +351 (21) 382-2000. Fax: (general) +351 (21) 382 0165; (engineering) +351 (21) 387 1381. Email: (general) rdpinternacional@rdp.pt; (reception reports and listener correspondence) isabelsaraiva@rdp.pt, or christianehaupt@rdp.pt; (Frequency Management) teresaabreu@rdp.pt or paulacarvalho@rdp.pt. Web: (includes Windows Media) www.rdp.pt/internacional. Contact: (administration) José Manuel Nunes, Chairman; or Jaime Marques de Almeida, Director; (general) Isabel Saraiva or Christiane Haupt, Listener's Service Department; (technical) Eng. Francisco Mascarenhas, Technical Director; (Frequency Management) Teresa Abreu, Frequency Manager; or Ms. Paula Carvalho. Free stickers. May also send literature from the Portuguese National Tourist Office.

**Radio Trans Europe** (transmission facilities), 6º esq., Rua Braamcamp 84, 1200 Lisbon, Portugal. Transmitters located at Sines, and used by RDP Internacional and Germany's Deutsche Welle (see).

# QATAR   World Time +3

**Qatar Radio & Television Corporation**, P.O. Box 3939, Doha, Qatar. Phone: (director) +974 86-48-05; (under secretary) +974 864-823; (engineering) +974 864-518; (main Arabic service audio feed) +974 895-895. Fax: +974 822 888 or +974 831 447. Contact: Jassim Mohamed Al-Qattan, Head of Public Relations. May send booklet on Qatar Broadcasting Service. Occasionally replies, and return postage helpful.

TECHNICAL OFFICE: Qatar Radio and Television Corporation, P.O. Box 1836, Doha, Qatar. Phone: +974 831-443, +974 864-057 or +974 894-613. Fax: +974 831 447. Contact: Hassan Al-Mass, Abdelwahab Al-Kawary; or Issa Ahmed Al-Hamadi, Head of Frequency Management.

# ROMANIA   World Time +2 (+3 midyear)

**📻 Radio România Actualitati**, Societatea Româna de Radiodifuziune, 60-62 Berthelot St., RO-70747 Bucharest, Romania. Phone: +40 (1) 615-9350. Fax: +40 (1) 223 2612.

**📻 Radio România International**

STATION: 60-62 Berthelot St., RO-70747 Bucharest, Romania;

P.O. Box 111, RO-70756 Bucharest, Romania; or Romanian embassies worldwide. Phone: (general) +40 (1) 222-2556, +40 (1) 303-1172, +40 (1) 303-1488 or +40 (1) 312-3645; (English Department) +40 (1) 303-1357; (engineering) +40 (1) 303-1193. Fax: (general) +40 (1) 223 2613 [if no connection, try via the office of the Director General of Radio România, but mark fax "Pentru RRI"; that fax is +40 (1) 222 5641]; (Engineering Services) +40 (1) 312 1056/7 or +40 (1) 615 6992. Email: (general) rri@rri.ro; (English Service) engl@rri.ro; (Nisipeanu) mnisipeanu@radio.rornet.ro; (Ianculescu) rianculescu@rri.ro. Web: (includes RealAudio) www.rri.ro. Contact: (communications in English or Romanian) Dan Balamat, "Listeners' Letterbox"; or Ioana Masariu, Head of the English Service; (radio enthusiasts' issues, English only) "DX Mailbox," English Department; (communications in French or Romanian) Doru Vasile Ionescu, Deputy General Director; (listeners' letters) Dan Dumitrescu; (technical) Sorin Floricu, Head of Broadcasting Department; Radu Ianculescu, Frequency Monitoring Engineer; or Marius Nisipeanu, Director, Production & Broadcasting. Free stickers, pennants, posters, pins and assorted other items. Listeners' Club. Annual contests. Replies slowly but regularly. Concerns about frequency management should be directed to the PTT (*see* below), with copies to the Romanian Autonomous Company (*see* farther below) and to a suitable official at RRI.

*TRANSMISSION AND FREQUENCY MANAGEMENT, PTT:* General Directorate of Regulations, Ministry of Communications, 14a Al. Libertatii, R-70060 Bucharest, Romania. Phone: +40 (1) 400-1312 or +40 (1) 400-177. Fax: +40 (1) 400 1230. Email: rianculescu@rri.ro. Contact: Mrs. Elena Danila, Head of Frequency Management Department.

*TRANSMISSION AND FREQUENCY MANAGEMENT, AUTONO-MOUS COMPANY:* Romanian Autonomous Company for Radio Communications, 14a Al. Libertatii, R-70060 Bucharest, Romania. Phone: +40 (1) 400-1072. Fax: +40 (1) 400 1228 or +40 (1) 335 5965. Email: marian@snr.ro. Contact: Mr. Marian Ionitá, Executive Director of Operations.

# RUSSIA (Times given for republics, oblasts and krays):

- World Time +2 (+3 midyear) Kaliningradskaya;
- World Time +3 (+4 midyear) Adygeya, Arkhangelskaya, Astrakhanskaya, Belgorodskaya, Bryanskaya, Chechnya, Chuvashiya, Dagestan, Ingushetiya, Kabardino-Balkariya, Kalmykiya, Kaluzhskaya, Karachayevo-Cherkesiya, Ivanovskaya, Karelia, Kirovskaya, Komi, Kostromskaya, Krasnodarskiy, Kurskaya, Leningradskaya (including St. Petersburg), Lipetskaya, Mariy-El, Mordoviya, Moskovskaya (including the capital, Moscow), Murmanskaya, Nenetskiy, Nizhegorodskaya, Novgorodskaya, Severnaya Osetiya, Orlovskaya, Penzenskaya, Pskovskaya, Rostovskaya, Ryazanskaya, Saratovskaya, Smolenskaya, Stavropolskiy, Tambovskaya, Tatarstan, Tulskaya, Tverskaya, Ulyanovskaya, Vladimirskaya, Volgogradskaya, Vologodskaya, Voronezhskaya, Yaroslavskaya;
- World Time +4 (+5 midyear) Samarskaya, Udmurtiya;
- World Time +5 (+6 midyear) Bashkortostan, Chelyabinskaya, Khanty-Mansiyskiy, Komi-Permyatskiy, Kurganskaya, Orenburgskaya, Permskaya, Sverdlovskaya, Tyumenskaya, Yamalo-Nenetskiy;
- World Time +6 (+7 midyear) Altayskiy, Novosibirskaya, Omskaya, Tomskaya;
- World Time +7 (+8 midyear) Evenkiyskiy, Kemerovskaya, Khakasiya, Krasnoyarskiy, Taymyrskiy, Tyva;
- World Time +8 (+9 midyear) Buryatiya, Irkutskaya, Ust-Ordynskiy;
- World Time +9 (+10 midyear) Aginskiy-Buryatskiy, Amurskaya, Chitinskaya, Sakha;
- World Time +10 (+11 midyear) Khabarovskiy, Primorskiy, Yevreyskaya;
- World Time +11 (+12 midyear) Magadanskaya, Sakhalinskaya;
- World Time +12 (+13 midyear) Chukotskiy, Kamchatskaya, Koryakskiy;

*VERIFICATION OF STATIONS USING TRANSMITTERS IN ST. PETERSBURG AND KALININGRAD:* Transmissions of certain world band stations—such as Radio Rossii and China Radio International—when emanating from transmitters located in St. Petersburg and Kaliningrad, may be verified directly from: World Band Verification QSL Service, Centre for Broadcasting and Radio Communications No. 2 (CRR-2), ul. Akademika Pavlova 13A, 197376 St. Petersburg, Russia. Phone: +7 (812) 234-1002. Fax: +7 (812) 234 2971 during working hours. Contact: Mikhail V. Sergeyev, Chief Engineer; or Mikhail Timofeyev, verifier. Free stickers. Two IRCs required for a reply, which upon request includes a copy of "Broadcast Schedule," which gives transmission details (excluding powers) for all transmissions emanating from three distinct transmitter locations: Kaliningrad-Bolshakovo, St. Petersburg and St. Petersburg-Popovka.

## Government Radio Agencies

*C.I.S. FREQUENCY MANAGEMENT ENGINEERING OFFICE:* General Radio Frequency Center, 7 Nikolskaya Str., 103012 Moscow, Russia. Phone/fax: +7 (095) 789-3587. Email: (Titov) titov@vr.ru. Web: www.mccbn.ru. Contact: (general) Mrs. Antonia Ostakhova, Interpreter, Mrs. Nina Bykova, Monitoring Coordinator; or Ms. Margarita Ovetchkina, Frequency Manager; (administration) Anatoliy T. Titov, Chief Director. This office is responsible for the operation of radio broadcasting in the Russian Federation, as well as for frequency usage of transmitters throughout much of the C.I.S. Correspondence should be concerned only with significant technical observations or engineering suggestions concerning frequency management improvement—not regular requests for verifications. Correspondence in Russian preferred, but English accepted.

*CENTRE FOR BROADCASTING AND RADIO COMMUNICATIONS NO. 2 (GPR-2)—see VERIFICATION OF STATIONS USING TRANSMITTERS IN ST. PETERSBURG AND KALININGRAD, above.*

*STATE RADIO COMPANY:* AS Radioagency Co., Pyatnitskaya 25, 115326 Moscow, Russia. Phone: (Staviskaia) +7 (095) 950-6115. Fax: (Staviskaia) +7 (095) 950 6851. Email: (Staviskaia) srm@vr.ru. Contact: Mrs. Rachel Staviskaia, Director of Technical Development.

*STATE TRANSMISSION AUTHORITY:* Russian Ministry of Telecommunication, ul. Tverskaya 7, 103375 Moscow, Russia. Phone: +7 (095) 201-6568. Fax: +7 (095) 292 7086 or +7 (095) 292 7128. Contact: Anatoly C. Batiouchkine.

*STATE TV AND RADIO COMPANY:* Russian State TV and Radio Company, Yamskogo polya, 5-ya ul. 19/21, 125124 Moscow, Russia. Phone: +7 (095) 213-1054, +7 (095) 213-1054 or +7 (095) 250-0511. Fax: +7 (095) 250 0105. Contact: Ivan Sitilenlov.

**Adygey Radio (Radio Maykop),** ul. Zhukovskogo 24, 352700 Maykop, Republic of Adygeya, Russia. Contact: A.T. Kerashev, Chairman. English accepted but Russian preferred. Return postage helpful.

**Amur Radio,** GTRK Amur, per Svyatitelya Innokentiya 15, 675000 Blagoveschensk, Russia. Contact: V.I. Kal'chenko, Chief Engineer.

**Arkhangel'sk Radio**, GTRK "Pomorye," ul. Popova 2, 163000 Arkhangel'sk, Arkhangel'skaya Oblast, Russia; or U1PR, Valentin G. Kalasnikov, ul. Suvorov 2, kv. 16, Arkhangel'sk, Arkhangel'skaya Oblast, Russia. Replies irregularly to correspondence in Russian.

**Buryat Radio**, Dom Radio, ul. Erbanova 7, 670013 Ulan-Ude, Republic of Buryatia, Russia. Contact: Z.A. Telin; Mrs. M.V. Urbaeva, 1st Vice-Chairman; or L.S. Shikhanova.

**Kabardino-Balkar Radio (Radio Nalchik)**, ul. Nogmova 38, 360000 Nalchik, Republic of Kabardino-Balkariya, Russia. Contact: Kamal Makitov, Vice-Chairman. Replies to correspondence in Russian.

**Kamchatka Radio**, RTV Center, Dom Radio, ul. Sovietskaya 62-G, 683000 Petropavlovsk-Kamchatskiy, Kamchatskaya Oblast, Russia. Contact: A. Borodin, Chief OTK; or V.I. Aibabin. $1 required. Replies in Russian to correspondence in Russian or English. Currently inactive on shortwave, apart from a special program for fishermen—*see* next item.

**Kamchatka Rybatskaya**—a special service for fishermen off the coasts of China, Japan and western North America; *see* "Kamchatka Radio," above, for contact details.

**Khabarovsk Radio** (when operating), RTV Center, ul. Lenina 71, 680013 Khabarovsk, Khabarovskiy Kray, Russia; or Dom Radio, pl. Slavy, 682632 Khabarovsk, Khabarovskiy Kray, Russia. Web: (program schedule only) www.khb.ru/Afisha/Radio/kabar.htm. Contact: (technical) V.N. Kononov, Glavnyy Inzhener.

**Khanty-Mansiysk Radio**, Dom Radio, ul. Mira 7, 626200 Khanty-Mansiysk, Khanty-Mansiyiskiy Avt. Okrug, Tyumenskaya Oblast, Russia. Contact: (technical) Vladimir Sokolov, Engineer.

**Koryak Radio**, Koryakskaya GTRK "Palana," ul. Obukhova 4, 684620 Palana, Koryakskiy avt. Okrug, Russia.

**Krasnoyarsk Radio**, Krasnoyarskaya GTRK, "Tsentr Rossii," ul. Mechnikova 44A, 666001 Krasnoyarsk 28, Krasnoyarskiy Kray, Russia. Email: postmaster@telegid.krasnoyarsk.su. Contact: Valeriy Korotchenko; or Anatoliy A. Potehin, RAØAKE. Free local information booklets in English/Russian. Replies in Russian to correspondence in English or Russian. Return postage helpful.

**Magadan Radio**, RTV Center, ul. Kommuny 8/12, 685013 Magadan, Magadanskaya Oblast, Russia. Contact: Viktor Loktionov or V.G. Kuznetsov. Return postage helpful. Occasionally replies to correspondence in Russian.

**Mariy Radio**, Mari Yel, ul. Osipenko 50, 424014 Yoshkar-Ola, Russia. Contact: V. F. Melnikov, Director. Replies in Russian to correspondence in English or Russian. Return postage useful.

**Mayak**—*see* Radiostantsiya Mayak.

**Murmansk Radio**, Sopka Varnichnaya, 183042 Murmansk, Murmanskaya Oblast, Russia; or RTV Center, Sopka Varnichaya, 183042 Murmansk, Murmanskaya Oblast, Russia. Phone: +7 (8152) 561-527. Phone/fax: +7 (8152) 459-770. Fax: +7 (8152) 231 913. Email: tvmurman@sampo.ru; tvmurman@sampo.karelia.ru; murmantv@com.mels.ru. Web: www.sampo.ru/~tvmurman/radio/rmain.html. Contact: D. Peredeni (chairman).

**Perm Radio**, Permskaya Gosudarstvennaya Telekinoradiokompaniya, ul. Technicheskaya 21, 614600 Perm, Permskaya Oblast, Russia; or ul. Krupskoy 26, 614060 Perm, Permskaya Oblast, Russia. Contact: M. Levin, Senior Editor; or A. Losev, Acting Chief Editor.

**Radio Gardarika**, Radio Studio Dom Radio, Ligovsky Prospekt 174, 197002 St. Petersburg, Russia. Email: studiosw@metroclub.ru. Contact: Dmitry Vasyliev, Shortwave Project Manager. Replies to correspondence in Russian and English. Return postage helpful.

**Radio Maykop**—*see* Adygey Radio, above.

**Radio Mix-Master**, Office 1, ul. Oktyabr'skaya 20/1, 677027 Yakutsk, Respublika Sakha, Russia. Phone: +7 (4112) 420-302. Email: mix_radio@rambler.ru. Web: (includes MP3) http://mixmaster.ykt.ru.

**Radio Nalchik**—*see* Radio Kabardino-Balkar, above.

**Radio Rossii** (Russia's Radio), Yamskogo polya 5-ya ul. 19/21, 125124 Moscow, Russia. Phone: +7 (095) 213-1054, +7 (095) 250-0511 or +7 (095) 251-4050. Fax: +7 (095) 250 0105, +7 (095) 233 6449 or +7 (095) 214 4767. Email: webmaster@radiorus.ru. Web: (includes Windows Media) www.radiorus.ru. Contact: Sergei Yerofeyev, Director of International Operations [sic]; or Sergei Davidov, Director. Free English-language information sheet. For verification of reception from transmitters located in St. Petersburg and Kaliningrad, *see NOTE*, above, shortly after the country heading, "RUSSIA."

**Radio Samorodinka**, P.O. Box 898, Center, 101000 Moscow, Russia. Contact: Lev Stepanovich Shiskin, Editor. This station may be licensed as other than a regular broadcaster.

**Radio Studio**—*see* Radio Gardarika.

**Radiostantsiya Mayak**, ul. Pyatnitskaya 25, 115326 Moscow, Russia. Phone: +7 (095) 950-6767. Fax: +7 (095) 959 4204. Email: inform@radiomayak.ru. Web: (includes Windows Media) www.radiomayak.ru. Although no longer operating officially on shortwave from Russia, the station's programs can still be heard on the world bands via outlets such as Belarusian Radio's Program 2 and one or two regional stations in western Siberia. Unofficially, Mayak broadcasts are also aired over certain military transmitters in Belarus which operate in the 2, 3 and 5 MHz bands. Correspondence in Russian preferred, but English increasingly accepted.

**Radiostantsiya Tikhiy Okean** ("Radio Station Pacific Ocean") (when operating), RTV Center, ul. Uborevieha 20A, 690000 Vladivostok, Primorskiy Kray, Russia.

**Sakha Radio**, GTRK Respubliki Sakha, ul. Ordzhonikidze 48, 677007 Yakutsk, Respublika Sakha, Russia. Contact: (general) Alexandra Borisova; Lia Sharoborina, Advertising Editor; or Albina Danilova, Producer, "Your Letters"; (technical) Sergei Bobnev, Technical Director. Russian books $15; audio cassettes $10. Free station stickers and original Yakutian souvenirs. Replies to correspondence in English.

**Sakhalin Radio**, GTRK "Sakhalin," ul. Komsomolskaya 211, 693000 Yuzhno-Sakhalinsk, Sakhalinskaya Oblast, Russia. Phone: (Director of Radio) +7 (42422) 729-349. Phone/fax: (GTRK parent company) +7 (42422) 35286. Email: gtrk@sakhalin.ru; (Romanov) romanov@gtrk.sakhalin.su. Web: www.gtrk.ru/RV/radio.htm. Contact: S. Romanov, Director of Radio.

**Tatarstan Awazy**—*see* Voice of Tatarstan.

**Tyumen' Radio**, RTV Center, ul. Permyakova 6, 625013 Tyumen', Tyumenskaya Oblast, Russia. Email: regtumc@sbtx.tmn.ru. Contact: (general) Liliya Vycherova, Advertising Manager; (technical) V.D. Kizerov, Engineer, Technical Center. Sometimes replies to correspondence in Russian. Return postage helpful.

**Voice of Russia**, ul. Pyatnitskaya 25, Moscow 115326, Russia. Phone: (Chairman) +7 (095) 950-6331; (International Relations Department) +7 (095) 950-6440; (Technical Department) +7 (095) 950-6115. Fax: (Chairman & World Service in English) +7 (095) 230 2828; Email: letters@vor.ru. Web: (includes RealAudio) www.vor.ru. Contact: (Letters Department, World Service in English) Olga Troshina, Tanya Stukova, Elena

Osipova or Elena Frolovskaya; (Chairman) Armen Oganesyan; (International Relations Department) Victor Kopytin, Director; (Technical Department) Ms. Rachel Staviskaya, Director; (World Service in English) Vladimir Zhamkin, Director. For language services other than English contact the International Relations Department.

**Voice of Tatarstan**, ul. Maksima Gor'kogo 15, 420015 Kazan, Tatarstan, Russia. Phone: (general) +7 (8432) 384-846; (editorial) +7 (8432) 367-493. Fax: +7 (8432) 361 283. Email: root@gtrkrt.kazan.su; postmaster@stvcrt.kazan.su. Contact: Hania Hazipovna Galinova.
*ADDRESS FOR RECEPTION REPORTS:* QSL Manager, P.O. Box 134, 420136 Kazan, Tatarstan, Russia. Contact: Ildus Ibatullin, QSL Manager. Offers an honorary diploma in return for 12 correct reports in a given year. The diploma costs 2 IRCs for Russia and 4 IRCs elsewhere. All reports to the QSL Manager address listed above. Accepts reports in English and Russian. Return postage helpful.

## RWANDA   World Time +2

**Deutsche Welle—Relay Station Kigali**—Correspondence should be directed to the main offices in Cologne, Germany (*see*).
📻**Radio Rwanda**, B.P. 83, Kigali, Rwanda. Phone: +250 76540. Fax: +250 76185. Email: (Rwandan Information Office) imvaho2002@yahoo.fr. Web: (includes RealAudio) www.orinfor.gov.rw/radiorwanda.htm. Contact: Marcel Singirankabo. $1 required. Rarely replies, with correspondence in French preferred.

## SAO TOME E PRINCIPE   World Time exactly

**Voice of America/IBB—São Tomé Relay Station**, P.O. Box 522, São Tomé, São Tomé e Príncipe. Contact: Manuel Neves, Transmitter Plant Technician. Replies direct if $1 included with correspondence, otherwise all communications should be directed to the usual VOA or IBB addresses in Washington (*see* USA).

## SAUDI ARABIA   World Time +3

📻**Broadcasting Service of the Kingdom of Saudi Arabia**, P.O. Box 61718, Riyadh-11575, Saudi Arabia. Phone: (general) +966 (1) 404-2795; (administration) +966 (1) 442-5493. Fax: (general) +966 (1) 402 8177. Web: (Holy Quran domestic service, RealAudio only) http://radio.kacst.edu.sa/ithaa.ram. Contact: (general) Mutlaq A. Albegami. Free travel information and book on Saudi history. For technical contacts including Engineering and Frequency Management, see the next entry.
**Saudi Arabian Radio & Television**, P.O. Box 8525, Riyadh-11492, Saudi Arabia. Phone: (technical & frequency managementl) +966 (1) 442-5170. Fax: (technical & frequency management) +966 (1) 404 1692. Email: alsamnan@yahoo.com or inform.eng@suhuf.net.sa. Contact: Suleiman Al-Samnan, Director of Engineering and Frequency Management; Suleiman Al-Kalifa, General Manager; Suleiman Al Haidari, Engineer; or Youssef Dhim.

## SEYCHELLES   World Time +4

**BBC World Service—Indian Ocean Relay Station**, P.O. Box 448, Victoria, Mahé, Seychelles; or Grand Anse, Mahé,

Seychelles. Phone: +248 78-269. Fax: +248 78 500. Contact: (administration) Peter J. Loveday, Station Manager; (technical) Peter Lee, Resident Engineer; Nigel Bird, Resident Engineer; or Steve Welch, Assistant Resident Engineer. Nontechnical correspondence should be sent to the BBC World Service in London (*see*).
**Far East Broadcasting Association—FEBA Radio**
*MAIN OFFICE:* P.O. Box 234, Mahé, Seychelles, Indian Ocean. Phone: (main office) +248 282-2000. Fax: +248 242 146. Email: mmaillet@feba.org.sc. Web: www.feba.org.uk. Contact: (general) Hugh Barton, Seychelles Director; or Andy Platts, Head of Engineering; (reception reports) N. Nugashe, QSL Secretary; Regina Duval; or Doreen Dugathe. Free stickers, pennants and station information sheet. $1 or one IRC helpful. Also, *see* FEBC Radio International—USA and United Kingdom.
*CANADA OFFICE:* 6850 Antrim Avenue, Burnaby BC, V5J 4M4 Canada. Phone: +1 (604) 430-8439. Fax: +1 (604) 430 5272. Email: dpatter@axionet.com.
*INDIA OFFICE:* FEBA India, P.O. Box 2526, 7 Commissariat Road, Bangalore-560 025, India. Phone: +91 (80) 558-5019. Fax: +91 (80) 558 5098. Email: febindia@giasbg01.vsn1.net.in. Contact: Peter Muthl Raj.

## SIERRA LEONE   World Time exactly

**Radio UNAMSIL** (when operating), Mammy Yoko Hotel, Aberdeen, Freetown, Sierra Leone. Email: info@unamsil.org; or patrickcoker@unamsil.org. Web: (UNAMSIL parent organization) www.unamsil.org. Contact: Patrick Coker. Station of the United Nations Mission in Sierra Leone.
**Sierra Leone Broadcasting Service**, New England, Freetown, Sierra Leone. Phone: +232 (22) 240-123; +232 (22) 240-173; +232 (22) 240-497 or 232 (22) 241-919. Fax: +232 (22) 240 922. Contact: Cyril Juxon-Smith, Officer in Charge; or Henry Goodaig Hjax, Assistant Engineer.

## SINGAPORE   World Time +8

**BBC World Service—Far Eastern Relay Station**, VT Merlin Communications, 51 Turut Track, Singapore 718930, Singapore. Phone: + 65 6793-7511. Fax: +65 6793 7834. Contact: (technical) Far East Resident Engineer. Nontechnical correspondence should be sent to the BBC World Service in London (*see*).
📻**MediaCorp Radio**, Farrer Road, P.O. Box 968, Singapore 912899, Singapore; or (street address) Caldecott Broadcast Centre, Caldecott Hill, Andrew Road, Singapore 299939, Singapore. Phone: (general) +65 6251-8622; (Fern) +65 6359-7577; (transmitting station) +65 6793-7651. Fax: +65 6256 9533. Email: (Fern) cherfern@mediacorpradio.com. Web: (includes Windows Media) www.mediacorpradio.com. Contact: (general) Peh Cher Fern, Corporate Communications Senior Executive. Free regular and Post-It stickers, pens, umbrellas, mugs, towels, wallets and lapel pins. Do not include currency in envelope. Successor to the former Radio Corporation of Singapore.
**Radio Nederland via Singapore**—All correspondence should be directed to the regular address in the Netherlands (*see*).
**Radio Japan via Singapore**—All correspondence should be directed to the regular address in Japan (*see*).
📻**Radio Singapore International**, Farrer Road, P.O. Box 5300, Singapore 912899, Singapore; or (street address) Caldecott Broadcast Centre, Annex Building Level 1, Andrew Road, Singapore 299939, Singapore. Phone: (general) + 65 6359-7662;

A visiting American enjoys the BBC World Service during an interlude at South Africa's Kruger National Park. The BBC has had a long history of positive influence in southern Africa.    H. Johnson

(English Service) + 65 6359-7675. Fax: +65 6259 1357 or +65 6259 1380. Email: info@rsi.com.sg; or (English Service) english@rsi.com.sg. Web: (includes Windows Media) www.rsi.com.sg. Contact: (general) Augustine Anthuvan, Assistant Programme Manager, English Service; (technical) Lim Wing Kee, RSI Engineering. Free souvenir T-shirts and key chains to selected listeners. Do not include currency in envelope.

## SLOVAKIA    World Time +1 (+2 midyear)

📻Radio Slovakia International, Mýtna 1, P.O. Box 55, 81755 Bratislava 15, Slovakia. Phone: (Editor-in-Chief) +421 (2) 5727-3730; (English Service) +421 (2) 5727-3736 or +421 (2) 5727-2737; (technical) +421 (2) 5727-3251. Fax: +421 (2) 5249 6282 or +421 (2) 5249 8247; (technical) +421 (2) 5249 7659. Email: (English Section) englishsection@slovakradio sk; for other language sections, the format is rsi_language@slovakradio.sk, where the language is written in English (e.g. rsi_german@slovakradio.sk); (Frequency Manager) chocholata@slovakradio.sk. Web: (includes RealAudio and online reception-report form) www.rsi.sk. Contact: Oxana Ferjenčíková, Director of English Broadcasting; (administration) PhDr. Karol Palkovič, Head of External Broadcasting; or Dr. Slavomira Kubickova, Head of International Relations; (technical) Ms. Edita Chocholatá, Frequency Manager; Jozef Krátky, Ing. May exchange stamps, recipes and coins. Free pennants, pocket calendars, T-shirts (occasionally) and other souvenirs and publications.

## SOLOMON ISLANDS    World Time +11

Solomon Islands Broadcasting Corporation (Radio Happy Isles), P.O. Box 654, Honiara, Solomon Islands. Phone: +677 20051. Fax: +677 23159 or +677 25652. Email: sibcnews@solomon.com.sb. Web: (SIBC news in text format) www.sibconline.com.sb. Contact: (general) Julian Maka'a, Producer, "Listeners From Far Away"; Cornelius Teasi; or Silas Hule; (administration) Johnson Honimae, General Manager; (techni-

cal) John Babera, Chief Engineer. IRC or $1 helpful. Problems with the domestic mail system may cause delays.

## SOMALIA    World Time +3

Radio Baidoa (when operating)
RAHANWEIN RESISTANCE ARMY SPONSORING ORGANIZATION: Email: info@arlaadi.com. Web: www.arlaadi.com; www.arlaadinet.com.
Radio Banaadir—see Radio Banadir, below.
Radio Banadir (when operating), Kaaraan (Beexaani), Mogadishu, Somalia. Phone: +2525 944-156 or +2525 960-368. Email: radiobanadir@somalinternet.com. Web: (includes RealAudio) www.radiobanadir.com.
Radio Baydhabo—see Radio Baidoa, above.
Radio Galkayo (when operating), 2 Griffith Avenue, Roseville NSW 2069, Australia. Phone/fax: +61 (2) 9417-1066. Web: (includes RealAudio and online email form) www.radiogalkayo.com. Contact: Sam Voron, Australian Director. $5, AUS$5 or 5 IRCs required. A community radio station in the Mudug region of northeastern Somalia, and operated by the Somali International Amateur Radio Club. Seeks volunteers and donations of radio equipment and airline tickets.

## SOMALILAND    World Time +3

NOTE: "Somaliland," claimed as an independent nation, is diplomatically recognized only as part of Somalia.
📻Radio Hargeysa, P.O. Box 14, Hargeysa, Somaliland, Somalia. Email: no known direct mail address, but try admin@radiohargeysa.com or radio@somaliland.com. Web: (includes RealAudio) www.radiohargeysa.com; (RealAudio archives only) www.radiosomaliland.com. Contact: Sulayman Abdel-Rahman, announcer. More likely to respond to correspondence in Somali or Arabic.

## SOUTH AFRICA    World Time +2

BBC World Service via South Africa—For verification direct from the South African transmitters, contact Sentech (see below). Nontechnical correspondence should be sent to the BBC World Service in London (see).
📻Channel Africa, P.O. Box 91313, Auckland Park 2006, South Africa. Phone: (executive editor) +27 (11) 714-2255; (technical) +27 (11) 714-2614. Fax: (executive editor) +27 (11) 714 2072. Email: (general) africancan@channelafrica.org; (news desk) news.africa@channelafrica.org; (technical) meyerhelen@channelafrica.org. Web: (includes Windows Media) www.channelafrica.org. Contact: (general) Promise Zamesa, Executive Editor; (technical) Mrs. Helen Meyer, Supervisor Operations. Reception reports are best directed to Sentech (see), which operates the transmission facilities.
Radio Veritas, P.O. Box 53687, Troyeville 2139, South Africa; or (street address) 36 Beelaerts Street, Troyeville 2094, South Africa. Phone: +27 (11) 624-2516; (studio) +27 (11) 614-6225. Fax: +27 (11) 614 7711. Email: info@radioveritas.co.za; (Fr. Blaser) eblaser@iafrica.com. Web: www.radioveritas.co.za. Contact: Fr. Emil Blaser OP, Director. Return postage helpful. Reception reports can also be directed to Sentech (see), which operates the transmission facilities.
📻Radiosondergrense (Radio Without Boundaries), Posbus 91312, Auckland Park 2006, South Africa. Phone: (general) +27 (89) 110-2525; (live studio on-air line) +27 (89) 110-4553; (station manager) +27 (11) 714-2702. Fax: (general) +27 (11) 714 6445; (station manager) +27 (11) 714 3472. Email: (gen-

eral) info@rsg.co.za; (Myburgh) sarel@rsg.co.za. Web: (includes Windows Media) www.rsg.co.za. Contact: Sarel Myburgh, Station Manager. Reception reports are best directed to Sentech (*see*, below), which operates the shortwave transmission facilities. A domestic service of the South African Broadcasting Corporation, and formerly known as Afrikaans Stereo. The shortwave operation is scheduled to be eventually replaced by a satellite and FM network.

**Sentech (Pty) Ltd**, Shortwave Services, Private Bag X06, Honeydew 2040, South Africa. Phone: (general) +27 (11) 475-5600; (shortwave) +27 (11) 475-1596; (Otto) +27 (11) 471-4658 or +27 (11) 471-4537. Fax: (general) +27 (11) 475 5112; (Otto) +27 (11) 471 4758 or +27 (11) 471 4754. Email: (Otto) ottok@sentech.co.za; (Smuts) smutsn@sentech.co.za. Web: (general) www.sentech.co.za; (schedules, unofficial) http://home.mweb.co.za/an/andre46. Contact: Mr. Neël Smuts, Managing Director; Rodgers Gamuti, Client Manager; or Kathy Otto, HF Coverage Planner. Sentech issues its own verification cards, and is the best place to send reception reports for world band stations broadcasting via South African transmission facilities.

**Trans World Radio Africa**
*NONTECHNICAL CORRESPONDENCE:* Trans World Radio—South Africa, Private Bag 987, Pretoria 0001, South Africa. Phone: +27 (12) 807-0053. Fax: +27 (12) 807 1266. Web: (includes online email form) www.twrafrica.org.
*TECHNICAL CORRESPONDENCE:* Reception reports and other technical correspondence are best directed to Sentech (*see*, above) or to TWR's Swaziland office (*see*). Also, *see* USA.

## SPAIN  World Time +1 (+2 midyear)

**☞Radio Exterior de España (Spanish National Radio, World Service)**
*MAIN OFFICE:* Apartado de Correos 156.202, E-28080 Madrid, Spain. Phone: (general) +34 (91) 346-1081/1083; (Audience Relations) +34 (91) 346-1149. Fax: +34 (91) 346 1815. Email: (Director) dir_ree.rne@rtve.es; (Spanish programming) audiencia_ree.rne@rtve.es; (foreign language programming, including English) lenguas_extranjeras.rne@rtve.es; (reception reports) dxree.rne@rtve.es. Web: (includes RealAudio and Windows Media) www.rtve.es/rne/ree. Contact: (Audience Relations) Pilar Salvador M.; (Assistant Director) Pedro Fernández Céspedes; (Director) Javier Garrigós. Free stickers and tourist information. Reception reports can be sent to: Radio Exterior de España, Relaciones con la Audiencia, Sección DX, Apartado de Correos 156.202, E-28080 Madrid, Spain or to the email address listed above.
*TRANSCRIPTION SERVICE:* Radio Nacional de España, Servicio de Transcripciones, Apartado 156.200, Casa de la Radio (Prado del Rey), E-28223 Madrid, Spain.
*HF FREQUENCY PLANNING OFFICE:* Prado del Rey. Pozuelo de Alarcom, E-28223 Madrid, Spain. Phone: (Huerta) +34 (91) 346-1276 or (Almarza) +34 (91) 346-1978. Fax: +34 (91) 346 1402. Email: (Almarza) planif_red2.rne@rtve.es; or (Huerta) plan_red.rne@rtve.es. Contact: Fernando Almarza, Frequency Planning; or José Maria Huerta, Frequency Manager.
*NOBLEJAS TRANSMITTER SITE:* Centro Emisor de RNE en Onda Corta, Ctra. Dos Barrios s/n, E-45350 Noblejas-Toledo, Spain.
*COSTA RICA RELAY FACILITY—see* Costa Rica.
*MOSCOW OFFICE:* P.O Box 88, 109044 Moscow, Russia.
*WASHINGTON NEWS BUREAU:* National Press Building, 529 14th Street NW, Suite 1288, Washington DC 20045 USA. Phone: +1 (202) 783-0768. Contact: Luz María Rodríguez.

## SRI LANKA  World Time +6:00

**Deutsche Welle—Relay Station Sri Lanka**, 92/2 D.S. Senanayake Mawatha, Colombo 08, Sri Lanka. Phone: +94 (1) 699-449. Fax: +94 (1) 699 450. Contact: R. Groschkus, Resident Engineer. Nontechnical correspondence should be sent to Deutsche Welle in Germany (*see*).

**Radio Japan/NHK**, c/o SLBC, P.O. Box 574, Torrington Square, Colombo 7, Sri Lanka. This address for technical correspondence only. General nontechnical listener correspondence should be sent to the usual Radio Japan address in Japan. News-oriented correspondence may also be sent to the NHK Bangkok Bureau (*see* Radio Japan, Japan).

**Sri Lanka Broadcasting Corporation** (also announces as "Radio Sri Lanka" in the external service), P.O. Box 574, Independence (Torrington) Square, Colombo 7, Sri Lanka. Phone: (general) +94 (1) 697-491 or +94 (1) 697-493; (Director General) +94 (1) 696-140. Fax: (general) +94 (1) 697 150 or +94 (1) 698 576; (Director General) +94 (1) 695 488; (Sooriya, Phone/fax) +94 (1) 696-1311. Email: slbc@sri.lanka.net; slbcweb@sri.lanka.net. Web: (general) www.infolanka.com/people/sisira/slbc.html. Contact: Icumar Ratnayake, Controller, "Mailbag Program"; (SLBC administration) Eric Fernando, Director General; Newton Gunaratne, Deputy Director-General; (technical) H.M.N.R. Jayawardena, Engineer -Training and Frequency Management; Wimala Sooriya, Deputy Director - Engineering; or A.M.W. Gunaratne, Station Engineer, Ekala.

**Voice of America/IBB—Iranawila Relay Station**.
*ADDRESS:* International Broadcasting Bureau, Sri Lanka Transmission Station, c/o U.S. Embassy, 210 Galle Road, Colombo 3, Sri Lanka. Contact: Gary Wise, Station Manager. Nontechnical correspondence should be sent to the VOA address in Washington.

## SUDAN  World Time +3

**Sudan National Radio Corporation**, P.O. Box 572, Omdurman, Sudan. Phone: +249 (11) 553-151 or +249 (11) 552-100. Email: snrc@sudanmail.net. Contact: (general) Mohammed Elfatih El Sumoal; (technical) Abbas Sidig, Director General, Engineering and Technical Affairs; Mohammed Elmahdi Khalil, Administrator, Engineering and Technical Affairs; Saleh Al-Hay; or Adil Didahammed, Engineering Department. Replies irregularly. Return postage necessary.

**"Voice of New Sudan's" 10 kW transmitter sometimes changes frequency to avoid Sudanese government jammers.** clandestineradio.com

**Announcer auditions cassettes at Radio Apinte, Suriname.** George Cheng, Jr., Radio Apintie

# SURINAME World Time –3

☞**Radio Apintie**, Postbus 595, Paramaribo, Suriname. Phone: +597 400-500, +597 400-450 or +597 401-400. Fax: +597 400 684. Email: apintie@sr.net. Web: (includes Windows Media) www.apintie.sr. Contact: Charles E. Vervuurt, Director. Free pennant. Return postage or $1 required. Email reception reports preferred, since local mail service is unreliable.

# SWAZILAND World Time +2

**Trans World Radio—Swaziland**
MAIN OFFICE: P.O. Box 64, Manzini, Swaziland. Phone: +268 505-2781/2/3. Fax: +268 505 5333. Email: (James Burnett, Regional Engineer and Frequency Manager) jburnett@twr.org; (Chief Engineer) sstavrop@twr.org; (Mrs. L. Stavropoulos, DX Secretary) lstavrop@twr.org; (Greg Shaw, Follow-up Department) gshaw@twr.org. Web: (transmission schedule) www.gospelcom.net/twr/broadcasts/africa.htm. Contact: (general) Greg Shaw, Follow-up Department; G.J. Alary, Station Director; or Joseph Ndzinisa, Program Manager; (technical) Mrs. L. Stavropoulos, DX Secretary; Chief Engineer; or James Burnett, Regional Engineer. Free stickers, postcards and calendars. A free Bible Study course is available. May swap canceled stamps. $1, return postage or 3 IRCs required. Also, see USA.
AFRICA REGIONAL OFFICE: P.O. Box 4232,Kempton Park 1610, South Africa. Contact: Stephen Boakye-Yiadom, African Regional Director.
CÔTE D'IVOIRE OFFICE: B.P. 2131, Abidjan 06, Côte d'Ivoire.
KENYA OFFICE: P.O. Box 21514 Nairobi, Kenya.
MALAWI OFFICE: P. O. Box 52 Lilongwe, Malawi.
SOUTH AFRICA OFFICE: P.O. Box 36000, Menlo Park 0102, South Africa.
ZIMBABWE OFFICE: P.O. Box H-74, Hatfield, Harare, Zimbabwe.

# SWEDEN World Time +1 (+2 midyear)

**IBRA Radio** (program producer)
MAIN OFFICE: International Broadcasting Association, Box 396, SE-105 36 Stockholm, Sweden; or Box 4033, SE-14104 Huddinge, Sweden. Phone: +46 (8) 619-2540. Fax: +46 (8) 619 2539. Email: hq@ibra.se; or ibra@ibra.se. Web: www.ibra.se; www.ibra.org. Contact: Mikael Stjernberg, Public Relations Manager; or Helene Hasslof. Free pennants and stickers. IBRA Radio's programs are aired over various world band stations, including Trans World Radio (Monaco); and also broadcast via transmitters in Germany and Russia. Accepts emailed reception reports.
CYPRUS OFFICE: P.O. Box 7420, 3315 Limassol, Cyprus. Contact: Rashad Saleem. Free schedules, calendars and stickers.
☞**Radio Sweden**
MAIN OFFICE: SE-105 10 Stockholm, Sweden. Phone: (general) +46 (8) 784-7200, +46 (8) 784-7207, +46 (8) 784-7288 or +46 (8) 784-5000; (listener voice mail) +46 (8) 784-7287; (technical department) +46 (8) 784-7286. Fax: (general) +46 (8) 667 6283; (polling to receive schedule) +46 8 660 2990. Email: (general) radiosweden@sr.se; (In Touch) intouch@p6.sr.se; (schedule on demand) english@rs.sr.se; (Roxström) sarah.roxstrom@rs.sr.se; (Hagström) nidia.hagstrom@rs.sr.se; (Wood) george.wood@p6.sr.se; (Sounds Nordic) sono@p6.sr.se); (Beckman, technical manager) rolf-b@stab.sr.se. Web: (includes RealAudio) www.sr.se/rs.Contact: (general) Nidia Hagström, Host, "In Touch with Stockholm" [include your telephone number]; Sarah Roxström, Head, English Service; Greta Grandin, Program Assistant, English Service; Gabby Katz, Presenter of Heartbeat; Bill Schiller, Spectrum presenter; George Wood; Olimpia Seldon, Assistant to the Director; or Charlotte Adler, Public Relations and Information; (administration) Finn Norgren, Director General; (technical) Rolf Erik Beckman, Head, Technical Department; or Anders Baecklin, Editor, Technical Administration. T-shirts (three sizes) $10 or £8. Payment for T-shirts may be made by international money order, Swedish postal giro account No. 43 36 56-6 or internationally negotiable bank check.
NEW YORK NEWS BUREAU: Swedish Broadcasting, 747 Third Avenue, 8th floor, New York NY 10022 USA. Phone: +1 (212) 644-1224. Fax: +1 (212) 644 1227. Contact: Elizabeth Johansson.
WASHINGTON NEWS BUREAU: Swedish Broadcasting, 2030 M Street NW, Suite 700, Washington DC 20036 USA. Phone: +1 (202) 785-1727. Contact: Folke Rydén, Lisa Carlsson or Steffan Ekendahl.
TRANSMISSION AUTHORITY: TERACOM, Svensk Rundradio AB, P.O. Box 17666, SE-118 92 Stockholm, Sweden. Phone: (general) +46 (8) 555-420-00; (Nilsson) +46 (8) 555-420-66. Fax: (general) +46 (8) 555 420 01; (Nilsson) +46 (8) 555 20 60. Email: (general) info@teracom.se; (Nilsson) magnus.nilsson@teracom.se. Web: www.teracom.se. Contact: (Frequency Planning Dept.—Head Office): Magnus Nilsson; (Engineering) H. Widenstedt, Chief Engineer. Free stickers; sometimes free T-shirts to those monitoring during special test transmissions. Seeks monitoring feedback for new frequency usages.

# SWITZERLAND World Time +1 (+2 midyear)

**European Broadcasting Union**, 17A Ancienne Route, CH-1218 Grand-Saconnex, Geneva, Switzerland; or Case Postal 67, CH-1218 Grand-Saconnex, Geneva, Switzerland. Phone: +41 (22) 717-2111. Fax: +41 (22) 747 4000. Email: ebu@ebu.ch. Web: www.ebu.ch. Contact: Mr. Jean Stock, Secretary-General; or Robin Levey, Strategic Information Service Database Manager. Umbrella organization for broadcasters in 49 European and Mediterranean countries.
**International Telecommunication Union**, Place des Nations, CH-1211 Geneva 20, Switzerland. Phone: (switchboard) +41 (22) 730-5111. Fax: (general) +41 (22) 733 7256; (Broadcasting Services Division) +41 (22) 730 5785. Email: (schedules and reference tables) brmail@itu.int. Web: www.itu.int. The ITU is the world's official regulatory body for all telecommunica-

tion activities, including world band radio. Offers a wide range of official multilingual telecommunication publications in print and/or digital formats.

☞**Radio Réveil**, Paroles, Les Chapons 4, CH-2022 Bevaix, Switzerland. Phone: +41 (32) 846-1655. Fax: +41 (32) 846 2547. Email: contact@paroles.ch. Web (includes RealAudio): www.paroles.ch. An evangelical radio ministry, part of the larger Radio Réveil Paroles de Vie organization, which apart from broadcasting to much of Europe on longwave, mediumwave and FM, also targets an African audience via the shortwave facilities of Germany's Deutsche Telekom (see).

☞**Swiss Radio International (Swissinfo/SRI)**

*MAIN OFFICE:* Giacomettistrasse 1, CH-3000 Berne 15, Switzerland. Phone: (general) +41 (31) 350-9222; (English Department) +41 (31) 350-9790; (French Department) +41 (31) 350-9555; (German Department) +41 (31) 350-9535; (Italian Department) +41 (31) 350-9531; (Frequency Management) +41 (31) 350-9734. Fax: (general) +41 (31) 350 9569; (administration) +41 (31) 350 9744 or +41 (31) 350 9581; (Communication and Marketing) +41 (31) 350 9544; (Programme Department) +41 (31) 350 9569; (English Department) +41 (31) 350 9580; (French Department) +41 (31) 350 9664; (German Department) +41 (31) 350 9562; (Italian Department) +41 (31) 350 9678; (Frequency Management) +41 (31) 350 9745. Email: (general) format is language@sri.ch (e.g. english@sri.ch, german@sri.ch); (marketing) marketing@swissinfo.org; (technical) technical@swissinfo.org; (Frequency Management) ulrich.wegmueller@sri.ch. Web: (includes RealAudio and MP3) www.swissinfo.org. Contact: (general) Nancy Thoeni; Marlies Schmutz, Listeners' Letters, German Programmes; Thérèse Schafter, Listeners' Letters, French Programmes; Esther Niedhammer, Listeners' Letters, Italian Programmes; Beatrice Lombard, Promotion; Giovanni D'Amico, Audience Officer; (administration) Ulrich Kündig, General Manager; Nicolas Lombard, Director; Walter Fankhauser, Head, Communication and Marketing Services; Rose-Marie Malinverni, Head, Editorial Co-ordination Unit; Ron Grünig, Head, English Programmes; James Jeanneret, Head, German Programmes; Diana Zanotta, German Service; Philippe Zahne, Head, French Programmes; Fabio Mariani, Head, Italian Programmes; (technical) Paul Badertscher, Head, Engineering Services; or Ulrich Wegmüller, Frequency Manager. Free station flyers, posters, stickers and pennants. Sells CDs of Swiss music, plus audio and video (PAL/NTSC) cassettes; also, Swiss watches and clocks, microphone lighters, briefcases, umbrellas, letter openers, books, T-shirts, sweatshirts and Swiss Army knives. VISA/EURO/AX or cash, but no personal checks. For catalog, write to SRI Enterprises, c/o the above address, fax +41 (31) 350 9581, or email shopping@sri.srg-ssr.ch. Swiss Radio International will gradually phase out its shortwave transmissions by the end of October 2004 in favor of alternative delivery systems such as the internet and to a lesser extent direct satellite broadcasting in English.

*WASHINGTON NEWS BUREAU:* 2030 M Street NW, Washington DC 20554 USA. Phone: (general) +1 (202) 775-0894 or +1 (202) 429-9668; (French-language radio) +1 (202) 296-0277; (German-language radio) +1 (202) 7477. Fax: +1 (202) 833 2777. Contact: Christophe Erbeck, reporter.

## SYRIA World Time +2 (+3 midyear)

**Ministry of Information**, Maza-Dar-Al-Baath, Damascus, Syria. Phone: +963 (11) 662-0975. Fax: +963 (11) 662 0052. Contact: Mr. Michel Barra.

**Radio Damascus**, Syrian Radio and Television, P.O. Box 4702, Damascus, Syria. Phone: +963 (11) 221-7653. Fax: +963 (11)

222 2692. Contact: Mr. Afaf, Director General; Mr. Adnan Al-Massri; Mr. Mazen Al-Achhab, Head of Frequency Department; Adnan Salhab; Lisa Arslanian; or Mrs. Wafa Ghawi. Free stickers, paper pennants and *The Syria Times* newspaper. Replies can be highly erratic, but as of late have been more regular, if sometimes slow.

## TAIWAN—*see* CHINA (TAIWAN)

## TAJIKISTAN World Time +5

**Radio Tajikistan**, Chapaev Street 31, 734025 Dushanbe, Tajikistan; or English Service, International Service, Radio Tajikistan, P.O. Box 108, 734025 Dushanbe, Tajikistan. Phone: (Director) +7 (3772) 210-877 or +7 (3772) 277-417; (English Department) +7 (3772) 277-417; (Ramazonov) +7 (3772) 277-667 or +7 (3772) 277-347. Fax: +7 (3772) 211 198. Note that the country and city codes are scheduled to be changed in the near future, so the current +7 (3772) should then become +992 (372). Email: treng@td.silk.org. Web: http://radio.tojikiston.com. Contact: (administration) Mansur Sultanov, Director - Tajik Radio; Nasrullo Ramazonov, Foreign Relations Department. Correspondence in Russian or Tajik preferred. There is no official policy for verification of listeners' reports, so try sending reception reports and correspondence in English to the attention of Mr. Ramazonov, who is currently the sole English speaker at the station. Caution should be exercised when contacting him via email, as it is his personal account and he is charged for both incoming and outgoing mail. In addition, all email is routinely monitored and censored. Return postage of 5$ has been requested on at least one occasion, but enclosing currency notes is risky due to the high level of postal theft in the country. IRCs are not exchangeable, so including small souvenirs with your letter may help produce a reply.

*TRANSMISSION FACILITIES:* Television and Radiocommunications Ltd., ul. Internationalskaya 85, 734001 Dushanbe, Tajikistan. Phone: +7 (3772) 244-646. Fax: +7 (3772) 212 517. Email: nodir@uralnet.ru. Contact: Rakhmatillo Masharipovich Masharipov, Director General.

**Tajik Radio**, ul. Chapaeva 31, 734025 Dushanbe, Tajikistan. Contact information as for Radio Tajikistan, above.

## TANZANIA World Time +3

**Radio Tanzania**, Nyerere Road, P.O. Box 9191, Dar es Salaam, Tanzania. Phone: +255 (51) 860-760. Fax: +255 (51) 865 577. Email: radiotanzania@raha.com. Contact: (general) Abdul Ngarawa, Director of Broadcasting; Mrs. Edda Sanga, Controller of Programs; Ms. Penzi Nyamungumi, Head of English Service and International Relations Unit; or Ahmed Jongo, Producer, "Your Answer"; (technical) Taha Usi, Chief Engineer; or Emmanuel Mangula, Deputy Chief Engineer. Replies to correspondence in English.

**Voice of Tanzania Zanzibar**, Department of Broadcasting, Radio Tanzania Zanzibar, P.O. Box 2503, Zanzibar, Tanzania— if this address brings no reply, try P.O. Box 1178; (Ali Bakari Muomba, personal address) P.O. Box 2068, Zanzibar, Tanzania. Phone: +255 (54) 231-088. Fax: + 255 (54) 257 207. Contact: (general) Seti Suleiman, Director; Ndaro Nyamwolha; Ali Bakari Muombwa; Abdulrah'man M. Said; or Kassim S. Kassim; (technical) Khalid Hassan Rajab, Shortwave Transmitter Engineer; Nassor M. Suleiman, Maintenance Engineer. $1 return postage helpful.

## THAILAND   World Time +7

**BBC World Service—Asia Relay Station**, P.O. Box 20, Muang, Nakhon Sawan 60000, Thailand. Contact: Jaruwan Meesaurtong, Personal Assistant. Verifies reception reports.
**Radio Thailand World Service**, 236 Vibhavadi Rangsit Highway, Din Daeng, Huaykhwang, Bangkok 10400, Thailand. Phone: +66 (2) 2777-895, +66 (2) 277-1814, +66 (2) 274-9098. Phone/fax: +66 (2) 277-6139, +66 (2) 274-9099. Email: (general) radio_thailand@hotmail.com; (Samosorn) amporns@ mozart.inet.co.th. Web: www.geocities.com/hsk9th. Contact: Mrs. Amporn Samosorn, Chief of External Services; or Patra Lamjiack. Free pennants. Replies irregularly, especially to those who persist.

## TUNISIA   World Time +1

📷**Radiodiffusion Télévision Tunisienne**, 71 Avenue de la Liberté, TN-1070 Tunis, Tunisia. Phone: +216 (1) 801-177. Fax: +216 (1) 781 927. Email: info@radiotunis.com. Web: (includes RealAudio) www.radiotunis.com/news.html. Contact: Mongai Caffai, Director General; Mohamed Abdelkafi, Director; Kamel Cherif, Directeur; Masmoudi Mahmoud; Mr. Bechir Betteib; or Smaoui Sadok, Le Sous-Directeur Technique. Replies irregularly and slowly to correspondence in French or Arabic. $1 helpful. For reception reports try: Le Chef de Service du Controle de la Récepcion de l'Office National de la Télediffusion, O.N.T, Cité Ennassim I, Bourjel, B.P. 399, TN-1080 Tunis, Tunisia. Phone: +216 (1) 801-177. Fax: +216 (1) 781 927. Email: ont.@ati.tn. Contact: Abdesselem Slim.

## TURKEY   World Time +2 (+3 midyear)

**Meteoroloji Sesi Radyosu** (Voice of Meteorology), T.C. Tarim Bakanliği, Devlet Meteoroloji İşleri, Genel Müdürlüğü, P.K. 401, Ankara, Turkey. Phone: +90 (312) 359-7545, X-281. Fax: +90 (312) 314 1196. Contact: (nontechnical) Gühekin Takinalp; Recep Yilmaz, Head of Forecasting Department; or Abdullah Gölpinar; (technical) Mehmet Örmeci, Director General. Free tourist literature. Return postage helpful.
**Türkiye Polis Radyosu** (Turkish Police Radio) (when operating), T.C. Içişleri Bakanliği, Emniyet Genel Müdürlüğü, Ankara, Turkey. Contact: Fatih Umutlu. Tourist literature for return postage. Replies irregularly.
📷**Voice of Turkey** (Turkish Radio-Television Corporation External Service)
*MAIN OFFICE, NONTECHNICAL:* TRT External Services Department, TRT Sitesi, Turan Güneş Blv., Or-An Çankaya, 06450 Ankara, Turkey; or P.K. 333, Yeniş̧ehir, 06443 Ankara, Turkey. Phone: (general) +90 (312) 490-9800/9801; (English Service) +90 (312) 490-9842. Fax: +90 (312) 490 9835/45/46. Email: (general) infotsr@tsr.gov.tr; (Turkish broadcasts) turkceyayin@ tsr.gov.tr; (English Service) englishservice@tsr.gov.tr; same format applies for Arabic, French, German and Russian services, e.g. germanservice@tsr.gov.tr. Web: (includes RealAudio) www.trt.net.tr. *WARNING: this site can only be viewed using Microsoft's Internet Explorer, and is not easy to navigate.* Contact: (English and non-technical) Mr. Osman Erkan, Chief, English Service; Ms. Refside Morali, Host of "Letterbox" & "DX Corner"; (other languages) Mr. Rafet Esit, Director, Foreign Languages Section; (administration) Mr. Danyal Gurdal, Head, External Services Department. Technical correspondence, such as on reception quality should be directed to: Ms. Sedef Somaltin (*see* next entry below). On-air language courses offered in Arabic and German, but no printed course material. Free stickers, pennants, and tourist literature.
*MAIN OFFICE, TECHNICAL (FOR EMIRLER AND ÇAKIRLAR TRANSMITTER SITES AND FOR FREQUENCY MANAGEMENT):* TRT Teknik Yardimcilik, TRT Sitesi, Kat: 5/C, 06450 ORAN, Ankara, Turkey. Phone: +90 (312) 490-1730/2. Fax: +90 (312) 490 1733. Email: utis@turnet.net.tr or utis2@trt.net.tr; (Ms. Somaltin) sedef.somaltin@trt.net.tr. Contact: Mr. O. Haluk Buran, TRT Deputy Director General (Head of Engineering); Ms. Sedef Somaltin, Engineer; or Ms. Kiymet Erdal, Engineer.
*SAN FRANCISCO OFFICE, SCHEDULES:* 2654 17th Avenue, San Francisco CA 94116 USA. Phone: +1 (415) 564-9968. Email: GPoppin@aol.com. Contact: George Poppin. This address, a volunteer office, only provides TRT schedules to listeners. All other correspondence should be sent directly to Ankara.

## TURKMENISTAN   World Time +5

**Radio Turkmenistan**, National TV and Radio Broadcasting Company, Mollanepes St. 3, 744000 Ashgabat, Turkmenistan. Phone: +993 (12) 251-515. Fax: +993 (12) 251 421. Contact: (administration) Yu M. Pashaev, Deputy Chairman of State Television and Radio Company; (technical) G. Khanmamedov; Kakali Karayev, Chief of Technical Department; or A.A Armanklichev, Deputy Chief, Technical Department. This country is currently under strict censorship and media people are closely watched. A lot of foreign mail addressed to a particular person may attract the attention of the security services. Best is not to address your mail to particular individuals but to the station itself.

## UGANDA   World Time +3

**Radio Uganda**
*GENERAL OFFICE:* P.O. Box 7142, Kampala, Uganda. Phone: +256 (41) 257-256. Fax: +256 (41) 256 888. Email: ugabro@infocom.co.ug. Contact: (general) Charles Byekwaso, Controller of Programmes; Machel Rachel Makibuuka; or Mrs. Florence Sewanyana, Head of Public Relations. $1 or return postage required. Replies infrequently and slowly. Correspondence to this address has sometimes been returned with the annotation "storage period overdue"—presumably because the mail is not collected on a regular basis.
*ENGINEERING DIVISION:* P.O. Box 2038, Kampala, Uganda. Phone: +256 (41) 256-647. Contact: Leopold B. Lubega, Principal Broadcasting Engineer; or Rachel Nakibuuka, Secretary. Four IRCs or $2 required. Enclosing a self addressed envelope may also help to get a reply.

## UKRAINE   World Time +2 (+3 midyear)

*WARNING-MAIL THEFT:* For the time being, letters to Ukrainian stations, especially containing funds or IRCs, are more likely to arrive safely if sent by registered mail.
**Government Transmission Authority:** RRT/Concern of Broadcasting, Radiocommunication and Television, 10 Dorogajtshaya St., 254112 Kyiv, Ukraine. Phone: +380 (44) 226-2262 or +380 (44) 444-6900. Fax: +380 (44) 440 8722; or +380 (44) 452 6784. Email: (Kurilov) ak@cbrt.freenet.kiev.ua. Contact: Mr. Mykola Kyryliuk, Deputy Director, Technical Operations & Management Centre; Alexej M. Kurilov; Alexey Karpenko; Alexander Serdiuk, Director, Technical Operations & Management Centre; Nikolai P. Kiriliuk, Head of Operative Management Service; or Mrs. Liudmila Deretskaya, Interpreter.

This agency is responsible for choosing the frequencies used by Radio Ukraine International.

**Radio Ukraine International**, Kreshchatik str., 26, 252001 Kyiv, Ukraine. Phone: +380 (44) 228-2534, +380 (44) 229-1757, +380 (44) 229-1883 or (phone/fax) +380 (44) 228-7356. Fax: +380 (44) 229 4585 or +380 (44) 229 3477. Email: (QSL cards & complete schedules) vsru@nrcu.gov.ua; (reception reports) egorov@nrcu.gov.ua; mo@ukrradio.ru.kiev.ua. Web: www.nrcu.gov.ua/eng/program/vsru/vsru.html. Contact: (administration) Inna Chichinadze, Vice-Director of RUI; or Yulia McGuffie, Deputy Editor-in-Chief. Free stickers, calendars and Ukrainian stamps.

# UNITED ARAB EMIRATES   World Time +4

**UAE Radio in Dubai**, P.O. Box 1695, Dubai, United Arab Emirates. Phone: +971 (4) 370-255. Fax: +971 (4) 374 111, +971 (4) 370 283 or +971 (4) 371 079. Contact: Ms. Khulud Halaby; or Sameer Aga, Producer, "Cassette Club Cinarabic"; (technical) K.F. Fenner, Chief Engineer—Radio; or Ahmed Al Muhaideb, Assistant Controller, Engineering. Free pennants. Replies irregularly.

# UNITED KINGDOM   World Time exactly (+1 midyear)

**Adventist World Radio**, 39 Brendon Street, London W1H 5HD, United Kingdom. Phone: +44 (1344) 401-401. Fax: +44 (1344) 401 419. Email: english@awr.org. Web: www.awr.org. Contact: Bert Smit, European Regional Director; or Victor Hulbert, Director English Listener Mail. All mail addressed to AWR and written in English is processed at this address. Also, see AWR listings under Germany, Guam, Guatemala, Kenya, Madagascar and USA.

**BBC Monitoring**, Caversham Park, Reading, Berkshire RG4 8TZ, United Kingdom. Phone: (switchboard) +44 (118) 948-6000; (Foreign Media Unit—monitoring) +44 (118) 948-6261; Marketing Department) +44 (118) 948-6289. Fax: (Foreign Media Unit) +44 (118) 946 1993; (Marketing Department) +44 (118) 946 3823. Email: (Marketing Department) marketing@mon.bbc.co.uk; (Foreign Media Unit/World Media) fmu@mon.bbc.co.uk; (Kenny) dave_kenny@mon.bbc.co.uk; (publications and real time services) marketing@ mon.bbc.co.uk. Web: www.monitor.bbc.co.uk. Contact: (administration) Andrew Hills, Director of Monitoring; (Foreign Media Unit) Chris McWhinnie, Editor "World Media," Dave Kenny, Chief Sub Editor, "World Media," or Peter Feuilherade; (Publication Sales) Stephen Innes, Marketing. BBC Monitoring produces the weekly publication *World Media* which reports political, economic, legal, organisational, programming and technical developments in the world's electronic media. Its reports are based on material broadcast or published by radio and TV stations, news agencies, Websites and publications; other information issued but not necessarily broadcast by such sources and by other relevant bodies; and information obtained by BBC Monitoring's own observations of foreign media. Available on yearly subscription, costing £410.00. Price excludes postage overseas. *World Media* is also available online through the Internet or via a direct dial-in bulletin board at an annual cost of £425.00. VISA/MC/AX. The Technical Operations Unit provides detailed observations of broadcasts on the long, medium, short wave, satellite bands and Internet. This unit provides tailored channel occupancy observations, reception reports, and updates the *MediaNet* source information database (constantly updated on over 100 countries) and the *Broadcast Research Log* (a record of broadcasting developments compiled daily).

**⬛BBC World Service**

*MAIN OFFICE, NONTECHNICAL:* Bush House, Strand, London WC2B 4PH, United Kingdom. Phone: (general) +44 (20) 7240-3456; (Press Office) +44 (20) 7557-2947/1; (International Marketing) +44 (20) 7557-1143. Fax: (Audience Relations) +44 (20) 7557 1258; ("Write On" listeners' letters program) +44 (20) 7436 2800; (Audience and Market Research) +44 (20) 7557 1254; (International Marketing) +44 (20) 7557 1254. Email: (general listener correspondence) worldservice.letters@ bbc.co.uk; ("Write On") writeon@bbc.co.uk. Web: (general, including RealAudio and Windows Media) www.bbc.co.uk/ worldservice/; (RealAudio) www.broadcast.com/bbc; (entertainment and information) www.beeb.com. Contact: Patrick Condren, Presenter, of "Write On"; Alan Booth, Controller, Marketing & Communications; Miles Palmer, Head of Business Development; or Mark Byford, Chief Executive. Offers *BBC On Air* magazine (see below). Also, see Antigua, Ascension, Oman, Seychelles, Singapore and Thailand. Does not verify reception reports due to budget limitations.

*SAN FRANCISCO OFFICE, SCHEDULES:* 2654 17th Avenue, San Francisco CA 94116 USA. Phone: +1 (415) 564-9968. Email: GPoppin@aol.com. Contact: George Poppin. This address, a volunteer office, only provides BBC World Service schedules to listeners. All other correspondence should be sent directly to the main office in London.

*TECHNICAL: See* VT Merlin Communications.

*BBC WORLD SERVICE—PUBLICATION AND PRODUCT SALES*
BBC World Service Shop, Bush House Arcade, Strand, London WC2B 4PH, United Kingdom. Phone: +44 (20) 7557-2576. Fax: +44 (20) 7240 4811. Sells numerous audio/video (video PAL/ VHS only) cassettes, publications, portable world band radios, T-shirts, sweatshirts and other BBC souvenirs available by mail order to UK addresses only.

"BBC On Air" monthly program magazine, Room 310 NW, Bush House, Strand, London WC2B 4PH, United Kingdom. Phone: (editorial office) +44 (20) 7557-2211; (Circulation Manager) +44 (20) 7557-2855; (advertising) +44 (20) 7557-2873; (subscription voice mail) +44 (20) 7557-2211. Fax: +44 (20) 7240 4899. Email: on.air.magazine@bbc.co.uk. Contact: (editorial) Dionne St. Hill, Editor; (subscriptions) Rosemarie Reid, Circulation Manager; (advertising) Adam Ford. Subscription $32 or £20 per year. VISA/MC/AX/Barclay/EURO/Access, Postal Order, International Money Draft or cheque in pounds sterling.

**Commonwealth Broadcasting Association**, CBA Secretariat, 17 Fleet Street, London EC4Y 1AA, United Kingdom. Phone: +44 (20) 7583-5550. Fax: +44 (20) 7583 5549. Email: cba@cba.org.uk. Web: www.cba.org.uk. Publishes the annual *Commonwealth Broadcaster Directory* and the quarterly *Commonwealth Broadcaster* (online subscription form available).

**Far East Broadcasting Association (FEBA)**, Ivy Arch Road, Worthing, West Sussex BN14 8BX, United Kingdom. Phone: +44 (1903) 237-281. Fax: +44 (1903) 205 294. Email: reception@feba.org.uk or (Richard Whittington) rwhittington@ feba.org.uk. Web: www.feba.org.uk. Contact: Tony Ford or Richard Whittington, Schedule Engineer. This office is the headquarters for FEBA worldwide.

**High Adventure Ministries Global Broadcasting Network—"European Beacon,"** P.O. Box 2801, Eastbourne, East Sussex BN21 2EQ, United Kingdom. Phone: +44 (1323) 639-798. Fax: +44 (1323) 722 716. Email: hamukmartin@hotmail.com. Contact: Martin Thompson. Broadcasts via transmitters of Deutsche Telekom (see) in Jülich, Germany. Also, see High Adventure Radio, USA.

**⬛IBC-Tamil**, P.O. Box 1505, London SW8 2ZH, United Kingdom. Phone: +44 (20) 7787-8000. Fax: +44 (20) 7787 8010.

Email: radio@ibctamil.co.uk. Web: (includes RealAudio, registration required) www.ibctamil.co.uk. Contact: A.C. Tarcisius, Managing Director; S. Shivaranjith, Manager; K. Pillai; or Public Relations Officer.

**Radio Ezra** (when operating), P.O. Box 16, Stockton on Tees TS18 3GN, United Kingdom. Fax: +44 (1642) 887 546. Email: info@radioezra.com. Web: www.radioezra.com. Contact: John D. Hill. Broadcasts irregularly using different Russian transmission facilities. Verifies reception reports. $1 or one IRC appreciated. Describes itself as a "counter-missionary station."

**Radio Voice of Afghanistan** (if reactivated), Afghan Broadcasting Company, P.O. Box 36467, London EC2A 2DW, United Kingdom, or (street address) The Studio Centre, Nicon House, 21 Worship Street, London EC2A 2DW, United Kingdom. Phone: (switchboard) +44 (20) 7382-9610; (listener line) +44 (20) 7588-0828. Fax: +44 (20) 7382 9608. Email: afbc2001@hotmail.com. Web: www.afghanbroadcasting.com. Aired originally via a transmitter in Moldova, but later switched to facilities in Moosbrunn, Austria. Broadcasts suspended on July 22, 2002 (initially, for three months).

**Salama Radio**, The Studio, P.O. Box 126, Chessington, Surrey KT9 2WJ, United Kingdom. Phone/fax: +44 (208) 395-7425. Email: admin@salamaradio.org. Web: www.salamaradio.org. Contact: Dr. Jacob Abdalla, President, Harvestime Ministries; Mrs. Margaret Perera, International Director, Harvestime Ministries.

*NIGERIA ADDRESS:* P.O. Box 287, Jos, Plateau State, Nigeria. Commenced operation on July 6, 2001, via the U.K. facilities of VT Merlin Communications (*see*, below). A radio project of Harvestime Ministries.

**Tamil Broadcasting Corporation—London** ("TBC-London"), P.O. Box 383, Harrow, HA1 3FW, United Kingdom. Phone: +44 (20) 8864-0909. Fax: +44 (20) 8864 0700. Email: tbcradio@hotmail.com. Broadcasts to Sri Lanka and southern India from the Jülich facilities of Germany's Deutsche Telekom (*see*).

**VT Merlin International** (formerly Merlin Communications International Limited), 20 Lincoln's Inn Fields, London WC2A 3ES, United Kingdom. Phone: +44 (171) 969-0000. Fax: +44 (171) 396 6223. Email: marketing@merlincommunications.com. Web: www.merlincommunications.com or www.vtplc.com/merlin. Contact: Fiona Lowry, Chief Executive; Rory Maclachlan, Director of International Communications & Digital Services; Kevin Cawood, Director of Global Facilities; Ciaran Fitzgerald, Head of Engineering & Operations; Richard Hurd, Head of Transmission Sales; Chris Clarkson, Head of Critical Communications Services; or Laura Jelf, Marketing Manager. VT Merlin Communications (formerly Merlin Communications International) is a world class provider of critical communications services to the broadcast, defense and space communications industries worldwide. Operating the world's leading commercial shortwave network. VT Merlin Communications delivers over one thousand hours of both short and mediumwave broadcasts every day for international and religious broadcasters worldwide. Customers include the BBC World Service, Australian Broadcasting Corporation, NHK (Radio Japan), Voice of America, Radio Canada International and Radio Netherlands. Merlin's range of critical communications services include both total facilities management and packaged services for radio communications and satellite ground segment support, as well as project & programme management. VT Merlin Communications has extensive experience in the design, build, finance, operation, maintenance and support of technical facilities both in the UK and overseas. VT Merlin provides these services to prestigious customers including the UK Ministry of Defense

(MoD), BBC World Service, the European Space Agency (ESA) and QinetiQ. Does not verify reception reports.

⬛**Wales Radio International**, Preseli Radio Productions, Pros Kairon, Crymych, Pembrokeshire, SA41 3QE, Wales, United Kingdom. Phone: +44 (1437) 563-361. Fax: +44 (1239) 831 390. Email: jenny@wri.cymru.net. Web: (includes MP3) http://wri.cymru.net. Contact: Jenny O'Brien. A weekly broadcast via the facilities of VT Merlin Communications (*see*, above).

⬛**World Radio Network**, P.O. Box 1212, London SW8 2ZF, United Kingdom. Phone: +44 (20) 7896-9000. Fax: + 44 (20) 7896 9007. Email: (general) email@wrn.org; (WRN Boutique) boutique@wrn.org; (Cohen) jeffc@wrn.org; (Ayris) tim.ayris@wrn.org. Web: (includes RealAudio and Windows Media) www.wrn.org. Contact: Karl Miosga, Managing Director; Kimberly Rivers, Sales Manager; Jeffrey Cohen, Director of Development; Tim Ashburner, Director of Technical Operations; Tim Ayris, Marketing and Rebroadcasting Manager. Sells numerous items such as Polo and T-shirts, baseball caps, pen knives and dual-time wristwatches. Provides Webcasts and program placement via satellite for nearly two dozen international broadcasters.

## UNITED NATIONS   World Time –5 (–4 midyear)

⬛**Radio UNMEE**

Web: (MP3) www.un.org/Depts/dpko/unmee/radio.htm; (UNMEE general information) www.un.org/Depts/dpko/unmee/unmeeN.htm.

*NEW YORK OFFICE:* Same contact details as United Nations Radio, below.

*ERITREA OFFICE:* P.O. Box 5805, Asmara, Eritrea. Phone: +291 (1) 151-908. Email: kellyb@un.org.

*ETHIOPIA OFFICE:* ECA Building, P.O. Box 3001, Addis Ababa, Ethiopia. Phone: +251 (1) 443-396. Email: walkera@un.org.

Radio service of the United Nations Mission in Eritrea and Ethiopia (UNMEE). Aired via facilities in the United Arab Emirates, and also relayed over Eritrea's national radio, Voice of the Broad Masses of Eritrea.

⬛**United Nations Radio**, Secretariat Building, Room S-850-M, United Nations, New York NY 10017 USA; or write to the station over which UN Radio was heard. Phone: +1 (212) 963-5201. Fax: +1 (212) 963 1307. Email: (general) unradio@un.org; (comments on programs) audio-visual@un.org; (reception reports) smithd@un.org. Web: (general) www.un.org/av/radio; (RealAudio) www.wrn.org/ondemand/unitednations.html; www.internetbroadcast.com/un. Contact: (general) Sylvester E. Rowe, Chief, Radio and Video Service; or Ayman El-Amir, Chief, Radio Section, Department of Public Information; (reception reports) David Smith; (technical and nontechnical) Sandra Guy, Secretary. Free stamps and *UN Frequency* publication. Reception reports (including those sent by email) are verified with a QSL card.

*GENEVA OFFICE:* Room G209, Palais des Nations, CH-1211 Geneva 10, Switzerland. Phone: +41 (22) 917-4222. Fax: +41 (22) 917 0123.

*PARIS OFFICE:* UNESCO Radio, 7 Place de Fontenoy, F-75007 Paris, France. Fax: +33 (1) 45 67 30 72. Contact: Erin Faherty, Executive Radio Producer.

## URUGUAY   World Time –3

**Banda Oriental**—*see* Radio Sarandí del Yí.

⬛**Emisora Ciudad de Montevideo**, Canelones 2061, 11200 Montevideo, Uruguay. Phone: +598 (2) 402-0142 or +598 (2)

402-4242. Fax: +598 (2) 402 0700. Email: online form. Web: (includes MP3) www.emisoraciudaddemontevideo.com.uy. Contact: Aramazd Yizmeyian, Director General. Free stickers. Return postage helpful.

**La Voz de Artigas** (when operating), Av. Lecueder 483, 55000 Artigas, Uruguay. Phone: +598 (772) 2447 or +598 (772) 3445. Fax: +598 (772) 4744. Email: lavozart@adinet.com.uy. Contact: (general) Sra. Solange Murillo Ricciardi, Co-Propietario; or Luis Murillo; (technical) Roberto Murillo Ricciardi, Director. Free stickers and pennants. Replies to correspondence written in English, Spanish, French, Italian and Portuguese.

**Radiodifusion Nacional**—*see* S.O.D.R.E.

☞**Radio Monte Carlo**, Av. 18 de Julio 1224 piso 1, 11100 Montevideo, Uruguay. Phone: +598 (2) 901-4433 or +598 (2) 908-3987. Fax: +598 (2) 901 7762. Email: cx20@netgate.com.uy. Contact: Ana Ferreira de Errázquin, Secretaria, Departamento de Prensa de la Cooperativa de Radioemisoras; Gustavo Cirino, Jefe Técnico; Déborah Ibarra, Secretaria; Emilia Sánchez Vega, Secretaria; or Ulises Graceras. Correspondence in Spanish preferred.

☞**Radio Oriental**—Same mailing address as Radio Monte Carlo, above. Phone: +598 (2) 901-4433 or +598 (2) 900-5612. Fax: +598 (2) 901 7762. Contact: (technical) José A. Porro, Technician. Correspondence in Spanish preferred.

**Radio Sarandí del Yí**, Sarandí 328, 97100 Sarandí del Yí, Uruguay. Phone/fax: +598 (367) 9155. Email: (owner) norasan@adinet.com.uy. Contact: Nora San Martín de Porro, Propietaria.

**Radio Universo**, Ferrer 1265, 27000 Castillos, Dpto. de Rocha, Uruguay. Email: am1480@adinet.com.uy. Contact: Juan Héber Brañas, Propietario. Currently only on 1480 kHz mediumwave AM, but has been granted a license to operate on shortwave.

**S.O.D.R.E.**, Radiodifusión Nacional, Casilla 1412, 11000 Montevideo, Uruguay. Phone: +598 (2) 916-1933; (technical) +598 (2) 915-7865. Email: info@sodre.gub.uy. Web: www.sodre.gub.uy. Contact: (management) Julio César Ocampos, Director de Radiodifusión Nacional; (technical) José Cuello, División Técnica Radio. Reception reports may also be sent to the "Radioactividades" program (*see*, below).

*MEDIA PROGRAM:* "Radioactividades," Casilla 7011, 11000 Montevideo, Uruguay. Fax: +598 (2) 575 4640. Email: radioact@chasque.apc.org. Web: www.chasque.org/radioact.

# USA

World Time –4 Atlantic, including Puerto Rico and Virgin Islands; –5 (–4 midyear) Eastern, excluding Indiana; –5 Indiana, except northwest and southwest portions; –6 (–5 midyear) Central, including northwest and southwest Indiana; –7 (–6 midyear) Mountain, except Arizona; –7 Arizona; –8 (–7 midyear) Pacific; –9 (–8 midyear) Alaska, except Aleutian Islands; –10 (–9 midyear) Aleutian Islands; –10 Hawaii; –11 Samoa

☞**Adventist World Radio**

*HEADQUARTERS:* 12501 Old Columbia Pike, Silver Spring MD 20904 USA. Email: english@awr.org. Web: www.awr.org; (Chinese service, English/Chinese text) www.vohc.com—worth a visit just for the graphics. Send all letters and reception reports to: AWR, 39 Brendon Street, London W1H 5HD, United Kingdom.

*INTERNATIONAL RELATIONS:* Box 29235, Indianapolis IN 46229 USA. Phone/fax: +1 (317) 891-8540. Contact: Dr. Adrian M. Peterson, International Relations Coordinator. Provides publications with regular news releases and technical information. Sometimes issues special verification cards. QSL stamps and certificates also available from this address in return for reception reports.

*DX PROGRAM:* "Wavescan," prepared by Adrian Peterson; aired on all AWR facilities and other stations. Also available in RealAudio at the AWR Website, www.awr.org. Also, *see* AWR listings under Germany, Guam, Guatemala, Kenya, Madagascar and United Kingdom.

☞**AFRTS-Armed Forces Radio and Television Service (Shortwave)**, Naval Media Center, NDW Anacostia Annex, 2713 Mitscher Road SW, Washington DC 20373-5819 USA. For verification of reception, be sure to mark the envelope, "Attn: Short Wave Reception Reports." Email: (verifications) qsl@mediacen.navy.mil. Web: www.myafn.net; (AFRTS parent organization) www.afrts.osd.mil; (2-minute news clips in RealAudio): www.defenselink.mil/news/radio/; (Naval Media Center) www.mediacen.navy.mil. The Naval Media Center is responsible for all AFRTS broadcasts aired on shortwave.

FLORIDA ADDRESS: NCTS-Jacksonville-Detachment Key West, Building A 1004, Naval Air Station Boca Chica, Key West, FL 33040 USA.

**Aurora Communications**, Mile 129, Sterling Highway, Ninilchik, Alaska, USA. Plans to commence broadcasts to Russia when circumstances allow.

**BBC World Service via WYFR—Family Radio**. For verification direct from WYFR's transmitters, contact WYFR—Family

# Upgrade Your Receiver With Synchronous Detection!

**M**ake your receiver even better, with sideband-selectable synchronous detection that fights selective-fade distortion and minimizes adjacent-channel interference.

**S**E-3 MkIII is available with turnkey or do-it-yourself installation for your:

NRD-515, 525, 535, 345
Icom R-70/71, R-9000, R-8500
Kenwood R5000
Collins, Ten-Tec 340
Drake R-7 (A), R-8 (A/B)
Watkins Johnson HF1000/WJ-8711A
AOR, Yaesu, Racal, and any classic tube radio.

**S**E-3 MkIII: $449, Deluxe SE-3: $549. Rack version: add $49.00. Custom filters and special modifications are available.

**O**n-line Acrobat catalog at www.sherweng.com.

**Sherwood Engineering Inc.**
1268 South Ogden Street
Denver, CO 80210
Voice: (303) 722-2257
Fax: (303) 744-8876
Web: www.sherweng.com
E-mail: robert@sherweng.com

Radio (*see* below). Nontechnical correspondence should be sent to the BBC World Service in London (*see*).

**Broadcasting Board of Governors (BBG)**, 330 Independence Avenue SW, Room 3360, Washington DC 20237 USA. Phone: +1 (202) 619-2538. Fax: +1 (202) 619 1241. Email: pubaff@ibb.gov. Web: www.ibb.gov/bbg. Contact: Kathleen Harrington, Public Relations. The BBG, created in 1994 and headed by nine members nominated by the President, is the overseeing agency for all official non-military United States international broadcasting operations, including the VOA, RFE-RL, Radio Martí and Radio Free Asia.

**⚘Christian Science Publishing Society—Shortwave Broadcasts (all locations)**, Shortwave Broadcasts, P.O. Box 1524, Boston MA 02117-1524 USA. Phone: +1 (617) 450-2929; general-toll free within U.S. (800) 288-7090, extension 2929 for Shortwave Helpline to request printed schedules and information. Email: (letters & reception reports) letterbox@csps.com. Web: (includes RealAudio) www.tfccs.com/GV/shortwave/shortwave_schedule.jhtml. Free schedules and information about Christian Science religion. *The Christian Science Monitor* newspaper and a full line of Christian Science books are available from: 1 Norway Street, Boston MA 02115 USA. *Science and Health with Key to the Scriptures* by Mary Baker Eddy is available in English $12.95 paperback; $24-26 in French, German, Portuguese, Russian or Spanish paperback; from Science and Health, P.O. Box 1875, Boston MA 02117 USA.

**Christian Science Publishing Society—WSHB Cypress Creek**, 1030 Shortwave Lane, Pineland SC 29934 USA. Phone: (general) +1 (803) 625-5551; (station manager) +1 (803) 625-5555; (engineer) +1 (803) 625-5554. Fax: +1 (803) 625 5559. Email: (English religious questions) Sentinel@csps.com; (Station Manager) evansc@wshb.com; (Chief Engineer) centgrafd@wshb.com; (QSL Coordinator) riehmc@wshb.com. Web: www.tfccs.com/GV/shortwave/shortwave_schedule.jhtml. Contact: Catherine Aitken-Smith, Broadcast Director; (technical) C. Ed Evans, Station Manager; Damian Centgraf, Chief Engineer; Tony Kobatake, Transmission Engineer; Tina Hammers, Frequency & Production Coordinator; or Cindy Riehm, QSL Coordinator. Visitors welcome at WSHB from 9 to 4 Monday through Friday; for other times, contact transmitter site beforehand to make arrangements. 1030 Shortwave Lane address for technical feedback on South Carolina transmissions only; other inquiries should be directed to the Boston address.

**⚘Family Radio Worldwide**:
*NONTECHNICAL:* Family Stations, Inc., 290 Hegenberger Road, Oakland CA 94621-1436 USA; or P.O. Box 2140 Oakland CA 94621-9985 USA. Phone: (toll-free, U.S. only) 1-800-543-1495; (elsewhere) +1 (510) 568-6200; (engineering) +1 (510) 568-6200 ext. 240. Fax: (main office) +1 (510) 568 6200; (engineering) +1 (510) 562 1023. Email: (general) famradio@familyradio.com; (international department) international@familyradio.com; (shortwave program schedules) shortwave@familyradio.com. Web: (includes RealAudio and MP3) www.familyradio.com. Contact: (general) Harold Camping, General Manager; or Thomas Schaff, Shortwave Program Manager. Free gospel tracts (33 languages), books, booklets, quarterly *Family Radio News* magazine and frequency schedule. 2 IRCs helpful.
*TECHNICAL:* WYFR—Family Radio, 10400 NW 240th Street, Okeechobee FL 34972 USA. Phone: +1 (941) 763-0281. Fax: +1 (941) 763 1034. Email: (technical) fsiyfr@okeechobee.com; (frequency schedule) wyfr@okeechobee.com. Contact: Dan Elyea, Engineering Manager; or Edward F. Dearborn, Assistant Engineering Manager; (frequency schedule) Evelyn Marcy.

**FEBC Radio International**
*INTERNATIONAL HEADQUARTERS:* Far East Broadcasting Company, Inc., P.O. Box 1, La Mirada CA 90637 USA. Phone: +1 (310) 947-4651. Fax: +1 (310) 943 0160. Email: febc@febc.org. Web: www.febc.org. Operates world band stations in the Northern Mariana Islands, the Philippines and the Seychelles. Does not verify reception reports from this address.
*RUSSIAN OFFICE:* P.O. Box 2128, Khabarovsk 680020, Russia. Email: khabarovsk@febc.org.

**Federal Communications Commission**, 445 12th Street SW, Washington DC 20554 USA. Phone: +1 (202) 418-0190; (toll-free within U.S.) 1-888-225-5322. Fax: +1 (202) 418 0232. Email: (general information and inquiries) fccinfo@fcc.gov; (Freedom of Information Act requests) FOIA@fcc.gov; (Polzin) tpolzin@fcc.gov. Web: (general) www.fcc.gov; (high frequency operating schedules) www.fcc.gov/ib/pnd/neg/hf_web/seasons.html; (FTP) ftp://ftp.fcc.gov/pub. Contact: (International Bureau, technical) Thomas E. Polzin.

**⚘Fundamental Broadcasting Network**, Grace Missionary Baptist Church, 520 Roberts Road, Newport NC 28570 USA. Phone: +1 (252) 223-6088; (toll-free, within the United States) 1-800-245-9685; (Robinson) +1 (252) 223-4600. Web: (text) www.clis.com/fbn/; (RealAudio) www.worthwhile.com/fbn. Email: fbn@bmd.clis.com. Alternative address: Morehead City NC 28557 USA. Phone: +1 (252) 240-1600. Fax: +1 (252) 726 2251. Contact: Pastor Clyde Eborn; (technical) David Robinson, Chief Engineer. Verifies reception reports if 1 IRC or (within USA) an SASE is included. Accepts email reports. Plans to eventually broadcast in Chinese, French, and Russian in addition to the current English and Spanish.

**George Jacobs and Associates, Inc.**, 8701 Georgia Avenue, Suite 711, Silver Spring MD 20910 USA. Phone: +1 (301) 587-8800. Fax: +1 (301) 587 8801. Email: gja@gjainc.com; or gjainc_20910@yahoo.com. Web: www.gjainc.com. Contact: (technical) Bob German or Mrs. Anne Case; (administration) George Jacobs, P.E. This firm provides frequency management and other engineering services for a variety of private U.S. world band stations.

**High Adventure Ministries Global Broadcasting Network**
*MAIN OFFICE:* P.O. Box 100, Simi Valley CA 93062 USA. Phone: +1 (805) 520-9460; toll-free (within USA) 1-800-517-4673. Fax: +1 (805) 520 7823. Email: mail@highadventure.net. Web: www.highadventure.org. Contact: (listeners' correspondence) Pat Kowalick, "Listeners' Letterbox"; (nontechnical) Ralph McDevitt, Program Manager; (administration, High Adventure Ministries) George Otis, President and Chairman; (administration, KVOH) Paul Johnson, General Manager, KVOH; (technical) Paul Hunter, Director of Engineering. Free program schedules and *Voice of Hope* book. Sells books, audio and video cassettes, T-shirts and world band radios. Booklist available on request. VISA/MC. A new site is currently under construction in northern Nigeria which will eventually be home to FM, mediumwave AM and shortwave transmitters. Also, *see* Palau and United Kingdom. Return postage (IRCs) required. Replies as time permits.
*WESTERN AUSTRALIA OFFICE, NONTECHNICAL:* P.O. Box 545, Balcatta WA 6194, Australia. Phone: +61 (8) 9345-1300. Fax: +61 (8) 9345 5407. Email: caron@hatikvahfilm.com. Contact: Caron Hedgeland.
*CANADA OFFICE, NONTECHNICAL:* Box 425, Station 'E', Toronto, M6H 4E3 Canada. Phone: +1 (905) 898-5447. Fax: +1 (905) 898 5447. Email: hiadvcan@home.com. Contact: Don McLaughlin, Director.
*HONG KONG OFFICE:* P.O. Box 7014, KCPO, Hong Kong, China.

*MIDDLE EAST OFFICE:* P.O. Box 53379, Limassol, Cyprus. Phone: +972 (9) 767-0835. Fax: +972 (9) 765 1407. Email: gronberg@zahav.net.il. Contact: Isaac Gronberg.

*SINGAPORE OFFICE, NONTECHNICAL:* 265B/C South Bridge Road -Eu Yan Sang Annexe, Singapore 058814, Singapore. Phone: + 65 221-2054. Fax: +65 221 2059. Email: csarch@singnet.com.sg. Contact: Cyril Seah.

*U.K. OFFICE:* P.O. Box 2801, Eastbourne, East Sussex BN21 2EQ, United Kingdom. Phone: +44 (1323) 639-798. Fax: +44 (1323) 722 716. Email: hamukmartin@hotmail.com. Contact: Martin Thompson.

**International Broadcasting Bureau (IBB)**—Reports to the Broadcasting Board of Governors (*see*), and includes, among others, the Voice of America, RFE-RL, Radio Martí and Radio Free Asia. IBB Engineering (Office of Engineering and Technical Operations) provides broadcast services for these stations. Contact: (administration) Brian Conniff, Director; or Joseph O'Connell, Director of External Affairs. Web: www.ibb.gov/ibbpage.html.

*FREQUENCY AND MONITORING OFFICE, TECHNICAL:*
IBB/EOF: Spectrum Management Division, International Broadcasting Bureau (IBB), Room 4611 Cohen Bldg., 330 Independence Avenue SW, Washington DC 20237 USA. Phone: +1 (202) 619-1669. Fax: +1 (202) 619 1680. Email: (scheduling) dferguson@ibb.gov; (monitoring) bw@his.com. Web: (general) http://monitor.ibb.gov; (email reception report form) http://monitor.ibb.gov/now_you_try_it.html. Contact: Dan Ferguson (dferguson@ibb.gov); or Bill Whitacre (bw@his.com).

**KAIJ**
*ADMINISTRATION OFFICE:* Two-if-by-Sea Broadcasting Co., 22720 SE 410th St., Enumclaw WA 89022 USA. Phone/fax: (Mike Parker, California) +1 (818) 606-1254; (Washington State office, if and when operating) +1 (206) 825 4517. Contact: Mike Parker (mark envelope, "please forward"). Relays programs of Dr. Gene Scott's University Network (*see*). Replies occasionally.
*STUDIO:* Faith Center, 1615 S. Glendale Avenue, Glendale CA 91025 USA. Phone: +1 (818) 246-8121. Contact: Dr. Gene Scott, President.
*TRANSMITTER SITE:* RR#3 Box 120, Frisco TX 75034 USA; or Highway 380 West, Prosper TX 75078 USA (physical location: Highway 380, 3.6 miles west of State Rt. 289, near Denton TX; transmitters and antennas located on Belt Line Road along the lake in Coppell TX). Phone: +1 (972) 346-2758. Contact: Walt Green or Fred Bithell. Station encourages mail to be sent to the administration office, which seldom replies, or the studio (*see* above).

**KIMF** (under construction): International Fellowship of Churches, Radio Station KIMF, 9746 6th Street, Rancho Cucamonga CA 91730 USA.
*ALTERNATIVE ADDRESS:* IMF World Missions, P.O. Box 6321, San Bernardino CA 92412, USA. Phone +1 (909) 370-4515. Fax: +1 (909) 370 4862. Email: jkpimf@msn.com. Contact: Dr. James K. Planck, President.
*TRANSMITTER SITE:* Intersection Spring Mesa Road & State Road 506, Pinon NM, USA.

**KJES—King Jesus Eternal Savior**
*STATION:* The Lord's Ranch, 230 High Valley Road, Vado NM 88072 USA. Phone: +1 (505) 233-2090. Fax: +1 (505) 233 3019. Email: KJES@aol.com. Contact: Michael Reuter, Manager. $1 or return postage appreciated.
*SPONSORING ORGANIZATION:* Our Lady's Youth Center, P.O. Box 1422, El Paso TX 79948 USA. Phone: +1 (915) 533-9122.

**KNLS—New Life Station**
*OPERATIONS CENTER:* 605 Bradley Ct., Franklin TN 37067 USA

(letters sent to the Alaska transmitter site are usually forwarded to Franklin). Phone: +1 (615) 371-8707 ext.140. Fax: +1 (615) 371 8791. Email: knls@aol.com. Web: (includes sample programs in RealAudio) www.knls.org. Contact: (general) Dale Ward, Executive Producer; L. Wesley Jones, Director of Follow-Up Teaching; or Mike Osborne, Senior Producer, English Language Service; (technical) F.M. Perry, Frequency Coordinator. Free *Alaska Calling!* newsletter and station pennants. Free spiritual literature and bibles in Russian, Mandarin and English. Free Alaska books, tapes, postcards and cloth patches. Two free DX books for beginners. Special, individually numbered, limited edition, verification cards issued for each new transmission period to the first 200 listeners providing confirmed reception reports. Stamp and postcard exchange. Return postage appreciated.

*TRANSMITTER SITE:* P.O. Box 473, Anchor Point AK 99556 USA. Phone: +1 (907) 235-8262. Fax: +1 (907) 235 2326. Contact: (technical) Kevin Chambers, Chief Engineer.

**KRSI—Radio Sedaye Iran**, Suite 207, 9744 Wilshire Boulevard, Beverly Hills CA 90212-1812 USA. Phone: +1 (310) 888-2818. Fax: +1 (310) 859 8444. Web: (includes Windows Media and online email form) www.krsi.net. Normally operates via a closed broadcasting system and the Internet, but started shortwave broadcasts during 2000. Hires airtime via facilities in Moldova or France (occasionally both).

**KTBN—Trinity Broadcasting Network**:
*GENERAL CORRESPONDENCE:* P.O. Box A, Santa Ana CA 92711 USA. Phone: +1 (714) 832-2950. Fax: +1 (714) 730 0661. Email: comments@tbn.org. Web: (Trinity Broadcasting Network, including RealAudio) www.tbn.org; (KTBN) www.tbn.org/watch/how2watch/sw_radio/index.htm. Contact: Dr. Paul F. Crouch, Managing Director. Monthly TBN newsletter. Free booklets, stickers and small souvenirs sometimes available.

*TECHNICAL CORRESPONDENCE:* Engineering/QSL Department, 2442 Michelle Drive, Tustin CA 92780-7015 USA. Phone: +1 (714) 665-2145. Fax: +1 (714) 730 0661. Email: lreyes@tbn.org. Contact: Laura Reyes, QSL Manager; or Ben Miller, Vice President, Engineering. Responds to reception reports. Write to: Trinity Broadcasting Network, Attention: Superpower KTBN Radio QSL Manager, Laura Reyes, 2442 Michelle Drive, Tustin CA 92780 USA. Return postage (IRC or SASE) helpful. Although a California operation, KTBN's shortwave transmitter is located at Salt Lake City, Utah.

**KVOH—Voice of Hope**. *See* High Adventure Ministries Global Broadcasting Network.

**KWHR-World Harvest Radio:**
*ADMINISTRATION OFFICE: see* WHRI, USA, below.
*TRANSMITTER:* Although located 6½ miles southwest of Naalehu, 8 miles north of South Cape, and 2000 feet west of South Point (Ka La) Road (the antennas are easily visible from this road) on Big Island, Hawaii, the operators of this rural transmitter site maintain no post office box in or near Naalehu, and their telephone number is unlisted, Best bet is to contact them via their administration office (*see* WHRI, below), or to drive in unannounced (it's just off South Point Road) the next time you vacation on Big Island.

**Leinwoll (Stanley)—Telecommunication Consultant**, 305 E. 86th Street, Suite 21S-W, New York NY 10028 USA. Phone: +1 (212) 987-0456. Fax: +1 (212) 987 3532. Email: stanL00011@aol.com. Contact: Stanley Leinwoll, President. This firm provides frequency management and other engineering services for some private U.S. world band stations, but does not correspond with the general public.

**National Association of Shortwave Broadcasters**, 10400 NW 20th Street, Okeechobee, FL 34972 USA; P.O. Box 8700, Cary NC 27512 USA. Phone: +1 (863) 763-0281. Fax: +1 (863) 763 8867. Email: nasbmem@rocketmail.com. Web: www.shortwave.org. Contact: Dan Elyea, Secretary-Treasurer. Association of most private U.S. world band stations, as well as a group of other international broadcasters, equipment manufacturers and organizations related to shortwave broadcasting. Includes committees on various subjects, such as digital shortwave radio. Interfaces with the Federal Communications Commission's International Bureau and other broadcasting-related organizations to advance the interests of its members. Publishes *NASB Newsletter* for members and associate members; free sample upon request on letterhead of an appropriate organization. Annual one-day convention held near Washington DC's National Airport early each spring; non-members wishing to attend should contact the Secretary-Treasurer in advance; convention fee typically $50 per person.

**Overcomer Ministry** ("Voice of the Last Day Prophet of God"), P.O. Box 691, Walterboro SC 29488 USA. Phone: (0900-1700 local time, Sunday through Friday) +1 (803) 538-3892. Email: (general) brotherstair@overcomerministry.com; (reception reports) overcomer@overcomerministry.com. Web: (includes RealAudio) www.overcomerministry.com. Contact: Brother R.G. Stair. Sample "Overcomer" newsletter and various pamphlets free upon request. Sells a Sangean shortwave radio for $50, plus other items of equipment and various publications at appropriate prices. Via Deutsche Telekom, Germany, and WWCR, USA.

**Radio Africa International**, General Board of Global Ministries, United Methodist Church, 475 Riverside Drive, New York NY 10115 USA. Phone: (toll-free within U.S.) 1-800-862-4246; (Media Contact) +1 (212) 870 3803. Fax: +1 (212) 870 3748. Email: radio@gbgm-umc.org. Web: (GBGM-UMC parent organization) www.gbgm-umc.org. Contact: Donna Niemann, Executive Producer; Raphael Mbadinga, Senior Producer. Sells calendars, magazines, books, videos and CDs of Christian music. Transmits via Jülich, Germany.

**Radio Free Afghanistan**—a service of Radio Free Europe-Radio Liberty (*see*). Web: (includes RealAudio) www.rferl.org/bd/af.

**Radio Free Asia**, Suite 300, 2025 M Street NW, Washington DC 20036 USA. Phone: (general) +1 (202) 530-4999; (vice president of programming) +1 (202) 530-4907; (president) +1 (202) 457-4901; (chief technology officer) +1 (202) 530-4958. Fax: +1 (202) 530 7794 or +1 (202) 721 7468. Email: (individuals) the format is lastnameinitial@rfa.org; so to reach, say the CTO, David Baden, it would be badend@rfa.org; (language sections) the format is language@rfa.org; so to contact, say, the Vietnamese section, address your message to vietnamese@rfa.org; (general) communications@rfa.org. Web: (includes audio in AudioActive and Real formats) www.rfa.org. Contact: (administration) Richard Richter, President; or Daniel Southerland, Vice President of Editoral; (technical) David Baden, Chief Technology Officer; (on-air operations) AJ Janitschek, Manager of Production Support; (reception reports) Ms. Tetiana Iwanciw, Executive Assistant for Technical Operations. RFA, originally created in 1996 as the Asia Pacific Network, is funded as a private nonprofit U.S. corporation by a grant from the Broadcasting Board of Governors (*see*), a politically bipartisan body appointed by the President of the United States. The purpose of RFA is to deliver accurate and timely news, information, and commentary, and to provide a forum for a variety of opinions and voices from within Asian countries. RFA focuses on events occurring in those countries. RFA seeks to promote the rights of freedom of opinion and expression—including the freedom to seek, receive and impart information and ideas through any medium regardless of frontiers.

*CHINA OFFICE:* P.O. Box 28840, Hong Kong, S.A.R. China. (or send to: 904, Massmutal Tower, 38 Gloucester Road, Wanchai, Hong Kong, China).

*JAPAN OFFICE:* P.O. Box 49, Central Post Office, Tokyo 100-91, Japan.

**Radio Free Europe-Radio Liberty/RFE-RL**
*PRAGUE HEADQUARTERS:* Vinohradská 1, 110 00 Prague 1, Czech Republic. Phone: +420 (2) 2112-1111; (president) +420 (2) 2112-3000; (news desk) +420 (2) 2112-3629; (public relations) +420 (2) 2112-3012; (technical operations) +420 (2) 2112-3700; (broadcast operations) +420 (2) 2112-3550; (affiliate relations). +420 (2) 2112-2539. Fax: +420 (2) 2112 3013; (president) +420 (2) 2112 3002; (news desk) +420 (2) 2112 3613; (public relations) +420 (2) 2112 2995; (technical operations) +420 (2) 2112 3702; (broadcast operations) +420 (2) 2112 3540; (affiliate operations) +420 (2) 2112 4563. Email: the format is lastnameinitial@rferl.org; so to reach, say, Luke Springer, it would be springerl@rferl.org. Web: (general, including RealAudio) www.rferl.org; (broadcast services) www.rferl.org/bd. Contact: Thomas A. Dine, President; Kestutis Girnius, Managing Editor, News and Current Affairs; Luke Springer, Deputy Director, Technology; Jana Horakova, Public Relations Coordinator; Uldis Grava, Marketing Director; or Christopher Carzoli, Broadcast Operations Director.

*WASHINGTON OFFICE:* 1201 Connecticut Avenue NW, Washington DC 20036 USA. Phone: +1 (202) 457-6900; (newsdesk) +1 (202) 457-6950; (technical) +1 (202) 457-6963. Fax: +1 (202) 457 6992; (news desk) +1 (202) 457 6997; (technical) +1 (202) 457 6913. Email and Web: *see* above. Contact: Jane Lester, Secretary of the Corporation; Ken Morehouse, Director of Technology Systems; or Paul Goble, Director of Communications; (news) Oleh Zwadiuk, Washington Bureau Chief. A private nonprofit corporation funded by a grant from the Broadcasting Board of Governors, RFE/RL broadcasts in 21 languages (but not English) from transmission facilities now part of the International Broadcasting Bureau (IBB), *see*.

**Radio Free Iraq**—a service of Radio Free Europe-Radio Liberty (*see*, above). Web: (includes RealAudio) www.rferl.org/bd/iq.

**Radio Martí**, Office of Cuba Broadcasting, 4201 N.W. 77th Avenue, Miami FL 33166 USA. Phone: +1 (305) 437-7000; (Director) +1 (305) 437-7117; (Technical Operations) +1 (305) 437-7051. Fax: +1 (305) 437 7016. Email: (Spanish) rcotta@ocb.ibb.gov; (English) webmaster@ocb.ibb.gov. Web: (includes RealAudio) www.ibb.gov/marti. Contact: (technical) Michael Pallone, Director of Technical Operations; or Tom Warden, Chief of Radio Operations.

**Radio Sawa**—the Middle East Radio Network (MERN) of the Voice of America (*see*). Web: (includes RealAudio and Windows Media) www.radiosawa.com.

**Remants Hope Ministry**, 4155 Strider Cir., Kannapolis NC 28081 USA. Phone: +1 (704) 932-4951. Email: remnantshope@hotmail.com. Web: http://home.bellsouth.net/p/s/community.dll?ep=16&groupid=26396&ck=. Contact: Pastor Tim Butler. To North America over WWRB, and irregularly to Europe via Jülich, Germany.

**TNT—Tomorrow's News Today**, P.O. Box 2100, Bowling Green KY 42102-2100 USA. Sponsored by Yahweh's Philadelphia Remnant Assembly. To North America via WWCR and WWRB, and irregularly to Europe from facilities in Eastern Europe. The

European broadcasts can be verified via: TDP, P.O. Box 1, 2310 Rijkevorsel, Belgium.

◪**Trans World Radio**, International Headquarters, P.O. Box 8700, Cary NC 27512-8700 USA. Phone: +1 (919) 460-3700; toll-free (U.S. only) 1-800-456-7897. Fax: +1 (919) 460 3702. Email: info2@twr.org. Web: (includes RealAudio) www.gospelcom.net/twr. Contact: (general) Jon Vaught, Public Relations; Richard Greene, Director, Public Relations; Joe Fort, Director, Broadcaster Relations; or Bill Danick; (technical) Glenn W. Sink, Assistant Vice President, International Operations. Free "Towers to Eternity" publication for those living in the U.S. Technical correspondence should be sent to the office nearest the country where the transmitter is located—Guam, Monaco or Swaziland. For information on offices in Asia and Australasia, refer to the entry under "Guam."

*CANADIAN OFFICE:* P.O. Box 444, Niagara Falls ON, L2E 6T8 Canada. Web: http://twrcan.ca.

◪**University Network**, P.O. Box 1, Los Angeles CA 90053 USA. Phone: (toll-free within U.S.) 1-800-338-3030; (elsewhere, call collect) +1 (818) 240-8151. Web: (includes RealAudio and Windows Media) www.drgenescott.com. Contact: Dr. Gene Scott. Sells audio and video tapes and books relating to Dr. Scott's teaching. Free copies of *The Truth About* and *The University Cathedral Pulpit* publications. Transmits over KAIJ and WWCR (USA); Caribbean Beacon (Anguilla, West Indies); the former AWR facilities in Cahuita, Costa Rica; and a transmitter in Samara, Russia.

◪**USA Radio Network**, 2290 Springlake Road, Suite 107, Dallas TX 75234 USA. Toll-free phone (within the U.S.) 1-800-829-8111. Email: (complaints/suggestions) tim@usaradio.com; (technical) david@usaradio.com. Web: (includes RealAudio and MP3) www.usaradio.com. Contact: (general) Tim Maddoux. Does not broadcast direct on shortwave, but some of its news and other programs are heard via U.S. stations KWHR, WHRA, WHRI and WWCR.

◪**Voice of America—All Transmitter Locations**

*MAIN OFFICE:* 330 Independence Avenue SW, Washington DC 20237 USA. If contacting the VOA directly is impractical, write c/o the American Embassy in your country. Phone: (to hear VOA-English live) +1 (202) 619-1979; (Office of External Affairs) +1 (202) 619-2358 or +1 (202) 619-2039; (Audience Mail Division) +1 (202) 619-2770; (Africa Division) +1 (202) 619-1666 or +1 (202) 619-2879; (Office of Research) +1 (202) 619-4965; (administration) +1 (202) 619-1088. Fax: (general information for listeners outside the United States) +1 (202) 376 1066; (Public Liaison for listeners within the United States) +1 (202) 619 1241; (Office of External Affairs) +1 (202) 205 0634 or +1 (202) 205 2875; (Africa Division) +1 (202) 619 1664; (Audience Mail Division and Office of Research) +1 (202) 619 0211; (administration) +1 (202) 619 0085. Email: (general business) pubaff@voa.gov; (reception reports and schedule requests) letters@voa.gov; (automatic reply back email schedules for "VOA News Now") schedule@voanews.com or cwschedule@voa.gov; ("VOA News Now") newsnow@voanews.com; (VOA Special English) special@voa.gov; (VOA English to Africa) africanews@voa.gov. Web: (includes RealAudio) www.voa.gov. Contact: Mrs. Betty Lacy Thompson, Chief, Audience Mail Division, B/K. G759A Cohen; Larry James, Director, English Programs Division; Leo Sarkisian; Rita Rochelle, Africa Division; George Mackenzie, Audience Research Officer; (reception reports) Mrs. Irene Greene, QSL Desk, Audience Mail Division, Room G-759-C. Free stickers and calendars. If you're an American and miffed because you can't receive these goodies from the VOA, don't blame the station—they're only following the law. The VOA occasionally hosts international broadcasting conventions, and as of 1996 has been accepting limited supplemental funding from the U.S. Agency for International Development (AID). Also, *see* Ascension, Botswana, Greece, Morocco, Philippines, São Tomé e Príncipe, Sri Lanka and Thailand.

**Voice of America/IBB—Delano Relay Station**, Rt. 1, Box 1350, Delano CA 93215 USA; (physical address) 11015 Melcher Road, Delano CA 93215 USA. Phone: +1 (805) 725-0150. Fax: +1 (805) 725 6511. Email: (Vodenik) k9hsp@juno.com. Contact: (technical) Brent Boyd, Manager; or John Vodenik, Chief Engineer. Photos of this facility can be seen at the following Website: www.hawkins.pair.com/voadelano.shtml. Nontechnical correspondence should be sent to the VOA address in Washington.

**Voice of America/IBB—Greenville Relay Station**, P.O. Box 1826, Greenville NC 27834 USA. Phone: +1 (919) 752-7115. Fax: +1 (919) 752 5959. Contact: (technical) Bruce Hunter, Manager; or Glenn Ruckleson. Nontechnical correspondence should be sent to the VOA address in Washington.

**WBCQ—"The Planet,"** 97 High Street, Kennebunk ME 04043 USA. Phone: +1 (207) 985-7547; (transmitter site, urgent technical matters only) +1 (207) 538-9180. Email: wbcq@gwi.net. Web: http://theplanet.wbcq.net. Contact: Allan H. Weiner, Owner; or Elayne Star, Assistant Manager. Verifies reception reports if 1 IRC or (within USA) an SASE is included.

◪**WEWN—EWTN Global Catholic Radio**

*TRANSMISSION FACILITY AND STATION MAILING ADDRESS:* 1500 High Road, P.O. Box 176, Vandiver AL 35176 USA.

*ENGINEERING AND MARKETING OFFICES:* 5817 Old Leeds Rd., Irondale AL 35210 USA. Phone: (general) +1 (205) 271-2900; (Station Manager) +1 (205) 271-2943; (Chief Engineer) +1 (205) 271-2959; (Marketing Manager) +1 (205) 271-2982; (Program Director, English) +1 (205) 271-2944; (Program Director, Spanish) +1 (205) 271-2900 ext. 2073; (Frequency Manager) +1 (205) 795-5779. Fax: (general) +1 (205) 271 2926; (Marketing) +1 (205) 271 2925; (Engineering and Frequency Management) +1 (205) 271 2953. Email: (general) wewn@ewtn.com; (technical) radio@ewtn.com; (Spanish) rcm@ewtn.com. To contact individuals, the format is initiallastname@ewtn.com; so to reach, say, Thom Price, it would be tprice@ewtn.com. Web: (includes RealAudio and online reception-report form) www.ewtn.com/wewn. Contact: (general) Thom Price, Director of English Programming; or Doug Archer, Director of Spanish Programming; (marketing) Bernard Lockhart, Radio Marketing Manager; (administration) William Steltemeier, President; or Frank Leurck, Station Manager; (technical) Terry Borders, Vice President Engineering; Glen Tapley, Frequency Manager; or Dennis Dempsey, Chief Engineer. Listener correspondence welcomed; responds to correspondence on-air and by mail. Free bumper stickers, program schedules and (sometimes) other booklets or publications. Sells numerous religious books, CDs, audio and video cassettes, T-shirts, sweatshirts and various other religious articles; list available upon request (VISA/MC). IRC or return postage appreciated for correspondence. Although a Catholic entity, WEWN is not an official station of the Vatican, which operates its own Vatican Radio (*see*). Rather, WEWN reflects the activities of Mother M. Angelica and the Eternal Word Foundation, Inc. Donations and bequests accepted by the Eternal Word Foundation.

◪**WHRA-World Harvest Radio:**

*ADMINISTRATION OFFICE: see* WHRI, USA, below.

*TRANSMITTER:* Located in Greenbush, Maine, but all technical and other correspondence should be sent to WHRI (*see* next entry).

**Elder and Mrs. Jacob Meyer with WMLK's newly purchased transmitter.** WMLK

📻**WHRI—World Harvest Radio**, WHRI/WHRA/KWHR, LeSEA Broadcasting, P.O. Box 12, South Bend IN 46624 USA. Phone: +1 (219) 291-8200. Fax: (station) +1 (219) 291 9043. Email: whr@lesea.com; (Joe Brashier) jbrashier@lesea.com; (Joe Hill) jhill@lesea.com. Web: (including RealAudio): www.whr.org; (LeSEA Broadcasting parent organization) www.lesea.com. Contact: (listener contact) Loren Holycross; (general) Pete Sumrall, Vice President; or Joe Hill, Operations Manager; (programming or sales) Joe Hill or Joe Brashier; (technical) Douglas Garlinger, Chief Engineer. World Harvest Radio T-shirts available from 61300 S. Ironwood Road, South Bend IN 46614 USA. Return postage appreciated.
*ENGINEERING DEPARTMENT:* P.O. Box 50450, Indianapolis, IN 46250 USA.
*"EDXP NEWS REPORTS":* Web: www.members.tripod.com/-bpadula.html. Special news reports concentrating on shortwave broadcasts to and from Asia, the Far East, Australia, the Pacific and the Indian sub-continent, compiled by EDXP and aired on the first Friday of each month, (UTC) and repeated on the following Saturday and Sunday within the *"Dxing with Cumbre"* program, over the World Harvest Radio shortwave and RealAudio Networks. Special EDXP QSLs will be offered for the shortwave releases (not for RealAudio). Reports of the EDXP feature should be sent to: Bob Padula, EDXP QSL Service, 404 Mont Albert Road, Surrey Hills, Victoria 3127, Aus-

tralia. Return postage appreciated. Outside of Australia, 1 IRC or $1; within Australia, four 50c Australian stamps. Email reports welcome at: edxp@bigpond.com, and verified with Web-delivered animated QSLs.
**WINB—World International Broadcasters**, 2900 Windsor Road, P.O. Box 88, Red Lion PA 17356 USA. Phone: (all departments) +1 (717) 244-5360. Fax: +1 (717) 246 0363. Email: info@winb.com. Web: www.winb.com. Contact: (general) Mrs. Sally Spyker, Manager; (sales & Frequency Manager) Hans Johnson; (technical) Fred W. Wise, Technical Director; or John H. Norris, Owner. Return postage helpful outside United States. No giveaways or items for sale.
**WJIE Shortwave**, P.O. Box 197309, Louisville KY 40259 USA. Phone: +1 (502) 965-1220. Fax: +1 (502) 964 4228. Email: wjiesw@hotmail.com. Web: www.wjiesw.com. Transmitting equipment purchased from former world band station WJCR.
**WMLK—Assemblies of Yahweh**, 190 Frantz Road, P.O. Box C, Bethel PA 19507 USA. Toll-free telephone (U.S only) 1-800-523-3827; (elsewhere) +1 (717) 933-4518 or +1 (717) 933-4880. Email: (general) aoy@wmlkradio.com; (technical) technician@wmlkradio.com; (Elder Meyer) jacobmeyer@wmlkradio.com; (McAvin) garymcavin@wmlkradio.com. Web: www.wmlkradio.com; (Assemblies of Yahweh parent organization) www.assembliesofyahweh.com. Contact: (general) Elder Jacob O. Meyer, Manager and Producer of "The Open Door to the Living World"; (technical) Gary McAvin, Station Manager. Free *The Sacred Name Broadcaster* magazine published monthly, stickers and religious material. Bibles, audio and video (VHS) tapes and religious paperback books offered. Enclosing return postage ($1 or IRCs) helps speed things up.
**WRMI—Radio Miami International**, 175 Fontainebleau Blvd., Suite 1N4, Miami FL 33172 USA; or P.O. Box 526852, Miami FL 33152 USA. Phone: (general) +1 (305) 559-9764; (Engineering) +1 (305) 827-2234. Fax: (general) +1 (305) 559 8186; ( Engineering) +1 (305) 819 8756. Email: info@wrmi.net. Web: www.wrmi.net. Contact: (technical and nontechnical) Jeff White, General Manager/Sales Manager; (technical) Indalecio "Kiko" Espinosa, Chief Engineer. Free station stickers and tourist brochures. Sells "public access" airtime to nearly anyone to say virtually anything for $1 or more per minute.
**WRNO WORLDWIDE** (when reactivated)
*TRANSMITTER SITE:* 4539 I-10 Service Road North, Metairie LA 70006 USA.
*GOOD NEWS WORLDWIDE, PARENT ORGANIZATION:* P.O. Box 895, Fort Worth TX 76101 USA. Phone: +1 (817) 801-8322. Fax: +1 (817) 492 7015. Email: hope@goodnewsworld.org. Web: www.goodnewsworld.org. Currently inactive due to change of ownership after previous transmitter was destroyed by fire.
**WSHB**—*see* Christian Science Publishing Society, above.
📻**WTJC**, Fundamental Broadcasting Network, Grace Missionary Baptist Church, 520 Roberts Road, Newport NC 28570 USA.Phone: +1 (252) 223-6088; (toll free, within the United States) 1-800-245-9685; (Robinson) +1 (252) 223-4600. Email: (general) fbn@clis.com; (technical, David Robinson) davidwr@clis.com. Web: (includes RealAudio) www.fbnradio.com. Contact: Pastor Clyde Eborn; (technical) David Robinson, Chief Engineer. Verifies reception reports if an IRC or (within the USA) an SASE is included. Accepts email reports. Station is operated by FBN, a religious and educational non-commercial broadcasting network.
**WWBS**, P.O. Box 18174. Macon GA 31209 USA. Phone: +1 (912) 477-3433. Email: (general) wwbsradio@aol.com. Contact: Charles C. Josey; or Joanne Josey. Include return postage if you want your reception reports verified.

**WWCR—World Wide Christian Radio**, F.W. Robbert Broadcasting Co., 1300 WWCR Avenue, Nashville TN 37218 USA. Phone: (general) +1 (615) 255-1300. Fax: +1 (615) 255 1311. Email: (general) wwcr@wwcr.com; ("Ask WWCR" program) askwwcr@wwcr.com. Web: www.wwcr.com. Contact: (administration) George McClintock, K4BTY, General Manager; Adam W. Lock, Sr., WA2JAL, Head of Operations; or Dawn Keen, Program Director; (technical) William Hair, Chief Engineer. Free program guides, updated monthly. Return postage helpful. For items sold on the air and tapes of programs, contact the producers of the programs, and *not* WWCR. Replies as time permits. Carries programs from various political organizations, which may be contacted directly.

**WWRB—World Wide Religious Broadcasters**, c/o Southeast Radio Church, Box 7, Manchester TN 37349-0007 USA. Phone/fax: +1 (931) 841-0492. Email: dfrantz@tennessee.com. Web: www.wwrb.org. Contact: Dave Frantz, Chief Engineer. In its previous incarnation as WWFV, verification policy was that reception reports were to be sent to individual broadcasters (i.e. program producers) with a request to forward the report to the station, which in turn would then verify it.

**WWV/WWVB** (official time and frequency stations): NIST Radio Station WWV, 2000 East County Road #58, Ft. Collins CO 80524 USA. Phone: +1 (303) 497-3914. Fax: +1 (303) 497 4063. Email: nist.radio@boulder.nist.gov; (Deutch) deutch@boulder.nist.gov. Contact: Matt Deutch, Engineer-in-Charge. Web: http://tf.nist.gov. Along with branch sister station WWVH in Hawaii (*see* below), WWV and WWVB are the official time and frequency stations of the United States, operating over longwave (WWVB) on 60 kHz, and over shortwave (WWV) on 2500, 5000, 10000, 15000 and 20000 kHz.

*PARENT ORGANIZATION:* National Institute of Standards and Technology, Time and Frequency Division, 325 Broadway, Boulder CO 80305-3328 USA. Phone: +1 (303) 497-5453. Email: (Lowe) lowe@boulder.nist.gov. Contact: John Lowe, Group Leader.

**WWVH** (official time and frequency station): NIST Radio Station WWVH, P.O. Box 417, Kekaha, Kauai HI 96752 USA. Phone: +1 (808) 335-4361; (live audio) +1 (808) 335-4363. Fax: +1 (808) 335 4747. Email: nistwwvh@gte.net. Contact: (technical) Dean T. Okayama, Engineer-in-Charge. Along with headquarters sister stations WWV and WWVB (*see* preceding), WWVH is the official time and frequency station of the United States, operating on 2500, 5000, 10000 and 15000 kHz.

**WYFR—Family Radio**—*see* Family Radio Worldwide.

## UZBEKISTAN    World Time +5

*WARNING—MAIL THEFT:* Due to increasing local mail theft, Radio Tashkent suggests that those wishing to correspond should try using one of the drop-mailing addresses listed below.

**Radio Tashkent**, 49 Khorazm Street, 700047 Tashkent, Uzbekistan. Phone: (Head of International Service) +998 (71) 133-8920; (Correspondence Section) +998 (71) 139-9657; (Shekhar) +998 (71) 139-0752 or +998 (71) 139-9521. Fax: +998 (71) 144 0021. Email: (Shekhar) alex@kirsh.silk.org. Contact: Sherzat Gulyamov, Head of International Service; Mrs. Alfia Ruzmatova, Head of Correspondence Section; Babur Turdieav, Head of English Service; Alok Shekhar, Announcer - Hindi Service. Correspondence is welcomed in English, German, Russian, Uzbek and nine other languages broadcast by Radio Tashkent. Reception reports are verified with colorful QSL cards. Free pennants, badges, wallet calendars and postcards. Has quizzes from time to time with prizes and souve-

nirs. Books in English by Uzbek writers are apparently available for purchase. Station offers free membership to the "Salum Aleikum Listeners' Club" for regular listeners.

*TRANSMISSION FACILITIES:* Pochta va Telekommunikasiyalar Agentligi, Aleksey Tolstoy küçä 1, 700000 Tashkent, Uzbekistan. Phone: +998 (71) 133-6645. Fax: +998 (71) 144 2603. Contact: Fatrullah Fazullahyev, Director General.

**Uzbek Radio** (if reactivated), Khorazm küçä 49, 700047 Tashkent, Uzbekistan. Phone: (general) +998 (71) 144-1210; (Director) +998 (71) 133-8920 or 998 (71) 139-9636; (technical) +998 (71) 136-2290. Fax: (general) +998 (71) 144 0021; (Director) +998 (71) 133 8920. Email: uzradio@eanetways.com. Contact: (administration) Fakhriddin N. Nizom, Director; (technical) Komoljon Rajapov, Chief Engineer. Uzbek Radio's shortwave relays were suspended in 2001.

## VANUATU    World Time +12 (+11 midyear)

**Radio Vanuatu**, Information and Public Relations, Private Mail Bag 049, Port Vila, Vanuatu. Phone: +678 22999 or +678 23026. Fax: +678 22026. Contact: Maxwell E. Maltok, General Manager; Ambong Thompson, Head of Programmes; or Allan Kalfabun, Sales and Marketing Consultant, who is interested in exchanging letters and souvenirs from other countries; (technical) K.J. Page, Principal Engineer; Marianne Berukilkilu, Technical Manager; or Willie Daniel, Technician.

## VATICAN CITY STATE    World Time +1 (+2 midyear)

☞**Radio Vaticana (Vatican Radio)**

*MAIN AND PROMOTION OFFICES:* 00120 Città del Vaticano, Vatican City State. Phone: (general) +39 (06) 6988-3551; (Director General) +39 (06) 6988-3945; (Programme Director) +39 (06) 6988-3996; (Publicity and Promotion Department) +39 (06) 6988-3045; (technical, general) +39 (06) 6988-4897; (frequency management) +39 (06) 6988-5258. Fax: (general) +39 (06) 6988 4565; (frequency management) +39 (06) 6988 5062. Email: sedoc@vatiradio.va; sedoc@vaticanradio-us.org; (Director General) dirigen@vatiradio.va; (frequency management) mc6790@mclink.it; or gestfreq@vatiradio.va; (technical direction, general) sectec@vatiradio.va; (Programme Director) dirpro@vatiradio.va; (Publicity and Promotion Department) promo@vatiradio.va; (English Section) englishpr@vatiradio.va, (French Section) magfra@vatiradio.va; (German Section) deutsch@vatiradio.va; (Japanese Section) japan@vatiradio.va. Web: (general, including multilingual news and live broadcasts in RealAudio) www.vatican.va/news_services/radio/; www.vaticanradio.org; (RealAudio in English and other European languages, plus text) www.wrn.org/vatican-radio. Contact: (general) Elisabetta Vitalini Sacconi, Promotion Office and schedules; Eileen O'Neill, Head of Program Development, English Service; Fr. Lech Rynkiewicz S.J., Head of Promotion Office; Fr. Federico Lombardi, S.J., Program Director; Solange de Maillardoz, Head of International Relations; Sean Patrick Lovett, Head of English Service; or Veronica Scarisbrick, Producer, "On the Air;" (administration) Fr. Pasquale Borgomeo, S.J., Director General; (technical) Umberto Tolaini, Frequency Manager, Direzione Tecnica; Sergio Salvatori, Assistant Frequency Manager, Direzione Tecnica; Fr. Eugenio Matis S.J., Technical Director; or Giovanni Serra, Frequency Management Department. Correspondence sought on religious and programming matters, rather than the technical minutiae of radio. Free station stickers and paper pennants. Music CDs $13; *Pope John Paul II: The Pope of the Rosary* double CD/cassette $19.98 plus shipping; "Sixty Years . . . a Single Day" PAL video on Vatican Radio for 15,000 lire, including postage, from the Promotion Office.

*INDIA OFFICE:* Loyola College, P.B. No 3301, Chennai-600 03, India. Fax: +91 (44) 825 7340. Email: (Tamil) tamil@vatiradio.va; (Hindi) hindi@vatiradio.va; (English) india@vatiradio.va.

*REGIONAL OFFICE, INDIA:* Pastoral Orientation Centre, P.B. No 2251, Palarivattom, India. Fax: +91 (484) 336 227. Email: (Malayalam) malayalam@vatiradio.va.

*JAPAN OFFICE:* 2-10-10 Shiomi, Koto-ku, Tokyo 135, Japan. Fax: +81 (3) 5632 4457.

*POLAND OFFICE:* Warszawskie Biuro Sekcji Polskiej Radia Watykanskiego, ul. Skwer Ks. Kard. S, Warsaw, Poland. Phone: +48 (22) 838-8796.

## VENEZUELA    World Time –4

**Ecos del Torbes**, Apartado 152, San Cristóbal 5001-A, Táchira, Venezuela. Phone: (general) +58 (276) 438-244; (studio): +58 (276) 421-949. Contact: (general) Licenciada Dinorah González Zerpa, Gerente; Simón Zaidman Krenter; (technical) Ing. Iván Escobar S., Jefe Técnico.

**Observatorio Cagigal—YVTO**, Apartado 6745, Armada 84-DHN, Caracas 103, Venezuela. Phone: +58 (212) 481-2761. Email: armdhn@ven.net. Contact: Jesús Alberto Escalona, Director Técnico; or Gregorio Pérez Moreno, Director. $1 or return postage helpful.

**Radio Amazonas**, Av. Simón Bolívar 4, Puerto Ayacucho 7101, Amazonas, Venezuela; or if no reply try Francisco José Ocaña at: Urb. 23 de Enero, Calle Nicolás Briceño, No. 18-266, Barinas 5201-A, Venezuela. Contact: Luis Jairo, Director; or Santiago Sangil Gonzales, Gerente. Francisco José Ocaña is a keen collector of U.S. radio station stickers. Sending a few stickers with your letter as well as enclosing $2 may help.

**Radio Nacional de Venezuela** (when operating), Final Calle Las Marías, El Pedregal de Chapellín, 1050 Caracas, Venezuela. If this fails, try: Director de la Onda Corta, Sr. Miguel Angel Cariel, Apartado Postal 3979, Caracas 1010-A, Venezuela. Phone: +58 (212) 730-6022 or +58 (212) 730-6666. Email: rnb2000@hotmail.com. Contact: Miguel Angel Cariel, Director de la Onda Corta. The transmitter site is actually located at Campo Carabobo, near Valencia, some three hours drive from Caracas.

**Radio Táchira**, Apartado 152, San Cristóbal 5001-A, Táchira, Venezuela. Phone: +58 (276) 430-009. Contact: Desirée González Zerpa, Directora; Sra. Albertina, Secretaria; or Eleázar Silva Malavé, Gerente.

**Radio Valera**, Av. 10 No. 9-31, Valera 3102, Trujillo, Venezuela. Phone: +58 (271) 53-744. Contact: Gladys Barroeta; or Mariela Leal. Replies to correspondence in Spanish. Return postage required. This station has been on the same world band frequency for almost 50 years, which is a record for Latin America.

## VIETNAM    World Time +7

**Bac Thai Broadcasting Service**—contact via Voice of Vietnam—Overseas Service, below.

**Lai Chau Broadcasting Service**—contact via Voice of Vietnam—Overseas Service, below.

**Lam Dong Broadcasting Service**, Da Lat, Vietnam. Contact: Hoang Van Trung. Replies slowly to correspondence in Vietnamese, but French may also suffice.

**Son La Broadcasting Service**, Son La, Vietnam. Contact: Nguyen Hang, Director. Replies slowly to correspondence in Vietnamese, but French may also suffice.

**Voice of Vietnam—Domestic Service** (Dài Tiêng Nói Viêt Nam, TNVN)—Addresses and contact numbers as for all sections of Voice of Vietnam—Overseas Service, below. Contact: Phan Quang, Director General.

**🔊Voice of Vietnam—Overseas Service**

*TRANSMISSION FACILITY (MAIN ADDRESS FOR NONTECHNICAL CORRESPONDENCE AND GENERAL VERIFICATIONS):* 58 Quán Sú, Hànôi, Vietnam. Phone: +84 (4) 824-0044 or +84 (4) 825-5669. Fax: +84 (4) 826 1122. Email: qhqt.vov@hn.vnn.vn. Web: (English text) www.vov.org.vn/docs1/english/; (Vietnamese text and RealAudio in English and Vietnamese) www.vov.org.vn. Contact: Ms. Hoang Minh Nguyet, Director of International Relations; or Mr. Pham Van Ly. Free paper pennant and, occasionally upon request, Vietnamese stamps. $1 helpful, but IRCs apparently of no use. Replies slowly. Try not to send stamps on correspondence to Vietnam. They're often cut off the envelopes and the station doesn't receive the letters. Machine-franked envelopes stand a better chance of getting through.

*STUDIOS (NONTECHNICAL CORRESPONDENCE AND GENERAL VERIFICATIONS):* 45 Ba Trieu Street, Hànôi, Vietnam. Phone: (director) +84 (4) 825-7870; (English service) +84 (4) 934-2456; (newsroom) +84 (4) 825-5761 or +84 (4) 825-5862. Fax: (English service) +84 (4) 826 6707. Email: btdn.vov@hn.vnn.vn. Contact Dinh The Loc, Director.

*TECHNICAL CORRESPONDENCE:* Office of Radio Reception Quality, Central Department of Radio and Television Broadcast Engineering, Vietnam General Corporation of Posts and Telecommunications, Hànôi, Vietnam.

**Yen Bai Broadcasting Station**—contact via Voice of Vietnam, Overseas Service, above.

## WESTERN SAHARA    World Time exactly

**Radio Nacional de la República Arabe Saharaui Democrática**, Directeur d'Information, Frente Polisario, B.P. 10, El-Mouradia, 16000 Algiers, Algeria; or c/o Ambassade de la République Arabe Saharaui Démocratique, 1 Av. Franklin Roosevelt, 16000 Algiers, Algeria. Phone (Algeria): +213 (2) 747-907. Fax, when operating (Algeria): +213 (2) 747 984. Email: rasdradio@yahoo.es. Web: (includes a RealAudio recording made in the station's studios) http://web.jet.es/rasd/amateur4.htm. Contact: Mohammed Baali. Two IRCs helpful. Pro-Polisario Front, and supported by the Algerian government. Operates from Rabuni, near Tindouf, on the Algerian side of the border with Western Sahara.

## YEMEN    World Time +3

**🔊Republic of Yemen Radio**, Ministry of Information, P.O. Box 2182 (or P.O. Box 2371), Sana'a-al Hasbah, Yemen. Phone: (general) +967 (1) 230-654; (engineering) +967 ((1) 230-751. Fax: (general) +967 (1) 230 761; (engineering) +967 (1) 251 628. Email: yradio@y.net.ye or hussein3itu@y.net.ye. Web: (includes RealAudio) www.yradio.gov.ye. Contact: (general) English Service; (administration) Mohammed Dahwan, General Director of Sana'a Radio; Adel Affara; or Abdulrahman Al-Haimi; (technical) Engineer Mohammed H. Bather, Technical Director; or Mohamed Al Sammann, Chairman of Engineering Sector.

## YUGOSLAVIA    World Time +1 (+2 midyear)

**Radiotelevizija Srbije**, Hilendarska 2/IV, 11000 Beograd, Serbia, Yugoslavia. Phone: +381 (11) 322-1850 or +381 (11) 321-1119. Fax: +381 (11) 324 8808. Email: (Simic) momas@afrodita.rcub.bg.ac.yu. Web: www.rts.co.yu. Contact: Momcilo Simic.

**Radio Beograd**, Hilandarska 2a, 11000 Beograd, Serbia, Yugoslavia. Phone: +381 (11) 324-8888 or +381 (11) 324-9337. Email: info@radiobeograd.co.yu. Web: (includes RealAudio) www.radiobeograd.co.yu. A service of Radiotelevizija Srbije (*see*, above). Currently inactive on shortwave except for relays via Radio Yugoslavia (when operating—*see*, below), following the destruction of its transmitter by NATO forces in 1999.

**Radio Yugoslavia**, Hilendarska 2/IV, P.O. Box 200, 11000 Beograd, Serbia, Yugoslavia. Phone: +381 (11) 324-4455. Fax: +381 (11) 323 2014. Email: radioyu@bitsyu.net. Web: (includes RealAudio) www.radioyu.org. Contact: (general) Nikola Ivanovic, Director; Aleksandar Georgiev; Aleksandar Popovic, Head of Public Relations; Pance Zafirovski, Head of Programs; or Slobodan Topović, Producer, "Post Office Box 200/Radio Hams' Corner"; (technical) B. Miletic, Operations Manager of HF Broadcasting; Technical Department; or Rodoljub Medan, Chief Engineer. Free pennants, stickers, pins and tourist information. $1 helpful. Currently off the air due to a dispute with Bosnia, where the transmitters are located.

## ZAMBIA    World Time +2

**Radio Christian Voice**
*STATION:* Private Bag E606, Lusaka, Zambia. Phone: +260 (1) 274-251. Fax: +260 (1) 274 526. Email: cvoice@zamnet.zm. Web: (includes RealAudio) www.christianvoice.org. Contact: Philip Haggar, Station Manager; Beatrice Phiri; or Lenganji Nanyangwe, Assistant to Station Manager. Free calendars and stickers pens, as available. Free religious books and items under selected circumstances. Sells T-shirts and sundry other items. $1 or 2 IRCs appreciated for reply. Broadcasts Christian teachings and music, as well as news and programs on farming, sport, education, health, business and children's affairs.
*U. K. OFFICE:* Christian Voice International, P.O. Box 3040, West Bromwich, West Midlands, B70 0AY, United Kingdom. Phone:+44 (121) 224-1614. Fax: +44 (121) 224 1613. Email: mail@christianvoice.org; (Joynes) sandra@christianvoice.org. Web: (includes RealAudio) www.christianvoice.org. Contact: Sandra Joynes, Office Administrator.
**Radio Zambia**, Mass Media Complex, Alick Nkhata Road, P.O. Box 50015, Lusaka 10101, Zambia. Phone: (general) +260 (1) 254-989, +260 (1) 253-301 or +260 (1) 252-005; (Public Relations) +260 (1) 254-989, X-216; (engineering) +260 (1) 250-380. Fax: +260 (1) 254 317 or +260 (1) 254 013. Email: znbc@microlink.zm (zambroad@zamnet.zm may also work). Web: www.znbc.co.zm. Contact: (general) Keith M. Nalumango, Director of Programmes; or Lawson Chishimba, Public Relations Manager; (administration) Duncan H. Mbazima, Director-General; (technical) Patrick Nkula, Director of Engineering; or Malolela Lusambo. Free *Zamwaves* newsletter. Sometimes gives away stickers, postcards and small publications. $1 required, and postal correspondence should be sent via registered mail. Tours given of the station Tuesdays to Fridays between 9:00 AM and noon local time; inquire in advance. Used to reply slowly and irregularly, but seems to be better now.

## ZIMBABWE    World Time +2

**Zimbabwe Broadcasting Corporation**, P.O. Box HG444, Highlands, Harare, Zimbabwe; or P.O. Box 2271, Harare, Zimbabwe. Phone: +263 (4) 498-610 or +263 (4) 498-630. Fax: +263 (4) 498 613. Email: zbc@zbc.co.zw; (general enquiries) pr@zbc.co.zw; (news) hnn@zbc.co.zw; (Engineering) hbt@zbc.co.zw. Web: (includes Windows Media) www.zbc.co.zw. Contact: (general) Rugare Sangomoyo; or Lydia Muzenda; (administration) Alum Mpofu, Chief Executive Officer; (news details) Munyaradzi Hwengwere; (Broadcasting Technology, Engineering) Craig Matambo. $1 helpful.

---

*CREDITS: Craig Tyson (Australia), Editor, with Tony Jones (Paraguay). Also, Marie Lamb (USA) and Lawrence Magne (USA). Special thanks to colleagues Gabriel Iván Barrera (Argentina), David Crystal (Israel), Jose Jacob (India), Richard Lam (Singapore), Gary Neal (USA), Fotios Padazopulos (USA) George Poppin (USA) and Célio Romais (Brazil); also the following organizations for their support and cooperation:* Cumbre DX/Hans Johnson (USA), Jembatan DX/ Juichi Yamada (Japan), Radio Nuevo Mundo/ Tetsuya Hirahara (Japan) and RUS-DX/Anatoly Klepov (Russia).

**VERIFICATIONS**

You have spent a lot of time and effort on your QSL collection, but what will happen to it if you leave the listening hobby or pass away? It will probably be lost or discarded. **The Committee to Preserve Radio Verifications**—a committee of the Association of North American Radio Clubs—will preserve this valuable material for future hobbyists to enjoy and appreciate. The CPRV colletion is housed at the Library of American Broadcasting, University of Maryland, U.S.A.

For information, send an SASE or two IRCs to:

Committee to Preserve Radio Verifications
Jerry Berg, Chair
38 Eastern Avenue
Lexington, MA 02421, U.S.A.

Visit our website at
http://www.ontheshortwaves.com

# Worldwide Broadcasts in English— 2003

## Country-by-Country Guide to Best-Heard Stations

Dozens of countries reach out to us in English, and this section gives the times and frequencies where you're likely to hear them. If you want to know which shows are on hour-by-hour, check out "What's On Tonight."

• **When and where:** "Best Times and Frequencies," earlier in this edition, pinpoints where each world band segment is found and gives tuning tips. Best is late afternoon and evening, when most programs are beamed your way. Tune world band segments within the 5730-10000 kHz range in winter, 5730-15800 kHz during summer. Around breakfast, you can also explore segments within the 5730-17900 kHz range for fewer but intriguing catches.

- **Strongest (and weakest) frequencies:** Frequencies shown in italics—say, *5965* kHz—tend to be best, as they are from transmitters that may be located near you. However, other frequencies beamed your way might do almost as well. Some signals not beamed to you can also be heard, especially when they are targeted to nearby parts of the world. Frequencies with no target zones are typically for domestic coverage, so they are unlikely to be heard unless you're in or near that country.

## Program Times

Some stations shift broadcast times by one hour midyear, typically April through October. These are indicated by ▣ (one hour earlier) and ▣ (one hour later). Frequencies used seasonally are labeled ▣ for summer (midyear, typically April through October), and ▣ for winter. Stations may also extend their hours of transmission, or air special programs, for national holidays, emergencies or sports events.

Times and days of the week are in World Time, explained in "Setting Your World Time Clock" earlier in this edition, as well as in PASSPORT's glossary.

## Indigenous Music

Broadcasts in other than English? Turn to the next section, "Voices from Home," or the Blue Pages. Keep in mind that stations for kinsfolk abroad sometimes carry delightful chunks of native music. They make for enjoyable listening, regardless of language.

## Schedules for Entire Year

To be as useful as possible over the months to come, PASSPORT's schedules consist not just of observed activity, but also that which we have creatively opined will take place during the forthcoming year. This predictive material is based on decades of experience and is original from us. Although inherently not as exact as real-time data, over the years it's been of tangible value to PASSPORT readers.

**Best is late afternoon and evening, when many English programs are beamed your way.**

## ALBANIA
### RADIO TIRANA
| | |
|---|---|
| 0245-0300 & | |
| 0330-0400 ▣ | Tu-Su 6115 & Tu-Su 7160 (E North Am) |
| 1845-1900 | ▣ M-Sa 9520 (W Europe) |
| 1945-2000 ▣ | M-Sa 7210 (W Europe) |
| 1945-2000 ▣ | M-Sa 9510 (W Europe) |
| 2230-2300 ▣ | M-Sa 7130 & M-Sa 9540 (W Europe) |

## ARGENTINA
### RADIO ARGENTINA AL EXTERIOR-RAE
| | |
|---|---|
| 0200-0300 | Tu-Sa 6060 (C America & S America), Tu-Sa 11710 (Americas) |
| 1800-1900 | M-F 9690 (Europe & N Africa), M-F 15345 (Europe) |

## ARMENIA
### VOICE OF ARMENIA
| | |
|---|---|
| 0910-0930 ▣ | Su 4810 (E Europe, Mideast & W Asia), Su 15270 (Europe) |
| 2040-2100 ▣ | M-Sa 4810 (E Europe, Mideast & W Asia), M-Sa 9960 (Europe) |

## AUSTRALIA
### RADIO AUSTRALIA
| | |
|---|---|
| 0000-0100 | 21740 (Pacific & N America) |
| 0000-0130 | 17775 (SE Asia) |
| 0000-0200 | 17795 (Pacific & W North Am) |
| 0000-0700 | 15240 (Pacific & E Asia) |
| 0000-0800 | 9660 (Pacific), 17580 (Pacific & W North Am) |
| 0000-0900 | 12080 (S Pacific), 15415 (SE Asia) |
| 0030-0400 | 17750 (SE Asia) |
| 0100-0900 | 21725 (E Asia) |
| 0200-0700 | 15515 (Pacific & N America) |
| 0430-0500 & | |
| 0530-0800 | 17750 (SE Asia) |
| 0700-0900 | 15240 (Pacific & W North Am) |
| 0800-0900 | 5995 & 9710 (Pacific) |
| 0805-1100 | 9580 (Pacific & W North Am) |
| 0830-0900 | 17750 (SE Asia) |
| 0900-1400 | 21820 (Asia & Europe) |
| 0930-1100 | 11880/17750 (E Asia & SE Asia) |
| 1100-1200 | 12080 (S Pacific) |
| 1100-1330 | 11880 (E Asia & SE Asia) |
| 1100-1400 | 5995 (Pacific), 6020 (Pacific & W North Am) |
| 1100-2130 | 9580 (Pacific & N America) |
| 1200-1700 | 11650 (Pacific) |
| 1330-1700 | 11660 (SE Asia) |
| 1400-1800 | 5995 (Pacific & W North Am), 6080 (SE Asia) |
| 1530-1900 | 9475 (E Asia & SE Asia) |
| 1700-2100 | 9815 (Pacific & E Asia) |
| 1700-2200 | 11880 (Pacific & W North Am) |
| 1800-2000 | 6080 (Pacific & E Asia), 7240 (Pacific) |
| 1900-2130 | 9500 (E Asia & SE Asia) |
| 2000-2100 | F/Sa 6080 & F/Sa 7240 (Pacific) |
| 2000-2200 | 12080 (S Pacific) |
| 2100-2200 | 7240 & 9660 (Pacific) |
| 2100-2400 | 17715 (Pacific & W North Am), 21740 (Pacific & N America) |
| 2200-2400 | 13620, 15230 & 15240 (SE Asia), 17795 (Pacific & W North Am) |
| 2300-2400 | 9660 (Pacific), 12080 (S Pacific) |
| 2330-2400 | 11695 & 15415 (SE Asia) |

### VOICE INTERNATIONAL—(S Asia & SE Asia)
| | |
|---|---|
| 0800-1500 | 13685 |
| 1500-2000 | 11930 |

## AUSTRIA
### RADIO AUSTRIA INTERNATIONAL
| | |
|---|---|
| 0130-0200 | ▣ 9870 (E North Am) |
| 0230-0300 | ▣ 7325 (E North Am) |
| 0530-0600 | ▣ 6155 & ▣ 13730 (Europe) |
| 0630-0700 ▣ | 17870 (Mideast) |
| 0630-0700 | ▣ 6155 & ▣ 13730 (Europe) |
| 1130-1200 | ▣ 6155 & ▣ 13730 (Europe), ▣ 21780 (S Asia, SE Asia & Australasia) |
| 1230-1300 | ▣ 6155 & ▣ 13730 (Europe), ▣ 21770 (S Asia, SE Asia & Australasia) |
| 1330-1400 | ▣ 6155 & ▣ 13730 (Europe) |
| 1430-1500 | ▣ 6155 & ▣ 13730 (Europe) |
| 1830-1900 | ▣ 5945 & ▣ 6155 (Europe) |
| 1930-2000 | ▣ 5945 & ▣ 6155 (Europe) |
| 2130-2200 | ▣ 5945 & ▣ 6155 (Europe) |
| 2230-2300 | ▣ 5945 & ▣ 6155 (Europe) |

## BANGLADESH
### BANGLADESH BETAR
| | |
|---|---|
| 1230-1300 | 7185 & 9550 (SE Asia) |
| 1530-1545 | 15519 (Mideast & Europe) |
| 1745-1815 & | |
| 1815-1900 | 7185, 9550 & 15519 (Irr) (Europe) |

## BELARUS

### RADIO BELARUS/RADIO MINSK

0300-0330 ▣ W/F-M 5970 (W Europe & Atlantic), M/W/F-Su 7210 (N Europe)

2030-2100 &
2130-2200 ▣ Tu/Th 7105 (Europe), Tu/Th 7210 (N Europe)

## BELGIUM

### RADIO VLAANDEREN INTERNATIONAAL

0400-0430    ▣ *11985* & ▣ *15565* (W North Am)

0800-0830 ▣ *5985* (W Europe)

1130-1200    *9865/7390* (E Asia & Australasia)

1730-1800    ▣ *13690* (S Europe)

1830-1900 ▣ *9925* (Europe), *13710* (S Europe & Mideast)

1830-1900    ▣ *13685* (S Europe)

1930-2000    ▣ *13690* (S Europe)

2030-2100 ▣ *9925* (Europe)

2230-2300    ▣ *13700* & ▣ *15565* (N America)

## BULGARIA

### RADIO BULGARIA

0000-0100 ▣ 9400 (E North Am)

0000-0100    ▣ 7400 (E North Am)

0200-0300    ▣ 11700 (E North Am)

0300-0400 ▣ 9400 (E North Am)

0300-0400    ▣ 7400 (E North Am)

1200-1300 ▣ 15700 & 17500 (Europe)

1900-2000    ▣ 9400 & ▣ 11700 (Europe)

2000-2100    ▣ 5845 & ▣ 7535 (Europe)

2100-2200    ▣ 9400 & ▣ 11700 (Europe)

2200-2300    ▣ 7535 & ▣ 7545 (Europe)

2300-2400    ▣ 11700 (E North Am)

## CANADA

### CANADIAN BROADCASTING CORP—(E North Am)

0000-0300 ▣ Su 9625

0200-0300 ▣ Tu-Sa 9625

0300-0310 &
0330-0609 ▣ M 9625

0400-0609 ▣ Su 9625

0500-0609 ▣ Tu-Sa 9625

1200-1255 ▣ M-F 9625

1200-1505 ▣ Sa 9625

1200-1700 ▣ Su 9625

1600-1615 &
1700-1805 ▣ Sa 9625

1800-2400 ▣ Su 9625

1945-2015,
2200-2225 &
2240-2330 ▣ M-F 9625

### CFRX-CFRB—(E North Am)

24 Hr    6070

### CFVP-CKMX—(W North Am)

0600-0400 ▣ 6030

### CKZN—(E North Am)

24 Hr    6160

### CKZU-CBU—(W North Am)

24 Hr    6160

### RADIO CANADA INTERNATIONAL

0000-0100 ▣ 9590 (N America & C America), 9755 (E North Am & C America)

0000-0100    ▣ 5960 (E North Am & C America), ▣ *9640* (E Asia), *11895* (SE Asia)

0100-0200    ▣ 5960 (N America), ▣ 13670 (E North Am & C America), ▣ 15170 & ▣ 15305 (C America & S America)

0200-0300    ▣ 6040 (E North Am & C America), ▣ 11725 (C America & S America), ▣ *15150*, ▣ *15260* & 17860 (S Asia)

1200-1300    *9660* (E Asia), ▣ *11730* & ▣ *15190* (E Asia & SE Asia)

1200-1500    ▣ M-F 17820 (C America)

1300-1400 ▣ M-F 9515 (N America & C America), M-F 13655 (E North Am & C America)

1300-1400    ▣ M-F 17710 (C America)

1300-1600    ▣ Sa/Su 17800 (C America)

1400-1600 ▣ 9515 (N America & C America), 13655 (E North Am & C America)

1400-1600    ▣ 17710 (C America)

1500-1600    ▣ *15360*, ▣ *15455*, ▣ *17720* & ▣ *17820* (S Asia)

1600-1700 ▣ Sa/Su 9515 (N America & C America), Sa/Su 13655 (E North Am & C America)

1600-1700    ▣ Sa/Su 17710 (C America)

2000-2100    ▣ *5995* (S Europe & N Africa), ▣ *11690* (Europe), ▣ *11965* (N Africa & W Africa), ▣ *12015* (E Africa), ▣ *15470* (Mideast & E Africa)

2000-2130    ▣ *5850* (W Europe), ▣ 15325 (W Africa), ▣ 17870 (W Europe & N Africa)

For yachting, the Tecsun HAM 2000/Grundig Satellit 800 has the audio punch needed to overcome surf noise. Enough weight to stay put in normal seas, too.

Tecsun

| | |
|---|---|
| 2100-2130 | **S** *7235* & **S** *13690* (N Africa & W Africa) |
| 2100-2200 ▭ | *7235* (N Africa) |
| 2100-2200 | **W** *7425* (Mideast & E Africa), **W** *9805* (C Africa & E Africa), **W** *12015* (W Europe), **W** *13650* (N Africa) |
| 2100-2230 | **W** *5850* (Europe & Mideast), **W** *9770* (W Europe) |
| 2200-2230 | **W** *6045* (W Europe & N Africa), **W** *9805* (N Africa & W Africa), **S** 11920 & **S** 15170 (C America & S America), **S** 17880 (S America) |
| 2200-2400 | **S** 6175 (N America & C America), **S** 13670 (E North Am & C America), **S** 17695 (E North Am, C America & S America) |
| 2300-2330 | **W** 11865 (C America & S America) |
| 2300-2400 ▭ | 9590 (N America & C America), 9755 (E North Am & C America) |
| 2300-2400 | **W** 5960 (E North Am & C America) |

## CHINA

### CHINA RADIO INTERNATIONAL

| | |
|---|---|
| 0100-0200 | *9580* (E North Am), *9790* (W North Am) |

| | |
|---|---|
| 0300-0400 | *9690* (N America & C America) |
| 0400-0500 | *9730* (W North Am) |
| 0500-0600 ▭ | *9560* (W North Am) |
| 0900-1100 | 11730 & 15210 (Australasia) |
| 1200-1300 | 9730 (SE Asia), 9760 & 15415 (Australasia) |
| 1200-1400 | 11760 (Australasia), 11980 (SE Asia) |
| 1300-1400 | *9570* (E North Am), 11900 (Australasia), 15180 (SE Asia) |
| 1400-1500 | 9700, 11675, **W** 11765, **S** 11825 & **S** 15110 (S Asia) |
| 1400-1600 ▭ | 7405 (W North Am) |
| 1400-1600 | *13685* (E Africa & S Africa), *15125* (C Africa & E Africa), *17720* (W North Am) |
| 1500-1600 | 7160 & 9785 (S Asia) |
| 1600-1700 | **W** 7190 (E Africa), **S** 9565 (S Africa), **S** 9870 (E Africa), **W** 13650 (S Africa) |
| 1700-1800 | **W** 7150 (E Africa), 9570 (E Africa & S Africa), 9670 (Mideast & W Asia), 9695 (S Africa), **S** 11920 (E Africa), **S** 15265 (S Africa) |
| 1900-2000 | **W** 6165, **W** 9585 & **S** 13790 (Mideast) |
| 1900-2100 | 9440 (N Africa) |
| 2000-2130 | *11735/11640* (E Africa & S Africa), *13630/13640* (E Africa) |
| 2000-2200 | **W** 5965, **W** 9840, **S** 11790 & **S** 15110 (Europe) |
| 2200-2300 | **W** *7170* & **S** *9880/7175* (W Europe) |
| 2300-2400 | *5990* (C America), *13680* (N America & C America) |

## CHINA (TAIWAN)

### RADIO TAIPEI INTERNATIONAL

| | |
|---|---|
| 0200-0300 | *5950* (E North Am), *11740* (C America), 15465 (E Asia) |
| 0200-0400 | *9680* (W North Am), 15320 (SE Asia) |
| 0300-0400 | *5950* (N America & C America), 11875 (SE Asia) |
| 0700-0800 | *5950* (W North Am & C America) |
| 1100-1200 | 7445 (SE Asia), 11985 (E Asia) |
| 1200-1300 | 7130 (E Asia), 9610 (Australasia) |
| 1400-1500 | 15265 (SE Asia) |
| 1600-1800 | 11550 (S Asia) |

| | |
|---|---|
| 1800-1900 | *3955* (W Europe) |
| 2200-2300 | ▥ *5810*, ▥ *9355* & ▤ *15600* (Europe) |

## COSTA RICA
### RADIO FOR PEACE INTERNATIONAL

| | |
|---|---|
| 2200-0500 | 15039 (N America) |
| 2200-0800 | 7445 (N America & Europe) |

## CROATIA
### VOICE OF CROATIA

| | |
|---|---|
| 0000-0018 & | |
| 0142-0200 ▭ | *9925* (S America) |
| 0200-0218 ▭ | *9885/9925* (E North Am) |
| 0342-0400 ▭ | *9925/9885* (E North Am) |
| 0400-0418 ▭ | *9925* (W North Am) |
| 0400-0418 | ▥ *9885/7285* (W North Am) |
| 0542-0600 ▭ | *9925* (W North Am) |
| 0542-0600 | ▥ *9885/7285* (W North Am) |
| 0600-0618 & | |
| 0742-0800 ▭ | *9470/11665* (Australasia) |
| 0800-0818 & | |
| 0942-1000 ▭ | *13820* (Australasia) |

## CUBA
### RADIO HABANA CUBA

| | |
|---|---|
| 0100-0500 | 6000 (E North Am), 9820 (N America), 11705 USB (E North Am & Europe) |
| 0500-0700 | 9550 (E North Am), 9820 (W North Am), 9830 USB (E North Am & Europe) |
| 2030-2130 | 13660 USB & 13750 (Europe & E North Am) |
| 2230-2330 | 9550 (C America) |

## CZECH REPUBLIC
### RADIO PRAGUE

| | |
|---|---|
| 0000-0030 | ▤ 7345 (N America & C America), ▤ 11615 (Americas) |
| 0100-0130 | 6200 (N America & C America), 7345 (N America) |
| 0200-0230 | ▥ 6200 (N America & C America), ▥ 7345 (N America) |
| 0300-0330 | ▤ 7345 (N America), ▤ 9870 (W North Am & C America) |
| 0330-0400 | ▤ 11600 (Mideast), ▤ 15620 (Mideast & S Asia) |
| 0400-0430 | ▥ 7345 (N America), ▥ 9435 (W North Am & C America) |

| | |
|---|---|
| 0430-0500 | ▥ 9865 (Mideast), ▥ 11600 (Mideast & S Asia) |
| 0700-0730 | ▤ 9880 (W Europe) |
| 0800-0830 ▭ | 11600 (W Europe) |
| 0800-0830 | ▥ 15255 (W Europe) |
| 0900-0930 | ▤ 21745 (S Asia & W Africa) |
| 1000-1030 | ▥ 21745 (S Asia & W Africa) |
| 1030-1100 | ▤ 9880 & ▤ 11615 (N Europe) |
| 1130-1200 | ▥ 11640 (N Europe), ▥ 21745 (E Africa & Mideast) |
| 1300-1330 | ▤ 13580 (N Europe), ▤ 21745/21735 (S Asia) |
| 1400-1430 | ▥ 21745 (N America & E Africa) |
| 1600-1630 | ▤ 21745 (E Africa) |
| 1700-1730 ▭ | 5930 (W Europe) |
| 1700-1730 | ▥ 17485 (W Africa & C Africa), ▤ 21745 (C Africa) |
| 1800-1830 ▭ | 5930 (W Europe) |
| 1800-1830 | ▥ 7315 (E Europe, Asia & Australasia) |
| 2000-2030 | ▤ 11600 (SE Asia & Australasia) |
| 2100-2130 ▭ | 5930 (W Europe) |
| 2100-2130 | ▥ 9430 (SE Asia & Australasia) |
| 2130-2200 | ▤ 11600 (SE Asia & Australasia), ▤ 15545 (W Africa) |
| 2230-2300 | ▥ 7345 (N America), ▥ 9435 (W Africa), ▤ 11600 (E North Am), ▤ 15545 (N America) |
| 2330-2400 | ▥ 7345 & ▥ 9435 (N America) |

## ECUADOR
### HCJB-VOICE OF THE ANDES

| | |
|---|---|
| 0100-0400 | 9745 (E North Am) |
| 0100-0600 | 11960 (N America), 21455 USB (Europe & Australasia) |
| 0230-0400 | ▥ 12040 & ▤ 21470 (Europe & S Asia) |
| 0400-0600 | 9745 (W North Am) |
| 0600-0800 | ▤ 11680 (Europe) |
| 0630-0700 | ▤ 21455 USB (Europe & Australasia) |
| 0700-0900 | ▥ 5965 (Europe) |
| 0700-1100 | 11755 (Australasia) |
| 0700-1430 | 21455 USB (Europe & Australasia) |
| 1100-1430 | 12005 (C America), 15115 (N America & S America) |
| 2000-2200 | ▥ 11895 & ▤ 17660 (Europe) |
| 2030-2200 | ▤ 21455 USB (Europe & Australasia) |

**The IBB control room at Biblis, Germany, routes VOA and kindred programs to transmission facilities.**

Nick Olguin

## EGYPT

**RADIO CAIRO**

| | |
|---|---|
| 0000-0030 | 9900 (E North Am) |
| 0200-0330 | 9475 (N America) |
| 1215-1330 | 17595 (S Asia) |
| 1630-1830 | 15255 (S Africa) |
| 2030-2200 | 15375 (W Africa) |
| 2115-2245 | 9990 (Europe) |
| 2300-2400 | 9900 (E North Am) |

## ETHIOPIA

**RADIO ETHIOPIA**

| | |
|---|---|
| 1030-1100 | M-F 5990, M-F 7110, M-F 9704 |
| 1600-1700 | 7165, 9560 & 11800 (E Africa) |

## FRANCE

**RADIO FRANCE INTERNATIONALE**

| | |
|---|---|
| 0400-0430 | [W] *11910*, [W] 11995, 13610 (Irr) & [S] 15155 (E Africa) |
| 0500-0530 | [W] 13610 (E Africa), [W] *15155* (E Africa & S Africa), [S] 17800 (E Africa) |
| 0600-0630 | [W] *11710* (W Africa), [W] 15155, 17800 & [S] 21620 (E Africa) |
| 0700-0800 | *15605* (W Africa) |
| 1200-1230 | *15540* (W Africa), 25820 (E Africa) |
| 1400-1500 | *11610* (S Asia), 17620 (Mideast) |
| 1600-1700 | 11615 (Irr) (N Africa), *11995* (W Africa), *12015* (S Africa), 17850 (C Africa & S Africa) |
| 1600-1730 | [W] 11615 & [S] 15605 (Mideast), [W] 15605 & [S] 17605 (E Africa) |

## GERMANY

**DEUTSCHE WELLE**

| | |
|---|---|
| 0100-0145 | [S] *6040* (N America & C America), [W] *6040* (E North Am & C America), [W] 6145 (N America & C America), [S] 9640 (E North Am), [W] *9640* (E North Am & C America), [W] *9700* (E North Am), [W] *9765* (N America), [S] *11810* (E North Am), [S] *13720* (E North Am & C America) |
| 0200-0245 | [W] 7285, [W] 9765, *11965*, [W] *13605*, [S] 13720 & [S] *15370* (S Asia) |
| 0300-0345 | [W] *6020* (W North Am), [W] 6045 (N America), [S] *9535* (W North Am), [S] *9640* (N America), [W] *9640* (E North Am & C America), [W] *9700* (N America), [S] *11935* (E North Am & C America), [W] *11985* & [S] *15105* (W North Am) |
| 0400-0445 | *6180* (E Africa), [W] *7195* (S Africa), [S] *7225* (E Africa & S Africa), [W] *9565* (S Africa), [W] 9710 & [S] *12045* (E Africa & S Africa), [S] 13690 (E Africa) |
| 0500-0545 | [W] 5960 & [W] *6120* (W North Am), [S] *9670* (N America), [W] *9670*, [S] *9785*, [W] *11795* & [S] *11985* (W North Am) |
| 0600-0645 | [W] *7225* & [W] 9565 (W Africa), [W] 11785 (C Africa), [S] *11925* (W Africa), [S] *13790* (E Africa & S Africa), [S] 17860 (W Africa) |
| 0600-1900 | 6140 (Europe) |
| 0900-0945 | *6160* (Australasia), *9510* (C America, W North Am & Australasia), [W] *9770* (E Asia), [W] *11785* & [S] *12035* (E Africa & S Africa), *15410* (S Africa), [S] *15470* (E Asia), [S] *17715* & [S] *17770* (SE Asia & Australasia), [S] *17800* (S Africa), [W] *17800* (W Africa), [S] *17820* (SE Asia), [W] *17820* (SE Asia & Australasia), [W] *17845* (SE Asia), [W] *17860* (S Africa), [W] 21560 (Mideast & E Africa), [S] *21560* (W Africa), [S] 21780 (E Africa & S Africa) |

| | |
|---|---|
| 1100-1145 | **S** *11785* (E Africa & C Africa), *15410* (S Africa), **W** *17800* (W Africa), **S** 17860 (W Africa & S Africa), **S** *21525*, **W** *21550*, **S** *21665* & **W** 21780 (W Africa) |
| 1600-1645 | **S** *6170* & *7225* (S Asia), *9735* (E Africa & S Africa), **S** *11665* (S Africa), **W** 11695 & **W** 13605 (S Asia, SE Asia & Australasia), **W** *15455* (S Africa), **S** 17595 (S Asia), 21840 (E Africa & S Africa) |
| 1900-1945 | **W** 11765, **S** *11805* & **W** *11810* (W Africa), **S** *11965* (E Africa & S Africa), **S** 13720 (W Africa), **W** 13780 (Africa), **W** *15275* & **S** *15390* (W Africa), **W** *15455* (S Africa), *17810* (E Africa & S Africa) |
| 2000-2045 | **S** 6140 (W Europe), **W** *6180* (Europe) |
| 2100-2145 | **S** *9670* (SE Asia & Australasia), 9765 (Australasia), **S** *9830* (W Africa), **W** 11645 (C Africa), **S** 11865 (W Africa), **S** *12035* (SE Asia & Australasia), **S** *15135* (W Africa & C America), **W** *15275* (SE Asia & Australasia), **W** *15410* (W Africa & C America), **W** *17560* (Australasia), **W** *17765* (W Africa & C America) |
| 2300-2345 | **W** *9470* (E Asia & SE Asia), 9815 & **S** *12000* (S Asia & SE Asia), **W** *13690* (SE Asia), **S** *17560* & **S** *21790* (S Asia & SE Asia) |
| 2300-2350 | **W** *9940* (SE Asia) |

## GHANA

### GHANA BROADCASTING CORPORATION

| | |
|---|---|
| 0530-0900 | 4915, 6130/3366 |
| 0900-1200 | 6130 |
| 1200-1700 | M-F 6130 |
| 1700-2400 | 3366, 4915 |

## GUAM

### KTWR-TRANS WORLD RADIO

| | |
|---|---|
| 0715-0900 | 15215 (SE Asia) |
| 0815-0930 | 15330 (Australasia & S Pacific) |
| 1445-1545 | 15330 (S Asia) |

## GUYANA

### VOICE OF GUYANA

| | |
|---|---|
| 24 Hr | 3290/5950 |

## HUNGARY

### RADIO BUDAPEST

| | |
|---|---|
| 0100-0130 | **S** 9560 (N America) |
| 0200-0230 | **W** 9835 (N America) |
| 0230-0300 | **S** 9570 (N America) |
| 0330-0400 | **W** 9835 (N America) |
| 1900-1930 | **S** 7130 (W Europe) |
| 2000-2030 | **▭** 6025 (Europe) |
| 2000-2030 | **W** 7135 (W Europe) |
| 2200-2230 | **▭** 3975 & 6025 (Europe) |

## INDIA

### ALL INDIA RADIO

| | |
|---|---|
| 0000-0045 | 9705 (SE Asia), 9950 (E Asia), 11620 & 13605 (E Asia & SE Asia) |
| 1000-1100 | 15235 (E Asia), 15260 (S Asia), 17510 (Australasia), 17800 (E Asia), 17895 (Australasia) |
| 1330-1500 | 9690, 11620 & 13710 (SE Asia) |
| 1745-1945 | 7410 (Europe), 9445 (W Africa), 9950 & 11620 (Europe), 11935 (E Africa), 13605 (W Africa), 15075 (E Africa), 15155 (W Africa), 17670 (E Africa) |
| 2045-2230 | 7410 & 9445 (Europe), 9575 & 9910 (Australasia), 9950 (Europe), 11620 (Europe & Australasia), 11715 (Australasia) |
| 2245-2400 | 9705 (SE Asia), 9950 (E Asia), 11620 & 13605 (E Asia & SE Asia) |

## INDONESIA

### VOICE OF INDONESIA

| | |
|---|---|
| 0100-0200 | 11785 (E Asia, SE Asia & Pacific) |
| 0800-0900 | 11785 (Australasia) |
| 2000-2100 | 11785 & 15150 (Europe) |

## IRAN

### VOICE OF THE ISLAMIC REPUBLIC

| | |
|---|---|
| 0030-0130 | **W** 6015 & **W** 6065 (C America), **W** 6135, **S** 9610 & **S** 9835 (E North Am & C America), **S** 11970 (C America) |
| 1100-1230 | **S** 15215 (S Asia), **W** 15265 & **S** 15275 (W Asia & S Asia), **W** 15375 (S Asia & SE Asia), 15385, **W** 15480, **S** 15585 & **S** 15600 (W Asia & S Asia), 21470 & 21730 (S Asia & SE Asia) |

| | |
|---|---|
| 1530-1630 | [W] 7115 (S Asia, SE Asia & Australasia), [W] 7180 (S Asia & SE Asia), [S] 7245, [W] 9605 & [S] 9635 (S Asia, SE Asia & Australasia), [W] 11640, 11775 & [W] 11835 (S Asia & SE Asia), [W] 11870 (S Asia, SE Asia & Australasia) |
| 1930-2030 | [W] 6110, [W] 7215 & [W] 7320 (Europe), [S] 9800 (S Africa), [S] 11670 (Europe), [W] 11695 & [S] 11750 (S Africa), [S] 11855 & [S] 13730 (Europe), 15140 (S Africa) |
| 2130-2230 | [S] 9570 (S Asia, SE Asia & Australasia), [S] 9670 (SE Asia & Australasia), [W] 9780 & [W] 11740 (Australasia), [S] 13665 (SE Asia & Australasia), [S] 13745 (S Asia, SE Asia & Australasia) |

## IRELAND

**RTE OVERSEAS**

| | |
|---|---|
| 0130-0200 | *6155* (C America) |
| 1000-1030 | *15280* (Australasia) |
| 1800-1830 | [W] *9895* & [S] *15585* (Mideast) |
| 1830-1900 | [W] *13640* (N America), *21630* (C Africa & S Africa) |

**Attending the August 2002 celebration of the Japan Shortwave Club's 50th anniversary were, front row: Dr. Kenro Wada, founder (left); Akira Ogawa, co-founder (third from right). Second row: Yoshinobu Sano, editor (moustache). Third row: Toshimichi Ohtake (left, glasses); Nobuya Kato, special verification signer (next to Ohtake).** T. Ohtake

## ISRAEL

**KOL ISRAEL**

| | |
|---|---|
| 0400-0415 | [S] 15640 (W Europe & E North Am) |
| 0500-0515 ⬅ | 9435 (W Europe & E North Am), 17600 (Australasia) |
| 0500-0515 | [W] 6280 & [W] 11605/7475 (W Europe & E North Am) |
| 1115-1130 ⬅ | 15640 & 17545 (W Europe & E North Am) |
| 1630-1645 | [S] 15615 (W Europe & E North Am) |
| 1730-1745 ⬅ | 17545 (W Europe & E North Am) |
| 1730-1745 | [W] 11605 (W Europe & E North Am) |
| 1900-1925 | [S] 11605, [S] 15615 & [S] 17545 (W Europe & E North Am) |
| 2000-2025 ⬅ | 15640 (S Africa & S America) |
| 2000-2025 | [W] 6280, [W] 9435, [W] 11605/7520 & [W] 13720 (W Europe & E North Am) |

## ITALY

**RAI INTERNATIONAL**

| | |
|---|---|
| 0055-0115 | 9675 (N America), 11800 (N America & C America) |
| 0445-0500 | [W] 5965, [W] 5975 & 7235 (S Europe & N Africa) |
| 1935-1955 | 5970, [S] 9750 & [W] 9760 (W Europe) |
| 2025-2045 | [S] 7125, [W] 7220, [S] 9635, [W] 9710, [S] 11800, [W] 11880 & [W] 11885 (Mideast) |

**RAI-RADIOTELEVISIONE ITALIANA**—(Europe, Mideast & N Africa)

| | |
|---|---|
| 0003-0012, 0103-0112, 0203-0212, 0303-0312 & 0403-0412 ⬅ | 6060 |

## JAPAN

**RADIO JAPAN/NHK**

| | |
|---|---|
| 0000-0015 | 13650 & 17810 (SE Asia) |
| 0000-0100 | *6145* (E North Am) |
| 0100-0200 | *11860* (SE Asia), *11880* (Mideast), 15325 (S Asia), 17560 (Mideast), 17685 (Australasia), 17810 (SE Asia), 17835 (S America), 17845 (E Asia) |
| 0300-0400 | 17825 (C America), 21610 (Australasia) |

| | |
|---|---|
| 0500-0600 | *5975* (W Europe), *6110* (W North Am), 11715 & 11760 (E Asia), 17810 (SE Asia) |
| 0500-0700 | *7230* (Europe), ◪ 9835 & ◪ 13630 (W North Am), 15195 (E Asia), 21755 (Australasia) |
| 0600-0700 | *11740* (SE Asia), 17870 (Pacific) |
| 1000-1100 | 21755 (Australasia) |
| 1000-1200 | 9695 (SE Asia), 15590 (Asia) |
| 1100-1200 | *6120* (E North Am) |
| 1400-1500 | 9505 (W North Am), *17755* (Mideast) |
| 1400-1600 | 7200 (SE Asia), ◪ 9845 & ◪ 11730 (S Asia) |
| 1500-1600 | 9750 (E Asia) |
| 1700-1800 | 9505 (W North Am), 11970 (Europe), *15355* (S Africa) |
| 2100-2200 | ◪ *6035* (Australasia), ◪ *6055* & ◪ *6090* (W Europe), *6180* & 11830 (Europe), ◪ 11850 (Australasia), *11855* (C Africa), ◪ *11920* (Australasia), 17825 (W North Am), ◪ 17860 (Australasia), 21670 (Pacific) |

## KOREA (DPR)

### VOICE OF KOREA

| | |
|---|---|
| 0100-0200 | 3560 & 6195 (E Asia), 6520/13760 (C America & S America), 7140 (E Asia), 7580/15180 (C America & S America), 9345 (E Asia), 11735 (C America & S America) |
| 0200-0300 | 4405 (E Asia), 9325/11845 & 11335/15230 (SE Asia) |
| 0300-0400 | 3560, 6195, 7140 & 9345 (E Asia) |
| 1000-1100 | 3560 (E Asia), 9335 (C America), 9850/13650 (SE Asia), 11710 (C America), 11735 (SE Asia) |
| 1300-1400 & 1500-1600 | 4405 (E Asia), 7505/13760 (Europe), 9335 (N America), 11335/15245 (Europe), 11710 (N America) |
| 1600-1700 | 3560 (E Asia), 9975 & 11735 (Mideast & Africa) |
| 1900-2000 | 4405 (E Asia), 7505/13760 & 11335/15245 (Europe), 11710 (N America) |
| 2100-2200 | 4405 (E Asia), 7505/13760 & 11335/15245 (Europe) |

## KOREA (REPUBLIC)

### RADIO KOREA INTERNATIONAL

| | |
|---|---|
| 0200-0300 | *9560* (W North Am), 15575 (N America) |
| 0800-0900 | 7550 (Europe), 9570 (Asia & Australasia), 13670 (Europe) |
| 1130-1230 | *9650* (E North Am) |
| 1300-1400 | 9570 & 13670 (SE Asia) |
| 1600-1700 | 5975 (E Asia), 9515 & 9870 (Mideast & Africa) |
| 1900-2000 | 5975 (E Asia), 7275 (Europe) |
| 2100-2130 | ◪ *3955* (W Europe) |
| 2100-2200 | 15575 (Europe) |
| 2200-2230 | ◪ *3955* (W Europe) |

## KUWAIT

### RADIO KUWAIT

| | |
|---|---|
| 0500-0800 | 15110 (S Asia & SE Asia) |
| 1800-2100 | 11990 (Europe & E North Am) |

## LITHUANIA

### RADIO VILNIUS

| | |
|---|---|
| 0030-0100 | ◪ *7325*, ◪ 11690 (E North Am) |
| 0930-1000 | 9710 (W Europe) |
| 2330-2400 | 9875 (E North Am) |

## MALAYSIA

### VOICE OF MALAYSIA

| | |
|---|---|
| 0300-0825 | 6175 & 9750 (SE Asia), 15295 (Australasia) |

## MALTA

### VOICE OF THE MEDITERRANEAN

| | |
|---|---|
| 0900-1000 | ◱ Su *9605/9630* (Europe) |
| 1730-1800 | ◪ M-Sa *9605* & ◪ M-Sa *9850* (Europe) |
| 1900-2000 | ◪ Sa-Th *12060* (Europe & N Africa) |
| 2000-2100 | ◪ Sa-Th *7440* (Europe) |

## MEXICO

### RADIO EDUCACION

| | |
|---|---|
| 0830-0900 | ◱ W 6185 |

### RADIO MEXICO INTERNACIONAL—(W North Am & C America)

| | |
|---|---|
| 0400-0430 & 0500-0530 | ◱ Tu-Su 9705 & Tu-Su 11770 |
| 1500-1530, 1600-1630 & 2200-2230 | ◱ 9705 & 11770 |
| 2300-2330 | ◱ M-F 9705 & M-F 11770 |

Lucy Borisova, program host at the Voice of Russia. The station has been woefully underfunded since the end of the Cold War, but a number of loyal staff have stayed on board to help shape its future.  VoR

## MONGOLIA
### VOICE OF MONGOLIA
| | |
|---|---|
| 1000-1030 | 12015/12085 (E Asia, SE Asia & Australasia) |
| 1500-1530 & | |
| 2000-2030 | 12015 (E Europe & W Asia) |

## NEPAL
### RADIO NEPAL
| | |
|---|---|
| 0215-0225 & | |
| 1415-1425 | 5005, 7165/6100/3230 |

## NETHERLANDS
### RADIO NEDERLAND
| | |
|---|---|
| 0000-0125 | *6165* (N America), *9845* (E North Am) |
| 0430-0530 | *6165 & 9590* (W North Am) |
| 0930-1130 | 🗓 *7260* (E Asia & Australasia), 9790 (Australasia), 🗓 *12065* (E Asia & Australasia), 🗓 *12065* (SE Asia), 🗓 *13710* (E Asia & Australasia) |
| 1130-1325 | 🗓 *5965* (E North Am), *6045 & 9860* (W Europe) |
| 1430-1625 | 🗓 *9890*, 🗓 *11835*, 🗓 *12070*, 🗓 *12075 & 🗓 12080* (S Asia), 15220 (W North Am), 🗓 *15595* (S Asia) |

| | |
|---|---|
| 1730-2025 | *6020* (S Africa), 🗓 *7120* (E Africa), 🗓 11655 (W Africa), 🗓 *11655* (E Africa) |
| 1830-2025 | 9895 & 13700 (W Africa), *17605 &* 🗓 *21590* (W Africa & C Africa) |
| 2330-2400 | *6165* (N America), *9845* (E North Am) |

## NEW ZEALAND
### RADIO NEW ZEALAND INTERNATIONAL—
(Pacific)
| | |
|---|---|
| 0000-0400 | 17675 |
| 0400-0500 | 🗓 17675/15340 |
| 0500-0700 | 🗓 11820 & 🗓 15340 |
| 0700-1005 | 🗓 11675 |
| 0700-1105 | 🗓 9885 |
| 1005-1205 | 🗓 15175 |
| 1105-1305 | 🗓 9850 |
| 1205-1305 | 🗓 6095 (Irr) |
| 1305-1650 | 6095 (Irr) |
| 1650-1750 | 🗓 M-F 6095 & 🗓 M-F 11980 |
| 1750-1850 | 🗓 M-F 11725 & 🗓 11980/15265 |
| 1850-2050 | 🗓 15265 |
| 1850-2215 | 🗓 15160 |
| 2050-2215 | 🗓 17675 |
| 2215-2400 | 17675 |

## NIGERIA
### VOICE OF NIGERIA
| | |
|---|---|
| 0500-1000 & | |
| 1900-2300 | 7255 (W Africa), 11770 (C Africa, E Africa & S Africa), 15120 (N Africa & Europe) |

## OMAN
### RADIO SULTANATE OF OMAN
| | |
|---|---|
| 0300-0400 | 15355 (E Africa) |
| 1400-1500 | 15140 (Europe & Mideast) |

## PAKISTAN
### RADIO PAKISTAN
| | |
|---|---|
| 0045-0115 🗓 | 11580/11650 & 15455 (S Asia) |
| 1600-1615 🗓 | 11570 (Mideast), 15100 (Mideast & N Africa), 15725 (E Africa & S Africa) |

## PAPUA NEW GUINEA
### NBC
| | |
|---|---|
| 0000-0730 | 9675 |
| 0700-0900 | 9675/4890 |

| | |
|---|---|
| 0900-1200 | 4890 |
| 1200-1900 | M-Sa 4890 |
| 1900-2200 | M-Sa 9675/4890 |
| 2200-2400 | 9675 |

## ROMANIA
### RADIO ROMANIA INTERNATIONAL

| | |
|---|---|
| 0200-0300 | [S] 9510 (E North Am), [W] 9550 (N America), 9570 (E North Am), [W] 11740 & [S] 11810 (E Asia), [W] 11830 & [S] 11940 (E North Am), [W] 11940 (Australasia), [S] 15105 (E Asia), [S] 15180 (Australasia), [W] 15290 (E Asia), [W] 15370 & [S] 17815 (Australasia) |
| 0400-0500 | [S] 9510 (E North Am), [W] 9550 (N America), [W] 11830 & [S] 11940 (E North Am), [W] 15335, 17735 & [S] 21480 (S Asia) |
| 0600-0700 | [W] 9530, [S] 9635, [W] 11830 & [S] 11940 (W North Am) |
| 0632-0641 | 9665 (Europe) |
| 0638-0656 | [S] 7105 (Europe) |
| 1400-1500 | [W] 11940, [S] 15250, [W] 15365, [S] 17735 & [W] 17790 (Europe) |
| 1700-1800 | [W] 9625, [S] 11740, [W] 11830, [W] 11940, [W] 15245, [S] 15365, [S] 15380 & [S] 17805 (Europe) |
| 1730-1800 | [W] 11740 (S Africa) |
| 2100-2200 | [W] 5955, 7105, [W] 7215, [S] 9510, [W] 9690, [S] 9725, [S] 11740 & [S] 11940 (Europe) |
| 2300-2400 | [W] 7195 (Europe), [W] 9510 (E North Am), 9570 (Europe), [S] 11740 (E North Am), [S] 11775 (Europe), [W] 11940 & [S] 15105 (E North Am) |

## RUSSIA
### VOICE OF RUSSIA

| | |
|---|---|
| 0100-0200 | [S] 11825 (E North Am) |
| 0100-0300 | [S] 9725 (E North Am), [S] 17595 (W North Am) |
| 0100-0500 | [S] 9665 (E North Am), [S] 12000 (W North Am) |
| 0200-0300 | [W] 9765 (E North Am) |
| 0200-0400 | [W] 7250 (E North Am) |
| 0200-0500 | [W] 7335 (C America), [W] 13665 (W North Am) |
| 0200-0600 | [W] 7180 (E North Am), [W] 12020 (W North Am) |
| 0300-0500 | [S] 11750 (E North Am), [S] 17565, [S] 17650, [S] 17660 & [S] 17690 (W North Am) |
| 0400-0600 | [W] 7125 (E North Am), [W] 12010, [W] 15595 & [W] 17595 (W North Am) |
| 0500-0900 | [S] 17635 (Australasia), [S] 17685 & [S] 17795 (SE Asia & Australasia) |
| 0530-0900 | [S] 15490 (SE Asia & Australasia) |
| 0600-0800 | [↔] 21790 (Australasia) |
| 0600-0800 | [W] 21485 (SE Asia) |
| 0600-0900 | [W] 17655 (SE Asia & Australasia) |
| 0600-1000 | [W] 11770 (SE Asia), [W] 15275, [W] 15470 & [W] 17665 (Australasia) |
| 0700-0900 | [S] 17675 (SE Asia & Australasia) |
| 0700-1000 | [W] 11820 (W Europe) |
| 0800-1000 | [↔] 17495 (SE Asia & Australasia), 17525 (Australasia) |
| 0800-1000 | [W] 21485/21810 (SE Asia) |
| 1400-1500 | [S] 9745 (C Asia & S Asia), [S] 12055 (SE Asia), [S] 15560 & [S] 17645 (S Asia & SE Asia) |
| 1400-1600 | [S] 7390 (E Asia & SE Asia) |
| 1500-1600 | [W] 6205 (SE Asia), [W] 7315 (W Asia & S Asia), [S] 7325 (Mideast), [W] 7350 (S Asia), 11500 (SE Asia) |
| 1500-1800 | [S] 11985 (Mideast) |
| 1500-1900 | [W] 7260 (N Pacific & W North Am) |
| 1600-1700 | [↔] 4940, 4965 & 4975 (W Asia & S Asia) |
| 1600-1700 | [W] 5890 (S Asia), [W] 6005 (Mideast), [W] 7305, [S] 7350 & [S] 11720 (S Asia), [S] 12055 (W Asia & S Asia), [S] 15540 (Mideast) |
| 1600-1900 | [W] 9830 (Mideast) |
| 1700-1800 | [W] 9470 (Mideast), [S] Sa/Su 9480 & [S] Sa/Su 11675 (N Europe) |
| 1700-1900 | [S] 9745 (E Africa) |
| 1700-2000 | [S] 9890 (Europe) |
| 1700-2100 | [S] 9775 (Europe) |
| 1800-1900 | [W] Sa/Su 5940 (N Europe), [S] 5950 (Europe), [W] Sa/Su 6175 (N Europe), [S] 7300, [S] 11630 & [S] 11870 (Europe) |
| 1800-2000 | [↔] 11510 (E Africa & S Africa) |
| 1800-2000 | [W] 7335 (E Africa), [W] 9775 (Europe) |
| 1800-2100 | [S] 9480 & [S] 11675 (N Europe) |
| 1800-2200 | [W] 7335 & [W] 7340 (Europe) |

| | |
|---|---|
| 1900-2000 | ▣ 7360 (Europe & N Africa), 7440 (Europe), ▣ 9875 (E Africa & S Africa) |
| 1900-2100 | ▣ 12030 & ▣ 12070 (Europe) |
| 1900-2200 | ▣ 5940 (N Europe), ▣ 5950 (Europe), ▣ 6175 (N Europe) |
| 2000-2100 | ▣ 15455 (Europe) |
| 2000-2200 ▣ | *15735* (S America) |
| 2000-2200 | ▣ 7390 (Europe) |
| 2030-2100 | ▣ 9775 (Europe) |
| 2100-2200 | ▣ 7300 (Europe) |

## SINGAPORE

**MEDIACORP RADIO**

| | |
|---|---|
| 1400-1600 & | |
| 2300-1100 | 6150 |

**RADIO SINGAPORE INTERNATIONAL—(SE Asia)**

| | |
|---|---|
| 1100-1400 | 6150 & 9600 |

## SLOVAKIA

**RADIO SLOVAKIA INTERNATIONAL**

| | |
|---|---|
| 0100-0130 | 5930, ▣ 6190 & ▣ 7230 (E North Am & C America), 9440 (S America) |
| 0700-0730 | ▣ 9440, 15460, 17550 & ▣ 21705/13715 (Australasia) |
| 1630-1700 | ▣ 5920 (W Europe) |
| 1730-1800 ▣ | 6055 & 7345 (W Europe) |
| 1730-1800 | ▣ 5915 (W Europe) |
| 1830-1900 | ▣ 5920 (W Europe) |
| 1930-2000 ▣ | 6055 & 7345 (W Europe) |
| 1930-2000 | ▣ 5915 (W Europe) |

An interview with a farmer for a program on agriculture is conducted near RVOG's area studio, "Sawtu Linjiila," in Ngaoundéré, Cameroon.   LWF

## SOLOMON ISLANDS

**SOLOMON ISLANDS BROADCASTING**

| | |
|---|---|
| 0000-0030 | 5020 |
| 0030-0035 | Sa/Su 5020 |
| 0035-0130 | 5020 |
| 0130-0145 | Sa/Su 5020 |
| 0145-0230 | 5020 |
| 0230-0245 | Sa/Su 5020 |
| 0240-0330 | 5020 |
| 0330-0335 | Sa/Su 5020 |
| 0335-0430 | 5020 |
| 0430-0435 | Sa/Su 5020 |
| 0435-0545 | 5020 |
| 0545-0600 | Sa/Su 5020 |
| 0600-0648 | 5020 |
| 0648-0700 | Sa/Su 5020 |
| 0700-0800 | 5020 |
| 0800-0830 | Sa/Su 5020 |
| 0830-0945 | 5020 |
| 0945-1000 | Su-F 5020 |
| 1000-1010 | 5020 |
| 1010-1030 | Sa/Su 5020 |
| 1030-1100, | |
| 1100-1900, | |
| 1900-1930 & | |
| 1945-2030 | 5020 |
| 2030-2045 | F/Sa 5020 |
| 2045-2130 | 5020 |
| 2130-2135 | F/Sa 5020 |
| 2135-2230 | 5020 |
| 2230-2235 | F/Sa 5020 |
| 2235-2330 | 5020 |
| 2330-2345 | F/Sa 5020 |
| 2345-2400 | 5020 |

## SOUTH AFRICA

**CHANNEL AFRICA**

| | |
|---|---|
| 0300-0330 | ▣ 6035 & ▣ 9525 (E Africa & C Africa) |
| 0400-0430 | 5955 (S Africa) |
| 0500-0530 | 11710 (W Africa & S Africa) |
| 0600-0630 | 15215 (W Africa & S Africa) |
| 1300-1455 | Sa/Su 11710/11720 (S Africa), Sa/Su 17780/17725 (E Africa), Sa/Su 21725/21760 (W Africa) |
| 1500-1530 | 17770/17725 (C Africa & E Africa) |
| 1600-1630 | 9525 (S Africa) |
| 1700-1730 | ▣ 17860 & ▣ 17870 (W Africa & S Africa) |
| 1800-1830 | 17870 (W Africa) |

## SPAIN

### RADIO EXTERIOR DE ESPAÑA

| | |
|---|---|
| 0000-0200 | ◧ 6055 & ◧ 15385 (N America & C America) |
| 0500-0600 | 6055 (N America & C America) |
| 2000-2100 | ◧ M-F 9570 & ◧ M-F 9595 (N Africa & W Africa), ◧ M-F 9680/9700 & ◧ M-F 15290 (Europe) |
| 2100-2200 | ◧ Sa/Su 9570 (N Africa & W Africa), ◧ Sa/Su 9840 (Europe) |
| 2200-2300 | ◧ Sa/Su 9595 (N Africa & W Africa), ◧ Sa/Su 9680 (Europe) |

## SRI LANKA

### SRI LANKA BROADCASTING CORPORATION

| | |
|---|---|
| 0025-0430 | 6005, 9770 & 15425 (S Asia) |
| 1230-1550 | 6005, 9770 & 15425 (S Asia) |
| 1900-2000 | Sa 6010 (W Europe) |

## SWEDEN

### RADIO SWEDEN

| | |
|---|---|
| 0130-0200 | ◧ 7430 & ◧ 9490 (S Asia) |
| 0230-0300 & | |
| 0330-0400 | 9490 (N America) |
| 1100-1130 | ◧ 17505 (E Asia & Australasia) |
| 1230-1300 | ◧ 18960 (N America) |
| 1230-1300 | ◧ 21530 (SE Asia & Australasia) |
| 1330-1400 | ◧ 17505 (E Asia & Australasia), 18960 (N America) |
| 1330-1400 | ◧ 9430 (E Asia & Australasia) |
| 1430-1500 | ◧ 17505 (Asia & Australasia), 18960 (N America) |
| 1730-1800 | ◧ Su 13580 (Europe & Africa) |
| 1830-1900 | ◧ M-Sa 6065 (Europe) |
| 1830-1900 | ◧ Su 5840 (W Europe & N Africa) |
| 2030-2100 | ◧ 6065 (Europe) |
| 2030-2100 | ◧ 9445 (Australasia) |
| 2130-2200 | ◧ 15255 (Australasia) |
| 2230-2300 | ◧ 6065 (Europe) |

## SWITZERLAND

### SWISS RADIO INTERNATIONAL

| | |
|---|---|
| 0730-0800 | ◧ 9885 (N Africa), ◧ 13790 (W Africa), ◧ 15545 (N Africa), ◧ 17665 (C Africa & S Africa), ◧ 17685 (N Africa & W Africa), ◧ 21750 (C Africa & S Africa) |
| 0830-0900 | 21770 (C Africa & S Africa) |

| | |
|---|---|
| 1730-1800 | ◧ 9755, ◧ 13790 & ◧ 15220 (Mideast), ◧ 15555 (Mideast & E Africa), ◧ 17735 (Mideast), ◧ 21720 (Mideast & E Africa) |
| 1930-2030 | ◧ 9775 (N Africa & W Africa), ◧ 13645 (E Africa), ◧ 13660 & ◧ 15220 (C Africa & S Africa), ◧ 15485 (E Africa), ◧ 17580 (N Africa & W Africa), ◧ 17660 & ◧ 17735 (S Africa) |
| 2330-2400 | 9885, ◧ 11660 & ◧ 11905 (S America) |

## SYRIA

### RADIO DAMASCUS

| | |
|---|---|
| 2005-2105 | 12085 & 13610 (Europe) |
| 2110-2210 | 12085 (N America), 13610 (Australasia) |

## THAILAND

### RADIO THAILAND

| | |
|---|---|
| 0000-0030 | ◧ 9680 & ◧ 9690 (E Africa & S Africa) |
| 0030-0100 | ◧ 13695 & ◧ 15395 (E North Am) |
| 0300-0330 | ◧ 15395 & ◧ 15460 (W North Am) |
| 0530-0600 | ◧ 13780 & ◧ 21795 (Europe) |
| 1230-1300 | ◧ 9810 & ◧ 9885 (SE Asia & Australasia) |
| 1400-1430 | ◧ 9530 & ◧ 9830 (SE Asia & Australasia) |
| 1900-2000 | ◧ 7155 & ◧ 9535 (N Europe) |
| 2030-2045 | ◧ 9535 & ◧ 9680 (Europe) |

## TURKEY

### VOICE OF TURKEY

| | |
|---|---|
| 0300-0350 | ◧ 7270 (Mideast), ◧ 9650 (N America), ◧ 11655 (Europe & N America) |
| 0400-0450 | ◧ 6020 (Europe & N America), ◧ 7240 (Mideast) |
| 1230-1325 | ◧ 17615 (S Asia, SE Asia & Australasia), ◧ 17830 (Europe) |
| 1330-1425 | ◧ 17690 (S Asia, SE Asia & Australasia), ◧ 17815 (Europe) |
| 1830-1920 | ◧ 11960 (Europe) |
| 1930-2020 | ◧ 7125 (Europe) |
| 2130-2220 | ◧ 9525 (S Asia, SE Asia & Australasia) |
| 2200-2250 | ◧ 11960 & ◧ 12000 (W Europe & E North Am) |

2300-2350   ▥ 6020 (Europe), ▥ 9655 (W Europe & E North Am)

## UKRAINE

**RADIO UKRAINE INTERNATIONAL**

0000-0100   ▣ 5905 (S Europe), ▣ 7320 (E Europe & W Asia), ▣ 12040 (E North Am)

0100-0200   ▥ 7375 (E North Am), ▥ 7420 (W Asia), ▥ 9610 (E Europe)

0300-0400   ▣ 7150 (N Europe), ▣ 12040 (E North Am)

0400-0500   ▥ 7285 (N Europe), ▥ 7375 (E North Am), ▥ 7420 (W Asia), ▥ 9610 (E Europe)

1100-1200   ▣ 11840 (W Asia), ▣ 15520 (N Europe)

1200-1300   ▥ 11720 (S Europe), ▥ 11825 (C Asia), ▥ 15520 (W Europe)

2100-2200   ▣ 5905 (S Europe), ▣ 6020 (Europe), ▣ 9950 (N Europe), ▣ 11705 & ▣ 11950 (W Europe)

2200-2300   ▥ 5905 (W Europe), ▥ 7240 (N Europe), ▥ 9560 (W Europe)

## UNITED ARAB EMIRATES

**UAE RADIO IN DUBAI**

0330-0350   12005, 13675 & 15400 (E North Am & C America)

0530-0550   15435 (Australasia), 17830 (E Asia), 21700 (Australasia)

1030-1050   13675 (Europe), 15370 (N Africa), 15395 & 21605 (Europe)

1330-1350   13630 (N Africa), 13675, 15395 & 21605 (Europe)

1600-1615   13630 (N Africa), 13675, 15395 & 21605 (Europe)

## UNITED KINGDOM

**BBC WORLD SERVICE**

0000-0030   *3915 (SE Asia), 11945 (E Asia)*

0000-0100   *7105 (SE Asia),* ▣ *11810 (W North Am & C America), 11955 (S Asia), 17615 (E Asia)*

0000-0200   *5965 (S Asia), 6195 (SE Asia), 9410 (W Asia)*

0000-0300   *9915 & 12095 (S America), 15310 & 17790 (S Asia)*

0000-0330   *15360 (E Asia & SE Asia)*

0000-0400   *5975 (C America & N America)*

0000-0530   *15280 (E Asia)*

0100-0300   ▣ *11835 (C America & W North Am),* ▥ *11860 (SE Asia), 11955 (S Asia)*

0100-0400   ▥ *9525 (C America & W North Am)*

0200-0300   ▣ *6195 (E Europe),* ▣ *9410 (E Europe & Mideast),* ▥ *9410 (W Asia), 9770 (E Africa)*

0200-0500   ▥ *11760 (Mideast)*

0300-0400   *6005 (S Africa),* ▥ *9410 (E Europe), 11730 &* ▣ *12035 (E Africa),* ▣ *21830 (W Asia & S Asia)*

0300-0500   *3255 (S Africa),* ▣ *7120 &* ▥ *11765 (W Africa),* ▣ *11835 (W North Am & C America),* ▣ *12095 (Mideast),* ▥ *12095 (E Africa),* ▣ *15575 (Mideast), 17760 (E Asia)*

0300-0530   *21660 (E Asia)*

0300-0600   *17790 (S Asia)*

0300-0700   *6195 (Europe), 7160 (C Africa)*

0300-0800   *15310 (S Asia)*

0300-2200   *6190 (S Africa)*

0330-0600   *15420 (E Africa)*

0400-0500   *5975 (C America & W North Am),* ▣ *12035 (Europe),* ▣ *17640 (E Africa), 21830 (W Asia & S Asia)*

0400-0600   ▥ *6135 (W North Am & C America)*

0400-0700 ⟵ *9410 (Europe)*

0400-0720   *6005 (W Africa)*

0400-0730   ▥ *15575 (Mideast)*

0500-0530   *17885 (E Africa)*

0500-0700   *11765 (W Africa), 17640 (E Africa)*

0500-0730   ▣ *15575 (Mideast & W Asia)*

0500-0800   *11760 (Mideast)*

0500-1030   *15360 (E Asia, SE Asia & Australasia), 17760 (E Asia & SE Asia)*

0500-1100   *9740 (SE Asia)*

0500-1700   *11940 (S Africa), 12095 (Europe)*

0530-0600   *M-F 17885 (E Africa)*

0530-1030   *21660 (E Asia & SE Asia)*

0600-0700   ▥ *15420 (E Africa),* ▣ *15565 (E Europe)*

0600-0800   *Sa/Su 17885 (E Africa)*

0600-0805   *17790 (S Asia)*

0700-0800   *11765 & 17830 (W Africa)*

0700-0900 ⟵ *9410 (W Europe)*

0700-1000   *15400 (W Africa)*

| | |
|---|---|
| 0700-1500 | 17640 (E Europe & W Asia) |
| 0700-1600 | 15485 (W Europe & N Africa) |
| 0700-1700 | 15565 (E Europe) |
| 0730-0900 | Sa/Su 15575 (Mideast & W Asia) |
| 0800-0900 | Ⓢ 21470 (S Africa), 21830 (W Asia & S Asia) |
| 0800-1000 | 17830 (W Africa & C Africa) |
| 0800-1400 | 15310 (S Asia), 17885 (E Africa) |
| 0900-1000 | 15190 (S America) |
| 0900-1100 | 9605, Ⓦ 11765 & 11945 (E Asia), 17790 (S Asia) |
| 0900-1300 | Ⓦ 15310 (Mideast), 21470 (S Africa) |
| 0900-1400 | 11760 (Mideast) |
| 0900-1500 | 15575 (Mideast & W Asia) |
| 0900-1700 | 6195 (SE Asia) |
| 1000-1100 | Sa/Su 15400 (W Africa), Sa/Su 17830 (W Africa & C Africa) |
| 1000-1400 | 6195 (C America & N America) |
| 1100-1130 | 15400 (W Africa), 17790 (S America) |
| 1100-1300 | 15280 (E Asia) |
| 1100-1600 | 9740 (E Asia, SE Asia & Australasia), Ⓢ 9815 (E Asia) |
| 1100-1700 | 15190 (Americas), 17705 (S Asia) |
| 1100-2100 | 17830 (W Africa & C Africa) |
| 1300-1900 | 21470 (S Africa) |
| 1400-1700 | 15310 (S Asia), 21660 (E Africa) |
| 1430-1700 | Ⓦ 6195 (W Europe) |
| 1500-1530 | 11860, 15420 & 21490 (E Africa) |
| 1500-1600 | Ⓦ 9410 (Europe) |
| 1500-1830 | 5975 (S Asia) |
| 1500-1900 | 15400 (W Africa) |
| 1600-1700 | Ⓢ 9410 (W Europe), Ⓢ 15485 (W Europe & N Africa) |
| 1600-1800 | 3915 & 7160 (SE Asia), 9740 (S Asia) |
| 1600-2100 | Ⓦ 9410 (N Europe) |
| 1615-1700 | Sa/Su 11860, Sa/Su 15420 & Sa/Su 21490 (E Africa) |
| 1700-1745 | Ⓢ 6005 & 9630 (E Africa) |
| 1700-1800 | Ⓢ 15485 (W Europe) |
| 1700-1830 | 9510 (S Asia) |
| 1700-1900 | 15420 (E Africa) |
| 1700-2000 | 6195 (W Europe), Ⓢ 9410 (Europe), 15575 (Mideast & W Asia) |
| 1700-2100 | Ⓢ 12095 (E Europe) |
| 1700-2200 | 3255 (S Africa) |
| 1830-2100 | 6005 & 9630 (E Africa) |
| 1900-2000 | Ⓦ 15400 (S Africa) |
| 2000-2100 | Ⓢ 9410 (W Europe), 15400 (W Africa & S Africa) |
| 2000-2300 | 6195 (Europe), 11835 (W Africa) |
| 2100-2200 | 3915 (S Asia & SE Asia), 6005 (S Africa), 9410 (W Europe), Ⓢ 11945 (E Asia) |
| 2100-2300 | 15400 (W Africa) |
| 2100-2400 | 5965 (E Asia), 5975 (C America & N America), 6195 (SE Asia), 12095 (S America) |
| 2115-2130 | M-F 11675 & M-F 15390 (C America) |
| 2130-2145 | Tu/F 11680 (Atlantic & S America) |
| 2200-2300 | 9660 (SE Asia), 12080 (S Pacific) |
| 2200-2400 | 7105 (SE Asia), 11955 (SE Asia & Australasia) |
| 2300-2400 | 3915 (SE Asia), Ⓦ 6195 (W Europe), 11945 & 15280 (E Asia) |

**WALES RADIO INTERNATIONAL**

| | |
|---|---|
| 0200-0230 | Ⓢ Sa 9795 (N America) |
| 0300-0330 | Ⓦ Sa 9735 (N America) |
| 1130-1200 | Ⓦ Sa 17625 (Australasia) |
| 1230-1300 | Ⓢ Sa 17845 (Australasia) |
| 2030-2100 | Ⓢ F 7325 (Europe) |
| 2130-2200 | Ⓦ F 6010/7325 (Europe) |

## UNITED NATIONS

**UNITED NATIONS RADIO**

| | |
|---|---|
| 1730-1745 | M-F 6125/7150 (S Africa), Ⓦ M-F 15495 (E Africa & Mideast), Ⓢ M-F 17570/15105 & Ⓦ M-F 17580/15105 (W Africa & C Africa), Ⓢ M-F 17710 (E Africa & Mideast) |

## USA

**ADVENTIST WORLD RADIO**

| | |
|---|---|
| 0030-0100 | 6035 & Ⓢ 6055 (S Asia) |
| 0100-0130 | Ⓦ 9835 (W Asia & S Asia) |
| 0200-0230 & | |
| 0230-0300 | Ⓢ 9820 (W Asia & S Asia) |
| 0330-0400 | Ⓢ 11775 (C Asia) |
| 0400-0430 | Ⓦ 9650 (E Africa) |
| 0430-0500 | Ⓢ 11975 & Ⓦ 12080 (E Africa), Ⓦ 15160 (C Asia) |
| 0500-0530 | 5960 & 6015 (S Africa) |
| 0530-0600 | Ⓦ 15345 (W Africa & C Africa) |
| 0530-0630 | Ⓢ 15105 (C Africa & E Africa) |
| 0600-0630 | Ⓦ 15345 (C Africa & E Africa) |
| 0830-0900 | Ⓦ 9660 (Europe), Ⓦ 17820 (W Africa) |

| | |
|---|---|
| 0830-0930 | [S] *17780* (W Africa) |
| 0900-0930 | [W] *17670* (W Africa) |
| 1000-1030 | [W] *11705* & [S] *11930* (SE Asia) |
| 1000-1100 | [S] *11560* & [W] *11900* (E Asia) |
| 1300-1330 | [S] *15385* (S Asia & SE Asia) |
| 1330-1400 | [S] *11705* & [W] *11755* (E Asia), [S] *15320* & [W] *15385* (S Asia), [W] *15660* (S Asia & SE Asia) |
| 1600-1700 | [W] *11560* (Mideast), [W] *15380* & [W] *15495* (S Asia) |
| 1630-1700 | [S] *9385* (Mideast), [S] *9600* (S Asia), [W] *9850* (Europe), [S] *11850* & [W] *11980* (S Asia) |
| 1730-1800 | [W] *9820* (Mideast & W Asia), [W] *13720* & [S] *17630* (Mideast) |
| 1800-1830 | [W] *5960*, [S] *5970* & *6095* (S Africa) |
| 1800-1900 | [S] *7170* & [W] *11985* (E Africa) |
| 1930-2000 | [S] *7130* (W Europe) |
| 2000-2030 | [W] *15295* (C Africa) |
| 2000-2100 | [W] *7135* (E Asia), [S] *9745* (W Africa & C Africa), [W] *11700* (E Asia) |
| 2030-2100 | [W] *5955* (W Europe), [W] *15295* (C Africa & E Africa) |
| 2100-2200 | [W] *9660* & [S] *15355* (W Africa) |
| 2130-2200 | [S] *11850*, [W] *11960* & *11980* (E Asia) |

## AFRTS-ARMED FORCES RADIO & TV SERVICE

| | |
|---|---|
| 24 Hr | *4319/12579* USB (S Asia), *5765/13362* USB (Pacific), *6350/10320* (Irr) USB (Atlantic), *6459* USB (C America), *12690* USB (Americas) |

## FAMILY RADIO

| | |
|---|---|
| 0000-0100 | 6085 (E North Am) |
| 0000-0445 | 9505 (W North Am) |
| 0100-0200 | *15060* (S Asia) |
| 0100-0445 | 6065 (E North Am) |
| 0400-0445 | 9985 (Europe) |
| 0400-0500 | [S] 9355 (Europe), [W] 11550 (Europe & Mideast) |
| 0445-0600 | [S] 9985 (Europe) |
| 0500-0600 | [S] 9355 & [S] 11580 (Europe) |
| 0600-0700 | [W] 11550 (Europe & Mideast) |
| 0600-0745 | 7355 (Europe) |
| 0700-0800 | [W] 9985 (W Africa), [W] 11580 (C Africa & S Africa), [S] 13695 (W Africa), [S] 15170 (C Africa & S Africa) |
| 1000-1245 | 5950 (E North Am) |

| | |
|---|---|
| 1100-1300 | [S] 5850 & [W] 11830 (W North Am) |
| 1200-1300 | 13695 (E North Am) |
| 1200-1345 | [W] 11970 (C America) |
| 1200-1700 | [S] 17750 (W North Am & C America) |
| 1300-1500 | *11550* (S Asia), [W] 11740 & [S] 11970 (E North Am), 17510 & 17575 (S America) |
| 1300-1700 | 11830 (W North Am) |
| 1400-1700 | [W] 17760 (W North Am & C America) |
| 1500-1600 | *6280* (S Asia) |
| 1500-1700 | [S] *15520/17800* & [W] 15520 (S Asia) |
| 1600-1700 | [S] 15600 (W North Am), 21525 (C Africa & S Africa) |
| 1600-1800 | 21455 (Europe) |
| 1600-1945 | 18980 (Europe) |
| 1700-1800 | *21680* (C Africa & E Africa) |
| 1900-1945 | [W] 15565 (Europe) |
| 1900-2100 | *3230* (S Africa) |
| 1945-2145 | [S] 18980 (Europe) |
| 2000-2100 | *15195* (C Africa) |
| 2000-2200 | 17575 (S America) |
| 2000-2245 | [W] 7580 (Europe), [W] 15565 & [S] 17845 (W Africa) |
| 2100-2200 | [W] 21525 (C Africa & S Africa) |
| 2100-2245 | [S] 15120 (C Africa & S Africa) |
| 2200-2345 | 11740 (W North Am) |
| 2300-2400 | [W] 15170 & [W] 15400 (S America) |

## HERALD BROADCASTING

| | |
|---|---|
| 0000-0057 | W/F-M 9430 (E North Am), M/W/F 15285 (C America & S America) |
| 0100-0157 | 9430 (N America), M 15285 (C America & S America) |
| 0200-0257 | M/Th 7535 (W North Am & C America), Su/M 9430 (N America) |
| 0300-0357 | [W] M 5850, M 7535 & [S] M 11550 (E Europe) |
| 0400-0457 | [W] M/Tu/Th/Sa 12020 & [S] M/Tu/Th/Sa 15195 (E Africa & C Africa) |
| 0500-0557 | M 7535 (E Europe), [S] 9840 & [W] 12020 (S Africa) |
| 0600-0657 | [W] M/W/F/Sa 7535 & [S] M/W/F/Sa 9450 (W Africa & C Africa) |
| 0700-0757 | [W] Tu/Th 7535 & [S] Tu/Th 9450 (W Africa) |
| 0800-0857 | [W] Sa/Su 7535 (Europe), Sa-Th 9845 (Australasia), [S] Sa/Su 9860 (Europe) |

| | |
|---|---|
| 0900-0957 | ▣ Tu/Th 7535 & ▣ Tu/Th 9860 (Europe) |
| 1000-1057 | M/W/Th 6095 (E North Am), Su 9455 (S America) |
| 1000-1100 | Th-Tu *11780* (E Asia) |
| 1100-1157 | Tu/F-Su 6095 (E North Am), M 9455 (C America & S America) |
| 1200-1257 | M/W/Th 6095 (E North Am), Sa 9455 (C America & S America) |
| 1200-1300 | ▣ *9585* & ▣ *9880* (SE Asia) |
| 1300-1357 | Sa-Th 9430 (N America), Tu/F 9455 (W North Am & C America) |
| 1300-1400 | ▣ *7460* & ▣ *9940* (S Asia) |
| 1600-1657 | Sa 18910 (E Africa) |
| 1700-1800 | Tu/Th/Sa 18910 (C Africa) |
| 1800-1857 | Su 15665 (E Europe), Su/W 18910 (S Africa) |
| 1900-1957 | Su/Tu/Th 15665 (E Europe), 18910 (S Africa) |
| 2000-2057 | ▣ Su/M/W/F 15665 & ▣ Su/M/W/F 18910 (Africa) |
| 2100-2157 | ▣ W/Sa-M 11650 & ▣ W/Sa-M 15665 (W Europe), ▣ F 15665 & ▣ F 18910 (W Africa & C Africa) |
| 2200-2257 | ▣ Su/Th 7510 & ▣ Su/Th 13770 (W Europe), W/Su 15285 (S America) |
| 2300-2357 | ▣ Su/W 7510 & ▣ Su/W 13770 (S Europe & W Africa), Su 15285 (S America) |

**KAIJ**—(N America)

| | |
|---|---|
| 0000-0200 | 5755/13815 |
| 0200-1200 | 5755 |
| 1200-1400 | 5755/13815 |
| 1400-2400 | 13815 |

**KJES**

| | |
|---|---|
| 0100-0230 | 7555 (W North Am) |
| 1300-1400 | 11715 (N America) |
| 1400-1500 | 11715 (W North Am) |
| 1800-1900 | 15385 (Australasia) |

**KNLS-NEW LIFE STATION**—(E Asia)

| | |
|---|---|
| 0800-0900 | ▣ 9615/11765 & ▣ 11765 |
| 1300-1400 | ▣ 9615/11765 & ▣ 11870/11565 |

**KTBN**—(E North Am)

| | |
|---|---|
| 0000-0100 | ▣ 7510 & ▣ 15590 |
| 0100-1500 | 7510 |
| 1500-1600 | ▣ 7510 & ▣ 15590 |
| 1600-2400 | 15590 |

**KWHR-WORLD HARVEST RADIO**

| | |
|---|---|
| 0000-0100 | Su-F 17510 (E Asia) |
| 0100-0200 | M-Sa 17510 (E Asia) |
| 0200-0400 | 17510 (E Asia) |
| 0400-0430 | 17780 (E Asia) |
| 0430-0500 | Su-F 17780 (E Asia) |
| 0500-0600 | 17780 (E Asia) |
| 0600-0630 | M-Sa 17780 (E Asia) |
| 0630-0800 | 17780 (E Asia) |
| 0700-1045 | 11565 (Australasia) |
| 0800-0900 | ▣ 9930 & ▣ 17780 (E Asia) |
| 0900-1000 | ▣ Su-F 9930 & ▣ Su-F 17780 (E Asia) |
| 1000-1030 | Su-F 9930 (E Asia & SE Asia) |
| 1045-1300 | Sa/Su 11565 (Australasia) |
| 1130-1230 | 9930 (E Asia & SE Asia) |
| 1230-1400 & | |
| 1500-1600 | Su 9930 (E Asia & SE Asia) |
| 1600-1630 | Sa 9930 (E Asia & SE Asia) |
| 2200-2230 | 17510 (E Asia) |
| 2230-2300 | Su-F 17510 (E Asia) |
| 2300-2400 | 17510 (E Asia) |

**RADIO AFRICA INTERNATIONAL**

| | |
|---|---|
| 1700-1900 | ▣ *11735* (W Africa & C Africa), *13820* (E Africa), ▣ *15265* (W Africa & C Africa) |

**UNIVERSITY NETWORK**

| | |
|---|---|
| 0000-0200 | 9940 (S Asia), *13749* (C America) |
| 0000-1200 | *5029* (C America), *6150* (C America & S America), *7375* (S America) |
| 24 Hr | *9725* (N America) |
| 0200-0400 | ▣ *9940* & ▣ *17765* (S Asia) |
| 0400-1400 | *17765* (S Asia) |
| 1200-2400 | *11869* (S America) |
| 1400-1700 | ▣ *9940* & ▣ *17765* (S Asia) |
| 1700-2400 | *9940* (S Asia) |
| 2100-2400 | *13749* (C America) |

**VOA-VOICE OF AMERICA**

| | |
|---|---|
| 0000-0100 | *7215*, ▣ *9770* & ▣ *9890* (SE Asia), Tu-Sa 11695 (C America & S America), *11760* (SE Asia), *15185* (SE Asia & S Pacific), *15290* (E Asia), *17740* (E Asia & S Pacific), *17820* (E Asia) |
| 0000-0130 | Tu-Sa 13790 (C America & S America) |
| 0000-0200 | Tu-Sa 5995, Tu-Sa 6130, Tu-Sa 7405, Tu-Sa 9455 & Tu-Sa 9775 (C America & S America) |
| 0100-0300 | *7115*, ▣ *7200*, ▣ *9635*, ▣ *9850*, 11705, ▣ *11725*, 11820, ▣ *13650*, 15250, ▣ *15300*, *17740* & *17820* (S Asia) |

| | |
|---|---|
| 0130-0200 | Tu-Sa 13740 (C America & S America) |
| 0300-0330 | W M-F 4960 (W Africa & C Africa), 7340 (C Africa & E Africa) |
| 0300-0400 | W 6035 (E Africa & S Africa), 7105 (S Africa) |
| 0300-0430 | 9885 (C Africa) |
| 0300-0500 | S 5855 (E Africa & S Africa), 6080 (S Africa), S 7275 (Africa), 7290 (C Africa & E Africa), W 7415 (C Africa & S Africa), 9575 (W Africa & S Africa), S 17895 (C Africa & E Africa) |
| 0400-0500 | S 4960 (W Africa & C Africa) |
| 0400-0600 | W 9775 (C Africa & E Africa) |
| 0400-0700 | W 7170 & S 9530 (N Africa), S 11965 (Mideast), 15205 (Mideast & S Asia) |
| 0500-0600 | W 9700 (N Africa) |
| 0500-0630 | 5970 (W Africa & C Africa), 6035 (W Africa & S Africa), 6080, S 7195 & W 7295 (W Africa), W 11835 (W Africa & S Africa), S 12080 (Africa), S 13670 (C Africa), W 13710 (Africa) |
| 0500-0700 | W 11825 (Mideast) |
| 0600-0630 | S 11995 (E Africa), W 11995 (C Africa) |
| 0600-0700 | W 5995, S 9680, S 11805 & W 11930 (N Africa) |
| 0630-0700 | Sa/Su 5970 (W Africa & C Africa), Sa/Su 6035 (W Africa & S Africa), Sa/Su 6080, S Sa/Su 7195 & W Sa/Su 7295 (W Africa), W Sa/Su 11835 (W Africa & S Africa), S Sa/Su 11995 (E Africa), W Sa/Su 11995 (C Africa), S Sa/Su 12080 (Africa), S Sa/Su 13670 (C Africa), W Sa/Su 13710 (Africa) |
| 0700-0730 | Sa 10869/6873 (Europe) |
| 0800-1000 | S 11930, W 11995, S 13610, W 13615 & 15150 (E Asia) |
| 1000-1100 | 5745, W 7370 & 9590 (C America) |
| 1000-1200 | W 5985 & S 9770 (Pacific & Australasia), W 11720 (E Asia & Australasia) |
| 1000-1300 | S 15240 & W 15250 (E Asia) |
| 1000-1500 | 15425 (SE Asia & Pacific) |
| 1100-1300 | W 6110 & S 6160 (SE Asia) |
| 1100-1400 | 9645 (SE Asia & Australasia) |
| 1100-1500 | 9760 (E Asia, S Asia & SE Asia), W 11705 & S 15160 (E Asia) |
| 1200-1330 | W 11715 (E Asia & Australasia) |
| 1300-1800 | W 6110 & S 6160 (S Asia & SE Asia) |
| 1400-1430 | Su 18275 (Europe) |
| 1400-1800 | 7125 & 9645 (S Asia), W 15205 (Mideast & S Asia), S 15255 (Mideast), W 15395 (S Asia) |
| 1500-1600 | S 9590 & S 9760 (S Asia & SE Asia), W 9760 (E Asia, S Asia & SE Asia), W 9795, S 9845 & 12040 (E Asia), W 15460 & S 15550 (SE Asia) |
| 1500-1700 | W 9575 (Mideast & S Asia), S 15205 (Europe, N Africa & Mideast) |
| 1600-1700 | 6035 (W Africa), 9760 (S Asia & SE Asia), 13600 (C Africa & E Africa), S 13710 & S 15225 (S Africa), S 15410 (C Africa & E Africa), W 15485 (S Africa), W 17640 & W 17715 (E Africa), S 17810 & W 17895 (Africa) |
| 1600-1800 | S 15445 (Africa), W 15445 (E Africa) |
| 1600-1900 | S 17895 (Africa) |
| 1600-2000 | W 13710 (C Africa & E Africa) |
| 1600-2200 | W 15240 (Africa) |
| 1700-1800 | M-F 5990 (E Asia), W M-F 6045 (E Asia & Australasia), S M-F 7170 (Australasia), S M-F 7215 (SE Asia), W M-F 9525 (E Asia, SE Asia & S Pacific), S M-F 9550 (E Asia & SE Asia), W M-F 9670 (E Asia, SE Asia & Australasia), S M-F 9770 (E Asia), W M-F 9785, W M-F 9795 & W M-F 11955 (S Asia & SE Asia), W M-F 12005 (SE Asia), W M-F 15255 (E Asia & S Pacific), W 17895 (C Africa & E Africa) |
| 1700-1900 | W 6040 (N Africa & Mideast) |
| 1700-2100 | S 9760 (N Africa & Mideast), W 9760 (Mideast & S Asia) |
| 1700-2200 | S 15410 (Africa) |
| 1800-1900 | S 7415 (C Africa & S Africa), 9770 (Mideast), W 9840 (Mideast & S Asia) |
| 1800-2000 | W 17895 (Africa) |

**The editorial staff of Radio Austria International's English section prepares the day's programs under an ever-present Union Jack.**
ROI

| | |
|---|---|
| 1800-2200 | *6035* (W Africa), *11975* (C Africa & E Africa), 15580 (W Africa & S Africa) |
| 1830-1900 | [S] Sa/Su *11690*, [W] Sa/Su *13675*, [S] Sa/Su *13730*, [W] Sa/Su *15160*, [S] Sa/Su *15525* & [W] Sa/Su *17640* (E Africa) |
| 1900-2000 | [W] M-F *5965*, [S] *6160* & [S] *7260* (Mideast), *9525* (Australasia), [S] *9550*, [S] *9680* & [W] *9785* (Mideast), M-F *9840* & [W] *11720* (Mideast & S Asia), [S] M-F *11780* (Mideast), [S] *11805* (S Pacific), [W] *11870* (Australasia), [S] M-F *11970* (SE Asia), [W] M-F *11970* (E Asia), [S] M-F *12015* (S Asia), [W] *12015*, [W] *13640*, [S] *13690* & M-F *13725* (Mideast), *15180* (Pacific), [W] M-F *15205* (Mideast), [S] M-F *15235* (SE Asia), [W] M-F *15410* (E Asia) |
| 1900-2030 | *4950* (W Africa & C Africa) |
| 1900-2100 | [W] *9690* (Mideast & S Asia), [S] *9770* (N Africa & Mideast) |
| 1900-2200 | [S] *7375* (C Africa & S Africa), *7415* (E Africa & S Africa), [S] *15445* (Africa) |
| 2000-2030 | *11855* (W Africa) |
| 2000-2100 | [S] *17745* & [W] *17885* (W Africa & C Africa) |
| 2000-2200 | *6095* (Mideast), [W] *13710* (Africa), 17895 (W Africa) |
| 2030-2100 | Sa/Su *4950* (W Africa & C Africa) |
| 2100-2200 | *6040* (Mideast), [S] *9535* (N Africa & Mideast), [W] *9595* (Mideast & S Asia), [W] *9670* (SE Asia & Australasia), *9760* (E Europe & Mideast), *11870* (Australasia) |
| 2100-2400 | [S] *9705* (SE Asia), *15185* (SE Asia & S Pacific), [W] *17735* & [S] *17740* (E Asia & S Pacific), *17820* (E Asia) |
| 2200-2230 | [S] M-F *5855* (C Africa & S Africa), M-F *6035* (W Africa), [S] M-F *7375* (C Africa & S Africa), M-F *7415* (E Africa & S Africa), [W] M-F *11655* (C Africa & S Africa), M-F 11975 (C Africa & E Africa), [W] M-F *13710* (Africa) |
| 2200-2400 | *7215* & [S] *9770* (SE Asia), [W] *9770* (SE Asia & Australasia), [W] *9890* & *11760* (SE Asia), *15290* (E Asia), *15305* (E Asia & SE Asia) |
| 2300-2400 | [W] *6045*, [W] *7140*, [S] *7190*, [S] *7200*, *9545*, *11925*, [S] *13775* & [W] *15395* (E Asia) |

| | |
|---|---|
| 2330-2400 | ▣ 7130, ▣ 7225, ▣ 7260, ▣ 9620, 11805, ▣ 13735, ▣ 13745 & 15205 (SE Asia) |

**WBCQ-"THE PLANET"—(N America)**

| | |
|---|---|
| 0000-0500 ▣ | 7415 & 9335 |
| 0500-0545 ▣ | Tu-Su 7415 |
| 0545-0700 ▣ | F/Su 7415 |
| 1300-1400 ▣ | Su 17495 |
| 1500-2200 ▣ | M-F 7415/9335 |
| 1800-1900 ▣ | M-Sa 17495 |
| 1900-2200 ▣ | M-F 17495 |
| 2200-2400 ▣ | 7415 & M-Sa 9335 |

**WEWN**

| | |
|---|---|
| 0000-1000 | 5825 (N America & C America) |
| 1000-1200 | ▣ 7520 (N America & C America) |
| 1000-1300 | ▣ 5825 (N America & C America) |
| 1000-1700 | 15745 (Europe) |
| 1200-1600 | ▣ 11875 (N America & C America) |
| 1300-1600 | ▣ 9955 (N America & C America) |
| 1600-2200 | 13615 (N America & C America) |
| 1700-2400 | 17595 (W Africa) |
| 2200-2400 | 9975 (N America & C America) |

**WHRA-WORLD HARVEST RADIO**

| | |
|---|---|
| 0000-0500 | 7580 (Europe & Mideast) |
| 0500-1000 | ▣ 7580 & ▣ 11730 (Africa) |
| 1500-2300 ▣ | 17650 (Africa) |
| 2300-2400 | 7580 (Europe & Mideast) |

**WHRI-WORLD HARVEST RADIO**

| | |
|---|---|
| 0000-1000 | 5745 (E North Am), 7315 (C America) |
| 1000-1045 | M-Sa 9495 (N America & C America) |
| 1000-1500 | 6040/9840 (E North Am) |
| 1045-1300 | 9495 (N America & C America) |
| 1300-1700 | 15105 (C America) |
| 1500-1600 | ▣ 6040/9840 (E North Am), ▣ 13760 (E North Am & W Europe) |
| 1600-1715 | 13760 (E North Am & W Europe) |
| 1700-1800 | ▣ 9495 (N America & C America), ▣ 15105 (C America) |
| 1715-1730 | M-Sa 13760 (E North Am & W Europe) |
| 1730-2000 | 13760 (E North Am & W Europe) |
| 1800-2400 | 9495 (N America & C America) |
| 2000-2400 | 5745 (E North Am) |

**WINB-WORLD INTERNATIONAL BROADCASTERS—(C America & W North Am)**

| | |
|---|---|
| 0000-0400 | 12160 |
| 1000-1200 | 13845 |
| 1200-2300 | 13570 |
| 2300-2400 | 13570/12160 |

**WJIE SHORTWAVE**

| | |
|---|---|
| 24 Hr | 7490 (E North Am), 13595 (W North Am) |

**WMLK—(Europe, Mideast & N America)**

| | |
|---|---|
| 1500-2100 | Su-F 9465 |

**WRMI-RADIO MIAMI INTERNATIONAL**

| | |
|---|---|
| 0000-0130 ▣ | 9955 (C America & S America) |
| 0130-0300 ▣ | Tu-Sa 7385 (N America), Su/M 9955 (C America & S America) |
| 0400-0545 ▣ | 7385 (N America) |
| 0545-0600 ▣ | M-Th/Sa 7385 (N America) |
| 0600-0630 ▣ | Tu-Sa 7385 (N America) |
| 0630-0700 ▣ | M-Sa 7385 (N America) |
| 0700-0715 & | |
| 0715-1030 ▣ | Tu-Sa 7385 (N America) |
| 1300-1500 ▣ | Su 9955 (C America) |
| 1300-2300 ▣ | 15725 (N America) |
| 1300-2400 ▣ | M-F 7385 (N America) |
| 2100-2300 ▣ | Sa/Su 9955 (C America) |
| 2300-2400 ▣ | Sa 9955 (C America) |

**WTJC**

| | |
|---|---|
| 0000-0130 ▣ | 9370 (N America) |
| 0130-0145 ▣ | Tu-Su 9370 (N America) |
| 0145-1105 ▣ | 9370 (N America) |
| 0800-0900 | Sa 9710 (E Europe) |
| 1100-1200 | Su 9710 (W Europe) |
| 1105-1120 ▣ | M-Sa 9370 (N America) |
| 1120-2400 ▣ | 9370 (N America) |

**WWBS—(E North Am)**

| | |
|---|---|
| 0000-0100 | ▣ Su/M 11910 |
| 0000-0200 | ▣ Su/M 11900 |
| 2300-2400 | ▣ Sa/Su 11910 |

**WWCR**

| | |
|---|---|
| 0000-0100 | 3210/9475 (E North Am) |
| 0000-0200 | 5935/13845 & 13845 (E North Am) |
| 0000-1200 | 5070 (E North Am) |
| 0000-1400 | 7465 (E North Am) |
| 0100-0900 | 3210 (E North Am) |
| 0200-1200 | 5935 (E North Am) |
| 0900-1000 | 3210/9475 (E North Am) |
| 1000-1100 ▣ | Su-F 9475 (E North Am) |
| 1200-1400 | 5070/12160 & 5935/13845 (E North Am) |
| 1400-2200 | 12160 (E North Am & Europe) |
| 1400-2300 | 9475 (E North Am & Europe) |
| 1400-2400 | 13845 (E North Am) |
| 2200-2400 | 5070/12160 (E North Am & Europe), 7465 (E North Am) |
| 2300-2400 | 3210/9475 (E North Am) |

**WWRB**

0000-0600 5085 (W North Am & C America)
1600-2400 12172 (W North Am)

## UZBEKISTAN

**RADIO TASHKENT**

0100-0130 [W] 5955 (S Asia), [W] 5975, [S] 7190 & [W] 7215 (Mideast & W Asia), [S] 9715 (Mideast & S Asia)
1200-1230 &
1330-1400 [W] 5060 & 5975 (S Asia), [W] 6025 & [S] 7285 (W Asia & S Asia), 9715 & [S] 15295 (S Asia), [S] 17775 (S Asia & SE Asia)
2030-2100 &
2130-2200 5025 (Europe), [W] 7105 & [S] 9540 (Mideast & W Asia), [S] 9545 (W Asia), 11905 (Europe)

## VATICAN STATE

**VATICAN RADIO**

0250-0310 7305 (E North Am), 9605 (E North Am & C America)
0600-0620 ⬅ 4005 (Europe), 5890 (W Europe)
0620-0700 ⬅ 5890 (W Europe)
0630-0645 [S] M-Sa 9645 (S Europe & N Africa)
0730-0745 ⬅ M-Sa 4005 (Europe), M-Sa 5890 (W Europe), M-Sa 7250 (Europe), M-Sa 11740 (W Europe & N Africa), M-Sa 15595 (Mideast)
0730-0745 [W] M-Sa 9645 (W Europe)
1120-1130 ⬅ M-Sa 7250 (Europe), M-Sa 11740 (W Europe), M-Sa 15595 (Mideast)
1615-1630 [S] 7250 (N Europe), [S] 11810 (Mideast)
1715-1730 ⬅ 4005 (Europe), 5890 & 9645 (W Europe)
1715-1730 [W] 7250 (Mideast)
2050-2110 ⬅ 4005 & 5890 (Europe)

## VIETNAM

**VOICE OF VIETNAM**

0100-0130,
0230-0300 &
0330-0400 *6175* (E North Am & C America)
1000-1030 9840 & 12020 (SE Asia)
1100-1130 7285 (SE Asia)

**Producer Mike Popham (glasses) and Giles Brooks, Senior Studio Manager, of the BBC World Service's "From Our Own Correspondent." One of the jewels of broadcast journalism, it has been selected by PASSPORT as among the best programs for 2003.**

BBC Audience Relations

1230-1300 9840 & 12020 (SE Asia)
1330-1400 &
1600-1630 [W] 7145/11575, [W] 9730, [S] 11640 & [S] 13740 (Europe)
1700-1730 [S] *9725* (W Europe)
1800-1830 [W] *5955* (W Europe), [W] 7145/11575, [W] 9730, [S] 11640 & [S] 13740 (Europe)
1900-1930 &
2030-2100 [W] 7145/11575, [W] 9730, [S] 11640 & [S] 13740 (Europe)
2330-2400 9840 & 12020 (SE Asia)

## YEMEN

**REPUBLIC OF YEMEN RADIO**—(Mideast & E Africa)

0600-0700 &
1800-1900 9780

## YUGOSLAVIA

**RADIO YUGOSLAVIA**

0000-0030 [S] M-Sa *9580/11870* (E North Am)
0100-0130 [W] M-Sa *7115* (E North Am)
0200-0230 [W] M-Sa *7130* (W North Am)
0430-0500 [S] *9580/11870* (W North Am)
1930-2000 ⬅ *6100* (Europe), *9720* (S Africa)
2200-2230 ⬅ *6185/6100* (Europe)

# Voices from Home—2003

## Country-by-Country Guide to Native Broadcasts

For some listeners, English offerings are merely icing on the cake. Their real interest is in eavesdropping on broadcasts for *nativos*—the home folks. These can be enjoyable regardless of language, especially when they offer traditional music.

Some you'll hear, many you won't, depending on your location and receiving equipment. Keep in mind that native-language broadcasts are sometimes weaker than those in English, so you may need more patience and better hardware. PASSPORT REPORTS shows which radios and antennas work best.

### When to Tune

Some broadcasts come in better during the day within world band segments from 9300 to 21850 kHz. However, signals from Latin

America and Africa peak near or during darkness, especially from 4700 to 5100 kHz. See "Best Times and Frequencies" for specifics.

Times and days of the week are in World Time, explained in "Setting Your World Time Clock" and PASSPORT's glossary; for local times in each country, see "Addresses PLUS." Midyear, some stations are an hour earlier (◨) or later (◪) because of daylight saving time, typically April through October. Those used only seasonally are labeled ▣ for summer (midyear) and ◪ for winter (January, etc.). Stations may also extend their hours for holidays, emergencies or sports events.

Frequencies in *italics* may be best, as they come from relay transmitters that might be near you, although other frequencies beamed your way might do almost as well. Some signals not beamed to you can also be heard, especially when they are targeted to nearby parts of the world. Frequencies with no target zones are usually for domestic coverage, so they are the least likely to be heard unless you're in or near that country.

**Woman village elder, Ethiopia.**

Nick Francis, theafricaguide.com

## Schedules for Entire Year

To be as useful as possible over the months to come, PASSPORT's schedules consist not just of observed activity, but also that which we have creatively opined will take place during the forthcoming year. This predictive material is based on decades of experience and is original from us. Although inherently not as exact as real-time data, over the years it's been of tangible value to PASSPORT readers.

**Schedules consist of predictive as well as observed activity.**

**Although seafaring Norway has cut back on foreign-language transmissions, the NRK continues to broadcast worldwide in Norwegian (see Blue Pages). Shown, historic Alesund.**

Corbis

## ALBANIA—Albanian
**RADIO TIRANA**
0000-0430 ▭ 7270 (E North Am)
0900-1000 ▭ 7110 (Europe)
1500-1800 ▭ 7270 (Europe)
2130-2300 ▭ 7295 (Europe)

## ARGENTINA—Spanish
**RADIO ARGENTINA AL EXTERIOR-RAE**
0900-1200   6060 (S America), 15345 (Americas)
1200-1400   M-F 15345 (Americas)
2200-2400   M-F 6060 (C America & S America), M-F 11710 & M-F 15345 (Europe)

**RADIO NACIONAL**
0000-0100   M 11710 (S America)
0000-0230   Su/M 6060 (C America & S America), Su/M 15345 (Americas)
0230-0300   M 6060 (C America & S America), M 15345 (Americas)
1700-2000   Su 6060 (S America), Su 15345 (Europe)
1800-2000   Su 11710 (S America)
2000-2200   Sa/Su 11710 (Irr) (S America)
2000-2400   Sa/Su 6060 (S America), Sa/Su 15345 (Europe)
2200-2400   Su 11710 (S America)

## ARMENIA—Armenian
**VOICE OF ARMENIA**
0300-0330 ▭ 4810 (Irr) (E Europe, Mideast & W Asia), 9965 (S America)
0400-0430 ▭ 9965 (Irr) (S America)
0800-0830 ▭ Su 4810 (E Europe, Mideast & W Asia), Su 15270 (Europe)
1600-1700 **S** 11685 (W Europe)
1930-2000 ▭ M-Sa 4810 (E Europe, Mideast & W Asia), M-Sa 9960 (Europe)

## AUSTRIA—German
**RADIO AUSTRIA INTERNATIONAL**
0000-0030 ▭ 13730 (S America)
0000-0030 **S** 9870 (C America & S America)
0100-0130 **S** 9870 (E North Am), **W** 9870 (C America & S America)
0200-0230 **W** 7325 (E North Am)
0400-0500 **S** 6155 & **S** 13730 (Europe)
0500-0530   6155 & 13730 (Europe)
0530-0600 **W** 6155 & **W** 13730 (Europe)
0600-0630 ▭ 17870 (Mideast)
0600-0630 &
0700-0730   6155 & 13730 (Europe)
0730-0800 **S** 6155 & **S** 13730 (Europe)
0800-1100   6155 & 13730 (Europe)
1100-1130 **S** 21780 (S Asia, SE Asia & Australasia)
1100-1200 **W** 6155 & **W** 13730 (Europe)
1200-1230 **W** 21770 (S Asia, SE Asia & Australasia)
1200-1300 **S** 6155 & **S** 13730 (Europe)
1300-1330   6155 & 13730 (Europe)
1330-1400 **W** 6155 & **W** 13730 (Europe)
1400-1430   6155 & 13730 (Europe)
1430-1500 **S** 6155 & **S** 13730 (Europe)
1500-1730   6155 & 13730 (Europe)
1600-1700 ▭ 17860 (W North Am)
1730-1800 **W** 6155 & **W** 13730 (Europe)
1800-1830   5945 & 6155 (Europe)
1900-1930 **S** Tu-Th/Sa 5945, **W** 5945, **S** Tu-Th/Sa 6155 & **W** 6155 (Europe)
2000-2030 **S** Su-F 5945, **W** Tu-Th/Sa 5945, **S** Su-F 6155 & **W** Tu-Th/Sa 6155 (Europe)
2100-2130 **S** 5945, **W** Su-F 5945, **S** 6155 & **W** Su-F 6155 (Europe)
2200-2215   5945 & 6155 (Europe)
2215-2230 &
2300-2315 **W** 5945 & **W** 6155 (Europe)

## BANGLADESH—Bangla
**BANGLADESH BETAR**
1200-1530 &
1545-1600   15519 (Mideast & Europe)
1600-1730   15519 (Mideast & Europe)
1630-1730   7185 & 9550 (Mideast)
1915-2000   7185, 9550 & 15519 (Irr) (Europe)

## BELGIUM
**RADIO VLAANDEREN INTERNATIONAAL**
**Dutch**
0430-0500 **W** 11985 & **S** 15565 (W North Am)
0500-0530 **S** 9925 (C Africa)
0600-0630 **W** 17730 (C Africa)
0600-0800 ▭ 13685 (S Europe & Mideast)
0600-0900 ▭ 15195 (Europe)
0800-0900 ▭ 13685 (S Europe)
1100-1130 **S** 15195 (S Europe), **S** 17670 (Europe)
1100-1200 ▭ Su 21630 (C Africa)
1200-1230 ▭ 21630 (C Africa)

1200-1230    9865/7390 (E Asia & Australasia), **W** 15195 (Europe), 17690 (SE Asia & Australasia)

1300-1600    **S** Su 15275 (W Europe), **S** 17670 (Europe)

1400-1700    **W** 13685 (Europe), **W** Su 15325 (W Europe)

1700-1800    **S** 15195 (Europe)

1800-1900    **W** 5910 (W Europe), **S** 7195 (S Africa), **W** 13685 (Europe), **S** 13690 (S Europe)

1800-2000    **S** Sa 5910 (W Europe)

1900-2000    13710 (S Europe & Mideast), 15325 (C Africa)

1900-2000    **W** 5910 (W Europe), 5960 (C Africa), **W** 13645 (S Africa), **W** 13685 (S Europe)

2000-2100    **W** Sa 5910 (W Europe)

2100-2200    9925 (Europe)

2100-2200    **W** 5910 & **W** 5960 (W Europe)

2300-2330    **W** 13700 & **S** 15565 (N America)

### RTBF INTERNATIONAL
**French**

0300-0400    **S** 9970 (S Europe)

0400-0530    M-F 9490 (C Africa)

0400-2200    9970 (S Europe)

0530-0600    9490 (C Africa)

0600-0812    17580 (C Africa)

0812-0906    Sa/Su 17580 (C Africa)

0906-1100    Sa 17580 (C Africa)

1100-1200    M-Sa 21565 (C Africa)

1200-1217    21565 (C Africa)

1217-1306    M-F 21565 (C Africa)

1600-1700    Su-F 17570 (C Africa)

1700-1816    17570 (C Africa)

## BRAZIL—Portuguese
### RADIO BANDEIRANTES
24 Hr    6090, 9645, 11925

### RADIO BRASIL CENTRAL
0000-0200    4985

0000-0330    11815

0200-0600    4985 (Irr)

0330-0600    11815 (Irr)

0600-2400    4985, 11815

### RADIO CULTURA
0000-0200    6170, 9615, 17815

0700-2400    9615, 17815

0800-2400    6170

### RADIO NACIONAL
0000-0230    6180, 11780

0230-0700    Su 6180, Su 11780

2105-2300    Sa/Su 6180, Sa/Su 11780

2300-2400    6180, 11780

### RADIO NACIONAL DA AMAZONIA
0700-2105    6180, 11780

2105-2300    M-F 6180, M-F 11780

## CANADA—French
### CANADIAN BROADCASTING CORP—(E North Am)
0100-0300    M 9625

0300-0400    Su 9625 & Tu-Sa 9625

1300-1310 &

1500-1555    M-F 9625

1700-1715    Su 9625

1900-1945    M-F 9625

1900-2310    Sa 9625

### RADIO CANADA INTERNATIONAL
0000-0100    **W** 11865 (C America & S America), **W** 13640 (E North Am & C America)

1100-1200    **S** 5990 (E North Am), **S** 11910 & **S** 15305 (E North Am & C America)

1200-1300    **S** Sa/Su 5990 (E North Am), **W** 11805, **S** Sa/Su 11910, **W** 13655, **S** Sa/Su 15305 & **W** 15425 (E North Am & C America)

1300-1400    **W** Sa/Su 11805, **W** Sa/Su 13655 & **W** Sa/Su 15425 (E North Am & C America)

1600-1700    **S** 9515, **S** 13650 & **S** 15305 (E North Am & C America)

1700-1800    **W** 17820 & **W** 21565 (C America)

1900-2000    **S** 5995 (S Europe & N Africa), **S** 15325 & **S** 17570 (N Africa & W Africa), **S** 17870 (W Europe & N Africa)

2000-2100    7235 (N Africa)

2000-2100    **W** 9770 (W Europe), **W** 11725 (W Africa), **W** 12015 (W Europe), **W** 13650 (N Africa), **W** 15325 (W Africa)

2130-2200    **S** 5850 (W Europe), **S** 7235 (N Africa & W Africa), **S** 9590 & **S** 11920 (E North Am & C America), **S** 13690 (N Africa & W Africa), **S** 15325 (W Africa), **S** 17870 (W Europe & N Africa), **S** 17880 (S America)

Forced by flooding to leave their village, a displaced woman and her baby stand in a field outside the southern city of Kismayo, Somalia.   R. Chalasani, UNICEF

| | |
|---|---|
| 2200-2300 | ▥ *9680* & ▥ *11705* (E Asia & SE Asia), ▤ *11810* & ▥ *13705* (E Asia), ▤ *17835* (E Asia & SE Asia) |
| 2230-2300 | ▥ *5850* (Europe & Mideast), ▥ *6045* (W Europe & N Africa), ▥ 9755 (E North Am & C America), ▥ 9770 (W Europe), ▥ *9805* (N Africa & W Africa) |
| 2300-2400 | ▤ 5960 (E North Am & C America), ▤ 15305 (C America & S America), ▤ 17880 (S America) |

## CHINA

### CENTRAL PEOPLE'S BROADCASTING STATION
**Chinese**

| | |
|---|---|
| 0000-0030 | 4800, ▥ 6110, 7335, ▥ 11710, ▤ 11960, ▥ 11990, 12045, 12055, ▤ 17605 |
| 0000-0100 | 3985, 6750, ▥ 7115, ▥ 7130, 7935, ▤ 9080, 9710, ▥ 9775, 9800, ▥ 9830, ▥ 9845, ▤ 11710, 11925, ▤ 17550, ▤ 17565, ▤ 17700 |
| 0000-0300 | 11835 |
| 0000-0400 | 11685, 12080 |
| 0000-0500 | 7230, 11660 |
| 0000-0600 | 6030, 7200, 9445, 9480, 9600, 9625, 9645, 9675, 9700, 9810, 11610, 11670, 11695, 11720, 11790, 11800, 11825, 13710, 13725, 15145, 15285, 15300, 15360, 15380, 15480, 15500, 15540, 15550, 17625, 17890 |

| | |
|---|---|
| 0030-0600 | 9590, 11915, 11960, 17605, 17660 |
| 0100-0400 | 15570 |
| 0100-0600 | 7140, 9080, 11710, 17550, 17565, 17700 |
| 0130-0500 | 17580 |
| 0200-0500 | 11630, 11890, 12055, 15390 |
| 0200-0600 | 13700 |
| 0500-0600 | Sa-Th 7230, W-M 11660, 11685, 11835, 12080, 15570 |
| 0600-0800 | Th-Tu 11685, W-M 11835, Th-Tu 12080, Th-Tu 15570 |
| 0600-0855 | W-M 6030, Th-Tu 7140, Th-Tu 7200, W/Th/Sa-M 7230, Th-Tu 9080, Th-Tu 9445, W-M 9480, W-M 9590, W-M 9600, Th-Tu 9625, W-M 9645, W-M 9675, Th-Tu 9700, W-M 9800, Th-Tu 9810, Th-Tu 11610, Th-M 11660, Th-Tu 11670, W-M 11695, W-M 11710, W-M 11720, Th-Tu 11790, Th-Tu 11800, W-M 11825, Th-Tu 11915, W-M 11960, Th-Tu 13710, Th-Tu 13725, W-M 15145, W-M 15285, W-M 15300, Th-Tu 15360, W-M 15380, W-M 15480, Th-Tu 15500, Th-Tu 15540, W-M 15550, W-M 17550, W-M 17565, W-M 17605, Th-Tu 17625, Th-Tu 17660, Th-Tu 17700, W-M 17890 |
| 0700-0855 | W-M 11630, W-M 11890, W-M 12055, W-M 15390, W-M 17580 |
| 0800-1730 | 13610 |
| 0855-1000 | 9700 |
| 0855-1030 | 7140, 9645, 9800 |
| 0855-1100 | 9600, 9675, 11670, 11695, 11825, 11960, 15480 |
| 0855-1130 | 9590, 17550, 17565, 17625, 17660, 17700 |
| 0855-1200 | 9810, 11710, 11720, 11790, 11915, 13725, 15145, 15380, 17890 |
| 0855-1230 | 9445, 15285, 15500, 15550 |
| 0855-1300 | 9080, 9480, 11610, 11660, 13710 |
| 0855-1330 | 11800, 17605 |
| 0855-1400 | 15360, 15540 |
| 0855-1500 | 15300 |
| 0855-1601 | 7200, 9625 |
| 0855-1730 | 6030, 7230 |

| | |
|---|---|
| 0900-1210 | 12080, 15570 |
| 0900-1300 | 11685, 11835 |
| 0900-1730 | 9710 |
| 1000-1100 | [S] 9820, 11630, [W] 11890, 12055, 15390, 17580 |
| 1000-1400 | 7935 |
| 1000-1601 | 7185 |
| 1030-1300 | [W] 4460, [S] 9645 |
| 1030-1601 | 3985 |
| 1030-1730 | [W] 6125, [S] 9800 |
| 1100-1200 | [W] 5030, [S] 9675 |
| 1100-1230 | [S] 15480 |
| 1100-1300 | [W] 4850, [S] 11670 |
| 1100-1400 | [W] 5955, [S] 11825 |
| 1100-1601 | 12020 |
| 1100-1730 | 4800, [W] 5320, 5880, 6110, 6750 |
| 1130-1330 | [W] 9845, [S] 17550 |
| 1130-1601 | 9745, 9775, 12045 |
| 1130-1730 | 9830 |
| 1200-1300 | [W] 6175, [S] 11720 |
| 1200-1400 | [W] 9455, 9820, 11630 |
| 1200-1600 | 11925 |
| 1200-1601 | 7335, 9525, [S] 9810, 9890 |
| 1200-1730 | 5030, 7290, 9460, 9655, 9720, 12030 |
| 1230-1400 | [W] 7345, [S] 15550 |
| 1230-1601 | [W] 5010, 7350, [S] 15500 |
| 1230-1730 | [S] 11860, 11970 |
| 1230-1804 | [W] 6790, 9170, [S] 11000 |
| 1300-1400 | [W] 7120, [W] 9890, [S] 11660, [S] 13700 |
| 1300-1601 | 4850, 7115, 7140, 9445, 11710 |
| 1300-1730 | 4460, 6095, 6175 |
| 1330-1601 | [W] 3290, [S] 11800 |
| 1330-1730 | 9845, 11990 |
| 1400-1600 | 5985, 7120 |
| 1400-1601 | [W] 5163, 9755, 11730 |
| 1400-1730 | 5955, 7130, 7345 |
| 1500-1730 | 9900 |
| 2000-2200 | 4460, 5955, 7290, 7345 |
| 2000-2230 | 5030, [W] 5320, 6095, 6125 |
| 2000-2300 | 6110, 6175, 7130, 7550, 9845, 9900, 11885 |
| 2000-2330 | 11990 |
| 2000-2400 | 4800, 5880, 6030, 6750, 7230, 7935, 9455, 9655, 9710, 9720, 9820, 9830, 9890, 11630, [S] 11860, 11925, 12030 |
| 2100-2300 | 5010, 7120, 9745, 9755, 11710 |
| 2100-2330 | [W] 3290, 5985, 7140, 9445, [S] 9810, [W] 11730, [S] 11800, [S] 15540 |
| 2100-2400 | 3985, 7115, 7200, 7335, 7350, 9525, 9625, 9775, 9880, 12045, 12055 |
| 2200-2300 | [W] 4850, [S] 11670 |
| 2200-2400 | [W] 4460, [W] 5955, [W] 6790, [W] 7290, [S] 9645, 9690, [S] 11000, [S] 11825, [S] 17890 |
| 2230-2300 | [S] 15550 |
| 2230-2330 | [W] 5030, [W] 6125, [S] 9675, 9800 |
| 2230-2400 | 9480, [W] 15480 |
| 2300-2400 | [W] 5010, [W] 6110, [W] 9745, [W] 9845, 11660, 11670, [W] 11710, 11720, [S] 11960, 15285, 15300, [S] 15500, 15550, [S] 17550, [S] 17625 |
| 2330-2400 | 9675, 9800, 9810, 11610, 11800, [W] 11990, 13710, 15360, 15540, [S] 17605 |

## CHINA RADIO INTERNATIONAL
### Chinese

| | |
|---|---|
| 0200-0300 | *9580* (E North Am), *9690* (N America & C America), 15435 (S America) |
| 0300-0400 | *9720* (W North Am) |
| 0900-1000 | [W] 6165 & [S] 9550 (E Asia), 11700 & 11875 (Australasia), [S] 11975 & [W] 15110 (E Asia), [S] 15250 (SE Asia), 15440 (Australasia) |
| 0900-1100 | 7360, 15340/11685 & 17785 (SE Asia) |

**Jonathan Izard presents "From Our Own Correspondent" over the BBC World Service.**

BBC Audience Relations

| | |
|---|---|
| 1200-1300 | *9570* (E North Am) |
| 1200-1400 | 11875 (Australasia), 15260, 15340/11685 & 17785 (SE Asia) |
| 1300-1400 | 9440 (SE Asia) |
| 1500-1600 | ▥ 7180, ▥ 7265, ▤ 11760 & ▤ 11825 (S Asia) |
| 1730-1830 | ▥ 6135 & ▥ 7120 (Europe), ▥ 7160 (W Africa & C Africa), ▥ 7315 (N Africa), 9645 (W Africa & C Africa), ▤ 9685 (Mideast & N Africa), ▥ 9745 (Mideast), ▤ 11660 (Europe), ▤ 11760 (Mideast & N Africa), ▤ 11835 (N Africa), ▤ 13610 (Europe) |
| 1830-2230 | ▤ 11660 (Europe) |
| 2000-2100 | ▥ 6165 & ▥ 7135 (Mideast), ▥ 7225 (Europe), ▥ 7245 (Mideast), ▥ 7660 (E Europe), ▥ 9585 & 9685 (Mideast), ▥ 9720 & ▤ 9765 (E Europe), ▤ 11610 & ▤ 11650 (Mideast & N Africa), ▤ 11870 (E Europe), ▤ 13775 (Europe), ▤ 13790 (Mideast) |
| 2230-2300 | ▥ 7150 & ▤ 15110 (E Asia), *15500* (E Africa) |
| 2230-2330 | 6140, 9460, ▥ 9515/9550, 11945, 15100, 15260 & 15400 (SE Asia) |
| 2230-2400 | *11975* (N Africa) |
| 2300-2400 | *7170* (W Africa) |
| **Cantonese** | |
| 1000-1100 | 15440 (Australasia), 17755 (SE Asia) |
| 1000-1200 | 11875 (Australasia) |
| 1100-1200 | 9590, 15340/11685 & 17785 (SE Asia) |
| 1700-1800 | ▥ 7220 (E Africa & S Africa), 9770 & ▤ 15580 (E Africa) |
| 1900-2000 | ▥ 7255 (Europe), ▥ 9720 & ▤ 9765 (E Europe), ▤ 11895 (Europe) |
| 2330-2400 | 6140, 9460, ▥ 9515/9550, 11945, 15100, 15260 & 15400 (SE Asia) |

## CHINA (TAIWAN)

### RADIO TAIPEI INTERNATIONAL
**Amoy**

| | |
|---|---|
| 0000-0100 | *15440* (W North Am & C America) |
| 0000-0200 | 11875 (SE Asia) |
| 0600-0700 | *9680* (W North Am) |

| | |
|---|---|
| 0600-0800 | 15580 (SE Asia) |
| 0800-0900 | 11715 (SE Asia) |
| 1000-1100 | 11605 (E Asia), 15465 (SE Asia) |
| 1300-1400 | 11635 & 15465 (SE Asia) |
| 2100-2200 | 15130 (Australasia) |
| **Chinese** | |
| 0100-0200 | ▥ *11825* & ▤ *17845* (S America) |
| 0400-0500 | *5950* (N America & C America), *9680* (W North Am), 15270 & 15320 (SE Asia) |
| 0900-1000 | 9610 (Australasia), 11520 (SE Asia), 11605 (E Asia), 11715, 11735 & 15525 (SE Asia) |
| 1200-1300 | 11605 (E Asia), 15465 (SE Asia) |
| 1900-2000 | ▥ *9355*, 9955, ▤ *15600*, ▤ *17750* & ▥ *17760* (Europe) |
| **Cantonese** | |
| 0100-0200 | *5950* (E North Am), *7520* (Europe), 15290 (SE Asia), *15440* (W North Am & C America) |
| 0200-0300 | 15610 (SE Asia) |
| 0300-0400 | *11740* (C America) |
| 0500-0600 | *5950* (N America & C America), *9680* (W North Am), 15320 & 15580 (SE Asia) |
| 1000-1100 | 9610 (Australasia), 11635, 11715 & 15525 (SE Asia) |
| 1000-1200 | 15270 (SE Asia) |
| 1200-1400 | 6105 & 6145 (E Asia), 11915 (SE Asia) |

## COLOMBIA—Spanish

### RADIO NACIONAL
| | |
|---|---|
| 1700-0445 | 9635 |

## CROATIA—Croatian

### CROATIAN RADIO—(Europe)
| | |
|---|---|
| 0500-1000 | ▭ 7365 |
| 0500-1815 | ▭ 9830 |
| 0500-2400 | ▭ 6165 |
| 0900-1000 | ▤ 13830 |
| 1000-2200 | 13830 |
| 2200-2300 | ▤ 13830 |

### VOICE OF CROATIA
| | |
|---|---|
| 0018-0142 | ▭ *9925* (S America) |
| 0218-0342 | ▭ *9885/9925* (E North Am) |
| 0418-0542 | ▭ *9925* (W North Am) |
| 0418-0542 | ▥ *9885/7285* (W North Am) |
| 0618-0742 | ▭ *9470/11665* (Australasia) |
| 0818-0942 | ▭ *13820* (Australasia) |

## CUBA—Spanish

### RADIO HABANA CUBA
| | |
|---|---|
| 0000-0100 | 6000 (E North Am), 9820 (N America) |
| 0000-0500 | 5965 (C America & W North Am), 9505 (C America), 9600 (S America), 11760 (Americas), 15230 (S America) |
| 0200-0500 | 9550 (E North Am) |
| 1100-1300 | 11705 (S America) |
| 1100-1400 | 6000 (C America) |
| 1100-1500 | 11760 (C America) |
| 1200-1400 | 9550 (C America & W North Am), 15250 (S America) |
| 1400-1830 | Su 6140 & Su 9505 (C America), Su 9820 (N America), Su 11705 & Su 11875 (S America) |
| 2100-2300 | 11705 USB (E North Am & Europe), 11760 & 13680 (Europe & N Africa) |
| 2100-2400 | 15230 (S America) |
| 2300-2400 | 6000 (E North Am) |

### RADIO REBELDE
| | |
|---|---|
| 24 Hr | 5025 |
| 1000-1300 | 9600 (C America) |
| 1100-1300 | 6140 (C America) |

## CZECH REPUBLIC—Czech

### RADIO PRAGUE
| | |
|---|---|
| 0030-0100 | W 7345 (N America), W 9440 (S America) |
| 0130-0200 | S 6200 (N America & C America), S 7345 (S America) |
| 0230-0300 | W 6200 (N America & C America), S 7345 (N America), W 7345 (S America), S 9870 (W North Am & C America) |
| 0330-0400 | W 7345 (N America), W 9435 (W North Am & C America) |
| 0830-0900 | S 11600 (W Europe), S 21745 (E Africa & Mideast) |
| 0930-1000 | W 15255 (W Europe), S 21745 (S Asia & W Africa), W 21745 (E Africa & Mideast) |
| 1030-1100 | W 21745 (S Asia & W Africa) |
| 1100-1130 | S 11615 (N Europe), S 21745 (S Asia) |
| 1200-1230 | W 11640 (N Europe), W 21745 (S Asia, SE Asia & Australasia) |
| 1330-1400 | ▭ 6055 (Europe), 7345 (W Europe) |
| 1330-1400 | S 13580 (N Europe), S 21745/21735 (S Asia) |
| 1430-1500 | W 21745 (N America & E Africa) |
| 1530-1600 | S 21745 (E Africa) |
| 1630-1700 | ▭ 5930 (W Europe) |
| 1630-1700 | W 17485 (W Africa & C Africa) |
| 1730-1800 | S 5930 (E Europe, SE Asia & Australasia), S 21745 (C Africa) |
| 1830-1900 | W 5930 (W Europe), W 7315 (E Europe, Asia & Australasia) |
| 1930-2000 | S 11600 (SE Asia & Australasia) |
| 2030-2100 | ▭ 5930 (W Europe) |
| 2030-2100 | W 9430 (SE Asia & Australasia) |
| 2100-2130 | S 11600 (SE Asia & Australasia), S 15545 (W Africa) |
| 2200-2230 | W 5930 (W Europe), W 9435 (W Europe & S America) |
| 2330-2400 | S 11615 (Americas), S 13580 (S America) |

## DENMARK—Danish

### RADIO DANMARK
| | |
|---|---|
| 0030-0055 | W 7470 (E North Am & C America), W 7490 (SE Asia), S 9930 (SE Asia & Australasia), S 9985 (E North Am & C America), S 11635 (N America) |
| 0130-0155 | W 7470 (E North Am & C America), W 7490 (S Asia), W 9945 (N America), S 9975 (S Asia), S 9985 (E North Am & C America), S 11635 (N America) |
| 0230-0255 | W 7470 (E North Am & C America), W 7490 (S Asia), W 9590 (N America), S 9975 (S Asia) |

**Prague is home to RFE-RL, as well as Radio Prague.**

Corbis

0330-0355   **W** 7470 (W North Am), **S** 7490 (E Europe & Mideast), **W** 7490 & **W** 9945 (Mideast & E Africa), **S** 9960 (W North Am), **S** 13800 (Mideast & E Africa)

0430-0455   **S** 7465 (Europe), **W** 7470 (W North Am), **S** 7490 (E Europe & Mideast), **W** 7490 (Mideast), **S** 9475 (W North Am), **W** 9945 & **S** 13800 (Mideast & E Africa)

0530-0555   **S** 7465 (Europe), **W** 7465 (E Europe & Mideast), **W** 7490 (E Europe & W Asia), **S** 11615 (Mideast), **S** 13800 (Africa)

0630-0655   **W** 5945 & 7180 (Europe), **S** 9590 (W Africa & Australasia), **W** 9590 (W Africa), **S** 13800 (Africa & Australasia), **W** 13800 (Africa)

0730-0755   7180 & 9590 (Europe), **S** 13800 (W Africa & Australasia)

0830-0855   **S** 11640 (Mideast), 13800 (S America & Australasia), **W** 15705 (E Asia & Australasia)

0930-0955   13800 (S America & Australasia), **W** 15705 & **S** 17505 (E Asia & Australasia), **W** 18950 (Mideast & S Asia)

1030-1055   13800 (Europe), **S** 21745 & **W** 21765 (S America)

1130-1155   13800 (Europe), **S** 18950 (E North Am & C America), **W** 21765 (S America)

1230-1255   **W** 12070 (E Asia), **W** 13800 (Europe), **S** 15705 (E Asia), **S** 15735 (N America), **W** 15735 & **S** 18920 (SE Asia & Australasia), 18950 (E North Am & C America)

1330-1355   9590 (Europe), **S** 15735 (N America), **S** 17525 (E Asia), **S** 18920 (SE Asia & Australasia)

1430-1455   **W** 13800 (Mideast & S Asia), **S** 15735 (S Asia), **S** 17525 (W North Am), **W** 17555 (N America)

1530-1555   **S** 13800 (Mideast & S Asia), **S** 15735 (S Asia), **W** 15735 (Mideast), **S** 17525 (W North Am)

1630-1655   **S** 9595 (Europe), **S** 13800 (S Asia), **W** 13800 & **S** 15735 (Mideast & E Africa), **S** 17525 (E North Am & C America), **W** 18950 (W North Am)

1730-1755   7490 (Europe), **W** 9980 (E Europe & W Asia), **S** 13800 (Mideast), **W** 13800 & **S** 15705 (Mideast & E Africa), **S** 17505 (N America), **W** 18950 (E North Am & C America)

1830-1855   7490 (Europe), **W** 9980 & **S** 11615 (Australasia), 13800 (Africa), **W** 15705 (N America)

1930-1955   7490 (Europe), **W** 9980 (Africa), **S** 11615 (Australasia), **S** 13800 (Africa), **W** 13800 & **S** 17505 (W North Am)

2030-2055   7490 (Europe), **S** 9510 & **W** 9980 (Australasia)

2130-2155   **W** 7490 (W Europe), 9510 (Australasia)

2230-2255   **W** 7470 (E Asia), **W** 7530 & **S** 9925 (S America), **S** 11620 (E Asia)

2330-2355   **W** 7470 (E North Am & C America), **W** 7490 (SE Asia & Australasia), **W** 7530 (S America), **S** 9920 (SE Asia & Australasia), **W** 9920 (E Asia), **S** 9945 (E North Am & C America), **S** 13710 (E Asia)

2330-2400   **S** 9985 (S America)

## EGYPT—Arabic

### EGYPTIAN RADIO

0000-0030  **▣** 9700 (N Africa), 11665 (C Africa & E Africa), 15285 (Mideast)

0150-2400  **▣** 12050 (Europe & E North Am)

0300-0600  **▣** 9855 (N Africa & Mideast)

0300-2400  **▣** 15285 (Mideast)

0350-0700  **▣** 9620 & 9770 (N Africa)

0350-1200  **▣** 9800 (Mideast)

0600-1400  **▣** 11720 (N Africa & Mideast)

0700-1100  **▣** 15115 (W Africa)

0700-1500  **▣** 11785 (N Africa)

1100-2400  **▣** 11540 (N Africa & Mideast)

1300-1800  **▣** 17675 (N Africa)

1800-2400  **▣** 9700 (N Africa)

1900-2400  **▣** 11665 (C Africa & E Africa)

### RADIO CAIRO

0000-0045  15590 (C America & S America), 17770 (S America)

0030-0430  9900 (E North Am)

1015-1215  17745 (Mideast & W Asia)

1100-1130  17800 (E Africa & S Africa)

1300-1600  15220 (C Africa)

In Ethiopia much of the population is beyond the reach of FM and television—sometimes even electricity—and the soil limits mediumwave AM travel during the day. World band portables thus are an essential and popular lifeline. LWF

| 2000-2200 | 11990 (Australasia) |
| 2330-2400 | 15590 (C America & S America), 17770 (S America) |

## FRANCE—French

### RADIO FRANCE INTERNATIONALE

| 0000-0030 | 🆆 *15440* & 🆂 *17710* (SE Asia) |
| 0000-0100 | 🆆 9805 & 🆂 11660 (S Asia & SE Asia), 🆆 *12025* (SE Asia), *15200* (S America), 🆂 *15535* (SE Asia) |
| 0100-0200 | 🆆 *15440* & 🆂 *17710* (S Asia) |
| 0130-0200 | 🆆 9790 (C America), 🆆 9800 (S America), *9800* & *11665* (C America), 🆂 11995 (S America) |
| 0200-0230 | *15200* (S America) |
| 0300-0400 | 🆆 5915 (Mideast & E Africa), 🆂 *5925* (C Africa & E Africa), 🆆 *5925* (S Africa), 🆆 5945 (E Europe & Mideast), 9550 (Mideast), 🆂 9825, 🆂 11700, 11995 & 🆂 13610 (E Africa) |
| 0300-0500 | 🆆 7315 (Mideast) |
| 0300-0600 | 9790 (Africa), 🆆 9845 (E Africa) |
| 0300-0700 | 7135 (Africa) |
| 0330-0500 | 🆂 9745 (E Europe) |
| 0400-0430 | 🆂 11995 (E Africa) |
| 0400-0445 | 🆂 7280 (E Europe) |
| 0400-0500 | 🆆 3965 (N Africa), *4890* (C Africa), 🆂 5925 (N Africa), 🆆 *9805* (C Africa), *11850* (Mideast) |
| 0400-0600 ▱ | 11685 (Mideast) |
| 0400-0600 | 🆆 9550 (Mideast), 11700 (C Africa & S Africa), 🆂 15135 (E Africa), 🆂 15605 (Mideast & W Asia) |
| 0430-0445 | 🆆 5990 (E Europe) |
| 0430-0500 ▱ | 7280 (E Europe) |
| 0430-0500 | 🆆 *11910*, 11995, 13610 (Irr) & 🆂 15155 (E Africa) |
| 0430-0600 ▱ | 6045 (E Europe) |
| 0500-0600 | *6175* (C Africa), 🆆 11995 (E Africa), 🆂 15300 (C Africa & S Africa), *15605* (N Africa & Mideast) |
| 0500-0700 | 🆆 11700 (C Africa & S Africa), 🆂 17620 (E Africa) |
| 0530-0600 | 🆆 13610 (E Africa), 🆆 *15155* (E Africa & S Africa), 🆂 17800 (E Africa) |
| 0600-0700 | 🆆 5925 (N Africa), 🆆 6175 (E Europe), 9790 (N Africa & W Africa), 🆂 *9790* (C Africa), 🆆 15135 (Mideast), 15300 (C Africa & S Africa), *15315* (Irr) (W Africa), 🆂 17650 (Mideast), 🆂 17850 (C Africa & S Africa) |

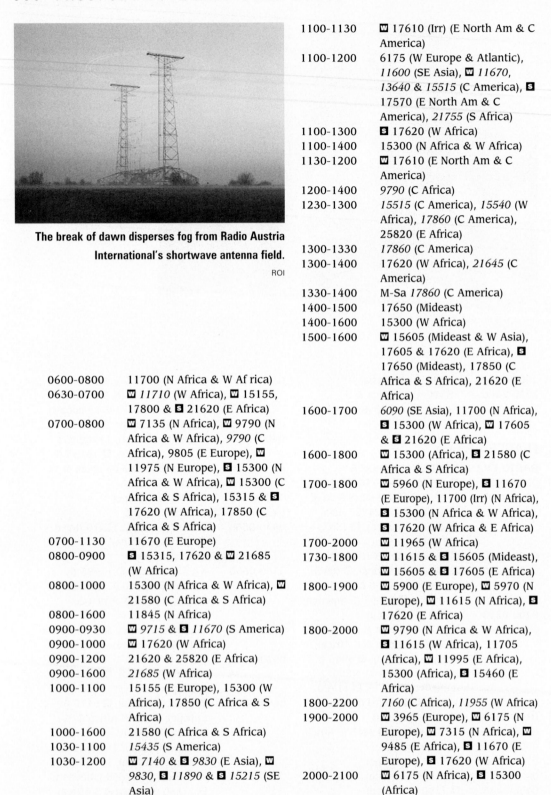

**The break of dawn disperses fog from Radio Austria International's shortwave antenna field.**

ROI

| Time | Frequencies |
|---|---|
| 0600-0800 | 11700 (N Africa & W Af rica) |
| 0630-0700 | 🔳 11710 (W Africa), 🔳 15155, 17800 & 🔳 21620 (E Africa) |
| 0700-0800 | 🔳 7135 (N Africa), 🔳 9790 (N Africa & W Africa), 9790 (C Africa), 9805 (E Europe), 🔳 11975 (N Europe), 🔳 15300 (N Africa & W Africa), 🔳 15300 (C Africa & S Africa), 15315 & 🔳 17620 (W Africa), 17850 (C Africa & S Africa) |
| 0700-1130 | 11670 (E Europe) |
| 0800-0900 | 🔳 15315, 17620 & 🔳 21685 (W Africa) |
| 0800-1000 | 15300 (N Africa & W Africa), 🔳 21580 (C Africa & S Africa) |
| 0800-1600 | 11845 (N Africa) |
| 0900-0930 | 🔳 9715 & 🔳 11670 (S America) |
| 0900-1000 | 🔳 17620 (W Africa) |
| 0900-1200 | 21620 & 25820 (E Africa) |
| 0900-1600 | 21685 (W Africa) |
| 1000-1100 | 15155 (E Europe), 15300 (W Africa), 17850 (C Africa & S Africa) |
| 1000-1600 | 21580 (C Africa & S Africa) |
| 1030-1100 | 15435 (S America) |
| 1030-1200 | 🔳 7140 & 🔳 9830 (E Asia), 🔳 9830, 🔳 11890 & 🔳 15215 (SE Asia) |
| 1100-1130 | 🔳 17610 (Irr) (E North Am & C America) |
| 1100-1200 | 6175 (W Europe & Atlantic), 11600 (SE Asia), 🔳 11670, 13640 & 15515 (C America), 🔳 17570 (E North Am & C America), 21755 (S Africa) |
| 1100-1300 | 🔳 17620 (W Africa) |
| 1100-1400 | 15300 (N Africa & W Africa) |
| 1130-1200 | 🔳 17610 (E North Am & C America) |
| 1200-1400 | 9790 (C Africa) |
| 1230-1300 | 15515 (C America), 15540 (W Africa), 17860 (C America), 25820 (E Africa) |
| 1300-1330 | 17860 (C America) |
| 1300-1400 | 17620 (W Africa), 21645 (C America) |
| 1330-1400 | M-Sa 17860 (C America) |
| 1400-1500 | 17650 (Mideast) |
| 1400-1600 | 15300 (W Africa) |
| 1500-1600 | 🔳 15605 (Mideast & W Asia), 17605 & 17620 (E Africa), 🔳 17650 (Mideast), 17850 (C Africa & S Africa), 21620 (E Africa) |
| 1600-1700 | 6090 (SE Asia), 11700 (N Africa), 🔳 15300 (W Africa), 🔳 17605 & 🔳 21620 (E Africa) |
| 1600-1800 | 🔳 15300 (Africa), 🔳 21580 (C Africa & S Africa) |
| 1700-1800 | 🔳 5960 (N Europe), 🔳 11670 (E Europe), 11700 (Irr) (N Africa), 🔳 15300 (N Africa & W Africa), 🔳 17620 (W Africa & E Africa) |
| 1700-2000 | 🔳 11965 (W Africa) |
| 1730-1800 | 🔳 11615 & 🔳 15605 (Mideast), 🔳 15605 & 🔳 17605 (E Africa) |
| 1800-1900 | 🔳 5900 (E Europe), 🔳 5970 (N Europe), 🔳 11615 (N Africa), 🔳 17620 (E Africa) |
| 1800-2000 | 🔳 9790 (N Africa & W Africa), 🔳 11615 (W Africa), 11705 (Africa), 🔳 11995 (E Africa), 15300 (Africa), 🔳 15460 (E Africa) |
| 1800-2200 | 7160 (C Africa), 11955 (W Africa) |
| 1900-2000 | 🔳 3965 (Europe), 🔳 6175 (N Europe), 🔳 7315 (N Africa), 🔳 9485 (E Africa), 🔳 11670 (E Europe), 🔳 17620 (W Africa) |
| 2000-2100 | 🔳 6175 (N Africa), 🔳 15300 (Africa) |

| | |
|---|---|
| 2000-2200 | [W] 5960 (S Europe), 7315 (N Africa), 9485 (E Africa), 9790 (N Africa & W Africa), [W] 9790 (C Africa & S Africa), 11995 (E Africa) |
| 2100-2200 | [W] 3965 (N Africa), [S] 5915 (E Europe), 6175 (N Africa), [S] 9805 (E Europe), [S] 15300 (C Africa & S Africa) |
| 2200-2300 | [W] 9790 (W Africa) |
| 2230-2300 | *17620 (S America)* |
| 2300-2400 | [W] 9805 & [S] 11660 (S Asia & SE Asia), [W] *12025 (SE Asia)*, [W] *12075 (E Asia)*, [W] *15440*, [S] *15535*, [S] *15595* & [S] *17710* (SE Asia) |
| 2330-2400 | [W] 9790 (C America), [W] 9800 (S America), [S] 11670 (C America), [S] 11995, *15200* & *17620 (S America)* |

## FRENCH GUIANA—French

**RFO-GUYANE**

| | |
|---|---|
| 24 Hr | 5055 |

## GABON—French

**AFRIQUE NUMERO UN**

| | |
|---|---|
| 0500-2300 | 9580 (C Africa) |
| 0700-1600 | 17630 (W Africa) |
| 1600-1900 | 15475 (W Africa & E North Am) |

## GERMANY—German

**BAYERISCHER RUNDFUNK**

| | |
|---|---|
| 24 Hr | 6085 |

**DEUTSCHE WELLE**

| | |
|---|---|
| 0000-0200 | 6075 (Europe), [W] 6100 (E North Am), [S] 7130 (N Africa & S America), 9545 (S America), [W] *11795 (SE Asia)*, [W] *12000 (S America)*, [W] *12045 (E North Am)*, [W] *13750 (SE Asia)*, [S] 13780 (E North Am), [S] *13780 (S America)*, [W] *13780 (C America)*, [S] 15275 (C America & S America), [S] *15410 (E North Am & S America)*, [W] *15410 (S America)*, [S] *17860* & [S] *17875 (SE Asia)* |
| 0000-0355 | [S] *11785 (C America)* |
| 0000-0400 | [W] 7130 (S Europe & S America) |
| 0000-0600 | 3995 (Europe) |
| 0200-0300 | [S] 9735 (N America) |
| 0200-0400 | [W] 6075 (Mideast & W Asia), [W] 6100 (C America), [W] 6145 (N America & C America), [W] *9870 (W Africa, C America & S America)*, [S] 11795 (E Africa), *15205 (S Asia)* |
| 0200-0600 | 6075 (Europe & N America), [S] 6100 (E North Am & C America) |
| 0300-0600 | [S] 9735 (N Europe & N America) |
| 0400-0555 | [S] 13780 (Africa) |
| 0400-0600 | [W] 6075 (E Europe & W Asia), [W] *6100 (W North Am)*, [W] 6145 (N America & C America), [W] 7225 (S Europe), [W] 9545 (Mideast & W Asia), [S] *9640 (N America & C America)*, [S] *9700 (S Africa)*, [W] 9735 (Mideast & Africa), [W] *11805 (S Africa)*, [S] 17810 (Africa) |
| 0500-0600 | [S] 9735 (Australasia) |
| 0600-0800 | [W] 3995 & 6075 (Europe), 9735 & *11985 (Australasia)*, [S] 21600 (C Africa & S Africa) |
| 0600-1000 | *9690* & 11795 (Australasia), 11865 (N Europe & E Europe), [S] 17845 (S Asia & SE Asia), *21640 (SE Asia & Australasia)*, [W] 21840 (Africa) |
| 0600-1800 | 13780 (Mideast) |
| 0600-2000 | 9545 (S Europe) |
| 0800-1000 | [S] 9735 (S Europe & N Africa), [W] 9735 (Australasia) |
| 0800-1400 | [W] 25740 (S Asia & SE Asia) |
| 0800-1800 | 6075 (Europe) |
| 0900-1200 | *15135 (E Africa)* |
| 1000-1400 | [W] *5905*, [W] *7400* & [S] *9900 (E Asia)*, [S] *13720 (S Asia & SE Asia)*, [W] *13810 (E Asia & SE Asia)*, [S] 17560 (Atlantic & W Africa), [W] 17845 (S Asia & SE Asia), [S] *17845 (SE Asia & Australasia)*, [S] *21640 (E Asia & SE Asia)*, [S] 21680 (E Europe & Asia), [S] 21790 (S Asia & SE Asia), [W] *21790 (E Asia & SE Asia)*, 21840 (Mideast) |
| 1100-1300 | [S] *17650 (W Europe)* |
| 1200-1400 | *15135 (S Africa)*, [W] *17570 (W Europe)*, [W] 17650 (E Europe & W Asia), *17730 (E North Am)*, [S] *17730* & [W] *17765 (S America)* |

| | |
|---|---|
| 1200-1600 | ◻ *7440* & ◻ *15480* (W Asia & C Asia) |
| 1400-1600 | 15275 (S Asia & SE Asia), ◻ 15275 (Atlantic & W Africa), ◻ 15275 (S Europe & Mideast) |
| 1400-1700 | ◻ *15515* (W North Am), *17730* (N America), *17765* (S America)*, ◻ *17875* (N America & C America) |
| 1400-1800 | *9655* (S Asia), ◻ *13720* (Mideast & W Asia), ◻ 13780 (S Asia & SE Asia), ◻ 17845 (Mideast), ◻ 17845 (S Asia & SE Asia), ◻ *21560* (Mideast) |
| 1600-1800 | ◻ 11795 & ◻ 15275 (S Asia) |
| 1800-2000 | ◻ 3995 (Europe), ◻ 13780 (Mideast) |
| 1800-2155 | ◻ *11765* (SE Asia & Australasia) |
| 1800-2200 | 6075 (Europe & E Africa), ◻ 7185 & ◻ 9735 (Africa), ◻ *9735* (S Africa), ◻ *11765* (Australasia), ◻ 11795 (E Africa & S Africa), ◻ *11795* (S Africa), ◻ *12045* (Australasia), ◻ 15275 (W Africa & S America), *17860* (W Africa & C America) |
| 2000-2200 | 9545 (Atlantic & S America), *17810* (N America & S America) |
| 2000-2400 | 3995 (Europe) |
| 2200-2400 | ◻ *5925* (E Asia), 6075 (Europe), 9545 (S America), ◻ *9610* (E Asia & SE Asia), ◻ 9715 (S Asia & SE Asia), ◻ *11785* (C America), ◻ *11795* (E Asia), ◻ *11795* & ◻ 11895 (SE Asia), ◻ *12000* (S America), ◻ *12045* (E North Am), ◻ *13690* (S Asia & SE Asia), ◻ 13780 (E North Am), ◻ *13780* (S America), ◻ *13780* (C America), ◻ *15250* (E Asia & SE Asia), ◻ *15250* (E Asia), ◻ *15275* (C America & S America), ◻ *15410* (E North Am & S America), ◻ *15410* (S America), *17860* (C America) |
| **DEUTSCHLANDFUNK**—(Europe) | |
| 24 Hr | 6190 |
| **DEUTSCHLANDRADIO**—(Europe) | |
| 24 Hr | 6005 |
| **SUDWESTRUNDFUNK**—(Europe) | |
| 24 Hr | 7265 |
| 0455-2305 | ◻ 6030 |

## HUNGARY—Hungarian

### RADIO BUDAPEST

| | |
|---|---|
| 0000-0100 | ◻ M 9580 (S America), ◻ 9800 (N America), ◻ M 11990 (S America) |
| 0100-0200 | ◻ 9835 (N America) |
| 0130-0230 | ◻ 9570 (N America) |
| 0230-0330 | ◻ 9835 (N America) |
| 0600-1300 | ◻ 6025 (Europe) |
| 1200-1300 | ◻ 21560 (Australasia) |
| 1300-1400 | ◻ M-Sa 6025 (Europe) |
| 1400-1500 | ◻ 6025 (Europe) |
| 1500-1700 | ◻ M-Sa 6025 (Europe) |
| 1900-2000 | ◻ 3975 & 6025 (Europe) |
| 1900-2000 | ◻ 6130 (Australasia) |
| 2000-2100 | ◻ 17690 (N America) |
| 2100-2200 | ◻ 15195 (Australasia) |
| 2200-2300 | ◻ 9825 (N America), ◻ 11755 & ◻ 15455 (S America) |
| 2300-2400 | ◻ 6025 (Europe) |
| 2300-2400 | ◻ 9580, ◻ Su 11755, ◻ 11990 & ◻ Su 15455 (S America) |

## INDIA—Hindi

### ALL INDIA RADIO

| | |
|---|---|
| 0000-0043 | 9425 (S Asia) |
| 0215-0300 | 15075 (Mideast) |
| 0315-0415 | 11835 & 13695 (Mideast), 15075 (Mideast & E Africa), 15185, 17630 & 17715 (E Africa) |
| 0430-0530 | 15075, 15185, 17630 & 17715 (E Africa) |
| 1350-2400 | 9425 (S Asia) |
| 1615-1730 | 7410 (Mideast & W Asia), 9950 (E Africa), 11585 (Mideast), 12025 (Mideast & W Asia), 13605 (E Africa), 13770 (Mideast), 15075 & 17670 (E Africa) |
| 1945-2045 | 7410, 9950 & 11620 (Europe) |
| 2300-2400 | 9910, 11740 & 13795 (SE Asia) |

## IRAN—Persian

### VOICE OF THE ISLAMIC REPUBLIC

| | |
|---|---|
| 0000-0630 | 15084 (Europe & C America) |
| 0130-0300 | 7275 (W Asia & S Asia) |
| 0300-0400 | ◻ 7275 (W Asia & S Asia) |
| 0730-1200 | 15084 (Europe & C America), ◻ 15215 & ◻ 15365 (W Asia & S Asia) |
| 0930-1030 | ◻ 15115 (E Asia) |

| | |
|---|---|
| 0930-1030 | 17785 (Europe) |
| 0930-1100 | 13695 (W Asia) |
| 1300-2400 | 15084 (Europe & C America) |
| 1630-1730 | 9765 (Europe) |
| 1930-2030 | 7105 (W Europe), 9775 (Australasia) |

## ISRAEL
### KOL ISRAEL
**Arabic**

| | |
|---|---|
| 0400-2215 ▣ | 5915 (Mideast & N Africa), 12150 (Mideast & W Asia) |

**Hebrew**

| | |
|---|---|
| 0000-0330 | 11585 (W Europe & E North Am) |
| 0000-0400 | ▣ 13850 (W Europe & E North Am) |
| 0000-0500 | ▣ 9310 & ▣ 15760 (W Europe & E North Am) |
| 0000-0600 | ▣ 7545 (W Europe & N America) |
| 0330-0500 | ▣ 11590 (W Europe & E North Am) |
| 0330-0600 | ▣ 11585 (W Europe & E North Am) |
| 0400-0600 | ▣ 17535 (W Europe & E North Am) |
| 0500-1800 | 15760 (W Europe & E North Am) |
| 0600-1900 | 17535 (W Europe & E North Am) |
| 1600-1700 | ▣ 11585 (W Europe & E North Am) |
| 1700-2400 | 11585 (W Europe & E North Am) |
| 1800-2400 | ▣ 9310 & ▣ 15760 (W Europe & E North Am) |
| 1900-2300 | ▣ 9390 (W Europe & E North Am) |
| 1900-2400 | ▣ 17535 (W Europe & E North Am) |
| 2100-2215 ▣ | 15640 (S America) |
| 2300-2400 | ▣ 7545 (W Europe & N America) |

**Yiddish**

| | |
|---|---|
| 1100-1130 | ▣ 15655 (E Europe) |
| 1200-1230 | ▣ 15615 (E Europe) |
| 1600-1625 | ▣ 11605 & ▣ 15650 (E Europe) |
| 1700-1725 ▣ | 9435 (E Europe) |
| 1700-1725 | ▣ 11605 & ▣ 15640 (E Europe) |
| 1800-1825 ▣ | 9435 (E Europe) |

## ITALY—Italian
### RAI INTERNATIONAL

| | |
|---|---|
| 0000-0055 | 9675 (N America), 9840 & 11755 (S America), 11800 (N America & C America) |
| 0130-0230 | 6110 (S America), 11765 (C America) |

| | |
|---|---|
| 0130-0315 | 9675 (N America), 9840 & 11755 (S America), 11800 (E North Am & C America) |
| 0435-0445 | ▣ 5965, ▣ 5975 & 7235 (S Europe & N Africa) |
| 0455-0530 | 15250 & 17780 (E Africa) |
| 0630-1300 | 9670 (Europe & N Africa), 11800 (E Europe), 17710 & 21520 (E Africa) |
| 1000-1100 | 11920 (Australasia) |
| 1350-1730 ▣ | Su 9670 (N Europe), Su/Holidays 17780 (N America), Su/Holidays 21520 (E Africa), Su/Holidays 21535 (S America), Su/Holidays 21710 (C Africa & S Africa) |
| 1400-1430 | M-Sa 17780 (N America), M-Sa 21520 (E North Am) |
| 1500-1525 | M-Sa 9670 (S Europe & N Africa), 11880 (Mideast) |
| 1555-1625 | M-Sa 9670 (Europe), ▣ 11855 & ▣ 11880 (W Europe) |
| 1700-1800 | ▣ 9670, ▣ M-Sa 9670 & 11910 (S Europe & N Africa), ▣ 15230 (C Africa & S Africa), 15320 (S Africa), 15330 (E Africa), ▣ 17660 & ▣ 17720 (C Africa & S Africa) |
| 1830-1905 | ▣ 15250, 17780 & ▣ 21520 (N America) |
| 2240-2400 | 9675 (N America), 9840 & 11755 (S America), 11800 (N America & C America) |

### RAI-RADIOTELEVISIONE ITALIANA

| | |
|---|---|
| 0000-0003, 0012-0103, 0112-0203, 0212-0303, 0312-0403 & | |
| 0412-0500 ▣ | 6060 (Europe, Mideast & N Africa) |
| 0500-2300 ▣ | 6060 (Europe, N Africa & Mideast), 7175 (Europe, Mideast & N Africa), 9515 (Europe, N Africa & Mideast) |
| 2300-2400 ▣ | 6060 (Europe, Mideast & N Africa) |

## JAPAN—Japanese
### RADIO JAPAN/NHK

| | |
|---|---|
| 0200-0300 | 11860 (SE Asia), 17825 (C America), 17845 (E Asia), 21610 (Australasia) |

| | |
|---|---|
| 0200-0400 | *5960* (E North Am), 15325 (S Asia), 17560 (Mideast), 17685 (Australasia), 17835 (S America), 17875 (W North Am) |
| 0200-0500 | 15195 (E Asia), 17810 (SE Asia) |
| 0300-0400 | *9660* (S America), *11890* (S Asia), *11930* (Mideast & W Asia) |
| 0700-0800 | 6145, 6165 & 15195 (E Asia), 17870 (Pacific) |
| 0700-0900 | 17860 (SE Asia) |
| 0700-1000 | *11740* (SE Asia), *11920* & 21755 (Australasia) |
| 0800-1000 | *9530* (S America), 9825 (Pacific & S America), 9835 (W North Am), *11710* (Europe), 12030 (C America), 15590 (S Asia), *17650* (W Africa), *21550* (Mideast) |
| 0800-1500 | 9750 (E Asia) |
| 0900-1500 | 11815 (SE Asia) |
| 1300-1500 | *11705* (E North Am) |
| 1500-1700 | 9505 (W North Am), [W] 9535 & [S] 11895 (C America), *12045* (S Asia) |
| 1600-1700 | 9750 (E Asia), [W] 9845 & [S] 11730 (S Asia) |
| 1600-1800 | 7140 (Australasia), *21630* (C Africa) |
| 1600-1900 | 6035 (E Asia), 7200 (SE Asia) |
| 1700-1800 | *9750* (Europe), *21600* (S America) |
| 1700-1900 | *6175* (W Europe), 9835 (Pacific & S America), *11880* (Mideast) |
| 1800-1900 | *15355* (S Africa) |
| 1900-2000 | [W] 11665 (SE Asia) |
| 1900-2100 | 6165 (E Asia) |
| 1900-2400 | 11910 (E Asia), [S] 13680 (SE Asia) |
| 2000-2100 | [S] *6035* (Australasia), 11830 (Europe), [W] 11850, [W] *11920* & [S] 17860 (Australasia) |
| 2000-2200 | [W] 7225 & 11665 (SE Asia) |
| 2200-2300 | *6110* (E North Am), *6115* (W Europe), *11895* (C America), *15220* (S America), 17825 (W North Am) |
| 2200-2400 | [W] 11665 (SE Asia) |

**RADIO TAMPA**

| | |
|---|---|
| 0000-0800 | 3925, Sa/Su 9760 |
| 0000-0900 | Sa/Su 3945, Sa/Su 6115 |
| 0000-1400 | 6055, 9595 |
| 0800-1400 & 2030-2300 | 3925 |
| 2030-2400 | 6055, 9595 |
| 2300-2400 | 3925, F/Sa 3945, F/Sa 6115, F/Sa 9760 |

## KOREA (DPR)—Korean

**KOREAN CENTRAL BROADCASTING STATION**

| | |
|---|---|
| 0000-0630 | 6100 |
| 0000-0930 | 9665 |
| 0000-1800 | 2850, 11680 |
| 0900-0950 | 4405, 7140 & 9345 (E Asia), 11335/15245 (E Europe) |
| 1200-1250 | 3560 (E Asia), 9335 (C America), 9850/13650 (SE Asia), 11710 (C America), 11735 (SE Asia) |
| 1400-1450 | 3560 (E Asia), 9850/13650 & 11735 (SE Asia) |
| 1500-1800 | 6100 |
| 1700-1750 | 4405 (E Asia), 7505/13760 (Europe), 9335 (N America), 11335/15245 (Europe), 11710 (N America) |
| 2000-2050 | 3560 (E Asia), 6520/9640 (C Africa), 6575 & 9325 (E Europe), 9975 & 11735 (Mideast & Africa) |
| 2000-2400 | 2850, 6100, 9665, 11680 |
| 2300-2350 | 3560, 4405, 7140, 9345 & 9975 (E Asia), 11335/15245 (Europe), 11735 (E Asia) |

**RADIO PYONGYANG**

| | |
|---|---|
| 0000-0050 | 3560, 7140 & 9345 (E Asia) |
| 0000-0100 | 6195 (E Asia) |
| 0000-0925 | 6250 (E Asia) |
| 0700-0750 | 4405, 7140 & 9345 (E Asia) |
| 0900-0950 | 3560 & 6575/11735 (E Asia), 9325 (E Europe & Asia), 9975 (E Asia) |
| 1000-1050 & 1200-1250 | 4405, 7140 & 9345 (E Asia) |
| 1300-1350 | 6575 & 9325 (E Europe) |
| 1500-1900 & 2100-2400 | 6250 (E Asia) |

## KOREA (REPUBLIC)—Korean

**RADIO KOREA INTERNATIONAL**

| | |
|---|---|
| 0000-0100 | 15575 (N America) |
| 0100-0300 | 7275/11810 (E Asia) |
| 0300-0400 | 15575 (N America) |
| 0700-0800 | *9535* (Europe), 9570 (Asia & Australasia) |
| 0900-1000 | 7550 (Europe) |

| | |
|---|---|
| 0900-1100 | 5975 & 7275 (E Asia), 9570 (Asia & Australasia), 13670 (Europe) |
| 1100-1130 | *9650* (E North Am) |
| 1700-1900 | 5975 (E Asia), 7550 (Europe) |
| 1800-1900 | 7275 & 15575 (Europe) |
| 1900-2000 | 9870 (Mideast & Africa) |
| 2100-2200 | 5975 (E Asia) |
| 2300-2400 | 9640 (SE Asia) |

## KUWAIT—Arabic
**RADIO KUWAIT**

| | |
|---|---|
| 0000-0530 | 11675 (W North Am) |
| 0200-1305 | 6055 & 15495 (Mideast) |
| 0400-0740 | 15505 (E Europe & W Asia) |
| 0800-0925 | 15110 (S Asia & SE Asia) |
| 0930-1605 | 13620 (Europe & E North Am) |
| 1015-1740 | 15505 (W Africa & C Africa) |
| 1200-1505 | 17885 (SE Asia) |
| 1315-1600 | 15110 (S Asia & SE Asia) |
| 1315-2130 | 9880 (Mideast) |
| 1615-1800 | 11990 (Europe & E North Am) |
| 1745-2130 | 15505 (Europe & E North Am) |
| 1745-2400 | 15495 (W Africa & C Africa) |
| 1815-2400 | 9855 (Europe & E North Am) |
| 2145-2400 | 11675 (W North Am) |

## LIBYA—Arabic
**RADIO JAMAHIRIYA**

| | |
|---|---|
| 0000-0130, 0145-0350 & 1000-1030 | 15435 & 17725/15415 (Africa) |
| 1000-1400 | *21695* (E Africa) |
| 1045-1730 | 15435 & 17725/15415 (Africa) |
| 1100-1130 | *17695,* [W] *21640* & [S] *21810* (W Africa) |
| 1100-1500 | *21675* (C Africa) |
| 1500-1600 | *17695,* [W] *21640* & [S] *21810* (W Africa) |
| 1600-1800 | [W] *15220* (W Africa) |
| 1600-1900 | [W] *15615,* [S] *15660* & [S] *17695* (W Africa) |
| 1700-1800 | [W] *15660* (E Africa), *17880* (C Africa) |
| 1700-1900 | [S] *17635* (E Africa) |
| 1745-2030 | 15435 & 17725/15415 (Africa) |
| 1800-1900 | [W] *9415* (W Africa), [W] *15660* (C Africa) |
| 1800-2000 | [W] *11635* & [S] *15205* (C Africa) |
| 1800-2030 | [W] *11715* (E Africa) |
| 1900-2030 | [S] *15315* (E Africa) |
| 2000-2130 | *11635* (C Africa) |

| | |
|---|---|
| 2045-2330 & 2345-2400 | 15435 & 17725/15415 (Africa) |

## LITHUANIA—Lithuanian
**RADIO VILNIUS**

| | |
|---|---|
| 0000-0030 | [W] 7325 & [S] 11690 (E North Am) |
| 0900-0930 | 9710 (W Europe) |
| 2300-2330 | 9875 (E North Am) |

## MEXICO—Spanish
**RADIO EDUCACION**

| | |
|---|---|
| 0000-0830 [▭] | 6185 |
| 0830-0900 [▭] | Th-Tu 6185 |
| 0900-1200 [▭] | 6185 |

**RADIO MEXICO INTERNACIONAL**—(W North Am & C America)

| | |
|---|---|
| 0000-0400 [▭] | 9705 & 11770 |
| 0400-0430 [▭] | M 9705 & M 11770 |
| 0430-0500 [▭] | 9705 & 11770 |
| 0530-0600 [▭] | Tu/Th/Sa 9705 & Tu/Th/Sa 11770 |
| 1300-1500 & 1530-1600 [▭] | 9705 & 11770 |
| 1630-1700 [▭] | Su/M/W/F 9705 & Su/M/W/F 11770 |
| 1700-2200 [▭] | 9705 & 11770 |
| 2230-2300 [▭] | Su/M/W/F 9705 & Su/M/W/F 11770 |
| 2300-2330 [▭] | Sa/Su 9705 & Sa/Su 11770 |
| 2330-2400 [▭] | 9705 & 11770 |

## MOROCCO
**RADIO MEDI UN**—(Europe & N Africa)
**French & Arabic**

| | |
|---|---|
| 0500-0400 | 9575 |

**RTV MAROCAINE**
**Arabic**

| | |
|---|---|
| 0000-0500 | [W] 7185 (N Africa), [S] 11920 (N Africa & Mideast) |
| 0900-2200 | 15345 (N Africa & Mideast) |
| 1100-1500 | 15335 (Europe) |
| 2200-2400 | [S] 7135 & [W] 7160 (Europe) |

## NETHERLANDS—Dutch
**RADIO NEDERLAND**

| | |
|---|---|
| 0000-0025 | [S] *7280* (SE Asia), [W] *7280* & [S] *9590* (SE Asia & Australasia), [W] *9590,* [W] *15565,* [W] *17570* & [S] *17590* (SE Asia) |

0130-0225 [S] *6010* (E North Am), [W] *6020* & [S] 11730 (E North Am & C America), *15315* (S America)
0330-0425 *6165* (N America), *9590* (W North Am), [S] *9845* & [W] *9860* (E Africa), *15560* (Mideast)
0600-0700 ⇦ 7125 (Europe)
0600-0700 [W] 6015 (W Europe)
0600-1800 ⇦ 5955 (W Europe), 9895 (S Europe)
0700-0800 [W] *9625*, [S] *9820* & *11655* (Australasia)
0700-0900 ⇦ 11935 (S Europe)
0800-1100 [S] 13700 (S Europe)
0930-1015 M-Sa *6020* (C America)
1030-1125 *9720/9885* (Australasia), *13820* (E Asia), [S] *17575* & [W] *17580* (Australasia), *21480* (SE Asia)
1100-1300 13700 (S Europe)
1300-1700 [S] 13700 (S Europe)
1330-1425 [W] *7375*, [W] *9885* & [S] *9890* (E Asia & SE Asia), [S] *12065* (SE Asia & Australasia), [W] *12070* (S Asia), [S] *13695* (E Asia & SE Asia), [W] 13700 (Mideast & S Asia), *17580* & *21480* (S Asia)
1600-1800 [W] 13700 (N Africa & W Africa)
1630-1725 *6020* (S Africa), *11655* (E Africa)
1730-1825 [S] 9895 & [S] 13700 (S Europe & Mideast), [S] 15560 (S Africa & E Africa)
1830-1925 [W] 11695 (Mideast & E Africa), [W] 13765 & [W] *21590* (W Africa)
2030-2125 *5835* (Europe), [W] 6015 (S Europe), [S] *6015* (S Africa), [S] 6020 (W Europe & N Africa), [W] *6020* (S Africa), [S] *7120* (C Africa & W Africa), 9895 (S Europe & N Africa), [S] 11655 (W Africa), [W] *11655* (W Africa & C Africa), *15315* & *17605* (W Africa), *21590* (W Africa & C Africa)
2130-2225 [W] *6020* (C America), [S] 9895 (C America & S America), [W] 9895 (E North Am), [W] 11730 (C America & S America), [S] 13700 (S America), [W] *13700* & [S] *15155* (E North Am), *15315* (S America)
2330-2400 [S] *7280* (SE Asia), [W] *7280* & [S] *9590* (SE Asia & Australasia), [W] *9590*, [W] *15565*, [W] *17570* & [S] *17590* (SE Asia)

## OMAN—Arabic

**RADIO SULTANATE OF OMAN**

0000-0200 9760 (Europe & Mideast)
0200-0300 [W] 15355 (E Africa)
0200-0400 6085 (Mideast)
0400-0600 9515/9740 (Mideast), 17590 (E Africa)
0600-1000 17630 (Europe & Mideast)
0600-1400 13640 (Mideast)
1400-1800 [S] 13725 & 15375 (E Africa)
1500-1800 15140 (Europe & Mideast)
1800-2000 6190 & 15355 (E Africa)
2000-2200 6085 (E Africa), 13640 (Europe & Mideast)
2200-2400 13755 (Europe & Mideast)
2300-2400 [S] 9760 (Europe & Mideast)

## PARAGUAY—Spanish

**RADIO NACIONAL**

0800-0900 ⇨ M-Sa 9737 (S America)
0900-1300 ⇨ 9737 (S America)
2000-0300 ⇨ 9737 (S America & E North Am)

## PORTUGAL—Portuguese

**RDP INTERNATIONAL-RADIO PORTU GAL**

0000-0200 [S] Tu-Sa 13660 & [S] Tu-Sa 15295 (S America)
0000-0300 ⇦ Tu-Sa 9715 (E North Am), Tu-Sa 11655 (W North Am), Tu-Sa 13700 (C America)
0000-0300 [W] Tu-Sa 11980 & [W] Tu-Sa 13770 (S America)
0500-0800 [S] M-F 9840 (Europe)
0500-0900 [S] M-F 11950 (W Europe)
0500-1200 [S] M-F 15555 (W Europe)
0600-0800 ⇦ M-F 15585 (W North Am)
0600-0800 [W] M-F 11675 (W North Am)
0600-0900 [W] M-F 9580 & [W] M-F 9755 (Europe)
0600-1300 ⇦ M-F 9815 & M-F 11960 (W Europe)
0645-0800 [S] M-F 11850 (Europe)
0700-0800 [W] Sa/Su 12020 & [S] Sa/Su 13640 (Europe)
0700-1300 [S] Sa/Su 9840 (Europe)
0700-1400 [S] Sa/Su 13610 (W Europe)
0745-0900 [W] M-F 11660 (Europe)
0800-0900 [W] Sa/Su 11875 (W Europe)
0800-1100 ⇦ Sa/Su 21655 (W Africa & S America), Sa/Su 21830 (E Africa & S Africa)

0800-1200 | [W] 12020 & [S] 13640 (Europe)
0800-1300 | [W] M-F 15140 (W Europe)
0800-1500 | [W] Sa/Su 15575 (W Europe)
0800-1700 | [W] Sa/Su 17680 (E Africa & S Africa)
0900-1300 | [W] 11875 (W Europe)
0930-1100 | [◻] Sa/Su 11995 (Europe)
1100-1300 | [◻] 21655 & M-F 21725 (W Africa & S America), 21830 (E Africa & S Africa)
1200-1400 | [W] Sa/Su 12020 & [S] Sa/Su 13640 (Europe)
1200-2000 | [S] Sa/Su/Holidays 17575 (N America), [S] Sa/Su/Holidays 17615/21690 (C America)
1300-1500 | [W] Sa/Su 11875 (W Europe), [S] M-F 17760 (Mideast & S Asia)
1300-1700 | [◻] Sa/Su 21655 (W Africa & S America), Sa/Su 21800 (S America)
1300-1800 | [◻] Sa/Su 21830 (E Africa & S Africa)
1300-1800 | [W] Sa/Su/Holidays 17745 (C America)
1300-2100 | [W] Sa/Su/Holidays 15540 (N America)
1400-1600 | [◻] M-F 21810 (S Asia)
1400-1600 | [S] Sa/Su 13770 (Europe), [W] M-F 15265 (Mideast & S Asia), [S] Sa/Su 15555 (W Europe)
1500-2100 | [W] Sa/Su 13660 (Europe), [W] Sa/Su 13790 (W Europe)
1600-1900 | [S] 13770, [S] 15445 & [S] M-F 15525 (Europe), [S] 15555 (W Europe), [S] M-F 17650 & [S] M-F 17770 (Europe)
1700-2000 | [◻] 17680 (E Africa & S Africa), 21655 (W Africa & S America), 21800 (S America)
1700-2000 | [W] M-F 11555 (Irr) (Europe), [W] M-F 11800 & [W] M-F 11960 (W Europe), [W] M-F 13585 & [W] M-F 13625 (Europe)
1800-2000 | [W] 17745 (C America)
1900-2000 | [S] Sa/Su 13770 (Europe)
1900-2300 | [S] 11945 (Irr) (S Africa), [S] 13720 (Irr) (W Europe), [S] 15445 (Irr) (Europe), [S] 15555 (Irr) (W Europe), [S] 21540 (Irr) (C America)
2000-2100 | [W] Sa/Su/Holidays 17745 (C America)
2000-2300 | [S] M-F 15480 (Irr) (N America), [S] 17575 (Irr) (E North Am), [S] Sa/Su 21655 (Irr) (W Africa & S America)
2000-2400 | [◻] M-F 13625 (Irr) (Europe), 17680 (Irr) (E Africa & S Africa), 21800 (Irr) (S America)
2000-2400 | [W] M-F 11675 (Irr) (Europe), [W] M-F 11800 (Irr) (W Europe), [W] M-F 11860 (Irr) & [W] M-F 13585 (Irr) (Europe), [W] 13770 (Irr) (C America), [W] M-F 13820 (Irr) (Europe)
2100-2400 | [W] Sa/Su 13660 (Irr) (Europe), [W] 15540 (Irr) (N America)
2300-2400 | [S] M-F 13660 & [S] M-F 15295 (S America)

## RUSSIA—Russian
### VOICE OF RUSSIA

0100-0300 | [S] *11750* (E North Am), [S] 12060 & [S] 12070 (S America), [S] 17565, [S] 17620, [S] 17660 & [S] 17690 (W North Am)
0200-0300 | [S] 7330 & 9480 (S America), [S] 17650 (W North Am)
0200-0400 | [W] *7125* (E North Am), [W] 7260 (Atlantic & C America), [W] 9810 (S America), [W] 12010, [W] 15595, [W] 17565 & [W] 17595 (W North Am)
0300-0400 | [W] 7350 & [W] 9480 (S America)
1200-1300 | [S] 7390 & [S] 11870 (E Asia), [S] 13720 (E Asia & SE Asia)
1200-1400 | [S] 9745 (C Asia & S Asia), [S] 11640 (SE Asia), [S] 15470 (E Asia), [S] 15560 (S Asia & SE Asia)
1200-1500 | [S] 9470 (E Asia & SE Asia), [S] 9920 (C Asia & S Asia)
1300-1400 | [W] 6145 & [S] 7330 (E Asia), [S] 17645 (S Asia & SE Asia)
1300-1500 | [W] 7105 (C Asia), [W] 7155 & [W] 9450 (E Asia), [S] 9490 & [W] 9490 (SE Asia), [W] 15460 (S Asia & SE Asia)
1300-1900 | [W] 6185 (C Asia)
1300-2100 | [S] 7370 (Europe)
1400-1500 | [W] 6205 (SE Asia), [W] 7315 (W Asia & S Asia)
1400-1700 | [S] 11830 (Mideast)
1400-1800 | [S] 7315 (W Asia & S Asia)

| | |
|---|---|
| 1400-1900 | ☑ 6045 (W Europe & Atlantic) |
| 1400-2000 | ◐ 9820 (Europe) |
| 1500-1600 | ☑ 5890, ◐ 7350 & ◐ 9745 (S Asia), ◐ 12005 (Mideast), ◐ 12055 (S Asia), ◐ 15540 (Mideast), ◐ 15560 (S Asia & SE Asia), ◐ 17580 (Mideast & E Africa) |
| 1500-1700 | ☑ 7440 (Europe) |
| 1500-1900 | ☑ 5995 (C Asia) |
| 1500-2100 | ☑ 7170 (W Europe) |
| 1500-2200 | ☑ 7445 (E Europe & Mideast) |
| 1600-1700 | ☑ 7315 (W Asia & S Asia), ☑ 9470 (Mideast), ☑ 12030 (E Europe & Mideast) |
| 1600-1800 | ◐ 7420 (Europe), ◐ 9875 (W Asia) |
| 1700-1800 | ◐ 5950, ◐ 7300 & ◐ 11630 (Europe), ◐ 15540 (Mideast) |
| 1700-2100 | ◐ 12055 (Mideast & E Africa) |
| 1800-1900 | ☑ 5950 & ◐ 7360 (Europe), ☑ 7360 (Europe & N Africa) |
| 1900-2000 | ◐ 5950, ◐ 11745 & ◐ 15350 (Europe), ◐ 17685 (S Europe) |
| 1930-2000 | ◐ 11630 (Europe) |
| 2000-2100 | ☑ 6145, ☑ 7310 & ☑ 7380 (Europe), ◐ 7390 (Europe & W Africa), ◐ 9450 (S Europe), ◐ 9890 (Europe), ◐ 12000 (Europe & W Africa) |
| 2000-2200 | ☑ 7355 (E Asia) |
| 2030-2100 | ☑ 7360 (Europe & N Africa) |
| 2100-2200 | ☑ 6045 (W Europe & Atlantic), ☑ 7370 (S Europe), ☑ 9480 (Europe & W Africa) |

## SAUDI ARABIA—Arabic
### BROADCASTING SERVICE OF THE KINGDOM

| | |
|---|---|
| 0300-0600 | 9580 (Mideast & E Africa), 11820 (N Africa), 15170 (E Europe & W Asia), 15435 (W Asia), 21495 (C Asia & E Asia) |
| 0300-0900 | 9675 (Mideast) |
| 0600-0800 | 17895 (C Asia) |
| 0600-0900 | 15380 (Mideast), 17620/17500 (W Asia), 17760 (N Africa) |
| 0600-1500 | 21505 (N Africa), 21705 (W Europe) |
| 0600-1700 | 11855 (Mideast & E Africa) |
| 0900-1200 | 11935 (Mideast), 17615 (SE Asia), 21495 (E Asia & SE Asia) |
| 0900-1600 | 9675 (Mideast) |
| 1200-1400 | 15380 (Mideast), 21600 (SE Asia) |
| 1200-1500 | 17585 (W Asia), 17895 (N Africa) |
| 1200-1600 | 17760 (N Africa) |
| 1500-1800 | 11785 (W Asia), 13710 & 15315 (N Africa), 15435 (W Europe) |
| 1600-1800 | 11710 (N Africa), 15205 (W Europe), 17560 (C Africa & W Africa) |
| 1700-2200 | 9580 (Mideast & E Africa) |
| 1800-2100 | 11950 (W Asia) |
| 1800-2300 | 9555 (N Africa), 9870 & 11820 (W Europe), 11915 (N Africa), 15230 (C Africa & W Africa) |

## SINGAPORE—Chinese
### MEDIACORP RADIO

| | |
|---|---|
| 1400-1600 & 2300-1100 | 6000 |

### RADIO SINGAPORE INTERNATIONAL—(SE Asia)

| | |
|---|---|
| 1100-1400 | 6000 & 9560 |

## SLOVAKIA—Slovak
### RADIO SLOVAKIA INTERNATIONAL

| | |
|---|---|
| 0130-0200 | 5930, ◐ 6190 & ☑ 7230 (E North Am & C America), 9440 (S America) |
| 0730-0800 | ◐ 9440, 15460, 17550 & ☑ 21705/13715 (Australasia) |
| 1530-1600 | ◐ 5920 (W Europe) |
| 1630-1700 ▭ | 6055 & 7345 (W Europe) |
| 1630-1700 | ☑ 5915 (W Europe) |
| 1900-1930 | ◐ 5920 (W Europe) |
| 2000-2030 ▭ | 6055 & 7345 (W Europe) |
| 2000-2030 | ☑ 5915 (W Europe) |

## SPAIN
### RADIO EXTERIOR DE ESPAÑA
### Galician, Catalan and Basque

| | |
|---|---|
| 1240-1255 | ◐ M-F *9765* (C America), ◐ M-F *15170* (W North Am), ◐ M-F 15585 (Europe), ◐ M-F 21540 (C Africa & S Africa), ◐ M-F 21570 (S America), ◐ M-F 21610 (Mideast), ◐ M-F 21700 (N America) |

**Somali bride-to-be. Throughout the Horn of Africa infibulation is still routinely performed on prepubertal girls. The hope is that they will be disinclined to have extramarital affairs, but studies suggest biological urges are only slightly diminished.** UN

| | |
|---|---|
| 1340-1355 | ▣ M-F *9765* (C America), ▣ M-F *15170* (W North Am), ▣ M-F 15585 (Europe), ▣ M-F 17595 (N America & C America), ▣ M-F 21540 (C Africa & S Africa), ▣ M-F 21570 (S America), ▣ M-F 21610 (Mideast) |

**Spanish**

| | |
|---|---|
| 0000-0200 | ▣ 11680 & ▣ 11945 (S America) |
| 0000-0400 | ▣ *6020* & ▣ *11815* (C America) |
| 0000-0500 | 9540 (N America & C America), 9620 (S America), ▣ 15160 (C America & S America) |
| 0200-0500 | 6055 (N America & C America) |
| 0200-0600 | ▣ *3350* (C America), ▣ *6125* (W North Am & C America), ▣ *11880/3210* (C America & W North Am) |
| 0500-0600 | ▣ 9710 & ▣ 12035 (Europe) |
| 0500-0700 | ▣ 11890 & ▣ 17665 (Mideast) |
| 0600-0700 | 9710 (Europe) |
| 0600-0800 | 12035 (Europe) |
| 0600-1300 | ▣ 13720 (W Europe) |
| 0700-0900 | 17770 & 21610 (Australasia) |
| 0800-0900 | ▣ 12035 (Europe) |
| 0800-1000 | M-F 21570 (S America) |
| 0900-1240 | 15585 (Europe), 21540 (C Africa & S Africa), 21610 (Mideast) |

| | |
|---|---|
| 1000-1200 | *9660* (E Asia) |
| 1000-1240 | 21570 (S America), ▣ M-F 21700 (N America) |
| 1000-1300 | M-F *11815* & ▣ M-F 17595 (C America) |
| 1100-1240 | ▣ M-F *9765* (C America), M-F *15170* (W North Am) |
| 1100-1400 | ▣ M-F *5970* (C America) |
| 1200-1400 | *11910* (SE Asia) |
| 1200-1500 | Su *15170* (W North Am & C America), Sa/Su 21700 (C America & S America) |
| 1200-1600 | ▣ Su *9765* & ▣ Su *11815* (C America), ▣ Su *15125* (C America & S America) |
| 1240-1255 | ▣ M-F *15170* (W North Am), ▣ Sa/Su 15585 & ▣ 15585 (Europe), ▣ Sa/Su 21540 & ▣ 21540 (C Africa & S Africa), ▣ Sa/Su 21570 & ▣ 21570 (S America), ▣ Sa/Su 21610 & ▣ 21610 (Mideast) |
| 1255-1340 | M-F *15170* (W North Am), 15585 (Europe), 21540 (C Africa & S Africa), 21570 (S America), 21610 (Mideast) |
| 1255-1400 | ▣ M-F *9765* (C America) |
| 1300-1340 | M-F 17595 (N America & C America) |

Monte-Carlo is home to casino gambling, topless
bathing and TV porn. Trans World Radio helps balance
this out with daily doses of Christian outreach.

Corbis

| | |
|---|---|
| 1300-1400 | 🅦 Sa/Su 13720 (W Europe) |
| 1340-1355 | 🅢 M-F *15170* (W North Am), 🅢 15585 & 🅦 Sa/Su 15585 (Europe), 🅢 M-F 17595 (N America & C America), 🅢 21540 & 🅦 Sa/Su 21540 (C Africa & S Africa), 🅢 21570 & 🅦 Sa/Su 21570 (S America), 🅢 21610 & 🅦 Sa/Su 21610 (Mideast) |
| 1355-1500 | M-F 17595 (N America & C America), 21610 (Mideast) |
| 1355-1700 | 15585 (Europe), 21570 (S America) |
| 1400-1500 | 🅢 M-Sa 17755 & 🅦 21540 (C Africa & S Africa) |
| 1500-1600 | 🅦 Su *9765* (C America), Su *17850* (W North Am) |
| 1500-1700 | M-Sa 15375/15385 (W Africa & C Africa), 17755 (C Africa & S Africa), 21610 & 🅦 21770 (Mideast) |

| | |
|---|---|
| 1500-1800 | 21700 (C America & S America) |
| 1600-2300 | Sa/Su *9765* & 🅢 Sa/Su *11815* (C America), 🅦 Sa/Su *15125* (C America & S America), Sa/Su *17850* (W North Am) |
| 1700-1900 | 17715 (S America), 🅢 M-Sa 17755 & 🅦 17755 (C Africa & S Africa) |
| 1700-2000 | Sa/Su 9665 (Europe) |
| 1700-2300 | 7275 (Europe) |
| 1800-2100 | Sa/Su 21700 (Irr) (C America & S America) |
| 1900-2100 | 🅦 Su 17755 & Su 17755 (C Africa & S Africa) |
| 1900-2300 | 15110 (N America & C America) |
| 2000-2100 | 🅢 Sa 9665 & 🅦 Sa/Su 9665 (Europe) |
| 2100-2200 | 🅦 Sa 9665 (Europe), 🅦 M-F 11665 (C Africa) |
| 2200-2300 | 7270 (N Africa & W Africa), 🅦 Sa 11665 (C Africa) |
| 2300-2400 | 9540 (N America & C America), 9620, 🅢 11680 & 🅦 11945 (S America), 🅢 15160 (C America & S America) |

## SWEDEN—Swedish

### RADIO SWEDEN

| | |
|---|---|
| 0000-0030 | *9490* (S America) |
| 0100-0130 | 🅦 7430 & 🅢 13640 (S Asia) |
| 0130-0200 | 🅢 13625 (S Asia) |
| 0200-0230 & | |
| 0300-0330 | *9490* (N America) |
| 0400-0430 | 🅢 9490 & 🅢 15245 (N America) |
| 0430-0500 | 🅢 M-F 9490 (W Europe & W Africa) |
| 0500-0700 ⬛ | M-F 6065 (Europe), M-F 17505 (Mideast & E Africa) |
| 0600-0800 ⬛ | M-F 9490 (Europe, N Africa & Mideast) |
| 0700-0900 ⬛ | Sa 9490 (Europe & N Africa), Sa 17505 (Africa) |
| 0700-0900 | 🅦 Sa 6065 (Europe) |
| 0800-1000 ⬛ | Su 9490 (Europe & N Africa), Su 17505 (Africa) |
| 0800-1000 | 🅦 Su 6065 (Europe) |
| 1000-1010 | 🅢 21530 (E Asia & Australasia) |
| 1010-1030 | 🅢 Sa/Su 21530 (E Asia & Australasia) |
| 1030-1040 | 🅢 21530 (SE Asia & Australasia) |
| 1040-1100 | 🅢 Sa/Su 21530 (SE Asia & Australasia) |

1100-1110 ◧ 6065/9490 (Europe), 21810 (Africa)
1100-1110 W 17505 (E Asia & Australasia)
1110-1130 ◧ Sa/Su 6065/9490 (Europe), Sa/Su 21810 (Africa)
1110-1130 W Sa/Su 17505 (E Asia & Australasia)
1130-1140 ◧ 18960 (N America), 21810 (S America)
1130-1140 W 12065 (E Asia & Australasia), W 17505 (SE Asia & Australasia)
1140-1200 ◧ Sa/Su 18960 (N America), Sa/Su 21810 (S America)
1140-1200 W Sa/Su 12065 (E Asia & Australasia), W Sa/Su 17505 (SE Asia & Australasia)
1200-1230 S 17505 (E Asia & Australasia), W 18960 (N America)
1300-1330 ◧ 18960 (N America)
1300-1330 W 12065 (E Asia & Australasia)
1315-1330 W M-F 17505 (SE Asia & Australasia)
1400-1430 ◧ 17505 (E Asia & Australasia), 18960 (N America)
1415-1430 W M-F 12065 (E Asia & Australasia)
1500-1530 ◧ 17505 (Asia & Australasia), 18960 (N America)
1500-1530 S 13580 (E Europe & Mideast)
1545-1600 ◧ 18960 (N America)
1545-1600 S 13580 (Mideast), S 17485 (W Europe & W Africa)
1545-1700 ◧ 6065 (Europe)
1600-1615 S M-F 17485 (W Europe & W Africa)
1600-1630 W 5840 (E Europe)
1600-1645 S M-F 13580 (Mideast)
1645-1700 W 12065 (Europe & Mideast), W 13840 (Atlantic & W Africa)
1645-1715 W 17705 (Atlantic & W Africa)
1700-1710 ◧ M-F 6065 (Europe)
1700-1715 W M-F 12065 (Europe & Mideast), W M-F 13840 (Atlantic & W Africa)
1800-1830 S 11905 (E Europe & S Asia), S 17505 (S Europe & Africa)
1800-1900 ◧ Su 6065 (Europe)
1900-1930 ◧ 6065 (Europe)
1900-1930 W 9765 (Europe & N Africa), W 12065 (Europe & Mideast)
2000-2030 W 9445 (Australasia)
2000-2100 S 13580 (Europe & Africa)

2100-2130 S 15255 (Australasia)
2100-2200 W 12065 (Atlantic & S America)
2100-2230 ◧ 6065 (Europe)
2200-2230 W 7325 (Europe & Africa)

# SWITZERLAND

## SWISS RADIO INTERNATIONAL

### French
0600-0630 W 9885 (N Africa), W 13790 (W Africa), S 15545 (N Africa), W 17665 (C Africa & S Africa), S 17685 (N Africa & W Africa), S 21750 (C Africa & S Africa)
1000-1030 21770 (C Africa & S Africa)
1800-1815 W 9755, W 13790 & S 15220 (Mideast), W 15555 (Mideast & E Africa), S 17735 (Mideast), S 21720 (Mideast & E Africa)
2100-2130 W 9775 (N Africa & W Africa), S 13645 (E Africa), W 13660 & S 15220 (C Africa & S Africa), W 15485 (E Africa), S 17580 (N Africa & W Africa), W 17660 & S 17735 (S Africa)
2200-2230 9885, W 11660 & S 11905 (S America)

### German
0630-0700 W 9885 (N Africa), W 13790 (W Africa), S 15545 (N Africa), W 17665 (C Africa & S Africa), S 17685 (N Africa & W Africa), S 21750 (C Africa & S Africa)
0930-1000 21770 (C Africa & S Africa)
2030-2100 W 9775 (N Africa & W Africa), S 13645 (E Africa), W 13660 & S 15220 (C Africa & S Africa), W 15485 (E Africa), S 17580 (N Africa & W Africa), W 17660 & S 17735 (S Africa)
2230-2300 9885, W 11660 & S 11905 (S America)

### Italian
0700-0730 W 9885 (N Africa), W 13790 (W Africa), S 15545 (N Africa), W 17665 (C Africa & S Africa), S 17685 (N Africa & W Africa), S 21750 (C Africa & S Africa)
0900-0930 21770 (C Africa & S Africa)
1630-1700 W 9755, W 13790 & S 15220 (Mideast), W 15555 (Mideast & E Africa), S 17735 (Mideast), S 21720 (Mideast & E Africa)

1830-1900    ◩ *9775* (N Africa & W Africa), ⬛ 13645 (E Africa), ◩ 13660 & ⬛ 15220 (C Africa & S Africa), ◩ 15485 (E Africa), ⬛ 17580 (N Africa & W Africa), ◩ *17660* & ⬛ *17735* (S Africa)

2300-2330    9885, ◩ *11660* & ⬛ *11905* (S America)

## SYRIA—Arabic

**RADIO DAMASCUS**—(S America)
2215-2315    12085 & 13610
**SYRIAN BROADCASTING SERVICE**
0600-1600 ▭    13610
0600-1700 ▭    12085

## THAILAND—Thai

**RADIO THAILAND**
0100-0200    ◩ 13695 & ⬛ 15395 (E North Am)
0330-0430    ⬛ 15395 & ◩ 15460 (W North Am)
1000-1100    ◩ 7285 & ⬛ 11805 (SE Asia & Australasia)
1330-1400    ◩ 7145 & ⬛ 11955 (E Asia)
1800-1900    ⬛ 9690 & ◩ 11855 (Mideast)
2045-2115    ◩ 9535 & ⬛ 9680 (Europe)

## TUNISIA—Arabic

**RTV TUNISIENNE**
0200-0500    9720 & 12005 (N Africa & Mideast)
0400-0700    7190 (N Africa)
0400-0800    7275 (W Europe)
1200-1700    ◩ 15450 & 17735 (N Africa & Mideast)
1400-1700    11730 (W Europe)
1400-1900    11950 (N Africa)
1700-2100    9720 & 12005 (N Africa & Mideast)
1700-2300    7225 (W Europe)
1900-2300    7190 (N Africa)

## TURKEY—Turkish

**VOICE OF TURKEY**
0000-0400    ⬛ 5960 (Mideast), ⬛ 11885 (Europe & N America)
0000-0500    ◩ 6120 (Mideast), ◩ 7300 (Europe & N America)
0000-0800 ▭    9460 (Europe, E North Am & C America)

0400-0900    ⬛ 11750 (Mideast), ⬛ 15545 (Mideast & W Asia)
0500-0800 ▭    17690 (W Asia & C Asia)
0500-1000    ◩ 11925 (Mideast), ◩ 17570 (Mideast & W Asia)
0500-1700 ▭    11955 (Mideast)
0800-1700 ▭    15350 (Europe)
0800-2200 ▭    9460 (Europe)
1000-1300 ▭    21715 (W Asia, S Asia & Australasia)
1000-1500    ⬛ F 17630 (N Africa)
1100-1600    ◩ F 17860 (N Africa)
1200-1600    ⬛ 15405 (S Asia, SE Asia & Australasia)
1300-1700    ◩ 13615 (S Asia, SE Asia & Australasia)
1600-2400    ⬛ 5960 (Mideast)
1700-2200    ⬛ 7215 (N Africa & W Africa)
1700-2300 ▭    5980 (Europe), 9560 (S Asia, SE Asia & Australasia)
1700-2400    ◩ 6120 (Mideast)
1800-2300    ◩ 6185 (N Africa & W Africa)
2200-2400 ▭    9460 (Europe, E North Am & C America)
2200-2400    ⬛ 11885 (Europe & N America)
2300-2400    ◩ 7300 (Europe & N America)

## UKRAINE—Ukrainian

**RADIO UKRAINE**
0000-0100    ◩ 7375 (E North Am), ◩ 9610 (E Europe)
0000-0400    ⬛ 9640 (W Asia)
0030-1500    ◩ 11840 (W Asia)
0100-0300    ⬛ 7320 (E Europe & W Asia), ⬛ 12040 (E North Am)
0200-0300    ⬛ 7150 (N Europe)
0200-0400    ◩ 7375 (E North Am), ◩ 7420 (W Asia), ◩ 9610 (E Europe)
0300-0400    ◩ 7285 (N Europe)
0400-0600    ⬛ 7150 (N Europe)
0400-0800    ⬛ 7410 (W Europe)
0400-0900    ⬛ 9620 (S Europe)
0400-1100    ⬛ 11840 (W Asia)
0500-0700    ◩ 7285 (N Europe), ◩ 7420 (W Asia)
0500-1000    ⬛ 11705 (W Europe)
0600-1200    ◩ 11720 (S Europe), ◩ 11825 (C Asia)
0600-1300    ◩ 9600 (W Europe)
0600-1600    ⬛ 13590 (W Europe)
0700-1500    ◩ 6020 (Europe)

| | |
|---|---|
| 0800-1100 | [S] 15520 (N Europe) |
| 0800-1200 | [W] 15520 (W Europe) |
| 1100-1700 | [S] 12045 (W Asia) |
| 1200-1300 | [S] 11840 (W Asia) |
| 1200-1400 | [S] 15520 (N Europe) |
| 1300-1400 | [W] 11720 (S Europe) |
| 1300-1500 | [W] 15520 (W Europe) |
| 1300-1600 | [W] 11825 (C Asia) |
| 1400-1800 | [W] 7420 & [S] 9640 (W Asia) |
| 1400-1900 | [W] 9610 (E Europe) |
| 1600-1700 | [S] 5905 (S Europe), [S] 6020 (Europe) |
| 1600-1800 | [W] 5905 & [W] 9560 (W Europe) |
| 1600-2100 | [S] 7150 (N Europe) |
| 1700-2200 | [W] 7285 (N Europe) |
| 1800-2000 | [S] 5905 (S Europe), [S] 6020 (Europe), [S] 11950 (W Europe) |
| 1900-2000 | [W] 7420 (W Asia) |
| 1900-2100 | [W] 5905, [W] 9560 & [S] 11705 (W Europe) |
| 2000-2200 | [W] 7240 (N Europe) |
| 2200-2300 | [S] 5905 (S Europe), [S] 6020 (Europe), [S] 9950 (N Europe), [S] 11705 & [S] 11950 (W Europe) |
| 2300-2400 | [W] 5905 (W Europe), [W] 7240 (N Europe), [W] 9560 (W Europe), [S] 12040 (E North Am) |

## UNITED ARAB EMIRATES—Arabic

**UAE RADIO IN DUBAI**

| | |
|---|---|
| 0000-0200 | 11950 (Irr), 13675 (Irr) (E North Am & C America) |
| 0230-0330 | 12005, 13675 & 15400 (E North Am & C America) |
| 0400-0530 | 15435 (Australasia), 17830 (E Asia), 21700 (Australasia) |
| 0600-1030 | 13675, 15395 & 21605 (Europe) |
| 1050-1200 | 15370 (N Africa) |
| 1050-1330 | 13675, 15395 & 21605 (Europe) |
| 1200-1330 | 13630 (N Africa) |
| 1350-1600 | 13630 (N Africa), 13675, 15395 & 21605 (Europe) |
| 1615-1630 | 21605 (Europe) |
| 1615-2050 | 13675 & 15395 (Europe) |
| 1630-2050 | 11950, 13630 (N Africa) |
| 2050-2400 | 11950 (Irr), 13675 (Irr) (E North Am & C America) |

## VENEZUELA—Spanish

**ECOS DEL TORBES**

| | |
|---|---|
| 0900-0400 | 4980 |
| 1200-2200 | 9640 |
| 2200-2400 | 9640 (Irr) |

**RADIO NACIONAL**—(C America)

| | |
|---|---|
| 0000-0100, 0300-0400, 1100-1200, 1400-1500, 1800-1900 & 2100-2200 | 9540 (Irr) |

**RADIO TACHIRA**

| | |
|---|---|
| 1000-1400 & 2100-0400 | 4830 |

## VIETNAM—Vietnamese

**VOICE OF VIETNAM**

| | |
|---|---|
| 0000-0100 | [W] 7145/11575, [W] 9730, [S] 11640 & [S] 13740 (C Africa) |
| 0000-1600 | 5925, 5975, 6020, 7210, 9530 |
| 0130-0230 | *6175* (E North Am & C America) |
| 0150-1000 | 9875 |
| 0400-0500 | *6175* (W North Am) |
| 1600-1700 | F 5975, F 9530 |
| 1700-1800 | [W] 7145/11575, [W] 9730, [S] 11640 & [S] 13740 (Europe) |
| 1730-1830 | [S] *9725* (W Europe) |
| 1830-1930 | [W] *5955* (W Europe) |
| 1930-2030 | [S] *9725* (S Europe) |
| 2030-2130 | [W] *5970* (S Europe) |
| 2200-2400 | 5925, 5975, 6020, 7210, 9530 |

## YEMEN—Arabic

**REPUBLIC OF YEMEN RADIO**

| | |
|---|---|
| 0300-0600 | 9780 (Mideast & E Africa) |
| 0300-1500 | 5950 (Mideast) |
| 0700-1800 & 1900-2208 | 9780 |
| 2208-2308 | 9780 (Irr) |

## YUGOSLAVIA—Serbian

**RADIO YUGOSLAVIA**

| | |
|---|---|
| 0000-0030 | [S] Su *9580/11870* (E North Am) |
| 0030-0100 | [W] *7115* & [S] *9580/11870* (E North Am) |
| 0100-0130 | [W] Su *7115* (E North Am) |
| 0130-0200 | [W] *7115* (E North Am) |
| 1400-1600 ⬅ | *7200* (Europe) |
| 2030-2100 ⬅ | *6100* (Europe) |
| 2030-2100 ➡ | *7230* (Australasia) |
| 2100-2130 ⬅ | Sa *6100* (Europe) |
| 2100-2130 ➡ | Sa *7230* (Australasia) |
| 2330-2400 | [S] *9580/11870* (E North Am) |

# Weird Words

## PASSPORT's Ultimate Glossary of World Band Terms and Abbreviations

A rich variety of terms and abbreviations is used in world band radio. Some are specialized and benefit from explanation; several are foreign words that need translation; and yet others are simply adaptations of everyday usage.

Here, then, is PASSPORT's A-Z guide to what's what in world band buzzwords. For a thorough analysis of terms and norms used in evaluating world band radios, see the Radio Database International White Paper, *How to Interpret Receiver Specifications and Lab Tests*.

**A.** Summer schedule season for world band stations. See ◨. See HFCC. Cf. B.

**Active Antenna.** An antenna that electronically amplifies signals. Active, or amplified, antennas are typically mounted indoors, but some models can also be mounted outdoors. Active antennas take up relatively little space, but their amplification circuits may introduce certain types of problems that can result in unwanted sounds being heard. See Passive Antenna.

**Adjacent-Channel Rejection.** See Selectivity.

**AGC.** See Automatic Gain Control.

**AGC Threshold.** The threshold at which the automatic gain control (AGC), see, chooses to act relates to both listening pleasure and audible sensitivity. If the threshold is too low, the AGC will tend to act on internal receiver noise and minor static, desensitizing the receiver. However, if the threshold is too high, variations in loudness will be uncomfortable to the ear, forcing the listener to manually twiddle with the volume control to do, in effect, what the AGC should be doing automatically. Measured in µV (microvolts).

**Alt. Freq.** Alternative frequency or channel. Frequency or channel that may be used in place of the regularly scheduled one.

**Amateur Radio.** See Hams.

**AM Band.** The popular radio band that runs from 520–1705 kHz within the mediumwave spectrum, or Medium Frequency (MF) range of the radio spectrum, from 0.3-3.0 MHz (300-3,000 kHz). Outside North America, it is usually called the mediumwave (MW) band. However, in parts of Latin America it is sometimes called, by the general public and a few stations, *onda larga*—longwave—strictly speaking, a misnomer.

**Amplified Antenna.** See Active Antenna.

**Analog Frequency Readout.** This type of received-frequency indication is used on radios having needle-and-dial or "slide-rule" tuning. It is much less handy than digital frequency readout. See Synthesizer. Cf. Digital Frequency Display.

**Arrestor.** See MOV.

**Audio Quality.** At Passport, audio quality refers to what in computer testing is called "benchmark" quality. This means, primarily, the freedom from distortion of a signal fed through a receiver's entire circuitry—*not* just the audio stage—from the antenna input through to the speaker terminals. A lesser characteristic of audio quality is the audio bandwidth needed for pleasant world band reception of music. Also, see Enhanced Fidelity.

**Automatic Gain Control (AGC).** Smooths out fluctuations in signal strength brought about by fading, a regular occurrence with world band signals. See AGC Threshold.

**AV.** A Voz—Portuguese for "The Voice." In Passport, this term is also used to represent "The Voice of."

**B.** Winter schedule season for world band stations. See ◨. See HFCC. Cf. A.

**Bandwidth.** A key variable that determines selectivity (see), bandwidth is the amount of radio signal at –6 dB a radio's circuitry will let pass, and thus be heard. With world band channel spacing at 5 kHz, the best single bandwidths are usually in the vicinity of 3 to 6 kHz. Better radios offer two or more selectable bandwidths: at least one of 5 to 9 kHz or so for when a station is in the clear, and one or more others between 2 to 6 kHz for when a station is hemmed in by other signals next to it. Proper selectivity is a key determinant of the aural quality of what you hear, and some newer models of tabletop receivers have dozens of bandwidths. Synchronous selectable sideband (see) allows wider bandwidths to be used to provide improved fidelity.

**Baud.** Measurement of the speed by which radioteletype (see), radiofax (see) and other digital data are transmitted. Baud is properly written entirely in lower case, and thus is abbreviated as b (baud), kb (kilobaud) or Mb (Megabaud). Baud rate standards are usually set by the international CCITT regulatory body.

**BC.** Broadcaster, Broadcasters, Broadcasting, Broadcasting Company, Broadcasting Corporation.

**Birdie.** A silent spurious signal, similar to a station's open carrier, created by circuit interaction within a receiver. The fewer and weaker the birdies within a receiver's tuning range, the better, although in reality birdies rarely degrade reception.

**Blocking.** The ability of a receiver to avoid being desensitized by powerful adjacent signals or signals from other nearby frequencies. Measured in dB (decibels) at 100 kHz signal spacing.

**Boat Anchor.** Radio slang for a classic or vintage tube-type communications receiver. These huge, heavy monsters were manufactured mainly from before World War II through the mid-1970s, although a few continued to be available up to a decade later. The definitive reference for collectors of elder receivers is *Shortwave Receivers Past & Present* by Universal Radio.

**Broadcast.** A radio or television transmission meant for the general public. *Compare* Utility Stations, Hams.

**BS.** Broadcasting Station, Broadcasting Service.

**Cd.** Ciudad—Spanish for "City."

**Channel.** An everyday term to indicate where a station is supposed to be located on the dial. World band channels are spaced exactly 5 kHz apart. Stations operating outside this norm are "off-channel" (for these, Passport provides resolution to better than 1 kHz to aid in station identification).

**Chugging, Chuffing.** The sound made by some synthesized tuning systems when the tuning knob is turned. Called "chugging" or "chuffing," as it is suggestive of the rhythmic "chuf, chuf" sound of steam locomotives or "chugalug" gulping of beverages.

**Cl.** Club, Clube.

**Coordinated Universal Time.** See UTC.

**Cult.** Cultura, Cultural.

**Default.** The setting at which a control of a digitally operated electronic device, including many world band radios, normally operates, and to which it will eventually return (e.g., when the radio is next switched on).

**Digital Frequency Display, Digital Frequency Readout.** Indicates that a receiver displays the tuned frequency digitally, usually in kilohertz (see). Because this is so much handier than an analog frequency readout, all models included in Passport REPORTS have digital frequency readout. See Synthesizer.

**Digital Radio Mondiale (DRM).** International organization (www.drm.org) heavily involved in the effort to convert world band transmissions from traditional analog mode to digital mode. See Mode.

**Digital Signal Processing (DSP).** Where digital circuitry and software are used to perform radio circuit functions traditionally done using analog circuits. Used on certain world band receivers; also, available as an add-on accessory for audio processing only.

**Dipole Antenna.** See Passive Antenna.

**Distortion.** See Overall Distortion.

**Domestic Service.** See DS.

**DS.** Domestic Service—Broadcasting intended primarily for audiences in the broadcaster's home country. However, some domestic programs are beamed on world band to expatriates and other kinfolk abroad, as well as interested foreigners. *Compare* ES.

**DSP.** See Digital Signal Processing.

**DX, DXers, DXing.** From an old telegraph abbreviation for "distance"; thus, to DX is to communicate over a great distance. DXers are those who specialize in finding distant or exotic stations that are considered to be rare catches. Few world band listeners are considered to be regular DXers, but many others seek out DX stations every now and then—usually by bandscanning, which is greatly facilitated by Passport's Blue Pages.

**Dynamic Range.** The ability of a receiver to handle weak signals in the presence of strong competing signals within or near the same world band segment (see World Band Spectrum). Sets with inferior dynamic range sometimes "overload," especially with external antennas, causing a mishmash of false signals up and down—and even beyond—the segment being received. Dynamic range is closely related to the third-order intercept point, or IP3. Where possible, Passport measures dynamic range and IP3 at the traditional 20 kHz and more challenging 5 kHz signal-separation points.

**Earliest Heard (or Latest Heard).** See key at the bottom of each Blue Page. If the Passport monitoring team cannot establish the definite sign-on (or sign-off) time of a station, the earliest (or latest) time that the station could be traced is indicated by a left-facing or right-facing "arrowhead flag." This means that the station almost certainly operates beyond the time shown by that "flag." It also means that, unless you live relatively close to the station, you're unlikely to be able to hear it beyond that "flagged" time.

**EBS.** Economic Broadcasting Station, a type of station found in China.

**ECSS (Exalted-Carrier Selectable Sideband).** Manual tuning of a conventional AM-mode signal, using a receiver's single-sideband circuitry to zero-beat *(see)* the receiver's BFO with the transmitted signal's carrier. The better-sounding of the signal's sidebands is then selected by the listener. *See* Synchronous Detector.

**Ed, Educ.** Educational, Educação, Educadora.

**Electrical Noise.** *See* Noise.

**Em.** Emissora, Emisora, Emissor, Emetteur—in effect, "station" in various languages.

**Enhanced Fidelity.** Radios with good audio performance and certain types of high-tech circuitry can improve the fidelity of world band signals. Among the newer fidelity-enhancing techniques is synchronous detection *(see* Synchronous Detector), especially when coupled with selectable sideband. Another potential technological advance to improve fidelity is digital world band transmission, which is actively being researched and tested *(see* Digital Radio Mondiale*)*.

**EP.** Emissor Provincial—Portuguese for "Provincial Station."

**ER.** Emissor Regional—Portuguese for "Regional Station."

**Ergonomics.** How handy and comfortable—intuitive—a set is to operate, especially hour after hour.

**ES.** External Service—Broadcasting intended primarily for audiences abroad. *Compare* DS.

**External Service.** *See* ES.

**F.** Friday.

**Fax.** *See* Radiofax.

**Feeder, Shortwave.** A utility transmission from the broadcaster's home country to a relay site or placement facility some distance away. Although these specialized transmissions carry world band programming, most are not intended to be received by the general public. Many world band radios can process these quasi-broadcasts anyway. Feeders operate in lower sideband (LSB), upper sideband (USB) or independent sideband (termed ISL if heard on the lower side, ISU if heard on the upper side) modes. Nearly all shortwave feeders have now been replaced by satellite and Internet audio feeders, but an important newcomer—Armed Forces Radio & Television Service—has taken to the air in recent years; the AFRTS is beamed to U.S. Navy ships, where radio operators retransmit the audio shipboard. *See* Single Sideband, Utility Stations, NBFM.

**First IF Rejection.** A relatively uncommon source of false signals occurs when powerful transmitters operate on the same frequency as a receiver's first intermediate frequency (IF). The ability of receiving circuitry to avoid such transmitters' causing reception problems is called "IF rejection."

**FM.** *See* NBFM.

**Frequency.** The standard term to indicate where a station is located within the radio spectrum—regardless of whether it is "on-channel" or "off-channel" *(see* Channel). Below 30 MHz this is customarily expressed in kilohertz (kHz, *see*), but some receivers display in Megahertz (MHz, *see*). These differ only in the placement of a decimal; e.g., 5970 kHz is the same as 5.97 MHz. Either measurement is equally valid, but to minimize confusion PASSPORT and most stations designate frequencies only in kHz.

**Frequency Synthesizer.** *See* Synthesizer, Frequency.

**Front-End Selectivity.** The ability of the initial stage of receiving circuitry to admit only limited frequency ranges into succeeding stages of circuitry. Good front-end selectivity keeps signals from other, powerful bands or segments from being superimposed upon the frequency range you're tuning. For example, a receiver with good front-end selectivity will receive only shortwave signals within the range 3200-3400 kHz. However, a receiver with mediocre front-end selectivity might allow powerful local mediumwave AM stations from 520-1700 kHz to be heard "ghosting in" between 3200 and 3400 kHz, along with the desired shortwave signals. Obviously, mediumwave AM signals don't belong on shortwave. Receivers with inadequate front-end selectivity can benefit from the addition of a preselector *(see)* or a high-pass filter.

**GMT.** Greenwich Mean Time—*See* World Time.

**Hams.** Government-licensed amateur radio hobbyists who *transmit* to each other by radio, often by single sideband *(see)*, within special amateur bands. Many of these bands are within the shortwave spectrum *(see)*. This spectrum is also used by world band radio, but

world band radio and ham radio, which laymen sometimes confuse with each other, are two very separate entities. The easiest way is to think of hams as making something like phone calls, whereas world band stations are like long-distance versions of ordinary mediumwave AM stations.

**Harmonic, Harmonic Radiation, Harmonic Signal.** Usually, an unwanted weak spurious repeat of a signal in multiple(s) of the fundamental, or "real," frequency. Thus, the third harmonic of a mediumwave AM station on 1120 kHz might be heard faintly on 4480 kHz within the world band spectrum. Stations almost always try to minimize harmonic radiation, as it wastes energy and spectrum space. However, in rare cases stations have been known to amplify a harmonic signal so they can operate inexpensively on a second frequency. Also, *see* Subharmonic.

**Hash.** Electrical noise. *See* Noise.

**High Fidelity.** *See* Enhanced Fidelity.

**HFCC (High Frequency Co-ordination Conference).** Founded in 1990 and headquartered in Prague, the HFCC (www.hfcc.org) helps coordinate frequency usage by some 60 broadcasting organizations from more than 30 countries. These represent about 75 to 80 percent of the global output for international shortwave broadcasting. Coordination meetings take place twice yearly: once each for the "A" (summer) and "B" (winter) schedule seasons.

**IBS.** International Broadcasting Services, Ltd., publishers of PASSPORT TO WORLD BAND RADIO and other publications.

**Image.** A common type of spurious signal found on low-cost radios where a strong signal appears at reduced strength, usually on a frequency 900 kHz or 910 kHz lower down. For example, the BBC on 5875 kHz might repeat on 4975 kHz, its "image frequency." *See* Spurious-Signal Rejection.

**Independent Sideband.** *See* Single Sideband.

**Interference.** Sounds from other signals, notably on the same ("co-channel") frequency or nearby channels, that are disturbing the one you are trying to hear. Worthy radios reduce interference by having good selectivity *(see)*. Nearby television sets and cable television wiring may also generate a special type of radio interference called TVI, a "growl" heard every 15 kHz or so. Sometimes referred to as QRM, a term based on Morse-code shorthand.

**International Reply Coupon (IRC).** Sold by selected post offices in most parts of the world, IRCs amount to official international "scrip" that may be exchanged for postage in most countries of the world. Because they amount to an international form of postage repayment, they are handy for listeners trying to encourage foreign stations to write them back. However, IRCs are very costly for the amount in stamps that is provided in return. Too, an increasing number of countries are not forthcoming about "cashing in" IRCs. Specifics on this and related matters are provided in the Addresses PLUS section of this book.

**International Telecommunication Union (ITU).** The regulatory body, headquartered in Geneva, for all international telecommunications, including world band radio. Sometimes incorrectly referred to as the "International Telecommunications Union." In recent years, the ITU has become increasingly ineffective as a regulatory body for world band radio, with much of its former role having been taken up by the HFCC *(see)*.

**Internet Radio.** *See* Web radio.

**Inverted-L Antenna.** *See* Passive Antenna.

**Ionosphere.** *See* Propagation.

**IP3.** Third-order intercept point. *See* Dynamic Range.

**IRC.** *See* International Reply Coupon.

**Irr.** Irregular operation or hours of operation; i.e., schedule tends to be unpredictable.

**ISB.** Independent sideband. *See* Single Sideband.

**ISL.** Independent sideband, lower. *See* Feeder.

**ISU.** Independent sideband, upper. *See* Feeder.

**ITU.** *See* International Telecommunication Union.

**Jamming.** Deliberate interference to a transmission with the intent of discouraging listening. However, shortwave broadcasts are uniquely resistant to jamming. This ability to avoid "gatekeeping" is a major reason why shortwave continues to be the workhorse for international broadcasting. For now, jamming is practiced much less than it was during the Cold War.

**Keypad.** On a world band radio, like a cell phone, a keypad can be used to control many variables. Radio keypads are used primarily so you can enter a station's frequency for reception, and the best keypads have real keys (not a membrane) in the standard telephone format of 3x4 with "zero" under the "8" key. Many keypads are also used for presets, but this means you have to remember code numbers for stations (e.g., BBC 5975 kHz is "07"); handier radios have separate keys for presets, while some others use LCD-displayed "pages" to access presets.

**kHz.** Kilohertz, the most common unit for measuring where a station is located on the world band dial if it is below 30,000 kHz. Formerly known as "kilocycles per second," or kc/s. 1,000 kilohertz equals one Megahertz. *See* Frequency. *Cf.* MHz.

**Kilohertz.** *See* kHz.

**kW.** Kilowatt(s), the most common unit of measurement for transmitter power (*see*).

**LCD.** Liquid-crystal display. LCDs, if properly designed, are fairly easily seen in bright light, but require illumination under darker conditions. LCDs—typically monochrome and gray on gray—also tend to have mediocre contrast, and sometimes can be read from only a certain angle or angles, but they consume nearly no battery power.

**LED.** Light-emitting diode. LEDs have a long life and are very easily read in the dark or in normal room light, but consume more battery power than LCDs and are hard to read in bright ambient light.

**Location.** The physical location of a station's transmitter, which may be different from the studio location. Transmitter location is useful as a guide to reception quality. For example, if you're in eastern North America and wish to listen to the Voice of Russia, a transmitter located in St. Petersburg will almost certainly provide better reception than, say, one located in Siberia.

**Longwave Band.** The 148.5–283.5 kHz portion of the low-frequency (LF) radio spectrum used in Europe, the Near East, North Africa, Russia and Mongolia for domestic broadcasting. As a practical matter, these longwave signals, which have nothing to do with world band or other shortwave signals, are not usually audible in other parts of the world.

**Longwire Antenna.** *See* Passive Antenna.

**Loop Antenna.** Round (like a hula hoop) or square antenna often used for reception of longwave, mediumwave AM and even shortwave signals. These can be highly directive below around 2 MHz, and even up to roughly 6 MHz. For this reason, most such antennas can be rotated and even tilted manually or with an antenna rotor. Loops tend to have low gain, and thus need electrical amplification in order to reach their potential. When properly designed and mounted, they can produce superior signal-to-noise ratios that help with weak-signal (DX) reception. Strictly speaking, ferrite-rod antennas, found inside nearly every mediumwave AM radio as well as some specialty outboard antennas, are not "loops." However, in everyday parlance these tiny antennas are referred to as "loops" or "loopsticks."

**LSB.** Lower Sideband. *See* Feeder, Single Sideband.

**LV.** La Voix, La Voz—French and Spanish for "The Voice." In PASSPORT, this term is also used to represent "The Voice of."

**M.** Monday.

**Mediumwave Band, Mediumwave AM Band, Mediumwave Spectrum.** *See* AM Band.

**Megahertz.** *See* MHz.

**Memory, Memories.** *See* Preset.

**Meters.** An outdated unit of measurement used for individual world band segments of the shortwave spectrum. The frequency range covered by a given meters designation—also known as "wavelength"—can be gleaned from the following formula: *frequency (kHz) = 299,792 ÷ meters*. Thus, 49 meters comes out to a frequency of 6118 kHz—well within the range of frequencies included in that segment (*see* World Band Spectrum). Inversely, meters can be derived from the following: *meters = 299,792 ÷ frequency (kHz)*. The figure 299,792 is based on the speed of light as agreed upon internationally in 1983. However, in practice this awkward figure is usually rounded to 300,000 for computational purposes.

**MHz.** Megahertz, a common unit to measure where a station is located on the dial, especially above 30 MHz, although in the purest sense all measurements above 3 MHz are supposed to be in MHz. Formerly known as "Megacycles per second," or Mc/s. One Megahertz equals 1,000 kilohertz. *See* Frequency. *Cf.* kHz.

**Mode.** Method of transmission of radio signals. World band radio broadcasts are almost always in the analog AM mode, the same mode used in the mediumwave AM band (*see*). The AM mode consists of three components: two "sidebands," plus one "carrier" that resides between the two sidebands. Each sideband contains the same programming as the other, and the carrier carries no programming, so a few stations have experimented with the single-sideband (SSB) mode. SSB contains only one sideband, either the lower sideband (LSB) or upper sideband (USB), and a reduced carrier. It requires special radio circuitry to be demodulated, or made intelligible, which is the main reason SSB is unlikely to be widely adopted as a world band mode. However, major efforts are currently underway to implement digital-mode world band transmissions (*see* Digital Radio Mondiale). There are yet other modes used on shortwave, but not for world band. These include CW (Morse-type code), radiofax, RTTY (radioteletype) and narrow-band FM used by utility and ham stations. Narrow-band FM is not used for music, and is different from usual FM. *See* Single Sideband, NBFM, ISB, ISL, ISU, LSB and USB.

**MOV.** Often used in power-line and antenna surge arrestors to shunt static and line-power surges to ground. MOVs perform well and are inexpensive, but tend to lose their effectiveness with use; costlier alternatives are thus sometimes worth considering. On rare occasion they also appear to have been implicated in starting fires, so a UL or other recognized certification is helpful. For both these reasons MOV-based arrestors should be replaced at least once every decade that they are in service.

**N.** New, Nueva, Nuevo, Nouvelle, Nacional, National, Nationale.

**Nac.** Nacional. Spanish and Portuguese for "National."

**Narrow-band FM.** *See* NBFM.

**Nat, Natl, Nat'l.** National, Nationale.

**NBFM.** Narrow-band FM, used within the shortwave spectrum by some "utility" stations, including (between 25-30 MHz) point-to-point broadcast station remote links. These links are documented by Guido Schotmans at http://dxing.hypermart.net.

**Noise.** Static, buzzes, pops and the like caused by the earth's atmosphere (typically lightning), and to a lesser extent by galactic noise. Also, electrical noise emanates from such man-made sources as electric blankets, fish-tank heaters, heating pads, electrical and gasoline motors, light dimmers, flickering light bulbs, non-incandescent lights, computers and computer peripherals, office machines, electric fences, and faulty electric utility wiring and related components. Sometimes referred to as QRN, a term based on Morse-code shorthand.

**Noise Floor.** *See* Sensitivity.

**Notch Filter, Tunable.** A useful feature for reducing or rejecting annoying heterodyne interference—the whistles, howls and squeals for which shortwave has traditionally been notorious.

**Other.** Programs are in a language other than one of the world's primary languages.

**Overall Distortion.** Nothing makes listening quite so tiring as distortion. PASSPORT has devised techniques to measure overall cumulative distortion from signal input through audio output—not just distortion within the audio stage. This level of distortion is thus equal to what is heard by the ear.

**Overloading.** *See* Dynamic Range.

**Passive Antenna.** An antenna that is not electronically amplified. Typically, these are mounted outdoors, although the "tape-measure" type that comes as an accessory with some portables is usually strung indoors. For world band reception, virtually all outboard models for consumers are made from wire, rather than rods or tubular elements. The two most common designs are the inverted-L (so-called "longwire") and trapped dipole (mounted either horizontally or as a "sloper"). These antennas are preferable to active antennas (*see*), and are reviewed in detail in the Radio Database International White Paper, PASSPORT *Evaluation of Popular Outdoor Antennas (Unamplified)*.

**PBS.** In China, People's Broadcasting Station.

**Phase Noise.** Synthesizers and other circuits can create a "rushing" noise that is usually noticed only when the receiver is tuned alongside the edge of a powerful broadcast or other carrier. In effect, the signal becomes "modulated" by the noise. Phase noise is a useful measurement if you tune weak signals alongside powerful signals. Measured in dBc (decibels below carrier).

**PLL (Phase-Locked Loop).** With world band receivers, a PLL circuit means that the radio can be tuned digitally, often using a number of handy tuning techniques, such as a keypad *(see)* and presets *(see)*.

**Power.** Transmitter power *before* antenna gain, expressed in kilowatts (kW). The present range of world band powers is 0.01 to 1,000 kW.

**Power Lock.** *See* Travel Power Lock.

**PR.** People's Republic.

**Preselector.** A circuit—outboard as an accessory, or inboard as part of the receiver—that effectively limits the range of frequencies which can enter a receiver's circuitry or the circuitry of an active antenna *(see)*; that is, which improves front-end selectivity *(see)*. For example, a preselector may let in the range 15000-16000 kHz, thus helping ensure that your receiver or active antenna will not encounter problems within that range caused by signals from, say, 5730-6250 kHz or local mediumwave AM signals (520-1705 kHz). This range usually can be varied, manually or automatically, according to the frequency to which the receiver is being tuned. A preselector may be passive (unamplified) or active (amplified).

**Preset.** Allows you to select a station pre-stored in a radio's memory. The handiest presets require only one push of a button, as on a car radio.

**Propagation.** World band signals travel, like a basketball, up and down from the station to your radio. The "floor" below is the earth's surface, whereas the "player's hand" on high is the *ionosphere*, a gaseous layer that envelops the planet. While the earth's surface remains pretty much the same from day to day, the ionosphere—nature's own passive "satellite"—varies in how it propagates radio signals, depending on how much sunlight hits the "bounce points."

Thus, some world band segments do well mainly by day, whereas others are best by night. During winter there's less sunlight, so the "night bands" become unusually active, whereas the "day bands" become correspondingly less useful *(see* World Band Spectrum). Day-to-day changes in the sun's weather also cause short-term changes in world band radio reception; this explains why some days you can hear rare signals.

Additionally, the 11-year sunspot cycle has a long term effect on propagation, with sunspot maximum greatly enhancing reception on higher world band segments.

**PS.** Provincial Station, Pangsong.

**Pto.** Puerto, Porto.

**QRM.** *See* Interference.

**QRN.** *See* Noise.

**QSL.** *See* Verification.

**R.** Radio, Radiodiffusion, Radiodifusora, Radiodifusão, Radiophonikos, Radiostantsiya, Radyo, Radyosu, and so forth.

**Radiofax, Radio Facsimile.** Like ordinary telefax (facsimile by telephone lines), but by radio.

**Radioteletype (RTTY).** Characters, but not illustrations, transmitted by radio. *See* Baud.

**RDI.** Radio Database International®, a registered trademark of International Broadcasting Services, Ltd.

**Receiver.** Synonym for a radio, but sometimes—especially when called a "communications receiver"—implying a radio with superior tough-signal or utility-signal performance.

**Reduced Carrier.** *See* Single Sideband.

**Reg.** Regional.

**Relay.** A retransmission facility, often highlighted in "Worldwide Broadcasts in English" and "Voices from Home" in PASSPORT's WorldScan® section. Relay facilities are generally considered to be located outside the broadcaster's country. Being closer to the target audience, they usually provide superior reception. *See* Feeder.

**Rep.** Republic, République, República.

**RN.** *See* R and N.

**RS.** Radio Station, Radiostantsiya, Radiostudiya, Radiophonikos Stathmos.

**RT, RTV.** Radiodiffusion Télévision, Radio Télévision, and so forth.

**RTTY.** *See* Radioteletype.

🄴 Transmission aired summer (midyear) only; see "HFCC." *Cf.* 🆆

**S.** San, Santa, Santo, São, Saint, Sainte. Also, South.

**Sa.** Saturday.

**Scan, Scanning.** Circuitry within a radio that allows it to bandscan or memory scan automatically.

**Season, Schedule Season.** *See* HFCC.

**Segments.** *See* Shortwave Spectrum.

**Selectivity.** The ability of a radio to reject interference *(see)* from signals on adjacent channels. Thus, also known as adjacent-channel rejection, a key variable in radio quality. *See* Bandwidth. *See* Shape Factor. *See* Ultimate Rejection. *See* Synchronous Detector.

**Sensitivity.** The ability of a radio to receive weak signals; thus, also known as weak-signal sensitivity. Of special importance if you are listening during the day or tuning domestic tropical band broadcasts—or if you are located in such parts of the world as Western North America, Hawaii or Australasia, where signals tend to be relatively weak. The best measurement of sensitivity is the noise floor.

**Shape Factor.** Skirt selectivity helps reduce interference and increase audio fidelity. It is important if you will be tuning stations that are weaker than adjacent-channel signals. Skirt selectivity is measured by the shape factor, the ratio between the bandwidth at -6 dB (adjacent signal at about the same strength as the received station) and -60 dB (adjacent signal relatively much stronger). A good shape factor provides the best defense against adjacent powerful signals' muscling their way in to disturb reception of the desired signal.

**Shortwave Spectrum.** The shortwave spectrum—also known as the High Frequency (HF) spectrum—is that portion of the radio spectrum from 3 MHz through 30 MHz (3,000-30,000 kHz). The shortwave spectrum is occupied not only by world band broadcasts *(see* World Band Segments), but also hams *(see)* and utility stations *(see)*.

**Sideband.** *See* Mode.

**Single Sideband, Independent Sideband.** Spectrum- and power-conserving modes of transmission commonly used mainly by utility stations and hams. These transmitted signals consist of one full sideband (lower sideband, LSB; or upper sideband, USB) and a vestigial carrier, but no second sideband. Very few broadcasters use, or are expected ever to use, these modes, although some quasi-broadcasts, such as the American AFRTS, operate in the single-sideband mode. Many world band radios are already capable of demodulating single-sideband transmissions, and some can even process independent-sideband signals. Certain single-sideband transmissions operate with a minimum of carrier reduction, which allows them to be listened to, albeit with some distortion, on ordinary radios not equipped to demodulate single sideband. Properly designed synchronous detectors *(see)* may prevent such distortion. *See* Feeder, Mode.

**Site.** *See* Location.

**Skirt Selectivity.** *See* Shape Factor.

**Slew Controls.** Elevator-button-type up and down controls to tune a radio. On many radios with synthesized tuning, slewing is used in lieu of tuning by knob. Better is when slew controls are complemented by a tuning knob, which is more versatile.

**Sloper Antenna.** *See* Passive Antenna.

**SPR.** Spurious (false) extra signal from a transmitter actually operating on another frequency. One such type is harmonic *(see)*.

**Spurious-Signal Rejection.** The ability of a radio receiver to avoid producing false, or "ghost," signals that might otherwise interfere with the clarity of the station you're trying to hear. *See* Image.

**St, Sta, Sto.** Abbreviations for words that mean "Saint."

**Stability.** The ability of a receiver to rest exactly the tuned frequency without drifting.

**Static.** *See* Noise.

**Static Arrestor.** *See* MOV.

**Su.** Sunday.

**Subharmonic.** A harmonic heard at 1.5 or 0.5 times the operating frequency. This anomaly is caused by the way signals are generated within vintage-model transmitters, and thus cannot take place with modern transmitters. For example, the subharmonic of a station on 3360 kHz might be heard faintly on 5040 or 1680 kHz. Also, *see* Harmonic.

**Sunspot Cycle.** *See* Propagation.

**Surge Arrestor.** *See* MOV.

**Synchronous Detector.** World band radios are increasingly coming equipped with this high-tech circuit that greatly reduces fading distortion. Better synchronous detectors also allow for synchronous selectable sideband; that is, the highly desirable ability to select the less-interfered of the two sidebands of a world band or other AM-mode signal. *See* Mode.

**Synchronous Selectable Sideband.** *See* Synchronous Detector.

**Synthesizer, Frequency.** Better world band receivers utilize a digital frequency synthesizer to tune signals. Among other things, such synthesizers allow for pushbutton tuning and presets, and display the exact frequency digitally—pluses that make tuning to the world considerably easier. Virtually a "must" feature. *See* Analog Frequency Readout. *See* Digital Frequency Display.

**Target.** Where a transmission is beamed, a/k/a target zone.

**Th.** Thursday.

**Third Order Intercept Point.** *See* Dynamic Range.

**Travel Power Lock.** Control which disables the on/off switch to prevent a radio from switching on accidentally.

**Transmitter Power.** *See* Power.

**Trap Dipole Antenna, Trapped Dipole Antenna.** *See* Passive Antenna.

**Tu.** Tuesday.

**Ultimate Rejection, Ultimate Selectivity.** The point at which a receiver is no longer able to reject adjacent-channel interference. Ultimate rejection is important if you listen to signals that are markedly weaker than are adjacent signals. *See* Selectivity.

**Universal Day.** *See* World Time.

**Universal Time.** *See* World Time.

**URL.** Universal Resource Locator; i.e., the Internet address for a given Webpage.

**USB.** Upper Sideband. *See* Feeder. *See* Single Sideband.

**UTC.** Coordinated Universal Time—and, no, it's *never* "Universal Time Coordinated," although for everyday use it's okay to refer simply to "Universal Time." *See* World Time.

**Utility Stations.** Most signals within the shortwave spectrum are not world band stations. Rather, they are utility stations—radio telephones, ships at sea, aircraft, ionospheric sounders, over-the-horizon radar and the like—that transmit strange sounds (growls, gurgles, dih-dah sounds, etc.). Although these can be picked up on many receivers, they are rarely intended to be utilized by the general public. *Compare* Broadcast, Hams and Feeders.

**v.** Variable frequency; i.e., one that is unstable or drifting because of a transmitter malfunction or, less often, to avoid jamming or other interference.

**Verification.** A "QSL" card or letter from a station verifying that a listener indeed heard that particular station. In order to stand a chance of qualifying for a verification card or letter, you should respond shortly after having heard the transmission. You need to provide the station heard with, at a minimum, the following information in a three-number "SIO" code, in which "SIO 555" is best and "SIO 111" is worst:

- **S**ignal strength, with 5 being of excellent quality, comparable to that of a local mediumwave AM station, and 1 being inaudible or at least so weak as to be virtually unintelligible. 2 (faint, but somewhat intelligible), 3 (moderate strength) and 4 (good strength) represent the signal-strength levels usually encountered with world band stations.
- **I**nterference from other stations, with 5 indicating no interference whatsoever, and 1 indicating such extreme interference that the desired signal is virtually drowned out. 2 (heavy interference), 3 (moderate interference) and 4 (slight interference) represent the differing degrees of interference more typically encountered with world band signals. If possible, indicate the names of the interfering station(s) and the channel(s) they are on. Otherwise, at least describe what the interference sounds like.
- **O**verall quality of the signal, with 5 being best, 1 worst.
- In addition to providing SIO findings, you should indicate which programs you've heard, as well as comments on how you liked or disliked those programs. Refer to the Addresses PLUS section of

this edition for information on where and to whom your report should be sent, and whether return postage should be included.

- Because of the hassle involved, few stations wish to receive tape recordings of their transmissions.

**Vo.** Voice of.

◨ Transmission aired winter only; *see* HFCC. *Cf.* ◧

**W.** Wednesday.

**Wavelength.** *See* Meters.

**Weak-Signal Sensitivity.** *See* Sensitivity.

**Webcasting.** *See* Web Radio.

**Web Radio, Webcasts.** Broadcasts aired to the public over the Internet's World Wide Web. These thousands of stations worldwide include simulcast FM, mediumwave AM and world band stations, as well as Web-only "stations." Thus far listening to Webcasts for more than brief periods has been limited by phone-line and related costs except within the United States. Although Webcasting was originally completely unfettered, it is increasingly subject to official gatekeeping, or censorship, as well as copyright and union restrictions. Accordingly, it has been in a state of gradual decline since early 2001. Where Webcasting is headed is anybody's guess, but recent trends suggest that the same entities which are major forces in terrestrial broadcasting will also eventually dominate Webcasting.

**World Band Radio.** Similar to regular mediumwave AM band and FM band radio, except that world band stations can be heard over enormous distances, and thus often carry news, music and entertainment programs created especially for audiences abroad. World band is also especially difficult to "jam" (*see* Jamming), making it uniquely effective in outflanking official censorship. Some world band stations have regular audiences in the tens of millions, and even over 100 million. Some 600 million people worldwide are believed to listen to world band radio.

**World Band Segments.** Fourteen slices within the world band spectrum (*see*) and mediumwave spectrum (*see* AM Band) that are used almost exclusively for transmission of world band broadcasts. *See* "Best Times and Frequencies" within this edition.

**World Band Spectrum.** The portion of the shortwave spectrum not (*see*) and mediumwave spectrum between 2.3-26.1 MHz.

**World Day.** *See* World Time.

**World Time.** Also known as Coordinated Universal Time (UTC), Greenwich Mean Time (GMT), Zulu time (Z) and "military time." With over 150 countries on world band radio, if each announced its own local time you would need a calculator to figure it all out. To get around this, a single international time—World Time—is used. The differences between World Time and local time are detailed in the Addresses PLUS and Setting Your World Time Clock sections of this edition. World Time can also be determined simply by listening to time announcements given on the hour by world band stations—or minute by minute by WWV and WWVH in the United States on such frequencies as 5000, 10000 and 15000 kHz, or CHU in Canada on 3330, 7335 and 14670 kHz. A 24-hour clock format is used, so "1800 World Time" means 6:00 PM World Time. If you're in, say, North America, Eastern Time is five hours behind World Time winters and four hours behind World Time summers, so 1800 World Time would be 1:00 PM EST or 2:00 PM EDT. The easiest solution is to use a 24-hour digital clock set to World Time. Many radios already have these built in, and World Time clocks are also available as accessories. World Time also applies to the days of the week. So if it's 9:00 PM (21:00) Wednesday in New York during the winter, it's 0200 *Thursday* World Time.

**WS.** World Service.

**Zero beat.** When tuning a world band or other AM-mode signal in the single-sideband mode, there is a whistle, or "beat," whose pitch is the result of the difference in frequency between the receiver's internally generated carrier (BFO, or beat-frequency oscillator) and the station's transmitted carrier. By tuning carefully, the listener can reduce the difference between these two carriers to the point where the whistle is deeper and deeper, to the point where it no longer audible. This silent sweet spot is known as "zero beat." *See* ECSS.

Printed in Canada

# PASSPORT's Blue Pages— 2003

## Channel-by-Channel Guide to World Band Schedules

If you scan the world band airwaves, you'll discover lots more stations than those aimed your way. That's because shortwave signals are capriciously scattered by the heavens, so you can often hear stations not targeted to your area.

## Blue Pages Help Identify Stations

But just dialing around can be frustrating if you don't have a "map"—PASSPORT's Blue Pages. Let's say that you've stumbled across something Asian-sounding on 7410 kHz at 2035 World Time. The Blue Pages show All India Radio beamed to Western Europe, with a hefty 500 kW of power from Bangalore. These clues suggest this is probably what you're hearing, even if you're not in Europe. You can also see that English from India will begin on that same channel in about ten minutes.

## Schedules for Entire Year

Times and days of the week are in World Time; for local times in each country, see "Addresses PLUS." Some stations are shown as one hour earlier (◨) or later (◧) midyear—typically April through October. Stations may also extend their hours for holidays, emergencies or sports events.

To be as useful as possible over the months to come, PASSPORT's schedules consist not just of observed activity, but also that which we have creatively opined will take place during the forthcoming year. This predictive material is based on decades of experience and is original from us. Although inherently not as exact as real-time data, over the years it's been of tangible value to PASSPORT readers.

## Guide to Blue Pages Format

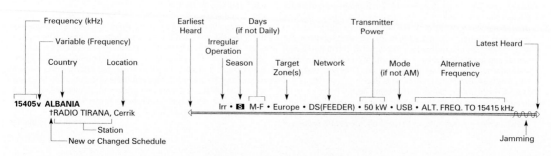

Frequency (kHz) — Variable (Frequency) — Country — Location — Earliest Heard — Irregular Operation — Season — Days (if not Daily) — Target Zone(s) — Network — Transmitter Power — Mode (if not AM) — Alternative Frequency — Latest Heard

**15405v ALBANIA** †RADIO TIRANA, Cerrik — Station — New or Changed Schedule

Irr • **S** M-F • Europe • DS(FEEDER) • 50 kW • USB • ALT. FREQ. TO 15415 kHz — Jamming

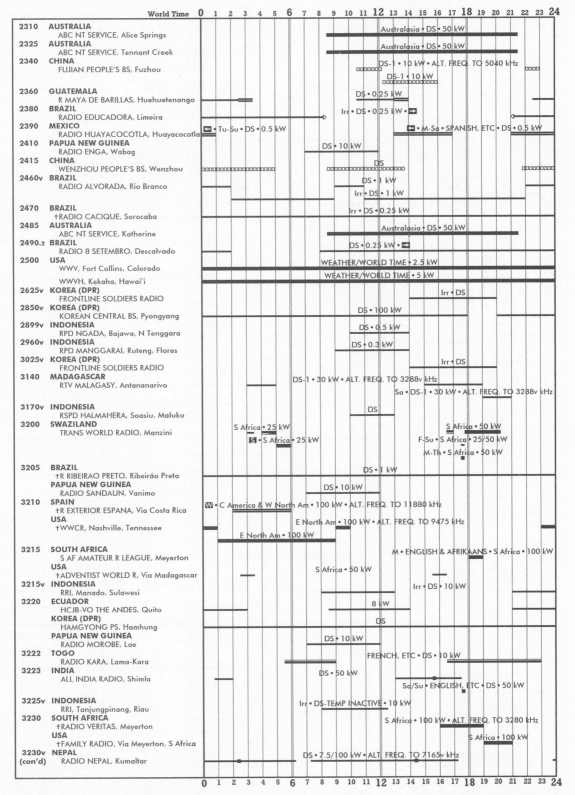

World Time

| kHz | | |
|---|---|---|
| 2310 | **AUSTRALIA** | ABC NT SERVICE, Alice Springs |
| 2325 | **AUSTRALIA** | ABC NT SERVICE, Tennant Creek |
| 2340 | **CHINA** | FUJIAN PEOPLE'S BS, Fuzhou |
| 2360 | **GUATEMALA** | R MAYA DE BARILLAS, Huehuetenango |
| 2380 | **BRAZIL** | RADIO EDUCADORA, Limeira |
| 2390 | **MEXICO** | RADIO HUAYACOCOTLA, Huayacocotla |
| 2410 | **PAPUA NEW GUINEA** | RADIO ENGA, Wabag |
| 2415 | **CHINA** | WENZHOU PEOPLE'S BS, Wenzhou |
| 2460v | **BRAZIL** | RADIO ALVORADA, Rio Branco |
| 2470 | **BRAZIL** | †RADIO CACIQUE, Sorocaba |
| 2485 | **AUSTRALIA** | ABC NT SERVICE, Katherine |
| 2490.2 | **BRAZIL** | RADIO 8 SETEMBRO, Descalvado |
| 2500 | **USA** | WWV, Fort Collins, Colorado |
| | | WWVH, Kekaha, Hawai'i |
| 2625v | **KOREA (DPR)** | FRONTLINE SOLDIERS RADIO |
| 2850v | **KOREA (DPR)** | KOREAN CENTRAL BS, Pyongyang |
| 2899v | **INDONESIA** | RPD NGADA, Bajawa, N Tenggara |
| 2960v | **INDONESIA** | RPD MANGGARAI, Ruteng, Flores |
| 3025v | **KOREA (DPR)** | FRONTLINE SOLDIERS RADIO |
| 3140 | **MADAGASCAR** | RTV MALAGASY, Antananarivo |
| 3170v | **INDONESIA** | RSPD HALMAHERA, Soasiu, Maluku |
| 3200 | **SWAZILAND** | TRANS WORLD RADIO, Manzini |
| 3205 | **BRAZIL** | †R RIBEIRÃO PRETO, Ribeirão Preto |
| | **PAPUA NEW GUINEA** | RADIO SANDAUN, Vanimo |
| 3210 | **SPAIN** | †R EXTERIOR ESPANA, Via Costa Rica |
| | **USA** | †WWCR, Nashville, Tennessee |
| 3215 | **SOUTH AFRICA** | S AF AMATEUR R LEAGUE, Meyerton |
| | **USA** | †ADVENTIST WORLD R, Via Madagascar |
| 3215v | **INDONESIA** | RRI, Manado, Sulawesi |
| 3220 | **ECUADOR** | HCJB-VO THE ANDES, Quito |
| | **KOREA (DPR)** | HAMGYONG PS, Hamhung |
| | **PAPUA NEW GUINEA** | RADIO MOROBE, Lae |
| 3222 | **TOGO** | RADIO KARA, Lama-Kara |
| 3223 | **INDIA** | ALL INDIA RADIO, Shimla |
| 3225v | **INDONESIA** | RRI, Tanjungpinang, Riau |
| 3230 | **SOUTH AFRICA** | †RADIO VERITAS, Meyerton |
| | **USA** | †FAMILY RADIO, Via Meyerton, S Africa |
| 3230v | **NEPAL** | RADIO NEPAL, Kumaltar |
| (con'd) | | |

Bar-chart annotations (left to right by frequency):

- 2310 AUSTRALIA: Australasia • DS • 50 kW
- 2325 AUSTRALIA: Australasia • DS • 50 kW
- 2340 CHINA: DS-1 • 10 kW • ALT. FREQ. TO 5040 kHz / DS-1 • 10 kW
- 2360 GUATEMALA: DS • 0.25 kW
- 2380 BRAZIL: Irr • DS • 0.25 kW •
- 2390 MEXICO: Tu-Su • DS • 0.5 kW / M-Sa • SPANISH, ETC • DS • 0.5 kW
- 2410 PAPUA NEW GUINEA: DS • 10 kW
- 2415 CHINA: DS
- 2460v BRAZIL: DS • 1 kW / Irr • DS • 1 kW
- 2470 BRAZIL: Irr • DS • 0.25 kW
- 2485 AUSTRALIA: Australasia • DS • 50 kW
- 2490.2 BRAZIL: DS • 0.25 kW •
- 2500 USA: WEATHER/WORLD TIME • 2.5 kW
- WWVH: WEATHER/WORLD TIME • 5 kW
- 2625v KOREA: Irr • DS
- 2850v KOREA: DS • 100 kW
- 2899v INDONESIA: DS • 0.5 kW
- 2960v INDONESIA: DS • 0.3 kW
- 3025v KOREA: Irr • DS
- 3140 MADAGASCAR: DS-1 • 30 kW • ALT. FREQ. TO 3288v kHz / Sa • DS-1 • 30 kW • ALT. FREQ. TO 3288v kHz
- 3170v INDONESIA: DS
- 3200 SWAZILAND: S Africa • 25 kW / S Africa • 25 kW / S Africa • 50 kW / F-Su • S Africa • 25/50 kW / M-Th • S Africa • 50 kW
- 3205 BRAZIL: DS • 1 kW
- PAPUA NEW GUINEA: DS • 10 kW
- 3210 SPAIN: C America & W North Am • 100 kW • ALT. FREQ. TO 11880 kHz
- USA: E North Am • 100 kW • ALT. FREQ. TO 9475 kHz / E North Am • 100 kW
- 3215 SOUTH AFRICA: M • ENGLISH & AFRIKAANS • S Africa • 100 kW
- USA: S Africa • 50 kW
- 3215v INDONESIA: Irr • DS • 10 kW
- 3220 ECUADOR: 8 kW
- KOREA: DS
- PAPUA NEW GUINEA: DS • 10 kW
- 3222 TOGO: FRENCH, ETC • DS • 10 kW
- 3223 INDIA: DS • 50 kW / Sa/Su • ENGLISH, ETC • DS • 50 kW
- 3225v INDONESIA: Irr • DS-TEMP INACTIVE • 10 kW
- 3230 SOUTH AFRICA: S Africa • 100 kW • ALT. FREQ. TO 3280 kHz
- USA: S Africa • 100 kW
- 3230v NEPAL: DS • 7.5/100 kW • ALT. FREQ. TO 7165v kHz

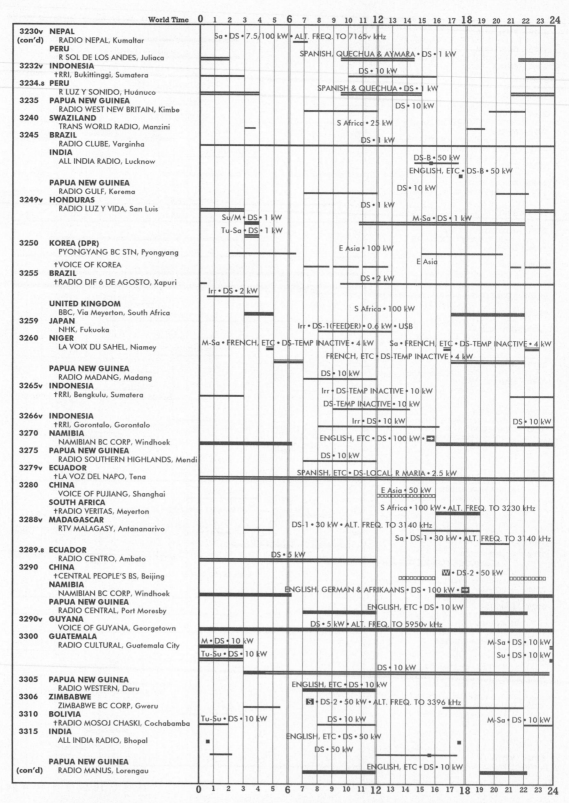

World Time 0 1 2 3 4 5 6 7 8 9 10 11 12 13 14 15 16 17 18 19 20 21 22 23 24

| 3230v | NEPAL |
| (con'd) | RADIO NEPAL, Kumaltar |
| | PERU |
| | R SOL DE LOS ANDES, Juliaca |
| 3232v | INDONESIA |
| | †RRI, Bukittinggi, Sumatera |
| 3234.8 | PERU |
| | R LUZ Y SONIDO, Huánuco |
| 3235 | PAPUA NEW GUINEA |
| | RADIO WEST NEW BRITAIN, Kimbe |
| 3240 | SWAZILAND |
| | TRANS WORLD RADIO, Manzini |
| 3245 | BRAZIL |
| | RADIO CLUBE, Varginha |
| | INDIA |
| | ALL INDIA RADIO, Lucknow |
| | PAPUA NEW GUINEA |
| | RADIO GULF, Kerema |
| 3249v | HONDURAS |
| | RADIO LUZ Y VIDA, San Luis |
| 3250 | KOREA (DPR) |
| | PYONGYANG BC STN, Pyongyang |
| | †VOICE OF KOREA |
| 3255 | BRAZIL |
| | †RADIO DIF 6 DE AGOSTO, Xapuri |
| | UNITED KINGDOM |
| | BBC, Via Meyerton, South Africa |
| 3259 | JAPAN |
| | NHK, Fukuoka |
| 3260 | NIGER |
| | LA VOIX DU SAHEL, Niamey |
| | PAPUA NEW GUINEA |
| | RADIO MADANG, Madang |
| 3265v | INDONESIA |
| | †RRI, Bengkulu, Sumatera |
| 3266v | INDONESIA |
| | †RRI, Gorontalo, Gorontalo |
| 3270 | NAMIBIA |
| | NAMIBIAN BC CORP, Windhoek |
| 3275 | PAPUA NEW GUINEA |
| | RADIO SOUTHERN HIGHLANDS, Mendi |
| 3279v | ECUADOR |
| | †LA VOZ DEL NAPO, Tena |
| 3280 | CHINA |
| | VOICE OF PUJIANG, Shanghai |
| | SOUTH AFRICA |
| | †RADIO VERITAS, Meyerton |
| 3288v | MADAGASCAR |
| | RTV MALAGASY, Antananarivo |
| 3289.8 | ECUADOR |
| | RADIO CENTRO, Ambato |
| 3290 | CHINA |
| | †CENTRAL PEOPLE'S BS, Beijing |
| | NAMIBIA |
| | NAMIBIAN BC CORP, Windhoek |
| | PAPUA NEW GUINEA |
| | RADIO CENTRAL, Port Moresby |
| 3290v | GUYANA |
| | VOICE OF GUYANA, Georgetown |
| 3300 | GUATEMALA |
| | RADIO CULTURAL, Guatemala City |
| 3305 | PAPUA NEW GUINEA |
| | RADIO WESTERN, Daru |
| 3306 | ZIMBABWE |
| | ZIMBABWE BC CORP, Gweru |
| 3310 | BOLIVIA |
| | †RADIO MOSOJ CHASKI, Cochabamba |
| 3315 | INDIA |
| | ALL INDIA RADIO, Bhopal |
| | PAPUA NEW GUINEA |
| (con'd) | RADIO MANUS, Lorengau |

Labels within the chart:
- Sa • DS • 7.5/100 kW • ALT. FREQ. TO 7165v kHz
- SPANISH, QUECHUA & AYMARA • DS • 1 kW
- DS • 10 kW
- SPANISH & QUECHUA • DS • 1 kW
- DS • 10 kW
- S Africa • 25 kW
- DS • 1 kW
- DS-B • 50 kW
- ENGLISH, ETC • DS-B • 50 kW
- DS • 10 kW
- DS • 1 kW
- Su/M • DS • 1 kW
- Tu-Sa • DS • 1 kW
- M-Sa • DS • 1 kW
- E Asia • 100 kW
- E Asia
- DS • 2 kW
- Irr • DS • 2 kW
- S Africa • 100 kW
- Irr • DS-1(FEEDER) • 0.6 kW • USB
- M-Sa • FRENCH, ETC • DS-TEMP INACTIVE • 4 kW
- Sa • FRENCH, ETC • DS-TEMP INACTIVE • 4 kW
- FRENCH, ETC • DS-TEMP INACTIVE • 4 kW
- DS • 10 kW
- Irr • DS-TEMP INACTIVE • 10 kW
- DS-TEMP INACTIVE • 10 kW
- Irr • DS • 10 kW
- DS • 10 kW
- ENGLISH, ETC • DS • 100 kW • ➡
- DS • 10 kW
- SPANISH, ETC • DS-LOCAL, R MARIA • 2.5 kW
- E Asia • 50 kW
- S Africa • 100 kW • ALT. FREQ. TO 3230 kHz
- DS-1 • 30 kW • ALT. FREQ. TO 3140 kHz
- Sa • DS-1 • 30 kW • ALT. FREQ. TO 3140 kHz
- DS • 5 kW
- W • DS-2 • 50 kW
- ENGLISH, GERMAN & AFRIKAANS • DS • 100 kW • ➡
- ENGLISH, ETC • DS • 10 kW
- DS • 5 kW • ALT. FREQ. TO 5950v kHz
- M • DS • 10 kW
- M-Sa • DS • 10 kW
- Tu-Su • DS • 10 kW
- Su • DS • 10 kW
- DS • 10 kW
- ENGLISH, ETC • DS • 10 kW
- S • DS-2 • 50 kW • ALT. FREQ. TO 3396 kHz
- Tu-Su • DS • 10 kW
- DS • 10 kW
- M-Sa • DS • 10 kW
- ENGLISH, ETC • DS • 50 kW
- DS • 50 kW
- ENGLISH, ETC • DS • 10 kW

0 1 2 3 4 5 6 7 8 9 10 11 12 13 14 15 16 17 18 19 20 21 22 23 24

ENGLISH ▬▬   ARABIC ⌇⌇⌇   CHINESE □□□   FRENCH ══   GERMAN ▬▬   RUSSIAN ══   SPANISH ══   OTHER ──

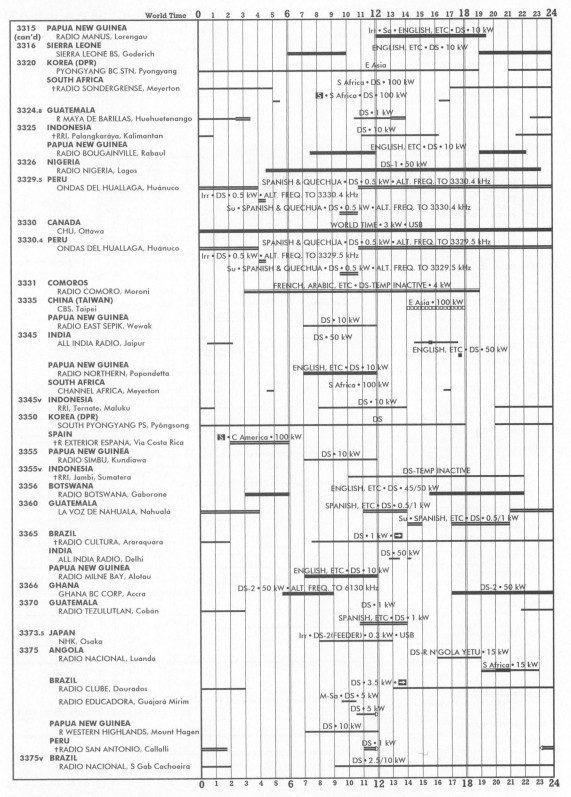

| World Time | | |
|---|---|---|
| **3315** | **PAPUA NEW GUINEA** | |
| (con'd) | RADIO MANUS, Lorengau | Irr • Sa • ENGLISH, ETC • DS • 10 kW |
| **3316** | **SIERRA LEONE** | |
| | SIERRA LEONE BS, Goderich | ENGLISH, ETC • DS • 10 kW |
| **3320** | **KOREA (DPR)** | |
| | PYONGYANG BC STN, Pyongyang | E Asia |
| | **SOUTH AFRICA** | |
| | †RADIO SONDERGRENSE, Meyerton | S Africa • DS • 100 kW |
| | | S • S Africa • DS • 100 kW |
| **3324.8** | **GUATEMALA** | |
| | R MAYA DE BARILLAS, Huehuetenango | DS • 1 kW |
| **3325** | **INDONESIA** | |
| | †RRI, Palangkaráya, Kalimantan | DS • 10 kW |
| | **PAPUA NEW GUINEA** | |
| | RADIO BOUGAINVILLE, Rabaul | ENGLISH, ETC • DS • 10 kW |
| **3326** | **NIGERIA** | |
| | RADIO NIGERIA, Lagos | DS-1 • 50 kW |
| **3329.5** | **PERU** | |
| | ONDAS DEL HUALLAGA, Huánuco | SPANISH & QUECHUA • DS • 0.5 kW • ALT. FREQ. TO 3330.4 kHz |
| | | Irr • DS • 0.5 kW • ALT. FREQ. TO 3330.4 kHz |
| | | Su • SPANISH & QUECHUA • DS • 0.5 kW • ALT. FREQ. TO 3330.4 kHz |
| **3330** | **CANADA** | |
| | CHU, Ottawa | WORLD TIME • 3 kW • USB |
| **3330.4** | **PERU** | |
| | ONDAS DEL HUALLAGA, Huánuco | SPANISH & QUECHUA • DS • 0.5 kW • ALT. FREQ. TO 3329.5 kHz |
| | | Irr • DS • 0.5 kW • ALT. FREQ. TO 3329.5 kHz |
| | | Su • SPANISH & QUECHUA • DS • 0.5 kW • ALT. FREQ. TO 3329.5 kHz |
| **3331** | **COMOROS** | |
| | RADIO COMORO, Moroni | FRENCH, ARABIC, ETC • DS-TEMP INACTIVE • 4 kW |
| **3335** | **CHINA (TAIWAN)** | |
| | CBS, Taipei | E Asia • 100 kW |
| | **PAPUA NEW GUINEA** | |
| | RADIO EAST SEPIK, Wewak | DS • 10 kW |
| **3345** | **INDIA** | |
| | ALL INDIA RADIO, Jaipur | DS • 50 kW |
| | | ENGLISH, ETC • DS • 50 kW |
| | **PAPUA NEW GUINEA** | |
| | RADIO NORTHERN, Popondetta | ENGLISH, ETC • DS • 10 kW |
| | **SOUTH AFRICA** | |
| | CHANNEL AFRICA, Meyerton | S Africa • 100 kW |
| **3345v** | **INDONESIA** | |
| | RRI, Ternate, Maluku | DS • 10 kW |
| **3350** | **KOREA (DPR)** | |
| | SOUTH PYONGYANG PS, Pyŏngsong | DS |
| | **SPAIN** | |
| | †R EXTERIOR ESPANA, Via Costa Rica | S • C America • 100 kW |
| **3355** | **PAPUA NEW GUINEA** | |
| | RADIO SIMBU, Kundiawa | DS • 10 kW |
| **3355v** | **INDONESIA** | |
| | †RRI, Jambi, Sumatera | DS-TEMP INACTIVE |
| **3356** | **BOTSWANA** | |
| | RADIO BOTSWANA, Gaborone | ENGLISH, ETC • DS • 45/50 kW |
| **3360** | **GUATEMALA** | |
| | LA VOZ DE NAHUALA, Nahualá | SPANISH, ETC • DS • 0.5/1 kW |
| | | Su • SPANISH, ETC • DS • 0.5/1 kW |
| **3365** | **BRAZIL** | |
| | †RADIO CULTURA, Araraquara | DS • 1 kW • ➡ |
| | **INDIA** | |
| | ALL INDIA RADIO, Delhi | DS • 50 kW |
| | **PAPUA NEW GUINEA** | |
| | RADIO MILNE BAY, Alotau | ENGLISH, ETC • DS • 10 kW |
| **3366** | **GHANA** | |
| | GHANA BC CORP, Accra | DS-2 • 50 kW • ALT. FREQ. TO 6130 kHz    DS-2 • 50 kW |
| **3370** | **GUATEMALA** | |
| | RADIO TEZULUTLAN, Cobán | DS • 1 kW |
| | | SPANISH, ETC • DS • 1 kW |
| **3373.5** | **JAPAN** | |
| | NHK, Osaka | Irr • DS-2(FEEDER) • 0.3 kW • USB |
| **3375** | **ANGOLA** | |
| | RADIO NACIONAL, Luanda | DS-R N'GOLA YETU • 15 kW |
| | | S Africa • 15 kW |
| | **BRAZIL** | |
| | RADIO CLUBE, Dourados | DS • 3.5 kW • ➡ |
| | RADIO EDUCADORA, Guajará Mirim | M-Sa • DS • 5 kW |
| | | DS • 5 kW |
| | **PAPUA NEW GUINEA** | |
| | R WESTERN HIGHLANDS, Mount Hagen | DS • 10 kW |
| | **PERU** | |
| | †RADIO SAN ANTONIO, Callalli | DS • 1 kW |
| **3375v** | **BRAZIL** | |
| | RADIO NACIONAL, S Gab Cachoeira | DS • 2.5/10 kW |

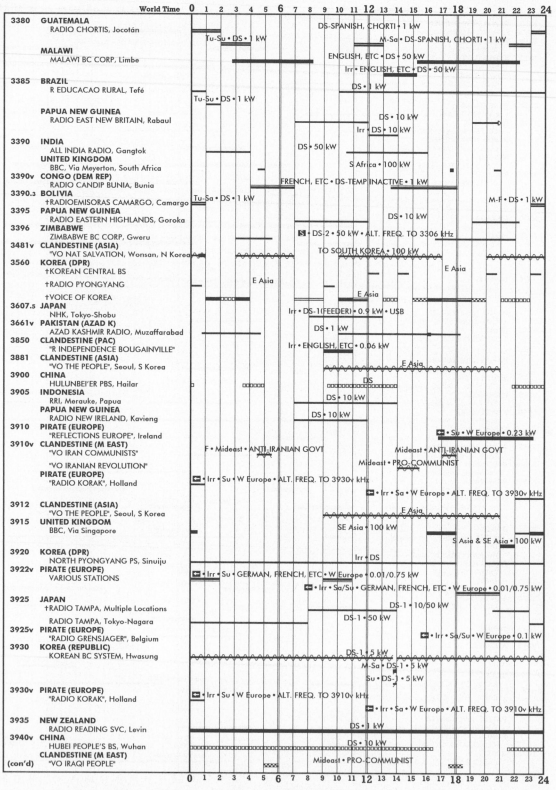

| World Time | Station | Details |
|---|---|---|
| 3380 | **GUATEMALA** — RADIO CHORTIS, Jocotán | DS-SPANISH, CHORTI • 1 kW / Tu-Su • DS • 1 kW / M-Sa • DS-SPANISH, CHORTI • 1 kW |
|  | **MALAWI** — MALAWI BC CORP, Limbe | ENGLISH, ETC • DS • 50 kW / Irr • ENGLISH, ETC • DS • 50 kW |
| 3385 | **BRAZIL** — R EDUCACAO RURAL, Tefé | DS • 1 kW / Tu-Su • DS • 1 kW |
|  | **PAPUA NEW GUINEA** — RADIO EAST NEW BRITAIN, Rabaul | DS • 10 kW / Irr • DS • 10 kW |
| 3390 | **INDIA** — ALL INDIA RADIO, Gangtok | DS • 50 kW |
|  | **UNITED KINGDOM** — BBC, Via Meyerton, South Africa | S Africa • 100 kW |
| 3390v | **CONGO (DEM REP)** — RADIO CANDIP BUNIA, Bunia | FRENCH, ETC • DS-TEMP INACTIVE • 1 kW |
| 3390.3 | **BOLIVIA** — †RADIOEMISORAS CAMARGO, Camargo | Tu-Sa • DS • 1 kW / M-F • DS • 1 kW |
| 3395 | **PAPUA NEW GUINEA** — RADIO EASTERN HIGHLANDS, Goroka | DS • 10 kW |
| 3396 | **ZIMBABWE** — ZIMBABWE BC CORP, Gweru | Ⓢ • DS-2 • 50 kW • ALT. FREQ. TO 3306 kHz |
| 3481v | **CLANDESTINE (ASIA)** — "VO NAT SALVATION, Wonsan, N Korea" | TO SOUTH KOREA • 100 kW |
| 3560 | **KOREA (DPR)** — †KOREAN CENTRAL BS | E Asia |
|  | †RADIO PYONGYANG | E Asia |
|  | †VOICE OF KOREA | E Asia |
| 3607.5 | **JAPAN** — NHK, Tokyo-Shobu | Irr • DS-1 (FEEDER) • 0.9 kW • USB |
| 3661v | **PAKISTAN (AZAD K)** — AZAD KASHMIR RADIO, Muzaffarabad | DS • 1 kW |
| 3850 | **CLANDESTINE (PAC)** — "R INDEPENDENCE BOUGAINVILLE" | Irr • ENGLISH, ETC • 0.06 kW |
| 3881 | **CLANDESTINE (ASIA)** — "VO THE PEOPLE", Seoul, S Korea | E Asia |
| 3900 | **CHINA** — HULUNBEI'ER PBS, Hailar | DS |
| 3905 | **INDONESIA** — RRI, Merauke, Papua | DS • 10 kW |
|  | **PAPUA NEW GUINEA** — RADIO NEW IRELAND, Kavieng | DS • 10 kW |
| 3910 | **PIRATE (EUROPE)** — "REFLECTIONS EUROPE", Ireland | • Su • W Europe • 0.23 kW |
| 3910v | **CLANDESTINE (M EAST)** — "VO IRAN COMMUNISTS" | F • Mideast • ANTI-IRANIAN GOVT / Mideast • ANTI-IRANIAN GOVT |
|  | "VO IRANIAN REVOLUTION" | Mideast • PRO-COMMUNIST |
|  | **PIRATE (EUROPE)** — "RADIO KORAK", Holland | • Irr • Su • W Europe • ALT. FREQ. TO 3930v kHz / • Irr • Sa • W Europe • ALT. FREQ. TO 3930v kHz |
| 3912 | **CLANDESTINE (ASIA)** — "VO THE PEOPLE", Seoul, S Korea | E Asia |
| 3915 | **UNITED KINGDOM** — BBC, Via Singapore | SE Asia • 100 kW / S Asia & SE Asia • 100 kW |
| 3920 | **KOREA (DPR)** — NORTH PYONGYANG PS, Sinuiju | Irr • DS |
| 3922v | **PIRATE (EUROPE)** — VARIOUS STATIONS | • Irr • Su • GERMAN, FRENCH, ETC • W Europe • 0.01/0.75 kW / • Irr • Sa/Su • GERMAN, FRENCH, ETC • W Europe • 0.01/0.75 kW |
| 3925 | **JAPAN** — †RADIO TAMPA, Multiple Locations | DS-1 • 10/50 kW |
|  | RADIO TAMPA, Tokyo-Nagara | DS-1 • 50 kW |
| 3925v | **PIRATE (EUROPE)** — "RADIO GRENSJAGER", Belgium | • Irr • Sa/Su • W Europe • 0.1 kW |
| 3930 | **KOREA (REPUBLIC)** — KOREAN BC SYSTEM, Hwasung | DS-1 • 5 kW / M-Sa • DS-1 • 5 kW / Su • DS-1 • 5 kW |
| 3930v | **PIRATE (EUROPE)** — "RADIO KORAK", Holland | • Irr • Su • W Europe • ALT. FREQ. TO 3910v kHz / • Irr • Sa • W Europe • ALT. FREQ. TO 3910v kHz |
| 3935 | **NEW ZEALAND** — RADIO READING SVC, Levin | DS • 1 kW |
| 3940v | **CHINA** — HUBEI PEOPLE'S BS, Wuhan | DS • 10 kW |
|  | **CLANDESTINE (M EAST)** (con'd) — "VO IRAQI PEOPLE" | Mideast • PRO-COMMUNIST |

ENGLISH ▬▬   ARABIC ▧▧   CHINESE ▫▫▫   FRENCH ═══   GERMAN ▬▬   RUSSIAN ═══   SPANISH ▬▬   OTHER ▬▬

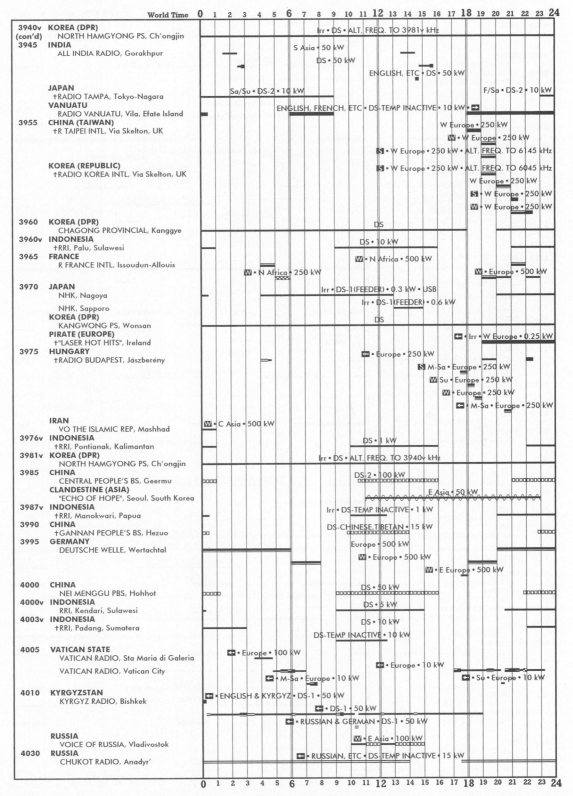

| | | |
|---|---|---|
| 3940v (con'd) | KOREA (DPR) | NORTH HAMGYONG PS, Ch'ongjin |
| 3945 | INDIA | ALL INDIA RADIO, Gorakhpur |
| | JAPAN | †RADIO TAMPA, Tokyo-Nagara |
| | VANUATU | RADIO VANUATU, Vila, Efate Island |
| 3955 | CHINA (TAIWAN) | †R TAIPEI INTL, Via Skelton, UK |
| | KOREA (REPUBLIC) | †RADIO KOREA INTL, Via Skelton, UK |
| 3960 | KOREA (DPR) | CHAGONG PROVINCIAL, Kanggye |
| 3960v | INDONESIA | †RRI, Palu, Sulawesi |
| 3965 | FRANCE | R FRANCE INTL, Issoudun-Allouis |
| 3970 | JAPAN | NHK, Nagoya |
| | | NHK, Sapporo |
| | KOREA (DPR) | KANGWONG PS, Wonsan |
| | PIRATE (EUROPE) | †"LASER HOT HITS", Ireland |
| 3975 | HUNGARY | †RADIO BUDAPEST, Jászberény |
| | IRAN | VO THE ISLAMIC REP, Mashhad |
| 3976v | INDONESIA | †RRI, Pontianak, Kalimantan |
| 3981v | KOREA (DPR) | NORTH HAMGYONG PS, Ch'ongjin |
| 3985 | CHINA | CENTRAL PEOPLE'S BS, Geermu |
| | CLANDESTINE (ASIA) | "ECHO OF HOPE", Seoul, South Korea |
| 3987v | INDONESIA | †RRI, Manokwari, Papua |
| 3990 | CHINA | †GANNAN PEOPLE'S BS, Hezuo |
| 3995 | GERMANY | DEUTSCHE WELLE, Wertachtal |
| 4000 | CHINA | NEI MENGGU PBS, Hohhot |
| 4000v | INDONESIA | RRI, Kendari, Sulawesi |
| 4003v | INDONESIA | †RRI, Padang, Sumatera |
| 4005 | VATICAN STATE | VATICAN RADIO, Sta Maria di Galeria |
| | | VATICAN RADIO, Vatican City |
| 4010 | KYRGYZSTAN | KYRGYZ RADIO, Bishkek |
| | RUSSIA | VOICE OF RUSSIA, Vladivostok |
| 4030 | RUSSIA | CHUKOT RADIO, Anadyr' |

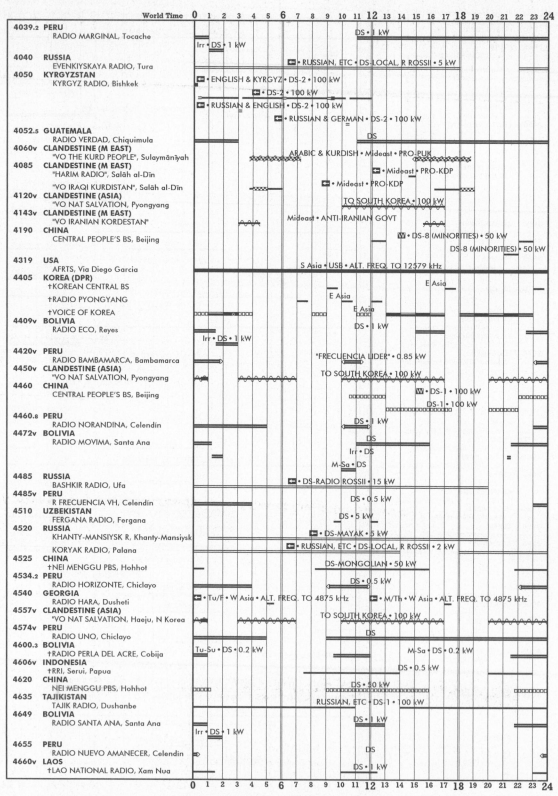

| | | |
|---|---|---|
| 4039.2 | **PERU** | |
| | RADIO MARGINAL, Tocache | DS • 1 kW / Irr • DS • 1 kW |
| 4040 | **RUSSIA** | |
| | EVENKIYSKAYA RADIO, Tura | RUSSIAN, ETC • DS-LOCAL, R ROSSII • 5 kW |
| 4050 | **KYRGYZSTAN** | |
| | KYRGYZ RADIO, Bishkek | ENGLISH & KYRGYZ • DS-2 • 100 kW / DS-2 • 100 kW / RUSSIAN & ENGLISH • DS-2 • 100 kW / RUSSIAN & GERMAN • DS-2 • 100 kW |
| 4052.5 | **GUATEMALA** | |
| | RADIO VERDAD, Chiquimula | DS |
| 4060v | **CLANDESTINE (M EAST)** | |
| | "VO THE KURD PEOPLE", Sulaymānīyah | ARABIC & KURDISH • Mideast • PRO-PUK |
| 4085 | **CLANDESTINE (M EAST)** | |
| | "HARIM RADIO", Salāh al-Dīn | Mideast • PRO-KDP |
| | "VO IRAQI KURDISTAN", Salāh al-Dīn | Mideast • PRO-KDP |
| 4120v | **CLANDESTINE (ASIA)** | |
| | "VO NAT SALVATION, Pyongyang | TO SOUTH KOREA • 100 kW |
| 4143v | **CLANDESTINE (M EAST)** | |
| | "VO IRANIAN KORDESTAN" | Mideast • ANTI-IRANIAN GOVT |
| 4190 | **CHINA** | |
| | CENTRAL PEOPLE'S BS, Beijing | W • DS-8 (MINORITIES) • 50 kW / DS-8 (MINORITIES) • 50 kW |
| 4319 | **USA** | |
| | AFRTS, Via Diego Garcia | S Asia • USB • ALT. FREQ. TO 12579 kHz |
| 4405 | **KOREA (DPR)** | |
| | †KOREAN CENTRAL BS | E Asia |
| | †RADIO PYONGYANG | E Asia |
| | †VOICE OF KOREA | E Asia |
| 4409v | **BOLIVIA** | |
| | RADIO ECO, Reyes | DS • 1 kW / Irr • DS • 1 kW |
| 4420v | **PERU** | |
| | RADIO BAMBAMARCA, Bambamarca | "FRECUENCIA LIDER" • 0.85 kW |
| 4450v | **CLANDESTINE (ASIA)** | |
| | "VO NAT SALVATION, Pyongyang | TO SOUTH KOREA • 100 kW |
| 4460 | **CHINA** | |
| | CENTRAL PEOPLE'S BS, Beijing | W • DS-1 • 100 kW / DS-1 • 100 kW |
| 4460.8 | **PERU** | |
| | RADIO NORANDINA, Celendin | DS • 1 kW |
| 4472v | **BOLIVIA** | |
| | RADIO MOVIMA, Santa Ana | DS / Irr • DS / M-Sa • DS |
| 4485 | **RUSSIA** | |
| | BASHKIR RADIO, Ufa | DS-RADIO ROSSII • 15 kW |
| 4485v | **PERU** | |
| | R FRECUENCIA VH, Celendin | DS • 0.5 kW |
| 4510 | **UZBEKISTAN** | |
| | FERGANA RADIO, Fergana | DS • 5 kW |
| 4520 | **RUSSIA** | |
| | KHANTY-MANSIYSK R, Khanty-Mansiysk | DS-MAYAK • 5 kW |
| | KORYAK RADIO, Palana | RUSSIAN, ETC • DS-LOCAL, R ROSSII • 2 kW |
| 4525 | **CHINA** | |
| | †NEI MENGGU PBS, Hohhot | DS-MONGOLIAN • 50 kW |
| 4534.2 | **PERU** | |
| | RADIO HORIZONTE, Chiclayo | DS • 0.5 kW |
| 4540 | **GEORGIA** | |
| | RADIO HARA, Dusheti | Tu/F • W Asia • ALT. FREQ. TO 4875 kHz / M/Th • W Asia • ALT. FREQ. TO 4875 kHz |
| 4557v | **CLANDESTINE (ASIA)** | |
| | "VO NAT SALVATION, Haeju, N Korea | TO SOUTH KOREA • 100 kW |
| 4574v | **PERU** | |
| | RADIO UNO, Chiclayo | DS |
| 4600.3 | **BOLIVIA** | |
| | †RADIO PERLA DEL ACRE, Cobija | Tu-Su • DS • 0.2 kW / M-Sa • DS • 0.2 kW |
| 4606v | **INDONESIA** | |
| | †RRI, Serui, Papua | DS • 0.5 kW |
| 4620 | **CHINA** | |
| | NEI MENGGU PBS, Hohhot | DS • 50 kW |
| 4635 | **TAJIKISTAN** | |
| | TAJIK RADIO, Dushanbe | RUSSIAN, ETC • DS-1 • 100 kW |
| 4649 | **BOLIVIA** | |
| | RADIO SANTA ANA, Santa Ana | DS • 1 kW / Irr • DS • 1 kW |
| 4655 | **PERU** | |
| | RADIO NUEVO AMANECER, Celendin | DS |
| 4660v | **LAOS** | |
| | †LAO NATIONAL RADIO, Xam Nua | DS • 1 kW |

World Time   0  1  2  3  4  5  6  7  8  9  10  11  12  13  14  15  16  17  18  19  20  21  22  23  24

ENGLISH ▬▬   ARABIC ⨯⨯⨯   CHINESE □□□   FRENCH ▬▬   GERMAN ▬▬   RUSSIAN ══   SPANISH ▬▬   OTHER ▬▬

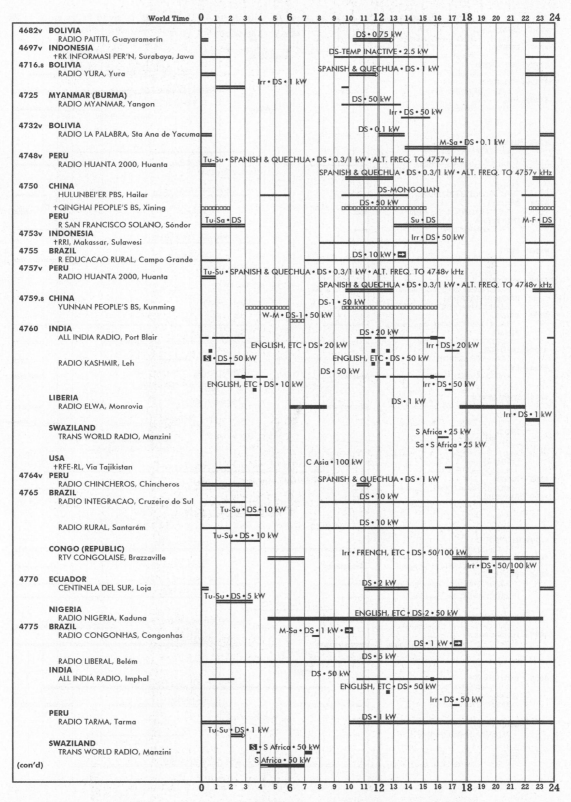

| | World Time | | |
|---|---|---|---|
| 4682v | BOLIVIA | RADIO PAITITI, Guayaramerín | DS • 0.75 kW |
| 4697v | INDONESIA | †RK INFORMASI PER'N, Surabaya, Jawa | DS-TEMP INACTIVE • 2.5 kW |
| 4716.8 | BOLIVIA | RADIO YURA, Yura | SPANISH & QUECHUA • DS • 1 kW |
| | | | Irr • DS • 1 kW |
| 4725 | MYANMAR (BURMA) | RADIO MYANMAR, Yangon | DS • 50 kW |
| | | | Irr • DS • 50 kW |
| 4732v | BOLIVIA | RADIO LA PALABRA, Sta Ana de Yacuma | DS • 0.1 kW |
| | | | M-Sa • DS • 0.1 kW |
| 4748v | PERU | RADIO HUANTA 2000, Huanta | Tu-Su • SPANISH & QUECHUA • DS • 0.3/1 kW • ALT. FREQ. TO 4757v kHz |
| | | | SPANISH & QUECHUA • DS • 0.3/1 kW • ALT. FREQ. TO 4757v kHz |
| 4750 | CHINA | HULUNBEI'ER PBS, Hailar | DS-MONGOLIAN |
| | | †QINGHAI PEOPLE'S BS, Xining | DS • 50 kW |
| | PERU | R SAN FRANCISCO SOLANO, Sóndor | Tu-Sa • DS / Su • DS / M-F • DS |
| 4753v | INDONESIA | †RRI, Makassar, Sulawesi | Irr • DS • 50 kW |
| 4755 | BRAZIL | R EDUCACAO RURAL, Campo Grande | DS • 10 kW • ➡ |
| 4757v | PERU | RADIO HUANTA 2000, Huanta | Tu-Su • SPANISH & QUECHUA • DS • 0.3/1 kW • ALT. FREQ. TO 4748v kHz |
| | | | SPANISH & QUECHUA • DS • 0.3/1 kW • ALT. FREQ. TO 4748v kHz |
| 4759.8 | CHINA | YUNNAN PEOPLE'S BS, Kunming | DS-1 • 50 kW |
| | | | W-M • DS-1 • 50 kW |
| 4760 | INDIA | ALL INDIA RADIO, Port Blair | DS • 20 kW |
| | | | ENGLISH, ETC • DS • 20 kW / Irr • DS • 20 kW |
| | | RADIO KASHMIR, Leh | S • DS • 50 kW |
| | | | ENGLISH, ETC • DS • 50 kW |
| | | | DS • 50 kW |
| | | | ENGLISH, ETC • DS • 10 kW / Irr • DS • 50 kW |
| | LIBERIA | RADIO ELWA, Monrovia | DS • 1 kW |
| | | | Irr • DS • 1 kW |
| | SWAZILAND | TRANS WORLD RADIO, Manzini | S Africa • 25 kW |
| | | | Sa • S Africa • 25 kW |
| | USA | †RFE-RL, Via Tajikistan | C Asia • 100 kW |
| 4764v | PERU | RADIO CHINCHEROS, Chincheros | SPANISH & QUECHUA • DS • 1 kW |
| 4765 | BRAZIL | RADIO INTEGRACAO, Cruzeiro do Sul | DS • 10 kW |
| | | | Tu-Su • DS • 10 kW |
| | | RADIO RURAL, Santarém | DS • 10 kW |
| | | | Tu-Su • DS • 10 kW |
| | CONGO (REPUBLIC) | RTV CONGOLAISE, Brazzaville | Irr • FRENCH, ETC • DS • 50/100 kW |
| | | | Irr • DS • 50/100 kW |
| 4770 | ECUADOR | CENTINELA DEL SUR, Loja | DS • 2 kW |
| | | | Tu-Su • DS • 5 kW |
| | NIGERIA | RADIO NIGERIA, Kaduna | ENGLISH, ETC • DS-2 • 50 kW |
| 4775 | BRAZIL | RADIO CONGONHAS, Congonhas | M-Sa • DS • 1 kW • ➡ |
| | | | DS • 1 kW • ➡ |
| | | RADIO LIBERAL, Belém | DS • 5 kW |
| | INDIA | ALL INDIA RADIO, Imphal | DS • 50 kW |
| | | | ENGLISH, ETC • DS • 50 kW |
| | | | Irr • DS • 50 kW |
| | PERU | RADIO TARMA, Tarma | DS • 1 kW |
| | | | Tu-Su • DS • 1 kW |
| | SWAZILAND | TRANS WORLD RADIO, Manzini | S • S Africa • 50 kW |
| | | | S Africa • 50 kW |
| (con'd) | | | |

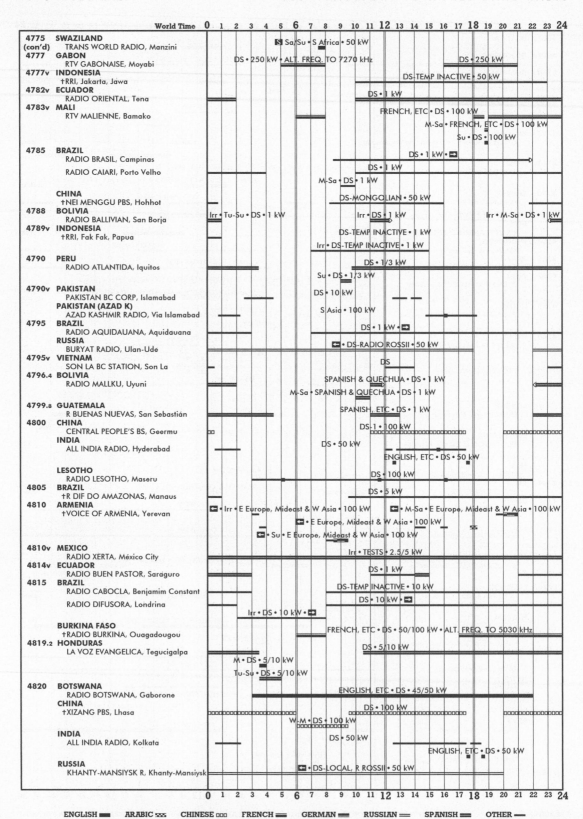

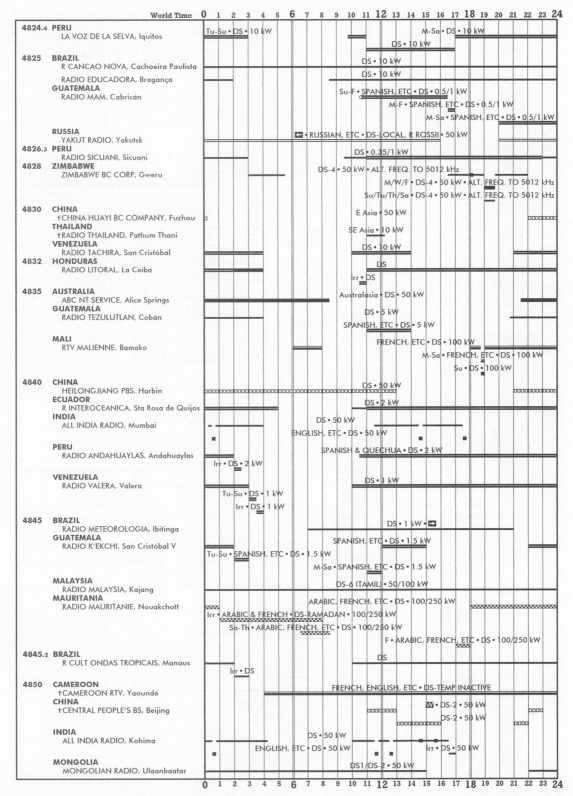

World Time 0 1 2 3 4 5 6 7 8 9 10 11 12 13 14 15 16 17 18 19 20 21 22 23 24

**4824.4 PERU**
LA VOZ DE LA SELVA, Iquitos
Tu-Su • DS • 10 kW — M-Sa • DS • 10 kW
DS • 10 kW

**4825 BRAZIL**
R CANCAO NOVA, Cachoeira Paulista — DS • 10 kW
RADIO EDUCADORA, Bragança — DS • 10 kW
**GUATEMALA**
RADIO MAM, Cabricán
Su-F • SPANISH, ETC • DS • 0.5/1 kW
M-F • SPANISH, ETC • DS • 0.5/1 kW
M-Sa • SPANISH, ETC • DS • 0.5/1 kW
**RUSSIA**
YAKUT RADIO, Yakutsk — RUSSIAN, ETC • DS-LOCAL, R ROSSII • 50 kW

**4826.3 PERU**
RADIO SICUANI, Sicuani — DS • 0.35/1 kW
**4828 ZIMBABWE**
ZIMBABWE BC CORP, Gweru
DS-4 • 50 kW • ALT. FREQ. TO 5012 kHz
M/W/F • DS-4 • 50 kW • ALT. FREQ. TO 5012 kHz
Su/Tu/Th/Sa • DS-4 • 50 kW • ALT. FREQ. TO 5012 kHz

**4830 CHINA**
†CHINA HUAYI BC COMPANY, Fuzhou — E Asia • 50 kW
**THAILAND**
†RADIO THAILAND, Pathum Thani — SE Asia • 10 kW
**VENEZUELA**
RADIO TACHIRA, San Cristóbal — DS • 10 kW
**4832 HONDURAS**
RADIO LITORAL, La Ceiba — DS
Irr • DS

**4835 AUSTRALIA**
ABC NT SERVICE, Alice Springs — Australasia • DS • 50 kW
**GUATEMALA**
RADIO TEZULUTLAN, Cobán — DS • 5 kW
SPANISH, ETC • DS • 5 kW
**MALI**
RTV MALIENNE, Bamako
FRENCH, ETC • DS • 100 kW
M-Sa • FRENCH, ETC • DS • 100 kW
Su • DS • 100 kW

**4840 CHINA**
HEILONGJIANG PBS, Harbin — DS • 50 kW
**ECUADOR**
R INTEROCEANICA, Sta Rosa de Quijos — DS • 2 kW
**INDIA**
ALL INDIA RADIO, Mumbai
DS • 50 kW
ENGLISH, ETC • DS • 50 kW
**PERU**
RADIO ANDAHUAYLAS, Andahuaylas
SPANISH & QUECHUA • DS • 2 kW
Irr • DS • 2 kW
**VENEZUELA**
RADIO VALERA, Valera
DS • 1 kW
Tu-Su • DS • 1 kW
Irr • DS • 1 kW

**4845 BRAZIL**
RADIO METEOROLOGIA, Ibitinga — DS • 1 kW
**GUATEMALA**
RADIO K'EKCHI, San Cristóbal V
SPANISH, ETC • DS • 1.5 kW
Tu-Su • SPANISH, ETC • DS • 1.5 kW
M-Sa • SPANISH, ETC • DS • 1.5 kW
**MALAYSIA**
RADIO MALAYSIA, Kajang — DS-6 (TAMIL) • 50/100 kW
**MAURITANIA**
RADIO MAURITANIE, Nouakchott
ARABIC, FRENCH, ETC • DS • 100/250 kW
Irr • ARABIC & FRENCH • DS-RAMADAN • 100/250 kW
Sa-Th • ARABIC, FRENCH, ETC • DS • 100/250 kW
F • ARABIC, FRENCH, ETC • DS • 100/250 kW

**4845.2 BRAZIL**
R CULT ONDAS TROPICAIS, Manaus — DS
Irr • DS

**4850 CAMEROON**
†CAMEROON RTV, Yaoundé — FRENCH, ENGLISH, ETC • DS-TEMP INACTIVE
**CHINA**
†CENTRAL PEOPLE'S BS, Beijing
W • DS-2 • 50 kW
DS-2 • 50 kW
**INDIA**
ALL INDIA RADIO, Kohima
DS • 50 kW
ENGLISH, ETC • DS • 50 kW
Irr • DS • 50 kW
**MONGOLIA**
MONGOLIAN RADIO, Ulaanbaatar — DS1/DS-2 • 50 kW

0 1 2 3 4 5 6 7 8 9 10 11 12 13 14 15 16 17 18 19 20 21 22 23 24

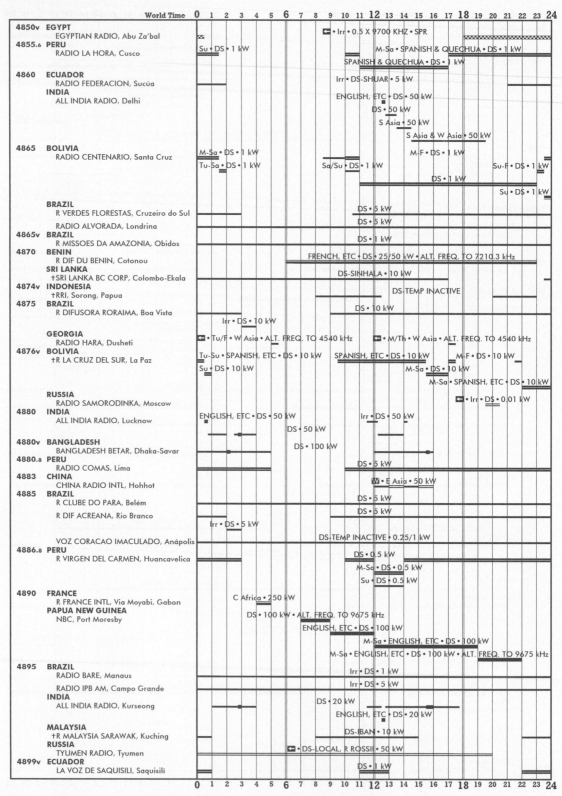

| World Time | 0 1 2 3 4 5 6 7 8 9 10 11 12 13 14 15 16 17 18 19 20 21 22 23 24 |
|---|---|

**4850v EGYPT**
EGYPTIAN RADIO, Abu Za'bal — Irr • 0.5 X 9700 KHZ • SPR

**4855.6 PERU**
RADIO LA HORA, Cusco — Su • DS • 1 kW — M-Sa • SPANISH & QUECHUA • DS • 1 kW
SPANISH & QUECHUA • DS • 1 kW

**4860 ECUADOR**
RADIO FEDERACION, Sucúa — Irr • DS-SHUAR • 5 kW

**INDIA**
ALL INDIA RADIO, Delhi — ENGLISH, ETC • DS • 50 kW
DS • 50 kW
S Asia • 50 kW
S Asia & W Asia • 50 kW

**4865 BOLIVIA**
RADIO CENTENARIO, Santa Cruz — M-Sa • DS • 1 kW — M-F • DS • 1 kW
Tu-Sa • DS • 1 kW — Sa/Su • DS • 1 kW — Su-F • DS • 1 kW
DS • 1 kW
Su • DS • 1 kW

**BRAZIL**
R VERDES FLORESTAS, Cruzeiro do Sul — DS • 5 kW
RADIO ALVORADA, Londrina — DS • 5 kW

**4865v BRAZIL**
R MISSOES DA AMAZONIA, Obidos — DS • 1 kW

**4870 BENIN**
R DIF DU BENIN, Cotonou — FRENCH, ETC • DS • 25/50 kW • ALT. FREQ. TO 7210.3 kHz

**SRI LANKA**
†SRI LANKA BC CORP, Colombo-Ekala — DS-SINHALA • 10 kW

**4874v INDONESIA**
†RRI, Sorong, Papua — DS-TEMP INACTIVE

**4875 BRAZIL**
R DIFUSORA RORAIMA, Boa Vista — DS • 10 kW
Irr • DS • 10 kW

**GEORGIA**
RADIO HARA, Dusheti — Tu/F • W Asia • ALT. FREQ. TO 4540 kHz — M/Th • W Asia • ALT. FREQ. TO 4540 kHz

**4876v BOLIVIA**
†R LA CRUZ DEL SUR, La Paz — Tu-Su • SPANISH, ETC • DS • 10 kW — SPANISH, ETC • DS • 10 kW — M-F • DS • 10 kW
Su • DS • 10 kW — M-Sa • DS • 10 kW
M-Sa • SPANISH, ETC • DS • 10 kW

**RUSSIA**
RADIO SAMORODINKA, Moscow — Irr • DS • 0.01 kW

**4880 INDIA**
ALL INDIA RADIO, Lucknow — ENGLISH, ETC • DS • 50 kW — Irr • DS • 50 kW
DS • 50 kW

**4880v BANGLADESH**
BANGLADESH BETAR, Dhaka-Savar — DS • 100 kW

**4880.8 PERU**
RADIO COMAS, Lima — DS • 5 kW

**4883 CHINA**
CHINA RADIO INTL, Hohhot — W • E Asia • 50 kW

**4885 BRAZIL**
R CLUBE DO PARA, Belém — DS • 5 kW
R DIF ACREANA, Rio Branco — DS • 5 kW
Irr • DS • 5 kW
VOZ CORACAO IMACULADO, Anápolis — DS-TEMP INACTIVE • 0.25/1 kW

**4886.8 PERU**
R VIRGEN DEL CARMEN, Huancavelica — DS • 0.5 kW
M-Sa • DS • 0.5 kW
Su • DS • 0.5 kW

**4890 FRANCE**
R FRANCE INTL, Via Moyabi, Gabon — C Africa • 250 kW

**PAPUA NEW GUINEA**
NBC, Port Moresby — DS • 100 kW • ALT. FREQ. TO 9675 kHz
ENGLISH, ETC • DS • 100 kW
M-Sa • ENGLISH, ETC • DS • 100 kW
M-Sa • ENGLISH, ETC • DS • 100 kW • ALT. FREQ. TO 9675 kHz

**4895 BRAZIL**
RADIO BARE, Manaus — Irr • DS • 1 kW
RADIO IPB AM, Campo Grande — Irr • DS • 5 kW

**INDIA**
ALL INDIA RADIO, Kurseong — DS • 20 kW
ENGLISH, ETC • DS • 20 kW

**MALAYSIA**
†R MALAYSIA SARAWAK, Kuching — DS-IBAN • 10 kW

**RUSSIA**
TYUMEN RADIO, Tyumen — DS-LOCAL, R ROSSII • 50 kW

**4899v ECUADOR**
LA VOZ DE SAQUISILI, Saquisili — DS • 1 kW

| | 0 1 2 3 4 5 6 7 8 9 10 11 12 13 14 15 16 17 18 19 20 21 22 23 24 |
|---|---|

ENGLISH ▬   ARABIC ⌇⌇⌇   CHINESE ▫▫▫   FRENCH ═══   GERMAN ▬▬   RUSSIAN ═══   SPANISH ▬▬   OTHER ▬

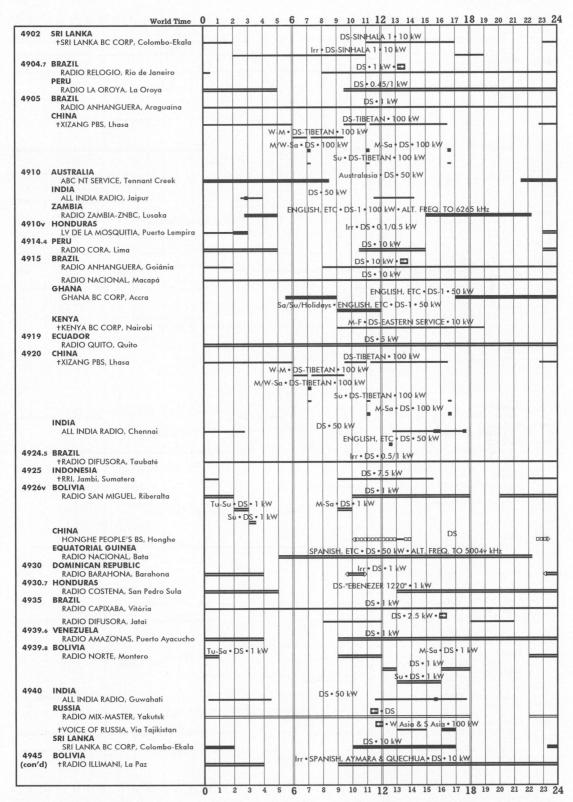

World Time 0 1 2 3 4 5 6 7 8 9 10 11 12 13 14 15 16 17 18 19 20 21 22 23 24

| 4902 | SRI LANKA |
| | †SRI LANKA BC CORP, Colombo-Ekala | DS-SINHALA 1 • 10 kW |
| | | Irr • DS-SINHALA 1 • 10 kW |
| 4904.7 | BRAZIL |
| | RADIO RELOGIO, Rio de Janeiro | DS • 1 kW • |
| | PERU |
| | RADIO LA OROYA, La Oroya | DS • 0.45/1 kW |
| 4905 | BRAZIL |
| | RADIO ANHANGUERA, Araguaína | DS • 1 kW |
| | CHINA |
| | †XIZANG PBS, Lhasa | DS-TIBETAN • 100 kW |
| | | W-M • DS-TIBETAN • 100 kW |
| | | M/W-Sa • DS • 100 kW     M-Sa • DS • 100 kW |
| | | Su • DS-TIBETAN • 100 kW |
| 4910 | AUSTRALIA |
| | ABC NT SERVICE, Tennant Creek | Australasia • DS • 50 kW |
| | INDIA |
| | ALL INDIA RADIO, Jaipur | DS • 50 kW |
| | ZAMBIA |
| | RADIO ZAMBIA-ZNBC, Lusaka | ENGLISH, ETC • DS-1 • 100 kW • ALT. FREQ. TO 6265 kHz |
| 4910v | HONDURAS |
| | LV DE LA MOSQUITIA, Puerto Lempira | Irr • DS • 0.1/0.5 kW |
| 4914.4 | PERU |
| | RADIO CORA, Lima | DS • 10 kW |
| 4915 | BRAZIL |
| | RADIO ANHANGUERA, Goiânia | DS • 10 kW • |
| | RADIO NACIONAL, Macapá | DS • 10 kW |
| | GHANA |
| | GHANA BC CORP, Accra | ENGLISH, ETC • DS-1 • 50 kW |
| | | Sa/Su/Holidays • ENGLISH, ETC • DS-1 • 50 kW |
| | KENYA |
| | †KENYA BC CORP, Nairobi | M-F • DS-EASTERN SERVICE • 10 kW |
| 4919 | ECUADOR |
| | RADIO QUITO, Quito | DS • 5 kW |
| 4920 | CHINA |
| | †XIZANG PBS, Lhasa | DS-TIBETAN • 100 kW |
| | | W-M • DS-TIBETAN • 100 kW |
| | | M/W-Sa • DS-TIBETAN • 100 kW |
| | | Su • DS-TIBETAN • 100 kW |
| | | M-Sa • DS • 100 kW |
| | INDIA |
| | ALL INDIA RADIO, Chennai | DS • 50 kW |
| | | ENGLISH, ETC • DS • 50 kW |
| 4924.5 | BRAZIL |
| | †RADIO DIFUSORA, Taubaté | Irr • DS • 0.5/1 kW |
| 4925 | INDONESIA |
| | †RRI, Jambi, Sumatera | DS • 7.5 kW |
| 4926v | BOLIVIA |
| | RADIO SAN MIGUEL, Riberalta | DS • 1 kW |
| | | Tu-Su • DS • 1 kW     M-Sa • DS • 1 kW |
| | | Su • DS • 1 kW |
| | CHINA |
| | HONGHE PEOPLE'S BS, Honghe | DS |
| | EQUATORIAL GUINEA |
| | RADIO NACIONAL, Bata | SPANISH, ETC • DS • 50 kW • ALT. FREQ. TO 5004v kHz |
| 4930 | DOMINICAN REPUBLIC |
| | RADIO BARAHONA, Barahona | Irr • DS • 1 kW |
| 4930.7 | HONDURAS |
| | RADIO COSTENA, San Pedro Sula | DS-"EBENEZER 1220" • 1 kW |
| 4935 | BRAZIL |
| | RADIO CAPIXABA, Vitória | DS • 1 kW |
| | RADIO DIFUSORA, Jataí | DS • 2.5 kW • |
| 4939.6 | VENEZUELA |
| | RADIO AMAZONAS, Puerto Ayacucho | DS • 1 kW |
| 4939.8 | BOLIVIA |
| | RADIO NORTE, Montero | Tu-Sa • DS • 1 kW     M-Sa • DS • 1 kW |
| | | DS • 1 kW |
| | | Su • DS • 1 kW |
| 4940 | INDIA |
| | ALL INDIA RADIO, Guwahati | DS • 50 kW |
| | RUSSIA |
| | RADIO MIX-MASTER, Yakutsk | DS |
| | †VOICE OF RUSSIA, Via Tajikistan | W Asia & S Asia • 100 kW |
| | SRI LANKA |
| | SRI LANKA BC CORP, Colombo-Ekala | DS • 10 kW |
| 4945 | BOLIVIA |
| (con'd) | †RADIO ILLIMANI, La Paz | Irr • SPANISH, AYMARA & QUECHUA • DS • 10 kW |

0 1 2 3 4 5 6 7 8 9 10 11 12 13 14 15 16 17 18 19 20 21 22 23 24

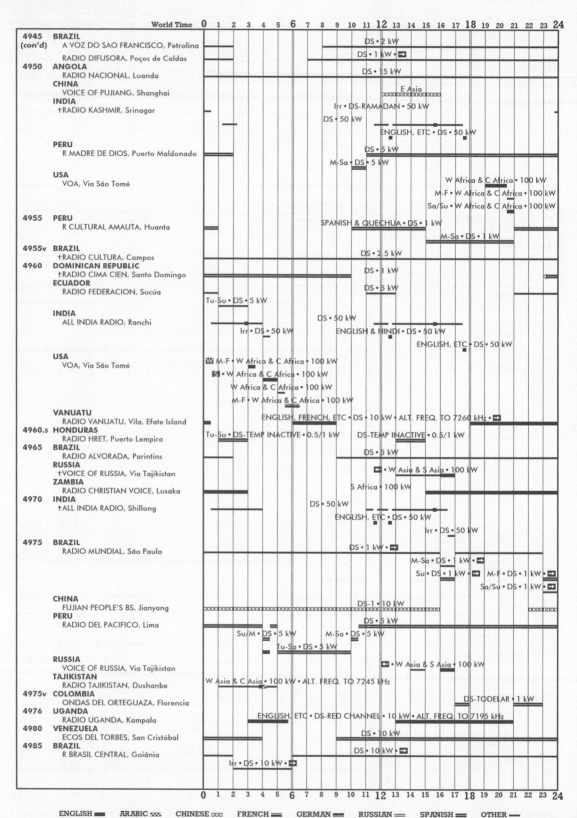

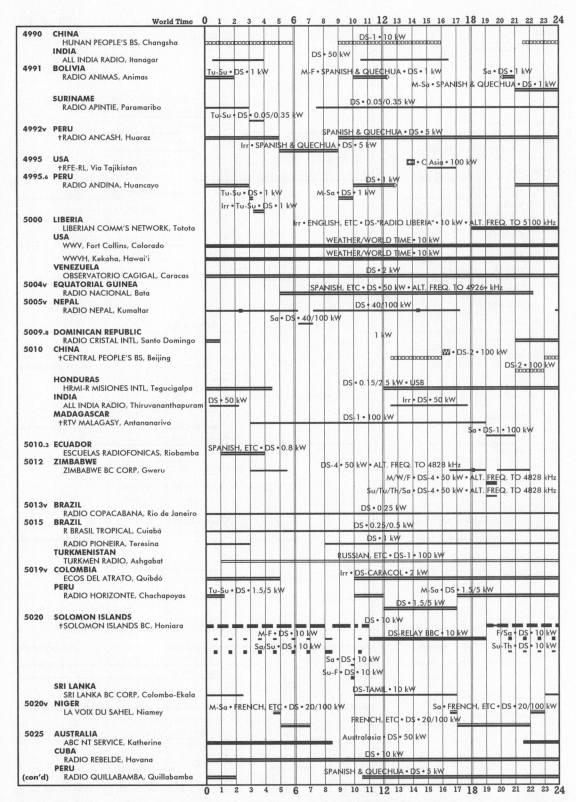

World Time 0 1 2 3 4 5 6 7 8 9 10 11 12 13 14 15 16 17 18 19 20 21 22 23 24

**4990  CHINA**
HUNAN PEOPLE'S BS, Changsha — DS-1 • 10 kW
**INDIA**
ALL INDIA RADIO, Itanagar
**4991  BOLIVIA**
RADIO ANIMAS, Animas — Tu-Su • DS • 1 kW / M-F • SPANISH & QUECHUA • DS • 1 kW / Sa • DS • 1 kW / M-Sa • SPANISH & QUECHUA • DS • 1 kW

**SURINAME**
RADIO APINTIE, Paramaribo — DS • 0.05/0.35 kW / Tu-Su • DS • 0.05/0.35 kW

**4992v  PERU**
†RADIO ANCASH, Huaraz — SPANISH & QUECHUA • DS • 5 kW / Irr • SPANISH & QUECHUA • DS • 5 kW

**4995  USA**
†RFE-RL, Via Tajikistan — • C Asia • 100 kW
**4995.6  PERU**
RADIO ANDINA, Huancayo — DS • 1 kW / Tu-Su • DS • 1 kW / M-Sa • DS • 1 kW / Irr • Tu-Su • DS • 1 kW

**5000  LIBERIA**
LIBERIAN COMM'S NETWORK, Totota — Irr • ENGLISH, ETC • DS • "RADIO LIBERIA" • 10 kW • ALT. FREQ. TO 5100 kHz
**USA**
WWV, Fort Collins, Colorado — WEATHER/WORLD TIME • 10 kW
WWVH, Kekaha, Hawai'i — WEATHER/WORLD TIME • 10 kW
**VENEZUELA**
OBSERVATORIO CAGIGAL, Caracas — DS • 2 kW
**5004v  EQUATORIAL GUINEA**
RADIO NACIONAL, Bata — SPANISH, ETC • DS • 50 kW • ALT. FREQ. TO 4926v kHz
**5005v  NEPAL**
RADIO NEPAL, Kumaltar — DS • 40/100 kW / Sa • DS • 40/100 kW

**5009.8  DOMINICAN REPUBLIC**
RADIO CRISTAL INTL, Santo Domingo — 1 kW
**5010  CHINA**
†CENTRAL PEOPLE'S BS, Beijing — W • DS-2 • 100 kW / DS-2 • 100 kW

**HONDURAS**
HRMI-R MISIONES INTL, Tegucigalpa — DS • 0.15/2.5 kW • USB
**INDIA**
ALL INDIA RADIO, Thiruvananthapuram — DS • 50 kW / Irr • DS • 50 kW
**MADAGASCAR**
†RTV MALAGASY, Antananarivo — DS-1 • 100 kW / Sa • DS-1 • 100 kW

**5010.3  ECUADOR**
ESCUELAS RADIOFONICAS, Riobamba — SPANISH, ETC • DS • 0.8 kW
**5012  ZIMBABWE**
ZIMBABWE BC CORP, Gweru — DS-4 • 50 kW • ALT. FREQ. TO 4828 kHz / M/W/F • DS-4 • 50 kW • ALT. FREQ. TO 4828 kHz / Su/Tu/Th/Sa • DS-4 • 50 kW • ALT. FREQ. TO 4828 kHz

**5013v  BRAZIL**
RADIO COPACABANA, Rio de Janeiro — DS • 0.25 kW
**5015  BRAZIL**
R BRASIL TROPICAL, Cuiabá — DS • 0.25/0.5 kW

RADIO PIONEIRA, Teresina — DS • 1 kW
**TURKMENISTAN**
TURKMEN RADIO, Ashgabat — RUSSIAN, ETC • DS-1 • 100 kW
**5019v  COLOMBIA**
ECOS DEL ATRATO, Quibdó — Irr • DS-CARACOL • 2 kW
**PERU**
RADIO HORIZONTE, Chachapoyas — Tu-Su • DS • 1.5/5 kW / M-Sa • DS • 1.5/5 kW / DS • 1.5/5 kW

**5020  SOLOMON ISLANDS**
†SOLOMON ISLANDS BC, Honiara — DS • 10 kW / M-F • DS • 10 kW / DS-RELAY BBC • 10 kW / F/Sa • DS • 10 kW / Sa/Su • DS • 10 kW / Su-Th • DS • 10 kW / Sa • DS • 10 kW / Su-F • DS • 10 kW

**SRI LANKA**
SRI LANKA BC CORP, Colombo-Ekala — DS-TAMIL • 10 kW
**5020v  NIGER**
LA VOIX DU SAHEL, Niamey — M-Sa • FRENCH, ETC • DS • 20/100 kW / Sa • FRENCH, ETC • DS • 20/100 kW / FRENCH, ETC • DS • 20/100 kW

**5025  AUSTRALIA**
ABC NT SERVICE, Katherine — Australasia • DS • 50 kW
**CUBA**
RADIO REBELDE, Havana — DS • 10 kW
**PERU**
(con'd)  RADIO QUILLABAMBA, Quillabamba — SPANISH & QUECHUA • DS • 5 kW

0 1 2 3 4 5 6 7 8 9 10 11 12 13 14 15 16 17 18 19 20 21 22 23 24

SEASONAL S OR W    1-HR TIMESHIFT MIDYEAR ⬅ OR ➡    JAMMING / OR ∧    EARLIEST HEARD ◁    LATEST HEARD ▷    NEW FOR 2003 †

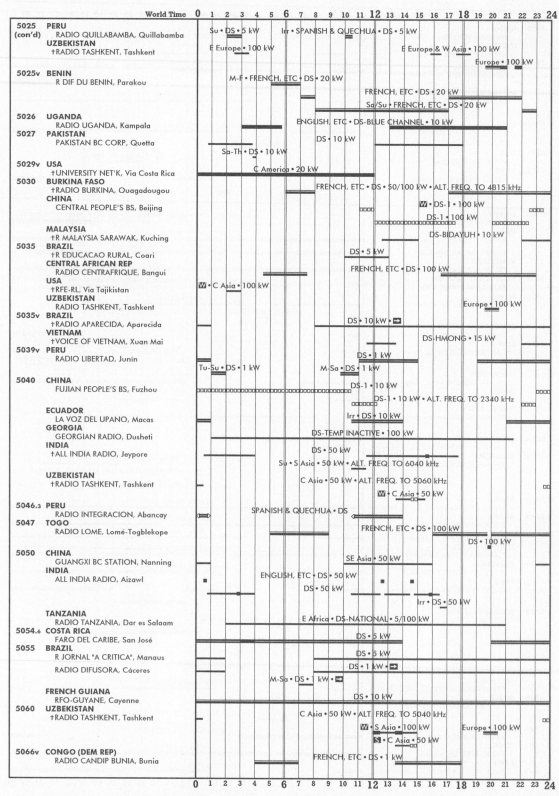

| World Time | 0 | 1 | 2 | 3 | 4 | 5 | 6 | 7 | 8 | 9 | 10 | 11 | 12 | 13 | 14 | 15 | 16 | 17 | 18 | 19 | 20 | 21 | 22 | 23 | 24 |

**5025 PERU**
(con'd) RADIO QUILLABAMBA, Quillabamba — Su • DS • 5 kW ; Irr • SPANISH & QUECHUA • DS • 5 kW
**UZBEKISTAN**
†RADIO TASHKENT, Tashkent — E Europe • 100 kW ; E Europe & W Asia • 100 kW ; Europe • 100 kW

**5025v BENIN**
R DIF DU BENIN, Parakou — M-F • FRENCH, ETC • DS • 20 kW ; FRENCH, ETC • DS • 20 kW ; Sa/Su • FRENCH, ETC • DS • 20 kW

**5026 UGANDA**
RADIO UGANDA, Kampala — ENGLISH, ETC • DS-BLUE CHANNEL • 10 kW
**5027 PAKISTAN**
PAKISTAN BC CORP, Quetta — DS • 10 kW ; Sa-Th • DS • 10 kW

**5029v USA**
†UNIVERSITY NET'K, Via Costa Rica — C America • 20 kW
**5030 BURKINA FASO**
†RADIO BURKINA, Ouagadougou — FRENCH, ETC • DS • 50/100 kW • ALT. FREQ. TO 4815 kHz
**CHINA**
CENTRAL PEOPLE'S BS, Beijing — W • DS-1 • 100 kW ; DS-1 • 100 kW

**MALAYSIA**
†R MALAYSIA SARAWAK, Kuching — DS-BIDAYUH • 10 kW
**5035 BRAZIL**
†R EDUCACAO RURAL, Coari — DS • 5 kW
**CENTRAL AFRICAN REP**
RADIO CENTRAFRIQUE, Bangui — FRENCH, ETC • DS • 100 kW
**USA**
†RFE-RL, Via Tajikistan — W • C Asia • 100 kW
**UZBEKISTAN**
RADIO TASHKENT, Tashkent — Europe • 100 kW
**5035v BRAZIL**
†RADIO APARECIDA, Aparecida — DS • 10 kW • ▭
**VIETNAM**
†VOICE OF VIETNAM, Xuan Mai — DS-HMONG • 15 kW
**5039v PERU**
RADIO LIBERTAD, Junín — DS • 1 kW ; Tu-Su • DS • 1 kW ; M-Sa • DS • 1 kW

**5040 CHINA**
FUJIAN PEOPLE'S BS, Fuzhou — DS-1 • 10 kW ; DS-1 • 10 kW • ALT. FREQ. TO 2340 kHz

**ECUADOR**
LA VOZ DEL UPANO, Macas — Irr • DS • 10 kW
**GEORGIA**
GEORGIAN RADIO, Dusheti — DS-TEMP INACTIVE • 100 kW
**INDIA**
†ALL INDIA RADIO, Jeypore — DS • 50 kW ; Su • S Asia • 50 kW • ALT. FREQ. TO 6040 kHz
**UZBEKISTAN**
†RADIO TASHKENT, Tashkent — C Asia • 50 kW • ALT. FREQ. TO 5060 kHz ; W • C Asia • 50 kW

**5046.3 PERU**
RADIO INTEGRACION, Abancay — ◁▭ SPANISH & QUECHUA • DS
**5047 TOGO**
RADIO LOME, Lomé-Togblekope — FRENCH, ETC • DS • 100 kW ; DS • 100 kW

**5050 CHINA**
GUANGXI BC STATION, Nanning — SE Asia • 50 kW
**INDIA**
ALL INDIA RADIO, Aizawl — ENGLISH, ETC • DS • 50 kW ; DS • 50 kW ; Irr • DS • 50 kW

**TANZANIA**
RADIO TANZANIA, Dar es Salaam — E Africa • DS-NATIONAL • 5/100 kW
**5054.6 COSTA RICA**
FARO DEL CARIBE, San José — DS • 5 kW
**5055 BRAZIL**
R JORNAL "A CRITICA", Manaus — DS • 5 kW

RADIO DIFUSORA, Cáceres — DS • 1 kW • ▭ ; M-Sa • DS • 1 kW • ▭

**FRENCH GUIANA**
RFO-GUYANE, Cayenne — DS • 10 kW
**5060 UZBEKISTAN**
†RADIO TASHKENT, Tashkent — C Asia • 50 kW • ALT. FREQ. TO 5040 kHz ; W • S Asia • 100 kW ; S • C Asia • 50 kW ; Europe • 100 kW

**5066v CONGO (DEM REP)**
RADIO CANDIP BUNIA, Bunia — FRENCH, ETC • DS • 1 kW

| | 0 | 1 | 2 | 3 | 4 | 5 | 6 | 7 | 8 | 9 | 10 | 11 | 12 | 13 | 14 | 15 | 16 | 17 | 18 | 19 | 20 | 21 | 22 | 23 | 24 |

ENGLISH ▬  ARABIC ⌇⌇  CHINESE □□□  FRENCH ═  GERMAN ▬  RUSSIAN ═  SPANISH ═  OTHER ▬

World Time

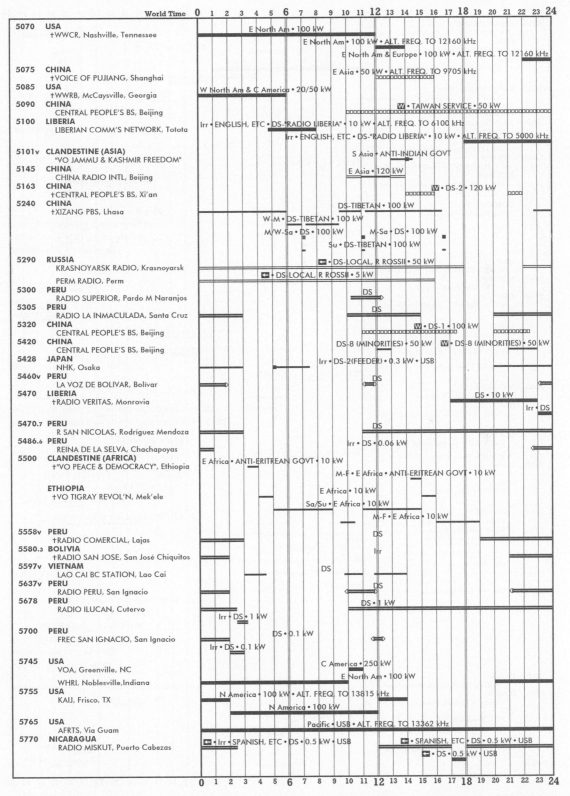

| Freq | Station | Transmission notes |
|---|---|---|
| 5070 | USA †WWCR, Nashville, Tennessee | E North Am • 100 kW; E North Am • 100 kW • ALT. FREQ. TO 12160 kHz; E North Am & Europe • 100 kW • ALT. FREQ. TO 12160 kHz |
| 5075 | CHINA †VOICE OF PUJIANG, Shanghai | E Asia • 50 kW • ALT. FREQ. TO 9705 kHz |
| 5085 | USA †WWRB, McCaysville, Georgia | W North Am & C America • 20/50 kW |
| 5090 | CHINA CENTRAL PEOPLE'S BS, Beijing | W • TAIWAN SERVICE • 50 kW |
| 5100 | LIBERIA LIBERIAN COMM'S NETWORK, Totota | Irr • ENGLISH, ETC • DS-"RADIO LIBERIA" • 10 kW • ALT. FREQ. TO 6100 kHz; Irr • ENGLISH, ETC • DS-"RADIO LIBERIA" • 10 kW • ALT. FREQ. TO 5000 kHz |
| 5101v | CLANDESTINE (ASIA) "VO JAMMU & KASHMIR FREEDOM" | S Asia • ANTI-INDIAN GOVT |
| 5145 | CHINA CHINA RADIO INTL, Beijing | E Asia • 120 kW |
| 5163 | CHINA †CENTRAL PEOPLE'S BS, Xi'an | W • DS-2 • 120 kW |
| 5240 | CHINA †XIZANG PBS, Lhasa | DS-TIBETAN • 100 kW; W-M • DS-TIBETAN • 100 kW; M/W-Sa • DS • 100 kW; M-Sa • DS • 100 kW; Su • DS-TIBETAN • 100 kW |
| 5290 | RUSSIA KRASNOYARSK RADIO, Krasnoyarsk | DS-LOCAL, R ROSSII • 50 kW |
| | PERM RADIO, Perm | DS-LOCAL, R ROSSII • 5 kW |
| 5300 | PERU RADIO SUPERIOR, Pardo M Naranjos | DS |
| 5305 | PERU RADIO LA INMACULADA, Santa Cruz | DS |
| 5320 | CHINA CENTRAL PEOPLE'S BS, Beijing | W • DS-1 • 100 kW |
| 5420 | CHINA CENTRAL PEOPLE'S BS, Beijing | DS-8 (MINORITIES) • 50 kW; W • DS-8 (MINORITIES) • 50 kW |
| 5428 | JAPAN NHK, Osaka | Irr • DS-2(FEEDER) • 0.3 kW • USB |
| 5460v | PERU LA VOZ DE BOLIVAR, Bolivar | DS |
| 5470 | LIBERIA †RADIO VERITAS, Monrovia | DS • 10 kW; Irr • DS |
| 5470.7 | PERU R SAN NICOLAS, Rodríguez Mendoza | DS |
| 5486.6 | PERU REINA DE LA SELVA, Chachapoyas | Irr • DS • 0.06 kW |
| 5500 | CLANDESTINE (AFRICA) †"VO PEACE & DEMOCRACY", Ethiopia | E Africa • ANTI-ERITREAN GOVT • 10 kW; M-F • E Africa • ANTI-ERITREAN GOVT • 10 kW |
| | ETHIOPIA †VO TIGRAY REVOL'N, Mek'ele | E Africa • 10 kW; Sa/Su • E Africa • 10 kW; M-F • E Africa • 10 kW |
| 5558v | PERU †RADIO COMERCIAL, Lajas | DS |
| 5580.3 | BOLIVIA †RADIO SAN JOSE, San José Chiquitos | Irr |
| 5597v | VIETNAM LAO CAI BC STATION, Lao Cai | DS |
| 5637v | PERU RADIO PERU, San Ignacio | DS |
| 5678 | PERU RADIO ILUCAN, Cutervo | DS • 1 kW; Irr • DS • 1 kW |
| 5700 | PERU FREC SAN IGNACIO, San Ignacio | DS • 0.1 kW; Irr • DS • 0.1 kW |
| 5745 | USA VOA, Greenville, NC | C America • 250 kW; E North Am • 100 kW |
| | WHRI, Noblesville, Indiana | |
| 5755 | USA KAIJ, Frisco, TX | N America • 100 kW • ALT. FREQ. TO 13815 kHz; N America • 100 kW |
| 5765 | USA AFRTS, Via Guam | Pacific • USB • ALT. FREQ. TO 13362 kHz |
| 5770 | NICARAGUA RADIO MISKUT, Puerto Cabezas | Irr • SPANISH, ETC • DS • 0.5 kW • USB; SPANISH, ETC • DS • 0.5 kW • USB; DS • 0.5 kW • USB |

0 1 2 3 4 5 6 7 8 9 10 11 12 13 14 15 16 17 18 19 20 21 22 23 24

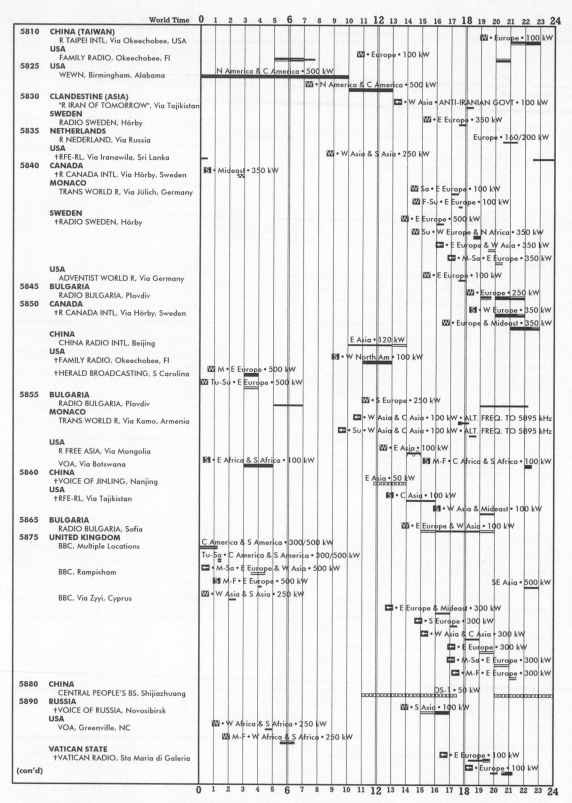

World Time 0 1 2 3 4 5 6 7 8 9 10 11 12 13 14 15 16 17 18 19 20 21 22 23 24

**5810 CHINA (TAIWAN)**
R TAIPEI INTL, Via Okeechobee, USA — W • Europe • 100 kW
**USA**
FAMILY RADIO, Okeechobee, Fl — W • Europe • 100 kW
**5825 USA**
WEWN, Birmingham, Alabama — N America & C America • 500 kW — W • N America & C America • 500 kW

**5830 CLANDESTINE (ASIA)**
"R IRAN OF TOMORROW", Via Tajikistan — • W Asia • ANTI-IRANIAN GOVT • 100 kW
**SWEDEN**
RADIO SWEDEN, Hörby — W • E Europe • 350 kW
**5835 NETHERLANDS**
R NEDERLAND, Via Russia — Europe • 160/200 kW
**USA**
†RFE-RL, Via Iranawila, Sri Lanka — W • W Asia & S Asia • 250 kW
**5840 CANADA**
†R CANADA INTL, Via Hörby, Sweden — S • Mideast • 350 kW
**MONACO**
TRANS WORLD R, Via Jülich, Germany — W Sa • E Europe • 100 kW — W F-Su • E Europe • 100 kW

**SWEDEN**
†RADIO SWEDEN, Hörby — W • E Europe • 500 kW — W Su • W Europe & N Africa • 350 kW — • E Europe & W Asia • 350 kW — • M-Sa • E Europe • 350 kW

**USA**
ADVENTIST WORLD R, Via Germany — W • E Europe • 100 kW
**5845 BULGARIA**
RADIO BULGARIA, Plovdiv — W • Europe • 250 kW
**5850 CANADA**
†R CANADA INTL, Via Hörby, Sweden — S • W Europe • 350 kW — W • Europe & Mideast • 350 kW

**CHINA**
CHINA RADIO INTL, Beijing — E Asia • 120 kW
**USA**
†FAMILY RADIO, Okeechobee, Fl — S • W North Am • 100 kW
†HERALD BROADCASTING, S Carolina — W M • E Europe • 500 kW — W Tu-Su • E Europe • 500 kW

**5855 BULGARIA**
RADIO BULGARIA, Plovdiv — W • S Europe • 250 kW
**MONACO**
TRANS WORLD R, Via Kamo, Armenia — • W Asia & C Asia • 100 kW • ALT. FREQ. TO 5895 kHz — • Su • W Asia & C Asia • 100 kW • ALT. FREQ. TO 5895 kHz

**USA**
R FREE ASIA, Via Mongolia — W • E Asia • 100 kW
VOA, Via Botswana — S • E Africa & S Africa • 100 kW — S M-F • C Africa & S Africa • 100 kW
**5860 CHINA**
†VOICE OF JINLING, Nanjing — E Asia • 50 kW
**USA**
†RFE-RL, Via Tajikistan — S • C Asia • 100 kW — S • W Asia & Mideast • 100 kW

**5865 BULGARIA**
RADIO BULGARIA, Sofia — W • E Europe & W Asia • 100 kW
**5875 UNITED KINGDOM**
BBC, Multiple Locations — C America & S America • 300/500 kW — Tu-Sa • C America & S America • 300/500 kW
BBC, Rampisham — • M-Sa • E Europe & W Asia • 500 kW — S M-F • E Europe • 500 kW — SE Asia • 500 kW
BBC, Via Zyyi, Cyprus — W • W Asia & S Asia • 250 kW — • E Europe & Mideast • 300 kW — • S Europe • 300 kW — • W Asia & C Asia • 300 kW — • E Europe • 300 kW — • M-Sa • E Europe • 300 kW — • M-F • E Europe • 300 kW

**5880 CHINA**
CENTRAL PEOPLE'S BS, Shijiazhuang — DS-1 • 50 kW
**5890 RUSSIA**
†VOICE OF RUSSIA, Novosibirsk — W • S Asia • 100 kW
**USA**
VOA, Greenville, NC — W • W Africa & S Africa • 250 kW — W M-F • W Africa & S Africa • 250 kW

**VATICAN STATE**
†VATICAN RADIO, Sta Maria di Galeria — • E Europe • 100 kW — • Europe • 100 kW

(con'd)

0 1 2 3 4 5 6 7 8 9 10 11 12 13 14 15 16 17 18 19 20 21 22 23 24

ENGLISH ▬ ARABIC ▨ CHINESE ⬚ FRENCH ▭ GERMAN ▬ RUSSIAN ═ SPANISH ▭ OTHER ▬

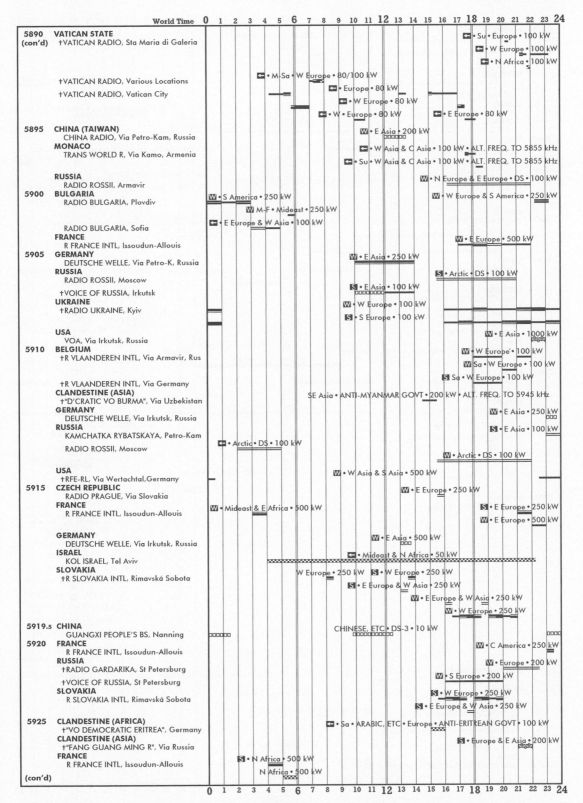

World Time  0  1  2  3  4  5  6  7  8  9  10  11  12  13  14  15  16  17  18  19  20  21  22  23  24

**5890 VATICAN STATE**
(con'd)  †VATICAN RADIO, Sta Maria di Galeria
- ▣ • Su • Europe • 100 kW
- ▣ • W Europe • 100 kW
- ▣ • N Africa • 100 kW

†VATICAN RADIO, Various Locations
- ▣ • M-Sa • W Europe • 80/100 kW
- ▣ • Europe • 80 kW

†VATICAN RADIO, Vatican City
- ▣ • W Europe • 80 kW
- ▣ • W Europe • 80 kW
- ▣ • E Europe • 80 kW

**5895 CHINA (TAIWAN)**
CHINA RADIO, Via Petro-Kam, Russia
- W • E Asia • 200 kW

**MONACO**
TRANS WORLD R, Via Kamo, Armenia
- ▣ • W Asia & C Asia • 100 kW • ALT. FREQ. TO 5855 kHz
- ▣ • Su • W Asia & C Asia • 100 kW • ALT. FREQ. TO 5855 kHz

**RUSSIA**
RADIO ROSSII, Armavir
- W • N Europe & E Europe • DS • 100 kW

**5900 BULGARIA**
RADIO BULGARIA, Plovdiv
- W • S America • 250 kW
- W • W Europe & S America • 250 kW
- W • M-F • Mideast • 250 kW
- ▣ • E Europe & W Asia • 100 kW

RADIO BULGARIA, Sofia

**FRANCE**
R FRANCE INTL, Issoudun-Allouis
- W • E Europe • 500 kW

**5905 GERMANY**
DEUTSCHE WELLE, Via Petro-K, Russia
- W • E Asia • 250 kW

**RUSSIA**
RADIO ROSSII, Moscow
- S • Arctic • DS • 100 kW

†VOICE OF RUSSIA, Irkutsk
- S • E Asia • 100 kW

**UKRAINE**
†RADIO UKRAINE, Kyiv
- W • W Europe • 100 kW
- S • S Europe • 100 kW

**USA**
VOA, Via Irkutsk, Russia
- W • E Asia • 1000 kW

**5910 BELGIUM**
†R VLAANDEREN INTL, Via Armavir, Rus
- W • W Europe • 100 kW
- W Sa • W Europe • 100 kW
- S Sa • W Europe • 100 kW

†R VLAANDEREN INTL, Via Germany

**CLANDESTINE (ASIA)**
†"D'CRATIC VO BURMA", Via Uzbekistan
- SE Asia • ANTI-MYANMAR GOVT • 200 kW • ALT. FREQ. TO 5945 kHz

**GERMANY**
DEUTSCHE WELLE, Via Irkutsk, Russia
- W • E Asia • 250 kW

**RUSSIA**
KAMCHATKA RYBATSKAYA, Petro-Kam
- S • E Asia • 100 kW

RADIO ROSSII, Moscow
- ▣ • Arctic • DS • 100 kW
- W • Arctic • DS • 100 kW

**USA**
†RFE-RL, Via Wertachtal, Germany
- W • W Asia & S Asia • 500 kW

**5915 CZECH REPUBLIC**
RADIO PRAGUE, Via Slovakia
- W • E Europe • 250 kW

**FRANCE**
R FRANCE INTL, Issoudun-Allouis
- W • Mideast & E Africa • 500 kW
- S • E Europe • 250 kW
- W • E Europe • 500 kW

**GERMANY**
DEUTSCHE WELLE, Via Irkutsk, Russia
- W • E Asia • 500 kW

**ISRAEL**
KOL ISRAEL, Tel Aviv
- ▣ • Mideast & N Africa • 50 kW

**SLOVAKIA**
†R SLOVAKIA INTL, Rimavská Sobota
- W Europe • 250 kW
- S • W Europe • 250 kW
- S • E Europe & W Asia • 250 kW
- W • E Europe & W Asia • 250 kW
- W • W Europe • 250 kW

**5919.5 CHINA**
GUANGXI PEOPLE'S BS, Nanning
- CHINESE, ETC • DS-3 • 10 kW

**5920 FRANCE**
R FRANCE INTL, Issoudun-Allouis
- W • C America • 250 kW

**RUSSIA**
†RADIO GARDARIKA, St Petersburg
- W • Europe • 200 kW

†VOICE OF RUSSIA, St Petersburg
- W • S Europe • 200 kW

**SLOVAKIA**
R SLOVAKIA INTL, Rimavská Sobota
- S • W Europe • 250 kW
- S • E Europe & W Asia • 250 kW

**5925 CLANDESTINE (AFRICA)**
†"VO DEMOCRATIC ERITREA", Germany
- ▣ • Sa • ARABIC, ETC • Europe • ANTI-ERITREAN GOVT • 100 kW

**CLANDESTINE (ASIA)**
†"FANG GUANG MING R", Via Russia
- S • Europe & E Asia • 200 kW

**FRANCE**
R FRANCE INTL, Issoudun-Allouis
- S • N Africa • 500 kW
- N Africa • 500 kW

(con'd)

0  1  2  3  4  5  6  7  8  9  10  11  12  13  14  15  16  17  18  19  20  21  22  23  24

SEASONAL ▣ OR ▣      1-HR TIMESHIFT MIDYEAR ▣ OR ▣      JAMMING / OR /\      EARLIEST HEARD ◁      LATEST HEARD ▷      NEW FOR 2003 †

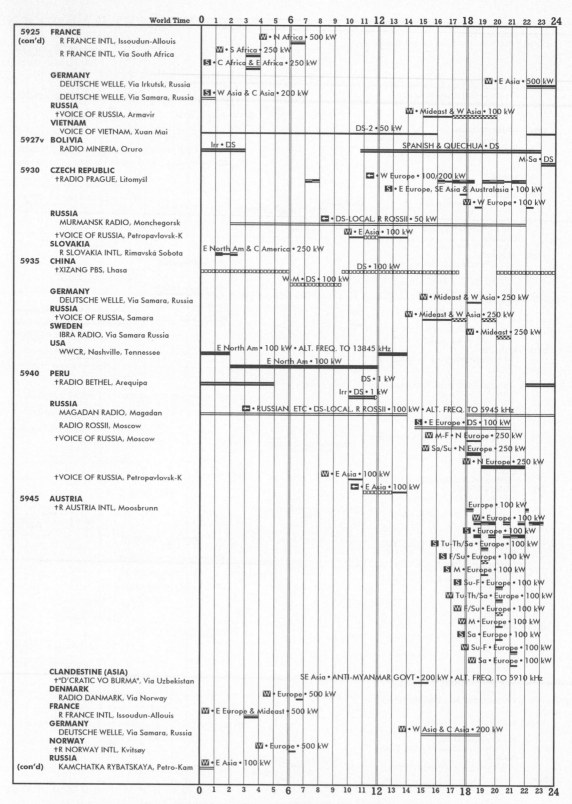

World Time 0 1 2 3 4 5 6 7 8 9 10 11 12 13 14 15 16 17 18 19 20 21 22 23 24

**5925** **FRANCE**
**(con'd)**    R FRANCE INTL, Issoudun-Allouis   W • N Africa • 500 kW

   R FRANCE INTL, Via South Africa   W • S Africa • 250 kW

                          S • C Africa & E Africa • 250 kW

   **GERMANY**
   DEUTSCHE WELLE, Via Irkutsk, Russia   W • E Asia • 500 kW

   DEUTSCHE WELLE, Via Samara, Russia   S • W Asia & C Asia • 200 kW
   **RUSSIA**
   †VOICE OF RUSSIA, Armavir   W • Mideast & W Asia • 100 kW
   **VIETNAM**
   VOICE OF VIETNAM, Xuan Mai   DS-2 • 50 kW
**5927v** **BOLIVIA**
   RADIO MINERIA, Oruro   Irr • DS     SPANISH & QUECHUA • DS

                                                  M-Sa • DS

**5930** **CZECH REPUBLIC**
   †RADIO PRAGUE, Litomyšl   ← • W Europe • 100/200 kW

                                  S • E Europe, SE Asia & Australasia • 100 kW

                                        W • W Europe • 100 kW

   **RUSSIA**
   MURMANSK RADIO, Monchegorsk   ← • DS-LOCAL, R ROSSII • 50 kW

   †VOICE OF RUSSIA, Petropavlovsk-K   W • E Asia • 100 kW
   **SLOVAKIA**
   R SLOVAKIA INTL, Rimavská Sobota   E North Am & C America • 250 kW
**5935** **CHINA**
   †XIZANG PBS, Lhasa   DS • 100 kW

                              W-M • DS • 100 kW

   **GERMANY**
   DEUTSCHE WELLE, Via Samara, Russia   W • Mideast & W Asia • 250 kW
   **RUSSIA**
   †VOICE OF RUSSIA, Samara   W • Mideast & W Asia • 250 kW
   **SWEDEN**
   IBRA RADIO, Via Samara Russia   W • Mideast • 250 kW
   **USA**
   WWCR, Nashville, Tennessee   E North Am • 100 kW • ALT. FREQ. TO 13845 kHz

                                E North Am • 100 kW

**5940** **PERU**
   †RADIO BETHEL, Arequipa   DS • 1 kW

                                Irr • DS • 1 kW

   **RUSSIA**
   MAGADAN RADIO, Magadan   ← • RUSSIAN, ETC • DS-LOCAL, R ROSSII • 100 kW • ALT. FREQ. TO 5945 kHz

   RADIO ROSSII, Moscow   S • E Europe • DS • 100 kW

   †VOICE OF RUSSIA, Moscow   W M-F • N Europe • 250 kW

                                  W Sa/Su • N Europe • 250 kW

                                    W • N Europe • 250 kW

   †VOICE OF RUSSIA, Petropavlovsk-K   W • E Asia • 100 kW

                              ← • E Asia • 100 kW

**5945** **AUSTRIA**
   †R AUSTRIA INTL, Moosbrunn   Europe • 100 kW

                                  W • Europe • 100 kW

                                  S • Europe • 100 kW

                            S Tu-Th/Sa • Europe • 100 kW

                            S F/Su • Europe • 100 kW

                              S M • Europe • 100 kW

                                S Su-F • Europe • 100 kW

                              W Tu-Th/Sa • Europe • 100 kW

                            W F/Su • Europe • 100 kW

                              W M • Europe • 100 kW

                            S Sa • Europe • 100 kW

                              W Su-F • Europe • 100 kW

                              W Sa • Europe • 100 kW

   **CLANDESTINE (ASIA)**
   †"D'CRATIC VO BURMA", Via Uzbekistan   SE Asia • ANTI-MYANMAR GOVT • 200 kW • ALT. FREQ. TO 5910 kHz
   **DENMARK**
   RADIO DANMARK, Via Norway   W • Europe • 500 kW
   **FRANCE**
   R FRANCE INTL, Issoudun-Allouis   W • E Europe & Mideast • 500 kW
   **GERMANY**
   DEUTSCHE WELLE, Via Samara, Russia   W • W Asia & C Asia • 200 kW
   **NORWAY**
   †R NORWAY INTL, Kvitsøy   W • Europe • 500 kW
   **RUSSIA**
**(con'd)**    KAMCHATKA RYBATSKAYA, Petro-Kam   W • E Asia • 100 kW

0 1 2 3 4 5 6 7 8 9 10 11 12 13 14 15 16 17 18 19 20 21 22 23 24

ENGLISH ▬  ARABIC ∞∞  CHINESE □□□  FRENCH ▬▬  GERMAN ▬  RUSSIAN ══  SPANISH ▬  OTHER ▬

World Time  0  1  2  3  4  5  6  7  8  9  10  11  12  13  14  15  16  17  18  19  20  21  22  23  24

| Freq | Country / Station | Schedule |
|------|-------------------|----------|
| 5945 (con'd) | RUSSIA MAGADAN RADIO, Magadan | • RUSSIAN, ETC • DS-LOCAL, R ROSSII • 100 kW • ALT. FREQ. TO 5940 kHz |
| 5950 | CHINA HEILONGJIANG EBS, Harbin | DS • 50 kW |
| | HEILONGJIANG KOREAN BS, Harbin | Su • DS • 50 kW     Su-F • DS • 50 kW |
| | | DS • 50 kW |
| | CHINA (TAIWAN) CBS, Via Okeechobee, USA | E North Am • NEWS NETWORK • 100 kW |
| | R TAIPEI INTL, Via Okeechobee, USA | E North Am • 100 kW |
| | | N America & C America • 100 kW |
| | | W North Am & C America • 100 kW |
| | IRAN VO THE ISLAMIC REP, Mashhad | W • C Asia • 500 kW |
| | RUSSIA †VOICE OF RUSSIA, Armavir | W • Europe • 500 kW |
| | †VOICE OF RUSSIA, Samara | S • Europe • 250 kW |
| | USA FAMILY RADIO, Okeechobee, Fl | E North Am • 100 kW |
| | YEMEN REP OF YEMEN RADIO, San'ā | Mideast • DS • 300 kW |
| 5950v | GUYANA VOICE OF GUYANA, Georgetown | DS • 5 kW • ALT. FREQ. TO 3290v kHz |
| 5952v | BOLIVIA RADIO PIO DOCE, Llallagua-Siglo XX | SPANISH, ETC • DS • 1 kW |
| | | Tu-Su • SPANISH, ETC • DS • 1 kW |
| 5954v | COSTA RICA RADIO CASINO, Limón | DS • 0.7 kW |
| 5955 | BRAZIL RADIO GAZETA, São Paulo | SPANISH, ETC • DS • 10 kW |
| | CHINA CENTRAL PEOPLE'S BS, Shijiazhuang | W • DS-1 • 50 kW |
| | | DS-1 • 50 kW |
| | COLOMBIA CARACOL V'VICENCIO, Villavicencio | Irr • DS-CARACOL • 5 kW |
| | | DS-CARACOL • 5 kW |
| | GERMANY DEUTSCHE WELLE, Nauen | S • E Europe & W Asia • 500 kW |
| | DEUTSCHE WELLE, Wertachtal | S • E Europe & W Asia • 500 kW |
| | IRAN VO THE ISLAMIC REP, Mashhad | C Asia • 500 kW |
| | ITALY RAI INTERNATIONAL, Rome | W • N Europe • 100 kW |
| | JAPAN RADIO JAPAN/NHK, Tokyo-Yamata | E Asia • 300 kW |
| | NETHERLANDS R NEDERLAND, Flevoland | • W Europe • 500 kW |
| | ROMANIA †RADIO ROMANIA INTL, Bucharest | Europe • 50 kW     W • Europe • 250 kW |
| | | W • Europe • 50 kW |
| | SOUTH AFRICA CHANNEL AFRICA, Meyerton | S Africa • 500 kW |
| | TURKEY †VOICE OF TURKEY, Ankara-Emirler | W • C Asia • 500 kW |
| | | W • E Europe & Asia • 500 kW |
| | USA †ADVENTIST WORLD R, Via Slovakia | W • W Europe • 250 kW |
| | RFE-RL, Via Biblis, Germany | W • E Europe • 100 kW |
| | †RFE-RL, Via Kavála, Greece | S • E Europe • 250 kW |
| | | W • W Asia • 250 kW |
| | †RFE-RL, Via Lampertheim, Germany | W • E Europe • 100 kW |
| | VOA, Via Iranawila, Sri Lanka | S • SE Asia • 250 kW |
| | †VOA, Via Kavála, Greece | W • S Asia • 250 kW     W • SE Asia • 250 kW |
| | VOA, Via Philippines | SE Asia • 250 kW |
| | UZBEKISTAN RADIO TASHKENT, Tashkent | W • S Asia • 100 kW |
| | VIETNAM VOICE OF VIETNAM, Via Austria | W • W Europe • 100 kW |
| 5955v | GUATEMALA RADIO CULTURAL, Guatemala City | M • DS • 1 kW     M-Sa • DS • 1 kW |
| | | Tu-Su • DS • 1 kW     Su • DS • 1 kW |
| | | DS • 1 kW |
| 5958v | CHINA YUNNAN PEOPLE'S BS, Kunming | M-Sa • DS-EDUCATIONAL • 50 kW |
| | | DS-EDUCATIONAL • 50 kW |

0  1  2  3  4  5  6  7  8  9  10  11  12  13  14  15  16  17  18  19  20  21  22  23  24

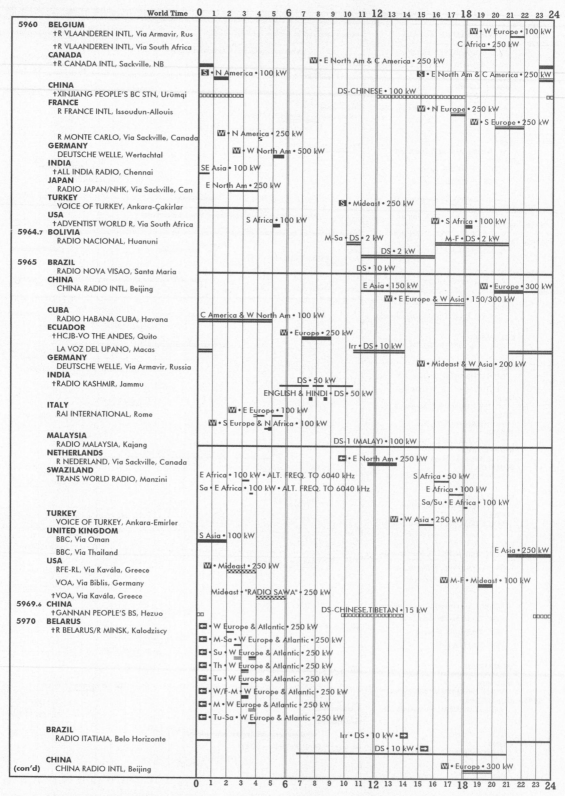

| | | World Time | 0 1 2 3 4 5 6 7 8 9 10 11 12 13 14 15 16 17 18 19 20 21 22 23 24 |
|---|---|---|---|

**5960 BELGIUM**
  †R VLAANDEREN INTL, Via Armavir, Rus — W • W Europe • 100 kW
  †R VLAANDEREN INTL, Via South Africa — C Africa • 250 kW
**CANADA**
  †R CANADA INTL, Sackville, NB — W • E North Am & C America • 250 kW / S • N America • 100 kW / S • E North Am & C America • 250 kW
**CHINA**
  †XINJIANG PEOPLE'S BC STN, Urümqi — DS-CHINESE • 100 kW
**FRANCE**
  R FRANCE INTL, Issoudun-Allouis — W • N Europe • 250 kW / W • S Europe • 250 kW
  R MONTE CARLO, Via Sackville, Canada — W • N America • 250 kW
**GERMANY**
  DEUTSCHE WELLE, Wertachtal — W • W North Am • 500 kW
**INDIA**
  †ALL INDIA RADIO, Chennai — SE Asia • 100 kW
**JAPAN**
  RADIO JAPAN/NHK, Via Sackville, Can — E North Am • 250 kW
**TURKEY**
  VOICE OF TURKEY, Ankara-Çakirlar — S • Mideast • 250 kW
**USA**
  †ADVENTIST WORLD R, Via South Africa — S Africa • 100 kW / W • S Africa • 100 kW
**5964.7 BOLIVIA**
  RADIO NACIONAL, Huanuni — M-Sa • DS • 2 kW / M-F • DS • 2 kW / DS • 2 kW

**5965 BRAZIL**
  RADIO NOVA VISAO, Santa Maria — DS • 10 kW
**CHINA**
  CHINA RADIO INTL, Beijing — E Asia • 150 kW / W • Europe • 300 kW / W • E Europe & W Asia • 150/300 kW
**CUBA**
  RADIO HABANA CUBA, Havana — C America & W North Am • 100 kW
**ECUADOR**
  †HCJB-VO THE ANDES, Quito — W • Europe • 250 kW
  LA VOZ DEL UPANO, Macas — Irr • DS • 10 kW
**GERMANY**
  DEUTSCHE WELLE, Via Armavir, Russia — W • Mideast & W Asia • 200 kW
**INDIA**
  †RADIO KASHMIR, Jammu — DS • 50 kW / ENGLISH & HINDI • DS • 50 kW
**ITALY**
  RAI INTERNATIONAL, Rome — W • E Europe • 100 kW / W • S Europe & N Africa • 100 kW
**MALAYSIA**
  RADIO MALAYSIA, Kajang — DS-1 (MALAY) • 100 kW
**NETHERLANDS**
  R NEDERLAND, Via Sackville, Canada — ← • E North Am • 250 kW
**SWAZILAND**
  TRANS WORLD RADIO, Manzini — E Africa • 100 kW • ALT. FREQ. TO 6040 kHz / Sa • E Africa • 100 kW • ALT. FREQ. TO 6040 kHz / S Africa • 50 kW / E Africa • 100 kW / Sa/Su • E Africa • 100 kW
**TURKEY**
  VOICE OF TURKEY, Ankara-Emirler — W • W Asia • 250 kW
**UNITED KINGDOM**
  BBC, Via Oman — S Asia • 100 kW
  BBC, Via Thailand — E Asia • 250 kW
**USA**
  RFE-RL, Via Kavála, Greece — W • Mideast • 250 kW
  VOA, Via Biblis, Germany — W M-F • Mideast • 100 kW
  †VOA, Via Kavála, Greece — Mideast • "RADIO SAWA" • 250 kW
**5969.6 CHINA**
  †GANNAN PEOPLE'S BS, Hezuo — DS-CHINESE,TIBETAN • 15 kW
**5970 BELARUS**
  †R BELARUS/R MINSK, Kalodziscy — ← • W Europe & Atlantic • 250 kW / ← • M-Sa • W Europe & Atlantic • 250 kW / ← • Su • W Europe & Atlantic • 250 kW / ← • Th • W Europe & Atlantic • 250 kW / ← • Tu • W Europe & Atlantic • 250 kW / ← • W/F-M • W Europe & Atlantic • 250 kW / ← • M • W Europe & Atlantic • 250 kW / ← • Tu-Sa • W Europe & Atlantic • 250 kW
**BRAZIL**
  RADIO ITATIAIA, Belo Horizonte — Irr • DS • 10 kW • → / DS • 10 kW • →
**CHINA**
**(con'd)**   CHINA RADIO INTL, Beijing — W • Europe • 300 kW

| | World Time | 0 1 2 3 4 5 6 7 8 9 10 11 12 13 14 15 16 17 18 19 20 21 22 23 24 |
|---|---|---|

ENGLISH ▬    ARABIC ░    CHINESE ▫▫▫    FRENCH ▬    GERMAN ▬    RUSSIAN ══    SPANISH ▬    OTHER ▬

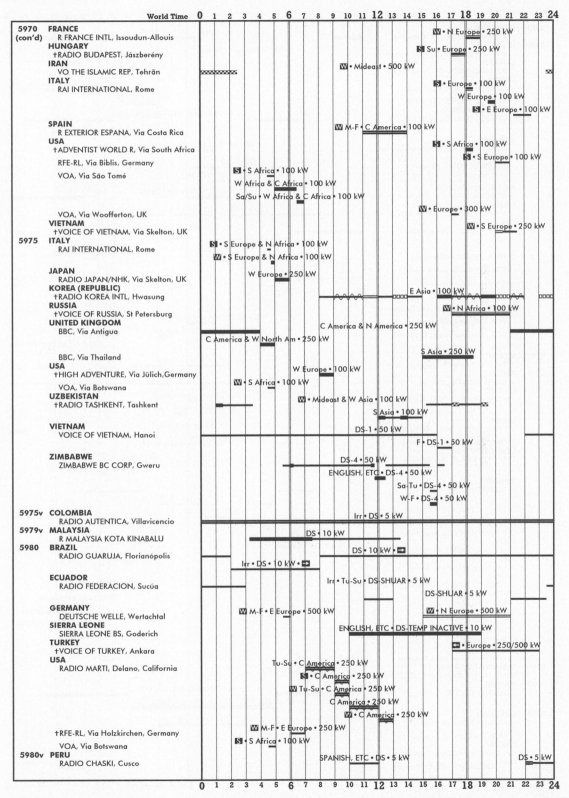

| | |
|---|---|
| **5970** | **FRANCE** |
| **(con'd)** | R FRANCE INTL, Issoudun-Allouis · W • N Europe • 250 kW |
| | **HUNGARY** |
| | †RADIO BUDAPEST, Jászberény · S • Su • Europe • 250 kW |
| | **IRAN** |
| | VO THE ISLAMIC REP, Tehrän · W • Mideast • 500 kW |
| | **ITALY** |
| | RAI INTERNATIONAL, Rome · S • Europe • 100 kW / W Europe • 100 kW / S • E Europe • 100 kW |
| | **SPAIN** |
| | R EXTERIOR ESPANA, Via Costa Rica · W • M-F • C America • 100 kW |
| | **USA** |
| | †ADVENTIST WORLD R, Via South Africa · S • S Africa • 100 kW / S • S Europe • 100 kW |
| | RFE-RL, Via Biblis, Germany |
| | VOA, Via São Tomé · S • S Africa • 100 kW / W Africa & C Africa • 100 kW / Sa/Su • W Africa & C Africa • 100 kW |
| | VOA, Via Woofferton, UK · W • Europe • 300 kW |
| | **VIETNAM** |
| | †VOICE OF VIETNAM, Via Skelton, UK · W • S Europe • 250 kW |
| **5975** | **ITALY** |
| | RAI INTERNATIONAL, Rome · S • S Europe & N Africa • 100 kW / W • S Europe & N Africa • 100 kW |
| | **JAPAN** |
| | RADIO JAPAN/NHK, Via Skelton, UK · W Europe • 250 kW |
| | **KOREA (REPUBLIC)** |
| | †RADIO KOREA INTL, Hwasung · E Asia • 100 kW |
| | **RUSSIA** |
| | †VOICE OF RUSSIA, St Petersburg · W • N Africa • 100 kW |
| | **UNITED KINGDOM** |
| | BBC, Via Antigua · C America & N America • 250 kW / C America & W North Am • 250 kW |
| | BBC, Via Thailand · S Asia • 250 kW |
| | **USA** |
| | †HIGH ADVENTURE, Via Jülich, Germany · W Europe • 100 kW |
| | VOA, Via Botswana · W • S Africa • 100 kW |
| | **UZBEKISTAN** |
| | †RADIO TASHKENT, Tashkent · W • Mideast & W Asia • 100 kW / S Asia • 100 kW |
| | **VIETNAM** |
| | VOICE OF VIETNAM, Hanoi · DS-1 • 50 kW / F • DS-1 • 50 kW |
| | **ZIMBABWE** |
| | ZIMBABWE BC CORP, Gweru · DS-4 • 50 kW / ENGLISH, ETC • DS-4 • 50 kW / Sa-Tu • DS-4 • 50 kW / W-F • DS-4 • 50 kW |
| **5975v** | **COLOMBIA** |
| | RADIO AUTENTICA, Villavicencio · Irr • DS • 5 kW |
| **5979v** | **MALAYSIA** |
| | R MALAYSIA KOTA KINABALU · DS • 10 kW |
| **5980** | **BRAZIL** |
| | RADIO GUARUJA, Florianópolis · DS • 10 kW • / Irr • DS • 10 kW • |
| | **ECUADOR** |
| | RADIO FEDERACION, Sucúa · Irr • Tu-Su • DS-SHUAR • 5 kW / DS-SHUAR • 5 kW |
| | **GERMANY** |
| | DEUTSCHE WELLE, Wertachtal · W • M-F • E Europe • 500 kW / W • N Europe • 500 kW |
| | **SIERRA LEONE** |
| | SIERRA LEONE BS, Goderich · ENGLISH, ETC • DS-TEMP INACTIVE • 10 kW |
| | **TURKEY** |
| | †VOICE OF TURKEY, Ankara · • Europe • 250/500 kW |
| | **USA** |
| | RADIO MARTI, Delano, California · Tu-Su • C America • 250 kW / S • C America • 250 kW / W • Tu-Su • C America • 250 kW / C America • 250 kW / W • C America • 250 kW |
| | †RFE-RL, Via Holzkirchen, Germany · W • M-F • E Europe • 250 kW |
| | VOA, Via Botswana · S • S Africa • 100 kW |
| **5980v** | **PERU** |
| | RADIO CHASKI, Cusco · SPANISH, ETC • DS • 5 kW / DS • 5 kW |

World Time   0 1 2 3 4 5 6 7 8 9 10 11 12 13 14 15 16 17 18 19 20 21 22 23 24

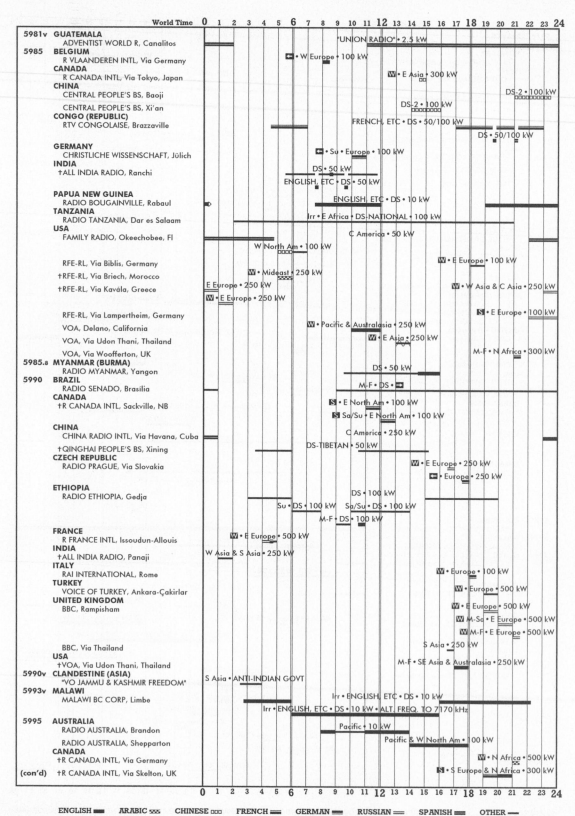

| World Time | | |
|---|---|---|
| **5981v GUATEMALA** | | |
| ADVENTIST WORLD R, Canalitos | "UNION RADIO" • 2.5 kW | |
| **5985 BELGIUM** | | |
| R VLAANDEREN INTL, Via Germany | W Europe • 100 kW | |
| **CANADA** | | |
| R CANADA INTL, Via Tokyo, Japan | W • E Asia • 300 kW | |
| **CHINA** | | |
| CENTRAL PEOPLE'S BS, Baoji | DS-2 • 100 kW | |
| CENTRAL PEOPLE'S BS, Xi'an | DS-2 • 100 kW | |
| **CONGO (REPUBLIC)** | | |
| RTV CONGOLAISE, Brazzaville | FRENCH, ETC • DS 50/100 kW | |
| | DS • 50/100 kW | |
| **GERMANY** | | |
| CHRISTLICHE WISSENSCHAFT, Jülich | Su • Europe • 100 kW | |
| **INDIA** | | |
| †ALL INDIA RADIO, Ranchi | DS • 50 kW | |
| | ENGLISH, ETC • DS • 50 kW | |
| **PAPUA NEW GUINEA** | | |
| RADIO BOUGAINVILLE, Rabaul | ENGLISH, ETC • DS • 10 kW | |
| **TANZANIA** | | |
| RADIO TANZANIA, Dar es Salaam | Irr • E Africa • DS-NATIONAL • 100 kW | |
| **USA** | | |
| FAMILY RADIO, Okeechobee, Fl | C America • 50 kW | |
| | W North Am • 100 kW | |
| RFE-RL, Via Biblis, Germany | W • E Europe • 100 kW | |
| †RFE-RL, Via Briech, Morocco | W • Mideast • 250 kW | |
| †RFE-RL, Via Kavála, Greece | E Europe • 250 kW     W • W Asia & C Asia • 250 kW | |
| | W • E Europe • 250 kW | |
| | S • E Europe • 100 kW | |
| RFE-RL, Via Lampertheim, Germany | | |
| VOA, Delano, California | W • Pacific & Australasia • 250 kW | |
| VOA, Via Udon Thani, Thailand | W • E Asia • 250 kW | |
| VOA, Via Woofferton, UK | M-F • N Africa • 300 kW | |
| **5985.8 MYANMAR (BURMA)** | | |
| RADIO MYANMAR, Yangon | DS • 50 kW | |
| **5990 BRAZIL** | | |
| RADIO SENADO, Brasilia | M-F • DS | |
| **CANADA** | | |
| †R CANADA INTL, Sackville, NB | S • E North Am • 100 kW | |
| | Sa/Su • E North Am • 100 kW | |
| **CHINA** | | |
| CHINA RADIO INTL, Via Havana, Cuba | C America • 250 kW | |
| †QINGHAI PEOPLE'S BS, Xining | DS-TIBETAN • 50 kW | |
| **CZECH REPUBLIC** | | |
| RADIO PRAGUE, Via Slovakia | W • E Europe • 250 kW | |
| | • Europe • 250 kW | |
| **ETHIOPIA** | | |
| RADIO ETHIOPIA, Gedja | DS • 100 kW | |
| | Su • DS • 100 kW     Sa/Su • DS • 100 kW | |
| | M-F • DS • 100 kW | |
| **FRANCE** | | |
| R FRANCE INTL, Issoudun-Allouis | W • E Europe • 500 kW | |
| **INDIA** | | |
| †ALL INDIA RADIO, Panaji | W Asia & S Asia • 250 kW | |
| **ITALY** | | |
| RAI INTERNATIONAL, Rome | W • Europe • 100 kW | |
| **TURKEY** | | |
| VOICE OF TURKEY, Ankara-Çakirlar | W • Europe • 500 kW | |
| **UNITED KINGDOM** | | |
| BBC, Rampisham | W • E Europe • 500 kW | |
| | W M-Sa • E Europe • 500 kW | |
| | W M-F • E Europe • 500 kW | |
| BBC, Via Thailand | S Asia • 250 kW | |
| **USA** | | |
| †VOA, Via Udon Thani, Thailand | M-F • SE Asia & Australasia • 250 kW | |
| **5990v CLANDESTINE (ASIA)** | | |
| "VO JAMMU & KASHMIR FREEDOM" | S Asia • ANTI-INDIAN GOVT | |
| **5993v MALAWI** | | |
| MALAWI BC CORP, Limbe | Irr • ENGLISH, ETC • DS • 10 kW | |
| | Irr • ENGLISH, ETC • DS • 10 kW • ALT. FREQ. TO 7170 kHz | |
| **5995 AUSTRALIA** | | |
| RADIO AUSTRALIA, Brandon | Pacific • 10 kW | |
| RADIO AUSTRALIA, Shepparton | Pacific & W North Am • 100 kW | |
| **CANADA** | | |
| †R CANADA INTL, Via Germany | W • N Africa • 500 kW | |
| (con'd) †R CANADA INTL, Via Skelton, UK | S • S Europe & N Africa • 300 kW | |

0  1  2  3  4  5  6  7  8  9  10  11  12  13  14  15  16  17  18  19  20  21  22  23  24

ENGLISH ▬▬   ARABIC ▨▨   CHINESE □□□   FRENCH ▬▬   GERMAN ▬▬   RUSSIAN ══   SPANISH ──   OTHER ──

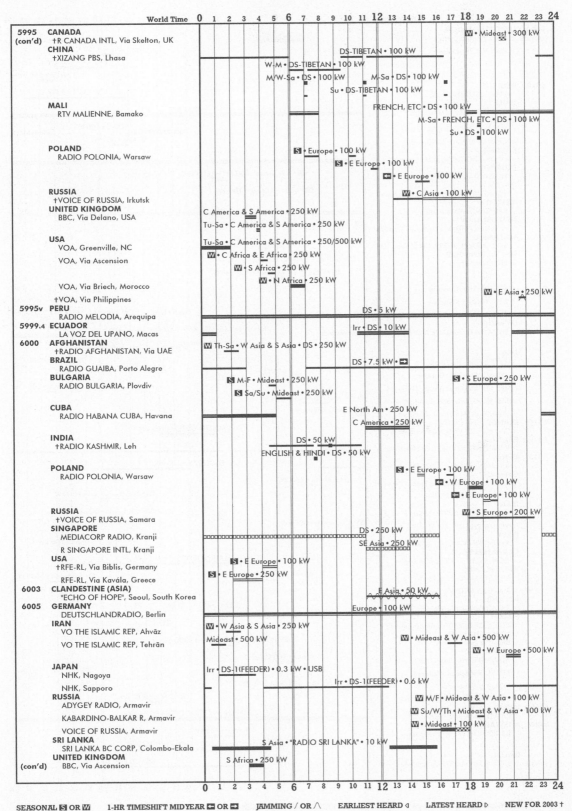

World Time 0 1 2 3 4 5 6 7 8 9 10 11 12 13 14 15 16 17 18 19 20 21 22 23 24

**5995 CANADA** (con'd)
  †R CANADA INTL, Via Skelton, UK — W • Mideast • 300 kW
**CHINA**
  †XIZANG PBS, Lhasa — DS-TIBETAN • 100 kW / W-M • DS-TIBETAN • 100 kW / M/W-Sa • DS • 100 kW / M-Sa • DS • 100 kW / Su • DS-TIBETAN • 100 kW
**MALI**
  RTV MALIENNE, Bamako — FRENCH, ETC • DS • 100 kW / M-Sa • FRENCH, ETC • DS • 100 kW / Su • DS • 100 kW
**POLAND**
  RADIO POLONIA, Warsaw — S • Europe • 100 kW / S • E Europe • 100 kW / ⇐ • E Europe • 100 kW
**RUSSIA**
  †VOICE OF RUSSIA, Irkutsk — W • C Asia • 100 kW
**UNITED KINGDOM**
  BBC, Via Delano, USA — C America & S America • 250 kW / Tu-Sa • C America & S America • 250 kW
**USA**
  VOA, Greenville, NC — Tu-Sa • C America & S America • 250/500 kW
  VOA, Via Ascension — W • C Africa & E Africa • 250 kW / W • S Africa • 250 kW / W • N Africa • 250 kW
  VOA, Via Briech, Morocco
  †VOA, Via Philippines — W • E Asia • 250 kW
**5995v PERU**
  RADIO MELODIA, Arequipa — DS • 5 kW
**5999.4 ECUADOR**
  LA VOZ DEL UPANO, Macas — Irr • DS • 10 kW
**6000 AFGHANISTAN**
  †RADIO AFGHANISTAN, Via UAE — W Th-Sa • W Asia & S Asia • DS • 250 kW
**BRAZIL**
  RADIO GUAIBA, Porto Alegre — DS • 7.5 kW • ⇒
**BULGARIA**
  RADIO BULGARIA, Plovdiv — S M-F • Mideast • 250 kW / S Sa/Su • Mideast • 250 kW / S • S Europe • 250 kW
**CUBA**
  RADIO HABANA CUBA, Havana — E North Am • 250 kW / C America • 250 kW
**INDIA**
  †RADIO KASHMIR, Leh — DS • 50 kW / ENGLISH & HINDI • DS • 50 kW
**POLAND**
  RADIO POLONIA, Warsaw — S • E Europe • 100 kW / ⇐ • W Europe • 100 kW / ⇐ • E Europe • 100 kW
**RUSSIA**
  †VOICE OF RUSSIA, Samara — W • S Europe • 200 kW
**SINGAPORE**
  MEDIACORP RADIO, Kranji — DS • 250 kW / SE Asia • 250 kW
  R SINGAPORE INTL, Kranji
**USA**
  †RFE-RL, Via Biblis, Germany — S • E Europe • 100 kW
  RFE-RL, Via Kavála, Greece — S • E Europe • 250 kW
**6003 CLANDESTINE (ASIA)**
  "ECHO OF HOPE", Seoul, South Korea — E Asia • 50 kW
**6005 GERMANY**
  DEUTSCHLANDRADIO, Berlin — Europe • 100 kW
**IRAN**
  VO THE ISLAMIC REP, Ahvāz — W • W Asia & S Asia • 250 kW
  VO THE ISLAMIC REP, Tehrān — Mideast • 500 kW / W • Mideast & W Asia • 500 kW / W • W Europe • 500 kW
**JAPAN**
  NHK, Nagoya — Irr • DS-1(FEEDER) • 0.3 kW • USB
  NHK, Sapporo — Irr • DS-1(FEEDER) • 0.6 kW
**RUSSIA**
  ADYGEY RADIO, Armavir — W M/F • Mideast & W Asia • 100 kW
  KABARDINO-BALKAR R, Armavir — W Su/W/Th • Mideast & W Asia • 100 kW
  VOICE OF RUSSIA, Armavir — W • Mideast • 100 kW
**SRI LANKA**
  SRI LANKA BC CORP, Colombo-Ekala — S Asia • "RADIO SRI LANKA" • 10 kW
**UNITED KINGDOM** (con'd)
  BBC, Via Ascension — S Africa • 250 kW

World Time 0 1 2 3 4 5 6 7 8 9 10 11 12 13 14 15 16 17 18 19 20 21 22 23 24

SEASONAL S OR W    1-HR TIMESHIFT MIDYEAR ⇐ OR ⇒    JAMMING / OR ∧    EARLIEST HEARD ◁    LATEST HEARD ▷    NEW FOR 2003 †

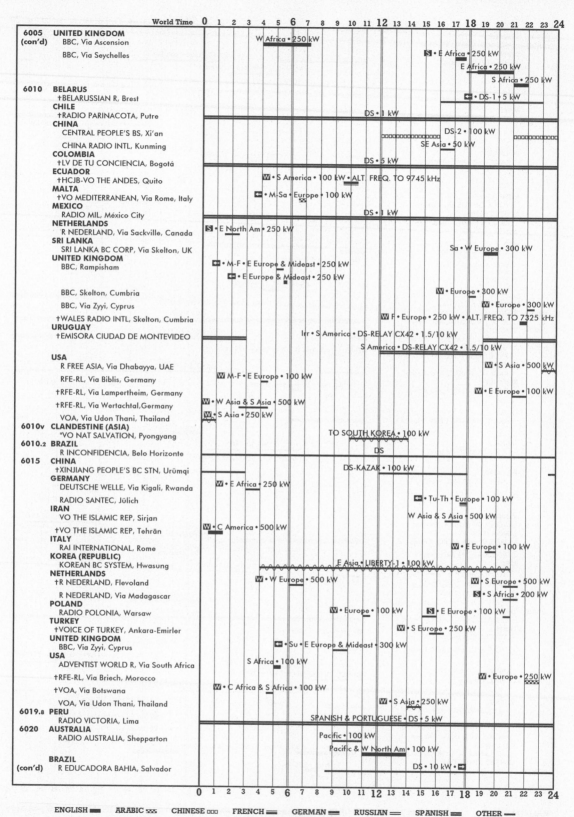

| World Time | Station details |
|---|---|
| **6005** **UNITED KINGDOM** | |
| (con'd) BBC, Via Ascension | W Africa • 250 kW |
| BBC, Via Seychelles | S • E Africa • 250 kW |
| | E Africa • 250 kW |
| | S Africa • 250 kW |
| **6010** **BELARUS** | |
| †BELARUSSIAN R, Brest | DS-1 • 5 kW |
| **CHILE** | |
| †RADIO PARINACOTA, Putre | DS • 1 kW |
| **CHINA** | |
| CENTRAL PEOPLE'S BS, Xi'an | DS-2 • 100 kW |
| CHINA RADIO INTL, Kunming | SE Asia • 50 kW |
| **COLOMBIA** | |
| †LV DE TU CONCIENCIA, Bogotá | DS • 5 kW |
| **ECUADOR** | |
| †HCJB-VO THE ANDES, Quito | W • S America • 100 kW • ALT. FREQ. TO 9745 kHz |
| **MALTA** | |
| †VO MEDITERRANEAN, Via Rome, Italy | M-Sa • Europe • 100 kW |
| **MEXICO** | |
| RADIO MIL, México City | DS • 1 kW |
| **NETHERLANDS** | |
| R NEDERLAND, Via Sackville, Canada | S • E North Am • 250 kW |
| **SRI LANKA** | |
| SRI LANKA BC CORP, Via Skelton, UK | Sa • W Europe • 300 kW |
| **UNITED KINGDOM** | |
| BBC, Rampisham | M-F • E Europe & Mideast • 250 kW |
| | E Europe & Mideast • 250 kW |
| BBC, Skelton, Cumbria | W • Europe • 300 kW |
| BBC, Via Zyyi, Cyprus | W • Europe • 300 kW |
| †WALES RADIO INTL, Skelton, Cumbria | F • Europe • 250 kW • ALT. FREQ. TO 7325 kHz |
| **URUGUAY** | |
| †EMISORA CIUDAD DE MONTEVIDEO | Irr • S America • DS-RELAY CX42 • 1.5/10 kW |
| | S America • DS-RELAY CX42 • 1.5/10 kW |
| **USA** | |
| R FREE ASIA, Via Dhabayya, UAE | W • S Asia • 500 kW |
| RFE-RL, Via Biblis, Germany | W M-F • E Europe • 100 kW |
| †RFE-RL, Via Lampertheim, Germany | W • E Europe • 100 kW |
| †RFE-RL, Via Wertachtal, Germany | W • W Asia & S Asia • 500 kW |
| VOA, Via Udon Thani, Thailand | W • S Asia • 250 kW |
| **6010v** **CLANDESTINE (ASIA)** | |
| "VO NAT SALVATION, Pyongyang | TO SOUTH KOREA • 100 kW |
| **6010.2** **BRAZIL** | |
| R INCONFIDENCIA, Belo Horizonte | DS |
| **6015** **CHINA** | |
| †XINJIANG PEOPLE'S BC STN, Urümqi | DS-KAZAK • 100 kW |
| **GERMANY** | |
| DEUTSCHE WELLE, Via Kigali, Rwanda | W • E Africa • 250 kW |
| RADIO SANTEC, Jülich | Tu-Th • Europe • 100 kW |
| **IRAN** | |
| VO THE ISLAMIC REP, Sirjan | W Asia & S Asia • 500 kW |
| †VO THE ISLAMIC REP, Tehrān | W • C America • 500 kW |
| **ITALY** | |
| RAI INTERNATIONAL, Rome | W • E Europe • 100 kW |
| **KOREA (REPUBLIC)** | |
| KOREAN BC SYSTEM, Hwasung | E Asia • LIBERTY-1 • 100 kW |
| **NETHERLANDS** | |
| †R NEDERLAND, Flevoland | W • W Europe • 500 kW |
| | W • S Europe • 500 kW |
| R NEDERLAND, Via Madagascar | S • S Africa • 200 kW |
| **POLAND** | |
| RADIO POLONIA, Warsaw | W • Europe • 100 kW |
| | S • E Europe • 100 kW |
| **TURKEY** | |
| †VOICE OF TURKEY, Ankara-Emirler | W • S Europe • 250 kW |
| **UNITED KINGDOM** | |
| BBC, Via Zyyi, Cyprus | Su • E Europe & Mideast • 300 kW |
| **USA** | |
| ADVENTIST WORLD R, Via South Africa | S Africa • 100 kW |
| †RFE-RL, Via Briech, Morocco | W • Europe • 250 kW |
| †VOA, Via Botswana | W • C Africa & S Africa • 100 kW |
| VOA, Via Udon Thani, Thailand | W • S Asia • 250 kW |
| **6019.8** **PERU** | |
| RADIO VICTORIA, Lima | SPANISH & PORTUGUESE • DS • 5 kW |
| **6020** **AUSTRALIA** | |
| RADIO AUSTRALIA, Shepparton | Pacific • 100 kW |
| | Pacific & W North Am • 100 kW |
| **BRAZIL** | |
| (con'd) R EDUCADORA BAHIA, Salvador | DS • 10 kW • E |

ENGLISH ▬  ARABIC ▨  CHINESE ▫▫▫  FRENCH ▭▭  GERMAN ▬▬  RUSSIAN ═══  SPANISH ▭▭  OTHER —

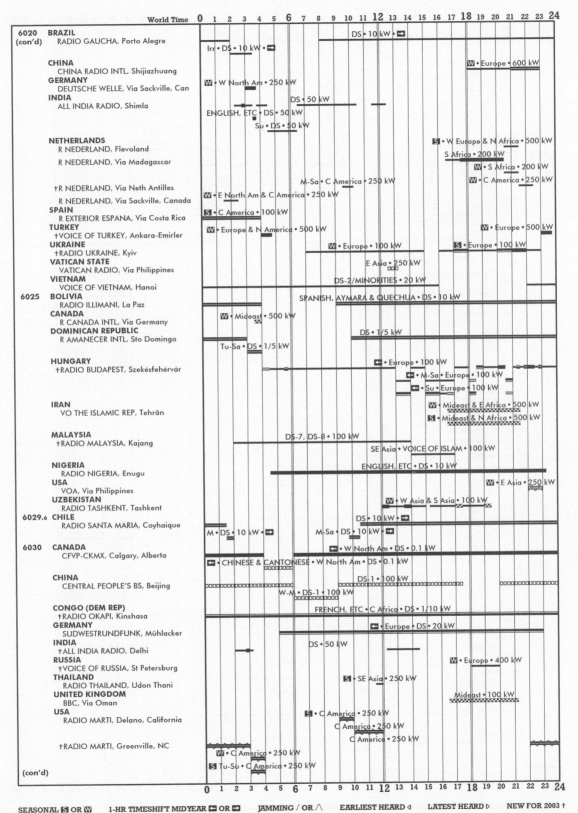

World Time 0 1 2 3 4 5 6 7 8 9 10 11 12 13 14 15 16 17 18 19 20 21 22 23 24

| 6020 | BRAZIL |
| (con'd) | RADIO GAUCHA, Porto Alegre |
| | DS • 10 kW • ➡ |
| | Irr • DS • 10 kW • ➡ |
| | CHINA |
| | CHINA RADIO INTL, Shijiazhuang — W • Europe • 600 kW |
| | GERMANY |
| | DEUTSCHE WELLE, Via Sackville, Can — W • W North Am • 250 kW |
| | INDIA |
| | ALL INDIA RADIO, Shimla — DS • 50 kW |
| | ENGLISH, ETC • DS • 50 kW |
| | Su • DS • 50 kW |
| | NETHERLANDS |
| | R NEDERLAND, Flevoland — S • W Europe & N Africa • 500 kW |
| | R NEDERLAND, Via Madagascar — S Africa • 200 kW |
| | — W • S Africa • 200 kW |
| | M-Sa • C America • 250 kW — W • C America • 250 kW |
| | †R NEDERLAND, Via Neth Antilles |
| | R NEDERLAND, Via Sackville, Canada — W • E North Am & C America • 250 kW |
| | SPAIN |
| | R EXTERIOR ESPANA, Via Costa Rica — S • C America • 100 kW |
| | TURKEY |
| | †VOICE OF TURKEY, Ankara-Emirler — W • Europe & N America • 500 kW — W • Europe • 500 kW |
| | UKRAINE |
| | †RADIO UKRAINE, Kyiv — W • Europe • 100 kW — S • Europe • 100 kW |
| | VATICAN STATE |
| | VATICAN RADIO, Via Philippines — E Asia • 250 kW |
| | VIETNAM |
| | VOICE OF VIETNAM, Hanoi — DS-2/MINORITIES • 20 kW |
| 6025 | BOLIVIA |
| | RADIO ILLIMANI, La Paz — SPANISH, AYMARA & QUECHUA • DS • 10 kW |
| | CANADA |
| | R CANADA INTL, Via Germany — W • Mideast • 500 kW |
| | DOMINICAN REPUBLIC |
| | R AMANECER INTL, Sto Domingo — DS • 1/5 kW |
| | Tu-Sa • DS • 1/5 kW |
| | HUNGARY |
| | †RADIO BUDAPEST, Szekésfehérvár — ⬅ • Europe • 100 kW |
| | — ⬅ • M-Sa • Europe • 100 kW |
| | — ⬅ • Su • Europe • 100 kW |
| | IRAN |
| | VO THE ISLAMIC REP, Tehrān — W • Mideast & E Africa • 500 kW |
| | — S • Mideast & N Africa • 500 kW |
| | MALAYSIA |
| | †RADIO MALAYSIA, Kajang — DS-7, DS-8 • 100 kW |
| | SE Asia • VOICE OF ISLAM • 100 kW |
| | NIGERIA |
| | RADIO NIGERIA, Enugu — ENGLISH, ETC • DS • 10 kW |
| | USA |
| | VOA, Via Philippines — W • E Asia • 250 kW |
| | UZBEKISTAN |
| | RADIO TASHKENT, Tashkent — W • W Asia & S Asia • 100 kW |
| 6029.6 | CHILE |
| | RADIO SANTA MARIA, Coyhaique — DS • 10 kW • ➡ |
| | M • DS • 10 kW • ➡ M-Sa • DS • 10 kW • ➡ |
| 6030 | CANADA |
| | CFVP-CKMX, Calgary, Alberta — ⬅ • W North Am • DS • 0.1 kW |
| | — ⬅ • CHINESE & CANTONESE • W North Am • DS • 0.1 kW |
| | CHINA |
| | CENTRAL PEOPLE'S BS, Beijing — DS-1 • 100 kW |
| | W-M • DS-1 • 100 kW |
| | CONGO (DEM REP) |
| | †RADIO OKAPI, Kinshasa — FRENCH, ETC • C Africa • DS • 1/10 kW |
| | GERMANY |
| | SUDWESTRUNDFUNK, Mühlacker — ⬅ • Europe • DS • 20 kW |
| | INDIA |
| | †ALL INDIA RADIO, Delhi — DS • 50 kW |
| | RUSSIA |
| | †VOICE OF RUSSIA, St Petersburg — W • Europe • 400 kW |
| | THAILAND |
| | RADIO THAILAND, Udon Thani — S • SE Asia • 250 kW |
| | UNITED KINGDOM |
| | BBC, Via Oman — Mideast • 100 kW |
| | USA |
| | RADIO MARTI, Delano, California — S • C America • 250 kW |
| | C America • 250 kW |
| | C America • 250 kW |
| | †RADIO MARTI, Greenville, NC |
| | W • C America • 250 kW |
| | S Tu-Su • C America • 250 kW |
| (con'd) | |

0 1 2 3 4 5 6 7 8 9 10 11 12 13 14 15 16 17 18 19 20 21 22 23 24

SEASONAL S OR W    1-HR TIMESHIFT MIDYEAR ⬅ OR ➡    JAMMING / OR ∧    EARLIEST HEARD ◁    LATEST HEARD ▷    NEW FOR 2003 †

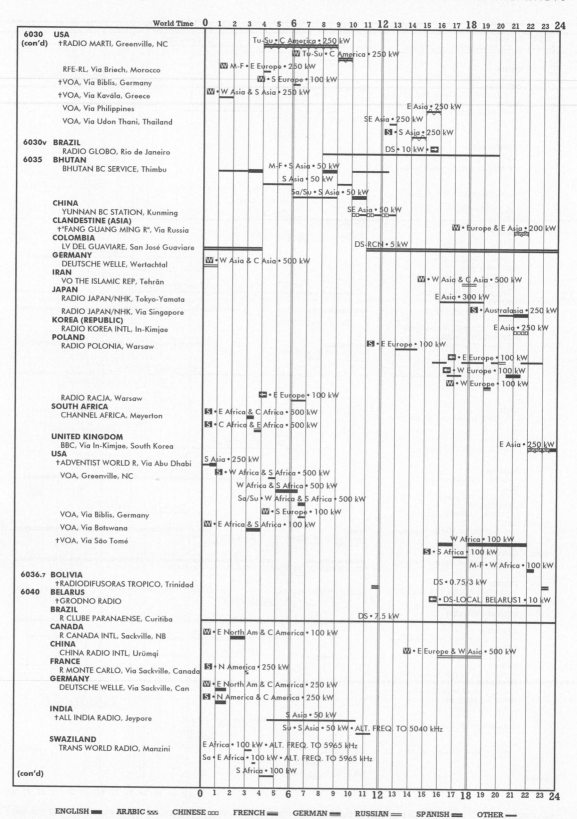

World Time 0 1 2 3 4 5 6 7 8 9 10 11 12 13 14 15 16 17 18 19 20 21 22 23 24

**6030 USA**
(con'd)　†RADIO MARTI, Greenville, NC
　　　　　Tu-Su • C America • 250 kW
　　　　　W Tu-Su • C America • 250 kW

　　RFE-RL, Via Briech, Morocco
　　　　　W M-F • E Europe • 250 kW
　　†VOA, Via Biblis, Germany
　　　　　W • S Europe • 100 kW
　　†VOA, Via Kavála, Greece
　　　　　W • W Asia & S Asia • 250 kW
　　VOA, Via Philippines
　　　　　E Asia • 250 kW
　　VOA, Via Udon Thani, Thailand
　　　　　SE Asia • 250 kW
　　　　　S • S Asia • 250 kW

**6030v BRAZIL**
　　RADIO GLOBO, Rio de Janeiro
　　　　　DS • 10 kW
**6035 BHUTAN**
　　BHUTAN BC SERVICE, Thimbu
　　　　　M-F • S Asia • 50 kW
　　　　　S Asia • 50 kW
　　　　　Sa/Su • S Asia • 50 kW

**CHINA**
　　YUNNAN BC STATION, Kunming
　　　　　SE Asia • 50 kW
**CLANDESTINE (ASIA)**
　　†"FANG GUANG MING R", Via Russia
　　　　　W • Europe & E Asia • 200 kW
**COLOMBIA**
　　LV DEL GUAVIARE, San José Guaviare
　　　　　DS-RCN • 5 kW
**GERMANY**
　　DEUTSCHE WELLE, Wertachtal
　　　　　W • W Asia & C Asia • 500 kW
**IRAN**
　　VO THE ISLAMIC REP, Tehrän
　　　　　W • W Asia & C Asia • 500 kW
**JAPAN**
　　RADIO JAPAN/NHK, Tokyo-Yamata
　　　　　E Asia • 300 kW
　　RADIO JAPAN/NHK, Via Singapore
　　　　　S • Australasia • 250 kW
**KOREA (REPUBLIC)**
　　RADIO KOREA INTL, In-Kimjae
　　　　　E Asia • 250 kW
**POLAND**
　　RADIO POLONIA, Warsaw
　　　　　S • E Europe • 100 kW
　　　　　• E Europe • 100 kW
　　　　　• W Europe • 100 kW
　　　　　W • W Europe • 100 kW

　　RADIO RACJA, Warsaw
　　　　　• E Europe • 100 kW
**SOUTH AFRICA**
　　CHANNEL AFRICA, Meyerton
　　　　　S • E Africa & C Africa • 500 kW
　　　　　S • C Africa & E Africa • 500 kW

**UNITED KINGDOM**
　　BBC, Via In-Kimjae, South Korea
　　　　　E Asia • 250 kW
**USA**
　　†ADVENTIST WORLD R, Via Abu Dhabi
　　　　　S Asia • 250 kW
　　VOA, Greenville, NC
　　　　　S • W Africa & S Africa • 500 kW
　　　　　W Africa & S Africa • 500 kW
　　　　　Sa/Su • W Africa & S Africa • 500 kW
　　VOA, Via Biblis, Germany
　　　　　W • S Europe • 100 kW
　　VOA, Via Botswana
　　　　　W • E Africa & S Africa • 100 kW
　　†VOA, Via São Tomé
　　　　　W Africa • 100 kW
　　　　　S • S Africa • 100 kW
　　　　　M-F • W Africa • 100 kW

**6036.7 BOLIVIA**
　　†RADIODIFUSORAS TROPICO, Trinidad
　　　　　DS • 0.75/3 kW
**6040 BELARUS**
　　†GRODNO RADIO
　　　　　• DS-LOCAL BELARUS1 • 10 kW
**BRAZIL**
　　R CLUBE PARANAENSE, Curitiba
　　　　　DS • 7.5 kW
**CANADA**
　　R CANADA INTL, Sackville, NB
　　　　　W • E North Am & C America • 100 kW
**CHINA**
　　CHINA RADIO INTL, Urümqi
　　　　　W • E Europe & W Asia • 500 kW
**FRANCE**
　　R MONTE CARLO, Via Sackville, Canada
　　　　　S • N America • 250 kW
**GERMANY**
　　DEUTSCHE WELLE, Via Sackville, Can
　　　　　W • E North Am & C America • 250 kW
　　　　　S • N America & C America • 250 kW

**INDIA**
　　†ALL INDIA RADIO, Jeypore
　　　　　S Asia • 50 kW
　　　　　Su • S Asia • 50 kW • ALT. FREQ. TO 5040 kHz

**SWAZILAND**
　　TRANS WORLD RADIO, Manzini
　　　　　E Africa • 100 kW • ALT. FREQ. TO 5965 kHz
　　　　　Sa • E Africa • 100 kW • ALT. FREQ. TO 5965 kHz
　　　　　S Africa • 100 kW

(con'd)

0 1 2 3 4 5 6 7 8 9 10 11 12 13 14 15 16 17 18 19 20 21 22 23 24

ENGLISH ▬　ARABIC ░░░　CHINESE ▫▫▫　FRENCH ▬　GERMAN ▬　RUSSIAN ▬　SPANISH ▬　OTHER ▬

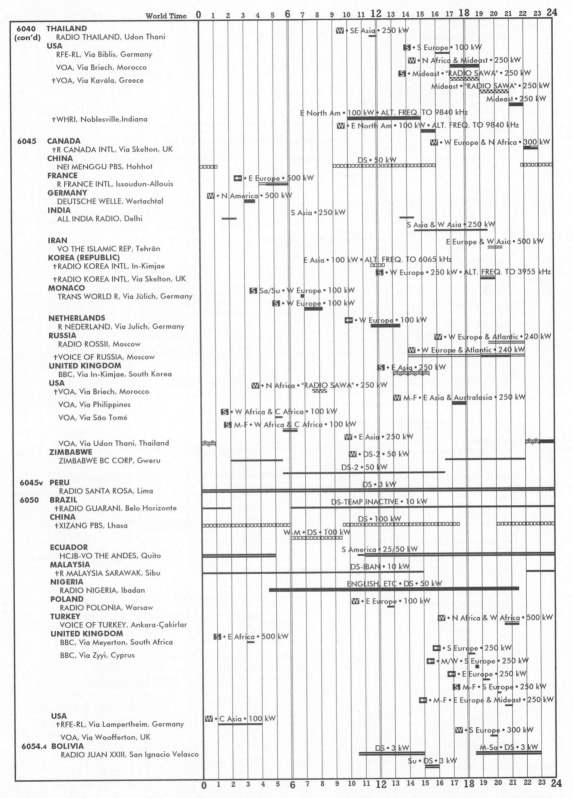

| | | |
|---|---|---|
| **6040** | **THAILAND** | |
| **(con'd)** | RADIO THAILAND, Udon Thani | W • SE Asia • 250 kW |
| | **USA** | |
| | RFE-RL, Via Biblis, Germany | S • S Europe • 100 kW |
| | VOA, Via Briech, Morocco | W • N Africa & Mideast • 250 kW |
| | †VOA, Via Kavála, Greece | S • Mideast • "RADIO SAWA" • 250 kW |
| | | Mideast • "RADIO SAWA" • 250 kW |
| | | Mideast • 250 kW |
| | †WHRI, Noblesville, Indiana | E North Am • 100 kW • ALT. FREQ. TO 9840 kHz |
| | | W • E North Am • 100 kW • ALT. FREQ. TO 9840 kHz |
| **6045** | **CANADA** | |
| | †R CANADA INTL, Via Skelton, UK | W • W Europe & N Africa • 300 kW |
| | **CHINA** | DS • 50 kW |
| | NEI MENGGU PBS, Hohhot | |
| | **FRANCE** | |
| | R FRANCE INTL, Issoudun-Allouis | ⇦ • E Europe • 500 kW |
| | **GERMANY** | |
| | DEUTSCHE WELLE, Wertachtal | W • N America • 500 kW |
| | **INDIA** | S Asia • 250 kW |
| | ALL INDIA RADIO, Delhi | S Asia & W Asia • 250 kW |
| | **IRAN** | |
| | VO THE ISLAMIC REP, Tehrān | E Europe & W Asia • 500 kW |
| | **KOREA (REPUBLIC)** | E Asia • 100 kW • ALT. FREQ. TO 6065 kHz |
| | †RADIO KOREA INTL, In-Kimjae | |
| | †RADIO KOREA INTL, Via Skelton, UK | S • W Europe • 250 kW • ALT. FREQ. TO 3955 kHz |
| | **MONACO** | S • Sa/Su • W Europe • 100 kW |
| | TRANS WORLD R, Via Jülich, Germany | S • W Europe • 100 kW |
| | **NETHERLANDS** | |
| | R NEDERLAND, Via Julich, Germany | ⇦ • W Europe • 100 kW |
| | **RUSSIA** | W • W Europe & Atlantic • 240 kW |
| | RADIO ROSSII, Moscow | W • W Europe & Atlantic • 240 kW |
| | †VOICE OF RUSSIA, Moscow | |
| | **UNITED KINGDOM** | S • E Asia • 250 kW |
| | BBC, Via In-Kimjae, South Korea | |
| | **USA** | W • N Africa • "RADIO SAWA" • 250 kW |
| | †VOA, Via Briech, Morocco | W • M-F • E Asia & Australasia • 250 kW |
| | VOA, Via Philippines | S • W Africa & C Africa • 100 kW |
| | VOA, Via São Tomé | S • M-F • W Africa & C Africa • 100 kW |
| | VOA, Via Udon Thani, Thailand | W • E Asia • 250 kW |
| | **ZIMBABWE** | W • DS-2 • 50 kW |
| | ZIMBABWE BC CORP, Gweru | DS-2 • 50 kW |
| **6045v** | **PERU** | DS • 3 kW |
| | RADIO SANTA ROSA, Lima | |
| **6050** | **BRAZIL** | DS-TEMP INACTIVE • 10 kW |
| | †RADIO GUARANI, Belo Horizonte | |
| | **CHINA** | DS • 100 kW |
| | †XIZANG PBS, Lhasa | |
| | | W-M • DS • 100 kW |
| | **ECUADOR** | S America • 25/50 kW |
| | HCJB-VO THE ANDES, Quito | |
| | **MALAYSIA** | DS-IBAN • 10 kW |
| | †R MALAYSIA SARAWAK, Sibu | |
| | **NIGERIA** | ENGLISH, ETC • DS • 50 kW |
| | RADIO NIGERIA, Ibadan | |
| | **POLAND** | W • E Europe • 100 kW |
| | RADIO POLONIA, Warsaw | |
| | **TURKEY** | W • N Africa & W Africa • 500 kW |
| | VOICE OF TURKEY, Ankara-Çakirlar | |
| | **UNITED KINGDOM** | S • E Africa • 500 kW |
| | BBC, Via Meyerton, South Africa | ⇦ • S Europe • 250 kW |
| | BBC, Via Zyyi, Cyprus | ⇦ • M/W • S Europe • 250 kW |
| | | ⇦ • E Europe • 250 kW |
| | | S • M-F • S Europe • 250 kW |
| | | ⇦ • M-F • E Europe & Mideast • 250 kW |
| | **USA** | W • C Asia • 100 kW |
| | †RFE-RL, Via Lampertheim, Germany | |
| | VOA, Via Woofferton, UK | W • S Europe • 300 kW |
| **6054.4** | **BOLIVIA** | DS • 3 kW |
| | RADIO JUAN XXIII, San Ignacio Velasco | M-Sa • DS • 3 kW |
| | | Su • DS • 3 kW |

SEASONAL S OR W     1-HR TIMESHIFT MIDYEAR ⇦ OR ⇨     JAMMING / OR ∧     EARLIEST HEARD ◁     LATEST HEARD ▷     NEW FOR 2003 †

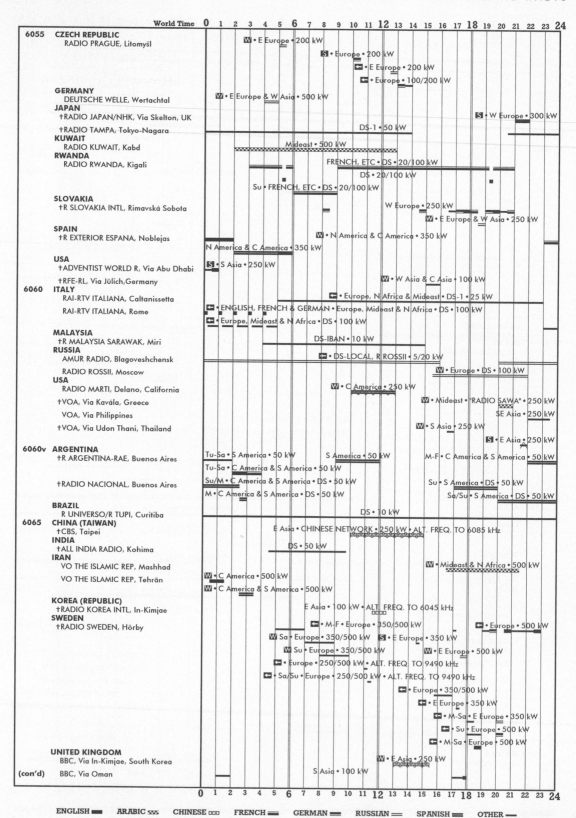

| | | |
|---|---|---|
| **6055** | **CZECH REPUBLIC** | |
| | RADIO PRAGUE, Litomyšl | W • E Europe • 200 kW |
| | | S • Europe • 200 kW |
| | | E Europe • 200 kW |
| | | Europe • 100/200 kW |
| | **GERMANY** | |
| | DEUTSCHE WELLE, Wertachtal | W • E Europe & W Asia • 500 kW |
| | **JAPAN** | |
| | †RADIO JAPAN/NHK, Via Skelton, UK | S • W Europe • 300 kW |
| | †RADIO TAMPA, Tokyo-Nagara | DS-1 • 50 kW |
| | **KUWAIT** | |
| | RADIO KUWAIT, Kabd | Mideast • 500 kW |
| | **RWANDA** | |
| | RADIO RWANDA, Kigali | FRENCH, ETC • DS 20/100 kW |
| | | DS 20/100 kW |
| | | Su • FRENCH, ETC • DS • 20/100 kW |
| | **SLOVAKIA** | |
| | †R SLOVAKIA INTL, Rimavská Sobota | W Europe • 250 kW |
| | | W • E Europe & W Asia • 250 kW |
| | **SPAIN** | |
| | †R EXTERIOR ESPANA, Noblejas | W • N America & C America • 350 kW |
| | | N America & C America • 350 kW |
| | **USA** | |
| | †ADVENTIST WORLD R, Via Abu Dhabi | S • S Asia • 250 kW |
| | †RFE-RL, Via Jülich, Germany | W • W Asia & C Asia • 100 kW |
| **6060** | **ITALY** | |
| | RAI-RTV ITALIANA, Caltanissetta | Europe, N Africa & Mideast • DS-1 • 25 kW |
| | RAI-RTV ITALIANA, Rome | ENGLISH, FRENCH & GERMAN • Europe, Mideast & N Africa • DS • 100 kW |
| | | Europe, Mideast & N Africa • DS • 100 kW |
| | **MALAYSIA** | |
| | †R MALAYSIA SARAWAK, Miri | DS-IBAN • 10 kW |
| | **RUSSIA** | |
| | AMUR RADIO, Blagoveshchensk | DS-LOCAL, R ROSSII • 5/20 kW |
| | RADIO ROSSII, Moscow | W • Europe • DS • 100 kW |
| | **USA** | |
| | RADIO MARTI, Delano, California | W • C America • 250 kW |
| | †VOA, Via Kavála, Greece | W • Mideast • "RADIO SAWA" • 250 kW |
| | VOA, Via Philippines | SE Asia • 250 kW |
| | †VOA, Via Udon Thani, Thailand | W • S Asia • 250 kW |
| | | S • E Asia • 250 kW |
| **6060v** | **ARGENTINA** | |
| | †R ARGENTINA-RAE, Buenos Aires | Tu-Sa • S America • 50 kW    S America • 50 kW    M-F • C America & S America • 50 kW |
| | | Tu-Sa • C America & S America • 50 kW |
| | †RADIO NACIONAL, Buenos Aires | Su/M • C America & S America • DS • 50 kW    Su • S America • DS • 50 kW |
| | | M • C America & S America • DS • 50 kW    Sa/Su • S America • DS • 50 kW |
| | **BRAZIL** | |
| | R UNIVERSO/R TUPI, Curitiba | DS • 10 kW |
| **6065** | **CHINA (TAIWAN)** | |
| | †CBS, Taipei | E Asia • CHINESE NETWORK • 250 kW • ALT. FREQ. TO 6085 kHz |
| | **INDIA** | |
| | †ALL INDIA RADIO, Kohima | DS • 50 kW |
| | **IRAN** | |
| | VO THE ISLAMIC REP, Mashhad | W • Mideast & N Africa • 500 kW |
| | VO THE ISLAMIC REP, Tehrān | W • C America • 500 kW |
| | | W • C America & S America • 500 kW |
| | **KOREA (REPUBLIC)** | |
| | †RADIO KOREA INTL, In-Kimjae | E Asia • 100 kW • ALT. FREQ. TO 6045 kHz |
| | **SWEDEN** | |
| | †RADIO SWEDEN, Hörby | M-F • Europe • 350/500 kW    Europe • 500 kW |
| | | W Sa • Europe • 350/500 kW    S • E Europe • 350 kW |
| | | W Su • Europe • 350/500 kW    W • E Europe • 500 kW |
| | | Europe • 250/500 kW • ALT. FREQ. TO 9490 kHz |
| | | Sa/Su • Europe • 250/500 kW • ALT. FREQ. TO 9490 kHz |
| | | Europe • 350/500 kW |
| | | E Europe • 350 kW |
| | | M-Sa • E Europe • 350 kW |
| | | Su • Europe • 500 kW |
| | | M-Sa • Europe • 500 kW |
| | **UNITED KINGDOM** | |
| | BBC, Via In-Kimjae, South Korea | W • E Asia • 250 kW |
| **(con'd)** | BBC, Via Oman | S Asia • 100 kW |

ENGLISH ▬   ARABIC ≈≈≈   CHINESE □□□   FRENCH ═   GERMAN ▭   RUSSIAN ══   SPANISH ▭   OTHER ▬

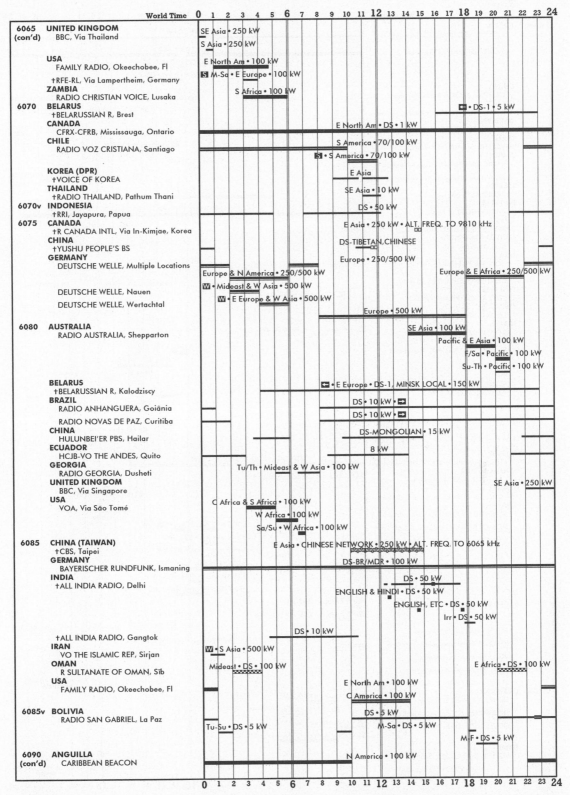

World Time

**6065 UNITED KINGDOM** (con'd)
BBC, Via Thailand
- SE Asia • 250 kW
- S Asia • 250 kW

**USA**
FAMILY RADIO, Okeechobee, Fl
- E North Am • 100 kW
- **S** M-Sa • E Europe • 100 kW

**†RFE-RL, Via Lampertheim, Germany**
**ZAMBIA**
RADIO CHRISTIAN VOICE, Lusaka
- S Africa • 100 kW

**6070 BELARUS**
†BELARUSSIAN R, Brest
- • DS-1 • 5 kW

**CANADA**
CFRX-CFRB, Mississauga, Ontario
- E North Am • DS • 1 kW

**CHILE**
RADIO VOZ CRISTIANA, Santiago
- S America • 70/100 kW
- **S** • S America • 70/100 kW

**KOREA (DPR)**
†VOICE OF KOREA
- E Asia

**THAILAND**
†RADIO THAILAND, Pathum Thani
- SE Asia • 10 kW

**6070v INDONESIA**
†RRI, Jayapura, Papua
- DS • 50 kW

**6075 CANADA**
†R CANADA INTL, Via In-Kimjae, Korea
- E Asia • 250 kW • ALT. FREQ. TO 9810 kHz

**CHINA**
†YUSHU PEOPLE'S BS
- DS-TIBETAN, CHINESE

**GERMANY**
DEUTSCHE WELLE, Multiple Locations
- Europe • 250/500 kW
- Europe & N America • 250/500 kW
- Europe & E Africa • 250/500 kW

DEUTSCHE WELLE, Nauen
- **W** • Mideast & W Asia • 500 kW

DEUTSCHE WELLE, Wertachtal
- **W** • E Europe & W Asia • 500 kW
- Europe • 500 kW

**6080 AUSTRALIA**
RADIO AUSTRALIA, Shepparton
- SE Asia • 100 kW
- Pacific & E Asia • 100 kW
- F/Sa • Pacific • 100 kW
- Su-Th • Pacific • 100 kW

**BELARUS**
†BELARUSSIAN R, Kalodziscy
- • E Europe • DS-1, MINSK LOCAL • 150 kW

**BRAZIL**
RADIO ANHANGUERA, Goiânia
- DS • 10 kW •

RADIO NOVAS DE PAZ, Curitiba
- DS • 10 kW •

**CHINA**
HULUNBEI'ER PBS, Hailar
- DS-MONGOLIAN • 15 kW

**ECUADOR**
HCJB-VO THE ANDES, Quito
- 8 kW

**GEORGIA**
RADIO GEORGIA, Dusheti
- Tu/Th • Mideast & W Asia • 100 kW

**UNITED KINGDOM**
BBC, Via Singapore
- SE Asia • 250 kW

**USA**
VOA, Via São Tomé
- C Africa & S Africa • 100 kW
- W Africa • 100 kW
- Sa/Su • W Africa • 100 kW

**6085 CHINA (TAIWAN)**
†CBS, Taipei
- E Asia • CHINESE NETWORK • 250 kW • ALT. FREQ. TO 6065 kHz

**GERMANY**
BAYERISCHER RUNDFUNK, Ismaning
- DS-BR/MDR • 100 kW

**INDIA**
†ALL INDIA RADIO, Delhi
- DS • 50 kW
- ENGLISH & HINDI • DS • 50 kW
- ENGLISH, ETC • DS • 50 kW
- Irr • DS • 50 kW

†ALL INDIA RADIO, Gangtok
- DS • 10 kW

**IRAN**
VO THE ISLAMIC REP, Sirjan
- **W** • S Asia • 500 kW

**OMAN**
R SULTANATE OF OMAN, Sib
- Mideast • DS • 100 kW
- E Africa • DS • 100 kW

**USA**
FAMILY RADIO, Okeechobee, Fl
- E North Am • 100 kW
- C America • 100 kW

**6085v BOLIVIA**
RADIO SAN GABRIEL, La Paz
- DS • 5 kW
- Tu-Su • DS • 5 kW
- M-Sa • DS • 5 kW
- M-F • DS • 5 kW

**6090 ANGUILLA** (con'd)
CARIBBEAN BEACON
- N America • 100 kW

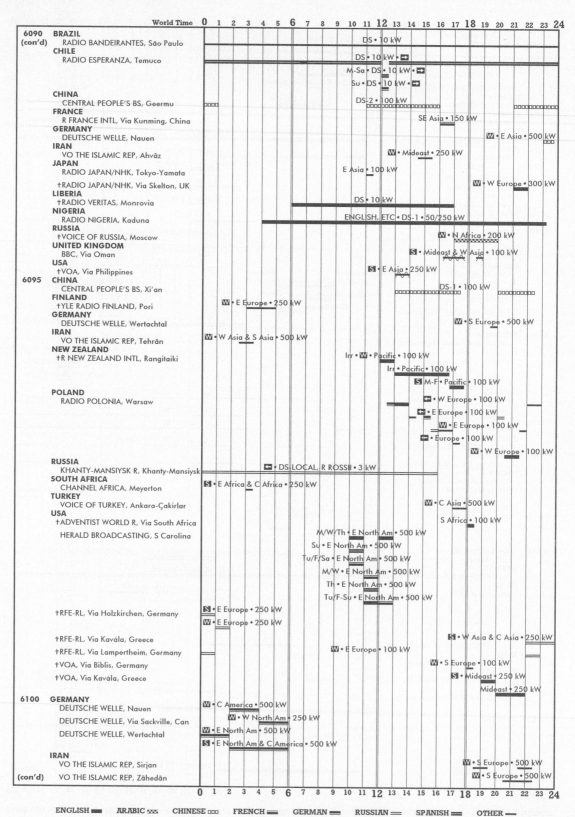

World Time  0  1  2  3  4  5  6  7  8  9  10  11  12  13  14  15  16  17  18  19  20  21  22  23  24

**6090  BRAZIL**
(con'd)  RADIO BANDEIRANTES, São Paulo — DS • 10 kW
**CHILE**
   RADIO ESPERANZA, Temuco — DS • 10 kW • ▭
      M-Sa • DS • 10 kW • ▭
      Su • DS • 10 kW • ▭
**CHINA**
   CENTRAL PEOPLE'S BS, Geermu — DS-2 • 100 kW
**FRANCE**
   R FRANCE INTL, Via Kunming, China — SE Asia • 150 kW
**GERMANY**
   DEUTSCHE WELLE, Nauen — W • E Asia • 500 kW
**IRAN**
   VO THE ISLAMIC REP, Ahvāz — W • Mideast • 250 kW
**JAPAN**
   RADIO JAPAN/NHK, Tokyo-Yamata — E Asia • 100 kW
   †RADIO JAPAN/NHK, Via Skelton, UK — W • W Europe • 300 kW
**LIBERIA**
   †RADIO VERITAS, Monrovia — DS • 10 kW
**NIGERIA**
   RADIO NIGERIA, Kaduna — ENGLISH, ETC • DS-1 • 50/250 kW
**RUSSIA**
   †VOICE OF RUSSIA, Moscow — W • N Africa • 200 kW
**UNITED KINGDOM**
   BBC, Via Oman — S • Mideast & W Asia • 100 kW
**USA**
   †VOA, Via Philippines — S • E Asia • 250 kW
**6095  CHINA**
   CENTRAL PEOPLE'S BS, Xi'an — DS-1 • 100 kW
**FINLAND**
   †YLE RADIO FINLAND, Pori — W • E Europe • 250 kW
**GERMANY**
   DEUTSCHE WELLE, Wertachtal — W • S Europe • 500 kW
**IRAN**
   VO THE ISLAMIC REP, Tehrān — W • W Asia & S Asia • 500 kW
**NEW ZEALAND**
   †R NEW ZEALAND INTL, Rangitaiki — Irr • W • Pacific • 100 kW
      Irr • Pacific • 100 kW
      S M-F • Pacific • 100 kW
**POLAND**
   RADIO POLONIA, Warsaw — ▭ • W Europe • 100 kW
      ▭ • E Europe • 100 kW
      W • E Europe • 100 kW
      ▭ • Europe • 100 kW
      W • W Europe • 100 kW
**RUSSIA**
   KHANTY-MANSIYSK R, Khanty-Mansiysk — ▭ • DS-LOCAL, R ROSSII • 3 kW
**SOUTH AFRICA**
   CHANNEL AFRICA, Meyerton — S • E Africa & C Africa • 250 kW
**TURKEY**
   VOICE OF TURKEY, Ankara-Çakirlar — W • C Asia • 500 kW
**USA**
   †ADVENTIST WORLD R, Via South Africa — S Africa • 100 kW
   HERALD BROADCASTING, S Carolina — M/W/Th • E North Am • 500 kW
      Su • E North Am • 500 kW
      Tu/F/Sa • E North Am • 500 kW
      M/W • E North Am • 500 kW
      Th • E North Am • 500 kW
      Tu/F-Su • E North Am • 500 kW
   †RFE-RL, Via Holzkirchen, Germany — S • E Europe • 250 kW
      W • E Europe • 250 kW
   †RFE-RL, Via Kavála, Greece — S • W Asia & C Asia • 250 kW
   †RFE-RL, Via Lampertheim, Germany — W • E Europe • 100 kW
   †VOA, Via Biblis, Germany — W • S Europe • 100 kW
   †VOA, Via Kavála, Greece — S • Mideast • 250 kW
      Mideast • 250 kW
**6100  GERMANY**
   DEUTSCHE WELLE, Nauen — W • C America • 500 kW
   DEUTSCHE WELLE, Via Sackville, Can — W • W North Am • 250 kW
   DEUTSCHE WELLE, Wertachtal — W • E North Am • 500 kW
      S • E North Am & C America • 500 kW
**IRAN**
   VO THE ISLAMIC REP, Sirjan — W • S Europe • 500 kW
(con'd)  VO THE ISLAMIC REP, Zāhedān — W • S Europe • 500 kW

0  1  2  3  4  5  6  7  8  9  10  11  12  13  14  15  16  17  18  19  20  21  22  23  24

ENGLISH ▬▬   ARABIC ⌇⌇⌇   CHINESE □□□   FRENCH ▭▭   GERMAN ▬▬   RUSSIAN ══   SPANISH ▬▬   OTHER ▬▬

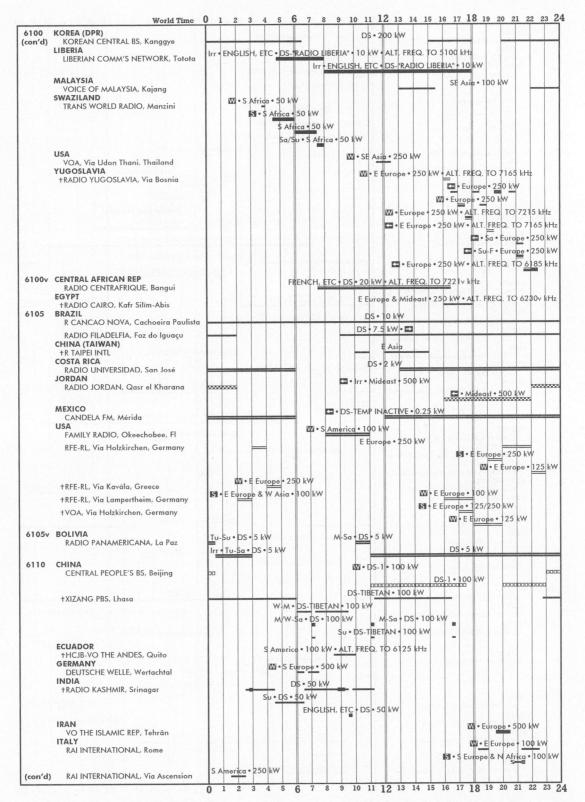

World Time | 0 1 2 3 4 5 6 7 8 9 10 11 12 13 14 15 16 17 18 19 20 21 22 23 24

**6100** KOREA (DPR)
**(con'd)** KOREAN CENTRAL BS, Kanggye — DS • 200 kW
LIBERIA
LIBERIAN COMM'S NETWORK, Totota — Irr • ENGLISH, ETC • DS-"RADIO LIBERIA" • 10 kW • ALT. FREQ. TO 5100 kHz
Irr • ENGLISH, ETC • DS-"RADIO LIBERIA" • 10 kW

MALAYSIA
VOICE OF MALAYSIA, Kajang — SE Asia • 100 kW
SWAZILAND
TRANS WORLD RADIO, Manzini — W • S Africa • 50 kW
S • S Africa • 50 kW
S Africa • 50 kW
Sa/Su • S Africa • 50 kW

USA
VOA, Via Udon Thani, Thailand — W • SE Asia • 250 kW
YUGOSLAVIA
†RADIO YUGOSLAVIA, Via Bosnia — W • E Europe • 250 kW • ALT. FREQ. TO 7165 kHz
⇦ • Europe • 250 kW
W • Europe • 250 kW
W • Europe • 250 kW • ALT. FREQ. TO 7215 kHz
⇦ • E Europe • 250 kW • ALT. FREQ. TO 7165 kHz
⇦ • Sa • Europe • 250 kW
⇦ • Su-F • Europe • 250 kW
⇦ • Europe • 250 kW • ALT. FREQ. TO 6185 kHz

**6100v** CENTRAL AFRICAN REP
RADIO CENTRAFRIQUE, Bangui — FRENCH, ETC • DS • 20 kW • ALT. FREQ. TO 7221v kHz
EGYPT
†RADIO CAIRO, Kafr Silim-Abis — E Europe & Mideast • 250 kW • ALT. FREQ. TO 6230v kHz
**6105** BRAZIL
R CANCAO NOVA, Cachoeira Paulista — DS • 10 kW
RADIO FILADELFIA, Foz do Iguaçu — DS • 7.5 kW • ⇨
CHINA (TAIWAN)
†R TAIPEI INTL — E Asia
COSTA RICA
RADIO UNIVERSIDAD, San José — DS • 2 kW
JORDAN
RADIO JORDAN, Qasr el Kharana — ⇦ • Irr • Mideast • 500 kW
⇦ • Mideast • 500 kW

MEXICO
CANDELA FM, Mérida — ⇦ • DS-TEMP INACTIVE • 0.25 kW
USA
FAMILY RADIO, Okeechobee, Fl — W • S America • 100 kW
E Europe • 250 kW
RFE-RL, Via Holzkirchen, Germany — S • E Europe • 250 kW
W • E Europe • 125 kW
†RFE-RL, Via Kavála, Greece — W • E Europe • 250 kW
†RFE-RL, Via Lampertheim, Germany — S • E Europe & W Asia • 100 kW
W • E Europe • 100 kW
†VOA, Via Holzkirchen, Germany — S • E Europe • 125/250 kW
W • E Europe • 125 kW

**6105v** BOLIVIA
RADIO PANAMERICANA, La Paz — Tu-Su • DS • 5 kW
M-Sa • DS • 5 kW
Irr • Tu-Sa • DS • 5 kW
DS • 5 kW

**6110** CHINA
CENTRAL PEOPLE'S BS, Beijing — W • DS-1 • 100 kW
DS-1 • 100 kW
†XIZANG PBS, Lhasa — DS-TIBETAN • 100 kW
W-M • DS-TIBETAN • 100 kW
M/W-Sa • DS • 100 kW
M-Sa • DS • 100 kW
Su • DS-TIBETAN • 100 kW

ECUADOR
†HCJB-VO THE ANDES, Quito — S America • 100 kW • ALT. FREQ. TO 6125 kHz
GERMANY
DEUTSCHE WELLE, Wertachtal — W • S Europe • 500 kW
INDIA
†RADIO KASHMIR, Srinagar — DS • 50 kW
Su • DS • 50 kW
ENGLISH, ETC • DS • 50 kW

IRAN
VO THE ISLAMIC REP, Tehrān — W • Europe • 500 kW
ITALY
RAI INTERNATIONAL, Rome — W • E Europe • 100 kW
S • S Europe & N Africa • 100 kW

**(con'd)** RAI INTERNATIONAL, Via Ascension — S America • 250 kW

0 1 2 3 4 5 6 7 8 9 10 11 12 13 14 15 16 17 18 19 20 21 22 23 24

SEASONAL S OR W    1-HR TIMESHIFT MIDYEAR ⇦ OR ⇨    JAMMING / OR ∧    EARLIEST HEARD ◁    LATEST HEARD ▷    NEW FOR 2003 †

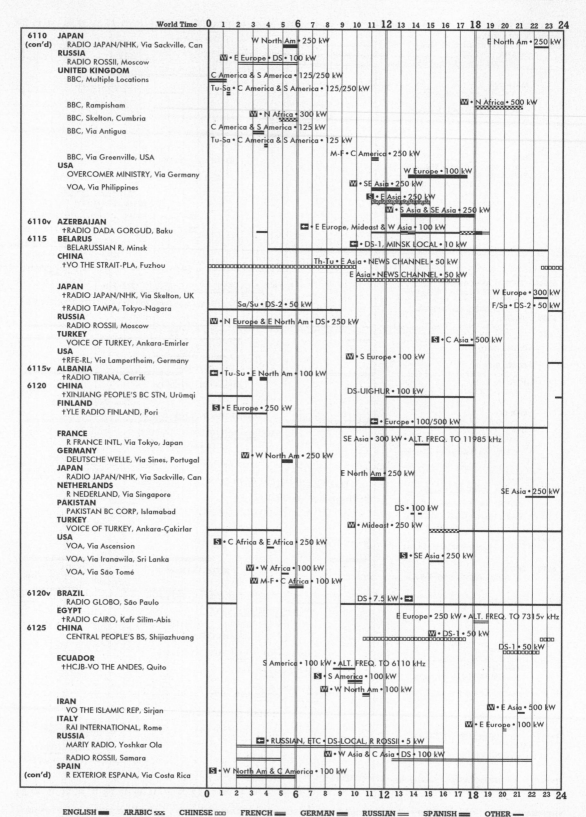

| | | |
|---|---|---|
| 6110 | JAPAN | |
| (con'd) | RADIO JAPAN/NHK, Via Sackville, Can | W North Am • 250 kW ... E North Am • 250 kW |
| | RUSSIA | |
| | RADIO ROSSII, Moscow | W • E Europe • DS • 100 kW |
| | UNITED KINGDOM | |
| | BBC, Multiple Locations | C America & S America • 125/250 kW |
| | | Tu-Sa • C America & S America • 125/250 kW |
| | BBC, Rampisham | W • N Africa • 500 kW |
| | BBC, Skelton, Cumbria | W • N Africa • 300 kW |
| | BBC, Via Antigua | C America & S America • 125 kW |
| | | Tu-Sa • C America & S America • 125 kW |
| | BBC, Via Greenville, USA | M-F • C America • 250 kW |
| | USA | |
| | OVERCOMER MINISTRY, Via Germany | W Europe • 100 kW |
| | VOA, Via Philippines | W • SE Asia • 250 kW |
| | | S • E Asia • 250 kW |
| | | W • S Asia & SE Asia • 250 kW |
| 6110v | AZERBAIJAN | |
| | †RADIO DADA GORGUD, Baku | E Europe, Mideast & W Asia • 100 kW |
| 6115 | BELARUS | |
| | BELARUSSIAN R, Minsk | DS-1, MINSK LOCAL • 10 kW |
| | CHINA | |
| | †VO THE STRAIT-PLA, Fuzhou | Th-Tu • E Asia • NEWS CHANNEL • 50 kW |
| | | E Asia • NEWS CHANNEL • 50 kW |
| | JAPAN | |
| | †RADIO JAPAN/NHK, Via Skelton, UK | W Europe • 300 kW |
| | †RADIO TAMPA, Tokyo-Nagara | Sa/Su • DS-2 • 50 kW ... F/Sa • DS-2 • 50 kW |
| | RUSSIA | |
| | RADIO ROSSII, Moscow | W • N Europe & E North Am • DS • 250 kW |
| | TURKEY | |
| | VOICE OF TURKEY, Ankara-Emirler | S • C Asia • 500 kW |
| | USA | |
| | †RFE-RL, Via Lampertheim, Germany | W • S Europe • 100 kW |
| 6115v | ALBANIA | |
| | †RADIO TIRANA, Cerrik | Tu-Su • E North Am • 100 kW |
| 6120 | CHINA | |
| | †XINJIANG PEOPLE'S BC STN, Urümqi | DS-UIGHUR • 100 kW |
| | FINLAND | |
| | †YLE RADIO FINLAND, Pori | S • E Europe • 250 kW |
| | | Europe • 100/500 kW |
| | FRANCE | |
| | R FRANCE INTL, Via Tokyo, Japan | SE Asia • 300 kW • ALT. FREQ. TO 11985 kHz |
| | GERMANY | |
| | DEUTSCHE WELLE, Via Sines, Portugal | W • W North Am • 250 kW |
| | JAPAN | |
| | RADIO JAPAN/NHK, Via Sackville, Can | E North Am • 250 kW |
| | NETHERLANDS | |
| | R NEDERLAND, Via Singapore | SE Asia • 250 kW |
| | PAKISTAN | |
| | PAKISTAN BC CORP, Islamabad | DS • 100 kW |
| | TURKEY | |
| | VOICE OF TURKEY, Ankara-Çakirlar | W • Mideast • 250 kW |
| | USA | |
| | VOA, Via Ascension | S • C Africa & E Africa • 250 kW |
| | VOA, Via Iranawila, Sri Lanka | S • SE Asia • 250 kW |
| | VOA, Via São Tomé | W • W Africa • 100 kW |
| | | W M-F • C Africa • 100 kW |
| 6120v | BRAZIL | |
| | RADIO GLOBO, São Paulo | DS • 7.5 kW • |
| | EGYPT | |
| | †RADIO CAIRO, Kafr Silïm-Abis | E Europe • 250 kW • ALT. FREQ. TO 7315v kHz |
| 6125 | CHINA | |
| | CENTRAL PEOPLE'S BS, Shijiazhuang | W • DS-1 • 50 kW |
| | | DS-1 • 50 kW |
| | ECUADOR | |
| | †HCJB-VO THE ANDES, Quito | S America • 100 kW • ALT. FREQ. TO 6110 kHz |
| | | S • S America • 100 kW |
| | | W • W North Am • 100 kW |
| | IRAN | |
| | VO THE ISLAMIC REP, Sirjan | W • E Asia • 500 kW |
| | ITALY | |
| | RAI INTERNATIONAL, Rome | W • E Europe • 100 kW |
| | RUSSIA | |
| | MARIY RADIO, Yoshkar Ola | RUSSIAN, ETC • DS-LOCAL, R ROSSII • 5 kW |
| | RADIO ROSSII, Samara | W • W Asia & C Asia • DS • 100 kW |
| | SPAIN | |
| (con'd) | R EXTERIOR ESPANA, Via Costa Rica | S • W North Am & C America • 100 kW |

ENGLISH ▬  ARABIC ≋  CHINESE □□□  FRENCH ═  GERMAN ▬  RUSSIAN ═  SPANISH ▬  OTHER ▬

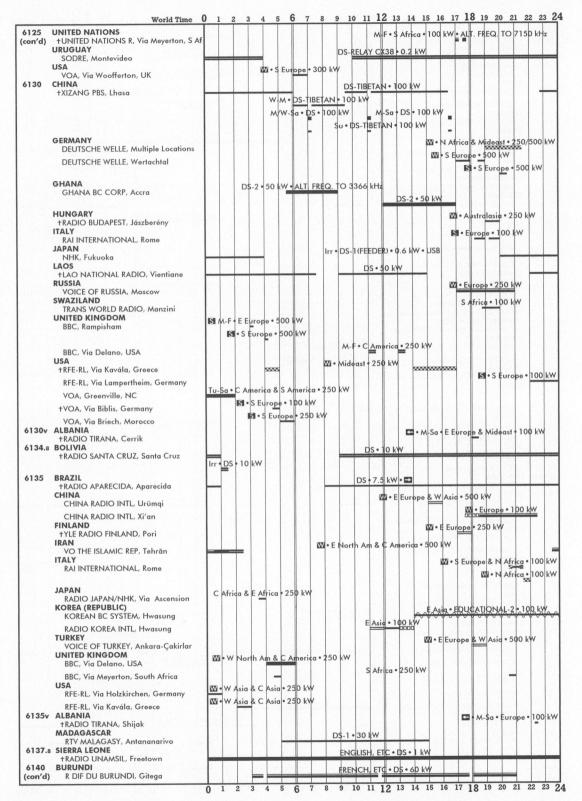

World Time: 0 1 2 3 4 5 6 7 8 9 10 11 12 13 14 15 16 17 18 19 20 21 22 23 24

**6125** **UNITED NATIONS**
(con'd) †UNITED NATIONS R, Via Meyerton, S Af — M-F • S Africa • 100 kW • ALT. FREQ. TO 7150 kHz
**URUGUAY**
SODRE, Montevideo — DS-RELAY CX38 • 0.2 kW
**USA**
VOA, Via Woofferton, UK — W • S Europe • 300 kW
**6130** **CHINA**
†XIZANG PBS, Lhasa — DS-TIBETAN • 100 kW
W-M • DS-TIBETAN • 100 kW
M/W-Sa • DS • 100 kW    M-Sa • DS • 100 kW
Su • DS-TIBETAN • 100 kW
**GERMANY**
DEUTSCHE WELLE, Multiple Locations — W • N Africa & Mideast • 250/500 kW
DEUTSCHE WELLE, Wertachtal — W • S Europe • 500 kW
S • S Europe • 500 kW
**GHANA**
GHANA BC CORP, Accra — DS-2 • 50 kW • ALT. FREQ. TO 3366 kHz
DS-2 • 50 kW
**HUNGARY**
†RADIO BUDAPEST, Jászberény — W • Australasia • 250 kW
**ITALY**
RAI INTERNATIONAL, Rome — S • Europe • 100 kW
**JAPAN**
NHK, Fukuoka — Irr • DS-1(FEEDER) • 0.6 kW • USB
**LAOS**
†LAO NATIONAL RADIO, Vientiane — DS • 50 kW
**RUSSIA**
VOICE OF RUSSIA, Moscow — W • Europe • 250 kW
**SWAZILAND**
TRANS WORLD RADIO, Manzini — S Africa • 100 kW
**UNITED KINGDOM**
BBC, Rampisham — S M-F • E Europe • 500 kW
S • S Europe • 500 kW

BBC, Via Delano, USA — M-F • C America • 250 kW
**USA**
†RFE-RL, Via Kavála, Greece — W • Mideast • 250 kW
RFE-RL, Via Lampertheim, Germany — S • S Europe • 100 kW
VOA, Greenville, NC — Tu-Sa • C America & S America • 250 kW
†VOA, Via Biblis, Germany — S • S Europe • 100 kW
VOA, Via Briech, Morocco — S • S Europe • 250 kW
**6130v** **ALBANIA**
†RADIO TIRANA, Cerrik — M-Sa • E Europe & Mideast • 100 kW
**6134.8** **BOLIVIA**
†RADIO SANTA CRUZ, Santa Cruz — DS • 10 kW
Irr • DS • 10 kW

**6135** **BRAZIL**
†RADIO APARECIDA, Aparecida — DS • 7.5 kW •
**CHINA**
CHINA RADIO INTL, Urümqi — W • E Europe & W Asia • 500 kW
CHINA RADIO INTL, Xi'an — W • Europe • 100 kW
**FINLAND**
†YLE RADIO FINLAND, Pori — W • E Europe • 250 kW
**IRAN**
VO THE ISLAMIC REP, Tehrān — W • E North Am & C America • 500 kW
**ITALY**
RAI INTERNATIONAL, Rome — W • S Europe & N Africa • 100 kW
W • N Africa • 100 kW
**JAPAN**
RADIO JAPAN/NHK, Via Ascension — C Africa & E Africa • 250 kW
**KOREA (REPUBLIC)**
KOREAN BC SYSTEM, Hwasung — E Asia • EDUCATIONAL-2 • 100 kW
RADIO KOREA INTL, Hwasung — E Asia • 100 kW
**TURKEY**
VOICE OF TURKEY, Ankara-Çakirlar — W • E Europe & W Asia • 500 kW
**UNITED KINGDOM**
BBC, Via Delano, USA — W • W North Am & C America • 250 kW
BBC, Via Meyerton, South Africa — S Africa • 250 kW
**USA**
RFE-RL, Via Holzkirchen, Germany — W • W Asia & C Asia • 250 kW
RFE-RL, Via Kavála, Greece — W • W Asia & C Asia • 250 kW
**6135v** **ALBANIA**
†RADIO TIRANA, Shijak — M-Sa • Europe • 100 kW
**MADAGASCAR**
RTV MALAGASY, Antananarivo — DS-1 • 30 kW
**6137.8** **SIERRA LEONE**
†RADIO UNAMSIL, Freetown — ENGLISH, ETC • DS • 1 kW
**6140** **BURUNDI**
(con'd) R DIF DU BURUNDI, Gitega — FRENCH, ETC • DS • 60 kW

0 1 2 3 4 5 6 7 8 9 10 11 12 13 14 15 16 17 18 19 20 21 22 23 24

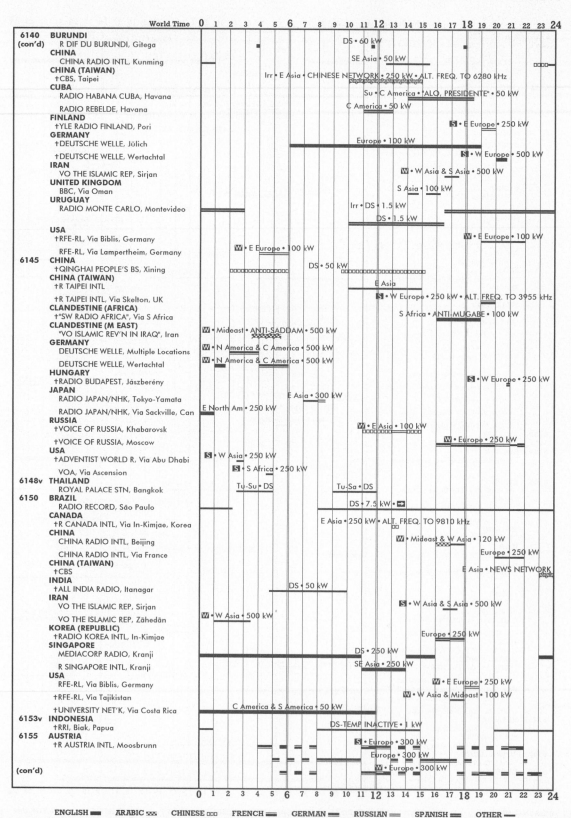

World Time    0  1  2  3  4  5  6  7  8  9  10  11  12  13  14  15  16  17  18  19  20  21  22  23  24

**6140 BURUNDI**
**(con'd)**
R DIF DU BURUNDI, Gitega — DS • 60 kW
**CHINA**
CHINA RADIO INTL, Kunming — SE Asia • 50 kW
**CHINA (TAIWAN)**
†CBS, Taipei — Irr • E Asia • CHINESE NETWORK • 250 kW • ALT. FREQ. TO 6280 kHz
**CUBA**
RADIO HABANA CUBA, Havana — Su • C America • "ALO, PRESIDENTE" • 50 kW
RADIO REBELDE, Havana — C America • 50 kW
**FINLAND**
†YLE RADIO FINLAND, Pori — S • E Europe • 250 kW
**GERMANY**
†DEUTSCHE WELLE, Jülich — Europe • 100 kW
†DEUTSCHE WELLE, Wertachtal — S • W Europe • 500 kW
**IRAN**
VO THE ISLAMIC REP, Sirjan — W • W Asia & S Asia • 500 kW
**UNITED KINGDOM**
BBC, Via Oman — S Asia • 100 kW
**URUGUAY**
RADIO MONTE CARLO, Montevideo — Irr • DS • 1.5 kW
DS • 1.5 kW
**USA**
†RFE-RL, Via Biblis, Germany — W • E Europe • 100 kW
RFE-RL, Via Lampertheim, Germany — W • E Europe • 100 kW
**6145 CHINA**
†QINGHAI PEOPLE'S BS, Xining — DS • 50 kW
**CHINA (TAIWAN)**
†R TAIPEI INTL — E Asia
†R TAIPEI INTL, Via Skelton, UK — S • W Europe • 250 kW • ALT. FREQ. TO 3955 kHz
**CLANDESTINE (AFRICA)**
†"SW RADIO AFRICA", Via S Africa — S Africa • ANTI-MUGABE • 100 kW
**CLANDESTINE (M EAST)**
"VO ISLAMIC REV'N IN IRAQ", Iran — W • Mideast • ANTI-SADDAM • 500 kW
**GERMANY**
DEUTSCHE WELLE, Multiple Locations — W • N America & C America • 500 kW
DEUTSCHE WELLE, Wertachtal — W • N America & C America • 500 kW
**HUNGARY**
†RADIO BUDAPEST, Jászberény — S • W Europe • 250 kW
**JAPAN**
RADIO JAPAN/NHK, Tokyo-Yamata — E Asia • 300 kW
RADIO JAPAN/NHK, Via Sackville, Can — E North Am • 250 kW
**RUSSIA**
†VOICE OF RUSSIA, Khabarovsk — W • E Asia • 100 kW
†VOICE OF RUSSIA, Moscow — W • Europe • 250 kW
**USA**
†ADVENTIST WORLD R, Via Abu Dhabi — S • W Asia • 250 kW
VOA, Via Ascension — S • S Africa • 250 kW
**6148v THAILAND**
ROYAL PALACE STN, Bangkok — Tu-Su • DS / Tu-Sa • DS
**6150 BRAZIL**
RADIO RECORD, São Paulo — DS • 7.5 kW •
**CANADA**
†R CANADA INTL, Via In-Kimjae, Korea — E Asia • 250 kW • ALT. FREQ. TO 9810 kHz
**CHINA**
CHINA RADIO INTL, Beijing — W • Mideast & W Asia • 120 kW
CHINA RADIO INTL, Via France — Europe • 250 kW
**CHINA (TAIWAN)**
†CBS — E Asia • NEWS NETWORK
**INDIA**
†ALL INDIA RADIO, Itanagar — DS • 50 kW
**IRAN**
VO THE ISLAMIC REP, Sirjan — S • W Asia & S Asia • 500 kW
VO THE ISLAMIC REP, Zāhedān — W • W Asia • 500 kW
**KOREA (REPUBLIC)**
†RADIO KOREA INTL, In-Kimjae — Europe • 250 kW
**SINGAPORE**
MEDIACORP RADIO, Kranji — DS • 250 kW
R SINGAPORE INTL, Kranji — SE Asia • 250 kW
**USA**
RFE-RL, Via Biblis, Germany — W • E Europe • 250 kW
†RFE-RL, Via Tajikistan — W • W Asia & Mideast • 100 kW
†UNIVERSITY NET'K, Via Costa Rica — C America & S America • 50 kW
**6153v INDONESIA**
†RRI, Biak, Papua — DS-TEMP INACTIVE • 1 kW
**6155 AUSTRIA**
†R AUSTRIA INTL, Moosbrunn — S • Europe • 300 kW
Europe • 300 kW
W • Europe • 300 kW

**(con'd)**

0  1  2  3  4  5  6  7  8  9  10  11  12  13  14  15  16  17  18  19  20  21  22  23  24

ENGLISH ▬   ARABIC ⬚⬚⬚   CHINESE □□□   FRENCH ═══   GERMAN ▬▬   RUSSIAN ══   SPANISH ═══   OTHER ▬▬

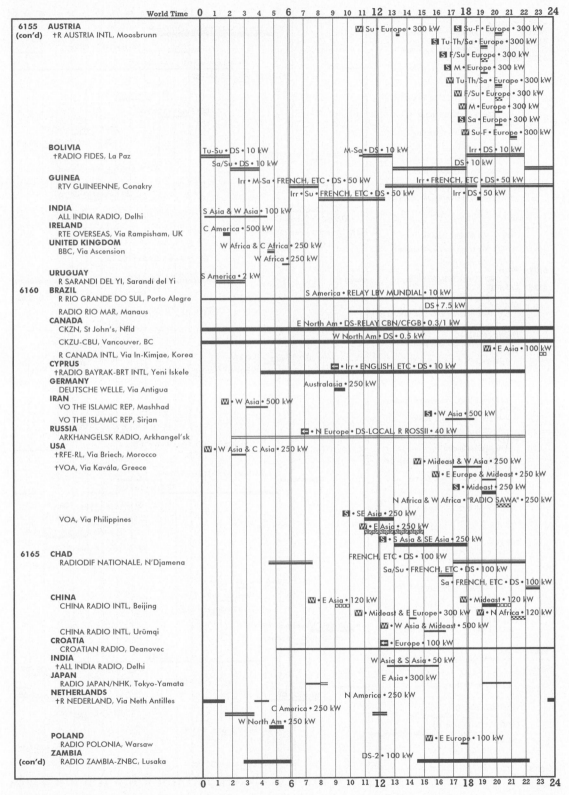

World Time

**6155 AUSTRIA**
(con'd)  †R AUSTRIA INTL, Moosbrunn
- W • Su • Europe • 300 kW
- S • Su-F • Europe • 300 kW
- S • Tu-Th/Sa • Europe • 300 kW
- S • F/Su • Europe • 300 kW
- S • M • Europe • 300 kW
- W • Tu-Th/Sa • Europe • 300 kW
- W • F/Su • Europe • 300 kW
- W • M • Europe • 300 kW
- S • Sa • Europe • 300 kW
- W • Su-F • Europe • 300 kW

**BOLIVIA**
  †RADIO FIDES, La Paz
- Tu-Su • DS • 10 kW
- M-Sa • DS • 10 kW
- Irr • DS • 10 kW
- Sa/Su • DS • 10 kW
- DS • 10 kW

**GUINEA**
  RTV GUINEENNE, Conakry
- Irr • M-Sa • FRENCH, ETC • DS • 50 kW
- Irr • FRENCH, ETC • DS • 50 kW
- Irr • Su • FRENCH, ETC • DS • 50 kW
- Irr • DS • 50 kW

**INDIA**
  ALL INDIA RADIO, Delhi — S Asia & W Asia • 100 kW
**IRELAND**
  RTE OVERSEAS, Via Rampisham, UK — C America • 500 kW
**UNITED KINGDOM**
  BBC, Via Ascension
- W Africa & C Africa • 250 kW
- W Africa • 250 kW

**URUGUAY**
  R SARANDI DEL YI, Sarandí del Yi — S America • 2 kW

**6160 BRAZIL**
  R RIO GRANDE DO SUL, Porto Alegre — S America • RELAY LBV MUNDIAL • 10 kW

  RADIO RIO MAR, Manaus — DS • 7.5 kW

**CANADA**
  CKZN, St John's, Nfld — E North Am • DS-RELAY CBN/CFGB • 0.3/1 kW

  CKZU-CBU, Vancouver, BC — W North Am • DS • 0.5 kW

  R CANADA INTL, Via In-Kimjae, Korea — W • E Asia • 100 kW
**CYPRUS**
  †RADIO BAYRAK-BRT INTL, Yeni Iskele — ⇐ • Irr • ENGLISH, ETC • DS • 10 kW
**GERMANY**
  DEUTSCHE WELLE, Via Antigua — Australasia • 250 kW
**IRAN**
  VO THE ISLAMIC REP, Mashhad — W • W Asia • 500 kW

  VO THE ISLAMIC REP, Sirjan — S • W Asia • 500 kW
**RUSSIA**
  ARKHANGELSK RADIO, Arkhangel'sk — ⇐ • N Europe • DS-LOCAL R ROSSII • 40 kW
**USA**
  †RFE-RL, Via Briech, Morocco — W • W Asia & C Asia • 250 kW

  †VOA, Via Kavála, Greece
- W • Mideast & W Asia • 250 kW
- W • E Europe & Mideast • 250 kW
- S • Mideast • 250 kW
- N Africa & W Africa • "RADIO SAWA" • 250 kW

  VOA, Via Philippines
- S • SE Asia • 250 kW
- W • E Asia • 250 kW
- W • S Asia & SE Asia • 250 kW

**6165 CHAD**
  RADIODIF NATIONALE, N'Djamena
- FRENCH, ETC • DS • 100 kW
- Sa/Su • FRENCH, ETC • DS • 100 kW
- Sa • FRENCH, ETC • DS • 100 kW

**CHINA**
  CHINA RADIO INTL, Beijing
- W • E Asia • 120 kW
- W • Mideast • 120 kW
- W • Mideast & E Europe • 300 kW
- W • N Africa • 120 kW

  CHINA RADIO INTL, Urümqi — W • W Asia & Mideast • 500 kW
**CROATIA**
  CROATIAN RADIO, Deanovec — ⇐ • Europe • 100 kW
**INDIA**
  †ALL INDIA RADIO, Delhi — W Asia & S Asia • 50 kW
**JAPAN**
  RADIO JAPAN/NHK, Tokyo-Yamata — E Asia • 300 kW
**NETHERLANDS**
  †R NEDERLAND, Via Neth Antilles
- N America • 250 kW
- C America • 250 kW
- W North Am • 250 kW

**POLAND**
  RADIO POLONIA, Warsaw — W • E Europe • 100 kW
**ZAMBIA**
(con'd)  RADIO ZAMBIA-ZNBC, Lusaka — DS-2 • 100 kW

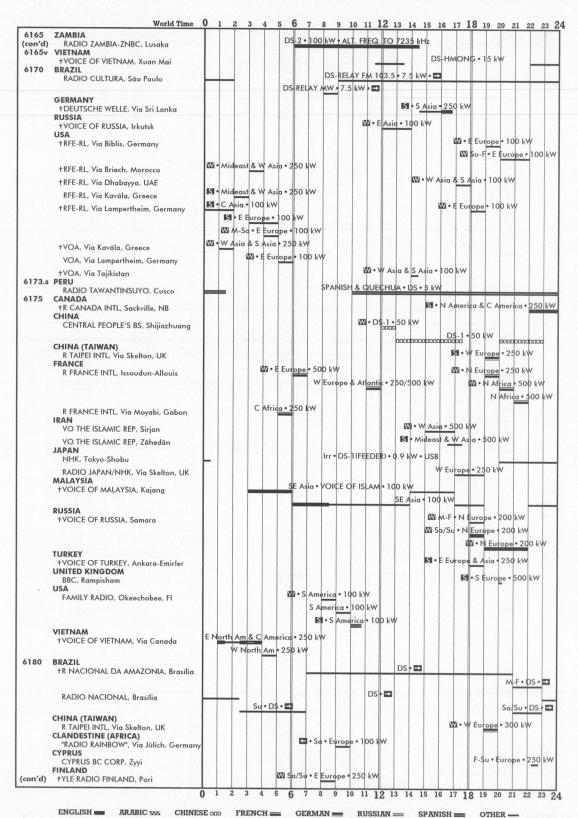

| World Time | | |
|---|---|---|
| **6165 ZAMBIA** | | |
| (con'd)  RADIO ZAMBIA-ZNBC, Lusaka | DS-2 • 100 kW • ALT. FREQ. TO 7235 kHz | |
| **6165v VIETNAM** | | |
| †VOICE OF VIETNAM, Xuan Mai | DS-HMONG • 15 kW | |
| **6170 BRAZIL** | | |
| RADIO CULTURA, São Paulo | DS-RELAY FM 103.5 • 7.5 kW • ⇨ | |
| | DS-RELAY MW • 7.5 kW • ⇨ | |
| **GERMANY** | | |
| †DEUTSCHE WELLE, Via Sri Lanka | S • S Asia • 250 kW | |
| **RUSSIA** | | |
| †VOICE OF RUSSIA, Irkutsk | W • E Asia • 100 kW | |
| **USA** | | |
| †RFE-RL, Via Biblis, Germany | W • E Europe • 100 kW | |
| | W • Su-F • E Europe • 100 kW | |
| †RFE-RL, Via Briech, Morocco | W • Mideast & W Asia • 250 kW | |
| †RFE-RL, Via Dhabayya, UAE | W • W Asia & S Asia • 100 kW | |
| RFE-RL, Via Kavála, Greece | S • Mideast & W Asia • 250 kW | |
| †RFE-RL, Via Lampertheim, Germany | S • C Asia • 100 kW   W • E Europe • 100 kW | |
| | S • E Europe • 100 kW | |
| | M-Sa • E Europe • 100 kW | |
| †VOA, Via Kavála, Greece | W • W Asia & S Asia • 250 kW | |
| VOA, Via Lampertheim, Germany | W • E Europe • 100 kW | |
| †VOA, Via Tajikistan | W • W Asia & S Asia • 100 kW | |
| **6173.8 PERU** | | |
| RADIO TAWANTINSUYO, Cusco | SPANISH & QUECHUA • DS • 5 kW | |
| **6175 CANADA** | | |
| †R CANADA INTL, Sackville, NB | S • N America & C America • 250 kW | |
| **CHINA** | | |
| CENTRAL PEOPLE'S BS, Shijiazhuang | W • DS-1 • 50 kW | |
| | DS-1 • 50 kW | |
| **CHINA (TAIWAN)** | | |
| R TAIPEI INTL, Via Skelton, UK | S • W Europe • 250 kW | |
| **FRANCE** | | |
| R FRANCE INTL, Issoudun-Allouis | W • E Europe • 500 kW   W • N Europe • 250 kW | |
| | W Europe & Atlantic • 250/500 kW   W • N Africa • 500 kW | |
| | N Africa • 500 kW | |
| R FRANCE INTL, Via Moyabi, Gabon | C Africa • 250 kW | |
| **IRAN** | | |
| VO THE ISLAMIC REP, Sirjan | W • W Asia • 500 kW | |
| VO THE ISLAMIC REP, Zāhedān | S • Mideast & W Asia • 500 kW | |
| **JAPAN** | | |
| NHK, Tokyo-Shobu | Irr • DS-1 (FEEDER) • 0.9 kW • USB | |
| RADIO JAPAN/NHK, Via Skelton, UK | W Europe • 250 kW | |
| **MALAYSIA** | | |
| †VOICE OF MALAYSIA, Kajang | SE Asia • VOICE OF ISLAM • 100 kW | |
| | SE Asia • 100 kW | |
| **RUSSIA** | | |
| †VOICE OF RUSSIA, Samara | W M-F • N Europe • 200 kW | |
| | W Sa/Su • N Europe • 200 kW | |
| | W • N Europe • 200 kW | |
| **TURKEY** | | |
| †VOICE OF TURKEY, Ankara-Emirler | S • E Europe & Asia • 250 kW | |
| **UNITED KINGDOM** | | |
| BBC, Rampisham | S • S Europe • 500 kW | |
| **USA** | | |
| FAMILY RADIO, Okeechobee, Fl | W • S America • 100 kW | |
| | S America • 100 kW | |
| | S • S America • 100 kW | |
| **VIETNAM** | | |
| †VOICE OF VIETNAM, Via Canada | E North Am & C America • 250 kW | |
| | W North Am • 250 kW | |
| **6180 BRAZIL** | | |
| †R NACIONAL DA AMAZONIA, Brasília | DS • ⇨ | |
| | M-F • DS • ⇨ | |
| RADIO NACIONAL, Brasília | DS • ⇨ | |
| | Su • DS • ⇨   Sa/Su • DS • ⇨ | |
| **CHINA (TAIWAN)** | | |
| R TAIPEI INTL, Via Skelton, UK | W • W Europe • 300 kW | |
| **CLANDESTINE (AFRICA)** | | |
| "RADIO RAINBOW", Via Jülich, Germany | ⇨ • Sa • Europe • 100 kW | |
| **CYPRUS** | | |
| CYPRUS BC CORP, Zyyi | F-Su • Europe • 250 kW | |
| **FINLAND** | | |
| (con'd) †YLE RADIO FINLAND, Pori | W Sa/Su • E Europe • 250 kW | |

ENGLISH ▬  ARABIC ▨▨▨  CHINESE ▢▢▢  FRENCH ▬▬  GERMAN ▬  RUSSIAN ═  SPANISH ▬  OTHER ▬

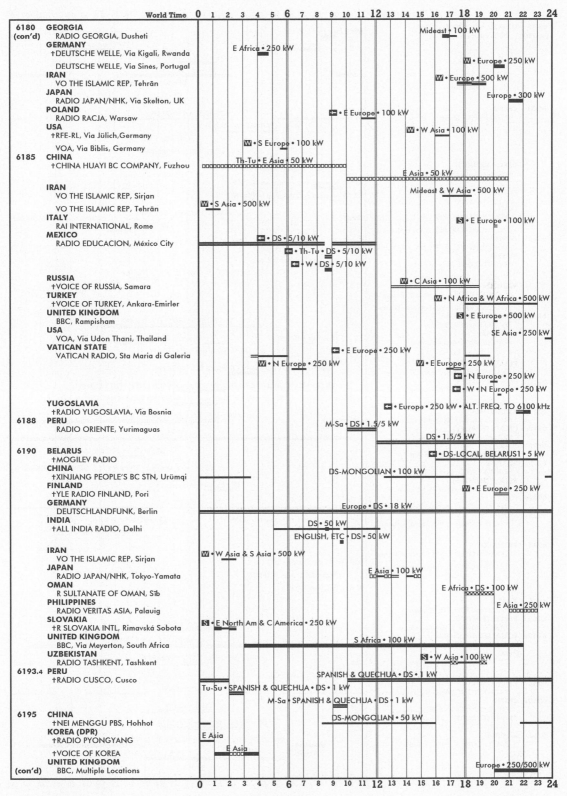

World Time   0 1 2 3 4 5 6 7 8 9 10 11 12 13 14 15 16 17 18 19 20 21 22 23 24

| | | |
|---|---|---|
| **6180** | **GEORGIA** | |
| (con'd) | RADIO GEORGIA, Dusheti | Mideast • 100 kW |
| | **GERMANY** | |
| | †DEUTSCHE WELLE, Via Kigali, Rwanda | E Africa • 250 kW |
| | DEUTSCHE WELLE, Via Sines, Portugal | W • Europe • 250 kW |
| | **IRAN** | |
| | VO THE ISLAMIC REP, Tehrān | W • Europe • 500 kW |
| | **JAPAN** | |
| | RADIO JAPAN/NHK, Via Skelton, UK | Europe • 300 kW |
| | **POLAND** | |
| | RADIO RACJA, Warsaw | • E Europe • 100 kW |
| | **USA** | |
| | †RFE-RL, Via Jülich, Germany | W • W Asia • 100 kW |
| | VOA, Via Biblis, Germany | W • S Europe • 100 kW |
| **6185** | **CHINA** | |
| | †CHINA HUAYI BC COMPANY, Fuzhou | Th-Tu • E Asia • 50 kW    E Asia • 50 kW |
| | **IRAN** | |
| | VO THE ISLAMIC REP, Sirjan | Mideast & W Asia • 500 kW |
| | VO THE ISLAMIC REP, Tehrān | W • S Asia • 500 kW |
| | **ITALY** | |
| | RAI INTERNATIONAL, Rome | S • E Europe • 100 kW |
| | **MEXICO** | |
| | RADIO EDUCACION, México City | • DS • 5/10 kW |
| | | • Th-Tu • DS • 5/10 kW |
| | | • W • DS • 5/10 kW |
| | **RUSSIA** | |
| | †VOICE OF RUSSIA, Samara | W • C Asia • 100 kW |
| | **TURKEY** | |
| | †VOICE OF TURKEY, Ankara-Emirler | W • N Africa & W Africa • 500 kW |
| | **UNITED KINGDOM** | |
| | BBC, Rampisham | S • E Europe • 500 kW |
| | **USA** | |
| | VOA, Via Udon Thani, Thailand | SE Asia • 250 kW |
| | **VATICAN STATE** | |
| | VATICAN RADIO, Sta Maria di Galeria | • E Europe • 250 kW |
| | | W • N Europe • 250 kW    W • E Europe • 250 kW |
| | | • N Europe • 250 kW |
| | | • W • N Europe • 250 kW |
| | **YUGOSLAVIA** | • Europe • 250 kW • ALT. FREQ. TO 6100 kHz |
| | †RADIO YUGOSLAVIA, Via Bosnia | |
| **6188** | **PERU** | M-Sa • DS • 1.5/5 kW |
| | RADIO ORIENTE, Yurimaguas | DS • 1.5/5 kW |
| **6190** | **BELARUS** | |
| | †MOGILEV RADIO | • DS-LOCAL, BELARUS1 • 5 kW |
| | **CHINA** | |
| | †XINJIANG PEOPLE'S BC STN, Urümqi | DS-MONGOLIAN • 100 kW |
| | **FINLAND** | |
| | †YLE RADIO FINLAND, Pori | W • E Europe • 250 kW |
| | **GERMANY** | |
| | DEUTSCHLANDFUNK, Berlin | Europe • DS • 18 kW |
| | **INDIA** | |
| | †ALL INDIA RADIO, Delhi | DS • 50 kW |
| | | ENGLISH, ETC • DS • 50 kW |
| | **IRAN** | |
| | VO THE ISLAMIC REP, Sirjan | W • W Asia & S Asia • 500 kW |
| | **JAPAN** | |
| | RADIO JAPAN/NHK, Tokyo-Yamata | E Asia • 100 kW |
| | **OMAN** | |
| | R SULTANATE OF OMAN, Sīb | E Africa • DS • 100 kW |
| | **PHILIPPINES** | |
| | RADIO VERITAS ASIA, Palauig | E Asia • 250 kW |
| | **SLOVAKIA** | |
| | †R SLOVAKIA INTL, Rimavská Sobota | S • E North Am & C America • 250 kW |
| | **UNITED KINGDOM** | |
| | BBC, Via Meyerton, South Africa | S Africa • 100 kW |
| | **UZBEKISTAN** | |
| | RADIO TASHKENT, Tashkent | S • W Asia • 100 kW |
| **6193.4** | **PERU** | SPANISH & QUECHUA • DS • 1 kW |
| | †RADIO CUSCO, Cusco | Tu-Su • SPANISH & QUECHUA • DS • 1 kW |
| | | M-Sa • SPANISH & QUECHUA • DS • 1 kW |
| **6195** | **CHINA** | |
| | †NEI MENGGU PBS, Hohhot | DS-MONGOLIAN • 50 kW |
| | **KOREA (DPR)** | |
| | †RADIO PYONGYANG | E Asia |
| | †VOICE OF KOREA | E Asia |
| | **UNITED KINGDOM** | |
| (con'd) | BBC, Multiple Locations | Europe • 250/500 kW |

0 1 2 3 4 5 6 7 8 9 10 11 12 13 14 15 16 17 18 19 20 21 22 23 24

SEASONAL S OR W    1-HR TIMESHIFT MIDYEAR ⬅ OR ➡    JAMMING / OR ∧    EARLIEST HEARD ◀    LATEST HEARD ▶    NEW FOR 2003 †

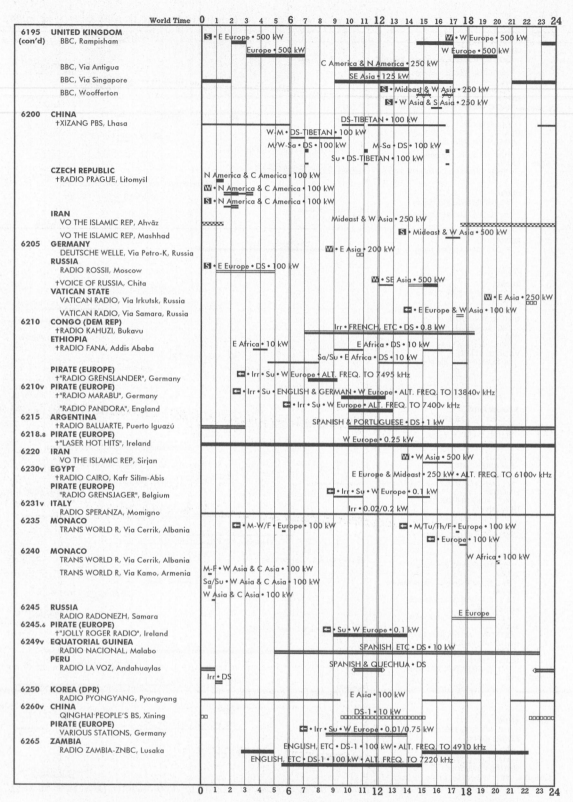

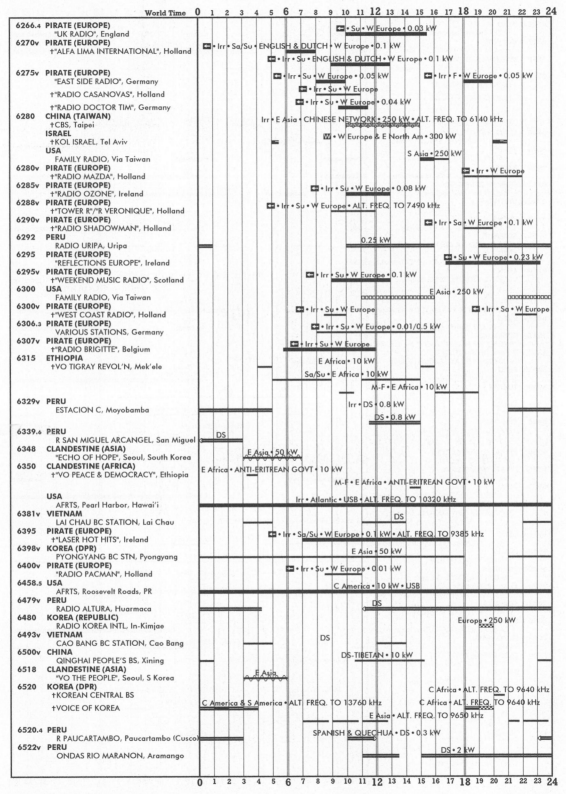

World Time  0  1  2  3  4  5  6  7  8  9  10  11  12  13  14  15  16  17  18  19  20  21  22  23  24

| Freq | Station | |
|---|---|---|
| 6266.4 | **PIRATE (EUROPE)** | |
| | "UK RADIO", England | ◧ • Su • W Europe • 0.03 kW |
| 6270v | **PIRATE (EUROPE)** | |
| | †"ALFA LIMA INTERNATIONAL", Holland | ◧ • Irr • Sa/Su • ENGLISH & DUTCH • W Europe • 0.1 kW |
| | | ◧ • Irr • Su • ENGLISH & DUTCH • W Europe • 0.1 kW |
| 6275v | **PIRATE (EUROPE)** | |
| | "EAST SIDE RADIO", Germany | ◧ • Irr • Su • W Europe • 0.05 kW   ◧ • Irr • F • W Europe • 0.05 kW |
| | †"RADIO CASANOVAS", Holland | ◧ • Irr • Su • W Europe |
| | †"RADIO DOCTOR TIM", Germany | ◧ • Irr • Su • W Europe • 0.04 kW |
| 6280 | **CHINA (TAIWAN)** | |
| | †CBS, Taipei | Irr • E Asia • CHINESE NETWORK • 250 kW • ALT. FREQ. TO 6140 kHz |
| | **ISRAEL** | |
| | †KOL ISRAEL, Tel Aviv | W • W Europe & E North Am • 300 kW |
| | **USA** | |
| | FAMILY RADIO, Via Taiwan | S Asia • 250 kW |
| 6280v | **PIRATE (EUROPE)** | |
| | †"RADIO MAZDA", Holland | ◧ • Irr • W Europe |
| 6285v | **PIRATE (EUROPE)** | |
| | †"RADIO OZONE", Ireland | ◧ • Irr • Su • W Europe • 0.08 kW |
| 6288v | **PIRATE (EUROPE)** | |
| | †"TOWER R"/"R VERONIQUE", Holland | ◧ • Irr • Su • W Europe • ALT. FREQ. TO 7490 kHz |
| 6290v | **PIRATE (EUROPE)** | |
| | †"RADIO SHADOWMAN", Holland | ◧ • Irr • Sa • W Europe • 0.1 kW |
| 6292 | **PERU** | |
| | RADIO URIPA, Uripa | 0.25 kW |
| 6295 | **PIRATE (EUROPE)** | |
| | "REFLECTIONS EUROPE", Ireland | ◧ • Su • W Europe • 0.23 kW |
| 6295v | **PIRATE (EUROPE)** | |
| | †"WEEKEND MUSIC RADIO", Scotland | ◧ • Irr • Su • W Europe • 0.1 kW |
| 6300 | **USA** | |
| | FAMILY RADIO, Via Taiwan | E Asia • 250 kW |
| 6300v | **PIRATE (EUROPE)** | |
| | †"WEST COAST RADIO", Holland | ◧ • Irr • Su • W Europe     ◧ • Irr • Sa • W Europe |
| 6306.3 | **PIRATE (EUROPE)** | |
| | VARIOUS STATIONS, Germany | ◧ • Irr • Su • W Europe • 0.01/0.5 kW |
| 6307v | **PIRATE (EUROPE)** | |
| | †"RADIO BRIGITTE", Belgium | ◧ • Irr • Su • W Europe |
| 6315 | **ETHIOPIA** | |
| | †VO TIGRAY REVOL'N, Mek'ele | E Africa • 10 kW |
| | | Sa/Su • E Africa • 10 kW |
| | | M–F • E Africa • 10 kW |
| 6329v | **PERU** | |
| | ESTACION C, Moyobamba | Irr • DS • 0.8 kW |
| | | DS • 0.8 kW |
| 6339.6 | **PERU** | |
| | R SAN MIGUEL ARCANGEL, San Miguel | DS |
| 6348 | **CLANDESTINE (ASIA)** | |
| | "ECHO OF HOPE", Seoul, South Korea | E Asia • 50 kW |
| 6350 | **CLANDESTINE (AFRICA)** | |
| | †"VO PEACE & DEMOCRACY", Ethiopia | E Africa • ANTI-ERITREAN GOVT • 10 kW |
| | | M–F • E Africa • ANTI-ERITREAN GOVT • 10 kW |
| | **USA** | |
| | AFRTS, Pearl Harbor, Hawai'i | Irr • Atlantic • USB • ALT. FREQ. TO 10320 kHz |
| 6381v | **VIETNAM** | |
| | LAI CHAU BC STATION, Lai Chau | DS |
| 6395 | **PIRATE (EUROPE)** | |
| | †"LASER HOT HITS", Ireland | ◧ • Irr • Sa/Su • W Europe • 0.1 kW • ALT. FREQ. TO 9385 kHz |
| 6398v | **KOREA (DPR)** | |
| | PYONGYANG BC STN, Pyongyang | E Asia • 50 kW |
| 6400v | **PIRATE (EUROPE)** | |
| | "RADIO PACMAN", Holland | ◧ • Irr • Su • W Europe • 0.01 kW |
| 6458.5 | **USA** | |
| | AFRTS, Roosevelt Roads, PR | C America • 10 kW • USB |
| 6479v | **PERU** | |
| | RADIO ALTURA, Huarmaca | DS |
| 6480 | **KOREA (REPUBLIC)** | |
| | RADIO KOREA INTL, In-Kimjae | Europe • 250 kW |
| 6493v | **VIETNAM** | |
| | CAO BANG BC STATION, Cao Bang | DS |
| 6500v | **CHINA** | |
| | QINGHAI PEOPLE'S BS, Xining | DS-TIBETAN • 10 kW |
| 6518 | **CLANDESTINE (ASIA)** | |
| | "VO THE PEOPLE", Seoul, S Korea | E Asia |
| 6520 | **KOREA (DPR)** | |
| | †KOREAN CENTRAL BS | C Africa • ALT. FREQ. TO 9640 kHz |
| | †VOICE OF KOREA | C America & S America • ALT. FREQ. TO 13760 kHz    C Africa • ALT. FREQ. TO 9640 kHz |
| | | E Asia • ALT. FREQ. TO 9650 kHz |
| 6520.4 | **PERU** | |
| | R PAUCARTAMBO, Paucartambo (Cusco) | SPANISH & QUECHUA • DS • 0.3 kW |
| 6522v | **PERU** | |
| | ONDAS RIO MARANON, Aramango | DS • 2 kW |

0  1  2  3  4  5  6  7  8  9  10  11  12  13  14  15  16  17  18  19  20  21  22  23  24

SEASONAL Ⓢ OR Ⓦ     1-HR TIMESHIFT MIDYEAR ◧ OR ▣     JAMMING / OR ∧     EARLIEST HEARD ◁     LATEST HEARD ▷     NEW FOR 2003 †

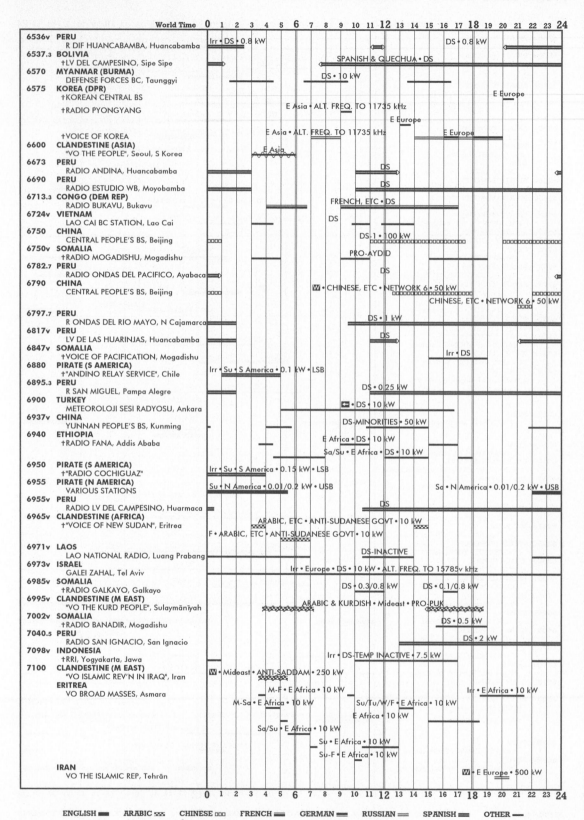

World Time  0 1 2 3 4 5 6 7 8 9 10 11 12 13 14 15 16 17 18 19 20 21 22 23 24

**6536v PERU**
R DIF HUANCABAMBA, Huancabamba — Irr • DS • 0.8 kW ... DS • 0.8 kW

**6537.3 BOLIVIA**
†LV DEL CAMPESINO, Sipe Sipe — SPANISH & QUECHUA • DS

**6570 MYANMAR (BURMA)**
DEFENSE FORCES BC, Taunggyi — DS • 10 kW

**6575 KOREA (DPR)**
†KOREAN CENTRAL BS — E Europe
†RADIO PYONGYANG — E Asia • ALT. FREQ. TO 11735 kHz ... E Europe
†VOICE OF KOREA — E Asia • ALT. FREQ. TO 11735 kHz ... E Europe

**6600 CLANDESTINE (ASIA)**
"VO THE PEOPLE", Seoul, S Korea — E Asia

**6673 PERU**
RADIO ANDINA, Huancabamba — DS

**6690 PERU**
RADIO ESTUDIO WB, Moyobamba — DS

**6713.3 CONGO (DEM REP)**
RADIO BUKAVU, Bukavu — FRENCH, ETC • DS

**6724v VIETNAM**
LAO CAI BC STATION, Lao Cai — DS

**6750 CHINA**
CENTRAL PEOPLE'S BS, Beijing — DS-1 • 100 kW

**6750v SOMALIA**
†RADIO MOGADISHU, Mogadishu — PRO-AYDID

**6782.7 PERU**
RADIO ONDAS DEL PACIFICO, Ayabaca — DS

**6790 CHINA**
CENTRAL PEOPLE'S BS, Beijing — W • CHINESE, ETC • NETWORK 6 • 50 kW ... CHINESE, ETC • NETWORK 6 • 50 kW

**6797.7 PERU**
R ONDAS DEL RIO MAYO, N Cajamarca — DS • 1 kW

**6817v PERU**
LV DE LAS HUARINJAS, Huancabamba — DS

**6847v SOMALIA**
†VOICE OF PACIFICATION, Mogadishu — Irr • DS

**6880 PIRATE (S AMERICA)**
†"ANDINO RELAY SERVICE", Chile — Irr • Su • S America • 0.1 kW • LSB

**6895.3 PERU**
R SAN MIGUEL, Pampa Alegre — DS • 0.25 kW

**6900 TURKEY**
METEOROLOJI SESI RADYOSU, Ankara — ◻ • DS • 10 kW

**6937v CHINA**
YUNNAN PEOPLE'S BS, Kunming — DS-MINORITIES • 50 kW

**6940 ETHIOPIA**
†RADIO FANA, Addis Ababa — E Africa • DS • 10 kW ... Sa/Su • E Africa • DS • 10 kW

**6950 PIRATE (S AMERICA)**
†"RADIO COCHIGUAZ" — Irr • Su • S America • 0.15 kW • LSB

**6955 PIRATE (N AMERICA)**
VARIOUS STATIONS — Su • N America • 0.01/0.2 kW • USB ... Sa • N America • 0.01/0.2 kW • USB

**6955v PERU**
RADIO LV DEL CAMPESINO, Huarmaca — DS

**6965v CLANDESTINE (AFRICA)**
†"VOICE OF NEW SUDAN", Eritrea — ARABIC, ETC • ANTI-SUDANESE GOVT • 10 kW ... F • ARABIC, ETC • ANTI-SUDANESE GOVT • 10 kW

**6971v LAOS**
LAO NATIONAL RADIO, Luang Prabang — DS-INACTIVE

**6973v ISRAEL**
GALEI ZAHAL, Tel Aviv — Irr • Europe • DS • 10 kW • ALT. FREQ. TO 15785v kHz

**6985v SOMALIA**
†RADIO GALKAYO, Galkayo — DS • 0.3/0.8 kW ... DS • 0.1/0.8 kW

**6995v CLANDESTINE (M EAST)**
"VO THE KURD PEOPLE", Sulaymānīyah — ARABIC & KURDISH • Mideast • PRO-PUK

**7002v SOMALIA**
†RADIO BANADIR, Mogadishu — DS • 0.5 kW

**7040.5 PERU**
RADIO SAN IGNACIO, San Ignacio — DS • 2 kW

**7098v INDONESIA**
†RRI, Yogyakarta, Jawa — Irr • DS-TEMP INACTIVE • 7.5 kW

**7100 CLANDESTINE (M EAST)**
"VO ISLAMIC REV'N IN IRAQ", Iran — W • Mideast • ANTI-SADDAM • 250 kW

**ERITREA**
VO BROAD MASSES, Asmara — M-F • E Africa • 10 kW ... Irr • E Africa • 10 kW
M-Sa • E Africa • 10 kW ... Su/Tu/W/F • E Africa • 10 kW
E Africa • 10 kW
Sa/Su • E Africa • 10 kW
Su • E Africa • 10 kW
Su-F • E Africa • 10 kW

**IRAN**
VO THE ISLAMIC REP, Tehrān — W • E Europe • 500 kW

0 1 2 3 4 5 6 7 8 9 10 11 12 13 14 15 16 17 18 19 20 21 22 23 24

ENGLISH ▬   ARABIC ⋙   CHINESE ▭▭▭   FRENCH ══   GERMAN ▬   RUSSIAN ═══   SPANISH ═══   OTHER ▬

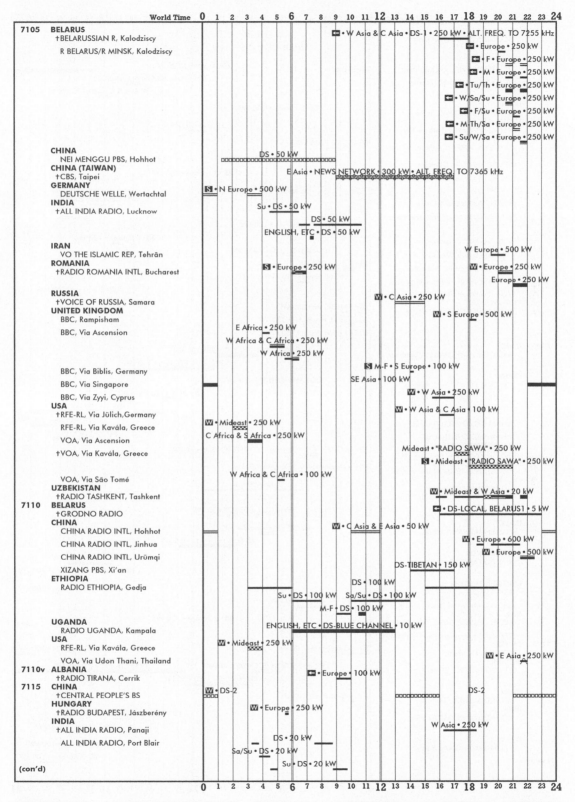

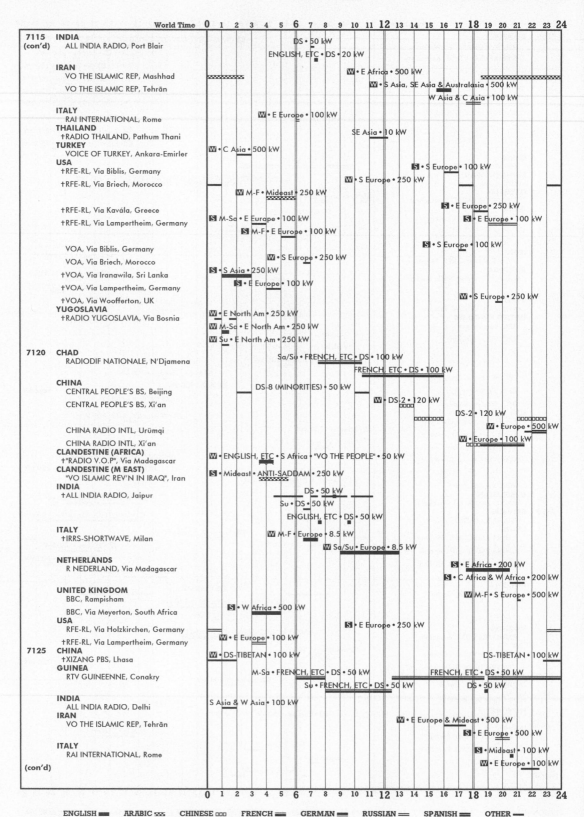

World Time   0  1  2  3  4  5  6  7  8  9  10  11  12  13  14  15  16  17  18  19  20  21  22  23  24

**7115  INDIA**
(con'd)   ALL INDIA RADIO, Port Blair — DS • 50 kW
          ENGLISH, ETC • DS • 20 kW

**IRAN**
          VO THE ISLAMIC REP, Mashhad — W • E Africa • 500 kW
          VO THE ISLAMIC REP, Tehrān — W • S Asia, SE Asia & Australasia • 500 kW
                                        W Asia & C Asia • 100 kW

**ITALY**
          RAI INTERNATIONAL, Rome — W • E Europe • 100 kW
**THAILAND**
          †RADIO THAILAND, Pathum Thani — SE Asia • 10 kW
**TURKEY**
          VOICE OF TURKEY, Ankara-Emirler — W • C Asia • 500 kW
**USA**
          †RFE-RL, Via Biblis, Germany — S • S Europe • 100 kW
          †RFE-RL, Via Briech, Morocco — W • S Europe • 250 kW

          †RFE-RL, Via Kavála, Greece — W M-F • Mideast • 250 kW
                                         S • E Europe • 250 kW
          †RFE-RL, Via Lampertheim, Germany — S M-Sa • E Europe • 100 kW
                                               S • E Europe • 100 kW
                                               S M-F • E Europe • 100 kW
          VOA, Via Biblis, Germany — S • S Europe • 100 kW
          VOA, Via Briech, Morocco — W • S Europe • 250 kW
          †VOA, Via Iranawila, Sri Lanka — S • S Asia • 250 kW
          †VOA, Via Lampertheim, Germany — S • E Europe • 100 kW
          †VOA, Via Woofferton, UK — W • S Europe • 250 kW
**YUGOSLAVIA**
          †RADIO YUGOSLAVIA, Via Bosnia — W • E North Am • 250 kW
                                           W M-Sa • E North Am • 250 kW
                                           W Su • E North Am • 250 kW

**7120  CHAD**
          RADIODIF NATIONALE, N'Djamena — Sa/Su • FRENCH, ETC • DS • 100 kW
                                           FRENCH, ETC • DS • 100 kW

**CHINA**
          CENTRAL PEOPLE'S BS, Beijing — DS-8 (MINORITIES) • 50 kW
          CENTRAL PEOPLE'S BS, Xi'an — W • DS-2 • 120 kW
                                        DS-2 • 120 kW
          CHINA RADIO INTL, Urümqi — W • Europe • 500 kW
          CHINA RADIO INTL, Xi'an — W • Europe • 100 kW
**CLANDESTINE (AFRICA)**
          †"RADIO V.O.P", Via Madagascar — W • ENGLISH, ETC • S Africa • "VO THE PEOPLE" • 50 kW
**CLANDESTINE (M EAST)**
          "VO ISLAMIC REV'N IN IRAQ", Iran — S • Mideast • ANTI-SADDAM • 250 kW
**INDIA**
          †ALL INDIA RADIO, Jaipur — DS • 50 kW
                                      Su • DS • 50 kW
                                      ENGLISH, ETC • DS • 50 kW
**ITALY**
          †IRRS-SHORTWAVE, Milan — W M-F • Europe • 8.5 kW
                                    W Sa/Su • Europe • 8.5 kW

**NETHERLANDS**
          R NEDERLAND, Via Madagascar — S • E Africa • 200 kW
                                         S • C Africa & W Africa • 200 kW

**UNITED KINGDOM**
          BBC, Rampisham — W M-F • S Europe • 500 kW
          BBC, Via Meyerton, South Africa — S • W Africa • 500 kW
**USA**
          RFE-RL, Via Holzkirchen, Germany — S • E Europe • 250 kW
          †RFE-RL, Via Lampertheim, Germany — W • E Europe • 100 kW
**7125  CHINA**
          †XIZANG PBS, Lhasa — W • DS-TIBETAN • 100 kW       DS-TIBETAN • 100 kW
**GUINEA**
          RTV GUINEENNE, Conakry — M-Sa • FRENCH, ETC • DS • 50 kW    FRENCH, ETC • DS • 50 kW
                                    Su • FRENCH, ETC • DS • 50 kW       DS • 50 kW

**INDIA**
          ALL INDIA RADIO, Delhi — S Asia & W Asia • 100 kW
**IRAN**
          VO THE ISLAMIC REP, Tehrān — W • E Europe & Mideast • 500 kW
                                        S • E Europe • 500 kW

**ITALY**
          RAI INTERNATIONAL, Rome — S • Mideast • 100 kW
                                     W • E Europe • 100 kW

(con'd)

0  1  2  3  4  5  6  7  8  9  10  11  12  13  14  15  16  17  18  19  20  21  22  23  24

ENGLISH ▬   ARABIC ▨   CHINESE ▯▯▯   FRENCH ═   GERMAN ▬   RUSSIAN ═   SPANISH ═   OTHER ▬

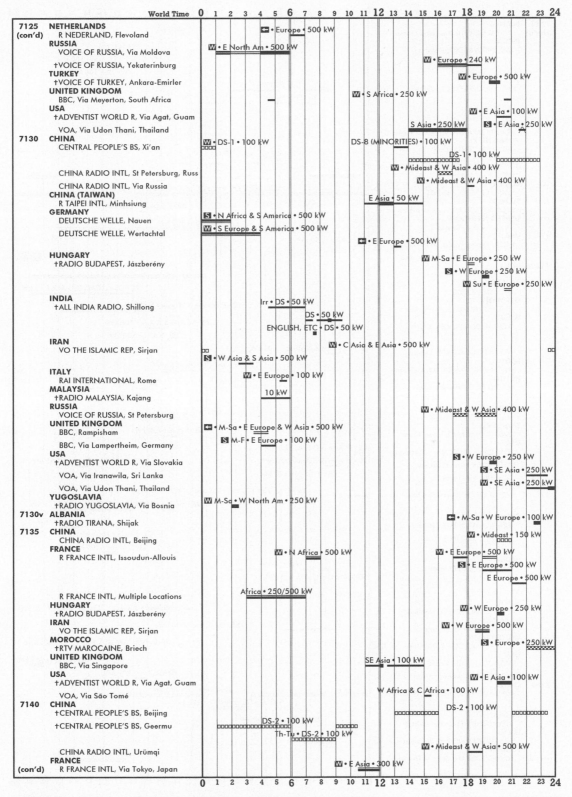

World Time    0  1  2  3  4  5  6  7  8  9  10  11  12  13  14  15  16  17  18  19  20  21  22  23  24

| Freq | Station | |
|---|---|---|
| 7125 (con'd) | **NETHERLANDS** R NEDERLAND, Flevoland | ⇆ • Europe • 500 kW |
| | **RUSSIA** VOICE OF RUSSIA, Via Moldova | W • E North Am • 500 kW |
| | †VOICE OF RUSSIA, Yekaterinburg | W • Europe • 240 kW |
| | **TURKEY** †VOICE OF TURKEY, Ankara-Emirler | W • Europe • 500 kW |
| | **UNITED KINGDOM** BBC, Via Meyerton, South Africa | W • S Africa • 250 kW |
| | **USA** †ADVENTIST WORLD R, Via Agat, Guam | W • E Asia • 100 kW |
| | VOA, Via Udon Thani, Thailand | S Asia • 250 kW / S • E Asia • 250 kW |
| 7130 | **CHINA** CENTRAL PEOPLE'S BS, Xi'an | W • DS-1 • 100 kW / DS-8 (MINORITIES) • 100 kW |
| | | DS-1 • 100 kW |
| | CHINA RADIO INTL, St Petersburg, Russ | W • Mideast & W Asia • 400 kW |
| | CHINA RADIO INTL, Via Russia | W • Mideast & W Asia • 400 kW |
| | **CHINA (TAIWAN)** R TAIPEI INTL, Minhsiung | E Asia • 50 kW |
| | **GERMANY** DEUTSCHE WELLE, Nauen | S • N Africa & S America • 500 kW |
| | DEUTSCHE WELLE, Wertachtal | W • S Europe & S America • 500 kW |
| | | ⇆ • E Europe • 500 kW |
| | **HUNGARY** †RADIO BUDAPEST, Jászberény | W M-Sa • E Europe • 250 kW |
| | | S • W Europe • 250 kW |
| | | W Su • E Europe • 250 kW |
| | **INDIA** †ALL INDIA RADIO, Shillong | Irr • DS • 50 kW |
| | | DS • 50 kW |
| | | ENGLISH, ETC • DS • 50 kW |
| | **IRAN** VO THE ISLAMIC REP, Sirjan | W • C Asia & E Asia • 500 kW |
| | | S • W Asia & S Asia • 500 kW |
| | **ITALY** RAI INTERNATIONAL, Rome | W • E Europe • 100 kW |
| | **MALAYSIA** †RADIO MALAYSIA, Kajang | 10 kW |
| | **RUSSIA** VOICE OF RUSSIA, St Petersburg | W • Mideast & W Asia • 400 kW |
| | **UNITED KINGDOM** BBC, Rampisham | ⇆ • M-Sa • E Europe & W Asia • 500 kW |
| | BBC, Via Lampertheim, Germany | S M-F • E Europe • 100 kW |
| | **USA** †ADVENTIST WORLD R, Via Slovakia | S • W Europe • 250 kW |
| | VOA, Via Iranawila, Sri Lanka | S • SE Asia • 250 kW |
| | VOA, Via Udon Thani, Thailand | W • SE Asia • 250 kW |
| | **YUGOSLAVIA** †RADIO YUGOSLAVIA, Via Bosnia | W M-Sa • W North Am • 250 kW |
| 7130v | **ALBANIA** †RADIO TIRANA, Shijak | ⇆ • M-Sa • W Europe • 100 kW |
| 7135 | **CHINA** CHINA RADIO INTL, Beijing | W • Mideast • 150 kW |
| | **FRANCE** R FRANCE INTL, Issoudun-Allouis | W • N Africa • 500 kW / W • E Europe • 500 kW |
| | | S • E Europe • 500 kW |
| | | E Europe • 500 kW |
| | R FRANCE INTL, Multiple Locations | Africa • 250/500 kW |
| | **HUNGARY** †RADIO BUDAPEST, Jászberény | W • W Europe • 250 kW |
| | **IRAN** VO THE ISLAMIC REP, Sirjan | W • W Europe • 500 kW |
| | **MOROCCO** †RTV MAROCAINE, Briech | S • Europe • 250 kW |
| | **UNITED KINGDOM** BBC, Via Singapore | SE Asia • 100 kW |
| | **USA** †ADVENTIST WORLD R, Via Agat, Guam | W • E Asia • 100 kW |
| | VOA, Via São Tomé | W Africa & C Africa • 100 kW |
| 7140 | **CHINA** †CENTRAL PEOPLE'S BS, Beijing | DS-2 • 100 kW |
| | †CENTRAL PEOPLE'S BS, Geermu | DS-2 • 100 kW |
| | | Th-Tu • DS-2 • 100 kW |
| | CHINA RADIO INTL, Urümqi | W • Mideast & W Asia • 500 kW |
| (con'd) | **FRANCE** R FRANCE INTL, Via Tokyo, Japan | W • E Asia • 300 kW |

0  1  2  3  4  5  6  7  8  9  10  11  12  13  14  15  16  17  18  19  20  21  22  23  24

SEASONAL S OR W    1-HR TIMESHIFT MIDYEAR ⇆ OR ⇒    JAMMING / OR ∧    EARLIEST HEARD ◁    LATEST HEARD ▷    NEW FOR 2003 †

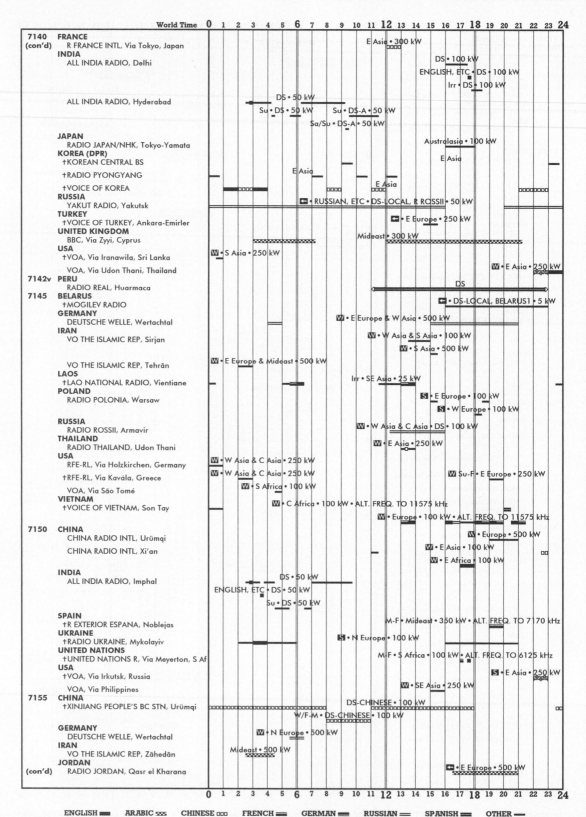

| | | World Time | 0 1 2 3 4 5 6 7 8 9 10 11 12 13 14 15 16 17 18 19 20 21 22 23 24 |
|---|---|---|---|

**7140 FRANCE**
(con'd)  R FRANCE INTL, Via Tokyo, Japan — E Asia • 300 kW
**INDIA**
  ALL INDIA RADIO, Delhi — DS • 100 kW / ENGLISH, ETC • DS • 100 kW / Irr • DS • 100 kW
  ALL INDIA RADIO, Hyderabad — DS • 50 kW / Su • DS • 50 kW / Su • DS-A • 50 kW / Sa/Su • DS-A • 50 kW
**JAPAN**
  RADIO JAPAN/NHK, Tokyo-Yamata — Australasia • 100 kW
**KOREA (DPR)**
  †KOREAN CENTRAL BS — E Asia
  †RADIO PYONGYANG — E Asia / E Asia
  †VOICE OF KOREA
**RUSSIA**
  YAKUT RADIO, Yakutsk — RUSSIAN, ETC • DS-LOCAL, R ROSSII • 50 kW
**TURKEY**
  †VOICE OF TURKEY, Ankara-Emirler — E Europe • 250 kW
**UNITED KINGDOM**
  BBC, Via Zyyi, Cyprus — Mideast • 300 kW
**USA**
  †VOA, Via Iranawila, Sri Lanka — W • S Asia • 250 kW
  VOA, Via Udon Thani, Thailand — W • E Asia • 250 kW
**7142v PERU**
  RADIO REAL, Huarmaca — DS
**7145 BELARUS**
  †MOGILEV RADIO — DS-LOCAL, BELARUS1 • 5 kW
**GERMANY**
  DEUTSCHE WELLE, Wertachtal — W • E Europe & W Asia • 500 kW
**IRAN**
  VO THE ISLAMIC REP, Sirjan — W • W Asia & S Asia • 100 kW / W • S Asia • 500 kW
  VO THE ISLAMIC REP, Tehrān — W • E Europe & Mideast • 500 kW
**LAOS**
  †LAO NATIONAL RADIO, Vientiane — Irr • SE Asia • 25 kW
**POLAND**
  RADIO POLONIA, Warsaw — S • E Europe • 100 kW / S • W Europe • 100 kW
**RUSSIA**
  RADIO ROSSII, Armavir — W • W Asia & C Asia • DS • 100 kW
**THAILAND**
  RADIO THAILAND, Udon Thani — W • E Asia • 250 kW
**USA**
  RFE-RL, Via Holzkirchen, Germany — W • W Asia & C Asia • 250 kW
  †RFE-RL, Via Kavála, Greece — W • W Asia & C Asia • 250 kW / Su-F • E Europe • 250 kW
  VOA, Via São Tomé — W • S Africa • 100 kW
**VIETNAM**
  †VOICE OF VIETNAM, Son Tay — W • C Africa • 100 kW • ALT. FREQ. TO 11575 kHz / W • Europe • 100 kW • ALT. FREQ. TO 11575 kHz
**7150 CHINA**
  CHINA RADIO INTL, Urümqi — W • Europe • 500 kW
  CHINA RADIO INTL, Xi'an — W • E Asia • 100 kW / W • E Africa • 100 kW
**INDIA**
  ALL INDIA RADIO, Imphal — DS • 50 kW / ENGLISH, ETC • DS • 50 kW / Su • DS • 50 kW
**SPAIN**
  †R EXTERIOR ESPANA, Noblejas — M-F • Mideast • 350 kW • ALT. FREQ. TO 7170 kHz
**UKRAINE**
  †RADIO UKRAINE, Mykolayiv — S • N Europe • 100 kW
**UNITED NATIONS**
  †UNITED NATIONS R, Via Meyerton, S Af — M-F • S Africa • 100 kW • ALT. FREQ. TO 6125 kHz
**USA**
  †VOA, Via Irkutsk, Russia — S • E Asia • 250 kW
  VOA, Via Philippines — W • SE Asia • 250 kW
**7155 CHINA**
  †XINJIANG PEOPLE'S BC STN, Urümqi — DS-CHINESE • 100 kW / W/F-M • DS-CHINESE • 100 kW
**GERMANY**
  DEUTSCHE WELLE, Wertachtal — W • N Europe • 500 kW
**IRAN**
  VO THE ISLAMIC REP, Zāhedān — Mideast • 500 kW
**JORDAN**
(con'd)  RADIO JORDAN, Qasr el Kharana — E Europe • 500 kW

| | 0 1 2 3 4 5 6 7 8 9 10 11 12 13 14 15 16 17 18 19 20 21 22 23 24 |
|---|---|

ENGLISH ▬  ARABIC ⧉  CHINESE ⋯  FRENCH ▬  GERMAN ▬  RUSSIAN ═  SPANISH ▬  OTHER ▬

World Time  0  1  2  3  4  5  6  7  8  9  10  11  12  13  14  15  16  17  18  19  20  21  22  23  24

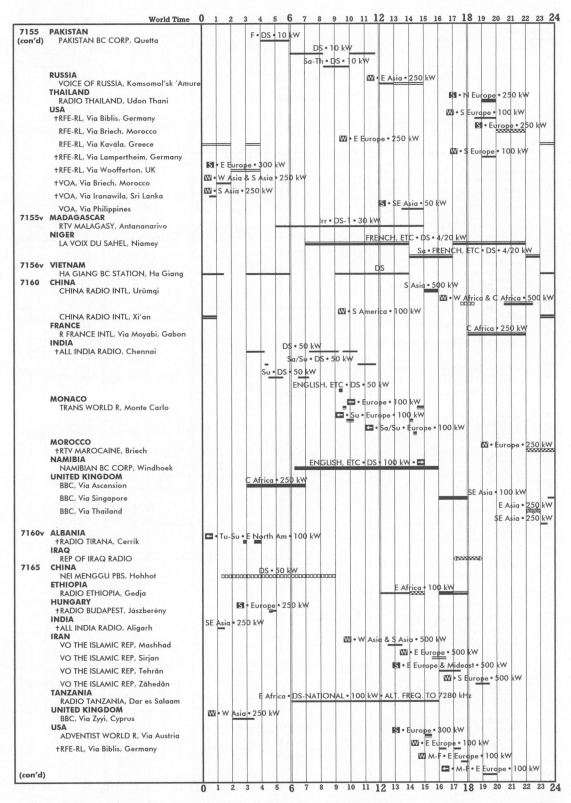

| 7155 | PAKISTAN | |
|---|---|---|
| (con'd) | PAKISTAN BC CORP, Quetta | F • DS • 10 kW |
| | | DS • 10 kW |
| | | Sa-Th • DS • 10 kW |
| | RUSSIA | |
| | VOICE OF RUSSIA, Komsomol'sk 'Amure | W • E Asia • 250 kW |
| | THAILAND | |
| | RADIO THAILAND, Udon Thani | S • N Europe • 250 kW |
| | USA | |
| | †RFE-RL, Via Biblis, Germany | W • S Europe • 100 kW |
| | RFE-RL, Via Briech, Morocco | S • Europe • 250 kW |
| | RFE-RL, Via Kavála, Greece | W • E Europe • 250 kW |
| | †RFE-RL, Via Lampertheim, Germany | W • S Europe • 100 kW |
| | †RFE-RL, Via Woofferton, UK | S • E Europe • 300 kW |
| | †VOA, Via Briech, Morocco | W • W Asia & S Asia • 250 kW |
| | †VOA, Via Iranawila, Sri Lanka | W • S Asia • 250 kW |
| | VOA, Via Philippines | S • SE Asia • 50 kW |
| 7155v | MADAGASCAR | |
| | RTV MALAGASY, Antananarivo | Irr • DS-1 • 30 kW |
| | NIGER | |
| | LA VOIX DU SAHEL, Niamey | FRENCH, ETC • DS • 4/20 kW |
| | | Sa • FRENCH, ETC • DS • 4/20 kW |
| 7156v | VIETNAM | |
| | HA GIANG BC STATION, Ha Giang | DS |
| 7160 | CHINA | |
| | CHINA RADIO INTL, Urümqi | S Asia • 500 kW |
| | | W • W Africa & C Africa • 500 kW |
| | CHINA RADIO INTL, Xi'an | W • S America • 100 kW |
| | FRANCE | |
| | R FRANCE INTL, Via Moyabi, Gabon | C Africa • 250 kW |
| | INDIA | |
| | †ALL INDIA RADIO, Chennai | DS • 50 kW |
| | | Sa/Su • DS • 50 kW |
| | | Su • DS • 50 kW |
| | | ENGLISH, ETC • DS • 50 kW |
| | MONACO | |
| | TRANS WORLD R, Monte Carlo | ☐ • Europe • 100 kW |
| | | ☐ • Su • Europe • 100 kW |
| | | ☐ • Sa/Su • Europe • 100 kW |
| | MOROCCO | |
| | †RTV MAROCAINE, Briech | W • Europe • 250 kW |
| | NAMIBIA | |
| | NAMIBIAN BC CORP, Windhoek | ENGLISH, ETC • DS • 100 kW • ☐ |
| | UNITED KINGDOM | |
| | BBC, Via Ascension | C Africa • 250 kW |
| | BBC, Via Singapore | SE Asia • 100 kW |
| | BBC, Via Thailand | E Asia • 250 kW |
| | | SE Asia • 250 kW |
| 7160v | ALBANIA | |
| | †RADIO TIRANA, Cerrik | ☐ • Tu-Su • E North Am • 100 kW |
| | IRAQ | |
| | REP OF IRAQ RADIO | |
| 7165 | CHINA | |
| | NEI MENGGU PBS, Hohhot | DS • 50 kW |
| | ETHIOPIA | |
| | RADIO ETHIOPIA, Gedja | E Africa • 100 kW |
| | HUNGARY | |
| | †RADIO BUDAPEST, Jászberény | S • Europe • 250 kW |
| | INDIA | |
| | †ALL INDIA RADIO, Aligarh | SE Asia • 250 kW |
| | IRAN | |
| | VO THE ISLAMIC REP, Mashhad | W • W Asia & S Asia • 500 kW |
| | VO THE ISLAMIC REP, Sirjan | W • E Europe • 500 kW |
| | VO THE ISLAMIC REP, Tehrān | S • E Europe & Mideast • 500 kW |
| | VO THE ISLAMIC REP, Zāhedān | W • S Europe • 500 kW |
| | TANZANIA | |
| | RADIO TANZANIA, Dar es Salaam | E Africa • DS-NATIONAL • 100 kW • ALT. FREQ. TO 7280 kHz |
| | UNITED KINGDOM | |
| | BBC, Via Zyyi, Cyprus | W • W Asia • 250 kW |
| | USA | |
| | ADVENTIST WORLD R, Via Austria | S • Europe • 300 kW |
| | | W • E Europe • 100 kW |
| | †RFE-RL, Via Biblis, Germany | W • M-F • E Europe • 100 kW |
| | | ☐ • M-F • E Europe • 100 kW |
| (con'd) | | |

0  1  2  3  4  5  6  7  8  9  10  11  12  13  14  15  16  17  18  19  20  21  22  23  24

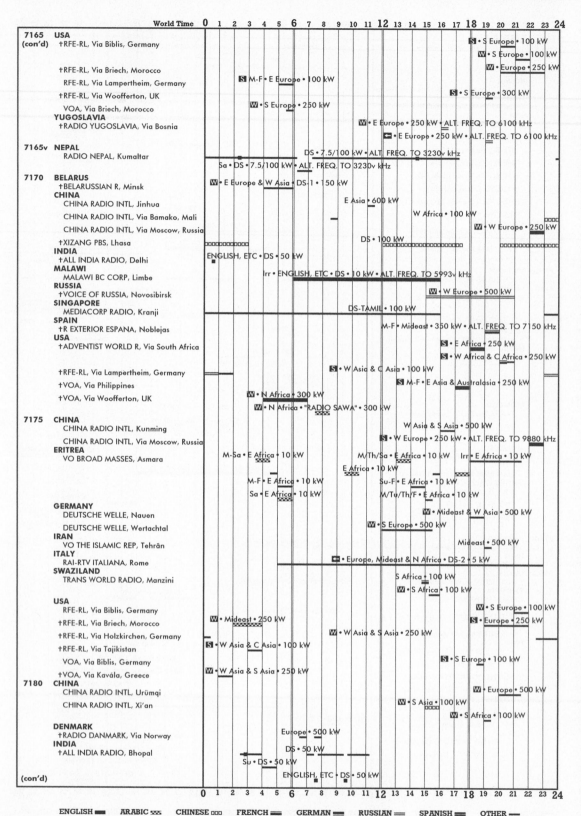

World Time  0  1  2  3  4  5  6  7  8  9  10  11  12  13  14  15  16  17  18  19  20  21  22  23  24

**7165 USA**
(con'd)  †RFE-RL, Via Biblis, Germany — S • S Europe • 100 kW / W • S Europe • 100 kW / W • Europe • 250 kW

†RFE-RL, Via Briech, Morocco
RFE-RL, Via Lampertheim, Germany — S • M-F • E Europe • 100 kW
†RFE-RL, Via Woofferton, UK — S • S Europe • 300 kW
VOA, Via Briech, Morocco — W • S Europe • 250 kW
**YUGOSLAVIA**
†RADIO YUGOSLAVIA, Via Bosnia — W • E Europe • 250 kW • ALT. FREQ. TO 6100 kHz / • E Europe • 250 kW • ALT. FREQ. TO 6100 kHz

**7165v NEPAL**
RADIO NEPAL, Kumaltar — DS • 7.5/100 kW • ALT. FREQ. TO 3230v kHz / Sa • DS • 7.5/100 kW • ALT. FREQ. TO 3230v kHz

**7170 BELARUS**
†BELARUSSIAN R, Minsk — W • E Europe & W Asia • DS-1 • 150 kW
**CHINA**
CHINA RADIO INTL, Jinhua — E Asia • 600 kW
CHINA RADIO INTL, Via Bamako, Mali — W Africa • 100 kW
CHINA RADIO INTL, Via Moscow, Russia — W • W Europe • 250 kW
†XIZANG PBS, Lhasa — DS • 100 kW
**INDIA**
†ALL INDIA RADIO, Delhi — ENGLISH, ETC • DS • 50 kW
**MALAWI**
MALAWI BC CORP, Limbe — Irr • ENGLISH, ETC • DS • 10 kW • ALT. FREQ. TO 5993v kHz
**RUSSIA**
†VOICE OF RUSSIA, Novosibirsk — W • W Europe • 500 kW
**SINGAPORE**
MEDIACORP RADIO, Kranji — DS-TAMIL • 100 kW
**SPAIN**
†R EXTERIOR ESPANA, Noblejas — M-F • Mideast • 350 kW • ALT. FREQ. TO 7150 kHz
**USA**
†ADVENTIST WORLD R, Via South Africa — S • E Africa • 250 kW / S • W Africa & C Africa • 250 kW

†RFE-RL, Via Lampertheim, Germany — S • W Asia & C Asia • 100 kW
†VOA, Via Philippines — S • M-F • E Asia & Australasia • 250 kW
†VOA, Via Woofferton, UK — W • N Africa • 300 kW / W • N Africa • "RADIO SAWA" • 300 kW

**7175 CHINA**
CHINA RADIO INTL, Kunming — W Asia & S Asia • 500 kW
CHINA RADIO INTL, Via Moscow, Russia — S • W Europe • 250 kW • ALT. FREQ. TO 9880 kHz
**ERITREA**
VO BROAD MASSES, Asmara — M-Sa • E Africa • 10 kW / M/Th/Sa • E Africa • 10 kW / Irr • E Africa • 10 kW / E Africa • 10 kW / M-F • E Africa • 10 kW / Su-F • E Africa • 10 kW / Sa • E Africa • 10 kW / M/Tu/Th/F • E Africa • 10 kW

**GERMANY**
DEUTSCHE WELLE, Nauen — W • Mideast & W Asia • 500 kW
DEUTSCHE WELLE, Wertachtal — W • S Europe • 500 kW
**IRAN**
VO THE ISLAMIC REP, Tehrān — Mideast • 500 kW
**ITALY**
RAI-RTV ITALIANA, Rome — • Europe, Mideast & N Africa • DS-2 • 5 kW
**SWAZILAND**
TRANS WORLD RADIO, Manzini — S Africa • 100 kW / W • S Africa • 100 kW

**USA**
RFE-RL, Via Biblis, Germany — W • S Europe • 100 kW
†RFE-RL, Via Briech, Morocco — W • Mideast • 250 kW / S • Europe • 250 kW
†RFE-RL, Via Holzkirchen, Germany — W • W Asia & S Asia • 250 kW
†RFE-RL, Via Tajikistan — S • W Asia & C Asia • 100 kW
VOA, Via Biblis, Germany — S • S Europe • 100 kW
†VOA, Via Kavála, Greece — W • W Asia & S Asia • 250 kW
**7180 CHINA**
CHINA RADIO INTL, Urümqi — W • Europe • 500 kW
CHINA RADIO INTL, Xi'an — W • S Asia • 100 kW / W • S Africa • 100 kW

**DENMARK**
†RADIO DANMARK, Via Norway — Europe • 500 kW
**INDIA**
†ALL INDIA RADIO, Bhopal — DS • 50 kW / Su • DS • 50 kW / ENGLISH, ETC • DS • 50 kW

(con'd)

0  1  2  3  4  5  6  7  8  9  10  11  12  13  14  15  16  17  18  19  20  21  22  23  24

ENGLISH ▬   ARABIC ▨   CHINESE ▦   FRENCH ▬   GERMAN ▬   RUSSIAN ═   SPANISH ═   OTHER ▬

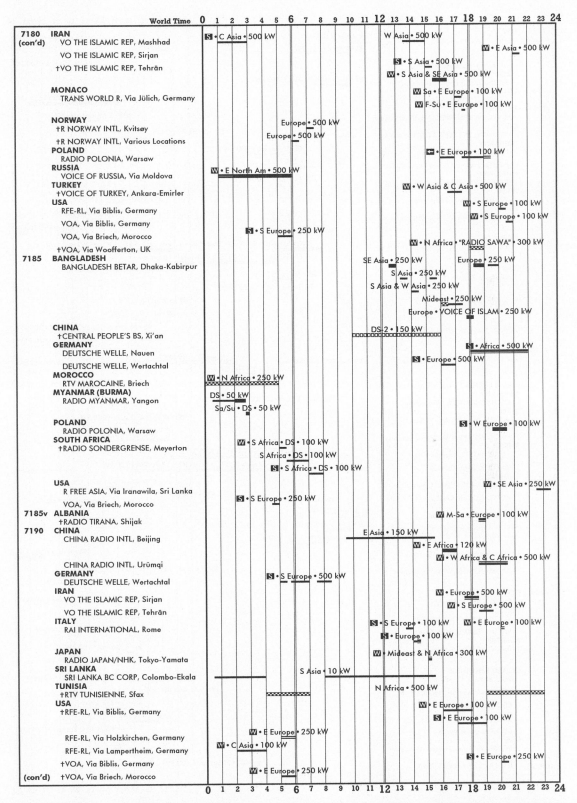

World Time 0 1 2 3 4 5 6 7 8 9 10 11 12 13 14 15 16 17 18 19 20 21 22 23 24

| Freq | Station | Schedule |
|---|---|---|
| 7180 (con'd) | **IRAN** | |
| | VO THE ISLAMIC REP, Mashhad | S • C Asia • 500 kW W Asia • 500 kW W • E Asia • 500 kW |
| | VO THE ISLAMIC REP, Sirjan | S • S Asia • 500 kW |
| | †VO THE ISLAMIC REP, Tehrān | W • S Asia & SE Asia • 500 kW |
| | **MONACO** | |
| | TRANS WORLD R, Via Jülich, Germany | W Sa • E Europe • 100 kW W F-Su • E Europe • 100 kW |
| | **NORWAY** | |
| | †R NORWAY INTL, Kvitsøy | Europe • 500 kW |
| | †R NORWAY INTL, Various Locations | Europe • 500 kW |
| | **POLAND** | |
| | RADIO POLONIA, Warsaw | • E Europe • 100 kW |
| | **RUSSIA** | |
| | VOICE OF RUSSIA, Via Moldova | W • E North Am • 500 kW |
| | **TURKEY** | |
| | †VOICE OF TURKEY, Ankara-Emirler | W • W Asia & C Asia • 500 kW |
| | **USA** | |
| | RFE-RL, Via Biblis, Germany | W • S Europe • 100 kW |
| | VOA, Via Biblis, Germany | W • S Europe • 100 kW |
| | VOA, Via Briech, Morocco | S • S Europe • 250 kW |
| | †VOA, Via Woofferton, UK | W • N Africa • "RADIO SAWA" • 300 kW |
| 7185 | **BANGLADESH** | |
| | BANGLADESH BETAR, Dhaka-Kabirpur | SE Asia • 250 kW Europe • 250 kW |
| | | S Asia • 250 kW |
| | | S Asia & W Asia • 250 kW |
| | | Mideast • 250 kW |
| | | Europe • VOICE OF ISLAM • 250 kW |
| | **CHINA** | |
| | †CENTRAL PEOPLE'S BS, Xi'an | DS-2 • 150 kW |
| | **GERMANY** | |
| | DEUTSCHE WELLE, Nauen | S • Africa • 500 kW |
| | DEUTSCHE WELLE, Wertachtal | S • Europe • 500 kW |
| | **MOROCCO** | |
| | RTV MAROCAINE, Briech | W • N Africa • 250 kW |
| | **MYANMAR (BURMA)** | |
| | RADIO MYANMAR, Yangon | DS • 50 kW |
| | | Sa/Su • DS • 50 kW |
| | **POLAND** | |
| | RADIO POLONIA, Warsaw | S • W Europe • 100 kW |
| | **SOUTH AFRICA** | |
| | †RADIO SONDERGRENSE, Meyerton | W • S Africa • DS • 100 kW |
| | | S Africa • DS • 100 kW |
| | | S • S Africa • DS • 100 kW |
| | **USA** | |
| | R FREE ASIA, Via Iranawila, Sri Lanka | W • SE Asia • 250 kW |
| | VOA, Via Briech, Morocco | S • S Europe • 250 kW |
| 7185v | **ALBANIA** | |
| | †RADIO TIRANA, Shijak | W M-Sa • Europe • 100 kW |
| 7190 | **CHINA** | |
| | CHINA RADIO INTL, Beijing | E Asia • 150 kW W • E Africa • 120 kW |
| | CHINA RADIO INTL, Urümqi | W • W Africa & C Africa • 500 kW |
| | **GERMANY** | |
| | DEUTSCHE WELLE, Wertachtal | S • S Europe • 500 kW |
| | **IRAN** | |
| | VO THE ISLAMIC REP, Sirjan | W • Europe • 500 kW |
| | VO THE ISLAMIC REP, Tehrān | W • S Europe • 500 kW |
| | **ITALY** | |
| | RAI INTERNATIONAL, Rome | S • S Europe • 100 kW W • E Europe • 100 kW |
| | | S • Europe • 100 kW |
| | **JAPAN** | |
| | RADIO JAPAN/NHK, Tokyo-Yamata | W • Mideast & N Africa • 300 kW |
| | **SRI LANKA** | |
| | SRI LANKA BC CORP, Colombo-Ekala | S Asia • 10 kW |
| | **TUNISIA** | |
| | †RTV TUNISIENNE, Sfax | N Africa • 500 kW |
| | **USA** | |
| | †RFE-RL, Via Biblis, Germany | W • E Europe • 100 kW |
| | | S • E Europe • 100 kW |
| | RFE-RL, Via Holzkirchen, Germany | W • E Europe • 250 kW |
| | RFE-RL, Via Lampertheim, Germany | W • C Asia • 100 kW |
| | †VOA, Via Biblis, Germany | S • E Europe • 250 kW |
| (con'd) | †VOA, Via Briech, Morocco | W • E Europe • 250 kW |

0 1 2 3 4 5 6 7 8 9 10 11 12 13 14 15 16 17 18 19 20 21 22 23 24

SEASONAL S OR W 1-HR TIMESHIFT MIDYEAR ⬅ OR ➡ JAMMING / OR /\ EARLIEST HEARD ◁ LATEST HEARD ▷ NEW FOR 2003 †

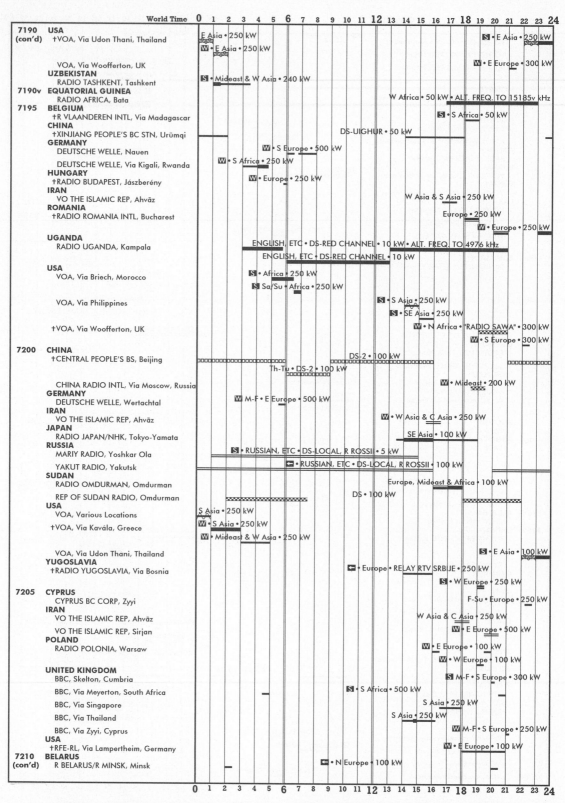

| | | World Time | 0 1 2 3 4 5 6 7 8 9 10 11 12 13 14 15 16 17 18 19 20 21 22 23 24 |
|---|---|---|---|

**7190 USA**
(con'd)  †VOA, Via Udon Thani, Thailand — E Asia • 250 kW · W • E Asia • 250 kW · S • E Asia • 250 kW

VOA, Via Woofferton, UK — W • E Europe • 300 kW
**UZBEKISTAN**
RADIO TASHKENT, Tashkent — S • Mideast & W Asia • 240 kW
**7190v EQUATORIAL GUINEA**
RADIO AFRICA, Bata — W Africa • 50 kW • ALT. FREQ. TO 15185v kHz
**7195 BELGIUM**
†R VLAANDEREN INTL, Via Madagascar — S • S Africa • 50 kW
**CHINA**
†XINJIANG PEOPLE'S BC STN, Urümqi — DS-UIGHUR • 50 kW
**GERMANY**
DEUTSCHE WELLE, Nauen — W • S Europe • 500 kW
DEUTSCHE WELLE, Via Kigali, Rwanda — W • S Africa • 250 kW
**HUNGARY**
†RADIO BUDAPEST, Jászberény — W • Europe • 250 kW
**IRAN**
VO THE ISLAMIC REP, Ahvāz — W Asia & S Asia • 250 kW
**ROMANIA**
†RADIO ROMANIA INTL, Bucharest — Europe • 250 kW · W • Europe • 250 kW
**UGANDA**
RADIO UGANDA, Kampala — ENGLISH, ETC • DS-RED CHANNEL • 10 kW • ALT. FREQ. TO 4976 kHz / ENGLISH, ETC • DS-RED CHANNEL • 10 kW
**USA**
VOA, Via Briech, Morocco — S • Africa • 250 kW · Sa/Su • Africa • 250 kW
VOA, Via Philippines — S • S Asia • 250 kW · S • SE Asia • 250 kW
†VOA, Via Woofferton, UK — W • N Africa • "RADIO SAWA" • 300 kW · W • S Europe • 300 kW
**7200 CHINA**
†CENTRAL PEOPLE'S BS, Beijing — DS-2 • 100 kW · Th-Tu • DS-2 • 100 kW
CHINA RADIO INTL, Via Moscow, Russia — W • Mideast • 200 kW
**GERMANY**
DEUTSCHE WELLE, Wertachtal — W • M-F • E Europe • 500 kW
**IRAN**
VO THE ISLAMIC REP, Ahvāz — W • W Asia & C Asia • 250 kW
**JAPAN**
RADIO JAPAN/NHK, Tokyo-Yamata — SE Asia • 100 kW
**RUSSIA**
MARIY RADIO, Yoshkar Ola — S • RUSSIAN, ETC • DS-LOCAL, R ROSSII • 5 kW
YAKUT RADIO, Yakutsk — RUSSIAN, ETC • DS-LOCAL, R ROSSII • 100 kW
**SUDAN**
RADIO OMDURMAN, Omdurman — Europe, Mideast & Africa • 100 kW
REP OF SUDAN RADIO, Omdurman — DS • 100 kW
**USA**
VOA, Various Locations — S Asia • 250 kW
†VOA, Via Kavála, Greece — W • S Asia • 250 kW · W • Mideast & W Asia • 250 kW
VOA, Via Udon Thani, Thailand — S • E Asia • 100 kW
**YUGOSLAVIA**
†RADIO YUGOSLAVIA, Via Bosnia — Europe • RELAY RTV SRBIJE • 250 kW · S • W Europe • 250 kW
**7205 CYPRUS**
CYPRUS BC CORP, Zyyi — F-Su • Europe • 250 kW
**IRAN**
VO THE ISLAMIC REP, Ahvāz — W Asia & C Asia • 250 kW
VO THE ISLAMIC REP, Sirjan — W • E Europe • 500 kW
**POLAND**
RADIO POLONIA, Warsaw — W • E Europe • 100 kW · W • W Europe • 100 kW
**UNITED KINGDOM**
BBC, Skelton, Cumbria — S • M-F • S Europe • 300 kW
BBC, Via Meyerton, South Africa — S • S Africa • 500 kW
BBC, Via Singapore — S Asia • 250 kW
BBC, Via Thailand — S Asia • 250 kW
BBC, Via Zyyi, Cyprus — W • M-F • S Europe • 250 kW
**USA**
†RFE-RL, Via Lampertheim, Germany — W • E Europe • 100 kW
**7210 BELARUS**
(con'd)  R BELARUS/R MINSK, Minsk — N Europe • 100 kW

| 0 1 2 3 4 5 6 7 8 9 10 11 12 13 14 15 16 17 18 19 20 21 22 23 24 |
|---|

**ENGLISH** ▬▬  **ARABIC** ⬚⬚⬚  **CHINESE** ▫▫▫  **FRENCH** ▬▬  **GERMAN** ▬▬  **RUSSIAN** ══  **SPANISH** ══  **OTHER** ▬▬

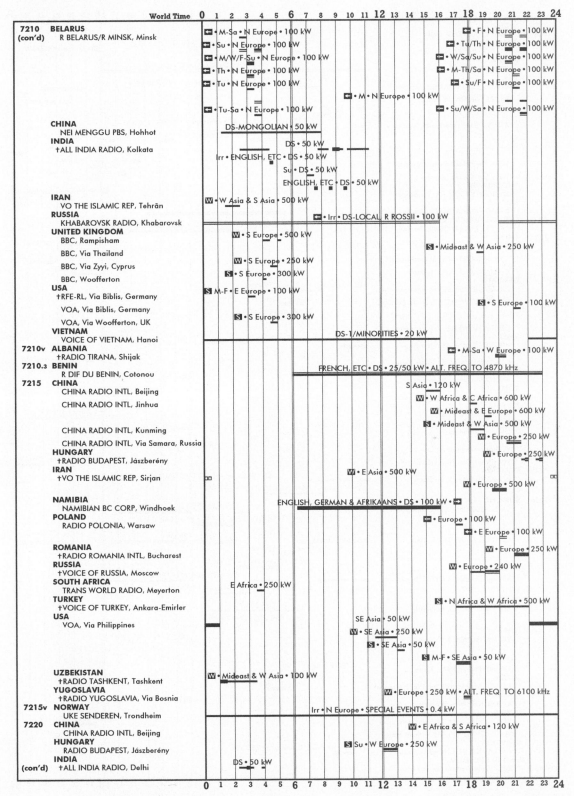

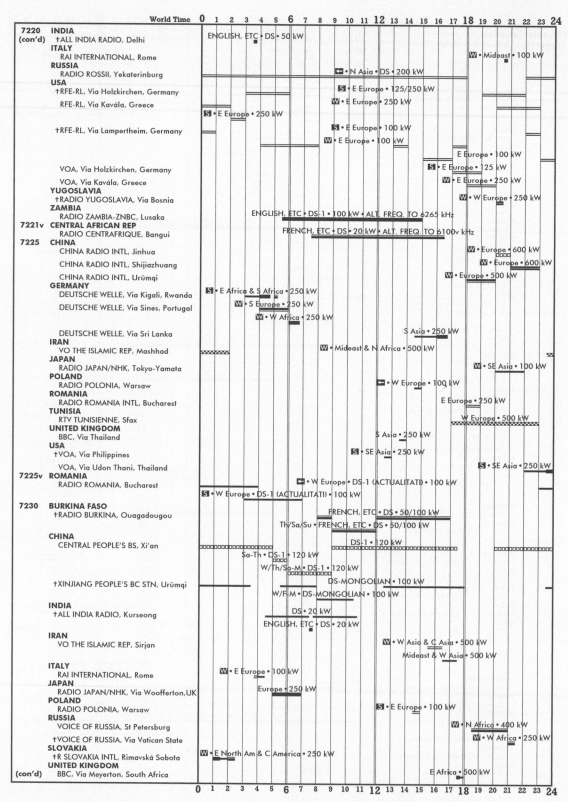

**World Time** 0 1 2 3 4 5 6 7 8 9 10 11 12 13 14 15 16 17 18 19 20 21 22 23 24

| 7220 | INDIA |
| (con'd) | †ALL INDIA RADIO, Delhi — ENGLISH, ETC • DS • 50 kW |
| | ITALY |
| | RAI INTERNATIONAL, Rome — W • Mideast • 100 kW |
| | RUSSIA |
| | RADIO ROSSII, Yekaterinburg — N Asia • DS • 200 kW |
| | USA |
| | †RFE-RL, Via Holzkirchen, Germany — S • E Europe • 125/250 kW |
| | RFE-RL, Via Kavála, Greece — W • E Europe • 250 kW |
| | | S • E Europe • 250 kW |
| | †RFE-RL, Via Lampertheim, Germany — S • E Europe • 100 kW |
| | | W • E Europe • 100 kW |
| | | E Europe • 100 kW |
| | VOA, Via Holzkirchen, Germany — S • E Europe • 125 kW |
| | VOA, Via Kavála, Greece — W • E Europe • 250 kW |
| | YUGOSLAVIA |
| | †RADIO YUGOSLAVIA, Via Bosnia — W • W Europe • 250 kW |
| | ZAMBIA |
| | RADIO ZAMBIA-ZNBC, Lusaka — ENGLISH, ETC • DS-1 • 100 kW • ALT. FREQ. TO 6265 kHz |
| 7221v | **CENTRAL AFRICAN REP** |
| | RADIO CENTRAFRIQUE, Bangui — FRENCH, ETC • DS 20 kW • ALT. FREQ. TO 6100v kHz |
| 7225 | **CHINA** |
| | CHINA RADIO INTL, Jinhua — W • Europe • 600 kW |
| | CHINA RADIO INTL, Shijiazhuang — W • Europe • 600 kW |
| | CHINA RADIO INTL, Urümqi — W • Europe • 500 kW |
| | **GERMANY** |
| | DEUTSCHE WELLE, Via Kigali, Rwanda — S • E Africa & S Africa • 250 kW |
| | DEUTSCHE WELLE, Via Sines, Portugal — W • S Europe • 250 kW |
| | | W • W Africa • 250 kW |
| | DEUTSCHE WELLE, Via Sri Lanka — S Asia • 250 kW |
| | **IRAN** |
| | VO THE ISLAMIC REP, Mashhad — W • Mideast & N Africa • 500 kW |
| | **JAPAN** |
| | RADIO JAPAN/NHK, Tokyo-Yamata — W • SE Asia • 100 kW |
| | **POLAND** |
| | RADIO POLONIA, Warsaw — W Europe • 100 kW |
| | **ROMANIA** |
| | RADIO ROMANIA INTL, Bucharest — E Europe • 250 kW |
| | **TUNISIA** |
| | RTV TUNISIENNE, Sfax — W Europe • 500 kW |
| | **UNITED KINGDOM** |
| | BBC, Via Thailand — S Asia • 250 kW |
| | **USA** |
| | †VOA, Via Philippines — S • SE Asia • 250 kW |
| | VOA, Via Udon Thani, Thailand — S • SE Asia • 250 kW |
| 7225v | **ROMANIA** |
| | RADIO ROMANIA, Bucharest — W Europe • DS-1 (ACTUALITATI) • 100 kW |
| | | S • W Europe • DS-1 (ACTUALITATI) • 100 kW |
| 7230 | **BURKINA FASO** |
| | †RADIO BURKINA, Ouagadougou — FRENCH, ETC • DS • 50/100 kW |
| | | Th/Sa/Su • FRENCH, ETC • DS • 50/100 kW |
| | **CHINA** |
| | CENTRAL PEOPLE'S BS, Xi'an — DS-1 • 120 kW |
| | | Sa-Th • DS-1 • 120 kW |
| | | W/Th/Sa-M • DS-1 • 120 kW |
| | †XINJIANG PEOPLE'S BC STN, Urümqi — DS-MONGOLIAN • 100 kW |
| | | W/F-M • DS-MONGOLIAN • 100 kW |
| | **INDIA** |
| | †ALL INDIA RADIO, Kurseong — DS • 20 kW |
| | | ENGLISH, ETC • DS • 20 kW |
| | **IRAN** |
| | VO THE ISLAMIC REP, Sirjan — W • W Asia & C Asia • 500 kW |
| | | Mideast & W Asia • 500 kW |
| | **ITALY** |
| | RAI INTERNATIONAL, Rome — W • E Europe • 100 kW |
| | **JAPAN** |
| | RADIO JAPAN/NHK, Via Woofferton, UK — Europe • 250 kW |
| | **POLAND** |
| | RADIO POLONIA, Warsaw — S • E Europe • 100 kW |
| | **RUSSIA** |
| | VOICE OF RUSSIA, St Petersburg — W • N Africa • 400 kW |
| | †VOICE OF RUSSIA, Via Vatican State — W • W Africa • 250 kW |
| | **SLOVAKIA** |
| | †R SLOVAKIA INTL, Rimavská Sobota — W • E North Am & C America • 250 kW |
| | **UNITED KINGDOM** |
| (con'd) | BBC, Via Meyerton, South Africa — E Africa • 500 kW |

0 1 2 3 4 5 6 7 8 9 10 11 12 13 14 15 16 17 18 19 20 21 22 23 24

ENGLISH ▬▬   ARABIC ▨▨▨   CHINESE ▫▫▫   FRENCH ══   GERMAN ▬▬   RUSSIAN ══   SPANISH ══   OTHER ──

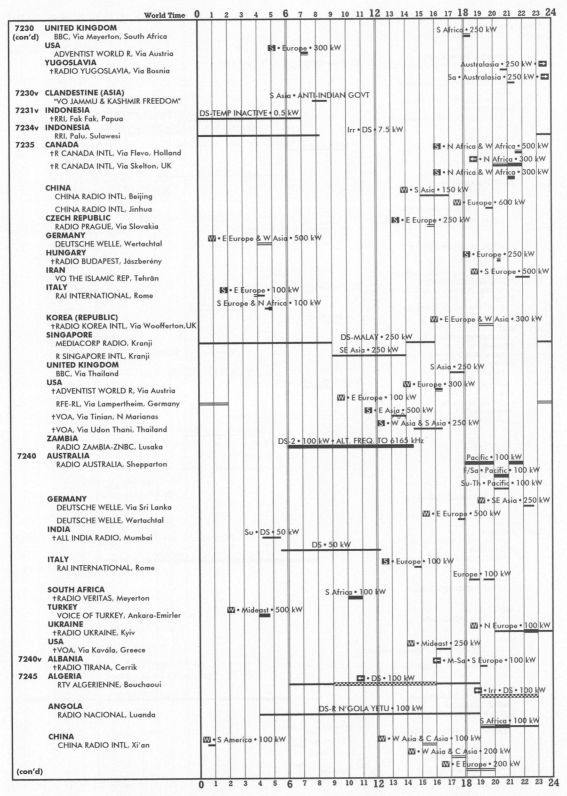

| | | World Time | | |
|---|---|---|---|---|
| 7230 (con'd) | **UNITED KINGDOM** | BBC, Via Meyerton, South Africa | | S Africa • 250 kW |
| | **USA** | ADVENTIST WORLD R, Via Austria | S • Europe • 300 kW | |
| | **YUGOSLAVIA** | †RADIO YUGOSLAVIA, Via Bosnia | | Australasia • 250 kW ➡<br>Sa • Australasia • 250 kW • ➡ |
| 7230v | **CLANDESTINE (ASIA)** | "VO JAMMU & KASHMIR FREEDOM" | S Asia • ANTI-INDIAN GOVT | |
| 7231v | **INDONESIA** | †RRI, Fak Fak, Papua | DS-TEMP INACTIVE • 0.5 kW | |
| 7234v | **INDONESIA** | RRI, Palu, Sulawesi | Irr • DS • 7.5 kW | |
| 7235 | **CANADA** | †R CANADA INTL, Via Flevo, Holland | | S • N Africa & W Africa • 500 kW |
| | | †R CANADA INTL, Via Skelton, UK | | ➡ • N Africa • 300 kW<br>S • N Africa & W Africa • 300 kW |
| | **CHINA** | CHINA RADIO INTL, Beijing | | W • S Asia • 150 kW |
| | | CHINA RADIO INTL, Jinhua | | W • Europe • 600 kW |
| | **CZECH REPUBLIC** | RADIO PRAGUE, Via Slovakia | | S • E Europe • 250 kW |
| | **GERMANY** | DEUTSCHE WELLE, Wertachtal | W • E Europe & W Asia • 500 kW | |
| | **HUNGARY** | †RADIO BUDAPEST, Jászberény | | S • Europe • 250 kW |
| | **IRAN** | VO THE ISLAMIC REP, Tehrān | | W • S Europe • 500 kW |
| | **ITALY** | RAI INTERNATIONAL, Rome | S • E Europe • 100 kW<br>S Europe & N Africa • 100 kW | |
| | **KOREA (REPUBLIC)** | †RADIO KOREA INTL, Via Woofferton, UK | | W • E Europe & W Asia • 300 kW |
| | **SINGAPORE** | MEDIACORP RADIO, Kranji | DS-MALAY • 250 kW | |
| | | R SINGAPORE INTL, Kranji | SE Asia • 250 kW | |
| | **UNITED KINGDOM** | BBC, Via Thailand | | S Asia • 250 kW |
| | **USA** | †ADVENTIST WORLD R, Via Austria | | W • Europe • 300 kW |
| | | RFE-RL, Via Lampertheim, Germany | W • E Europe • 100 kW | |
| | | †VOA, Via Tinian, N Marianas | S • E Asia • 500 kW | |
| | | †VOA, Via Udon Thani, Thailand | S • W Asia & S Asia • 250 kW | |
| | **ZAMBIA** | RADIO ZAMBIA-ZNBC, Lusaka | DS-2 • 100 kW • ALT. FREQ. TO 6165 kHz | |
| 7240 | **AUSTRALIA** | RADIO AUSTRALIA, Shepparton | | Pacific • 100 kW<br>F/Sa • Pacific • 100 kW<br>Su-Th • Pacific • 100 kW |
| | **GERMANY** | DEUTSCHE WELLE, Via Sri Lanka | | W • SE Asia • 250 kW |
| | | DEUTSCHE WELLE, Wertachtal | | W • E Europe • 500 kW |
| | **INDIA** | †ALL INDIA RADIO, Mumbai | Su • DS • 50 kW<br>DS • 50 kW | |
| | **ITALY** | RAI INTERNATIONAL, Rome | S • Europe • 100 kW<br>Europe • 100 kW | |
| | **SOUTH AFRICA** | †RADIO VERITAS, Meyerton | S Africa • 100 kW | |
| | **TURKEY** | VOICE OF TURKEY, Ankara-Emirler | W • Mideast • 500 kW | |
| | **UKRAINE** | †RADIO UKRAINE, Kyiv | | W • N Europe • 100 kW |
| | **USA** | †VOA, Via Kavála, Greece | W • Mideast • 250 kW | |
| 7240v | **ALBANIA** | †RADIO TIRANA, Cerrik | | ➡ • M-Sa • S Europe • 100 kW |
| 7245 | **ALGERIA** | RTV ALGERIENNE, Bouchaoui | ➡ • DS • 100 kW | ➡ • Irr • DS • 100 kW |
| | **ANGOLA** | RADIO NACIONAL, Luanda | DS-R N'GOLA YETU • 100 kW | S Africa • 100 kW |
| | **CHINA** | CHINA RADIO INTL, Xi'an | W • S America • 100 kW | W • W Asia & C Asia • 100 kW<br>W • W Asia & C Asia • 200 kW<br>W • E Europe • 200 kW |
| (con'd) | | | | |

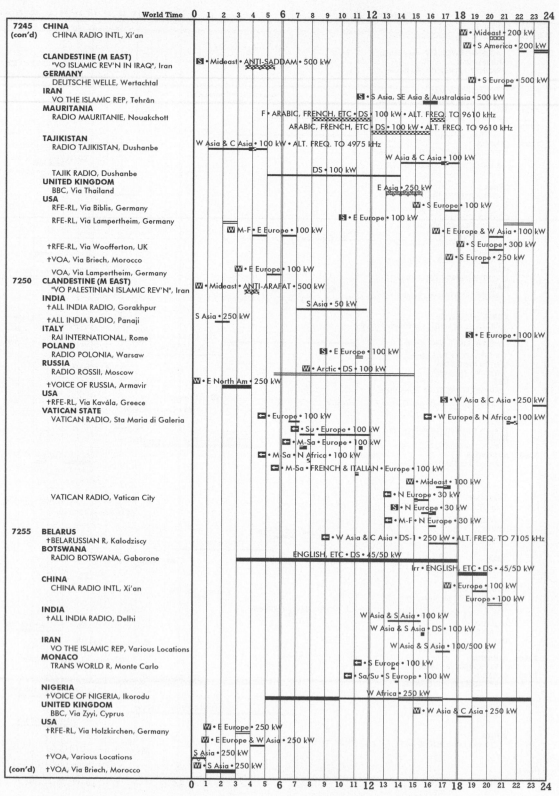

| World Time | Broadcaster | Schedule |
|---|---|---|
| 7245 (con'd) | **CHINA**<br>CHINA RADIO INTL, Xi'an | W • Mideast • 200 kW<br>W • S America • 200 kW |
| | **CLANDESTINE (M EAST)**<br>"VO ISLAMIC REV'N IN IRAQ", Iran | S • Mideast • ANTI-SADDAM • 500 kW |
| | **GERMANY**<br>DEUTSCHE WELLE, Wertachtal | W • S Europe • 500 kW |
| | **IRAN**<br>VO THE ISLAMIC REP, Tehrān | S • S Asia, SE Asia & Australasia • 500 kW |
| | **MAURITANIA**<br>RADIO MAURITANIE, Nouakchott | F • ARABIC, FRENCH, ETC • DS • 100 kW • ALT. FREQ. TO 9610 kHz<br>ARABIC, FRENCH, ETC • DS • 100 kW • ALT. FREQ. TO 9610 kHz |
| | **TAJIKISTAN**<br>RADIO TAJIKISTAN, Dushanbe | W Asia & C Asia • 100 kW • ALT. FREQ. TO 4975 kHz<br>W Asia & C Asia • 100 kW |
| | TAJIK RADIO, Dushanbe | DS • 100 kW |
| | **UNITED KINGDOM**<br>BBC, Via Thailand | E Asia • 250 kW |
| | **USA**<br>RFE-RL, Via Biblis, Germany | W • S Europe • 100 kW |
| | RFE-RL, Via Lampertheim, Germany | S • E Europe • 100 kW<br>W • M-F • E Europe • 100 kW<br>W • E Europe & W Asia • 100 kW |
| | †RFE-RL, Via Woofferton, UK | W • S Europe • 300 kW |
| | †VOA, Via Briech, Morocco | W • S Europe • 250 kW |
| | VOA, Via Lampertheim, Germany | W • E Europe • 100 kW |
| 7250 | **CLANDESTINE (M EAST)**<br>"VO PALESTINIAN ISLAMIC REV'N", Iran | W • Mideast • ANTI-ARAFAT • 500 kW |
| | **INDIA**<br>†ALL INDIA RADIO, Gorakhpur | S Asia • 50 kW |
| | †ALL INDIA RADIO, Panaji | S Asia • 250 kW |
| | **ITALY**<br>RAI INTERNATIONAL, Rome | S • E Europe • 100 kW |
| | **POLAND**<br>RADIO POLONIA, Warsaw | S • E Europe • 100 kW |
| | **RUSSIA**<br>RADIO ROSSII, Moscow | W • Arctic • DS • 100 kW |
| | †VOICE OF RUSSIA, Armavir | W • E North Am • 250 kW |
| | **USA**<br>†RFE-RL, Via Kavála, Greece | S • W Asia & C Asia • 250 kW |
| | **VATICAN STATE**<br>VATICAN RADIO, Sta Maria di Galeria | • Europe • 100 kW<br>• W Europe & N Africa • 100 kW • 100 kW<br>• Su • Europe • 100 kW<br>• M-Sa • Europe • 100 kW<br>• M-Sa • N Africa • 100 kW<br>• M-Sa • FRENCH & ITALIAN • Europe • 100 kW |
| | VATICAN RADIO, Vatican City | W • Mideast • 100 kW<br>• N Europe • 30 kW<br>S • N Europe • 30 kW<br>• M-F • N Europe • 30 kW |
| 7255 | **BELARUS**<br>†BELARUSSIAN R, Kalodziscy | • W Asia & C Asia • DS-1 • 250 kW • ALT. FREQ. TO 7105 kHz |
| | **BOTSWANA**<br>RADIO BOTSWANA, Gaborone | ENGLISH, ETC • DS • 45/50 kW<br>Irr • ENGLISH, ETC • DS • 45/50 kW |
| | **CHINA**<br>CHINA RADIO INTL, Xi'an | W • Europe • 100 kW<br>Europe • 100 kW |
| | **INDIA**<br>†ALL INDIA RADIO, Delhi | W Asia & S Asia • 100 kW<br>W Asia & S Asia • DS • 100 kW |
| | **IRAN**<br>VO THE ISLAMIC REP, Various Locations | W Asia & S Asia • 100/500 kW |
| | **MONACO**<br>TRANS WORLD R, Monte Carlo | • S Europe • 100 kW<br>• Sa/Su • S Europe • 100 kW |
| | **NIGERIA**<br>†VOICE OF NIGERIA, Ikorodu | W Africa • 250 kW |
| | **UNITED KINGDOM**<br>BBC, Via Zyyi, Cyprus | W • W Asia & C Asia • 250 kW |
| | **USA**<br>†RFE-RL, Via Holzkirchen, Germany | W • E Europe • 250 kW<br>W • E Europe & W Asia • 250 kW |
| | †VOA, Various Locations | S Asia • 250 kW |
| (con'd) | †VOA, Via Briech, Morocco | W • S Asia • 250 kW |

ENGLISH ▬▬    ARABIC ≋≋≋    CHINESE □□□    FRENCH ══    GERMAN ▬▬    RUSSIAN ══    SPANISH ══    OTHER ▬

World Time 0 1 2 3 4 5 6 7 8 9 10 11 12 13 14 15 16 17 18 19 20 21 22 23 24

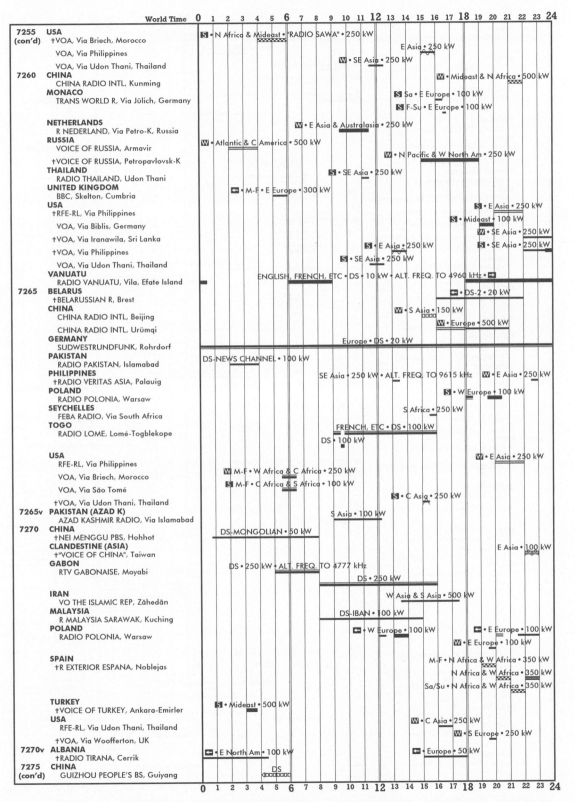

| | |
|---|---|
| **7255** **USA** | |
| (con'd) †VOA, Via Briech, Morocco | S • N Africa & Mideast • "RADIO SAWA" • 250 kW |
| VOA, Via Philippines | E Asia • 250 kW |
| VOA, Via Udon Thani, Thailand | W • SE Asia • 250 kW |
| **7260 CHINA** | |
| CHINA RADIO INTL, Kunming | W • Mideast & N Africa • 500 kW |
| **MONACO** | |
| TRANS WORLD R, Via Jülich, Germany | S Sa • E Europe • 100 kW |
| | S F-Su • E Europe • 100 kW |
| **NETHERLANDS** | |
| R NEDERLAND, Via Petro-K, Russia | W • E Asia & Australasia • 250 kW |
| **RUSSIA** | |
| VOICE OF RUSSIA, Armavir | W • Atlantic & C America • 500 kW |
| †VOICE OF RUSSIA, Petropavlovsk-K | W • N Pacific & W North Am • 250 kW |
| **THAILAND** | |
| RADIO THAILAND, Udon Thani | S • SE Asia • 250 kW |
| **UNITED KINGDOM** | |
| BBC, Skelton, Cumbria | ⇦ • M-F • E Europe • 300 kW |
| **USA** | |
| †RFE-RL, Via Philippines | S • E Asia • 250 kW |
| VOA, Via Biblis, Germany | S • Mideast • 100 kW |
| †VOA, Via Iranawila, Sri Lanka | W • SE Asia • 250 kW |
| †VOA, Via Philippines | S • E Asia • 250 kW    S • SE Asia • 250 kW |
| VOA, Via Udon Thani, Thailand | S • SE Asia • 250 kW |
| **VANUATU** | |
| RADIO VANUATU, Vila, Efate Island | ENGLISH, FRENCH, ETC • DS • 10 kW • ALT. FREQ. TO 4960 kHz • ⇨ |
| **7265 BELARUS** | |
| †BELARUSSIAN R, Brest | ⇦ • DS-2 • 20 kW |
| **CHINA** | |
| CHINA RADIO INTL, Beijing | W • S Asia • 150 kW |
| CHINA RADIO INTL, Urümqi | W • Europe • 500 kW |
| **GERMANY** | |
| SUDWESTRUNDFUNK, Rohrdorf | Europe • DS • 20 kW |
| **PAKISTAN** | |
| RADIO PAKISTAN, Islamabad | DS-NEWS CHANNEL • 100 kW |
| **PHILIPPINES** | |
| †RADIO VERITAS ASIA, Palauig | SE Asia • 250 kW • ALT. FREQ. TO 9615 kHz    W • E Asia • 250 kW |
| **POLAND** | |
| RADIO POLONIA, Warsaw | S • W Europe • 100 kW |
| **SEYCHELLES** | |
| FEBA RADIO, Via South Africa | S Africa • 250 kW |
| **TOGO** | |
| RADIO LOME, Lomé-Togblekope | FRENCH, ETC • DS • 100 kW |
| | DS • 100 kW |
| **USA** | |
| RFE-RL, Via Philippines | W • E Asia • 250 kW |
| VOA, Via Briech, Morocco | W • M-F • W Africa & C Africa • 250 kW |
| VOA, Via São Tomé | S • M-F • C Africa & S Africa • 100 kW |
| †VOA, Via Udon Thani, Thailand | S • C Asia • 250 kW |
| **7265v PAKISTAN (AZAD K)** | |
| AZAD KASHMIR RADIO, Via Islamabad | S Asia • 100 kW |
| **7270 CHINA** | |
| †NEI MENGGU PBS, Hohhot | DS-MONGOLIAN • 50 kW |
| **CLANDESTINE (ASIA)** | |
| †"VOICE OF CHINA", Taiwan | E Asia • 100 kW |
| **GABON** | |
| RTV GABONAISE, Moyabi | DS • 250 kW • ALT. FREQ. TO 4777 kHz |
| | DS • 250 kW |
| **IRAN** | |
| VO THE ISLAMIC REP, Zāhedān | W Asia & S Asia • 500 kW |
| **MALAYSIA** | |
| R MALAYSIA SARAWAK, Kuching | DS-IBAN • 100 kW |
| **POLAND** | |
| RADIO POLONIA, Warsaw | ⇦ • W Europe • 100 kW    ⇦ • E Europe • 100 kW |
| | W • E Europe • 100 kW |
| **SPAIN** | |
| †R EXTERIOR ESPANA, Noblejas | M-F • N Africa & W Africa • 350 kW |
| | N Africa & W Africa • 350 kW |
| | Sa/Su • N Africa & W Africa • 350 kW |
| **TURKEY** | |
| †VOICE OF TURKEY, Ankara-Emirler | S • Mideast • 500 kW |
| **USA** | |
| RFE-RL, Via Udon Thani, Thailand | W • C Asia • 250 kW |
| †VOA, Via Woofferton, UK | W • S Europe • 250 kW |
| **7270v ALBANIA** | |
| †RADIO TIRANA, Cerrik | ⇦ • E North Am • 100 kW    ⇦ • Europe • 50 kW |
| **7275 CHINA** | |
| (con'd) GUIZHOU PEOPLE'S BS, Guiyang | DS |

0 1 2 3 4 5 6 7 8 9 10 11 12 13 14 15 16 17 18 19 20 21 22 23 24

SEASONAL S OR W    1-HR TIMESHIFT MIDYEAR ⇦ OR ⇨    JAMMING / OR ∧    EARLIEST HEARD ◁    LATEST HEARD ▷    NEW FOR 2003 †

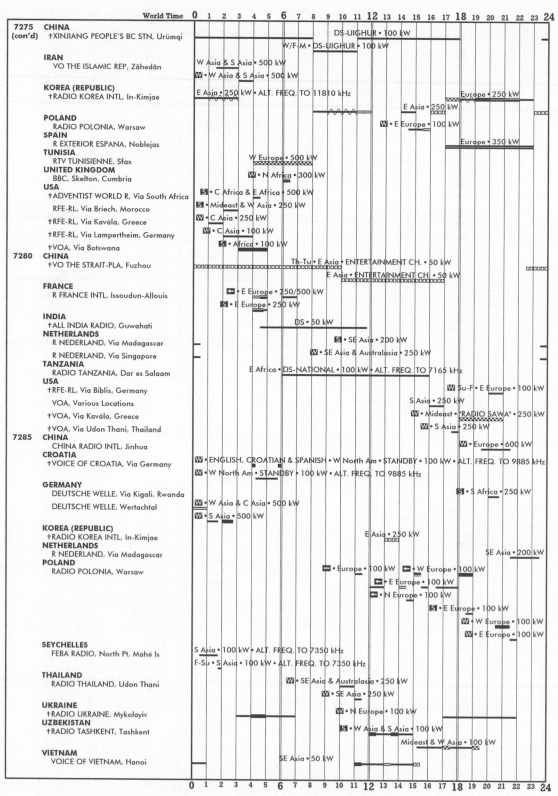

| | World Time | 0 1 2 3 4 5 6 7 8 9 10 11 12 13 14 15 16 17 18 19 20 21 22 23 24 |
|---|---|---|

**7275 (con'd)  CHINA**
†XINJIANG PEOPLE'S BC STN, Urümqi — DS-UIGHUR • 100 kW / W/F-M • DS-UIGHUR • 100 kW

**IRAN**
VO THE ISLAMIC REP, Zāhedān — W Asia & S Asia • 500 kW / W • W Asia & S Asia • 500 kW

**KOREA (REPUBLIC)**
†RADIO KOREA INTL, In-Kimjae — E Asia • 250 kW • ALT. FREQ. TO 11810 kHz / E Asia • 250 kW / Europe • 250 kW

**POLAND**
RADIO POLONIA, Warsaw — W • E Europe • 100 kW

**SPAIN**
R EXTERIOR ESPANA, Noblejas — Europe • 350 kW

**TUNISIA**
RTV TUNISIENNE, Sfax — W Europe • 500 kW

**UNITED KINGDOM**
BBC, Skelton, Cumbria — W • N Africa • 300 kW

**USA**
†ADVENTIST WORLD R, Via South Africa — S • C Africa & E Africa • 500 kW / S • Mideast & W Asia • 250 kW

RFE-RL, Via Briech, Morocco — W • C Asia • 250 kW

†RFE-RL, Via Kavála, Greece — W • C Asia • 100 kW

†RFE-RL, Via Lampertheim, Germany — S • Africa • 100 kW

†VOA, Via Botswana

**7280  CHINA**
†VO THE STRAIT-PLA, Fuzhou — Th-Tu • E Asia • ENTERTAINMENT CH. • 50 kW / E Asia • ENTERTAINMENT CH. • 50 kW

**FRANCE**
R FRANCE INTL, Issoudun-Allouis — E Europe • 250/500 kW / S • E Europe • 250 kW

**INDIA**
†ALL INDIA RADIO, Guwahati — DS • 50 kW

**NETHERLANDS**
R NEDERLAND, Via Madagascar — S • SE Asia • 200 kW

R NEDERLAND, Via Singapore — W • SE Asia & Australasia • 250 kW

**TANZANIA**
RADIO TANZANIA, Dar es Salaam — E Africa • DS-NATIONAL • 100 kW • ALT. FREQ. TO 7165 kHz

**USA**
†RFE-RL, Via Biblis, Germany — W • Su-F • E Europe • 100 kW

VOA, Various Locations — S Asia • 250 kW

†VOA, Via Kavála, Greece — W • Mideast • "RADIO SAWA" • 250 kW

†VOA, Via Udon Thani, Thailand — W • S Asia • 250 kW

**7285  CHINA**
CHINA RADIO INTL, Jinhua — W • Europe • 600 kW

**CROATIA**
†VOICE OF CROATIA, Via Germany — W • ENGLISH, CROATIAN & SPANISH • W North Am • STANDBY • 100 kW • ALT. FREQ. TO 9885 kHz / W • W North Am • STANDBY • 100 kW • ALT. FREQ. TO 9885 kHz

**GERMANY**
DEUTSCHE WELLE, Via Kigali, Rwanda — S • S Africa • 250 kW

DEUTSCHE WELLE, Wertachtal — W • W Asia & C Asia • 500 kW / W • S Asia • 500 kW

**KOREA (REPUBLIC)**
†RADIO KOREA INTL, In-Kimjae — E Asia • 250 kW

**NETHERLANDS**
R NEDERLAND, Via Madagascar — SE Asia • 200 kW

**POLAND**
RADIO POLONIA, Warsaw — Europe • 100 kW / W Europe • 100 kW / E Europe • 100 kW / N Europe • 100 kW / S • E Europe • 100 kW / W • W Europe • 100 kW / W • E Europe • 100 kW

**SEYCHELLES**
FEBA RADIO, North Pt, Mahé Is — S Asia • 100 kW • ALT. FREQ. TO 7350 kHz / F-Su • S Asia • 100 kW • ALT. FREQ. TO 7350 kHz

**THAILAND**
RADIO THAILAND, Udon Thani — W • SE Asia & Australasia • 250 kW / W • SE Asia • 250 kW

**UKRAINE**
†RADIO UKRAINE, Mykolayiv — W • N Europe • 100 kW

**UZBEKISTAN**
†RADIO TASHKENT, Tashkent — S • W Asia & S Asia • 100 kW / Mideast & W Asia • 100 kW

**VIETNAM**
VOICE OF VIETNAM, Hanoi — SE Asia • 50 kW

| | 0 1 2 3 4 5 6 7 8 9 10 11 12 13 14 15 16 17 18 19 20 21 22 23 24 |
|---|---|

ENGLISH ▬   ARABIC ⌇⌇⌇   CHINESE □□□   FRENCH ▭▭   GERMAN ▬▬   RUSSIAN ══   SPANISH ▭▭   OTHER ──

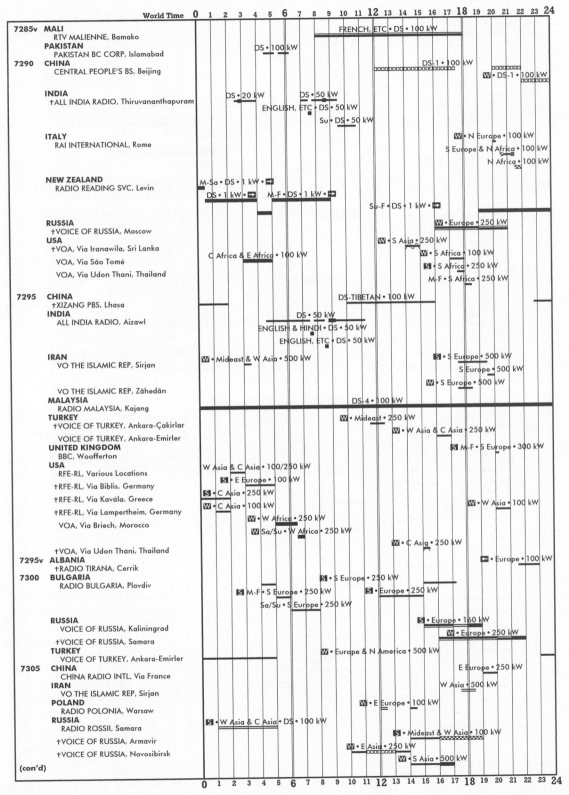

| | | |
|---|---|---|
| **7285v** | **MALI** | |
| | RTV MALIENNE, Bamako | FRENCH, ETC • DS • 100 kW |
| | **PAKISTAN** | |
| | PAKISTAN BC CORP, Islamabad | DS • 100 kW |
| **7290** | **CHINA** | |
| | CENTRAL PEOPLE'S BS, Beijing | DS-1 • 100 kW / W • DS-1 • 100 kW |
| | **INDIA** | |
| | †ALL INDIA RADIO, Thiruvananthapuram | DS • 20 kW / DS • 50 kW / ENGLISH, ETC • DS • 50 kW / Su • DS • 50 kW |
| | **ITALY** | |
| | RAI INTERNATIONAL, Rome | W • N Europe • 100 kW / S Europe & N Africa • 100 kW / N Africa • 100 kW |
| | **NEW ZEALAND** | |
| | RADIO READING SVC, Levin | M-Sa • DS • 1 kW • / DS • 1 kW • / M-F • DS • 1 kW • / Su-F • DS • 1 kW • |
| | **RUSSIA** | |
| | †VOICE OF RUSSIA, Moscow | W • Europe • 250 kW |
| | **USA** | |
| | †VOA, Via Iranawila, Sri Lanka | W • S Asia • 250 kW |
| | VOA, Via São Tomé | C Africa & E Africa • 100 kW / W • S Africa • 100 kW |
| | VOA, Via Udon Thani, Thailand | S • S Africa • 250 kW / M-F • S Africa • 250 kW |
| **7295** | **CHINA** | |
| | †XIZANG PBS, Lhasa | DS-TIBETAN • 100 kW |
| | **INDIA** | |
| | ALL INDIA RADIO, Aizawl | DS • 50 kW / ENGLISH & HINDI • DS • 50 kW / ENGLISH, ETC • DS • 50 kW |
| | **IRAN** | |
| | VO THE ISLAMIC REP, Sirjan | W • Mideast & W Asia • 500 kW / S • S Europe • 500 kW / S Europe • 500 kW |
| | VO THE ISLAMIC REP, Zāhedān | W • S Europe • 500 kW |
| | **MALAYSIA** | |
| | RADIO MALAYSIA, Kajang | DS-4 • 100 kW |
| | **TURKEY** | |
| | †VOICE OF TURKEY, Ankara-Çakirlar | W • Mideast • 250 kW |
| | VOICE OF TURKEY, Ankara-Emirler | W • W Asia & C Asia • 250 kW |
| | **UNITED KINGDOM** | |
| | BBC, Woofferton | S • M-F • S Europe • 300 kW |
| | **USA** | |
| | RFE-RL, Various Locations | W Asia & C Asia • 100/250 kW |
| | †RFE-RL, Via Biblis, Germany | S • E Europe • 100 kW |
| | †RFE-RL, Via Kavála, Greece | S • C Asia • 250 kW |
| | †RFE-RL, Via Lampertheim, Germany | W • C Asia • 100 kW / W • W Asia • 100 kW |
| | VOA, Via Briech, Morocco | W • W Africa • 250 kW / W • Sa/Su • W Africa • 250 kW |
| | †VOA, Via Udon Thani, Thailand | W • C Asia • 250 kW |
| **7295v** | **ALBANIA** | |
| | †RADIO TIRANA, Cerrik | • Europe • 100 kW |
| **7300** | **BULGARIA** | |
| | RADIO BULGARIA, Plovdiv | S • S Europe • 250 kW / S • M-F • S Europe • 250 kW / Sa/Su • S Europe • 250 kW / S • Europe • 250 kW |
| | **RUSSIA** | |
| | VOICE OF RUSSIA, Kaliningrad | S • Europe • 160 kW |
| | †VOICE OF RUSSIA, Samara | W • Europe • 250 kW |
| | **TURKEY** | |
| | VOICE OF TURKEY, Ankara-Emirler | W • Europe & N America • 500 kW |
| **7305** | **CHINA** | |
| | CHINA RADIO INTL, Via France | E Europe • 250 kW |
| | **IRAN** | |
| | VO THE ISLAMIC REP, Sirjan | W Asia • 500 kW |
| | **POLAND** | |
| | RADIO POLONIA, Warsaw | W • E Europe • 100 kW |
| | **RUSSIA** | |
| | RADIO ROSSII, Samara | S • W Asia & C Asia • DS • 100 kW |
| | †VOICE OF RUSSIA, Armavir | S • Mideast & W Asia • 100 kW |
| | †VOICE OF RUSSIA, Novosibirsk | W • E Asia • 250 kW / W • S Asia • 500 kW |

**(con'd)**

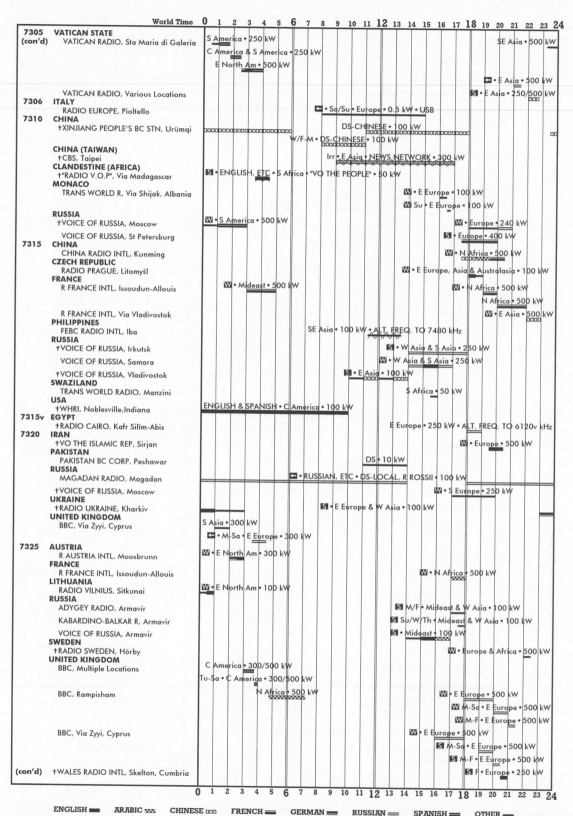

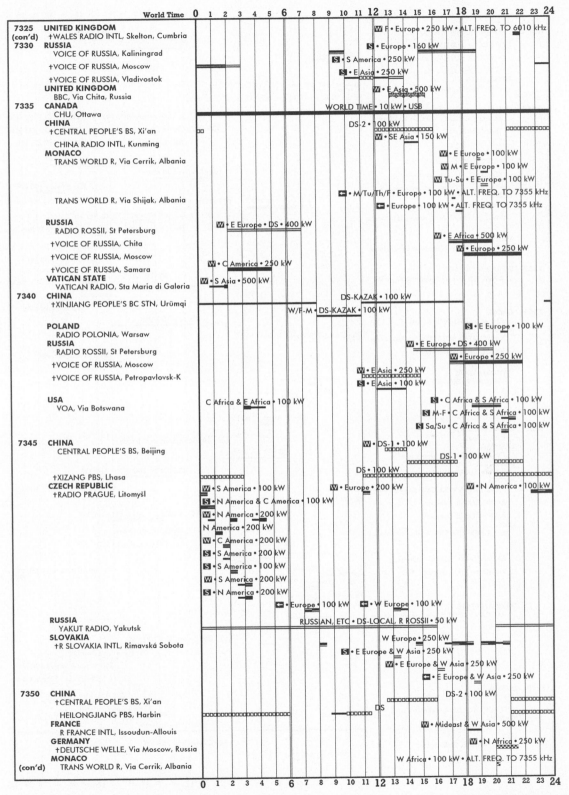

World Time 0 1 2 3 4 5 6 7 8 9 10 11 12 13 14 15 16 17 18 19 20 21 22 23 24

**7325** **UNITED KINGDOM**
(con'd)  †WALES RADIO INTL, Skelton, Cumbria W F • Europe • 250 kW • ALT. FREQ. TO 6010 kHz
**7330** **RUSSIA**
 VOICE OF RUSSIA, Kaliningrad S • Europe • 160 kW
 †VOICE OF RUSSIA, Moscow S • S America • 250 kW
 †VOICE OF RUSSIA, Vladivostok S • E Asia • 250 kW
**UNITED KINGDOM**
 BBC, Via Chita, Russia W • E Asia • 500 kW
**7335** **CANADA**
 CHU, Ottawa WORLD TIME • 10 kW • USB
**CHINA**
 †CENTRAL PEOPLE'S BS, Xi'an DS-2 • 100 kW
 CHINA RADIO INTL, Kunming W • SE Asia • 150 kW
**MONACO**
 TRANS WORLD R, Via Cerrik, Albania W • E Europe • 100 kW
 W M • E Europe • 100 kW
 W Tu-Su • E Europe • 100 kW
 • M/Tu/Th/F • Europe • 100 kW • ALT. FREQ. TO 7355 kHz
 TRANS WORLD R, Via Shijak, Albania • Europe • 100 kW • ALT. FREQ. TO 7355 kHz
**RUSSIA**
 RADIO ROSSII, St Petersburg W • E Europe • DS • 400 kW
 †VOICE OF RUSSIA, Chita W • E Africa • 500 kW
 †VOICE OF RUSSIA, Moscow W • Europe • 250 kW
 †VOICE OF RUSSIA, Samara W • C America • 250 kW
**VATICAN STATE**
 VATICAN RADIO, Sta Maria di Galeria W • S Asia • 500 kW
**7340** **CHINA**
 †XINJIANG PEOPLE'S BC STN, Urümqi DS-KAZAK • 100 kW
 W/F-M • DS-KAZAK • 100 kW
**POLAND**
 RADIO POLONIA, Warsaw S • E Europe • 100 kW
**RUSSIA**
 RADIO ROSSII, St Petersburg W • E Europe • DS • 400 kW
 †VOICE OF RUSSIA, Moscow W • Europe • 250 kW
 †VOICE OF RUSSIA, Petropavlovsk-K W • E Asia • 250 kW
 S • E Asia • 100 kW
**USA**
 VOA, Via Botswana C Africa & E Africa • 100 kW
 S • C Africa & S Africa • 100 kW
 S M-F • C Africa & S Africa • 100 kW
 S Sa/Su • C Africa & S Africa • 100 kW
**7345** **CHINA**
 CENTRAL PEOPLE'S BS, Beijing W • DS-1 • 100 kW
 DS-1 • 100 kW
 DS • 100 kW
 †XIZANG PBS, Lhasa
**CZECH REPUBLIC**
 †RADIO PRAGUE, Litomyšl W • S America • 100 kW W • Europe • 200 kW W • N America • 100 kW
 S • N America & C America • 100 kW
 W • N America • 200 kW
 N America • 200 kW
 W • C America • 200 kW
 S • S America • 200 kW
 S • S America • 100 kW
 W • S America • 200 kW
 S • N America • 200 kW
 • Europe • 100 kW • W Europe • 100 kW
**RUSSIA**
 YAKUT RADIO, Yakutsk RUSSIAN, ETC • DS-LOCAL, R ROSSII • 50 kW
**SLOVAKIA**
 †R SLOVAKIA INTL, Rimavská Sobota W Europe • 250 kW
 S • E Europe & W Asia • 250 kW
 W • E Europe & W Asia • 250 kW
 • E Europe & W Asia • 250 kW
**7350** **CHINA**
 †CENTRAL PEOPLE'S BS, Xi'an DS-2 • 100 kW
 HEILONGJIANG PBS, Harbin DS
**FRANCE**
 R FRANCE INTL, Issoudun-Allouis W • Mideast & W Asia • 500 kW
**GERMANY**
 †DEUTSCHE WELLE, Via Moscow, Russia W • N Africa • 250 kW
**MONACO**
(con'd)  TRANS WORLD R, Via Cerrik, Albania W Africa • 100 kW • ALT. FREQ. TO 7355 kHz

0 1 2 3 4 5 6 7 8 9 10 11 12 13 14 15 16 17 18 19 20 21 22 23 24

SEASONAL S OR W 1-HR TIMESHIFT MIDYEAR ⇐ OR ⇒ JAMMING / OR ∧ EARLIEST HEARD ◁ LATEST HEARD ▷ NEW FOR 2003 †

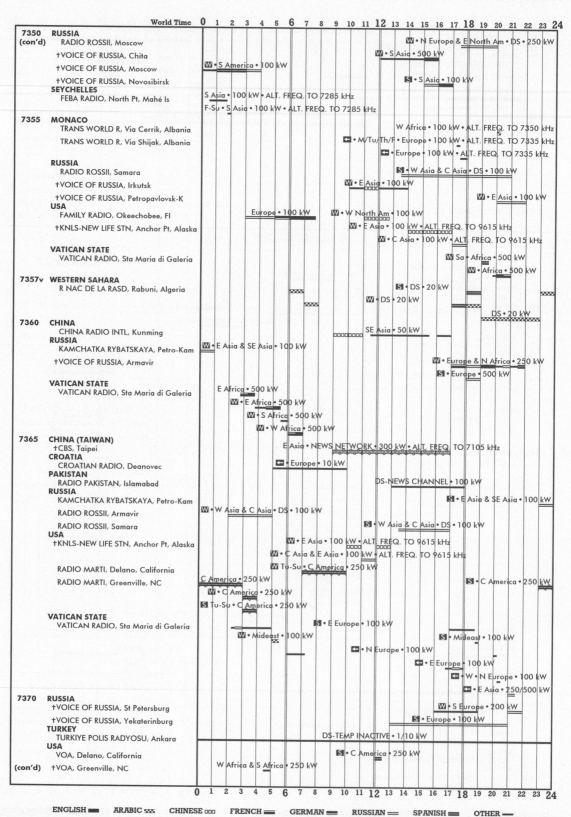

| World Time | 0 | 1 | 2 | 3 | 4 | 5 | 6 | 7 | 8 | 9 | 10 | 11 | 12 | 13 | 14 | 15 | 16 | 17 | 18 | 19 | 20 | 21 | 22 | 23 | 24 |

**7350 RUSSIA**
**(con'd)**  RADIO ROSSII, Moscow — W • N Europe & E North Am • DS • 250 kW
†VOICE OF RUSSIA, Chita — W • S Asia • 500 kW
†VOICE OF RUSSIA, Moscow — W • S America • 100 kW
†VOICE OF RUSSIA, Novosibirsk — S • S Asia • 100 kW
**SEYCHELLES**
FEBA RADIO, North Pt, Mahé Is — S Asia • 100 kW • ALT. FREQ. TO 7285 kHz
F-Su • S Asia • 100 kW • ALT. FREQ. TO 7285 kHz

**7355 MONACO**
TRANS WORLD R, Via Cerrik, Albania — W Africa • 100 kW • ALT. FREQ. TO 7350 kHz
TRANS WORLD R, Via Shijak, Albania — • M/Tu/Th/F • Europe • 100 kW • ALT. FREQ. TO 7335 kHz
— • Europe • 100 kW • ALT. FREQ. TO 7335 kHz
**RUSSIA**
RADIO ROSSII, Samara — S • W Asia & C Asia • DS • 100 kW
†VOICE OF RUSSIA, Irkutsk — W • E Asia • 100 kW
†VOICE OF RUSSIA, Petropavlovsk-K — W • E Asia • 100 kW
**USA**
FAMILY RADIO, Okeechobee, Fl — Europe • 100 kW
W • W North Am • 100 kW
†KNLS-NEW LIFE STN, Anchor Pt, Alaska — W • E Asia • 100 kW • ALT. FREQ. TO 9615 kHz
W • C Asia • 100 kW • ALT. FREQ. TO 9615 kHz
**VATICAN STATE**
VATICAN RADIO, Sta Maria di Galeria — W Sa • Africa • 500 kW
W • Africa • 500 kW

**7357v WESTERN SAHARA**
R NAC DE LA RASD, Rabuni, Algeria — S • DS • 20 kW
W • DS • 20 kW
DS • 20 kW

**7360 CHINA**
CHINA RADIO INTL, Kunming — SE Asia • 50 kW
**RUSSIA**
KAMCHATKA RYBATSKAYA, Petro-Kam — W • E Asia & SE Asia • 100 kW
†VOICE OF RUSSIA, Armavir — W • Europe & N Africa • 250 kW
S • Europe • 500 kW
**VATICAN STATE**
VATICAN RADIO, Sta Maria di Galeria — E Africa • 500 kW
W • E Africa • 500 kW
W • S Africa • 500 kW
W • W Africa • 500 kW

**7365 CHINA (TAIWAN)**
†CBS, Taipei — E Asia • NEWS NETWORK • 300 kW • ALT. FREQ. TO 7105 kHz
**CROATIA**
CROATIAN RADIO, Deanovec — — • Europe • 10 kW
**PAKISTAN**
RADIO PAKISTAN, Islamabad — DS • NEWS CHANNEL • 100 kW
**RUSSIA**
KAMCHATKA RYBATSKAYA, Petro-Kam — S • E Asia & SE Asia • 100 kW
RADIO ROSSII, Armavir — W • W Asia & C Asia • DS • 100 kW
RADIO ROSSII, Samara — S • W Asia & C Asia • DS • 100 kW
**USA**
†KNLS-NEW LIFE STN, Anchor Pt, Alaska — W • E Asia • 100 kW • ALT. FREQ. TO 9615 kHz
W • C Asia & E Asia • 100 kW • ALT. FREQ. TO 9615 kHz
W Tu-Su • C America • 250 kW
RADIO MARTI, Delano, California — C America • 250 kW
RADIO MARTI, Greenville, NC — S • C America • 250 kW
W • C America • 250 kW
S Tu-Su • C America • 250 kW
**VATICAN STATE**
VATICAN RADIO, Sta Maria di Galeria — S • E Europe • 100 kW
W • Mideast • 100 kW
S • Mideast • 100 kW
— • N Europe • 100 kW
— • E Europe • 100 kW
— • W • N Europe • 100 kW
— • E Asia • 250/500 kW

**7370 RUSSIA**
†VOICE OF RUSSIA, St Petersburg — W • S Europe • 200 kW
†VOICE OF RUSSIA, Yekaterinburg — S • Europe • 100 kW
**TURKEY**
TURKIYE POLIS RADYOSU, Ankara — DS • TEMP INACTIVE • 1/10 kW
**USA**
VOA, Delano, California — S • C America • 250 kW
**(con'd)**  †VOA, Greenville, NC — W Africa & S Africa • 250 kW

| 0 | 1 | 2 | 3 | 4 | 5 | 6 | 7 | 8 | 9 | 10 | 11 | 12 | 13 | 14 | 15 | 16 | 17 | 18 | 19 | 20 | 21 | 22 | 23 | 24 |

ENGLISH ▬  ARABIC ▨  CHINESE ▫▫▫  FRENCH ═  GERMAN ▭  RUSSIAN ═  SPANISH ▭  OTHER ▬

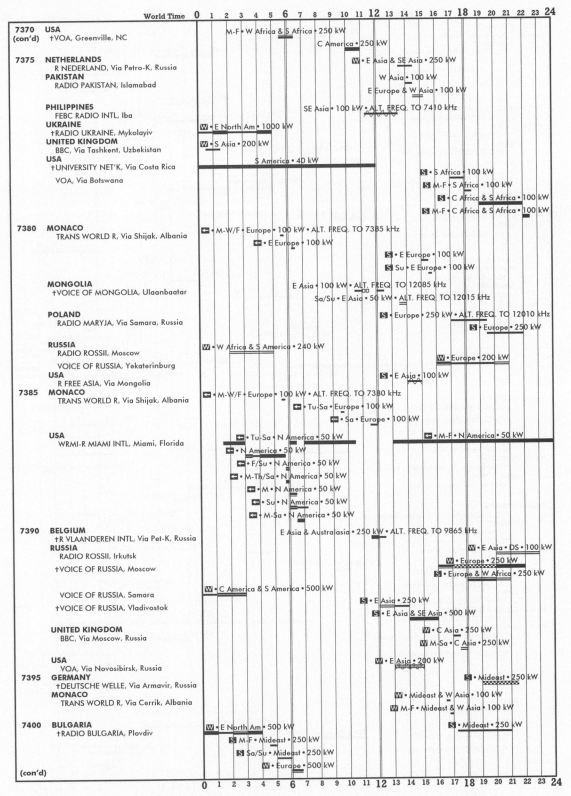

World Time  0  1  2  3  4  5  6  7  8  9  10  11  12  13  14  15  16  17  18  19  20  21  22  23  24

**7370** **USA**
(con'd)  †VOA, Greenville, NC
M-F • W Africa & S Africa • 250 kW
C America • 250 kW

**7375** **NETHERLANDS**
R NEDERLAND, Via Petro-K, Russia
W • E Asia & SE Asia • 250 kW
**PAKISTAN**
RADIO PAKISTAN, Islamabad
W Asia • 100 kW
E Europe & W Asia • 100 kW

**PHILIPPINES**
FEBC RADIO INTL, Iba
SE Asia • 100 kW • ALT. FREQ. TO 7410 kHz
**UKRAINE**
†RADIO UKRAINE, Mykolayiv
W • E North Am • 1000 kW
**UNITED KINGDOM**
BBC, Via Tashkent, Uzbekistan
W • S Asia • 200 kW
**USA**
†UNIVERSITY NET'K, Via Costa Rica
S America • 40 kW

VOA, Via Botswana
S • S Africa • 100 kW
S M-F • S Africa • 100 kW
S • C Africa & S Africa • 100 kW
S M-F • C Africa & S Africa • 100 kW

**7380** **MONACO**
TRANS WORLD R, Via Shijak, Albania
M-W/F • Europe • 100 kW • ALT. FREQ. TO 7385 kHz
E Europe • 100 kW
S • E Europe • 100 kW
S Su • E Europe • 100 kW

**MONGOLIA**
†VOICE OF MONGOLIA, Ulaanbaatar
E Asia • 100 kW • ALT. FREQ. TO 12085 kHz
Sa/Su • E Asia • 50 kW • ALT. FREQ. TO 12015 kHz

**POLAND**
RADIO MARYJA, Via Samara, Russia
S • Europe • 250 kW • ALT. FREQ. TO 12010 kHz
S • Europe • 250 kW

**RUSSIA**
RADIO ROSSII, Moscow
W • W Africa & S America • 240 kW

VOICE OF RUSSIA, Yekaterinburg
W • Europe • 200 kW
**USA**
R FREE ASIA, Via Mongolia
S • E Asia • 100 kW

**7385** **MONACO**
TRANS WORLD R, Via Shijak, Albania
M-W/F • Europe • 100 kW • ALT. FREQ. TO 7380 kHz
Tu-Sa • Europe • 100 kW
Sa • Europe • 100 kW

**USA**
WRMI-R MIAMI INTL, Miami, Florida
Tu-Sa • N America • 50 kW
M-F • N America • 50 kW
N America • 50 kW
F/Su • N America • 50 kW
M-Th/Sa • N America • 50 kW
M • N America • 50 kW
Su • N America • 50 kW
M-Sa • N America • 50 kW

**7390** **BELGIUM**
†R VLAANDEREN INTL, Via Pet-K, Russia
E Asia & Australasia • 250 kW • ALT. FREQ. TO 9865 kHz
**RUSSIA**
RADIO ROSSII, Irkutsk
W • E Asia • DS • 100 kW
†VOICE OF RUSSIA, Moscow
W • Europe • 250 kW
S • Europe & W Africa • 250 kW

VOICE OF RUSSIA, Samara
W • C America & S America • 500 kW
†VOICE OF RUSSIA, Vladivostok
S • E Asia • 250 kW
S • E Asia & SE Asia • 500 kW

**UNITED KINGDOM**
BBC, Via Moscow, Russia
W • C Asia • 250 kW
W M-Sa • C Asia • 250 kW

**USA**
VOA, Via Novosibirsk, Russia
W • E Asia • 200 kW
**7395** **GERMANY**
†DEUTSCHE WELLE, Via Armavir, Russia
S • Mideast • 250 kW
**MONACO**
TRANS WORLD R, Via Cerrik, Albania
W • Mideast & W Asia • 100 kW
W M-F • Mideast & W Asia • 100 kW

**7400** **BULGARIA**
†RADIO BULGARIA, Plovdiv
W • E North Am • 500 kW
S • Mideast • 250 kW
M-F • Mideast • 250 kW
Sa/Su • Mideast • 250 kW
W • Europe • 500 kW

(con'd)

0  1  2  3  4  5  6  7  8  9  10  11  12  13  14  15  16  17  18  19  20  21  22  23  24

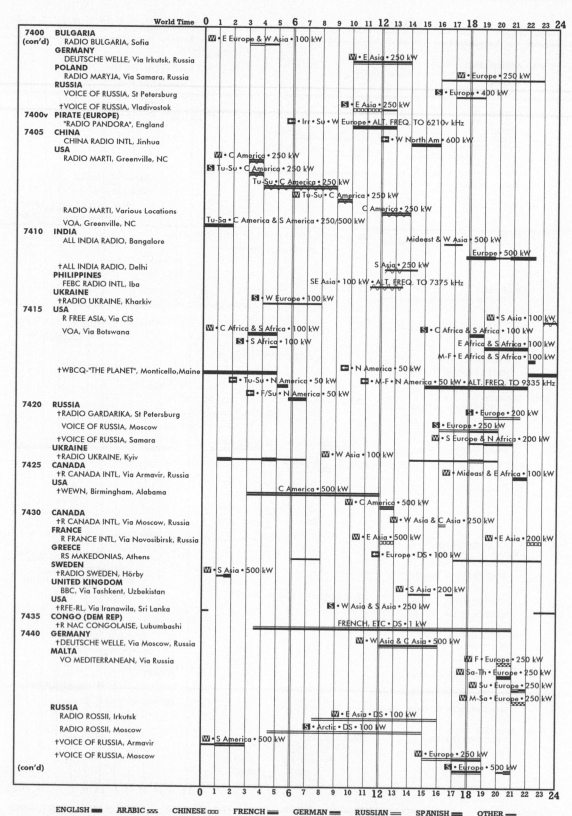

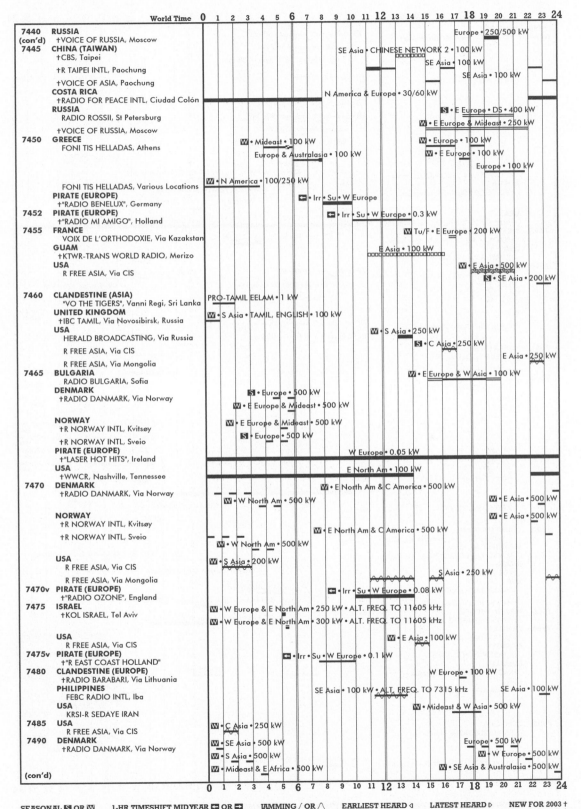

| World Time | 0 1 2 3 4 5 6 7 8 9 10 11 12 13 14 15 16 17 18 19 20 21 22 23 24 |
|---|---|
| **7440** RUSSIA | |
| (con'd) †VOICE OF RUSSIA, Moscow | Europe • 250/500 kW |
| **7445** CHINA (TAIWAN) | SE Asia • CHINESE NETWORK 2 • 100 kW |
| †CBS, Taipei | |
| †R TAIPEI INTL, Paochung | SE Asia • 100 kW |
| †VOICE OF ASIA, Paochung | SE Asia • 100 kW |
| COSTA RICA | |
| †RADIO FOR PEACE INTL, Ciudad Colón | N America & Europe • 30/60 kW |
| RUSSIA | S • E Europe • DS • 400 kW |
| RADIO ROSSII, St Petersburg | W • E Europe & Mideast • 250 kW |
| †VOICE OF RUSSIA, Moscow | |
| **7450** GREECE | W • Mideast • 100 kW    W • Europe • 100 kW |
| FONI TIS HELLADAS, Athens | Europe & Australasia • 100 kW   W • E Europe • 100 kW |
| | Europe • 100 kW |
| FONI TIS HELLADAS, Various Locations | W • N America • 100/250 kW |
| PIRATE (EUROPE) | |
| †"RADIO BENELUX", Germany | ⇦ • Irr • Su • W Europe |
| **7452** PIRATE (EUROPE) | |
| †"RADIO MI AMIGO", Holland | ⇦ • Irr • Su • W Europe • 0.3 kW |
| **7455** FRANCE | W • Tu/F • E Europe • 200 kW |
| VOIX DE L'ORTHODOXIE, Via Kazakstan | |
| GUAM | E Asia • 100 kW |
| †KTWR-TRANS WORLD RADIO, Merizo | |
| USA | W • E Asia • 500 kW |
| R FREE ASIA, Via CIS | S • SE Asia • 200 kW |
| **7460** CLANDESTINE (ASIA) | PRO-TAMIL EELAM • 1 kW |
| "VO THE TIGERS", Vanni Regi, Sri Lanka | |
| UNITED KINGDOM | W • S Asia • TAMIL, ENGLISH • 100 kW |
| †IBC TAMIL, Via Novosibirsk, Russia | |
| USA | W • S Asia • 250 kW |
| HERALD BROADCASTING, Via Russia | S • C Asia • 250 kW |
| R FREE ASIA, Via CIS | E Asia • 250 kW |
| R FREE ASIA, Via Mongolia | |
| **7465** BULGARIA | W • E Europe & W Asia • 100 kW |
| RADIO BULGARIA, Sofia | |
| DENMARK | S • Europe • 500 kW |
| †RADIO DANMARK, Via Norway | W • E Europe & Mideast • 500 kW |
| NORWAY | W • E Europe & Mideast • 500 kW |
| †R NORWAY INTL, Kvitsøy | |
| †R NORWAY INTL, Sveio | S • Europe • 500 kW |
| PIRATE (EUROPE) | W Europe • 0.05 kW |
| †"LASER HOT HITS", Ireland | |
| USA | E North Am • 100 kW |
| †WWCR, Nashville, Tennessee | |
| **7470** DENMARK | W • E North Am & C America • 500 kW |
| †RADIO DANMARK, Via Norway | W • W North Am • 500 kW    W • E Asia • 500 kW |
| NORWAY | W • E Asia • 500 kW |
| †R NORWAY INTL, Kvitsøy | W • E North Am & C America • 500 kW |
| †R NORWAY INTL, Sveio | W • W North Am • 500 kW |
| USA | W • S Asia • 200 kW |
| R FREE ASIA, Via CIS | |
| R FREE ASIA, Via Mongolia | S Asia • 250 kW |
| **7470v** PIRATE (EUROPE) | ⇦ • Irr • Su • W Europe • 0.08 kW |
| †"RADIO OZONE", England | |
| **7475** ISRAEL | W • W Europe & E North Am • 250 kW • ALT. FREQ. TO 11605 kHz |
| †KOL ISRAEL, Tel Aviv | W • W Europe & E North Am • 300 kW • ALT. FREQ. TO 11605 kHz |
| USA | W • E Asia • 100 kW |
| R FREE ASIA, Via CIS | |
| **7475v** PIRATE (EUROPE) | ⇦ • Irr • Su • W Europe • 0.1 kW |
| †"R EAST COAST HOLLAND" | |
| **7480** CLANDESTINE (EUROPE) | W Europe • 100 kW |
| †RADIO BARABARI, Via Lithuania | |
| PHILIPPINES | SE Asia • 100 kW • ALT. FREQ. TO 7315 kHz   SE Asia • 100 kW |
| FEBC RADIO INTL, Iba | |
| USA | W • Mideast & W Asia • 500 kW |
| KRSI-R SEDAYE IRAN | |
| **7485** USA | W • C Asia • 250 kW |
| R FREE ASIA, Via CIS | |
| **7490** DENMARK | W • SE Asia • 500 kW    Europe • 500 kW |
| †RADIO DANMARK, Via Norway | W • S Asia • 500 kW    W • W Europe • 500 kW |
| | W • Mideast & E Africa • 500 kW   W • SE Asia & Australasia • 500 kW |
| (con'd) | 0 1 2 3 4 5 6 7 8 9 10 11 12 13 14 15 16 17 18 19 20 21 22 23 24 |

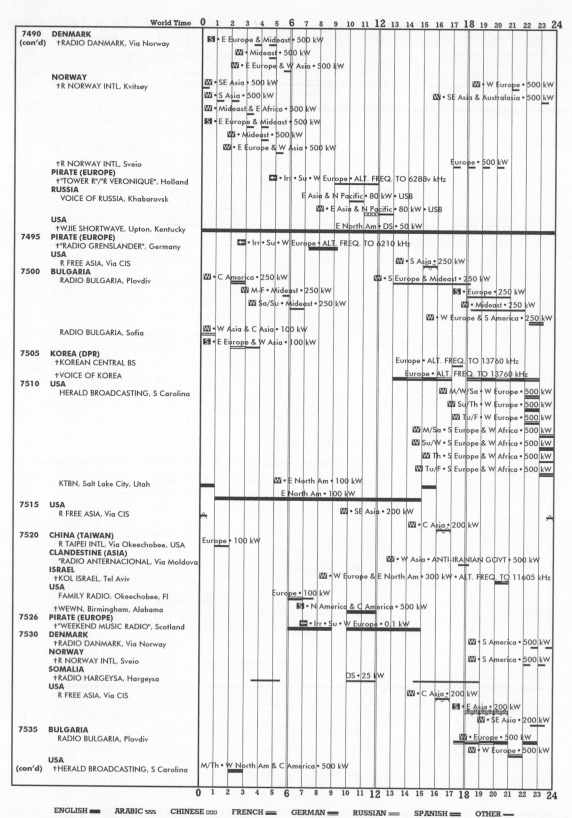

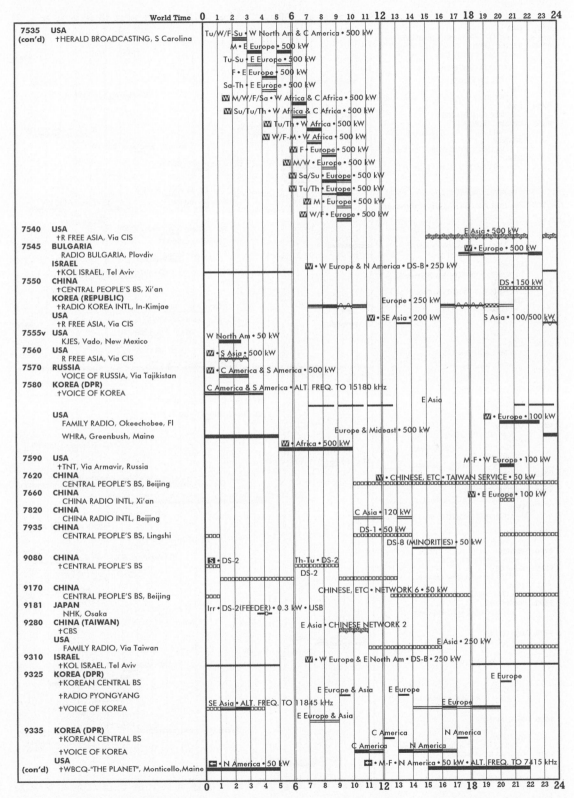

| World Time | Station | Details |
|---|---|---|
| 7535 (con'd) | USA †HERALD BROADCASTING, S Carolina | Tu/W/F-Su • W North Am & C America • 500 kW; M • E Europe • 500 kW; Tu-Su • E Europe • 500 kW; F • E Europe • 500 kW; Sa-Th • E Europe • 500 kW; W M/W/F/Sa • W Africa & C Africa • 500 kW; W Su/Tu/Th • W Africa & C Africa • 500 kW; W Tu/Th • W Africa • 500 kW; W W/F-M • W Africa • 500 kW; W F • Europe • 500 kW; W M/W • Europe • 500 kW; W Sa/Su • Europe • 500 kW; W Tu/Th • Europe • 500 kW; W M • Europe • 500 kW; W W/F • Europe • 500 kW |
| 7540 | USA †R FREE ASIA, Via CIS | E Asia • 500 kW |
| 7545 | BULGARIA RADIO BULGARIA, Plovdiv | W • Europe • 500 kW |
| | ISRAEL †KOL ISRAEL, Tel Aviv | W • W Europe & N America • DS-B • 250 kW |
| 7550 | CHINA †CENTRAL PEOPLE'S BS, Xi'an | DS • 150 kW |
| | KOREA (REPUBLIC) †RADIO KOREA INTL, In-Kimjae | Europe • 250 kW |
| | USA †R FREE ASIA, Via CIS | W • SE Asia • 200 kW; S Asia • 100/500 kW |
| 7555v | USA KJES, Vado, New Mexico | W North Am • 50 kW |
| 7560 | USA R FREE ASIA, Via CIS | W • S Asia • 500 kW |
| 7570 | RUSSIA VOICE OF RUSSIA, Via Tajikistan | W • C America & S America • 500 kW |
| 7580 | KOREA (DPR) †VOICE OF KOREA | C America & S America • ALT. FREQ. TO 15180 kHz; E Asia |
| | USA FAMILY RADIO, Okeechobee, Fl | W • Europe • 100 kW |
| | WHRA, Greenbush, Maine | Europe & Mideast • 500 kW; W • Africa • 500 kW |
| 7590 | USA †TNT, Via Armavir, Russia | M-F • W Europe • 100 kW |
| 7620 | CHINA CENTRAL PEOPLE'S BS, Beijing | W • CHINESE, ETC • TAIWAN SERVICE • 50 kW |
| 7660 | CHINA CHINA RADIO INTL, Xi'an | W • E Europe • 100 kW |
| 7820 | CHINA CHINA RADIO INTL, Beijing | C Asia • 120 kW |
| 7935 | CHINA CENTRAL PEOPLE'S BS, Lingshi | DS-1 • 50 kW; DS-8 (MINORITIES) • 50 kW |
| 9080 | CHINA †CENTRAL PEOPLE'S BS | S • DS-2; Th-Tu • DS-2; DS-2 |
| 9170 | CHINA CENTRAL PEOPLE'S BS, Beijing | CHINESE, ETC • NETWORK 6 • 50 kW |
| 9181 | JAPAN NHK, Osaka | Irr • DS-2(FEEDER) • 0.3 kW • USB |
| 9280 | CHINA (TAIWAN) †CBS | E Asia • CHINESE NETWORK 2 |
| | USA FAMILY RADIO, Via Taiwan | E Asia • 250 kW |
| 9310 | ISRAEL †KOL ISRAEL, Tel Aviv | W • W Europe & E North Am • DS-B • 250 kW |
| 9325 | KOREA (DPR) †KOREAN CENTRAL BS | E Europe |
| | †RADIO PYONGYANG | E Europe & Asia; E Europe; E Europe |
| | †VOICE OF KOREA | SE Asia • ALT. FREQ. TO 11845 kHz; E Europe & Asia |
| 9335 | KOREA (DPR) †KOREAN CENTRAL BS | C America; N America |
| | †VOICE OF KOREA | C America; N America |
| | USA (con'd) †WBCQ-"THE PLANET", Monticello, Maine | N America • 50 kW; M-F • N America • 50 kW • ALT. FREQ. TO 7415 kHz |

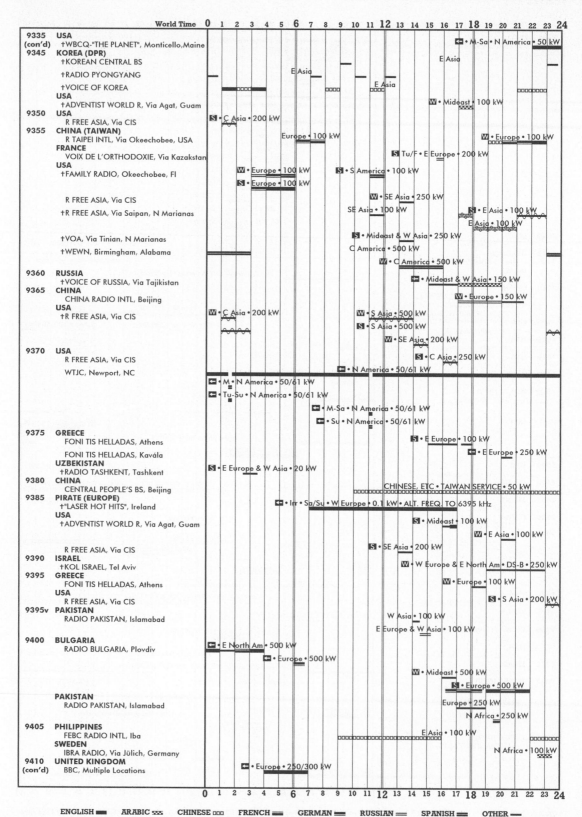

ENGLISH ▬  ARABIC ⋙  CHINESE ▯▯▯  FRENCH ═  GERMAN ▬  RUSSIAN ═  SPANISH ▭  OTHER ─

**World Time** 0 1 2 3 4 5 6 7 8 9 10 11 12 13 14 15 16 17 18 19 20 21 22 23 24

| | |
|---|---|
| **9410** | **UNITED KINGDOM** |
| **(con'd)** | BBC, Skelton, Cumbria |
| | ⇦ • W Europe • 300 kW |
| | W Asia • 250 kW |
| | S • W Europe • 250 kW |
| | BBC, Via Zyyi, Cyprus |
| | W • W Asia • 250 kW |
| | W • N Europe • 250 kW |
| | S • E Europe & Mideast • 250 kW |
| | S • Europe • 250 kW |
| | W • E Europe • 250 kW |
| | W Europe • 250 kW |
| | ⇦ • Su • E Europe & Mideast • 300 kW |
| | ⇦ • M-Th • E Europe • 300 kW |
| | W • Europe • 300 kW |
| | BBC, Woofferton |
| **9415** | **BULGARIA** |
| | RADIO BULGARIA, Plovdiv |
| | W • S America • 250 kW |
| | **CHINA (TAIWAN)** |
| | †R TAIPEI INTL |
| | E Asia |
| | S Asia |
| | **LIBYA** |
| | †RADIO JAMAHIRIYA, Via France |
| | W • W Africa • 500 kW |
| **9420** | **GREECE** |
| | FONI TIS HELLADAS, Athens |
| | N America • 100 kW |
| | W • Mideast • 100 kW |
| | W • Europe • 100 kW |
| | S • Mideast • 100 kW |
| | S • Europe, N America & Australasia • 100 kW |
| | FONI TIS HELLADAS, Kavála |
| | Mideast • 250 kW • ALT. FREQ. TO 9425 kHz |
| | E Europe • 250 kW |
| | E Europe • 250 kW • ALT. FREQ. TO 9425 kHz |
| | **PHILIPPINES** |
| | FEBC RADIO INTL, Iba |
| | E Asia • 50 kW |
| **9425** | **GREECE** |
| | FONI TIS HELLADAS, Athens |
| | S • Europe & Australasia • 100 kW |
| | W • Europe • 100 kW |
| | Mideast • 100 kW |
| | S • C America & Australasia • 100 kW |
| | FONI TIS HELLADAS, Kavála |
| | Mideast • 250 kW • ALT. FREQ. TO 9420 kHz |
| | E Europe • 250 kW • ALT. FREQ. TO 9420 kHz |
| | Australasia • 250 kW |
| | **INDIA** |
| | †ALL INDIA RADIO, Bangalore |
| | ENGLISH, ETC • S Asia • DS • 500 kW |
| **9430** | **CLANDESTINE (ASIA)** |
| | "D'CRATIC VO BURMA", Via Germany |
| | W • SE Asia • ANTI-MYANMAR GOVT • 100 kW |
| | **CZECH REPUBLIC** |
| | RADIO PRAGUE, Litomyšl |
| | W • W Europe • 100 kW |
| | W • SE Asia & Australasia • 100 kW |
| | S • E Europe • 250 kW |
| | †RADIO PRAGUE, Via Slovakia |
| | **FRANCE** |
| | R FRANCE INTL, Issoudun-Allouis |
| | Mideast & W Asia • 500 kW |
| | **GUAM** |
| | †KTWR-TRANS WORLD RADIO, Merizo |
| | SE Asia • 100 kW |
| | E Asia • 100 kW |
| | **INDIA** |
| | †TRANS WORLD R, Via Uzbekistan |
| | S • S Asia • 250 kW |
| | **PAKISTAN** |
| | PAKISTAN BC CORP, Islamabad |
| | DS • 100 kW |
| | **SWEDEN** |
| | †RADIO SWEDEN, Hörby |
| | W • E Asia & Australasia • 500 kW |
| | **USA** |
| | HERALD BROADCASTING, S Carolina |
| | Th • E North Am • 500 kW |
| | Sa-Th • N America • 500 kW |
| | Tu • E North Am • 500 kW |
| | W/F-M • E North Am • 500 kW |
| | N America • 500 kW |
| | F • N America • 500 kW |
| | Sa • N America • 500 kW |
| | Su/M • N America • 500 kW |
| | Th • N America • 500 kW |
| | Tu • N America • 500 kW |
| | W • N America • 500 kW |
| **9435** | **CZECH REPUBLIC** |
| | RADIO PRAGUE, Litomyšl |
| | W • W North Am & C America • 100 kW |
| | W • W Europe & S America • 100 kW |
| | W • W Africa • 100 kW |
| | W • N America • 100 kW |
| | **GERMANY** |
| | RADIO SANTEC, Jülich |
| | Su • S Asia • 100 kW |
| | **INDIA** |
| | †TRANS WORLD R, Via Irkutsk, Russia |
| | S • S Asia • 250 kW |
| | S • Sa • S Asia • 250 kW |
| | S • Su-F • S Asia • 250 kW |
| | S • M/Tu • S Asia • 250 kW |
| **(con'd)** | |

0 1 2 3 4 5 6 7 8 9 10 11 12 13 14 15 16 17 18 19 20 21 22 23 24

SEASONAL S OR W      1-HR TIMESHIFT MIDYEAR ⇦ OR ⇨      JAMMING / OR ⋀      EARLIEST HEARD ◁      LATEST HEARD ▷      NEW FOR 2003 †

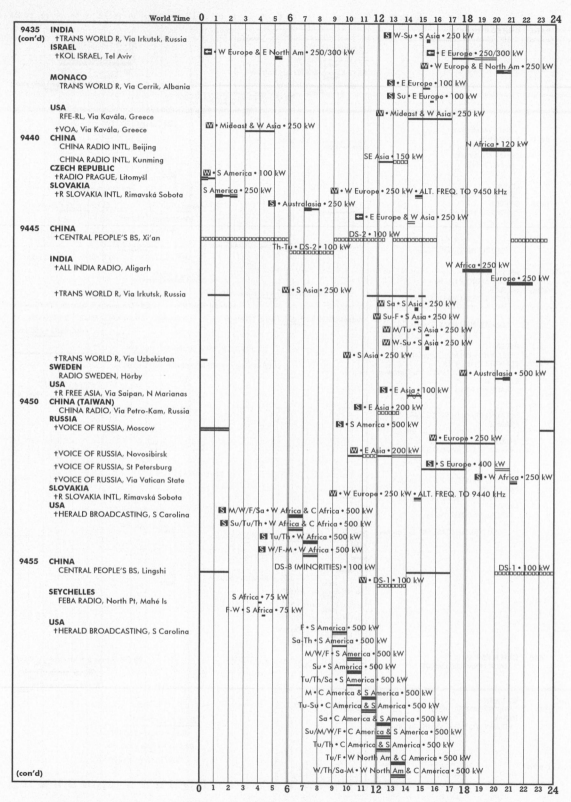

World Time  0  1  2  3  4  5  6  7  8  9  10  11  12  13  14  15  16  17  18  19  20  21  22  23  24

**9435 INDIA**
(con'd) †TRANS WORLD R, Via Irkutsk, Russia
**ISRAEL**
  †KOL ISRAEL, Tel Aviv

**MONACO**
  TRANS WORLD R, Via Cerrik, Albania

**USA**
  RFE-RL, Via Kavála, Greece
  †VOA, Via Kavála, Greece
**9440 CHINA**
  CHINA RADIO INTL, Beijing
  CHINA RADIO INTL, Kunming
**CZECH REPUBLIC**
  †RADIO PRAGUE, Litomyšl
**SLOVAKIA**
  †R SLOVAKIA INTL, Rimavská Sobota

**9445 CHINA**
  †CENTRAL PEOPLE'S BS, Xi'an

**INDIA**
  †ALL INDIA RADIO, Aligarh

  †TRANS WORLD R, Via Irkutsk, Russia

  †TRANS WORLD R, Via Uzbekistan
**SWEDEN**
  RADIO SWEDEN, Hörby
**USA**
  †R FREE ASIA, Via Saipan, N Marianas
**9450 CHINA (TAIWAN)**
  CHINA RADIO, Via Petro-Kam, Russia
**RUSSIA**
  †VOICE OF RUSSIA, Moscow

  †VOICE OF RUSSIA, Novosibirsk
  †VOICE OF RUSSIA, St Petersburg
  †VOICE OF RUSSIA, Via Vatican State
**SLOVAKIA**
  †R SLOVAKIA INTL, Rimavská Sobota
**USA**
  †HERALD BROADCASTING, S Carolina

**9455 CHINA**
  CENTRAL PEOPLE'S BS, Lingshi

**SEYCHELLES**
  FEBA RADIO, North Pt, Mahé Is

**USA**
  †HERALD BROADCASTING, S Carolina

(con'd)

0  1  2  3  4  5  6  7  8  9  10  11  12  13  14  15  16  17  18  19  20  21  22  23  24

ENGLISH ▬   ARABIC ▨   CHINESE ▫▫▫   FRENCH ═   GERMAN ▭   RUSSIAN ═   SPANISH ─   OTHER ▬

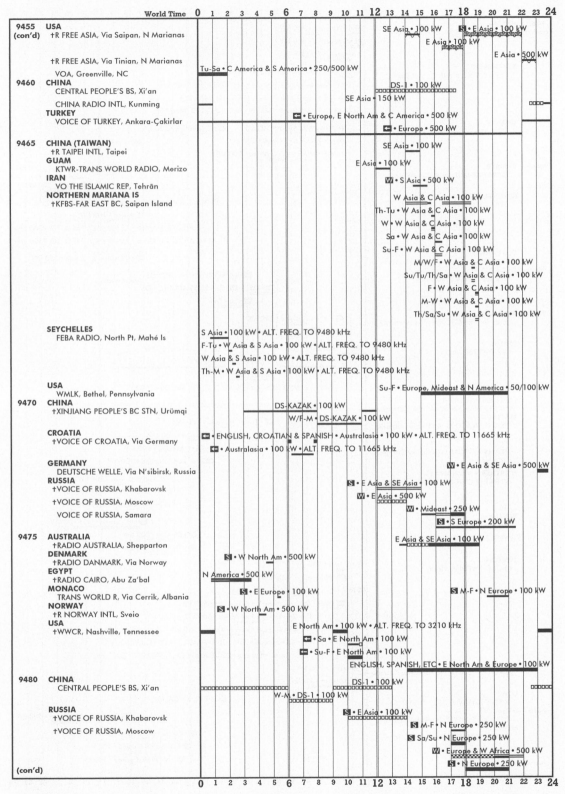

| World Time | 0 | 1 | 2 | 3 | 4 | 5 | 6 | 7 | 8 | 9 | 10 | 11 | 12 | 13 | 14 | 15 | 16 | 17 | 18 | 19 | 20 | 21 | 22 | 23 | 24 |

**9455 USA**
(con'd)  †R FREE ASIA, Via Saipan, N Marianas — SE Asia • 100 kW; S • E Asia • 100 kW; E Asia • 100 kW; E Asia • 500 kW

†R FREE ASIA, Via Tinian, N Marianas

VOA, Greenville, NC — Tu-Sa • C America & S America • 250/500 kW

**9460 CHINA**
CENTRAL PEOPLE'S BS, Xi'an — DS-1 • 100 kW
CHINA RADIO INTL, Kunming — SE Asia • 150 kW

**TURKEY**
VOICE OF TURKEY, Ankara-Çakirlar — ◄ • Europe, E North Am & C America • 500 kW; ◄ • Europe • 500 kW

**9465 CHINA (TAIWAN)**
†R TAIPEI INTL, Taipei — SE Asia • 100 kW
**GUAM**
KTWR-TRANS WORLD RADIO, Merizo — E Asia • 100 kW
**IRAN**
VO THE ISLAMIC REP, Tehrān — W • S Asia • 500 kW
**NORTHERN MARIANA IS**
†KFBS-FAR EAST BC, Saipan Island — W Asia & C Asia • 100 kW

Th-Tu • W Asia & C Asia • 100 kW
W • W Asia & C Asia • 100 kW
Sa • W Asia & C Asia • 100 kW
Su-F • W Asia & C Asia • 100 kW
M/W/F • W Asia & C Asia • 100 kW
Su/Tu/Th/Sa • W Asia & C Asia • 100 kW
F • W Asia & C Asia • 100 kW
M-W • W Asia & C Asia • 100 kW
Th/Sa/Su • W Asia & C Asia • 100 kW

**SEYCHELLES**
FEBA RADIO, North Pt, Mahé Is — S Asia • 100 kW • ALT. FREQ. TO 9480 kHz
F-Tu • W Asia & S Asia • 100 kW • ALT. FREQ. TO 9480 kHz
W Asia & S Asia • 100 kW • ALT. FREQ. TO 9480 kHz
Th-M • W Asia & S Asia • 100 kW • ALT. FREQ. TO 9480 kHz

**USA**
WMLK, Bethel, Pennsylvania — Su-F • Europe, Mideast & N America • 50/100 kW

**9470 CHINA**
†XINJIANG PEOPLE'S BC STN, Urümqi — DS-KAZAK • 100 kW; W/F-M • DS-KAZAK • 100 kW

**CROATIA**
†VOICE OF CROATIA, Via Germany — ◄ • ENGLISH, CROATIAN & SPANISH • Australasia • 100 kW • ALT. FREQ. TO 11665 kHz
◄ • Australasia • 100 kW • ALT. FREQ. TO 11665 kHz

**GERMANY**
DEUTSCHE WELLE, Via N'sibirsk, Russia — W • E Asia & SE Asia • 500 kW
**RUSSIA**
†VOICE OF RUSSIA, Khabarovsk — S • E Asia & SE Asia • 100 kW
†VOICE OF RUSSIA, Moscow — W • E Asia • 500 kW
VOICE OF RUSSIA, Samara — W • Mideast • 250 kW; S • S Europe • 200 kW

**9475 AUSTRALIA**
†RADIO AUSTRALIA, Shepparton — E Asia & SE Asia • 100 kW
**DENMARK**
†RADIO DANMARK, Via Norway — S • W North Am • 500 kW
**EGYPT**
†RADIO CAIRO, Abu Za'bal — N America • 500 kW
**MONACO**
TRANS WORLD R, Via Cerrik, Albania — S • E Europe • 100 kW; S M-F • N Europe • 100 kW
**NORWAY**
†R NORWAY INTL, Sveio — S • W North Am • 500 kW
**USA**
†WWCR, Nashville, Tennessee — E North Am • 100 kW • ALT. FREQ. TO 3210 kHz
◄ • Sa • E North Am • 100 kW
◄ • Su-F • E North Am • 100 kW
ENGLISH, SPANISH, ETC • E North Am & Europe • 100 kW

**9480 CHINA**
CENTRAL PEOPLE'S BS, Xi'an — DS-1 • 100 kW; W-M • DS-1 • 100 kW

**RUSSIA**
†VOICE OF RUSSIA, Khabarovsk — S • E Asia • 100 kW
†VOICE OF RUSSIA, Moscow — S M-F • N Europe • 250 kW; S Sa/Su • N Europe • 250 kW; W • Europe & W Africa • 500 kW; S • N Europe • 250 kW

(con'd)

| World Time | 0 | 1 | 2 | 3 | 4 | 5 | 6 | 7 | 8 | 9 | 10 | 11 | 12 | 13 | 14 | 15 | 16 | 17 | 18 | 19 | 20 | 21 | 22 | 23 | 24 |

SEASONAL Ⓢ OR Ⓦ     1-HR TIMESHIFT MIDYEAR ⇐ OR ⇒     JAMMING / OR ∧     EARLIEST HEARD ◁     LATEST HEARD ▷     NEW FOR 2003 †

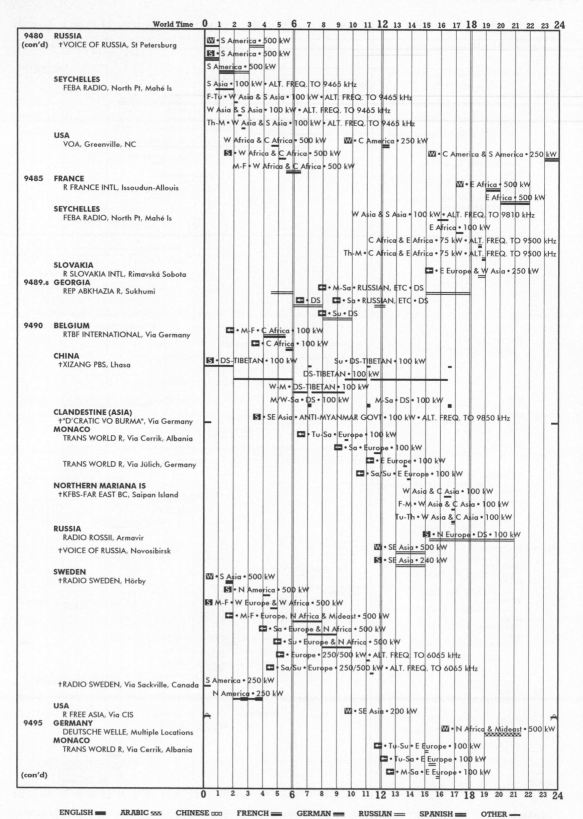

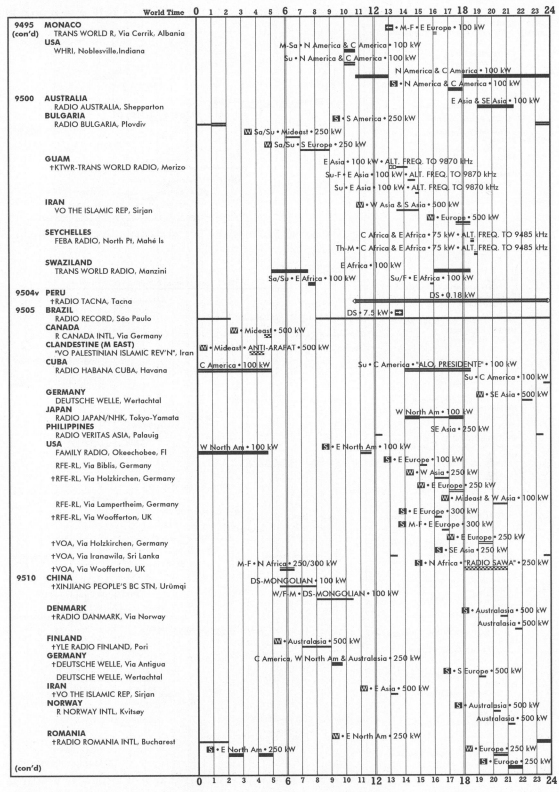

World Time

| 9495 (con'd) | MONACO TRANS WORLD R, Via Cerrik, Albania | ▭⊡ • M-F • E Europe • 100 kW |
| | USA WHRI, Noblesville, Indiana | M-Sa • N America & C America • 100 kW |
| | | Su • N America & C America • 100 kW |
| | | N America & C America • 100 kW |
| | | 𝕊 • N America & C America • 100 kW |
| 9500 | AUSTRALIA RADIO AUSTRALIA, Shepparton | E Asia & SE Asia • 100 kW |
| | BULGARIA RADIO BULGARIA, Plovdiv | 𝕊 • S America • 250 kW |
| | | 𝕎 Sa/Su • Mideast • 250 kW |
| | | 𝕎 Sa/Su • S Europe • 250 kW |
| | GUAM †KTWR-TRANS WORLD RADIO, Merizo | E Asia • 100 kW • ALT. FREQ. TO 9870 kHz |
| | | Su-F • E Asia • 100 kW • ALT. FREQ. TO 9870 kHz |
| | | Su • E Asia • 100 kW • ALT. FREQ. TO 9870 kHz |
| | IRAN VO THE ISLAMIC REP, Sirjan | 𝕎 • W Asia & S Asia • 500 kW |
| | | 𝕎 • Europe • 500 kW |
| | SEYCHELLES FEBA RADIO, North Pt, Mahé Is | C Africa & E Africa • 75 kW • ALT. FREQ. TO 9485 kHz |
| | | Th-M • C Africa & E Africa • 75 kW • ALT. FREQ. TO 9485 kHz |
| | SWAZILAND TRANS WORLD RADIO, Manzini | E Africa • 100 kW |
| | | Sa/Su • E Africa • 100 kW   Su/F • E Africa • 100 kW |
| 9504v | PERU †RADIO TACNA, Tacna | DS • 0.18 kW |
| 9505 | BRAZIL RADIO RECORD, São Paulo | DS • 7.5 kW • ▭⊡ |
| | CANADA R CANADA INTL, Via Germany | 𝕎 • Mideast • 500 kW |
| | CLANDESTINE (M EAST) "VO PALESTINIAN ISLAMIC REV'N", Iran | 𝕎 • Mideast • ANTI-ARAFAT • 500 kW |
| | CUBA RADIO HABANA CUBA, Havana | C America • 100 kW   Su • C America • "ALO, PRESIDENTE" • 100 kW |
| | | Su • C America • 100 kW |
| | GERMANY DEUTSCHE WELLE, Wertachtal | 𝕎 • SE Asia • 500 kW |
| | JAPAN RADIO JAPAN/NHK, Tokyo-Yamata | W North Am • 100 kW |
| | PHILIPPINES RADIO VERITAS ASIA, Palauig | SE Asia • 250 kW |
| | USA FAMILY RADIO, Okeechobee, Fl | W North Am • 100 kW   𝕊 • E North Am • 100 kW |
| | RFE-RL, Via Biblis, Germany | 𝕊 • E Europe • 100 kW |
| | †RFE-RL, Via Holzkirchen, Germany | 𝕎 • W Asia • 250 kW |
| | | 𝕎 • E Europe • 250 kW |
| | RFE-RL, Via Lampertheim, Germany | 𝕎 • Mideast & W Asia • 100 kW |
| | †RFE-RL, Via Woofferton, UK | 𝕊 • E Europe • 300 kW |
| | | 𝕊 M-F • E Europe • 300 kW |
| | †VOA, Via Holzkirchen, Germany | 𝕎 • E Europe • 250 kW |
| | †VOA, Via Iranawila, Sri Lanka | 𝕊 • SE Asia • 250 kW |
| | †VOA, Via Woofferton, UK | 𝕊 • N Africa • "RADIO SAWA" • 250 kW |
| | | M-F • N Africa • 250/300 kW |
| 9510 | CHINA †XINJIANG PEOPLE'S BC STN, Urümqi | DS-MONGOLIAN • 100 kW |
| | | W/F-M • DS-MONGOLIAN • 100 kW |
| | DENMARK †RADIO DANMARK, Via Norway | 𝕊 • Australasia • 500 kW |
| | | Australasia • 500 kW |
| | FINLAND †YLE RADIO FINLAND, Pori | 𝕎 • Australasia • 500 kW |
| | GERMANY †DEUTSCHE WELLE, Via Antigua | C America, W North Am & Australasia • 250 kW |
| | DEUTSCHE WELLE, Wertachtal | 𝕊 • S Europe • 500 kW |
| | IRAN †VO THE ISLAMIC REP, Sirjan | 𝕎 • E Asia • 500 kW |
| | NORWAY R NORWAY INTL, Kvitsøy | 𝕊 • Australasia • 500 kW |
| | | Australasia • 500 kW |
| | ROMANIA †RADIO ROMANIA INTL, Bucharest | 𝕎 • E North Am • 250 kW |
| | | 𝕊 • E North Am • 250 kW   𝕎 • Europe • 250 kW |
| | | 𝕊 • Europe • 250 kW |

(con'd)

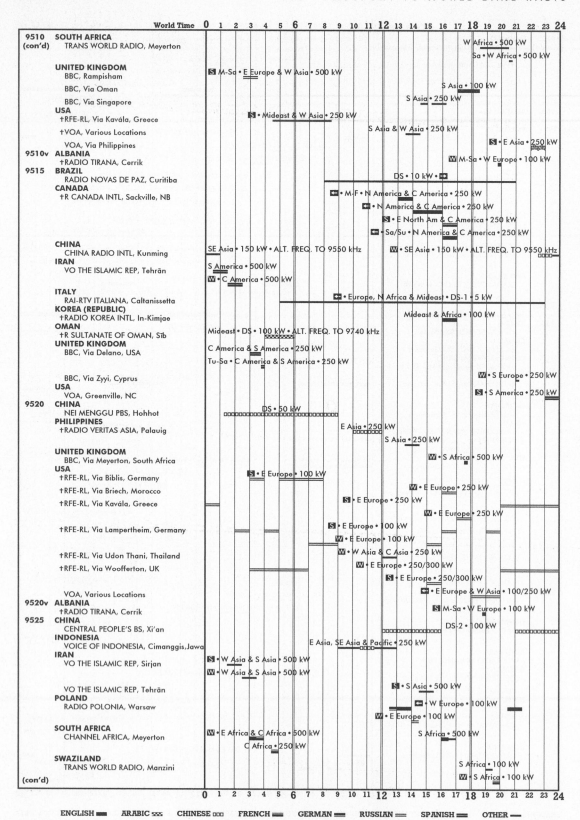

World Time  0  1  2  3  4  5  6  7  8  9  10  11  12  13  14  15  16  17  18  19  20  21  22  23  24

**9510 SOUTH AFRICA**
(con'd)    TRANS WORLD RADIO, Meyerton

**UNITED KINGDOM**
BBC, Rampisham
BBC, Via Oman
BBC, Via Singapore
**USA**
†RFE-RL, Via Kavála, Greece
†VOA, Various Locations
VOA, Via Philippines
**9510v ALBANIA**
†RADIO TIRANA, Cerrik
**9515 BRAZIL**
RADIO NOVAS DE PAZ, Curitiba
**CANADA**
†R CANADA INTL, Sackville, NB

**CHINA**
CHINA RADIO INTL, Kunming
**IRAN**
VO THE ISLAMIC REP, Tehrän

**ITALY**
RAI-RTV ITALIANA, Caltanissetta
**KOREA (REPUBLIC)**
†RADIO KOREA INTL, In-Kimjae
**OMAN**
†R SULTANATE OF OMAN, Sïb
**UNITED KINGDOM**
BBC, Via Delano, USA

BBC, Via Zyyi, Cyprus
**USA**
VOA, Greenville, NC
**9520 CHINA**
NEI MENGGU PBS, Hohhot
**PHILIPPINES**
†RADIO VERITAS ASIA, Palauig

**UNITED KINGDOM**
BBC, Via Meyerton, South Africa
**USA**
†RFE-RL, Via Biblis, Germany
†RFE-RL, Via Briech, Morocco

†RFE-RL, Via Kavála, Greece

†RFE-RL, Via Lampertheim, Germany

†RFE-RL, Via Udon Thani, Thailand
†RFE-RL, Via Woofferton, UK

VOA, Various Locations
**9520v ALBANIA**
†RADIO TIRANA, Cerrik
**9525 CHINA**
CENTRAL PEOPLE'S BS, Xi'an
**INDONESIA**
VOICE OF INDONESIA, Cimanggis,Jawa
**IRAN**
VO THE ISLAMIC REP, Sirjan

VO THE ISLAMIC REP, Tehrän
**POLAND**
RADIO POLONIA, Warsaw

**SOUTH AFRICA**
CHANNEL AFRICA, Meyerton

**SWAZILAND**
TRANS WORLD RADIO, Manzini
(con'd)

W Africa • 500 kW
Sa • W Africa • 500 kW

S M-Sa • E Europe & W Asia • 500 kW
S Asia • 100 kW
S Asia • 250 kW
S • Mideast & W Asia • 250 kW
S Asia & W Asia • 250 kW
S • E Asia • 250 kW
W M-Sa • W Europe • 100 kW
DS • 10 kW •
• M-F • N America & C America • 250 kW
• N America & C America • 250 kW
S • E North Am & C America • 250 kW
• Sa/Su • N America & C America • 250 kW
SE Asia • 150 kW • ALT. FREQ. TO 9550 kHz    W • SE Asia • 150 kW • ALT. FREQ. TO 9550 kHz
S America • 500 kW
W • C America • 500 kW
• Europe, N Africa & Mideast • DS-1 • 5 kW
Mideast & Africa • 100 kW
Mideast • DS • 100 kW • ALT. FREQ. TO 9740 kHz
C America & S America • 250 kW
Tu-Sa • C America & S America • 250 kW
W • S Europe • 250 kW
S • S America • 250 kW
DS • 50 kW
E Asia • 250 kW
S Asia • 250 kW
W • S Africa • 500 kW
S • E Europe • 100 kW
W • E Europe • 250 kW
S • E Europe • 250 kW
W • E Europe • 250 kW
S • E Europe • 100 kW
W • E Europe • 100 kW
W • W Asia & C Asia • 250 kW
W • E Europe • 250/300 kW
S • E Europe • 250/300 kW
• E Europe & W Asia • 100/250 kW
S M-Sa • W Europe • 100 kW
DS-2 • 100 kW
E Asia, SE Asia & Pacific • 250 kW
S • W Asia & S Asia • 500 kW
W • W Asia & S Asia • 500 kW
S • S Asia • 500 kW
• W Europe • 100 kW
W • E Europe • 100 kW
W • E Africa & C Africa • 500 kW
S Africa • 500 kW
C Africa • 250 kW
S Africa • 100 kW
W • S Africa • 100 kW

0  1  2  3  4  5  6  7  8  9  10  11  12  13  14  15  16  17  18  19  20  21  22  23  24

ENGLISH ▬  ARABIC ∿∿  CHINESE □□□  FRENCH ▬  GERMAN ▬  RUSSIAN ═  SPANISH ▬  OTHER ▬

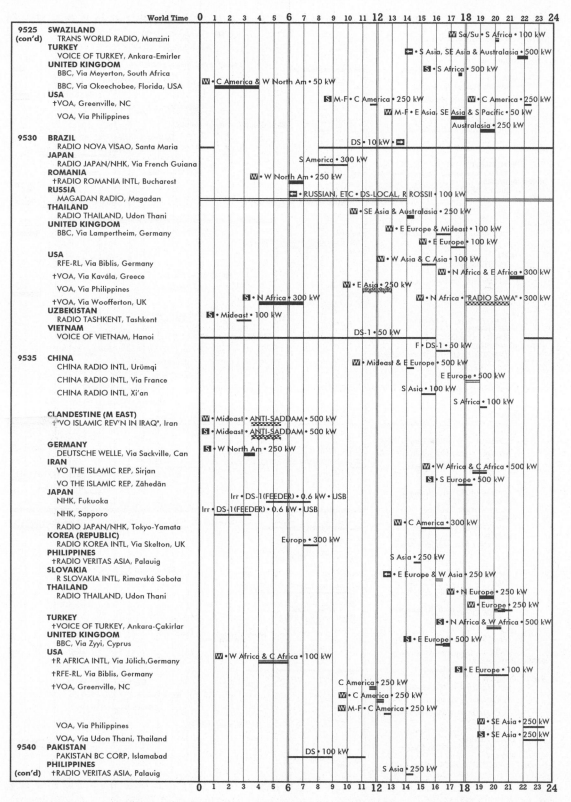

World Time 0 1 2 3 4 5 6 7 8 9 10 11 12 13 14 15 16 17 18 19 20 21 22 23 24

**9525**
**(con'd)** SWAZILAND
    TRANS WORLD RADIO, Manzini — W Sa/Su • S Africa • 100 kW
    TURKEY
      VOICE OF TURKEY, Ankara-Emirler — ⬌ S Asia, SE Asia & Australasia • 500 kW
    UNITED KINGDOM
      BBC, Via Meyerton, South Africa — S • S Africa • 500 kW
      BBC, Via Okeechobee, Florida, USA — W • C America & W North Am • 50 kW
    USA
      †VOA, Greenville, NC — S M-F • C America • 250 kW | W • C America • 250 kW
      VOA, Via Philippines — W M-F • E Asia, SE Asia & S Pacific • 50 kW | Australasia • 250 kW

**9530** BRAZIL
    RADIO NOVA VISAO, Santa Maria — DS • 10 kW • ➡
    JAPAN
      RADIO JAPAN/NHK, Via French Guiana — S America • 300 kW
    ROMANIA
      †RADIO ROMANIA INTL, Bucharest — W • W North Am • 250 kW
    RUSSIA
      MAGADAN RADIO, Magadan — ⬌ • RUSSIAN, ETC • DS-LOCAL, R ROSSII • 100 kW
    THAILAND
      RADIO THAILAND, Udon Thani — W • SE Asia & Australasia • 250 kW
    UNITED KINGDOM
      BBC, Via Lampertheim, Germany — W • E Europe & Mideast • 100 kW | W • E Europe • 100 kW
    USA
      RFE-RL, Via Biblis, Germany — W • W Asia & C Asia • 100 kW | W • N Africa & E Africa • 300 kW
      †VOA, Via Kavála, Greece — W • E Asia • 250 kW
      VOA, Via Philippines — S • N Africa • 300 kW | W • N Africa • "RADIO SAWA" • 300 kW
      †VOA, Via Woofferton, UK
    UZBEKISTAN
      RADIO TASHKENT, Tashkent — S • Mideast • 100 kW
    VIETNAM
      VOICE OF VIETNAM, Hanoi — DS-1 • 50 kW | F • DS-1 • 50 kW

**9535** CHINA
    CHINA RADIO INTL, Urümqi — W • Mideast & E Europe • 500 kW
    CHINA RADIO INTL, Via France — E Europe • 500 kW
    CHINA RADIO INTL, Xi'an — S Asia • 100 kW | S Africa • 100 kW
    CLANDESTINE (M EAST)
      †"VO ISLAMIC REV'N IN IRAQ", Iran — W • Mideast • ANTI-SADDAM • 500 kW | S • Mideast • ANTI-SADDAM • 500 kW
    GERMANY
      DEUTSCHE WELLE, Via Sackville, Can — S • W North Am • 250 kW
    IRAN
      VO THE ISLAMIC REP, Sirjan — W • W Africa & C Africa • 500 kW
      VO THE ISLAMIC REP, Zāhedān — S • S Europe • 500 kW
    JAPAN
      NHK, Fukuoka — Irr • DS-1(FEEDER) • 0.6 kW • USB
      NHK, Sapporo — Irr • DS-1 (FEEDER) • 0.6 kW • USB
      RADIO JAPAN/NHK, Tokyo-Yamata — W • C America • 300 kW
    KOREA (REPUBLIC)
      RADIO KOREA INTL, Via Skelton, UK — Europe • 300 kW
    PHILIPPINES
      †RADIO VERITAS ASIA, Palauig — S Asia • 250 kW
    SLOVAKIA
      R SLOVAKIA INTL, Rimavská Sobota — ⬌ • E Europe & W Asia • 250 kW
    THAILAND
      RADIO THAILAND, Udon Thani — W • N Europe • 250 kW | W • Europe • 250 kW
    TURKEY
      †VOICE OF TURKEY, Ankara-Çakirlar — S • N Africa & W Africa • 500 kW
    UNITED KINGDOM
      BBC, Via Zyyi, Cyprus — S • E Europe • 500 kW
    USA
      †R AFRICA INTL, Via Jülich, Germany — W • W Africa & C Africa • 100 kW
      †RFE-RL, Via Biblis, Germany — S • E Europe • 100 kW
      †VOA, Greenville, NC — C America • 250 kW | W • C America • 250 kW | W M-F • C America • 250 kW
      VOA, Via Philippines — W • SE Asia • 250 kW | S • SE Asia • 250 kW

**9540** PAKISTAN
    PAKISTAN BC CORP, Islamabad — DS • 100 kW
    PHILIPPINES
**(con'd)** †RADIO VERITAS ASIA, Palauig — S Asia • 250 kW

0 1 2 3 4 5 6 7 8 9 10 11 12 13 14 15 16 17 18 19 20 21 22 23 24

SEASONAL S OR W    1-HR TIMESHIFT MIDYEAR ⬌ OR ➡    JAMMING / OR ∧    EARLIEST HEARD ◁    LATEST HEARD ▷    NEW FOR 2003 †

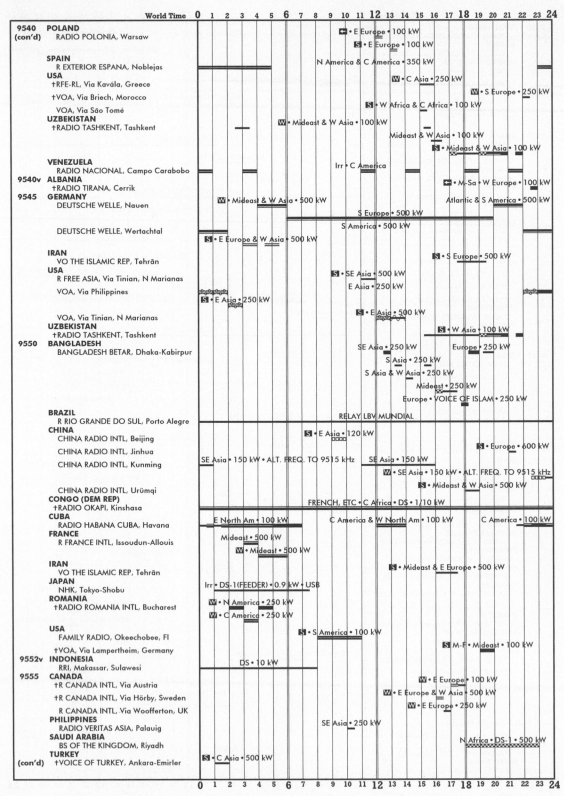

| | | |
|---|---|---|
| **9540** | **POLAND** | |
| (con'd) | RADIO POLONIA, Warsaw | ⊡ • E Europe • 100 kW |
| | | S • E Europe • 100 kW |
| | **SPAIN** | |
| | R EXTERIOR ESPANA, Noblejas | N America & C America • 350 kW |
| | **USA** | |
| | †RFE-RL, Via Kavála, Greece | W • C Asia • 250 kW |
| | †VOA, Via Briech, Morocco | W • S Europe • 250 kW |
| | VOA, Via São Tomé | S • W Africa & C Africa • 100 kW |
| | **UZBEKISTAN** | |
| | †RADIO TASHKENT, Tashkent | W • Mideast & W Asia • 100 kW |
| | | Mideast & W Asia • 100 kW |
| | | S • Mideast & W Asia • 100 kW |
| | **VENEZUELA** | |
| | RADIO NACIONAL, Campo Carabobo | Irr • C America |
| **9540v** | **ALBANIA** | |
| | †RADIO TIRANA, Cerrik | ⊡ • M-Sa • W Europe • 100 kW |
| **9545** | **GERMANY** | |
| | DEUTSCHE WELLE, Nauen | W • Mideast & W Asia • 500 kW |
| | | Atlantic & S America • 500 kW |
| | | S Europe • 500 kW |
| | DEUTSCHE WELLE, Wertachtal | S America • 500 kW |
| | | S • E Europe & W Asia • 500 kW |
| | **IRAN** | |
| | VO THE ISLAMIC REP, Tehrān | S • S Europe • 500 kW |
| | **USA** | |
| | R FREE ASIA, Via Tinian, N Marianas | S • SE Asia • 500 kW |
| | VOA, Via Philippines | E Asia • 250 kW |
| | | S • E Asia • 250 kW |
| | VOA, Via Tinian, N Marianas | S • E Asia • 500 kW |
| | **UZBEKISTAN** | |
| | †RADIO TASHKENT, Tashkent | S • W Asia • 100 kW |
| **9550** | **BANGLADESH** | |
| | BANGLADESH BETAR, Dhaka-Kabirpur | SE Asia • 250 kW |
| | | Europe • 250 kW |
| | | S Asia • 250 kW |
| | | S Asia & W Asia • 250 kW |
| | | Mideast • 250 kW |
| | | Europe • VOICE OF ISLAM • 250 kW |
| | **BRAZIL** | |
| | R RIO GRANDE DO SUL, Porto Alegre | RELAY LBV MUNDIAL |
| | **CHINA** | |
| | CHINA RADIO INTL, Beijing | S • E Asia • 120 kW |
| | CHINA RADIO INTL, Jinhua | S • Europe • 600 kW |
| | CHINA RADIO INTL, Kunming | SE Asia • 150 kW • ALT. FREQ. TO 9515 kHz |
| | | SE Asia • 150 kW |
| | | W • SE Asia • 150 kW • ALT. FREQ. TO 9515 kHz |
| | CHINA RADIO INTL, Urümqi | S • Mideast & W Asia • 500 kW |
| | **CONGO (DEM REP)** | |
| | †RADIO OKAPI, Kinshasa | FRENCH, ETC • C Africa • DS • 1/10 kW |
| | **CUBA** | |
| | RADIO HABANA CUBA, Havana | E North Am • 100 kW |
| | | C America & W North Am • 100 kW |
| | | C America • 100 kW |
| | **FRANCE** | |
| | R FRANCE INTL, Issoudun-Allouis | Mideast • 500 kW |
| | | W • Mideast • 500 kW |
| | **IRAN** | |
| | VO THE ISLAMIC REP, Tehrān | S • Mideast & E Europe • 500 kW |
| | **JAPAN** | |
| | NHK, Tokyo-Shobu | Irr • DS-1(FEEDER) • 0.9 kW • USB |
| | **ROMANIA** | |
| | †RADIO ROMANIA INTL, Bucharest | W • N America • 250 kW |
| | | W • C America • 250 kW |
| | **USA** | |
| | FAMILY RADIO, Okeechobee, Fl | S • S America • 100 kW |
| | †VOA, Via Lampertheim, Germany | S • M-F • Mideast • 100 kW |
| **9552v** | **INDONESIA** | |
| | RRI, Makassar, Sulawesi | DS • 10 kW |
| **9555** | **CANADA** | |
| | †R CANADA INTL, Via Austria | W • E Europe • 100 kW |
| | †R CANADA INTL, Via Hörby, Sweden | W • E Europe & W Asia • 500 kW |
| | R CANADA INTL, Via Woofferton, UK | W • E Europe • 250 kW |
| | **PHILIPPINES** | |
| | RADIO VERITAS ASIA, Palauig | SE Asia • 250 kW |
| | **SAUDI ARABIA** | |
| | BS OF THE KINGDOM, Riyadh | N Africa • DS-1 • 500 kW |
| | **TURKEY** | |
| (con'd) | †VOICE OF TURKEY, Ankara-Emirler | S • C Asia • 500 kW |

ENGLISH ▬  ARABIC ⋙  CHINESE ⸱⸱⸱  FRENCH ═  GERMAN ▬  RUSSIAN ═  SPANISH ▬  OTHER ─

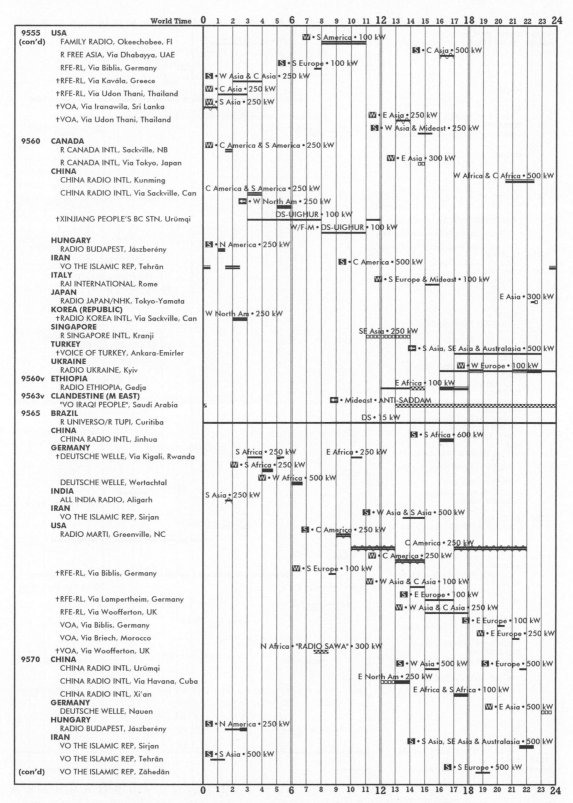

| | World Time | 0 | 1 | 2 | 3 | 4 | 5 | 6 | 7 | 8 | 9 | 10 | 11 | 12 | 13 | 14 | 15 | 16 | 17 | 18 | 19 | 20 | 21 | 22 | 23 | 24 |

**9555 USA**
**(con'd)**
    FAMILY RADIO, Okeechobee, Fl — W • S America • 100 kW
    R FREE ASIA, Via Dhabayya, UAE — S • C Asia • 500 kW
    RFE-RL, Via Biblis, Germany — S • S Europe • 100 kW
    †RFE-RL, Via Kavála, Greece — S • W Asia & C Asia • 250 kW
    †RFE-RL, Via Udon Thani, Thailand — W • C Asia • 250 kW
    †VOA, Via Iranawila, Sri Lanka — W • S Asia • 250 kW
    †VOA, Via Udon Thani, Thailand — W • E Asia • 250 kW
                        S • W Asia & Mideast • 250 kW

**9560 CANADA**
    R CANADA INTL, Sackville, NB — W • C America & S America • 250 kW
    R CANADA INTL, Via Tokyo, Japan — W • E Asia • 300 kW
**CHINA**
    CHINA RADIO INTL, Kunming — W Africa & C Africa • 500 kW
    CHINA RADIO INTL, Via Sackville, Can — C America & S America • 250 kW
                  • W North Am • 250 kW
    †XINJIANG PEOPLE'S BC STN, Urümqi — DS-UIGHUR • 100 kW
                W/F-M • DS-UIGHUR • 100 kW
**HUNGARY**
    RADIO BUDAPEST, Jászberény — S • N America • 250 kW
**IRAN**
    VO THE ISLAMIC REP, Tehrān — S • C America • 500 kW
**ITALY**
    RAI INTERNATIONAL, Rome — W • S Europe & Mideast • 100 kW
**JAPAN**
    RADIO JAPAN/NHK, Tokyo-Yamata — E Asia • 300 kW
**KOREA (REPUBLIC)**
    †RADIO KOREA INTL, Via Sackville, Can — W North Am • 250 kW
**SINGAPORE**
    R SINGAPORE INTL, Kranji — SE Asia • 250 kW
**TURKEY**
    †VOICE OF TURKEY, Ankara-Emirler — • S Asia, SE Asia & Australasia • 500 kW
**UKRAINE**
    RADIO UKRAINE, Kyiv — W • W Europe • 100 kW
**9560v ETHIOPIA**
    RADIO ETHIOPIA, Gedja — E Africa • 100 kW
**9563v CLANDESTINE (M EAST)**
    "VO IRAQI PEOPLE", Saudi Arabia — • Mideast • ANTI-SADDAM
**9565 BRAZIL**
    R UNIVERSO/R TUPI, Curitiba — DS • 15 kW
**CHINA**
    CHINA RADIO INTL, Jinhua — S • S Africa • 600 kW
**GERMANY**
    †DEUTSCHE WELLE, Via Kigali, Rwanda — S Africa • 250 kW   E Africa • 250 kW
         W • S Africa • 250 kW
    DEUTSCHE WELLE, Wertachtal — W • W Africa • 500 kW
**INDIA**
    ALL INDIA RADIO, Aligarh — S Asia • 250 kW
**IRAN**
    VO THE ISLAMIC REP, Sirjan — S • W Asia & S Asia • 500 kW
**USA**
    RADIO MARTI, Greenville, NC — S • C America • 250 kW
                     C America • 250 kW
                     W • C America • 250 kW
    †RFE-RL, Via Biblis, Germany — W • S Europe • 100 kW
                     W • W Asia & C Asia • 100 kW
    †RFE-RL, Via Lampertheim, Germany — S • E Europe • 100 kW
    RFE-RL, Via Woofferton, UK — W • W Asia & C Asia • 250 kW
    VOA, Via Biblis, Germany — S • E Europe • 100 kW
    VOA, Via Briech, Morocco — W • E Europe • 250 kW
    †VOA, Via Woofferton, UK — N Africa • "RADIO SAWA" • 300 kW
**9570 CHINA**
    CHINA RADIO INTL, Urümqi — S • W Asia • 500 kW   S • Europe • 500 kW
    CHINA RADIO INTL, Via Havana, Cuba — E North Am • 250 kW
    CHINA RADIO INTL, Xi'an — E Africa & S Africa • 100 kW
**GERMANY**
    DEUTSCHE WELLE, Nauen — W • E Asia • 500 kW
**HUNGARY**
    RADIO BUDAPEST, Jászberény — S • N America • 250 kW
**IRAN**
    VO THE ISLAMIC REP, Sirjan — S • S Asia, SE Asia & Australasia • 500 kW
    VO THE ISLAMIC REP, Tehrān — S • S Asia • 500 kW
**(con'd)**    VO THE ISLAMIC REP, Zāhedān — S • S Europe • 500 kW

| | World Time | 0 | 1 | 2 | 3 | 4 | 5 | 6 | 7 | 8 | 9 | 10 | 11 | 12 | 13 | 14 | 15 | 16 | 17 | 18 | 19 | 20 | 21 | 22 | 23 | 24 |

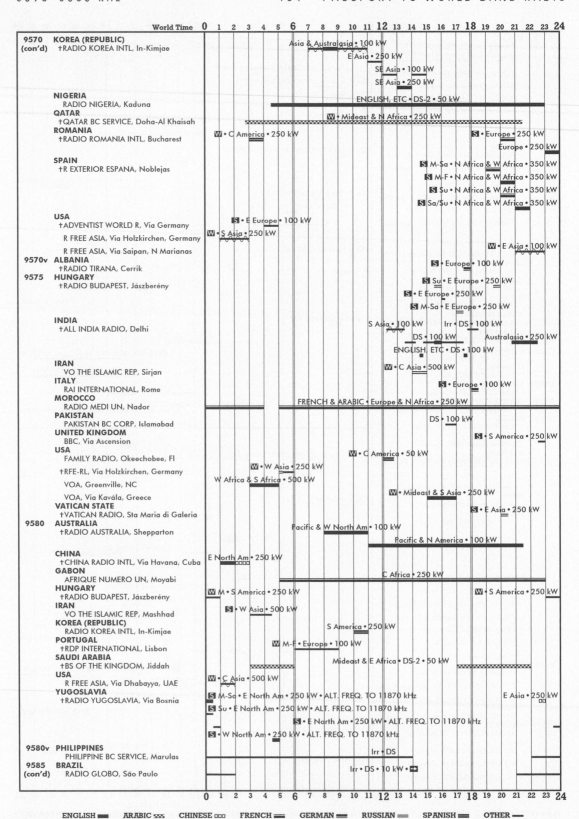

| | | World Time | 0 1 2 3 4 5 6 7 8 9 10 11 12 13 14 15 16 17 18 19 20 21 22 23 24 |
|---|---|---|---|

**9570** **KOREA (REPUBLIC)**
**(con'd)** †RADIO KOREA INTL, In-Kimjae — Asia & Australasia • 100 kW; E Asia • 250 kW; SE Asia • 100 kW; SE Asia • 250 kW

**NIGERIA**
RADIO NIGERIA, Kaduna — ENGLISH, ETC • DS-2 • 50 kW

**QATAR**
†QATAR BC SERVICE, Doha-Al Khaisah — W • Mideast & N Africa • 250 kW

**ROMANIA**
†RADIO ROMANIA INTL, Bucharest — W • C America • 250 kW; S • Europe • 250 kW; Europe • 250 kW

**SPAIN**
†R EXTERIOR ESPANA, Noblejas — S M-Sa • N Africa & W Africa • 350 kW; S M-F • N Africa & W Africa • 350 kW; S Su • N Africa & W Africa • 350 kW; S Sa/Su • N Africa & W Africa • 350 kW

**USA**
†ADVENTIST WORLD R, Via Germany — S • E Europe • 100 kW
R FREE ASIA, Via Holzkirchen, Germany — W • S Asia • 250 kW
R FREE ASIA, Via Saipan, N Marianas — W • E Asia • 100 kW

**9570v** **ALBANIA**
†RADIO TIRANA, Cerrik — S • Europe • 100 kW

**9575** **HUNGARY**
†RADIO BUDAPEST, Jászberény — S Su • E Europe • 250 kW; S • E Europe • 250 kW; S M-Sa • E Europe • 250 kW

**INDIA**
†ALL INDIA RADIO, Delhi — S Asia • 100 kW; Irr • DS • 100 kW; DS • 100 kW; Australasia • 250 kW; ENGLISH, ETC • DS • 100 kW

**IRAN**
VO THE ISLAMIC REP, Sirjan — W • C Asia • 500 kW

**ITALY**
RAI INTERNATIONAL, Rome — S • Europe • 100 kW

**MOROCCO**
RADIO MEDI UN, Nador — FRENCH & ARABIC • Europe & N Africa • 250 kW

**PAKISTAN**
PAKISTAN BC CORP, Islamabad — DS • 100 kW

**UNITED KINGDOM**
BBC, Via Ascension — S • S America • 250 kW

**USA**
FAMILY RADIO, Okeechobee, Fl — W • C America • 50 kW
†RFE-RL, Via Holzkirchen, Germany — W • W Asia • 250 kW
VOA, Greenville, NC — W Africa & S Africa • 500 kW
VOA, Via Kavála, Greece — W • Mideast & S Asia • 250 kW

**VATICAN STATE**
†VATICAN RADIO, Sta Maria di Galeria — S • E Asia • 250 kW

**9580** **AUSTRALIA**
†RADIO AUSTRALIA, Shepparton — Pacific & W North Am • 100 kW; Pacific & N America • 100 kW

**CHINA**
†CHINA RADIO INTL, Via Havana, Cuba — E North Am • 250 kW

**GABON**
AFRIQUE NUMERO UN, Moyabi — C Africa • 250 kW

**HUNGARY**
†RADIO BUDAPEST, Jászberény — W M • S America • 250 kW; W • S America • 250 kW

**IRAN**
VO THE ISLAMIC REP, Mashhad — S • W Asia • 500 kW

**KOREA (REPUBLIC)**
RADIO KOREA INTL, In-Kimjae — S America • 250 kW

**PORTUGAL**
†RDP INTERNATIONAL, Lisbon — W M-F • Europe • 100 kW

**SAUDI ARABIA**
†BS OF THE KINGDOM, Jiddah — Mideast & E Africa • DS-2 • 50 kW

**USA**
R FREE ASIA, Via Dhabayya, UAE — W • C Asia • 500 kW

**YUGOSLAVIA**
†RADIO YUGOSLAVIA, Via Bosnia — S M-Sa • E North Am • 250 kW • ALT. FREQ. TO 11870 kHz; S Su • E North Am • 250 kW • ALT. FREQ. TO 11870 kHz; S • E North Am • 250 kW • ALT. FREQ. TO 11870 kHz; S • W North Am • 250 kW • ALT. FREQ. TO 11870 kHz; E Asia • 250 kW

**9580v** **PHILIPPINES**
PHILIPPINE BC SERVICE, Marulas — Irr • DS

**9585** **BRAZIL**
**(con'd)** RADIO GLOBO, São Paulo — Irr • DS • 10 kW •

| World Time | 0 1 2 3 4 5 6 7 8 9 10 11 12 13 14 15 16 17 18 19 20 21 22 23 24 |
|---|---|

ENGLISH ▬  ARABIC ▨  CHINESE ▭  FRENCH ═  GERMAN ▬  RUSSIAN ═  SPANISH ▬  OTHER ─

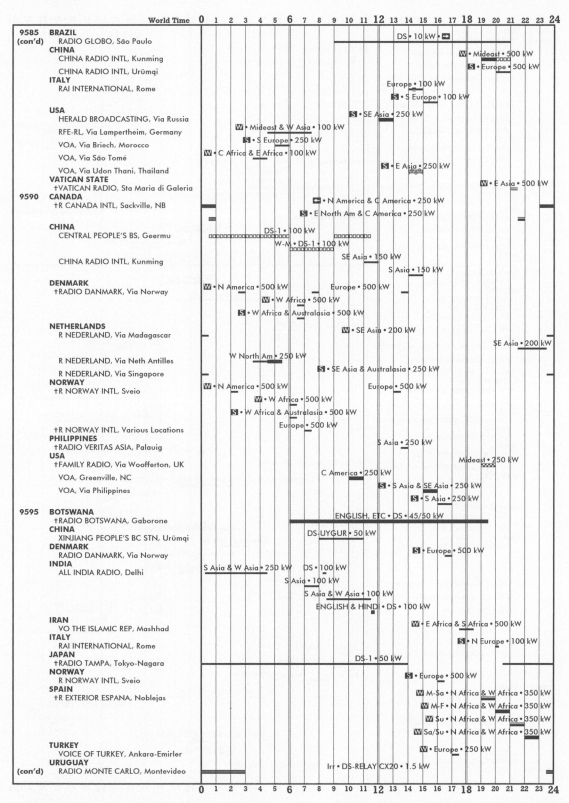

| World Time | 0 | 1 | 2 | 3 | 4 | 5 | 6 | 7 | 8 | 9 | 10 | 11 | 12 | 13 | 14 | 15 | 16 | 17 | 18 | 19 | 20 | 21 | 22 | 23 | 24 |

**9585**
**(con'd)**

**BRAZIL**
　RADIO GLOBO, São Paulo — DS • 10 kW ➡
**CHINA**
　CHINA RADIO INTL, Kunming — W • Mideast • 500 kW
　CHINA RADIO INTL, Urümqi — S • Europe • 500 kW
**ITALY**
　RAI INTERNATIONAL, Rome — Europe • 100 kW
　　　S • S Europe • 100 kW
**USA**
　HERALD BROADCASTING, Via Russia — S • SE Asia • 250 kW
　RFE-RL, Via Lampertheim, Germany — W • Mideast & W Asia • 100 kW
　VOA, Via Briech, Morocco — S • S Europe • 250 kW
　VOA, Via São Tomé — W • C Africa & E Africa • 100 kW
　VOA, Via Udon Thani, Thailand — S • E Asia • 250 kW
**VATICAN STATE**
　†VATICAN RADIO, Sta Maria di Galeria — W • E Asia • 500 kW

**9590**　**CANADA**
　†R CANADA INTL, Sackville, NB — ➡ • N America & C America • 250 kW
　　　➡ • E North Am & C America • 250 kW
**CHINA**
　CENTRAL PEOPLE'S BS, Geermu — DS-1 • 100 kW
　　　W-M • DS-1 • 100 kW
　CHINA RADIO INTL, Kunming — SE Asia • 150 kW
　　　S Asia • 150 kW
**DENMARK**
　†RADIO DANMARK, Via Norway — W • N America • 500 kW　Europe • 500 kW
　　　W • W Africa • 500 kW
　　　S • W Africa & Australasia • 500 kW
**NETHERLANDS**
　R NEDERLAND, Via Madagascar — W • SE Asia • 200 kW
　　　SE Asia • 200 kW
　R NEDERLAND, Via Neth Antilles — W North Am • 250 kW
　R NEDERLAND, Via Singapore — S • SE Asia & Australasia • 250 kW
**NORWAY**
　†R NORWAY INTL, Sveio — W • N America • 500 kW　Europe • 500 kW
　　　W • W Africa • 500 kW
　　　S • W Africa & Australasia • 500 kW
　　　Europe • 500 kW
　†R NORWAY INTL, Various Locations
**PHILIPPINES**
　†RADIO VERITAS ASIA, Palauig — S Asia • 250 kW
**USA**
　†FAMILY RADIO, Via Woofferton, UK — Mideast • 250 kW
　VOA, Greenville, NC — C America • 250 kW
　VOA, Via Philippines — S • S Asia & SE Asia • 250 kW
　　　S • S Asia • 250 kW

**9595**　**BOTSWANA**
　†RADIO BOTSWANA, Gaborone — ENGLISH, ETC • DS • 45/50 kW
**CHINA**
　XINJIANG PEOPLE'S BC STN, Urümqi — DS-UYGUR • 50 kW
**DENMARK**
　RADIO DANMARK, Via Norway — S • Europe • 500 kW
**INDIA**
　ALL INDIA RADIO, Delhi — S Asia & W Asia • 250 kW　DS • 100 kW
　　　S Asia • 100 kW
　　　S Asia & W Asia • 100 kW
　　　ENGLISH & HINDI • DS • 100 kW
**IRAN**
　VO THE ISLAMIC REP, Mashhad — W • E Africa & S Africa • 500 kW
**ITALY**
　RAI INTERNATIONAL, Rome — S • N Europe • 100 kW
**JAPAN**
　†RADIO TAMPA, Tokyo-Nagara — DS-1 • 50 kW
**NORWAY**
　R NORWAY INTL, Sveio — S • Europe • 500 kW
**SPAIN**
　†R EXTERIOR ESPANA, Noblejas — W M-Sa • N Africa & W Africa • 350 kW
　　　W M-F • N Africa & W Africa • 350 kW
　　　W Su • N Africa & W Africa • 350 kW
　　　W Sa/Su • N Africa & W Africa • 350 kW
　　　W • Europe • 250 kW
**TURKEY**
　VOICE OF TURKEY, Ankara-Emirler
**URUGUAY**
**(con'd)**　RADIO MONTE CARLO, Montevideo — Irr • DS-RELAY CX20 • 1.5 kW

| World Time | 0 | 1 | 2 | 3 | 4 | 5 | 6 | 7 | 8 | 9 | 10 | 11 | 12 | 13 | 14 | 15 | 16 | 17 | 18 | 19 | 20 | 21 | 22 | 23 | 24 |

SEASONAL **S** OR **W**　　1-HR TIMESHIFT MIDYEAR ⬅ OR ➡　　JAMMING / OR ∧　　EARLIEST HEARD ◁　　LATEST HEARD ▷　　NEW FOR 2003 †

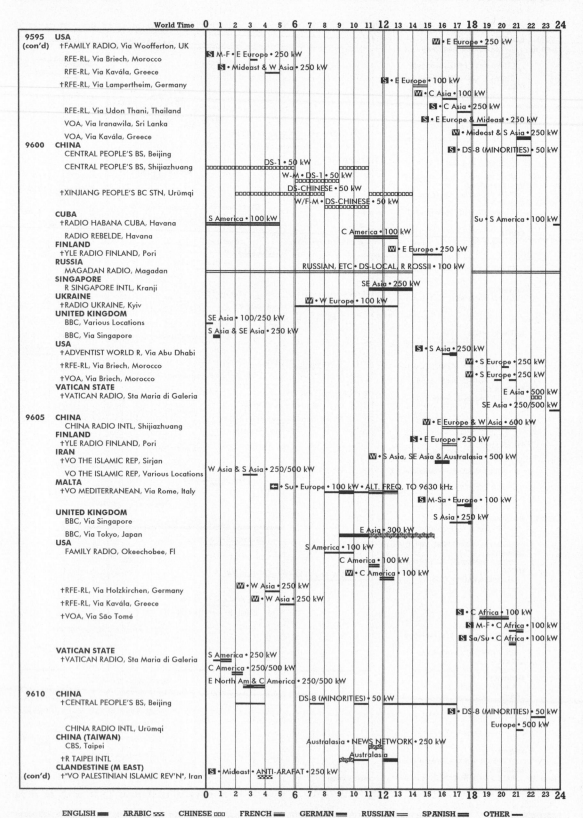

| World Time | 0 | 1 | 2 | 3 | 4 | 5 | 6 | 7 | 8 | 9 | 10 | 11 | 12 | 13 | 14 | 15 | 16 | 17 | 18 | 19 | 20 | 21 | 22 | 23 | 24 |

**9595**
(con'd) **USA**
  †FAMILY RADIO, Via Woofferton, UK — W • E Europe • 250 kW
  RFE-RL, Via Briech, Morocco — S M-F • E Europe • 250 kW
  RFE-RL, Via Kavála, Greece — S • Mideast & W Asia • 250 kW
  †RFE-RL, Via Lampertheim, Germany — S • E Europe • 100 kW
    W • C Asia • 100 kW
    S • C Asia • 250 kW
  RFE-RL, Via Udon Thani, Thailand — S • E Europe & Mideast • 250 kW
  VOA, Via Iranawila, Sri Lanka — W • Mideast & S Asia • 250 kW
  VOA, Via Kavála, Greece
**9600** **CHINA** — S • DS-8 (MINORITIES) • 50 kW
  CENTRAL PEOPLE'S BS, Beijing
  CENTRAL PEOPLE'S BS, Shijiazhuang — DS-1 • 50 kW
    W-M • DS-1 • 50 kW
  †XINJIANG PEOPLE'S BC STN, Urümqi — DS-CHINESE • 50 kW
    W/F-M • DS-CHINESE • 50 kW
  **CUBA**
  †RADIO HABANA CUBA, Havana — S America • 100 kW    Su • S America • 100 kW
  RADIO REBELDE, Havana — C America • 100 kW
**FINLAND**
  †YLE RADIO FINLAND, Pori — W • E Europe • 250 kW
**RUSSIA**
  MAGADAN RADIO, Magadan — RUSSIAN, ETC • DS-LOCAL, R ROSSII • 100 kW
**SINGAPORE**
  R SINGAPORE INTL, Kranji — SE Asia • 250 kW
**UKRAINE**
  †RADIO UKRAINE, Kyiv — W • W Europe • 100 kW
**UNITED KINGDOM**
  BBC, Various Locations — SE Asia • 100/250 kW
  BBC, Via Singapore — S Asia & SE Asia • 250 kW
**USA**
  †ADVENTIST WORLD R, Via Abu Dhabi — S • S Asia • 250 kW
  †RFE-RL, Via Briech, Morocco — W • S Europe • 250 kW
  †VOA, Via Briech, Morocco — W • S Europe • 250 kW
**VATICAN STATE**
  †VATICAN RADIO, Sta Maria di Galeria — E Asia • 500 kW
    SE Asia • 250/500 kW
**9605** **CHINA**
  CHINA RADIO INTL, Shijiazhuang — W • E Europe & W Asia • 600 kW
**FINLAND**
  †YLE RADIO FINLAND, Pori — S • E Europe • 250 kW
**IRAN**
  †VO THE ISLAMIC REP, Sirjan — W • S Asia, SE Asia & Australasia • 500 kW
  VO THE ISLAMIC REP, Various Locations — W Asia & S Asia • 250/500 kW
**MALTA**
  †VO MEDITERRANEAN, Via Rome, Italy — ← • Su • Europe • 100 kW • ALT. FREQ. TO 9630 kHz
    S M-Sa • Europe • 100 kW
**UNITED KINGDOM**
  BBC, Via Singapore — S Asia • 250 kW
  BBC, Via Tokyo, Japan — E Asia • 300 kW
**USA**
  FAMILY RADIO, Okeechobee, Fl — S America • 100 kW
    C America • 100 kW
    W • C America • 100 kW
  †RFE-RL, Via Holzkirchen, Germany — W • W Asia • 250 kW
  †RFE-RL, Via Kavála, Greece — W • W Asia • 250 kW
  †VOA, Via São Tomé — S • C Africa • 100 kW
    S M-F • C Africa • 100 kW
    S Sa/Su • C Africa • 100 kW
**VATICAN STATE**
  †VATICAN RADIO, Sta Maria di Galeria — S America • 250 kW
    C America • 250/500 kW
    E North Am & C America • 250/500 kW
**9610** **CHINA**
  †CENTRAL PEOPLE'S BS, Beijing — DS-8 (MINORITIES) • 50 kW
    S • DS-8 (MINORITIES) • 50 kW
    Europe • 500 kW
  CHINA RADIO INTL, Urümqi
**CHINA (TAIWAN)**
  CBS, Taipei — Australasia • NEWS NETWORK • 250 kW
  †R TAIPEI INTL — Australasia
**CLANDESTINE (M EAST)**
(con'd) †"VO PALESTINIAN ISLAMIC REV'N", Iran — S • Mideast • ANTI-ARAFAT • 250 kW

| | 0 | 1 | 2 | 3 | 4 | 5 | 6 | 7 | 8 | 9 | 10 | 11 | 12 | 13 | 14 | 15 | 16 | 17 | 18 | 19 | 20 | 21 | 22 | 23 | 24 |

ENGLISH ▬    ARABIC ░░░    CHINESE ░░░    FRENCH ▬    GERMAN ▬    RUSSIAN ═    SPANISH ▬    OTHER ▬

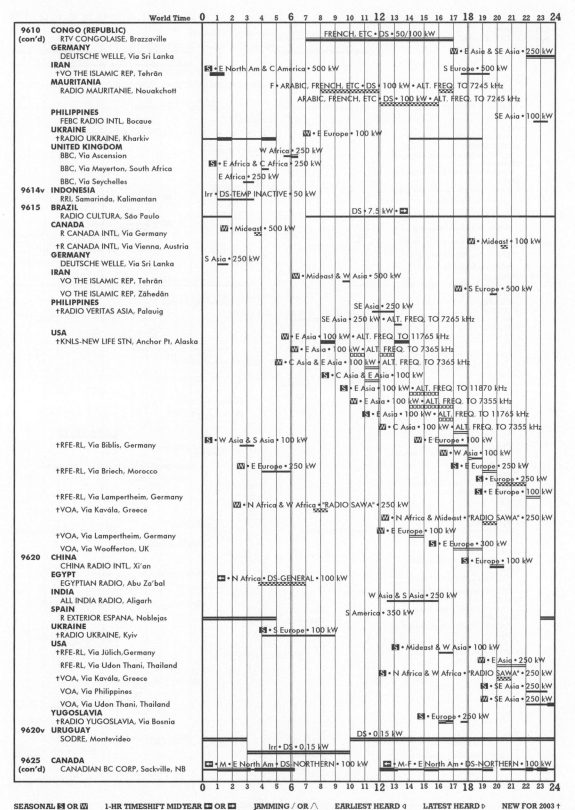

World Time 0 1 2 3 4 5 6 7 8 9 10 11 12 13 14 15 16 17 18 19 20 21 22 23 24

**9610** **CONGO (REPUBLIC)**
**(con'd)** RTV CONGOLAISE, Brazzaville — FRENCH, ETC • DS • 50/100 kW
**GERMANY**
DEUTSCHE WELLE, Via Sri Lanka — W • E Asia & SE Asia • 250 kW
**IRAN**
†VO THE ISLAMIC REP, Tehrān — S • E North Am & C America • 500 kW / S Europe • 500 kW
**MAURITANIA**
RADIO MAURITANIE, Nouakchott — F • ARABIC, FRENCH, ETC • DS • 100 kW • ALT. FREQ. TO 7245 kHz
— ARABIC, FRENCH, ETC • DS • 100 kW • ALT. FREQ. TO 7245 kHz
**PHILIPPINES**
FEBC RADIO INTL, Bocaue — SE Asia • 100 kW
**UKRAINE**
†RADIO UKRAINE, Kharkiv — W • E Europe • 100 kW
**UNITED KINGDOM**
BBC, Via Ascension — W Africa • 250 kW
BBC, Via Meyerton, South Africa — S • E Africa & C Africa • 250 kW
BBC, Via Seychelles — E Africa • 250 kW
**9614v** **INDONESIA**
RRI, Samarinda, Kalimantan — Irr • DS-TEMP INACTIVE • 50 kW
**9615** **BRAZIL**
RADIO CULTURA, São Paulo — DS • 7.5 kW • →
**CANADA**
R CANADA INTL, Via Germany — W • Mideast • 500 kW
†R CANADA INTL, Via Vienna, Austria — W • Mideast • 100 kW
**GERMANY**
DEUTSCHE WELLE, Via Sri Lanka — S Asia • 250 kW
**IRAN**
VO THE ISLAMIC REP, Tehrān — W • Mideast & W Asia • 500 kW
VO THE ISLAMIC REP, Zāhedān — W • S Europe • 500 kW
**PHILIPPINES**
†RADIO VERITAS ASIA, Palauig — SE Asia • 250 kW
— SE Asia • 250 kW • ALT. FREQ. TO 7265 kHz
**USA**
†KNLS-NEW LIFE STN, Anchor Pt, Alaska — W • E Asia • 100 kW • ALT. FREQ. TO 11765 kHz
— W • E Asia • 100 kW • ALT. FREQ. TO 7365 kHz
— W • C Asia & E Asia • 100 kW • ALT. FREQ. TO 7365 kHz
— S • C Asia & E Asia • 100 kW
— S • E Asia • 100 kW • ALT. FREQ. TO 11870 kHz
— W • E Asia • 100 kW • ALT. FREQ. TO 7355 kHz
— S • E Asia • 100 kW • ALT. FREQ. TO 11765 kHz
— W • C Asia • 100 kW • ALT. FREQ. TO 7355 kHz
†RFE-RL, Via Biblis, Germany — S • W Asia & S Asia • 100 kW / W • E Europe • 100 kW
— W • W Asia • 100 kW
†RFE-RL, Via Briech, Morocco — W • E Europe • 250 kW / S • E Europe • 250 kW
— S • Europe • 250 kW
— S • E Europe • 100 kW
†RFE-RL, Via Lampertheim, Germany
†VOA, Via Kavála, Greece — W • N Africa & W Africa • "RADIO SAWA" • 250 kW
— W • N Africa & Mideast • "RADIO SAWA" • 250 kW
†VOA, Via Lampertheim, Germany — W • E Europe • 100 kW
VOA, Via Woofferton, UK — S • E Europe • 300 kW
**9620** **CHINA**
CHINA RADIO INTL, Xi'an — S • Europe • 100 kW
**EGYPT**
EGYPTIAN RADIO, Abu Za'bal — ← • N Africa • DS-GENERAL • 100 kW
**INDIA**
ALL INDIA RADIO, Aligarh — W Asia & S Asia • 250 kW
**SPAIN**
R EXTERIOR ESPANA, Noblejas — S America • 350 kW
**UKRAINE**
†RADIO UKRAINE, Kyiv — S • S Europe • 100 kW
**USA**
†RFE-RL, Via Jülich, Germany — S • Mideast & W Asia • 100 kW
RFE-RL, Via Udon Thani, Thailand — W • E Asia • 250 kW
†VOA, Via Kavála, Greece — S • N Africa & W Africa • "RADIO SAWA" • 250 kW
VOA, Via Philippines — S • SE Asia • 250 kW
VOA, Via Udon Thani, Thailand — W • SE Asia • 250 kW
**YUGOSLAVIA**
†RADIO YUGOSLAVIA, Via Bosnia — S • Europe • 250 kW
**9620v** **URUGUAY**
SODRE, Montevideo — DS • 0.15 kW
— Irr • DS • 0.15 kW
**9625** **CANADA**
**(con'd)** CANADIAN BC CORP, Sackville, NB — ← • M • E North Am • DS-NORTHERN • 100 kW / ← • M-F • E North Am • DS-NORTHERN • 100 kW

0 1 2 3 4 5 6 7 8 9 10 11 12 13 14 15 16 17 18 19 20 21 22 23 24

SEASONAL S OR W   1-HR TIMESHIFT MIDYEAR ← OR →   JAMMING / OR /\   EARLIEST HEARD ◁   LATEST HEARD ▷   NEW FOR 2003 †

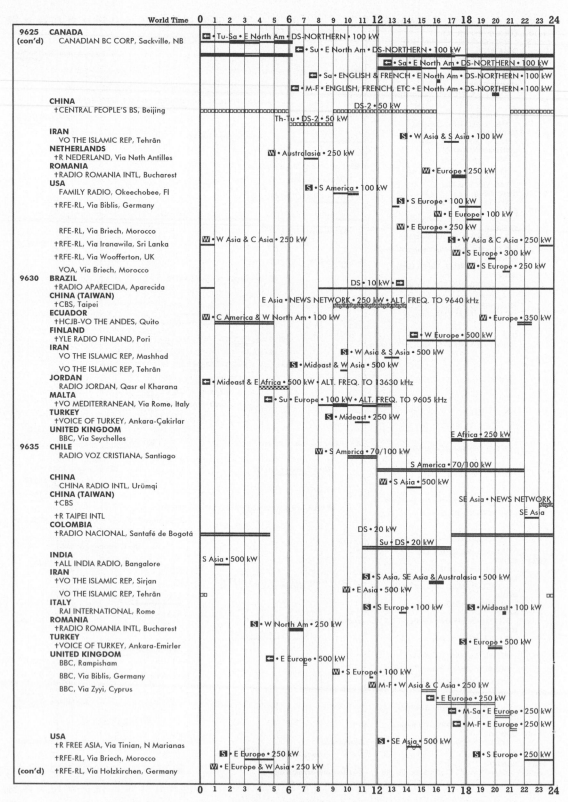

**World Time** 0 1 2 3 4 5 6 7 8 9 10 11 12 13 14 15 16 17 18 19 20 21 22 23 24

**9625** **CANADA**
**(con'd)**  CANADIAN BC CORP, Sackville, NB

**CHINA**
  †CENTRAL PEOPLE'S BS, Beijing

**IRAN**
  VO THE ISLAMIC REP, Tehrān
**NETHERLANDS**
  †R NEDERLAND, Via Neth Antilles
**ROMANIA**
  †RADIO ROMANIA INTL, Bucharest
**USA**
  FAMILY RADIO, Okeechobee, Fl

  †RFE-RL, Via Biblis, Germany

  RFE-RL, Via Briech, Morocco

  †RFE-RL, Via Iranawila, Sri Lanka

  †RFE-RL, Via Woofferton, UK

  VOA, Via Briech, Morocco

**9630** **BRAZIL**
  †RADIO APARECIDA, Aparecida
**CHINA (TAIWAN)**
  †CBS, Taipei
**ECUADOR**
  †HCJB-VO THE ANDES, Quito
**FINLAND**
  †YLE RADIO FINLAND, Pori
**IRAN**
  VO THE ISLAMIC REP, Mashhad

  VO THE ISLAMIC REP, Tehrān
**JORDAN**
  RADIO JORDAN, Qasr el Kharana
**MALTA**
  †VO MEDITERRANEAN, Via Rome, Italy
**TURKEY**
  †VOICE OF TURKEY, Ankara-Çakirlar
**UNITED KINGDOM**
  BBC, Via Seychelles
**9635** **CHILE**
  RADIO VOZ CRISTIANA, Santiago

**CHINA**
  CHINA RADIO INTL, Urümqi
**CHINA (TAIWAN)**
  †CBS

  †R TAIPEI INTL
**COLOMBIA**
  †RADIO NACIONAL, Santafé de Bogotá

**INDIA**
  †ALL INDIA RADIO, Bangalore
**IRAN**
  †VO THE ISLAMIC REP, Sirjan

  VO THE ISLAMIC REP, Tehrān
**ITALY**
  RAI INTERNATIONAL, Rome
**ROMANIA**
  †RADIO ROMANIA INTL, Bucharest
**TURKEY**
  †VOICE OF TURKEY, Ankara-Emirler
**UNITED KINGDOM**
  BBC, Rampisham

  BBC, Via Biblis, Germany

  BBC, Via Zyyi, Cyprus

**USA**
  †R FREE ASIA, Via Tinian, N Marianas

  †RFE-RL, Via Briech, Morocco
**(con'd)**  †RFE-RL, Via Holzkirchen, Germany

0 1 2 3 4 5 6 7 8 9 10 11 12 13 14 15 16 17 18 19 20 21 22 23 24

ENGLISH ▬▬   ARABIC ✕✕✕   CHINESE ▫▫▫   FRENCH ══   GERMAN ▬▬   RUSSIAN ══   SPANISH ══   OTHER ▬

World Time | 0 1 2 3 4 5 6 7 8 9 10 11 12 13 14 15 16 17 18 19 20 21 22 23 24

**9635 USA**
(con'd) †RFE-RL, Via Kavála, Greece — W • E Europe • 250 kW
    †VOA, Via Briech, Morocco — W • S Europe • 250 kW
    VOA, Via Kavála, Greece — S • S Asia • 250 kW

**9635v MALI**
    RTV MALIENNE, Bamako — FRENCH, ETC • DS • 100 kW

**9639.8 VENEZUELA**
    ECOS DEL TORBES, San Cristóbal — DS • 1 kW · Irr • DS • 1 kW

**9640 CANADA**
    †R CANADA INTL, Via In-Kimjae, Korea — S • E Asia • 100 kW
**CHINA**
    CHINA RADIO INTL, Urümqi — S • Europe • 500 kW · Europe • 500 kW

**CHINA (TAIWAN)**
    †CBS, Taipei — Irr • E Asia • NEWS NETWORK • 250 kW • ALT. FREQ. TO 9670 kHz
    E Asia • NEWS NETWORK • 250 kW • ALT. FREQ. TO 9630 kHz

**GERMANY**
    †DEUTSCHE WELLE, Via Antigua — S • N America • 250 kW
    DEUTSCHE WELLE, Via Sackville, Can — S • N America & C America • 250 kW
    DEUTSCHE WELLE, Via Sines, Portugal — W • E North Am & C America • 250 kW
    DEUTSCHE WELLE, Wertachtal — S • E North Am • 500 kW · W • S Europe • 500 kW
**IRAN**
    VO THE ISLAMIC REP, Tehrãn — W • Mideast & E Africa • 500 kW · W • Mideast & E Europe • 500 kW
**KOREA (DPR)**
    †KOREAN CENTRAL BS — C Africa • ALT. FREQ. TO 6520 kHz
    †VOICE OF KOREA — C Africa • ALT. FREQ. TO 6520 kHz
**KOREA (REPUBLIC)**
    †RADIO KOREA INTL, In-Kimjae — SE Asia • 250 kW
**UKRAINE**
    †RADIO UKRAINE, Kyiv — S • W Asia • 100 kW

**9644.6 COSTA RICA**
    FARO DEL CARIBE, San José — DS • 5 kW

**9645 BRAZIL**
    RADIO BANDEIRANTES, São Paulo — DS • 10 kW
**CHINA**
    CENTRAL PEOPLE'S BS, Beijing — DS-1 • 100 kW · W-M • DS-1 • 100 kW · S • DS-1 • 100 kW
    CHINA RADIO INTL, Kunming — W Africa & C Africa • 500 kW
**LEBANON**
    VOICE OF CHARITY, Via Vatican City — W • Mideast • 100 kW
**USA**
    RFE-RL, Via Briech, Morocco — W • Europe • 250 kW
    †VOA, Via Iranawila, Sri Lanka — W • S Asia • 250 kW · S Asia • 250 kW
    †VOA, Via Philippines — W • S Asia • 250 kW
    VOA, Via Udon Thani, Thailand — SE Asia & Australasia • 250 kW
**VATICAN STATE**
    †VATICAN RADIO, Sta Maria di Galeria — W • Mideast • 250 kW · Sa • Africa • 250 kW
    S • M-Sa • S Europe & N Africa • 100 kW · Africa • 500 kW
    ⇆ • Europe • 100 kW · ⇆ • E Europe • 100 kW
    S • M-Sa • N Africa • 100 kW
    W • M-Sa • W Europe • 100 kW
    W • M-Sa • S Europe & N Africa • 100 kW
    ⇆ • Su • E Europe • 100 kW · ⇆ • W Europe • 100 kW
    ⇆ • Su • W Europe • 100 kW
    ⇆ • M-F • W Europe • 100 kW
    ⇆ • Africa • 250 kW

**9650 CHINA (TAIWAN)**
    †CBS, Taipei — E Asia • NEWS NETWORK • 250 kW • ALT. FREQ. TO 9685 kHz
**GERMANY**
    DEUTSCHE WELLE, Wertachtal — S • S Europe • 500 kW · S • E Europe • 500 kW
**GUINEA**
    RTV GUINEENNE, Conakry — M-Sa • FRENCH, ETC • DS-TEMP INACTIVE • 50 kW · DS-TEMP INACTIVE • 50 kW
    Su • FRENCH, ETC • DS-TEMP INACTIVE • 50 kW
    FRENCH, ETC • DS-TEMP INACTIVE • 50 kW
**IRAN**
    VO THE ISLAMIC REP, Sirjan — W • C America • 500 kW
**KOREA (DPR)**
    †VOICE OF KOREA — E Asia • ALT. FREQ. TO 6520 kHz
**KOREA (REPUBLIC)**
    †RADIO KOREA INTL, Via Sackville, Can — E North Am • 250 kW
**SOUTH AFRICA**
(con'd) †RADIO SONDERGRENSE, Meyerton — W • S Africa • DS • 100 kW

0 1 2 3 4 5 6 7 8 9 10 11 12 13 14 15 16 17 18 19 20 21 22 23 24

SEASONAL S OR W    1-HR TIMESHIFT MIDYEAR ⇆ OR ⇆    JAMMING / OR ∧    EARLIEST HEARD ◁    LATEST HEARD ▷    NEW FOR 2003 †

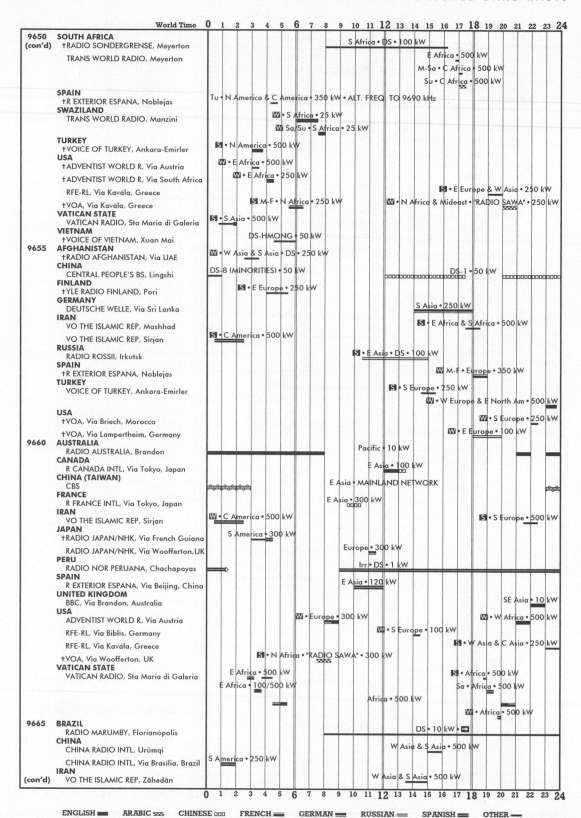

| World Time | | |
|---|---|---|
| **9650** SOUTH AFRICA | | |
| (con'd) †RADIO SONDERGRENSE, Meyerton | S Africa • DS • 100 kW | |
| TRANS WORLD RADIO, Meyerton | E Africa • 500 kW | |
| | M-Sa • C Africa • 500 kW | |
| | Su • C Africa • 500 kW | |
| SPAIN | | |
| †R EXTERIOR ESPANA, Noblejas | Tu • N America & C America • 350 kW • ALT. FREQ. TO 9690 kHz | |
| SWAZILAND | | |
| TRANS WORLD RADIO, Manzini | W • S Africa • 25 kW | |
| | W Sa/Su • S Africa • 25 kW | |
| TURKEY | | |
| †VOICE OF TURKEY, Ankara-Emirler | S • N America • 500 kW | |
| USA | | |
| †ADVENTIST WORLD R, Via Austria | W • E Africa • 500 kW | |
| †ADVENTIST WORLD R, Via South Africa | W • E Africa • 250 kW | |
| RFE-RL, Via Kavála, Greece | S • E Europe & W Asia • 250 kW | |
| †VOA, Via Kavála, Greece | S M-F • N Africa • 250 kW ; W • N Africa & Mideast • "RADIO SAWA" • 250 kW | |
| VATICAN STATE | | |
| VATICAN RADIO, Sta Maria di Galeria | S • S Asia • 500 kW | |
| VIETNAM | | |
| †VOICE OF VIETNAM, Xuan Mai | DS-HMONG • 50 kW | |
| **9655** AFGHANISTAN | | |
| †RADIO AFGHANISTAN, Via UAE | W • W Asia & S Asia • DS • 250 kW | |
| CHINA | | |
| CENTRAL PEOPLE'S BS, Lingshi | DS-8 (MINORITIES) • 50 kW ; DS-1 • 50 kW | |
| FINLAND | | |
| †YLE RADIO FINLAND, Pori | S • E Europe • 250 kW | |
| GERMANY | | |
| DEUTSCHE WELLE, Via Sri Lanka | S Asia • 250 kW | |
| IRAN | | |
| VO THE ISLAMIC REP, Mashhad | S • E Africa & S Africa • 500 kW | |
| VO THE ISLAMIC REP, Sirjan | S • C America • 500 kW | |
| RUSSIA | | |
| RADIO ROSSII, Irkutsk | S • E Asia • DS • 100 kW | |
| SPAIN | | |
| †R EXTERIOR ESPANA, Noblejas | W M-F • Europe • 350 kW | |
| TURKEY | | |
| VOICE OF TURKEY, Ankara-Emirler | S • S Europe • 250 kW | |
| | W • W Europe & E North Am • 500 kW | |
| USA | | |
| †VOA, Via Briech, Morocco | W • S Europe • 250 kW | |
| †VOA, Via Lampertheim, Germany | W • E Europe • 100 kW | |
| **9660** AUSTRALIA | | |
| RADIO AUSTRALIA, Brandon | Pacific • 10 kW | |
| CANADA | | |
| R CANADA INTL, Via Tokyo, Japan | E Asia • 100 kW | |
| CHINA (TAIWAN) | | |
| CBS | E Asia • MAINLAND NETWORK | |
| FRANCE | | |
| R FRANCE INTL, Via Tokyo, Japan | E Asia • 300 kW | |
| IRAN | | |
| VO THE ISLAMIC REP, Sirjan | W • C America • 500 kW ; S • S Europe • 500 kW | |
| JAPAN | | |
| †RADIO JAPAN/NHK, Via French Guiana | S America • 300 kW | |
| RADIO JAPAN/NHK, Via Woofferton, UK | Europe • 300 kW | |
| PERU | | |
| RADIO NOR PERUANA, Chachapoyas | Irr • DS • 1 kW | |
| SPAIN | | |
| R EXTERIOR ESPANA, Via Beijing, China | E Asia • 120 kW | |
| UNITED KINGDOM | | |
| BBC, Via Brandon, Australia | SE Asia • 10 kW | |
| USA | | |
| ADVENTIST WORLD R, Via Austria | W • Europe • 300 kW ; W • W Africa • 500 kW | |
| RFE-RL, Via Biblis, Germany | W • S Europe • 100 kW | |
| RFE-RL, Via Kavála, Greece | S • W Asia & C Asia • 250 kW | |
| †VOA, Via Woofferton, UK | S • N Africa • "RADIO SAWA" • 300 kW | |
| VATICAN STATE | | |
| VATICAN RADIO, Sta Maria di Galeria | E Africa • 500 kW ; S • Africa • 500 kW | |
| | E Africa • 100/500 kW ; Sa • Africa • 500 kW | |
| | Africa • 500 kW | |
| | W • Africa • 500 kW | |
| **9665** BRAZIL | | |
| RADIO MARUMBY, Florianópolis | DS • 10 kW • ➡ | |
| CHINA | | |
| CHINA RADIO INTL, Urümqi | W Asia & S Asia • 500 kW | |
| CHINA RADIO INTL, Via Brasília, Brazil | S America • 250 kW | |
| IRAN | | |
| (con'd) VO THE ISLAMIC REP, Zāhedān | W Asia & S Asia • 500 kW | |

ENGLISH ▬    ARABIC ▨    CHINESE □□□    FRENCH ▬    GERMAN ▬    RUSSIAN ═    SPANISH ▬    OTHER ──

World Time    0 1 2 3 4 5 6 7 8 9 10 11 12 13 14 15 16 17 18 19 20 21 22 23 24

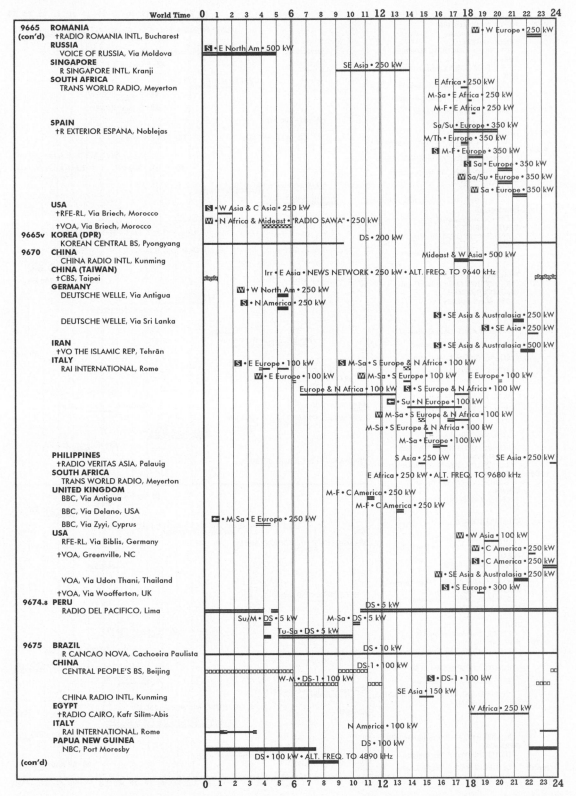

**9665**   **ROMANIA**
**(con'd)**    †RADIO ROMANIA INTL, Bucharest — Ⓦ • W Europe • 250 kW
    **RUSSIA**
     VOICE OF RUSSIA, Via Moldova — Ⓢ • E North Am • 500 kW
    **SINGAPORE**
     R SINGAPORE INTL, Kranji — SE Asia • 250 kW
    **SOUTH AFRICA**
     TRANS WORLD RADIO, Meyerton — E Africa • 250 kW
      M-Sa • E Africa • 250 kW
      M-F • E Africa • 250 kW
    **SPAIN**
     †R EXTERIOR ESPANA, Noblejas — Sa/Su • Europe • 350 kW
      M/Th • Europe • 350 kW
      Ⓢ M-F • Europe • 350 kW
      Ⓢ Sa • Europe • 350 kW
      Ⓦ Sa/Su • Europe • 350 kW
      Ⓢ Sa • Europe • 350 kW
    **USA**
     †RFE-RL, Via Briech, Morocco — Ⓢ • W Asia & C Asia • 250 kW
     †VOA, Via Briech, Morocco — Ⓦ • N Africa & Mideast • "RADIO SAWA" • 250 kW
**9665v**   **KOREA (DPR)**
     KOREAN CENTRAL BS, Pyongyang — DS • 200 kW
**9670**   **CHINA**
     CHINA RADIO INTL, Kunming — Mideast & W Asia • 500 kW
    **CHINA (TAIWAN)**
     †CBS, Taipei — Irr • E Asia • NEWS NETWORK • 250 kW • ALT. FREQ. TO 9640 kHz
    **GERMANY**
     DEUTSCHE WELLE, Via Antigua — Ⓦ • W North Am • 250 kW
      Ⓢ • N America • 250 kW
     DEUTSCHE WELLE, Via Sri Lanka — Ⓢ • SE Asia & Australasia • 250 kW
      Ⓢ • SE Asia • 250 kW
    **IRAN**
     †VO THE ISLAMIC REP, Tehrān — Ⓢ • SE Asia & Australasia • 500 kW
    **ITALY**
     RAI INTERNATIONAL, Rome — Ⓢ • E Europe • 100 kW   Ⓢ M-Sa • S Europe & N Africa • 100 kW
      Ⓦ • E Europe • 100 kW   Ⓦ M-Sa • S Europe • 100 kW   E Europe • 100 kW
      Europe & N Africa • 100 kW   Ⓢ • S Europe & N Africa • 100 kW
      ⇦ • Su • N Europe • 100 kW
      Ⓦ M-Sa • S Europe & N Africa • 100 kW
      M-Sa • S Europe & N Africa • 100 kW
      M-Sa • Europe • 100 kW
    **PHILIPPINES**
     †RADIO VERITAS ASIA, Palauig — S Asia • 250 kW   SE Asia • 250 kW
    **SOUTH AFRICA**
     TRANS WORLD RADIO, Meyerton — E Africa • 250 kW • ALT. FREQ. TO 9680 kHz
    **UNITED KINGDOM**
     BBC, Via Antigua — M-F • C America • 250 kW
     BBC, Via Delano, USA — M-F • C America • 250 kW
     BBC, Via Zyyi, Cyprus — ⇦ • M-Sa • E Europe • 250 kW
    **USA**
     RFE-RL, Via Biblis, Germany — Ⓦ • W Asia • 100 kW
     †VOA, Greenville, NC — Ⓦ • C America • 250 kW
      Ⓢ • C America • 250 kW
     VOA, Via Udon Thani, Thailand — Ⓦ • SE Asia & Australasia • 250 kW
     †VOA, Via Woofferton, UK — Ⓢ • S Europe • 300 kW
**9674.8**   **PERU**
     RADIO DEL PACIFICO, Lima — DS • 5 kW
      Su/M • DS • 5 kW   M-Sa • DS • 5 kW
      Tu-Sa • DS • 5 kW
**9675**   **BRAZIL**
     R CANCAO NOVA, Cachoeira Paulista — DS • 10 kW
    **CHINA**
     CENTRAL PEOPLE'S BS, Beijing — DS-1 • 100 kW
      W-M • DS-1 • 100 kW   Ⓢ • DS-1 • 100 kW
     CHINA RADIO INTL, Kunming — SE Asia • 150 kW
    **EGYPT**
     †RADIO CAIRO, Kafr Silim-Abis — W Africa • 250 kW
    **ITALY**
     RAI INTERNATIONAL, Rome — N America • 100 kW
    **PAPUA NEW GUINEA**
     NBC, Port Moresby — DS • 100 kW
      DS • 100 kW • ALT. FREQ. TO 4890 kHz

**(con'd)**

0 1 2 3 4 5 6 7 8 9 10 11 12 13 14 15 16 17 18 19 20 21 22 23 24

SEASONAL Ⓢ OR Ⓦ    1-HR TIMESHIFT MIDYEAR ⇦ OR ⇨    JAMMING / OR ∧    EARLIEST HEARD ◁    LATEST HEARD ▷    NEW FOR 2003 †

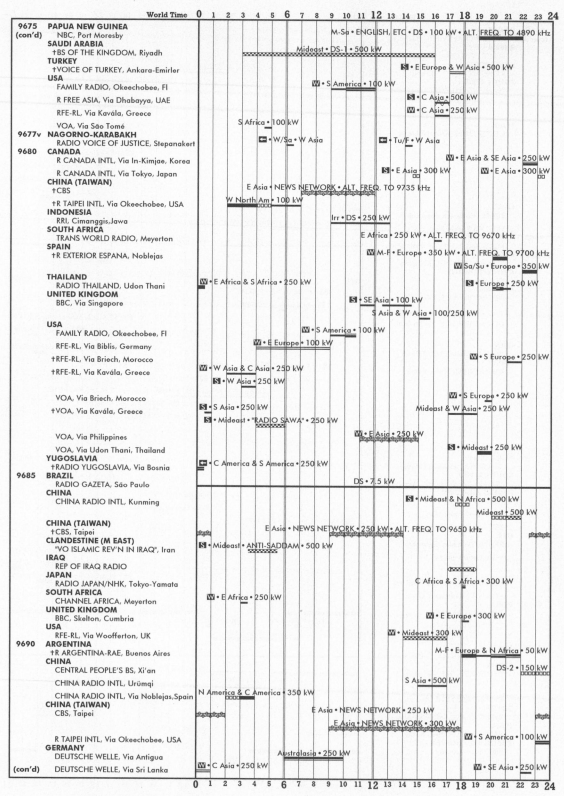

| | World Time | 0 1 2 3 4 5 6 7 8 9 10 11 12 13 14 15 16 17 18 19 20 21 22 23 24 |
|---|---|---|

**9675** **PAPUA NEW GUINEA**
(con'd)   NBC, Port Moresby — M-Sa • ENGLISH, ETC • DS • 100 kW • ALT. FREQ. TO 4890 kHz
**SAUDI ARABIA**
   †BS OF THE KINGDOM, Riyadh — Mideast • DS-1 • 500 kW
**TURKEY**
   †VOICE OF TURKEY, Ankara-Emirler — S • E Europe & W Asia • 500 kW
**USA**
   FAMILY RADIO, Okeechobee, Fl — W • S America • 100 kW
   R FREE ASIA, Via Dhabayya, UAE — S • C Asia • 500 kW
   RFE-RL, Via Kavála, Greece — W • C Asia • 250 kW
   VOA, Via São Tomé — S Africa • 100 kW
**9677v NAGORNO-KARABAKH**
   RADIO VOICE OF JUSTICE, Stepanakert — W/Sa • W Asia / Tu/F • W Asia
**9680 CANADA**
   R CANADA INTL, Via In-Kimjae, Korea — W • E Asia & SE Asia • 250 kW
   R CANADA INTL, Via Tokyo, Japan — S • E Asia • 300 kW / W • E Asia • 300 kW
**CHINA (TAIWAN)**
   †CBS — E Asia • NEWS NETWORK • ALT. FREQ. TO 9735 kHz
   †R TAIPEI INTL, Via Okeechobee, USA — W North Am • 100 kW
**INDONESIA**
   RRI, Cimanggis, Jawa — Irr • DS • 250 kW
**SOUTH AFRICA**
   TRANS WORLD RADIO, Meyerton — E Africa • 250 kW • ALT. FREQ. TO 9670 kHz
**SPAIN**
   †R EXTERIOR ESPAÑA, Noblejas — W M-F • Europe • 350 kW • ALT. FREQ. TO 9700 kHz
   W Sa/Su • Europe • 350 kW
**THAILAND**
   RADIO THAILAND, Udon Thani — W • E Africa & S Africa • 250 kW / S • Europe • 250 kW
**UNITED KINGDOM**
   BBC, Via Singapore — S • SE Asia • 100 kW
   S Asia & W Asia • 100/250 kW
**USA**
   FAMILY RADIO, Okeechobee, Fl — W • S America • 100 kW
   RFE-RL, Via Biblis, Germany — W • E Europe • 100 kW
   †RFE-RL, Via Briech, Morocco — W • S Europe • 250 kW
   †RFE-RL, Via Kavála, Greece — W • W Asia & C Asia • 250 kW / S • W Asia • 250 kW
   VOA, Via Briech, Morocco — W • S Europe • 250 kW
   †VOA, Via Kavála, Greece — S • S Asia • 250 kW / Mideast & W Asia • 250 kW
   VOA, Via Philippines — S • Mideast • "RADIO SAWA" • 250 kW
   VOA, Via Udon Thani, Thailand — W • E Asia • 250 kW / S • Mideast • 250 kW
**YUGOSLAVIA**
   †RADIO YUGOSLAVIA, Via Bosnia — C America & S America • 250 kW
**9685 BRAZIL**
   RADIO GAZETA, São Paulo — DS • 7.5 kW
**CHINA**
   CHINA RADIO INTL, Kunming — S • Mideast & N Africa • 500 kW
   Mideast • 500 kW
**CHINA (TAIWAN)**
   †CBS, Taipei — E Asia • NEWS NETWORK • 250 kW • ALT. FREQ. TO 9650 kHz
**CLANDESTINE (M EAST)**
   "VO ISLAMIC REV'N IN IRAQ", Iran — S • Mideast • ANTI-SADDAM • 500 kW
**IRAQ**
   REP OF IRAQ RADIO
**JAPAN**
   RADIO JAPAN/NHK, Tokyo-Yamata — C Africa & S Africa • 300 kW
**SOUTH AFRICA**
   CHANNEL AFRICA, Meyerton — W • E Africa • 250 kW
**UNITED KINGDOM**
   BBC, Skelton, Cumbria — W • E Europe • 300 kW
**USA**
   RFE-RL, Via Woofferton, UK — W • Mideast • 300 kW
**9690 ARGENTINA**
   †R ARGENTINA-RAE, Buenos Aires — M-F • Europe & N Africa • 50 kW
**CHINA**
   CENTRAL PEOPLE'S BS, Xi'an — DS-2 • 150 kW
   CHINA RADIO INTL, Urümqi — S Asia • 500 kW
   CHINA RADIO INTL, Via Noblejas, Spain — N America & C America • 350 kW
**CHINA (TAIWAN)**
   CBS, Taipei — E Asia • NEWS NETWORK • 250 kW
   E Asia • NEWS NETWORK • 300 kW
   R TAIPEI INTL, Via Okeechobee, USA — W • S America • 100 kW
**GERMANY**
   DEUTSCHE WELLE, Via Antigua — Australasia • 250 kW / W • C Asia • 250 kW
(con'd)   DEUTSCHE WELLE, Via Sri Lanka — W • SE Asia • 250 kW

| | World Time | 0 1 2 3 4 5 6 7 8 9 10 11 12 13 14 15 16 17 18 19 20 21 22 23 24 |
|---|---|---|

ENGLISH ▬▬   ARABIC ⌇⌇⌇   CHINESE □□□   FRENCH ═══   GERMAN ▬▬   RUSSIAN ═══   SPANISH ▬▬   OTHER ▬▬

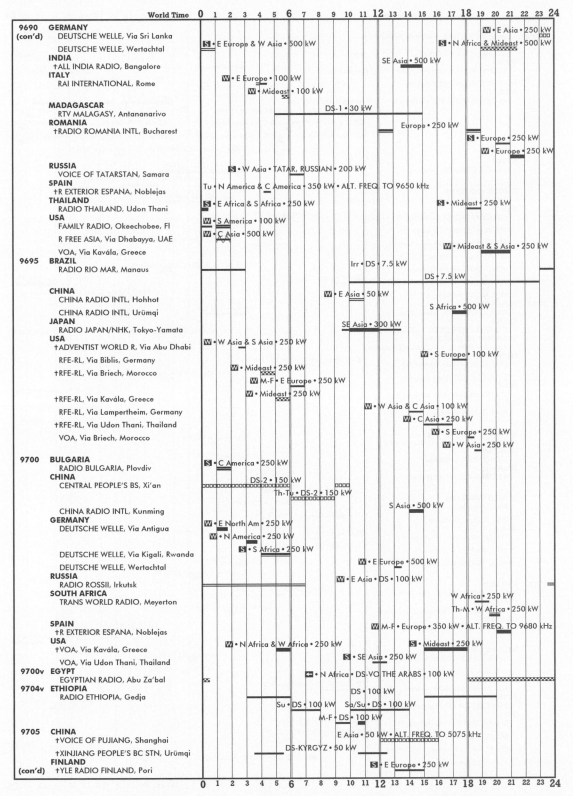

World Time: 0 1 2 3 4 5 6 7 8 9 10 11 12 13 14 15 16 17 18 19 20 21 22 23 24

**9690 GERMANY**
**(con'd)** DEUTSCHE WELLE, Via Sri Lanka — Ⓦ • E Asia • 250 kW
        Ⓢ • E Europe & W Asia • 500 kW
    DEUTSCHE WELLE, Wertachtal — Ⓢ • N Africa & Mideast • 500 kW
**INDIA**
    †ALL INDIA RADIO, Bangalore — SE Asia • 500 kW
**ITALY**
    RAI INTERNATIONAL, Rome — Ⓦ • E Europe • 100 kW
    Ⓦ • Mideast • 100 kW

**MADAGASCAR**
    RTV MALAGASY, Antananarivo — DS-1 • 30 kW
**ROMANIA**
    †RADIO ROMANIA INTL, Bucharest — Europe • 250 kW
    Ⓢ • Europe • 250 kW
    Ⓦ • Europe • 250 kW

**RUSSIA**
    VOICE OF TATARSTAN, Samara — Ⓢ • W Asia • TATAR, RUSSIAN • 200 kW
**SPAIN**
    †R EXTERIOR ESPANA, Noblejas — Tu • N America & C America • 350 kW • ALT. FREQ. TO 9650 kHz
**THAILAND**
    RADIO THAILAND, Udon Thani — Ⓢ • E Africa & S Africa • 250 kW
    Ⓢ • Mideast • 250 kW
**USA**
    FAMILY RADIO, Okeechobee, Fl — Ⓦ • S America • 100 kW
    R FREE ASIA, Via Dhabayya, UAE — Ⓦ • C Asia • 500 kW
    VOA, Via Kavála, Greece — Ⓦ • Mideast & S Asia • 250 kW
**9695 BRAZIL**
    RADIO RIO MAR, Manaus — Irr • DS • 7.5 kW
    DS • 7.5 kW

**CHINA**
    CHINA RADIO INTL, Hohhot — Ⓦ • E Asia • 50 kW
    CHINA RADIO INTL, Urümqi — S Africa • 500 kW
**JAPAN**
    RADIO JAPAN/NHK, Tokyo-Yamata — SE Asia • 300 kW
**USA**
    †ADVENTIST WORLD R, Via Abu Dhabi — Ⓦ • W Asia & S Asia • 250 kW
    RFE-RL, Via Biblis, Germany — Ⓦ • S Europe • 100 kW
    †RFE-RL, Via Briech, Morocco — Ⓦ • Mideast • 250 kW
    Ⓦ • M-F • E Europe • 250 kW
    †RFE-RL, Via Kavála, Greece — Ⓦ • Mideast • 250 kW
    RFE-RL, Via Lampertheim, Germany — Ⓦ • W Asia & C Asia • 100 kW
    †RFE-RL, Via Udon Thani, Thailand — Ⓦ • C Asia • 250 kW
    VOA, Via Briech, Morocco — Ⓦ • S Europe • 250 kW
    Ⓦ • W Asia • 250 kW

**9700 BULGARIA**
    RADIO BULGARIA, Plovdiv — Ⓢ • C America • 250 kW
**CHINA**
    CENTRAL PEOPLE'S BS, Xi'an — DS-2 • 150 kW
    Th-Tu • DS-2 • 150 kW
    CHINA RADIO INTL, Kunming — S Asia • 500 kW
**GERMANY**
    DEUTSCHE WELLE, Via Antigua — Ⓦ • E North Am • 250 kW
    Ⓦ • N America • 250 kW
    DEUTSCHE WELLE, Via Kigali, Rwanda — Ⓢ • S Africa • 250 kW
    DEUTSCHE WELLE, Wertachtal — Ⓦ • E Europe • 500 kW
**RUSSIA**
    RADIO ROSSII, Irkutsk — Ⓦ • E Asia • DS • 100 kW
**SOUTH AFRICA**
    TRANS WORLD RADIO, Meyerton — W Africa • 250 kW
    Th-M • W Africa • 250 kW
**SPAIN**
    †R EXTERIOR ESPANA, Noblejas — Ⓦ • M-F • Europe • 350 kW • ALT. FREQ. TO 9680 kHz
**USA**
    †VOA, Via Kavála, Greece — Ⓦ • N Africa & W Africa • 250 kW
    Ⓢ • Mideast • 250 kW
    VOA, Via Udon Thani, Thailand — Ⓢ • SE Asia • 250 kW
**9700v EGYPT**
    EGYPTIAN RADIO, Abu Za'bal — N Africa • DS-VO THE ARABS • 100 kW
**9704v ETHIOPIA**
    RADIO ETHIOPIA, Gedja — DS • 100 kW
    Su • DS • 100 kW
    Sa/Su • DS • 100 kW
    M-F • DS • 100 kW

**9705 CHINA**
    †VOICE OF PUJIANG, Shanghai — E Asia • 50 kW • ALT. FREQ. TO 5075 kHz
    †XINJIANG PEOPLE'S BC STN, Urümqi — DS-KYRGYZ • 50 kW
**FINLAND**
**(con'd)** †YLE RADIO FINLAND, Pori — Ⓢ • E Europe • 250 kW

0 1 2 3 4 5 6 7 8 9 10 11 12 13 14 15 16 17 18 19 20 21 22 23 24

SEASONAL Ⓢ OR Ⓦ    1-HR TIMESHIFT MIDYEAR ◁▷ OR ▷    JAMMING / OR ∧    EARLIEST HEARD ◁    LATEST HEARD ▷    NEW FOR 2003 †

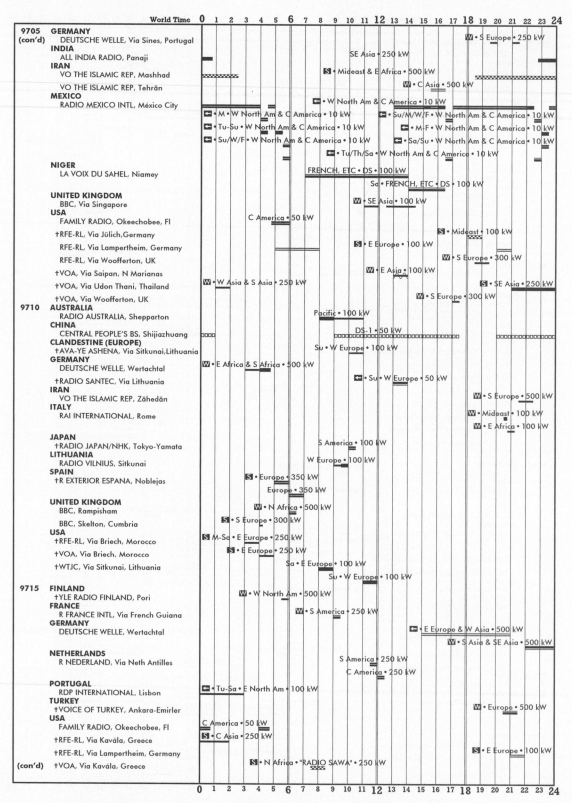

ENGLISH ▬  ARABIC ▨  CHINESE ▢▢▢  FRENCH ▬  GERMAN ▬  RUSSIAN ═  SPANISH ▬  OTHER ▬

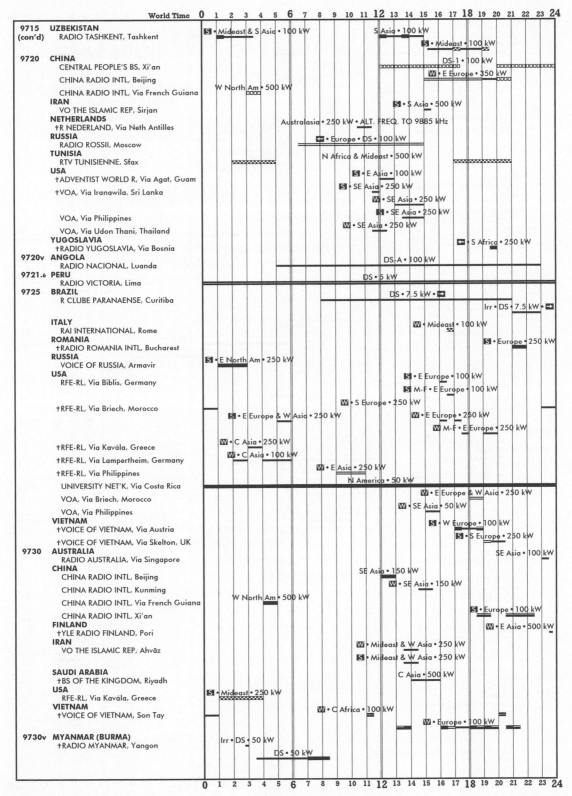

World Time

| | 0 1 2 3 4 5 6 7 8 9 10 11 12 13 14 15 16 17 18 19 20 21 22 23 24 |

**9715** **UZBEKISTAN**
(con'd)     RADIO TASHKENT, Tashkent
- S • Mideast & S Asia • 100 kW
- S Asia • 100 kW
- S • Mideast • 100 kW

**9720** **CHINA**
CENTRAL PEOPLE'S BS, Xi'an — DS-1 • 100 kW
CHINA RADIO INTL, Beijing — W • E Europe • 350 kW
CHINA RADIO INTL, Via French Guiana — W North Am • 500 kW
**IRAN**
VO THE ISLAMIC REP, Sirjan — S • S Asia • 500 kW
**NETHERLANDS**
†R NEDERLAND, Via Neth Antilles — Australasia • 250 kW • ALT. FREQ. TO 9885 kHz
**RUSSIA**
RADIO ROSSII, Moscow — ⊏ • Europe • DS • 100 kW
**TUNISIA**
RTV TUNISIENNE, Sfax — N Africa & Mideast • 500 kW
**USA**
†ADVENTIST WORLD R, Via Agat, Guam — S • E Asia • 100 kW
†VOA, Via Iranawila, Sri Lanka — S • SE Asia • 250 kW
— W • SE Asia • 250 kW
VOA, Via Philippines — S • SE Asia • 250 kW
VOA, Via Udon Thani, Thailand — W • SE Asia • 250 kW
**YUGOSLAVIA**
†RADIO YUGOSLAVIA, Via Bosnia — ⊏ • S Africa • 250 kW

**9720v** **ANGOLA**
RADIO NACIONAL, Luanda — DS-A • 100 kW

**9721.6** **PERU**
RADIO VICTORIA, Lima — DS • 5 kW

**9725** **BRAZIL**
R CLUBE PARANAENSE, Curitiba — DS • 7.5 kW • ⊐
— Irr • DS • 7.5 kW • ⊐
**ITALY**
RAI INTERNATIONAL, Rome — W • Mideast • 100 kW
**ROMANIA**
†RADIO ROMANIA INTL, Bucharest — S • Europe • 250 kW
**RUSSIA**
VOICE OF RUSSIA, Armavir — S • E North Am • 250 kW
**USA**
RFE-RL, Via Biblis, Germany — S • E Europe • 100 kW
— S • M-F • E Europe • 100 kW
†RFE-RL, Via Briech, Morocco — W • S Europe • 250 kW
— S • E Europe & W Asia • 250 kW
— W • E Europe • 250 kW
— W • M-F • E Europe • 250 kW
†RFE-RL, Via Kavála, Greece — W • C Asia • 250 kW
†RFE-RL, Via Lampertheim, Germany — W • C Asia • 100 kW
†RFE-RL, Via Philippines — W • E Asia • 250 kW
UNIVERSITY NET'K, Via Costa Rica — N America • 50 kW
VOA, Via Briech, Morocco — W • E Europe & W Asia • 250 kW
VOA, Via Philippines — W • SE Asia • 50 kW
**VIETNAM**
†VOICE OF VIETNAM, Via Austria — S • W Europe • 100 kW
†VOICE OF VIETNAM, Via Skelton, UK — S • S Europe • 250 kW

**9730** **AUSTRALIA**
RADIO AUSTRALIA, Via Singapore — SE Asia • 100 kW
**CHINA**
CHINA RADIO INTL, Beijing — SE Asia • 150 kW
CHINA RADIO INTL, Kunming — W • SE Asia • 150 kW
CHINA RADIO INTL, Via French Guiana — W North Am • 500 kW
CHINA RADIO INTL, Xi'an — S • Europe • 100 kW
**FINLAND**
†YLE RADIO FINLAND, Pori — W • E Asia • 500 kW
**IRAN**
VO THE ISLAMIC REP, Ahvāz — W • Mideast & W Asia • 250 kW
— S • Mideast & W Asia • 250 kW
**SAUDI ARABIA**
†BS OF THE KINGDOM, Riyadh — C Asia • 500 kW
**USA**
RFE-RL, Via Kavála, Greece — S • Mideast • 250 kW
**VIETNAM**
†VOICE OF VIETNAM, Son Tay — W • C Africa • 100 kW
— W • Europe • 100 kW

**9730v** **MYANMAR (BURMA)**
†RADIO MYANMAR, Yangon — Irr • DS • 50 kW
— DS • 50 kW

| | 0 1 2 3 4 5 6 7 8 9 10 11 12 13 14 15 16 17 18 19 20 21 22 23 24 |

SEASONAL S OR W     1-HR TIMESHIFT MIDYEAR ⊏ OR ⊐     JAMMING / OR ∧     EARLIEST HEARD ◁     LATEST HEARD ▷     NEW FOR 2003 †

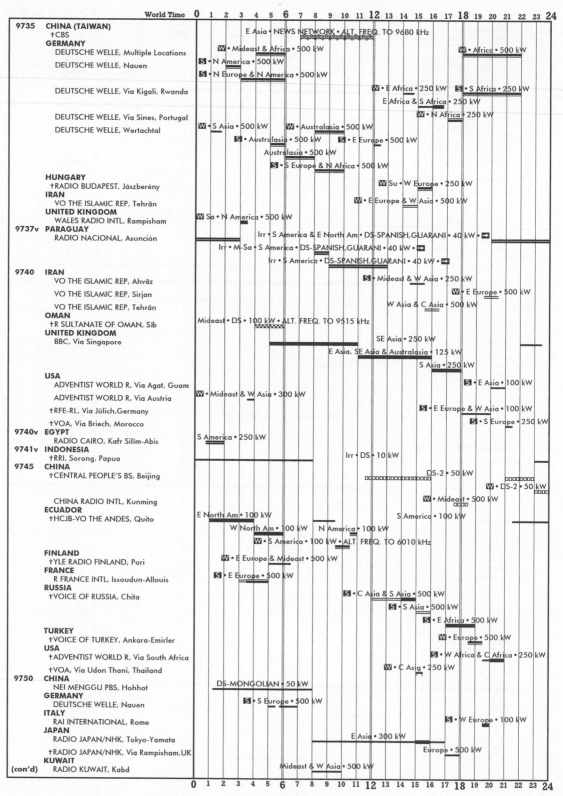

| World Time | | | | | |
| --- | --- | --- | --- | --- | --- |

**9735 CHINA (TAIWAN)**
 †CBS — E Asia • NEWS NETWORK • ALT. FREQ. TO 9680 kHz

**GERMANY**
 DEUTSCHE WELLE, Multiple Locations — W • Mideast & Africa • 500 kW ... W • Africa • 500 kW
 DEUTSCHE WELLE, Nauen — S • N America • 500 kW
  S • N Europe & N America • 500 kW
 DEUTSCHE WELLE, Via Kigali, Rwanda — W • E Africa • 250 kW ... S • S Africa • 250 kW
  E Africa & S Africa • 250 kW
 DEUTSCHE WELLE, Via Sines, Portugal — W • N Africa • 250 kW
 DEUTSCHE WELLE, Wertachtal — W • S Asia • 500 kW    W • Australasia • 500 kW
  S • Australasia • 500 kW    W • E Europe • 500 kW
  Australasia • 500 kW
  S • S Europe & N Africa • 500 kW

**HUNGARY**
 †RADIO BUDAPEST, Jászberény — W Su • W Europe • 250 kW

**IRAN**
 VO THE ISLAMIC REP, Tehrān — W • E Europe & W Asia • 500 kW

**UNITED KINGDOM**
 WALES RADIO INTL, Rampisham — W Sa • N America • 500 kW

**9737v PARAGUAY**
 RADIO NACIONAL, Asunción — Irr • S America & E North Am • DS-SPANISH,GUARANI • 40 kW • →
  Irr • M-Sa • S America • DS-SPANISH,GUARANI • 40 kW • →
  Irr • S America • DS-SPANISH,GUARANI • 40 kW • →

**9740 IRAN**
 VO THE ISLAMIC REP, Ahvāz — S • Mideast & W Asia • 250 kW
 VO THE ISLAMIC REP, Sirjan — W • E Europe • 500 kW
 VO THE ISLAMIC REP, Tehrān — W Asia & C Asia • 500 kW

**OMAN**
 †R SULTANATE OF OMAN, Sīb — Mideast • DS • 100 kW • ALT. FREQ. TO 9515 kHz

**UNITED KINGDOM**
 BBC, Via Singapore — SE Asia • 250 kW
  E Asia, SE Asia & Australasia • 125 kW
  S Asia • 250 kW

**USA**
 ADVENTIST WORLD R, Via Agat, Guam — S • E Asia • 100 kW
 ADVENTIST WORLD R, Via Austria — W • Mideast & W Asia • 300 kW
 †RFE-RL, Via Jülich, Germany — S • E Europe & W Asia • 100 kW
 †VOA, Via Briech, Morocco — S • S Europe • 250 kW

**9740v EGYPT**
 RADIO CAIRO, Kafr Silīm-Abis — S America • 250 kW

**9741v INDONESIA**
 †RRI, Sorong, Papua — Irr • DS • 10 kW

**9745 CHINA**
 †CENTRAL PEOPLE'S BS, Beijing — DS-2 • 50 kW
  W • DS-2 • 50 kW

 CHINA RADIO INTL, Kunming — W • Mideast • 500 kW

**ECUADOR**
 †HCJB-VO THE ANDES, Quito — E North Am • 100 kW    S America • 100 kW
  W North Am • 100 kW    N America • 100 kW
  W • S America • 100 kW • ALT. FREQ. TO 6010 kHz

**FINLAND**
 †YLE RADIO FINLAND, Pori — W • E Europe & Mideast • 500 kW

**FRANCE**
 R FRANCE INTL, Issoudun-Allouis — S • E Europe • 500 kW

**RUSSIA**
 †VOICE OF RUSSIA, Chita — S • C Asia & S Asia • 500 kW
  S • S Asia • 500 kW

**TURKEY**
 †VOICE OF TURKEY, Ankara-Emirler — S • E Africa • 500 kW
  W • Europe • 500 kW

**USA**
 †ADVENTIST WORLD R, Via South Africa — S • W Africa & C Africa • 250 kW
 †VOA, Via Udon Thani, Thailand — W • C Asia • 250 kW

**9750 CHINA**
 NEI MENGGU PBS, Hohhot — DS-MONGOLIAN • 50 kW

**GERMANY**
 DEUTSCHE WELLE, Nauen — S • S Europe • 500 kW

**ITALY**
 RAI INTERNATIONAL, Rome — S • W Europe • 100 kW

**JAPAN**
 RADIO JAPAN/NHK, Tokyo-Yamata — E Asia • 300 kW
 †RADIO JAPAN/NHK, Via Rampisham, UK — Europe • 500 kW

**KUWAIT**
**(con'd)** RADIO KUWAIT, Kabd — Mideast & W Asia • 500 kW

ENGLISH ▪▪▪ ARABIC ⊠⊠⊠ CHINESE □□□ FRENCH ▬▬ GERMAN ▬▬ RUSSIAN ══ SPANISH ▬▬ OTHER ▬▬

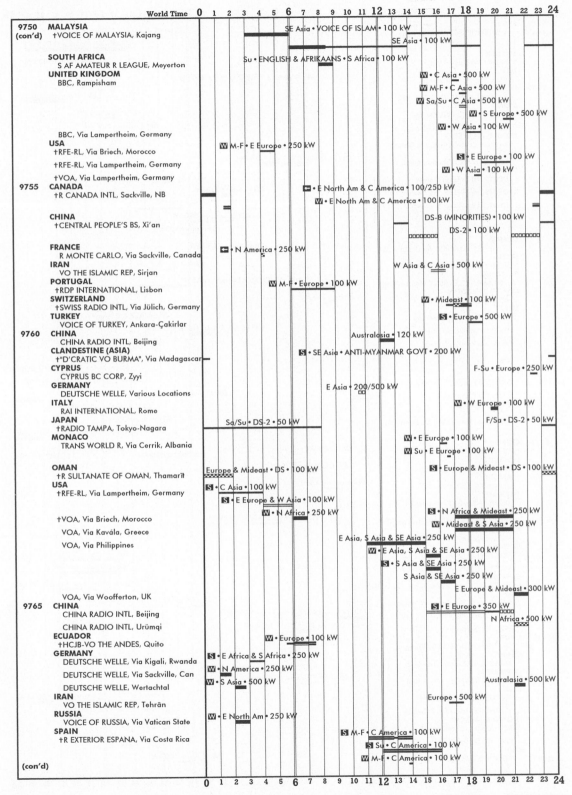

| World Time | 0 1 2 3 4 5 6 7 8 9 10 11 12 13 14 15 16 17 18 19 20 21 22 23 24 |
|---|---|

**9750 MALAYSIA**
**(con'd)** †VOICE OF MALAYSIA, Kajang — SE Asia • VOICE OF ISLAM • 100 kW; SE Asia • 100 kW

**SOUTH AFRICA**
 S AF AMATEUR R LEAGUE, Meyerton — Su • ENGLISH & AFRIKAANS • S Africa • 100 kW
**UNITED KINGDOM**
 BBC, Rampisham — W • C Asia • 500 kW; W M-F • C Asia • 500 kW; W Sa/Su • C Asia • 500 kW; W • S Europe • 500 kW; W • W Asia • 100 kW

 BBC, Via Lampertheim, Germany
**USA**
 †RFE-RL, Via Briech, Morocco — W M-F • E Europe • 250 kW
 †RFE-RL, Via Lampertheim, Germany — S • E Europe • 100 kW
 †VOA, Via Lampertheim, Germany — W • W Asia • 100 kW

**9755 CANADA**
 †R CANADA INTL, Sackville, NB — ⬅ • E North Am & C America • 100/250 kW; W • E North Am & C America • 100 kW

**CHINA**
 †CENTRAL PEOPLE'S BS, Xi'an — DS-8 (MINORITIES) • 100 kW; DS-2 • 100 kW

**FRANCE**
 R MONTE CARLO, Via Sackville, Canada — ⬅ • N America • 250 kW
**IRAN**
 VO THE ISLAMIC REP, Sirjan — W Asia & C Asia • 500 kW
**PORTUGAL**
 †RDP INTERNATIONAL, Lisbon — W M-F • Europe • 100 kW
**SWITZERLAND**
 †SWISS RADIO INTL, Via Jülich, Germany — W • Mideast • 100 kW
**TURKEY**
 VOICE OF TURKEY, Ankara-Çakirlar — S • Europe • 500 kW

**9760 CHINA**
 CHINA RADIO INTL, Beijing — Australasia • 120 kW
**CLANDESTINE (ASIA)**
 †"D'CRATIC VO BURMA", Via Madagascar — S • SE Asia • ANTI-MYANMAR GOVT • 200 kW
**CYPRUS**
 CYPRUS BC CORP, Zyyi — F-Su • Europe • 250 kW
**GERMANY**
 DEUTSCHE WELLE, Various Locations — E Asia • 200/500 kW
**ITALY**
 RAI INTERNATIONAL, Rome — W • W Europe • 100 kW
**JAPAN**
 †RADIO TAMPA, Tokyo-Nagara — Sa/Su • DS-2 • 50 kW; F/Sa • DS-2 • 50 kW
**MONACO**
 TRANS WORLD R, Via Cerrik, Albania — W • E Europe • 100 kW; W Su • E Europe • 100 kW

**OMAN**
 †R SULTANATE OF OMAN, Thamarīt — Europe & Mideast • DS • 100 kW; S • Europe & Mideast • DS • 100 kW
**USA**
 †RFE-RL, Via Lampertheim, Germany — S • C Asia • 100 kW; S • E Europe & W Asia • 100 kW; W • N Africa • 250 kW

 †VOA, Via Briech, Morocco — S • N Africa & Mideast • 250 kW
 VOA, Via Kavála, Greece — W • Mideast & S Asia • 250 kW
 VOA, Via Philippines — E Asia, S Asia & SE Asia • 250 kW; W • E Asia, S Asia & SE Asia • 250 kW; S • S Asia & SE Asia • 250 kW; S Asia & SE Asia • 250 kW

 VOA, Via Woofferton, UK — E Europe & Mideast • 300 kW
**9765 CHINA**
 CHINA RADIO INTL, Beijing — S • E Europe • 350 kW
 CHINA RADIO INTL, Urümqi — N Africa • 500 kW
**ECUADOR**
 †HCJB-VO THE ANDES, Quito — W • Europe • 100 kW
**GERMANY**
 DEUTSCHE WELLE, Via Kigali, Rwanda — S • E Africa & S Africa • 250 kW
 DEUTSCHE WELLE, Via Sackville, Can — W • N America • 250 kW
 DEUTSCHE WELLE, Wertachtal — W • S Asia • 500 kW; Australasia • 500 kW
**IRAN**
 VO THE ISLAMIC REP, Tehrān — Europe • 500 kW
**RUSSIA**
 VOICE OF RUSSIA, Via Vatican State — W • E North Am • 250 kW
**SPAIN**
 †R EXTERIOR ESPANA, Via Costa Rica — S M-F • C America • 100 kW; S Su • C America • 100 kW; W M-F • C America • 100 kW

**(con'd)**

| 0 1 2 3 4 5 6 7 8 9 10 11 12 13 14 15 16 17 18 19 20 21 22 23 24 |
|---|

SEASONAL S OR W    1-HR TIMESHIFT MIDYEAR ⬅ OR ➡    JAMMING / OR /\    EARLIEST HEARD ◁    LATEST HEARD ▷    NEW FOR 2003 †

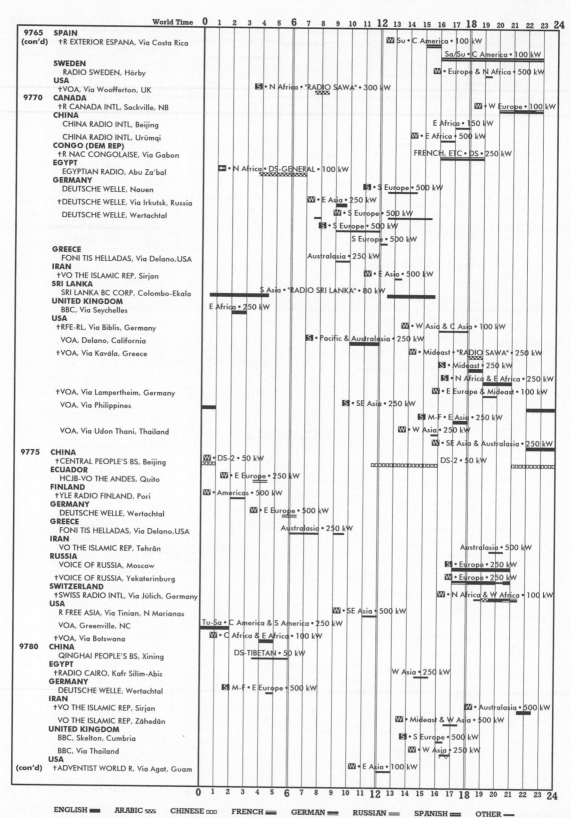

| | World Time | 0 | 1 | 2 | 3 | 4 | 5 | 6 | 7 | 8 | 9 | 10 | 11 | 12 | 13 | 14 | 15 | 16 | 17 | 18 | 19 | 20 | 21 | 22 | 23 | 24 |

**SPAIN**
**9765 (con'd)**
†R EXTERIOR ESPANA, Via Costa Rica — W • Su • C America • 100 kW; Sa/Su • C America • 100 kW

**SWEDEN**
RADIO SWEDEN, Hörby — W • Europe & N Africa • 500 kW

**USA**
†VOA, Via Woofferton, UK — S • N Africa • "RADIO SAWA" • 300 kW

**9770 CANADA**
†R CANADA INTL, Sackville, NB — W • W Europe • 100 kW

**CHINA**
CHINA RADIO INTL, Beijing — E Africa • 150 kW

CHINA RADIO INTL, Urümqi — W • E Africa • 500 kW

**CONGO (DEM REP)**
†R NAC CONGOLAISE, Via Gabon — FRENCH, ETC • DS • 250 kW

**EGYPT**
EGYPTIAN RADIO, Abu Za'bal — • N Africa • DS-GENERAL • 100 kW

**GERMANY**
DEUTSCHE WELLE, Nauen — S • S Europe • 500 kW

†DEUTSCHE WELLE, Via Irkutsk, Russia — W • E Asia • 250 kW

DEUTSCHE WELLE, Wertachtal — W • S Europe • 500 kW; S • S Europe • 500 kW; S Europe • 500 kW

**GREECE**
FONI TIS HELLADAS, Via Delano, USA — Australasia • 250 kW

**IRAN**
†VO THE ISLAMIC REP, Sirjan — W • E Asia • 500 kW

**SRI LANKA**
SRI LANKA BC CORP, Colombo-Ekala — S Asia • "RADIO SRI LANKA" • 80 kW

**UNITED KINGDOM**
BBC, Via Seychelles — E Africa • 250 kW

**USA**
†RFE-RL, Via Biblis, Germany — W • W Asia & C Asia • 100 kW

VOA, Delano, California — S • Pacific & Australasia • 250 kW

†VOA, Via Kavála, Greece — W • Mideast • "RADIO SAWA" • 250 kW; S • Mideast • 250 kW; S • N Africa & E Africa • 250 kW

†VOA, Via Lampertheim, Germany — W • E Europe & Mideast • 100 kW

VOA, Via Philippines — S • SE Asia • 250 kW; M-F • E Asia • 250 kW

VOA, Via Udon Thani, Thailand — W • W Asia • 250 kW; W • SE Asia & Australasia • 250 kW

**9775 CHINA**
†CENTRAL PEOPLE'S BS, Beijing — W • DS-2 • 50 kW; DS-2 • 50 kW

**ECUADOR**
HCJB-VO THE ANDES, Quito — W • E Europe • 250 kW

**FINLAND**
†YLE RADIO FINLAND, Pori — W • Americas • 500 kW

**GERMANY**
DEUTSCHE WELLE, Wertachtal — W • E Europe • 500 kW

**GREECE**
FONI TIS HELLADAS, Via Delano, USA — Australasia • 250 kW

**IRAN**
VO THE ISLAMIC REP, Tehrān — Australasia • 500 kW

**RUSSIA**
VOICE OF RUSSIA, Moscow — S • Europe • 250 kW

†VOICE OF RUSSIA, Yekaterinburg — W • Europe • 250 kW

**SWITZERLAND**
†SWISS RADIO INTL, Via Jülich, Germany — W • N Africa & W Africa • 100 kW

**USA**
R FREE ASIA, Via Tinian, N Marianas — W • SE Asia • 500 kW

VOA, Greenville, NC — Tu-Sa • C America & S America • 250 kW

†VOA, Via Botswana — W • C Africa & E Africa • 100 kW

**9780 CHINA**
QINGHAI PEOPLE'S BS, Xining — DS-TIBETAN • 50 kW

**EGYPT**
†RADIO CAIRO, Kafr Silim-Abis — W Asia • 250 kW

**GERMANY**
DEUTSCHE WELLE, Wertachtal — S • M-F • E Europe • 500 kW

**IRAN**
†VO THE ISLAMIC REP, Sirjan — W • Australasia • 500 kW

VO THE ISLAMIC REP, Zāhedān — W • Mideast & W Asia • 500 kW

**UNITED KINGDOM**
BBC, Skelton, Cumbria — S • S Europe • 500 kW

BBC, Via Thailand — W • W Asia • 250 kW

**USA**
**(con'd)** †ADVENTIST WORLD R, Via Agat, Guam — W • E Asia • 100 kW

| | 0 | 1 | 2 | 3 | 4 | 5 | 6 | 7 | 8 | 9 | 10 | 11 | 12 | 13 | 14 | 15 | 16 | 17 | 18 | 19 | 20 | 21 | 22 | 23 | 24 |

ENGLISH ▬▬  ARABIC ⟩⟩⟩  CHINESE □□□  FRENCH ▬▬  GERMAN ▬▬  RUSSIAN ══  SPANISH ▬▬  OTHER ▬▬

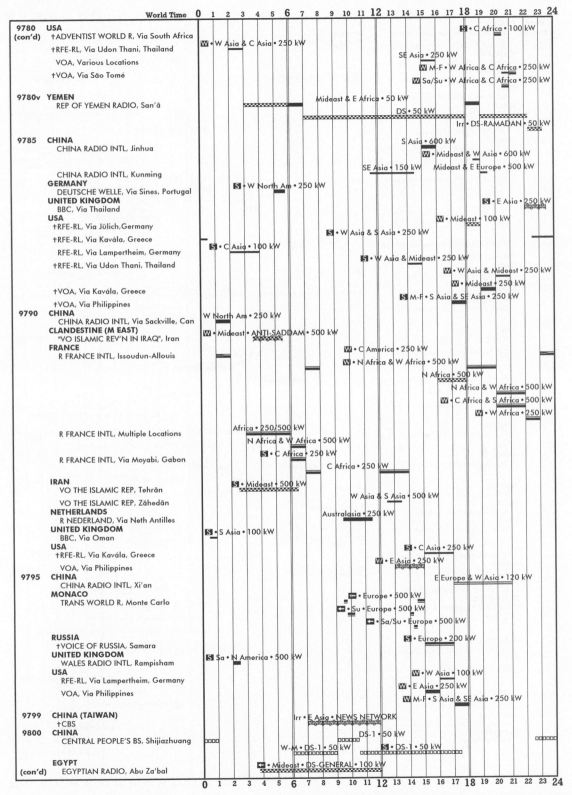

**World Time**

| | |
|---|---|
| **9780** (con'd) | **USA** |
| | †ADVENTIST WORLD R, Via South Africa |
| | C Africa • 100 kW |
| | †RFE-RL, Via Udon Thani, Thailand |
| | W • W Asia & C Asia • 250 kW |
| | VOA, Various Locations |
| | SE Asia • 250 kW |
| | †VOA, Via São Tomé |
| | W M-F • W Africa & C Africa • 250 kW |
| | W Sa/Su • W Africa & C Africa • 250 kW |
| **9780v** | **YEMEN** |
| | REP OF YEMEN RADIO, San'ā |
| | Mideast & E Africa • 50 kW |
| | DS • 50 kW |
| | Irr • DS-RAMADAN • 50 kW |
| **9785** | **CHINA** |
| | CHINA RADIO INTL, Jinhua |
| | S Asia • 600 kW |
| | W • Mideast & W Asia • 600 kW |
| | SE Asia • 150 kW   Mideast & E Europe • 500 kW |
| | CHINA RADIO INTL, Kunming |
| | **GERMANY** |
| | DEUTSCHE WELLE, Via Sines, Portugal |
| | S • W North Am • 250 kW |
| | **UNITED KINGDOM** |
| | BBC, Via Thailand |
| | S • E Asia • 250 kW |
| | **USA** |
| | †RFE-RL, Via Jülich, Germany |
| | W • Mideast • 100 kW |
| | †RFE-RL, Via Kavála, Greece |
| | S • W Asia & S Asia • 250 kW |
| | RFE-RL, Via Lampertheim, Germany |
| | S • C Asia • 100 kW |
| | †RFE-RL, Via Udon Thani, Thailand |
| | S • W Asia & Mideast • 250 kW |
| | W • W Asia & Mideast • 250 kW |
| | W • Mideast • 250 kW |
| | †VOA, Via Kavála, Greece |
| | †VOA, Via Philippines |
| | S M-F • S Asia & SE Asia • 250 kW |
| **9790** | **CHINA** |
| | CHINA RADIO INTL, Via Sackville, Can |
| | W North Am • 250 kW |
| | **CLANDESTINE (M EAST)** |
| | "VO ISLAMIC REV'N IN IRAQ", Iran |
| | W • Mideast • ANTI-SADDAM • 500 kW |
| | **FRANCE** |
| | R FRANCE INTL, Issoudun-Allouis |
| | W • C America • 250 kW |
| | W • N Africa & W Africa • 500 kW |
| | N Africa • 500 kW |
| | N Africa & W Africa • 500 kW |
| | W • C Africa & S Africa • 500 kW |
| | W • W Africa • 250 kW |
| | R FRANCE INTL, Multiple Locations |
| | Africa • 250/500 kW |
| | N Africa & W Africa • 500 kW |
| | R FRANCE INTL, Via Moyabi, Gabon |
| | S • C Africa • 250 kW |
| | C Africa • 250 kW |
| | **IRAN** |
| | VO THE ISLAMIC REP, Tehrān |
| | S • Mideast • 500 kW |
| | VO THE ISLAMIC REP, Zāhedān |
| | W Asia & S Asia • 500 kW |
| | **NETHERLANDS** |
| | R NEDERLAND, Via Neth Antilles |
| | Australasia • 250 kW |
| | **UNITED KINGDOM** |
| | BBC, Via Oman |
| | S • S Asia • 100 kW |
| | **USA** |
| | †RFE-RL, Via Kavála, Greece |
| | S • C Asia • 250 kW |
| | VOA, Via Philippines |
| | W • E Asia • 250 kW |
| **9795** | **CHINA** |
| | CHINA RADIO INTL, Xi'an |
| | E Europe & W Asia • 120 kW |
| | **MONACO** |
| | TRANS WORLD R, Monte Carlo |
| | • Europe • 500 kW |
| | • Su • Europe • 500 kW |
| | • Sa/Su • Europe • 500 kW |
| | **RUSSIA** |
| | †VOICE OF RUSSIA, Samara |
| | S • Europe • 200 kW |
| | **UNITED KINGDOM** |
| | WALES RADIO INTL, Rampisham |
| | S Sa • N America • 500 kW |
| | **USA** |
| | RFE-RL, Via Lampertheim, Germany |
| | W • W Asia • 100 kW |
| | VOA, Via Philippines |
| | W • E Asia • 250 kW |
| | W M-F • S Asia & SE Asia • 250 kW |
| **9799** | **CHINA (TAIWAN)** |
| | †CBS |
| | Irr • E Asia • NEWS NETWORK |
| **9800** | **CHINA** |
| | CENTRAL PEOPLE'S BS, Shijiazhuang |
| | DS-1 • 50 kW |
| | W-M • DS-1 • 50 kW   S • DS-1 • 50 kW |
| **(con'd)** | **EGYPT** |
| | EGYPTIAN RADIO, Abu Za'bal |
| | • Mideast • DS-GENERAL • 100 kW |

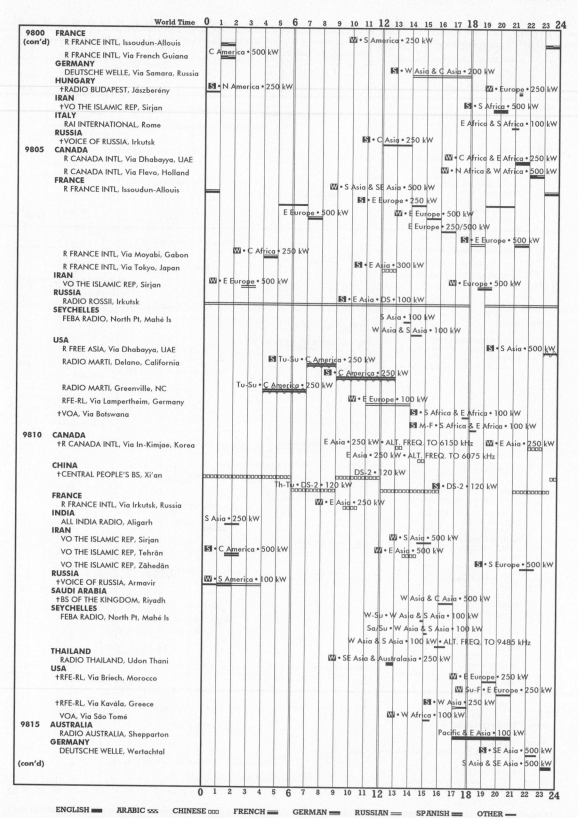

World Time 0 1 2 3 4 5 6 7 8 9 10 11 12 13 14 15 16 17 18 19 20 21 22 23 24

**9800**
**(con'd)** **FRANCE**
     R FRANCE INTL, Issoudun-Allouis      W • S America • 250 kW
     R FRANCE INTL, Via French Guiana      C America • 500 kW
   **GERMANY**
     DEUTSCHE WELLE, Via Samara, Russia    S • W Asia & C Asia • 200 kW
   **HUNGARY**
     †RADIO BUDAPEST, Jászberény    S • N America • 250 kW      W • Europe • 250 kW
   **IRAN**
     †VO THE ISLAMIC REP, Sirjan      S • S Africa • 500 kW
   **ITALY**
     RAI INTERNATIONAL, Rome      E Africa & S Africa • 100 kW
   **RUSSIA**
**9805**    †VOICE OF RUSSIA, Irkutsk      S • C Asia • 250 kW
   **CANADA**
     R CANADA INTL, Via Dhabayya, UAE      W • C Africa & E Africa • 250 kW
     R CANADA INTL, Via Flevo, Holland      W • N Africa & W Africa • 500 kW
   **FRANCE**
     R FRANCE INTL, Issoudun-Allouis      W • S Asia & SE Asia • 500 kW
         S • E Europe • 250 kW
         E Europe • 500 kW    W • E Europe • 500 kW
         E Europe • 250/500 kW
         S • E Europe • 500 kW
     R FRANCE INTL, Via Moyabi, Gabon    W • C Africa • 250 kW
     R FRANCE INTL, Via Tokyo, Japan      S • E Asia • 300 kW
   **IRAN**
     VO THE ISLAMIC REP, Sirjan    W • E Europe • 500 kW      W • Europe • 500 kW
   **RUSSIA**
     RADIO ROSSII, Irkutsk      S • E Asia • DS • 100 kW
   **SEYCHELLES**
     FEBA RADIO, North Pt, Mahé Is      S Asia • 100 kW
         W Asia & S Asia • 100 kW
   **USA**
     R FREE ASIA, Via Dhabayya, UAE      S • S Asia • 500 kW
     RADIO MARTI, Delano, California    S Tu-Su • C America • 250 kW
         S • C America • 250 kW
     RADIO MARTI, Greenville, NC    Tu-Su • C America • 250 kW
     RFE-RL, Via Lampertheim, Germany      W • E Europe • 100 kW
     †VOA, Via Botswana      S • S Africa & E Africa • 100 kW
         S M-F • S Africa & E Africa • 100 kW
**9810** **CANADA**
     †R CANADA INTL, Via In-Kimjae, Korea      E Asia • 250 kW • ALT. FREQ. TO 6150 kHz      W • E Asia • 250 kW
         E Asia • 250 kW • ALT. FREQ. TO 6075 kHz
   **CHINA**
     †CENTRAL PEOPLE'S BS, Xi'an      DS-2 • 120 kW
         Th-Tu • DS-2 • 120 kW      S • DS-2 • 120 kW
   **FRANCE**
     R FRANCE INTL, Via Irkutsk, Russia      W • E Asia • 250 kW
   **INDIA**
     ALL INDIA RADIO, Aligarh    S Asia • 250 kW
   **IRAN**
     VO THE ISLAMIC REP, Sirjan      W • S Asia • 500 kW
     VO THE ISLAMIC REP, Tehrān    S • C America • 500 kW      W • E Asia • 500 kW
     VO THE ISLAMIC REP, Zāhedān      S • S Europe • 500 kW
   **RUSSIA**
     †VOICE OF RUSSIA, Armavir    W • S America • 100 kW
   **SAUDI ARABIA**
     †BS OF THE KINGDOM, Riyadh      W Asia & C Asia • 500 kW
   **SEYCHELLES**
     FEBA RADIO, North Pt, Mahé Is      W-Su • W Asia & S Asia • 100 kW
         Sa/Su • W Asia & S Asia • 100 kW
         W Asia & S Asia • 100 kW • ALT. FREQ. TO 9485 kHz
   **THAILAND**
     RADIO THAILAND, Udon Thani      W • SE Asia & Australasia • 250 kW
   **USA**
     †RFE-RL, Via Briech, Morocco      W • E Europe • 250 kW
         W Su-F • E Europe • 250 kW
     †RFE-RL, Via Kavála, Greece      S • W Asia • 250 kW
     VOA, Via São Tomé      W • W Africa • 100 kW
**9815** **AUSTRALIA**
     RADIO AUSTRALIA, Shepparton      Pacific & E Asia • 100 kW
   **GERMANY**
     DEUTSCHE WELLE, Wertachtal      S • SE Asia • 500 kW
**(con'd)**      S Asia & SE Asia • 500 kW

0 1 2 3 4 5 6 7 8 9 10 11 12 13 14 15 16 17 18 19 20 21 22 23 24

ENGLISH ▬▬    ARABIC ░░░    CHINESE □□□    FRENCH ▬▬    GERMAN ▬▬    RUSSIAN ══    SPANISH ▬▬    OTHER ▬▬

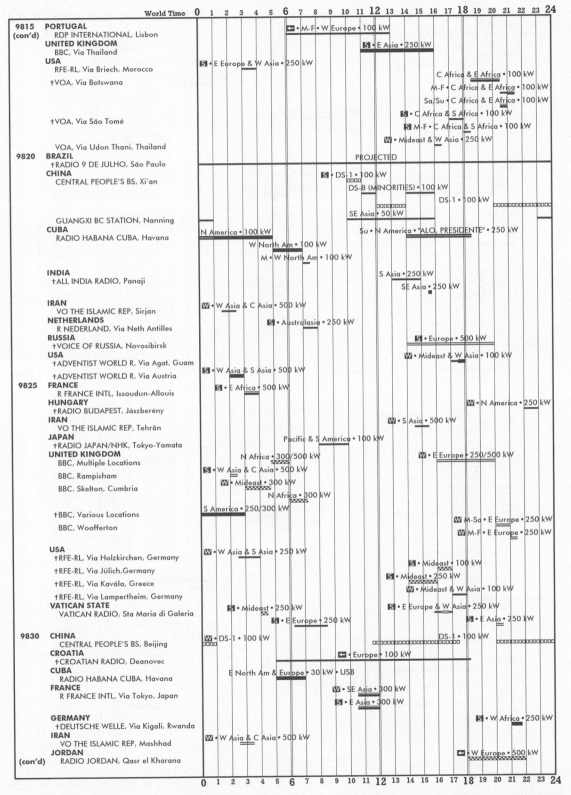

World Time   0 1 2 3 4 5 6 7 8 9 10 11 12 13 14 15 16 17 18 19 20 21 22 23 24

| Freq | Station | Schedule |
|---|---|---|
| 9815 (con'd) | **PORTUGAL** RDP INTERNATIONAL, Lisbon | M-F • W Europe • 100 kW |
| | **UNITED KINGDOM** BBC, Via Thailand | S • E Asia • 250 kW |
| | **USA** RFE-RL, Via Briech, Morocco | S • E Europe & W Asia • 250 kW |
| | †VOA, Via Botswana | C Africa & E Africa • 100 kW; M-F • C Africa & E Africa • 100 kW; Sa/Su • C Africa & E Africa • 100 kW |
| | †VOA, Via São Tomé | S • C Africa & S Africa • 100 kW; S • M-F • C Africa & S Africa • 100 kW; W • Mideast & W Asia • 250 kW |
| | VOA, Via Udon Thani, Thailand | |
| 9820 | **BRAZIL** †RADIO 9 DE JULHO, São Paulo | PROJECTED |
| | **CHINA** CENTRAL PEOPLE'S BS, Xi'an | S • DS-1 • 100 kW; DS-8 (MINORITIES) • 100 kW; DS-1 • 100 kW |
| | GUANGXI BC STATION, Nanning | SE Asia • 50 kW |
| | **CUBA** RADIO HABANA CUBA, Havana | N America • 100 kW; Su • N America • "ALO, PRESIDENTE" • 250 kW; W North Am • 100 kW; M • W North Am • 100 kW |
| | **INDIA** †ALL INDIA RADIO, Panaji | S Asia • 250 kW; SE Asia • 250 kW |
| | **IRAN** VO THE ISLAMIC REP, Sirjan | W • W Asia & C Asia • 500 kW |
| | **NETHERLANDS** R NEDERLAND, Via Neth Antilles | S • Australasia • 250 kW |
| | **RUSSIA** †VOICE OF RUSSIA, Novosibirsk | S • Europe • 500 kW |
| | **USA** †ADVENTIST WORLD R, Via Agat, Guam | W • Mideast & W Asia • 100 kW; S • W Asia & S Asia • 500 kW |
| | †ADVENTIST WORLD R, Via Austria | |
| 9825 | **FRANCE** R FRANCE INTL, Issoudun-Allouis | S • E Africa • 500 kW |
| | **HUNGARY** †RADIO BUDAPEST, Jászberény | W • N America • 250 kW |
| | **IRAN** VO THE ISLAMIC REP, Tehrān | W • S Asia • 500 kW |
| | **JAPAN** †RADIO JAPAN/NHK, Tokyo-Yamata | Pacific & S America • 100 kW |
| | **UNITED KINGDOM** BBC, Multiple Locations | N Africa • 300/500 kW; W • E Europe • 250/500 kW |
| | BBC, Rampisham | S • W Asia & C Asia • 500 kW |
| | BBC, Skelton, Cumbria | W • Mideast • 300 kW; N Africa • 300 kW |
| | †BBC, Various Locations | S America • 250/300 kW; W M-Sa • E Europe • 250 kW; W M-F • E Europe • 250 kW |
| | BBC, Woofferton | |
| | **USA** †RFE-RL, Via Holzkirchen, Germany | W • W Asia & S Asia • 250 kW |
| | †RFE-RL, Via Jülich, Germany | S • Mideast • 100 kW |
| | †RFE-RL, Via Kavála, Greece | S • Mideast • 250 kW |
| | †RFE-RL, Via Lampertheim, Germany | W • Mideast & W Asia • 100 kW |
| | **VATICAN STATE** VATICAN RADIO, Sta Maria di Galeria | S • Mideast • 250 kW; S • E Europe & W Asia • 250 kW; S • E Europe • 250 kW; S • E Asia • 250 kW |
| 9830 | **CHINA** CENTRAL PEOPLE'S BS, Beijing | W • DS-1 • 100 kW; DS-1 • 100 kW |
| | **CROATIA** †CROATIAN RADIO, Deanovec | Europe • 100 kW |
| | **CUBA** RADIO HABANA CUBA, Havana | E North Am & Europe • 30 kW • USB |
| | **FRANCE** R FRANCE INTL, Via Tokyo, Japan | W • SE Asia • 300 kW; S • E Asia • 300 kW |
| | **GERMANY** †DEUTSCHE WELLE, Via Kigali, Rwanda | S • W Africa • 250 kW |
| | **IRAN** VO THE ISLAMIC REP, Mashhad | W • W Asia & C Asia • 500 kW |
| | **JORDAN** (con'd) RADIO JORDAN, Qasr el Kharana | W Europe • 500 kW |

0 1 2 3 4 5 6 7 8 9 10 11 12 13 14 15 16 17 18 19 20 21 22 23 24

SEASONAL S OR W    1-HR TIMESHIFT MIDYEAR ⇦ OR ⇨    JAMMING / OR ∧    EARLIEST HEARD ◁    LATEST HEARD ▷    NEW FOR 2003 †

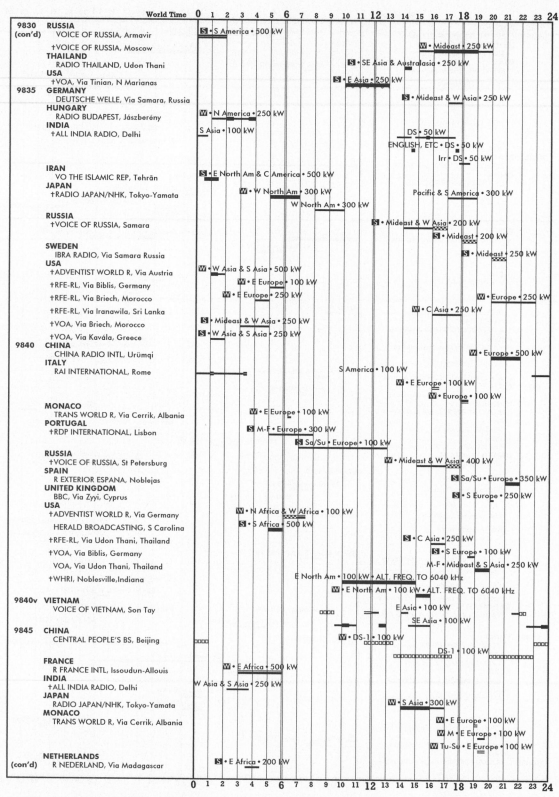

| World Time | | |
|---|---|---|
| **9830** (con'd) | **RUSSIA** | |
| | VOICE OF RUSSIA, Armavir | S • S America • 500 kW |
| | †VOICE OF RUSSIA, Moscow | W • Mideast • 250 kW |
| | **THAILAND** | |
| | RADIO THAILAND, Udon Thani | S • SE Asia & Australasia • 250 kW |
| | **USA** | |
| | †VOA, Via Tinian, N Marianas | S • E Asia • 250 kW |
| **9835** | **GERMANY** | |
| | DEUTSCHE WELLE, Via Samara, Russia | S • Mideast & W Asia • 250 kW |
| | **HUNGARY** | |
| | RADIO BUDAPEST, Jászberény | W • N America • 250 kW |
| | **INDIA** | |
| | †ALL INDIA RADIO, Delhi | S Asia • 100 kW |
| | | DS • 50 kW |
| | | ENGLISH, ETC • DS • 50 kW |
| | | Irr • DS • 50 kW |
| | **IRAN** | |
| | VO THE ISLAMIC REP, Tehrān | S • E North Am & C America • 500 kW |
| | **JAPAN** | |
| | †RADIO JAPAN/NHK, Tokyo-Yamata | W • W North Am • 300 kW |
| | | Pacific & S America • 300 kW |
| | | W North Am • 300 kW |
| | **RUSSIA** | |
| | †VOICE OF RUSSIA, Samara | S • Mideast & W Asia • 200 kW |
| | | S • Mideast • 200 kW |
| | **SWEDEN** | |
| | IBRA RADIO, Via Samara Russia | S • Mideast • 250 kW |
| | **USA** | |
| | †ADVENTIST WORLD R, Via Austria | W • W Asia & S Asia • 500 kW |
| | †RFE-RL, Via Biblis, Germany | W • E Europe • 100 kW |
| | †RFE-RL, Via Briech, Morocco | W • E Europe • 250 kW |
| | | W • Europe • 250 kW |
| | †RFE-RL, Via Iranawila, Sri Lanka | W • C Asia • 250 kW |
| | †VOA, Via Briech, Morocco | S • Mideast & W Asia • 250 kW |
| | †VOA, Via Kavála, Greece | S • W Asia & S Asia • 250 kW |
| **9840** | **CHINA** | |
| | CHINA RADIO INTL, Urümqi | W • Europe • 500 kW |
| | **ITALY** | |
| | RAI INTERNATIONAL, Rome | S America • 100 kW |
| | | W • E Europe • 100 kW |
| | | W • Europe • 100 kW |
| | **MONACO** | |
| | TRANS WORLD R, Via Cerrik, Albania | W • E Europe • 100 kW |
| | **PORTUGAL** | |
| | †RDP INTERNATIONAL, Lisbon | S • M-F • Europe • 300 kW |
| | | S • Sa/Su • Europe • 100 kW |
| | **RUSSIA** | |
| | †VOICE OF RUSSIA, St Petersburg | W • Mideast & W Asia • 400 kW |
| | **SPAIN** | |
| | R EXTERIOR ESPANA, Noblejas | S • Sa/Su • Europe • 350 kW |
| | **UNITED KINGDOM** | |
| | BBC, Via Zyyi, Cyprus | S • S Europe • 250 kW |
| | **USA** | |
| | †ADVENTIST WORLD R, Via Germany | W • N Africa & W Africa • 100 kW |
| | HERALD BROADCASTING, S Carolina | S • S Africa • 500 kW |
| | †RFE-RL, Via Udon Thani, Thailand | S • C Asia • 250 kW |
| | †VOA, Via Biblis, Germany | S • S Europe • 100 kW |
| | VOA, Via Udon Thani, Thailand | M-F • Mideast & S Asia • 250 kW |
| | †WHRI, Noblesville, Indiana | E North Am • 100 kW • ALT. FREQ. TO 6040 kHz |
| | | W • E North Am • 100 kW • ALT. FREQ. TO 6040 kHz |
| **9840v** | **VIETNAM** | |
| | VOICE OF VIETNAM, Son Tay | E Asia • 100 kW |
| | | SE Asia • 100 kW |
| **9845** | **CHINA** | |
| | CENTRAL PEOPLE'S BS, Beijing | W • DS-1 • 100 kW |
| | | DS-1 • 100 kW |
| | **FRANCE** | |
| | R FRANCE INTL, Issoudun-Allouis | W • E Africa • 500 kW |
| | **INDIA** | |
| | †ALL INDIA RADIO, Delhi | W Asia & S Asia • 250 kW |
| | **JAPAN** | |
| | RADIO JAPAN/NHK, Tokyo-Yamata | W • S Asia • 300 kW |
| | **MONACO** | |
| | TRANS WORLD R, Via Cerrik, Albania | W • E Europe • 100 kW |
| | | W M • E Europe • 100 kW |
| | | W Tu-Su • E Europe • 100 kW |
| | **NETHERLANDS** | |
| (con'd) | R NEDERLAND, Via Madagascar | S • E Africa • 200 kW |

0　1　2　3　4　5　6　7　8　9　10　11　12　13　14　15　16　17　18　19　20　21　22　23　24

ENGLISH ▬　ARABIC ∾∾　CHINESE □□□　FRENCH ═══　GERMAN ▬▬　RUSSIAN ══　SPANISH ▭▭　OTHER ▬

World Time 0 1 2 3 4 5 6 7 8 9 10 11 12 13 14 15 16 17 18 19 20 21 22 23 24

**9845** **NETHERLANDS**
(con'd)   R NEDERLAND, Via Neth Antilles — E North Am • 250 kW; C America & W North Am • 250 kW

**PAKISTAN**
  PAKISTAN BC CORP, Islamabad — DS • 100 kW
**RUSSIA**
  RADIO ROSSII, Moscow — S • N Europe & E North Am • DS • 250 kW
  RADIO ROSSII, St Petersburg — S • E Europe • DS • 400 kW
**USA**
  †ADVENTIST WORLD R, Via South Africa — S • W Africa & C Africa • 500 kW
  HERALD BROADCASTING, S Carolina — F • Australasia • 500 kW; Sa-Th • Australasia • 500 kW

  R FREE ASIA, Via Palau — W • E Asia • 80 kW
  RFE-RL, Via Briech, Morocco — W • E Europe • 250 kW
  †RFE-RL, Via Lampertheim, Germany — W • Mideast • 100 kW
  †RFE-RL, Via Udon Thani, Thailand — S • W Asia & S Asia • 250 kW
  VOA, Via Philippines — W • E Asia • 250 kW; S • E Asia • 250 kW

**9850** **CLANDESTINE (ASIA)**
  †"D'CRATIC VO BURMA", Via Germany — S • SE Asia • ANTI-MYANMAR GOVT • 100 kW • ALT. FREQ. TO 9490 kHz
**GERMANY**
  DEUTSCHE WELLE, Wertachtal — W • E Europe & Mideast • 500 kW
**HUNGARY**
  †RADIO BUDAPEST, Jászberény — Su • Europe • 250 kW
**KOREA (DPR)**
  †KOREAN CENTRAL BS — SE Asia • ALT. FREQ. TO 13650 kHz
  †VOICE OF KOREA — SE Asia • ALT. FREQ. TO 13650 kHz
**MALTA**
  †VO MEDITERRANEAN, Via Rome, Italy — M-Sa • Europe • 100 kW
**NEW ZEALAND**
  †R NEW ZEALAND INTL, Rangitaiki — S • Pacific • 100 kW
**USA**
  †ADVENTIST WORLD R, Via Austria — W • Europe • 300 kW
  †RFE-RL, Via Biblis, Germany — S • W Asia • 100 kW
  VOA, Via Kavála, Greece — W • S Asia • 250 kW
**9855** **CHINA**
  CHINA RADIO INTL, Beijing — E Asia • 120 kW
**EGYPT**
  EGYPTIAN RADIO, Kafr Silim-Abis — N Africa & Mideast • DS-VO THE ARABS • 250 kW
**KUWAIT**
  RADIO KUWAIT, Kabd — Europe & E North Am • 500 kW
**MONACO**
  TRANS WORLD R, Monte Carlo — S Sa • E Europe • 500 kW; S F-Su • E Europe • 500 kW

**USA**
  RFE-RL, Via Biblis, Germany — S • E Europe • 100 kW
  †VOA, Via Kavála, Greece — W • S Asia • 250 kW
  VOA, Via Philippines — W • S Asia • 250 kW
**VIETNAM**
  †VOICE OF VIETNAM, Xuan Mai — DS-HMONG • 50 kW
**9860** **CHINA**
  CHINA RADIO INTL, Beijing — Europe • 150 kW; S America • 150 kW

  CHINA RADIO INTL, Urümqi — W • Europe • 500 kW
**IRAN**
  VO THE ISLAMIC REP, Tehrān — Mideast & E Africa • 500 kW
**NETHERLANDS**
  R NEDERLAND, Via Madagascar — W • E Africa • 200 kW
  R NEDERLAND, Via Wertachtal, Germany — W Europe • 125 kW
**RUSSIA**
  RADIO ROSSII, Moscow — W • N Europe & E North Am • DS • 250 kW
  †VOICE OF RUSSIA, Armavir — W • C America & S America • 250 kW
  †VOICE OF RUSSIA, Moscow — S • S America • 500 kW
**USA**
  HERALD BROADCASTING, S Carolina — S F • Europe • 500 kW; S M/W • Europe • 500 kW; S Sa/Su • Europe • 500 kW; S Tu/Th • Europe • 500 kW; S M • Europe • 500 kW; S W/F • Europe • 500 kW

**9865** **BELGIUM**
  †R VLAANDEREN INTL, Via Pet-K, Russia — E Asia & Australasia • 250 kW • ALT. FREQ. TO 7390 kHz
**CZECH REPUBLIC**
(con'd)   RADIO PRAGUE, Litomyšl — S • E Europe • 100 kW

0 1 2 3 4 5 6 7 8 9 10 11 12 13 14 15 16 17 18 19 20 21 22 23 24

SEASONAL S OR W   1-HR TIMESHIFT MIDYEAR ⬅ OR ➡   JAMMING / OR ∧   EARLIEST HEARD ◁   LATEST HEARD ▷   NEW FOR 2003 †

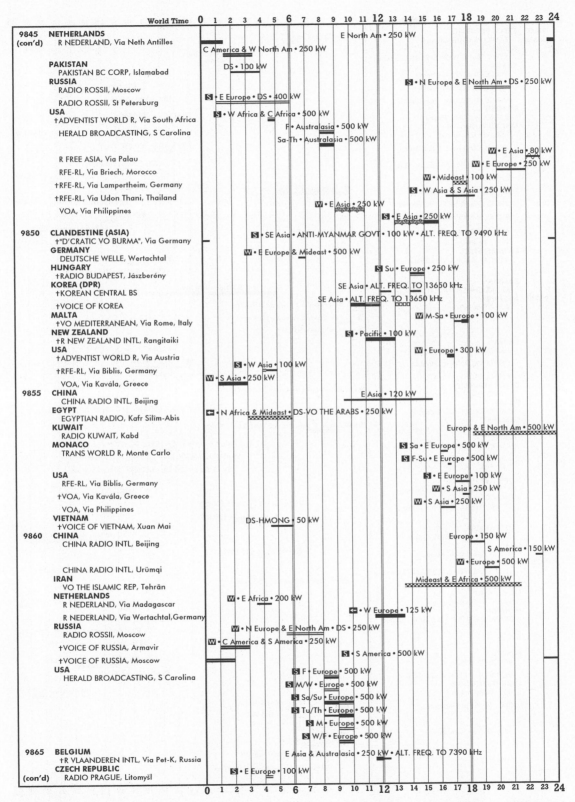

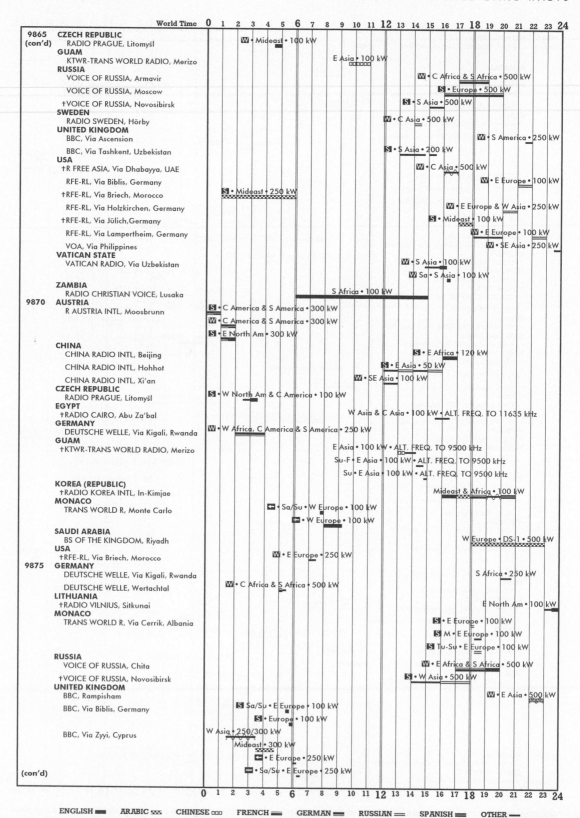

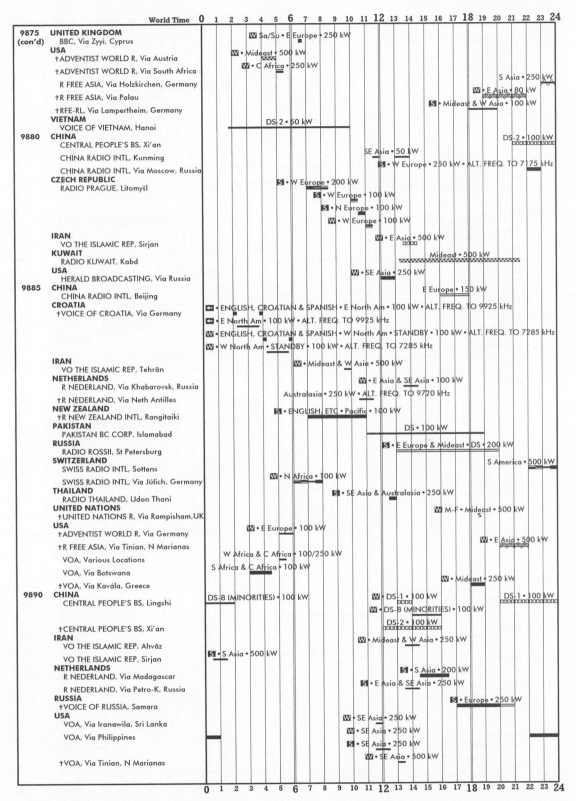

World Time | 0 1 2 3 4 5 6 7 8 9 10 11 12 13 14 15 16 17 18 19 20 21 22 23 24

**9875**
**(con'd)** UNITED KINGDOM
BBC, Via Zyyi, Cyprus — W • Sa/Su • E Europe • 250 kW
USA
†ADVENTIST WORLD R, Via Austria — W • Mideast • 500 kW
†ADVENTIST WORLD R, Via South Africa — W • C Africa • 250 kW
R FREE ASIA, Via Holzkirchen, Germany — S Asia • 250 kW
†R FREE ASIA, Via Palau — W • E Asia • 80 kW
†RFE-RL, Via Lampertheim, Germany — S • Mideast & W Asia • 100 kW
VIETNAM
VOICE OF VIETNAM, Hanoi — DS-2 • 50 kW

**9880** CHINA
CENTRAL PEOPLE'S BS, Xi'an — DS-2 • 100 kW
CHINA RADIO INTL, Kunming — SE Asia • 50 kW
CHINA RADIO INTL, Via Moscow, Russia — S • W Europe • 250 kW • ALT. FREQ. TO 7175 kHz
CZECH REPUBLIC
RADIO PRAGUE, Litomyšl — S • W Europe • 200 kW
— S • W Europe • 100 kW
— S • N Europe • 100 kW
— W • W Europe • 100 kW
IRAN
VO THE ISLAMIC REP, Sirjan — W • E Asia • 500 kW
KUWAIT
RADIO KUWAIT, Kabd — Mideast • 500 kW
USA
HERALD BROADCASTING, Via Russia — W • SE Asia • 250 kW

**9885** CHINA
CHINA RADIO INTL, Beijing — E Europe • 150 kW
CROATIA
†VOICE OF CROATIA, Via Germany — ⇇ • ENGLISH, CROATIAN & SPANISH • E North Am • 100 kW • ALT. FREQ. TO 9925 kHz
— ⇇ • E North Am • 100 kW • ALT. FREQ. TO 9925 kHz
— W • ENGLISH, CROATIAN & SPANISH • W North Am • STANDBY • 100 kW • ALT. FREQ. TO 7285 kHz
— W • W North Am • STANDBY • 100 kW • ALT. FREQ. TO 7285 kHz
IRAN
VO THE ISLAMIC REP, Tehrān — W • Mideast & W Asia • 500 kW
NETHERLANDS
R NEDERLAND, Via Khabarovsk, Russia — W • E Asia & SE Asia • 100 kW
†R NEDERLAND, Via Neth Antilles — Australasia • 250 kW • ALT. FREQ. TO 9720 kHz
NEW ZEALAND
†R NEW ZEALAND INTL, Rangitaiki — S • ENGLISH, ETC • Pacific • 100 kW
PAKISTAN
PAKISTAN BC CORP, Islamabad — DS • 100 kW
RUSSIA
RADIO ROSSII, St Petersburg — S • E Europe & Mideast • DS • 200 kW
SWITZERLAND
SWISS RADIO INTL, Sottens — S America • 500 kW
SWISS RADIO INTL, Via Jülich, Germany — W • N Africa • 100 kW
THAILAND
RADIO THAILAND, Udon Thani — S • SE Asia & Australasia • 250 kW
UNITED NATIONS
†UNITED NATIONS R, Via Rampisham, UK — W • M-F • Mideast • 500 kW
USA
†ADVENTIST WORLD R, Via Germany — W • E Europe • 100 kW
†R FREE ASIA, Via Tinian, N Marianas — W • E Asia • 500 kW
VOA, Various Locations — W Africa & C Africa • 100/250 kW
VOA, Via Botswana — S Africa & C Africa • 100 kW
†VOA, Via Kavála, Greece — W • Mideast • 250 kW

**9890** CHINA
CENTRAL PEOPLE'S BS, Lingshi — DS-8 (MINORITIES) • 100 kW — W • DS-1 • 100 kW — DS-1 • 100 kW
— W • DS-8 (MINORITIES) • 100 kW
†CENTRAL PEOPLE'S BS, Xi'an — DS-2 • 100 kW
IRAN
VO THE ISLAMIC REP, Ahvāz — W • Mideast & W Asia • 250 kW
VO THE ISLAMIC REP, Sirjan — S • S Asia • 500 kW
NETHERLANDS
R NEDERLAND, Via Madagascar — S • S Asia • 200 kW
R NEDERLAND, Via Petro-K, Russia — S • E Asia & SE Asia • 250 kW
RUSSIA
†VOICE OF RUSSIA, Samara — S • Europe • 250 kW
USA
VOA, Via Iranawila, Sri Lanka — W • SE Asia • 250 kW
VOA, Via Philippines — W • SE Asia • 250 kW
— S • SE Asia • 250 kW
†VOA, Via Tinian, N Marianas — W • SE Asia • 500 kW

0 1 2 3 4 5 6 7 8 9 10 11 12 13 14 15 16 17 18 19 20 21 22 23 24

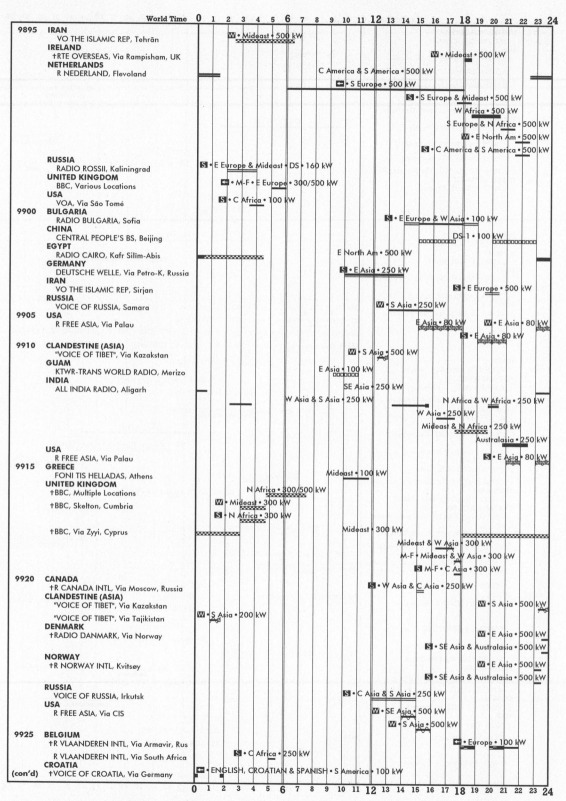

| | World Time | 0 1 2 3 4 5 6 7 8 9 10 11 12 13 14 15 16 17 18 19 20 21 22 23 24 |
|---|---|---|
| 9895 | IRAN | |
| | VO THE ISLAMIC REP, Tehrān | W • Mideast • 500 kW |
| | IRELAND | |
| | †RTE OVERSEAS, Via Rampisham, UK | W • Mideast • 500 kW |
| | NETHERLANDS | |
| | R NEDERLAND, Flevoland | C America & S America • 500 kW |
| | | S Europe • 500 kW |
| | | S • S Europe & Mideast • 500 kW |
| | | W Africa • 500 kW |
| | | S Europe & N Africa • 500 kW |
| | | W • E North Am • 500 kW |
| | | S • C America & S America • 500 kW |
| | RUSSIA | |
| | RADIO ROSSII, Kaliningrad | S • E Europe & Mideast • DS • 160 kW |
| | UNITED KINGDOM | |
| | BBC, Various Locations | M-F • E Europe • 300/500 kW |
| | USA | |
| | VOA, Via São Tomé | S • C Africa • 100 kW |
| 9900 | BULGARIA | |
| | RADIO BULGARIA, Sofia | S • E Europe & W Asia • 100 kW |
| | CHINA | |
| | CENTRAL PEOPLE'S BS, Beijing | DS-1 • 100 kW |
| | EGYPT | |
| | RADIO CAIRO, Kafr Silīm-Abis | E North Am • 500 kW |
| | GERMANY | |
| | DEUTSCHE WELLE, Via Petro-K, Russia | S • E Asia • 250 kW |
| | IRAN | |
| | VO THE ISLAMIC REP, Sirjan | S • E Europe • 500 kW |
| | RUSSIA | |
| | VOICE OF RUSSIA, Samara | W • S Asia • 250 kW |
| 9905 | USA | |
| | R FREE ASIA, Via Palau | E Asia • 80 kW    W • E Asia • 80 kW |
| | | S • E Asia • 80 kW |
| 9910 | CLANDESTINE (ASIA) | |
| | "VOICE OF TIBET", Via Kazakstan | W • S Asia • 500 kW |
| | GUAM | |
| | KTWR-TRANS WORLD RADIO, Merizo | E Asia • 100 kW |
| | INDIA | |
| | ALL INDIA RADIO, Aligarh | SE Asia • 250 kW |
| | | W Asia & S Asia • 250 kW    N Africa & W Africa • 250 kW |
| | | W Asia • 250 kW |
| | | Mideast & N Africa • 250 kW |
| | | Australasia • 250 kW |
| | USA | |
| | R FREE ASIA, Via Palau | S • E Asia • 80 kW |
| 9915 | GREECE | |
| | FONI TIS HELLADAS, Athens | Mideast • 100 kW |
| | UNITED KINGDOM | |
| | †BBC, Multiple Locations | N Africa • 300/500 kW |
| | †BBC, Skelton, Cumbria | W • Mideast • 300 kW |
| | | S • N Africa • 300 kW |
| | †BBC, Via Zyyi, Cyprus | Mideast • 300 kW |
| | | Mideast & W Asia • 300 kW |
| | | M-F • Mideast & W Asia • 300 kW |
| | | S • M-F • C Asia • 300 kW |
| 9920 | CANADA | |
| | †R CANADA INTL, Via Moscow, Russia | S • W Asia & C Asia • 250 kW |
| | CLANDESTINE (ASIA) | |
| | "VOICE OF TIBET", Via Kazakstan | W • S Asia • 500 kW |
| | "VOICE OF TIBET", Via Tajikistan | W • S Asia • 200 kW |
| | DENMARK | |
| | †RADIO DANMARK, Via Norway | W • E Asia • 500 kW |
| | | S • SE Asia & Australasia • 500 kW |
| | NORWAY | |
| | †R NORWAY INTL, Kvitsøy | W • E Asia • 500 kW |
| | | S • SE Asia & Australasia • 500 kW |
| | RUSSIA | |
| | VOICE OF RUSSIA, Irkutsk | S • C Asia & S Asia • 250 kW |
| | USA | |
| | R FREE ASIA, Via CIS | W • SE Asia • 500 kW |
| | | W • S Asia • 500 kW |
| 9925 | BELGIUM | |
| | †R VLAANDEREN INTL, Via Armavir, Rus | S • Europe • 100 kW |
| | R VLAANDEREN INTL, Via South Africa | S • C Africa • 250 kW |
| | CROATIA | |
| (con'd) | †VOICE OF CROATIA, Via Germany | ENGLISH, CROATIAN & SPANISH • S America • 100 kW |

| World Time | 0 1 2 3 4 5 6 7 8 9 10 11 12 13 14 15 16 17 18 19 20 21 22 23 24 |
|---|---|

ENGLISH ▬   ARABIC ≈≈≈   CHINESE □□□   FRENCH ═══   GERMAN ▬▬   RUSSIAN ═══   SPANISH ═══   OTHER ▬▬

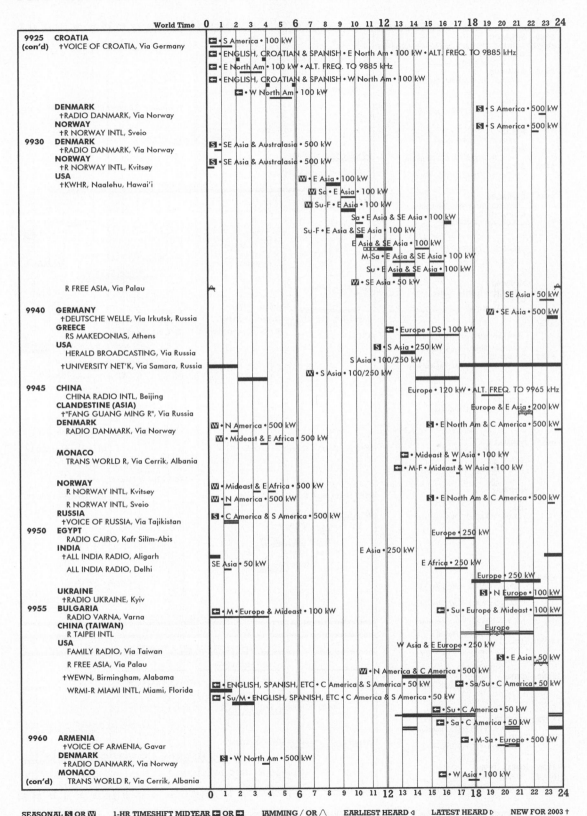

| | World Time | 0 1 2 3 4 5 6 7 8 9 10 11 12 13 14 15 16 17 18 19 20 21 22 23 24 |
|---|---|---|

**9925 CROATIA**
**(con'd) †VOICE OF CROATIA, Via Germany**
- ⮂ • S America • 100 kW
- ⮂ • ENGLISH, CROATIAN & SPANISH • E North Am • 100 kW • ALT. FREQ. TO 9885 kHz
- ⮂ • E North Am • 100 kW • ALT. FREQ. TO 9885 kHz
- ⮂ • ENGLISH, CROATIAN & SPANISH • W North Am • 100 kW
- ⮂ • W North Am • 100 kW

**DENMARK**
**†RADIO DANMARK, Via Norway**
- S • S America • 500 kW

**NORWAY**
**†R NORWAY INTL, Sveio**
- S • S America • 500 kW

**9930 DENMARK**
**†RADIO DANMARK, Via Norway**
- S • SE Asia & Australasia • 500 kW

**NORWAY**
**†R NORWAY INTL, Kvitsøy**
- S • SE Asia & Australasia • 500 kW

**USA**
**†KWHR, Naalehu, Hawai'i**
- W • E Asia • 100 kW
- Sa • E Asia • 100 kW
- W • Su-F • E Asia • 100 kW
- Sa • E Asia & SE Asia • 100 kW
- Su-F • E Asia & SE Asia • 100 kW
- E Asia & SE Asia • 100 kW
- M-Sa • E Asia & SE Asia • 100 kW
- Su • E Asia & SE Asia • 100 kW
- W • SE Asia • 50 kW

**R FREE ASIA, Via Palau**
- SE Asia • 50 kW

**9940 GERMANY**
**†DEUTSCHE WELLE, Via Irkutsk, Russia**
- W • SE Asia • 500 kW

**GREECE**
**RS MAKEDONIAS, Athens**
- ⮂ • Europe • DS • 100 kW

**USA**
**HERALD BROADCASTING, Via Russia**
- S • S Asia • 250 kW

**†UNIVERSITY NET'K, Via Samara, Russia**
- S Asia • 100/250 kW
- W • S Asia • 100/250 kW

**9945 CHINA**
**CHINA RADIO INTL, Beijing**
- Europe • 120 kW • ALT. FREQ. TO 9965 kHz

**CLANDESTINE (ASIA)**
**†"FANG GUANG MING R", Via Russia**
- Europe & E Asia • 200 kW

**DENMARK**
**RADIO DANMARK, Via Norway**
- W • N America • 500 kW
- S • E North Am & C America • 500 kW
- W • Mideast & E Africa • 500 kW

**MONACO**
**TRANS WORLD R, Via Cerrik, Albania**
- ⮂ • Mideast & W Asia • 100 kW
- ⮂ • M-F • Mideast & W Asia • 100 kW

**NORWAY**
**R NORWAY INTL, Kvitsøy**
- W • Mideast & E Africa • 500 kW

**R NORWAY INTL, Sveio**
- W • N America • 500 kW
- S • E North Am & C America • 500 kW

**RUSSIA**
**†VOICE OF RUSSIA, Via Tajikistan**
- S • C America & S America • 500 kW

**9950 EGYPT**
**RADIO CAIRO, Kafr Silim-Abis**
- Europe • 250 kW

**INDIA**
**†ALL INDIA RADIO, Aligarh**
- E Asia • 250 kW
- E Africa • 250 kW

**ALL INDIA RADIO, Delhi**
- SE Asia • 50 kW
- Europe • 250 kW

**UKRAINE**
**†RADIO UKRAINE, Kyiv**
- S • N Europe • 100 kW

**9955 BULGARIA**
**RADIO VARNA, Varna**
- ⮂ • M • Europe & Mideast • 100 kW
- ⮂ • Su • Europe & Mideast • 100 kW

**CHINA (TAIWAN)**
**R TAIPEI INTL**
- Europe

**USA**
**FAMILY RADIO, Via Taiwan**
- W Asia & E Europe • 250 kW

**R FREE ASIA, Via Palau**
- S • E Asia • 50 kW

**†WEWN, Birmingham, Alabama**
- W • N America & C America • 500 kW

**WRMI-R MIAMI INTL, Miami, Florida**
- ⮂ • ENGLISH, SPANISH, ETC • C America & S America • 50 kW
- ⮂ • Sa/Su • C America • 50 kW
- ⮂ • Su/M • ENGLISH, SPANISH, ETC • C America & S America • 50 kW
- ⮂ • Su • C America • 50 kW
- ⮂ • Sa • C America • 50 kW

**9960 ARMENIA**
**†VOICE OF ARMENIA, Gavar**
- ⮂ • M-Sa • Europe • 500 kW

**DENMARK**
**†RADIO DANMARK, Via Norway**
- S • W North Am • 500 kW

**MONACO**
**(con'd) TRANS WORLD R, Via Cerrik, Albania**
- ⮂ • W Asia • 100 kW

| | 0 1 2 3 4 5 6 7 8 9 10 11 12 13 14 15 16 17 18 19 20 21 22 23 24 |
|---|---|

SEASONAL S OR W    1-HR TIMESHIFT MIDYEAR ⮂ OR ⮂    JAMMING / OR ∧    EARLIEST HEARD ◁    LATEST HEARD ▷    NEW FOR 2003 †

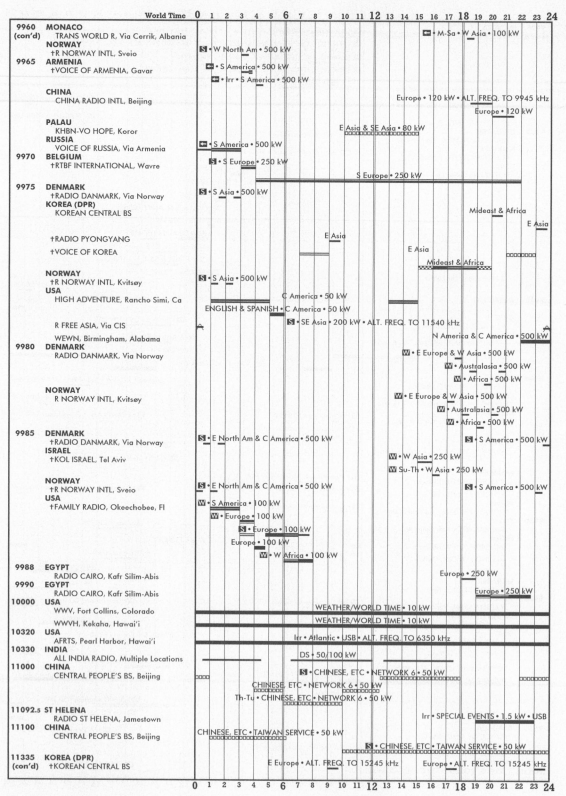

| World Time | 0 1 2 3 4 5 6 7 8 9 10 11 12 13 14 15 16 17 18 19 20 21 22 23 24 |
|---|---|

**9960** **MONACO**
(con'd)   TRANS WORLD R, Via Cerrik, Albania — M-Sa • W Asia • 100 kW
**NORWAY**
    †R NORWAY INTL, Sveio — S • W North Am • 500 kW
**9965** **ARMENIA**
    †VOICE OF ARMENIA, Gavar — S America • 500 kW
        Irr • S America • 500 kW

**CHINA**
    CHINA RADIO INTL, Beijing — Europe • 120 kW • ALT. FREQ. TO 9945 kHz
        Europe • 120 kW

**PALAU**
    KHBN-VO HOPE, Koror — E Asia & SE Asia • 80 kW
**RUSSIA**
    VOICE OF RUSSIA, Via Armenia — S America • 500 kW
**9970** **BELGIUM**
    †RTBF INTERNATIONAL, Wavre — S • S Europe • 250 kW
        S Europe • 250 kW

**9975** **DENMARK**
    †RADIO DANMARK, Via Norway — S • S Asia • 500 kW
**KOREA (DPR)**
    KOREAN CENTRAL BS — Mideast & Africa
        E Asia

    †RADIO PYONGYANG — E Asia
    †VOICE OF KOREA — E Asia
        Mideast & Africa

**NORWAY**
    †R NORWAY INTL, Kvitsøy — S • S Asia • 500 kW
**USA**
    HIGH ADVENTURE, Rancho Simi, Ca — C America • 50 kW
        ENGLISH & SPANISH • C America • 50 kW
    R FREE ASIA, Via CIS — S • SE Asia • 200 kW • ALT. FREQ. TO 11540 kHz
    WEWN, Birmingham, Alabama — N America & C America • 500 kW
**9980** **DENMARK**
    RADIO DANMARK, Via Norway — W • E Europe & W Asia • 500 kW
        W • Australasia • 500 kW
        W • Africa • 500 kW
**NORWAY**
    R NORWAY INTL, Kvitsøy — W • E Europe & W Asia • 500 kW
        W • Australasia • 500 kW
        W • Africa • 500 kW

**9985** **DENMARK**
    †RADIO DANMARK, Via Norway — S • E North Am & C America • 500 kW       S • S America • 500 kW
**ISRAEL**
    †KOL ISRAEL, Tel Aviv — W • W Asia • 250 kW
        W Su-Th • W Asia • 250 kW
**NORWAY**
    †R NORWAY INTL, Sveio — S • E North Am & C America • 500 kW       S • S America • 500 kW
**USA**
    †FAMILY RADIO, Okeechobee, Fl — W • S America • 100 kW
        W • Europe • 100 kW
        S • Europe • 100 kW
        Europe • 100 kW
        W • W Africa • 100 kW

**9988** **EGYPT**
    RADIO CAIRO, Kafr Silîm-Abis — Europe • 250 kW
**9990** **EGYPT**
    RADIO CAIRO, Kafr Silîm-Abis — Europe • 250 kW
**10000** **USA**
    WWV, Fort Collins, Colorado — WEATHER/WORLD TIME • 10 kW
    WWVH, Kekaha, Hawai'i — WEATHER/WORLD TIME • 10 kW
**10320** **USA**
    AFRTS, Pearl Harbor, Hawai'i — Irr • Atlantic • USB • ALT. FREQ. TO 6350 kHz
**10330** **INDIA**
    ALL INDIA RADIO, Multiple Locations — DS • 50/100 kW
**11000** **CHINA**
    CENTRAL PEOPLE'S BS, Beijing — S • CHINESE, ETC • NETWORK 6 • 50 kW
        CHINESE, ETC • NETWORK 6 • 50 kW
        Th-Tu • CHINESE, ETC • NETWORK 6 • 50 kW

**11092.5 ST HELENA**
    RADIO ST HELENA, Jamestown — Irr • SPECIAL EVENTS • 1.5 kW • USB
**11100** **CHINA**
    CENTRAL PEOPLE'S BS, Beijing — CHINESE, ETC • TAIWAN SERVICE • 50 kW
        S • CHINESE, ETC • TAIWAN SERVICE • 50 kW

**11335** **KOREA (DPR)**
(con'd)   †KOREAN CENTRAL BS — E Europe • ALT. FREQ. TO 15245 kHz       Europe • ALT. FREQ. TO 15245 kHz

| 0 1 2 3 4 5 6 7 8 9 10 11 12 13 14 15 16 17 18 19 20 21 22 23 24 |
|---|

ENGLISH ▬   ARABIC ≋   CHINESE ▫▫▫   FRENCH —   GERMAN ▬   RUSSIAN ═   SPANISH ▬   OTHER —

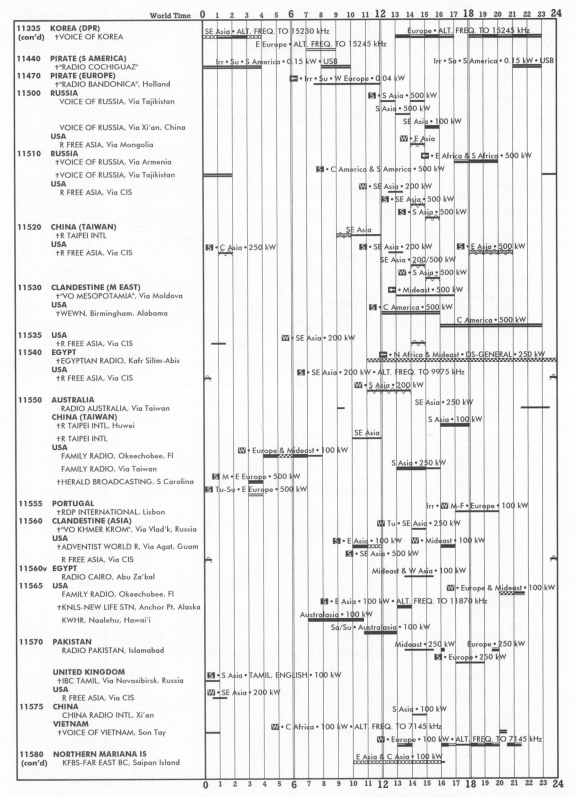

World Time: 0 1 2 3 4 5 6 7 8 9 10 11 12 13 14 15 16 17 18 19 20 21 22 23 24

**11335 KOREA (DPR)**
**(con'd)** †VOICE OF KOREA
- SE Asia • ALT. FREQ. TO 15230 kHz
- Europe • ALT. FREQ. TO 15245 kHz
- E Europe • ALT. FREQ. TO 15245 kHz

**11440 PIRATE (S AMERICA)**
†"RADIO COCHIGUAZ"
- Irr • Su • S America • 0.15 kW • USB
- Irr • Sa • S America • 0.15 kW • USB

**11470 PIRATE (EUROPE)**
†"RADIO BANDONICA", Holland
- Irr • Su • W Europe • 0.04 kW

**11500 RUSSIA**
VOICE OF RUSSIA, Via Tajikistan
- S • S Asia • 500 kW
- S Asia • 500 kW
- SE Asia • 100 kW

VOICE OF RUSSIA, Via Xi'an, China
**USA**
R FREE ASIA, Via Mongolia
- W • E Asia

**11510 RUSSIA**
†VOICE OF RUSSIA, Via Armenia
- ← • E Africa & S Africa • 500 kW

†VOICE OF RUSSIA, Via Tajikistan
- S • C America & S America • 500 kW
**USA**
R FREE ASIA, Via CIS
- W • SE Asia • 200 kW
- S • SE Asia • 500 kW
- S • S Asia • 500 kW

**11520 CHINA (TAIWAN)**
†R TAIPEI INTL
- SE Asia
**USA**
†R FREE ASIA, Via CIS
- S • C Asia • 250 kW
- S • SE Asia • 200 kW
- S • E Asia • 500 kW
- SE Asia • 200/500 kW
- W • S Asia • 500 kW

**11530 CLANDESTINE (M EAST)**
†"VO MESOPOTAMIA", Via Moldova
- ← • Mideast • 500 kW
**USA**
†WEWN, Birmingham, Alabama
- S • C America • 500 kW
- C America • 500 kW

**11535 USA**
†R FREE ASIA, Via CIS
- W • SE Asia • 200 kW
**11540 EGYPT**
†EGYPTIAN RADIO, Kafr Silim-Abis
- ← • N Africa & Mideast • DS-GENERAL • 250 kW
**USA**
†R FREE ASIA, Via CIS
- S • SE Asia • 200 kW • ALT. FREQ. TO 9975 kHz
- W • S Asia • 200 kW

**11550 AUSTRALIA**
RADIO AUSTRALIA, Via Taiwan
- SE Asia • 250 kW
**CHINA (TAIWAN)**
†R TAIPEI INTL, Huwei
- S Asia • 100 kW

†R TAIPEI INTL
- SE Asia
**USA**
FAMILY RADIO, Okeechobee, Fl
- W • Europe & Mideast • 100 kW

FAMILY RADIO, Via Taiwan
- S Asia • 250 kW

†HERALD BROADCASTING, S Carolina
- S • M • E Europe • 500 kW
- S Tu-Su • E Europe • 500 kW

**11555 PORTUGAL**
†RDP INTERNATIONAL, Lisbon
- Irr • W M-F • Europe • 100 kW
**11560 CLANDESTINE (ASIA)**
†"VO KHMER KROM", Via Vlad'k, Russia
- W Tu • SE Asia • 250 kW
**USA**
†ADVENTIST WORLD R, Via Agat, Guam
- S • E Asia • 100 kW
- W • Mideast • 100 kW

R FREE ASIA, Via CIS
- S • SE Asia • 500 kW
**11560v EGYPT**
RADIO CAIRO, Abu Za'bal
- Mideast & W Asia • 100 kW
**11565 USA**
FAMILY RADIO, Okeechobee, Fl
- W • Europe & Mideast • 100 kW

†KNLS-NEW LIFE STN, Anchor Pt, Alaska
- S • E Asia • 100 kW • ALT. FREQ. TO 11870 kHz

KWHR, Naalehu, Hawai'i
- Australasia • 100 kW
- Sa/Su • Australasia • 100 kW

**11570 PAKISTAN**
RADIO PAKISTAN, Islamabad
- Mideast • 250 kW
- Europe • 250 kW
- S • Europe • 250 kW

**UNITED KINGDOM**
†IBC TAMIL, Via Novosibirsk, Russia
- S • S Asia • TAMIL, ENGLISH • 100 kW
**USA**
R FREE ASIA, Via CIS
- W • SE Asia • 200 kW
**11575 CHINA**
CHINA RADIO INTL, Xi'an
- S Asia • 100 kW
**VIETNAM**
†VOICE OF VIETNAM, Son Tay
- W • C Africa • 100 kW • ALT. FREQ. TO 7145 kHz
- W • Europe • 100 kW • ALT. FREQ. TO 7145 kHz

**11580 NORTHERN MARIANA IS**
**(con'd)** KFBS-FAR EAST BC, Saipan Island
- E Asia & C Asia • 100 kW

World Time: 0 1 2 3 4 5 6 7 8 9 10 11 12 13 14 15 16 17 18 19 20 21 22 23 24

SEASONAL **S** OR **W**    1-HR TIMESHIFT MIDYEAR ← OR →    JAMMING / OR ∧    EARLIEST HEARD ◁    LATEST HEARD ▷    NEW FOR 2003 †

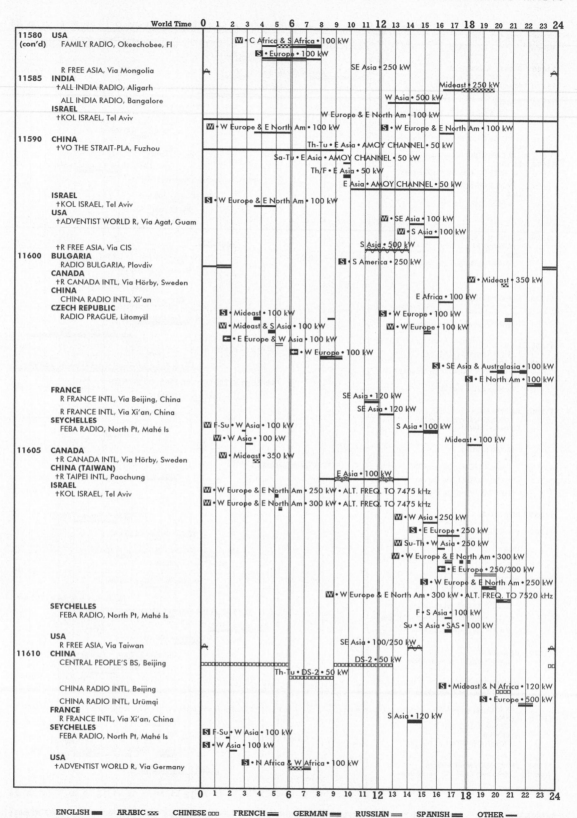

World Time

| | |
|---|---|
| 11580 **USA** | |
| (con'd) FAMILY RADIO, Okeechobee, Fl | W • C Africa & S Africa • 100 kW |
| | S • Europe • 100 kW |
| R FREE ASIA, Via Mongolia | SE Asia • 250 kW |
| 11585 **INDIA** | |
| †ALL INDIA RADIO, Aligarh | Mideast • 250 kW |
| ALL INDIA RADIO, Bangalore | W Asia • 500 kW |
| **ISRAEL** | |
| †KOL ISRAEL, Tel Aviv | W Europe & E North Am • 100 kW |
| | W • W Europe & E North Am • 100 kW     S • W Europe & E North Am • 100 kW |
| 11590 **CHINA** | |
| †VO THE STRAIT-PLA, Fuzhou | Th-Tu • E Asia • AMOY CHANNEL • 50 kW |
| | Sa-Tu • E Asia • AMOY CHANNEL • 50 kW |
| | Th/F • E Asia • 50 kW |
| | E Asia • AMOY CHANNEL • 50 kW |
| **ISRAEL** | |
| †KOL ISRAEL, Tel Aviv | S • W Europe & E North Am • 100 kW |
| **USA** | |
| †ADVENTIST WORLD R, Via Agat, Guam | W • SE Asia • 100 kW |
| | W • S Asia • 100 kW |
| †R FREE ASIA, Via CIS | S Asia • 500 kW |
| 11600 **BULGARIA** | |
| RADIO BULGARIA, Plovdiv | S • S America • 250 kW |
| **CANADA** | |
| †R CANADA INTL, Via Hörby, Sweden | W • Mideast • 350 kW |
| **CHINA** | |
| CHINA RADIO INTL, Xi'an | E Africa • 100 kW |
| **CZECH REPUBLIC** | |
| RADIO PRAGUE, Litomyšl | S • Mideast • 100 kW     S • W Europe • 100 kW |
| | W • Mideast & S Asia • 100 kW     W • W Europe • 100 kW |
| | ← • E Europe & W Asia • 100 kW |
| | ← • W Europe • 100 kW |
| | S • SE Asia & Australasia • 100 kW |
| | S • E North Am • 100 kW |
| **FRANCE** | |
| R FRANCE INTL, Via Beijing, China | SE Asia • 120 kW |
| R FRANCE INTL, Via Xi'an, China | SE Asia • 120 kW |
| **SEYCHELLES** | |
| FEBA RADIO, North Pt, Mahé Is | W • F-Su • W Asia • 100 kW     S Asia • 100 kW |
| | W • W Asia • 100 kW     Mideast • 100 kW |
| 11605 **CANADA** | |
| †R CANADA INTL, Via Hörby, Sweden | W • Mideast • 350 kW |
| **CHINA (TAIWAN)** | |
| †R TAIPEI INTL, Paochung | E Asia • 100 kW |
| **ISRAEL** | |
| †KOL ISRAEL, Tel Aviv | W • W Europe & E North Am • 250 kW • ALT. FREQ. TO 7475 kHz |
| | W • W Europe & E North Am • 300 kW • ALT. FREQ. TO 7475 kHz |
| | W • W Asia • 250 kW |
| | S • E Europe • 250 kW |
| | W • Su-Th • W Asia • 250 kW |
| | W • W Europe & E North Am • 300 kW |
| | ← • E Europe • 250/300 kW |
| | S • W Europe & E North Am • 250 kW |
| | W • W Europe & E North Am • 300 kW • ALT. FREQ. TO 7520 kHz |
| **SEYCHELLES** | |
| FEBA RADIO, North Pt, Mahé Is | F • S Asia • 100 kW |
| | Su • S Asia • SAS • 100 kW |
| **USA** | |
| R FREE ASIA, Via Taiwan | SE Asia • 100/250 kW |
| 11610 **CHINA** | |
| CENTRAL PEOPLE'S BS, Beijing | DS-2 • 50 kW |
| | Th-Tu • DS-2 • 50 kW |
| CHINA RADIO INTL, Beijing | S • Mideast & N Africa • 120 kW |
| CHINA RADIO INTL, Urümqi | S • Europe • 500 kW |
| **FRANCE** | |
| R FRANCE INTL, Via Xi'an, China | S Asia • 120 kW |
| **SEYCHELLES** | |
| FEBA RADIO, North Pt, Mahé Is | S • F-Su • W Asia • 100 kW |
| | S • W Asia • 100 kW |
| **USA** | |
| †ADVENTIST WORLD R, Via Germany | S • N Africa & W Africa • 100 kW |

ENGLISH ▬    ARABIC ▨    CHINESE ▫▫▫    FRENCH ▬    GERMAN ▬    RUSSIAN ═    SPANISH ▬    OTHER ▬

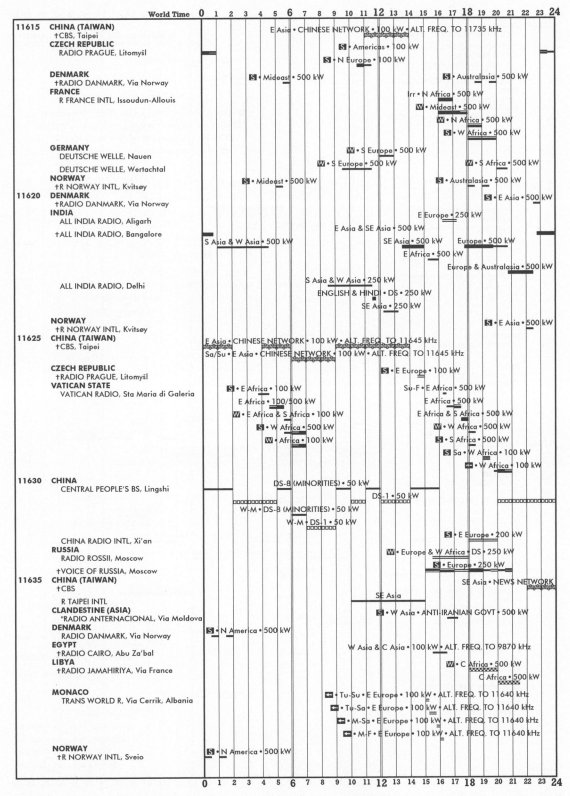

World Time   0 1 2 3 4 5 6 7 8 9 10 11 12 13 14 15 16 17 18 19 20 21 22 23 24

**11615**   **CHINA (TAIWAN)**
    †CBS, Taipei
   E Asia • CHINESE NETWORK • 100 kW • ALT. FREQ. TO 11735 kHz
   **CZECH REPUBLIC**
    RADIO PRAGUE, Litomyšl
   S • Americas • 100 kW
   S • N Europe • 100 kW

   **DENMARK**
    †RADIO DANMARK, Via Norway
   S • Mideast • 500 kW    S • Australasia • 500 kW
   **FRANCE**
    R FRANCE INTL, Issoudun-Allouis
   Irr • N Africa • 500 kW
   W • Mideast • 500 kW
   W • N Africa • 500 kW
   S • W Africa • 500 kW

   **GERMANY**
    DEUTSCHE WELLE, Nauen
   W • S Europe • 500 kW
    DEUTSCHE WELLE, Wertachtal
   W • S Europe • 500 kW    W • S Africa • 500 kW
   **NORWAY**
    †R NORWAY INTL, Kvitsøy
   S • Mideast • 500 kW    S • Australasia • 500 kW

**11620**   **DENMARK**
    †RADIO DANMARK, Via Norway
   S • E Asia • 500 kW
   **INDIA**
    ALL INDIA RADIO, Aligarh
   E Europe • 250 kW
    †ALL INDIA RADIO, Bangalore
   E Asia & SE Asia • 500 kW
   S Asia & W Asia • 500 kW
   SE Asia • 500 kW    Europe • 500 kW
   E Africa • 500 kW
   Europe & Australasia • 500 kW

    ALL INDIA RADIO, Delhi
   S Asia & W Asia • 250 kW
   ENGLISH & HINDI • DS • 250 kW
   SE Asia • 250 kW

   **NORWAY**
    †R NORWAY INTL, Kvitsøy
   S • E Asia • 500 kW
**11625**   **CHINA (TAIWAN)**
    †CBS, Taipei
   E Asia • CHINESE NETWORK • 100 kW • ALT. FREQ. TO 11645 kHz
   Sa/Su • E Asia • CHINESE NETWORK • 100 kW • ALT. FREQ. TO 11645 kHz

   **CZECH REPUBLIC**
    †RADIO PRAGUE, Litomyšl
   S • E Europe • 100 kW
   **VATICAN STATE**
    VATICAN RADIO, Sta Maria di Galeria
   S • E Africa • 100 kW    Su-F • E Africa • 500 kW
   E Africa • 100/500 kW    E Africa • 500 kW
   W • E Africa & S Africa • 100 kW    E Africa & S Africa • 500 kW
   S • W Africa • 500 kW    W • W Africa • 500 kW
   W • Africa • 100 kW    S • S Africa • 500 kW
   S • Sa • W Africa • 100 kW
   ⟷ • W Africa • 100 kW

**11630**   **CHINA**
    CENTRAL PEOPLE'S BS, Lingshi
   DS-8 (MINORITIES) • 50 kW
   DS-1 • 50 kW
   W-M • DS-8 (MINORITIES) • 50 kW
   W-M • DS-1 • 50 kW

    CHINA RADIO INTL, Xi'an
   S • E Europe • 200 kW
   **RUSSIA**
    RADIO ROSSII, Moscow
   W • Europe & W Africa • DS • 250 kW
    †VOICE OF RUSSIA, Moscow
   S • Europe • 250 kW
**11635**   **CHINA (TAIWAN)**
    †CBS
   SE Asia • NEWS NETWORK

    R TAIPEI INTL
   SE Asia
   **CLANDESTINE (ASIA)**
    "RADIO ANTERNACIONAL, Via Moldova
   S • W Asia • ANTI-IRANIAN GOVT • 500 kW
   **DENMARK**
    RADIO DANMARK, Via Norway
   S • N America • 500 kW
   **EGYPT**
    †RADIO CAIRO, Abu Za'bal
   W Asia & C Asia • 100 kW • ALT. FREQ. TO 9870 kHz
   **LIBYA**
    †RADIO JAMAHIRIYA, Via France
   W • C Africa • 500 kW
   C Africa • 500 kW

   **MONACO**
    TRANS WORLD R, Via Cerrik, Albania
   ⟷ • Tu-Su • E Europe • 100 kW • ALT. FREQ. TO 11640 kHz
   ⟷ • Tu-Sa • E Europe • 100 kW • ALT. FREQ. TO 11640 kHz
   ⟷ • M-Sa • E Europe • 100 kW • ALT. FREQ. TO 11640 kHz
   ⟷ • M-F • E Europe • 100 kW • ALT. FREQ. TO 11640 kHz

   **NORWAY**
    †R NORWAY INTL, Sveio
   S • N America • 500 kW

0 1 2 3 4 5 6 7 8 9 10 11 12 13 14 15 16 17 18 19 20 21 22 23 24

SEASONAL S OR W    1-HR TIMESHIFT MIDYEAR ⟷ OR ⟶    JAMMING / OR ∧    EARLIEST HEARD ◁    LATEST HEARD ▷    NEW FOR 2003 †

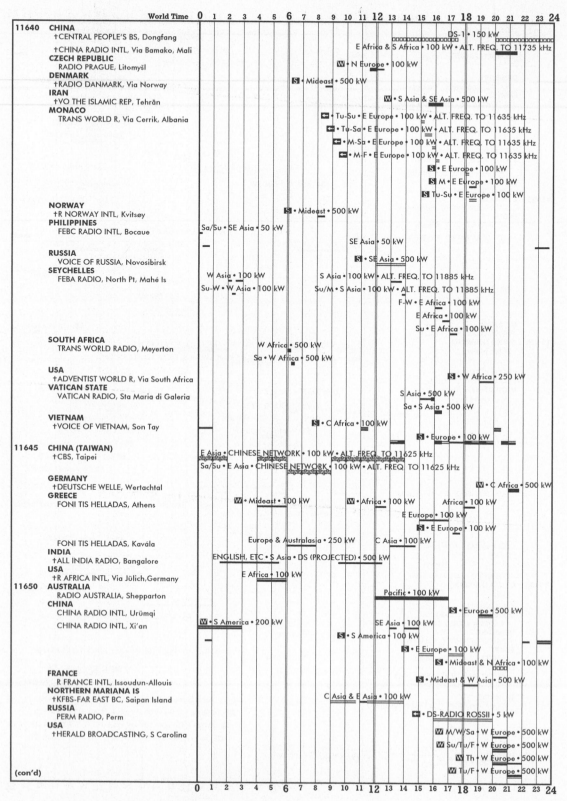

ENGLISH ▬   ARABIC ▨▨▨   CHINESE ▫▫▫   FRENCH ▭▭   GERMAN ▬▬   RUSSIAN ══   SPANISH ══   OTHER ▬

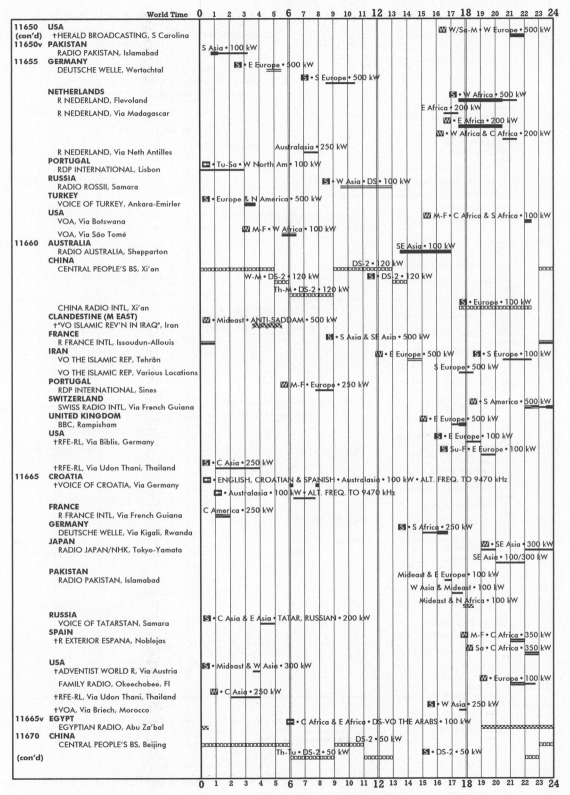

World Time 0 1 2 3 4 5 6 7 8 9 10 11 12 13 14 15 16 17 18 19 20 21 22 23 24

| | | |
|---|---|---|
| **11650** | **USA** | |
| (con'd) | †HERALD BROADCASTING, S Carolina | W • W/Sa-M • W Europe • 500 kW |
| **11650v** | **PAKISTAN** | |
| | RADIO PAKISTAN, Islamabad | S Asia • 100 kW |
| **11655** | **GERMANY** | |
| | DEUTSCHE WELLE, Wertachtal | S • E Europe • 500 kW |
| | | S • S Europe • 500 kW |
| | **NETHERLANDS** | |
| | R NEDERLAND, Flevoland | S • W Africa • 500 kW |
| | R NEDERLAND, Via Madagascar | E Africa • 200 kW |
| | | W • E Africa • 200 kW |
| | | W • W Africa & C Africa • 200 kW |
| | R NEDERLAND, Via Neth Antilles | Australasia • 250 kW |
| | **PORTUGAL** | |
| | RDP INTERNATIONAL, Lisbon | ⮜ • Tu-Sa • W North Am • 100 kW |
| | **RUSSIA** | |
| | RADIO ROSSII, Samara | S • W Asia • DS • 100 kW |
| | **TURKEY** | |
| | VOICE OF TURKEY, Ankara-Emirler | S • Europe & N America • 500 kW |
| | **USA** | |
| | VOA, Via Botswana | W • M-F • C Africa & S Africa • 100 kW |
| | VOA, Via São Tomé | W • M-F • W Africa • 100 kW |
| **11660** | **AUSTRALIA** | |
| | RADIO AUSTRALIA, Shepparton | SE Asia • 100 kW |
| | **CHINA** | |
| | CENTRAL PEOPLE'S BS, Xi'an | DS-2 • 120 kW |
| | | W-M • DS-2 • 120 kW   S • DS-2 • 120 kW |
| | | Th-M • DS-2 • 120 kW |
| | CHINA RADIO INTL, Xi'an | S • Europe • 100 kW |
| | **CLANDESTINE (M EAST)** | |
| | †"VO ISLAMIC REV'N IN IRAQ", Iran | W • Mideast • ANTI-SADDAM • 500 kW |
| | **FRANCE** | |
| | R FRANCE INTL, Issoudun-Allouis | S • S Asia & SE Asia • 500 kW |
| | **IRAN** | |
| | VO THE ISLAMIC REP, Tehrān | W • E Europe • 500 kW   S • S Europe • 100 kW |
| | VO THE ISLAMIC REP, Various Locations | S Europe • 500 kW |
| | **PORTUGAL** | |
| | RDP INTERNATIONAL, Sines | W • M-F • Europe • 250 kW |
| | **SWITZERLAND** | |
| | SWISS RADIO INTL, Via French Guiana | W • S America • 500 kW |
| | **UNITED KINGDOM** | |
| | BBC, Rampisham | W • E Europe • 500 kW |
| | **USA** | |
| | †RFE-RL, Via Biblis, Germany | S • E Europe • 100 kW |
| | | S • Su-F • E Europe • 100 kW |
| | †RFE-RL, Via Udon Thani, Thailand | S • C Asia • 250 kW |
| **11665** | **CROATIA** | |
| | †VOICE OF CROATIA, Via Germany | ⮜ • ENGLISH, CROATIAN & SPANISH • Australasia • 100 kW • ALT. FREQ. TO 9470 kHz |
| | | ⮜ • Australasia • 100 kW • ALT. FREQ. TO 9470 kHz |
| | **FRANCE** | |
| | R FRANCE INTL, Via French Guiana | C America • 250 kW |
| | **GERMANY** | |
| | DEUTSCHE WELLE, Via Kigali, Rwanda | S • S Africa • 250 kW |
| | **JAPAN** | |
| | RADIO JAPAN/NHK, Tokyo-Yamata | W • SE Asia • 300 kW |
| | | SE Asia • 100/300 kW |
| | **PAKISTAN** | |
| | RADIO PAKISTAN, Islamabad | Mideast & E Europe • 100 kW |
| | | W Asia & Mideast • 100 kW |
| | | Mideast & N Africa • 100 kW |
| | **RUSSIA** | |
| | VOICE OF TATARSTAN, Samara | S • C Asia & E Asia • TATAR, RUSSIAN • 200 kW |
| | **SPAIN** | |
| | †R EXTERIOR ESPANA, Noblejas | W • M-F • C Africa • 350 kW |
| | | W • Sa • C Africa • 350 kW |
| | **USA** | |
| | †ADVENTIST WORLD R, Via Austria | S • Mideast & W Asia • 300 kW |
| | FAMILY RADIO, Okeechobee, Fl | W • Europe • 100 kW |
| | †RFE-RL, Via Udon Thani, Thailand | W • C Asia • 250 kW |
| | †VOA, Via Briech, Morocco | S • W Asia • 250 kW |
| **11665v** | **EGYPT** | |
| | EGYPTIAN RADIO, Abu Za'bal | ⮜ • C Africa & E Africa • DS-VO THE ARABS • 100 kW |
| **11670** | **CHINA** | |
| | CENTRAL PEOPLE'S BS, Beijing | DS-2 • 50 kW |
| | | Th-Tu • DS-2 • 50 kW   S • DS-2 • 50 kW |
| (con'd) | | |

0 1 2 3 4 5 6 7 8 9 10 11 12 13 14 15 16 17 18 19 20 21 22 23 24

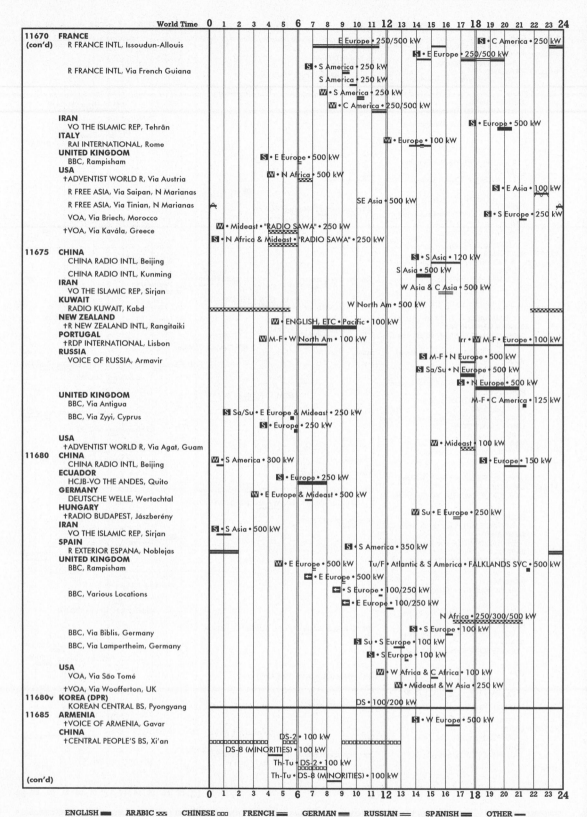

| | World Time | 0 1 2 3 4 5 6 7 8 9 10 11 12 13 14 15 16 17 18 19 20 21 22 23 24 |
|---|---|---|
| **11670** | **FRANCE** | |
| (con'd) | R FRANCE INTL, Issoudun-Allouis | E Europe • 250/500 kW  S • C America • 250 kW |
| | | S • E Europe • 250/500 kW |
| | R FRANCE INTL, Via French Guiana | S • S America • 250 kW |
| | | S America • 250 kW |
| | | W • S America • 250 kW |
| | | W • C America • 250/500 kW |
| | **IRAN** | |
| | VO THE ISLAMIC REP, Tehrān | S • Europe • 500 kW |
| | **ITALY** | |
| | RAI INTERNATIONAL, Rome | W • Europe • 100 kW |
| | **UNITED KINGDOM** | |
| | BBC, Rampisham | S • E Europe • 500 kW |
| | **USA** | |
| | †ADVENTIST WORLD R, Via Austria | W • N Africa • 500 kW |
| | R FREE ASIA, Via Saipan, N Marianas | S • E Asia • 100 kW |
| | R FREE ASIA, Via Tinian, N Marianas | SE Asia • 500 kW |
| | VOA, Via Briech, Morocco | S • S Europe • 250 kW |
| | †VOA, Via Kavála, Greece | W • Mideast • "RADIO SAWA" • 250 kW |
| | | S • N Africa & Mideast • "RADIO SAWA" • 250 kW |
| **11675** | **CHINA** | |
| | CHINA RADIO INTL, Beijing | S • S Asia • 120 kW |
| | CHINA RADIO INTL, Kunming | S Asia • 500 kW |
| | **IRAN** | |
| | VO THE ISLAMIC REP, Sirjan | W Asia & C Asia • 500 kW |
| | **KUWAIT** | |
| | RADIO KUWAIT, Kabd | W North Am • 500 kW |
| | **NEW ZEALAND** | |
| | †R NEW ZEALAND INTL, Rangitaiki | W • ENGLISH, ETC • Pacific • 100 kW |
| | **PORTUGAL** | |
| | †RDP INTERNATIONAL, Lisbon | W M-F • W North Am • 100 kW   Irr • W M-F • Europe • 100 kW |
| | **RUSSIA** | |
| | VOICE OF RUSSIA, Armavir | S • M-F • N Europe • 500 kW |
| | | S • Sa/Su • N Europe • 500 kW |
| | | S • N Europe • 500 kW |
| | | M-F • C America • 125 kW |
| | **UNITED KINGDOM** | |
| | BBC, Via Antigua | S • Sa/Su • E Europe & Mideast • 250 kW |
| | BBC, Via Zyyi, Cyprus | S • Europe • 250 kW |
| | **USA** | |
| | †ADVENTIST WORLD R, Via Agat, Guam | W • Mideast • 100 kW |
| **11680** | **CHINA** | |
| | CHINA RADIO INTL, Beijing | W • S America • 300 kW   S • Europe • 150 kW |
| | **ECUADOR** | |
| | HCJB-VO THE ANDES, Quito | S • Europe • 250 kW |
| | **GERMANY** | |
| | DEUTSCHE WELLE, Wertachtal | W • E Europe & Mideast • 500 kW |
| | **HUNGARY** | |
| | †RADIO BUDAPEST, Jászberény | W • Su • E Europe • 250 kW |
| | **IRAN** | |
| | VO THE ISLAMIC REP, Sirjan | S • S Asia • 500 kW |
| | **SPAIN** | |
| | R EXTERIOR ESPAÑA, Noblejas | S • S America • 350 kW |
| | **UNITED KINGDOM** | |
| | BBC, Rampisham | W • E Europe • 500 kW   Tu/F • Atlantic & S America • FALKLANDS SVC • 500 kW |
| | | ← • E Europe • 500 kW |
| | BBC, Various Locations | ← • S Europe • 100/250 kW |
| | | ← • E Europe • 100/250 kW |
| | | N Africa • 250/300/500 kW |
| | BBC, Via Biblis, Germany | S • S Europe • 100 kW |
| | BBC, Via Lampertheim, Germany | S • Su • S Europe • 100 kW |
| | | S • S Europe • 100 kW |
| | **USA** | |
| | VOA, Via São Tomé | W • W Africa & C Africa • 100 kW |
| | †VOA, Via Woofferton, UK | W • Mideast & W Asia • 250 kW |
| **11680v** | **KOREA (DPR)** | |
| | KOREAN CENTRAL BS, Pyongyang | DS • 100/200 kW |
| **11685** | **ARMENIA** | |
| | †VOICE OF ARMENIA, Gavar | S • W Europe • 500 kW |
| | **CHINA** | |
| | †CENTRAL PEOPLE'S BS, Xi'an | DS-2 • 100 kW |
| | | DS-8 (MINORITIES) • 100 kW |
| | | Th-Tu • DS-2 • 100 kW |
| | | Th-Tu • DS-8 (MINORITIES) • 100 kW |
| (con'd) | | 0 1 2 3 4 5 6 7 8 9 10 11 12 13 14 15 16 17 18 19 20 21 22 23 24 |

ENGLISH ▬   ARABIC ▨   CHINESE ▨   FRENCH ▬   GERMAN ▬   RUSSIAN ▬   SPANISH ▬   OTHER ▬

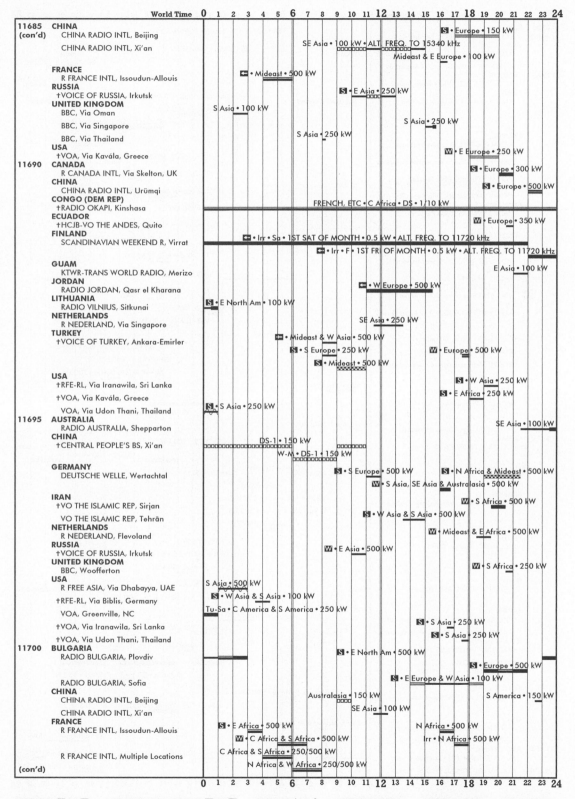

World Time: 0 1 2 3 4 5 6 7 8 9 10 11 12 13 14 15 16 17 18 19 20 21 22 23 24

**11685 CHINA** (con'd)
- CHINA RADIO INTL, Beijing — S • Europe • 150 kW
- CHINA RADIO INTL, Xi'an — SE Asia • 100 kW • ALT. FREQ. TO 15340 kHz / Mideast & E Europe • 100 kW

**FRANCE**
- R FRANCE INTL, Issoudun-Allouis — ⇦ • Mideast • 500 kW

**RUSSIA**
- †VOICE OF RUSSIA, Irkutsk — S • E Asia • 250 kW

**UNITED KINGDOM**
- BBC, Via Oman — S Asia • 100 kW
- BBC, Via Singapore — S Asia • 250 kW
- BBC, Via Thailand — S Asia • 250 kW

**USA**
- †VOA, Via Kavála, Greece — W • E Europe • 250 kW

**11690 CANADA**
- R CANADA INTL, Via Skelton, UK — S • Europe • 300 kW

**CHINA**
- CHINA RADIO INTL, Urümqi — S • Europe • 500 kW

**CONGO (DEM REP)**
- †RADIO OKAPI, Kinshasa — FRENCH, ETC • C Africa • DS • 1/10 kW

**ECUADOR**
- †HCJB-VO THE ANDES, Quito — W • Europe • 350 kW

**FINLAND**
- SCANDINAVIAN WEEKEND R, Virrat — ⇦ • Irr • Sa • 1ST SAT OF MONTH • 0.5 kW • ALT. FREQ. TO 11720 kHz / ⇦ • Irr • F • 1ST FRI OF MONTH • 0.5 kW • ALT. FREQ. TO 11720 kHz

**GUAM**
- KTWR-TRANS WORLD RADIO, Merizo — E Asia • 100 kW

**JORDAN**
- RADIO JORDAN, Qasr el Kharana — ⇦ • W Europe • 500 kW

**LITHUANIA**
- RADIO VILNIUS, Sitkunai — S • E North Am • 100 kW

**NETHERLANDS**
- R NEDERLAND, Via Singapore — SE Asia • 250 kW

**TURKEY**
- †VOICE OF TURKEY, Ankara-Emirler — ⇦ • Mideast & W Asia • 500 kW / S • S Europe • 250 kW / W • Europe • 500 kW / S • Mideast • 500 kW

**USA**
- †RFE-RL, Via Iranawila, Sri Lanka — S • W Asia • 250 kW
- †VOA, Via Kavála, Greece — S • E Africa • 250 kW
- VOA, Via Udon Thani, Thailand — S • S Asia • 250 kW

**11695 AUSTRALIA**
- RADIO AUSTRALIA, Shepparton — SE Asia • 100 kW

**CHINA**
- †CENTRAL PEOPLE'S BS, Xi'an — DS-1 • 150 kW / W-M • DS-1 • 150 kW

**GERMANY**
- DEUTSCHE WELLE, Wertachtal — S • S Europe • 500 kW / S • N Africa & Mideast • 500 kW / W • S Asia, SE Asia & Australasia • 500 kW

**IRAN**
- †VO THE ISLAMIC REP, Sirjan — W • S Africa • 500 kW
- VO THE ISLAMIC REP, Tehrān — S • W Asia & S Asia • 500 kW

**NETHERLANDS**
- R NEDERLAND, Flevoland — W • Mideast & E Africa • 500 kW

**RUSSIA**
- †VOICE OF RUSSIA, Irkutsk — W • E Asia • 500 kW

**UNITED KINGDOM**
- BBC, Woofferton — W • S Africa • 250 kW

**USA**
- R FREE ASIA, Via Dhabayya, UAE — S Asia • 500 kW
- †RFE-RL, Via Biblis, Germany — S • W Asia & S Asia • 100 kW
- VOA, Greenville, NC — Tu-Sa • C America & S America • 250 kW
- †VOA, Via Iranawila, Sri Lanka — S • S Asia • 250 kW
- †VOA, Via Udon Thani, Thailand — S • S Asia • 250 kW

**11700 BULGARIA**
- RADIO BULGARIA, Plovdiv — S • E North Am • 500 kW / S • Europe • 500 kW
- RADIO BULGARIA, Sofia — S • E Europe & W Asia • 100 kW

**CHINA**
- CHINA RADIO INTL, Beijing — Australasia • 150 kW / S America • 150 kW
- CHINA RADIO INTL, Xi'an — SE Asia • 100 kW

**FRANCE**
- R FRANCE INTL, Issoudun-Allouis — S • E Africa • 500 kW / W • C Africa & S Africa • 500 kW / N Africa • 500 kW / Irr • N Africa • 500 kW
- R FRANCE INTL, Multiple Locations — C Africa & S Africa • 250/500 kW / N Africa & W Africa • 250/500 kW

(con'd)

World Time: 0 1 2 3 4 5 6 7 8 9 10 11 12 13 14 15 16 17 18 19 20 21 22 23 24

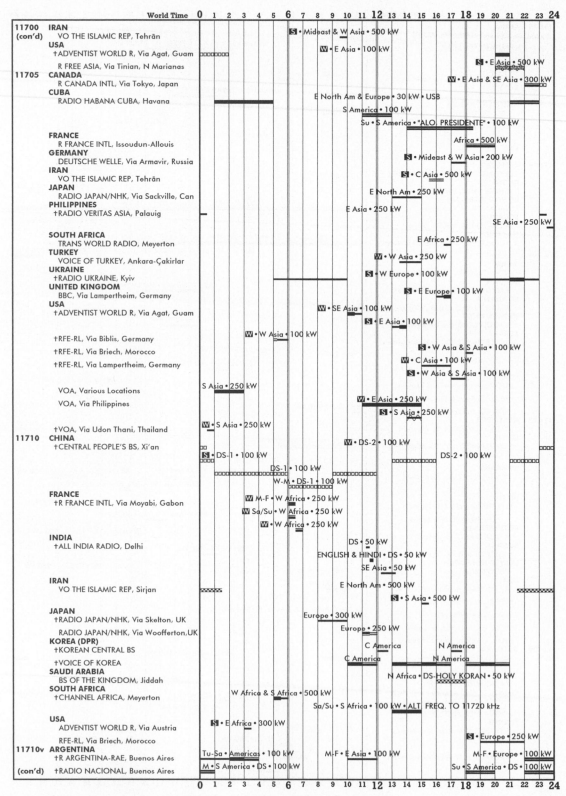

| | World Time | 0 1 2 3 4 5 6 7 8 9 10 11 12 13 14 15 16 17 18 19 20 21 22 23 24 |
|---|---|---|
| 11700 (con'd) | IRAN | |
| | VO THE ISLAMIC REP, Tehrān | **S** • Mideast & W Asia • 500 kW |
| | USA | |
| | †ADVENTIST WORLD R, Via Agat, Guam | **W** • E Asia • 100 kW |
| | R FREE ASIA, Via Tinian, N Marianas | **S** • E Asia • 500 kW |
| 11705 | CANADA | |
| | R CANADA INTL, Via Tokyo, Japan | **W** • E Asia & SE Asia • 300 kW |
| | CUBA | |
| | RADIO HABANA CUBA, Havana | E North Am & Europe • 30 kW • USB |
| | | S America • 100 kW |
| | | Su • S America • "ALO, PRESIDENTE" • 100 kW |
| | FRANCE | |
| | R FRANCE INTL, Issoudun-Allouis | Africa • 500 kW |
| | GERMANY | |
| | DEUTSCHE WELLE, Via Armavir, Russia | **S** • Mideast & W Asia • 200 kW |
| | IRAN | |
| | VO THE ISLAMIC REP, Tehrān | **S** • C Asia • 500 kW |
| | JAPAN | |
| | RADIO JAPAN/NHK, Via Sackville, Can | E North Am • 250 kW |
| | PHILIPPINES | |
| | †RADIO VERITAS ASIA, Palauig | E Asia • 250 kW |
| | | SE Asia • 250 kW |
| | SOUTH AFRICA | |
| | TRANS WORLD RADIO, Meyerton | E Africa • 250 kW |
| | TURKEY | |
| | VOICE OF TURKEY, Ankara-Çakirlar | **W** • W Asia • 250 kW |
| | UKRAINE | |
| | †RADIO UKRAINE, Kyiv | **S** • W Europe • 100 kW |
| | UNITED KINGDOM | |
| | BBC, Via Lampertheim, Germany | **S** • E Europe • 100 kW |
| | USA | |
| | †ADVENTIST WORLD R, Via Agat, Guam | **W** • SE Asia • 100 kW |
| | | **S** • E Asia • 100 kW |
| | †RFE-RL, Via Biblis, Germany | **W** • W Asia • 100 kW |
| | †RFE-RL, Via Briech, Morocco | **S** • W Asia & S Asia • 100 kW |
| | †RFE-RL, Via Lampertheim, Germany | **W** • C Asia • 100 kW |
| | | **S** • W Asia & S Asia • 100 kW |
| | VOA, Various Locations | S Asia • 250 kW |
| | VOA, Via Philippines | **W** • E Asia • 250 kW |
| | | **S** • S Asia • 250 kW |
| | †VOA, Via Udon Thani, Thailand | **W** • S Asia • 250 kW |
| 11710 | CHINA | |
| | †CENTRAL PEOPLE'S BS, Xi'an | **W** • DS-2 • 100 kW |
| | | DS-2 • 100 kW |
| | | **S** • DS-1 • 100 kW |
| | | DS-1 • 100 kW |
| | | W-M • DS-1 • 100 kW |
| | FRANCE | |
| | †R FRANCE INTL, Via Moyabi, Gabon | **W** M-F • W Africa • 250 kW |
| | | **W** Sa/Su • W Africa • 250 kW |
| | | **W** • W Africa • 250 kW |
| | INDIA | |
| | †ALL INDIA RADIO, Delhi | DS • 50 kW |
| | | ENGLISH & HINDI • DS • 50 kW |
| | | SE Asia • 50 kW |
| | IRAN | |
| | VO THE ISLAMIC REP, Sirjan | E North Am • 500 kW |
| | | **S** • S Asia • 500 kW |
| | JAPAN | |
| | †RADIO JAPAN/NHK, Via Skelton, UK | Europe • 300 kW |
| | RADIO JAPAN/NHK, Via Woofferton, UK | Europe • 250 kW |
| | KOREA (DPR) | |
| | †KOREAN CENTRAL BS | C America |
| | | N America |
| | †VOICE OF KOREA | C America |
| | | N America |
| | SAUDI ARABIA | |
| | BS OF THE KINGDOM, Jiddah | N Africa • DS-HOLY KORAN • 50 kW |
| | SOUTH AFRICA | |
| | †CHANNEL AFRICA, Meyerton | W Africa & S Africa • 500 kW |
| | | Sa/Su • S Africa • 100 kW • ALT FREQ. TO 11720 kHz |
| | USA | |
| | ADVENTIST WORLD R, Via Austria | **S** • E Africa • 300 kW |
| | RFE-RL, Via Briech, Morocco | **S** • Europe • 250 kW |
| 11710v | ARGENTINA | |
| | †R ARGENTINA-RAE, Buenos Aires | Tu-Sa • Americas • 100 kW |
| | | M-F • E Asia • 100 kW |
| | | M-F • Europe • 100 kW |
| (con'd) | †RADIO NACIONAL, Buenos Aires | M • S America • DS • 100 kW |
| | | Su • S America • DS • 100 kW |

ENGLISH ▬   ARABIC ⋙   CHINESE ▭▭▭   FRENCH ▬   GERMAN ▬   RUSSIAN ═   SPANISH ▬   OTHER ▬

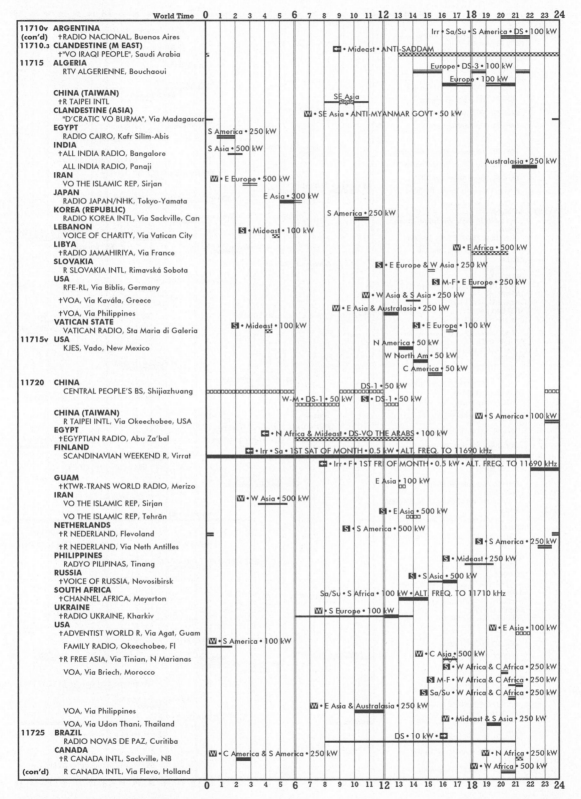

World Time  0  1  2  3  4  5  6  7  8  9  10  11  12  13  14  15  16  17  18  19  20  21  22  23  24

| | |
|---|---|
| **11710v** ARGENTINA | |
| (con'd) †RADIO NACIONAL, Buenos Aires | Irr • Sa/Su • S America • DS • 100 kW |
| **11710.3** CLANDESTINE (M EAST) | |
| †"VO IRAQI PEOPLE", Saudi Arabia | ◰ • Mideast • ANTI-SADDAM |
| **11715** ALGERIA | |
| RTV ALGERIENNE, Bouchaoui | Europe • DS-3 • 100 kW |
| | Europe • 100 kW |
| CHINA (TAIWAN) | |
| †R TAIPEI INTL | SE Asia |
| CLANDESTINE (ASIA) | |
| "D'CRATIC VO BURMA", Via Madagascar | W • SE Asia • ANTI-MYANMAR GOVT • 50 kW |
| EGYPT | |
| RADIO CAIRO, Kafr Silim-Abis | S America • 250 kW |
| INDIA | |
| †ALL INDIA RADIO, Bangalore | S Asia • 500 kW |
| ALL INDIA RADIO, Panaji | Australasia • 250 kW |
| IRAN | |
| VO THE ISLAMIC REP, Sirjan | W • E Europe • 500 kW |
| JAPAN | |
| RADIO JAPAN/NHK, Tokyo-Yamata | E Asia • 300 kW |
| KOREA (REPUBLIC) | |
| RADIO KOREA INTL, Via Sackville, Can | S America • 250 kW |
| LEBANON | |
| VOICE OF CHARITY, Via Vatican City | S • Mideast • 100 kW |
| LIBYA | |
| †RADIO JAMAHIRIYA, Via France | W • E Africa • 500 kW |
| SLOVAKIA | |
| R SLOVAKIA INTL, Rimavská Sobota | S • E Europe & W Asia • 250 kW |
| USA | |
| RFE-RL, Via Biblis, Germany | S M-F • E Europe • 250 kW |
| †VOA, Via Kavála, Greece | W • W Asia & S Asia • 250 kW |
| †VOA, Via Philippines | W • E Asia & Australasia • 250 kW |
| VATICAN STATE | |
| VATICAN RADIO, Sta Maria di Galeria | S • Mideast • 100 kW      S • E Europe • 100 kW |
| **11715v** USA | |
| KJES, Vado, New Mexico | N America • 50 kW |
| | W North Am • 50 kW |
| | C America • 50 kW |
| **11720** CHINA | |
| CENTRAL PEOPLE'S BS, Shijiazhuang | DS-1 • 50 kW |
| | W-M • DS-1 • 50 kW    S • DS-1 • 50 kW |
| CHINA (TAIWAN) | |
| R TAIPEI INTL, Via Okeechobee, USA | W • S America • 100 kW |
| EGYPT | |
| †EGYPTIAN RADIO, Abu Za'bal | ◰ • N Africa & Mideast • DS-VO THE ARABS • 100 kW |
| FINLAND | |
| SCANDINAVIAN WEEKEND R, Virrat | ◰ • Irr • Sa • 1ST SAT OF MONTH • 0.5 kW • ALT. FREQ. TO 11690 kHz |
| | ◰ • Irr • F • 1ST FRI OF MONTH • 0.5 kW • ALT. FREQ. TO 11690 kHz |
| GUAM | |
| †KTWR-TRANS WORLD RADIO, Merizo | E Asia • 100 kW |
| IRAN | |
| VO THE ISLAMIC REP, Sirjan | W • W Asia • 500 kW |
| VO THE ISLAMIC REP, Tehrān | S • E Asia • 500 kW |
| NETHERLANDS | |
| †R NEDERLAND, Flevoland | S • S America • 500 kW |
| †R NEDERLAND, Via Neth Antilles | S • S America • 250 kW |
| PHILIPPINES | |
| RADYO PILIPINAS, Tinang | S • Mideast • 250 kW |
| RUSSIA | |
| †VOICE OF RUSSIA, Novosibirsk | S • S Asia • 500 kW |
| SOUTH AFRICA | |
| †CHANNEL AFRICA, Meyerton | Sa/Su • S Africa • 100 kW • ALT FREQ. TO 11710 kHz |
| UKRAINE | |
| †RADIO UKRAINE, Kharkiv | W • S Europe • 100 kW |
| USA | |
| †ADVENTIST WORLD R, Via Agat, Guam | W • E Asia • 100 kW |
| FAMILY RADIO, Okeechobee, Fl | W • S America • 100 kW |
| †R FREE ASIA, Via Tinian, N Marianas | W • C Asia • 500 kW |
| VOA, Via Briech, Morocco | S • W Africa & C Africa • 250 kW |
| | S M-F • W Africa & C Africa • 250 kW |
| | S Sa/Su • W Africa & C Africa • 250 kW |
| VOA, Via Philippines | W • E Asia & Australasia • 250 kW |
| VOA, Via Udon Thani, Thailand | W • Mideast & S Asia • 250 kW |
| **11725** BRAZIL | |
| RADIO NOVAS DE PAZ, Curitiba | DS • 10 kW • ◰ |
| CANADA | |
| †R CANADA INTL, Sackville, NB | W • C America & S America • 250 kW    W • N Africa • 250 kW |
| (con'd) R CANADA INTL, Via Flevo, Holland | W • W Africa • 500 kW |

0  1  2  3  4  5  6  7  8  9  10  11  12  13  14  15  16  17  18  19  20  21  22  23  24

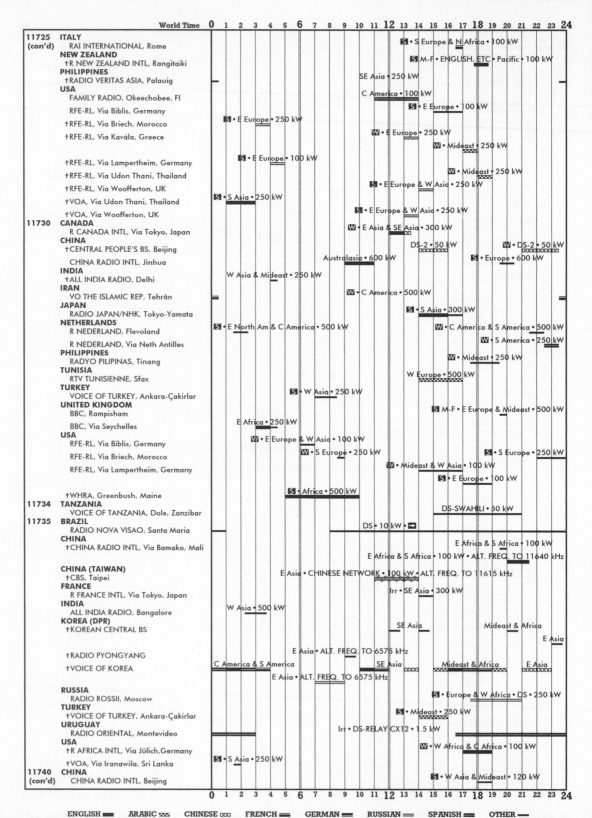

| World Time | 0 | 1 | 2 | 3 | 4 | 5 | 6 | 7 | 8 | 9 | 10 | 11 | 12 | 13 | 14 | 15 | 16 | 17 | 18 | 19 | 20 | 21 | 22 | 23 | 24 |

**11725 ITALY**
(con'd)     RAI INTERNATIONAL, Rome — Ⓢ • S Europe & N Africa • 100 kW
**NEW ZEALAND**
     †R NEW ZEALAND INTL, Rangitaiki — Ⓦ M-F • ENGLISH, ETC • Pacific • 100 kW
**PHILIPPINES**
     †RADIO VERITAS ASIA, Palauig — SE Asia • 250 kW
**USA**
     FAMILY RADIO, Okeechobee, Fl — C America • 100 kW
     RFE-RL, Via Biblis, Germany — Ⓢ • E Europe • 100 kW
     †RFE-RL, Via Briech, Morocco — Ⓢ • E Europe • 250 kW
     †RFE-RL, Via Kavála, Greece — Ⓦ • E Europe • 250 kW / Ⓦ • Mideast • 250 kW
     †RFE-RL, Via Lampertheim, Germany — Ⓢ • E Europe • 100 kW
     †RFE-RL, Via Udon Thani, Thailand — Ⓦ • Mideast • 250 kW
     †RFE-RL, Via Woofferton, UK — Ⓢ • E Europe & W Asia • 250 kW
     †VOA, Via Udon Thani, Thailand — Ⓢ • S Asia • 250 kW
     †VOA, Via Woofferton, UK — Ⓢ • E Europe & W Asia • 250 kW
**11730 CANADA**
     R CANADA INTL, Via Tokyo, Japan — Ⓦ • E Asia & SE Asia • 300 kW
**CHINA**
     †CENTRAL PEOPLE'S BS, Beijing — DS-2 • 50 kW / Ⓦ • DS-2 • 50 kW
     CHINA RADIO INTL, Jinhua — Australasia • 600 kW / Ⓢ • Europe • 600 kW
**INDIA**
     †ALL INDIA RADIO, Delhi — W Asia & Mideast • 250 kW
**IRAN**
     VO THE ISLAMIC REP, Tehrän — Ⓦ • C America • 500 kW
**JAPAN**
     RADIO JAPAN/NHK, Tokyo-Yamata — Ⓢ • S Asia • 300 kW
**NETHERLANDS**
     R NEDERLAND, Flevoland — Ⓢ • E North Am & C America • 500 kW / Ⓦ • C America & S America • 500 kW
     R NEDERLAND, Via Neth Antilles — Ⓦ • S America • 250 kW
**PHILIPPINES**
     RADYO PILIPINAS, Tinang — Ⓦ • Mideast • 250 kW
**TUNISIA**
     RTV TUNISIENNE, Sfax — W Europe • 500 kW
**TURKEY**
     VOICE OF TURKEY, Ankara-Çakirlar — Ⓢ • W Asia • 250 kW
**UNITED KINGDOM**
     BBC, Rampisham — Ⓢ M-F • E Europe & Mideast • 500 kW
     BBC, Via Seychelles — E Africa • 250 kW
**USA**
     RFE-RL, Via Biblis, Germany — Ⓦ • E Europe & W Asia • 100 kW
     RFE-RL, Via Briech, Morocco — Ⓦ • S Europe • 250 kW / Ⓢ • S Europe • 250 kW
     RFE-RL, Via Lampertheim, Germany — Ⓦ • Mideast & W Asia • 100 kW / Ⓢ • E Europe • 100 kW
     †WHRA, Greenbush, Maine — Ⓢ • Africa • 500 kW
**11734 TANZANIA**
     VOICE OF TANZANIA, Dole, Zanzibar — DS-SWAHILI • 50 kW
**11735 BRAZIL**
     RADIO NOVA VISAO, Santa Maria — DS • 10 kW • ➡
**CHINA**
     †CHINA RADIO INTL, Via Bamako, Mali — E Africa & S Africa • 100 kW / E Africa & S Africa • 100 kW • ALT. FREQ. TO 11640 kHz
**CHINA (TAIWAN)**
     †CBS, Taipei — E Asia • CHINESE NETWORK • 100 kW • ALT. FREQ. TO 11615 kHz
**FRANCE**
     R FRANCE INTL, Via Tokyo, Japan — Irr • SE Asia • 300 kW
**INDIA**
     ALL INDIA RADIO, Bangalore — W Asia • 500 kW
**KOREA (DPR)**
     †KOREAN CENTRAL BS — SE Asia / Mideast & Africa / E Asia
     †RADIO PYONGYANG — E Asia • ALT. FREQ. TO 6575 kHz
     †VOICE OF KOREA — C America & S America / SE Asia / Mideast & Africa / E Asia / E Asia • ALT. FREQ. TO 6575 kHz
**RUSSIA**
     RADIO ROSSII, Moscow — Ⓢ • Europe & W Africa • DS • 250 kW
**TURKEY**
     †VOICE OF TURKEY, Ankara-Çakirlar — Ⓢ • Mideast • 250 kW
**URUGUAY**
     RADIO ORIENTAL, Montevideo — Irr • DS-RELAY CX12 • 1.5 kW
**USA**
     †R AFRICA INTL, Via Jülich, Germany — Ⓦ • W Africa & C Africa • 100 kW
     †VOA, Via Iranawila, Sri Lanka — Ⓢ • S Asia • 250 kW
**11740 CHINA**
(con'd)     CHINA RADIO INTL, Beijing — Ⓢ • W Asia & Mideast • 120 kW

| World Time | 0 | 1 | 2 | 3 | 4 | 5 | 6 | 7 | 8 | 9 | 10 | 11 | 12 | 13 | 14 | 15 | 16 | 17 | 18 | 19 | 20 | 21 | 22 | 23 | 24 |

ENGLISH ▬  ARABIC ⌇⌇⌇  CHINESE □□□  FRENCH ▬▬  GERMAN ▬▬  RUSSIAN ══  SPANISH ▬▬  OTHER ▬

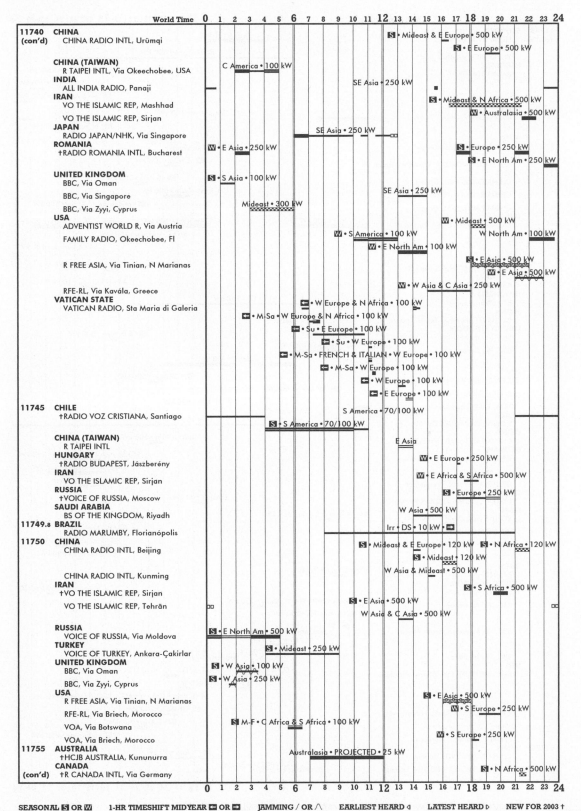

World Time | 0 1 2 3 4 5 6 7 8 9 10 11 12 13 14 15 16 17 18 19 20 21 22 23 24

**11740** **CHINA**
**(con'd)** CHINA RADIO INTL, Urümqi
- S • Mideast & E Europe • 500 kW
- S • E Europe • 500 kW

**CHINA (TAIWAN)**
R TAIPEI INTL, Via Okeechobee, USA
- C America • 100 kW
**INDIA**
ALL INDIA RADIO, Panaji
- SE Asia • 250 kW
**IRAN**
VO THE ISLAMIC REP, Mashhad
- S • Mideast & N Africa • 500 kW
VO THE ISLAMIC REP, Sirjan
- W • Australasia • 500 kW
**JAPAN**
RADIO JAPAN/NHK, Via Singapore
- SE Asia • 250 kW
**ROMANIA**
†RADIO ROMANIA INTL, Bucharest
- W • E Asia • 250 kW
- S • Europe • 250 kW
- S • E North Am • 250 kW

**UNITED KINGDOM**
BBC, Via Oman
- S • S Asia • 100 kW
BBC, Via Singapore
- SE Asia • 250 kW
BBC, Via Zyyi, Cyprus
- Mideast • 300 kW
**USA**
ADVENTIST WORLD R, Via Austria
- W • Mideast • 500 kW
FAMILY RADIO, Okeechobee, Fl
- W • S America • 100 kW
- W North Am • 100 kW
- W • E North Am • 100 kW

R FREE ASIA, Via Tinian, N Marianas
- S • E Asia • 500 kW
- W • E Asia • 500 kW

RFE-RL, Via Kavála, Greece
- W • W Asia & C Asia • 250 kW
**VATICAN STATE**
VATICAN RADIO, Sta Maria di Galeria
- ← W Europe & N Africa • 100 kW
- ← • M-Sa • W Europe & N Africa • 100 kW
- ← • Su • E Europe • 100 kW
- ← • Su • W Europe • 100 kW
- ← • M-Sa • FRENCH & ITALIAN • W Europe • 100 kW
- ← • M-Sa • W Europe • 100 kW
- ← W Europe • 100 kW
- ← • E Europe • 100 kW

**11745** **CHILE**
†RADIO VOZ CRISTIANA, Santiago
- S America • 70/100 kW
- S • S America • 70/100 kW

**CHINA (TAIWAN)**
R TAIPEI INTL
- E Asia
**HUNGARY**
†RADIO BUDAPEST, Jászberény
- W • E Europe • 250 kW
**IRAN**
VO THE ISLAMIC REP, Sirjan
- W • E Africa & S Africa • 500 kW
**RUSSIA**
†VOICE OF RUSSIA, Moscow
- S • Europe • 250 kW
**SAUDI ARABIA**
BS OF THE KINGDOM, Riyadh
- W Asia • 500 kW
**11749.8** **BRAZIL**
RADIO MARUMBY, Florianópolis
- Irr • DS • 10 kW • →
**11750** **CHINA**
CHINA RADIO INTL, Beijing
- S • Mideast & E Europe • 120 kW
- S • N Africa • 120 kW
- S • Mideast • 120 kW

CHINA RADIO INTL, Kunming
- W Asia & Mideast • 500 kW
**IRAN**
†VO THE ISLAMIC REP, Sirjan
- S • S Africa • 500 kW
VO THE ISLAMIC REP, Tehrān
- S • E Asia • 500 kW
- W Asia & C Asia • 500 kW

**RUSSIA**
VOICE OF RUSSIA, Via Moldova
- S • E North Am • 500 kW
**TURKEY**
VOICE OF TURKEY, Ankara-Çakirlar
- S • Mideast • 250 kW
**UNITED KINGDOM**
BBC, Via Oman
- S • W Asia • 100 kW
BBC, Via Zyyi, Cyprus
- S • W Asia • 250 kW
**USA**
R FREE ASIA, Via Tinian, N Marianas
- S • E Asia • 500 kW
RFE-RL, Via Briech, Morocco
- W • S Europe • 250 kW
VOA, Via Botswana
- S • M-F • C Africa & S Africa • 100 kW
VOA, Via Briech, Morocco
- W • S Europe • 250 kW
**11755** **AUSTRALIA**
†HCJB AUSTRALIA, Kununurra
- Australasia • PROJECTED • 25 kW
**CANADA**
**(con'd)** †R CANADA INTL, Via Germany
- S • N Africa • 500 kW

0 1 2 3 4 5 6 7 8 9 10 11 12 13 14 15 16 17 18 19 20 21 22 23 24

SEASONAL S OR W     1-HR TIMESHIFT MIDYEAR ← OR →     JAMMING / OR ∧     EARLIEST HEARD ◁     LATEST HEARD ▷     NEW FOR 2003 †

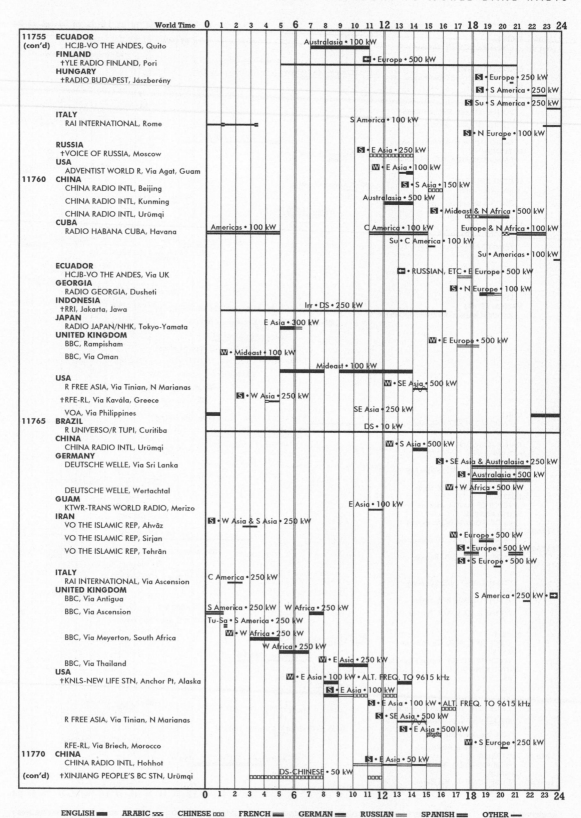

| | World Time | 0 | 1 | 2 | 3 | 4 | 5 | 6 | 7 | 8 | 9 | 10 | 11 | 12 | 13 | 14 | 15 | 16 | 17 | 18 | 19 | 20 | 21 | 22 | 23 | 24 |

**11755 ECUADOR**
(con'd) HCJB-VO THE ANDES, Quito — Australasia • 100 kW
**FINLAND**
†YLE RADIO FINLAND, Pori — • Europe • 500 kW
**HUNGARY**
†RADIO BUDAPEST, Jászberény — S • Europe • 250 kW / S • S America • 250 kW / S • Su • S America • 250 kW

**ITALY**
RAI INTERNATIONAL, Rome — S America • 100 kW / S • N Europe • 100 kW

**RUSSIA**
†VOICE OF RUSSIA, Moscow — S • E Asia • 250 kW
**USA**
ADVENTIST WORLD R, Via Agat, Guam — W • E Asia • 100 kW

**11760 CHINA**
CHINA RADIO INTL, Beijing — S • S Asia • 150 kW
CHINA RADIO INTL, Kunming — Australasia • 500 kW
CHINA RADIO INTL, Urümqi — S • Mideast & N Africa • 500 kW
**CUBA**
RADIO HABANA CUBA, Havana — Americas • 100 kW / C America • 100 kW / Europe & N Africa • 100 kW / Su • C America • 100 kW / Su • Americas • 100 kW

**ECUADOR**
HCJB-VO THE ANDES, Via UK — • RUSSIAN, ETC • E Europe • 500 kW
**GEORGIA**
RADIO GEORGIA, Dusheti — S • N Europe • 100 kW
**INDONESIA**
†RRI, Jakarta, Jawa — Irr • DS • 250 kW
**JAPAN**
RADIO JAPAN/NHK, Tokyo-Yamata — E Asia • 300 kW
**UNITED KINGDOM**
BBC, Rampisham — W • E Europe • 500 kW
BBC, Via Oman — W • Mideast • 100 kW / Mideast • 100 kW

**USA**
R FREE ASIA, Via Tinian, N Marianas — W • SE Asia • 500 kW
†RFE-RL, Via Kavála, Greece — S • W Asia • 250 kW
VOA, Via Philippines — SE Asia • 250 kW

**11765 BRAZIL**
R UNIVERSO/R TUPI, Curitiba — DS • 10 kW
**CHINA**
CHINA RADIO INTL, Urümqi — W • S Asia • 500 kW
**GERMANY**
DEUTSCHE WELLE, Via Sri Lanka — S • SE Asia & Australasia • 250 kW / S • Australasia • 500 kW
DEUTSCHE WELLE, Wertachtal — W • W Africa • 500 kW
**GUAM**
KTWR-TRANS WORLD RADIO, Merizo — E Asia • 100 kW
**IRAN**
VO THE ISLAMIC REP, Ahväz — S • W Asia & S Asia • 250 kW
VO THE ISLAMIC REP, Sirjan — W • Europe • 500 kW
VO THE ISLAMIC REP, Tehrän — S • Europe • 500 kW / S • S Europe • 500 kW

**ITALY**
RAI INTERNATIONAL, Via Ascension — C America • 250 kW
**UNITED KINGDOM**
BBC, Via Antigua — S America • 250 kW • 
BBC, Via Ascension — S America • 250 kW / W Africa • 250 kW / Tu-Sa • S America • 250 kW
BBC, Via Meyerton, South Africa — W • W Africa • 250 kW / W Africa • 250 kW
BBC, Via Thailand — W • E Asia • 250 kW
**USA**
†KNLS-NEW LIFE STN, Anchor Pt, Alaska — W • E Asia • 100 kW • ALT. FREQ. TO 9615 kHz / S • E Asia • 100 kW / S • E Asia • 100 kW • ALT. FREQ. TO 9615 kHz
R FREE ASIA, Via Tinian, N Marianas — S • SE Asia • 500 kW / S • E Asia • 500 kW
RFE-RL, Via Briech, Morocco — W • S Europe • 250 kW

**11770 CHINA**
CHINA RADIO INTL, Hohhot — S • E Asia • 50 kW
(con'd) †XINJIANG PEOPLE'S BC STN, Urümqi — DS-CHINESE • 50 kW

| | 0 | 1 | 2 | 3 | 4 | 5 | 6 | 7 | 8 | 9 | 10 | 11 | 12 | 13 | 14 | 15 | 16 | 17 | 18 | 19 | 20 | 21 | 22 | 23 | 24 |

ENGLISH ▬   ARABIC ▨   CHINESE ▫▫▫   FRENCH ═   GERMAN ▬   RUSSIAN ═   SPANISH ═   OTHER ▬

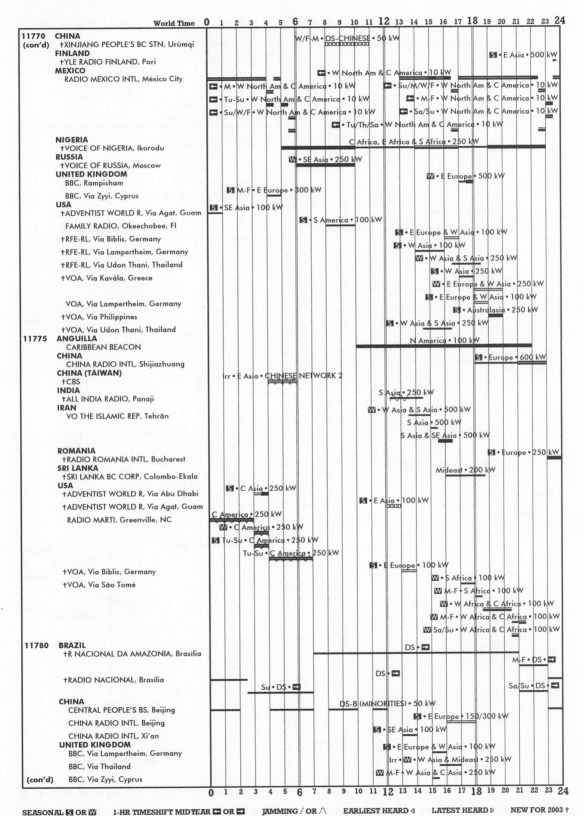

World Time 0 1 2 3 4 5 6 7 8 9 10 11 12 13 14 15 16 17 18 19 20 21 22 23 24

**11770 (con'd)**

**CHINA**
†XINJIANG PEOPLE'S BC STN, Urümqi — W/F-M • DS-CHINESE • 50 kW

**FINLAND**
†YLE RADIO FINLAND, Pori — [S] • E Asia • 500 kW

**MEXICO**
RADIO MEXICO INTL, México City
- ⬅ • W North Am & C America • 10 kW
- ⬅ • M • W North Am & C America • 10 kW
- ⬅ • Su/M/W/F • W North Am & C America • 10 kW
- ⬅ • Tu-Su • W North Am & C America • 10 kW
- ⬅ • M-F • W North Am & C America • 10 kW
- ⬅ • Su/W/F • W North Am & C America • 10 kW
- ⬅ • Sa/Su • W North Am & C America • 10 kW
- ⬅ • Tu/Th/Sa • W North Am & C America • 10 kW

**NIGERIA**
†VOICE OF NIGERIA, Ikorodu — C Africa, E Africa & S Africa • 250 kW

**RUSSIA**
†VOICE OF RUSSIA, Moscow — [W] • SE Asia • 250 kW

**UNITED KINGDOM**
BBC, Rampisham — [W] • E Europe • 500 kW
BBC, Via Zyyi, Cyprus — [S] M-F • E Europe • 300 kW

**USA**
†ADVENTIST WORLD R, Via Agat, Guam — [S] • SE Asia • 100 kW
FAMILY RADIO, Okeechobee, Fl — [S] • S America • 100 kW
†RFE-RL, Via Biblis, Germany — [S] • E Europe & W Asia • 100 kW
†RFE-RL, Via Lampertheim, Germany — [S] • W Asia • 100 kW
†RFE-RL, Via Udon Thani, Thailand — [W] • W Asia & S Asia • 250 kW
†VOA, Via Kavála, Greece
- [S] • W Asia • 250 kW
- [W] • E Europe & W Asia • 250 kW

VOA, Via Lampertheim, Germany — [S] • E Europe & W Asia • 100 kW
†VOA, Via Philippines — [S] • Australasia • 250 kW
†VOA, Via Udon Thani, Thailand — [S] • W Asia & S Asia • 250 kW

**11775**

**ANGUILLA**
CARIBBEAN BEACON — N America • 100 kW

**CHINA**
CHINA RADIO INTL, Shijiazhuang — [S] • Europe • 600 kW

**CHINA (TAIWAN)**
†CBS — Irr • E Asia • CHINESE NETWORK 2

**INDIA**
†ALL INDIA RADIO, Panaji — S Asia • 250 kW

**IRAN**
VO THE ISLAMIC REP, Tehrān
- [W] • W Asia & S Asia • 500 kW
- S Asia • 500 kW
- S Asia & SE Asia • 500 kW

**ROMANIA**
†RADIO ROMANIA INTL, Bucharest — [S] • Europe • 250 kW

**SRI LANKA**
†SRI LANKA BC CORP, Colombo-Ekala — Mideast • 200 kW

**USA**
†ADVENTIST WORLD R, Via Abu Dhabi — [S] • C Asia • 250 kW
†ADVENTIST WORLD R, Via Agat, Guam — [S] • E Asia • 100 kW
RADIO MARTI, Greenville, NC
- C America • 250 kW
- [W] • C America • 250 kW
- [S] Tu-Su • C America • 250 kW
- Tu-Su • C America • 250 kW

†VOA, Via Biblis, Germany — [S] • E Europe • 100 kW
†VOA, Via São Tomé
- [W] • S Africa • 100 kW
- [W] M-F • S Africa • 100 kW
- [W] • W Africa & C Africa • 100 kW
- [W] M-F • W Africa & C Africa • 100 kW
- [W] Sa/Su • W Africa & C Africa • 100 kW

**11780**

**BRAZIL**
†R NACIONAL DA AMAZONIA, Brasília
- DS • ➡
- M-F • DS • ➡

†RADIO NACIONAL, Brasília
- DS • ➡
- Su • DS • ➡
- Sa/Su • DS • ➡

**CHINA**
CENTRAL PEOPLE'S BS, Beijing — DS-8 (MINORITIES) • 50 kW
CHINA RADIO INTL, Beijing — [S] • E Europe • 150/300 kW
CHINA RADIO INTL, Xi'an — [S] • SE Asia • 100 kW

**UNITED KINGDOM**
BBC, Via Lampertheim, Germany — [S] • E Europe & W Asia • 100 kW
BBC, Via Thailand — Irr • [W] • W Asia & Mideast • 250 kW
BBC, Via Zyyi, Cyprus — [W] M-F • W Asia & C Asia • 250 kW

(con'd)

0 1 2 3 4 5 6 7 8 9 10 11 12 13 14 15 16 17 18 19 20 21 22 23 24

SEASONAL [S] OR [W] 1-HR TIMESHIFT MIDYEAR ⬅ OR ➡ JAMMING / OR ∧ EARLIEST HEARD ◁ LATEST HEARD ▷ NEW FOR 2003 †

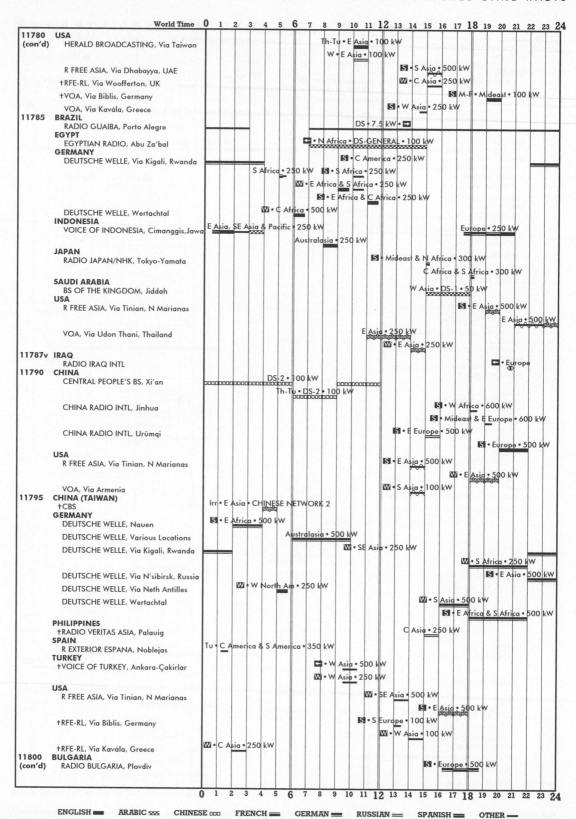

| | |
|---|---|
| **11780** **USA** | |
| **(con'd)** HERALD BROADCASTING, Via Taiwan | Th-Tu • E Asia • 100 kW |
| | W • E Asia • 100 kW |
| R FREE ASIA, Via Dhabayya, UAE | S • S Asia • 500 kW |
| †RFE-RL, Via Woofferton, UK | W • C Asia • 250 kW |
| †VOA, Via Biblis, Germany | S • M-F • Mideast • 100 kW |
| VOA, Via Kavála, Greece | S • W Asia • 250 kW |
| **11785** **BRAZIL** | |
| RADIO GUAIBA, Porto Alegre | DS • 7.5 kW • |
| **EGYPT** | |
| EGYPTIAN RADIO, Abu Za'bal | • N Africa • DS-GENERAL • 100 kW |
| **GERMANY** | |
| DEUTSCHE WELLE, Via Kigali, Rwanda | S • C America • 250 kW |
| | S Africa • 250 kW S • S Africa • 250 kW |
| | W • E Africa & S Africa • 250 kW |
| | S • E Africa & C Africa • 250 kW |
| DEUTSCHE WELLE, Wertachtal | W • C Africa • 500 kW |
| **INDONESIA** | |
| VOICE OF INDONESIA, Cimanggis, Jawa | E Asia, SE Asia & Pacific • 250 kW    Europe • 250 kW |
| | Australasia • 250 kW |
| **JAPAN** | |
| RADIO JAPAN/NHK, Tokyo-Yamata | S • Mideast & N Africa • 300 kW |
| | C Africa & S Africa • 300 kW |
| **SAUDI ARABIA** | |
| BS OF THE KINGDOM, Jiddah | W Asia • DS-1 • 50 kW |
| **USA** | |
| R FREE ASIA, Via Tinian, N Marianas | S • E Asia • 500 kW |
| | E Asia • 500 kW |
| VOA, Via Udon Thani, Thailand | E Asia • 250 kW |
| | W • E Asia • 250 kW |
| **11787v** **IRAQ** | |
| RADIO IRAQ INTL | • Europe |
| **11790** **CHINA** | |
| CENTRAL PEOPLE'S BS, Xi'an | DS-2 • 100 kW |
| | Th-Tu • DS-2 • 100 kW |
| CHINA RADIO INTL, Jinhua | S • W Africa • 600 kW |
| | S • Mideast & E Europe • 600 kW |
| CHINA RADIO INTL, Urümqi | S • E Europe • 500 kW |
| | S • Europe • 500 kW |
| **USA** | |
| R FREE ASIA, Via Tinian, N Marianas | S • E Asia • 500 kW |
| | W • E Asia • 500 kW |
| VOA, Via Armenia | W • S Asia • 100 kW |
| **11795** **CHINA (TAIWAN)** | |
| †CBS | Irr • E Asia • CHINESE NETWORK 2 |
| **GERMANY** | |
| DEUTSCHE WELLE, Nauen | S • E Africa • 500 kW |
| DEUTSCHE WELLE, Various Locations | Australasia • 500 kW |
| DEUTSCHE WELLE, Via Kigali, Rwanda | W • SE Asia • 250 kW |
| | W • S Africa • 250 kW |
| DEUTSCHE WELLE, Via N'sibirsk, Russia | S • E Asia • 500 kW |
| DEUTSCHE WELLE, Via Neth Antilles | W • W North Am • 250 kW |
| DEUTSCHE WELLE, Wertachtal | W • S Asia • 500 kW |
| | S • E Africa & S Africa • 500 kW |
| **PHILIPPINES** | |
| †RADIO VERITAS ASIA, Palauig | C Asia • 250 kW |
| **SPAIN** | |
| R EXTERIOR ESPANA, Noblejas | Tu • C America & S America • 350 kW |
| **TURKEY** | |
| †VOICE OF TURKEY, Ankara-Çakirlar | • W Asia • 500 kW |
| | W • W Asia • 250 kW |
| **USA** | |
| R FREE ASIA, Via Tinian, N Marianas | W • SE Asia • 500 kW |
| | S • E Asia • 500 kW |
| †RFE-RL, Via Biblis, Germany | S • S Europe • 100 kW |
| | W • W Asia • 100 kW |
| †RFE-RL, Via Kavála, Greece | W • C Asia • 250 kW |
| **11800** **BULGARIA** | |
| **(con'd)** RADIO BULGARIA, Plovdiv | S • Europe • 500 kW |

World Time: 0 1 2 3 4 5 6 7 8 9 10 11 12 13 14 15 16 17 18 19 20 21 22 23 24

ENGLISH ▬  ARABIC ▨  CHINESE ▢▢▢  FRENCH ▬  GERMAN ▬  RUSSIAN ═  SPANISH ▬  OTHER ▬

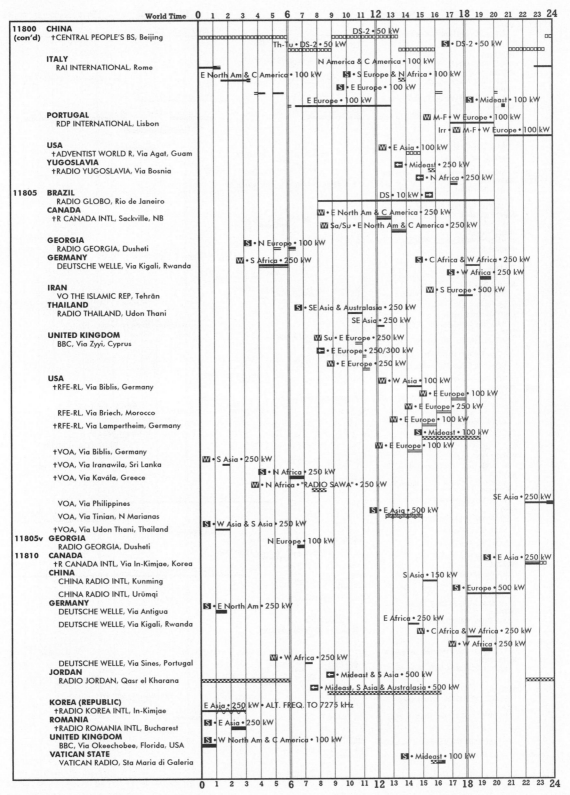

World Time 0 1 2 3 4 5 6 7 8 9 10 11 12 13 14 15 16 17 18 19 20 21 22 23 24

**11800 CHINA**
(con'd) †CENTRAL PEOPLE'S BS, Beijing
DS-2 • 50 kW
Th-Tu • DS-2 • 50 kW
ⓈDS-2 • 50 kW

**ITALY**
RAI INTERNATIONAL, Rome
N America & C America • 100 kW
E North Am & C America • 100 kW
Ⓢ S Europe & N Africa • 100 kW
Ⓢ E Europe • 100 kW
E Europe • 100 kW
Ⓢ Mideast • 100 kW

**PORTUGAL**
RDP INTERNATIONAL, Lisbon
Ⓦ M-F • W Europe • 100 kW
Irr • Ⓦ M-F • W Europe • 100 kW

**USA**
†ADVENTIST WORLD R, Via Agat, Guam
Ⓦ • E Asia • 100 kW
**YUGOSLAVIA**
†RADIO YUGOSLAVIA, Via Bosnia
⇦ • Mideast • 250 kW
⇦ • N Africa • 250 kW

**11805 BRAZIL**
RADIO GLOBO, Rio de Janeiro
DS • 10 kW • ⇨
**CANADA**
†R CANADA INTL, Sackville, NB
Ⓦ • E North Am & C America • 250 kW
Ⓦ Sa/Su • E North Am & C America • 250 kW

**GEORGIA**
RADIO GEORGIA, Dusheti
Ⓢ • N Europe • 100 kW
**GERMANY**
DEUTSCHE WELLE, Via Kigali, Rwanda
Ⓦ • S Africa • 250 kW
Ⓢ • C Africa & W Africa • 250 kW
Ⓢ • W Africa • 250 kW

**IRAN**
VO THE ISLAMIC REP, Tehrān
Ⓦ • S Europe • 500 kW
**THAILAND**
RADIO THAILAND, Udon Thani
Ⓢ • SE Asia & Australasia • 250 kW
SE Asia • 250 kW

**UNITED KINGDOM**
BBC, Via Zyyi, Cyprus
Ⓦ Su • E Europe • 250 kW
⇦ • E Europe • 250/300 kW
Ⓦ • E Europe • 250 kW

**USA**
†RFE-RL, Via Biblis, Germany
Ⓦ • W Asia • 100 kW
Ⓦ • E Europe • 100 kW

RFE-RL, Via Briech, Morocco
Ⓦ • E Europe • 250 kW
†RFE-RL, Via Lampertheim, Germany
Ⓦ • E Europe • 100 kW
Ⓢ • Mideast • 100 kW

†VOA, Via Biblis, Germany
Ⓦ • E Europe • 100 kW
†VOA, Via Iranawila, Sri Lanka
Ⓦ • S Asia • 250 kW
†VOA, Via Kavála, Greece
Ⓢ • N Africa • 250 kW
Ⓦ • N Africa • "RADIO SAWA" • 250 kW

VOA, Via Philippines
SE Asia • 250 kW
VOA, Via Tinian, N Marianas
Ⓢ • E Asia • 500 kW
†VOA, Via Udon Thani, Thailand
Ⓢ • W Asia & S Asia • 250 kW
**11805v GEORGIA**
RADIO GEORGIA, Dusheti
N Europe • 100 kW
**11810 CANADA**
†R CANADA INTL, Via In-Kimjae, Korea
Ⓢ • E Asia • 250 kW
**CHINA**
CHINA RADIO INTL, Kunming
S Asia • 150 kW
CHINA RADIO INTL, Urümqi
Ⓢ • Europe • 500 kW
**GERMANY**
DEUTSCHE WELLE, Via Antigua
Ⓢ • E North Am • 250 kW
DEUTSCHE WELLE, Via Kigali, Rwanda
E Africa • 250 kW
Ⓦ • C Africa & W Africa • 250 kW
Ⓦ • W Africa • 250 kW

DEUTSCHE WELLE, Via Sines, Portugal
Ⓦ • W Africa • 250 kW
**JORDAN**
RADIO JORDAN, Qasr el Kharana
⇦ • Mideast & S Asia • 500 kW
⇦ • Mideast, S Asia & Australasia • 500 kW

**KOREA (REPUBLIC)**
†RADIO KOREA INTL, In-Kimjae
E Asia • 250 kW • ALT. FREQ. TO 7275 kHz
**ROMANIA**
†RADIO ROMANIA INTL, Bucharest
Ⓢ • E Asia • 250 kW
**UNITED KINGDOM**
BBC, Via Okeechobee, Florida, USA
Ⓢ • W North Am & C America • 100 kW
**VATICAN STATE**
VATICAN RADIO, Sta Maria di Galeria
Ⓢ • Mideast • 100 kW

0 1 2 3 4 5 6 7 8 9 10 11 12 13 14 15 16 17 18 19 20 21 22 23 24

SEASONAL Ⓢ OR Ⓦ 1-HR TIMESHIFT MIDYEAR ⇦ OR ⇨ JAMMING / OR /\ EARLIEST HEARD ◁ LATEST HEARD ▷ NEW FOR 2003 †

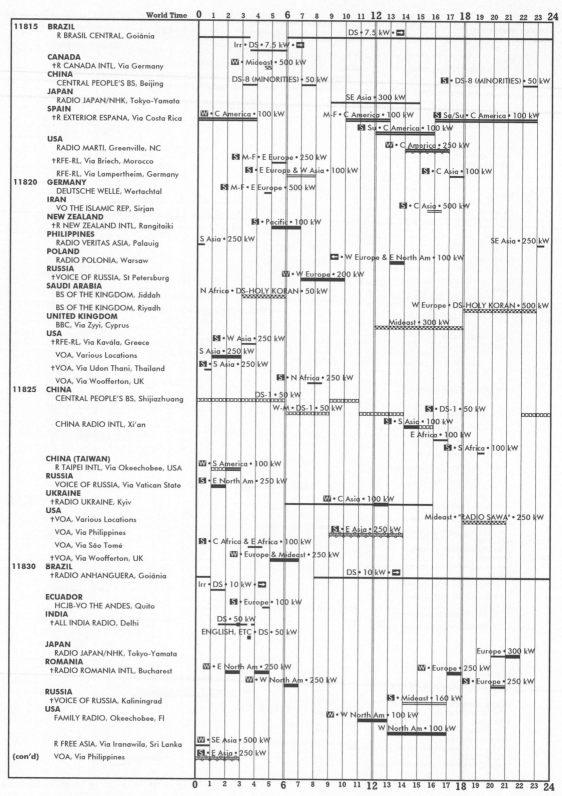

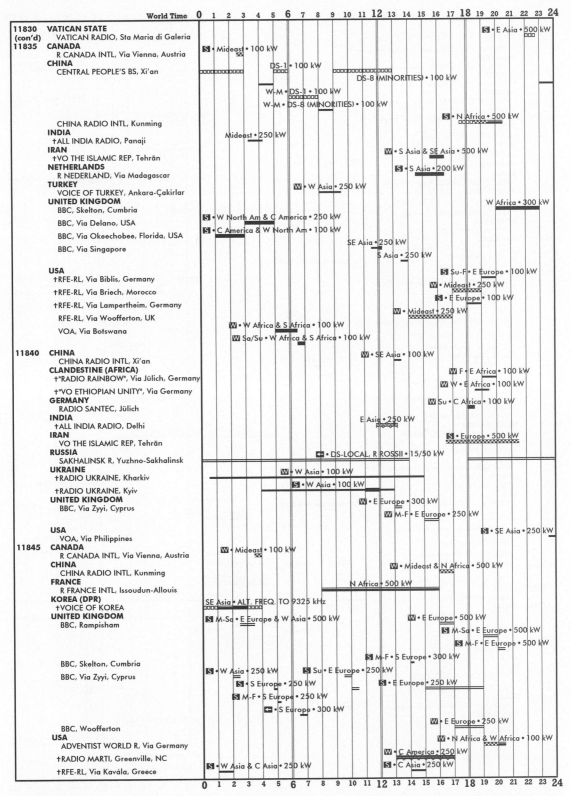

World Time: 0 1 2 3 4 5 6 7 8 9 10 11 12 13 14 15 16 17 18 19 20 21 22 23 24

| Freq | Station | Details |
|---|---|---|
| 11830 (con'd) | **VATICAN STATE** | |
| | VATICAN RADIO, Sta Maria di Galeria | S • E Asia • 500 kW |
| 11835 | **CANADA** | |
| | R CANADA INTL, Via Vienna, Austria | S • Mideast • 100 kW |
| | **CHINA** | |
| | CENTRAL PEOPLE'S BS, Xi'an | DS-1 • 100 kW / DS-8 (MINORITIES) • 100 kW |
| | | W-M • DS-1 • 100 kW |
| | | W-M • DS-8 (MINORITIES) • 100 kW |
| | CHINA RADIO INTL, Kunming | S • N Africa • 500 kW |
| | **INDIA** | |
| | †ALL INDIA RADIO, Panaji | Mideast • 250 kW |
| | **IRAN** | |
| | †VO THE ISLAMIC REP, Tehrān | W • S Asia & SE Asia • 500 kW |
| | **NETHERLANDS** | |
| | R NEDERLAND, Via Madagascar | S • S Asia • 200 kW |
| | **TURKEY** | |
| | VOICE OF TURKEY, Ankara-Çakirlar | W • W Asia • 250 kW |
| | **UNITED KINGDOM** | |
| | BBC, Skelton, Cumbria | W Africa • 300 kW |
| | BBC, Via Delano, USA | S • W North Am & C America • 250 kW |
| | BBC, Via Okeechobee, Florida, USA | S • C America & W North Am • 100 kW |
| | BBC, Via Singapore | SE Asia • 250 kW |
| | | S Asia • 250 kW |
| | **USA** | |
| | †RFE-RL, Via Biblis, Germany | S • Su-F • E Europe • 100 kW |
| | †RFE-RL, Via Briech, Morocco | W • Mideast • 250 kW |
| | †RFE-RL, Via Lampertheim, Germany | S • E Europe • 100 kW |
| | RFE-RL, Via Woofferton, UK | W • Mideast • 250 kW |
| | VOA, Via Botswana | W • W Africa & S Africa • 100 kW |
| | | W Sa/Su • W Africa & S Africa • 100 kW |
| 11840 | **CHINA** | |
| | CHINA RADIO INTL, Xi'an | W • SE Asia • 100 kW |
| | **CLANDESTINE (AFRICA)** | |
| | †"RADIO RAINBOW", Via Jülich, Germany | W F • E Africa • 100 kW |
| | †"VO ETHIOPIAN UNITY", Via Germany | W W • E Africa • 100 kW |
| | **GERMANY** | |
| | RADIO SANTEC, Jülich | W Su • C Africa • 100 kW |
| | **INDIA** | |
| | †ALL INDIA RADIO, Delhi | E Asia • 250 kW |
| | **IRAN** | |
| | VO THE ISLAMIC REP, Tehrān | S • Europe • 500 kW |
| | **RUSSIA** | |
| | SAKHALINSK R, Yuzhno-Sakhalinsk | ⬌ • DS-LOCAL, R ROSSII • 15/50 kW |
| | **UKRAINE** | |
| | †RADIO UKRAINE, Kharkiv | W • W Asia • 100 kW |
| | †RADIO UKRAINE, Kyiv | S • W Asia • 100 kW |
| | **UNITED KINGDOM** | |
| | BBC, Via Zyyi, Cyprus | W • E Europe • 300 kW |
| | | W M-F • E Europe • 250 kW |
| | **USA** | |
| | VOA, Via Philippines | S • SE Asia • 250 kW |
| 11845 | **CANADA** | |
| | R CANADA INTL, Via Vienna, Austria | W • Mideast • 100 kW |
| | **CHINA** | |
| | CHINA RADIO INTL, Kunming | W • Mideast & N Africa • 500 kW |
| | **FRANCE** | |
| | R FRANCE INTL, Issoudun-Allouis | N Africa • 500 kW |
| | **KOREA (DPR)** | |
| | †VOICE OF KOREA | SE Asia • ALT. FREQ. TO 9325 kHz |
| | **UNITED KINGDOM** | |
| | BBC, Rampisham | S M-Sa • E Europe & W Asia • 500 kW |
| | | W • E Europe • 500 kW |
| | | S M-Sa • E Europe • 500 kW |
| | | S M-F • E Europe • 500 kW |
| | | S M-F • S Europe • 300 kW |
| | BBC, Skelton, Cumbria | S • W Asia • 250 kW |
| | BBC, Via Zyyi, Cyprus | S Su • E Europe • 250 kW |
| | | S • S Europe • 250 kW    S • E Europe • 250 kW |
| | | S M-F • S Europe • 250 kW |
| | | ⬌ • S Europe • 300 kW |
| | BBC, Woofferton | W • E Europe • 250 kW |
| | **USA** | |
| | ADVENTIST WORLD R, Via Germany | W • N Africa & W Africa • 100 kW |
| | †RADIO MARTI, Greenville, NC | W • C America • 250 kW |
| | †RFE-RL, Via Kavála, Greece | S • W Asia & C Asia • 250 kW    S • C Asia • 250 kW |

SEASONAL S OR W    1-HR TIMESHIFT MIDYEAR ⬅ OR ➡    JAMMING / OR ∧    EARLIEST HEARD ◁    LATEST HEARD ▷    NEW FOR 2003 †

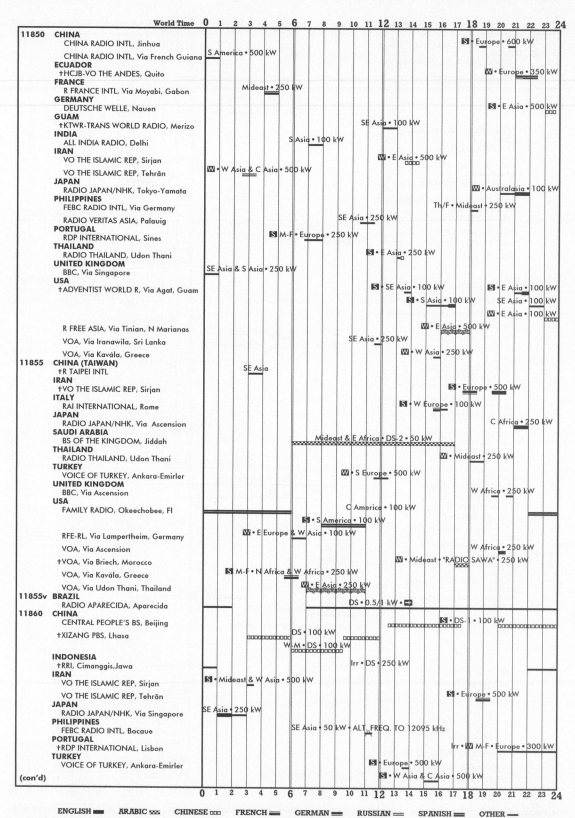

| | | |
|---|---|---|
| **11850** | **CHINA** | |
| | CHINA RADIO INTL, Jinhua | S • Europe • 600 kW |
| | CHINA RADIO INTL, Via French Guiana | S America • 500 kW |
| | **ECUADOR** | |
| | †HCJB-VO THE ANDES, Quito | W • Europe • 350 kW |
| | **FRANCE** | |
| | R FRANCE INTL, Via Moyabi, Gabon | Mideast • 250 kW |
| | **GERMANY** | |
| | DEUTSCHE WELLE, Nauen | S • E Asia • 500 kW |
| | **GUAM** | |
| | †KTWR-TRANS WORLD RADIO, Merizo | SE Asia • 100 kW |
| | **INDIA** | |
| | ALL INDIA RADIO, Delhi | S Asia • 100 kW |
| | **IRAN** | |
| | VO THE ISLAMIC REP, Sirjan | W • E Asia • 500 kW |
| | VO THE ISLAMIC REP, Tehrān | W • W Asia & C Asia • 500 kW |
| | **JAPAN** | |
| | RADIO JAPAN/NHK, Tokyo-Yamata | W • Australasia • 100 kW |
| | **PHILIPPINES** | |
| | FEBC RADIO INTL, Via Germany | Th/F • Mideast • 250 kW |
| | RADIO VERITAS ASIA, Palauig | SE Asia • 250 kW |
| | **PORTUGAL** | |
| | RDP INTERNATIONAL, Sines | S • M-F • Europe • 250 kW |
| | **THAILAND** | |
| | RADIO THAILAND, Udon Thani | S • E Asia • 250 kW |
| | **UNITED KINGDOM** | |
| | BBC, Via Singapore | SE Asia & S Asia • 250 kW |
| | **USA** | |
| | †ADVENTIST WORLD R, Via Agat, Guam | S • SE Asia • 100 kW — S • E Asia • 100 kW |
| | | S • S Asia • 100 kW — SE Asia • 100 kW |
| | | W • E Asia • 100 kW |
| | R FREE ASIA, Via Tinian, N Marianas | W • E Asia • 500 kW |
| | VOA, Via Iranawila, Sri Lanka | SE Asia • 250 kW |
| | VOA, Via Kavála, Greece | W • W Asia • 250 kW |
| **11855** | **CHINA (TAIWAN)** | |
| | †R TAIPEI INTL | SE Asia |
| | **IRAN** | |
| | †VO THE ISLAMIC REP, Sirjan | S • Europe • 500 kW |
| | **ITALY** | |
| | RAI INTERNATIONAL, Rome | S • W Europe • 100 kW |
| | **JAPAN** | |
| | RADIO JAPAN/NHK, Via Ascension | C Africa • 250 kW |
| | **SAUDI ARABIA** | |
| | BS OF THE KINGDOM, Jiddah | Mideast & E Africa • DS-2 • 50 kW |
| | **THAILAND** | |
| | RADIO THAILAND, Udon Thani | W • Mideast • 250 kW |
| | **TURKEY** | |
| | VOICE OF TURKEY, Ankara-Emirler | W • S Europe • 500 kW |
| | **UNITED KINGDOM** | |
| | BBC, Via Ascension | W Africa • 250 kW |
| | **USA** | |
| | FAMILY RADIO, Okeechobee, Fl | C America • 100 kW |
| | | S • S America • 100 kW |
| | RFE-RL, Via Lampertheim, Germany | W • E Europe & W Asia • 100 kW |
| | VOA, Via Ascension | W Africa • 250 kW |
| | †VOA, Via Briech, Morocco | W • Mideast • "RADIO SAWA" • 250 kW |
| | VOA, Via Kavála, Greece | S • M-F • N Africa & W Africa • 250 kW |
| | VOA, Via Udon Thani, Thailand | W • E Asia • 250 kW |
| **11855v** | **BRAZIL** | |
| | RADIO APARECIDA, Aparecida | DS • 0.5/1 kW • |
| **11860** | **CHINA** | |
| | CENTRAL PEOPLE'S BS, Beijing | S • DS-1 • 100 kW |
| | †XIZANG PBS, Lhasa | DS • 100 kW |
| | | W•M • DS • 100 kW |
| | **INDONESIA** | |
| | †RRI, Cimanggis, Jawa | Irr • DS • 250 kW |
| | **IRAN** | |
| | VO THE ISLAMIC REP, Sirjan | S • Mideast & W Asia • 500 kW |
| | VO THE ISLAMIC REP, Tehrān | S • Europe • 500 kW |
| | **JAPAN** | |
| | RADIO JAPAN/NHK, Via Singapore | SE Asia • 250 kW |
| | **PHILIPPINES** | |
| | FEBC RADIO INTL, Bocaue | SE Asia • 50 kW • ALT. FREQ. TO 12095 kHz |
| | **PORTUGAL** | |
| | †RDP INTERNATIONAL, Lisbon | Irr • W • M-F • Europe • 300 kW |
| | **TURKEY** | |
| | VOICE OF TURKEY, Ankara-Emirler | S • Europe • 500 kW |
| | | S • W Asia & C Asia • 500 kW |
| **(con'd)** | | |

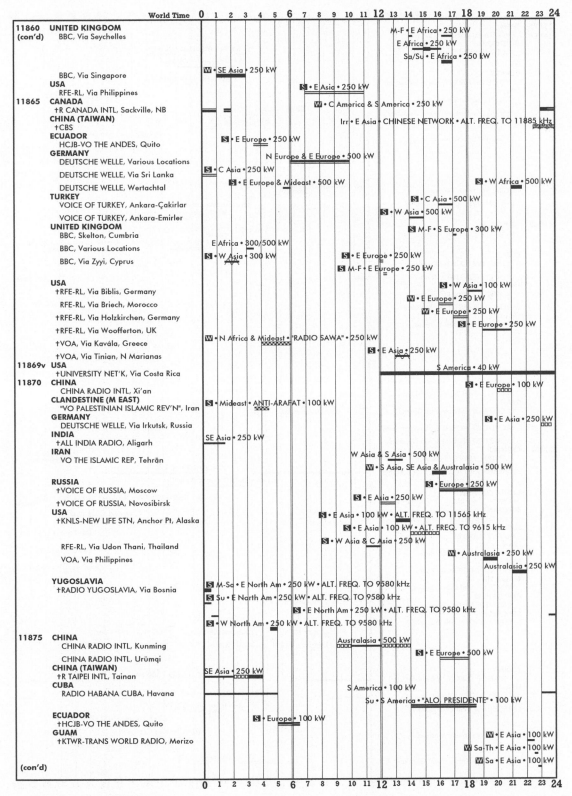

World Time: 0 1 2 3 4 5 6 7 8 9 10 11 12 13 14 15 16 17 18 19 20 21 22 23 24

**11860 UNITED KINGDOM**
(con'd)   BBC, Via Seychelles — M-F • E Africa • 250 kW; E Africa • 250 kW; Sa/Su • E Africa • 250 kW

BBC, Via Singapore — W • SE Asia • 250 kW
**USA**
  RFE-RL, Via Philippines — S • E Asia • 250 kW

**11865 CANADA**
  †R CANADA INTL, Sackville, NB — W • C America & S America • 250 kW
**CHINA (TAIWAN)**
  †CBS — Irr • E Asia • CHINESE NETWORK • ALT. FREQ. TO 11885 kHz
**ECUADOR**
  HCJB-VO THE ANDES, Quito — S • E Europe • 250 kW
**GERMANY**
  DEUTSCHE WELLE, Various Locations — N Europe & E Europe • 500 kW

  DEUTSCHE WELLE, Via Sri Lanka — S • C Asia • 250 kW; S • W Africa • 500 kW

  DEUTSCHE WELLE, Wertachtal — S • E Europe & Mideast • 500 kW
**TURKEY**
  VOICE OF TURKEY, Ankara-Çakirlar — S • C Asia • 500 kW

  VOICE OF TURKEY, Ankara-Emirler — S • W Asia • 500 kW
**UNITED KINGDOM**
  BBC, Skelton, Cumbria — S • M-F • S Europe • 300 kW

  BBC, Various Locations — E Africa • 300/500 kW

  BBC, Via Zyyi, Cyprus — S • W Asia • 300 kW; S • E Europe • 250 kW; S • M-F • E Europe • 250 kW

**USA**
  †RFE-RL, Via Biblis, Germany — S • W Asia • 100 kW

  RFE-RL, Via Briech, Morocco — W • E Europe • 250 kW

  †RFE-RL, Via Holzkirchen, Germany — W • E Europe • 250 kW

  †RFE-RL, Via Woofferton, UK — S • E Europe • 250 kW

  †VOA, Via Kavála, Greece — W • N Africa & Mideast • "RADIO SAWA" • 250 kW

  †VOA, Via Tinian, N Marianas — S • E Asia • 250 kW
**11869v USA**
  †UNIVERSITY NET'K, Via Costa Rica — S America • 40 kW
**11870 CHINA**
  CHINA RADIO INTL, Xi'an — S • E Europe • 100 kW
**CLANDESTINE (M EAST)**
  "VO PALESTINIAN ISLAMIC REV'N", Iran — S • Mideast • ANTI-ARAFAT • 100 kW
**GERMANY**
  DEUTSCHE WELLE, Via Irkutsk, Russia — S • E Asia • 250 kW
**INDIA**
  †ALL INDIA RADIO, Aligarh — SE Asia • 250 kW
**IRAN**
  VO THE ISLAMIC REP, Tehrān — W Asia & S Asia • 500 kW; W • S Asia, SE Asia & Australasia • 500 kW

**RUSSIA**
  †VOICE OF RUSSIA, Moscow — S • Europe • 250 kW

  †VOICE OF RUSSIA, Novosibirsk — S • E Asia • 250 kW
**USA**
  †KNLS-NEW LIFE STN, Anchor Pt, Alaska — S • E Asia • 100 kW • ALT. FREQ. TO 11565 kHz; S • E Asia • 100 kW • ALT. FREQ. TO 9615 kHz

  RFE-RL, Via Udon Thani, Thailand — S • W Asia & C Asia • 250 kW

  VOA, Via Philippines — W • Australasia • 250 kW; Australasia • 250 kW

**YUGOSLAVIA**
  †RADIO YUGOSLAVIA, Via Bosnia — S • M-Sa • E North Am • 250 kW • ALT. FREQ. TO 9580 kHz; S • Su • E North Am • 250 kW • ALT. FREQ. TO 9580 kHz; S • E North Am • 250 kW • ALT. FREQ. TO 9580 kHz; S • W North Am • 250 kW • ALT. FREQ. TO 9580 kHz

**11875 CHINA**
  CHINA RADIO INTL, Kunming — Australasia • 500 kW

  CHINA RADIO INTL, Urümqi — S • E Europe • 500 kW
**CHINA (TAIWAN)**
  †R TAIPEI INTL, Tainan — SE Asia • 250 kW
**CUBA**
  RADIO HABANA CUBA, Havana — S America • 100 kW; Su • S America • "ALO, PRESIDENTE" • 100 kW

**ECUADOR**
  †HCJB-VO THE ANDES, Quito — S • Europe • 100 kW
**GUAM**
  †KTWR-TRANS WORLD RADIO, Merizo — W • E Asia • 100 kW; W • Sa-Th • E Asia • 100 kW; W • Sa • E Asia • 100 kW

(con'd)

World Time: 0 1 2 3 4 5 6 7 8 9 10 11 12 13 14 15 16 17 18 19 20 21 22 23 24

SEASONAL Ⓢ OR Ⓦ    1-HR TIMESHIFT MIDYEAR ⬅ OR ➡    JAMMING / OR ∧    EARLIEST HEARD ◁    LATEST HEARD ▷    NEW FOR 2003 †

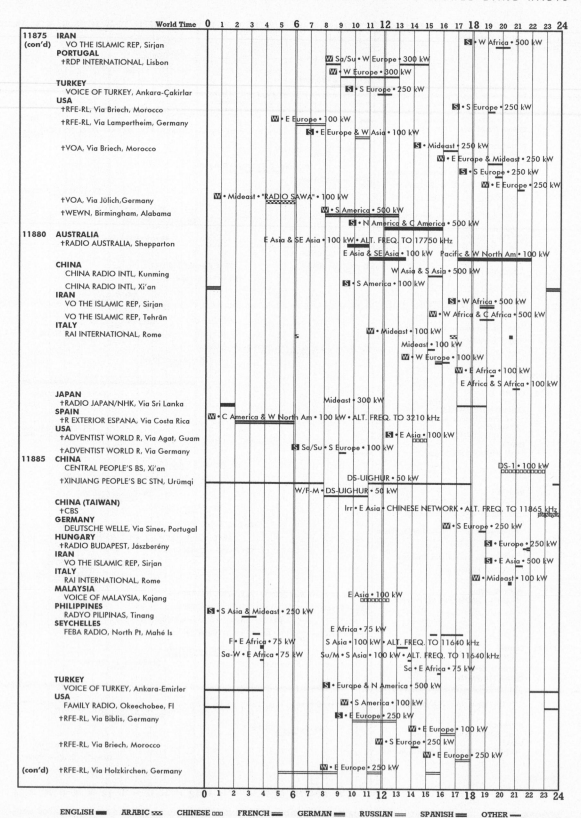

World Time  0  1  2  3  4  5  6  7  8  9  10  11  12  13  14  15  16  17  18  19  20  21  22  23  24

**11875 IRAN**
**(con'd)**  VO THE ISLAMIC REP, Sirjan — Ⓢ • W Africa • 500 kW
**PORTUGAL**
†RDP INTERNATIONAL, Lisbon — Ⓦ Sa/Su • W Europe • 300 kW / Ⓦ • W Europe • 300 kW
**TURKEY**
VOICE OF TURKEY, Ankara-Çakirlar — Ⓢ • S Europe • 250 kW
**USA**
†RFE-RL, Via Briech, Morocco — Ⓢ • S Europe • 250 kW
†RFE-RL, Via Lampertheim, Germany — Ⓦ • E Europe • 100 kW / Ⓢ • E Europe & W Asia • 100 kW
†VOA, Via Briech, Morocco — Ⓢ • Mideast • 250 kW / Ⓦ • E Europe & Mideast • 250 kW / Ⓢ • S Europe • 250 kW / Ⓦ • E Europe • 250 kW
†VOA, Via Jülich, Germany — Ⓦ • Mideast • "RADIO SAWA" • 100 kW
†WEWN, Birmingham, Alabama — Ⓦ • S America • 500 kW / Ⓢ • N America & C America • 500 kW

**11880 AUSTRALIA**
†RADIO AUSTRALIA, Shepparton — E Asia & SE Asia • 100 kW • ALT. FREQ. TO 17750 kHz / E Asia & SE Asia • 100 kW   Pacific & W North Am • 100 kW
**CHINA**
CHINA RADIO INTL, Kunming — W Asia & S Asia • 500 kW
CHINA RADIO INTL, Xi'an — Ⓢ • S America • 100 kW
**IRAN**
VO THE ISLAMIC REP, Sirjan — Ⓢ • W Africa • 500 kW
VO THE ISLAMIC REP, Tehrān — Ⓦ • W Africa & C Africa • 500 kW
**ITALY**
RAI INTERNATIONAL, Rome — Ⓦ • Mideast • 100 kW / Mideast • 100 kW / Ⓦ • W Europe • 100 kW / Ⓦ • E Africa • 100 kW / E Africa & S Africa • 100 kW
**JAPAN**
†RADIO JAPAN/NHK, Via Sri Lanka — Mideast • 300 kW
**SPAIN**
†R EXTERIOR ESPANA, Via Costa Rica — Ⓦ • C America & W North Am • 100 kW • ALT. FREQ. TO 3210 kHz
**USA**
†ADVENTIST WORLD R, Via Agat, Guam — Ⓢ • E Asia • 100 kW
†ADVENTIST WORLD R, Via Germany — Ⓢ Sa/Su • S Europe • 100 kW

**11885 CHINA**
CENTRAL PEOPLE'S BS, Xi'an — DS-1 • 100 kW
†XINJIANG PEOPLE'S BC STN, Urümqi — DS-UIGHUR • 50 kW / W/F-M • DS-UIGHUR • 50 kW
**CHINA (TAIWAN)**
†CBS — Irr • E Asia • CHINESE NETWORK • ALT. FREQ. TO 11865 kHz
**GERMANY**
DEUTSCHE WELLE, Via Sines, Portugal — Ⓦ • S Europe • 250 kW
**HUNGARY**
†RADIO BUDAPEST, Jászberény — Ⓢ • Europe • 250 kW
**IRAN**
VO THE ISLAMIC REP, Sirjan — Ⓢ • E Asia • 500 kW
**ITALY**
RAI INTERNATIONAL, Rome — Ⓦ • Mideast • 100 kW
**MALAYSIA**
VOICE OF MALAYSIA, Kajang — E Asia • 100 kW
**PHILIPPINES**
RADYO PILIPINAS, Tinang — Ⓢ • S Asia & Mideast • 250 kW
**SEYCHELLES**
FEBA RADIO, North Pt, Mahé Is — E Africa • 75 kW / F • E Africa • 75 kW / S Asia • 100 kW • ALT. FREQ. TO 11640 kHz / Sa-W • E Africa • 75 kW / Su/M • S Asia • 100 kW • ALT. FREQ. TO 11640 kHz / Sa • E Africa • 75 kW
**TURKEY**
VOICE OF TURKEY, Ankara-Emirler — Ⓢ • Europe & N America • 500 kW
**USA**
FAMILY RADIO, Okeechobee, Fl — Ⓦ • S America • 100 kW
†RFE-RL, Via Biblis, Germany — Ⓢ • E Europe • 250 kW / Ⓦ • E Europe • 100 kW
†RFE-RL, Via Briech, Morocco — Ⓦ • S Europe • 250 kW / Ⓦ • E Europe • 250 kW
**(con'd)** †RFE-RL, Via Holzkirchen, Germany — Ⓦ • E Europe • 250 kW

0  1  2  3  4  5  6  7  8  9  10  11  12  13  14  15  16  17  18  19  20  21  22  23  24

ENGLISH ▬   ARABIC ░   CHINESE □□□   FRENCH ▬   GERMAN ▬   RUSSIAN ═   SPANISH ▬   OTHER ▬

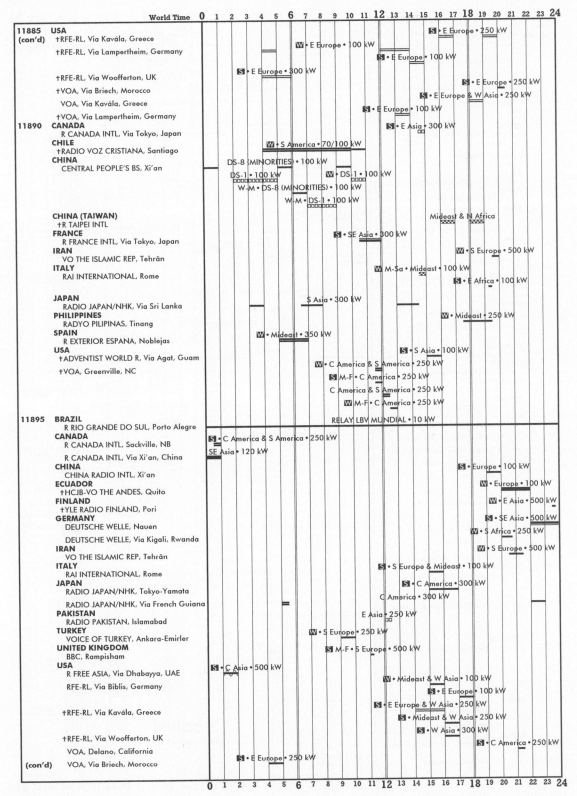

| | | World Time | 0 1 2 3 4 5 6 7 8 9 10 11 12 13 14 15 16 17 18 19 20 21 22 23 24 |
|---|---|---|---|

**11885 USA**
(con'd) †RFE-RL, Via Kavála, Greece — S • E Europe • 250 kW
†RFE-RL, Via Lampertheim, Germany — W • E Europe • 100 kW / S • E Europe • 100 kW
†RFE-RL, Via Woofferton, UK — S • E Europe • 300 kW / S • E Europe • 250 kW
†VOA, Via Briech, Morocco — S • E Europe & W Asia • 250 kW
VOA, Via Kavála, Greece — W • E Europe & W Asia • 250 kW
†VOA, Via Lampertheim, Germany — S • E Europe • 100 kW

**11890 CANADA**
R CANADA INTL, Via Tokyo, Japan — S • E Asia • 300 kW
**CHILE**
†RADIO VOZ CRISTIANA, Santiago — W • S America • 70/100 kW
**CHINA**
CENTRAL PEOPLE'S BS, Xi'an — DS-8 (MINORITIES) • 100 kW
DS-1 • 100 kW / W • DS-1 • 100 kW
W-M • DS-8 (MINORITIES) • 100 kW
W-M • DS-1 • 100 kW

**CHINA (TAIWAN)**
†R TAIPEI INTL — Mideast & N Africa
**FRANCE**
R FRANCE INTL, Via Tokyo, Japan — S • SE Asia • 300 kW
**IRAN**
VO THE ISLAMIC REP, Tehrān — W • S Europe • 500 kW
**ITALY**
RAI INTERNATIONAL, Rome — W M-Sa • Mideast • 100 kW
S • E Africa • 100 kW
**JAPAN**
RADIO JAPAN/NHK, Via Sri Lanka — S Asia • 300 kW
**PHILIPPINES**
RADYO PILIPINAS, Tinang — W • Mideast • 250 kW
**SPAIN**
R EXTERIOR ESPANA, Noblejas — W • Mideast • 350 kW
**USA**
†ADVENTIST WORLD R, Via Agat, Guam — S • S Asia • 100 kW
†VOA, Greenville, NC — W • C America & S America • 250 kW
M-F • C America • 250 kW
C America & S America • 250 kW
W M-F • C America • 250 kW

**11895 BRAZIL**
R RIO GRANDE DO SUL, Porto Alegre — RELAY LBV MUNDIAL • 10 kW
**CANADA**
R CANADA INTL, Sackville, NB — S • C America & S America • 250 kW
R CANADA INTL, Via Xi'an, China — SE Asia • 120 kW
**CHINA**
CHINA RADIO INTL, Xi'an — S • Europe • 100 kW
**ECUADOR**
†HCJB-VO THE ANDES, Quito — W • Europe • 100 kW
**FINLAND**
†YLE RADIO FINLAND, Pori — W • E Asia • 500 kW
**GERMANY**
DEUTSCHE WELLE, Nauen — S • SE Asia • 500 kW
DEUTSCHE WELLE, Via Kigali, Rwanda — W • S Africa • 250 kW
**IRAN**
VO THE ISLAMIC REP, Tehrān — W • S Europe • 500 kW
**ITALY**
RAI INTERNATIONAL, Rome — S • S Europe & Mideast • 100 kW
**JAPAN**
RADIO JAPAN/NHK, Tokyo-Yamata — S • C America • 300 kW
RADIO JAPAN/NHK, Via French Guiana — C America • 300 kW
**PAKISTAN**
RADIO PAKISTAN, Islamabad — E Asia • 250 kW
**TURKEY**
VOICE OF TURKEY, Ankara-Emirler — W • S Europe • 250 kW
**UNITED KINGDOM**
BBC, Rampisham — S M-F • S Europe • 500 kW
**USA**
R FREE ASIA, Via Dhabayya, UAE — S • C Asia • 500 kW
RFE-RL, Via Biblis, Germany — W • Mideast & W Asia • 100 kW
S • E Europe • 100 kW
†RFE-RL, Via Kavála, Greece — S • E Europe & W Asia • 250 kW
S • Mideast & W Asia • 250 kW
†RFE-RL, Via Woofferton, UK — S • W Asia • 300 kW
VOA, Delano, California — S • C America • 250 kW
(con'd) VOA, Via Briech, Morocco — S • E Europe • 250 kW

| | 0 1 2 3 4 5 6 7 8 9 10 11 12 13 14 15 16 17 18 19 20 21 22 23 24 |
|---|---|

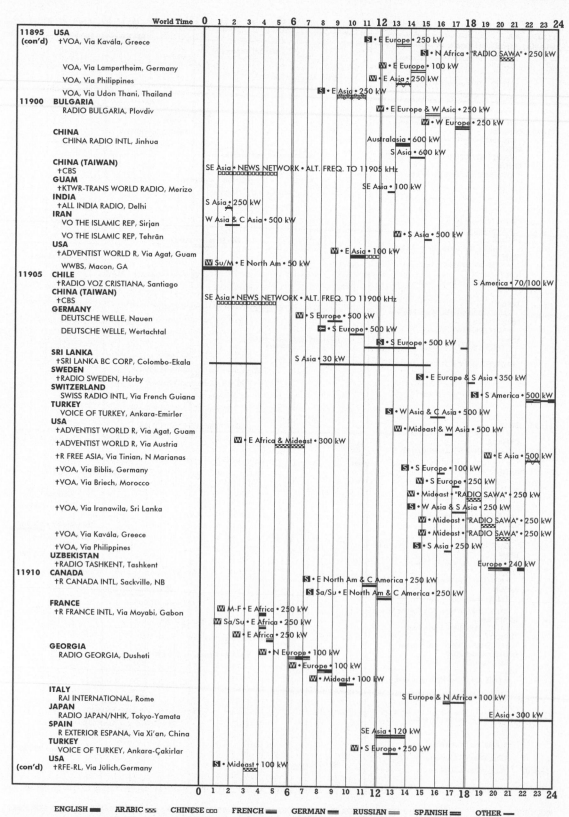

| World Time | | | |
|---|---|---|---|
| **11895 USA** | | | |
| (con'd) | †VOA, Via Kavála, Greece | S • E Europe • 250 kW | S • N Africa • "RADIO SAWA" • 250 kW |
| | VOA, Via Lampertheim, Germany | W • E Europe • 100 kW | |
| | VOA, Via Philippines | W • E Asia • 250 kW | |
| | VOA, Via Udon Thani, Thailand | S • E Asia • 250 kW | |
| **11900 BULGARIA** | RADIO BULGARIA, Plovdiv | W • E Europe & W Asia • 250 kW | |
| | | W • W Europe • 250 kW | |
| **CHINA** | CHINA RADIO INTL, Jinhua | Australasia • 600 kW | |
| | | S Asia • 600 kW | |
| **CHINA (TAIWAN)** | †CBS | SE Asia • NEWS NETWORK • ALT. FREQ. TO 11905 kHz | |
| **GUAM** | †KTWR-TRANS WORLD RADIO, Merizo | SE Asia • 100 kW | |
| **INDIA** | †ALL INDIA RADIO, Delhi | S Asia • 250 kW | |
| **IRAN** | VO THE ISLAMIC REP, Sirjan | W Asia & C Asia • 500 kW | |
| | VO THE ISLAMIC REP, Tehrān | W • S Asia • 500 kW | |
| **USA** | †ADVENTIST WORLD R, Via Agat, Guam | W • E Asia • 100 kW | |
| | WWBS, Macon, GA | W Su/M • E North Am • 50 kW | |
| **11905 CHILE** | †RADIO VOZ CRISTIANA, Santiago | S America • 70/100 kW | |
| **CHINA (TAIWAN)** | †CBS | SE Asia • NEWS NETWORK • ALT. FREQ. TO 11900 kHz | |
| **GERMANY** | DEUTSCHE WELLE, Nauen | W • S Europe • 500 kW | |
| | DEUTSCHE WELLE, Wertachtal | ⊞ • S Europe • 500 kW | |
| | | S • S Europe • 500 kW | |
| **SRI LANKA** | †SRI LANKA BC CORP, Colombo-Ekala | S Asia • 30 kW | |
| **SWEDEN** | †RADIO SWEDEN, Hörby | S • E Eurpe & S Asia • 350 kW | |
| **SWITZERLAND** | SWISS RADIO INTL, Via French Guiana | S • S America • 500 kW | |
| **TURKEY** | VOICE OF TURKEY, Ankara-Emirler | S • W Asia & C Asia • 500 kW | |
| **USA** | †ADVENTIST WORLD R, Via Agat, Guam | W • Mideast & W Asia • 500 kW | |
| | †ADVENTIST WORLD R, Via Austria | W • E Africa & Mideast • 300 kW | |
| | †R FREE ASIA, Via Tinian, N Marianas | W • E Asia • 500 kW | |
| | †VOA, Via Biblis, Germany | S • S Europe • 100 kW | |
| | †VOA, Via Briech, Morocco | W • S Europe • 250 kW | |
| | | W • Mideast • "RADIO SAWA" • 250 kW | |
| | †VOA, Via Iranawila, Sri Lanka | S • W Asia & S Asia • 250 kW | |
| | | W • Mideast • "RADIO SAWA" • 250 kW | |
| | †VOA, Via Kavála, Greece | W • Mideast • "RADIO SAWA" • 250 kW | |
| | †VOA, Via Philippines | S • S Asia • 250 kW | |
| **UZBEKISTAN** | †RADIO TASHKENT, Tashkent | Europe • 240 kW | |
| **11910 CANADA** | †R CANADA INTL, Sackville, NB | S • E North Am & C America • 250 kW | |
| | | S Sa/Su • E North Am & C America • 250 kW | |
| **FRANCE** | †R FRANCE INTL, Via Moyabi, Gabon | W M-F • E Africa • 250 kW | |
| | | W Sa/Su • E Africa • 250 kW | |
| | | W • E Africa • 250 kW | |
| **GEORGIA** | RADIO GEORGIA, Dusheti | W • N Europe • 100 kW | |
| | | W • Europe • 100 kW | |
| | | W • Mideast • 100 kW | |
| **ITALY** | RAI INTERNATIONAL, Rome | S Europe & N Africa • 100 kW | |
| **JAPAN** | RADIO JAPAN/NHK, Tokyo-Yamata | E Asia • 300 kW | |
| **SPAIN** | R EXTERIOR ESPANA, Via Xi'an, China | SE Asia • 120 kW | |
| **TURKEY** | VOICE OF TURKEY, Ankara-Çakirlar | W • S Europe • 250 kW | |
| **USA** | | | |
| (con'd) | †RFE-RL, Via Jülich, Germany | S • Mideast • 100 kW | |

ENGLISH ▬   ARABIC ᠁   CHINESE □□□   FRENCH ▬   GERMAN ▬   RUSSIAN ═   SPANISH ▬   OTHER ▬

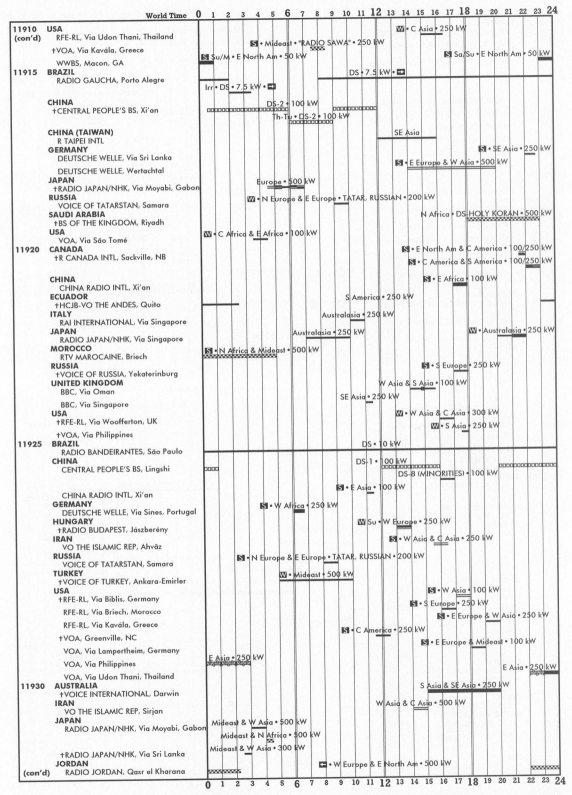

World Time 0 1 2 3 4 5 6 7 8 9 10 11 12 13 14 15 16 17 18 19 20 21 22 23 24

**11910 USA**
(con'd) RFE-RL, Via Udon Thani, Thailand — W • C Asia • 250 kW
†VOA, Via Kavála, Greece — S • Mideast • "RADIO SAWA" • 250 kW
WWBS, Macon, GA — S Su/M • E North Am • 50 kW ... S Sa/Su • E North Am • 50 kW
**11915 BRAZIL**
RADIO GAUCHA, Porto Alegre — DS • 7.5 kW • ⇒ ; Irr • DS • 7.5 kW • ⇒
**CHINA**
†CENTRAL PEOPLE'S BS, Xi'an — DS-2 • 100 kW ; Th-Tu • DS-2 • 100 kW
**CHINA (TAIWAN)**
R TAIPEI INTL — SE Asia
**GERMANY**
DEUTSCHE WELLE, Via Sri Lanka — S • SE Asia • 250 kW ; S • E Europe & W Asia • 500 kW
DEUTSCHE WELLE, Wertachtal
**JAPAN**
†RADIO JAPAN/NHK, Via Moyabi, Gabon — Europe • 500 kW
**RUSSIA**
VOICE OF TATARSTAN, Samara — W • N Europe & E Europe • TATAR, RUSSIAN • 200 kW
**SAUDI ARABIA**
†BS OF THE KINGDOM, Riyadh — N Africa • DS-HOLY KORAN • 500 kW
**USA**
VOA, Via São Tomé — W • C Africa & E Africa • 100 kW
**11920 CANADA**
†R CANADA INTL, Sackville, NB — S • E North Am & C America • 100/250 kW ; S • C America & S America • 100/250 kW
**CHINA**
CHINA RADIO INTL, Xi'an — S • E Africa • 100 kW
**ECUADOR**
†HCJB-VO THE ANDES, Quito — S America • 250 kW
**ITALY**
RAI INTERNATIONAL, Via Singapore — Australasia • 250 kW
**JAPAN**
RADIO JAPAN/NHK, Via Singapore — Australasia • 250 kW ; W • Australasia • 250 kW
**MOROCCO**
RTV MAROCAINE, Briech — S • N Africa & Mideast • 500 kW
**RUSSIA**
†VOICE OF RUSSIA, Yekaterinburg — S • S Europe • 250 kW
**UNITED KINGDOM**
BBC, Via Oman — W Asia & S Asia • 100 kW
BBC, Via Singapore — SE Asia • 250 kW
**USA**
†RFE-RL, Via Woofferton, UK — W • W Asia & C Asia • 300 kW
†VOA, Via Philippines — W • S Asia • 250 kW
**11925 BRAZIL**
RADIO BANDEIRANTES, São Paulo — DS • 10 kW
**CHINA**
CENTRAL PEOPLE'S BS, Lingshi — DS-1 • 100 kW ; DS-8 (MINORITIES) • 100 kW
CHINA RADIO INTL, Xi'an — S • E Asia • 100 kW
**GERMANY**
DEUTSCHE WELLE, Via Sines, Portugal — S • W Africa • 250 kW
**HUNGARY**
†RADIO BUDAPEST, Jászberény — W Su • W Europe • 250 kW
**IRAN**
VO THE ISLAMIC REP, Ahvāz — S • W Asia & C Asia • 250 kW
**RUSSIA**
VOICE OF TATARSTAN, Samara — S • N Europe & E Europe • TATAR, RUSSIAN • 200 kW
**TURKEY**
†VOICE OF TURKEY, Ankara-Emirler — W • Mideast • 500 kW
**USA**
†RFE-RL, Via Biblis, Germany — S • W Asia • 100 kW
RFE-RL, Via Briech, Morocco — S • S Europe • 250 kW
RFE-RL, Via Kavála, Greece — S • E Europe & W Asia • 250 kW
†VOA, Greenville, NC — S • C America • 250 kW
VOA, Via Lampertheim, Germany — S • E Europe & Mideast • 100 kW
VOA, Via Philippines — E Asia • 250 kW ; E Asia • 250 kW
VOA, Via Udon Thani, Thailand — S Asia & SE Asia • 250 kW
**11930 AUSTRALIA**
†VOICE INTERNATIONAL, Darwin — W Asia & C Asia • 500 kW
**IRAN**
VO THE ISLAMIC REP, Sirjan
**JAPAN**
RADIO JAPAN/NHK, Via Moyabi, Gabon — Mideast & W Asia • 500 kW ; Mideast & N Africa • 500 kW
†RADIO JAPAN/NHK, Via Sri Lanka — Mideast & W Asia • 300 kW
**JORDAN**
(con'd) RADIO JORDAN, Qasr el Kharana — ⇐ • W Europe & E North Am • 500 kW

SEASONAL S OR W    1-HR TIMESHIFT MIDYEAR ⇐ OR ⇒    JAMMING / OR ∧    EARLIEST HEARD ◁    LATEST HEARD ▷    NEW FOR 2003 †

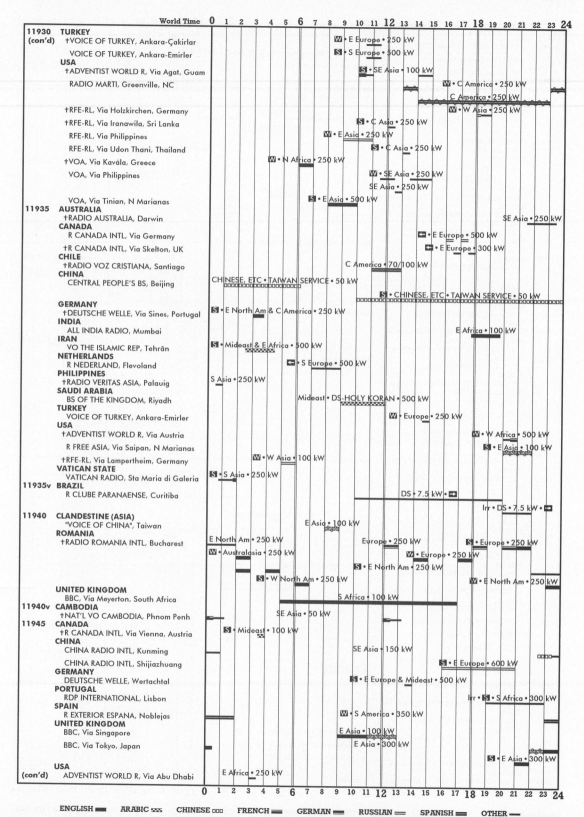

| | | World Time | Schedule |
|---|---|---|---|
| 11930 (con'd) | **TURKEY** | | |
| | †VOICE OF TURKEY, Ankara-Çakirlar | | W • E Europe • 250 kW |
| | VOICE OF TURKEY, Ankara-Emirler | | S • S Europe • 500 kW |
| | **USA** | | |
| | †ADVENTIST WORLD R, Via Agat, Guam | | S • SE Asia • 100 kW |
| | RADIO MARTI, Greenville, NC | | W • C America • 250 kW / C America • 250 kW |
| | †RFE-RL, Via Holzkirchen, Germany | | W • W Asia • 250 kW |
| | †RFE-RL, Via Iranawila, Sri Lanka | | S • C Asia • 250 kW |
| | RFE-RL, Via Philippines | | W • E Asia • 250 kW |
| | RFE-RL, Via Udon Thani, Thailand | | S • C Asia • 250 kW |
| | †VOA, Via Kavála, Greece | | W • N Africa • 250 kW |
| | VOA, Via Philippines | | W • SE Asia • 250 kW / SE Asia • 250 kW |
| | VOA, Via Tinian, N Marianas | | S • E Asia • 500 kW |
| 11935 | **AUSTRALIA** | | |
| | †RADIO AUSTRALIA, Darwin | | SE Asia • 250 kW |
| | **CANADA** | | |
| | R CANADA INTL, Via Germany | | ← • E Europe • 500 kW |
| | †R CANADA INTL, Via Skelton, UK | | ← • E Europe • 300 kW |
| | **CHILE** | | |
| | †RADIO VOZ CRISTIANA, Santiago | | C America • 70/100 kW |
| | **CHINA** | | |
| | CENTRAL PEOPLE'S BS, Beijing | | CHINESE, ETC • TAIWAN SERVICE • 50 kW / S • CHINESE, ETC • TAIWAN SERVICE • 50 kW |
| | **GERMANY** | | |
| | †DEUTSCHE WELLE, Via Sines, Portugal | | S • E North Am & C America • 250 kW |
| | **INDIA** | | |
| | ALL INDIA RADIO, Mumbai | | E Africa • 100 kW |
| | **IRAN** | | |
| | VO THE ISLAMIC REP, Tehrān | | S • Mideast & E Africa • 500 kW |
| | **NETHERLANDS** | | |
| | R NEDERLAND, Flevoland | | ← • S Europe • 500 kW |
| | **PHILIPPINES** | | |
| | †RADIO VERITAS ASIA, Palauig | | S Asia • 250 kW |
| | **SAUDI ARABIA** | | |
| | BS OF THE KINGDOM, Riyadh | | Mideast • DS-HOLY KORAN • 500 kW |
| | **TURKEY** | | |
| | VOICE OF TURKEY, Ankara-Emirler | | W • Europe • 250 kW |
| | **USA** | | |
| | †ADVENTIST WORLD R, Via Austria | | W • W Africa • 500 kW |
| | R FREE ASIA, Via Saipan, N Marianas | | S • E Asia • 100 kW |
| | †RFE-RL, Via Lampertheim, Germany | | W • W Asia • 100 kW |
| | **VATICAN STATE** | | |
| | VATICAN RADIO, Sta Maria di Galeria | | S • S Asia • 250 kW |
| 11935v | **BRAZIL** | | |
| | R CLUBE PARANAENSE, Curitiba | | DS • 7.5 kW • → / Irr • DS • 7.5 kW • → |
| 11940 | **CLANDESTINE (ASIA)** | | |
| | "VOICE OF CHINA", Taiwan | | E Asia • 100 kW |
| | **ROMANIA** | | |
| | †RADIO ROMANIA INTL, Bucharest | | E North Am • 250 kW / Europe • 250 kW / S • Europe • 250 kW |
| | | | W • Australasia • 250 kW / W • Europe • 250 kW |
| | | | S • E North Am • 250 kW |
| | | | S • W North Am • 250 kW / W • E North Am • 250 kW |
| | **UNITED KINGDOM** | | |
| | BBC, Via Meyerton, South Africa | | S Africa • 100 kW |
| 11940v | **CAMBODIA** | | |
| | †NAT'L VO CAMBODIA, Phnom Penh | | SE Asia • 50 kW |
| 11945 | **CANADA** | | |
| | †R CANADA INTL, Via Vienna, Austria | | S • Mideast • 100 kW |
| | **CHINA** | | |
| | CHINA RADIO INTL, Kunming | | SE Asia • 150 kW |
| | CHINA RADIO INTL, Shijiazhuang | | S • E Europe • 600 kW |
| | **GERMANY** | | |
| | DEUTSCHE WELLE, Wertachtal | | S • E Europe & Mideast • 500 kW |
| | **PORTUGAL** | | |
| | RDP INTERNATIONAL, Lisbon | | Irr • S • S Africa • 300 kW |
| | **SPAIN** | | |
| | R EXTERIOR ESPANA, Noblejas | | W • S America • 350 kW |
| | **UNITED KINGDOM** | | |
| | BBC, Via Singapore | | E Asia • 100 kW |
| | BBC, Via Tokyo, Japan | | E Asia • 300 kW / S • E Asia • 300 kW |
| (con'd) | **USA** ADVENTIST WORLD R, Via Abu Dhabi | | E Africa • 250 kW |

World Time: 0 1 2 3 4 5 6 7 8 9 10 11 12 13 14 15 16 17 18 19 20 21 22 23 24

ENGLISH ▬   ARABIC ⋙   CHINESE ☐☐☐   FRENCH ▭   GERMAN ▬   RUSSIAN ═   SPANISH ▬   OTHER ▬

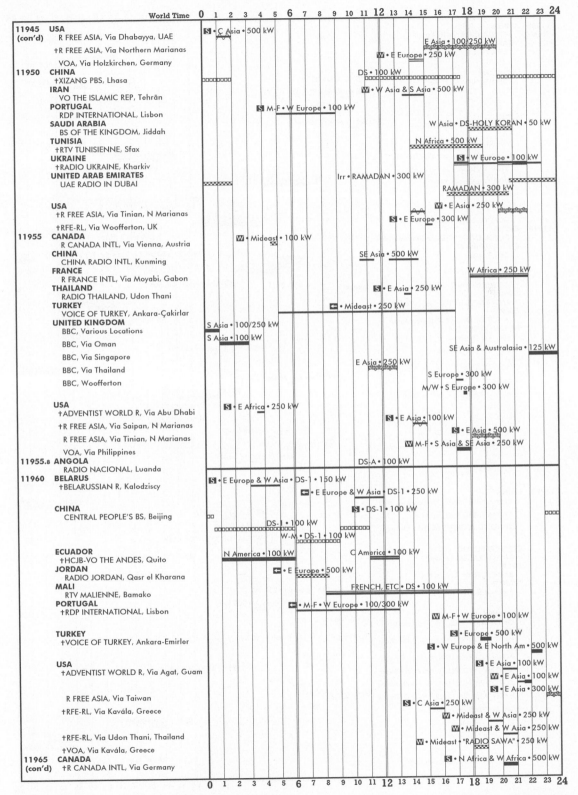

| World Time | 0 | 1 | 2 | 3 | 4 | 5 | 6 | 7 | 8 | 9 | 10 | 11 | 12 | 13 | 14 | 15 | 16 | 17 | 18 | 19 | 20 | 21 | 22 | 23 | 24 |

**11945** **USA**
(con'd)   R FREE ASIA, Via Dhabayya, UAE — S • C Asia • 500 kW

   †R FREE ASIA, Via Northern Marianas — E Asia • 100/250 kW

   VOA, Via Holzkirchen, Germany — W • E Europe • 250 kW

**11950** **CHINA**
   †XIZANG PBS, Lhasa — DS • 100 kW

   **IRAN**
   VO THE ISLAMIC REP, Tehrān — W • W Asia & S Asia • 500 kW

   **PORTUGAL**
   RDP INTERNATIONAL, Lisbon — S • M-F • W Europe • 100 kW

   **SAUDI ARABIA**
   BS OF THE KINGDOM, Jiddah — W Asia • DS-HOLY KORAN • 50 kW

   **TUNISIA**
   †RTV TUNISIENNE, Sfax — N Africa • 500 kW

   **UKRAINE**
   †RADIO UKRAINE, Kharkiv — S • W Europe • 100 kW

   **UNITED ARAB EMIRATES**
   UAE RADIO IN DUBAI — Irr • RAMADAN • 300 kW     RAMADAN • 300 kW

   **USA**
   †R FREE ASIA, Via Tinian, N Marianas — W • E Asia • 250 kW

   †RFE-RL, Via Woofferton, UK — S • E Europe • 300 kW

**11955** **CANADA**
   R CANADA INTL, Via Vienna, Austria — W • Mideast • 100 kW

   **CHINA**
   CHINA RADIO INTL, Kunming — SE Asia • 500 kW

   **FRANCE**
   R FRANCE INTL, Via Moyabi, Gabon — W Africa • 250 kW

   **THAILAND**
   RADIO THAILAND, Udon Thani — S • E Asia • 250 kW

   **TURKEY**
   VOICE OF TURKEY, Ankara-Çakirlar — ⇦ • Mideast • 250 kW

   **UNITED KINGDOM**
   BBC, Various Locations — S Asia • 100/250 kW

   BBC, Via Oman — S Asia • 100 kW

   BBC, Via Singapore — SE Asia & Australasia • 125 kW

   BBC, Via Thailand — E Asia • 250 kW

   BBC, Woofferton — S Europe • 300 kW   M/W • S Europe • 300 kW

   **USA**
   †ADVENTIST WORLD R, Via Abu Dhabi — S • E Africa • 250 kW

   †R FREE ASIA, Via Saipan, N Marianas — S • E Asia • 100 kW

   R FREE ASIA, Via Tinian, N Marianas — S • E Asia • 500 kW

   VOA, Via Philippines — W • M-F • S Asia & SE Asia • 250 kW

**11955.8** **ANGOLA**
   RADIO NACIONAL, Luanda — DS-A • 100 kW

**11960** **BELARUS**
   †BELARUSSIAN R, Kalodziscy — S • E Europe & W Asia • DS-1 • 150 kW

   ⇦ • E Europe & W Asia • DS-1 • 250 kW

   **CHINA**
   CENTRAL PEOPLE'S BS, Beijing — S • DS-1 • 100 kW

   DS-1 • 100 kW

   W-M • DS-1 • 100 kW

   **ECUADOR**
   †HCJB-VO THE ANDES, Quito — N America • 100 kW   C America • 100 kW

   **JORDAN**
   RADIO JORDAN, Qasr el Kharana — ⇦ • E Europe • 500 kW

   **MALI**
   RTV MALIENNE, Bamako — FRENCH, ETC • DS • 100 kW

   **PORTUGAL**
   †RDP INTERNATIONAL, Lisbon — ⇦ • M-F • W Europe • 100/300 kW

   **TURKEY**
   †VOICE OF TURKEY, Ankara-Emirler — W • M-F • W Europe • 100 kW

   S • Europe • 500 kW

   S • W Europe & E North Am • 500 kW

   **USA**
   †ADVENTIST WORLD R, Via Agat, Guam — S • E Asia • 100 kW

   W • E Asia • 100 kW

   S • E Asia • 300 kW

   R FREE ASIA, Via Taiwan — S • C Asia • 250 kW

   †RFE-RL, Via Kavála, Greece — W • Mideast & W Asia • 250 kW

   †RFE-RL, Via Udon Thani, Thailand — W • Mideast & W Asia • 250 kW

   †VOA, Via Kavála, Greece — W • Mideast • "RADIO SAWA" • 250 kW

**11965** **CANADA**
(con'd)   †R CANADA INTL, Via Germany — S • N Africa & W Africa • 500 kW

| 0 | 1 | 2 | 3 | 4 | 5 | 6 | 7 | 8 | 9 | 10 | 11 | 12 | 13 | 14 | 15 | 16 | 17 | 18 | 19 | 20 | 21 | 22 | 23 | 24 |

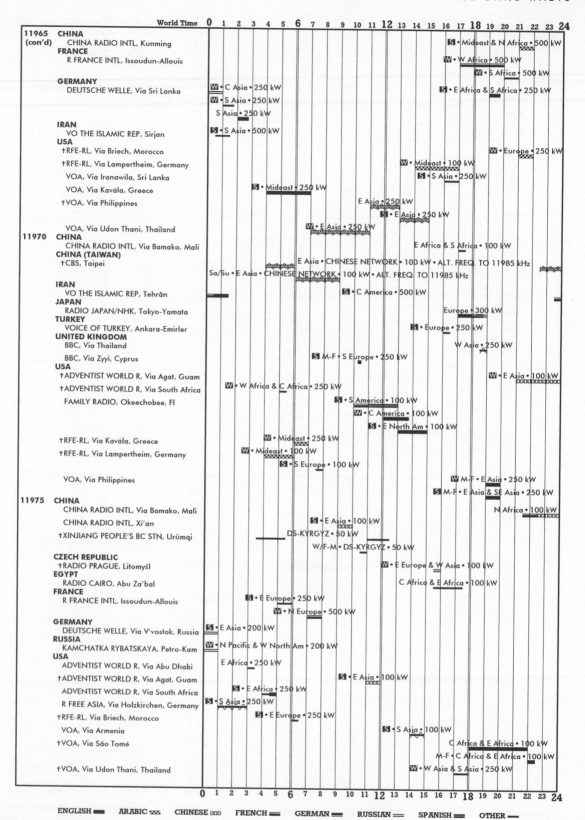

| | World Time | 0 1 2 3 4 5 6 7 8 9 10 11 12 13 14 15 16 17 18 19 20 21 22 23 24 |
|---|---|---|
| **11965** (con'd) | **CHINA** CHINA RADIO INTL, Kunming | S • Mideast & N Africa • 500 kW |
| | **FRANCE** R FRANCE INTL, Issoudun-Allouis | W • W Africa • 500 kW |
| | | W • S Africa • 500 kW |
| | **GERMANY** DEUTSCHE WELLE, Via Sri Lanka | W • C Asia • 250 kW |
| | | W • S Asia • 250 kW |
| | | S Asia • 250 kW |
| | **IRAN** VO THE ISLAMIC REP, Sirjan | S • S Asia • 500 kW |
| | **USA** †RFE-RL, Via Briech, Morocco | W • Europe • 250 kW |
| | †RFE-RL, Via Lampertheim, Germany | W • Mideast • 100 kW |
| | VOA, Via Iranawila, Sri Lanka | S • S Asia • 250 kW |
| | VOA, Via Kavála, Greece | S • Mideast • 250 kW |
| | †VOA, Via Philippines | E Asia • 250 kW |
| | | S • E Asia • 250 kW |
| | VOA, Via Udon Thani, Thailand | W • E Asia • 250 kW |
| **11970** | **CHINA** CHINA RADIO INTL, Via Bamako, Mali | E Africa & S Africa • 100 kW |
| | **CHINA (TAIWAN)** †CBS, Taipei | E Asia • CHINESE NETWORK • 100 kW • ALT. FREQ. TO 11985 kHz |
| | | Sa/Su • E Asia • CHINESE NETWORK • 100 kW • ALT. FREQ. TO 11985 kHz |
| | **IRAN** VO THE ISLAMIC REP, Tehrān | S • C America • 500 kW |
| | **JAPAN** RADIO JAPAN/NHK, Tokyo-Yamata | Europe • 300 kW |
| | **TURKEY** VOICE OF TURKEY, Ankara-Emirler | S • Europe • 250 kW |
| | **UNITED KINGDOM** BBC, Via Thailand | W Asia • 250 kW |
| | BBC, Via Zyyi, Cyprus | S • M-F • S Europe • 250 kW |
| | **USA** †ADVENTIST WORLD R, Via Agat, Guam | W • E Asia • 100 kW |
| | †ADVENTIST WORLD R, Via South Africa | W • W Africa & C Africa • 250 kW |
| | FAMILY RADIO, Okeechobee, Fl | S • S America • 100 kW |
| | | W • C America • 100 kW |
| | | S • E North Am • 100 kW |
| | †RFE-RL, Via Kavála, Greece | W • Mideast • 250 kW |
| | †RFE-RL, Via Lampertheim, Germany | W • Mideast • 100 kW |
| | | S • S Europe • 100 kW |
| | VOA, Via Philippines | W • M-F • E Asia • 250 kW |
| | | S • M-F • E Asia & SE Asia • 250 kW |
| **11975** | **CHINA** CHINA RADIO INTL, Via Bamako, Mali | N Africa • 100 kW |
| | CHINA RADIO INTL, Xi'an | S • E Asia • 100 kW |
| | †XINJIANG PEOPLE'S BC STN, Urümqi | DS-KYRGYZ • 50 kW |
| | | W/F-M • DS-KYRGYZ • 50 kW |
| | **CZECH REPUBLIC** †RADIO PRAGUE, Litomyšl | W • E Europe & W Asia • 100 kW |
| | **EGYPT** RADIO CAIRO, Abu Za'bal | C Africa & E Africa • 100 kW |
| | **FRANCE** R FRANCE INTL, Issoudun-Allouis | S • E Europe • 250 kW |
| | | W • N Europe • 500 kW |
| | **GERMANY** DEUTSCHE WELLE, Via V'vostok, Russia | S • E Asia • 200 kW |
| | **RUSSIA** KAMCHATKA RYBATSKAYA, Petro-Kam | W • N Pacific & W North Am • 200 kW |
| | **USA** ADVENTIST WORLD R, Via Abu Dhabi | E Africa • 250 kW |
| | †ADVENTIST WORLD R, Via Agat, Guam | S • E Asia • 100 kW |
| | ADVENTIST WORLD R, Via South Africa | S • E Africa • 250 kW |
| | R FREE ASIA, Via Holzkirchen, Germany | S • S Asia • 250 kW |
| | †RFE-RL, Via Briech, Morocco | S • E Europe • 250 kW |
| | VOA, Via Armenia | S • S Asia • 100 kW |
| | †VOA, Via São Tomé | C Africa & E Africa • 100 kW |
| | | M-F • C Africa & E Africa • 100 kW |
| | †VOA, Via Udon Thani, Thailand | W • W Asia & S Asia • 250 kW |

0 1 2 3 4 5 6 7 8 9 10 11 12 13 14 15 16 17 18 19 20 21 22 23 24

ENGLISH ▬    ARABIC ▧    CHINESE ▢▢▢    FRENCH ══    GERMAN ▬▬    RUSSIAN ══    SPANISH ══    OTHER ──

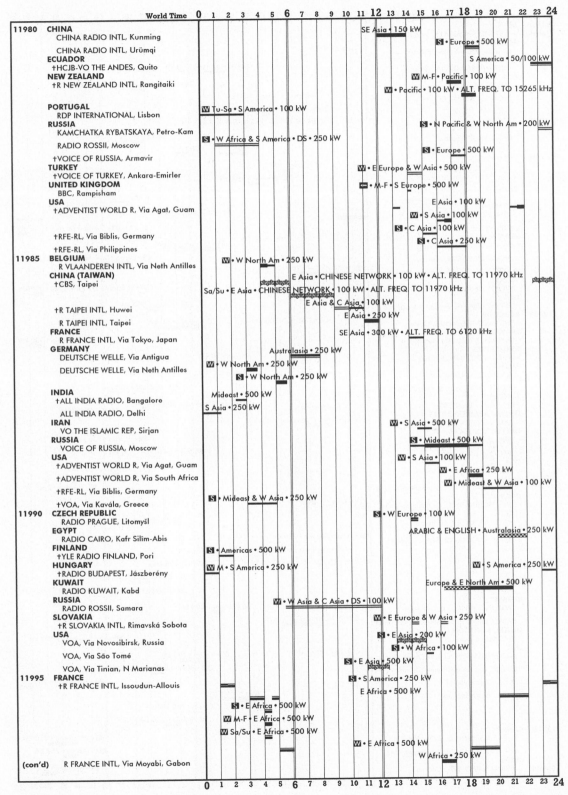

World Time  0 1 2 3 4 5 6 7 8 9 10 11 12 13 14 15 16 17 18 19 20 21 22 23 24

**11980 CHINA**
CHINA RADIO INTL, Kunming · SE Asia • 150 kW · Ⓢ • Europe • 500 kW
CHINA RADIO INTL, Urümqi
**ECUADOR** · S America • 50/100 kW
†HCJB-VO THE ANDES, Quito
**NEW ZEALAND** · Ⓦ M-F • Pacific • 100 kW
†R NEW ZEALAND INTL, Rangitaiki · Ⓦ • Pacific • 100 kW • ALT. FREQ. TO 15265 kHz

**PORTUGAL** · Ⓦ Tu-Sa • S America • 100 kW
RDP INTERNATIONAL, Lisbon
**RUSSIA** · Ⓢ • N Pacific & W North Am • 200 kW
KAMCHATKA RYBATSKAYA, Petro-Kam · Ⓢ • W Africa & S America • DS • 250 kW
RADIO ROSSII, Moscow · Ⓢ • Europe • 500 kW
†VOICE OF RUSSIA, Armavir
**TURKEY** · Ⓦ • E Europe & W Asia • 500 kW
†VOICE OF TURKEY, Ankara-Emirler
**UNITED KINGDOM** · ⬌ • M-F • S Europe • 500 kW
BBC, Rampisham
**USA** · E Asia • 100 kW
†ADVENTIST WORLD R, Via Agat, Guam · Ⓦ • S Asia • 100 kW
· Ⓢ • C Asia • 100 kW
†RFE-RL, Via Biblis, Germany · Ⓢ • C Asia • 250 kW
†RFE-RL, Via Philippines

**11985 BELGIUM** · Ⓦ • W North Am • 250 kW
R VLAANDEREN INTL, Via Neth Antilles
**CHINA (TAIWAN)** · E Asia • CHINESE NETWORK • 100 kW • ALT. FREQ. TO 11970 kHz
†CBS, Taipei · Sa/Su • E Asia • CHINESE NETWORK • 100 kW • ALT. FREQ. TO 11970 kHz
· E Asia & C Asia • 100 kW
†R TAIPEI INTL, Huwei · E Asia • 250 kW
R TAIPEI INTL, Taipei
**FRANCE** · SE Asia • 300 kW • ALT. FREQ. TO 6120 kHz
R FRANCE INTL, Via Tokyo, Japan
**GERMANY** · Australasia • 250 kW
DEUTSCHE WELLE, Via Antigua · Ⓦ • W North Am • 250 kW
DEUTSCHE WELLE, Via Neth Antilles · Ⓢ • W North Am • 250 kW
**INDIA** · Mideast • 500 kW
†ALL INDIA RADIO, Bangalore · S Asia • 250 kW
ALL INDIA RADIO, Delhi
**IRAN** · Ⓦ • S Asia • 500 kW
VO THE ISLAMIC REP, Sirjan
**RUSSIA** · Ⓢ • Mideast • 500 kW
VOICE OF RUSSIA, Moscow
**USA** · Ⓦ • S Asia • 100 kW
†ADVENTIST WORLD R, Via Agat, Guam · Ⓦ • E Africa • 250 kW
†ADVENTIST WORLD R, Via South Africa · Ⓦ • Mideast & W Asia • 100 kW
†RFE-RL, Via Biblis, Germany
†VOA, Via Kavála, Greece · Ⓢ • Mideast & W Asia • 250 kW

**11990 CZECH REPUBLIC** · Ⓢ • W Europe • 100 kW
RADIO PRAGUE, Litomyšl
**EGYPT** · ARABIC & ENGLISH • Australasia • 250 kW
RADIO CAIRO, Kafr Silîm-Abis
**FINLAND** · Ⓢ • Americas • 500 kW
†YLE RADIO FINLAND, Pori
**HUNGARY** · Ⓦ M • S America • 250 kW · Ⓦ • S America • 250 kW
†RADIO BUDAPEST, Jászberény
**KUWAIT** · Europe & E North Am • 500 kW
RADIO KUWAIT, Kabd
**RUSSIA** · Ⓦ • W Asia & C Asia • DS • 100 kW
RADIO ROSSII, Samara
**SLOVAKIA** · Ⓦ • E Europe & W Asia • 250 kW
†R SLOVAKIA INTL, Rimavská Sobota
**USA** · Ⓢ • E Asia • 200 kW
VOA, Via Novosibirsk, Russia · Ⓢ • W Africa • 100 kW
VOA, Via São Tomé · Ⓢ • E Asia • 500 kW
VOA, Via Tinian, N Marianas

**11995 FRANCE** · Ⓢ • S America • 250 kW
†R FRANCE INTL, Issoudun-Allouis · E Africa • 500 kW
· Ⓢ • E Africa • 500 kW
· Ⓦ M-F • E Africa • 500 kW
· Ⓦ Sa/Su • E Africa • 500 kW

· Ⓦ • E Africa • 500 kW
**(con'd)** R FRANCE INTL, Via Moyabi, Gabon · W Africa • 250 kW

0 1 2 3 4 5 6 7 8 9 10 11 12 13 14 15 16 17 18 19 20 21 22 23 24

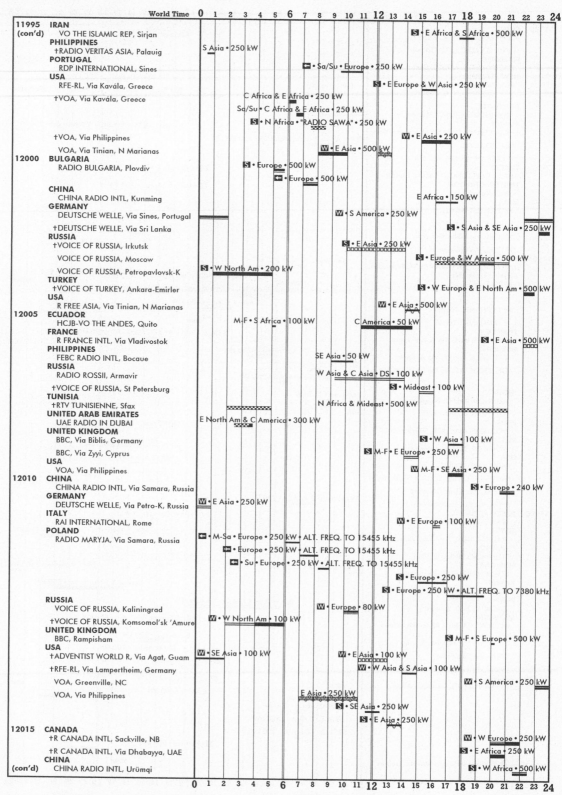

World Time

| 11995 | IRAN | | | |
| (con'd) | VO THE ISLAMIC REP, Sirjan | | | S • E Africa & S Africa • 500 kW |
| | PHILIPPINES | | | |
| | †RADIO VERITAS ASIA, Palauig | S Asia • 250 kW | | |
| | PORTUGAL | | | |
| | RDP INTERNATIONAL, Sines | | ⇦ • Sa/Su • Europe • 250 kW | |
| | USA | | | |
| | RFE-RL, Via Kavála, Greece | | S • E Europe & W Asia • 250 kW | |
| | †VOA, Via Kavála, Greece | C Africa & E Africa • 250 kW | | |
| | | Sa/Su • C Africa & E Africa • 250 kW | | |
| | | S • N Africa • "RADIO SAWA" • 250 kW | | |
| | †VOA, Via Philippines | | W • E Asia • 250 kW | |
| | VOA, Via Tinian, N Marianas | | W • E Asia • 500 kW | |
| 12000 | BULGARIA | | | |
| | RADIO BULGARIA, Plovdiv | S • Europe • 500 kW | | |
| | | ⇦ • Europe • 500 kW | | |
| | CHINA | | | |
| | CHINA RADIO INTL, Kunming | | E Africa • 150 kW | |
| | GERMANY | | | |
| | DEUTSCHE WELLE, Via Sines, Portugal | W • S America • 250 kW | | |
| | †DEUTSCHE WELLE, Via Sri Lanka | | S • S Asia & SE Asia • 250 kW | |
| | RUSSIA | | | |
| | †VOICE OF RUSSIA, Irkutsk | S • E Asia • 250 kW | | |
| | VOICE OF RUSSIA, Moscow | | S • Europe & W Africa • 500 kW | |
| | VOICE OF RUSSIA, Petropavlovsk-K | S • W North Am • 200 kW | | |
| | TURKEY | | | |
| | †VOICE OF TURKEY, Ankara-Emirler | | S • W Europe & E North Am • 500 kW | |
| | USA | | | |
| | R FREE ASIA, Via Tinian, N Marianas | | W • E Asia • 500 kW | |
| 12005 | ECUADOR | | | |
| | HCJB-VO THE ANDES, Quito | M-F • S Africa • 100 kW    C America • 50 kW | | |
| | FRANCE | | | |
| | R FRANCE INTL, Via Vladivostok | | S • E Asia • 500 kW | |
| | PHILIPPINES | | | |
| | FEBC RADIO INTL, Bocaue | SE Asia • 50 kW | | |
| | RUSSIA | | | |
| | RADIO ROSSII, Armavir | W Asia & C Asia • DS • 100 kW | | |
| | †VOICE OF RUSSIA, St Petersburg | | S • Mideast • 100 kW | |
| | TUNISIA | | | |
| | †RTV TUNISIENNE, Sfax | N Africa & Mideast • 500 kW | | |
| | UNITED ARAB EMIRATES | | | |
| | UAE RADIO IN DUBAI | E North Am & C America • 300 kW | | |
| | UNITED KINGDOM | | | |
| | BBC, Via Biblis, Germany | | S • W Asia • 100 kW | |
| | BBC, Via Zyyi, Cyprus | | S M-F • E Europe • 250 kW | |
| | USA | | | |
| | VOA, Via Philippines | | W M-F • SE Asia • 250 kW | |
| 12010 | CHINA | | | |
| | CHINA RADIO INTL, Via Samara, Russia | | S • Europe • 240 kW | |
| | GERMANY | | | |
| | DEUTSCHE WELLE, Via Petro-K, Russia | W • E Asia • 250 kW | | |
| | ITALY | | | |
| | RAI INTERNATIONAL, Rome | | W • E Europe • 100 kW | |
| | POLAND | | | |
| | RADIO MARYJA, Via Samara, Russia | ⇦ • M-Sa • Europe • 250 kW • ALT. FREQ. TO 15455 kHz | | |
| | | ⇦ • Europe • 250 kW • ALT. FREQ. TO 15455 kHz | | |
| | | ⇦ • Su • Europe • 250 kW • ALT. FREQ. TO 15455 kHz | | |
| | | | S • Europe • 250 kW | |
| | | | S • Europe • 250 kW • ALT. FREQ. TO 7380 kHz | |
| | RUSSIA | | | |
| | VOICE OF RUSSIA, Kaliningrad | W • Europe • 80 kW | | |
| | †VOICE OF RUSSIA, Komsomol'sk 'Amure | W • W North Am • 100 kW | | |
| | UNITED KINGDOM | | | |
| | BBC, Rampisham | | S M-F • S Europe • 500 kW | |
| | USA | | | |
| | †ADVENTIST WORLD R, Via Agat, Guam | W • SE Asia • 100 kW    W • E Asia • 100 kW | | |
| | †RFE-RL, Via Lampertheim, Germany | | W • W Asia & S Asia • 100 kW | |
| | VOA, Greenville, NC | | W • S America • 250 kW | |
| | VOA, Via Philippines | E Asia • 250 kW | | |
| | | | S • SE Asia • 250 kW | |
| | | | S • E Asia • 250 kW | |
| 12015 | CANADA | | | |
| | †R CANADA INTL, Sackville, NB | | W • W Europe • 250 kW | |
| | †R CANADA INTL, Via Dhabayya, UAE | | S • E Africa • 250 kW | |
| | CHINA | | | |
| (con'd) | CHINA RADIO INTL, Urümqi | | S • W Africa • 500 kW | |

ENGLISH ▬    ARABIC ⬚⬚⬚    CHINESE ⬚⬚⬚    FRENCH ▬▬    GERMAN ▬    RUSSIAN ═    SPANISH ▬    OTHER ▬

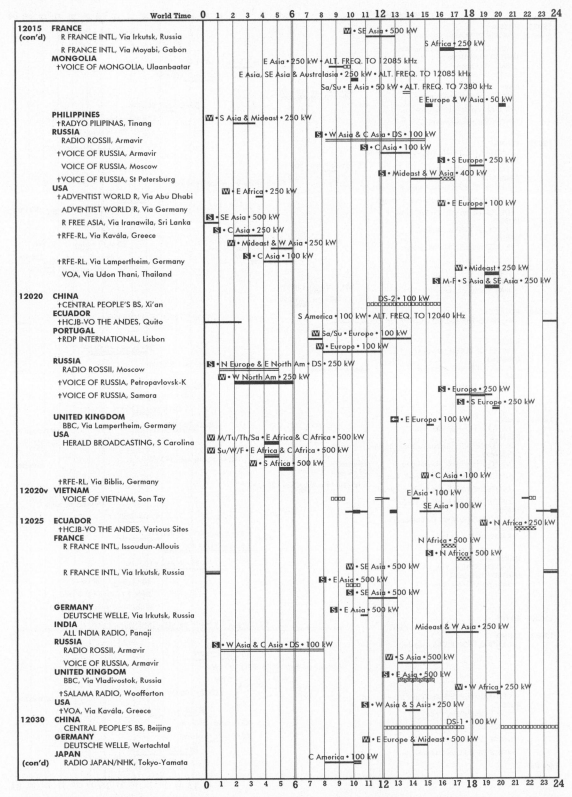

| | | |
|---|---|---|
| **12015** | **FRANCE** | |
| **(con'd)** | R FRANCE INTL, Via Irkutsk, Russia | W • SE Asia • 500 kW |
| | R FRANCE INTL, Via Moyabi, Gabon | S Africa • 250 kW |
| | **MONGOLIA** | |
| | †VOICE OF MONGOLIA, Ulaanbaatar | E Asia • 250 kW • ALT. FREQ. TO 12085 kHz |
| | | E Asia, SE Asia & Australasia • 250 kW • ALT. FREQ. TO 12085 kHz |
| | | Sa/Su • E Asia • 50 kW • ALT. FREQ. TO 7380 kHz |
| | | E Europe & W Asia • 50 kW |
| | **PHILIPPINES** | |
| | †RADYO PILIPINAS, Tinang | W • S Asia & Mideast • 250 kW |
| | **RUSSIA** | |
| | RADIO ROSSII, Armavir | S • W Asia & C Asia • DS • 100 kW |
| | †VOICE OF RUSSIA, Armavir | S • C Asia • 100 kW |
| | VOICE OF RUSSIA, Moscow | S • S Europe • 250 kW |
| | †VOICE OF RUSSIA, St Petersburg | S • Mideast & W Asia • 400 kW |
| | **USA** | |
| | †ADVENTIST WORLD R, Via Abu Dhabi | W • E Africa • 250 kW |
| | ADVENTIST WORLD R, Via Germany | W • E Europe • 100 kW |
| | R FREE ASIA, Via Iranawila, Sri Lanka | S • SE Asia • 500 kW |
| | †RFE-RL, Via Kavála, Greece | S • C Asia • 250 kW |
| | | W • Mideast & W Asia • 250 kW |
| | †RFE-RL, Via Lampertheim, Germany | S • C Asia • 100 kW |
| | VOA, Via Udon Thani, Thailand | W • Mideast • 250 kW |
| | | S M-F • S Asia & SE Asia • 250 kW |
| **12020** | **CHINA** | |
| | †CENTRAL PEOPLE'S BS, Xi'an | DS-2 • 100 kW |
| | **ECUADOR** | |
| | †HCJB-VO THE ANDES, Quito | S America • 100 kW • ALT. FREQ. TO 12040 kHz |
| | **PORTUGAL** | |
| | †RDP INTERNATIONAL, Lisbon | W Sa/Su • Europe • 100 kW |
| | | W • Europe • 100 kW |
| | **RUSSIA** | |
| | RADIO ROSSII, Moscow | S • N Europe & E North Am • DS • 250 kW |
| | †VOICE OF RUSSIA, Petropavlovsk-K | W • W North Am • 250 kW |
| | †VOICE OF RUSSIA, Samara | S • Europe • 250 kW |
| | | S • S Europe • 250 kW |
| | **UNITED KINGDOM** | |
| | BBC, Via Lampertheim, Germany | • E Europe • 100 kW |
| | **USA** | |
| | HERALD BROADCASTING, S Carolina | W M/Tu/Th/Sa • E Africa & C Africa • 500 kW |
| | | W Su/W/F • E Africa & C Africa • 500 kW |
| | | W • S Africa • 500 kW |
| | †RFE-RL, Via Biblis, Germany | W • C Asia • 100 kW |
| **12020v** | **VIETNAM** | |
| | VOICE OF VIETNAM, Son Tay | E Asia • 100 kW |
| | | SE Asia • 100 kW |
| **12025** | **ECUADOR** | |
| | †HCJB-VO THE ANDES, Various Sites | W • N Africa • 250 kW |
| | **FRANCE** | |
| | R FRANCE INTL, Issoudun-Allouis | N Africa • 500 kW |
| | | S • N Africa • 500 kW |
| | R FRANCE INTL, Via Irkutsk, Russia | W • SE Asia • 500 kW |
| | | S • E Asia • 500 kW |
| | | S • SE Asia • 500 kW |
| | **GERMANY** | |
| | DEUTSCHE WELLE, Via Irkutsk, Russia | S • E Asia • 500 kW |
| | **INDIA** | |
| | ALL INDIA RADIO, Panaji | Mideast & W Asia • 250 kW |
| | **RUSSIA** | |
| | RADIO ROSSII, Armavir | S • W Asia & C Asia • DS • 100 kW |
| | VOICE OF RUSSIA, Armavir | S • S Asia • 500 kW |
| | **UNITED KINGDOM** | |
| | BBC, Via Vladivostok, Russia | S • E Asia • 500 kW |
| | †SALAMA RADIO, Woofferton | W • W Africa • 250 kW |
| | **USA** | |
| | †VOA, Via Kavála, Greece | S • W Asia & S Asia • 250 kW |
| **12030** | **CHINA** | |
| | CENTRAL PEOPLE'S BS, Beijing | DS-1 • 100 kW |
| | **GERMANY** | |
| | DEUTSCHE WELLE, Wertachtal | W • E Europe & Mideast • 500 kW |
| | **JAPAN** | |
| **(con'd)** | RADIO JAPAN/NHK, Tokyo-Yamata | C America • 100 kW |

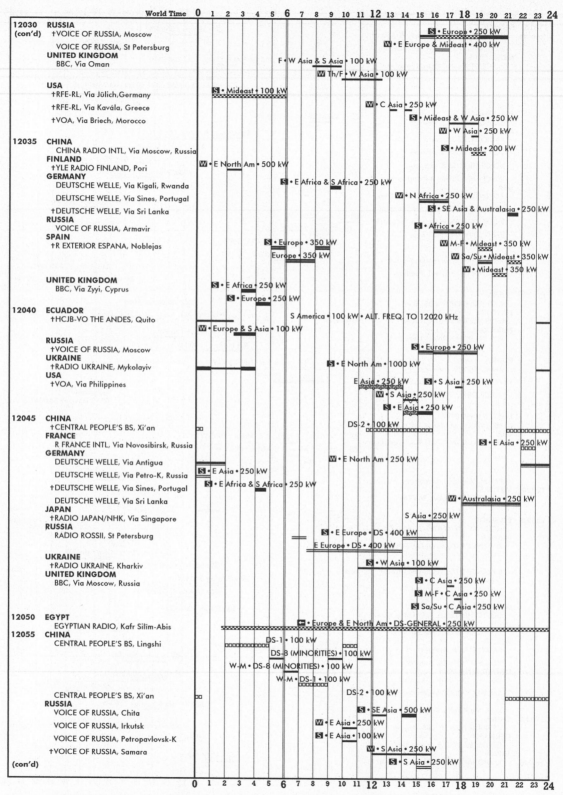

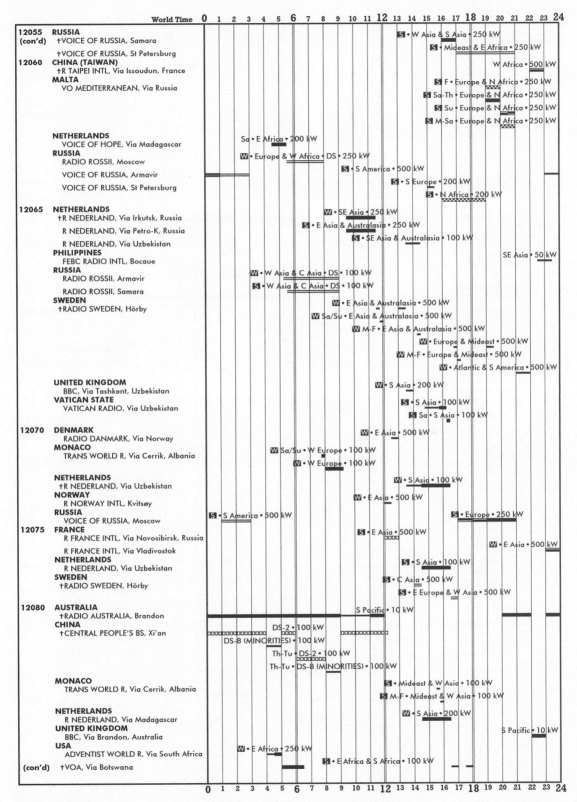

| World Time | 0 | 1 | 2 | 3 | 4 | 5 | 6 | 7 | 8 | 9 | 10 | 11 | 12 | 13 | 14 | 15 | 16 | 17 | 18 | 19 | 20 | 21 | 22 | 23 | 24 |

**12055 RUSSIA**
(con'd) †VOICE OF RUSSIA, Samara — Ⓢ • W Asia & S Asia • 250 kW
†VOICE OF RUSSIA, St Petersburg — Ⓢ • Mideast & E Africa • 250 kW

**12060 CHINA (TAIWAN)**
†R TAIPEI INTL, Via Issoudun, France — W Africa • 500 kW
**MALTA**
VO MEDITERRANEAN, Via Russia — Ⓢ F • Europe & N Africa • 250 kW
Ⓢ Sa-Th • Europe & N Africa • 250 kW
Ⓢ Su • Europe & N Africa • 250 kW
Ⓢ M-Sa • Europe & N Africa • 250 kW

**NETHERLANDS**
VOICE OF HOPE, Via Madagascar — Sa • E Africa • 200 kW
**RUSSIA**
RADIO ROSSII, Moscow — Ⓦ • Europe & W Africa • DS • 250 kW
VOICE OF RUSSIA, Armavir — Ⓢ • S America • 500 kW
VOICE OF RUSSIA, St Petersburg — Ⓢ • S Europe • 200 kW
Ⓢ • N Africa • 200 kW

**12065 NETHERLANDS**
†R NEDERLAND, Via Irkutsk, Russia — Ⓦ • SE Asia • 250 kW
R NEDERLAND, Via Petro-K, Russia — Ⓢ • E Asia & Australasia • 250 kW
R NEDERLAND, Via Uzbekistan — Ⓢ • SE Asia & Australasia • 100 kW
**PHILIPPINES**
FEBC RADIO INTL, Bocaue — SE Asia • 50 kW
**RUSSIA**
RADIO ROSSII, Armavir — Ⓦ • W Asia & C Asia • DS • 100 kW
RADIO ROSSII, Samara — Ⓢ • W Asia & C Asia • DS • 100 kW
**SWEDEN**
†RADIO SWEDEN, Hörby — Ⓦ • E Asia & Australasia • 500 kW
Ⓦ Sa/Su • E Asia & Australasia • 500 kW
Ⓦ M-F • E Asia & Australasia • 500 kW
Ⓦ • Europe & Mideast • 500 kW
Ⓦ M-F • Europe & Mideast • 500 kW
Ⓦ • Atlantic & S America • 500 kW

**UNITED KINGDOM**
BBC, Via Tashkent, Uzbekistan — Ⓦ • S Asia • 200 kW
**VATICAN STATE**
VATICAN RADIO, Via Uzbekistan — Ⓢ • S Asia • 100 kW
Ⓢ Sa • S Asia • 100 kW

**12070 DENMARK**
RADIO DANMARK, Via Norway — Ⓦ • E Asia • 500 kW
**MONACO**
TRANS WORLD R, Via Cerrik, Albania — Ⓦ Sa/Su • W Europe • 100 kW
Ⓦ • W Europe • 100 kW

**NETHERLANDS**
†R NEDERLAND, Via Uzbekistan — Ⓦ • S Asia • 100 kW
**NORWAY**
R NORWAY INTL, Kvitsøy — Ⓦ • E Asia • 500 kW
**RUSSIA**
VOICE OF RUSSIA, Moscow — Ⓢ • S America • 500 kW
Ⓢ • Europe • 250 kW
**12075 FRANCE**
R FRANCE INTL, Via Novosibirsk, Russia — Ⓢ • E Asia • 500 kW
R FRANCE INTL, Via Vladivostok — Ⓦ • E Asia • 500 kW
**NETHERLANDS**
R NEDERLAND, Via Uzbekistan — Ⓢ • S Asia • 100 kW
**SWEDEN**
†RADIO SWEDEN, Hörby — Ⓢ • C Asia • 500 kW
Ⓢ • E Europe & W Asia • 500 kW

**12080 AUSTRALIA**
†RADIO AUSTRALIA, Brandon — S Pacific • 10 kW
**CHINA**
†CENTRAL PEOPLE'S BS, Xi'an — DS-2 • 100 kW
DS-8 (MINORITIES) • 100 kW
Th-Tu • DS-2 • 100 kW
Th-Tu • DS-8 (MINORITIES) • 100 kW

**MONACO**
TRANS WORLD R, Via Cerrik, Albania — Ⓢ • Mideast & W Asia • 100 kW
Ⓢ M-F • Mideast & W Asia • 100 kW

**NETHERLANDS**
R NEDERLAND, Via Madagascar — Ⓦ • S Asia • 200 kW
**UNITED KINGDOM**
BBC, Via Brandon, Australia — S Pacific • 10 kW
**USA**
ADVENTIST WORLD R, Via South Africa — Ⓦ • E Africa • 250 kW
(con'd) †VOA, Via Botswana — Ⓢ • E Africa & S Africa • 100 kW

| 0 | 1 | 2 | 3 | 4 | 5 | 6 | 7 | 8 | 9 | 10 | 11 | 12 | 13 | 14 | 15 | 16 | 17 | 18 | 19 | 20 | 21 | 22 | 23 | 24 |

SEASONAL Ⓢ OR Ⓦ    1-HR TIMESHIFT MIDYEAR ⮂ OR ⮕    JAMMING / OR /\    EARLIEST HEARD ◁    LATEST HEARD ▷    NEW FOR 2003 †

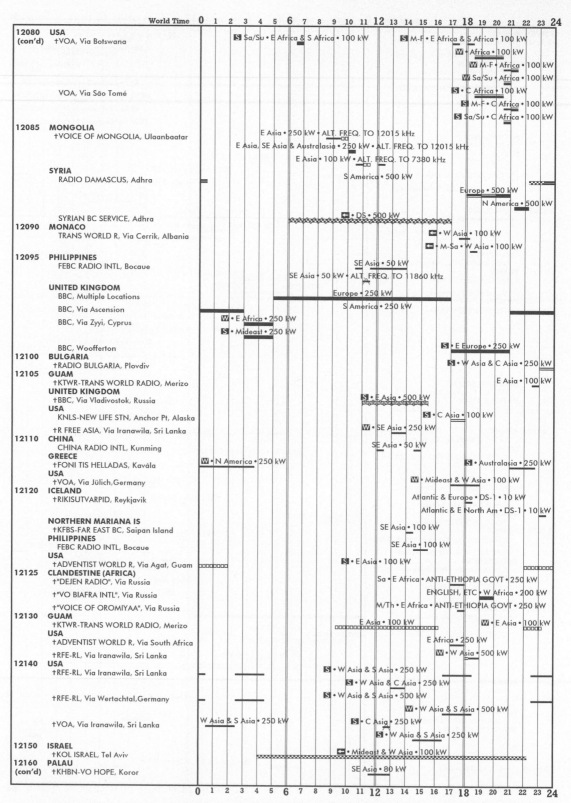

| | | World Time | 0 1 2 3 4 5 6 7 8 9 10 11 12 13 14 15 16 17 18 19 20 21 22 23 24 |
|---|---|---|---|

12080 USA
(con'd) †VOA, Via Botswana — S · Sa/Su · E Africa & S Africa · 100 kW — S · M-F · E Africa & S Africa · 100 kW — W · Africa · 100 kW — W · M-F · Africa · 100 kW — W · Sa/Su · Africa · 100 kW

VOA, Via São Tomé — S · C Africa · 100 kW — S · M-F · C Africa · 100 kW — S · Sa/Su · C Africa · 100 kW

12085 MONGOLIA
†VOICE OF MONGOLIA, Ulaanbaatar — E Asia · 250 kW · ALT. FREQ. TO 12015 kHz — E Asia, SE Asia & Australasia · 250 kW · ALT. FREQ. TO 12015 kHz — E Asia · 100 kW · ALT. FREQ. TO 7380 kHz

SYRIA
RADIO DAMASCUS, Adhra — S America · 500 kW — Europe · 500 kW — N America · 500 kW

SYRIAN BC SERVICE, Adhra — · DS · 500 kW
12090 MONACO
TRANS WORLD R, Via Cerrik, Albania — · W Asia · 100 kW — · M-Sa · W Asia · 100 kW

12095 PHILIPPINES
FEBC RADIO INTL, Bocaue — SE Asia · 50 kW — SE Asia · 50 kW · ALT. FREQ. TO 11860 kHz

UNITED KINGDOM
BBC, Multiple Locations — Europe · 250 kW
BBC, Via Ascension — S America · 250 kW
BBC, Via Zyyi, Cyprus — W · E Africa · 250 kW — S · Mideast · 250 kW

BBC, Woofferton — S · E Europe · 250 kW
12100 BULGARIA
†RADIO BULGARIA, Plovdiv — S · W Asia & C Asia · 250 kW
12105 GUAM
†KTWR-TRANS WORLD RADIO, Merizo — E Asia · 100 kW
UNITED KINGDOM
†BBC, Via Vladivostok, Russia — S · E Asia · 500 kW
USA
KNLS-NEW LIFE STN, Anchor Pt, Alaska — S · C Asia · 100 kW
†R FREE ASIA, Via Iranawila, Sri Lanka — W · SE Asia · 250 kW
12110 CHINA
CHINA RADIO INTL, Kunming — SE Asia · 50 kW
GREECE
†FONI TIS HELLADAS, Kavála — W · N America · 250 kW — S · Australasia · 250 kW
USA
†VOA, Via Jülich, Germany — W · Mideast & W Asia · 100 kW
12120 ICELAND
†RIKISUTVARPID, Reykjavik — Atlantic & Europe · DS-1 · 10 kW — Atlantic & E North Am · DS-1 · 10 kW

NORTHERN MARIANA IS
†KFBS-FAR EAST BC, Saipan Island — SE Asia · 100 kW
PHILIPPINES
FEBC RADIO INTL, Bocaue — SE Asia · 100 kW
USA
†ADVENTIST WORLD R, Via Agat, Guam — S · E Asia · 100 kW
12125 CLANDESTINE (AFRICA)
†"DEJEN RADIO", Via Russia — Sa · E Africa · ANTI-ETHIOPIA GOVT · 250 kW
†"VO BIAFRA INTL", Via Russia — ENGLISH, ETC · W Africa · 200 kW
†"VOICE OF OROMIYAA", Via Russia — M/Th · E Africa · ANTI-ETHIOPIA GOVT · 250 kW
12130 GUAM
†KTWR-TRANS WORLD RADIO, Merizo — E Asia · 100 kW — W · E Asia · 100 kW
USA
†ADVENTIST WORLD R, Via South Africa — E Africa · 250 kW
†RFE-RL, Via Iranawila, Sri Lanka — W · W Asia · 500 kW
12140 USA
†RFE-RL, Via Iranawila, Sri Lanka — S · W Asia & S Asia · 250 kW — S · W Asia & C Asia · 250 kW
†RFE-RL, Via Wertachtal, Germany — S · W Asia & S Asia · 500 kW — W · W Asia & S Asia · 500 kW
†VOA, Via Iranawila, Sri Lanka — W Asia & S Asia · 250 kW — S · C Asia · 250 kW — S · W Asia & S Asia · 250 kW
12150 ISRAEL
†KOL ISRAEL, Tel Aviv — · Mideast & W Asia · 100 kW
12160 PALAU
(con'd) †KHBN-VO HOPE, Koror — SE Asia · 80 kW

| | 0 1 2 3 4 5 6 7 8 9 10 11 12 13 14 15 16 17 18 19 20 21 22 23 24 |
|---|---|

ENGLISH ▬▬    ARABIC ≋≋    CHINESE □□□    FRENCH ═══    GERMAN ▬▬    RUSSIAN ══    SPANISH ══    OTHER ──

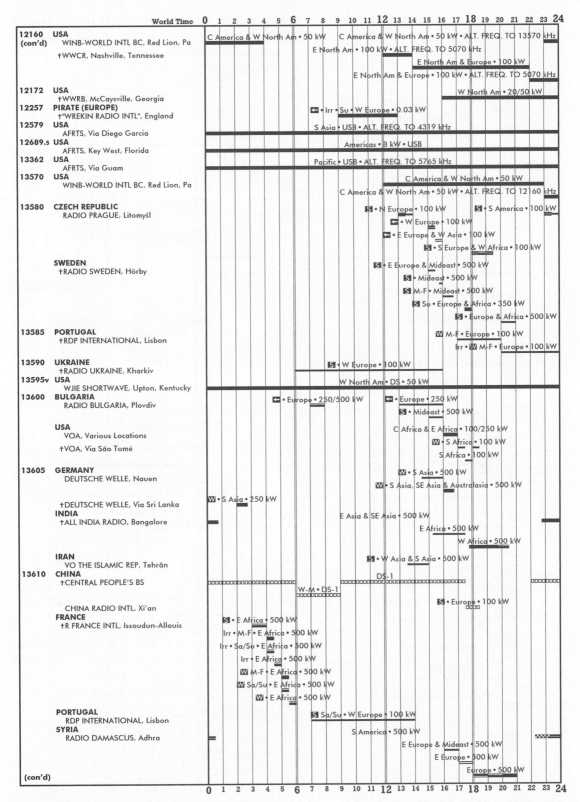

| World Time | | |
|---|---|---|
| **12160** (con'd) **USA** WINB-WORLD INTL BC, Red Lion, Pa | C America & W North Am • 50 kW | C America & W North Am • 50 kW • ALT. FREQ. TO 13570 kHz |
| †WWCR, Nashville, Tennessee | E North Am • 100 kW • ALT. FREQ. TO 5070 kHz | E North Am & Europe • 100 kW |
| | E North Am & Europe • 100 kW • ALT. FREQ. TO 5070 kHz | W North Am • 20/50 kW |
| **12172 USA** †WWRB, McCaysville, Georgia | | |
| **12257 PIRATE (EUROPE)** †"WREKIN RADIO INTL", England | Irr • Su • W Europe • 0.03 kW | |
| **12579 USA** AFRTS, Via Diego Garcia | S Asia • USB • ALT. FREQ. TO 4319 kHz | |
| **12689.5 USA** AFRTS, Key West, Florida | Americas • B kW • USB | |
| **13362 USA** AFRTS, Via Guam | Pacific • USB • ALT. FREQ. TO 5765 kHz | |
| **13570 USA** WINB-WORLD INTL BC, Red Lion, Pa | C America & W North Am • 50 kW | |
| | C America & W North Am • 50 kW • ALT. FREQ. TO 12160 kHz | |
| **13580 CZECH REPUBLIC** RADIO PRAGUE, Litomyšl | S • N Europe • 100 kW | S • S America • 100 kW |
| | W Europe • 100 kW | |
| | E Europe & W Asia • 100 kW | |
| | S • S Europe & W Africa • 100 kW | |
| **SWEDEN** †RADIO SWEDEN, Hörby | S • E Europe & Mideast • 500 kW | |
| | S • Mideast • 500 kW | |
| | S • M-F • Mideast • 500 kW | |
| | S • Su • Europe & Africa • 350 kW | |
| | S • Europe & Africa • 500 kW | |
| **13585 PORTUGAL** †RDP INTERNATIONAL, Lisbon | W M-F • Europe • 100 kW | |
| | Irr • W M-F • Europe • 100 kW | |
| **13590 UKRAINE** †RADIO UKRAINE, Kharkiv | S • W Europe • 100 kW | |
| **13595v USA** WJIE SHORTWAVE, Upton, Kentucky | W North Am • DS • 50 kW | |
| **13600 BULGARIA** RADIO BULGARIA, Plovdiv | Europe • 250/500 kW | Europe • 250 kW |
| | | S • Mideast • 500 kW |
| **USA** VOA, Various Locations | C Africa & E Africa • 100/250 kW | |
| †VOA, Via São Tomé | W • S Africa • 100 kW | |
| | S Africa • 100 kW | |
| **13605 GERMANY** DEUTSCHE WELLE, Nauen | W • S Asia • 500 kW | |
| | W • S Asia, SE Asia & Australasia • 500 kW | |
| †DEUTSCHE WELLE, Via Sri Lanka | W • S Asia • 250 kW | |
| **INDIA** †ALL INDIA RADIO, Bangalore | E Asia & SE Asia • 500 kW | |
| | E Africa • 500 kW | |
| | W Africa • 500 kW | |
| **IRAN** VO THE ISLAMIC REP, Tehrān | S • W Asia & S Asia • 500 kW | |
| **13610 CHINA** †CENTRAL PEOPLE'S BS | DS-1 | |
| | W-M • DS-1 | |
| CHINA RADIO INTL, Xi'an | S • Europe • 100 kW | |
| **FRANCE** †R FRANCE INTL, Issoudun-Allouis | S • E Africa • 500 kW | |
| | Irr • M-F • E Africa • 500 kW | |
| | Irr • Sa/Su • E Africa • 500 kW | |
| | Irr • E Africa • 500 kW | |
| | W M-F • E Africa • 500 kW | |
| | W Sa/Su • E Africa • 500 kW | |
| | W • E Africa • 500 kW | |
| **PORTUGAL** RDP INTERNATIONAL, Lisbon | S Sa/Su • W Europe • 100 kW | |
| **SYRIA** RADIO DAMASCUS, Adhra | S America • 500 kW | |
| | E Europe & Mideast • 500 kW | |
| | E Europe • 500 kW | |
| | Europe • 500 kW | |

(con'd)

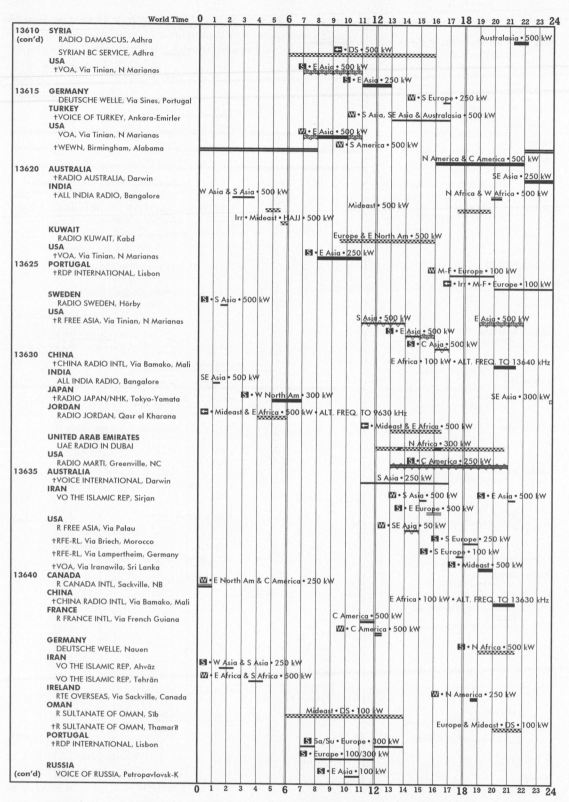

| | World Time | 0 1 2 3 4 5 6 7 8 9 10 11 12 13 14 15 16 17 18 19 20 21 22 23 24 |
|---|---|---|
| **13610** | **SYRIA** | |
| (con'd) | RADIO DAMASCUS, Adhra | Australasia • 500 kW |
| | SYRIAN BC SERVICE, Adhra | DS • 500 kW |
| | **USA** | |
| | †VOA, Via Tinian, N Marianas | S • E Asia • 500 kW |
| | | S • E Asia • 250 kW |
| **13615** | **GERMANY** | |
| | DEUTSCHE WELLE, Via Sines, Portugal | W • S Europe • 250 kW |
| | **TURKEY** | |
| | †VOICE OF TURKEY, Ankara-Emirler | W • S Asia, SE Asia & Australasia • 500 kW |
| | **USA** | |
| | VOA, Via Tinian, N Marianas | W • E Asia • 500 kW |
| | †WEWN, Birmingham, Alabama | W • S America • 500 kW |
| | | N America & C America • 500 kW |
| **13620** | **AUSTRALIA** | |
| | †RADIO AUSTRALIA, Darwin | SE Asia • 250 kW |
| | **INDIA** | |
| | †ALL INDIA RADIO, Bangalore | W Asia & S Asia • 500 kW     N Africa & W Africa • 500 kW |
| | | Mideast • 500 kW |
| | | Irr • Mideast • HAJJ • 500 kW |
| | **KUWAIT** | |
| | RADIO KUWAIT, Kabd | Europe & E North Am • 500 kW |
| | **USA** | |
| | †VOA, Via Tinian, N Marianas | S • E Asia • 250 kW |
| **13625** | **PORTUGAL** | |
| | †RDP INTERNATIONAL, Lisbon | W • M-F • Europe • 100 kW |
| | | Irr • M-F • Europe • 100 kW |
| | **SWEDEN** | |
| | RADIO SWEDEN, Hörby | S • S Asia • 500 kW |
| | **USA** | |
| | †R FREE ASIA, Via Tinian, N Marianas | S Asia • 500 kW      E Asia • 500 kW |
| | | S • E Asia • 500 kW |
| | | S • C Asia • 500 kW |
| **13630** | **CHINA** | |
| | †CHINA RADIO INTL, Via Bamako, Mali | E Africa • 100 kW • ALT. FREQ. TO 13640 kHz |
| | **INDIA** | |
| | ALL INDIA RADIO, Bangalore | SE Asia • 500 kW |
| | **JAPAN** | |
| | †RADIO JAPAN/NHK, Tokyo-Yamata | S • W North Am • 300 kW      SE Asia • 300 kW |
| | **JORDAN** | |
| | RADIO JORDAN, Qasr el Kharana | Mideast & E Africa • 500 kW • ALT. FREQ. TO 9630 kHz |
| | | Mideast & E Africa • 500 kW |
| | **UNITED ARAB EMIRATES** | |
| | UAE RADIO IN DUBAI | N Africa • 300 kW |
| | **USA** | |
| | RADIO MARTI, Greenville, NC | S • C America • 250 kW |
| **13635** | **AUSTRALIA** | |
| | †VOICE INTERNATIONAL, Darwin | S Asia • 250 kW |
| | **IRAN** | |
| | VO THE ISLAMIC REP, Sirjan | W • S Asia • 500 kW      S • E Asia • 500 kW |
| | | S • E Europe • 500 kW |
| | **USA** | |
| | R FREE ASIA, Via Palau | W • SE Asia • 50 kW |
| | †RFE-RL, Via Briech, Morocco | S • S Europe • 250 kW |
| | †RFE-RL, Via Lampertheim, Germany | S • S Europe • 100 kW |
| | †VOA, Via Iranawila, Sri Lanka | S • Mideast • 500 kW |
| **13640** | **CANADA** | |
| | R CANADA INTL, Sackville, NB | W • E North Am & C America • 250 kW |
| | **CHINA** | |
| | †CHINA RADIO INTL, Via Bamako, Mali | E Africa • 100 kW • ALT. FREQ. TO 13630 kHz |
| | **FRANCE** | |
| | R FRANCE INTL, Via French Guiana | C America • 500 kW |
| | | W • C America • 500 kW |
| | **GERMANY** | |
| | DEUTSCHE WELLE, Nauen | S • N Africa • 500 kW |
| | **IRAN** | |
| | VO THE ISLAMIC REP, Ahvāz | S • W Asia & S Asia • 250 kW |
| | VO THE ISLAMIC REP, Tehrān | W • E Africa & S Africa • 500 kW |
| | **IRELAND** | |
| | RTE OVERSEAS, Via Sackville, Canada | W • N America • 250 kW |
| | **OMAN** | |
| | R SULTANATE OF OMAN, Sīb | Mideast • DS • 100 kW |
| | †R SULTANATE OF OMAN, Thamarīt | Europe & Mideast • DS • 100 kW |
| | **PORTUGAL** | |
| | †RDP INTERNATIONAL, Lisbon | S • Sa/Su • Europe • 300 kW |
| | | S • Europe • 100/300 kW |
| | **RUSSIA** | |
| (con'd) | VOICE OF RUSSIA, Petropavlovsk-K | S • E Asia • 100 kW |

| World Time | 0 1 2 3 4 5 6 7 8 9 10 11 12 13 14 15 16 17 18 19 20 21 22 23 24 |
|---|---|

ENGLISH ▬▬   ARABIC ⋙   CHINESE ⬚⬚⬚   FRENCH ▬▬   GERMAN ▬▬   RUSSIAN ══   SPANISH ▬▬   OTHER ▬

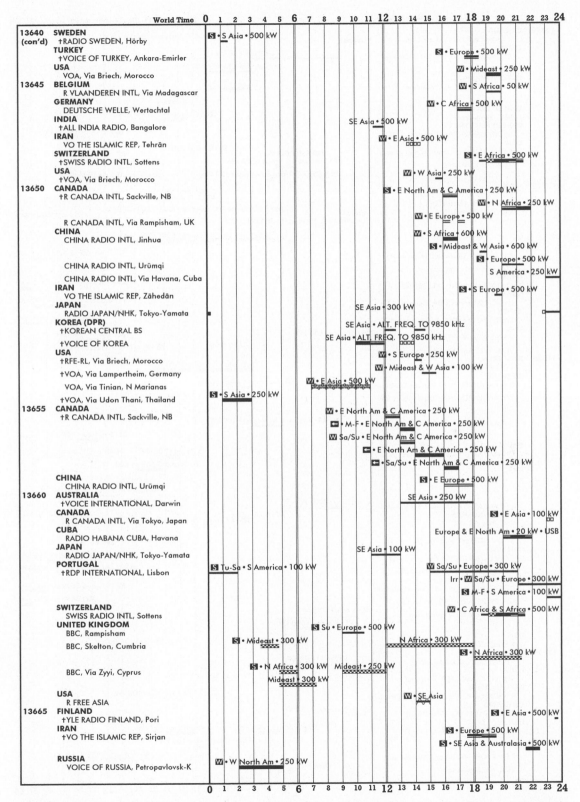

| World Time | Target • Power |
|---|---|
| **13640 SWEDEN** | |
| (con'd) †RADIO SWEDEN, Hörby | S • S Asia • 500 kW (0–6) |
| **TURKEY** | |
| †VOICE OF TURKEY, Ankara-Emirler | S • Europe • 500 kW (16–21) |
| **USA** | |
| VOA, Via Briech, Morocco | W • Mideast • 250 kW (18–20) |
| **13645 BELGIUM** | |
| R VLAANDEREN INTL, Via Madagascar | W • S Africa • 50 kW (18–19) |
| **GERMANY** | |
| DEUTSCHE WELLE, Wertachtal | W • C Africa • 500 kW (17–18) |
| **INDIA** | |
| †ALL INDIA RADIO, Bangalore | SE Asia • 500 kW (10–15) |
| **IRAN** | |
| VO THE ISLAMIC REP, Tehrān | W • E Asia • 500 kW (12–14) |
| **SWITZERLAND** | |
| †SWISS RADIO INTL, Sottens | S • E Africa • 500 kW (18–21) |
| **USA** | |
| †VOA, Via Briech, Morocco | W • W Asia • 250 kW (15–17) |
| **13650 CANADA** | |
| †R CANADA INTL, Sackville, NB | S • E North Am & C America • 250 kW (12–17) |
| | W • N Africa • 250 kW (20–22) |
| R CANADA INTL, Via Rampisham, UK | W • E Europe • 500 kW (15–17) |
| **CHINA** | |
| CHINA RADIO INTL, Jinhua | W • S Africa • 600 kW (15–17) |
| | S • Mideast & W Asia • 600 kW (16–20) |
| CHINA RADIO INTL, Urümqi | S • Europe • 500 kW (19–22) |
| CHINA RADIO INTL, Via Havana, Cuba | S America • 250 kW (21–24) |
| **IRAN** | |
| VO THE ISLAMIC REP, Zāhedān | S • S Europe • 500 kW (18–21) |
| **JAPAN** | |
| RADIO JAPAN/NHK, Tokyo-Yamata | SE Asia • 300 kW (11–15) |
| **KOREA (DPR)** | |
| †KOREAN CENTRAL BS | SE Asia • ALT. FREQ. TO 9850 kHz (10–16) |
| †VOICE OF KOREA | SE Asia • ALT. FREQ. TO 9850 kHz (9–16) |
| **USA** | |
| †RFE-RL, Via Briech, Morocco | W • S Europe • 250 kW (12–15) |
| | W • Mideast & W Asia • 100 kW (12–14) |
| †VOA, Via Lampertheim, Germany | W • E Asia • 500 kW (7–11) |
| VOA, Via Tinian, N Marianas | |
| †VOA, Via Udon Thani, Thailand | S • S Asia • 250 kW (0–6) |
| **13655 CANADA** | |
| †R CANADA INTL, Sackville, NB | W • E North Am & C America • 250 kW (10–14) |
| | ⇄ • M-F • E North Am & C America • 250 kW (11–14) |
| | W • Sa/Su • E North Am & C America • 250 kW (11–14) |
| | ⇄ • E North Am & C America • 250 kW (13–16) |
| | ⇄ • Sa/Su • E North Am & C America • 250 kW (13–17) |
| **CHINA** | |
| CHINA RADIO INTL, Urümqi | S • E Europe • 500 kW (15–17) |
| **13660 AUSTRALIA** | |
| †VOICE INTERNATIONAL, Darwin | SE Asia • 250 kW (13–16) |
| **CANADA** | |
| R CANADA INTL, Via Tokyo, Japan | S • E Asia • 100 kW (20–21) |
| **CUBA** | |
| RADIO HABANA CUBA, Havana | Europe & E North Am • 20 kW • USB (20–23) |
| **JAPAN** | |
| RADIO JAPAN/NHK, Tokyo-Yamata | SE Asia • 100 kW (11–14) |
| **PORTUGAL** | |
| †RDP INTERNATIONAL, Lisbon | S • Tu-Sa • S America • 100 kW (0–7) |
| | Irr • W • Sa/Su • Europe • 300 kW (18–22) |
| | S • M-F • S America • 100 kW (20–23) |
| **SWITZERLAND** | |
| SWISS RADIO INTL, Sottens | W • C Africa & S Africa • 500 kW (16–21) |
| **UNITED KINGDOM** | |
| BBC, Rampisham | S • Su • Europe • 500 kW (9–12) |
| BBC, Skelton, Cumbria | N Africa • 300 kW (13–17) |
| | S • N Africa • 300 kW (17–20) |
| BBC, Via Zyyi, Cyprus | S • N Africa • 300 kW (3–6) |
| | Mideast • 250 kW (9–11) |
| | Mideast • 300 kW (5–7) |
| **USA** | |
| R FREE ASIA | W • SE Asia (15–17) |
| **13665 FINLAND** | |
| †YLE RADIO FINLAND, Pori | S • E Asia • 500 kW (20–22) |
| **IRAN** | |
| †VO THE ISLAMIC REP, Sirjan | S • Europe • 500 kW (17–20) |
| | S • SE Asia & Australasia • 500 kW (17–22) |
| **RUSSIA** | |
| VOICE OF RUSSIA, Petropavlovsk-K | W • W North Am • 250 kW (1–6) |

World Time: 0 1 2 3 4 5 6 7 8 9 10 11 12 13 14 15 16 17 18 19 20 21 22 23 24

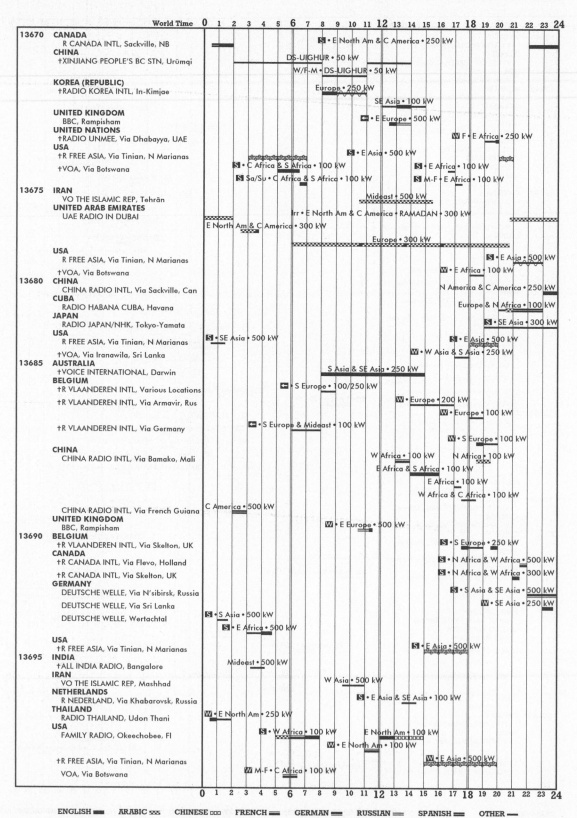

**13670 CANADA**
R CANADA INTL, Sackville, NB
**CHINA**
†XINJIANG PEOPLE'S BC STN, Urümqi

**KOREA (REPUBLIC)**
†RADIO KOREA INTL, In-Kimjae

**UNITED KINGDOM**
BBC, Rampisham
**UNITED NATIONS**
†RADIO UNMEE, Via Dhabayya, UAE
**USA**
†R FREE ASIA, Via Tinian, N Marianas
†VOA, Via Botswana

**13675 IRAN**
VO THE ISLAMIC REP, Tehrān
**UNITED ARAB EMIRATES**
UAE RADIO IN DUBAI

**USA**
R FREE ASIA, Via Tinian, N Marianas
†VOA, Via Botswana
**13680 CHINA**
CHINA RADIO INTL, Via Sackville, Can
**CUBA**
RADIO HABANA CUBA, Havana
**JAPAN**
RADIO JAPAN/NHK, Tokyo-Yamata
**USA**
R FREE ASIA, Via Tinian, N Marianas
†VOA, Via Iranawila, Sri Lanka
**13685 AUSTRALIA**
†VOICE INTERNATIONAL, Darwin
**BELGIUM**
†R VLAANDEREN INTL, Various Locations
†R VLAANDEREN INTL, Via Armavir, Rus

†R VLAANDEREN INTL, Via Germany

**CHINA**
CHINA RADIO INTL, Via Bamako, Mali

CHINA RADIO INTL, Via French Guiana
**UNITED KINGDOM**
BBC, Rampisham
**13690 BELGIUM**
†R VLAANDEREN INTL, Via Skelton, UK
**CANADA**
†R CANADA INTL, Via Flevo, Holland
†R CANADA INTL, Via Skelton, UK
**GERMANY**
DEUTSCHE WELLE, Via N'sibirsk, Russia
DEUTSCHE WELLE, Via Sri Lanka
DEUTSCHE WELLE, Wertachtal

**USA**
†R FREE ASIA, Via Tinian, N Marianas
**13695 INDIA**
†ALL INDIA RADIO, Bangalore
**IRAN**
VO THE ISLAMIC REP, Mashhad
**NETHERLANDS**
R NEDERLAND, Via Khabarovsk, Russia
**THAILAND**
RADIO THAILAND, Udon Thani
**USA**
FAMILY RADIO, Okeechobee, Fl

†R FREE ASIA, Via Tinian, N Marianas
VOA, Via Botswana

ENGLISH ▬   ARABIC ▨   CHINESE □□□   FRENCH ═   GERMAN ▬   RUSSIAN ▭   SPANISH ▭   OTHER ▬

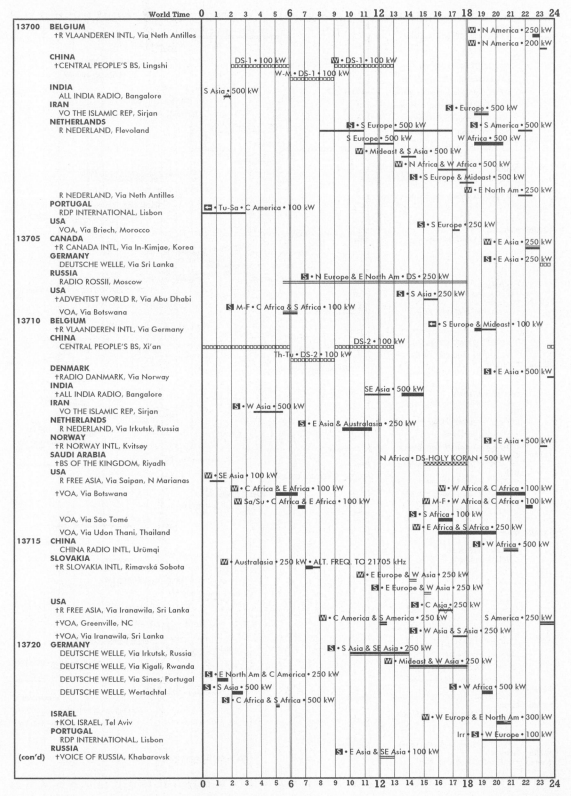

World Time 0 1 2 3 4 5 6 7 8 9 10 11 12 13 14 15 16 17 18 19 20 21 22 23 24

**13700 BELGIUM**
†R VLAANDEREN INTL, Via Neth Antilles
**W** • N America • 250 kW
**W** • N America • 200 kW

**CHINA**
†CENTRAL PEOPLE'S BS, Lingshi
DS-1 • 100 kW
**W** • DS-1 • 100 kW
W-M • DS-1 • 100 kW

**INDIA**
ALL INDIA RADIO, Bangalore
S Asia • 500 kW

**IRAN**
VO THE ISLAMIC REP, Sirjan
**S** • Europe • 500 kW

**NETHERLANDS**
R NEDERLAND, Flevoland
**S** • S Europe • 500 kW
**S** • S America • 500 kW
S Europe • 500 kW
W Africa • 500 kW
**W** • Mideast & S Asia • 500 kW
**W** • N Africa & W Africa • 500 kW
**S** • S Europe & Mideast • 500 kW
**W** • E North Am • 250 kW

R NEDERLAND, Via Neth Antilles

**PORTUGAL**
RDP INTERNATIONAL, Lisbon
➡ • Tu-Sa • C America • 100 kW

**USA**
VOA, Via Briech, Morocco
**S** • S Europe • 250 kW

**13705 CANADA**
†R CANADA INTL, Via In-Kimjae, Korea
**W** • E Asia • 250 kW

**GERMANY**
DEUTSCHE WELLE, Via Sri Lanka
**S** • E Asia • 250 kW

**RUSSIA**
RADIO ROSSII, Moscow
**S** • N Europe & E North Am • DS • 250 kW

**USA**
†ADVENTIST WORLD R, Via Abu Dhabi
**S** • S Asia • 250 kW

VOA, Via Botswana
**S** M-F • C Africa & S Africa • 100 kW

**13710 BELGIUM**
†R VLAANDEREN INTL, Via Germany
➡ • S Europe & Mideast • 100 kW

**CHINA**
CENTRAL PEOPLE'S BS, Xi'an
DS-2 • 100 kW
Th-Tu • DS-2 • 100 kW

**DENMARK**
†RADIO DANMARK, Via Norway
**S** • E Asia • 500 kW

**INDIA**
†ALL INDIA RADIO, Bangalore
SE Asia • 500 kW

**IRAN**
VO THE ISLAMIC REP, Sirjan
**S** • W Asia • 500 kW

**NETHERLANDS**
R NEDERLAND, Via Irkutsk, Russia
**S** • E Asia & Australasia • 250 kW

**NORWAY**
†R NORWAY INTL, Kvitsøy
**S** • E Asia • 500 kW

**SAUDI ARABIA**
†BS OF THE KINGDOM, Riyadh
N Africa • DS-HOLY KORAN • 500 kW

**USA**
R FREE ASIA, Via Saipan, N Marianas
**W** • SE Asia • 100 kW
**W** • W Africa & C Africa • 100 kW

†VOA, Via Botswana
**W** • C Africa & E Africa • 100 kW
**W** Sa/Su • C Africa & E Africa • 100 kW
**W** M-F • W Africa & C Africa • 100 kW

VOA, Via São Tomé
**S** • S Africa • 100 kW

VOA, Via Udon Thani, Thailand
**W** • E Africa & S Africa • 250 kW

**13715 CHINA**
CHINA RADIO INTL, Urümqi
**S** • W Africa • 500 kW

**SLOVAKIA**
†R SLOVAKIA INTL, Rimavská Sobota
**W** • Australasia • 250 kW • ALT. FREQ. TO 21705 kHz
**W** • E Europe & W Asia • 250 kW
**S** • E Europe & W Asia • 250 kW

**USA**
†R FREE ASIA, Via Iranawila, Sri Lanka
**S** • C Asia • 250 kW

†VOA, Greenville, NC
**W** • C America & S America • 250 kW
S America • 250 kW

†VOA, Via Iranawila, Sri Lanka
**S** • W Asia & S Asia • 250 kW

**13720 GERMANY**
DEUTSCHE WELLE, Via Irkutsk, Russia
**S** • S Asia & SE Asia • 250 kW

DEUTSCHE WELLE, Via Kigali, Rwanda
**W** • Mideast & W Asia • 250 kW

DEUTSCHE WELLE, Via Sines, Portugal
**S** • E North Am & C America • 250 kW

DEUTSCHE WELLE, Wertachtal
**S** • S Asia • 500 kW
**S** • C Africa & S Africa • 500 kW
**S** • W Africa • 500 kW

**ISRAEL**
†KOL ISRAEL, Tel Aviv
**W** • W Europe & E North Am • 300 kW

**PORTUGAL**
RDP INTERNATIONAL, Lisbon
Irr **S** • W Europe • 100 kW

**RUSSIA**
**(con'd)** †VOICE OF RUSSIA, Khabarovsk
**S** • E Asia & SE Asia • 100 kW

0 1 2 3 4 5 6 7 8 9 10 11 12 13 14 15 16 17 18 19 20 21 22 23 24

SEASONAL **S** OR **W**    1-HR TIMESHIFT MIDYEAR ➡ OR ➡    JAMMING / OR /\    EARLIEST HEARD ◁    LATEST HEARD ▷    NEW FOR 2003 †

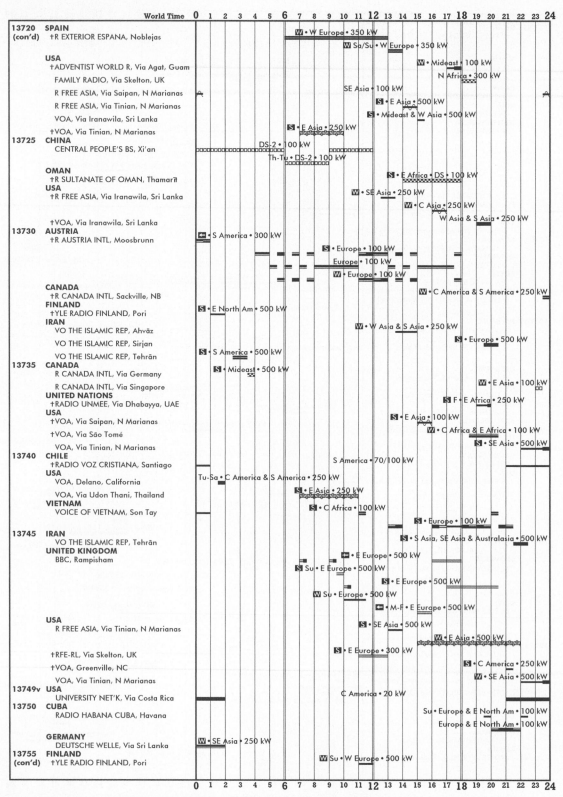

| World Time | | Frequency / Station |
|---|---|---|
| **13720** (con'd) | **SPAIN** | †R EXTERIOR ESPANA, Noblejas — W • W Europe • 350 kW; W Sa/Su • W Europe • 350 kW |
| | **USA** | †ADVENTIST WORLD R, Via Agat, Guam — W • Mideast • 100 kW; N Africa • 300 kW |
| | | FAMILY RADIO, Via Skelton, UK |
| | | R FREE ASIA, Via Saipan, N Marianas — SE Asia • 100 kW |
| | | R FREE ASIA, Via Tinian, N Marianas — S • E Asia • 500 kW |
| | | VOA, Via Iranawila, Sri Lanka — S • Mideast & W Asia • 500 kW |
| | | †VOA, Via Tinian, N Marianas — S • E Asia • 250 kW |
| **13725** | **CHINA** | CENTRAL PEOPLE'S BS, Xi'an — DS-2 • 100 kW; Th-Tu • DS-2 • 100 kW |
| | **OMAN** | †R SULTANATE OF OMAN, Thamarīt — S • E Africa • DS • 100 kW |
| | **USA** | †R FREE ASIA, Via Iranawila, Sri Lanka — W • SE Asia • 250 kW |
| | | — W • C Asia • 250 kW |
| | | †VOA, Via Iranawila, Sri Lanka — W Asia & S Asia • 250 kW |
| **13730** | **AUSTRIA** | †R AUSTRIA INTL, Moosbrunn — ◪ • S America • 300 kW; S • Europe • 100 kW; Europe • 100 kW; W • Europe • 100 kW |
| | **CANADA** | †R CANADA INTL, Sackville, NB — W • C America & S America • 250 kW |
| | **FINLAND** | †YLE RADIO FINLAND, Pori — S • E North Am • 500 kW |
| | **IRAN** | VO THE ISLAMIC REP, Ahvāz — W • W Asia & S Asia • 250 kW |
| | | VO THE ISLAMIC REP, Sirjan — S • Europe • 500 kW |
| | | VO THE ISLAMIC REP, Tehrān — S • S America • 500 kW |
| **13735** | **CANADA** | R CANADA INTL, Via Germany — S • Mideast • 500 kW |
| | | R CANADA INTL, Via Singapore — W • E Asia • 100 kW |
| | **UNITED NATIONS** | †RADIO UNMEE, Via Dhabayya, UAE — S F • E Africa • 250 kW |
| | **USA** | †VOA, Via Saipan, N Marianas — S • E Asia • 100 kW |
| | | †VOA, Via São Tomé — W • C Africa & E Africa • 100 kW |
| | | VOA, Via Tinian, N Marianas — S • SE Asia • 500 kW |
| **13740** | **CHILE** | †RADIO VOZ CRISTIANA, Santiago — S America • 70/100 kW |
| | **USA** | VOA, Delano, California — Tu-Sa • C America & S America • 250 kW |
| | | VOA, Via Udon Thani, Thailand — S • E Asia • 250 kW |
| | **VIETNAM** | VOICE OF VIETNAM, Son Tay — S • C Africa • 100 kW |
| **13745** | **IRAN** | VO THE ISLAMIC REP, Tehrān — S • Europe • 100 kW; S • S Asia, SE Asia & Australasia • 500 kW |
| | **UNITED KINGDOM** | BBC, Rampisham — ◪ • E Europe • 500 kW; S Su • E Europe • 500 kW; S • E Europe • 500 kW; W Su • Europe • 500 kW; ◪ • M-F • E Europe • 500 kW |
| | **USA** | R FREE ASIA, Via Tinian, N Marianas — S • SE Asia • 500 kW; W • E Asia • 500 kW |
| | | †RFE-RL, Via Skelton, UK — S • E Europe • 300 kW |
| | | †VOA, Greenville, NC — S • C America • 250 kW |
| | | VOA, Via Tinian, N Marianas — W • SE Asia • 500 kW |
| **13749v** | **USA** | UNIVERSITY NET'K, Via Costa Rica — C America • 20 kW |
| **13750** | **CUBA** | RADIO HABANA CUBA, Havana — Su • Europe & E North Am • 100 kW; Europe & E North Am • 100 kW |
| | **GERMANY** | DEUTSCHE WELLE, Via Sri Lanka — W • SE Asia • 250 kW |
| **13755** (con'd) | **FINLAND** | †YLE RADIO FINLAND, Pori — W Su • W Europe • 500 kW |

ENGLISH ▬   ARABIC ⠿   CHINESE ▭▭▭   FRENCH ═══   GERMAN ▬▬   RUSSIAN ══   SPANISH ═══   OTHER ▬▬

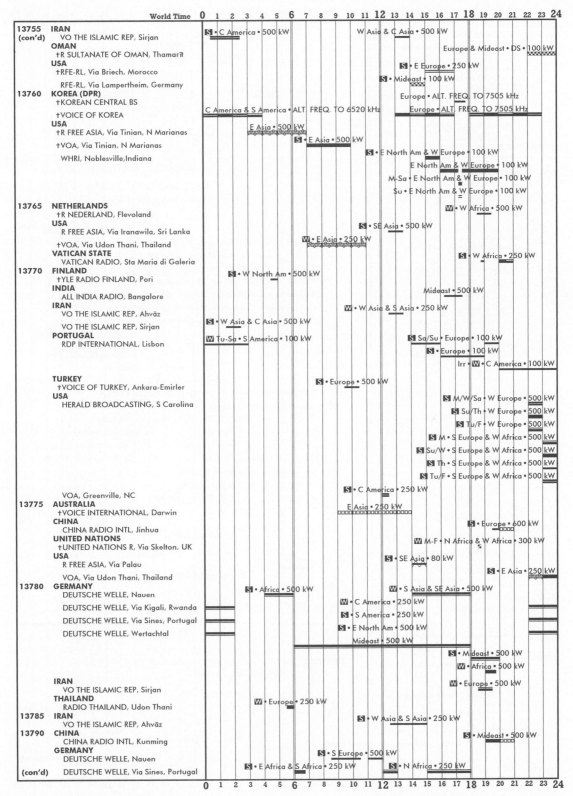

| World Time | 0 1 2 3 4 5 6 7 8 9 10 11 12 13 14 15 16 17 18 19 20 21 22 23 24 |
|---|---|
| **13755** **IRAN** (con'd)  VO THE ISLAMIC REP, Sirjan | ⑤ • C America • 500 kW     W Asia & C Asia • 500 kW |
| **OMAN** †R SULTANATE OF OMAN, Thamarīt | Europe & Mideast • DS • 100 kW |
| **USA** †RFE-RL, Via Briech, Morocco | ⑤ • E Europe • 250 kW |
| RFE-RL, Via Lampertheim, Germany | ⑤ • Mideast • 100 kW |
| **13760** **KOREA (DPR)** †KOREAN CENTRAL BS | Europe • ALT. FREQ. TO 7505 kHz |
| †VOICE OF KOREA | C America & S America • ALT FREQ. TO 6520 kHz     Europe • ALT. FREQ. TO 7505 kHz |
| **USA** †R FREE ASIA, Via Tinian, N Marianas | E Asia • 500 kW |
| †VOA, Via Tinian, N Marianas | ⑤ • E Asia • 500 kW |
| WHRI, Noblesville, Indiana | ⑤ • E North Am & W Europe • 100 kW   E North Am & W Europe • 100 kW   M-Sa • E North Am & W Europe • 100 kW   Su • E North Am & W Europe • 100 kW |
| **13765** **NETHERLANDS** †R NEDERLAND, Flevoland | W • W Africa • 500 kW |
| **USA** R FREE ASIA, Via Iranawila, Sri Lanka | ⑤ • SE Asia • 500 kW |
| †VOA, Via Udon Thani, Thailand | W • E Asia • 250 kW |
| **VATICAN STATE** VATICAN RADIO, Sta Maria di Galeria | ⑤ • W Africa • 250 kW |
| **13770** **FINLAND** †YLE RADIO FINLAND, Pori | ⑤ • W North Am • 500 kW |
| **INDIA** ALL INDIA RADIO, Bangalore | Mideast • 500 kW |
| **IRAN** VO THE ISLAMIC REP, Ahvāz | W • W Asia & S Asia • 250 kW |
| VO THE ISLAMIC REP, Sirjan | ⑤ • W Asia & C Asia • 500 kW |
| **PORTUGAL** RDP INTERNATIONAL, Lisbon | W Tu-Sa • S America • 100 kW     ⑤ Sa/Su • Europe • 100 kW   ⑤ • Europe • 100 kW   Irr W • C America • 100 kW |
| **TURKEY** †VOICE OF TURKEY, Ankara-Emirler | ⑤ • Europe • 500 kW |
| **USA** HERALD BROADCASTING, S Carolina | ⑤ M/W/Sa • W Europe • 500 kW   ⑤ Su/Th • W Europe • 500 kW   ⑤ Tu/F • W Europe • 500 kW   ⑤ M • S Europe & W Africa • 500 kW   ⑤ Su/W • S Europe & W Africa • 500 kW   ⑤ Th • S Europe & W Africa • 500 kW   ⑤ Tu/F • S Europe & W Africa • 500 kW |
| VOA, Greenville, NC | ⑤ • C America • 250 kW |
| **13775** **AUSTRALIA** †VOICE INTERNATIONAL, Darwin | E Asia • 250 kW |
| **CHINA** CHINA RADIO INTL, Jinhua | ⑤ • Europe • 600 kW |
| **UNITED NATIONS** †UNITED NATIONS R, Via Skelton, UK | W M-F • N Africa & W Africa • 300 kW |
| **USA** R FREE ASIA, Via Palau | ⑤ • SE Asia • 80 kW |
| VOA, Via Udon Thani, Thailand | ⑤ • E Asia • 250 kW |
| **13780** **GERMANY** DEUTSCHE WELLE, Nauen | ⑤ • Africa • 500 kW     W • S Asia & SE Asia • 500 kW |
| DEUTSCHE WELLE, Via Kigali, Rwanda | W • C America • 250 kW |
| DEUTSCHE WELLE, Via Sines, Portugal | ⑤ • S America • 250 kW |
| DEUTSCHE WELLE, Wertachtal | ⑤ • E North Am • 500 kW   Mideast • 500 kW   ⑤ • Mideast • 500 kW   W • Africa • 500 kW   W • Europe • 500 kW |
| **IRAN** VO THE ISLAMIC REP, Sirjan | |
| **THAILAND** RADIO THAILAND, Udon Thani | W • Europe • 250 kW |
| **13785** **IRAN** VO THE ISLAMIC REP, Ahvāz | ⑤ • W Asia & S Asia • 250 kW |
| **13790** **CHINA** CHINA RADIO INTL, Kunming | ⑤ • Mideast • 500 kW |
| **GERMANY** DEUTSCHE WELLE, Nauen | ⑤ • S Europe • 500 kW |
| (con'd)  DEUTSCHE WELLE, Via Sines, Portugal | ⑤ • E Africa & S Africa • 250 kW     ⑤ • N Africa • 250 kW |

SEASONAL ⑤ OR Ⓦ     1-HR TIMESHIFT MIDYEAR ⊟ OR ⊡     JAMMING / OR ⋀     EARLIEST HEARD ◁     LATEST HEARD ▷     NEW FOR 2003 †

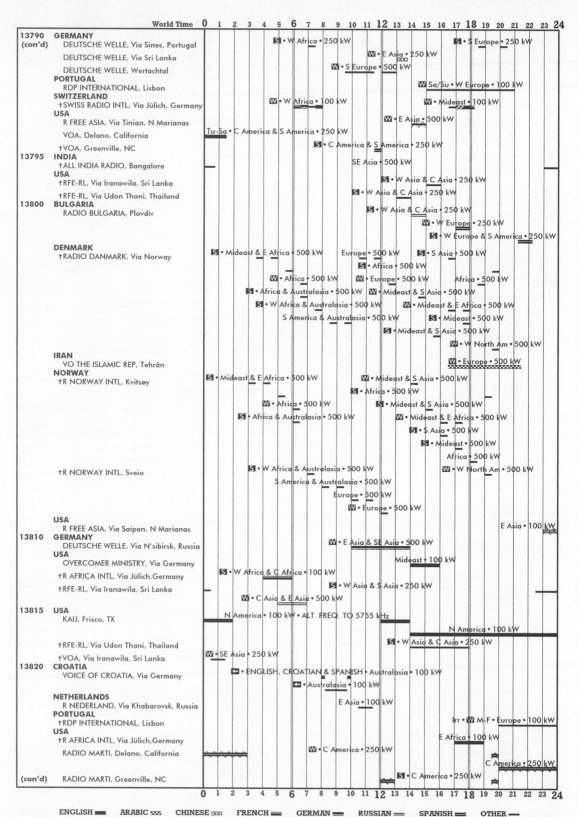

| | | World Time | 0 | 1 | 2 | 3 | 4 | 5 | 6 | 7 | 8 | 9 | 10 | 11 | 12 | 13 | 14 | 15 | 16 | 17 | 18 | 19 | 20 | 21 | 22 | 23 | 24 |

**13790 GERMANY**
(con'd)   DEUTSCHE WELLE, Via Sines, Portugal — S • W Africa • 250 kW / S • S Europe • 250 kW
DEUTSCHE WELLE, Via Sri Lanka — W • E Asia • 250 kW
DEUTSCHE WELLE, Wertachtal — W • S Europe • 500 kW
**PORTUGAL**
RDP INTERNATIONAL, Lisbon — W • Sa/Su • W Europe • 100 kW
**SWITZERLAND**
†SWISS RADIO INTL, Via Jülich, Germany — W • W Africa • 100 kW / W • Mideast • 100 kW
**USA**
R FREE ASIA, Via Tinian, N Marianas — W • E Asia • 500 kW
VOA, Delano, California — Tu-Sa • C America & S America • 250 kW
†VOA, Greenville, NC — S • C America & S America • 250 kW

**13795 INDIA**
†ALL INDIA RADIO, Bangalore — SE Asia • 500 kW
**USA**
†RFE-RL, Via Iranawila, Sri Lanka — S • W Asia & C Asia • 250 kW
†RFE-RL, Via Udon Thani, Thailand — S • W Asia & C Asia • 250 kW

**13800 BULGARIA**
RADIO BULGARIA, Plovdiv — S • W Asia & C Asia • 250 kW
— W • W Europe • 250 kW
— S • W Europe & S America • 250 kW

**DENMARK**
†RADIO DANMARK, Via Norway — S • Mideast & E Africa • 500 kW / Europe • 500 kW / S • S Asia • 500 kW
— S • Africa • 500 kW
— W • Africa • 500 kW / W • Europe • 500 kW / Africa • 500 kW
— S • Africa & Australasia • 500 kW / W • Mideast & S Asia • 500 kW
— S • W Africa & Australasia • 500 kW / W • Mideast & E Africa • 500 kW
— S America & Australasia • 500 kW / S • Mideast • 500 kW
— S • Mideast & S Asia • 500 kW
— W • W North Am • 500 kW
— S • Europe • 500 kW

**IRAN**
VO THE ISLAMIC REP, Tehrān
**NORWAY**
†R NORWAY INTL, Kvitsøy — S • Mideast & E Africa • 500 kW / W • Mideast & S Asia • 500 kW
— S • Africa • 500 kW
— W • Africa • 500 kW / S • Mideast & S Asia • 500 kW
— S • Africa & Australasia • 500 kW / W • Mideast & E Africa • 500 kW
— S • S Asia • 500 kW
— S • Mideast • 500 kW
— Africa • 500 kW
— W • W North Am • 500 kW

†R NORWAY INTL, Sveio — S • W Africa & Australasia • 500 kW
— S America & Australasia • 500 kW
— Europe • 500 kW
— W • Europe • 500 kW

**USA**
R FREE ASIA, Via Saipan, N Marianas — E Asia • 100 kW
**13810 GERMANY**
DEUTSCHE WELLE, Via N'sibirsk, Russia — W • E Asia & SE Asia • 500 kW
**USA**
OVERCOMER MINISTRY, Via Germany — Mideast • 100 kW
†R AFRICA INTL, Via Jülich, Germany — S • W Africa & C Africa • 100 kW
†RFE-RL, Via Iranawila, Sri Lanka — S • W Asia & S Asia • 250 kW
— W • C Asia & E Asia • 500 kW

**13815 USA**
KAIJ, Frisco, TX — N America • 100 kW • ALT. FREQ. TO 5755 kHz / N America • 100 kW

†RFE-RL, Via Udon Thani, Thailand — S • W Asia & C Asia • 250 kW
†VOA, Via Iranawila, Sri Lanka — W • SE Asia • 250 kW
**13820 CROATIA**
VOICE OF CROATIA, Via Germany — • ENGLISH, CROATIAN & SPANISH • Australasia • 100 kW
— • Australasia • 100 kW

**NETHERLANDS**
R NEDERLAND, Via Khabarovsk, Russia — E Asia • 100 kW
**PORTUGAL**
†RDP INTERNATIONAL, Lisbon — Irr • W M-F • Europe • 100 kW
**USA**
†R AFRICA INTL, Via Jülich, Germany — E Africa • 100 kW
RADIO MARTI, Delano, California — W • C America • 250 kW
— C America • 250 kW
(con'd)   RADIO MARTI, Greenville, NC — S • C America • 250 kW

| | World Time | 0 | 1 | 2 | 3 | 4 | 5 | 6 | 7 | 8 | 9 | 10 | 11 | 12 | 13 | 14 | 15 | 16 | 17 | 18 | 19 | 20 | 21 | 22 | 23 | 24 |

ENGLISH ▬▬   ARABIC ≋≋   CHINESE ▫▫▫   FRENCH ▬▬   GERMAN ▬▬   RUSSIAN ══   SPANISH ══   OTHER ▬▬

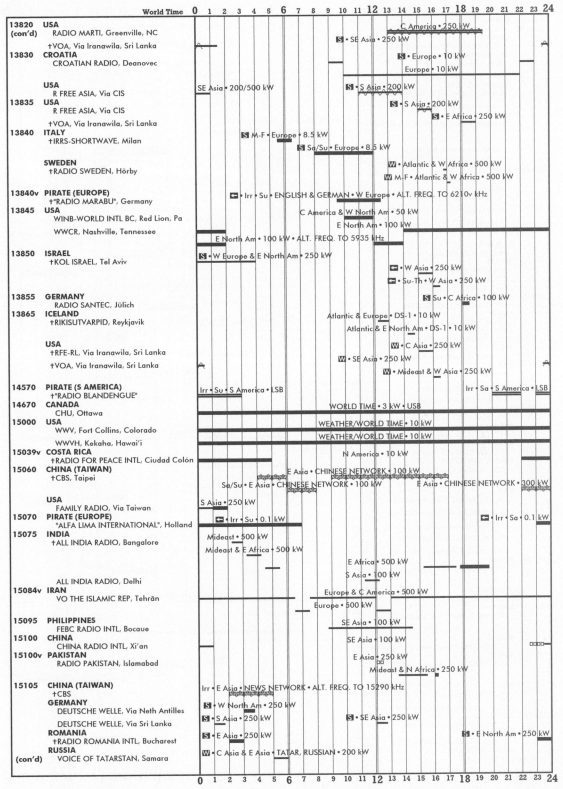

| Freq | Country / Station | |
|---|---|---|
| 13820 (con'd) | **USA** — RADIO MARTI, Greenville, NC | C America • 250 kW |
| | †VOA, Via Iranawila, Sri Lanka | S • SE Asia • 250 kW |
| 13830 | **CROATIA** — CROATIAN RADIO, Deanovec | S • Europe • 10 kW / Europe • 10 kW |
| | **USA** — R FREE ASIA, Via CIS | SE Asia • 200/500 kW / S • S Asia • 200 kW |
| 13835 | **USA** — R FREE ASIA, Via CIS | S • S Asia • 200 kW |
| | †VOA, Via Iranawila, Sri Lanka | S • E Africa • 250 kW |
| 13840 | **ITALY** — †IRRS-SHORTWAVE, Milan | S M-F • Europe • 8.5 kW / S Sa/Su • Europe • 8.5 kW |
| | **SWEDEN** — †RADIO SWEDEN, Hörby | W • Atlantic & W Africa • 500 kW / W M-F • Atlantic & W Africa • 500 kW |
| 13840v | **PIRATE (EUROPE)** — †"RADIO MARABU", Germany | ← • Irr • Su • ENGLISH & GERMAN • W Europe • ALT. FREQ. TO 6210v kHz |
| 13845 | **USA** — WINB-WORLD INTL BC, Red Lion, Pa | C America & W North Am • 50 kW |
| | WWCR, Nashville, Tennessee | E North Am • 100 kW / E North Am • 100 kW • ALT. FREQ. TO 5935 kHz |
| 13850 | **ISRAEL** — †KOL ISRAEL, Tel Aviv | S • W Europe & E North Am • 250 kW / ← • W Asia • 250 kW / ← • Su-Th • W Asia • 250 kW |
| 13855 | **GERMANY** — RADIO SANTEC, Jülich | S • C Africa • 100 kW |
| 13865 | **ICELAND** — †RIKISUTVARPID, Reykjavik | Atlantic & Europe • DS-1 • 10 kW / Atlantic & E North Am • DS-1 • 10 kW |
| | **USA** — †RFE-RL, Via Iranawila, Sri Lanka | W • C Asia • 250 kW |
| | †VOA, Via Iranawila, Sri Lanka | W • SE Asia • 250 kW / W • Mideast & W Asia • 250 kW |
| 14570 | **PIRATE (S AMERICA)** — †"RADIO BLANDENGUE" | Irr • Su • S America • LSB / Irr • Sa • S America • LSB |
| 14670 | **CANADA** — CHU, Ottawa | WORLD TIME • 3 kW • USB |
| 15000 | **USA** — WWV, Fort Collins, Colorado | WEATHER/WORLD TIME • 10 kW |
| | WWVH, Kekaha, Hawai'i | WEATHER/WORLD TIME • 10 kW |
| 15039v | **COSTA RICA** — †RADIO FOR PEACE INTL, Ciudad Colón | N America • 10 kW |
| 15060 | **CHINA (TAIWAN)** — †CBS, Taipei | E Asia • CHINESE NETWORK • 100 kW / Sa/Su • E Asia • CHINESE NETWORK • 100 kW / E Asia • CHINESE NETWORK • 300 kW |
| | **USA** — FAMILY RADIO, Via Taiwan | S Asia • 250 kW |
| 15070 | **PIRATE (EUROPE)** — "ALFA LIMA INTERNATIONAL", Holland | ← • Irr • Su • 0.1 kW / ← • Irr • Sa • 0.1 kW |
| 15075 | **INDIA** — †ALL INDIA RADIO, Bangalore | Mideast • 500 kW / Mideast & E Africa • 500 kW / E Africa • 500 kW / S Asia • 100 kW |
| | ALL INDIA RADIO, Delhi | |
| 15084v | **IRAN** — VO THE ISLAMIC REP, Tehrān | Europe & C America • 500 kW / Europe • 500 kW |
| 15095 | **PHILIPPINES** — FEBC RADIO INTL, Bocaue | SE Asia • 100 kW |
| 15100 | **CHINA** — CHINA RADIO INTL, Xi'an | SE Asia • 100 kW |
| 15100v | **PAKISTAN** — RADIO PAKISTAN, Islamabad | E Asia • 250 kW / Mideast & N Africa • 250 kW |
| 15105 | **CHINA (TAIWAN)** — †CBS | Irr • E Asia • NEWS NETWORK • ALT. FREQ. TO 15290 kHz |
| | **GERMANY** — DEUTSCHE WELLE, Via Neth Antilles | S • W North Am • 250 kW |
| | DEUTSCHE WELLE, Via Sri Lanka | S • S Asia • 250 kW / S • SE Asia • 250 kW |
| | **ROMANIA** — †RADIO ROMANIA INTL, Bucharest | S • E Asia • 250 kW / S • E North Am • 250 kW |
| (con'd) | **RUSSIA** — VOICE OF TATARSTAN, Samara | W • C Asia & E Asia • TATAR, RUSSIAN • 200 kW |

**SEASONAL** Ⓢ **OR** Ⓦ    **1-HR TIMESHIFT MIDYEAR** ← **OR** →    JAMMING / OR ∧    **EARLIEST HEARD** ◁    **LATEST HEARD** ▷    **NEW FOR 2003** †

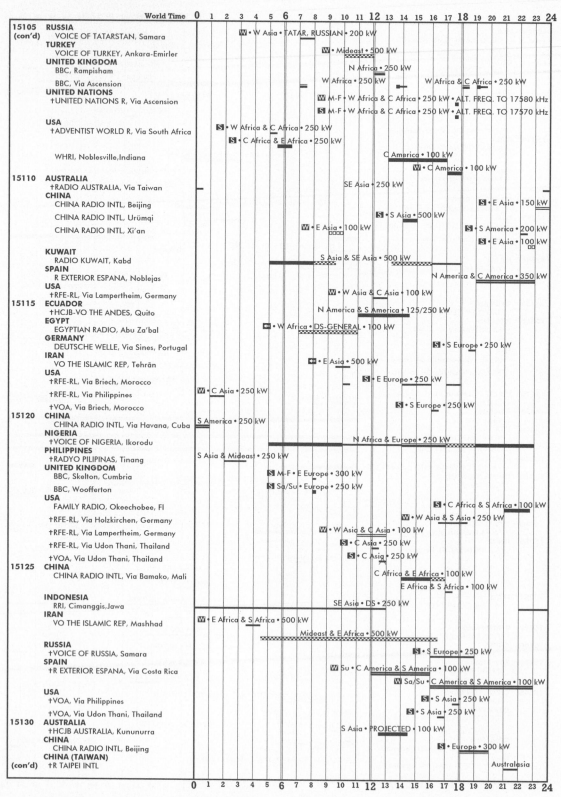

| | World Time | 0 1 2 3 4 5 6 7 8 9 10 11 12 13 14 15 16 17 18 19 20 21 22 23 24 |
|---|---|---|

**15105**
(con'd)  **RUSSIA**
  VOICE OF TATARSTAN, Samara — W • W Asia • TATAR, RUSSIAN • 200 kW
**TURKEY**
  VOICE OF TURKEY, Ankara-Emirler — W • Mideast • 500 kW
**UNITED KINGDOM**
  BBC, Rampisham — N Africa • 250 kW
  BBC, Via Ascension — W Africa • 250 kW / W Africa & C Africa • 250 kW
**UNITED NATIONS**
  †UNITED NATIONS R, Via Ascension — W M-F • W Africa & C Africa • 250 kW • ALT. FREQ. TO 17580 kHz / S M-F • W Africa & C Africa • 250 kW • ALT. FREQ. TO 17570 kHz
**USA**
  †ADVENTIST WORLD R, Via South Africa — S • W Africa & C Africa • 250 kW / S • C Africa & E Africa • 250 kW
  WHRI, Noblesville,Indiana — C America • 100 kW / W • C America • 100 kW

**15110**  **AUSTRALIA**
  †RADIO AUSTRALIA, Via Taiwan — SE Asia • 250 kW
**CHINA**
  CHINA RADIO INTL, Beijing — S • E Asia • 150 kW
  CHINA RADIO INTL, Urümqi — S • S Asia • 500 kW
  CHINA RADIO INTL, Xi'an — W • E Asia • 100 kW / S • S America • 200 kW / S • E Asia • 100 kW
**KUWAIT**
  RADIO KUWAIT, Kabd — S Asia & SE Asia • 500 kW
**SPAIN**
  R EXTERIOR ESPANA, Noblejas — N America & C America • 350 kW
**USA**
  †RFE-RL, Via Lampertheim, Germany — W • W Asia & C Asia • 100 kW

**15115**  **ECUADOR**
  †HCJB-VO THE ANDES, Quito — N America & S America • 125/250 kW
**EGYPT**
  EGYPTIAN RADIO, Abu Za'bal — ✈ • W Africa • DS-GENERAL • 100 kW
**GERMANY**
  DEUTSCHE WELLE, Via Sines, Portugal — S • S Europe • 250 kW
**IRAN**
  VO THE ISLAMIC REP, Tehrān — ✈ • E Asia • 500 kW
**USA**
  †RFE-RL, Via Briech, Morocco — S • E Europe • 250 kW
  †RFE-RL, Via Philippines — W • C Asia • 250 kW
  †VOA, Via Briech, Morocco — S • S Europe • 250 kW

**15120**  **CHINA**
  CHINA RADIO INTL, Via Havana, Cuba — S America • 250 kW
**NIGERIA**
  †VOICE OF NIGERIA, Ikorodu — N Africa & Europe • 250 kW
**PHILIPPINES**
  †RADYO PILIPINAS, Tinang — S Asia & Mideast • 250 kW
**UNITED KINGDOM**
  BBC, Skelton, Cumbria — S M-F • E Europe • 300 kW
  BBC, Woofferton — S Sa/Su • Europe • 250 kW
**USA**
  FAMILY RADIO, Okeechobee, Fl — S • C Africa & S Africa • 100 kW
  †RFE-RL, Via Holzkirchen, Germany — W • W Asia & S Asia • 250 kW
  †RFE-RL, Via Lampertheim, Germany — W • W Asia & C Asia • 100 kW
  †RFE-RL, Via Udon Thani, Thailand — S • C Asia • 250 kW
  †VOA, Via Udon Thani, Thailand — S • C Asia • 250 kW

**15125**  **CHINA**
  CHINA RADIO INTL, Via Bamako, Mali — C Africa & E Africa • 100 kW / E Africa & S Africa • 100 kW
**INDONESIA**
  RRI, Cimanggis,Jawa — SE Asia • DS • 250 kW
**IRAN**
  VO THE ISLAMIC REP, Mashhad — W • E Africa & S Africa • 500 kW / Mideast & E Africa • 500 kW
**RUSSIA**
  †VOICE OF RUSSIA, Samara — S • S Europe • 250 kW
**SPAIN**
  †R EXTERIOR ESPANA, Via Costa Rica — W Su • C America & S America • 100 kW / W Sa/Su • C America & S America • 100 kW
**USA**
  †VOA, Via Philippines — S • S Asia • 250 kW
  †VOA, Via Udon Thani, Thailand — S • S Asia • 250 kW

**15130**  **AUSTRALIA**
  †HCJB AUSTRALIA, Kununurra — S Asia • PROJECTED • 100 kW
**CHINA**
  CHINA RADIO INTL, Beijing — S • Europe • 300 kW
**CHINA (TAIWAN)**
(con'd)  †R TAIPEI INTL — Australasia

| | 0 1 2 3 4 5 6 7 8 9 10 11 12 13 14 15 16 17 18 19 20 21 22 23 24 |
|---|---|

ENGLISH ▬  ARABIC ⋙  CHINESE □□□  FRENCH ═  GERMAN ▬  RUSSIAN ══  SPANISH ══  OTHER ▬

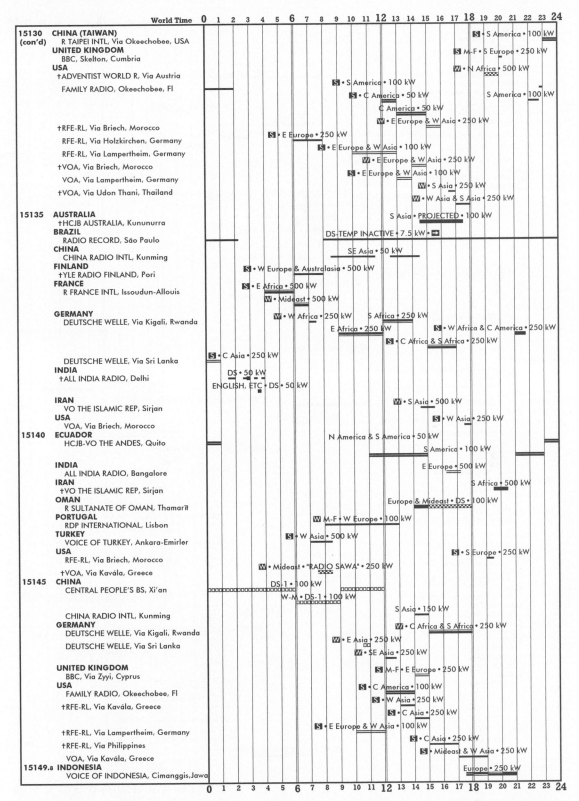

**World Time** 0 1 2 3 4 5 6 7 8 9 10 11 12 13 14 15 16 17 18 19 20 21 22 23 24

**15130** **CHINA (TAIWAN)**
(con'd)  R TAIPEI INTL, Via Okeechobee, USA — S · S America · 100 kW
**UNITED KINGDOM**
  BBC, Skelton, Cumbria — S · M-F · S Europe · 250 kW
**USA**
  †ADVENTIST WORLD R, Via Austria — W · N Africa · 500 kW
  — S · S America · 100 kW
  FAMILY RADIO, Okeechobee, Fl — S · C America · 50 kW — S America · 100 kW
  — C America · 50 kW
  — W · E Europe & W Asia · 250 kW
  †RFE-RL, Via Briech, Morocco — S · E Europe · 250 kW
  RFE-RL, Via Holzkirchen, Germany — S · E Europe & W Asia · 100 kW
  RFE-RL, Via Lampertheim, Germany — W · E Europe & W Asia · 250 kW
  †VOA, Via Briech, Morocco — S · E Europe & W Asia · 100 kW
  VOA, Via Lampertheim, Germany — W · S Asia · 250 kW
  †VOA, Via Udon Thani, Thailand — W · W Asia & S Asia · 250 kW

**15135** **AUSTRALIA**
  †HCJB AUSTRALIA, Kununurra — S Asia · PROJECTED · 100 kW
**BRAZIL**
  RADIO RECORD, São Paulo — DS · TEMP INACTIVE · 7.5 kW · ➡
**CHINA**
  CHINA RADIO INTL, Kunming — SE Asia · 50 kW
**FINLAND**
  †YLE RADIO FINLAND, Pori — S · W Europe & Australasia · 500 kW
**FRANCE**
  R FRANCE INTL, Issoudun-Allouis — S · E Africa · 500 kW
  — W · Mideast · 500 kW
**GERMANY**
  DEUTSCHE WELLE, Via Kigali, Rwanda — W · W Africa · 250 kW — S Africa · 250 kW
  — E Africa · 250 kW
  — W · W Africa & C America · 250 kW
  — S · C Africa & S Africa · 250 kW
  DEUTSCHE WELLE, Via Sri Lanka — S · C Asia · 250 kW
**INDIA**
  †ALL INDIA RADIO, Delhi — DS · 50 kW
  ENGLISH, ETC · DS · 50 kW
**IRAN**
  VO THE ISLAMIC REP, Sirjan — W · S Asia · 500 kW
**USA**
  VOA, Via Briech, Morocco — S · W Asia · 250 kW
**15140** **ECUADOR**
  HCJB-VO THE ANDES, Quito — N America & S America · 50 kW
  — S America · 100 kW
**INDIA**
  ALL INDIA RADIO, Bangalore — E Europe · 500 kW
**IRAN**
  †VO THE ISLAMIC REP, Sirjan — S Africa · 500 kW
**OMAN**
  R SULTANATE OF OMAN, Thamarīt — Europe & Mideast · DS · 100 kW
**PORTUGAL**
  RDP INTERNATIONAL, Lisbon — W · M-F · W Europe · 100 kW
**TURKEY**
  VOICE OF TURKEY, Ankara-Emirler — S · W Asia · 500 kW
**USA**
  RFE-RL, Via Briech, Morocco — S · S Europe · 250 kW
  †VOA, Via Kavála, Greece — W · Mideast · "RADIO SAWA" · 250 kW
**15145** **CHINA**
  CENTRAL PEOPLE'S BS, Xi'an — DS-1 · 100 kW
  W-M · DS-1 · 100 kW
  — S Asia · 150 kW
  CHINA RADIO INTL, Kunming — W · C Africa & S Africa · 250 kW
**GERMANY**
  DEUTSCHE WELLE, Via Kigali, Rwanda — W · E Asia · 250 kW
  DEUTSCHE WELLE, Via Sri Lanka — W · SE Asia · 250 kW
**UNITED KINGDOM**
  BBC, Via Zyyi, Cyprus — S · M-F · E Europe · 250 kW
**USA**
  FAMILY RADIO, Okeechobee, Fl — S · C America · 100 kW
  †RFE-RL, Via Kavála, Greece — S · W Asia · 250 kW
  — S · C Asia · 250 kW
  †RFE-RL, Via Lampertheim, Germany — S · E Europe & W Asia · 100 kW
  †RFE-RL, Via Philippines — S · C Asia · 250 kW
  VOA, Via Kavála, Greece — S · Mideast & W Asia · 250 kW
**15149.8** **INDONESIA**
  VOICE OF INDONESIA, Cimanggis, Jawa — Europe · 250 kW

0 1 2 3 4 5 6 7 8 9 10 11 12 13 14 15 16 17 18 19 20 21 22 23 24

SEASONAL S OR W    1-HR TIMESHIFT MIDYEAR ⬅ OR ➡    JAMMING / OR ∧    EARLIEST HEARD ◁    LATEST HEARD ▷    NEW FOR 2003 †

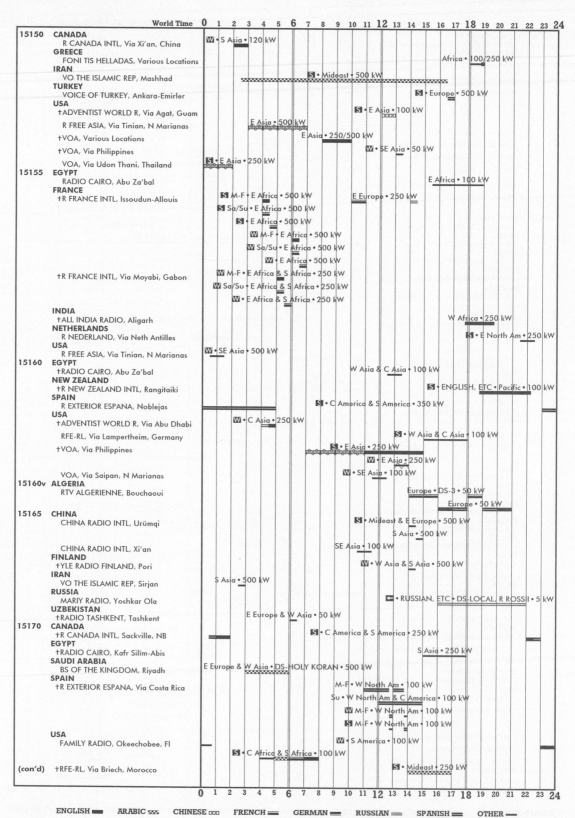

| | | World Time | 0 | 1 | 2 | 3 | 4 | 5 | 6 | 7 | 8 | 9 | 10 | 11 | 12 | 13 | 14 | 15 | 16 | 17 | 18 | 19 | 20 | 21 | 22 | 23 | 24 |

15150 **CANADA**
  R CANADA INTL, Via Xi'an, China — **W** • S Asia • 120 kW
**GREECE**
  FONI TIS HELLADAS, Various Locations — Africa • 100/250 kW
**IRAN**
  VO THE ISLAMIC REP, Mashhad — **S** • Mideast • 500 kW
**TURKEY**
  VOICE OF TURKEY, Ankara-Emirler — **S** • Europe • 500 kW
**USA**
  †ADVENTIST WORLD R, Via Agat, Guam — **S** • E Asia • 100 kW
  R FREE ASIA, Via Tinian, N Marianas — E Asia • 500 kW
  †VOA, Various Locations — E Asia • 250/500 kW
  †VOA, Via Philippines — **W** • SE Asia • 50 kW
  VOA, Via Udon Thani, Thailand — **S** • E Asia • 250 kW
15155 **EGYPT**
  RADIO CAIRO, Abu Za'bal — E Africa • 100 kW
**FRANCE**
  †R FRANCE INTL, Issoudun-Allouis — **S** • M-F • E Africa • 500 kW
  — E Europe • 250 kW
  — **S** • Sa/Su • E Africa • 500 kW
  — **S** • E Africa • 500 kW
  — **W** • M-F • E Africa • 500 kW
  — **W** • Sa/Su • E Africa • 500 kW
  — **W** • E Africa • 500 kW
  †R FRANCE INTL, Via Moyabi, Gabon — **W** • M-F • E Africa & S Africa • 250 kW
  — **W** • Sa/Su • E Africa & S Africa • 250 kW
  — **W** • E Africa & S Africa • 250 kW
**INDIA**
  †ALL INDIA RADIO, Aligarh — W Africa • 250 kW
**NETHERLANDS**
  R NEDERLAND, Via Neth Antilles — **S** • E North Am • 250 kW
**USA**
  R FREE ASIA, Via Tinian, N Marianas — **W** • SE Asia • 500 kW
15160 **EGYPT**
  †RADIO CAIRO, Abu Za'bal — W Asia & C Asia • 100 kW
**NEW ZEALAND**
  †R NEW ZEALAND INTL, Rangitaiki — **S** • ENGLISH, ETC • Pacific • 100 kW
**SPAIN**
  R EXTERIOR ESPANA, Noblejas — **S** • C America & S America • 350 kW
**USA**
  †ADVENTIST WORLD R, Via Abu Dhabi — **W** • C Asia • 250 kW
  RFE-RL, Via Lampertheim, Germany — **S** • W Asia & C Asia • 100 kW
  †VOA, Via Philippines — **S** • E Asia • 250 kW
  — **W** • E Asia • 250 kW
  VOA, Via Saipan, N Marianas — **W** • SE Asia • 100 kW
15160v **ALGERIA**
  RTV ALGERIENNE, Bouchaoui — Europe • DS-3 • 50 kW
  — Europe • 50 kW
15165 **CHINA**
  CHINA RADIO INTL, Urümqi — **S** • Mideast & E Europe • 500 kW
  — S Asia • 500 kW
  CHINA RADIO INTL, Xi'an — SE Asia • 100 kW
**FINLAND**
  †YLE RADIO FINLAND, Pori — **W** • W Asia & S Asia • 500 kW
**IRAN**
  VO THE ISLAMIC REP, Sirjan — S Asia • 500 kW
**RUSSIA**
  MARIY RADIO, Yoshkar Ola — **□** • RUSSIAN, ETC • DS-LOCAL, R ROSSII • 5 kW
**UZBEKISTAN**
  †RADIO TASHKENT, Tashkent — E Europe & W Asia • 50 kW
15170 **CANADA**
  †R CANADA INTL, Sackville, NB — **S** • C America & S America • 250 kW
**EGYPT**
  †RADIO CAIRO, Kafr Silim-Abis — S Asia • 250 kW
**SAUDI ARABIA**
  BS OF THE KINGDOM, Riyadh — E Europe & W Asia • DS-HOLY KORAN • 500 kW
**SPAIN**
  †R EXTERIOR ESPANA, Via Costa Rica — M-F • W North Am • 100 kW
  — Su • W North Am & C America • 100 kW
  — **W** • M-F • W North Am • 100 kW
  — **S** • M-F • W North Am • 100 kW
**USA**
  FAMILY RADIO, Okeechobee, Fl — **W** • S America • 100 kW
  — **S** • C Africa & S Africa • 100 kW
(con'd)  †RFE-RL, Via Briech, Morocco — **S** • Mideast • 250 kW

| | | | 0 | 1 | 2 | 3 | 4 | 5 | 6 | 7 | 8 | 9 | 10 | 11 | 12 | 13 | 14 | 15 | 16 | 17 | 18 | 19 | 20 | 21 | 22 | 23 | 24 |

ENGLISH ▬▬ ARABIC ▨▨ CHINESE ▫▫▫ FRENCH ▬▬ GERMAN ▬▬ RUSSIAN ══ SPANISH ▬▬ OTHER ──

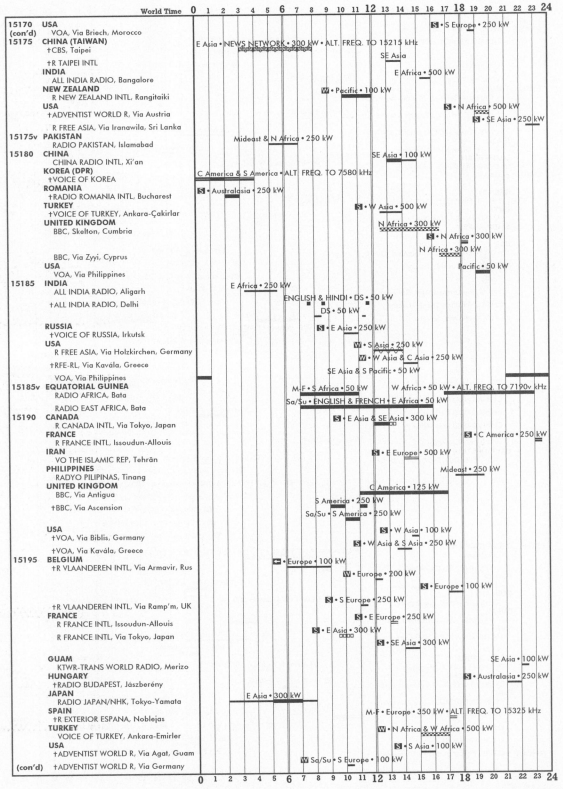

| | World Time | 0 1 2 3 4 5 6 7 8 9 10 11 12 13 14 15 16 17 18 19 20 21 22 23 24 |
|---|---|---|
| **15170** (con'd) | **USA** | |
| | VOA, Via Briech, Morocco | S • S Europe • 250 kW |
| **15175** | **CHINA (TAIWAN)** | |
| | †CBS, Taipei | E Asia • NEWS NETWORK • 300 kW • ALT. FREQ. TO 15215 kHz |
| | †R TAIPEI INTL | SE Asia |
| | **INDIA** | |
| | ALL INDIA RADIO, Bangalore | E Africa • 500 kW |
| | **NEW ZEALAND** | |
| | R NEW ZEALAND INTL, Rangitaiki | W • Pacific • 100 kW |
| | **USA** | |
| | †ADVENTIST WORLD R, Via Austria | S • N Africa • 500 kW |
| | R FREE ASIA, Via Iranawila, Sri Lanka | S • SE Asia • 250 kW |
| **15175v** | **PAKISTAN** | |
| | RADIO PAKISTAN, Islamabad | Mideast & N Africa • 250 kW |
| **15180** | **CHINA** | |
| | CHINA RADIO INTL, Xi'an | SE Asia • 100 kW |
| | **KOREA (DPR)** | |
| | †VOICE OF KOREA | C America & S America • ALT. FREQ. TO 7580 kHz |
| | **ROMANIA** | |
| | †RADIO ROMANIA INTL, Bucharest | S • Australasia • 250 kW |
| | **TURKEY** | |
| | †VOICE OF TURKEY, Ankara-Çakirlar | S • W Asia • 500 kW |
| | **UNITED KINGDOM** | |
| | BBC, Skelton, Cumbria | N Africa • 300 kW |
| | | S • N Africa • 300 kW |
| | BBC, Via Zyyi, Cyprus | N Africa • 300 kW |
| | **USA** | |
| | VOA, Via Philippines | Pacific • 50 kW |
| **15185** | **INDIA** | |
| | ALL INDIA RADIO, Aligarh | E Africa • 250 kW |
| | †ALL INDIA RADIO, Delhi | ENGLISH & HINDI • DS • 50 kW |
| | | DS • 50 kW |
| | **RUSSIA** | |
| | †VOICE OF RUSSIA, Irkutsk | S • E Asia • 250 kW |
| | **USA** | |
| | R FREE ASIA, Via Holzkirchen, Germany | W • S Asia • 250 kW |
| | †RFE-RL, Via Kavála, Greece | W • W Asia & C Asia • 250 kW |
| | VOA, Via Philippines | SE Asia & S Pacific • 50 kW |
| **15185v** | **EQUATORIAL GUINEA** | |
| | RADIO AFRICA, Bata | M-F • S Africa • 50 kW W Africa • 50 kW • ALT. FREQ. TO 7190v kHz |
| | RADIO EAST AFRICA, Bata | Sa/Su • ENGLISH & FRENCH • E Africa • 50 kW |
| **15190** | **CANADA** | |
| | R CANADA INTL, Via Tokyo, Japan | S • E Asia & SE Asia • 300 kW |
| | **FRANCE** | |
| | R FRANCE INTL, Issoudun-Allouis | S • C America • 250 kW |
| | **IRAN** | |
| | VO THE ISLAMIC REP, Tehrān | S • E Europe • 500 kW |
| | **PHILIPPINES** | |
| | RADYO PILIPINAS, Tinang | Mideast • 250 kW |
| | **UNITED KINGDOM** | |
| | BBC, Via Antigua | C America • 125 kW |
| | †BBC, Via Ascension | S America • 250 kW |
| | | Sa/Su • S America • 250 kW |
| | **USA** | |
| | †VOA, Via Biblis, Germany | S • W Asia • 100 kW |
| | †VOA, Via Kavála, Greece | S • W Asia & S Asia • 250 kW |
| **15195** | **BELGIUM** | |
| | †R VLAANDEREN INTL, Via Armavir, Rus | ← • Europe • 100 kW |
| | | W • Europe • 200 kW |
| | | S • Europe • 100 kW |
| | †R VLAANDEREN INTL, Via Ramp'm, UK | S • S Europe • 250 kW |
| | **FRANCE** | |
| | R FRANCE INTL, Issoudun-Allouis | S • E Europe • 250 kW |
| | R FRANCE INTL, Via Tokyo, Japan | S • E Asia • 300 kW |
| | | S • SE Asia • 300 kW |
| | **GUAM** | |
| | KTWR-TRANS WORLD RADIO, Merizo | SE Asia • 100 kW |
| | **HUNGARY** | |
| | †RADIO BUDAPEST, Jászberény | S • Australasia • 250 kW |
| | **JAPAN** | |
| | RADIO JAPAN/NHK, Tokyo-Yamata | E Asia • 300 kW |
| | **SPAIN** | |
| | †R EXTERIOR ESPANA, Noblejas | M-F • Europe • 350 kW • ALT. FREQ. TO 15325 kHz |
| | **TURKEY** | |
| | VOICE OF TURKEY, Ankara-Emirler | W • N Africa & W Africa • 500 kW |
| | **USA** | |
| | †ADVENTIST WORLD R, Via Agat, Guam | S • S Asia • 100 kW |
| (con'd) | †ADVENTIST WORLD R, Via Germany | W Sa/Su • S Europe • 100 kW |

| 0 1 2 3 4 5 6 7 8 9 10 11 12 13 14 15 16 17 18 19 20 21 22 23 24 |
|---|

SEASONAL S OR W    1-HR TIMESHIFT MIDYEAR ← OR →    JAMMING / OR ∧    EARLIEST HEARD ◁    LATEST HEARD ▷    NEW FOR 2003 †

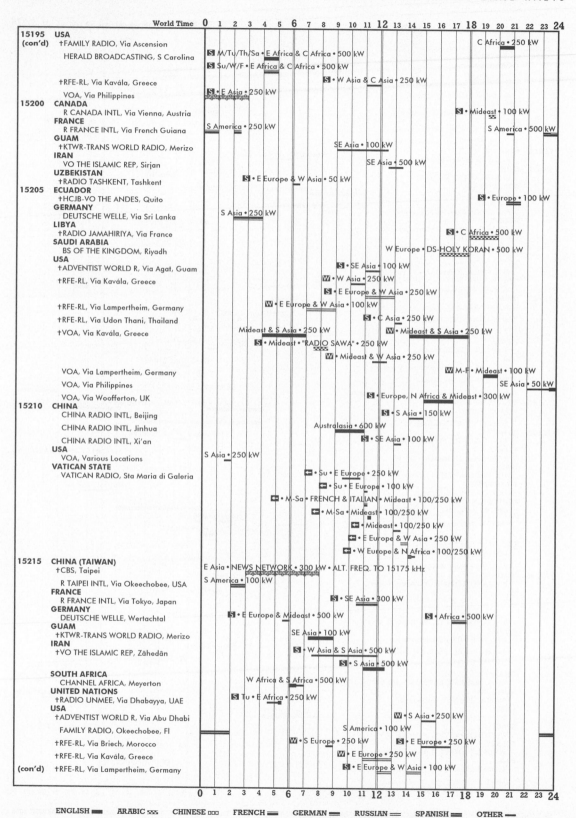

| World Time | 0 | 1 | 2 | 3 | 4 | 5 | 6 | 7 | 8 | 9 | 10 | 11 | 12 | 13 | 14 | 15 | 16 | 17 | 18 | 19 | 20 | 21 | 22 | 23 | 24 |

**15195 USA (con'd)**
- †FAMILY RADIO, Via Ascension — C Africa • 250 kW
- HERALD BROADCASTING, S Carolina — S • M/Tu/Th/Sa • E Africa & C Africa • 500 kW; S • Su/W/F • E Africa & C Africa • 500 kW
- †RFE-RL, Via Kavála, Greece — S • W Asia & C Asia • 250 kW
- VOA, Via Philippines — S • E Asia • 250 kW

**15200 CANADA**
- R CANADA INTL, Via Vienna, Austria — S • Mideast • 100 kW

**FRANCE**
- R FRANCE INTL, Via French Guiana — S America • 250 kW; S America • 500 kW

**GUAM**
- †KTWR-TRANS WORLD RADIO, Merizo — SE Asia • 100 kW

**IRAN**
- VO THE ISLAMIC REP, Sirjan — SE Asia • 500 kW

**UZBEKISTAN**
- †RADIO TASHKENT, Tashkent — S • E Europe & W Asia • 50 kW

**15205 ECUADOR**
- †HCJB-VO THE ANDES, Quito — S • Europe • 100 kW

**GERMANY**
- DEUTSCHE WELLE, Via Sri Lanka — S Asia • 250 kW

**LIBYA**
- †RADIO JAMAHIRIYA, Via France — S • C Africa • 500 kW

**SAUDI ARABIA**
- BS OF THE KINGDOM, Riyadh — W Europe • DS-HOLY KORAN • 500 kW

**USA**
- †ADVENTIST WORLD R, Via Agat, Guam — S • SE Asia • 100 kW
- †RFE-RL, Via Kavála, Greece — W • W Asia • 250 kW; S • E Europe & W Asia • 250 kW
- †RFE-RL, Via Lampertheim, Germany — W • E Europe & W Asia • 100 kW
- †RFE-RL, Via Udon Thani, Thailand — S • C Asia • 250 kW
- †VOA, Via Kavála, Greece — Mideast & S Asia • 250 kW; W • Mideast & S Asia • 250 kW; S • Mideast • "RADIO SAWA" • 250 kW; W • Mideast & W Asia • 250 kW
- VOA, Via Lampertheim, Germany — W • M-F • Mideast • 100 kW
- VOA, Via Philippines — SE Asia • 50 kW
- VOA, Via Woofferton, UK — S • Europe, N Africa & Mideast • 300 kW

**15210 CHINA**
- CHINA RADIO INTL, Beijing — S • S Asia • 150 kW
- CHINA RADIO INTL, Jinhua — Australasia • 600 kW
- CHINA RADIO INTL, Xi'an — S • SE Asia • 100 kW

**USA**
- VOA, Various Locations — S Asia • 250 kW

**VATICAN STATE**
- VATICAN RADIO, Sta Maria di Galeria — • Su • E Europe • 250 kW; • Su • E Europe • 100 kW; • M-Sa • FRENCH & ITALIAN • Mideast • 100/250 kW; • M-Sa • Mideast • 100/250 kW; Mideast • 100/250 kW; • E Europe & W Asia • 250 kW; • W Europe & N Africa • 100/250 kW

**15215 CHINA (TAIWAN)**
- †CBS, Taipei — E Asia • NEWS NETWORK • 300 kW • ALT. FREQ. TO 15175 kHz
- R TAIPEI INTL, Via Okeechobee, USA — S America • 100 kW

**FRANCE**
- R FRANCE INTL, Via Tokyo, Japan — S • SE Asia • 300 kW

**GERMANY**
- DEUTSCHE WELLE, Wertachtal — S • E Europe & Mideast • 500 kW; S • Africa • 500 kW

**GUAM**
- †KTWR-TRANS WORLD RADIO, Merizo — SE Asia • 100 kW

**IRAN**
- †VO THE ISLAMIC REP, Zāhedān — S • W Asia & S Asia • 500 kW; S • S Asia • 500 kW

**SOUTH AFRICA**
- CHANNEL AFRICA, Meyerton — W Africa & S Africa • 500 kW

**UNITED NATIONS**
- †RADIO UNMEE, Via Dhabayya, UAE — S • Tu • E Africa • 250 kW

**USA**
- †ADVENTIST WORLD R, Via Abu Dhabi — W • S Asia • 250 kW
- FAMILY RADIO, Okeechobee, Fl — S America • 100 kW
- †RFE-RL, Via Briech, Morocco — W • S Europe • 250 kW; S • E Europe • 250 kW
- †RFE-RL, Via Kavála, Greece — W • E Europe • 250 kW
- (con'd) †RFE-RL, Via Lampertheim, Germany — S • E Europe & W Asia • 100 kW

| | 0 | 1 | 2 | 3 | 4 | 5 | 6 | 7 | 8 | 9 | 10 | 11 | 12 | 13 | 14 | 15 | 16 | 17 | 18 | 19 | 20 | 21 | 22 | 23 | 24 |

ENGLISH ▬ ARABIC ▨ CHINESE ▢▢▢ FRENCH ▬ GERMAN ▬ RUSSIAN ═ SPANISH ▭ OTHER ▬

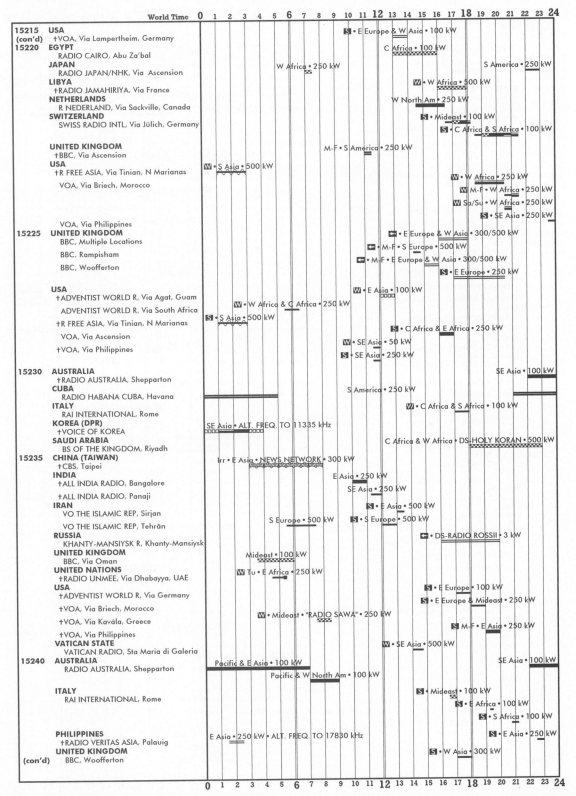

| World Time | 0 1 2 3 4 5 6 7 8 9 10 11 12 13 14 15 16 17 18 19 20 21 22 23 24 |
|---|---|
| **15215** **USA** | |
| (con'd) †VOA, Via Lampertheim, Germany | S • E Europe & W Asia • 100 kW |
| **15220** **EGYPT** | |
| RADIO CAIRO, Abu Za'bal | C Africa • 100 kW |
| **JAPAN** | |
| RADIO JAPAN/NHK, Via Ascension | W Africa • 250 kW          S America • 250 kW |
| **LIBYA** | |
| †RADIO JAMAHIRIYA, Via France | W • W Africa • 500 kW |
| **NETHERLANDS** | |
| R NEDERLAND, Via Sackville, Canada | W North Am • 250 kW |
| **SWITZERLAND** | |
| SWISS RADIO INTL, Via Jülich, Germany | S • Mideast • 100 kW |
| | S • C Africa & S Africa • 100 kW |
| **UNITED KINGDOM** | |
| †BBC, Via Ascension | M-F • S America • 250 kW |
| **USA** | |
| †R FREE ASIA, Via Tinian, N Marianas | W • S Asia • 500 kW |
| VOA, Via Briech, Morocco | W • W Africa • 250 kW |
| | W • M-F • W Africa • 250 kW |
| | W Sa/Su • W Africa • 250 kW |
| | S • SE Asia • 250 kW |
| VOA, Via Philippines | |
| **15225** **UNITED KINGDOM** | |
| BBC, Multiple Locations | ⮂ • E Europe & W Asia • 300/500 kW |
| BBC, Rampisham | ⮂ • M-F • S Europe • 500 kW |
| BBC, Woofferton | ⮂ • M-F • E Europe & W Asia • 300/500 kW |
| | S • E Europe • 250 kW |
| **USA** | |
| †ADVENTIST WORLD R, Via Agat, Guam | W • E Asia • 100 kW |
| ADVENTIST WORLD R, Via South Africa | W • W Africa & C Africa • 250 kW |
| †R FREE ASIA, Via Tinian, N Marianas | S • S Asia • 500 kW |
| VOA, Via Ascension | S • C Africa & E Africa • 250 kW |
| †VOA, Via Philippines | W • SE Asia • 50 kW |
| | S • SE Asia • 250 kW |
| **15230** **AUSTRALIA** | |
| †RADIO AUSTRALIA, Shepparton | SE Asia • 100 kW |
| **CUBA** | |
| RADIO HABANA CUBA, Havana | S America • 250 kW |
| **ITALY** | |
| RAI INTERNATIONAL, Rome | W • C Africa & S Africa • 100 kW |
| **KOREA (DPR)** | |
| †VOICE OF KOREA | SE Asia • ALT. FREQ. TO 11335 kHz |
| **SAUDI ARABIA** | |
| BS OF THE KINGDOM, Riyadh | C Africa & W Africa • DS-HOLY KORAN • 500 kW |
| **15235** **CHINA (TAIWAN)** | |
| †CBS, Taipei | Irr • E Asia • NEWS NETWORK • 300 kW |
| **INDIA** | |
| †ALL INDIA RADIO, Bangalore | E Asia • 250 kW |
| †ALL INDIA RADIO, Panaji | SE Asia • 250 kW |
| **IRAN** | |
| VO THE ISLAMIC REP, Sirjan | S • E Asia • 500 kW |
| VO THE ISLAMIC REP, Tehrān | S Europe • 500 kW    S • S Europe • 500 kW |
| **RUSSIA** | |
| KHANTY-MANSIYSK R, Khanty-Mansiysk | ⮂ • DS-RADIO ROSSII • 3 kW |
| **UNITED KINGDOM** | |
| BBC, Via Oman | Mideast • 100 kW |
| **UNITED NATIONS** | |
| †RADIO UNMEE, Via Dhabayya, UAE | W Tu • E Africa • 250 kW |
| **USA** | |
| †ADVENTIST WORLD R, Via Germany | S • E Europe • 100 kW |
| †VOA, Via Briech, Morocco | S • E Europe & Mideast • 250 kW |
| †VOA, Via Kavála, Greece | W • Mideast • "RADIO SAWA" • 250 kW |
| †VOA, Via Philippines | S M-F • E Asia • 250 kW |
| **VATICAN STATE** | |
| VATICAN RADIO, Sta Maria di Galeria | W • SE Asia • 500 kW |
| **15240** **AUSTRALIA** | |
| RADIO AUSTRALIA, Shepparton | Pacific & E Asia • 100 kW |
| | Pacific & W North Am • 100 kW |
| | SE Asia • 100 kW |
| **ITALY** | |
| RAI INTERNATIONAL, Rome | S • Mideast • 100 kW |
| | S • E Africa • 100 kW |
| | S • S Africa • 100 kW |
| **PHILIPPINES** | |
| †RADIO VERITAS ASIA, Palauig | E Asia • 250 kW • ALT. FREQ. TO 17830 kHz |
| | S • E Asia • 250 kW |
| **UNITED KINGDOM** | |
| (con'd) BBC, Woofferton | S • W Asia • 300 kW |

SEASONAL S OR W    1-HR TIMESHIFT MIDYEAR ⮂ OR ⮂    JAMMING / OR /\    EARLIEST HEARD ◁    LATEST HEARD ▷    NEW FOR 2003 †

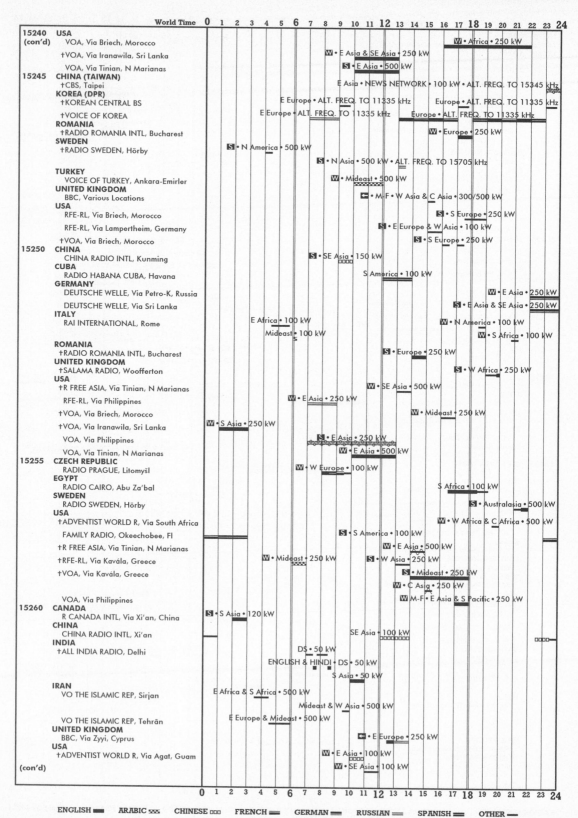

| World Time | | |
|---|---|---|
| **15240** USA | | |
| (con'd) VOA, Via Briech, Morocco | | W • Africa • 250 kW |
| †VOA, Via Iranawila, Sri Lanka | | W • E Asia & SE Asia • 250 kW |
| VOA, Via Tinian, N Marianas | | S • E Asia • 500 kW |
| **15245** CHINA (TAIWAN) | | |
| †CBS, Taipei | | E Asia • NEWS NETWORK • 100 kW • ALT. FREQ. TO 15345 kHz |
| KOREA (DPR) | | |
| †KOREAN CENTRAL BS | | E Europe • ALT. FREQ. TO 11335 kHz    Europe • ALT. FREQ. TO 11335 kHz |
| †VOICE OF KOREA | | E Europe • ALT. FREQ. TO 11335 kHz    Europe • ALT. FREQ. TO 11335 kHz |
| ROMANIA | | |
| †RADIO ROMANIA INTL, Bucharest | | W • Europe • 250 kW |
| SWEDEN | | |
| †RADIO SWEDEN, Hörby | | S • N America • 500 kW |
| TURKEY | | S • N Asia • 500 kW • ALT. FREQ. TO 15705 kHz |
| VOICE OF TURKEY, Ankara-Emirler | | W • Mideast • 500 kW |
| UNITED KINGDOM | | |
| BBC, Various Locations | | ← • M-F • W Asia & C Asia • 300/500 kW |
| USA | | |
| RFE-RL, Via Briech, Morocco | | S • S Europe • 250 kW |
| RFE-RL, Via Lampertheim, Germany | | S • E Europe & W Asia • 100 kW |
| †VOA, Via Briech, Morocco | | S • S Europe • 250 kW |
| **15250** CHINA | | |
| CHINA RADIO INTL, Kunming | | S • SE Asia • 150 kW |
| CUBA | | |
| RADIO HABANA CUBA, Havana | | S America • 100 kW |
| GERMANY | | |
| DEUTSCHE WELLE, Via Petro-K, Russia | | W • E Asia • 250 kW |
| DEUTSCHE WELLE, Via Sri Lanka | | S • E Asia & SE Asia • 250 kW |
| ITALY | | |
| RAI INTERNATIONAL, Rome | | E Africa • 100 kW    W • N America • 100 kW |
| | | Mideast • 100 kW    W • S Africa • 100 kW |
| ROMANIA | | |
| †RADIO ROMANIA INTL, Bucharest | | S • Europe • 250 kW |
| UNITED KINGDOM | | |
| †SALAMA RADIO, Woofferton | | S • W Africa • 250 kW |
| USA | | |
| †R FREE ASIA, Via Tinian, N Marianas | | W • SE Asia • 500 kW |
| RFE-RL, Via Philippines | | W • E Asia • 250 kW |
| †VOA, Via Briech, Morocco | | W • Mideast • 250 kW |
| †VOA, Via Iranawila, Sri Lanka | | W • S Asia • 250 kW |
| VOA, Via Philippines | | S • E Asia • 250 kW |
| VOA, Via Tinian, N Marianas | | W • E Asia • 500 kW |
| **15255** CZECH REPUBLIC | | |
| RADIO PRAGUE, Litomyšl | | W • W Europe • 100 kW |
| EGYPT | | |
| RADIO CAIRO, Abu Za'bal | | S Africa • 100 kW |
| SWEDEN | | |
| RADIO SWEDEN, Hörby | | S • Australasia • 500 kW |
| USA | | |
| †ADVENTIST WORLD R, Via South Africa | | W • W Africa & C Africa • 500 kW |
| FAMILY RADIO, Okeechobee, Fl | | S • S America • 100 kW |
| †R FREE ASIA, Via Tinian, N Marianas | | W • E Asia • 500 kW |
| †RFE-RL, Via Kavála, Greece | | W • Mideast • 250 kW    S • W Asia • 250 kW |
| †VOA, Via Kavála, Greece | | S • Mideast • 250 kW |
| VOA, Via Philippines | | W • C Asia • 250 kW |
| | | W • M-F • E Asia & S Pacific • 250 kW |
| **15260** CANADA | | |
| R CANADA INTL, Via Xi'an, China | | S • S Asia • 120 kW |
| CHINA | | |
| CHINA RADIO INTL, Xi'an | | SE Asia • 100 kW |
| INDIA | | |
| †ALL INDIA RADIO, Delhi | | DS • 50 kW |
| | | ENGLISH & HINDI • DS • 50 kW |
| | | S Asia • 50 kW |
| IRAN | | |
| VO THE ISLAMIC REP, Sirjan | | E Africa & S Africa • 500 kW |
| | | Mideast & W Asia • 500 kW |
| VO THE ISLAMIC REP, Tehrān | | E Europe & Mideast • 500 kW |
| UNITED KINGDOM | | |
| BBC, Via Zyyi, Cyprus | | ← • E Europe • 250 kW |
| USA | | |
| †ADVENTIST WORLD R, Via Agat, Guam | | W • E Asia • 100 kW |
| (con'd) | | W • SE Asia • 100 kW |

ENGLISH ▬▬  ARABIC ≋≋  CHINESE □□□  FRENCH ▬▬  GERMAN ▬▬  RUSSIAN ══  SPANISH ══  OTHER ▬

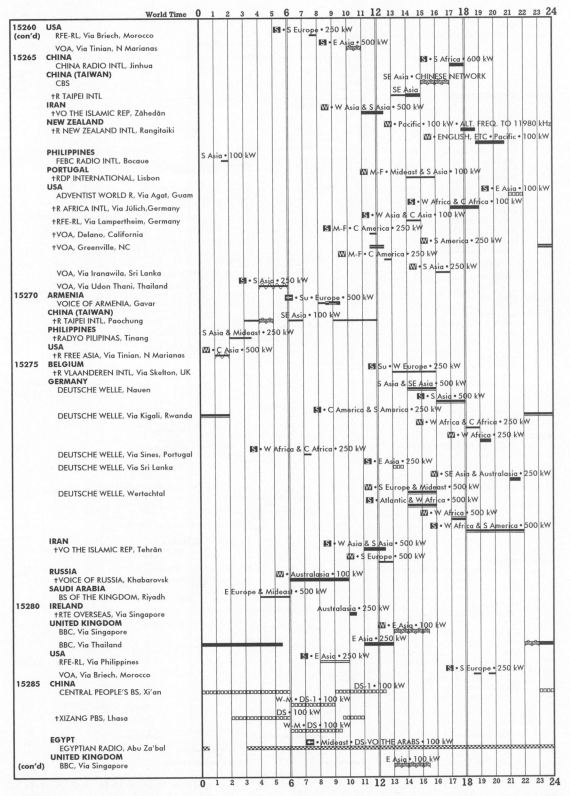

World Time

**15260 USA**
(con'd)
RFE-RL, Via Briech, Morocco — 🅂 S Europe • 250 kW
VOA, Via Tinian, N Marianas — 🅂 E Asia • 500 kW
**15265 CHINA**
CHINA RADIO INTL, Jinhua — 🅂 S Africa • 600 kW
**CHINA (TAIWAN)**
CBS — SE Asia • CHINESE NETWORK
†R TAIPEI INTL — SE Asia
**IRAN**
†VO THE ISLAMIC REP, Zāhedān — 🆆 • W Asia & S Asia • 500 kW
**NEW ZEALAND**
†R NEW ZEALAND INTL, Rangitaiki — 🆆 • Pacific • 100 kW • ALT. FREQ. TO 11980 kHz
🆆 • ENGLISH, ETC • Pacific • 100 kW
**PHILIPPINES**
FEBC RADIO INTL, Bocaue — S Asia • 100 kW
**PORTUGAL**
†RDP INTERNATIONAL, Lisbon — 🆆 M-F • Mideast & S Asia • 100 kW
**USA**
ADVENTIST WORLD R, Via Agat, Guam — 🅂 E Asia • 100 kW
†R AFRICA INTL, Via Jülich, Germany — 🅂 • W Africa & C Africa • 100 kW
†RFE-RL, Via Lampertheim, Germany — 🅂 • W Asia & C Asia • 100 kW
†VOA, Delano, California — 🅂 M-F • C America • 250 kW
†VOA, Greenville, NC — 🆆 • S America • 250 kW
🆆 M-F • C America • 250 kW
VOA, Via Iranawila, Sri Lanka — 🆆 • S Asia • 250 kW
VOA, Via Udon Thani, Thailand — 🅂 • S Asia • 250 kW
**15270 ARMENIA**
VOICE OF ARMENIA, Gavar — ⇔ • Su • Europe • 500 kW
**CHINA (TAIWAN)**
†R TAIPEI INTL, Paochung — SE Asia • 100 kW
**PHILIPPINES**
†RADYO PILIPINAS, Tinang — S Asia & Mideast • 250 kW
**USA**
†R FREE ASIA, Via Tinian, N Marianas — 🆆 • C Asia • 500 kW
**15275 BELGIUM**
†R VLAANDEREN INTL, Via Skelton, UK — 🅂 Su • W Europe • 250 kW
**GERMANY**
DEUTSCHE WELLE, Nauen — S Asia & SE Asia • 500 kW
🅂 • S Asia • 500 kW
DEUTSCHE WELLE, Via Kigali, Rwanda — 🅂 • C America & S America • 250 kW
🆆 • W Africa & C Africa • 250 kW
🆆 • W Africa • 250 kW
DEUTSCHE WELLE, Via Sines, Portugal — 🅂 • W Africa & C Africa • 250 kW
DEUTSCHE WELLE, Via Sri Lanka — 🅂 • E Asia • 250 kW
🆆 • SE Asia & Australasia • 250 kW
DEUTSCHE WELLE, Wertachtal — 🆆 • S Europe & Mideast • 500 kW
🅂 • Atlantic & W Africa • 500 kW
🆆 • W Africa • 500 kW
🅂 • W Africa & S America • 500 kW
**IRAN**
†VO THE ISLAMIC REP, Tehrān — 🅂 • W Asia & S Asia • 500 kW
🆆 • S Europe • 500 kW
**RUSSIA**
†VOICE OF RUSSIA, Khabarovsk — 🆆 • Australasia • 100 kW
**SAUDI ARABIA**
BS OF THE KINGDOM, Riyadh — E Europe & Mideast • 500 kW
**15280 IRELAND**
†RTE OVERSEAS, Via Singapore — Australasia • 250 kW
**UNITED KINGDOM**
BBC, Via Singapore — 🆆 • E Asia • 100 kW
BBC, Via Thailand — E Asia • 250 kW
**USA**
RFE-RL, Via Philippines — 🅂 • E Asia • 250 kW
VOA, Via Briech, Morocco — 🅂 • S Europe • 250 kW
**15285 CHINA**
CENTRAL PEOPLE'S BS, Xi'an — DS-1 • 100 kW
W-M • DS-1 • 100 kW
†XIZANG PBS, Lhasa — DS • 100 kW
W-M • DS • 100 kW
**EGYPT**
EGYPTIAN RADIO, Abu Za'bal — ⇔ • Mideast • DS-VO THE ARABS • 100 kW
**UNITED KINGDOM**
(con'd) BBC, Via Singapore — E Asia • 100 kW

SEASONAL 🅂 OR 🆆    1-HR TIMESHIFT MIDYEAR ⇔ OR ⇒    JAMMING / OR ∧    EARLIEST HEARD ◁    LATEST HEARD ▷    NEW FOR 2003 †

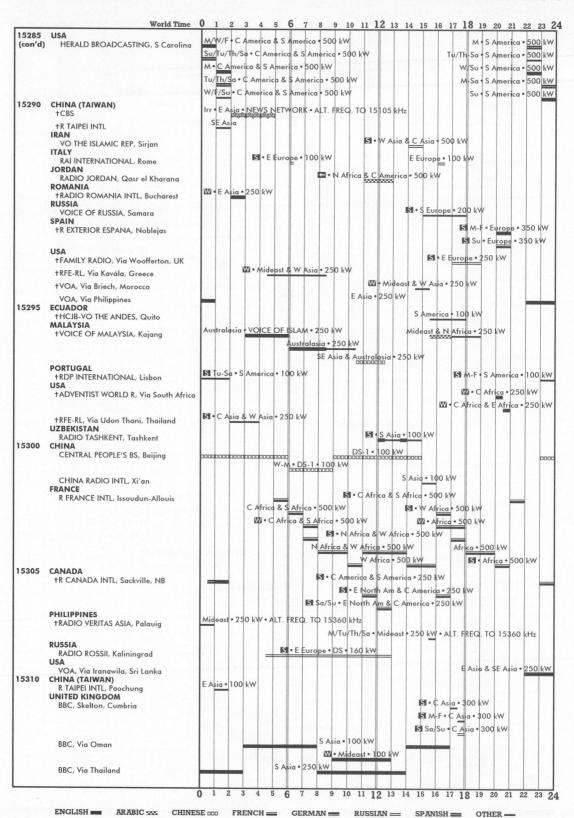

| | World Time | 0 1 2 3 4 5 6 7 8 9 10 11 12 13 14 15 16 17 18 19 20 21 22 23 24 |
|---|---|---|

**15285** USA
(con'd)   HERALD BROADCASTING, S Carolina
- M/W/F • C America & S America • 500 kW
- Su/Tu/Th/Sa • C America & S America • 500 kW
- M • C America & S America • 500 kW
- Tu/Th/Sa • C America & S America • 500 kW
- W/F/Su • C America & S America • 500 kW
- M • S America • 500 kW
- Tu/Th/Sa • S America • 500 kW
- W/Su • S America • 500 kW
- M-Sa • S America • 500 kW
- Su • S America • 500 kW

**15290** CHINA (TAIWAN)
  †CBS — Irr • E Asia • NEWS NETWORK • ALT. FREQ. TO 15105 kHz
  †R TAIPEI INTL — SE Asia
IRAN
  VO THE ISLAMIC REP, Sirjan — S • W Asia & C Asia • 500 kW
ITALY
  RAI INTERNATIONAL, Rome — S • E Europe • 100 kW ; E Europe • 100 kW
JORDAN
  RADIO JORDAN, Qasr el Kharana — • N Africa & C America • 500 kW
ROMANIA
  †RADIO ROMANIA INTL, Bucharest — W • E Asia • 250 kW
RUSSIA
  VOICE OF RUSSIA, Samara — S • S Europe • 200 kW
SPAIN
  †R EXTERIOR ESPANA, Noblejas — S • M-F • Europe • 350 kW ; S • Su • Europe • 350 kW

USA
  †FAMILY RADIO, Via Woofferton, UK — S • E Europe • 250 kW
  †RFE-RL, Via Kavála, Greece — W • Mideast & W Asia • 250 kW
  †VOA, Via Briech, Morocco — W • Mideast & W Asia • 250 kW
  VOA, Via Philippines — E Asia • 250 kW
**15295** ECUADOR
  †HCJB-VO THE ANDES, Quito — S America • 100 kW
MALAYSIA
  †VOICE OF MALAYSIA, Kajang — Australasia • VOICE OF ISLAM • 250 kW ; Mideast & N Africa • 250 kW
   — Australasia • 250 kW
   — SE Asia & Australasia • 250 kW

PORTUGAL
  †RDP INTERNATIONAL, Lisbon — S • Tu-Sa • S America • 100 kW ; S • M-F • S America • 100 kW
USA
  †ADVENTIST WORLD R, Via South Africa — W • C Africa • 250 kW ; W • C Africa & E Africa • 250 kW

  †RFE-RL, Via Udon Thani, Thailand — S • C Asia & W Asia • 250 kW
UZBEKISTAN
  RADIO TASHKENT, Tashkent — S • S Asia • 100 kW
**15300** CHINA
  CENTRAL PEOPLE'S BS, Beijing — DS-1 • 100 kW
   — W-M • DS-1 • 100 kW

  CHINA RADIO INTL, Xi'an — S Asia • 100 kW
FRANCE
  R FRANCE INTL, Issoudun-Allouis — S • C Africa & S Africa • 500 kW
   — C Africa & S Africa • 500 kW ; S • W Africa • 500 kW
   — W • C Africa & S Africa • 500 kW ; W • Africa • 500 kW
   — S • N Africa & W Africa • 500 kW
   — N Africa & W Africa • 500 kW ; Africa • 500 kW
   — W Africa • 500 kW ; S • Africa • 500 kW

**15305** CANADA
  †R CANADA INTL, Sackville, NB — S • C America & S America • 250 kW
   — S • E North Am & C America • 250 kW
   — Sa/Su • E North Am & C America • 250 kW

PHILIPPINES
  †RADIO VERITAS ASIA, Palauig — Mideast • 250 kW • ALT. FREQ. TO 15360 kHz
   — M/Tu/Th/Sa • Mideast • 250 kW • ALT. FREQ. TO 15360 kHz

RUSSIA
  RADIO ROSSII, Kaliningrad — S • E Europe • DS • 160 kW
USA
  VOA, Via Iranawila, Sri Lanka — E Asia & SE Asia • 250 kW
**15310** CHINA (TAIWAN)
  R TAIPEI INTL, Paochung — E Asia • 100 kW
UNITED KINGDOM
  BBC, Skelton, Cumbria — S • C Asia • 300 kW
   — S • M-F • C Asia • 300 kW
   — S • Sa/Su • C Asia • 300 kW

  BBC, Via Oman — S Asia • 100 kW
   — W • Mideast • 100 kW

  BBC, Via Thailand — S Asia • 250 kW

| | 0 1 2 3 4 5 6 7 8 9 10 11 12 13 14 15 16 17 18 19 20 21 22 23 24 |
|---|---|

ENGLISH ▬  ARABIC ▨  CHINESE ▢▢▢  FRENCH ▬  GERMAN ▬  RUSSIAN ═  SPANISH ▬  OTHER ▬

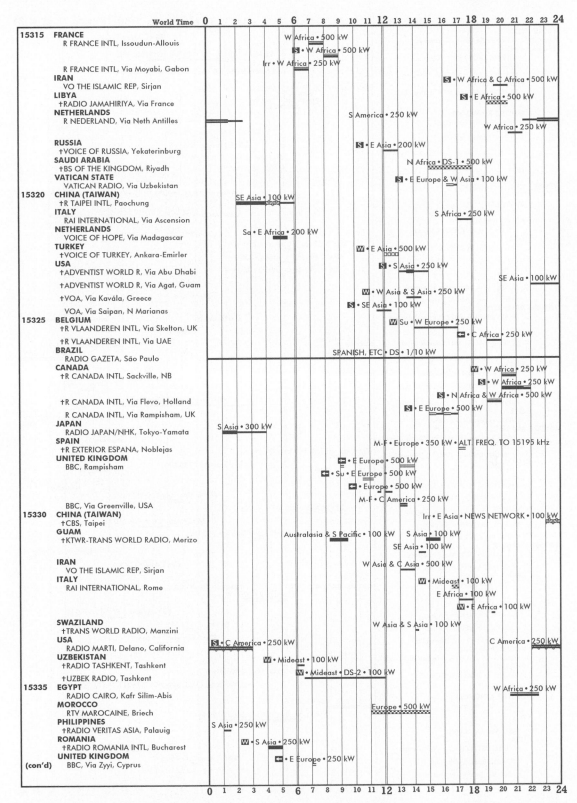

| kHz | Country / Station | Schedule (World Time 0–24) |
| --- | --- | --- |
| 15315 | **FRANCE** R FRANCE INTL, Issoudun-Allouis | W Africa • 500 kW; [S] • W Africa • 500 kW |
| | R FRANCE INTL, Via Moyabi, Gabon | Irr • W Africa • 250 kW |
| | **IRAN** VO THE ISLAMIC REP, Sirjan | [S] • W Africa & C Africa • 500 kW |
| | **LIBYA** †RADIO JAMAHIRIYA, Via France | [S] • E Africa • 500 kW |
| | **NETHERLANDS** R NEDERLAND, Via Neth Antilles | S America • 250 kW; W Africa • 250 kW |
| | **RUSSIA** †VOICE OF RUSSIA, Yekaterinburg | [S] • E Asia • 200 kW |
| | **SAUDI ARABIA** †BS OF THE KINGDOM, Riyadh | N Africa • DS-1 • 500 kW |
| | **VATICAN STATE** VATICAN RADIO, Via Uzbekistan | [S] • E Europe & W Asia • 100 kW |
| 15320 | **CHINA (TAIWAN)** †R TAIPEI INTL, Paochung | SE Asia • 100 kW |
| | **ITALY** RAI INTERNATIONAL, Via Ascension | S Africa • 250 kW |
| | **NETHERLANDS** VOICE OF HOPE, Via Madagascar | Sa • E Africa • 200 kW |
| | **TURKEY** †VOICE OF TURKEY, Ankara-Emirler | [W] • E Asia • 500 kW |
| | **USA** †ADVENTIST WORLD R, Via Abu Dhabi | [S] • S Asia • 250 kW |
| | †ADVENTIST WORLD R, Via Agat, Guam | SE Asia • 100 kW |
| | †VOA, Via Kavála, Greece | [W] • W Asia & S Asia • 250 kW |
| | VOA, Via Saipan, N Marianas | [S] • SE Asia • 100 kW |
| 15325 | **BELGIUM** †R VLAANDEREN INTL, Via Skelton, UK | [W] Su • W Europe • 250 kW |
| | †R VLAANDEREN INTL, Via UAE | ⬅ • C Africa • 250 kW |
| | **BRAZIL** RADIO GAZETA, São Paulo | SPANISH, ETC • DS • 1/10 kW |
| | **CANADA** †R CANADA INTL, Sackville, NB | [W] • W Africa • 250 kW; [S] • W Africa • 250 kW |
| | †R CANADA INTL, Via Flevo, Holland | [S] • N Africa & W Africa • 500 kW |
| | R CANADA INTL, Via Rampisham, UK | [S] • E Europe • 500 kW |
| | **JAPAN** RADIO JAPAN/NHK, Tokyo-Yamata | S Asia • 300 kW |
| | **SPAIN** †R EXTERIOR ESPANA, Noblejas | M-F • Europe • 350 kW • ALT. FREQ. TO 15195 kHz |
| | **UNITED KINGDOM** BBC, Rampisham | ⬅ • E Europe • 500 kW; ⬅ • Su • E Europe • 500 kW; ⬅ • Europe • 500 kW |
| | BBC, Via Greenville, USA | M-F • C America • 250 kW |
| 15330 | **CHINA (TAIWAN)** †CBS, Taipei | Irr • E Asia • NEWS NETWORK • 100 kW |
| | **GUAM** †KTWR-TRANS WORLD RADIO, Merizo | Australasia & S Pacific • 100 kW; S Asia • 100 kW; SE Asia • 100 kW |
| | **IRAN** VO THE ISLAMIC REP, Sirjan | W Asia & C Asia • 500 kW |
| | **ITALY** RAI INTERNATIONAL, Rome | [W] • Mideast • 100 kW; E Africa • 100 kW; [W] • E Africa • 100 kW |
| | **SWAZILAND** †TRANS WORLD RADIO, Manzini | W Asia & S Asia • 100 kW |
| | **USA** RADIO MARTI, Delano, California | [S] • C America • 250 kW; C America • 250 kW |
| | **UZBEKISTAN** †RADIO TASHKENT, Tashkent | [W] • Mideast • 100 kW |
| | †UZBEK RADIO, Tashkent | [W] • Mideast • DS-2 • 100 kW |
| 15335 | **EGYPT** RADIO CAIRO, Kafr Silîm-Abis | W Africa • 250 kW |
| | **MOROCCO** RTV MAROCAINE, Briech | Europe • 500 kW |
| | **PHILIPPINES** †RADIO VERITAS ASIA, Palauig | S Asia • 250 kW |
| | **ROMANIA** †RADIO ROMANIA INTL, Bucharest | [W] • S Asia • 250 kW |
| (con'd) | **UNITED KINGDOM** BBC, Via Zyyi, Cyprus | ⬅ • E Europe • 250 kW |

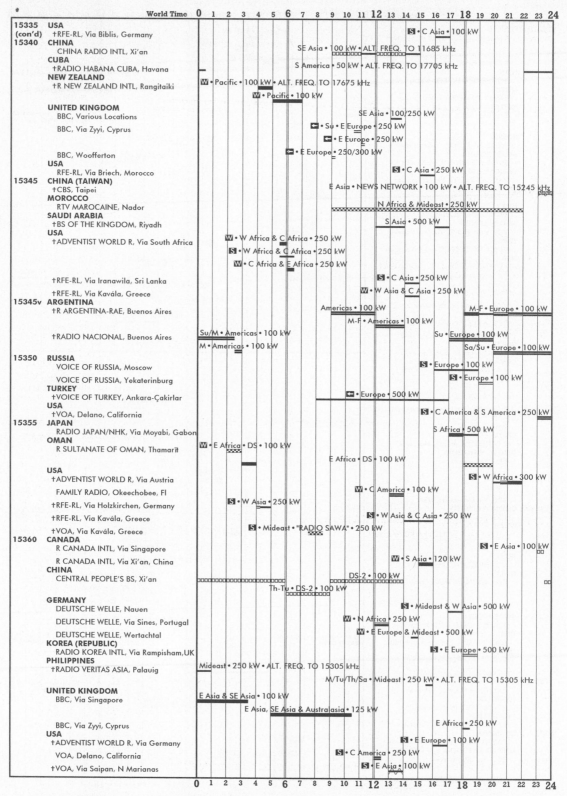

World Time  0  1  2  3  4  5  6  7  8  9  10  11  12  13  14  15  16  17  18  19  20  21  22  23  24

**15335 USA**
(con'd)  †RFE-RL, Via Biblis, Germany — S • C Asia • 100 kW
**15340 CHINA**
  CHINA RADIO INTL, Xi'an — SE Asia • 100 kW • ALT. FREQ. TO 11685 kHz
  **CUBA**
  †RADIO HABANA CUBA, Havana — S America • 50 kW • ALT. FREQ. TO 17705 kHz
  **NEW ZEALAND**
  †R NEW ZEALAND INTL, Rangitaiki — W • Pacific • 100 kW • ALT. FREQ. TO 17675 kHz
  W • Pacific • 100 kW

  **UNITED KINGDOM**
  BBC, Various Locations — SE Asia • 100/250 kW
  BBC, Via Zyyi, Cyprus — ← • Su • E Europe • 250 kW
  ← • E Europe • 250 kW

  BBC, Woofferton — ← • E Europe • 250/300 kW
  **USA**
  RFE-RL, Via Briech, Morocco — S • C Asia • 250 kW
**15345 CHINA (TAIWAN)**
  †CBS, Taipei — E Asia • NEWS NETWORK • 100 kW • ALT. FREQ. TO 15245 kHz
  **MOROCCO**
  RTV MAROCAINE, Nador — N Africa & Mideast • 250 kW
  **SAUDI ARABIA**
  †BS OF THE KINGDOM, Riyadh — S Asia • 500 kW
  **USA**
  †ADVENTIST WORLD R, Via South Africa — W • W Africa & C Africa • 250 kW
  S • W Africa & C Africa • 250 kW
  W • C Africa & E Africa • 250 kW

  †RFE-RL, Via Iranawila, Sri Lanka — S • C Asia • 250 kW
  †RFE-RL, Via Kavála, Greece — W • W Asia & C Asia • 250 kW
**15345v ARGENTINA**
  †R ARGENTINA-RAE, Buenos Aires — Americas • 100 kW          M-F • Europe • 100 kW
  M-F • Americas • 100 kW

  †RADIO NACIONAL, Buenos Aires — Su/M • Americas • 100 kW          Su • Europe • 100 kW
  M • Americas • 100 kW          Sa/Su • Europe • 100 kW
**15350 RUSSIA**
  VOICE OF RUSSIA, Moscow — S • Europe • 100 kW
  VOICE OF RUSSIA, Yekaterinburg — S • Europe • 100 kW
  **TURKEY**
  †VOICE OF TURKEY, Ankara-Çakirlar — ← • Europe • 500 kW
  **USA**
  †VOA, Delano, California — S • C America & S America • 250 kW
**15355 JAPAN**
  RADIO JAPAN/NHK, Via Moyabi, Gabon — S Africa • 500 kW
  **OMAN**
  R SULTANATE OF OMAN, Thamarit — W • E Africa • DS • 100 kW
  E Africa • DS • 100 kW
  **USA**
  †ADVENTIST WORLD R, Via Austria — S • W Africa • 300 kW
  FAMILY RADIO, Okeechobee, Fl — W • C America • 100 kW
  †RFE-RL, Via Holzkirchen, Germany — S • W Asia • 250 kW
  †RFE-RL, Via Kavála, Greece — S • W Asia & C Asia • 250 kW
  †VOA, Via Kavála, Greece — S • Mideast • "RADIO SAWA" • 250 kW
**15360 CANADA**
  R CANADA INTL, Via Singapore — S • E Asia • 100 kW
  R CANADA INTL, Via Xi'an, China — W • S Asia • 120 kW
  **CHINA**
  CENTRAL PEOPLE'S BS, Xi'an — DS-2 • 100 kW
  Th-Tu • DS-2 • 100 kW
  **GERMANY**
  DEUTSCHE WELLE, Nauen — S • Mideast & W Asia • 500 kW
  DEUTSCHE WELLE, Via Sines, Portugal — W • N Africa • 250 kW
  DEUTSCHE WELLE, Wertachtal — W • E Europe & Mideast • 500 kW
  **KOREA (REPUBLIC)**
  RADIO KOREA INTL, Via Rampisham, UK — S • E Europe • 500 kW
  **PHILIPPINES**
  †RADIO VERITAS ASIA, Palauig — Mideast • 250 kW • ALT. FREQ. TO 15305 kHz
  M/Tu/Th/Sa • Mideast • 250 kW • ALT. FREQ. TO 15305 kHz
  **UNITED KINGDOM**
  BBC, Via Singapore — E Asia & SE Asia • 100 kW
  E Asia, SE Asia & Australasia • 125 kW

  BBC, Via Zyyi, Cyprus — E Africa • 250 kW
  **USA**
  †ADVENTIST WORLD R, Via Germany — S • E Europe • 100 kW
  VOA, Delano, California — S • C America • 250 kW
  †VOA, Via Saipan, N Marianas — S • E Asia • 100 kW

0  1  2  3  4  5  6  7  8  9  10  11  12  13  14  15  16  17  18  19  20  21  22  23  24

ENGLISH ▬  ARABIC ⌇⌇⌇  CHINESE □□□  FRENCH ▬  GERMAN ▬  RUSSIAN ═  SPANISH ▬  OTHER ▬

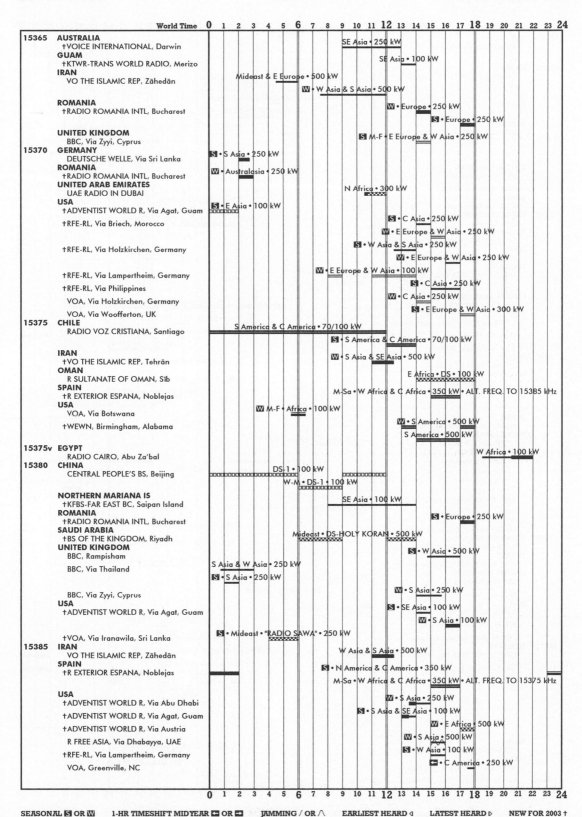

| | | World Time | | | |
|---|---|---|---|---|---|

**15365 AUSTRALIA**
  †VOICE INTERNATIONAL, Darwin — SE Asia • 250 kW
**GUAM**
  †KTWR-TRANS WORLD RADIO, Merizo — SE Asia • 100 kW
**IRAN**
  VO THE ISLAMIC REP, Zāhedān — Mideast & E Europe • 500 kW
    W • W Asia & S Asia • 500 kW
**ROMANIA**
  †RADIO ROMANIA INTL, Bucharest — W • Europe • 250 kW
    S • Europe • 250 kW
**UNITED KINGDOM**
  BBC, Via Zyyi, Cyprus — S M-F • E Europe & W Asia • 250 kW
**15370 GERMANY**
  DEUTSCHE WELLE, Via Sri Lanka — S • S Asia • 250 kW
**ROMANIA**
  †RADIO ROMANIA INTL, Bucharest — W • Australasia • 250 kW
**UNITED ARAB EMIRATES**
  UAE RADIO IN DUBAI — N Africa • 300 kW
**USA**
  †ADVENTIST WORLD R, Via Agat, Guam — S • E Asia • 100 kW
  †RFE-RL, Via Briech, Morocco — S • C Asia • 250 kW
    W • E Europe & W Asia • 250 kW
  †RFE-RL, Via Holzkirchen, Germany — S • W Asia & S Asia • 250 kW
    S • E Europe & W Asia • 250 kW
  †RFE-RL, Via Lampertheim, Germany — W • E Europe & W Asia • 100 kW
  †RFE-RL, Via Philippines — S • C Asia • 250 kW
  VOA, Via Holzkirchen, Germany — W • C Asia • 250 kW
  VOA, Via Woofferton, UK — S • E Europe & W Asia • 300 kW
**15375 CHILE**
  RADIO VOZ CRISTIANA, Santiago — S America & C America • 70/100 kW
    S • S America & C America • 70/100 kW
**IRAN**
  †VO THE ISLAMIC REP, Tehrān — W • S Asia & SE Asia • 500 kW
**OMAN**
  R SULTANATE OF OMAN, Sīb — E Africa • DS • 100 kW
**SPAIN**
  †R EXTERIOR ESPANA, Noblejas — M-Sa • W Africa & C Africa • 350 kW • ALT. FREQ. TO 15385 kHz
**USA**
  VOA, Via Botswana — W M-F • Africa • 100 kW
  †WEWN, Birmingham, Alabama — W • S America • 500 kW
    S America • 500 kW
**15375v EGYPT**
  RADIO CAIRO, Abu Za'bal — W Africa • 100 kW
**15380 CHINA**
  CENTRAL PEOPLE'S BS, Beijing — DS-1 • 100 kW
    W-M • DS-1 • 100 kW
**NORTHERN MARIANA IS**
  †KFBS-FAR EAST BC, Saipan Island — SE Asia • 100 kW
**ROMANIA**
  †RADIO ROMANIA INTL, Bucharest — S • Europe • 250 kW
**SAUDI ARABIA**
  †BS OF THE KINGDOM, Riyadh — Mideast • DS-HOLY KORAN • 500 kW
**UNITED KINGDOM**
  BBC, Rampisham — S • W Asia • 500 kW
  BBC, Via Thailand — S Asia & W Asia • 250 kW
    S • S Asia • 250 kW
  BBC, Via Zyyi, Cyprus — W • S Asia • 250 kW
**USA**
  †ADVENTIST WORLD R, Via Agat, Guam — S • SE Asia • 100 kW
    W • S Asia • 100 kW
  †VOA, Via Iranawila, Sri Lanka — S • Mideast • "RADIO SAWA" • 250 kW
**15385 IRAN**
  VO THE ISLAMIC REP, Zāhedān — W Asia & S Asia • 500 kW
**SPAIN**
  †R EXTERIOR ESPANA, Noblejas — S • N America & C America • 350 kW
    M-Sa • W Africa & C Africa • 350 kW • ALT. FREQ. TO 15375 kHz
**USA**
  †ADVENTIST WORLD R, Via Abu Dhabi — W • S Asia • 250 kW
  †ADVENTIST WORLD R, Via Agat, Guam — S • S Asia & SE Asia • 100 kW
  †ADVENTIST WORLD R, Via Austria — W • E Africa • 500 kW
  R FREE ASIA, Via Dhabayya, UAE — W • S Asia • 500 kW
  †RFE-RL, Via Lampertheim, Germany — S • W Asia • 100 kW
  VOA, Greenville, NC — C America • 250 kW

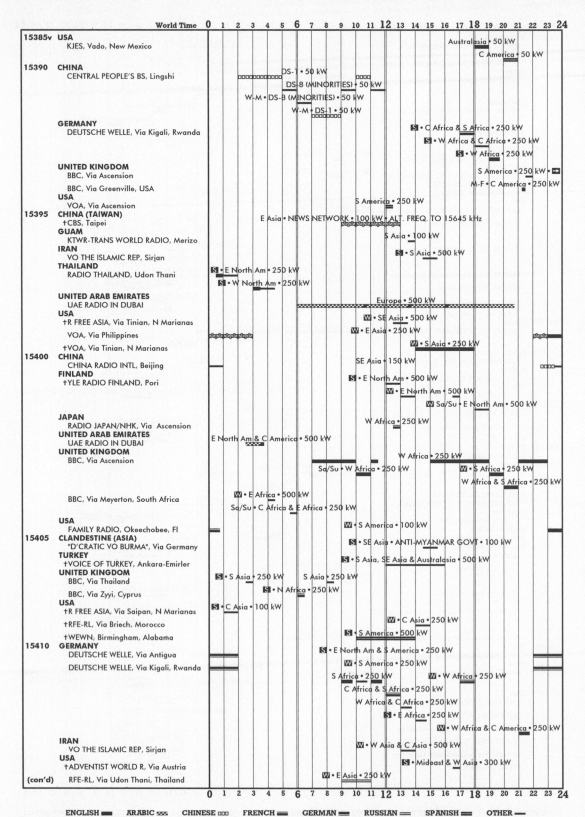

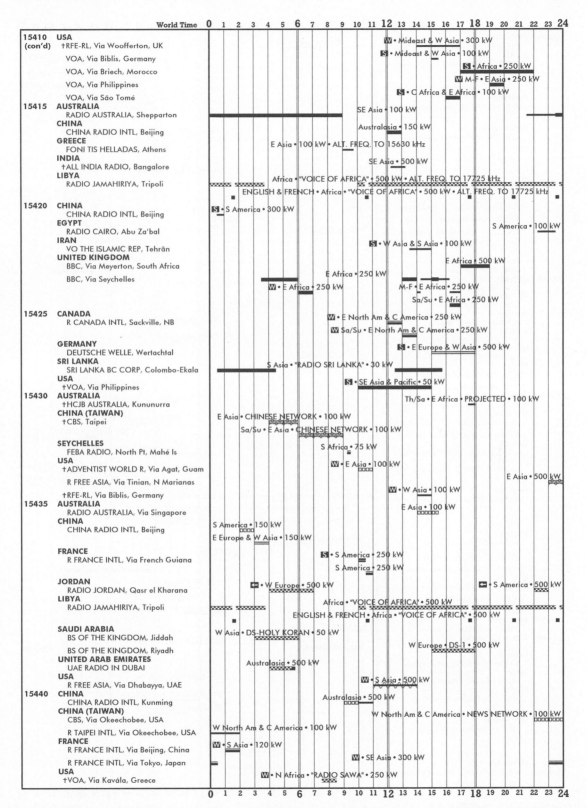

World Time | 0 1 2 3 4 5 6 7 8 9 10 11 12 13 14 15 16 17 18 19 20 21 22 23 24

**15410 USA**
(con'd) †RFE-RL, Via Woofferton, UK — **W** • Mideast & W Asia • 300 kW
VOA, Via Biblis, Germany — **S** • Mideast & W Asia • 100 kW
VOA, Via Briech, Morocco — **S** • Africa • 250 kW
VOA, Via Philippines — **W** M-F • E Asia • 250 kW
VOA, Via São Tomé — **S** • C Africa & E Africa • 100 kW

**15415 AUSTRALIA**
RADIO AUSTRALIA, Shepparton — SE Asia • 100 kW
**CHINA**
CHINA RADIO INTL, Beijing — Australasia • 150 kW
**GREECE**
FONI TIS HELLADAS, Athens — E Asia • 100 kW • ALT. FREQ. TO 15630 kHz
**INDIA**
†ALL INDIA RADIO, Bangalore — SE Asia • 500 kW
**LIBYA**
RADIO JAMAHIRIYA, Tripoli — Africa • "VOICE OF AFRICA" • 500 kW • ALT. FREQ. TO 17725 kHz
ENGLISH & FRENCH • Africa • "VOICE OF AFRICA" • 500 kW • ALT. FREQ. TO 17725 kHz

**15420 CHINA**
CHINA RADIO INTL, Beijing — **S** • S America • 300 kW
**EGYPT**
RADIO CAIRO, Abu Za'bal — S America • 100 kW
**IRAN**
VO THE ISLAMIC REP, Tehrān — **S** • W Asia & S Asia • 100 kW
**UNITED KINGDOM**
BBC, Via Meyerton, South Africa — E Africa • 500 kW
BBC, Via Seychelles — E Africa • 250 kW
**W** • E Africa • 250 kW
M-F • E Africa • 250 kW
Sa/Su • E Africa • 250 kW

**15425 CANADA**
R CANADA INTL, Sackville, NB — **W** • E North Am & C America • 250 kW
**W** Sa/Su • E North Am & C America • 250 kW
**GERMANY**
DEUTSCHE WELLE, Wertachtal — **S** • E Europe & W Asia • 500 kW
**SRI LANKA**
SRI LANKA BC CORP, Colombo-Ekala — S Asia • "RADIO SRI LANKA" • 30 kW
**USA**
†VOA, Via Philippines — **S** • SE Asia & Pacific • 50 kW

**15430 AUSTRALIA**
†HCJB AUSTRALIA, Kununurra — Th/Sa • E Africa • PROJECTED • 100 kW
**CHINA (TAIWAN)**
†CBS, Taipei — E Asia • CHINESE NETWORK • 100 kW
Sa/Su • E Asia • CHINESE NETWORK • 100 kW
**SEYCHELLES**
FEBA RADIO, North Pt, Mahé Is — S Africa • 75 kW
**USA**
†ADVENTIST WORLD R, Via Agat, Guam — **W** • E Asia • 100 kW
R FREE ASIA, Via Tinian, N Marianas — E Asia • 500 kW
†RFE-RL, Via Biblis, Germany — **W** • W Asia • 100 kW

**15435 AUSTRALIA**
RADIO AUSTRALIA, Via Singapore — E Asia • 100 kW
**CHINA**
CHINA RADIO INTL, Beijing — S America • 150 kW
E Europe & W Asia • 150 kW
**FRANCE**
R FRANCE INTL, Via French Guiana — **S** • S America • 250 kW
S America • 250 kW
**JORDAN**
RADIO JORDAN, Qasr el Kharana — ⬅ • W Europe • 500 kW
⬅ • S America • 500 kW
**LIBYA**
RADIO JAMAHIRIYA, Tripoli — Africa • "VOICE OF AFRICA" • 500 kW
ENGLISH & FRENCH • Africa • "VOICE OF AFRICA" • 500 kW
**SAUDI ARABIA**
BS OF THE KINGDOM, Jiddah — W Asia • DS-HOLY KORAN • 50 kW
BS OF THE KINGDOM, Riyadh — W Europe • DS-1 • 500 kW
**UNITED ARAB EMIRATES**
UAE RADIO IN DUBAI — Australasia • 500 kW
**USA**
R FREE ASIA, Via Dhabayya, UAE — **W** • S Asia • 500 kW

**15440 CHINA**
CHINA RADIO INTL, Kunming — Australasia • 500 kW
**CHINA (TAIWAN)**
CBS, Via Okeechobee, USA — W North Am & C America • NEWS NETWORK • 100 kW
R TAIPEI INTL, Via Okeechobee, USA — W North Am & C America • 100 kW
**FRANCE**
R FRANCE INTL, Via Beijing, China — **W** • S Asia • 120 kW
R FRANCE INTL, Via Tokyo, Japan — **W** • SE Asia • 300 kW
**USA**
†VOA, Via Kavála, Greece — **W** • N Africa • "RADIO SAWA" • 250 kW

0 1 2 3 4 5 6 7 8 9 10 11 12 13 14 15 16 17 18 19 20 21 22 23 24

SEASONAL **S** OR **W**    1-HR TIMESHIFT MIDYEAR ⬅ OR ➡    JAMMING / OR ∧    EARLIEST HEARD ◁    LATEST HEARD ▷    NEW FOR 2003 †

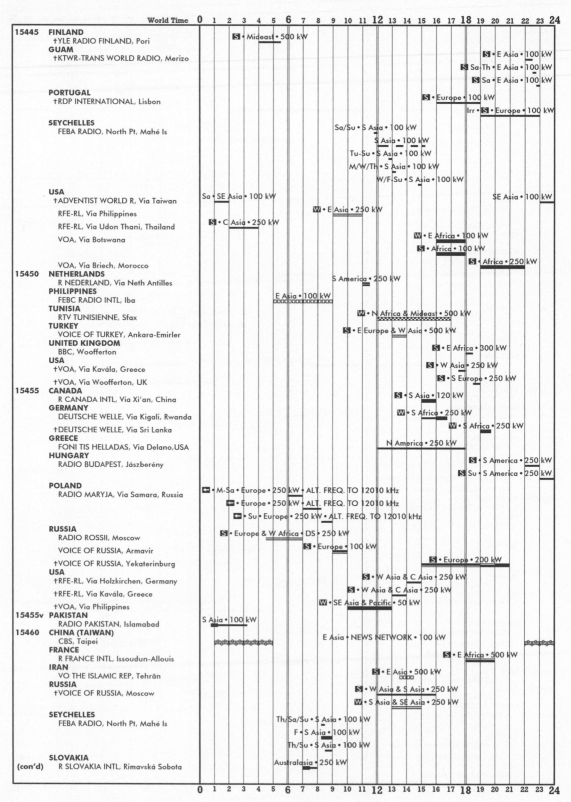

| | |
|---|---|
| 15445 | **FINLAND** |
| | †YLE RADIO FINLAND, Pori |
| | **GUAM** |
| | †KTWR-TRANS WORLD RADIO, Merizo |
| | **PORTUGAL** |
| | †RDP INTERNATIONAL, Lisbon |
| | **SEYCHELLES** |
| | FEBA RADIO, North Pt, Mahé Is |
| | **USA** |
| | †ADVENTIST WORLD R, Via Taiwan |
| | RFE-RL, Via Philippines |
| | RFE-RL, Via Udon Thani, Thailand |
| | VOA, Via Botswana |
| | VOA, Via Briech, Morocco |
| 15450 | **NETHERLANDS** |
| | R NEDERLAND, Via Neth Antilles |
| | **PHILIPPINES** |
| | FEBC RADIO INTL, Iba |
| | **TUNISIA** |
| | RTV TUNISIENNE, Sfax |
| | **TURKEY** |
| | VOICE OF TURKEY, Ankara-Emirler |
| | **UNITED KINGDOM** |
| | BBC, Woofferton |
| | **USA** |
| | †VOA, Via Kavála, Greece |
| | †VOA, Via Woofferton, UK |
| 15455 | **CANADA** |
| | R CANADA INTL, Via Xi'an, China |
| | **GERMANY** |
| | DEUTSCHE WELLE, Via Kigali, Rwanda |
| | †DEUTSCHE WELLE, Via Sri Lanka |
| | **GREECE** |
| | FONI TIS HELLADAS, Via Delano, USA |
| | **HUNGARY** |
| | RADIO BUDAPEST, Jászberény |
| | **POLAND** |
| | RADIO MARYJA, Via Samara, Russia |
| | **RUSSIA** |
| | RADIO ROSSII, Moscow |
| | VOICE OF RUSSIA, Armavir |
| | †VOICE OF RUSSIA, Yekaterinburg |
| | **USA** |
| | †RFE-RL, Via Holzkirchen, Germany |
| | †RFE-RL, Via Kavála, Greece |
| | †VOA, Via Philippines |
| 15455v | **PAKISTAN** |
| | RADIO PAKISTAN, Islamabad |
| 15460 | **CHINA (TAIWAN)** |
| | CBS, Taipei |
| | **FRANCE** |
| | R FRANCE INTL, Issoudun-Allouis |
| | **IRAN** |
| | VO THE ISLAMIC REP, Tehrān |
| | **RUSSIA** |
| | †VOICE OF RUSSIA, Moscow |
| | **SEYCHELLES** |
| | FEBA RADIO, North Pt, Mahé Is |
| | **SLOVAKIA** |
| (con'd) | R SLOVAKIA INTL, Rimavská Sobota |

ENGLISH ▰▰  ARABIC ⨯⨯⨯  CHINESE ▯▯▯  FRENCH ▰▰  GERMAN ▰▰  RUSSIAN ══  SPANISH ▰▰  OTHER ▬

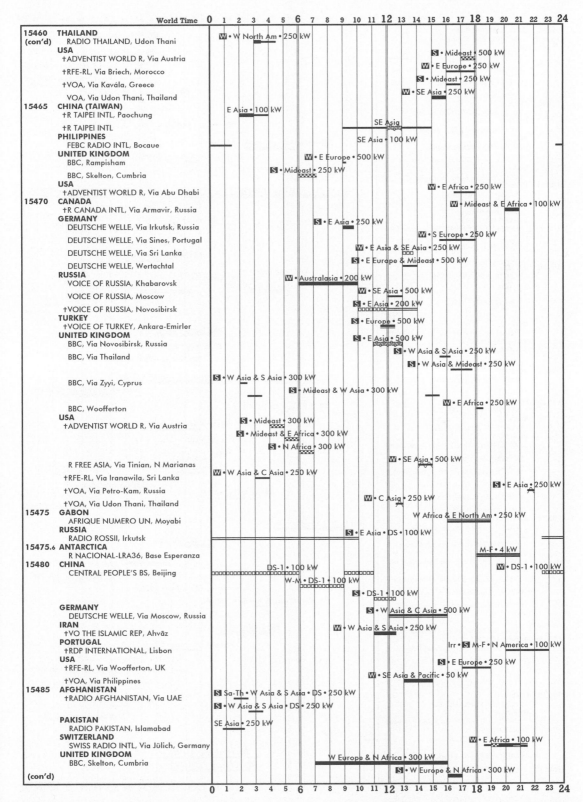

| kHz | Country / Station | Schedule |
|---|---|---|
| 15460 (con'd) | **THAILAND** — RADIO THAILAND, Udon Thani | W • W North Am • 250 kW |
| | **USA** — †ADVENTIST WORLD R, Via Austria | S • Mideast • 500 kW |
| | †RFE-RL, Via Briech, Morocco | W • E Europe • 250 kW |
| | †VOA, Via Kavála, Greece | S • Mideast • 250 kW |
| | VOA, Via Udon Thani, Thailand | W • SE Asia • 250 kW |
| 15465 | **CHINA (TAIWAN)** — †R TAIPEI INTL, Paochung | E Asia • 100 kW |
| | †R TAIPEI INTL | SE Asia |
| | **PHILIPPINES** — FEBC RADIO INTL, Bocaue | SE Asia • 100 kW |
| | **UNITED KINGDOM** — BBC, Rampisham | W • E Europe • 500 kW |
| | BBC, Skelton, Cumbria | S • Mideast • 250 kW |
| | **USA** — †ADVENTIST WORLD R, Via Abu Dhabi | W • E Africa • 250 kW |
| 15470 | **CANADA** — †R CANADA INTL, Via Armavir, Russia | W • Mideast & E Africa • 100 kW |
| | **GERMANY** — DEUTSCHE WELLE, Via Irkutsk, Russia | S • E Asia • 250 kW |
| | DEUTSCHE WELLE, Via Sines, Portugal | W • S Europe • 250 kW |
| | DEUTSCHE WELLE, Via Sri Lanka | W • E Asia & SE Asia • 250 kW |
| | DEUTSCHE WELLE, Wertachtal | S • E Europe & Mideast • 500 kW |
| | **RUSSIA** — VOICE OF RUSSIA, Khabarovsk | W • Australasia • 200 kW |
| | VOICE OF RUSSIA, Moscow | W • SE Asia • 500 kW |
| | †VOICE OF RUSSIA, Novosibirsk | S • E Asia • 200 kW |
| | **TURKEY** — †VOICE OF TURKEY, Ankara-Emirler | S • Europe • 500 kW |
| | **UNITED KINGDOM** — BBC, Via Novosibirsk, Russia | S • E Asia • 500 kW |
| | BBC, Via Thailand | S • W Asia & S Asia • 250 kW |
| | | S • W Asia & Mideast • 250 kW |
| | BBC, Via Zyyi, Cyprus | S • W Asia & S Asia • 300 kW |
| | | S • Mideast & W Asia • 300 kW |
| | BBC, Woofferton | W • E Africa • 250 kW |
| | **USA** — †ADVENTIST WORLD R, Via Austria | S • Mideast • 300 kW |
| | | S • Mideast & E Africa • 300 kW |
| | | S • N Africa • 300 kW |
| | R FREE ASIA, Via Tinian, N Marianas | W • SE Asia • 500 kW |
| | †RFE-RL, Via Iranawila, Sri Lanka | W • W Asia & C Asia • 250 kW |
| | †VOA, Via Petro-Kam, Russia | S • E Asia • 250 kW |
| | †VOA, Via Udon Thani, Thailand | W • C Asia • 250 kW |
| 15475 | **GABON** — AFRIQUE NUMERO UN, Moyabi | W Africa & E North Am • 250 kW |
| | **RUSSIA** — RADIO ROSSII, Irkutsk | S • E Asia • DS • 100 kW |
| 15475.6 | **ANTARCTICA** — R NACIONAL-LRA36, Base Esperanza | M-F • 4 kW |
| 15480 | **CHINA** — CENTRAL PEOPLE'S BS, Beijing | DS-1 • 100 kW / W • DS-1 • 100 kW |
| | | W-M • DS-1 • 100 kW |
| | | S • DS-1 • 100 kW |
| | **GERMANY** — DEUTSCHE WELLE, Via Moscow, Russia | S • W Asia & C Asia • 500 kW |
| | **IRAN** — †VO THE ISLAMIC REP, Ahvãz | W • W Asia & S Asia • 250 kW |
| | **PORTUGAL** — †RDP INTERNATIONAL, Lisbon | Irr • S • M-F • N America • 100 kW |
| | **USA** — †RFE-RL, Via Woofferton, UK | S • E Europe • 250 kW |
| | †VOA, Via Philippines | W • SE Asia & Pacific • 50 kW |
| 15485 | **AFGHANISTAN** — †RADIO AFGHANISTAN, Via UAE | S • Sa-Th • W Asia & S Asia • DS • 250 kW |
| | | S • W Asia & S Asia • DS • 250 kW |
| | **PAKISTAN** — RADIO PAKISTAN, Islamabad | SE Asia • 250 kW |
| | **SWITZERLAND** — SWISS RADIO INTL, Via Jülich, Germany | W • E Africa • 100 kW |
| | **UNITED KINGDOM** — BBC, Skelton, Cumbria | W Europe & N Africa • 300 kW |
| | | S • W Europe & N Africa • 300 kW |
| (con'd) | | |

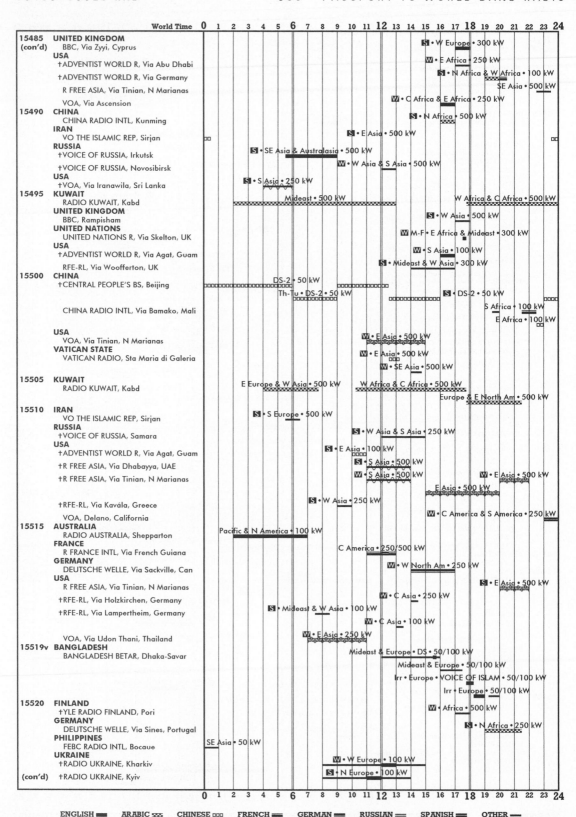

| | World Time | 0 | 1 | 2 | 3 | 4 | 5 | 6 | 7 | 8 | 9 | 10 | 11 | 12 | 13 | 14 | 15 | 16 | 17 | 18 | 19 | 20 | 21 | 22 | 23 | 24 |

**15485** **UNITED KINGDOM**
(con'd)   BBC, Via Zyyi, Cyprus — ⑤ • W Europe • 300 kW
**USA**
†ADVENTIST WORLD R, Via Abu Dhabi — Ⓦ • E Africa • 250 kW
†ADVENTIST WORLD R, Via Germany — ⑤ • N Africa & W Africa • 100 kW
R FREE ASIA, Via Tinian, N Marianas — SE Asia • 500 kW
VOA, Via Ascension — Ⓦ • C Africa & E Africa • 250 kW

**15490** **CHINA**
CHINA RADIO INTL, Kunming — ⑤ • N Africa • 500 kW
**IRAN**
VO THE ISLAMIC REP, Sirjan — ⑤ • E Asia • 500 kW
**RUSSIA**
†VOICE OF RUSSIA, Irkutsk — ⑤ • SE Asia & Australasia • 500 kW
†VOICE OF RUSSIA, Novosibirsk — Ⓦ • W Asia & S Asia • 500 kW
**USA**
†VOA, Via Iranawila, Sri Lanka — ⑤ • S Asia • 250 kW

**15495** **KUWAIT**
RADIO KUWAIT, Kabd — Mideast • 500 kW ... W Africa & C Africa • 500 kW
**UNITED KINGDOM**
BBC, Rampisham — ⑤ • W Asia • 500 kW
**UNITED NATIONS**
UNITED NATIONS R, Via Skelton, UK — Ⓦ M-F • E Africa & Mideast • 300 kW
**USA**
†ADVENTIST WORLD R, Via Agat, Guam — Ⓦ • S Asia • 100 kW
RFE-RL, Via Woofferton, UK — ⑤ • Mideast & W Asia • 300 kW

**15500** **CHINA**
†CENTRAL PEOPLE'S BS, Beijing — DS-2 • 50 kW
Th-Tu • DS-2 • 50 kW ⑤ DS-2 • 50 kW
CHINA RADIO INTL, Via Bamako, Mali — S Africa • 100 kW
E Africa • 100 kW
**USA**
VOA, Via Tinian, N Marianas — Ⓦ • E Asia • 500 kW
**VATICAN STATE**
VATICAN RADIO, Sta Maria di Galeria — Ⓦ • E Asia • 500 kW
Ⓦ • SE Asia • 500 kW

**15505** **KUWAIT**
RADIO KUWAIT, Kabd — E Europe & W Asia • 500 kW   W Africa & C Africa • 500 kW
Europe & E North Am • 500 kW

**15510** **IRAN**
VO THE ISLAMIC REP, Sirjan — ⑤ • S Europe • 500 kW
**RUSSIA**
†VOICE OF RUSSIA, Samara — ⑤ • W Asia & S Asia • 250 kW
**USA**
†ADVENTIST WORLD R, Via Agat, Guam — ⑤ • E Asia • 100 kW
†R FREE ASIA, Via Dhabayya, UAE — ⑤ • S Asia • 500 kW
†R FREE ASIA, Via Tinian, N Marianas — Ⓦ • S Asia • 500 kW   Ⓦ • E Asia • 500 kW
E Asia • 500 kW
†RFE-RL, Via Kavála, Greece — ⑤ • W Asia • 250 kW
VOA, Delano, California — Ⓦ • C America & S America • 250 kW

**15515** **AUSTRALIA**
RADIO AUSTRALIA, Shepparton — Pacific & N America • 100 kW
**FRANCE**
R FRANCE INTL, Via French Guiana — C America • 250/500 kW
**GERMANY**
DEUTSCHE WELLE, Via Sackville, Can — Ⓦ • W North Am • 250 kW
**USA**
R FREE ASIA, Via Tinian, N Marianas — ⑤ • E Asia • 500 kW
†RFE-RL, Via Holzkirchen, Germany — Ⓦ • C Asia • 250 kW
†RFE-RL, Via Lampertheim, Germany — ⑤ • Mideast & W Asia • 100 kW
Ⓦ • C Asia • 100 kW
VOA, Via Udon Thani, Thailand — Ⓦ • E Asia • 250 kW

**15519v** **BANGLADESH**
BANGLADESH BETAR, Dhaka-Savar — Mideast & Europe • DS • 50/100 kW
Mideast & Europe • 50/100 kW
Irr • Europe • VOICE OF ISLAM • 50/100 kW
Irr • Europe • 50/100 kW

**15520** **FINLAND**
†YLE RADIO FINLAND, Pori — Ⓦ • Africa • 500 kW
**GERMANY**
DEUTSCHE WELLE, Via Sines, Portugal — ⑤ • N Africa • 250 kW
**PHILIPPINES**
FEBC RADIO INTL, Bocaue — SE Asia • 50 kW
**UKRAINE**
†RADIO UKRAINE, Kharkiv — Ⓦ • W Europe • 100 kW
(con'd)   †RADIO UKRAINE, Kyiv — ⑤ • N Europe • 100 kW

| | | 0 | 1 | 2 | 3 | 4 | 5 | 6 | 7 | 8 | 9 | 10 | 11 | 12 | 13 | 14 | 15 | 16 | 17 | 18 | 19 | 20 | 21 | 22 | 23 | 24 |

ENGLISH ▬   ARABIC ⧖⧖   CHINESE ▭▭▭   FRENCH ▬▬   GERMAN ▬▬   RUSSIAN ══   SPANISH ▬▬   OTHER ▬

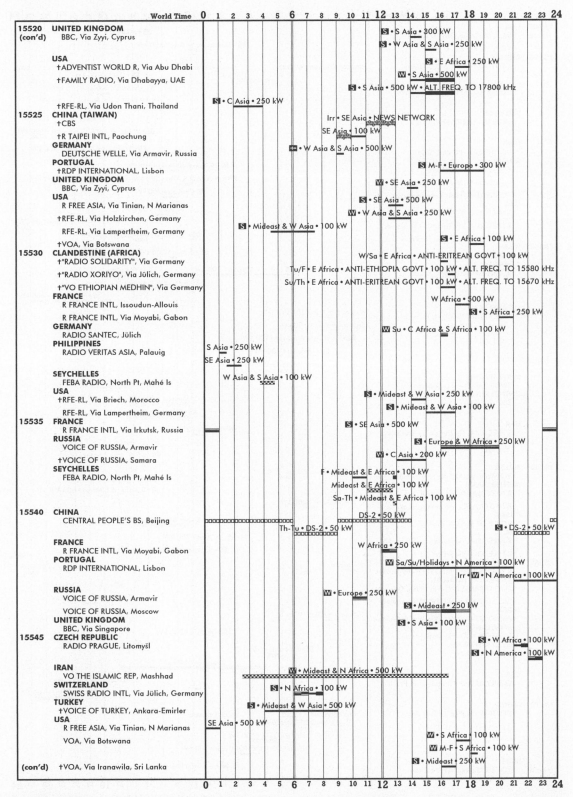

World Time 0 1 2 3 4 5 6 7 8 9 10 11 12 13 14 15 16 17 18 19 20 21 22 23 24

| 15520 | UNITED KINGDOM | |
| (con'd) | BBC, Via Zyyi, Cyprus | S • S Asia • 300 kW |
| | | S • W Asia & S Asia • 250 kW |
| | USA | |
| | †ADVENTIST WORLD R, Via Abu Dhabi | S • E Africa • 250 kW |
| | †FAMILY RADIO, Via Dhabayya, UAE | W • S Asia • 500 kW |
| | | S • S Asia • 500 kW • ALT. FREQ. TO 17800 kHz |
| | †RFE-RL, Via Udon Thani, Thailand | S • C Asia • 250 kW |
| 15525 | CHINA (TAIWAN) | Irr • SE Asia • NEWS NETWORK |
| | †CBS | |
| | †R TAIPEI INTL, Paochung | SE Asia • 100 kW |
| | GERMANY | |
| | DEUTSCHE WELLE, Via Armavir, Russia | • W Asia & S Asia • 500 kW |
| | PORTUGAL | |
| | †RDP INTERNATIONAL, Lisbon | S • M-F • Europe • 300 kW |
| | UNITED KINGDOM | |
| | BBC, Via Zyyi, Cyprus | W • SE Asia • 250 kW |
| | USA | |
| | R FREE ASIA, Via Tinian, N Marianas | S • SE Asia • 500 kW |
| | †RFE-RL, Via Holzkirchen, Germany | W • W Asia & S Asia • 250 kW |
| | RFE-RL, Via Lampertheim, Germany | S • Mideast & W Asia • 100 kW |
| | †VOA, Via Botswana | S • E Africa • 100 kW |
| 15530 | CLANDESTINE (AFRICA) | W/Sa • E Africa • ANTI-ERITREAN GOVT • 100 kW |
| | †"RADIO SOLIDARITY", Via Germany | |
| | †"RADIO XORIYO", Via Jülich, Germany | Tu/F • E Africa • ANTI-ETHIOPIA GOVT • 100 kW • ALT. FREQ. TO 15580 kHz |
| | †"VO ETHIOPIAN MEDHIN", Via Germany | Su/Th • E Africa • ANTI-ERITREAN GOVT • 100 kW • ALT. FREQ. TO 15670 kHz |
| | FRANCE | |
| | R FRANCE INTL, Issoudun-Allouis | W Africa • 500 kW |
| | R FRANCE INTL, Via Moyabi, Gabon | S • S Africa • 250 kW |
| | GERMANY | |
| | RADIO SANTEC, Jülich | W Su • C Africa & S Africa • 100 kW |
| | PHILIPPINES | |
| | RADIO VERITAS ASIA, Palauig | S Asia • 250 kW |
| | | SE Asia • 250 kW |
| | SEYCHELLES | |
| | FEBA RADIO, North Pt, Mahé Is | W Asia & S Asia • 100 kW |
| | USA | |
| | †RFE-RL, Via Briech, Morocco | S • Mideast & W Asia • 250 kW |
| | RFE-RL, Via Lampertheim, Germany | S • Mideast & W Asia • 100 kW |
| 15535 | FRANCE | |
| | R FRANCE INTL, Via Irkutsk, Russia | S • SE Asia • 500 kW |
| | RUSSIA | |
| | VOICE OF RUSSIA, Armavir | S • Europe & W Africa • 250 kW |
| | †VOICE OF RUSSIA, Samara | W • C Asia • 200 kW |
| | SEYCHELLES | |
| | FEBA RADIO, North Pt, Mahé Is | F • Mideast & E Africa • 100 kW |
| | | Mideast & E Africa • 100 kW |
| | | Sa-Th • Mideast & E Africa • 100 kW |
| 15540 | CHINA | |
| | CENTRAL PEOPLE'S BS, Beijing | DS-2 • 50 kW |
| | | Th-Tu • DS-2 • 50 kW |
| | | S • DS-2 • 50 kW |
| | FRANCE | |
| | R FRANCE INTL, Via Moyabi, Gabon | W Africa • 250 kW |
| | PORTUGAL | |
| | RDP INTERNATIONAL, Lisbon | W Sa/Su/Holidays • N America • 100 kW |
| | | Irr • W • N America • 100 kW |
| | RUSSIA | |
| | VOICE OF RUSSIA, Armavir | W • Europe • 250 kW |
| | VOICE OF RUSSIA, Moscow | S • Mideast • 250 kW |
| | UNITED KINGDOM | |
| | BBC, Via Singapore | S • S Asia • 100 kW |
| 15545 | CZECH REPUBLIC | |
| | RADIO PRAGUE, Litomyšl | S • W Africa • 100 kW |
| | | S • N America • 100 kW |
| | IRAN | |
| | VO THE ISLAMIC REP, Mashhad | W • Mideast & N Africa • 500 kW |
| | SWITZERLAND | |
| | SWISS RADIO INTL, Via Jülich, Germany | S • N Africa • 100 kW |
| | TURKEY | |
| | †VOICE OF TURKEY, Ankara-Emirler | S • Mideast & W Asia • 500 kW |
| | USA | |
| | R FREE ASIA, Via Tinian, N Marianas | SE Asia • 500 kW |
| | VOA, Via Botswana | W • S Africa • 100 kW |
| | | W • M-F • S Africa • 100 kW |
| | | S • Mideast • 250 kW |
| (con'd) | †VOA, Via Iranawila, Sri Lanka | |

0 1 2 3 4 5 6 7 8 9 10 11 12 13 14 15 16 17 18 19 20 21 22 23 24

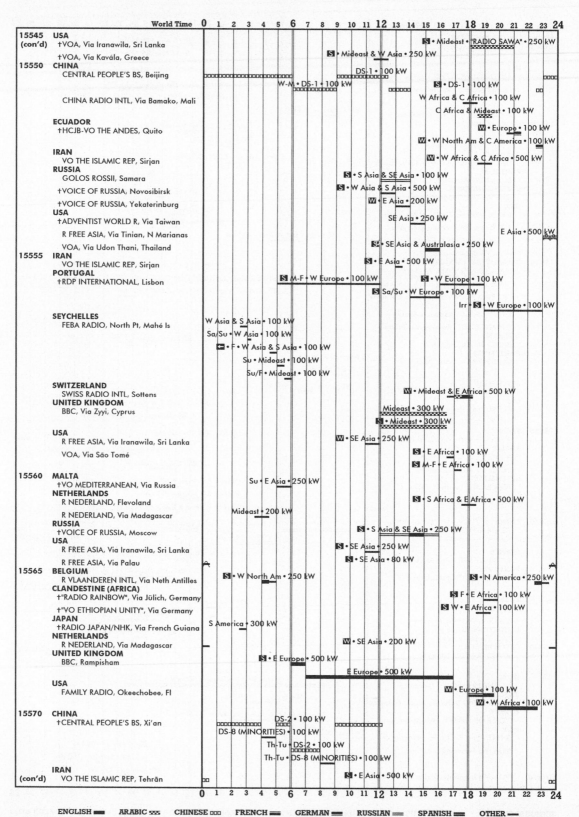

ENGLISH ▬   ARABIC ▨   CHINESE ▫   FRENCH ▬   GERMAN ▬   RUSSIAN ═   SPANISH ▬   OTHER ▬

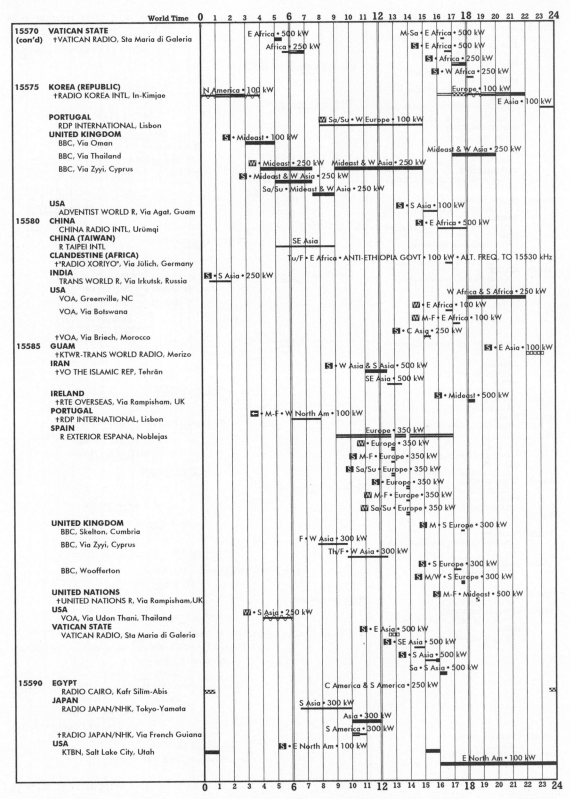

World Time  0 1 2 3 4 5 6 7 8 9 10 11 12 13 14 15 16 17 18 19 20 21 22 23 24

**15570** **VATICAN STATE**
(con'd) †VATICAN RADIO, Sta Maria di Galeria
- E Africa • 500 kW
- Africa • 250 kW
- M-Sa • E Africa • 500 kW
- S • E Africa • 500 kW
- S • Africa • 250 kW
- S • W Africa • 250 kW

**15575** **KOREA (REPUBLIC)**
†RADIO KOREA INTL, In-Kimjae
- N America • 100 kW
- Europe • 100 kW
- E Asia • 100 kW

**PORTUGAL**
RDP INTERNATIONAL, Lisbon
- W Sa/Su • W Europe • 100 kW

**UNITED KINGDOM**
BBC, Via Oman
- S • Mideast • 100 kW

BBC, Via Thailand
- Mideast & W Asia • 250 kW
- W • Mideast • 250 kW
- Mideast & W Asia • 250 kW

BBC, Via Zyyi, Cyprus
- S • Mideast & W Asia • 250 kW
- Sa/Su • Mideast & W Asia • 250 kW

**USA**
ADVENTIST WORLD R, Via Agat, Guam
- S • S Asia • 100 kW

**15580** **CHINA**
CHINA RADIO INTL, Urümqi
- S • E Africa • 500 kW

**CHINA (TAIWAN)**
R TAIPEI INTL
- SE Asia

**CLANDESTINE (AFRICA)**
†"RADIO XORIYO", Via Jülich, Germany
- Tu/F • E Africa • ANTI-ETHIOPIA GOVT • 100 kW • ALT. FREQ. TO 15530 kHz

**INDIA**
TRANS WORLD R, Via Irkutsk, Russia
- S • S Asia • 250 kW

**USA**
VOA, Greenville, NC
- W Africa & S Africa • 250 kW

VOA, Via Botswana
- W • E Africa • 100 kW
- W M-F • E Africa • 100 kW
- S • C Asia • 250 kW

†VOA, Via Briech, Morocco

**15585** **GUAM**
†KTWR-TRANS WORLD RADIO, Merizo
- S • E Asia • 100 kW

**IRAN**
†VO THE ISLAMIC REP, Tehrān
- S • W Asia & S Asia • 500 kW
- SE Asia • 500 kW

**IRELAND**
†RTE OVERSEAS, Via Rampisham, UK
- S • Mideast • 500 kW

**PORTUGAL**
†RDP INTERNATIONAL, Lisbon
- ← • M-F • W North Am • 100 kW

**SPAIN**
R EXTERIOR ESPANA, Noblejas
- Europe • 350 kW
- W • Europe • 350 kW
- S M-F • Europe • 350 kW
- S Sa/Su • Europe • 350 kW
- S • Europe • 350 kW
- W M-F • Europe • 350 kW
- W Sa/Su • Europe • 350 kW

**UNITED KINGDOM**
BBC, Skelton, Cumbria
- S M • S Europe • 300 kW

BBC, Via Zyyi, Cyprus
- F • W Asia • 300 kW
- Th/F • W Asia • 300 kW

BBC, Woofferton
- S • S Europe • 300 kW
- S M/W • S Europe • 300 kW

**UNITED NATIONS**
†UNITED NATIONS R, Via Rampisham, UK
- S M-F • Mideast • 500 kW

**USA**
VOA, Via Udon Thani, Thailand
- W • S Asia • 250 kW

**VATICAN STATE**
VATICAN RADIO, Sta Maria di Galeria
- S • E Asia • 500 kW
- S • SE Asia • 500 kW
- S • S Asia • 500 kW
- Sa • S Asia • 500 kW

**15590** **EGYPT**
RADIO CAIRO, Kafr Silim-Abis
- C America & S America • 250 kW

**JAPAN**
RADIO JAPAN/NHK, Tokyo-Yamata
- S Asia • 300 kW
- Asia • 300 kW
- S America • 300 kW

†RADIO JAPAN/NHK, Via French Guiana

**USA**
KTBN, Salt Lake City, Utah
- S • E North Am • 100 kW
- E North Am • 100 kW

0 1 2 3 4 5 6 7 8 9 10 11 12 13 14 15 16 17 18 19 20 21 22 23 24

SEASONAL S OR W    1-HR TIMESHIFT MIDYEAR ← OR →    JAMMING / OR ∧    EARLIEST HEARD ◁    LATEST HEARD ▷    NEW FOR 2003 †

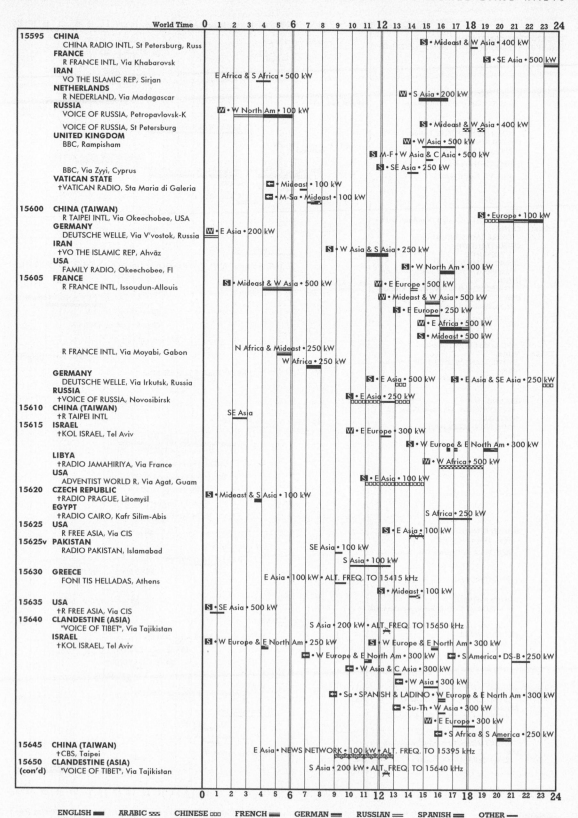

| World Time | 0 1 2 3 4 5 6 7 8 9 10 11 12 13 14 15 16 17 18 19 20 21 22 23 24 |
|---|---|

**15595 CHINA**
  CHINA RADIO INTL, St Petersburg, Russ — S • Mideast & W Asia • 400 kW
**FRANCE**
  R FRANCE INTL, Via Khabarovsk — S • SE Asia • 500 kW
**IRAN**
  VO THE ISLAMIC REP, Sirjan — E Africa & S Africa • 500 kW
**NETHERLANDS**
  R NEDERLAND, Via Madagascar — W • S Asia • 200 kW
**RUSSIA**
  VOICE OF RUSSIA, Petropavlovsk-K — W • W North Am • 100 kW
  VOICE OF RUSSIA, St Petersburg — S • Mideast & W Asia • 400 kW
**UNITED KINGDOM**
  BBC, Rampisham — W • W Asia • 500 kW
  — S • M-F • W Asia & C Asia • 500 kW
  BBC, Via Zyyi, Cyprus — S • SE Asia • 250 kW
**VATICAN STATE**
  †VATICAN RADIO, Sta Maria di Galeria — • Mideast • 100 kW
  — • M-Sa • Mideast • 100 kW

**15600 CHINA (TAIWAN)**
  R TAIPEI INTL, Via Okeechobee, USA — S • Europe • 100 kW
**GERMANY**
  DEUTSCHE WELLE, Via V'vostok, Russia — W • E Asia • 200 kW
**IRAN**
  †VO THE ISLAMIC REP, Ahvāz — S • W Asia & S Asia • 250 kW
**USA**
  FAMILY RADIO, Okeechobee, Fl — S • W North Am • 100 kW
**15605 FRANCE**
  R FRANCE INTL, Issoudun-Allouis — S • Mideast & W Asia • 500 kW
  — W • E Europe • 500 kW
  — W • Mideast & W Asia • 500 kW
  — S • E Europe • 250 kW
  — W • E Africa • 500 kW
  — S • Mideast • 500 kW
  R FRANCE INTL, Via Moyabi, Gabon — N Africa & Mideast • 250 kW
  — W Africa • 250 kW
**GERMANY**
  DEUTSCHE WELLE, Via Irkutsk, Russia — S • E Asia • 500 kW    S • E Asia & SE Asia • 250 kW
**RUSSIA**
  †VOICE OF RUSSIA, Novosibirsk — S • E Asia • 250 kW
**15610 CHINA (TAIWAN)**
  †R TAIPEI INTL — SE Asia
**15615 ISRAEL**
  †KOL ISRAEL, Tel Aviv — W • E Europe • 300 kW
  — S • W Europe & E North Am • 300 kW
**LIBYA**
  †RADIO JAMAHIRIYA, Via France — W • W Africa • 500 kW
**USA**
  ADVENTIST WORLD R, Via Agat, Guam — S • E Asia • 100 kW
**15620 CZECH REPUBLIC**
  †RADIO PRAGUE, Litomyšl — S • Mideast & S Asia • 100 kW
**EGYPT**
  †RADIO CAIRO, Kafr Silim-Abis — S Africa • 250 kW
**15625 USA**
  R FREE ASIA, Via CIS — S • E Asia • 100 kW
**15625v PAKISTAN**
  RADIO PAKISTAN, Islamabad — SE Asia • 100 kW
  — S Asia • 100 kW
**15630 GREECE**
  FONI TIS HELLADAS, Athens — E Asia • 100 kW • ALT. FREQ. TO 15415 kHz
  — S • Mideast • 100 kW
**15635 USA**
  †R FREE ASIA, Via CIS — S • SE Asia • 500 kW
**15640 CLANDESTINE (ASIA)**
  "VOICE OF TIBET", Via Tajikistan — S Asia • 200 kW • ALT. FREQ. TO 15650 kHz
**ISRAEL**
  †KOL ISRAEL, Tel Aviv — S • W Europe & E North Am • 250 kW    S • W Europe & E North Am • 300 kW
  — • W Europe & E North Am • 300 kW    • S America • DS-B • 250 kW
  — • W Asia & C Asia • 300 kW
  — • W Asia • 300 kW
  — • Sa • SPANISH & LADINO • W Europe & E North Am • 300 kW
  — • Su-Th • W Asia • 300 kW
  — W • E Europe • 300 kW
  — • S Africa & S America • 250 kW
**15645 CHINA (TAIWAN)**
  †CBS, Taipei — E Asia • NEWS NETWORK • 100 kW • ALT. FREQ. TO 15395 kHz
**15650 CLANDESTINE (ASIA)**
**(con'd)** "VOICE OF TIBET", Via Tajikistan — S Asia • 200 kW • ALT. FREQ. TO 15640 kHz

| 0 1 2 3 4 5 6 7 8 9 10 11 12 13 14 15 16 17 18 19 20 21 22 23 24 |
|---|

ENGLISH ▬  ARABIC ⬚⬚  CHINESE ▭▭▭  FRENCH ═  GERMAN ▬  RUSSIAN ══  SPANISH ▬  OTHER ▬

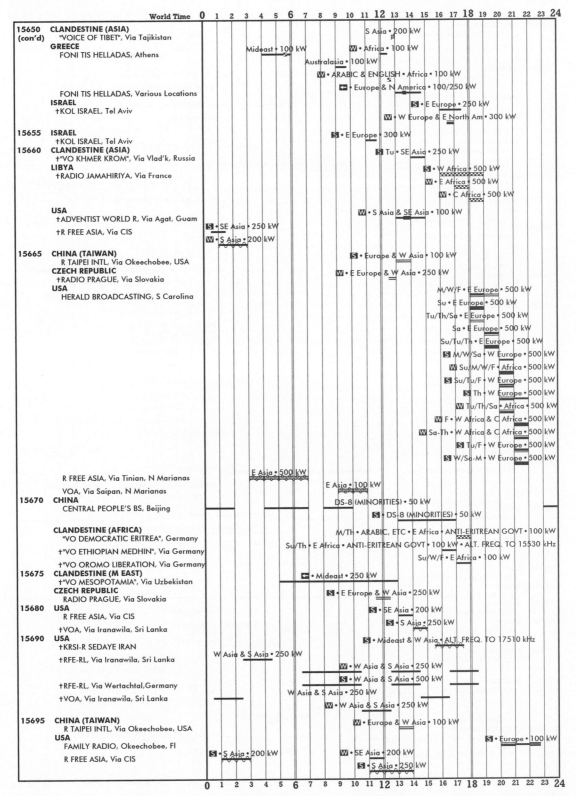

**World Time** 0 1 2 3 4 5 6 7 8 9 10 11 12 13 14 15 16 17 18 19 20 21 22 23 24

**15650 (con'd)**
CLANDESTINE (ASIA) "VOICE OF TIBET", Via Tajikistan — S Asia • 200 kW

GREECE
FONI TIS HELLADAS, Athens
- Mideast • 100 kW
- W • Africa • 100 kW
- Australasia • 100 kW
- W • ARABIC & ENGLISH • Africa • 100 kW

FONI TIS HELLADAS, Various Locations
- Europe & N America • 100/250 kW

ISRAEL
†KOL ISRAEL, Tel Aviv
- S • E Europe • 250 kW
- W • W Europe & E North Am • 300 kW

**15655** ISRAEL
†KOL ISRAEL, Tel Aviv — S • E Europe • 300 kW

**15660** CLANDESTINE (ASIA)
†"VO KHMER KROM", Via Vlad'k, Russia — S Tu • SE Asia • 250 kW

LIBYA
†RADIO JAMAHIRIYA, Via France
- S • W Africa • 500 kW
- W • E Africa • 500 kW
- W • C Africa • 500 kW

USA
†ADVENTIST WORLD R, Via Agat, Guam — W • S Asia & SE Asia • 100 kW

†R FREE ASIA, Via CIS
- S • SE Asia • 250 kW
- W • S Asia • 200 kW

**15665** CHINA (TAIWAN)
R TAIPEI INTL, Via Okeechobee, USA — S • Europe & W Asia • 100 kW

CZECH REPUBLIC
†RADIO PRAGUE, Via Slovakia — W • E Europe & W Asia • 250 kW

USA
HERALD BROADCASTING, S Carolina
- M/W/F • E Europe • 500 kW
- Su • E Europe • 500 kW
- Tu/Th/Sa • E Europe • 500 kW
- Sa • E Europe • 500 kW
- Su/Tu/Th • E Europe • 500 kW
- S M/W/Sa • W Europe • 500 kW
- W Su/M/W/F • Africa • 500 kW
- S Su/Tu/F • W Europe • 500 kW
- S Th • E Europe • 500 kW
- W Tu/Th/Sa • Africa • 500 kW
- W F • W Africa & C Africa • 500 kW
- W Sa-Th • W Africa & C Africa • 500 kW
- S Tu/F • W Europe • 500 kW
- S W/Sa-M • W Europe • 500 kW

R FREE ASIA, Via Tinian, N Marianas — E Asia • 500 kW

VOA, Via Saipan, N Marianas — E Asia • 100 kW

**15670** CHINA
CENTRAL PEOPLE'S BS, Beijing
- DS-8 (MINORITIES) • 50 kW
- S • DS-8 (MINORITIES) • 50 kW

CLANDESTINE (AFRICA)
"VO DEMOCRATIC ERITREA", Germany — M/TH • ARABIC, ETC • E Africa • ANTI-ERITREAN GOVT • 100 kW

†"VO ETHIOPIAN MEDHIN", Via Germany — Su/Th • E Africa • ANTI-ERITREAN GOVT • 100 kW • ALT. FREQ. TO 15530 kHz

†"VO OROMO LIBERATION, Via Germany — Su/W/F • E Africa • 100 kW

**15675** CLANDESTINE (M EAST)
†"VO MESOPOTAMIA", Via Uzbekistan — Mideast • 250 kW

CZECH REPUBLIC
RADIO PRAGUE, Via Slovakia — S • E Europe & W Asia • 250 kW

**15680** USA
R FREE ASIA, Via CIS — S • SE Asia • 200 kW

†VOA, Via Iranawila, Sri Lanka — S • S Asia • 250 kW

**15690** USA
†KRSI-R SEDAYE IRAN — S • Mideast & W Asia • ALT. FREQ. TO 17510 kHz

†RFE-RL, Via Iranawila, Sri Lanka
- W Asia & S Asia • 250 kW
- W • W Asia & S Asia • 250 kW

†RFE-RL, Via Wertachtal, Germany — S • W Asia & S Asia • 500 kW

†VOA, Via Iranawila, Sri Lanka
- W Asia & S Asia • 250 kW
- W • W Asia & S Asia • 250 kW

**15695** CHINA (TAIWAN)
R TAIPEI INTL, Via Okeechobee, USA — W • Europe & W Asia • 100 kW

USA
FAMILY RADIO, Okeechobee, Fl
- S • Europe • 100 kW
- S • S Asia • 200 kW
- W • SE Asia • 200 kW

R FREE ASIA, Via CIS — S • S Asia • 250 kW

0 1 2 3 4 5 6 7 8 9 10 11 12 13 14 15 16 17 18 19 20 21 22 23 24

SEASONAL S OR W    1-HR TIMESHIFT MIDYEAR ◄ OR ►    JAMMING / OR ∧    EARLIEST HEARD ◁    LATEST HEARD ▷    NEW FOR 2003 †

| World Time | Station details | Schedule |
|---|---|---|
| **15700** | **BULGARIA** RADIO BULGARIA, Plovdiv | ◄ • Europe • 500 kW / ◄ • Europe • 250 kW / S • W Europe • 250 kW |
| **15705** | **DENMARK** RADIO DANMARK, Via Norway | W • E Asia & Australasia • 500 kW / S • Mideast & E Africa • 500 kW / S • E Asia • 500 kW / W • N America • 500 kW |
| | **NORWAY** R NORWAY INTL, Kvitsøy | W • E Asia & Australasia • 500 kW / S • Mideast & E Africa • 500 kW / S • E Asia • 500 kW / W • N America • 500 kW |
| | R NORWAY INTL, Sveio | |
| | **SWEDEN** †RADIO SWEDEN, Hörby | S • N Asia • 500 kW • ALT. FREQ. TO 15245 kHz |
| **15710** | **CHINA** CENTRAL PEOPLE'S BS, Beijing | CHINESE, ETC • TAIWAN SERVICE • 50 kW |
| **15715** | **CHINA (TAIWAN)** R TAIPEI INTL, Via Okeechobee, USA | S • Europe • 100 kW |
| | **GERMANY** RADIO SANTEC, Jülich | S Su • C Africa & S Africa • 100 kW |
| | **USA** FAMILY RADIO, Okeechobee, Fl | S • Europe • 100 kW |
| **15725** | **PALAU** KHBN-VO HOPE, Koror | SE Asia • 50 kW |
| | **USA** ADVENTIST WORLD R, Via Agat, Guam | W • E Asia • 100 kW |
| | WRMI-R MIAMI INTL, Miami, Florida | ◄ • N America • 50 kW |
| **15725v** | **PAKISTAN** RADIO PAKISTAN, Islamabad | E Africa & S Africa • 100 kW / S • Mideast & N Africa • 100 kW |
| **15735** | **DENMARK** RADIO DANMARK, Via Norway | W • SE Asia & Australasia • 500 kW / S • N America • 500 kW / S • S Asia • 500 kW / W • Mideast • 500 kW / S • Mideast & E Africa • 500 kW |
| | **NORWAY** R NORWAY INTL, Kvitsøy | W • SE Asia & Australasia • 500 kW / S • S Asia • 500 kW / W • Mideast • 500 kW / S • Mideast & E Africa • 500 kW |
| | R NORWAY INTL, Sveio | S • N America • 500 kW |
| | **RUSSIA** VOICE OF RUSSIA, Via Armenia | ◄ • S America • 500 kW |
| **15745** | **USA** †WEWN, Birmingham, Alabama | S • S America • 500 kW / Europe • 500 kW / S America • 500 kW |
| **15750** | **USA** †VOA, Via Iranawila, Sri Lanka | S • Mideast & W Asia • 250 kW |
| **15760** | **ISRAEL** †KOL ISRAEL, Tel Aviv | S • W Europe & E North Am • DS-B • 250 kW / W Europe & E North Am • 250 kW |
| **15770** | **INDIA** †ALL INDIA RADIO, Aligarh | W Asia & Mideast • 250 kW / SE Asia • 250 kW / Irr • Mideast • HAJJ • 250 kW |
| **15775** | **USA** †VOA, Via Iranawila, Sri Lanka | W • E Africa • 250 kW |
| **15785v** | **ISRAEL** GALEI ZAHAL, Tel Aviv | Irr • Europe • DS • 10 kW • ALT. FREQ. TO 6973v kHz |
| **15795** | **INDIA** †ALL INDIA RADIO, Bangalore | SE Asia • 500 kW |
| **15880** | **CHINA** CENTRAL PEOPLE'S BS, Beijing | CHINESE, ETC • NETWORK 6 • 50 kW / Th-Tu • CHINESE, ETC • NETWORK 6 • 50 kW |
| **17485** | **CZECH REPUBLIC** RADIO PRAGUE, Litomyšl | W • W Africa & C Africa • 100 kW / W • C Africa & S Africa • 100 kW |
| | **SWEDEN** †RADIO SWEDEN, Hörby | S • W Europe & W Africa • 500 kW / S M-F • W Europe & W Africa • 500 kW |
| | **USA** †R FREE ASIA, Via CIS | S • S Asia • 500 kW |
| **17495** | **CLANDESTINE (ASIA)** †"D'CRATIC VO BURMA", Via Madagascar | SE Asia • ANTI-MYANMAR GOVT • 50 kW |
| **(con'd)** | **RUSSIA** VOICE OF RUSSIA, Via Tajikistan | ◄ • SE Asia & Australasia • 500 kW |

ENGLISH ■■■   ARABIC ░░░   CHINESE □□□   FRENCH ══   GERMAN ▬▬   RUSSIAN ══   SPANISH ══   OTHER ──

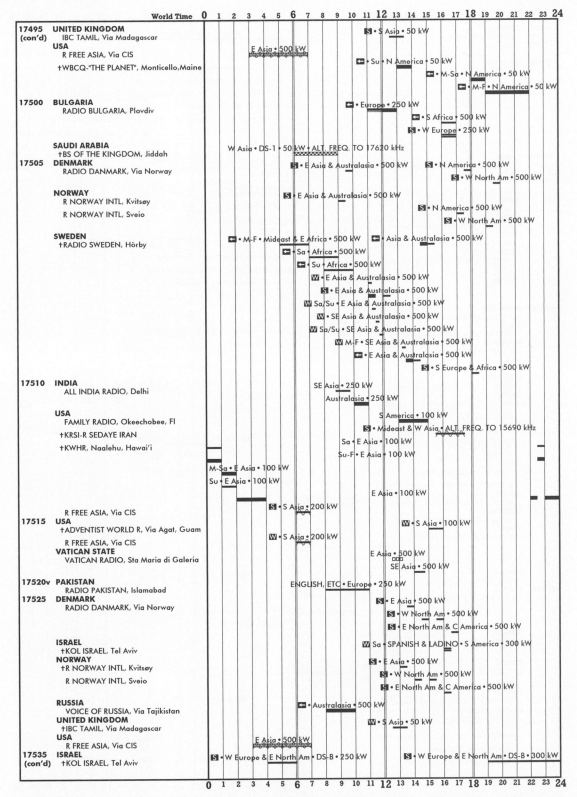

| World Time | | |
|---|---|---|
| **17495** (con'd) | **UNITED KINGDOM** IBC TAMIL, Via Madagascar | S • S Asia • 50 kW |
| | **USA** R FREE ASIA, Via CIS | E Asia • 500 kW |
| | †WBCQ-"THE PLANET", Monticello, Maine | Su • N America • 50 kW · M-Sa • N America • 50 kW · M-F • N America • 50 kW |
| **17500** | **BULGARIA** RADIO BULGARIA, Plovdiv | Europe • 250 kW · S Africa • 500 kW · W Europe • 250 kW |
| | **SAUDI ARABIA** †BS OF THE KINGDOM, Jiddah | W Asia • DS-1 • 50 kW • ALT. FREQ. TO 17620 kHz |
| **17505** | **DENMARK** RADIO DANMARK, Via Norway | S • E Asia & Australasia • 500 kW · S • N America • 500 kW · S • W North Am • 500 kW |
| | **NORWAY** R NORWAY INTL, Kvitsøy | S • E Asia & Australasia • 500 kW |
| | R NORWAY INTL, Sveio | S • N America • 500 kW · S • W North Am • 500 kW |
| | **SWEDEN** †RADIO SWEDEN, Hörby | • M-F • Mideast & E Africa • 500 kW · Asia & Australasia • 500 kW · Sa • Africa • 500 kW · Su • Africa • 500 kW · W • E Asia & Australasia • 500 kW · S • E Asia & Australasia • 500 kW · W Sa/Su • E Asia & Australasia • 500 kW · W • SE Asia & Australasia • 500 kW · W Sa/Su • SE Asia & Australasia • 500 kW · W M-F • SE Asia & Australasia • 500 kW · • E Asia & Australasia • 500 kW · S • S Europe & Africa • 500 kW |
| **17510** | **INDIA** ALL INDIA RADIO, Delhi | SE Asia • 250 kW · Australasia • 250 kW |
| | **USA** FAMILY RADIO, Okeechobee, Fl | S America • 100 kW |
| | †KRSI-R SEDAYE IRAN | S • Mideast & W Asia • ALT. FREQ. TO 15690 kHz |
| | †KWHR, Naalehu, Hawai'i | Sa • E Asia • 100 kW · Su-F • E Asia • 100 kW · M-Sa • E Asia • 100 kW · Su • E Asia • 100 kW · E Asia • 100 kW |
| | R FREE ASIA, Via CIS | |
| **17515** | **USA** †ADVENTIST WORLD R, Via Agat, Guam | S • S Asia • 200 kW · W • S Asia • 100 kW · W • S Asia • 200 kW |
| | R FREE ASIA, Via CIS | |
| | **VATICAN STATE** VATICAN RADIO, Sta Maria di Galeria | E Asia • 500 kW · SE Asia • 500 kW |
| **17520v** | **PAKISTAN** RADIO PAKISTAN, Islamabad | ENGLISH, ETC • Europe • 250 kW |
| **17525** | **DENMARK** RADIO DANMARK, Via Norway | S • E Asia • 500 kW · S • W North Am • 500 kW · S • E North Am & C America • 500 kW |
| | **ISRAEL** †KOL ISRAEL, Tel Aviv | W Sa • SPANISH & LADINO • S America • 300 kW |
| | **NORWAY** †R NORWAY INTL, Kvitsøy | S • E Asia • 500 kW · S • W North Am • 500 kW · S • E North Am & C America • 500 kW |
| | R NORWAY INTL, Sveio | |
| | **RUSSIA** VOICE OF RUSSIA, Via Tajikistan | • Australasia • 500 kW |
| | **UNITED KINGDOM** †IBC TAMIL, Via Madagascar | W • S Asia • 50 kW |
| | **USA** R FREE ASIA, Via CIS | E Asia • 500 kW |
| **17535** (con'd) | **ISRAEL** †KOL ISRAEL, Tel Aviv | S • W Europe & E North Am • DS-B • 250 kW · S • W Europe & E North Am • DS-B • 300 kW |

SEASONAL S OR W   1-HR TIMESHIFT MIDYEAR ⇐ OR ⇒   JAMMING / OR ∧   EARLIEST HEARD ◁   LATEST HEARD ▷   NEW FOR 2003 †

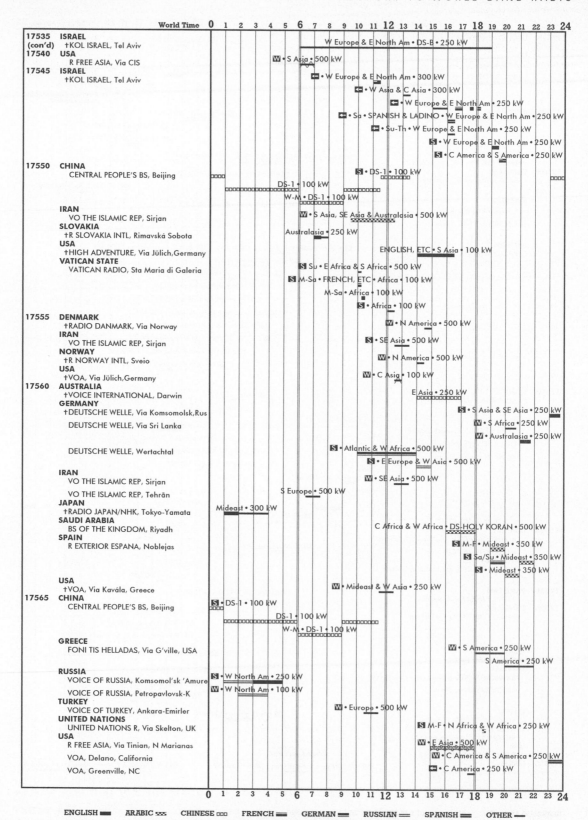

| World Time | 0 1 2 3 4 5 6 7 8 9 10 11 12 13 14 15 16 17 18 19 20 21 22 23 24 |
|---|---|
| **17535  ISRAEL** | |
| (con'd)  †KOL ISRAEL, Tel Aviv | W Europe & E North Am • DS-B • 250 kW |
| **17540  USA** | |
| R FREE ASIA, Via CIS | W • S Asia • 500 kW |
| **17545  ISRAEL** | |
| †KOL ISRAEL, Tel Aviv | • W Europe & E North Am • 300 kW |
| | • W Asia & C Asia • 300 kW |
| | • W Europe & E North Am • 250 kW |
| | • Sa • SPANISH & LADINO • W Europe & E North Am • 250 kW |
| | • Su-Th • W Europe & E North Am • 250 kW |
| | S • W Europe & E North Am • 250 kW |
| | S • C America & S America • 250 kW |
| **17550  CHINA** | |
| CENTRAL PEOPLE'S BS, Beijing | S • DS-1 • 100 kW |
| | DS-1 • 100 kW |
| | W-M • DS-1 • 100 kW |
| **IRAN** | |
| VO THE ISLAMIC REP, Sirjan | W • S Asia, SE Asia & Australasia • 500 kW |
| **SLOVAKIA** | |
| †R SLOVAKIA INTL, Rimavská Sobota | Australasia • 250 kW |
| **USA** | |
| †HIGH ADVENTURE, Via Jülich, Germany | ENGLISH, ETC • S Asia • 100 kW |
| **VATICAN STATE** | |
| VATICAN RADIO, Sta Maria di Galeria | S • Su • E Africa & S Africa • 500 kW |
| | S • M-Sa • FRENCH, ETC • Africa • 100 kW |
| | M-Sa • Africa • 100 kW |
| | S • Africa • 100 kW |
| **17555  DENMARK** | |
| †RADIO DANMARK, Via Norway | W • N America • 500 kW |
| **IRAN** | |
| VO THE ISLAMIC REP, Sirjan | S • SE Asia • 500 kW |
| **NORWAY** | |
| †R NORWAY INTL, Sveio | W • N America • 500 kW |
| **USA** | |
| †VOA, Via Jülich, Germany | W • C Asia • 100 kW |
| **17560  AUSTRALIA** | |
| †VOICE INTERNATIONAL, Darwin | E Asia • 250 kW |
| **GERMANY** | |
| †DEUTSCHE WELLE, Via Komsomolsk, Rus | S • S Asia & SE Asia • 250 kW |
| DEUTSCHE WELLE, Via Sri Lanka | W • S Africa • 250 kW |
| | W • Australasia • 250 kW |
| DEUTSCHE WELLE, Wertachtal | S • Atlantic & W Africa • 500 kW |
| | S • E Europe & W Asia • 500 kW |
| **IRAN** | |
| VO THE ISLAMIC REP, Sirjan | W • SE Asia • 500 kW |
| VO THE ISLAMIC REP, Tehrän | S Europe • 500 kW |
| **JAPAN** | |
| †RADIO JAPAN/NHK, Tokyo-Yamata | Mideast • 300 kW |
| **SAUDI ARABIA** | |
| BS OF THE KINGDOM, Riyadh | C Africa & W Africa • DS-HOLY KORAN • 500 kW |
| **SPAIN** | |
| R EXTERIOR ESPANA, Noblejas | S • M-F • Mideast • 350 kW |
| | S • Sa/Su • Mideast • 350 kW |
| | S • Mideast • 350 kW |
| **USA** | |
| †VOA, Via Kavála, Greece | W • Mideast & W Asia • 250 kW |
| **17565  CHINA** | |
| CENTRAL PEOPLE'S BS, Beijing | S • DS-1 • 100 kW |
| | DS-1 • 100 kW |
| | W-M • DS-1 • 100 kW |
| **GREECE** | |
| FONI TIS HELLADAS, Via G'ville, USA | W • S America • 250 kW |
| | S America • 250 kW |
| **RUSSIA** | |
| VOICE OF RUSSIA, Komsomol'sk 'Amure | S • W North Am • 250 kW |
| VOICE OF RUSSIA, Petropavlovsk-K | W • W North Am • 100 kW |
| **TURKEY** | |
| VOICE OF TURKEY, Ankara-Emirler | W • Europe • 500 kW |
| **UNITED NATIONS** | |
| UNITED NATIONS R, Via Skelton, UK | S • M-F • N Africa & W Africa • 250 kW |
| **USA** | |
| R FREE ASIA, Via Tinian, N Marianas | W • E Asia • 500 kW |
| VOA, Delano, California | W • C America & S America • 250 kW |
| VOA, Greenville, NC | • C America • 250 kW |

| | 0 1 2 3 4 5 6 7 8 9 10 11 12 13 14 15 16 17 18 19 20 21 22 23 24 |
|---|---|

ENGLISH ▬▬   ARABIC ﹌﹌   CHINESE □□□   FRENCH ▭▭   GERMAN ▬▬   RUSSIAN ══   SPANISH ▭▭   OTHER ▬▬

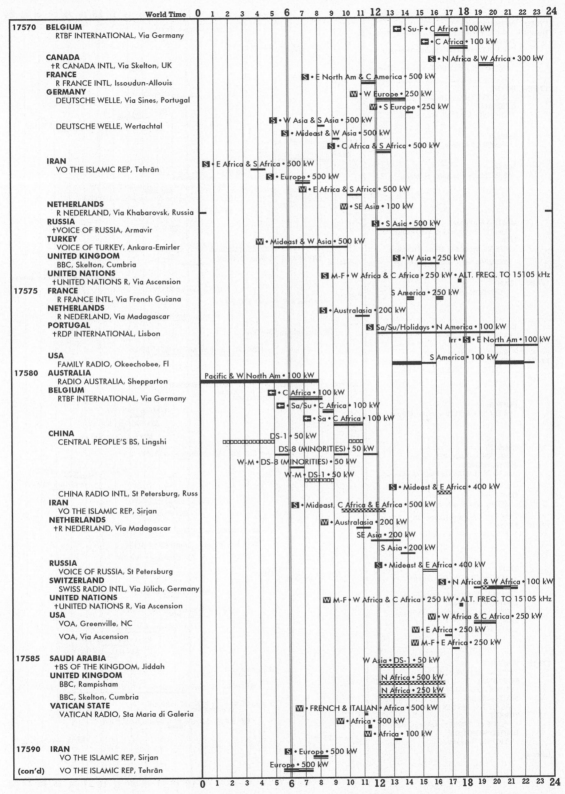

World Time 0 1 2 3 4 5 6 7 8 9 10 11 12 13 14 15 16 17 18 19 20 21 22 23 24

**17570 BELGIUM**
RTBF INTERNATIONAL, Via Germany — Su-F • C Africa • 100 kW / C Africa • 100 kW

**CANADA**
†R CANADA INTL, Via Skelton, UK — S • N Africa & W Africa • 300 kW

**FRANCE**
R FRANCE INTL, Issoudun-Allouis — S • E North Am & C America • 500 kW

**GERMANY**
DEUTSCHE WELLE, Via Sines, Portugal — W • W Europe • 250 kW / W • S Europe • 250 kW

DEUTSCHE WELLE, Wertachtal — S • W Asia & S Asia • 500 kW / S • Mideast & W Asia • 500 kW / S • C Africa & S Africa • 500 kW

**IRAN**
VO THE ISLAMIC REP, Tehrān — S • E Africa & S Africa • 500 kW / S • Europe • 500 kW / W • E Africa & S Africa • 500 kW

**NETHERLANDS**
R NEDERLAND, Via Khabarovsk, Russia — W • SE Asia • 100 kW

**RUSSIA**
†VOICE OF RUSSIA, Armavir — S • S Asia • 500 kW

**TURKEY**
VOICE OF TURKEY, Ankara-Emirler — W • Mideast & W Asia • 500 kW

**UNITED KINGDOM**
BBC, Skelton, Cumbria — S • W Asia • 250 kW

**UNITED NATIONS**
†UNITED NATIONS R, Via Ascension — S M-F • W Africa & C Africa • 250 kW • ALT. FREQ. TO 15105 kHz

**17575 FRANCE**
R FRANCE INTL, Via French Guiana — S America • 250 kW

**NETHERLANDS**
R NEDERLAND, Via Madagascar — S • Australasia • 200 kW

**PORTUGAL**
†RDP INTERNATIONAL, Lisbon — S Sa/Su/Holidays • N America • 100 kW / Irr • S • E North Am • 100 kW

**USA**
FAMILY RADIO, Okeechobee, Fl — S America • 100 kW

**17580 AUSTRALIA**
RADIO AUSTRALIA, Shepparton — Pacific & W North Am • 100 kW

**BELGIUM**
RTBF INTERNATIONAL, Via Germany — C Africa • 100 kW / Sa/Su • C Africa • 100 kW / Sa • C Africa • 100 kW

**CHINA**
CENTRAL PEOPLE'S BS, Lingshi — DS-1 • 50 kW / DS-8 (MINORITIES) • 50 kW / W-M • DS-8 (MINORITIES) • 50 kW / W-M • DS-1 • 50 kW

CHINA RADIO INTL, St Petersburg, Russ — S • Mideast & E Africa • 400 kW

**IRAN**
VO THE ISLAMIC REP, Sirjan — S • Mideast, C Africa & E Africa • 500 kW

**NETHERLANDS**
†R NEDERLAND, Via Madagascar — W • Australasia • 200 kW / SE Asia • 200 kW / S Asia • 200 kW

**RUSSIA**
VOICE OF RUSSIA, St Petersburg — S • Mideast & E Africa • 400 kW

**SWITZERLAND**
SWISS RADIO INTL, Via Jülich, Germany — S • N Africa & W Africa • 100 kW

**UNITED NATIONS**
†UNITED NATIONS R, Via Ascension — W M-F • W Africa & C Africa • 250 kW • ALT. FREQ. TO 15105 kHz

**USA**
VOA, Greenville, NC — W • W Africa & C Africa • 250 kW / W • E Africa • 250 kW

VOA, Via Ascension — W M-F • E Africa • 250 kW

**17585 SAUDI ARABIA**
†BS OF THE KINGDOM, Jiddah — W Asia • DS-1 • 50 kW

**UNITED KINGDOM**
BBC, Rampisham — N Africa • 500 kW

BBC, Skelton, Cumbria — N Africa • 250 kW

**VATICAN STATE**
VATICAN RADIO, Sta Maria di Galeria — W • FRENCH & ITALIAN • Africa • 500 kW / W • Africa • 500 kW / W • Africa • 100 kW

**17590 IRAN**
VO THE ISLAMIC REP, Sirjan — S • Europe • 500 kW

**(con'd)** VO THE ISLAMIC REP, Tehrān — Europe • 500 kW

0 1 2 3 4 5 6 7 8 9 10 11 12 13 14 15 16 17 18 19 20 21 22 23 24

SEASONAL S OR W     1-HR TIMESHIFT MIDYEAR ⇆ OR ⇥     JAMMING / OR ∧     EARLIEST HEARD ◁     LATEST HEARD ▷     NEW FOR 2003 †

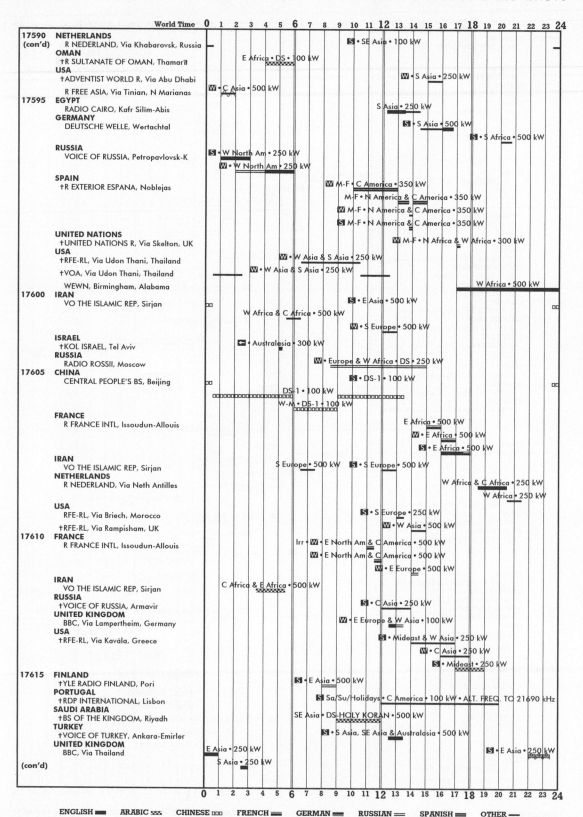

| | World Time | 0 1 2 3 4 5 6 7 8 9 10 11 12 13 14 15 16 17 18 19 20 21 22 23 24 |

**17590 NETHERLANDS**
(con'd) R NEDERLAND, Via Khabarovsk, Russia — S • SE Asia • 100 kW
**OMAN**
†R SULTANATE OF OMAN, Thamarīt — E Africa • DS • 100 kW
**USA**
†ADVENTIST WORLD R, Via Abu Dhabi — W • S Asia • 250 kW
R FREE ASIA, Via Tinian, N Marianas — W • C Asia • 500 kW
**17595 EGYPT**
RADIO CAIRO, Kafr Silīm-Abis — S Asia • 250 kW
**GERMANY**
DEUTSCHE WELLE, Wertachtal — S • S Asia • 500 kW / S • S Africa • 500 kW
**RUSSIA**
VOICE OF RUSSIA, Petropavlovsk-K — S • W North Am • 250 kW / W • W North Am • 250 kW
**SPAIN**
†R EXTERIOR ESPANA, Noblejas — W • M-F • C America • 350 kW / M-F • N America & C America • 350 kW / W • M-F • N America & C America • 350 kW / S • M-F • N America & C America • 350 kW
**UNITED NATIONS**
†UNITED NATIONS R, Via Skelton, UK — W • M-F • N Africa & W Africa • 300 kW
**USA**
†RFE-RL, Via Udon Thani, Thailand — W • W Asia & S Asia • 250 kW
†VOA, Via Udon Thani, Thailand — W • W Asia & S Asia • 250 kW
WEWN, Birmingham, Alabama — W Africa • 500 kW
**17600 IRAN**
VO THE ISLAMIC REP, Sirjan — S • E Asia • 500 kW / W Africa & C Africa • 500 kW / W • S Europe • 500 kW
**ISRAEL**
†KOL ISRAEL, Tel Aviv — Australasia • 300 kW
**RUSSIA**
RADIO ROSSII, Moscow — W • Europe & W Africa • DS • 250 kW
**17605 CHINA**
CENTRAL PEOPLE'S BS, Beijing — S • DS-1 • 100 kW / DS-1 • 100 kW / W-M • DS-1 • 100 kW
**FRANCE**
R FRANCE INTL, Issoudun-Allouis — E Africa • 500 kW / W • E Africa • 500 kW / S • E Africa • 500 kW
**IRAN**
VO THE ISLAMIC REP, Sirjan — S Europe • 500 kW / S • S Europe • 500 kW
**NETHERLANDS**
R NEDERLAND, Via Neth Antilles — W Africa & C Africa • 250 kW / W Africa • 250 kW
**USA**
RFE-RL, Via Briech, Morocco — S • S Europe • 250 kW
†RFE-RL, Via Rampisham, UK — W • W Asia • 500 kW
**17610 FRANCE**
R FRANCE INTL, Issoudun-Allouis — Irr • W • E North Am & C America • 500 kW / W • E North Am & C America • 500 kW / W • E Europe • 500 kW
**IRAN**
VO THE ISLAMIC REP, Sirjan — C Africa & E Africa • 500 kW
**RUSSIA**
†VOICE OF RUSSIA, Armavir — S • C Asia • 250 kW
**UNITED KINGDOM**
BBC, Via Lampertheim, Germany — W • E Europe & W Asia • 100 kW
**USA**
†RFE-RL, Via Kavála, Greece — S • Mideast & W Asia • 250 kW / W • C Asia • 250 kW / S • Mideast • 250 kW
**17615 FINLAND**
†YLE RADIO FINLAND, Pori — S • E Asia • 500 kW
**PORTUGAL**
†RDP INTERNATIONAL, Lisbon — S • Sa/Su/Holidays • C America • 100 kW • ALT. FREQ. TO 21690 kHz
**SAUDI ARABIA**
†BS OF THE KINGDOM, Riyadh — SE Asia • DS-HOLY KORAN • 500 kW
**TURKEY**
†VOICE OF TURKEY, Ankara-Emirler — S • S Asia, SE Asia & Australasia • 500 kW
**UNITED KINGDOM**
BBC, Via Thailand — E Asia • 250 kW / S Asia • 250 kW / S • E Asia • 250 kW

(con'd)

| | 0 1 2 3 4 5 6 7 8 9 10 11 12 13 14 15 16 17 18 19 20 21 22 23 24 |

ENGLISH ▬ ARABIC ⬚ CHINESE ⬚⬚ FRENCH ▬ GERMAN ▬ RUSSIAN ══ SPANISH ══ OTHER ▬

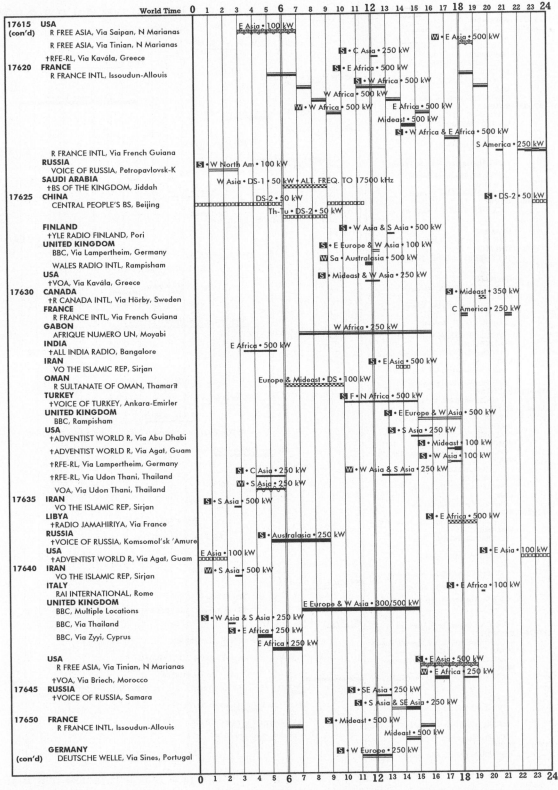

| World Time | 0 1 2 3 4 5 6 7 8 9 10 11 12 13 14 15 16 17 18 19 20 21 22 23 24 |
|---|---|
| **17615** USA | |
| (con'd) R FREE ASIA, Via Saipan, N Marianas | E Asia • 100 kW |
| R FREE ASIA, Via Tinian, N Marianas | W • E Asia • 500 kW |
| †RFE-RL, Via Kavála, Greece | S • C Asia • 250 kW |
| **17620** FRANCE | |
| R FRANCE INTL, Issoudun-Allouis | S • E Africa • 500 kW |
| | S • W Africa • 500 kW |
| | W Africa • 500 kW |
| | W • W Africa • 500 kW     E Africa • 500 kW |
| | Mideast • 500 kW |
| | S • W Africa & E Africa • 500 kW |
| | S America • 250 kW |
| R FRANCE INTL, Via French Guiana | |
| RUSSIA | |
| VOICE OF RUSSIA, Petropavlovsk-K | S • W North Am • 100 kW |
| SAUDI ARABIA | W Asia • DS-1 • 50 kW • ALT. FREQ. TO 17500 kHz |
| †BS OF THE KINGDOM, Jiddah | |
| **17625** CHINA | S • DS-2 • 50 kW |
| CENTRAL PEOPLE'S BS, Beijing | DS-2 • 50 kW |
| | Th-Tu • DS-2 • 50 kW |
| FINLAND | |
| †YLE RADIO FINLAND, Pori | S • W Asia & S Asia • 500 kW |
| UNITED KINGDOM | |
| BBC, Via Lampertheim, Germany | S • E Europe & W Asia • 100 kW |
| WALES RADIO INTL, Rampisham | W Sa • Australasia • 500 kW |
| USA | |
| †VOA, Via Kavála, Greece | S • Mideast & W Asia • 250 kW |
| **17630** CANADA | S • Mideast • 350 kW |
| †R CANADA INTL, Via Hörby, Sweden | |
| FRANCE | C America • 250 kW |
| R FRANCE INTL, Via French Guiana | |
| GABON | W Africa • 250 kW |
| AFRIQUE NUMERO UN, Moyabi | |
| INDIA | E Africa • 500 kW |
| †ALL INDIA RADIO, Bangalore | |
| IRAN | S • E Asia • 500 kW |
| VO THE ISLAMIC REP, Sirjan | |
| OMAN | Europe & Mideast • DS • 100 kW |
| R SULTANATE OF OMAN, Thamarīt | |
| TURKEY | S • F • N Africa • 500 kW |
| †VOICE OF TURKEY, Ankara-Emirler | |
| UNITED KINGDOM | S • E Europe & W Asia • 500 kW |
| BBC, Rampisham | |
| USA | S • S Asia • 250 kW |
| †ADVENTIST WORLD R, Via Abu Dhabi | S • Mideast • 100 kW |
| †ADVENTIST WORLD R, Via Agat, Guam | S • W Asia • 100 kW |
| †RFE-RL, Via Lampertheim, Germany | S • C Asia • 250 kW     W • W Asia & S Asia • 250 kW |
| †RFE-RL, Via Udon Thani, Thailand | W • S Asia • 250 kW |
| VOA, Via Udon Thani, Thailand | |
| **17635** IRAN | S • S Asia • 500 kW |
| VO THE ISLAMIC REP, Sirjan | |
| LIBYA | S • E Africa • 500 kW |
| †RADIO JAMAHIRIYA, Via France | |
| RUSSIA | S • Australasia • 250 kW |
| †VOICE OF RUSSIA, Komsomol'sk 'Amure | |
| USA | E Asia • 100 kW     S • E Asia • 100 kW |
| †ADVENTIST WORLD R, Via Agat, Guam | |
| **17640** IRAN | W • S Asia • 500 kW |
| VO THE ISLAMIC REP, Sirjan | |
| ITALY | S • E Africa • 100 kW |
| RAI INTERNATIONAL, Rome | |
| UNITED KINGDOM | E Europe & W Asia • 300/500 kW |
| BBC, Multiple Locations | S • W Asia & S Asia • 250 kW |
| BBC, Via Thailand | S • E Africa • 250 kW |
| BBC, Via Zyyi, Cyprus | E Africa • 250 kW |
| USA | |
| R FREE ASIA, Via Tinian, N Marianas | S • E Asia • 500 kW     W • E Africa • 250 kW |
| †VOA, Via Briech, Morocco | |
| **17645** RUSSIA | S • SE Asia • 250 kW |
| †VOICE OF RUSSIA, Samara | S • S Asia & SE Asia • 250 kW |
| **17650** FRANCE | S • Mideast • 500 kW |
| R FRANCE INTL, Issoudun-Allouis | Mideast • 500 kW |
| GERMANY | S • W Europe • 250 kW |
| (con'd) DEUTSCHE WELLE, Via Sines, Portugal | |

| | 0 1 2 3 4 5 6 7 8 9 10 11 12 13 14 15 16 17 18 19 20 21 22 23 24 |

SEASONAL ⓢ OR Ⓦ     1-HR TIMESHIFT MIDYEAR ⇦ OR ⇨     JAMMING / OR ∧     EARLIEST HEARD ◁     LATEST HEARD ▷     NEW FOR 2003 †

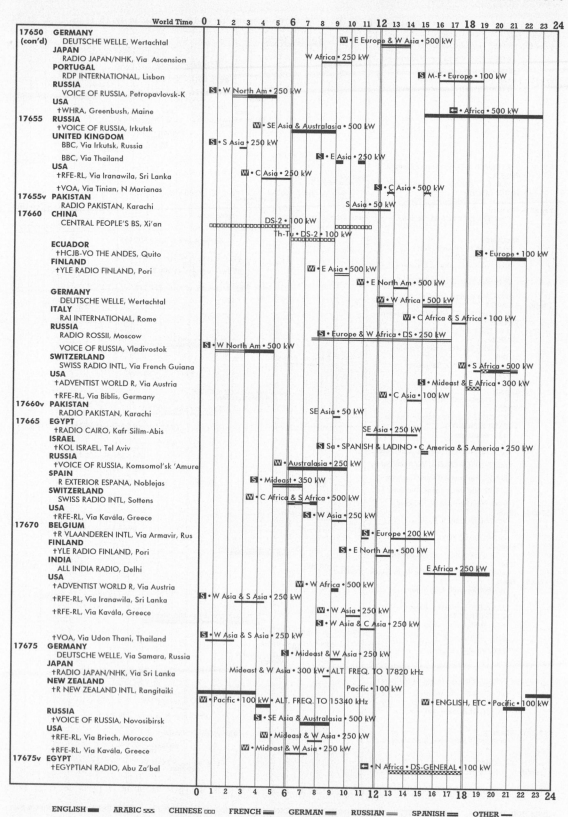

| Freq | Station | |
|---|---|---|
| 17650 (con'd) | **GERMANY** DEUTSCHE WELLE, Wertachtal | W • E Europe & W Asia • 500 kW |
| | **JAPAN** RADIO JAPAN/NHK, Via Ascension | W Africa • 250 kW |
| | **PORTUGAL** RDP INTERNATIONAL, Lisbon | S • M-F • Europe • 100 kW |
| | **RUSSIA** VOICE OF RUSSIA, Petropavlovsk-K | S • W North Am • 250 kW |
| | **USA** †WHRA, Greenbush, Maine | • Africa • 500 kW |
| 17655 | **RUSSIA** †VOICE OF RUSSIA, Irkutsk | W • SE Asia & Australasia • 500 kW |
| | **UNITED KINGDOM** BBC, Via Irkutsk, Russia | S • S Asia • 250 kW |
| | BBC, Via Thailand | S • E Asia • 250 kW |
| | **USA** †RFE-RL, Via Iranawila, Sri Lanka | W • C Asia • 250 kW |
| | †VOA, Via Tinian, N Marianas | S • C Asia • 500 kW |
| 17655v | **PAKISTAN** RADIO PAKISTAN, Karachi | S Asia • 50 kW |
| 17660 | **CHINA** CENTRAL PEOPLE'S BS, Xi'an | DS-2 • 100 kW  Th-Tu • DS-2 • 100 kW |
| | **ECUADOR** †HCJB-VO THE ANDES, Quito | S • Europe • 100 kW |
| | **FINLAND** †YLE RADIO FINLAND, Pori | W • E Asia • 500 kW |
| | **GERMANY** DEUTSCHE WELLE, Wertachtal | W • E North Am • 500 kW  W • W Africa • 500 kW |
| | **ITALY** RAI INTERNATIONAL, Rome | W • C Africa & S Africa • 100 kW |
| | **RUSSIA** RADIO ROSSII, Moscow | S • Europe & W Africa • DS • 250 kW |
| | VOICE OF RUSSIA, Vladivostok | S • W North Am • 500 kW |
| | **SWITZERLAND** SWISS RADIO INTL, Via French Guiana | W • S Africa • 500 kW |
| | **USA** †ADVENTIST WORLD R, Via Austria | S • Mideast & E Africa • 300 kW |
| | †RFE-RL, Via Biblis, Germany | W • C Asia • 100 kW |
| 17660v | **PAKISTAN** RADIO PAKISTAN, Karachi | SE Asia • 50 kW |
| 17665 | **EGYPT** †RADIO CAIRO, Kafr Silim-Abis | SE Asia • 250 kW |
| | **ISRAEL** †KOL ISRAEL, Tel Aviv | Sa • SPANISH & LADINO • C America & S America • 250 kW |
| | **RUSSIA** †VOICE OF RUSSIA, Komsomol'sk 'Amure | W • Australasia • 250 kW |
| | **SPAIN** R EXTERIOR ESPANA, Noblejas | S • Mideast • 350 kW |
| | **SWITZERLAND** SWISS RADIO INTL, Sottens | W • C Africa & S Africa • 500 kW |
| | **USA** †RFE-RL, Via Kavála, Greece | S • W Asia • 250 kW |
| 17670 | **BELGIUM** †R VLAANDEREN INTL, Via Armavir, Rus | S • Europe • 200 kW |
| | **FINLAND** †YLE RADIO FINLAND, Pori | S • E North Am • 500 kW |
| | **INDIA** ALL INDIA RADIO, Delhi | E Africa • 250 kW |
| | **USA** †ADVENTIST WORLD R, Via Austria | W • W Africa • 500 kW |
| | †RFE-RL, Via Iranawila, Sri Lanka | S • W Asia & S Asia • 250 kW |
| | †RFE-RL, Via Kavála, Greece | W • W Asia • 250 kW  S • W Asia & C Asia • 250 kW |
| | †VOA, Via Udon Thani, Thailand | S • W Asia & S Asia • 250 kW |
| 17675 | **GERMANY** DEUTSCHE WELLE, Via Samara, Russia | S • Mideast & W Asia • 250 kW |
| | **JAPAN** †RADIO JAPAN/NHK, Via Sri Lanka | Mideast & W Asia • 300 kW • ALT FREQ. TO 17820 kHz |
| | **NEW ZEALAND** †R NEW ZEALAND INTL, Rangitaiki | Pacific • 100 kW  W • Pacific • 100 kW • ALT. FREQ. TO 15340 kHz  W • ENGLISH, ETC • Pacific • 100 kW |
| | **RUSSIA** †VOICE OF RUSSIA, Novosibirsk | S • SE Asia & Australasia • 500 kW |
| | **USA** †RFE-RL, Via Briech, Morocco | W • Mideast & W Asia • 250 kW |
| | †RFE-RL, Via Kavála, Greece | W • Mideast & W Asia • 250 kW |
| 17675v | **EGYPT** †EGYPTIAN RADIO, Abu Za'bal | • N Africa • DS-GENERAL • 100 kW |

World Time: 0 1 2 3 4 5 6 7 8 9 10 11 12 13 14 15 16 17 18 19 20 21 22 23 24

ENGLISH ▬  ARABIC ⋙  CHINESE □□□  FRENCH ▬  GERMAN ▬  RUSSIAN ═  SPANISH ═  OTHER ▬

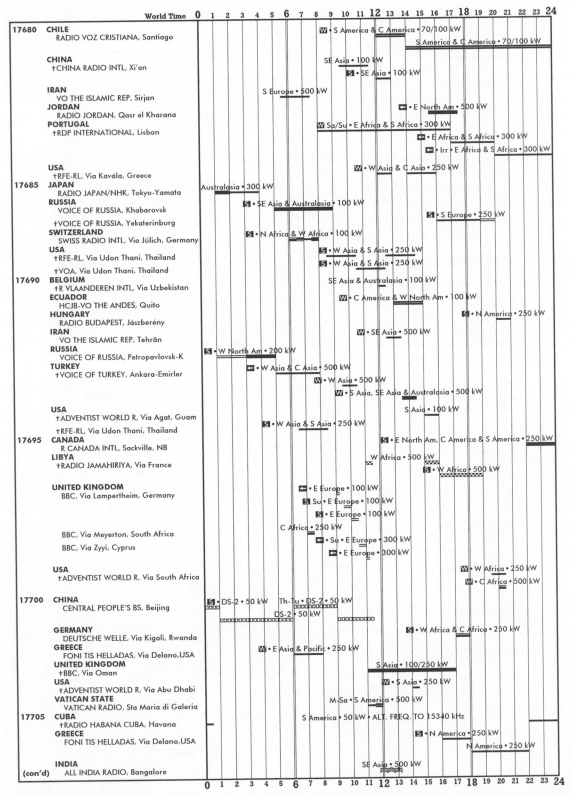

World Time

17680  **CHILE**
       RADIO VOZ CRISTIANA, Santiago

       **CHINA**
       †CHINA RADIO INTL, Xi'an

       **IRAN**
       VO THE ISLAMIC REP, Sirjan
       **JORDAN**
       RADIO JORDAN, Qasr el Kharana
       **PORTUGAL**
       †RDP INTERNATIONAL, Lisbon

       **USA**
       †RFE-RL, Via Kavála, Greece
17685  **JAPAN**
       RADIO JAPAN/NHK, Tokyo-Yamata
       **RUSSIA**
       VOICE OF RUSSIA, Khabarovsk

       †VOICE OF RUSSIA, Yekaterinburg
       **SWITZERLAND**
       SWISS RADIO INTL, Via Jülich, Germany
       **USA**
       †RFE-RL, Via Udon Thani, Thailand

       †VOA, Via Udon Thani, Thailand
17690  **BELGIUM**
       †R VLAANDEREN INTL, Via Uzbekistan
       **ECUADOR**
       HCJB-VO THE ANDES, Quito
       **HUNGARY**
       RADIO BUDAPEST, Jászberény
       **IRAN**
       VO THE ISLAMIC REP, Tehrān
       **RUSSIA**
       VOICE OF RUSSIA, Petropavlovsk-K
       **TURKEY**
       †VOICE OF TURKEY, Ankara-Emirler

       **USA**
       †ADVENTIST WORLD R, Via Agat, Guam

       †RFE-RL, Via Udon Thani, Thailand
17695  **CANADA**
       R CANADA INTL, Sackville, NB
       **LIBYA**
       †RADIO JAMAHIRIYA, Via France

       **UNITED KINGDOM**
       BBC, Via Lampertheim, Germany

       BBC, Via Meyerton, South Africa
       BBC, Via Zyyi, Cyprus

       **USA**
       †ADVENTIST WORLD R, Via South Africa

17700  **CHINA**
       CENTRAL PEOPLE'S BS, Beijing

       **GERMANY**
       DEUTSCHE WELLE, Via Kigali, Rwanda
       **GREECE**
       FONI TIS HELLADAS, Via Delano, USA
       **UNITED KINGDOM**
       †BBC, Via Oman
       **USA**
       †ADVENTIST WORLD R, Via Abu Dhabi
       **VATICAN STATE**
       VATICAN RADIO, Sta Maria di Galeria
17705  **CUBA**
       †RADIO HABANA CUBA, Havana
       **GREECE**
       FONI TIS HELLADAS, Via Delano, USA

       **INDIA**
(con'd)  ALL INDIA RADIO, Bangalore

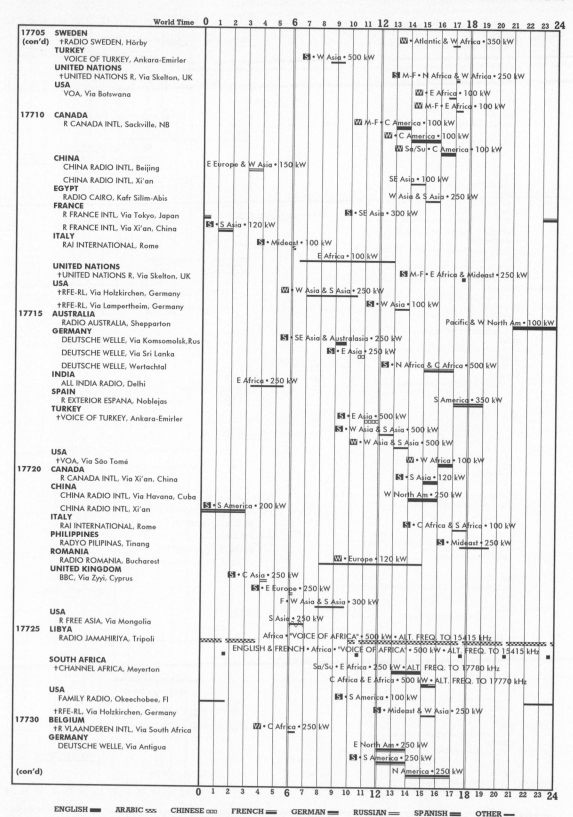

| World Time | 0 1 2 3 4 5 6 7 8 9 10 11 12 13 14 15 16 17 18 19 20 21 22 23 24 |
|---|---|

**17705 SWEDEN**
(con'd)    †RADIO SWEDEN, Hörby — W • Atlantic & W Africa • 350 kW
**TURKEY**
VOICE OF TURKEY, Ankara-Emirler — S • W Asia • 500 kW
**UNITED NATIONS**
†UNITED NATIONS R, Via Skelton, UK — S M-F • N Africa & W Africa • 250 kW
**USA**
VOA, Via Botswana — W • E Africa • 100 kW
— W M-F • E Africa • 100 kW

**17710 CANADA**
R CANADA INTL, Sackville, NB — W M-F • C America • 100 kW
— W • C America • 100 kW
— W Sa/Su • C America • 100 kW

**CHINA**
CHINA RADIO INTL, Beijing — E Europe & W Asia • 150 kW

CHINA RADIO INTL, Xi'an — SE Asia • 100 kW
**EGYPT**
RADIO CAIRO, Kafr Silim-Abis — W Asia & S Asia • 250 kW
**FRANCE**
R FRANCE INTL, Via Tokyo, Japan — S • SE Asia • 300 kW

R FRANCE INTL, Via Xi'an, China — S • S Asia • 120 kW
**ITALY**
RAI INTERNATIONAL, Rome — S • Mideast • 100 kW
— E Africa • 100 kW

**UNITED NATIONS**
†UNITED NATIONS R, Via Skelton, UK — S M-F • E Africa & Mideast • 250 kW
**USA**
†RFE-RL, Via Holzkirchen, Germany — W • W Asia & S Asia • 250 kW

†RFE-RL, Via Lampertheim, Germany — S • W Asia • 100 kW
**17715 AUSTRALIA**
RADIO AUSTRALIA, Shepparton — Pacific & W North Am • 100 kW
**GERMANY**
DEUTSCHE WELLE, Via Komsomolsk,Rus — S • SE Asia & Australasia • 250 kW

DEUTSCHE WELLE, Via Sri Lanka — S • E Asia • 250 kW

DEUTSCHE WELLE, Wertachtal — S • N Africa & C Africa • 500 kW
**INDIA**
ALL INDIA RADIO, Delhi — E Africa • 250 kW
**SPAIN**
R EXTERIOR ESPANA, Noblejas — S America • 350 kW
**TURKEY**
†VOICE OF TURKEY, Ankara-Emirler — S • E Asia • 500 kW
— S • W Asia & S Asia • 500 kW
— W • W Asia & S Asia • 500 kW

**USA**
†VOA, Via São Tomé — W • W Africa • 100 kW
**17720 CANADA**
R CANADA INTL, Via Xi'an, China — S • S Asia • 120 kW
**CHINA**
CHINA RADIO INTL, Via Havana, Cuba — W North Am • 250 kW

CHINA RADIO INTL, Xi'an — S • S America • 200 kW
**ITALY**
RAI INTERNATIONAL, Rome — S • C Africa & S Africa • 100 kW
**PHILIPPINES**
RADYO PILIPINAS, Tinang — S • Mideast • 250 kW
**ROMANIA**
RADIO ROMANIA, Bucharest — W • Europe • 120 kW
**UNITED KINGDOM**
BBC, Via Zyyi, Cyprus — S • C Asia • 250 kW
— S • E Europe • 250 kW
— F • W Asia & S Asia • 300 kW

**USA**
R FREE ASIA, Via Mongolia — S Asia • 250 kW
**17725 LIBYA**
RADIO JAMAHIRIYA, Tripoli — Africa • "VOICE OF AFRICA" • 500 kW • ALT. FREQ. TO 15415 kHz
— ENGLISH & FRENCH • Africa • "VOICE OF AFRICA" • 500 kW • ALT. FREQ. TO 15415 kHz

**SOUTH AFRICA**
†CHANNEL AFRICA, Meyerton — Sa/Su • E Africa • 250 kW • ALT. FREQ. TO 17780 kHz
— C Africa & E Africa • 500 kW • ALT. FREQ. TO 17770 kHz

**USA**
FAMILY RADIO, Okeechobee, Fl — S • S America • 100 kW

†RFE-RL, Via Holzkirchen, Germany — S • Mideast & W Asia • 250 kW
**17730 BELGIUM**
†R VLAANDEREN INTL, Via South Africa — W • C Africa • 250 kW
**GERMANY**
DEUTSCHE WELLE, Via Antigua — E North Am • 250 kW
— S • S America • 250 kW
— N America • 250 kW

(con'd)

| | 0 1 2 3 4 5 6 7 8 9 10 11 12 13 14 15 16 17 18 19 20 21 22 23 24 |
|---|---|

ENGLISH ▬  ARABIC ▨  CHINESE ▢▢▢  FRENCH ═  GERMAN ▬  RUSSIAN ═  SPANISH ▬  OTHER ▬

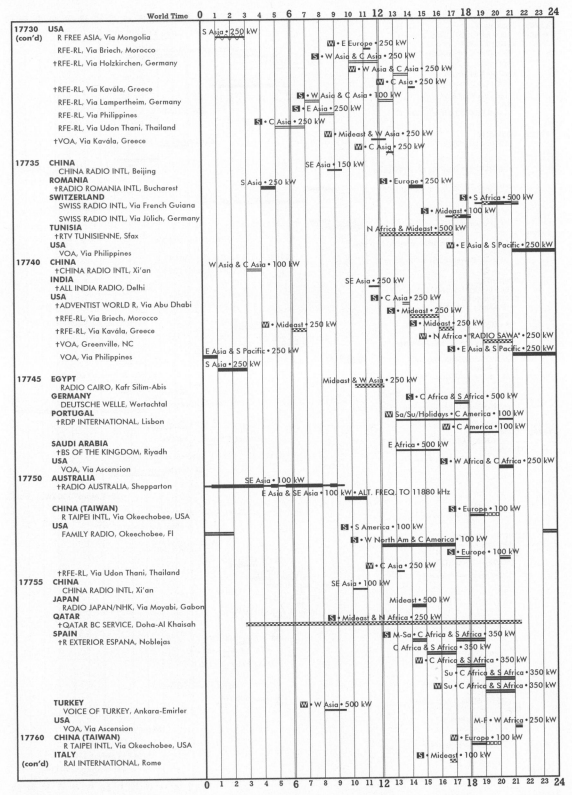

World Time | 0 1 2 3 4 5 6 7 8 9 10 11 12 13 14 15 16 17 18 19 20 21 22 23 24

**17730** **USA**
(con'd) R FREE ASIA, Via Mongolia — S Asia • 250 kW
RFE-RL, Via Briech, Morocco — W • E Europe • 250 kW
†RFE-RL, Via Holzkirchen, Germany — S • W Asia & C Asia • 250 kW
— W • W Asia & C Asia • 250 kW
— W • C Asia • 250 kW
†RFE-RL, Via Kavála, Greece — S • W Asia & C Asia • 100 kW
RFE-RL, Via Lampertheim, Germany — S • E Asia • 250 kW
RFE-RL, Via Philippines — S • C Asia • 250 kW
RFE-RL, Via Udon Thani, Thailand — W • Mideast & W Asia • 250 kW
†VOA, Via Kavála, Greece — W • C Asia • 250 kW

**17735** **CHINA**
CHINA RADIO INTL, Beijing — SE Asia • 150 kW
**ROMANIA**
†RADIO ROMANIA INTL, Bucharest — S Asia • 250 kW — S • Europe • 250 kW
**SWITZERLAND**
SWISS RADIO INTL, Via French Guiana — S • S Africa • 500 kW
SWISS RADIO INTL, Via Jülich, Germany — S • Mideast • 100 kW
**TUNISIA**
†RTV TUNISIENNE, Sfax — N Africa & Mideast • 500 kW
**USA**
VOA, Via Philippines — W • E Asia & S Pacific • 250 kW

**17740** **CHINA**
†CHINA RADIO INTL, Xi'an — W Asia & C Asia • 100 kW
**INDIA**
†ALL INDIA RADIO, Delhi — SE Asia • 250 kW
**USA**
†ADVENTIST WORLD R, Via Abu Dhabi — S • C Asia • 250 kW
†RFE-RL, Via Briech, Morocco — S • Mideast • 250 kW
†RFE-RL, Via Kavála, Greece — W • Mideast • 250 kW
— S • Mideast • 250 kW
†VOA, Greenville, NC — W • N Africa • "RADIO SAWA" • 250 kW
VOA, Via Philippines — E Asia & S Pacific • 250 kW — S • E Asia & S Pacific • 250 kW
— S Asia • 250 kW

**17745** **EGYPT**
RADIO CAIRO, Kafr Silim-Abis — Mideast & W Asia • 250 kW
**GERMANY**
DEUTSCHE WELLE, Wertachtal — S • C Africa & S Africa • 500 kW
**PORTUGAL**
†RDP INTERNATIONAL, Lisbon — W • Sa/Su/Holidays • C America • 100 kW
— W • C America • 100 kW
**SAUDI ARABIA**
†BS OF THE KINGDOM, Riyadh — E Africa • 500 kW
**USA**
VOA, Via Ascension — S • W Africa & C Africa • 250 kW

**17750** **AUSTRALIA**
†RADIO AUSTRALIA, Shepparton — SE Asia • 100 kW
— E Asia & SE Asia • 100 kW • ALT. FREQ. TO 11880 kHz
**CHINA (TAIWAN)**
R TAIPEI INTL, Via Okeechobee, USA — S • Europe • 100 kW
**USA**
FAMILY RADIO, Okeechobee, Fl — S • S America • 100 kW
— S • W North Am & C America • 100 kW
— S • Europe • 100 kW
†RFE-RL, Via Udon Thani, Thailand — W • C Asia • 250 kW

**17755** **CHINA**
CHINA RADIO INTL, Xi'an — SE Asia • 100 kW
**JAPAN**
RADIO JAPAN/NHK, Via Moyabi, Gabon — Mideast • 500 kW
**QATAR**
†QATAR BC SERVICE, Doha-Al Khaisah — S • Mideast & N Africa • 250 kW
**SPAIN**
†R EXTERIOR ESPANA, Noblejas — S • M-Sa • C Africa & S Africa • 350 kW
— C Africa & S Africa • 350 kW
— W • C Africa & S Africa • 350 kW
— Su • C Africa & S Africa • 350 kW
— W Su • C Africa & S Africa • 350 kW
**TURKEY**
VOICE OF TURKEY, Ankara-Emirler — W • W Asia • 500 kW
**USA**
VOA, Via Ascension — M-F • W Africa • 250 kW

**17760** **CHINA (TAIWAN)**
R TAIPEI INTL, Via Okeechobee, USA — W • Europe • 100 kW
**ITALY**
(con'd) RAI INTERNATIONAL, Rome — S • Mideast • 100 kW

0 1 2 3 4 5 6 7 8 9 10 11 12 13 14 15 16 17 18 19 20 21 22 23 24

SEASONAL S OR W    1-HR TIMESHIFT MIDYEAR ⇦ OR ⇨    JAMMING / OR ∧    EARLIEST HEARD ◁    LATEST HEARD ▷    NEW FOR 2003 †

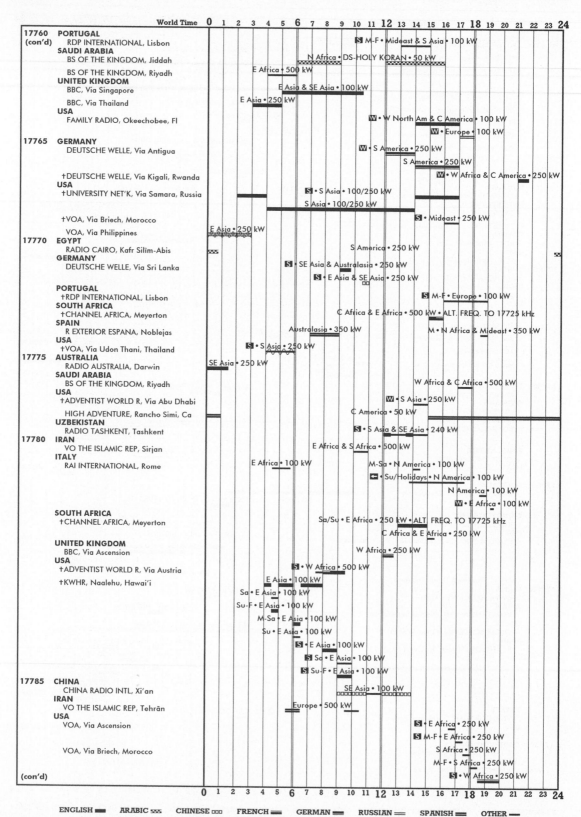

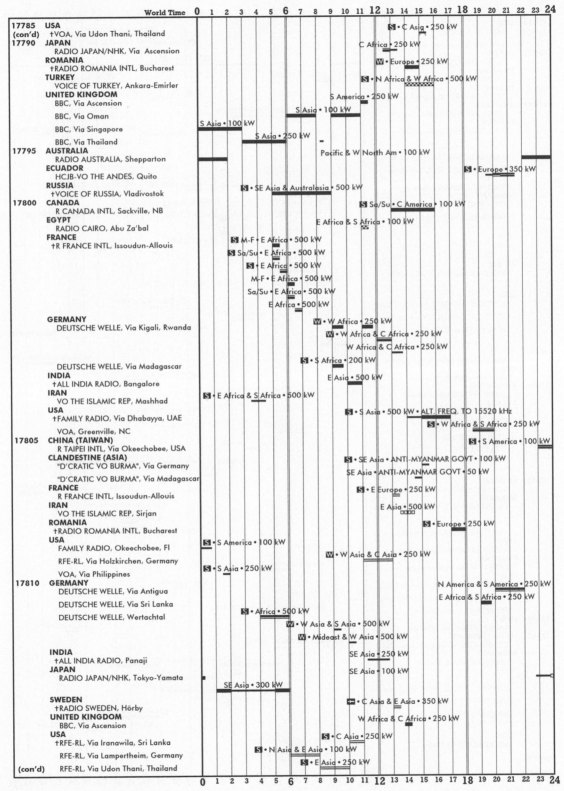

World Time

| Freq | Country / Station | Target • Power |
|---|---|---|

**17785** **USA**
(con'd)   †VOA, Via Udon Thani, Thailand — S • C Asia • 250 kW
**17790** **JAPAN**
    RADIO JAPAN/NHK, Via Ascension — C Africa • 250 kW
  **ROMANIA**
    †RADIO ROMANIA INTL, Bucharest — W • Europe • 250 kW
  **TURKEY**
    VOICE OF TURKEY, Ankara-Emirler — S • N Africa & W Africa • 500 kW
  **UNITED KINGDOM**
    BBC, Via Ascension — S America • 250 kW
    BBC, Via Oman — S Asia • 100 kW
    BBC, Via Singapore — S Asia • 100 kW
    BBC, Via Thailand — S Asia • 250 kW
**17795** **AUSTRALIA**
    RADIO AUSTRALIA, Shepparton — Pacific & W North Am • 100 kW
  **ECUADOR**
    HCJB-VO THE ANDES, Quito — S • Europe • 350 kW
  **RUSSIA**
    †VOICE OF RUSSIA, Vladivostok — S • SE Asia & Australasia • 500 kW
**17800** **CANADA**
    R CANADA INTL, Sackville, NB — S • Sa/Su • C America • 100 kW
  **EGYPT**
    RADIO CAIRO, Abu Za'bal — E Africa & S Africa • 100 kW
  **FRANCE**
    †R FRANCE INTL, Issoudun-Allouis — S • M-F • E Africa • 500 kW
          S • Sa/Su • E Africa • 500 kW
          S • E Africa • 500 kW
          M-F • E Africa • 500 kW
          Sa/Su • E Africa • 500 kW
          E Africa • 500 kW
  **GERMANY**
    DEUTSCHE WELLE, Via Kigali, Rwanda — W • W Africa • 250 kW
          W • W Africa & C Africa • 250 kW
          W Africa & C Africa • 250 kW
    DEUTSCHE WELLE, Via Madagascar — S • S Africa • 200 kW
  **INDIA**
    †ALL INDIA RADIO, Bangalore — E Asia • 500 kW
  **IRAN**
    VO THE ISLAMIC REP, Mashhad — S • E Africa & S Africa • 500 kW
  **USA**
    †FAMILY RADIO, Via Dhabayya, UAE — S • S Asia • 500 kW • ALT. FREQ. TO 15520 kHz
    VOA, Greenville, NC — S • W Africa & S Africa • 250 kW
**17805** **CHINA (TAIWAN)**
    R TAIPEI INTL, Via Okeechobee, USA — S • S America • 100 kW
  **CLANDESTINE (ASIA)**
    "D'CRATIC VO BURMA", Via Germany — S • SE Asia • ANTI-MYANMAR GOVT • 100 kW
    "D'CRATIC VO BURMA", Via Madagascar — SE Asia • ANTI-MYANMAR GOVT • 50 kW
  **FRANCE**
    R FRANCE INTL, Issoudun-Allouis — S • E Europe • 250 kW
  **IRAN**
    VO THE ISLAMIC REP, Sirjan — E Asia • 500 kW
  **ROMANIA**
    †RADIO ROMANIA INTL, Bucharest — S • Europe • 250 kW
  **USA**
    FAMILY RADIO, Okeechobee, Fl — S • S America • 100 kW
    RFE-RL, Via Holzkirchen, Germany — W • W Asia & C Asia • 250 kW
    VOA, Via Philippines — S • S Asia • 250 kW
**17810** **GERMANY**
    DEUTSCHE WELLE, Via Antigua — N America & S America • 250 kW
    DEUTSCHE WELLE, Via Sri Lanka — E Africa & S Africa • 250 kW
    DEUTSCHE WELLE, Wertachtal — S • Africa • 500 kW
          W • W Asia & S Asia • 500 kW
          W • Mideast & W Asia • 500 kW
  **INDIA**
    †ALL INDIA RADIO, Panaji — SE Asia • 250 kW
  **JAPAN**
    RADIO JAPAN/NHK, Tokyo-Yamata — SE Asia • 100 kW
          SE Asia • 300 kW
  **SWEDEN**
    †RADIO SWEDEN, Hörby — C Asia & E Asia • 350 kW
          W Africa & C Africa • 250 kW
  **UNITED KINGDOM**
    BBC, Via Ascension
  **USA**
    †RFE-RL, Via Iranawila, Sri Lanka — S • C Asia • 250 kW
    RFE-RL, Via Lampertheim, Germany — S • N Asia & E Asia • 100 kW
(con'd)   RFE-RL, Via Udon Thani, Thailand — S • E Asia • 250 kW

SEASONAL S OR W    1-HR TIMESHIFT MIDYEAR ⇦ OR ⇨    JAMMING / OR ∧    EARLIEST HEARD ◁    LATEST HEARD ▷    NEW FOR 2003 †

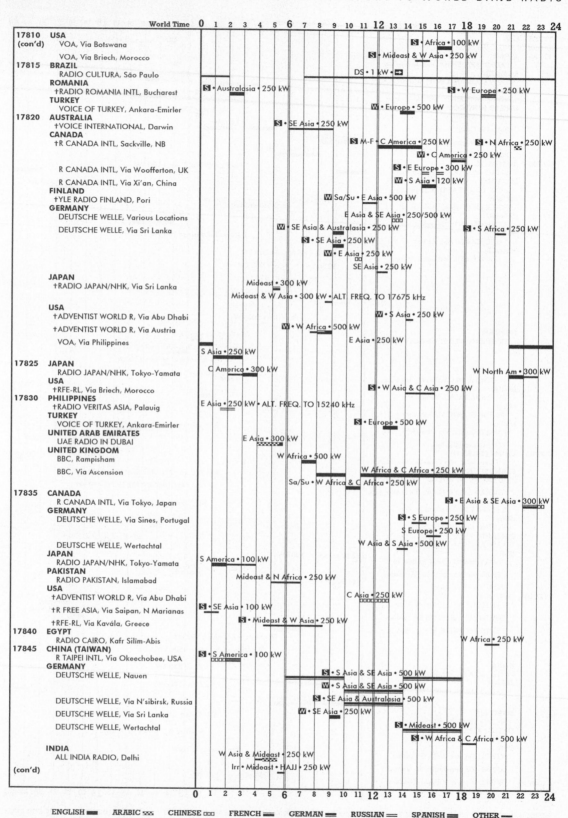

| | | |
|---|---|---|
| | World Time | 0 1 2 3 4 5 6 7 8 9 10 11 12 13 14 15 16 17 18 19 20 21 22 23 24 |

**17810  USA**
(con'd)    VOA, Via Botswana — ☒ • Africa • 100 kW
          VOA, Via Briech, Morocco — ☒ • Mideast & W Asia • 250 kW
**17815  BRAZIL**
          RADIO CULTURA, São Paulo — DS • 1 kW ☐➡
**ROMANIA**
          †RADIO ROMANIA INTL, Bucharest — ☒ • Australasia • 250 kW / ☒ • W Europe • 250 kW
**TURKEY**
          VOICE OF TURKEY, Ankara-Emirler — ☒ • Europe • 500 kW
**17820  AUSTRALIA**
          †VOICE INTERNATIONAL, Darwin — ☒ • SE Asia • 250 kW
**CANADA**
          †R CANADA INTL, Sackville, NB — ☒ M-F • C America • 250 kW / ☒ • N Africa • 250 kW
                                          ☒ • C America • 250 kW
          R CANADA INTL, Via Woofferton, UK — ☒ • E Europe • 300 kW
          R CANADA INTL, Via Xi'an, China — ☒ • S Asia • 120 kW
**FINLAND**
          †YLE RADIO FINLAND, Pori — ☒ Sa/Su • E Asia • 500 kW
**GERMANY**
          DEUTSCHE WELLE, Various Locations — E Asia & SE Asia • 250/500 kW
          DEUTSCHE WELLE, Via Sri Lanka — ☒ • SE Asia & Australasia • 250 kW / ☒ • S Africa • 250 kW
                                          ☒ • SE Asia • 250 kW
                                          ☒ • E Asia • 250 kW
                                          SE Asia • 250 kW
**JAPAN**
          †RADIO JAPAN/NHK, Via Sri Lanka — Mideast • 300 kW
                                            Mideast & W Asia • 300 kW • ALT FREQ. TO 17675 kHz
**USA**
          †ADVENTIST WORLD R, Via Abu Dhabi — ☒ • S Asia • 250 kW
          †ADVENTIST WORLD R, Via Austria — ☒ • W Africa • 500 kW
          VOA, Via Philippines — E Asia • 250 kW
                                 S Asia • 250 kW
**17825  JAPAN**
          RADIO JAPAN/NHK, Tokyo-Yamata — C America • 300 kW / W North Am • 300 kW
**USA**
          †RFE-RL, Via Briech, Morocco — ☒ • W Asia & C Asia • 250 kW
**17830  PHILIPPINES**
          †RADIO VERITAS ASIA, Palauig — E Asia • 250 kW • ALT. FREQ. TO 15240 kHz
**TURKEY**
          VOICE OF TURKEY, Ankara-Emirler — ☒ • Europe • 500 kW
**UNITED ARAB EMIRATES**
          UAE RADIO IN DUBAI — E Asia • 300 kW
**UNITED KINGDOM**
          BBC, Rampisham — W Africa • 500 kW
          BBC, Via Ascension — W Africa & C Africa • 250 kW
                               Sa/Su • W Africa & C Africa • 250 kW
**17835  CANADA**
          R CANADA INTL, Via Tokyo, Japan — ☒ • E Asia & SE Asia • 300 kW
**GERMANY**
          DEUTSCHE WELLE, Via Sines, Portugal — ☒ • S Europe • 250 kW
                                                S Europe • 250 kW
          DEUTSCHE WELLE, Wertachtal — W Asia & S Asia • 500 kW
**JAPAN**
          RADIO JAPAN/NHK, Tokyo-Yamata — S America • 100 kW
**PAKISTAN**
          RADIO PAKISTAN, Islamabad — Mideast & N Africa • 250 kW
**USA**
          †ADVENTIST WORLD R, Via Abu Dhabi — C Asia • 250 kW
          †R FREE ASIA, Via Saipan, N Marianas — ☒ • SE Asia • 100 kW
          †RFE-RL, Via Kavála, Greece — ☒ • Mideast & W Asia • 250 kW
**17840  EGYPT**
          RADIO CAIRO, Kafr Silim-Abis — W Africa • 250 kW
**17845  CHINA (TAIWAN)**
          R TAIPEI INTL, Via Okeechobee, USA — ☒ • S America • 100 kW
**GERMANY**
          DEUTSCHE WELLE, Nauen — ☒ • S Asia & SE Asia • 500 kW
                                  ☒ • S Asia & SE Asia • 500 kW
          DEUTSCHE WELLE, Via N'sibirsk, Russia — ☒ • SE Asia & Australasia • 500 kW
          DEUTSCHE WELLE, Via Sri Lanka — ☒ • SE Asia • 250 kW
          DEUTSCHE WELLE, Wertachtal — ☒ • Mideast • 500 kW
                                       ☒ • W Africa & C Africa • 500 kW
**INDIA**
          ALL INDIA RADIO, Delhi — W Asia & Mideast • 250 kW
                                   Irr • Mideast • HAJJ • 250 kW
(con'd)

0 1 2 3 4 5 6 7 8 9 10 11 12 13 14 15 16 17 18 19 20 21 22 23 24

ENGLISH ▬   ARABIC ░░░   CHINESE □□□   FRENCH ▭   GERMAN ▬   RUSSIAN ═   SPANISH ▭   OTHER ▬

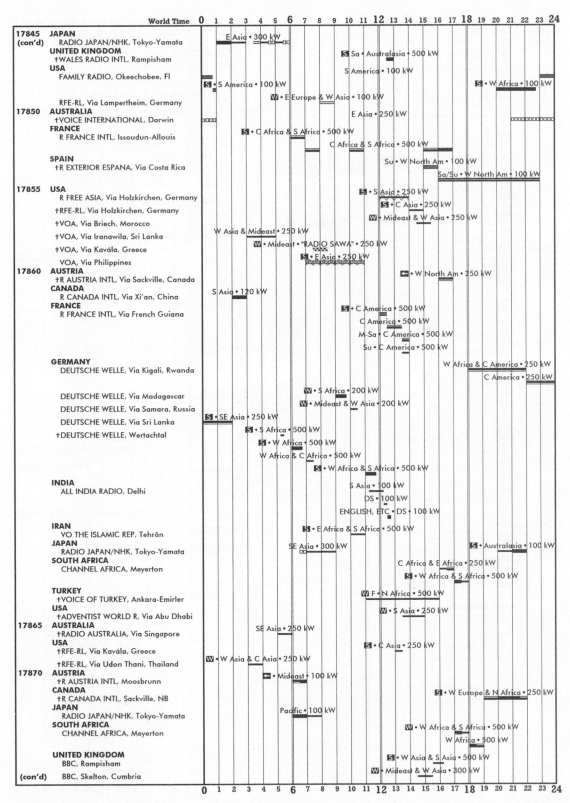

World Time

| 17845 | JAPAN |
| (con'd) | RADIO JAPAN/NHK, Tokyo-Yamata |
| | UNITED KINGDOM |
| | †WALES RADIO INTL, Rampisham |
| | USA |
| | FAMILY RADIO, Okeechobee, Fl |
| | RFE-RL, Via Lampertheim, Germany |
| 17850 | AUSTRALIA |
| | †VOICE INTERNATIONAL, Darwin |
| | FRANCE |
| | R FRANCE INTL, Issoudun-Allouis |
| | SPAIN |
| | †R EXTERIOR ESPANA, Via Costa Rica |
| 17855 | USA |
| | R FREE ASIA, Via Holzkirchen, Germany |
| | †RFE-RL, Via Holzkirchen, Germany |
| | †VOA, Via Briech, Morocco |
| | †VOA, Via Iranawila, Sri Lanka |
| | †VOA, Via Kavála, Greece |
| | VOA, Via Philippines |
| 17860 | AUSTRIA |
| | †R AUSTRIA INTL, Via Sackville, Canada |
| | CANADA |
| | R CANADA INTL, Via Xi'an, China |
| | FRANCE |
| | R FRANCE INTL, Via French Guiana |
| | GERMANY |
| | DEUTSCHE WELLE, Via Kigali, Rwanda |
| | DEUTSCHE WELLE, Via Madagascar |
| | DEUTSCHE WELLE, Via Samara, Russia |
| | DEUTSCHE WELLE, Via Sri Lanka |
| | †DEUTSCHE WELLE, Wertachtal |
| | INDIA |
| | ALL INDIA RADIO, Delhi |
| | IRAN |
| | VO THE ISLAMIC REP, Tehrān |
| | JAPAN |
| | RADIO JAPAN/NHK, Tokyo-Yamata |
| | SOUTH AFRICA |
| | CHANNEL AFRICA, Meyerton |
| | TURKEY |
| | †VOICE OF TURKEY, Ankara-Emirler |
| | USA |
| | †ADVENTIST WORLD R, Via Abu Dhabi |
| 17865 | AUSTRALIA |
| | †RADIO AUSTRALIA, Via Singapore |
| | USA |
| | †RFE-RL, Via Kavála, Greece |
| | †RFE-RL, Via Udon Thani, Thailand |
| 17870 | AUSTRIA |
| | †R AUSTRIA INTL, Moosbrunn |
| | CANADA |
| | †R CANADA INTL, Sackville, NB |
| | JAPAN |
| | RADIO JAPAN/NHK, Tokyo-Yamata |
| | SOUTH AFRICA |
| | CHANNEL AFRICA, Meyerton |
| | UNITED KINGDOM |
| | BBC, Rampisham |
| (con'd) | BBC, Skelton, Cumbria |

Schedule annotations (left to right):

- E Asia • 300 kW
- S • Australasia • 500 kW
- S America • 100 kW
- S • S America • 100 kW
- S • W Africa • 100 kW
- W • E Europe & W Asia • 100 kW
- E Asia • 250 kW
- S • C Africa & S Africa • 500 kW
- C Africa & S Africa • 500 kW
- Su • W North Am • 100 kW
- Sa/Su • W North Am • 100 kW
- S • S Asia • 250 kW
- S • C Asia • 250 kW
- W • Mideast & W Asia • 250 kW
- W Asia & Mideast • 250 kW
- W • Mideast • "RADIO SAWA" • 250 kW
- S • E Asia • 250 kW
- ⇦ • W North Am • 250 kW
- S Asia • 120 kW
- S • C America • 500 kW
- C America • 500 kW
- M-Sa • C America • 500 kW
- Su • C America • 500 kW
- W Africa & C America • 250 kW
- C America • 250 kW
- W • S Africa • 200 kW
- W • Mideast & W Asia • 200 kW
- S • SE Asia • 250 kW
- S • S Africa • 500 kW
- S • W Africa • 500 kW
- W Africa & C Africa • 500 kW
- S • W Africa & S Africa • 500 kW
- S Asia • 100 kW
- DS • 100 kW
- ENGLISH, ETC • DS • 100 kW
- S • E Africa & S Africa • 500 kW
- SE Asia • 300 kW
- S • Australasia • 100 kW
- C Africa & E Africa • 250 kW
- S • W Africa & S Africa • 500 kW
- W • F • N Africa • 500 kW
- W • S Asia • 250 kW
- SE Asia • 250 kW
- S • C Asia • 250 kW
- W • W Asia & C Asia • 250 kW
- ⇦ • Mideast • 100 kW
- S • W Europe & N Africa • 250 kW
- Pacific • 100 kW
- W • W Africa & S Africa • 500 kW
- W Africa • 500 kW
- S • W Asia & S Asia • 500 kW
- W • Mideast & W Asia • 300 kW

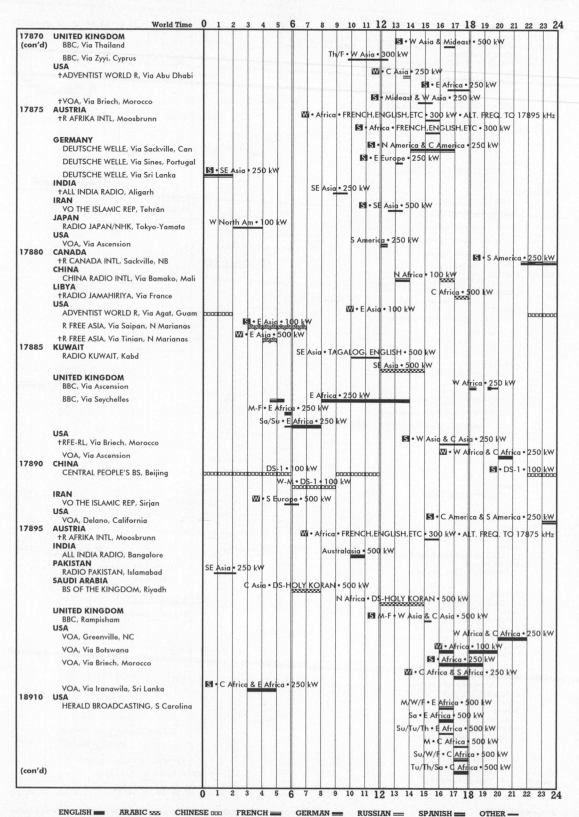

| | World Time | 0 1 2 3 4 5 6 7 8 9 10 11 12 13 14 15 16 17 18 19 20 21 22 23 24 |
|---|---|---|
| 17870 (con'd) | UNITED KINGDOM | |
| | BBC, Via Thailand | S • W Asia & Mideast • 500 kW |
| | BBC, Via Zyyi, Cyprus | Th/F • W Asia • 300 kW |
| | USA | |
| | †ADVENTIST WORLD R, Via Abu Dhabi | W • C Asia • 250 kW |
| | | S • E Africa • 250 kW |
| | †VOA, Via Briech, Morocco | S • Mideast & W Asia • 250 kW |
| 17875 | AUSTRIA | |
| | †R AFRIKA INTL, Moosbrunn | W • Africa • FRENCH,ENGLISH,ETC • 300 kW • ALT. FREQ. TO 17895 kHz |
| | | S • Africa • FRENCH,ENGLISH,ETC • 300 kW |
| | GERMANY | |
| | DEUTSCHE WELLE, Via Sackville, Can | S • N America & C America • 250 kW |
| | DEUTSCHE WELLE, Via Sines, Portugal | S • E Europe • 250 kW |
| | DEUTSCHE WELLE, Via Sri Lanka | S • SE Asia • 250 kW |
| | INDIA | |
| | †ALL INDIA RADIO, Aligarh | SE Asia • 250 kW |
| | IRAN | |
| | VO THE ISLAMIC REP, Tehrān | S • SE Asia • 500 kW |
| | JAPAN | |
| | RADIO JAPAN/NHK, Tokyo-Yamata | W North Am • 100 kW |
| | USA | |
| | VOA, Via Ascension | S America • 250 kW |
| 17880 | CANADA | |
| | †R CANADA INTL, Sackville, NB | S • S America • 250 kW |
| | CHINA | |
| | CHINA RADIO INTL, Via Bamako, Mali | N Africa • 100 kW |
| | LIBYA | |
| | †RADIO JAMAHIRIYA, Via France | C Africa • 500 kW |
| | USA | |
| | ADVENTIST WORLD R, Via Agat, Guam | W • E Asia • 100 kW |
| | R FREE ASIA, Via Saipan, N Marianas | S • E Asia • 100 kW |
| | †R FREE ASIA, Via Tinian, N Marianas | W • E Asia • 500 kW |
| 17885 | KUWAIT | |
| | RADIO KUWAIT, Kabd | SE Asia • TAGALOG, ENGLISH • 500 kW |
| | | SE Asia • 500 kW |
| | UNITED KINGDOM | |
| | BBC, Via Ascension | W Africa • 250 kW |
| | BBC, Via Seychelles | E Africa • 250 kW |
| | | M-F • E Africa • 250 kW |
| | | Sa/Su • E Africa • 250 kW |
| | USA | |
| | †RFE-RL, Via Briech, Morocco | S • W Asia & C Asia • 250 kW |
| | VOA, Via Ascension | W • W Africa & C Africa • 250 kW |
| 17890 | CHINA | |
| | CENTRAL PEOPLE'S BS, Beijing | DS-1 • 100 kW |
| | | S • DS-1 • 100 kW |
| | | W-M • DS-1 • 100 kW |
| | IRAN | |
| | VO THE ISLAMIC REP, Sirjan | W • S Europe • 500 kW |
| | USA | |
| | VOA, Delano, California | S • C America & S America • 250 kW |
| 17895 | AUSTRIA | |
| | †R AFRIKA INTL, Moosbrunn | W • Africa • FRENCH,ENGLISH,ETC • 300 kW • ALT. FREQ. TO 17875 kHz |
| | INDIA | |
| | ALL INDIA RADIO, Bangalore | Australasia • 500 kW |
| | PAKISTAN | |
| | RADIO PAKISTAN, Islamabad | SE Asia • 250 kW |
| | SAUDI ARABIA | |
| | BS OF THE KINGDOM, Riyadh | C Asia • DS-HOLY KORAN • 500 kW |
| | | N Africa • DS-HOLY KORAN • 500 kW |
| | UNITED KINGDOM | |
| | BBC, Rampisham | S • M-F • W Asia & C Asia • 500 kW |
| | USA | |
| | VOA, Greenville, NC | W Africa & C Africa • 250 kW |
| | VOA, Via Botswana | W • Africa • 100 kW |
| | VOA, Via Briech, Morocco | S • Africa • 250 kW |
| | | W • C Africa & S Africa • 250 kW |
| | VOA, Via Iranawila, Sri Lanka | S • C Africa & E Africa • 250 kW |
| 18910 | USA | |
| | HERALD BROADCASTING, S Carolina | M/W/F • E Africa • 500 kW |
| | | Sa • E Africa • 500 kW |
| | | Su/Tu/Th • E Africa • 500 kW |
| | | M • C Africa • 500 kW |
| | | Su/W/F • C Africa • 500 kW |
| | | Tu/Th/Sa • C Africa • 500 kW |
| (con'd) | | |

ENGLISH ■■    ARABIC ⋙    CHINESE ▭▭    FRENCH ▬▬    GERMAN ━━    RUSSIAN ══    SPANISH ▭▭    OTHER ▬▬

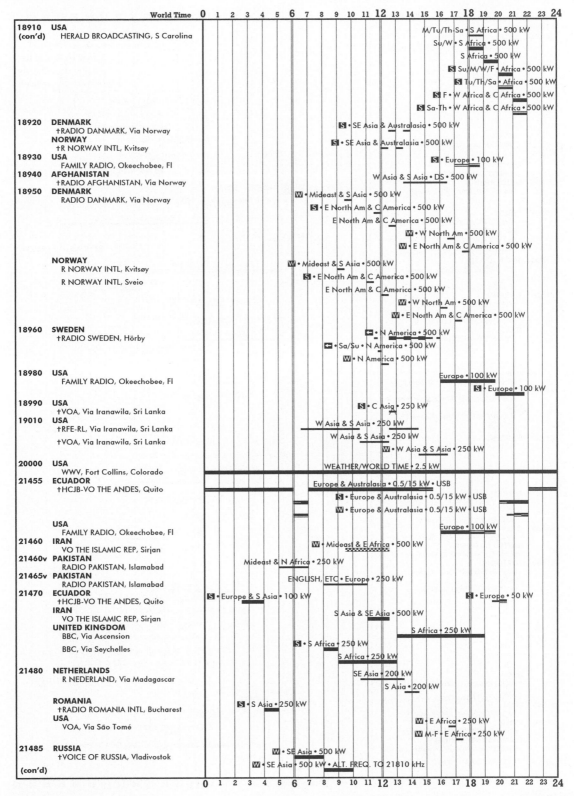

World Time | 0 1 2 3 4 5 6 7 8 9 10 11 12 13 14 15 16 17 18 19 20 21 22 23 24

**18910 USA**
(con'd)  HERALD BROADCASTING, S Carolina
- M/Tu/Th/Sa • S Africa • 500 kW
- Su/W • S Africa • 500 kW
- S Africa • 500 kW
- S Su/M/W/F • Africa • 500 kW
- S Tu/Th/Sa • Africa • 500 kW
- S F • W Africa & C Africa • 500 kW
- S Sa-Th • W Africa & C Africa • 500 kW

**18920 DENMARK**
†RADIO DANMARK, Via Norway
- S • SE Asia & Australasia • 500 kW

**NORWAY**
†R NORWAY INTL, Kvitsøy
- S • SE Asia & Australasia • 500 kW

**18930 USA**
FAMILY RADIO, Okeechobee, Fl
- S • Europe • 100 kW

**18940 AFGHANISTAN**
†RADIO AFGHANISTAN, Via Norway
- W Asia & S Asia • DS • 500 kW

**18950 DENMARK**
RADIO DANMARK, Via Norway
- W • Mideast & S Asia • 500 kW
- S • E North Am & C America • 500 kW
- E North Am & C America • 500 kW
- W • W North Am • 500 kW
- W • E North Am & C America • 500 kW

**NORWAY**
R NORWAY INTL, Kvitsøy
- W • Mideast & S Asia • 500 kW
- S • E North Am & C America • 500 kW

R NORWAY INTL, Sveio
- E North Am & C America • 500 kW
- W • W North Am • 500 kW
- W • E North Am & C America • 500 kW

**18960 SWEDEN**
†RADIO SWEDEN, Hörby
- ⇄ • N America • 500 kW
- ⇄ Sa/Su • N America • 500 kW
- W • N America • 500 kW

**18980 USA**
FAMILY RADIO, Okeechobee, Fl
- Europe • 100 kW
- S • Europe • 100 kW

**18990 USA**
†VOA, Via Iranawila, Sri Lanka
- S • C Asia • 250 kW

**19010 USA**
†RFE-RL, Via Iranawila, Sri Lanka
- W Asia & S Asia • 250 kW

†VOA, Via Iranawila, Sri Lanka
- W Asia & S Asia • 250 kW
- W • W Asia & S Asia • 250 kW

**20000 USA**
WWV, Fort Collins, Colorado
- WEATHER/WORLD TIME • 2.5 kW

**21455 ECUADOR**
†HCJB-VO THE ANDES, Quito
- Europe & Australasia • 0.5/15 kW • USB
- S • Europe & Australasia • 0.5/15 kW • USB
- W • Europe & Australasia • 0.5/15 kW • USB

**USA**
FAMILY RADIO, Okeechobee, Fl
- Europe • 100 kW

**21460 IRAN**
VO THE ISLAMIC REP, Sirjan
- W • Mideast & E Africa • 500 kW

**21460v PAKISTAN**
RADIO PAKISTAN, Islamabad
- Mideast & N Africa • 250 kW

**21465v PAKISTAN**
RADIO PAKISTAN, Islamabad
- ENGLISH, ETC • Europe • 250 kW

**21470 ECUADOR**
†HCJB-VO THE ANDES, Quito
- S • Europe & S Asia • 100 kW
- S • Europe • 50 kW

**IRAN**
VO THE ISLAMIC REP, Sirjan
- S Asia & SE Asia • 500 kW

**UNITED KINGDOM**
BBC, Via Ascension
- S Africa • 250 kW

BBC, Via Seychelles
- S • S Africa • 250 kW
- S Africa • 250 kW

**21480 NETHERLANDS**
R NEDERLAND, Via Madagascar
- SE Asia • 200 kW
- S Asia • 200 kW

**ROMANIA**
†RADIO ROMANIA INTL, Bucharest
- S • S Asia • 250 kW

**USA**
VOA, Via São Tomé
- W • E Africa • 250 kW
- W M-F • E Africa • 250 kW

**21485 RUSSIA**
†VOICE OF RUSSIA, Vladivostok
- W • SE Asia • 500 kW
- W • SE Asia • 500 kW • ALT. FREQ. TO 21810 kHz

(con'd)

0 1 2 3 4 5 6 7 8 9 10 11 12 13 14 15 16 17 18 19 20 21 22 23 24

SEASONAL S OR W    1-HR TIMESHIFT MIDYEAR ⇦ OR ⇨    JAMMING / OR /\    EARLIEST HEARD ◁    LATEST HEARD ▷    NEW FOR 2003 †

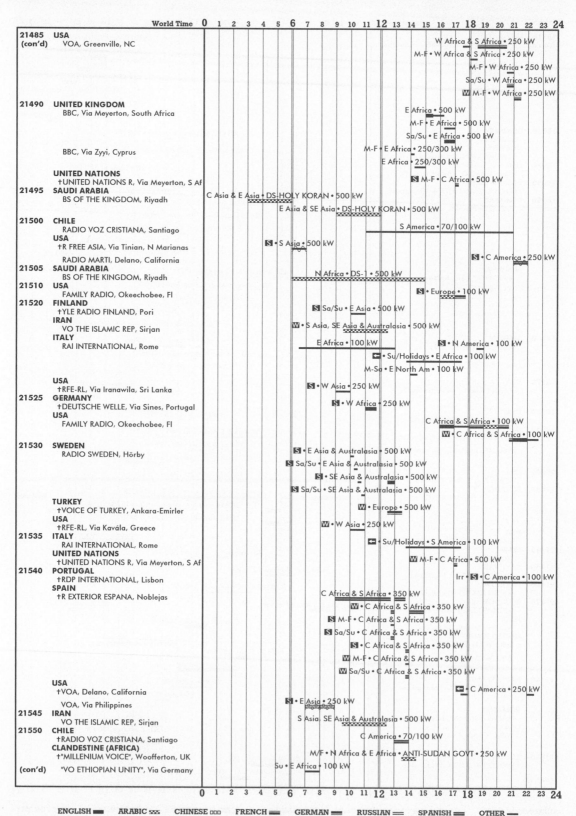

| World Time | 0 | 1 | 2 | 3 | 4 | 5 | 6 | 7 | 8 | 9 | 10 | 11 | 12 | 13 | 14 | 15 | 16 | 17 | 18 | 19 | 20 | 21 | 22 | 23 | 24 |

**21485** **USA**
(con'd)   VOA, Greenville, NC
- W Africa & S Africa • 250 kW
- M-F • W Africa & S Africa • 250 kW
- M-F • W Africa • 250 kW
- Sa/Su • W Africa • 250 kW
- W M-F • W Africa • 250 kW

**21490** **UNITED KINGDOM**
  BBC, Via Meyerton, South Africa
- E Africa • 500 kW
- M-F • E Africa • 500 kW
- Sa/Su • E Africa • 500 kW

  BBC, Via Zyyi, Cyprus
- M-F • E Africa • 250/300 kW
- E Africa • 250/300 kW

**UNITED NATIONS**
  †UNITED NATIONS R, Via Meyerton, S Af
- S M-F • C Africa • 500 kW

**21495** **SAUDI ARABIA**
  BS OF THE KINGDOM, Riyadh
- C Asia & E Asia • DS-HOLY KORAN • 500 kW
- E Asia & SE Asia • DS-HOLY KORAN • 500 kW

**21500** **CHILE**
  RADIO VOZ CRISTIANA, Santiago
- S America • 70/100 kW
**USA**
  †R FREE ASIA, Via Tinian, N Marianas
- S • S Asia • 500 kW
  RADIO MARTI, Delano, California
- S • C America • 250 kW

**21505** **SAUDI ARABIA**
  BS OF THE KINGDOM, Riyadh
- N Africa • DS-1 • 500 kW
**21510** **USA**
  FAMILY RADIO, Okeechobee, Fl
- S • Europe • 100 kW
**21520** **FINLAND**
  †YLE RADIO FINLAND, Pori
- S Sa/Su • E Asia • 500 kW
**IRAN**
  VO THE ISLAMIC REP, Sirjan
- W • S Asia, SE Asia & Australasia • 500 kW
**ITALY**
  RAI INTERNATIONAL, Rome
- E Africa • 100 kW
- S • N America • 100 kW
- • Su/Holidays • E Africa • 100 kW
- M-Sa • E North Am • 100 kW

**USA**
  †RFE-RL, Via Iranawila, Sri Lanka
- S • W Asia • 250 kW
**21525** **GERMANY**
  †DEUTSCHE WELLE, Via Sines, Portugal
- S • W Africa • 250 kW
**USA**
  FAMILY RADIO, Okeechobee, Fl
- C Africa & S Africa • 100 kW
- W • C Africa & S Africa • 100 kW

**21530** **SWEDEN**
  RADIO SWEDEN, Hörby
- S • E Asia & Australasia • 500 kW
- S Sa/Su • E Asia & Australasia • 500 kW
- S • SE Asia & Australasia • 500 kW
- S Sa/Su • SE Asia & Australasia • 500 kW

**TURKEY**
  †VOICE OF TURKEY, Ankara-Emirler
- W • Europe • 500 kW
**USA**
  †RFE-RL, Via Kavála, Greece
- W • W Asia • 250 kW
**21535** **ITALY**
  RAI INTERNATIONAL, Rome
- • Su/Holidays • S America • 100 kW
**UNITED NATIONS**
  †UNITED NATIONS R, Via Meyerton, S Af
- W M-F • C Africa • 500 kW
**21540** **PORTUGAL**
  †RDP INTERNATIONAL, Lisbon
- Irr • S • C America • 100 kW
**SPAIN**
  †R EXTERIOR ESPANA, Noblejas
- C Africa & S Africa • 350 kW
- W • C Africa & S Africa • 350 kW
- S M-F • C Africa & S Africa • 350 kW
- S Sa/Su • C Africa & S Africa • 350 kW
- S • C Africa & S Africa • 350 kW
- W M-F • C Africa & S Africa • 350 kW
- W Sa/Su • C Africa & S Africa • 350 kW

**USA**
  †VOA, Delano, California
- • C America • 250 kW
  VOA, Via Philippines
- S • E Asia • 250 kW
**21545** **IRAN**
  VO THE ISLAMIC REP, Sirjan
- S Asia, SE Asia & Australasia • 500 kW
**21550** **CHILE**
  †RADIO VOZ CRISTIANA, Santiago
- C America • 70/100 kW
**CLANDESTINE (AFRICA)**
  †"MILLENIUM VOICE", Woofferton, UK
- M/F • N Africa & E Africa • ANTI-SUDAN GOVT • 250 kW
(con'd)   "VO ETHIOPIAN UNITY", Via Germany
- Su • E Africa • 100 kW

| 0 | 1 | 2 | 3 | 4 | 5 | 6 | 7 | 8 | 9 | 10 | 11 | 12 | 13 | 14 | 15 | 16 | 17 | 18 | 19 | 20 | 21 | 22 | 23 | 24 |

ENGLISH ▬   ARABIC ∾   CHINESE □□□   FRENCH ═   GERMAN ▬   RUSSIAN ═   SPANISH ▭   OTHER ▬

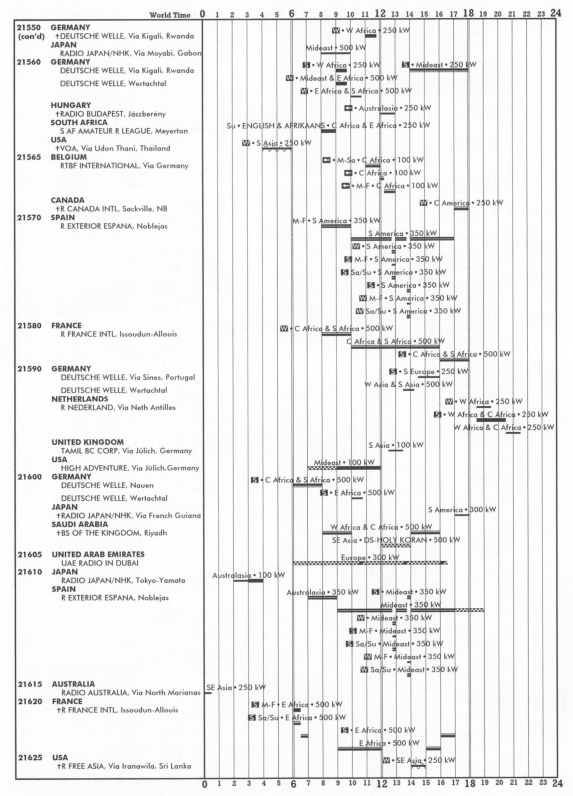

| | |
|---|---|
| 21550 (con'd) | **GERMANY** †DEUTSCHE WELLE, Via Kigali, Rwanda |
| | **JAPAN** RADIO JAPAN/NHK, Via Moyabi, Gabon |
| 21560 | **GERMANY** DEUTSCHE WELLE, Via Kigali, Rwanda |
| | DEUTSCHE WELLE, Wertachtal |
| | **HUNGARY** †RADIO BUDAPEST, Jászberény |
| | **SOUTH AFRICA** S AF AMATEUR R LEAGUE, Meyerton |
| | **USA** †VOA, Via Udon Thani, Thailand |
| 21565 | **BELGIUM** RTBF INTERNATIONAL, Via Germany |
| | **CANADA** †R CANADA INTL, Sackville, NB |
| 21570 | **SPAIN** R EXTERIOR ESPANA, Noblejas |
| 21580 | **FRANCE** R FRANCE INTL, Issoudun-Allouis |
| 21590 | **GERMANY** DEUTSCHE WELLE, Via Sines, Portugal |
| | DEUTSCHE WELLE, Wertachtal |
| | **NETHERLANDS** R NEDERLAND, Via Neth Antilles |
| | **UNITED KINGDOM** TAMIL BC CORP, Via Jülich, Germany |
| | **USA** HIGH ADVENTURE, Via Jülich, Germany |
| 21600 | **GERMANY** DEUTSCHE WELLE, Nauen |
| | DEUTSCHE WELLE, Wertachtal |
| | **JAPAN** †RADIO JAPAN/NHK, Via French Guiana |
| | **SAUDI ARABIA** †BS OF THE KINGDOM, Riyadh |
| 21605 | **UNITED ARAB EMIRATES** UAE RADIO IN DUBAI |
| 21610 | **JAPAN** RADIO JAPAN/NHK, Tokyo-Yamata |
| | **SPAIN** R EXTERIOR ESPANA, Noblejas |
| 21615 | **AUSTRALIA** RADIO AUSTRALIA, Via North Marianas |
| 21620 | **FRANCE** †R FRANCE INTL, Issoudun-Allouis |
| 21625 | **USA** †R FREE ASIA, Via Iranwila, Sri Lanka |

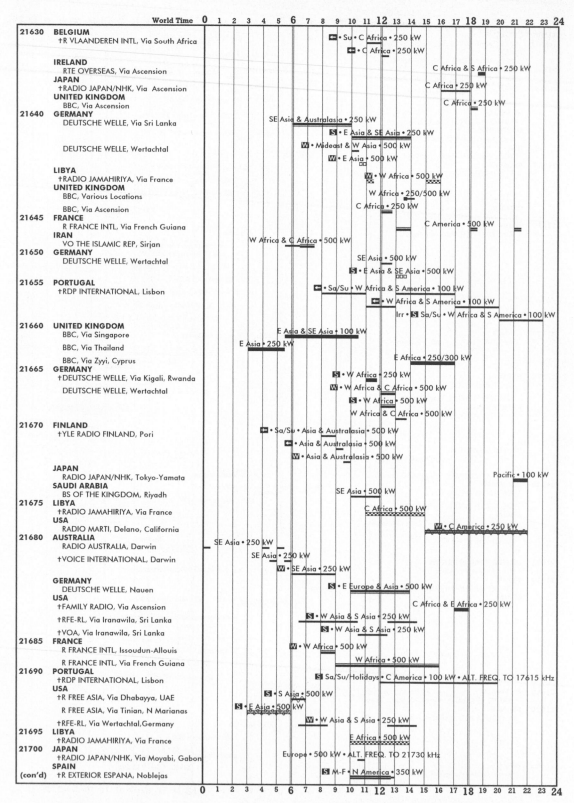

| World Time | 0 | 1 | 2 | 3 | 4 | 5 | 6 | 7 | 8 | 9 | 10 | 11 | 12 | 13 | 14 | 15 | 16 | 17 | 18 | 19 | 20 | 21 | 22 | 23 | 24 |

**21630 BELGIUM**
  †R VLAANDEREN INTL, Via South Africa — ⬅•Su•C Africa•250 kW / ⬅•C Africa•250 kW

**IRELAND**
  RTE OVERSEAS, Via Ascension — C Africa & S Africa•250 kW
**JAPAN**
  †RADIO JAPAN/NHK, Via Ascension — C Africa•250 kW
**UNITED KINGDOM**
  BBC, Via Ascension — C Africa•250 kW

**21640 GERMANY**
  DEUTSCHE WELLE, Via Sri Lanka — SE Asia & Australasia•250 kW / S•E Asia & SE Asia•250 kW
  DEUTSCHE WELLE, Wertachtal — W•Mideast & W Asia•500 kW / W•E Asia•500 kW

**LIBYA**
  †RADIO JAMAHIRIYA, Via France — W•W Africa•500 kW
**UNITED KINGDOM**
  BBC, Various Locations — W Africa•250/500 kW
  BBC, Via Ascension — C Africa•250 kW

**21645 FRANCE**
  R FRANCE INTL, Via French Guiana — C America•500 kW
**IRAN**
  VO THE ISLAMIC REP, Sirjan — W Africa & C Africa•500 kW

**21650 GERMANY**
  DEUTSCHE WELLE, Wertachtal — SE Asia•500 kW / S•E Asia & SE Asia•500 kW

**21655 PORTUGAL**
  †RDP INTERNATIONAL, Lisbon — ⬅•Sa/Su•W Africa & S America•100 kW / ⬅•W Africa & S America•100 kW / Irr•S•Sa/Su•W Africa & S America•100 kW

**21660 UNITED KINGDOM**
  BBC, Via Singapore — E Asia & SE Asia•100 kW
  BBC, Via Thailand — E Asia•250 kW
  BBC, Via Zyyi, Cyprus — E Africa•250/300 kW
**21665 GERMANY**
  †DEUTSCHE WELLE, Via Kigali, Rwanda — S•W Africa•250 kW
  DEUTSCHE WELLE, Wertachtal — W•W Africa & C Africa•500 kW / S•W Africa•500 kW / W Africa & C Africa•500 kW

**21670 FINLAND**
  †YLE RADIO FINLAND, Pori — ⬅•Sa/Su•Asia & Australasia•500 kW / ⬅•Asia & Australasia•500 kW / W•Asia & Australasia•500 kW

**JAPAN**
  RADIO JAPAN/NHK, Tokyo-Yamata — Pacific•100 kW
**SAUDI ARABIA**
  BS OF THE KINGDOM, Riyadh — SE Asia•500 kW
**21675 LIBYA**
  †RADIO JAMAHIRIYA, Via France — C Africa•500 kW
**USA**
  RADIO MARTI, Delano, California — W•C America•250 kW
**21680 AUSTRALIA**
  RADIO AUSTRALIA, Darwin — SE Asia•250 kW
  †VOICE INTERNATIONAL, Darwin — SE Asia•250 kW / W•SE Asia•250 kW

**GERMANY**
  DEUTSCHE WELLE, Nauen — S•E Europe & Asia•500 kW
**USA**
  †FAMILY RADIO, Via Ascension — C Africa & E Africa•250 kW
  †RFE-RL, Via Iranawila, Sri Lanka — S•W Asia & S Asia•250 kW
  †VOA, Via Iranawila, Sri Lanka — S•W Asia & S Asia•250 kW
**21685 FRANCE**
  R FRANCE INTL, Issoudun-Allouis — W•W Africa•500 kW
  R FRANCE INTL, Via French Guiana — W Africa•500 kW
**21690 PORTUGAL**
  †RDP INTERNATIONAL, Lisbon — S•Sa/Su/Holidays•C America•100 kW•ALT. FREQ. TO 17615 kHz
**USA**
  †R FREE ASIA, Via Dhabayya, UAE — S•S Asia•500 kW
  R FREE ASIA, Via Tinian, N Marianas — S•E Asia•500 kW
  †RFE-RL, Via Wertachtal, Germany — W•W Asia & S Asia•250 kW
**21695 LIBYA**
  †RADIO JAMAHIRIYA, Via France — E Africa•500 kW
**21700 JAPAN**
  †RADIO JAPAN/NHK, Via Moyabi, Gabon — Europe•500 kW•ALT. FREQ. TO 21730 kHz
**SPAIN**
**(con'd)** †R EXTERIOR ESPANA, Noblejas — S•M-F•N America•350 kW

| | 0 | 1 | 2 | 3 | 4 | 5 | 6 | 7 | 8 | 9 | 10 | 11 | 12 | 13 | 14 | 15 | 16 | 17 | 18 | 19 | 20 | 21 | 22 | 23 | 24 |

ENGLISH ▬   ARABIC ▨   CHINESE ▭▭▭   FRENCH ▬   GERMAN ▬   RUSSIAN ═   SPANISH ═   OTHER ▬

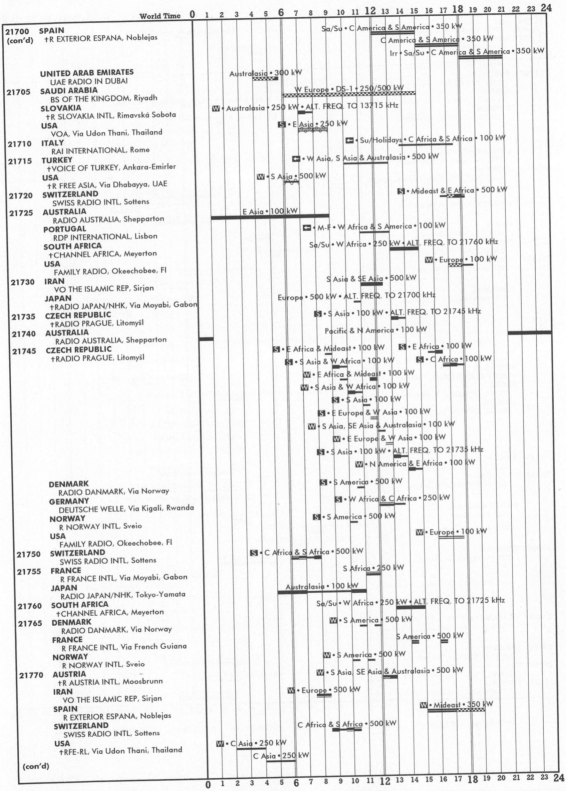

| Freq | Country / Station | Schedule |
|------|-------------------|----------|
| 21700 (con'd) | **SPAIN** †R EXTERIOR ESPANA, Noblejas | Sa/Su • C America & S America • 350 kW / C America & S America • 350 kW / Irr • Sa/Su • C America & S America • 350 kW |
| | **UNITED ARAB EMIRATES** UAE RADIO IN DUBAI | Australasia • 300 kW |
| 21705 | **SAUDI ARABIA** BS OF THE KINGDOM, Riyadh | W Europe • DS-1 • 250/500 kW |
| | **SLOVAKIA** †R SLOVAKIA INTL, Rimavská Sobota | W • Australasia • 250 kW • ALT. FREQ. TO 13715 kHz |
| | **USA** VOA, Via Udon Thani, Thailand | S • E Asia • 250 kW |
| 21710 | **ITALY** RAI INTERNATIONAL, Rome | Su/Holidays • C Africa & S Africa • 100 kW |
| 21715 | **TURKEY** †VOICE OF TURKEY, Ankara-Emirler | W Asia, S Asia & Australasia • 500 kW |
| | **USA** †R FREE ASIA, Via Dhabayya, UAE | W • S Asia • 500 kW |
| 21720 | **SWITZERLAND** SWISS RADIO INTL, Sottens | S • Mideast & E Africa • 500 kW |
| 21725 | **AUSTRALIA** RADIO AUSTRALIA, Shepparton | E Asia • 100 kW |
| | **PORTUGAL** RDP INTERNATIONAL, Lisbon | M-F • W Africa & S America • 100 kW |
| | **SOUTH AFRICA** †CHANNEL AFRICA, Meyerton | Sa/Su • W Africa • 250 kW • ALT. FREQ. TO 21760 kHz |
| | **USA** FAMILY RADIO, Okeechobee, Fl | W • Europe • 100 kW |
| 21730 | **IRAN** VO THE ISLAMIC REP, Sirjan | S Asia & SE Asia • 500 kW |
| | **JAPAN** †RADIO JAPAN/NHK, Via Moyabi, Gabon | Europe • 500 kW • ALT. FREQ. TO 21700 kHz |
| 21735 | **CZECH REPUBLIC** †RADIO PRAGUE, Litomyšl | S • S Asia • 100 kW • ALT. FREQ. TO 21745 kHz |
| 21740 | **AUSTRALIA** RADIO AUSTRALIA, Shepparton | Pacific & N America • 100 kW |
| 21745 | **CZECH REPUBLIC** †RADIO PRAGUE, Litomyšl | S • E Africa & Mideast • 100 kW / S • E Africa • 100 kW / S • S Asia & W Africa • 100 kW / S • C Africa • 100 kW / W • E Africa & Mideast • 100 kW / W • S Asia & W Africa • 100 kW / S • S Asia • 100 kW / S • E Europe & W Asia • 100 kW / W • S Asia, SE Asia & Australasia • 100 kW / W • E Europe & W Asia • 100 kW / S • S Asia • 100 kW • ALT. FREQ. TO 21735 kHz / W • N America & E Africa • 100 kW |
| | **DENMARK** RADIO DANMARK, Via Norway | S • S America • 500 kW |
| | **GERMANY** DEUTSCHE WELLE, Via Kigali, Rwanda | S • W Africa & C Africa • 250 kW |
| | **NORWAY** R NORWAY INTL, Sveio | S • S America • 500 kW |
| | **USA** FAMILY RADIO, Okeechobee, Fl | W • Europe • 100 kW |
| 21750 | **SWITZERLAND** SWISS RADIO INTL, Sottens | S • C Africa & S Africa • 500 kW |
| 21755 | **FRANCE** R FRANCE INTL, Via Moyabi, Gabon | S Africa • 250 kW |
| | **JAPAN** RADIO JAPAN/NHK, Tokyo-Yamata | Australasia • 100 kW |
| 21760 | **SOUTH AFRICA** †CHANNEL AFRICA, Meyerton | Sa/Su • W Africa • 250 kW • ALT. FREQ. TO 21725 kHz |
| 21765 | **DENMARK** RADIO DANMARK, Via Norway | W • S America • 500 kW |
| | **FRANCE** R FRANCE INTL, Via French Guiana | S America • 500 kW |
| | **NORWAY** R NORWAY INTL, Sveio | W • S America • 500 kW |
| 21770 | **AUSTRIA** †R AUSTRIA INTL, Moosbrunn | W • S Asia, SE Asia & Australasia • 500 kW |
| | **IRAN** VO THE ISLAMIC REP, Sirjan | W • Europe • 500 kW |
| | **SPAIN** R EXTERIOR ESPANA, Noblejas | W • Mideast • 350 kW |
| | **SWITZERLAND** SWISS RADIO INTL, Sottens | C Africa & S Africa • 500 kW |
| | **USA** †RFE-RL, Via Udon Thani, Thailand | W • C Asia • 250 kW / C Asia • 250 kW |

(con'd)

SEASONAL S OR W    1-HR TIMESHIFT MIDYEAR ⬅ OR ➡    JAMMING / OR ∧    EARLIEST HEARD ◁    LATEST HEARD ▷    NEW FOR 2003 †

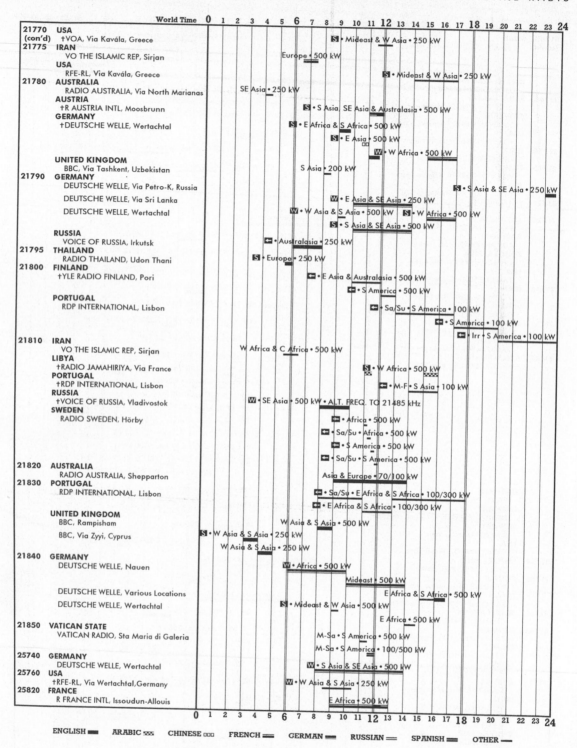

| World Time | 0 | 1 | 2 | 3 | 4 | 5 | 6 | 7 | 8 | 9 | 10 | 11 | 12 | 13 | 14 | 15 | 16 | 17 | 18 | 19 | 20 | 21 | 22 | 23 | 24 |

**21770 USA**
(con'd)   †VOA, Via Kavála, Greece — S • Mideast & W Asia • 250 kW
**21775 IRAN**
VO THE ISLAMIC REP, Sirjan — Europe • 500 kW
**USA**
RFE-RL, Via Kavála, Greece — S • Mideast & W Asia • 250 kW
**21780 AUSTRALIA**
RADIO AUSTRALIA, Via North Marianas — SE Asia • 250 kW
**AUSTRIA**
†R AUSTRIA INTL, Moosbrunn — S • S Asia, SE Asia & Australasia • 500 kW
**GERMANY**
†DEUTSCHE WELLE, Wertachtal — S • E Africa & S Africa • 500 kW
— S • E Asia • 500 kW
— W • W Africa • 500 kW
**UNITED KINGDOM**
BBC, Via Tashkent, Uzbekistan — S Asia • 200 kW
**21790 GERMANY**
DEUTSCHE WELLE, Via Petro-K, Russia — S • S Asia & SE Asia • 250 kW
DEUTSCHE WELLE, Via Sri Lanka — W • E Asia & SE Asia • 250 kW
DEUTSCHE WELLE, Wertachtal — W • W Asia & S Asia • 500 kW   S • W Africa • 500 kW
— S • S Asia & SE Asia • 500 kW
**RUSSIA**
VOICE OF RUSSIA, Irkutsk — ← • Australasia • 250 kW
**21795 THAILAND**
RADIO THAILAND, Udon Thani — S • Europe • 250 kW
**21800 FINLAND**
†YLE RADIO FINLAND, Pori — • E Asia & Australasia • 500 kW
**PORTUGAL**
RDP INTERNATIONAL, Lisbon — ← • S America • 500 kW
— ← • Sa/Su • S America • 100 kW
— ← • S America • 100 kW
— ← • Irr • S America • 100 kW
**21810 IRAN**
VO THE ISLAMIC REP, Sirjan — W Africa & C Africa • 500 kW
**LIBYA**
†RADIO JAMAHIRIYA, Via France — S • W Africa • 500 kW
**PORTUGAL**
†RDP INTERNATIONAL, Lisbon — ← • M-F • S Asia • 100 kW
**RUSSIA**
†VOICE OF RUSSIA, Vladivostok — W • SE Asia • 500 kW • ALT. FREQ. TO 21485 kHz
**SWEDEN**
RADIO SWEDEN, Hörby — ← • Africa • 500 kW
— ← • Sa/Su • Africa • 500 kW
— ← • S America • 500 kW
— ← • Sa/Su • S America • 500 kW
**21820 AUSTRALIA**
RADIO AUSTRALIA, Shepparton — Asia & Europe • 70/100 kW
**21830 PORTUGAL**
RDP INTERNATIONAL, Lisbon — ← • Sa/Su • E Africa & S Africa • 100/300 kW
— ← • E Africa & S Africa • 100/300 kW
**UNITED KINGDOM**
BBC, Rampisham — W Asia & S Asia • 500 kW
BBC, Via Zyyi, Cyprus — S • W Asia & S Asia • 250 kW
— W Asia & S Asia • 250 kW
**21840 GERMANY**
DEUTSCHE WELLE, Nauen — W • Africa • 500 kW
— Mideast • 500 kW
DEUTSCHE WELLE, Various Locations — E Africa & S Africa • 500 kW
DEUTSCHE WELLE, Wertachtal — S • Mideast & W Asia • 500 kW
— E Africa • 500 kW
**21850 VATICAN STATE**
VATICAN RADIO, Sta Maria di Galeria — M-Sa • S America • 500 kW
— M-Sa • S America • 100/500 kW
**25740 GERMANY**
DEUTSCHE WELLE, Wertachtal — W • S Asia & SE Asia • 500 kW
**25760 USA**
†RFE-RL, Via Wertachtal, Germany — W • W Asia & S Asia • 250 kW
**25820 FRANCE**
R FRANCE INTL, Issoudun-Allouis — E Africa • 500 kW

| 0 | 1 | 2 | 3 | 4 | 5 | 6 | 7 | 8 | 9 | 10 | 11 | 12 | 13 | 14 | 15 | 16 | 17 | 18 | 19 | 20 | 21 | 22 | 23 | 24 |

ENGLISH ▬   ARABIC ▨   CHINESE ▫▫▫   FRENCH ▬▬   GERMAN ▬   RUSSIAN ═══   SPANISH ▬▬   OTHER ▬